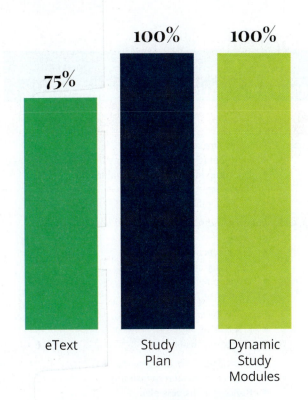

% of students who found learning tool helpful

Dynamic Study Mod... study chapter topics ... own by continuously assessing their **knowledge application** and performance in real time. These are available as graded assignments prior to class, and accessible on smartphones, tablets, and computers.

Pearson eText enhances student learning—both in and outside the classroom. Take notes, highlight, and bookmark important content, or engage with interactive lecture and example videos that bring learning to life (available with select titles). Accessible anytime, anywhere via MyLab or the app.

The **MyLab Gradebook** offers an easy way for students and instructors to view course performance. Item Analysis allows instructors to quickly see trends by analyzing details like the number of students who answered correctly/incorrectly, time on task, and median time spend on a question by question basis. And because it's correlated with the AACSB Standards, instructors can track students' progress toward outcomes that the organization has deemed important in preparing students to be **leaders.**

75%

of students would tell their instructor to keep using MyLab Entrepreneurship

For additional details visit: www.pearson.com/mylab/entrepreneurship

CASES

ESSENTIALS OF ENTREPRENEURSHIP AND SMALL BUSINESS MANAGEMENT, 9/E

Case #	Entrepreneur; Company Name	Related Topics	Chapter Reference
1	Bill, Melody, and Stephanie Cohen United Apparel Liquidators	*Industry: Discount retail clothing* • Developing a business strategy • Bootstrap marketing and social media marketing • Choosing the right location	5 9 14
2	Matt Meeker, Henrik Werdelin, and Carly Strife Bark & Co.	*Industry: Subscription-based gift boxes for dogs* • Entrepreneurship • Creativity and innovation • Developing a business strategy • Sources of financing	1 3 5 15
3	Jim Telikis and Saban Lomac Cousins Maine Lobster	*Industry: Restaurant (food truck)* • Franchising • Global expansion	8 16
4	Saul Garlick ThinkImpact	*Industry: Social entrepreneurship* • Ethics and social responsibility • Building a business plan • Forms of ownership • Sources of financing	2 5 6 15
5	Art, Ilene, Joseph, and Aaron Stadlen Intertech Construction Corporation	*Industry: Interior design and construction* • Financial analysis and management • Managing cash flow • Family business and management succession	12 13 17
6	Angela Crawford and Martin Rodriguez Bluffton Pharmacy—Part 1	*Industry: Pharmacy* • Financial analysis and management	12
7	Angela Crawford and Martin Rodriguez Bluffton Pharmacy—Part 2	*Industry: Pharmacy* • Managing cash flow	13
8	Max, Shelly, and Alfie Gitman Gitman Brothers	*Industry: Apparel (shirts and ties)* • Social media marketing • E-commerce and Web site design	9 10
9	James, Trish, and Palmer Higgins Seabreeze Property Services	*Industry: Landscape and snow removal* • Buying an existing business • Sources of financing	7 15
10	Jeff Braverman Nuts.com	*Industry: Snack foods* • Developing a business strategy • Bootstrap marketing and social media marketing • E-commerce • Family business	5 9 10 17

Ninth Edition

Essentials of Entrepreneurship and Small Business Management

Norman M. Scarborough

Presbyterian College

Jeffrey R. Cornwall

Belmont University

New York, NY

Vice President, Business, Economics, and UK Courseware:
 Donna Battista
Director of Portfolio Management: Stephanie Wall
Editorial Assistant: Linda Siebert Albelli
Vice President, Product Marketing: Roxanne McCarley
Product Marketer: Kaylee Carlson
Product Marketing Assistant: Marianela Silvestri
Manager of Field Marketing, Business Publishing: Adam Goldstein
Field Marketing Manager: Nicole Price
Vice President, Production and Digital Studio, Arts and Business:
 Etain O'Dea
Director of Production, Business: Jeff Holcomb
Managing Producer, Business: Melissa Feimer
Content Producer: Yasmita Hota

Operations Specialist: Carol Melville
Design Lead: Kathryn Foot
Manager, Learning Tools: Brian Surette
Content Developer, Learning Tools: Lindsey Sloan
Managing Producer, Digital Studio and GLP, Media Production
 and Development: Ashley Santora
Managing Producer, Digital Studio: Diane Lombardo
Digital Studio Producer: Monique Lawrence
Digital Studio Producer: Alana Coles
Project Manager: Susan McNally, Cenveo® Publisher Services
Interior and Cover Design: Cenveo® Publisher Services
Cover Art: Triloks/E+/Getty Images; Thomas Vogel/E+/Getty Image
Printer/Binder: LSC Communications, Inc./Menasha
Cover Printer: Phoenix Color/Hagerstown

Library of Congress Cataloging-in-Publication Data is on file with the Library of Congress.

2 18

ISBN 10:   0-13-474108-0
ISBN 13: 978-0-13-474108-6

To Cindy, whose patience is always tested during a writing project
of this magnitude. Your love, support, and understanding
are a vital part of every book.
You are the love of my life.

—NMS

To Ann, for her wisdom and love. Your encouragement
and support are the foundation for each new entrepreneurial
adventure we take.

—JRC

"May your own dreams be your only boundaries."

—The Reverend Purlie Victorious Judson,
in *Purlie*, Broadway Theater, 1970

Brief Contents

Contents

Preface

Entrepreneurship is a fast-growing and ever-changing discipline. People of all ages, backgrounds, and nationalities are launching businesses of their own and, in the process, are reshaping the world's economy. The purpose of this book is to open students' minds to the possibilities, the challenges, and the rewards of owning their own businesses and to provide the tools they will need to be successful if they choose the path of the entrepreneur. It is not an easy road to follow, but the rewards—both tangible and intangible—are well worth the risks. Not only may you be rewarded financially for your business ideas, but also like entrepreneurs the world over, you will be able to work at something you love!

New to This Edition

This edition includes many new features that reflect this dynamic and exciting field of study.

- This edition features separate chapters on "Forms of Business Ownership" and "Buying an Existing Business." In addition, we have reorganized the chapter on buying a business using a five-step process: the search stage, the due diligence stage, the valuation stage, the deal stage, and the transition stage. As members of the Baby Boom generation retire, the opportunities for you to buy a business are vast. This chapter covers the details of various valuation methods to help you determine the value of a business you might purchase.

- Almost every one of the real-world examples in this edition is new and is easy to spot because they are accompanied by an icon. These examples allow you to see how entrepreneurs are putting into practice the concepts that you are learning about in the book and in class. These examples are designed to help students remember the key concepts in the course. The business founders in these examples also reflect the diversity that makes entrepreneurship a vital part of the global economy.

ENTREPRENEURIAL PROFILE: Lauren Pears: Lady Dinah's Cat Emporium After a particularly bad day at work, Lauren Pears decided to leave her corporate job, began writing a business plan, and raised the necessary capital via crowdfunding to launch Lady Dinah's Cat Emporium, a café in London that is home to 13 rescued cats that each week host hundreds of human guests looking for feline companionship at high tea and a 90-minute respite from the hectic pace of life. Pears was confident that her business would succeed, but even she admits to being surprised at the 20,000 reservations the Cat Emporium received in only its first two weeks of operation. Pears drives business to her company's Web site primarily through social media. Every cat has his or her own Twitter handle and regularly tweets photos and comments about his or her activities (or, being cats, lack of activity). The cats and the Cat Emporium have 11,000 followers on Instagram, more than 55,000 likes on Facebook, and 19,000 followers on Twitter. Lady Dinah's Cat Emporium uses social media very effectively to connect with her audience; currently, there is a six-week waiting list for reservations.[57] ■

Roger Parkes/Alamy Stock Photo

ENTREPRENEURIAL PROFILE: Neil Parikh, Gabe Flateman, and Luke Sherwin: Casper Mattress Neil Parikh, Gabe Flateman, and Luke Sherwin, all in their mid-20s, believed that the $14 billion mattress industry, with its seemingly endless product variations, complicated delivery and return process, and high prices, was ripe for disruption. The trio of entrepreneurs decided to launch a business, Casper, in New York City that simplifies the process of buying a mattress. Casper produces only one mattress model that comes in six sizes and is priced from $500 to $950. Customers receive a 100-day trial period with every mattress. If a customer is dissatisfied at any time during the generous trial period, Casper picks up the mattress at no charge and provides a full refund. (Casper's return rate is extremely low, and the company donates returned mattresses to local charities.) Living in a large city where space is limited, the trio of entrepreneurs

- We have integrated discussions of social media into almost every chapter, including how entrepreneurs use social media in a wide range of applications, ranging from attracting investors and screening potential franchises to getting feedback from customers about a business idea and using it as a powerful, efficient marketing tool.

- We have updated the chapter on "Ethics and Entrepreneurship: Doing the Right Thing." This chapter provides students with a framework for making ethical decisions in business and with the opportunity to wrestle with some of the ethical dilemmas that entrepreneurs face, including the controversial issues surrounding employers' responses to employees' postings on social media sites. Encouraging you to think about and discuss these issues now prepares you for making the right business decisions later.

- We have updated Chapter 10, "E-Commerce and the Entrepreneur," to reflect the multichannel approach that businesses use to meet their customers wherever and whenever they want to shop. This chapter also includes coverage of the latest search engine optimization techniques and the steps business owners can take to avoid becoming victims of cybercrime.

- This edition provides expanded and updated coverage of important topics such as using the Business Model Canvas to refine a business idea, attracting capital using crowdfunding, identifying the keys to selecting the ideal location for a business, developing a process for hiring the right employees, creating a company culture that inspires employees to achieve their full potential, and others.

- To emphasize the practical nature of this book, we have updated the content of the very popular "Hands On: How To . . ." feature, which selects a concept from each chapter and explains how to put it into practice in your own company. These features include topics such as how to "Make Social Media Work for Your Business," "Create a Culture of Creativity and Innovation," "Build a Successful Global Company," "Make Your Small Business a Great Place to Work," and many others.

- Another feature that is popular with both students and professors is "You Be the Consultant." Every chapter contains at least one of these inserts describing a decision that an entrepreneur faces while asking you to play the role of consultant and to advise the entrepreneur on the best course of action. This feature includes the fascinating stories of how entrepreneurs came up with their business ideas (including Bill Mitchell, who began tailoring clothing for his college friends, which led him to start Billiam Jeans, a company that creates custom-made jeans for clients). Other topics explore deciding whether an entrepreneur should purchase one of the first outlets from a new franchise operation (John Rosatti and Lee Goldberg and BurgerFi), developing a strategy for providing "second mile service" to customers as a way of setting a company apart from its competition, understanding the psychology behind popular pricing strategies, helping an entrepreneur choose a location for his company's next retail store (Fan Bi, cofounder of custom shirtmaker Blank Label), and using social media to market a small company's services (Jeff Platt and SkyZone, an indoor wall-to-wall trampoline park franchise). Each one poses a problem or an opportunity and includes questions that focus attention on key issues to help you hone your analytical and critical thinking skills.

- This edition includes 10 new brief cases that cover a variety of topics (see the case matrix that appears on the inside cover). All of the cases are about small companies, and most are companies that you can research online. These cases challenge students to think critically about a variety of topics that are covered in the text—from developing a business strategy and building a brand to protecting intellectual property and financing a business.

- The content of every chapter reflects the most recent statistics, studies, surveys, and research about entrepreneurship and small business management. Students will learn how to launch and manage their businesses the *right* way by studying the most current concepts in entrepreneurship and small business management.

Ad Rank = Advertiser's Bid Price on Key Word x Advertiser's Quality Score
Example:

Advertiser	Key Word Bid Price	Quality Score	Ad Rank	Ad Position
A	$2.50	10	25	1st
B	$4.00	5	20	2nd
C	$6.00	2	12	3rd
D	$8.00	1	8	4th

Higher quality scores produce not only higher ad ranks and better ad positions but also result in lower costs per click.

How much does the advertiser pay when a customer clicks on its ad?
Ad Cost = Ad Rank of the Web site below yours ÷ Your Quality Score + $0.01

Example:

Advertiser	Key Word Bid Price	Quality Score	Ad Rank	Ad Cost per Click
A	$2.50	10	25	20 ÷ 10 + $.01 = **$2.01**
B	$4.00	5	20	12 ÷ 5 + $.01 = **$2.41**
C	$6.00	2	12	8 ÷ 2 + $.01 = **$4.01**
D	$8.00	1	8	Highest cost per click

This is what each advertiser pays when a shopper clicks on its ad that appears on Google's search engine results page.

FIGURE 10.10
How Google Determines a PPC Ad's Position and Cost

Source: Based on "What Is PPC? Learn the Basics of Pay-per-Click (PPC) Marketing, WordStream, January 2, 2017, www.wordstream.com/ppc.

Entrepreneurship has become a major force in the global economy. Policy makers across the world are discovering that economic growth and prosperity lie in the hands of entrepreneurs—those dynamic, driven men and women who are committed to achieving success by creating and marketing innovative, customer-focused new products and services. Not only are these entrepreneurs creating economic prosperity, but as social entrepreneurs many of them are also striving to make the world a better place in which to live. Those who possess this spirit of entrepreneurial leadership continue to lead the economic revolution that has proved time and again its ability to raise the standard of living for people everywhere. We hope that by using this book in your entrepreneurship or small business management course, you will join this economic revolution to bring about lasting, positive changes in your community and around the world. If you are interested in launching a business of your own, *Essentials of Entrepreneurship and Small Business Management* is the ideal book for you!

This ninth edition of *Essentials of Entrepreneurship and Small Business Management* introduces students to the process of creating a new venture and provides them with the knowledge they need to launch a business that has the greatest chance for success. One of the hallmarks of every edition of this book has been a very practical, "hands-on" approach to entrepreneurship. We strive to equip students with the tools they will need for entrepreneurial success. By combining this textbook with professors' expertise, students will be equipped to follow their dreams of becoming successful entrepreneurs.

Solving Teaching and Learning Challenges

Now in its ninth edition, *Essentials of Entrepreneurship and Small Business Management* has stood the test of time by presenting in an organized, concise manner the material needed to launch and manage a small business successfully in a hotly competitive environment. In writing this edition, we have worked hard to provide plenty of practical, "hands-on" tools and techniques to help you make your business ventures successful. Many people launch businesses every year, but only some of them succeed. This book provides the tools to help students learn the *right* way to launch and manage a small business with the staying power to succeed and grow.

ENTREPRENEURIAL PROFILE: Carolyn Yarina: CentriCycle As part of a class project in a freshman engineering class at the University of Michigan, Carolyn Yarina discovered that one of the greatest needs of rural health workers in developing nations is a centrifuge that could operate without electricity. By the end of the semester, Yarina and a team of students designed a human-powered centrifuge made from bicycle parts called the CentriCycle. The project stirred Yarina's interest in entrepreneurship, and she began taking courses in that field, including one on social entrepreneurship that enabled her to go to India. Soon, Yarina and fellow student Katie Kirsch teamed up with University of Michigan graduate Gillian Henker, who was developing Hemafuse, an auto-transfusion pump for blood, to create Sisu Global Health, a socially conscious, for-profit business that focuses on medical products designed

- Each chapter offers several insights from successful professionals, emphasizing concepts and valuable skills that students will explore in depth in the chapter.

- Each chapter includes a chapter summary (organized by learning objectives), discussion questions, and "Beyond the Classroom" questions that are designed to engage students and help them develop their analytical and critical thinking skills. On MyLab Entrepreneurship are flash cards for students to use to test their knowledge of key terms used throughout the book.

- Each chapter also includes a "Hands on: How to . . ." feature that provides students with practical insight into problems that entrepreneurs often face.

Chapter Summary by Learning Objective

1. Define the role of the entrepreneur in business in the United States and around the world.

- Entrepreneurship is thriving in the United States, but the current wave of entrepreneurship is not limited to the United States; many nations around the globe are seeing similar growth in their small business sectors. A variety of competitive, economic, and demographic shifts have created a world in which "small is beautiful."

- Capitalist societies depend on entrepreneurs to provide the drive and risk taking necessary for the system to supply people with the goods and services they need.

2. Describe the entrepreneurial profile.

- Entrepreneurs have some common characteristics, including a desire for responsibility, a preference for moderate risk, confidence in their ability to succeed, desire for immediate feedback, a high energy level, a future orientation, skill at organizing, and a value of achievement over money. In a phrase, they are tenacious high achievers.

3-A. Describe the benefits of entrepreneurship.

- Driven by their personal characteristics, entrepreneurs establish and manage small businesses to gain control over their lives, make a difference in the world, become self-fulfilled, reap unlimited profits, contribute to society, and do what they enjoy doing.

3-B. Describe the drawbacks of entrepreneurship.

- Entrepreneurs also face certain disadvantages, including uncertainty of income, the risk of losing their investments (and more), long hours and hard work, a lower quality of life until the business gets established, high stress levels, and complete decision-making responsibility.

4. Explain the forces that are driving the growth of entrepreneurship.

- Several factors are driving the boom in entrepreneurship, including the portrayal of entrepreneurs

as heroes, better entrepreneurial education, economic and demographic factors, a shift to a service economy, technological advances, more independent lifestyles, and increased international opportunities.

5. Explain the cultural diversity of entrepreneurship.

- Several groups are leading the nation's drive toward entrepreneurship: young people, women, minorities, immigrants, part-timers, home-based business owners, family business owners, copreneurs, corporate castoffs, corporate dropouts, social entrepreneurs, and retired Baby Boomers.

6. Describe the important role that small businesses play in our nation's economy.

- The small . . .

7. Put failure . . .

- Entrepre . . .

8. Explain ho . . . becoming . . .

- Entrepre . . .

Discussion Questions

7-1. What advantages can an entrepreneur who buys a business gain over one who starts a business "from scratch"?

7-2. How would you go about determining the value of the assets of a business if you were unfamiliar with them?

⭐ 7-3. Why do so many entrepreneurs run into trouble when they buy an existing business?

7-4. Outline the stages involved in buying a business.

7-5. What topics does the due diligence process address?

7-6. Briefly outline the process of valuing a business using the adjusted earnings, the capitalized earnings, and the discounted future earnings approaches.

⭐ 7-7. What determines the bargaining zone between a business seller and a buyer?

7-8. Explain the buyer's position in a typical negotiation for a business.

7-9. Explain the seller's position in a typical negotiation for a business.

7-10. What steps should a business buyer take to ensure a smooth transition after closing the deal to buy a business?

7-11. One entrepreneur who recently purchased a business advises buyers to expect some surprises in the deal, no matter how well prepared they may be. He says potential buyers must build some "wiggle room" into their plans to buy a company. What steps can a buyer take to ensure that he or she has sufficient wiggle room?

3-10. Your dinner guests are to arrive in five minutes, and you've just discovered that you forgot to chill the wine!! Wanting to maintain your reputation as the perfect host/hostess, you must tackle this problem with maximum creativity. What could you do? Generate as many solutions as you can in five minutes working alone and then work with two or three students in a small group to brainstorm the problem.

3-11. Work with a group of your classmates to think of as many alternative uses for the commercial lubricant WD-40 as you can. Remember to think *fluidly* (generating a quantity of ideas) and *flexibly* (generating unconventional ideas).

3-12. A Facebook group of more than 25,000 people is trying to convince Cadbury, the venerable British

confectioner (now owned by Kraft Foods), to produce a giant chocolate Cadbury Crème Egg that contains a filling made from fondant that resembles the yolk and white of a real egg. (Currently, giant Cadbury chocolate eggs, which are about the size of an ostrich egg, are hollow, a great disappointment to fans of the company's smaller chocolate eggs that are filled with creamy white and yolk-colored fondant.) A Cadbury spokesperson says that "creating a [chocolate] shell that is strong enough to contain the sheer weight of the fondant is technically challenging." Use the creativity-enhancing techniques described in this chapter to develop potential solutions that would allow Cadbury to manufacture a giant Crème Egg.

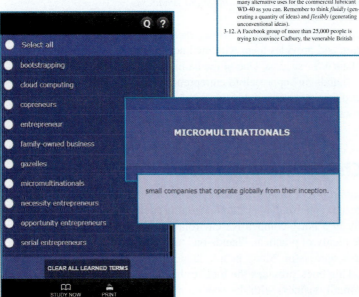

Q ?

○ Select all
○ bootstrapping
○ cloud computing
○ copreneurs
○ entrepreneur
○ family-owned business
○ gazelles
○ micromultinationals
○ necessity entrepreneurs
○ opportunity entrepreneurs
○ serial entrepreneurs

CLEAR ALL LEARNED TERMS

📖 STUDY NOW   PRINT

MICROMULTINATIONALS

small companies that operate globally from their inception.

Hands On . . . How To

Use Social Media to Market Your Business

The typical digital consumer now spends an average of 1 hour and 50 minutes each day on social media (and 80 percent of that time is on a mobile device). In addition, 77 percent of online shoppers use social media (Facebook, YouTube, Twitter, and Pinterest are the most popular apps), and more than one-third of online shoppers say that social media has influenced their purchases. Social media apps now offer users "shop now" and "buy now" features that enable them to make purchases directly from the app. In fact, nearly one-fourth of online shoppers have purchased a product on a social media network. Clearly, social media represents a tremendous marketing opportunity for small businesses; however, only 57 percent of small businesses have a social media presence. The accompanying graphic shows how these small businesses put social media tools to work for their companies.

At Sky Zone, an indoor wall-to-wall trampoline park franchise with 127 locations in the United States and 22 outlets in foreign countries, social media marketing emerged organically. CEO Jeff Platt says the company noticed that customers were planning trips to Sky Zone locations on Twitter, so the company joined in the conversations and posted special offers, such as "bring five people to Sky Zone, and we'll give you a free pass." Sky Zone also launched the Twitter campaign #I'dRatherBe@SkyZone to engage customers of all ages and to show people how much fun a Sky Zone adventure can be through posts, photos, and video. Platt was surprised to see how many people posted photos of their

How Small Businesses Use Social Media

- This edition once again emphasizes the importance of conducting a feasibility analysis and creating a business plan for a successful new venture. Chapter 4, "Conducting a Feasibility Analysis and Designing a Business Model," offers comprehensive coverage of how to conduct a feasibility study for a business idea and then how to create a sound business model for the ideas that pass the feasibility test. This content will enable students to avoid a common mistake that entrepreneurs make: failing to define and test a viable business model *before* they launch their businesses.

- This edition features an updated, attractive, full-color design and a layout that includes an in-margin glossary and learning objectives and is designed to be user friendly. Each chapter begins with learning objectives, which are repeated as in-margin markers within the chapter to guide your students as they study. Attention-grabbing graphics help visually-oriented students learn more effectively.

- Chapter 3, "Inside the Entrepreneurial Mind: From Ideas to Reality," explains the creative process entrepreneurs use to generate business ideas and to recognize entrepreneurial opportunities. This chapter helps students learn to think like entrepreneurs.

- Chapter 10, "E-Commerce and the Entrepreneur," serves as a practical guide to using the Internet as a marketing and business tool and offers helpful advice for engaging successfully in mobile commerce. The Internet will be at the core of many of the businesses students will start, and they must have a solid understanding of the pitfalls to avoid and how to build a successful e-commerce strategy.

- Chapter 14, "Sources of Financing: Equity and Debt," gives students a useful overview of the various financing sources that are available to entrepreneurs with plenty of practical advice for landing the financing they need to start or grow a business. In the difficult search for capital, many entrepreneurs take the first financing that becomes available, even though it often proves to be a poor choice. This chapter enables students to identify multiple sources of financing and evaluate the ones that are best for their particular situations.

- On MyLab Entrepreneurship, MediaShare for Business provides a robust video library and a powerful interface that help you connect course concepts to the business world.

- On MyLab Entrepreneurship, students can complete Auto-graded and Assisted-grading writing questions that cut down on your grading time so you can spend more time teaching.

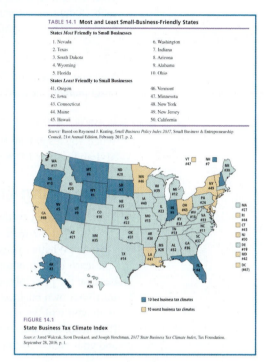

TABLE 14.1 Most and Least Small-Business-Friendly States

States *Most* Friendly to Small Businesses

1. Nevada	6. Washington
2. Texas	7. Indiana
3. South Dakota	8. Arizona
4. Wyoming	9. Alabama
5. Florida	10. Ohio

States *Least* Friendly to Small Businesses

41. Oregon	46. Vermont
42. Iowa	47. Minnesota
43. Connecticut	48. New York
44. Maine	49. New Jersey
45. Hawaii	50. California

Source: Based on Raymond J. Keating, *Small Business Policy Index 2017,* Small Business & Entrepreneurship Council, 21st Annual Edition, February 2017, p. 2.

- 10 best business tax climates
- 10 worst business tax climates

FIGURE 14.1
State Business Tax Climate Index

Source: Jared Walczak, Scott Drenkard, and Joseph Henchman, *2017 State Business Tax Climate Index,* Tax Foundation, September 28, 2016, p. 1.

RECOMMENDED ASSIGNMENTS

DBA Forms of Business Ownership	Ecoist Strategic Product Development	Fresher than Fresh Economics	Fresher than Fresh Economics	Johnny Cupcakes Financial and Cash Flow Mgmt MC2
MC2 (5:48)	MC2 (6:23)	StudentUpl (6:27)	StudentUpl (6:27)	

☐ Select All   ➕ Add Selected

MyLab Entrepreneurship

If your instructor is using MyLab Entrepreneurship, go to **www.pearson.com/mylab/entrepreneurship** for Auto-graded writing questions as well as the following Assisted-graded writing questions:

1. Briefly describe the role of the following groups in entrepreneurship: young people, women, minorities, immigrants, part-timers, home-based business owners, family business owners, copreneurs, corporate castoffs, corporate dropouts, social entrepreneurs, and retired Baby Boomers.
2. What contributions do small businesses make to our economy?

MyLab Entrepreneurship

Reach every student with MyLab

MyLab is the teaching and learning platform that empowers you to reach *every* student. By combining trusted author content with digital tools and a flexible platform, MyLab personalizes the learning experience and improves results for each student. Learn more at MyLab Entrepreneurship.

Deliver trusted content

You deserve teaching materials that meet your own high standards for your course. That's why we partner with highly respected authors to develop interactive content and course-specific resources that you can trust—and that keep your students engaged.

Empower each learner

Each student learns at a different pace. Personalized learning pinpoints the precise areas where each student needs practice, giving all students the support they need—when and where they need it—to be successful.

Teach your course your way

Your course is unique. So whether you'd like to build your own assignments, teach multiple sections, or set prerequisites, MyLab gives you the flexibility to easily create *your* course to fit *your* needs.

Improve student results

When you teach with MyLab, student performance improves. That's why instructors have chosen MyLab for over 15 years, touching the lives of over 50 million students.

Developing Employability Skills

In a recent survey by the Cooperative Institutional Research Program, 85 percent of college freshmen say that the main reason they decided to go to college is to secure a better job when they graduate. Whether you plan to pursue a career in entrepreneurship or some other field, the lessons you learn in your entrepreneurship course and from this book will help you secure a better job because the principles of entrepreneurship apply to *every* avenue of life. Whether you choose to start your own businesses or work for someone else in a for-profit or nonprofit organization, the skills you will learn in this course with the help of this book will be extremely valuable to you. Recent surveys show that employers value the following skill sets in the people they want to hire, and your course and this book will help you develop and enhance your abilities in these areas:

- *Critical Thinking and Problem Solving.* Every successful entrepreneur must engage in critical thinking and problem solving. Launching and running a successful company is a perpetual exercise in these areas. In this book, you can hone your critical thinking and problem-solving skills by tackling the "You Be the Consultant" and the "Beyond the Classroom" features that appear in every chapter. In addition, if one of the course requirements is to prepare a business plan, you will learn firsthand how to think critically and solve problems.

- *Communication Skills.* Successful entrepreneurs are good communicators. This book and the assignments you complete as part of the class will enhance your written and verbal communication skills. As part of entrepreneurs' search for capital, they must create well-written, coherent business plans and pitch their ideas to potential lenders and investors. Chapter 5, "Building a Solid Strategic Plan and Crafting a Winning Business Plan," teaches you how to write a plan that not only will help you build successful businesses but also will convince potential lenders and investors to put up financing for them. This chapter also explains how to make a successful business plan presentation. If the class involves developing a business plan (and perhaps participating in a business plan competition), you will learn important written and oral communication skills.

You Be the Consultant

College: The Ideal Place to Launch a Business

For growing numbers of students, college is not just a time of learning, partying, and growing into young adulthood; it is fast becoming a place for building a business. Today, more than 2,300 colleges and universities offer courses in entrepreneurship and small business management, and many of them have trouble meeting the demand for these classes. Today, entrepreneurship has become a mainstream activity on college campuses around the globe. Greater numbers of students are pursuing careers in entrepreneurship and see their college experience as an opportunity to get an early start not only by studying entrepreneurship but also by putting what they learn into practice. Bill Aulet, head of the Martin Trust Center for MIT Entrepreneurship, says that faculty members who teach entrepreneurship must nurture the spirit of a pirate in their students while teaching them how to execute their start-up plans with the precision of a Navy SEAL. In addition to regular classroom courses, colleges increasingly are building an extra dimension in their entrepreneurship programs, including internships with start-ups, consulting jobs with small businesses, mentoring relationships with other entrepreneurs, networking opportunities with potential investors, and participation in business plan competitions. Allan R. Cohen, the dean of the graduate program at Babson College, says that entrepreneurial education is a contact sport, and many colleges are adding boot camp–like courses to their curricula.

As the following examples prove, many college students expect to apply the entrepreneurial skills they are learning in their

and coaches often overlook talented athletes, who get only a handful of scholarship offers. That was the position that Samantha Weber found herself in during her last year of high school. Although things worked out well for Weber, who enrolled in Grove City College in Grove City, Pennsylvania, where she played varsity soccer for four years, the student-athlete decided to do something to help improve the recruiting process. During her senior year at Grove City College, while playing soccer and taking a full schedule of classes, Weber, just 21, created an athletic recruiting app, ProfilePasser, that connects high school athletes and college coaches at showcase tournaments. Student-athletes create their own profiles using the app, and when college coaches check in at a tournament, they have access to every player's profile and can use a search function to find athletes who fit a particular set of characteristics. ProfilePasser was one of only nine start-ups recently accepted into AlphaLab, Pittsburgh's leading business accelerator. Weber already has raised more than $25,000 in private financing and has attracted a "who's who" group of advisors, including her older sister, Alexa Andrzejewski, founder of Foodspotting, a company that OpenTable recently bought for $10 million.

FiscalNote

Students Jonathan Chen (University of Maryland), Timothy

Beyond the Classroom . . .

1-15. Choose an entrepreneur in your community and interview him or her. What's the "story" behind the business?

1-16. How well does the entrepreneur fit the entrepreneurial profile described in this chapter?

1-17. What advantages and disadvantages does the entrepreneur see in owning a business?

1-18. What advice would he or she offer to someone considering launching a business?

1-19. Select one of the categories under the section "The Cultural Diversity of Entrepreneurship" in this

chapter and research it in more detail. Find examples of business owners in that category and prepare a brief report for your class.

1-20. Search through recent business publications or their Web sites (especially those focusing on small companies, such as *Inc.* and *Entrepreneur*) and find an example of an entrepreneur, past or present, who exhibits the entrepreneurial spirit of striving for success in the face of failure. Prepare a brief report for your class.

- ***Teamwork.*** Research shows that businesses started by multiple founders have higher success rates than those started by solo entrepreneurs. Even if you choose to start businesses on your own, you will learn very quickly to rely on the help of other people to build it. In other words, you will learn the power of teamwork and collaboration. Chapter 17, "Building a New Venture Team and Planning for the Next Generation," will help you learn these skills.

- ***Leadership.*** One of an entrepreneur's most important skills is *leadership*. Effective leaders create a vision for their companies, convince other people to believe in and commit to it, develop a plan to implement the vision, and sustain the effort to accomplish it. Chapter 17, "Building a New Venture Team and Planning for the Next Generation," explains the behavior of successful leaders. Building a company will test and improve your leadership skills.

- ***Creativity.*** Whatever their business, employers are seeking creative talent. In Chapter 3, "Creativity and Innovation: Keys to Entrepreneurial Success," you will learn about the creative process and how to enhance both your personal creativity and the creativity of the people in your business. Throughout this book and course, you will experience the incredible creativity that entrepreneurs demonstrate.

- ***Ethics and Social Responsibility.*** One of a company's most valuable assets is its reputation. A company's reputation is critical to its success, but it also is quite fragile. One employee acting in an unethical fashion can destroy a company's good reputation. Employers seek employees in whom they can have confidence to do the right thing when faced with an ethical dilemma. In Chapter 2, "Ethics and Social Responsibility: Doing the Right Thing," you will learn basic principles of ethics and social responsibility. Often, entrepreneurs and employees fall into ethical traps that are cloaked in the garb of mundane decisions. This chapter will help you avoid these traps by making you aware of the issues and how to address them.

You may choose to use these skills in your own businesses or in someone else's business or nonprofit organization; either way, these skills are essential to your success. Moreover, it is only through the aggregate of your educational experiences that you will have the opportunity to develop many of these skills that employers have identified as critical to success in the workplace. As you can see, in this course, and specifically in this book, you will have the opportunity to develop and implement these skills.

The Pitch: Making the Business Plan Presentation

Entrepreneurs who are informed and prepared when requesting a loan or an investment impress lenders and investors. When entrepreneurs try to secure funding from lenders or investors, the written business plan most often precedes the opportunity to meet face-to-face. In recent years, some investors have moved away from requiring the submission of a formal business plan and instead have based their interest on the entrepreneur's presentation of the business model. However, even in these situations, sound planning is required.

Leadership: An Essential Part of an Entrepreneur's Job

To be successful, an entrepreneur must assume a wide range of roles, tasks, and responsibilities, but none is more important than the role of leader. Some entrepreneurs are uncomfortable assuming this role, but they must learn to be effective leaders if their companies are to grow and reach their potential. **Leadership** is the process of influencing and inspiring others to work to achieve a common goal and then giving them the power, the incentive, and the freedom to achieve it. Without leadership ability, entrepreneurs—and their companies—never rise above mediocrity. Entrepreneurs can learn to be effective leaders, but the task requires dedication, discipline, and hard work. In the past, business owners often relied on an autocratic management style, one built on command and control. Today's workforce is more knowledgeable, has more options, and is more skilled and, as a result, expects a different, more sophisticated style of leadership. Millennials, the 80 million Americans born between 1981 and 1997, now make up nearly 35 percent of the U.S. workforce and demand a more open, participative, inclusive, and flexible leadership typology.[1] Leadership is no lon-

Instructor Teaching Resources

Supplements available to instructors at www.pearsonhighered.com	Features of the supplement
Instructor's Manual	<ul><li>Chapter-by-chapter summaries</li><li>Additional examples and activities not included in the textbook</li><li>Teaching outlines</li><li>Sample syllabus</li><li>Case and chapter matrix</li><li>Solutions to all questions and problems in the book</li></ul>
Test Bank	More than 1,500 multiple-choice, true/false, and short-answer questions with these annotations: <ul><li>Difficulty level (1 for straight recall, 2 for some analysis, 3 for complex analysis)</li><li>Type (multiple choice, true/false, short answer, essay)</li><li>Learning outcome</li><li>AACSB learning standard (Written and Oral Communication, Ethical Understanding and Reasoning; Analytical Thinking; Information Technology; Interpersonal Relations and Teamwork; Diverse and Multicultural Work; Reflective Thinking; Application of Knowledge)</li></ul>

(continued)

Supplements available to instructors at www.pearsonhighered.com	Features of the supplement
Computerized TestGen	TestGen allows instructors to: • Customize, save, and generate classroom tests • Edit, add, or delete questions from the Test Item Files • Analyze test results • Organize a database of tests and student results
PowerPoints	Slides include all the graphs, tables, and equations in the textbook. PowerPoints meet accessibility standards for students with disabilities. Features include but are not limited to: • Keyboard and Screen Reader access • Alternative text for images • High-color contrast between background and foreground colors

This title is available as an eBook and can be purchased at most eBook retailers.

Essentials of Entrepreneurship and Small Business Management, 9/e, has stood the test of time and contains a multitude of both student- and instructor-friendly features. We trust that this edition will help the next generation of entrepreneurs to reach their full potential and achieve their dreams of success as independent business owners. It is their dedication, perseverance, and creativity that keep the world's economy moving forward.

Acknowledgments

Supporting every author is a staff of professionals who work extremely hard to bring a book to life. They handle the thousands of details involved in transforming a rough manuscript into the finished product you see before you. Their contributions are immeasurable, and I appreciate all they do to make this book successful. I have been blessed to work with the following outstanding publishing professionals:

- Dan Tylman, Portfolio Manager, who assisted us in many ways as we developed a revision plan for this edition. His input and vision proved to be a valuable resource.

- Susan McNally, Project Manager, who handled an arduous production process and, along the way, solved a plethora of problems for us.

We also extend a big "Thank You" to the corps of Pearson sales representatives, who work so hard to get our books into customers' hands and who represent the front line in our effort to serve our customers' needs. They are the unsung heroes of the publishing industry.

Special thanks to the following academic reviewers, whose ideas, suggestions, and thought-provoking input have helped to shape this and previous editions of our two books, *Essentials of Entrepreneurship and Small Business Management* and *Entrepreneurship and Effective Small Business Management*. We always welcome feedback from customers!

Lon Addams, *Weber State University*
Sol Ahiarah, *Buffalo State College*
Professor M. Ala, *California State University–Los Angeles*
Annamary Allen, *Broome Community College*
Tammy Yates Arthur, *Mississippi College*
Jay Azriel, *York College of Pennsylvania*
Bruce Bachenheimer, *Pace University*
Kevin Banning, *University of Florida*
Jeffrey Bell, *Dominican University*
Tom Bergman, *Northeastern State University*

Nancy Bowman, *Baylor University*
Jeff Brice, *Texas Southern University*
Michael S. Broida, *Miami University*
James Browne, *University of Southern Colorado*
Rochelle Brunson, *Alvin Community College*
John E. Butler, *University of Washington*
R. D. Butler, *Trenton State College*
Pamela Clark, *Angelo State University*
Richard Cuba, *University of Baltimore*
Kathy J. Daruty, *Los Angeles Pierce College*

Gita DeSouza, *Pennsylvania State University*

Stuart Devlin, *New Mexico State University*

John deYoung, *Cumberland Community College*

Michael Dickson, *Columbus State Community College*

Judy Dietert, *Southwest Texas State University*

Robert M. Donnelly, *St. Peter's College*

Steve Dunphy, *Indiana University Northwest*

Art Elkins, *University of Massachusetts*

W. Bruce Erickson, *University of Minnesota*

Frances Fabian, *University of Memphis*

Jan Feldbauer, *Austin Community College*

George J. Foegen, *Metropolitan State College of Denver*

Caroline E. W. Glackin, *Delaware State University*

Stephen O. Handley, *University of Washington–Bothell*

Charles Hubbard, *University of Arkansas*

Fred Hughes, *Faulkner University*

Samira B. Hussein, *Johnson County Community College*

Ralph Jagodka, *Mt. San Antonio College*

Theresa Janeczek, *Manchester Community College*

Robert Keimer, *Florida Institute of Technology*

E. L. (Betty) Kinarski, *Seattle University*

Kyoung-Nan Kwon, *Michigan State University*

Dick LaBarre, *Ferris State University*

Paul Lamberson, *Riverton, Wyoming*

Mary Lou Lockerby, *College of DuPage*

Martin K. Marsh, *California State University–Bakersfield*

Charles H. Matthews, *University of Cincinnati*

John McMahon, *Mississippi County Community College*

Michael L. Menefee, *Purdue University*

Julie Messing, *Kent State University*

William Meyer, *TRICOMP*

Milton Miller, *Carteret Community College*

John Moonen, *Daytona Beach Community College*

Linda Newell, *Saddleback College*

Marcella Norwood, *University of Houston*

David O'Dell, *McPherson State College*

John Phillips, *University of San Francisco*

Louis D. Ponthieu, *University of North Texas*

Ben Powell, *University of Alabama*

Frank Real, *St. Joseph's University*

William J. Riffe, *Kettering University*

Matthew W. Rutherford, *Virginia Commonwealth University*

Joseph Salamone, *State University of New York at Buffalo*

Manhula Salinath, *University of North Texas*

Nick Sarantakes, *Austin Community College*

Khaled Sartawi, *Fort Valley State University*

Terry J. Schindler, *University of Indianapolis*

Thomas Schramko, *University of Toledo*

Peter Mark Shaw, *Tidewater Community College*

Jack Sheeks, *Broward Community College*

Lakshmy Sivaratnam, *Johnson Community College*

Bill Snider, *Cuesta College*

Deborah Streeter, *Cornell University*

Ethné Swartz, *Fairleigh Dickinson University*

Yvette Swint-Blakely, *Lancing Community College*

John Todd, *University of Arkansas*

Charles Toftoy, *George Washington University*

Barry L. Van Hook, *Arizona State University*

Ina Kay Van Loo, *West Virginia University Institute of Technology*

William Vincent, *Mercer University*

Jim Walker, *Moorhead State University*

Bernard W. Weinrich, *St. Louis Community College*

Donald Wilkinson, *East Tennessee State University*

Gregory Worosz, *Schoolcraft College*

Bernard Zannini, *Northern Essex Community College*

We also are grateful to our colleagues who support us in the often grueling process of writing a book: Jerry Slice, Suzanne Smith, Jody Lipford, Tobin Turner, Cindy Lucking, Karen Mattison, and Rachel Childers of Presbyterian College and Mark Schenkel, Mark Phillips, and Jose Gonzalez of Belmont University.

Finally, we thank Cindy Scarborough and Ann Cornwall for their love, support, and understanding while we worked many long hours to complete this book. For them, this project represents a labor of love.

Special Note to Students

We trust that this edition of *Essentials of Entrepreneurship and Small Business Management* will encourage and challenge you to fulfill your aspirations as an entrepreneur and to make the most of your talents, experience, and abilities. We hope that you find this book to be of such value that it becomes a permanent addition to your personal library. We look forward to the day when we can write about your entrepreneurial success story on these pages.

Norman M. Scarborough
William Henry Scott III Chair in Entrepreneurship
Presbyterian College
Clinton, South Carolina
nmscarb@presby.edu

Jeffrey R. Cornwall
Jack C. Massey Chair in Entrepreneurship
Belmont University
Nashville, Tennessee
Jeff.cornwall@belmont.edu

1

The Foundations of Entrepreneurship

Dinis Tolipov/123RF

Learning Objectives

On completion of this chapter, you will be able to:

1. Define the role of the entrepreneur in business in the United States and around the world.

2. Describe the entrepreneurial profile.

3-A. Describe the benefits of entrepreneurship.

3-B. Describe the drawbacks of entrepreneurship.

4. Explain the forces that are driving the growth of entrepreneurship.

5. Explain the cultural diversity of entrepreneurship.

6. Describe the important role that small businesses play in our nation's economy.

7. Put failure into the proper perspective.

8. Explain how an entrepreneur can avoid becoming another failure statistic.

9. Discover how the skills of entrepreneurship, including critical thinking and problem solving, written and oral communication, teamwork and collaboration, leadership, creativity, and ethics and social responsibility, apply to every career choice and every avenue of life.

MyLab Entrepreneurship

⭐ **Improve Your Grade!**

If your instructor is using MyLab Entrepreneurship, visit **www.pearson.com/mylab/entrepreneurship** for videos, simulations, and writing exercises.

LO1

Define the role of the entrepreneur in business in the United States and around the world.

The World of the Entrepreneur

Welcome to the world of the entrepreneur! Despite economic swings, entrepreneurship is thriving in nearly every part of the world. Globally, nearly one in eight adults is actively engaged in launching a business.[1] In the United States alone, entrepreneurs launch more than 6.6 million businesses annually.[2] These people, who come from diverse backgrounds, are realizing that Great American Dream of owning and operating their own businesses. Some of them have chosen to leave the security of the corporate hierarchy in search of independence, others have been forced out of large corporations as a result of downsizing, and still others have from the start chosen the autonomy that owning a business offers. The impact these entrepreneurs make on the nation's economy goes far beyond their numbers, however. The resurgence of the entrepreneurial spirit they are spearheading is the most significant economic development in recent business history. These heroes of the business world are introducing innovative products and services, pushing back technological frontiers, creating new jobs, opening foreign markets, and, in the process, driving the U.S. economy.

Entrepreneurs, once shunned as people who could not handle a "real" job in the corporate world, now are the celebrities of the global economy. According to the Global Entrepreneurship Monitor, a global study of entrepreneurial activity across 60 nations, 68 percent of working adults around the world perceive entrepreneurs as having high status.[3] These entrepreneurs create companies, jobs, wealth, and innovative solutions to some of the world's most vexing problems, from relief for sore feet to renewable energy sources. "The story of entrepreneurship entails a never-ending search for new and imaginative ways to combine the factors of production into new methods, processes, technologies, products, or services," says one government economist who has conducted extensive research on entrepreneurship's impact.[4] In short, small business is "cool," and entrepreneurs are the rock stars of the business world.

One important indicator of the popularity of entrepreneurship is the keen interest expressed by young people in creating their own businesses. Globally, the highest rates of entrepreneurial activity are among people between the ages of 25 and 34, but entrepreneurship is the desired career path for many people who are still in college.[5] According to a recent study of global entrepreneurship, 65 percent of college students around the world aspire to be entrepreneurs, 27 percent of them immediately after graduation and 38 percent after gaining experience working for someone else. In the United States, 59 percent of college students in the survey expressed a desire to run their own businesses.[6] Although the percentage of people in the United States under 30 who own a share of a private company has declined to 3.6 percent from 6.1 percent in 2010, entrepreneurship remains the preferred career path for many young people (some of them while they are still in school), a more enticing option than joining the ranks of the pin-striped masses in major corporations.[7] When many young people hear the phrase "corporate America," they do not think of career opportunities; instead, negative images of the corporate world from the film *Office Space* come to mind. Others choose entrepreneurship out of necessity. The Kauffman Foundation reports that nearly one out of five entrepreneurs in the United States start businesses of their own because they cannot find jobs elsewhere.[8] The bottom line is that whatever drives your career choices, the probability that you will become an entrepreneur at some point in your life is quite high!

ENTREPRENEURIAL PROFILE: Riley Csernica and Chelsea Ex-Lubeskie: Tarian Braces While working on a class project in a bioengineering class at Clemson University, Riley Csernica and Chelsea Ex-Lubeskie were inspired to create a novel shoulder brace aimed at athletes. After graduating with degrees in biomedical engineering, Csernica and Ex-Lubeskie discovered that jobs in their field were extremely difficult to come by and began exploring the possibility of converting the shoulder brace they had developed as undergraduate students into a business. With the help of the business plan Csernica had built as part of a graduate course in Clemson's Entrepreneurship and Innovation program, the entrepreneurs, just 23 years old, launched Tarian Braces, a business based in Mt. Pleasant, South Carolina, that creates custom-fitted shoulder and ankle braces that give athletes better support and greater range of motion than traditional orthotic braces. To finance their business, Csernica and Ex-Lubeskie landed grants from South Carolina Launch and the National Science Foundation. They also competed in business plan competitions, where they met the director of The Harbor Accelerator, a business incubator in Mount Pleasant. They applied to be and were accepted as tenants of the incubator, where they continue to build their company, promoting it on social media, networking, calling on potential customers, and attending trade shows aimed at athletic trainers. Csernica and Ex-Lubeskie currently are developing new products for the shoulder (a commonly injured part of the body) and other joints, exploring other markets (for example, elderly people with physical impairments), and investigating the possibility of using 3-D printers to produce their braces. "College students should realize that starting a company is very difficult and requires a lot of sacrifice [both women still live with their parents so that they can funnel their resources into their business]," says Csernica. "However, there is no better time to give running your own company a shot. Working for ourselves is one of the most rewarding things Chelsea and I have ever done because we have the freedom to be our own bosses."[9] ■

Csernica and Ex-Lubeskie's journey is nothing new; entrepreneurship has been part of the fabric of the United States since its earliest days. Many of the nation's founding fathers were entrepreneurs. Thomas Jefferson started a nailery (a business that transformed iron into nails) in 1794 and purchased high-tech (at the time) nail-making machinery in 1796 to increase his company's production. Benjamin Franklin was an inventor and in 1729, at the age of 21, convinced several friends to finance his purchase of a newspaper that he renamed *The Pennsylvania Gazette*, a business that made him quite wealthy.[10] That same entrepreneurial spirit remains strong today. According to the Global Entrepreneurship Monitor, 12.6 percent of the U.S. population aged 18 to 64 is engaged in entrepreneurial activity. The level of entrepreneurial activity in the United States is slightly above the global average of 12.3 percent and is well above the average (8.7 percent) for innovation-driven economies (see Figure 1.1).[11]

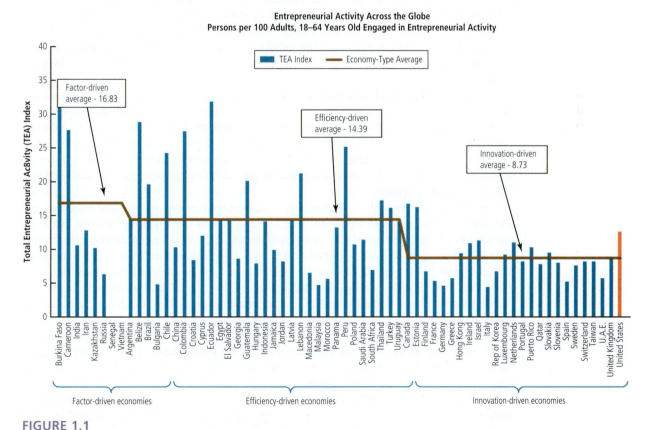

FIGURE 1.1

Entrepreneurial Activity Around the Globe

Source: Based on data from Donna Kelley, Slavica Singer, and Mike Herrington, *Global Entrepreneurship Monitor 2016/17 Global Report*, Global Entrepreneurship Monitor, 2017, pp. 39–102.

In recent years, large companies in the United States and elsewhere around the world have engaged in massive downsizing campaigns, dramatically cutting the number of managers and workers on their payrolls. This flurry of "pink slips" has spawned a new population of entrepreneurs—"castoffs" from large corporations (many of whom thought they would be lifetime ladder climbers in their companies) with solid management experience and many productive years left before retirement.

One casualty of this downsizing has been the long-standing notion of job security in large corporations, which all but destroyed the notion of loyalty and has made workers much more mobile. In the 1960s, the typical employee had worked for an average of four employers by the time he or she reached age 65; today, the average employee has had eight employers by the time he or she is 30.[12] Members of Generation X (those born between 1965 and 1980) and Generation Y (those born between 1981 and 2000), in particular, no longer see launching a business as being a risky career path. Having witnessed large companies lay off their parents after many years of service, these young people see entrepreneurship as the ideal way to create their own job security and career success. They are eager to control their own destinies.

This downsizing trend among large companies also has created a more significant philosophical change. It has ushered in an age in which "small is beautiful." Thirty years ago, competitive conditions favored large companies with their hierarchies and layers of management; today, with the pace of change constantly accelerating, fleet-footed, agile, small companies have the competitive advantage. These nimble competitors dart into and out of niche markets as they emerge and recede, they move faster to exploit opportunities the market presents, and they use modern technology to create within a matter of weeks or months products and services that once took years and all of the resources a giant corporation could muster. The balance has tipped in favor of small entrepreneurial companies. Alan Murray, editor of *Fortune* magazine, questions the necessity for large corporations, pointing out that today, from home (or anywhere there is an Internet connection), an entrepreneur can assemble a talented team of employees on LinkedIn, store intellectual property in the cloud, turn out products on 3-D printers, and reach customers around the world through the Internet. Howard Stevenson, Harvard's chaired professor of entrepreneurship, says, "Why is it so easy [for small companies] to compete against giant corporations? Because while [the giants] are studying the consequences, [entrepreneurs] are changing the world."[13]

Entrepreneurship also has become mainstream. Although launching a business is never easy, the resources available today make the job much simpler today than ever before. Thousands of colleges and universities offer courses in entrepreneurship, the Internet hosts a sea of information on launching a business, sources of capital that did not exist just a few years ago are now available, and business incubators hatch companies at impressive rates. Once looked down on as a choice for people unable to hold a corporate job, entrepreneurship is now an accepted and respected part of our culture.

Another significant shift in the bedrock of our nation's economic structure is influencing this swing in favor of small companies. The world is rapidly moving away from an industrial economy to a knowledge-based one. What matters now is not so much the traditional factors of production but *knowledge* and *information*. The final impact of this shift will be as dramatic as the move from an agricultural economy to an industrial one that occurred more than 200 years ago in the United States. A knowledge-based economy favors small businesses because the cost of managing and transmitting knowledge and information is very low, and computer and information technologies are driving these costs lower still.

Research suggests that entrepreneurial activity remains vibrant not only in the United States but elsewhere around the world as well. Entrepreneurs in every corner of the world are launching businesses thanks to technology that provides easy access to both local and global markets at start-up. Eastern European countries, China, Vietnam, and many other nations whose economies were state controlled and centrally planned are now fertile ground for growing small businesses. Table 1.1 shows some of the results from a recent study that ranks 137 nations according to the quality of the entrepreneurial environment they provide. Even countries that traditionally are not known as hotbeds of entrepreneurial activity, such as Malawi (which ranks 130th out of 137 nations in the GEDI survey), a growing country of nearly 18 million people in southeastern Africa, are home to promising start-up companies.

TABLE 1.1 **Entrepreneurship-Friendly Nations**

Which nations provide the best environment for cultivating entrepreneurship? A recent study ranked 137 countries on the quality of the entrepreneurial ecosystem in each nation using the Global Entrepreneurship and Development Index (GEDI), an index that includes a variety of factors that range from the availability of capital and workforce quality to attitudes toward entrepreneurs and technology available. The maximum GEDI score is 100.

GEDI Score, Top Ten Countries	GEDI Score, Bottom Ten Countries
1. United States 83.4	128. Venezuela 13.0
2. Switzerland 78.0	129. Nicaragua 12.7
3. Canada 75.6	130. Malawi 125
4. Sweden 75.5	131. Guinea 12.1
5. Denmark 74.1	132. Burkina Faso 11.9
6. Iceland 73.5	133. Bangladesh 11.8
7. Australia 72.5	134. Mauritania 11.6
8. United Kingdom 71.3	135. Sierra Leone 11.4
9. Ireland 71.0	136. Burundi 11.4
10. Netherlands 67.8	137. Chad 8.8

Source: Global Entrepreneurship Index, The Global Entrepreneurship and Development Institute, 2017, https://thegedi.org/global-entrepreneurship-and-development-index/.

ENTREPRENEURIAL PROFILE: Bellings Zkgaka Bellings Zkgaka lives in Usisya, a small village in Northern Malawi, where only 4 percent of residents complete high school and just 16 percent of the population is employed. Living in one of the most disadvantaged and remote regions of the world has not stifled Zkgaka's entrepreneurial spirit, however. To support his six children and three orphans he was raising, Zkgaka started a small grocery store. With a microloan of just £150 from Temwa, a nonprofit community development agency, Zkgaka was able to expand his store with a greater selection of goods, including ice pops, which have proved to be a popular item in the tropical heat. As sales and profits from his grocery store grew, Zkgaka spotted other entrepreneurial opportunities and opened a barber shop and a tailoring business. His companies now employ three people, and Zkgaka already is planning his next business venture: a restaurant. "There isn't one in my area," he says. "I want to set one up to employ more people, and I know some very good cooks!" Before starting his businesses, Zkgaka had great difficulty providing for his family; today, he is proud that his entrepreneurial ventures allow him to offer them a bright future.[14] ∎

Wherever they choose to start their companies, entrepreneurs continue to embark on one of the most exhilarating—and one of the most frightening—adventures ever known: launching a business. It's never easy, but it can be incredibly rewarding, both financially and emotionally. It can be both thrilling and dangerous, like living life without a safety net. Yet, true entrepreneurs see owning a business as the real measure of success. Lara Morgan started Pacific Direct, a British company that sells toiletries to the hotel industry, when she was just 23. Seventeen years later, she sold a majority share for £20 million and launched a second business, Company Shortcuts, a career coaching site aimed at entrepreneurs. "Running a business is not for the faint-hearted," says Morgan. "Yes, there are sacrifices to be made; yet I would change nothing of [my] journey. I have had the flexibility, freedom, and choice to do as I please because I choose to run my own company. It was by no means an easy road. I have been sued, risked my house as collateral, and have been through my own wars, not to mention weathering storms in the business and downturns created by wars. Yet, I am now wealthy beyond my wildest dreams." As an entrepreneur, she advises, "accept that you will make sacrifices, but the up side far outweighs the down side."[15] Like Lara Morgan, true entrepreneurs see owning a business as the real measure of success. Indeed, entrepreneurship often provides the only avenue for success to those who otherwise might have been denied the opportunity.

Who are these entrepreneurs, and what drives them to work so hard with no guarantee of success? What forces lead them to risk so much and to make so many sacrifices in an attempt to achieve an ideal? Why are they willing to give up the security of a steady paycheck working for someone else to become the last person to be paid in their own companies? This chapter will examine the entrepreneur, the driving force behind the U.S. economy.

LO2

Describe the entrepreneurial profile.

What Is an Entrepreneur?

Adapted from the French verb *entreprendre*, which means "to undertake" or "to attempt," the word "entrepreneur" was introduced in 1755 in economist Richard Cantillon's book *Essay on the Nature of Trade in General*. Cantillon defined an entrepreneur as a producer with nonfixed income and uncertain returns.[16] In a typical month, adults in the United States launch 550,000 new businesses, traveling down the path of entrepreneurship that Cantillon first wrote about more than 260 years ago. An **entrepreneur** is one who creates a new business in the face of risk and uncertainty for the purpose of achieving profit and growth by identifying significant opportunities and assembling the necessary resources to capitalize on them. Although many people come up with great business ideas, most of them never act on their ideas. Entrepreneurs do.

entrepreneur

one who creates a new business in the face of risk and uncertainty for the purpose of achieving profit and growth by identifying significant opportunities and assembling the necessary resources to capitalize on them.

Harvard Business School professor Howard Stevenson says that entrepreneurs spot opportunities, often a better way to do something, and do not feel constrained from pursuing it because they lack resources. In fact, entrepreneurs are *accustomed* to making do without resources.[17] In essence, entrepreneurs are *disrupters*, upsetting the traditional way of doing things by creating new ways to do them. They upend the status quo by playing the central role of entrepreneurs: catalysts who create change.

In his 1911 book *The Theory of Economic Development*, economist Joseph Schumpeter said that entrepreneurs are more than just business creators; they are change agents in society. The process of creative destruction, in which entrepreneurs create new ideas and new businesses that make existing ones obsolete, is a sign of a vibrant economy. Although this constant churn of businesses—some rising, others sinking, new ones succeeding, and many failing—concerns some people, in reality it is an indication of a healthy, growing, economic system that is creating new and better ways of serving people's needs and improving their quality of life and standard of living. Schumpeter compared the list of leading entrepreneurs to a popular hotel's guest list: always full of people but people who are forever changing.[18]

High levels of entrepreneurial activity translate into high levels of business formation and destruction and make an economy more flexible and capable of adapting to structural changes in the competitive landscape. "The United States has succeeded in part because of its dynamism, its high pace of job creation and destruction, and its high pace of churning workers," says John Haltiwanger, an economist who studies trends in entrepreneurship.[19] As disrupters, entrepreneurs are important change agents in the global economy, uprooting staid, old industries with fresh new business models that spot market opportunities and deliver the products and services that customers want.

Chance Yeh/Getty Images

ENTREPRENEURIAL PROFILE: Neil Parikh, Gabe Flateman, and Luke Sherwin: Casper Mattress Neil Parikh, Gabe Flateman, and Luke Sherwin, all in their mid-20s, believed that the $14 billion mattress industry, with its seemingly endless product variations, complicated delivery and return process, and high prices, was ripe for disruption. The trio of entrepreneurs decided to launch a business, Casper, in New York City that simplifies the process of buying a mattress. Casper produces only one mattress model that comes in six sizes and is priced from $500 to $950. Customers receive a 100-day trial period with every mattress. If a customer is dissatisfied at any time during the generous trial period, Casper picks up the mattress at no charge and provides a full refund. (Casper's return rate is extremely low, and the company donates returned mattresses to local charities.) Living in a large city where space is limited, the trio of entrepreneurs

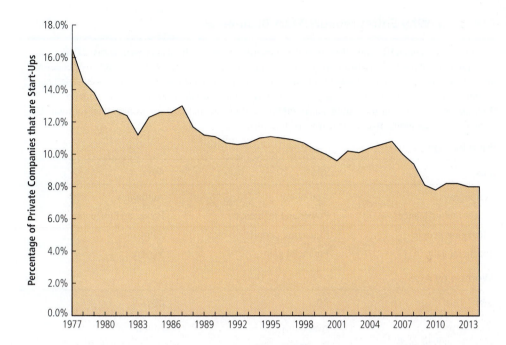

FIGURE 1.2

Percentage of Start-up Companies in the United States

Source: Business Dynamics Statistics Data Tables: Firm Age, U.S. Department of Commerce, U.S. Census Bureau, 2017, www.census.gov/ces/dataproducts/bds/data_firm.html.

focused their creative energy on packaging their company's mattresses for easy, compact shipping, which is free to customers. They developed a process for compressing a mattress so that it fits into a box roughly the size of a dorm refrigerator, which cost only one-tenth of what it costs to ship a full-size mattress. (Videos of "unboxing" a Casper mattress and watching it expand to its full size in less than a minute have become YouTube sensations.) By eliminating customers' pain points when buying mattresses, the entrepreneurs' have built a business model that works; Casper generated sales of $1 million in its first *month*. In its first full year of operation, sales were $20 million, and the company, now with 120 employees, has attracted $70 million in venture capital financing. Casper's founders are now focusing on other sleep products and use feedback from 15,000 customers who take part in the product development process. Casper recently invested 16 months of research, testing, and feedback from customers in developing a dual-layer pillow and followed a similar process to develop sheets that provide the perfect balance of softness and breathability.[20] ∎

Unfortunately, in the United States, the percentage of private companies that are start-up businesses (companies that are less than one year old), the primary source of the economy's healthy churn, has been declining since the late 1970s (see Figure 1.2). Although many entrepreneurs fail, some more than once, those who succeed earn the satisfaction of creating value for their customers and wealth for themselves—all while working at something that they love to do. Some of them create companies that change the world.

Researchers have invested a great deal of time and effort over the past few decades trying to paint a clear picture of "the entrepreneurial personality." Not surprisingly, the desire for autonomy is the single most important factor motivating entrepreneurs to start businesses (see Table 1.2). Although these studies have identified several characteristics entrepreneurs tend to exhibit, none of them has isolated a set of traits required for success.

We now turn to a brief summary of the entrepreneurial profile:[21]

1. *Desire for responsibility.* Entrepreneurs feel a deep sense of personal responsibility for the outcome of ventures they start. They prefer to be in control of their resources, and they use those resources to achieve self-determined goals. Deborah Sullivan, a lifelong serial entrepreneur, realized at the age of 16 that she did not want to spend her life working for others. "You're stuck by all of these different rules [when you work for someone else]," she says. "I wanted to create something for myself." Sullivan has been an entrepreneur since she was 22 years old, when she launched a hair salon and spa in Atlanta, Georgia. In 2012, at the age of 60, Sullivan started Consign Werks, a consignment shop in Greenville, South Carolina, which she says has been the most gratifying of her entrepreneurial ventures, perhaps

TABLE 1.2 Why Entrepreneurs Start Businesses

Noam Wasserman and Timothy Butler of the Harvard Business School surveyed nearly 2,000 entrepreneurs about their motivations for starting their businesses, analyzed the results by gender and age, and compared them to thousands of nonentrepreneurs. The primary motivator for entrepreneurs is autonomy, but security and a congenial work environment top the list for nonentrepreneurs. Entrepreneurs' source of motivation shifts slightly as they age, more so for women than for men. The following tables summarize the researchers' findings:

Men by Age

20s	30s	40s+
Autonomy	Autonomy	Autonomy
Power and influence	Power and influence	Power and influence
Managing people	Managing people	Altruism
Financial gain	Financial gain	Variety

Women by Age

20s	30s	40s+
Autonomy	Autonomy	Autonomy
Power and influence	Power and influence	Intellectual challenge
Managing people	Variety	Variety
Altruism	Altruism	Altruism

Source: Adapted from Leigh Buchanan, "The Motivation Matrix," *Inc.*, March 2012, pp. 60–62.

because she knew almost nothing about the business until she spent months researching and learning everything she could about consignment shops.[22]

2. *Preference for moderate risk.* Entrepreneurs are not wild risk takers but are instead *calculated* risk takers. Lee Lin, who left his job at a large investment bank to start RentHop, an online service that helps renters find the ideal apartment in New York City, says that entrepreneurs who risk everything typically do not stay in business very long. Lin says that to minimize risk, he manages his company's finances carefully and focuses on profitable growth opportunities.[23] A study of the founders of the businesses listed as *Inc.* magazine's fastest-growing companies found no correlation between risk tolerance and entrepreneurship. Researcher and former *Inc.* 500 chief executive officer Keith McFarland says that the belief that entrepreneurs are big risk takers just isn't true.[24] Unlike "high-rolling, riverboat" gamblers, entrepreneurs rarely gamble. Their goals may appear to be high—even impossible—in others' eyes, but entrepreneurs see the situation from a different perspective and believe that their goals are realistic and attainable.

Entrepreneurs usually spot opportunities in areas that reflect their passions, knowledge, backgrounds, or experiences, which increases their probability of success. Entrepreneurship is not like playing roulette, where chance determines whether one wins or loses. Instead, entrepreneurship involves recognizing and understanding opportunities in the market and taking calculated risks to capitalize on those opportunities by using their knowledge, skills, and abilities. Successful entrepreneurs do everything they can to stack the odds of winning in their favor. In other words, successful entrepreneurs are not as much risk *takers* as they are risk *eliminators*, systematically removing as many obstacles to the successful launch of their ventures as possible. Some of the most successful ways of eliminating risks include conducting a feasibility study for an idea, building and verifying a viable business model, and creating a sound business plan, which are the topics of Chapters 4 and 5.

3. *Willingness to break the rules.* Entrepreneurs have a different mindset from "adaptors," people who are conformists, abide by traditional rules, and thrive in a traditional corporate environment. Research shows that entrepreneurs are innovators who are willing to bend or

break the rules to disrupt business as usual.[25] The willingness of these mavericks to step outside the boundaries of traditional thinking is the source of their ability to innovate.

4. *Self-reliance.* Entrepreneurs must fill multiple roles to make their companies successful, especially in the early days of a start-up. Because their resources usually are limited, they end up performing many jobs themselves, even those that they know little about. Yet, entrepreneurs demonstrate a high level of self-reliance and do not shy away from the responsibility for making their businesses succeed. Perhaps that is why many entrepreneurs persist in building businesses even when others ridicule their ideas as follies.

5. *Confidence in their ability to succeed.* Entrepreneurs typically have an abundance of confidence in their ability to succeed and are confident that they chose the correct career path. They believe that they can accomplish just about anything! Entrepreneurs' high levels of optimism may explain why some of the most successful entrepreneurs have failed in business—often more than once—before finally succeeding. Milton Hershey, founder of one of the world's largest and most successful chocolate makers, started four candy businesses, all of which failed, before he launched the chocolate business that would make him famous.

 ENTREPRENEURIAL PROFILE: Kathryn Minshew, Alex Cavoulacos, and Melissa McCreery: The Muse At 24, Kathryn Minshew left her job at an elite management consulting firm to cofound PYP Media, a media company and career website aimed at young women. She and her cofounders ultimately split up, and Minshew lost her life savings, $20,000. Undaunted, Minshew, her co-founder Alexandra Cavoulacos and Melissa McCreery launched The Muse, a career-oriented website that provides free advice on topics ranging from interviewing skills to writing cover letters to negotiating a raise, job listings, explorations of various career paths, behind-the-scenes tours of companies that are hiring, one-on-one coaching services, and other helpful features. Minshew says that she and her cofounders survived the early days of their startup with a steady diet of ramen noodles and hope. The founders pitched The Muse to

Courtesy of The Muse

148 potential investors before landing a spot in – and a capital investment from – Y Combinator, the prestigious business accelerator in Silicon Valley. So far, Minshew and Cavoulacos (McCreery has since left the company to earn a PhD) have raised $28.7 million in financing, and The Muse attracts more than 6 million users each month. Looking back, Minshew says that PYP Media's failure was the best thing that ever happened to her because it set the stage for The Muse's success.[26] Like Minshew, smart entrepreneurs recognize that their failures can be the source of some of the lessons that lead them to their greatest successes. ∎

6. *Determination.* Some people call this characteristic "grit," the ability to focus intently on achieving a singular, long-term goal. It entails a combination of passion and perseverance. Studies show that grit is a reliable predictor of achievement and success, whether the goal involves launching a successful business, winning the Scripps National Spelling Bee, or excelling in professional sports.[27] (One recent study concludes that top performance in the National Football League's Combine, in which players who are entering the league's draft perform short physical and mental tasks, has no "consistent statistical relationship" to subsequent performance in the league.) Bob Mankoff, an aspiring cartoonist, demonstrated grit by submitting 2,000 cartoons to *The New Yorker* before the magazine ever accepted one. Mankoff went on to have a successful career as a cartoonist and is now the cartoon editor of *The New Yorker*.[28]

Successful entrepreneurs demonstrate high levels of determination, especially in the face of challenging circumstances. Research by Robert Fairlie of the University of California, Santa Cruz, shows that the Great Recession, which began in late 2007, spawned a surge in entrepreneurship and that the types of businesses entrepreneurs started were similar to those they start in prosperous times.[29] Perhaps that explains why 57 percent of the *Fortune* 500 companies were launched in either a recession, a "bear" market, or both.[30]

James Ransom/Food52

ENTREPRENEURIAL PROFILE: Amanda Hesser: Food52 Amanda Hesser took a circuitous route to entrepreneurship, working as a baker, a chef, and a leading food editor for *The New York Times* before launching her first business, a Web platform called Seawinkle that allowed users to consolidate their digital histories in one place. The business never gained traction, and Hesser decided to shut it down. Unfazed by the failure of her first venture, Hesser partnered with Merrill Stubbs to launch Food52, a Web site that provides a gathering place for foodies and includes recipes, captivating articles about food and its proper preparation, and food-related products. Like Seawinkle, Food52 struggled in its infancy and borrowed money from Stubbs's mother and Hesser's husband to stay afloat. Hesser and Stubbs persevered, however, eventually raising $9 million in capital from top-tier investors. Food52 employs 52 people, generates sales of more than $6 million annually, and is growing at nearly 900 percent a year.[31] ∎

7. *Desire for immediate feedback.* Entrepreneurs enjoy the challenge of running a business, and they like to know how they are doing and are constantly looking for feedback. Few things in life provide more meaningful feedback than an entrepreneur's business. Entrepreneurs have many ways, from sales and profits to the number of likes on Facebook and the number of followers on Instagram or Twitter, by which they measure their companies' success.

8. *High level of energy.* Entrepreneurs are more energetic than the average person. That energy may be a critical factor given the incredible effort required to launch a start-up company. Long hours and hard work are the rule rather than the exception, and the pace can be grueling. According to a survey by Bank of America, 72 percent of small business owners work more than 40 hours per week.[32] Another survey by Sage Software reports that 37 percent of business owners work more hours per week than they did just five years ago.[33] The phenomenon is not limited to the United States. A survey of British entrepreneurs reports that business owners there work an average of 52 hours per week, 63 percent more than the average worker.[34] Will Schroter, an entrepreneur who has launched numerous companies, including Go Big Network, an online community for entrepreneurs, says that he works at 1:30 in the morning because he is the founder of a start-up, and start-up founders often don't have time to sleep because their work is never-ending. He laughs, saying that he can catch up on his sleep when his company has grown and matured and has levels of managers to handle the immense workload that he now manages himself.[35]

9. *Competitiveness.* Entrepreneurs tend to exhibit competitive behavior, often early in life. They enjoy competitive games and sports and always want to keep score.

10. *Future orientation.* Entrepreneurs have a well-defined sense of searching for opportunities. They look ahead and are less concerned with what they did yesterday than with what they might do tomorrow. Not satisfied to sit back and revel in their success, real entrepreneurs stay focused on the future. Ever vigilant for new business opportunities, entrepreneurs *observe* the same events other people do, but they *see* something different. Dr. Rodney Perkins, an ear surgeon and medical entrepreneur, has started 16 health and life science companies, 3 of which have made initial public offerings, over the course of his career. Together, his companies are worth several billions of dollars. Now 80, Perkins, the quintessential entrepreneur, continues to look for the next opportunity. His most recent company, Soundhawk, based in Cupertino, California, markets an affordable smart listening system that integrates the latest advances in hearing science with the convenience of

modern wireless and mobile technology to help users hear better by filtering out background noise and amplifying only important sounds.[36]

Entrepreneurs see potential where most others see only problems or nothing at all, a characteristic that often makes them the objects of ridicule (at least until their ideas become huge successes). Whereas traditional managers are concerned with managing available *resources*, entrepreneurs are more interested in spotting and capitalizing on *opportunities*. In the United States, 84 percent of those engaged in entrepreneurial activity are **opportunity entrepreneurs**, people who start businesses because they spot an opportunity in the marketplace, compared to **necessity entrepreneurs**, those who start businesses because they cannot find work any other way.[37]

ENTREPRENEURIAL PROFILE: Morgan Hermand-Waiche: AdoreMe While attending business school, Morgan Hermand-Waiche wanted to surprise his girlfriend with a gift of fine lingerie but was surprised at the discrepancy between the prices of fine lingerie and his college student budget. Spotting an opportunity, Hermand-Waiche began researching the intimate apparel business. Using his experience and network of contacts at his family's fashion business in France, Hermand-Waiche developed a line of stylish, comfortable bras that he could sell to young women at an affordable price point. Because bras are difficult to produce (they typically contain 60 or more components), manufacturers he talked to would fill only large orders of 1 million units or more. Hermand-Waiche spent two years raising $11.5 million in investment capital before launching his e-commerce business, AdoreMe. Hermand-Waiche has since expanded the product line to include panties, loungewear, sleepwear, and bathing suits. AdoreMe now generates more than $43 million in annual sales and is opening stores in select markets across the United States.[38] ∎

Serial entrepreneurs, those who repeatedly start businesses and grow them to a sustainable size before striking out again, push this characteristic to the maximum. The majority of serial entrepreneurs are *leapfroggers*, people who start a company, manage its growth until they get bored, and then sell it to start another. A few are *jugglers* (or *parallel entrepreneurs*), people who start and manage several companies at once. Serial entrepreneurs instinctively know that the process of creating a company takes time, and many choose to pursue several ideas at the same time.[39] *The Entrepreneur State of Mind* study reports that 54 percent of business owners are serial entrepreneurs.[40] "The personality of the serial entrepreneur is almost like a curse," admits one entrepreneurial addict. "You see opportunities every day."[41] Serial entrepreneur Scott Painter has started 37 companies, not all of which have succeeded, including Pricelock, Advertise.com, and TrueCar. He started his first company, an auto detailing business, at age 14 and has been launching businesses ever since.[42]

It's almost as if serial entrepreneurs are addicted to launching businesses. "Starting a company is a very imaginative, innovative, energy-driven, fun process," says Dick Kouri, who has started 12 companies in his career and now teaches entrepreneurship at the University of North Carolina. "Serial entrepreneurs can't wait to do it again."[43]

11. *Skill at organizing.* Building a company "from scratch" is much like piecing together a giant jigsaw puzzle. Entrepreneurs know how to put together the right people to accomplish a task. Effectively combining people and jobs enables entrepreneurs to transform their visions into reality. "Great entrepreneurship is in the execution," says Eric Paley, an entrepreneur-turned-venture-capitalist.[44]

12. *Value of achievement over money.* One of the most common misconceptions about entrepreneurs is that they are driven wholly by the desire to make money. To the contrary, *achievement* seems to be entrepreneurs' primary motivating force; money is simply a way of "keeping score" of accomplishments—a symbol of achievement. What drives entrepreneurs goes much deeper than just the desire for wealth. Economist Joseph Schumpeter claimed that entrepreneurs have "the will to conquer, the impulse to fight, to prove oneself superior to others, to succeed for the sake, not of the fruits of success, but of success itself." Entrepreneurs, he says, experience "the joy of creating, of getting things done, or simply of exercising one's energy and ingenuity."[45]

opportunity entrepreneurs
entrepreneurs who start businesses because they spot an opportunity in the marketplace.

necessity entrepreneurs
entrepreneurs who start businesses because they cannot find work any other way.

serial entrepreneurs
entrepreneurs who repeatedly start businesses and grow them to a sustainable size before striking out again.

Other characteristics that entrepreneurs tend to exhibit include the following:

- *High degree of commitment.* Entrepreneurship is hard work, and launching a company successfully requires total commitment from an entrepreneur. Business founders often immerse themselves completely in their companies. Most entrepreneurs have to overcome seemingly insurmountable barriers to launch a company and to keep it growing. That requires commitment and fortitude. Phil Karlin, a former commercial lobster fisherman, invested his entire life savings to start North Fork Smoked Fish, a company in Greenport, New York, that sells smoked fish and seafood and fish patés made from fish caught fresh off the coast of Long Island to shoppers as well as some of New York City's top restaurants. At 54, Karlin recognizes the risk he has taken, but his experience coupled with the quality and uniqueness of the company's products gives him confidence that he will succeed.[46]

- *Tolerance for ambiguity.* Entrepreneurs tend to have a high tolerance for ambiguous, ever-changing situations, the environment in which they most often operate. This ability to handle uncertainty is critical because these business builders constantly make decisions using new, sometimes conflicting information gleaned from a variety of unfamiliar sources. Based on his research, entrepreneurial expert Amar Bhidé says that entrepreneurs exhibit a willingness to jump into ventures even when they cannot visualize what the ultimate outcome may be.[47]

- *Creativity.* One of the hallmarks of entrepreneurs is creativity. They constantly come up with new product or service ideas, unique ways to market their businesses, and innovative business models. Their minds are constantly at work developing unique business ideas. Jennifer Lewis, a professor of engineering and applied sciences, is the cofounder and CEO of Voxel8, a company that specializes in 3-D printing technology capable of producing finished electronic devices. Rather than produce components ready for assembly like traditional 3-D printers do, Voxel8's process uses materials such as conductive inks, flexible silicones, and high-strength epoxies to print embedded conductors, wires, and batteries into finished functional parts that require no assembly. Voxel8 recently landed $12 million in venture capital to continue developing and marketing its innovative technology.[48] You will learn more about the creative process and how to stimulate entrepreneurial creativity in Chapter 3.

- *Flexibility.* One hallmark of true entrepreneurs is their ability to adapt to the changing needs and preferences of their customers and the changing demands of the business environment. In this rapidly changing global economy, rigidity often leads to failure. Successful entrepreneurs learn to be masters of improvisation, reshaping and transforming their businesses as conditions demand. Research by Saras Sarasvathy, a professor at the University of Virginia's Darden School of Business, shows that entrepreneurs excel at effectual reasoning, which does not begin with a specific goal. Instead, effectual thinkers are like explorers setting out on voyages into uncharted waters. Like explorers, entrepreneurs set goals, but their goals are flexible. Sarasvathy compares entrepreneurs to iron chefs, who prepare sumptuous meals when handed a hodgepodge of ingredients and given the task of using their creativity to come up with an appetizing menu. Corporate CEOs, on the other hand, develop a plan to prepare a specific dish and then create a process for making that dish in the most efficient, expeditious fashion.[49]

- *Resourceful.* Entrepreneurs excel at getting the most out of the resources that are available—however limited they may be. They are the MacGyvers of the business world, able to accomplish almost any task using their street smarts, despite having only minimal resources. (*MacGyver* was a television show that ran from 1985 to 1992 and featured a secret agent whose extensive knowledge of science enabled him to develop innovative, spontaneous solutions to the catastrophic situations he often faced. For instance, MacGyver once used a lens from a pair of binoculars to reflect a laser beam back to its source and destroy the device.)

  Entrepreneurs rarely have "enough" resources; however, they know how to maximize the resources they have. They are skilled at **bootstrapping**, a strategy that

bootstrapping
a strategy that involves conserving money and cutting costs during start-up so that entrepreneurs can pour every available dollar into their businesses.

involves conserving money and cutting costs during start-up so that entrepreneurs can pour every available dollar into their businesses.

Mike McGregor/Contour/Getty Images

ENTREPRENEURIAL PROFILE: Sara Blakely: Spanx In 1998, Sara Blakely was a door-to-door fax salesperson. Tired of dealing with pantyhose that bunched up, she developed a slimming version of what she called *shapewear*, footless pantyhose designed to lie smoothly under a woman's clothing. She invested her life savings of $5,000 to create a company, Spanx, to market her invention. Her Atlanta apartment was the company's headquarters, and her bathroom was the order fulfillment center. Blakeley knew that she should file for a patent for her shapewear products but did not have enough money to hire a patent attorney, so she spent many evenings in the library at nearby Georgia Tech University, researching patent law. She wrote her own patent application (successfully) and spent weekends driving more than five hours to North Carolina, calling on hosiery mills, trying to convince one of them to manufacture her product. After a "show and tell" session with a Neiman Marcus buyer, Blakely landed her product in seven of the retailer's stores. Then Oprah Winfrey touted Spanx on her list of favorite things, and the company's sales took off. Today, the Spanx line includes more than 200 items, and because Blakely bootstrapped her company, which is valued at more than $1 billion, she still owns 100 percent of it. Spanx made Blakely the youngest self-made female billionaire in the world (and she has pledged to give away most of her wealth).[50] ■

- *Willingness to work hard.* Entrepreneurs work hard to build their companies, and there are no shortcuts around the workload. In his book *Outliers: The Story of Success*, Malcolm Gladwell observes that the secret to success in business (or sports, music, art, or any other field) is to invest at least 10,000 hours practicing and honing one's skills. For instance, Mark Cuban, billionaire owner of the Dallas Mavericks of the National Basketball Association and founder of Broadcast.com, the leading provider of multimedia and streaming on the Internet (which he sold to Yahoo! for $5.7 billion), says that he worked for seven years without taking a day off to launch his first business, Micro-Solutions, a computer systems integrator. Cuban spent his days making sales calls, and at night and on weekends he studied and practiced to learn everything he could about computers.[51] Entrepreneurs capitalize on opportunities through sheer hard work. A great idea may come to an entrepreneur in a flash, but building a successful business from a great idea takes time and lots of hard work.[52]
- *Tenacity.* Obstacles, obstructions, and defeat typically do not dissuade entrepreneurs from doggedly pursuing their visions. They simply keep trying. Hurricane Sandy nearly wiped out Jackie Summers' company, Jack from Brooklyn, which produces a unique artisanal alcoholic beverage called sorel in an old warehouse in Brooklyn's historic Red Hook district. Despite the loss of product, equipment, and sales, Summers persevered and rebuilt his business. Summers's spirit of tenacity, willingness to concentrate on a single insurmountable task each day, and accomplishment of each task allowed him to recover from the devastating loss.[53] Noting the obstacles that entrepreneurs must overcome, economist Joseph Schumpeter argued that success is "a feat not of intellect but of will."

What conclusion can we draw from the volumes of research conducted on the entrepreneurial personality? Entrepreneurs are not of one mold; no one set of characteristics can predict who will become entrepreneurs and whether they will succeed. Indeed, *diversity* seems to be a central characteristic of entrepreneurs. One astute observer of the entrepreneurial personality explains, "Business owners are a culture unto themselves—strong, individualistic people who scorn convention—and nowadays, they're driving the global economy."[54] Indeed, entrepreneurs tend to be nonconformists, a characteristic that seems to be central to their views of the world and to their success.

FIGURE 1.3

Most Important Qualities of an Entrepreneur

Source: Ryan Westwood, "What Traits Do We Need to Succeed as Entrepreneurs?" *Forbes*, September 4, 2015, www.forbes.com/sites/ ryanwestwood/2015/09/04/ what-traits-do-we-need-to- succeed-as-entrepreneurs/ #4d7f537f8ff4.

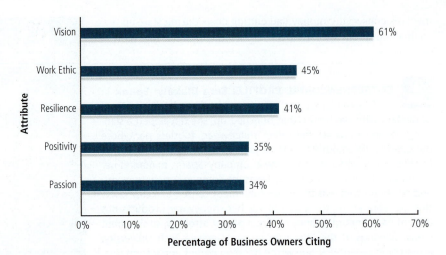

As you can see from the examples in this chapter, *anyone*, regardless of age, race, gender, color, national origin, or any other characteristic, can become an entrepreneur (although not everyone should). There are no limitations on this form of economic expression. Entrepreneurship is not a mystery; it is a practical discipline. Entrepreneurship is not a genetic trait; it is a skill that most people can learn. It has become a very common vocation. The editors of *Inc.* magazine claim, "Entrepreneurship is more mundane than it's sometimes portrayed. . . . You don't need to be a person of mythical proportions to be very, very successful in building a company."[55] Figure 1.3 summarizes the qualities that company founders say are most important to entrepreneurs.

LO3A

Describe the benefits of entrepreneurship.

The Benefits of Entrepreneurship

Surveys show that owners of small businesses believe they work harder, earn more money, and are more satisfied than if they worked for someone else. Before launching any business venture, every potential entrepreneur should consider the benefits of small business ownership.

Opportunity to Create Your Own Destiny

Owning a business provides entrepreneurs the independence and the opportunity to achieve what is important to them. Entrepreneurs want to "call the shots" in their lives, and they use their businesses to make that desire a reality. Numerous studies of entrepreneurs in several countries report that the primary incentive for starting their businesses is "being my own boss." "Owning your own business means you have some say in deciding what your destiny is going to be," says Kathy Mills, founder of Strategic Communications, a highly successful information technology company in Louisville, Kentucky.[56]

Opportunity to Make a Difference

social entrepreneurs
entrepreneurs who use their skills not only to create profitable businesses but also to achieve economic, social, and environmental goals for the common good.

Increasingly, entrepreneurs are starting businesses because they see an opportunity to make a difference in a cause that is important to them. Known as **social entrepreneurs**, these business builders seek innovative solutions to some of society's most vexing problems. They use their skills not only to create profitable business ventures but also to achieve social and environmental goals for society as a whole. Their businesses often have a triple bottom line that encompasses economic, social, and environmental objectives. These entrepreneurs see their businesses as mechanisms for achieving social goals that are important to them as individuals. Whether it is providing low-cost, sturdy housing for families in developing countries or establishing a recycling program to preserve Earth's limited resources, these entrepreneurs are finding ways to combine their concerns for social issues and their desire to earn a good living.

You Be the Consultant

Making the Most of an Opportunity

The inspiration for business ideas may strike entrepreneurs at any time and sometimes comes from unexpected sources. Many people come up with creative ideas for businesses, but what sets entrepreneurs apart is their willingness to act on their ideas.

Billiam Jeans

While Bill Mitchell was a student at Clemson University, he took up an atypical hobby: tailoring clothing for his friends. Mitchell reworked everything from ties and tuxedos to bridesmaid dresses and pants, even though he had no formal sewing training. Mitchell learned his sewing skills by reverse engineering, taking apart garments to see how they were put together. After his parents purchased a used sewing machine at a Goodwill store, Mitchell began making jeans for his friends, and within a year, he had a waiting list of 400 people. That prompted him to start Billiam (his college nickname) Jeans, a company that makes custom-fitted jeans, in his parents' basement.

Mitchell's business continued to grow, which prompted a move to the back of a climbing gym. He soon outgrew that space, which led him to sell his car to pay for a lease on a 1,600-square-foot storefront in a hip, historic section in Greenville, South Carolina, a city that a generation ago was a hub of the textile industry. Today, Mitchell, three employees, and two full-time interns make custom jeans aimed primarily at men between the ages of 30 and 50 on vintage cutting tables, rivet presses, and sewing machines that are at least 60 years old and often are repaired with screwdrivers, prayers, and tweezers, according to Mitchell. The company uses only one type of denim fabric, raw selvage denim, which is made on 100-year-old Draper looms in Greensboro, North Carolina, by one of the most renowned mills in the world, Cone Mills. The supply of this high-quality, finely woven denim fabric is limited, but jeans connoisseurs appreciate showing off the distinctive weave pattern when they turn up the cuffs on their custom-fitted jeans, which come in three leg styles and four different colors and start at $200. Billiam Jeans recently expanded its product line to include women's jeans and leather belts and bracelets and plans to add denim jackets, denim shorts, and chambray shirts.

Billiam Jeans is an anachronism, blending old-world techniques to make its denim products by hand and using modern marketing techniques, particularly social media marketing, to build the Billiam brand. Although sales have grown 330 percent each year for the last three years, Mitchell has not had to resort to outside financing. Several companies have approached Mitchell about distributing Billiam jeans internationally, but for now, he is content to have his company focus on local sales and grow organically.

ZVerse

John Carrington and Kevin Maloney left their corporate careers behind to start ZVerse, a company in Columbia, South Carolina, that specializes in translating two-dimensional images into three-dimensional works of art using the latest in 3-D printer technology. Launched in a business incubator, the entrepreneurs discovered a unique niche when representatives from the athletic department at Carrington's alma mater, the University of South Carolina, asked the company to create a unique gift to present to war heroes at a Salute to the Troops ceremony during halftime at a football game. Carrington and Maloney used their 3-D printing expertise to create a three-dimensional replica of the University of South Carolina football stadium that was so detailed that it included the image of a replay on the jumbo video screen. In the past, companies that sold stadium replicas to fans purchased them from foreign manufacturers and had to purchase large volumes of inventory, often 10,000 or more units. ZVerse's technology mastery allows the company to produce highly detailed replicas in small production runs, minimizing the risks that its retail customers take of being stuck with excess inventory. The sources of the company's competitive advantage are its speed, flexibility, and focus on customer service.

Spotting a large potential market, Carrington and Maloney decided not to become just another 3-D printing service company and negotiated licensing arrangements with 24 major universities from the Southeastern Conference and the Atlantic Coast Conference to sell replicas of their stadiums and mascots. ZVerse recently graduated from the incubator where it was hatched and moved into a large manufacturing facility that allows it to meet the rapidly growing demand for its unique products. Carrington and Maloney also successfully raised $1 million in venture capital to fuel the company's next round of growth. In two years, ZVerse's workforce grew from 3 employees to 16, and Carrington and Maloney are negotiating deals with other colleges and universities as well as NASCAR and Major League Baseball to produce replicas of race tracks and baseball stadiums. They also are working to license their proprietary process to other companies that are engaged in 3-D printing.

1. What benefits do entrepreneurs such as Bill Mitchell, John Carrington, and Kevin Maloney gain from creating businesses of their own rather than working for someone else?

2. What risks did these entrepreneurs take on when they started their businesses?

3. Is the way that these entrepreneurs discovered their business opportunities typical? Explain.

Sources: Based on Stephanie Burnette, "Decking Out Dad," *Greenville News*, June 7, 2014, pp. D1–D2; Ruta Fox, "Jeans Genius," *Town*, December 26, 2012, www.towncarolina.com/features/36-fashion/666-jeans-genius.html; Roddie Burris, "Tiny Stadium Replicas a Touchdown for S.C. Firm," *The State*, April 21, 2014, www.thestate.com/2014/04/21/3400897/tiny-stadium-replicasa-touchdown.html.

Courtesy of Katherine Kirsch, Chief Marketing Officer, Sisu Global Health Inc.

ENTREPRENEURIAL PROFILE: Carolyn Yarina: CentriCycle As part of a class project in a freshman engineering class at the University of Michigan, Carolyn Yarina discovered that one of the greatest needs of rural health workers in developing nations is a centrifuge that could operate without electricity. By the end of the semester, Yarina and a team of students designed a human-powered centrifuge made from bicycle parts called the CentriCycle. The project stirred Yarina's interest in entrepreneurship, and she began taking courses in that field, including one on social entrepreneurship that enabled her to go to India. Soon, Yarina and fellow student Katie Kirsch teamed up with University of Michigan graduate Gillian Henker, who was developing Hemafuse, an auto-transfusion pump for blood, to create Sisu Global Health, a socially conscious, for-profit business that focuses on medical products designed to meet the needs of healthcare professionals in developing countries. After field tests, the entrepreneurs redesigned the CentriCycle as a hand-operated device, but their goal remains the same: to use their business to improve the quality of healthcare in developing nations. Yarina, CEO of Sisu Global Health, says that she never expected to be the head of an entrepreneurial venture, but she now realizes that entrepreneurship involves more than merely making money; it involves making a positive impact on the world.[57] ■

Yarina, Kirsch, and Henker are just two of millions of social entrepreneurs who have started for-profit businesses with a broader goal of making the world a better place to live.

Opportunity to Reach Your Full Potential

Too many people find their work boring, unchallenging, and unexciting. But not entrepreneurs! To them, there is little difference between work and play; the two are synonymous. Entrepreneurs' businesses become their instruments for self-expression and self-actualization. They know that the only boundaries on their success are those imposed by their own creativity, enthusiasm, and vision, not limits artificially created by an organization (e.g., the "glass ceiling").

Owning a business gives them a sense of empowerment. While Elizabeth Elting was in college, she worked in the translation industry, where she saw plenty of room for improvement. After she met Phil Shawe at New York University's Stern School of Business, the pair decided to start TransPerfect Translations to provide timely, accurate translation services to companies around the globe. Launched from a dorm room, TransPerfect Translations now employs more than 2,000 people in 80 offices on six continents and generates annual sales of more than $350 million. Elting and Shawe have financed the companies' growth without any external financing. "We like not having to answer to other people, to spend time explaining exactly where we are to investors," says Elting. "We like it that it's just the two of us. There's nothing else we'd rather be doing every day."[58]

Opportunity to Reap Impressive Profits

Although money is not the primary force driving most entrepreneurs, the profits their businesses can earn are an important motivating factor in their decisions to launch companies. A recent survey by online lender OnDeck reports that 65 percent of small business owners believe that they are in a better financial position running their own businesses than working for a company in the same field.[59] Several studies, including one by the Institute for the Study of Labor, confirm this belief; the median salary for entrepreneurs is 18 percent higher than that for employed workers.[60] Entrepreneurs are not constrained by the boundaries that corporate hierarchies impose on their employees; they are free to create value by making the best use of their experience, skills, abilities, and ideas and, as a result, reap the financial benefits of their creative efforts. Most entrepreneurs never become superrich, but many of them do become quite wealthy. Indeed, nearly 75 percent of those on the *Forbes* list of the 400 richest Americans are first-generation entrepreneurs (and most of the others are part of successful family businesses)![61] In addition, the net worth of the entrepreneurs in the *Forbes* list of the 40 richest entrepreneurs under

You Be the Consultant

Decoding the DNA of the Entrepreneur

Management consulting firm Ernst & Young has developed the following model of an entrepreneur.

Nucleus

At the center of the model lie the entrepreneur's complementary characteristics of an opportunistic mindset and an attitude of tolerance of risk and failure.

Opportunistic mindset. One of the hallmarks of entrepreneurs is their ability to spot opportunities where others do not. They know that although disruptions create problems, they also create opportunities for those who are prepared to capitalize on them. Grace and Seung Paik and their three children ate many meals at restaurants while their house was being remodeled. Like most other young children, the little Paiks often grew restless, crumpled up their placemats, and wanted to run around the restaurant. To keep her children occupied while dining out, Seung created reusable placemats with chalkboards on one side so that the children could draw and doodle. When the food arrived, they simply flipped the mats over and had traditional placemats. When other parents began asking Seung where they could get similar placemats, she decided to launch a business selling them through local boutiques. Seung has expanded the

company's product line to include smocks, aprons, tote bags, chalk, baby bibs, and other items. Her company, Jaq Jaq Bird, has been featured on HGTV, CNBC, and Rachael Ray TV shows as well as on the Web site Daily Candy. It now sells its products through major retailers, including Nordstrom, Target, and The Container Store.

Tolerance of risk and failure. Most people are risk averse. Most entrepreneurs don't take extraordinary risks, but they accept risk as a natural part of achieving big goals. Mark Coker, CEO of Smashwords, a publisher of e-books, says that as an entrepreneur, he cannot afford to make too many mistakes; otherwise, his business will fail. However, he admits that if he is not making enough mistakes, that means he is not taking enough risks, and the business will fail. Keri Ferry was working long days in a private equity firm when she was inspired by retail models offering high-quality items at low prices directly to consumers. Ferry quit her job and launched 25 Bedford, a direct-to-consumer e-tail collection of quality mix-and-match professional separates aimed at young professional women like herself. Each piece in the collection, which is made in New York City's garment district, is simple, elegant, and designed to go with every other piece, maximizing the number of clothing combinations

(continued)

You Be the Consultant (continued)

a woman has. As an entrepreneur, Ferry, who financed 25 Bedford with money from family and friends, says that every morning when she makes out her to-do list, she realizes that she does not know how to do any of the items but she loves figuring things out. She also admits that her journey has required a willingness to take some risks.

Inner Ring

The inner ring of the model shows six characteristics that are integral parts of the entrepreneurial personality.

Drive, tenacity, and persistence. To bring their business ideas to life, entrepreneurs must demonstrate drive, tenacity, and persistence. Entrepreneurs must overcome countless obstacles on their way to building successful businesses.

Architect of own vision; passionate and focused. As you have learned in this chapter, entrepreneurs enjoy being in control of their own destinies, and they are passionate, even fanatical, about their business ideas. David Walsh, a former CIA operative and founder of Prescient Edge, a security integration and technology development business in McLean, Virginia, says that being solely responsible for every facet of his business can be a challenge, but it also means that there are no limits on his ability to create value. Jo Malone founded a highly successful cosmetics company at her kitchen table in London with four plastic mixing jugs for fragrances that she named after herself and ultimately sold to Estée Lauder. After a successful battle with cancer, Malone started a second company, Jo Loves, that sells a line of bath and body products, including unique fragrances, in a shop on London's Elizabeth Street. Malone's passion for her business and its products is driving her company's rapid growth. Malone says that successful entrepreneurs need three qualities: creativity, resilience, and passion.

Build an ecosystem of finance, people, and know-how. Smart entrepreneurs know that they cannot do everything themselves and build a team of professionals to nurture and protect the business. While attending the University of South Carolina, Allen Stephenson dreamed of starting a business. Having operated a successful lawn care business in high school, Stephenson had a head start on the road to entrepreneurship. His inspiration came one day as a result of a semester he spent abroad in Italy, where he saw firsthand fine clothing made with attention to detail; he took a pair of scissors to his collection of polo shirts, cut away what he considered to be the best features of each one, and stitched them back together into a model "Frankenstein" shirt. He spent the next year working with several textile industry veterans, perfecting his design for the perfect polo shirt and having samples made by 11 factories in four countries. Stephenson launched Southern Tide, ordered 5,500 shirts, and began calling on independent men's shops to sell them. Most shop owners declined, which prompted him to start giving the owners a few shirts to wear or to give to their best customers. The handouts accelerated sales quickly, and Stephenson made an important and selfless decision to bring in an experienced CEO, Jim Twining. "I was sure [the business] was going to work if I just kept working at it and getting the right people together," he says. "I knew it wouldn't work with what and who I alone knew at the time." Twining led Southern Tide in

a $1.8 million round of equity financing and developed a strategic plan to guide its growth. Today, Southern Tide's product line has grown well beyond the perfect polo shirt to include pants, T-shirts, hats, belts, shoes, swimwear, and more and is sold in nearly 600 stores in 43 states and on its Web site. Many publications, including *Inc.* and *Forbes*, have recognized Stephenson's Southern Tide as one of the fastest-growing small companies in the United States.

Seek out market niches and gaps. Entrepreneurs are adept at finding lucrative niches and gaps in the market that large businesses often overlook. After the real estate market collapsed, David Campbell left the industry and started Boxman Studios, a company based in Charlotte, North Carolina, that is focused on a unique market niche: transforming shipping containers into portable, upscale, turn-key hospitality suites aimed at companies participating in special events and marketing promotions or businesses establishing temporary pop-up shops. With annual sales of more than $4 million, Boxman Studios counts among its customers many small companies as well as major corporations such as Red Bull, Google, Razorfish, Ford, and Delta Air Lines.

Live what you believe; build success, culture, and values. As you have seen, entrepreneurs create company cultures that reflect their values and belief systems. "You live what you believe," says Turner Davila, founder of Katcon, an automotive supplier in Santa Catarina, Mexico. Entrepreneurs often build businesses that seek to achieve financial, social, and environmental goals that make their communities—and the world—better places to live.

Be a nonconformist and a team player. Entrepreneurs tend to be nonconformists, choosing to do things their own way. Just as many traditional managers would find the life of an entrepreneur unsettling, so too would entrepreneurs find the boundaries, rules, and traditions of corporate life stifling and boring. Yet successful entrepreneurs recognize the importance of being team players. They understand that accomplishing big goals requires a broad set of skills that no one person has. Sisters Sophie LaMontagne and Kallinis Berman were very close growing up but went their separate ways after college. LaMontagne became a biotech expert, and Berman worked in the fashion industry. In 2008, the sisters reunited to realize a dream that they had had since childhood: owning a bakery together. "We quit our jobs, borrowed our grandmother's cake recipes, and took a leap of faith," says LaMontagne. Today, the sisters are at the helm of Georgetown Cupcake, a bakery that has grown from a two-person shop outside of Washington, DC, to a 350-person operation with stores in New York City, Boston, Atlanta, and Los Angeles.

Outer Ring

The model's outer ring includes many of the entrepreneurial traits discussed in this chapter, including resilience, teamwork, innovation, passion, leadership, integrity, quality, customer focus, flexibility, and vision.

1. How do the characteristics at the model's nucleus—opportunistic mindset and tolerance of risk and failure—fit together in the entrepreneur's mind?

(continued)

You Be the Consultant

2. Work with a team of your classmates to interview at least one entrepreneur. Does he or she fit the model described here? Explain, giving specific examples from your interview.

Sources: Based on "Barbara Haislip, "No More Restless Children at Restaurants?" *Wall Street Journal*, May 2, 2016, p. R3; "The Inc. 500," *Inc.*, September 2014, p. 194; Alev Aktar, "Chic Staples," *Entrepreneur*, September 2014, p. 22; "The Inc. 500," *Inc.*, September 2014, p. 181; Dinah Eng, "The Sweet Smell of Jo Malone's

Success," *Fortune*, February 24, 2014, pp. 17–20; David Campbell, "How I Turned Old Containers into a Portable Party," *Inc.*, September 2014, p. 131; "Nature or Nurture? Decoding the DNA of the Entrepreneur," Ernst & Young, 2011, pp. 14–21; Amy Clarke Burns, "The Buzz About Honey," *Greenville News*, January 20, 2013, pp. 1E–2E; Lillia Callum-Penso, "An Original by Design," *Greenville News*, October 14, 2012, pp. 1E–2E; Lillia Callum-Penso, "Feeding a Passion," *Greenville News*, November 11, 2012, pp. 1E–2E; Julia Savacool, "The Sweet Success of Sisters," *USA Weekend*, August 3–5, 2012, pp. 6–7; Amy Clarke Burns, "Riding the Tide," *Greenville News*, August 5, 2012, pp. 1E–2E; Lillia Callum-Penso, "Crafting a Culture," *Greenville News*, July 29, 2012, pp. 1E–2E.

age 40 ranges from $50 billion (Mark Zuckerberg, founder of Facebook) to $270 million (Kyle Vogt, co-founder of Justin.tv, Twitch, and Cruise Automation).[62] People who own their own businesses are four times more likely to be millionaires than those who are employed by others. According to Russ Alan Prince and Lewis Schiff, authors of *The Middle Class Millionaire*, more than 80 percent of middle-class millionaires, those people with a net worth between $1 million and $10 million, own their own businesses or are part of professional partnerships. (They also work an average of 70 hours a week.)[63] Indeed, the typical millionaire's business is not a glamorous, high-tech enterprise; more often, it is something much less glamorous—scrap metal, welding, auctioneering, garbage collection, and the like.

ENTREPRENEURIAL PROFILE: Evan Spiegel and Bobby Murphy: Snapchat Evan Spiegel and Bobby Murphy met while attending Stanford University, where as freshmen they launched a business called FutureFreshmen, a business that never took off. In their junior year, they came up with the idea for a photo-sharing application they called Picaboo in which photos shared with friends would vanish from electronic devices and servers after a short time. The entrepreneurs changed the app's name to Snapchat, which grew slowly at first and then exploded as millions of people began using it. In 2013, Spiegel and Murphy rejected an offer from Facebook to purchase Snapchat for $3 billion. Today, Spiegel, whose net worth is $2.1 billion, and Murphy, whose net worth is $1.8 billion, own 15 percent of Snapchat, which is valued at $16 billion.[64] ∎

Opportunity to Contribute to Society and Be Recognized for Your Efforts

Playing a vital role in their local business systems and knowing that their work has a significant impact on the nation's economy is yet another reward for entrepreneurs. Often, small business owners are among the most respected and most trusted members of their communities. Business deals based on trust and mutual respect are the hallmark of many established small companies. These owners enjoy the trust and recognition they receive from the customers and the communities they have served faithfully over the years. A recent Gallup survey reports that 67 percent of adults have confidence in small businesses, compared to just 21 percent who have confidence in big businesses and just 8 percent who have confidence in Congress.[65] Another survey by the Public Affairs Council reports that 68 percent of adults prefer doing business with a small local company that charges somewhat higher prices than a large national company that offers lower prices.[66]

Opportunity to Do What You Enjoy and Have Fun at It

A common sentiment among small business owners is that their work *really* isn't work. In fact, a survey by consulting firm Deloitte reports that 60 percent of business owners say they do not plan to retire from their businesses unless they are forced to because of health reasons![67] Most successful entrepreneurs choose to enter their particular business fields because they have an interest in them and enjoy those lines of work. Many of them have made their avocations (hobbies) their vocations (work) and are glad they did! These entrepreneurs are living the advice Harvey McKay offers: "Find a job doing what you love, and you'll never have to work a day in your life."

The journey rather than the destination is the entrepreneur's greatest reward. "Rather than have money be your primary motivator," says Tony Hsieh, CEO of online shoe retailer Zappos, a company that Hsieh sold to Amazon for $1.2 billion, "think about what you would be so passionate about doing that you'd be happy doing it for 10 years, even if you never made any money from it. *That's* what you should be doing. Your passion is what's going to get you through the hard times. Your passion is going to be contagious and rub off onto employees and have a ripple effect on customers and business partners as well."[68]

ENTREPRENEURIAL PROFILE: Lily Wycoff: Lily Pottery The first time Lily Wycoff worked with ceramics was in a high school art class, and immediately she was hooked. What she did not realize at the time was the role that her love for art and ceramics would play in her career. After studying art at Bob Jones University in Greenville, South Carolina, Wycoff dreamed of starting her own business but decided to play it safe and took a job in marketing. In her spare time, she still practiced her art, making pottery using a wheel and kiln at her home. In 2007, Wycoff partnered with two other artists to hold a show, which prompted her to make ceramic jewelry for the first time. The simple clay pendants on leather strands she made sold out quickly, and Wycoff knew that the potential for a business existed. She quit her marketing job and opened a studio in Greenville with her longtime friend and fellow artist Barb Blair. Today, Wycoff owns Lily Pottery and has two locations from which she sells jewelry made from ceramics, metal, and other materials as well as clothing and home accessories. Although her employees now make the individual pieces of jewelry, Wycoff creates all the designs and oversees every aspect of the process. Through Lily Pottery, Wycoff's vocation is merely an extension of her avocation, and she enjoys making a living doing what she loves.[69] ■

LO3B

Describe the drawbacks of entrepreneurship.

The Potential Drawbacks of Entrepreneurship

Entrepreneurship is not a suitable career path for the timid. Individuals who prefer the security of a steady paycheck, a comprehensive benefits package, a two-week paid vacation, and the support of a corporate staff probably should not go into business for themselves. Owning a business has many benefits and provides many opportunities, but anyone planning to enter the world of entrepreneurship should be aware of its potential drawbacks. "Building a start-up is incredibly hard, stressful, chaotic, and—more often than not—results in failure," says entrepreneur Eric Ries. "So why become an entrepreneur? Three reasons: change the world, make customers' lives better, and create an organization of lasting value. If you want to do only one of these things, there are better options. Only start-ups combine all three."[70] Let's explore the "dark side" of entrepreneurship.

Uncertainty of Income

Opening and running a business provides no guarantee that an entrepreneur will earn enough money to survive. Although the mean and median incomes for entrepreneurs are higher than those for employees, so is the *variability* of entrepreneurs' incomes. In other words, some entrepreneurs earn far more through their companies than they could working for someone else, but other entrepreneurs' businesses barely earn enough to provide them with an adequate income. In the early days of a start-up, a business often cannot provide an attractive salary for its owner and meet all its financial obligations, and the entrepreneur may have to live on savings or a spouse's income. The regularity of income that comes with working for someone else is absent because the owner is always the last one to be paid. A recent survey by Citibank reports that 54 percent of small business owners have gone without a paycheck to help their businesses survive.[71]

Risk of Losing Your Entire Investment

Business failure can lead to financial ruin for an entrepreneur, and the small business failure rate is relatively high. According to research by the Bureau of Labor Statistics, 34 percent of new businesses fail within 2 years, and 52 percent shut down within 5 years. Within 10 years, 66 percent of new businesses have folded.[72] A failed business can be not only financially but also emotionally devastating. According to the Global Entrepreneurship Monitor, fear of failure prevents about 30 percent of adults in the United States from attempting to launch a business. Fear of failure equals entrepreneurial paralysis.[73] To Craig Dubitsky, founder of Hello, an oral-care-product manufacturer in Montclair, New Jersey, being scared is simply part of being an entrepreneur. However, he says, what is even scarier than launching a business is the regret associated with *not* bringing a business idea to life. Entrepreneurs simply conquer their fear and go "all in."[74]

Before launching their businesses, entrepreneurs should ask themselves whether they can cope financially and psychologically with the consequences of failure. They should consider the risk–reward trade-off before putting their financial and mental well-being at risk:

- What is the worst that could happen if I open my business and it fails?

- How likely is the worst to happen?

- What can I do to lower the risk of my business failing?

- If my business were to fail, what is my contingency plan for coping?

Just weeks after Jim Snediker's online flash sale business, Left of Trend, failed, he launched with four friends another business, Stock Mfg. Company, a company that manufactures premium men's casual clothing in a historic Chicago factory and sells directly to customers through its Web site and periodic pop-up shops across the United States.[75]

Long Hours and Hard Work

Business start-ups usually demand long hours and hard work from their owners. The average small business owner works 51 hours a week, compared to the 40.2 hours per week the typical U.S. production employee works.[76] Entrepreneurship is not a 9-to-5 job. A survey by OnDeck reports that 9 out of 10 business owners perform at least some work on weekends, and 80 percent report continuing to work in the evenings after leaving their businesses.[77] Adam Warren, founder of Syinc.tv and Sportyourself, companies that allows users to incorporate links to retailers' Web sites for the products that appear in their online photographs and receive payment when someone purchases a tagged item, says that his workday typically starts at 6:30 A.M. and does not end until 10 P.M. or later. "I'm thinking about the business all the time, but I don't see it as work. If you are passionate about your work, it's what you want to be doing anyway."[78]

In many start-ups, six- or seven-day workweeks with no paid vacations are the *norm*. A recent survey by Manta reports that only 43 percent of small business owners plan to take a summer vacation of at least one week. The primary reason entrepreneurs don't take vacations? They have no one to cover their workload.[79] The demands of owning a business make achieving a balance between work and life difficult for entrepreneurs. Sleep researcher James Maas of Cornell University estimates that entrepreneurs lose 700 hours of sleep in the year they launch their companies, which is equivalent to the amount of sleep that a parent loses in the first year of a baby's life.[80] Because they often must do everything themselves, owners experience intense, draining workdays. "I'm the owner, manager, secretary, and janitor," says Cynthia Malcolm, who owns a salon called the Hand Candy Mind and Body Escape in Cheviot, Ohio.[81] Many business owners start down the path of entrepreneurship thinking that they will own a business only to discover later that the business owns them!

Lower Quality of Life Until the Business Gets Established

The long hours and hard work needed to launch a company can take their toll on the remainder of an entrepreneur's life. Nearly three out of four (72 percent) business owners say that they have made significant personal sacrifices in their personal lives for their businesses. The most common regret: not spending enough time with their loved ones. (Interestingly, not starting their businesses sooner was second.)[82] Business owners often find that their roles as husbands and wives or fathers and mothers take a backseat to their roles as company founders. Marriages and friendships are too often casualties of small business ownership.

ENTREPRENEURIAL PROFILE: Tim Askew: Corporate Rain International Tim Askew, founder of Corporate Rain International, a provider of sales outsourcing services based in New Rochelle, New York, compares being married and an entrepreneur to standing with one foot atop two trains going in the same direction but moving farther apart. Askew and his wife of 16 years divorced not long after he started his business. Looking back, Askew admits that his first love was his company. He was so focused on building a successful business that he rarely joined his family on vacations, and when he was with his family, he was so preoccupied with thoughts of his company that he was mentally and emotionally absent.[83] ∎

High Levels of Stress

Starting and managing a business can be an incredibly rewarding experience, but it also can be a highly stressful one. Entrepreneurs often have made significant investments in their companies, have left behind the safety and security of a steady paycheck and benefits, and have mortgaged everything they own to get into business. Most start-ups take months, sometimes years, before they generate positive cash flow, which means their founders must continue to feed them cash during that stressful time. Rescue One Financial, a financial services company based in Irvine, California, generates more than $32 million in annual sales and is profitable, but in the early days, founder Bradley Smith had to borrow from his retirement account, max out a bank line of credit, borrow money from his father, and even sell his Rolex watch to keep the company from folding. Looking back, he says he was a psychological wreck, but his perseverance paid off in the form of a fast-growing, highly successful business.[84]

Business failure often means total financial ruin for entrepreneurs and their families, and that creates intense levels of stress and anxiety. Sometimes entrepreneurs unnecessarily bear the burden of managing alone because they cannot bring themselves to delegate authority and responsibility to others in the company, even though their employees are capable.

Complete Responsibility

It's great to be the boss, but many entrepreneurs find that they must make decisions on issues about which they are not really knowledgeable. Many business owners have difficulty finding advisers. When there is no one to ask, the pressure can build quickly. The realization that the decisions they make are the cause of their company's success or failure has a devastating effect on some people. Small business owners realize quickly that *they* are the business.

Discouragement

Launching a business is a substantial undertaking that requires a great deal of dedication, discipline, and tenacity. Along the way to building a successful business, entrepreneurs run headlong into many different obstacles, some of which appear to be insurmountable. In the face of such difficulties, discouragement and disillusionment are common emotions. Successful entrepreneurs know that every business encounters rough spots along the way, and they wade through difficult times with lots of hard work and an abundant reserve of optimism.

Despite the challenges that starting and running a business pose, entrepreneurs are very satisfied with their career choices. A recent Gallup poll survey reports that 84 percent of small business owners say that if they were choosing a career again, they would still become small business owners.[85] Many entrepreneurs are so happy with their work that they want to continue it indefinitely. In fact, 62 percent of entrepreneurs polled in a recent survey say that they never intend to fully retire, choosing instead to work either full- or part-time, and 4 percent say that they intend to start a new business.[86]

LO4

Explain the forces that are driving the growth of entrepreneurship.

Behind the Boom: What's Feeding the Entrepreneurial Fire

What forces are driving this entrepreneurial trend in our economy? Which factors have led to this age of entrepreneurship? Some of the most significant ones include the following:

- *Entrepreneurs as heroes.* An intangible but very important factor is the attitude that Americans have toward entrepreneurs. As a nation, we have raised them to hero status and have held out their accomplishments as models to follow. Business founders such as Kevin Plank (Under Armour), Mark Zuckerberg (Facebook), Oprah Winfrey (Harpo Productions and OWN [the Oprah Winfrey Network]), Jeff Bezos (Amazon), Robert Johnson (Black Entertainment Television), and Steve Jobs (Apple) are to entrepreneurship what Stephen Curry, Michael Phelps, and Tom Brady are to sports. The media reinforce entrepreneurs' hero status with television shows such as *Shark Tank* and *Dragons' Den*, both of which feature entrepreneurs who pitch their ideas to a panel of tough business experts who have the capital and the connections to make a budding business successful. More than 10 million people in 170 countries on six continents participate in 35,000 activities during Global Entrepreneurship Week, a celebration of entrepreneurship that is sponsored by the Kauffman Foundation.[87]

- *Entrepreneurial education.* Colleges and universities have discovered that entrepreneurship is an extremely popular course of study. Disillusioned with corporate America's downsized job offerings and less promising career paths, a rapidly growing number of students see owning a business as their best career option. Growing numbers of students enroll in college knowing that they want to start their own companies rather than consider entrepreneurship as a possibility later in life; indeed, many are starting companies while they are in college. More than 400,000 students are enrolled in entrepreneurship courses, and 491 colleges and universities offer majors in entrepreneurship.[88] Many colleges and universities have difficulty meeting the demand for courses in entrepreneurship and small business. A recent survey by CreativeLive demonstrates the importance of entrepreneurship education; 34 percent of employed adults who want to start their own businesses say that not knowing where to start the process is a major barrier to their entrepreneurial dreams.[89]

ENTREPRENEURIAL PROFILE: Gabe Jacobs, Amadou Crookes, and Mario Gomez-Hall: Cymbal In their senior year at Tufts University, Gabe Jacobs, Amadou Crookes, and Mario Gomez-Hall started a business, Cymbal, built around a music app they created to connect the digital music experience with social media. (Gomez-Hall and Crookes turned down job offers at Microsoft and Google to focus on building the company.) They describe Cymbal as "music discovery powered by friends, not algorithms" because, like Instagram, it includes a home feed, personal profile, followers, likes, comments, hashtags, and tags. A user's home feed becomes a living playlist that his or her friends help develop by sharing their favorite songs of the moment. The result, the cofounders say, is the soundtrack of your life. Within a few months, more than 17,000 users downloaded Cymbal, clearing the path for Jacobs, Crookes, and Gomez-Hall to raise $1.1 million in venture capital to fuel the company's growth.[90] ■

- *Demographic factors.* Globally, the rate of entrepreneurial activity is highest among people between the ages of 25 and 44 (see Figure 1.4). In the United States, the number of people in that age range currently is more than 84 million (26.4 percent of the U.S. population), which provides a strong demographic base for entrepreneurship.

- *Shift to a service economy.* The service sector accounts for 82.5 percent of the jobs and 80.1 percent of the private sector gross domestic product (GDP) in the United States, both

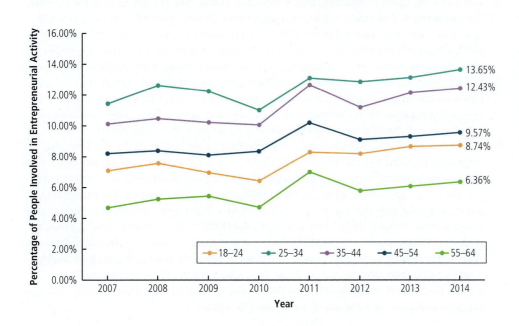

FIGURE 1.4

Global Entrepreneurial Activity by Age Group

Source: Based on Zoltán J. Ács, László Szerb, and Erkko Autio, *Global Entrepreneurship Index*, 2016, Global Entrepreneurship and Development Institute, p. 2.

of which represent a sharp rise from just a decade ago.[91] Because of their relatively low start-up costs, service businesses have become very popular among entrepreneurs. The booming service sector continues to provide many business opportunities, from educational services and computer maintenance to pet waste removal and smart phone repair.

- *Technology advancements.* With the help of modern technology such as portable computers and tablets, smart phones, copiers, 3-D printers, cloud storage, and productivity, communication, and social media apps, even one person working at home can look like a big business. At one time, the high cost of such technological wizardry made it impossible for small businesses to compete with larger companies that could afford the technology. Today, however, powerful computers, tablets, smart phones, and communication equipment are priced within the budgets of even the smallest businesses and have drastically reduced the cost of launching a business. Noting how technology has made testing an idea and starting a business much easier, David Kappos, head of the U.S. Patent and Trademark Office, says, "The distance between an idea and the marketplace has decreased dramatically."[92] With modern technology, entrepreneurs can run their companies from their homes—or almost anywhere—very effectively and look like any *Fortune* 500 company to customers and clients. Edith Elliott cofounded Noora Health, a company started at Stanford University that teaches patients and their family members simple healthcare skills that improve clinical outcomes and reduce readmissions after hospital visits. She splits her time between Stanford, California, where the company's headquarters are located, Boston, Massachusetts, and Bangalore, India.[93]

- *Independent lifestyle.* Entrepreneurship fits the way Americans want to live—with an independent and self-sustaining lifestyle. People want the freedom to choose where they live, the hours they work, and what they do. Although financial security remains an important goal for most entrepreneurs, many place top priority on lifestyle issues, such as more time with family and friends, more leisure time, and more control over work-related stress.

- *Outsourcing.* Entrepreneurs have discovered that they do not have to do everything themselves. Because of advances in technology, entrepreneurs can outsource many of the operations of their companies and retain only those in which they have a competitive advantage. Modern entrepreneurs use the "gig economy" to purchase the services they need on demand, eliminating the necessity of hiring staff to perform those duties. Doing so enhances their flexibility and adaptability to ever-changing market and competitive conditions.

- *The Internet, cloud computing, and mobile marketing.* The proliferation of the Internet, the vast network that links computers around the globe and opens up oceans of information to its users, has spawned thousands of entrepreneurial ventures since its beginning in 1993. **Cloud computing**, Internet-based subscription or pay-per-use software services that allow business owners to use a variety of business applications, from database management and inventory control to customer relationship management and accounting, has reduced business start-up and operating costs. Fast-growing small companies can substitute cloud computing applications for networks of computers and large office spaces, which allows entrepreneurs to build their companies without incurring high overhead costs.

Online retail sales, which currently account for 11 percent of total retail sales, are forecast to continue to grow rapidly (see Figure 1.5), creating many opportunities for Web-savvy entrepreneurs.[94] Apparel, accessories, books, music, travel services, event tickets, and electronic devices are among the best-selling items on the Internet, but entrepreneurs are learning that they can use this powerful tool to sell just about anything, including soil samples from Roswell, New Mexico, where a UFO allegedly crashed in 1947 (complete with a certificate of authenticity)![95] In fact, entrepreneurs are using the Web to sell services such as a matching service for people and dogs in need of a forever home (BarkBuddy), a service that rents upscale port-a-johns for swanky events (ElizaJ), and products such as customized tea blends (Design A Tea) and travel-size kits of individually packaged products that come in hundreds of variations (Minimus).[96]

cloud computing
Internet-based subscription or pay-per-use software services that allow business owners to use a variety of business applications, from database management and inventory control to customer relationship management and accounting.

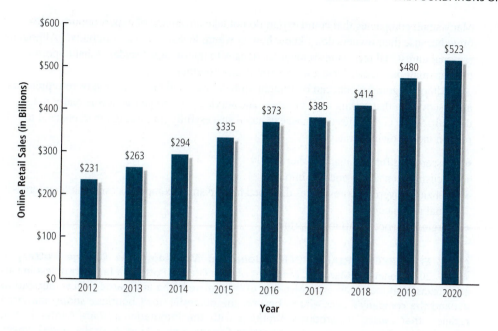

FIGURE 1.5

U.S. Online Retail Sales

Source: Based on data from Forrester Research, 2016.

Currently, about 54 percent of small businesses have Web sites, double the number that had Web sites in 1997, and 24 percent of business owners without Web sites say that they plan to build them in the near future.[97] Yet, 22 percent of small business owners say that they are not likely to launch a Web site. The most common reasons? A Web site is not relevant to their businesses, and the cost of creating and maintaining a site is too high.[98] Many entrepreneurs see the power of **mobile computing** and are putting it to use, but some small businesses have been slow to adopt the technology. More than 50 percent of Web searches are conducted on mobile devices, but 32 percent of small business Web sites are not mobile friendly.[99] Business owners whose Web sites are not mobile friendly are sacrificing sales; mobile e-commerce sales make up 30 percent of total e-commerce retail sales.[100] "It's almost as bad not to have a mobile-friendly Web site as it is not to have a site at all," says Max Elman, founder of Razorfrog Web Design.[101]

mobile computing
connecting wirelessly to a centrally located computing system via a small, portable communication device.

ENTREPRENEURIAL PROFILE: Antonio Swad: Pizza Patrón Pizza Patrón, a pizza chain of nearly 100 locations with a Latino flair founded in 1986 by Antonio Swad, recently updated its Web site with a responsive design that allows it to configure properly on devices of any size, including tablets and smart phones. The company, which is based in Dallas, Texas, made the move in response to customers' preference for placing pizza orders using mobile devices. Placing food orders from mobile devices is common, with 72 percent of mobile users having placed food orders via their smart phone or tablet.[102] Since making the change, traffic to Pizza Patrón's Web site is up 50 percent, and more than 75 percent of visits to the site were from users on mobile devices.[103] ∎

- *International opportunities.* No longer are small businesses limited to pursuing customers within their own borders. The shift to a global economy has opened the door to tremendous business opportunities for entrepreneurs willing to reach across the globe. Although the United States is an attractive market for entrepreneurs, approximately 95 percent of the world's population and more than 70 percent of its purchasing power lie outside U.S. borders.[104] The emergence of potential markets across the globe and crumbling barriers to international business because of trade agreements have opened the world to entrepreneurs who are looking for new customers. Whereas companies once had to grow into global markets, today small businesses can have a global scope from their inception. Called **micromultinationals**, these small companies focus more on serving customers' needs than on the countries in which their customers live. More than 297,000 small businesses export goods and services. In fact, small businesses make up 98 percent of all businesses engaged in exporting, yet they account for only 34 percent of the nation's export sales.[105]

micromultinationals
small companies that operate globally from their inception.

Many small companies that could export do not take advantage of export opportunities, often because their owners don't know how or where to start an export initiative. Although regional unrest and recessions remain challenges to international trade, global opportunities for small businesses have a long-term positive outlook.

Although going global can be fraught with dangers and problems, many entrepreneurs are discovering that selling their products and services in foreign markets is really not so difficult. Small companies that have expanded successfully into foreign markets tend to rely on the following strategies:

- Researching foreign markets thoroughly
- Focusing on a single country initially
- Utilizing government resources designed to help small companies establish an international presence
- Forging alliances with local partners

ENTREPRENEURIAL PROFILE: Jonathan Mercado: Blue Orange Pottery In 2011, Jonathan Mercado, president of Blue Orange Pottery, a family business in Laredo, Texas, that makes an expansive line of innovative home and garden décor, decided to expand the company's sales efforts beyond the domestic small boutique shops and large retailers that carried its products. Working with the International Trade Center in San Antonio, Blue Orange Pottery now exports to Canada, Switzerland, Australia, and Germany and is looking for new countries to target. Since beginning its export initiative, Blue Orange Pottery's sales have increased 30 percent.[106] ∎

The Cultural Diversity of Entrepreneurship

LO5

Explain the cultural diversity of entrepreneurship.

As we have seen, virtually anyone has the potential to become an entrepreneur. Indeed, diversity is a hallmark of entrepreneurship. We now explore the diverse mix of people who make up the rich fabric of entrepreneurship.

Young Entrepreneurs

Young people are enthusiastically embracing entrepreneurship as a career choice. Indeed, nearly half of all entrepreneurs globally are between the ages of 25 and 44.[107] A Gallup survey reports that 40 percent of students in grades 5 through 12 say that they plan to start their own businesses—and 38 percent said that their goal is to invent something that changes the world. (The percentage of minority students who expressed a desire for a career in entrepreneurship, 50 percent, was higher than for white students, 37 percent.)[108] Although entrepreneurial activity tends to increase with age, many members of the Millennial generation (or Generation Y, those born between 1981 and 2000) show high levels of interest in entrepreneurship. Disenchanted with their prospects in corporate America and willing to take a chance at controlling their own destinies, scores of young people are choosing entrepreneurship as their initial career path. People between the ages of 15 and 29, more than 65 million strong, are deciding that owning their own companies is the best way to create job security and to achieve the balance between work and life that they seek.

ENTREPRENEURIAL PROFILE: Sebastian Martinez: Are You Kidding? At age 5, Sebastian Martinez had a passion for wacky socks that he turned into a business, Are You Kidding?, that designs and markets colorful, funky socks. With the help of his older brother Brandon, 7, who is the company's director of sales, Are You Kidding? now generates annual sales of $15,000 through its Web site. Now 7 and 9, the Martinez brothers make sure the company lives up to its social responsibility, donating a portion of each sale to the American Cancer Society. The company recently donated $3,000 to the charity. Because of young people such as the Martinezes, the future of entrepreneurship looks very bright.[109] ∎

Courtesy of Are you Kidding?

🗨 You Be the Consultant

College: The Ideal Place to Launch a Business

For growing numbers of students, college is not just a time of learning, partying, and growing into young adulthood; it is fast becoming a place for building a business. Today, more than 2,300 colleges and universities offer courses in entrepreneurship and small business management, and many of them have trouble meeting the demand for these classes. Today, entrepreneurship has become a mainstream activity on college campuses around the globe. Greater numbers of students are pursuing careers in entrepreneurship and see their college experience as an opportunity to get an early start not only by studying entrepreneurship but also by putting what they learn into practice. Bill Aulet, head of the Martin Trust Center for MIT Entrepreneurship, says that faculty members who teach entrepreneurship must nurture the spirit of a pirate in their students while teaching them how to execute their start-up plans with the precision of a Navy SEAL. In addition to regular classroom courses, colleges increasingly are building an extra dimension in their entrepreneurship programs, including internships with start-ups, consulting jobs with small businesses, mentoring relationships with other entrepreneurs, networking opportunities with potential investors, and participation in business plan competitions. Allan R. Cohen, the dean of the graduate program at Babson College, says that entrepreneurial education is a contact sport, and many colleges are adding boot camp–like courses to their curricula.

As the following examples prove, many college students expect to apply the entrepreneurial skills they are learning in their classes and the abundant resources available to them by starting businesses while they are still in college. They also are a testament to college students' creativity and work ethic.

Cavebox

Like many other college students, Storm Anderson, 22, and Samuel George, 27, led busy lives, participating in many on- and off-campus activities at Indiana University. Their hectic schedules meant that they didn't have much time for shopping, and they often ran out of their personal care items. The young entrepreneurs say they had neither the time nor the inclination to keep track of their stock of toothpaste and realized that other young men felt the same way. In early 2014, Anderson and George launched Cavebox, a service aimed at 18- to 30-year-old men that ships one- or two-month supplies of personal hygiene products for as little as $25 so that men never have to leave their caves again to shop for personal care items. Customers can customize their Caveboxes, which include body, oral, skin, and hair care, along with other items, with their favorite brands, and shipping is free for boxes that cost $30 or more. The company's bulk purchases allow it to keep prices affordable. Anderson and George also offer a travel-size bag called the Cavebag for the man-on-the-go.

ProfilePasser

Many high school athletes dream of being recruited by a bevy of colleges, but the college recruiting process is extremely inefficient,

and coaches often overlook talented athletes, who get only a handful of scholarship offers. That was the position that Samantha Weber found herself in during her last year of high school. Although things worked out well for Weber, who enrolled in Grove City College in Grove City, Pennsylvania, where she played varsity soccer for four years, the student-athlete decided to do something to help improve the recruiting process. During her senior year at Grove City College, while playing soccer and taking a full schedule of classes, Weber, just 21, created an athletic recruiting app, ProfilePasser, that connects high school athletes and college coaches at showcase tournaments. Student-athletes create their own profiles using the app, and when college coaches check in at a tournament, they have access to every player's profile and can use a search function to find athletes who fit a particular set of characteristics. ProfilePasser was one of only nine start-ups recently accepted into AlphaLab, Pittsburgh's leading business accelerator. Weber already has raised more than $25,000 in private financing and has attracted a "who's who" group of advisors, including her older sister, Alexa Andrzejewski, founder of Foodspotting, a company that OpenTable recently bought for $10 million.

FiscalNote

Students Jonathan Chen (University of Maryland), Timothy Hwang (Princeton University), and Gerald Yao (Emory University), all 21, created a company, FiscalNote, that uses artificial intelligence and big data to unlock the massive amounts of data created by governments and courts in all 50 states, the District of Columbia, and Congress. FiscalNote's algorithms and statistical analysis tools allow clients to identify meaningful trends in government data and to predict with 90 percent accuracy whether proposed legislation will become law. The young entrepreneurs already have raised $1.2 million in equity capital from several high-profile investors.

A study by researchers at Babson College shows that students who take at least one entrepreneurship course are more likely to actually become entrepreneurs than those who do not. College can be one of the best places to start a business, but doing so requires discipline, good time management, and a willingness to make mistakes and learn from them. The recipe for success is the same as for entrepreneurs everywhere: Try something. Fail some. Learn something. Try again. Repeat.

1. One venture capitalist says that entrepreneurship can't be taught in a regular classroom any more than surfing can. His view is that students should get their feet wet in the real world of entrepreneurship. What do you think?

2. In addition to the normal obstacles of starting a business, what other barriers do collegiate entrepreneurs face?

3. What advantages do collegiate entrepreneurs have when launching a business?

(continued)

You Be the Consultant *(continued)*

4. What advice would you offer a fellow college student who is about to start a business?

5. Work with a team of your classmates to develop ideas about what your college or university could do to create a culture that supports entrepreneurship on your campus or in your community.

Sources: Based on Diana Ransom, "America's Coolest College Start-ups 2014," *Inc.*, 2014, www.inc.com/diana-ransom/coolest-college-startups-2014.html; "About Us," Cavebox, 2014, http://thecavebox.com/pages/about-us; Emily Niklas, "Student's Recruiter App Helps Athletes," *The Collegian*, November 1, 2013, pp. 1, 10; "About Our Company," FiscalNote, 2014, www.fiscalnote.com/about; Bill Aulet, "Teaching Entrepreneurship Is in the Start-up Phase," *Wall Street Journal*, September 12, 2013, p. A17; Jason Dailey, "Born or Made?" *Entrepreneur*, October 2013, pp. 65–72; Stewart Thornhill, "The Wrong Way to Judge an Entrepreneurship Course," *Bloomberg Businessweek*, February 5, 2014, www.businessweek.com/articles/2014-02-05/the-wrong-way-to-judge-an-entrepreneurship-course.

Women Entrepreneurs

Despite years of legislative effort, women still face discrimination in the workforce. However, small business has been a leader in offering women opportunities for economic expression through entrepreneurship. Increasing numbers of women are discovering that the best way to break the "glass ceiling" that prevents them from rising to the top of many organizations is to start their own companies. Women entrepreneurs have even broken through the comic strip barrier. Blondie Bumstead, long a typical suburban housewife married to Dagwood, now owns her own catering business with her best friend and neighbor, Tootsie Woodley!

In the United States, the number of women-owned businesses is growing 1.5 times faster than the national average for all U.S. businesses.[110] Women now own 31.1 percent of all privately held businesses in the United States, but their companies generate just 12 percent of business sales.[111] Although women-owned business are smaller and far less likely to attract equity capital investments than those that men start, they are just as likely to survive as businesses owned by men.[112] In addition, their impact is anything but small. The more than 11.3 million women-owned companies in the United States employ more than 9 million workers and generate sales of nearly $1.6 trillion a year (see Figure 1.6)![113]

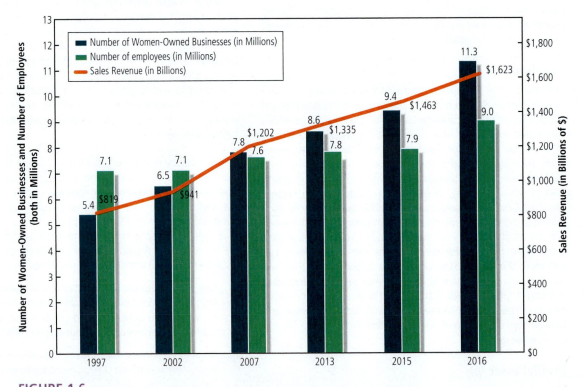

FIGURE 1.6

Characteristics of Women-Owned Businesses

Source: Based on data from the 2016 State of Women-Owned Businesses Report, American Express OPEN, 2016, p. 3.

ENTREPRENEURIAL PROFILE: Heather Tate McCartney: UV Couture After Heather Tate McCartney's father was diagnosed with melanoma, an aggressive form of skin cancer, she became alarmed because she also enjoyed spending time in the sun. She used sunscreen, but research revealed that most people do not apply sunscreen properly or often enough to be effective. McCartney began swimming in T-shirts and wrapping herself in towels to block the sun's harmful ultraviolet (UV) rays. The look was less than fashionable, so she came up with a line of summer clothing called UV Couture that offers an ultraviolet protection factor of 50, which blocks 99 percent of the sun's harmful rays. (Regular clothing blocks only 6 percent of the harmful UV rays.) Today, UV Couture, based in Ontario, Canada, sells a clothing line that includes shirts, cover-ups, jackets, dresses, skirts, leggings, hoodies, and other items priced from $39 to $165 on its Web site and through retailers.[114] ∎

Minority Enterprises

Like women, minorities also are choosing entrepreneurship more often than ever before. Hispanics, African Americans, and Asians are most likely to become entrepreneurs. Hispanics own 12.0 percent of all businesses in the United States, African-Americans own 9.4 percent, and Asians own 6.9 percent.[115] Companies started by Asian entrepreneurs have a significantly higher success rate than those started by other minority entrepreneurs.[116] Hispanics represent the fastest-growing segment of the U.S. population, and Hispanic entrepreneurs represent the largest and fastest-growing segment of minority-owned businesses in the United States (see Figure 1.7). More than 3.3 million Hispanic-owned companies employ more than 1.9 million people and generate more than $468 billion in annual sales.[117] The most recent Index of Startup Activity by the Kauffman Foundation shows that Hispanics are 59 percent more likely to start a business than whites.[118]

Minority entrepreneurs see owning their own businesses as an ideal way to battle discrimination, and minority-owned companies have come a long way in the last decade. Minority entrepreneurs own 29 percent of all businesses in the United States, generate $1 trillion in annual

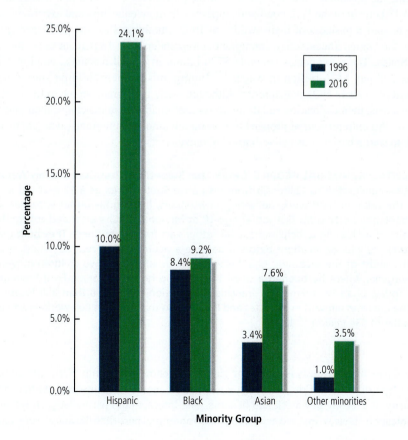

FIGURE 1.7

Percentage of New Entrepreneurs in the U.S. by Minority Group, 1996 and 2016

Source: Based on data from Robert Fairlie, Arnobio Morelix, and Inara Tareque, The Kauffman Index of Startup Activity, Kauffman Foundation, August 2017, p. 31.

revenues, and are twice as likely to export as non-minority entrepreneurs. Minority entrepreneurs start their businesses for the same reason that most entrepreneurs do: to control their own destinies.[119] The future is promising for this new generation of minority entrepreneurs, who are better educated, have more business experience, have more entrepreneurial role models, and are better prepared for business ownership than their predecessors.

ENTREPRENEURIAL PROFILE: Conchita Espinosa: Fru-Veg Distributors After working several years in the produce industry, Conchita Espinosa launched Fru-Veg Distributors, a distributor of fruits and vegetables that it imports from leading growers in Central and South America and Europe, with whom the company has had relationships for decades. Fru-Veg, based in Miami, Florida, has an office in Philadelphia and markets a wide variety of produce—ranging from apples and asparagus to stone fruit and tomatoes—to retail chains across the United States and Canada. Espinosa's company recently experienced a growth spurt, with sales increasing from $2.2 million to more than $40 million in just four years, landing it a spot on *Hispanic Business* magazine's list of the 100 fastest-growing Hispanic businesses in the United States.[120] ■

Immigrant Entrepreneurs

The United States, which has long been a melting pot of diverse cultures, is the leading destination in the world for immigrants, who are drawn by the promise of economic freedom and prosperity. The immigrant population in the United States is more diverse than in the past, with people coming from a larger number of countries. In 1960, 75 percent of the foreign-born population came from Europe; today, most immigrants come from Mexico, and just 12 percent of the immigrant population emigrates from Europe.[121] Immigrant entrepreneurs have created some of the most iconic U.S. companies since they began arriving in the nineteenth century, when Andrew Carnegie, whose family came to the United States from Scotland, became one of the wealthiest people of his era after launching the steel company that bore his name. One hundred fifty years later, Sergey Brin, a Russian immigrant, cofounded Google with his friend Larry Page.[122]

Unlike the unskilled "huddled masses" of the past, today's 41.3 million immigrants, which make up 13 percent of the U.S. population, arrive with more education and experience and often a desire to start a business of their own.[123] In 1992, immigrants owned just 9 percent of businesses in the United States; today, immigrant entrepreneurs own 18 percent of businesses in the United States. Their companies generate $776 billion in annual revenues, employ 4.7 million workers, and pay $126 billion in wages.[124] Immigrants or their children started more than 40 percent of *Fortune* 500 companies.[125] Although many immigrants come to the United States with few assets, their dedication and desire to succeed enable them to achieve their entrepreneurial dreams. An entrepreneurial propensity is common among immigrants, who are nearly twice as likely to start a business as native-born U.S. citizens.[126]

ENTREPRENEURIAL PROFILE: Derek Cha: SweetFrog Premium Frozen Yogurt Derek Cha immigrated to California from his native South Korea as a 12-year-old and quickly learned the value of hard work, delivering newspapers, helping his father with cleaning work after school, and landing his first job at age 16 at McDonald's. Cha attended college for a year and a half before leaving to help manage his father's art framing business. They built the venture into a company with 80 locations before it became a victim of the Great Recession. A year later, still in the midst of the recession, Cha, his wife Annah, and their two children moved to Richmond, Virginia, where he opened a small yogurt shop he named SweetFrog Premium Frozen Yogurt. Today, Cha's SweetFrog is a franchised operation with more than 350 locations (70 of which Cha operates himself) in 25 states and Puerto Rico that employs 800 workers and generates annual sales of $34 million.[127] ■

Part-Time Entrepreneurs

Starting a part-time business is a popular gateway to entrepreneurship. Part-time entrepreneurs have the best of both worlds: They can ease into business for themselves without sacrificing the security of a steady paycheck and benefits. The Internet (and particularly eBay) and mobile communication devices make establishing and running a part-time business very easy; many part-time entrepreneurs run online businesses from a spare bedroom in their homes or from wherever they are.

ENTREPRENEURIAL PROFILE: Will Waldron, Matt Sandler, and Five of Their Friends: Two Fingers Brewing Company Will Waldron, Matt Sandler, and five of their friends were working for an advertising agency, Karmarama, that moved into a building in Farringdon, London, which once had housed a bar (that was still in place). The team of young men decided to use the bar to raise money for a nonprofit organization in Great Britain that fights prostate cancer. That idea quickly morphed into brewing beer, which, with the blessing of their employer, led them to start a part-time microbrewery they named the Two Fingers Brewing Company. More than 500 guests showed up for their launch party, and the part-time entrepreneurs quickly sold out of beer. Today, the entrepreneurial team continues to hold their jobs with Karmarama and to operate Two Fingers Brewing Company part time out of the bar in the advertising company's workspace. They have refined their supply chain to ensure consistency and top quality and have expanded their distribution channel to include major chain stores, including Tesco, Morrisons, and Ocado. Ten pence for every bottle of Aurelio Golden Artisan Beer ("A beer for mankind") sold goes to Prostate Cancer UK. The team of entrepreneurs plans to continue working in advertising and running their brewery part-time for the foreseeable future.[128] ∎

A major advantage of going into business part-time is the lower risk in case the venture flops. Many part-timers are "testing the entrepreneurial waters" to see whether their business ideas will work, whether there is sufficient demand for their products and services, and whether they enjoy being self-employed. As they grow, many successful part-time enterprises absorb more of the entrepreneurs' time until they become full-time businesses. Starting part-time businesses on a small scale means that entrepreneurs can finance their companies themselves, allowing them to retain complete ownership.

Home-Based Businesses

Home-based businesses are booming! An entrepreneur starts a home-based business on average every 11 seconds.[129] Fifty-two percent of all small businesses are home based, and 75 percent of them have full-time employees.[130] Home-based businesses are an important economic force; they generate $427 billion a year in sales.[131] Many now-famous companies started as home-based businesses, including Apple Inc., Mary Kay Cosmetics, and Hershey Inc.[132] Several factors make the home the first choice location for many entrepreneurs:

- Operating a business from home keeps start-up and operating costs to a minimum. In fact, 51 percent of home-based entrepreneurs start their businesses with less than $5,000 in capital.[133]

- Home-based companies allow owners to maintain flexible life and work styles. Many home-based entrepreneurs relish being part of the "open-collar workforce." Women own 58 percent of all home-based businesses, compared to 31 percent of all small businesses.[134]

- Technology, which is transforming many ordinary homes into "electronic cottages," allows entrepreneurs to run a wide variety of businesses from their homes.

- Many entrepreneurs use the Internet to operate e-commerce businesses from their homes that literally span the globe. They also rely heavily on social media to promote their home-based businesses.

In the past, home-based businesses tended to be rather mundane cottage industries, such as making crafts or sewing. Today's home-based businesses are more diverse; modern "homepreneurs" are more likely to be running high-tech or service companies with annual sales of hundreds of thousands of dollars. Twenty percent of home-based businesses generate between $100,000 and $500,000 in annual revenue.[135]

ENTREPRENEURIAL PROFILE: Ryan Kuhlman and Lauren Tafuri: Preppi After Ryan Kuhlman and Lauren Tafuri experienced a small earthquake in Los Angeles, they realized the importance of having a kit of emergency supplies, so they began to assemble one for themselves. When they asked their friends what items were in their emergency kits, Kuhlman and

Tafuri discovered just how few people had made any preparation at all for emergencies—and spotted a business opportunity. They researched recommendations for items to include in an emergency kit from the Red Cross and other disaster response organizations. As part of a feasibility analysis to test the viability of their new product, Kuhlman and Tafuri used Photoshop to create a mockup of their emergency kit, which they named The Prepster, posted it on Instagram, and asked for feedback. The response led the budding entrepreneurs to launch a company, Preppi, from their downtown Los Angeles loft to market their stylish, chic emergency kit that contains nearly 170 items, including a tent, a blanket, a flashlight, a hand-crank radio/solar-powered phone charger, various personal grooming items, and even a deck of playing cards. The Prepster kits come in a variety of configurations, and prices start at $145 for an essentials version designed to last just 72 hours and go to $445 for a two-person, three-day survival kit. Kuhlman and Tafuri started their business by making only three kits, but after coverage from several major media outlets and celebrity blogs, sales have increased rapidly for the home-based business. The entrepreneurs are working on deals to distribute The Prepster through shops in New York City and Japan.[136] ■

Family Businesses

family-owned business

a business that includes two or more members of a family who have financial control of the company.

A **family-owned business** is a business that includes two or more members of a family who have financial control of the company. Family businesses are an integral part of the global economy. More than 80 percent of all companies in the world are family owned, and their contributions to the global economy are significant. Family-owned businesses account for 70 to 90 percent of global GDP. In the United States alone, family businesses make up 90 percent of all businesses, create 64 percent of the nation's gross domestic product, employ 62 percent of the private sector workforce, and account for 65 percent of all wages paid. Not all family-owned businesses are small, however; 33 percent of *Fortune* 500 companies are family businesses. Family-owned companies such as Wal-Mart, Ford, Mars, Cargill, and Winn-Dixie employ thousands of people and generate billions of dollars in annual revenue.[137] Family firms also create 78 percent of the U.S. economy's net new jobs and are responsible for many famous products, including Heinz ketchup, Levi's jeans, and classic toys such as the Slinky, the Radio Flyer wagon, and the Wiffle Ball.[138]

"When it works right," says one writer, "nothing succeeds like a family firm. The roots run deep, embedded in family values. The flash of the fast buck is replaced with long-term plans. Tradition counts."[139] Indeed, the life span of the typical family business is 24 years.[140] Despite their magnitude, family businesses face a major threat, a threat from within: management succession, passing the baton from one generation to the next. In a recent survey by PriceWaterhouseCoopers, only 16 percent of family business owners around the globe say that they have a thorough, documented succession plan in place.[141] Lack of succession planning explains why only 30 percent of family businesses survive to the second generation, just 12 percent make it to the third generation, and only 3 percent survive into the fourth generation and beyond. Business periodicals are full of stories describing bitter feuds among family members that have crippled or destroyed once thriving businesses. The co-owner of one family business explains the challenges of operating a family business this way: "The best part is working with family. The worst part is working with family."[142] To avoid the senseless destruction of thriving family businesses, owners should do the following:

- Work to build positive relationships among family members both at and away from work

- Demonstrate respect for other family members' abilities and talents

- Separate responsibilities in the company based on each person's interests, abilities, and talents

- Develop plans for minimizing the potentially devastating effects of estate taxes

- Develop plans for management succession long before retirement looms before them

ENTREPRENEURIAL PROFILE: Bobby Schlesinger: The Obadon Hotel Group Bobby Schlesinger and his brothers are the third generation of family members to operate The Obadon Hotel Group, a portfolio of luxury hotels scattered along the Florida coast. Schlesinger's grandfather, Gilbert, started the family business in the 1950s, when he began buying hotels and real estate along the East Coast. Schlesinger's father, Richard, stepped into the family business and in 2002 purchased the Brazilian Hotel, a Palm Beach landmark famous for luxury since the 1920s. After a $35 million upgrade, much of it designed by Schlesinger's mother, Leslie, the Brazilian became the centerpiece of the family's hotel business. Both of Schlesinger's older brothers joined the family business, but after graduating from college, Schlesinger worked in banking and as a sports agent. "It's not easy to be in a family business," explains his father. Then Schlesinger realized the treasure that the family business represented and stepped in to manage the daily operations of Obadon's four luxury hotels. "I went into [the family business] because there would be nothing that I would care about more, nothing I would work harder for, than to preserve the hard work that two generations of my family had done before me," he says.[143] ■

Copreneurs

Copreneurs are entrepreneurial couples who work together as co-owners of their businesses. Nearly 4 million couples operate businesses together in the United States, but unlike the traditional "Mom & Pop" (Pop as "boss" and Mom as "subordinate"), copreneurs divide their business responsibilities on the basis of their skills, experience, and abilities rather than on gender. Managing a small business with a spouse may appear to be a recipe for divorce, but most copreneurs say it's not. "There is nothing like sharing an intense, life-changing experience with someone to bring you closer," says Caterina Fake, who with her husband Sewart Butterfield launched Flickr, a photo-sharing Web site. "Late nights, early mornings, laughter, terror, white-knuckle meetings with people you desperately need to give you money, getting your first check from a paying user—how can you beat it?"[144] Successful copreneurs learn to build the foundation for a successful working relationship before they ever launch their companies. Some of the characteristics they rely on include the following:

copreneurs
entrepreneurial couples who work together as co-owners of their businesses.

- An assessment of whether their personalities will mesh—or conflict—in a business setting

- Mutual respect for each other and one another's talents

- Compatible business and life goals—a common vision

- Similar work ethic

- A view that they are full and equal partners, not a superior and a subordinate

- Complementary business skills that each acknowledges and appreciates and that lead to a unique business identity for each spouse

- The ability to keep lines of communication open, talking and listening to each other about personal as well as business issues

- A clear division of roles and authority, ideally based on each partner's skills and abilities, to minimize conflict and power struggles

- The ability to encourage each other and to lift up a disillusioned partner

- Separate work spaces that allow them to escape when the need arises

- Boundaries between their business life and their personal life so that one doesn't consume the other

- A sense of humor

- The realization that not every couple can work together

Although copreneuring isn't for everyone, it works extremely well for many couples and often leads to successful businesses. "Both spouses are working for a common purpose but also focusing on their unique talents," says a family business counselor. "With all these skills put together, one plus one equals more than two."[145]

ENTREPRENEURIAL PROFILE: Brook Harvey-Taylor and Billy Taylor: Pacifica As a teenager, Brook Harvey-Taylor was fascinated by fragrances and began mixing her own using essential oils she bought at a local food cooperative in Bozeman, Montana, that her mother started. Years later, she moved to Oregon to study aromatherapy and met her future husband,

Billy Taylor, a photographer and filmmaker. While driving home from a surfing trip, the couple decided to start a business making all-natural scented candles using their own capital and money borrowed from family members. As their company grew, the copreneurs expanded into perfumes and fragrances, again using the all-natural philosophy on which they founded their company. Today, their business, Pacifica, employees 110 workers, generates sales of more than $40 million, and produces a full line of innovative, vegan, cruelty-free beauty products, including cosmetics, skin care items, perfumes, and others. The U.S. Small Business Administration recently honored the copreneurs by naming them the National Small Business Persons of the Year.[146] ∎

Corporate Castoffs

Concentrating on shedding the excess bulk that took away their flexibility and speed, many large American corporations have been downsizing in an attempt to regain their competitive edge. For decades, one major corporation after another has announced layoffs—and not just among blue-collar workers. According to placement firm Challenger, Gray, and Christmas, from 2002 to 2017, corporations laid off an average of 68,711 employees per month.[147] Executives and line workers alike have experienced job cuts. Many of these corporate castoffs are deciding that the best defense against future job insecurity is an entrepreneurial offense. Some 20 percent of discharged corporate managers have become entrepreneurs, and many of those left behind in corporate America would like to join them. Given their experience in the corporate structure and their management skills, a significant number of castoffs buy franchises, which gives them the opportunity to exercise their entrepreneurial muscles within the corporate-style structure to which they are accustomed. After Kendall Titchener, 28, was laid off from her job as the social media and digital director at Cenovus Energy Inc. in Calgary, Canada, she immediately put together a business plan and launched Pixelated Pinto, a boutique digital marketing agency that targets start-up companies with its services. Titchener says that she never suspected that her job was at risk but is extremely pleased with her new career as an entrepreneur.[148]

Encore Entrepreneurs

The dramatic downsizing of corporate America, particularly during the Great Recession, has created another effect among the employees left after restructuring: a trust gap. The result of this trust gap is a growing number of dropouts from the corporate structure who then become entrepreneurs. One recent survey reports that 47 percent of working Millennials would like to leave their jobs in corporate America.[149] These entrepreneurs, known as **encore entrepreneurs**, may see their workdays grow longer and their incomes shrink, but those who strike out on their own often find their work more rewarding and more satisfying because they are doing what they enjoy and are in control. For corporate dropouts, the issue is not money; it is the opportunity to pursue their own vision and passion and to change the world, even if in only a small way.

encore entrepreneurs
people who drop out of the corporate world to become entrepreneurs.

ENTREPRENEURIAL PROFILE: Adam Herscher and Sean Anderson: Hasmetrics
After working for technology giant Microsoft in Redmond, Washington, for nine years after graduating from college, Adam Herscher grew weary of managing major new products for years only to have many of them canceled before they were released. Eventually, he realized that something was missing from his work life and that he was no longer engaged in his work. Herscher, who had dreamed of having his own business, took the bold step of walking away from a comfortable but unrewarding corporate management job that paid $254,895 annually to cofound with Sean Anderson, another Microsoft dropout, Hasmetrics, a small company (now with four employees) that provides unique customer experience management software, or as Herscher calls it, "customer happiness software." Herscher admits that most of his friends thought he was insane for leaving his high-paying corporate job, but he says it was the best decision of his life and encourages other would-be entrepreneurs caught in unrewarding corporate jobs to take the leap of faith into entrepreneurship.[150] ∎

Because they have college degrees, a working knowledge of business, and years of management experience, both corporate dropouts and castoffs may ultimately increase the small business survival rate. Although a college degree is not a prerequisite for entrepreneurial success, better-trained, more experienced entrepreneurs are more likely to succeed. Currently, nearly 72 percent of business owners in the United States have at least some college education (and 39 percent of business owners have earned a bachelor's degree or higher).[151]

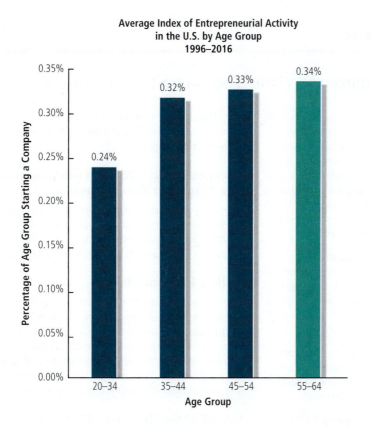

FIGURE 1.8

Entrepreneurial Activity in the U.S. by Age Group

Source: Based on data from Robert W. Fairlie, and Inara Tareque, 2017 Kauffman Index of Startup Activity, Kauffman Foundation, 2017, p. 34.

Retiring Baby Boomers

Self-employment rates tend to rise with age, and life spans are longer than ever before. Members of the Baby Boom Generation (born between 1946 and 1964) are retiring, but many of them are not idle; instead, they are launching businesses of their own. In fact, people 55 and older have demonstrated the greatest increase in entrepreneurial activity over the last 25 years of any age group. A study by the Kauffman Foundation shows that the average level of entrepreneurial activity over the last 21 years among people aged 55 to 64 actually is higher than that among people of any other age group (see Figure 1.8).[152] The trend shows no sign of slowing. A recent survey reports that 72 percent of 50-plus pre-retirees plan to work in some capacity in retirement.[153] The main reason that retirees give for starting their own post-retirement businesses is that they want to work on their own terms. One advantage that older entrepreneurs have is wisdom that has been forged by experience. Because people are living longer and healthier than ever before, many entrepreneurs start their entrepreneurial ventures late in life. At age 65, Colonel Harland Sanders, for example, began franchising the fried chicken business that he had started three years earlier, a company that became Kentucky Fried Chicken (now known as KFC).

To finance their businesses, most retirees use some of their invested "nest eggs," some of them through **rollovers-as-business-start-ups (ROBS)**, a system that allows entrepreneurs to tap their retirement funds to start businesses without incurring taxes or penalties. Others rely on the same sources of funds as younger entrepreneurs, including banks, private investors, and others.

rollovers-as-business-start-ups (ROBS)
a system that allows entrepreneurs to tap their retirement funds to start businesses without incurring taxes or penalties.

ENTREPRENEURIAL PROFILE: Marvin and Leslie Gay: Painting with a Twist At 71, Marvin Gay, a retired accountant, and his wife, Leslie, 61, used $70,000 of their savings to open a Painting with a Twist franchise, a business that combines art instruction with bring-your-own-wine parties, in St. Petersburg, Florida. Their first business was so successful that the couple opened a second location 18 months later, and, within a year, both locations were generating $750,000 in annual revenue and were profitable. The Gays are about to open a third Painting with a Twist location and once again will finance it from their savings. The Gays say that the real delight they get from their retirement business is watching customers enjoy learning to paint while sipping wine and hearing their boisterous laughter.[154] ■

Hands On . . . How To

Launch a Successful Business While You Are Still in College

Collegiate entrepreneurs are becoming increasingly common as colleges and universities offer more courses and a greater variety of courses in the areas of entrepreneurship and small business management. Launching a business while in college offers many advantages, including access to research and valuable advice, but starting an entrepreneurial career also poses challenges, including a lack of financial resources, business experience, and time. What are some of the most common myths that prevent young people (not just college students) from launching businesses?

- *I don't have enough money to launch a business.* One of the greatest benefits of the shift in the United States to a service economy is that service businesses usually are very inexpensive to start. One young entrepreneur worked with a friend to launch a Web development company while in high school, and their total start-up cost was just $80.

- *I don't have enough time.* Many companies that have grown into very successful, mature businesses were started by entrepreneurs in their spare time. Everyone has the same 24 hours in a day. What matters is what you do with those hours.

- *I'm not smart enough to start a company.* SAT scores and grades have little correlation to one's ability to launch a successful business. Quite a few successful entrepreneurs, including Michael Dell (Dell Inc.), Richard Branson (Virgin), Walt Disney (Disney), Mark Zuckerberg (Facebook), and Debbi Fields (Mrs. Fields Cookies), dropped out of college to start their businesses.

- *I'm not majoring in business.* Success in entrepreneurship is not limited to students who earn business degrees. *Anyone* has the potential to be a successful entrepreneur. At the University of Miami, only 20 percent of the students who have participated in The Launch Pad, the school's start-up accelerator, have been business majors.

- *I'm not creative enough to come up with a good idea for a business.* As you will learn in Chapter 3, *everyone* has the potential to be creative. Some of the most successful businesses were created when an entrepreneur recognized a simple need that people had and created a business to meet that need.

- *I don't have any experience.* Neither did Bill Gates (Microsoft) and Michael Dell (Dell Inc.) when they launched their companies, and things worked out pretty well for both of them. Business experience can be an important factor in a company's success, but every entrepreneur has to start somewhere to gain that experience.

- *I might fail.* Failure *is* a possibility. In fact, the survival rate of new companies after five years is 48 percent. Ask yourself this: What is the worst that can happen if I launch a business and it fails? Entrepreneurs do not allow the fear of failure to stop them from trying to realize their dreams.

If you want to become a successful collegiate entrepreneur, what can you do to increase the chances of your success? The following tips will help.

Recognize That Starting a Business at an Early Age May Be to Your Advantage

Young people tend to be highly creative, and that can provide a company with a competitive advantage. In addition, young people often accomplish things simply because they don't know that they are not supposed to be able to do them!

Build a Business Plan

One of the best ways to reduce the probability that your business will fail is to create a business plan. Doing so forces you to ask and then answer some tough questions about your idea and your proposed venture. "It's all about 'derisking' your idea," says Gregg Fairbrothers, who teaches entrepreneurship at Dartmouth's Tuck School of Business. "Identifying, unblinkingly, what could go wrong and taking whatever steps necessary to slash the odds that it will."

Use All of the Resources That Are Available to You

Many colleges and universities now offer courses in entrepreneurship and small business management and have faculty members who are experts in the field. In many cases, the people who are teaching these classes are veteran entrepreneurs themselves with tremendous reservoirs of knowledge and experience. Some colleges provide special dorms for budding entrepreneurs that serve as business incubators. Smart collegiate entrepreneurs tap into the pool of resources that their campuses offer.

Don't Go It Alone

Research at MIT's Sloan School of Business suggests that starting a business with cofounders increases the company's probability of success. Each additional founder up to four increases the likelihood that a start-up will succeed. Another study reports that solo entrepreneurs take 3.6 times as long to launch as teams of two or more cofounders. Cofounders bring complementary skill sets to the venture, share the burden of the huge volume of work required to launch, and provide an important support system when things get tough. Senthil Natarajan hoped to play baseball in college, but in his senior year of high school, he suffered four injuries to his pitching arm in just two months, ending his baseball career. While attending Rice University, Natarajan met Alex Dzeda, a fellow engineering student, and the duo came up with the idea for a wearable device that measures stress and muscle fatigue in a pitcher's arm, analyzes his or her throwing motion, and relays the information to a mobile device via Bluetooth. The young entrepreneurs pitched their idea in a business plan competition at Rice University and won first place. Then they competed in a national business plan competition with their patent-pending device and took third place. *Forbes* magazine recently named their company, Ziel Solutions, one of the 15 most innovative college start-ups in the United States.

(continued)

Hands On . . . How To

Find a Mentor

Most young entrepreneurs have not had the opportunity to gain a wealth of business experience, but they do have access to mentors who do. While a student at Chapman University in Orange, California, Mike Brown won the top prize at the annual Global Student Entrepreneur Awards for his company, ModBargains.com, a business that sells aftermarket products for modifying cars and trucks. Brown says that his first boss, who owns several businesses, served as his mentor. ModBargains.com, which Brown started with fellow car enthusiast Ron Hay, now has more than 4,000 products available and has surpassed annual sales of $1 million. Brown is now a volunteer entrepreneur-in-residence at Chapman University, where he mentors college students with entrepreneurial aspirations.

Learn to Be a "Bootstrapper"

Learning to start and manage a company with few resources is good training for any entrepreneur. In the early days of their start-ups, many successful entrepreneurs find creative ways to finance their businesses and to keep their operating expenses as low as possible. Because they lack the deep pockets of their larger rivals, entrepreneurs must use their creativity, ingenuity, and street smarts to market their companies effectively.

Manage Your Time Wisely

Taking college classes and running a business places a large workload on any collegiate entrepreneur, one that demands good time management skills. The most successful entrepreneurs recognize the importance of controlling their schedules (as much as possible) and working as efficiently as they can.

Remember to Have Fun

College is supposed to be one of the best times of your life! Starting and running a business also can be one of the most rewarding experiences of your life. Doing both can double the fun, but it also can create a great deal of stress. Balance is the key.

Sources: Based on Matt Hunckler, "Meet Fifteen of the Brightest College Entrepreneurs and Their Innovative Startups," *Forbes*, January 14, 2016, www.forbes.com/sites/matthunckler/2016/01/14/15-brightest-college-entrepreneurs/#683e29c92802; Colleen Taylor, "For Start-Ups Pitching VCs, Three Is the Magic Number," Gigaom, May 13, 2011, http://gigaom.com/2011/05/13/multiple-founder-startups/; "No Entrepreneur Is an Island: Cofounders Help Start-Ups Succeed," Nevada Institute for Renewable Energy and Commercialization, January 21, 2013, http://nirec.org/no-entrepreneur-is-an-island-co-founders-help-startups-succeed/; Michael Hughes, "Top 10 Articles to Help Entrepreneurs Find a Cofounder," CoFounders Lab, May 31, 2012, http://blog.cofounderslab.com/founders/how-to-find-a-co-founder; Millie Kerr, "Fashion's Final Frontier," *Entrepreneur*, May 2013, p. 78; Claire Martin, "Rolling Up Their Sleeves, as a Team," *New York Times*, May 18, 2013, www.nytimes.com/2013/05/19/business/at-ministry-of-supply-teamwork-in-making-high-tech-apparel.html?pagewanted=all&_r=0; Adam Bluestein and Amy Barrett, "Revitalize the American Dream: Bring on the Entrepreneurs!" *Inc.*, July/August 2010, pp. 76–88; David Whitford, "Can You Learn to Be an Entrepreneur?" *Fortune*, March 22, 2010, p. 66; Robert Sherman, "Student Entrepreneur Shares Hard-Won Lessons at YoungMoney.com," *Orange Entrepreneur*, Syracuse University, Fall 2007, p. 5; Daniel Jimenez, "The Best College Entrepreneurs of 2006," *Young Money*, July 2007, www.youngmoney.com/entrepreneur/student_entrepreneurs/070126; Michael Simmons, "Why Starting a Business Now May Be the Best Way to Achieve Your Dreams," *Young Money*, July 2003, www.youngmoney.com/entrepreneur/student_entrepreneurs/031010_01; and Scott Reeves, "How to Swing with Guerrilla Marketing," *Forbes*, June 8, 2006, www.forbes.com/2006/06/08/entrepreneurs-marketing-harley-davidson-cx_sr_0608askanexpert.html.

The Power of "Small" Business

Since 1982, the number of small businesses in the United States has increased 49 percent. Of the 28.8 million businesses in the United States, approximately 28.7 million, or 99.7 percent, are considered small. Although there is no universal definition of a small business (the U.S. Small Business Administration has more than 800 definitions of a small business, based on industry categories), a common delineation of a **small business** is one that employs fewer than 100 people. They thrive in virtually every industry, although the majority of small companies are concentrated in the service, construction, and retail industries (see Figure 1.9). Although they may be small businesses, their contributions to the economy are anything but small. For example, small companies employ 56.8 million people, or 48.0 percent of the nation's private sector workforce, even though they possess less than one-fourth of total business assets. Almost 90 percent of businesses with paid employees are small, employing fewer than 20 workers, but small companies account for 43 percent of total private payroll in the United States. Although nearly 80 percent of small companies have no employees other than the founder, the 20 percent that do have employees actually create more jobs than do big businesses. Small businesses created 63 percent of the net new jobs in the United States between 1993 and 2013.[155] The ability to create jobs is not distributed evenly across the small business sector, however. Research shows that the top-performing 5 percent of small companies create 67 percent of the net new jobs in the economy, and they do so across all industry sectors, not just in "hot" industries, such as high-tech. These young, job-creating small companies are known as **gazelles**, businesses that grow at 20 percent or more per year for four years and have at least $100,000 in annual sales. Nearly 85 percent of these high-impact companies are located in urban areas. Not surprisingly, cities with high levels of entrepreneurial activity boast higher levels of job creation than those that are

LO6

Describe the important role that small businesses play in our nation's economy.

small business
a business that employs fewer than 100 people.

gazelles
small companies that are growing at 20 percent or more per year with at least $100,000 in annual sales; they create 70 percent of net new jobs in the economy.

FIGURE 1.9

Small Businesses by Industry

Source: Based on data from "Statistics of U.S. Businesses, U.S. and States, NAICS Sectors, Small Employment Sizes," United States Census Bureau, 2013, www.census.gov/econ/susb/.

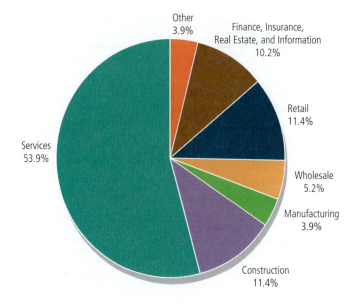

home to heavier concentrations of existing businesses.[156] "Mice" are small companies that never grow much and don't create many jobs. The majority of small companies are mice.[157] In fact, 75 percent of small business owners say that they are not seeking rapid growth for their businesses and want to keep them small.[158]

Small businesses also produce 48.5 percent of the U.S. private GDP and account for 47 percent of business sales.[159] In fact, the U.S small business sector is the world's third-largest "economy," trailing only the economies of the United States and China. Small companies make up 97.7 percent of exporting companies and account for 34 percent of the value of all exports.[160] One business writer describes the United States as "an entrepreneurial economy, a system built on nimble, low-overhead small companies with fluid workforces, rather than the massive conglomerates that upheld the economy for decades."[161]

Small companies also are incubators of new ideas, products, and services. Small firms actually create 16 times more patents per employee than large companies.[162] Traditionally, small businesses have played a vital role in innovation, and they continue to do so today. Many important inventions trace their roots to an entrepreneur, including the zipper, FM radio, the laser, the brassiere, air-conditioning, the escalator, the lightbulb, the personal computer, and the automatic transmission.

Putting Failure into Perspective

LO7

Put failure into the proper perspective.

Because of their limited resources, inexperienced management, and lack of financial stability, small businesses suffer relatively high mortality rates. As you learned earlier in this chapter, two years after start-up, 34 percent of small companies have failed, and after five years, 52 percent have failed.[163] Figure 1.10 shows the failure rate for small businesses over time, clear evidence of the constant "churn" that exists as entrepreneurs create new businesses and others close. New companies that replace old ones with better ideas, market approaches, and products actually are a sign of a healthy entrepreneurial economy.

Because they are building businesses in an environment filled with uncertainty and shaped by rapid change, entrepreneurs recognize that failure is likely to be part of their lives, but they are not paralyzed by that fear. "The excitement of building a new business from scratch is greater than the fear of failure," says one entrepreneur who failed in business several times before finally succeeding.[164] Entrepreneurs use their failures as a rallying point and as a means of refocusing their business ventures for success. They see failure for what it really is: an opportunity to learn what does not work! Successful entrepreneurs have the attitude that failures are simply stepping-stones along the path to success. Author J. K. Rowling was a penniless, unemployed,

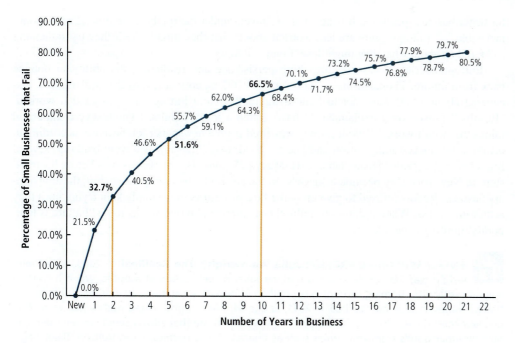

FIGURE 1.10

**Small Business
Failure Rate**

Source: Based on data from
"Survival Rates of Establishments, by Year Started and
Number of Years Since
Starting, 1994–2016," Business Employment Dynamics,
U.S. Bureau of Labor Statistics, www.bls.gov/bdm/
entrepreneurship/bdm_chart3
.htm.

single parent when she penned a book about a boy wizard and his adventures. She submitted her manuscript to 12 publishers, all of whom rejected it. Rowling persisted, however, and a small London publisher, Bloomsbury, finally decided to take a chance on *Harry Potter and the Philosopher's Stone* after a glowing review from the CEO's young daughter. The seven-book Harry Potter series went on to sell more than 450 million copies worldwide, making Rowling the first billionaire author.[165] Basketball legend Michael Jordan displayed the same attitude. "I've missed more than 9,000 shots in my career," he says. "I lost almost 300 games. Twenty-six times, I've been trusted to take the game-winning shot and *missed*. I've failed over and over and over again in my life. And that is why I succeed."[166]

Failure is a natural part of the creative process. The only people who never fail are those who never do anything or never attempt anything new. Baseball fans know that Babe Ruth held the record for career home runs (714) for many years, but how many know that he also held the record for strikeouts (1,330)? Successful entrepreneurs know that hitting an entrepreneurial home run requires a few strikeouts along the way, and they are willing to accept them. In an address at Harvard University's graduation, author J. K. Rowling told students, "You might never fail on the scale I did, but some failure in life is inevitable. It is impossible to live without failing at something, unless you live so cautiously that you might as well not have lived at all—in which case, you fail by default."[167] Although entrepreneurs don't always succeed, they are not willing to fail by default. Failure is an inevitable part of being an entrepreneur, and true entrepreneurs don't quit when they fail. One entrepreneur whose business burned through $800 million of investors' money before folding says, "If you're an entrepreneur, you don't give up when times get tough."[168]

One hallmark of successful entrepreneurs is the ability to fail *intelligently*, learning why they failed so that they can avoid making the same mistake again. They fail quickly, and often spectacularly, but the key is that they take away valuable lessons from their failures. James Dyson, whose company makes one of the best-selling vacuum cleaners in the world, made 5,127 prototypes of his bagless vacuum cleaner before he hit on one that worked. "There were 5,126 failures," he says, "but I learned from each one. That's how I came up with a solution. So I don't mind failure."[169] Like Dyson, other entrepreneurs know that business success depends on their ability not to avoid making mistakes but rather to be open to the lessons that each mistake teaches. They learn from their failures and use them as fuel to push themselves closer to their ultimate target. "Failure can teach not only what one is doing wrong but also how to do it right the next time," says one business writer. "It can be a useful, even transformational, force for better business practices. It is best not to shove it under the rug because it is, at some point, inevitable."[170] Entrepreneurs are less worried about what they might lose if they try something and fail than about what they might lose if they fail to try.

Entrepreneurial success requires both persistence and resilience, the ability to bounce back from failure. Thomas Edison, who earned 1,093 patents (a record that still stands), discovered about 1,800 ways not to build a lightbulb before hitting on a design that worked. "Results!" Edison once exclaimed. "I have gotten a lot of results. I know several thousand things that won't work."[171] Walt Disney was fired from a newspaper job because, according to his boss, he "lacked imagination and had no good ideas." Disney also went bankrupt several times before he created Disneyland. R. H. Macy failed in business seven times before his retail store in New York City became a success. In the spirit of true entrepreneurship, these visionary business leaders refused to give up in the face of failure; they simply kept trying until they achieved success. When it comes to failure, entrepreneurs' motto seems to be "Failure is temporary; quitting is permanent."

ENTREPRENEURIAL PROFILE: Julie Wainwright: The RealReal In 2000, Julie Wainwright was CEO of Pets.com, an online seller of pet food and supplies, when it crashed magnificently after burning through $147 million of investors' capital in 20 months and failing to find a business model that worked. In 2011, at age 54, Wainwright, undaunted by Pets.com's failure, launched The RealReal, an upscale consignment Web site that allows people to sell their like-new designer goods from companies such as Chanel, Gucci, Hermes, Louis Vuitton, Balenciaga, and others online. The RealReal, which receives about 130,000 designer items per month, verifies the authenticity of each item it lists for sale, so that buyers are assured of getting genuine designer products rather than fakes (which is a real problem for many other consignment Web sites). Wainwright has attracted $83 million in funding for The RealReal, which generates sales of more than $200 million annually and is now profitable.[172] ∎

LO8

Explain how an entrepreneur can avoid becoming another failure statistic.

How to Avoid the Pitfalls

Although failure can be a valuable part of the entrepreneurial process, no one sets out to fail in business. Now we must examine the ways to avoid becoming another failure statistic and gain insight into what makes a successful business.

Know Your Business in Depth

We have already emphasized the need for the right type of experience in the business you plan to start. Get the best education in your business area you possibly can *before* you set out on your own. Become a serious student of your industry. Read everything you can—trade journals, business periodicals, books, and research reports—relating to your industry and learn what it takes to succeed in it. Personal contact with suppliers, customers, trade associations, and others in the same industry is another excellent way to get that knowledge. Smart entrepreneurs join industry trade associations and attend trade shows to pick up valuable information and to make key contacts before they open their doors for business.

Build a Viable Business Model—And Test It

Before launching a business, an entrepreneur should define the business model on which he or she plans to build a company and test it, preferably with actual customers or potential customers, to verify that it can be successful. Does real market demand for the proposed product or service actually exist? Validating an idea before investing significant time and money to develop it is foolhardy. Grand assumptions about capturing market share and "hockey stick" revenue growth that never materialize have been the downfall of many start-up businesses. Creating a successful business model requires entrepreneurs to identify all of the model's vital components, including the resources, partners, and activities they must assemble; the customer segments they are targeting; the channels they will use to reach them; the value proposition they offer customers; and the sources of revenue and accompanying costs they will incur. We will discuss a useful tool for defining a viable business model, the Business Model Canvas, and the process of testing it in Chapter 4.

ENTREPRENEURIAL PROFILE: Parker Moore, Jon Rice, and Jonathon Peterson: Tux on Trux While participating in a Startup Weekend at the University of South Carolina's Darla Moore School of Business, Parker Moore recalled the convoluted, time-consuming experience of renting a tuxedo for his high school senior prom and decided that he had a better idea for providing tuxedo rentals. He partnered with friends Jon Rice and Jonathon Peterson to pitch the idea for Tux on Trux, a business that brings tuxedos to young men for special events. Tux on Trux schedules fitting sessions at a convenient location, such as a high school gym or a fraternity house, and then returns a week later to distribute the tuxedos. After the event is over, Tux on Trux meets its customers at the same location to pick up the tuxedos. The business model provides greater convenience for customers and allows the entrepreneurs to eliminate the significant overhead costs associated with maintaining a physical store. As a result, Tux on Trux is able to rent tuxedos at rates that are well below those of traditional rental shops, just $80 for a basic black tuxedo to $189 for more upscale models with all of the accoutrements. To test their business model, the young entrepreneurs set up a pilot program at a nearby high school. The test was successful, so they began marketing Tux on Trux to other high schools and, as an afterthought, pitched their service to the fraternities at their university. To their surprise, the service was even more popular among college students than among high school students. With a refined business model, the trio's business went from idea to market test to launch to profitability in just three months. The young entrepreneurs have expanded their service to cater to wedding parties as well and use social media as an essential marketing tool.[173] ■

Use Lean Start-up Principles

Entrepreneurs are accustomed to accomplishing big goals with few resources and often rely on the principles of the lean start-up. Whereas some entrepreneurs ask "*Can* we build this product or provide this service?" those who follow lean start-up principles ask "*Should* we build this product?" and "Can we build a viable business around this product or service?" The first step is to identify a customer need or a pain point and build a **minimum viable product (or service)** to address it. Getting the minimum viable product (or service) into customers' hands is an essential part of validating an idea because it produces valuable feedback that entrepreneurs use to improve and refine the product or service and the business model. The lean approach views an entrepreneur's idea and business model as hypotheses to be tested by subjecting them to potential customers for feedback. The goal is to minimize waste and maximize the customer's value proposition. Customer feedback tells entrepreneurs whether they are pulling the right levers and pushing the right buttons on their business models.

minimum viable product (or service)
the simplest version of a product or service that allows entrepreneurs to validate a business idea by producing valuable feedback that entrepreneurs use to improve and refine the product or service and the business model.

Know When to Pivot

Following lean start-up principles means that entrepreneurs often must make pivots in their business models and plans. A pivot is a course correction in which an entrepreneur keeps a company fixed on the original vision but changes the direction in which the company is moving. Successful entrepreneurs often start their companies with one product, service, market, or model in mind and then change course once market realities redirect them.

ENTREPRENEURIAL PROFILE: Alex White, Samir Rayani, and David Hoffman: Next Big Sound While Alex White, Samir Rayani, and David Hoffman were students at Northwestern University, they cofounded Next Big Sound, a Web site where people could create fantasy record labels and sign up-and-coming artists. Despite much media coverage, the company's revenue was small. The young entrepreneurs were on the verge of shutting down their business when they made a pivot and refocused Next Big Sound on tracking major social media to measure the popularity of artists and bands with a simple real-time dashboard. They focused their new business model on providing analytics for record labels, music producers, and artists themselves. Next Big Sound has attracted $7.9 million in financing, has thousands of customers in the music industry, has generated millions of dollars in sales, and recently began offering a similar service to book publishers through Next Big Book.[174] ■

Develop a Solid Business Plan

If an entrepreneur's business model passes the feasibility test, the next step is to prepare a business plan. A business plan explains *how* an entrepreneur intends to implement the business model. Without a sound business plan, a company merely drifts along without any real direction and often stalls out when it faces its first challenge. Yet entrepreneurs, who tend to be people of action, often jump right into a business venture without taking time to prepare a written plan outlining the essence of the business. Not only does a plan provide a pathway to success, but it also creates a benchmark against which an entrepreneur can measure actual company performance. Building a successful business begins with implementing a sound business plan with laser-like focus. One study of small businesses reports that the founders of top-performing companies were 78 percent more likely to have created a formal business plan before launching than founders of companies in the bottom tier.[175]

A business plan allows entrepreneurs to replace sometimes faulty assumptions with facts before making the decision to go into business. The planning process forces entrepreneurs to ask and then answer some difficult, challenging, and crucial questions about target customers, market potential, the competition, the cost of doing business, pricing, realistic revenue forecasts, and other matters. A study by Palo Alto Software concludes that entrepreneurs who prepare business plans achieve greater success in acquiring capital for their businesses (through both loans and investments) and in growing their companies than those who do not.[176] We will discuss the process of developing a business plan in Chapter 5.

ENTREPRENEURIAL PROFILE: Frank Mobley: Immedion At 43, Frank Mobley bowed to his independent streak, left a well-paying steady job with a successful data solutions business, and started his own data support and security company, Immedion. Building on his experience in the telecommunications and data solutions industries, Mobley saw a growing need among midsize companies for reliable servers that could store data securely and keep companies' Web sites up and running under any circumstances. He spent two months writing a business plan, which was all he had to convince investors to put up the $2.5 million he needed to launch Immedion. Mobley was able to use the business plan to sell his idea to investors, including friends, family members, and even his former employers. When Mobley started his company in Greenville, South Carolina, he had one data center and no clients. Today, Immedion has five data centers and more than 300 clients, and is growing rapidly. The company recently expanded into the Midwest by acquiring Appica, a provider of cloud and data center services in Cincinnati, Ohio.[177] ∎

Manage Financial Resources

The best defense against financial problems is to develop a practical information system and then use that information to make business decisions. No entrepreneur can maintain control over a business unless he or she is able to judge its financial health.

The first step in managing financial resources effectively is to have adequate start-up capital. Too many entrepreneurs start their businesses undercapitalized. Wise entrepreneurs follow the old axiom "Estimate how much capital you need to get the business going and then double that figure" because launching a business almost always costs more (and takes longer) than any entrepreneur expects. Jake Burton, founder of Burton Snowboards, a company that dominates the snowboard industry with 58 percent market share, made that mistake when he started his now-successful company in 1977, straight out of college. "I lost [my start-up capital] before I knew what had happened," he says. "I underestimated the cost and time it would take to get the business going."[178]

The most valuable financial resource to any small business is *cash*. Although earning a profit is essential to its long-term survival, a business must have an adequate supply of cash to pay its bills and obligations. Some entrepreneurs count on growing sales to supply their company's cash needs, but this almost never happens. Growing companies usually consume more cash than they generate, and the faster they grow, the more cash they gobble up! Business history is littered with failed companies whose founders had no idea how much cash their businesses were generating and were spending cash as if they were certain there was "plenty more where that came from." Four years after former professional baseball player Curt Schilling launched 38 Studios, a company that he started to produce massive multiplayer online games, the company ran short of cash and defaulted on a $1.1 million interest payment that was part of a $75 million guaranteed loan. The company soon folded, 400 people lost their jobs, lenders lost $110 million, and Schilling himself lost $50 million.[179] We will discuss cash management techniques in Chapter 13.

Understand Financial Statements

Every business owner must depend on records and financial statements to know the condition of his or her business. All too often, entrepreneurs use these only for tax purposes and not as vital management control devices. To truly understand what is going on in the business, an owner must have at least a basic understanding of accounting and finance.

When analyzed and interpreted properly, these financial statements are reliable indicators of a small firm's health. They can be quite helpful in signaling potential problems. For example, declining sales, slipping profits, rising debt, and deteriorating working capital are all symptoms of potentially lethal problems that require immediate attention. We will discuss financial statement analysis in Chapter 12.

Build the Right Team

One of the most important steps to creating a successful start-up is assembling the right entrepreneurial team to refine the business model and implement the business plan. Entrepreneurship is increasingly becoming a team sport. One study of small businesses reports that top-performing companies are 59 percent more likely to have multiple founders than businesses in the bottom tier.[180] Another study suggests that companies started by two to four cofounders are more likely to succeed than those started by a single founder. (Three founders appears to be the "sweet spot.") Each additional cofounder up to four increases the odds of a company's success.[181]

Learn to Manage People Effectively

No matter what kind of business you launch, you must learn to manage people. Every business depends on a foundation of well-trained, motivated employees. No business owner can do everything alone. The people an entrepreneur hires ultimately determine the heights to which the company can climb—or the depths to which it can plunge. Attracting and retaining a corps of quality employees is no easy task, however, and is a challenge for every small business owner. In a recent talent shortage survey, Manpower Group reports that 40 percent of global employers (and 46 percent of employers in the United States) say they have difficulty filling vacant jobs, which represents a nine-year high.[182]

Entrepreneurs quickly learn that treating their employees with respect and compassion usually translates into their employees treating customers in the same fashion. Successful entrepreneurs value their employees and constantly find ways to show it. The Muse, the career-oriented Web site started by Kathryn Minshew, Alex Cavoulacos, and Melissa McCreery, is growing so quickly that the company must hire many new employees from the outside; however, Minshew and Cavoulacos emphasize promoting from within and rewarding employees with meaningful assignments. The Muse uses a team-based approach, and Minshew says that managers push employees to grow and look for chances to help employees learn new skills and develop new talents. Mark Wasmund started with The Muse as an account executive, and one year later was promoted to the company's West Coast sales manager position, managing 16 account executives.[183] We will discuss the techniques of managing and motivating people effectively in Chapter 17.

Set Your Business Apart from the Competition

The formula for almost certain business failure involves becoming a "me-too business"—merely copying whatever the competition is doing. Most successful entrepreneurs find a way to differentiate their companies from competitors even if they sell similar products or services. This is especially important for small companies going up against larger, more powerful rivals with greater financial resources. Ideally, the basis for differentiating a company from its competitors is founded in what it does best. For small companies, that basis often is customer service, convenience, speed, quality, or whatever else is important to attracting and keeping satisfied customers. We will discuss the strategies for creating a unique footprint in the marketplace in Chapters 5 and 9.

Maintain a Positive Attitude

Achieving business success requires an entrepreneur to maintain a positive mental attitude toward business and the discipline to stick with it. Successful entrepreneurs recognize that their most valuable resource is their time, and they learn to manage it effectively to make themselves and their companies more productive. None of this, of course, is possible without passion—passion for their businesses, their products or services, their customers, and their communities. Passion enables a failed business owner to get back up, try again, and make it to the top! One business writer says that growing a successful business requires entrepreneurs to have great faith in themselves and their ideas, great doubt concerning the challenges and inevitable obstacles they will face as they build their businesses, and great effort—lots of hard work—to make their dreams become reality.[184]

Developing Skills for Your Career

If you're not an entrepreneurship or business major, you may be thinking that this course is not relevant to you. We assure you that it is. Whether you plan to pursue a career in entrepreneurship or some other field, the lessons you learn in this course will help you because the principles of entrepreneurship apply to *every* avenue of life. Whether you choose to start your own business or work for someone else in either a for-profit or non-profit organization, the skills you will learn in this course with the help of this book will be extremely valuable to you. Recent surveys show that employers value the following skill sets in the people they want to hire, and, as you will discover, this course and this book will help you develop and enhance your abilities in the following areas.

Critical Thinking and Problem Solving

Every successful entrepreneur must engage in critical thinking and problem solving. Launching a running a successful company is a perpetual exercise in these areas. In this book, you can hone your critical thinking and problem solving skills by tackling the "You Be the Consultant" and the "Beyond the Classroom" features that appear in every chapter. In addition, if one of your course requirements is to prepare a business plan, you will learn firsthand how to think critically and solve problems.

Written and Oral Communication

Successful entrepreneurs are good communicators. As part of their search for capital, they must create well-written, coherent business plans and pitch their ideas to potential lenders and investors. Chapter 5, Crafting a Business Plan and Building a Solid Strategic Plan, teaches you how to write a plan that not only will help you build a successful business but also convince potential lenders and investors to put up financing for it. This chapter also explains how to make a successful business plan presentation. If you develop a business plan (and perhaps participate in a business plan competition), you will learn important written and oral communication skills.

Teamwork and Collaboration

Research shows that businesses started by multiple founders have higher success rates than those started by solo entrepreneurs. Even if you choose to start a business by yourself, you will learn very quickly that you must rely on the help of other people to build it. In other words, you will learn the power of teamwork and collaboration. Chapter 17, Building a New Venture Team and Planning for the Next Generation, will help you learn these skills.

Leadership

One of an entrepreneur's most important skills is *leadership*. Effective leaders create a vision for their companies, convince other people to believe in and commit to it, develop a plan to implement the vision, and sustain the effort to accomplish it. In Chapter 17, Building a New Venture Team and Planning for the Next Generation, you will also learn the behaviors of successful leaders. Building a company will test and improve your leadership skills.

Creativity

Whatever their business, employers are seeking creative talent. In Chapter 3, Creativity and Innovation: Keys to Entrepreneurial Success, you will learn about the creative process and how to enhance both your personal creativity and the creativity of the people in your company.

Throughout this book and course, you will experience the incredible creativity that entrepreneurs demonstrate. Sometimes their ideas are so innovative that people call them "crazy." Many of those entrepreneurs whom people mocked and called "crazy" built successful businesses that changed the world.

Ethics and Social Responsibility

Employers seek employees whom they are confident will do the right thing when faced with an ethical dilemma. A company's reputation is critical to its success, but it also is quite fragile. One employee acting in an unethical fashion can destroy a company's good reputation. In Chapter 2, Ethics and Social Responsibility: Doing the Right Thing, you will learn basic principles of ethics and social responsibility. Often, entrepreneurs and employees fall into ethical traps that are cloaked in the garb of mundane decisions. This chapter will help you avoid these traps by making you aware of the issues and how to address them.

Throughout your career, you may choose to use these skills in your own business or in someone else's business or non-profit organization; either way, they are essential to your success. Moreover, it is only through the aggregate of your educational experience that you will have the opportunity to develop many of these skills that employers have identified as critical to success in the workplace. As you can see, in this course, and specifically in this book, you will have the opportunity to develop and practice these skills.

Conclusion

As you can see, entrepreneurship lies at the heart of this nation's free enterprise system; small companies truly are the backbone of our economy. Their contributions are as many and as diverse as the businesses themselves. Indeed, diversity is one of the strengths of the U.S. small business sector. Although there are no secrets to becoming a successful entrepreneur, there are steps that entrepreneurs can take to enhance the probability of their success. The remainder of this book will explore those steps and how to apply them to the process of launching a successful business with an emphasis on building a sound business plan.

- Chapter 2, "Ethics and Social Responsibility: Doing the Right Thing," describes a framework for making ethical decisions and ensuring that a business lives up to its social responsibility. Chapter 3, "Creativity and Innovation: Keys to Entrepreneurial Success," explores the creative process that lies at the heart of entrepreneurship and offers practical tips on how you can stimulate your own creativity and that of your employees.

- Section II, "The Entrepreneurial Journey Begins" (Chapters 4 to 8), discusses the classic start-up questions every entrepreneur faces, particularly conducting a feasibility analysis, creating a business model, developing a strategy, building a business plan, choosing a form of ownership, and alternative methods for becoming a business owner (franchising and buying an existing business).

- Section III, "Launching the Business" (Chapters 9 to 14), focuses first on creating an effective bootstrap marketing plan for a small company. These chapters address creating an effective e-commerce strategy and establishing pricing and credit strategies. This section also explains how to develop the financial component of a business plan, including creating projected financial statements and forecasting cash flow. These chapters also offer existing business owners practical financial management tools and explain how to find the sources of funding, both debt and equity, necessary to launch a business. Finally, this section includes a chapter on selecting the right location and designing an appropriate layout for a business.

- Section IV, "Putting the Business Plan to Work: Sources of Funds" (Chapters 15 to 17), explains how to find the sources of funding, both debt and equity, necessary to launch a business and how to penetrate global markets successfully. This section also provides useful techniques for assembling a strong new venture team and leading its members to success and discusses the importance of creating a management succession plan to ensure that a company successfully makes the transition to the next generation of owners.

As you can see, the journey down the road of entrepreneurship will be a fascinating and exciting one. Let's get started!

> **MyLab Entrepreneurship**
>
> If your instructor is using MyLab Entrepreneurship, go to **www.pearson.com/mylab/ entrepreneurship** to complete the problems marked with this icon ⭐.

Chapter Summary by Learning Objective

1. Define the role of the entrepreneur in business in the United States and around the world.

- Entrepreneurship is thriving in the United States, but the current wave of entrepreneurship is not limited to the United States; many nations around the globe are seeing similar growth in their small business sectors. A variety of competitive, economic, and demographic shifts have created a world in which "small is beautiful."

- Capitalist societies depend on entrepreneurs to provide the drive and risk taking necessary for the system to supply people with the goods and services they need.

2. Describe the entrepreneurial profile.

- Entrepreneurs have some common characteristics, including a desire for responsibility, a preference for moderate risk, confidence in their ability to succeed, desire for immediate feedback, a high energy level, a future orientation, skill at organizing, and a value of achievement over money. In a phrase, they are tenacious high achievers.

3-A. Describe the benefits of entrepreneurship.

- Driven by their personal characteristics, entrepreneurs establish and manage small businesses to gain control over their lives, make a difference in the world, become self-fulfilled, reap unlimited profits, contribute to society, and do what they enjoy doing.

3-B. Describe the drawbacks of entrepreneurship.

- Entrepreneurs also face certain disadvantages, including uncertainty of income, the risk of losing their investments (and more), long hours and hard work, a lower quality of life until the business gets established, high stress levels, and complete decision-making responsibility.

4. Explain the forces that are driving the growth of entrepreneurship.

- Several factors are driving the boom in entrepreneurship, including the portrayal of entrepreneurs

as heroes, better entrepreneurial education, economic and demographic factors, a shift to a service economy, technological advances, more independent lifestyles, and increased international opportunities.

5. Explain the cultural diversity of entrepreneurship.

- Several groups are leading the nation's drive toward entrepreneurship: young people, women, minorities, immigrants, part-timers, home-based business owners, family business owners, copreneurs, corporate castoffs, corporate dropouts, social entrepreneurs, and retired Baby Boomers.

6. Describe the important role that small businesses play in our nation's economy.

- The small business sector's contributions are many. Small businesses make up 99.7 percent of all businesses, employ 51 percent of the private sector workforce, have created two-thirds to three-fourths of the net new jobs in the economy, produce 51 percent of the country's private GDP, and account for 47 percent of all business sales.

7. Put failure into the proper perspective.

- Entrepreneurs recognize that failure is a natural part of the creative process. Successful entrepreneurs have the attitude that failures are simply stepping-stones along the path to success, and they refuse to be paralyzed by a fear of failure.

8. Explain how an entrepreneur can avoid becoming another failure statistic.

- Entrepreneurs can employ several general tactics to avoid these pitfalls. They should know their businesses in depth, prepare a solid business plan, manage financial resources effectively, understand financial statements, learn to manage people, set their businesses apart from the competition, and maintain a positive attitude.

MyLab Entrepreneurship

If your instructor is using MyLab Entrepreneurship, go to **www.pearson.com/mylab/entrepreneurship** for Auto-graded writing questions as well as the following Assisted-graded writing questions:

1. Briefly describe the role of the following groups in entrepreneurship: young people, women, minorities, immigrants, part-timers, home-based business owners, family business owners, copreneurs, corporate castoffs, corporate dropouts, social entrepreneurs, and retired Baby Boomers.
2. What contributions do small businesses make to our economy?

Discussion Questions

1-1. What forces have led to the boom in entrepreneurship in the United States and around the globe?

1-2. What is an entrepreneur? Give a brief description of the entrepreneurial profile.

1-3. *Inc.* magazine claims, "Entrepreneurship is more mundane than it's sometimes portrayed … you don't need to be a person of mythical proportions to be very, very successful in building a company." Do you agree? Explain.

1-4. What are the major benefits of business ownership?

1-5. Which of the potential drawbacks to business ownership are most critical?

1-6. Describe the small business failure rate.

1-7. Outline the causes of business failure. Which problems cause most business failures?

1-8. How does a typical entrepreneur view the possibility of business failure?

1-9. How can a small business owner avoid the common pitfalls that often lead to business failures?

1-10. Why is it important to study the small business failure rate and to understand the causes of business failures?

1-11. Explain the typical entrepreneur's attitude toward risk.

1-12. Are you interested in someday launching a small business?

1-13. If you are interested in launching a business, when do you intend to start it?

1-14. If you intend to start a business, what steps can you take to increase the likelihood that it will succeed?

Beyond the Classroom . . .

1-15. Choose an entrepreneur in your community and interview him or her. What's the "story" behind the business?

1-16. How well does the entrepreneur fit the entrepreneurial profile described in this chapter?

1-17. What advantages and disadvantages does the entrepreneur see in owning a business?

1-18. What advice would he or she offer to someone considering launching a business?

1-19. Select one of the categories under the section "The Cultural Diversity of Entrepreneurship" in this chapter and research it in more detail. Find examples of business owners in that category and prepare a brief report for your class.

1-20. Search through recent business publications or their Web sites (especially those focusing on small companies, such as *Inc.* and *Entrepreneur*) and find an example of an entrepreneur, past or present, who exhibits the entrepreneurial spirit of striving for success in the face of failure. Prepare a brief report for your class.

Endnotes

[1] Donna Kelley, Slavica Singer, and Mike Herrington, *Global Entrepreneurship Monitor 2016/17 Global Report*, Global Entrepreneurship Monitor, 2017, p. 7.

[2] Robert W. Fairlie, Amobio Morelix, E.J. Reedy, and Joshua Russell, *The 2016 Kauffman Index of Startup Activity*, 2016, Kauffman Foundation, p. 5.

[3] Donna Kelley, Slavica Singer, and Mike Herrington, *Global Entrepreneurship Monitor 2016/2017 Global Report*, Global Entrepreneurship Monitor, 2017, p. 8.

[4] Akbar Sadeghi, "The Births and Deaths of Business Establishments in the United States," *Monthly Labor Review*, December 2008, p. 3.

[5] *EY Megatrends 2015*, Ernst and Young, 2015, www.ey.com/GL/en/Issues/Business-environment/ey-megatrends-that-will-shape-our-future-3-entrepreneurship-rising.

[6] *EY Global Job Creation and Youth Entrepreneurship Survey 2015*, Ernst and Young, 2015, p. 12.

[7]Ruth Simon, "Sparking Entrepreneurial Spirit in Teens," *Wall Street Journal*, January 22, 2015, p. B6.

[8]Robert W. Fairlie, Amobio Morelix, E.J. Reedy, and Joshua Russell, "Opportunity Share of New Entrepreneurs," *The 2015 Kauffman Index of Startup Activity*, Kauffman Foundation, 2015, p. 26.

[9]Personal interview with Riley Csernica, Tarian Orthotics, July 25, 2014; "About Tarian," Tarian Orthotics, www.tarianorthotics.com/company.

[10]Katie Morell, "Fourth of July Special: Small Businesses of the Founding Fathers," *Open Forum*, July 4, 2012, www.openforum.com/articles/fourth-of-july-special-small-businesses-of-the-founding-fathers.

[11]José Ernesto Amorós and Niels Bosma, *Global Entrepreneurship Monitor: 2013 Global Report*, Babson College, Universidad del Desarollo, and Universiti Tun Abdul Razak, pp. 30–31.

[12]Adrian Woolridge, "Global Heroes," *The Economist*, March 14, 2009, p. 8.

[13]Howard H. Stevens, "We Create Entrepreneurs," *Success*, September 1995, p. 51.

[14]"Inspiration from a Serial Entrepreneur in One of the World's Poorest Villages," *Business Zone*, October 22, 2014, www.businesszone.co.uk/inspiration-from-a-serial-entrepreneur-in-one-of-the-worlds-poorest-villages.

[15]Lara Morgan, "Unfit and Happy or Fit and Miserable? A Millionaire Entrepreneur Talks About Work–Life Balance," *Business Zone*, June 20, 2014, www.businesszone.co.uk/topic/business-trends/unexercised-and-happy-or-fit-and-miserable-entrepreneurs-and-work-life-balance.

[16]Michelle Juergen, "Entrepreneur: A Powerful Team Gains a Cultural Foothold," *Entrepreneur*, June 2012, p. 144.

[17]Eric Schurenberg, "What's an Entrepreneur? The Best Answer Ever," *Inc.*, January 9, 2012, www.inc.com/eric-schurenberg/the-best-definition-of-entepreneurship.html.

[18]Thomas K. McCraw, "Mapping the Entrepreneurial Psyche," *Inc.*, August 2007, pp. 73–74.

[19]Ben Casselman, "Risk-Averse Culture Infects U.S. Workers, Entrepreneurs," *Wall Street Journal*, June 3, 2013, pp. A1, A14.

[20]Liz Welch, "Selling a Better Night's Sleep," *Inc.*, March 2016, pp. 92–93, 97; Ilan Mochari, "How This Mattress Startup Made $20 Million in 10 Months," *Inc.*, April 22, 2015, www.inc.com/ilan-mochari/2015-30-under-30-casper.html.

[21]David McClelland, *The Achieving Society* (Princeton, NJ: Van Nostrand, 1961), p. 16.

[22]Angelia Davis, "More Women of Color Finding Fulfillment in Self Employment," *Greenville News*, March 4, 2013, www.greenvilleonline.com/apps/pbcs.dll/article?AID=2013304270007&template=artiphone.

[23]Darren Dahl, "So Long, Wall Street," *Inc.*, June 2013, p. 25.

[24]Rod Kurtz, "What It Takes," *Inc. 500*, Fall 2004, p. 120.

[25]Joe Robinson, "The Rule Breakers," *Entrepreneur*, October 2015, pp. 49–56.

[26]Connie Loizos, "The Muse Raises $16 Million for It's Next-Gen Website," *TechCrunch*, June 22, 2016, https://techcrunch.com/2016/06/22/the-muse-raises-16-million-for-its-next-gen-career-site/; Vivian Giang, "11 Famous Entrepreneurs Share How They Overcame Their Biggest Failure," *Fast Company*, May 1, 2014, http://www.fastcompany.com/3029883/bottom-line/11-famous-entrepreneurs-share-how-they-overcame-their-biggest-failure; Amy White, "Need Help Up the Ladder? Let The Muse Be Your Guide," *Inc.*, June 24, 2014, http://www.inc.com/amy-whyte/35-under-35-the-muse-kathryn-minshew-2014.html.

[27]Jonah Lehrer, "Measurements That Mislead," *Wall Street Journal*, April 2, 2011, http://online.wsj.com/article/SB1 0001424052748704471904576230931647955902.html; Jonah Lehrer, "Which Traits Predict Success? (The Importance of Grit)," *Wired*, March 14, 2011, www.wired.com/wiredscience/2011/03/what-is-success-true-grit.

[28]Emily Esfahani Smith, "The Virtue of Hard Things," *Wall Street Journal*, May 4, 2016, p. A11.

[29]"How the Great Recession Spurred Entrepreneurship," *Strategy+Business*, June 21, 2013, www.strategy-business.com/article/re00240?gko=d3750.

[30]Dane Stangler, *The Economic Future Just Happened*, Ewing Marion Kauffman Foundation, 2009, p. 4.

[31]Jon Fine, "The Right Recipe for a Startup," *Inc.*, March 2015, pp. 27–29.

[32]"Small Business Owner Report," Bank of America, Spring 2013, p. 2.

[33]"Sage Reinvention of Small Business Study Summary Report," Sage Software, July 2013, p. 2.

[34]Jack Torrance, "Entrepreneurs Work 63% Longer Than Average Workers," *Real Business*, August 13, 2013, http://realbusiness.co.uk/article/22838-entrepreneurs-work-63-longer-than-average-workers.

[35]Will Schroter, "Sleep Sounds Nice, but for Start-up Founders, It's an Unaffordable Luxury," BizJournals.com, September 3, 2007, www.bizjournals.com/extraedge/consultants/go_big/2007/09/03/column10.html.

[36]Brittany Shoot, "Can You Hear Me Now?" *Entrepreneur*, May 2015, p. 78; "Dr. Rodney Perkins," *How Did I Get Here?* Bloomberg, June 3, 2016, www.bloomberg.com/graphics/2015-how-did-i-get-here/dr-rodney-perkins.html.

[37]Robert W. Fairlie, E.J. Reedy, Amobio Morelix, and Joshua Russell, *Kaufmann Index of Startup Activity*, Kauffman Foundation, 2016, p. 27.

[38]Matthew Flamm, "Look Out, Victoria's Secret: Lingerie e-Tailer Is Launching a Brick-and-Mortar Shop," *Crain's New York Business*, February 24, 2016, www.crainsnewyork.com/article/20160224/TECHNOLOGY/160229942/look-out-victorias-secret-lingerie-e-tailer-is-opening-a-brick-and-mortar-shop; Amy Westervelt, "It All Began with Impressing a Girl," *Wall Street Journal*, January 25, 2016, p. R6.

[39]Sarah Max, "Entrepreneurs Help Build Start-ups by the Batch," *New York Times*, May 27, 2013, http://dealbook.nytimes.com/2013/05/27/entrepreneurs-help-build-start-ups-by-the-batch/.

[40]Siamak Taghaddos, "Results Are In: Entrepreneur State of Mind 2010," *Grasslands: The Entrepreneurial Blog*, April 12, 2010, http://grasshopper.com/blog/founders/2010/04/12/results-are-in-the-entrepreneur-state-of-mind-2010.

[41]Meg Cadoux Hirshberg, "Once More into the Breach," *Inc.*, September 2010, p. 41.

[42]Michal Lev-Ram, "Can This Man Take the Haggling Out of Car Buying?" *Fortune*, March 17, 2014, p. 32; Paul Keegan, "The War and Truce Between TrueCar and Auto Dealers," *Inc.*, November 2014, www.inc.com/magazine/201411/paul-keegan/collision-course-truecar-disrupter-gets-disrupted.html.

[43]Stephanie Clifford, "They Just Can't Stop Themselves," *Inc.*, March 2005, p. 104.

[44]Eric Paley, "A Great Idea Is Never Enough," *Inc.*, June 2013, p. 45.

[45]Joseph A. Schumpeter, *Theorie de wirtschaftlichen Entwicklung*. Leipzig: Duncker und Humblot (1912).

[46]Veronica Dagher, "An Entrepreneur Goes All In," *Wall Street Journal*, March 28, 2016, p. R8; "About Us," North Fork Smoked Fish, June 3, 2016, http://northforksmokedfish.com/about_us/.

[47]George Gendron, "The Origin of the Entrepreneurial Species," *Inc.*, February 2000, p. 107.

[48]Michael Molitch-Hou, "CEO Jennifer Lewis on the Future of Electronics 3D Printing and Voxel8's Huge $12 Million Funding," *3D Printing Industry*, July 24, 2015, http://3dprintingindustry.com/news/voxel8-ceo-jennifer-lewis-on-how-12m-in-funding-will-fuel-the-future-of-electronics-3d-printing-54053/.

[49]S. K. Murphy, "Saras Sarasvathy's Effectual Reasoning Model for Expert Entrepreneurs," *SKMurphy*, February 7, 2010, www.skmurphy.com/blog/2010/02/07/saras-sarasvathys-effectual-reasoning-model-for-expert-entrepreneurs; Leigh Buchanan, "How Great Entrepreneurs Think," *Inc.*, February 2011, pp. 54–61.

[50]Christopher Ross, "Sara Blakely," *Wall Street Journal Magazine*, September 2014, p. 111; "The World's 100 Most Powerful Women: Sara Blakely," *Forbes*, 2016, www.forbes.com/profile/sara-blakely/; Clare O'Conner, "Spanx Inventor Sara Blakely on Hustling Her Way to a Billion Dollar Business," *Forbes*, October 21, 2014, www.forbes.com/sites/clareoconnor/2014/10/21/spanx-inventor-sara-blakely-on-hustling-her-way-to-a-billion-dollar-business/#6cafc80a478f.

[51]Scott Edward Walker, "What Makes a Great Entrepreneur?" *Venture Beat*, January 17, 2011, http://venturebeat.com/2011/01/17/what-makes-a-great-entrepreneur; Steven Swinford, "Malcolm Gladwell Says That if You Want to Shine, Put in 10,000 Hours," *Sunday Times*, October 19, 2008, http://entertainment.timesonline.co.uk/tol/arts_and_entertainment/books/article4969415.ece.

[52]Eric Paley, "A Great Idea Is Never Enough," *Inc.*, June 2013, p. 45.

[53]"Best Inspirational Words from Business Leaders in 2012," *Entrepreneur*, December 31, 2012, www.entrepreneur.com/slideshow/225285#8.

[54]Dan Goodgame, "Our Roving Editor," *FSB*, April 2008, p. 10.

[55]John Case, "The Origins of Entrepreneurship," *Inc.*, June 1989, p. 52.

[56]Issie Lapowsky, "Why I Could Not Have Done It Alone," *Inc.*, September 5, 2012, www.inc.com/magazine/201209/issie-lapowsky/how-i-did-itinc-500-kathy-mills-of-strategic-communications.html.

[57]Jason Daley, "The Old College Try," *Entrepreneur*, October 2014, pp. 73–77.

[58]Leigh Buchanan, "What Do Entrepreneurs Do After Leading Their Companies to the Inc. 500?" *Inc.*, September 2012, pp. 187–193; "About TransPerfect," TransPerfect Translations, www.transperfect.com/about/_about_us.html.

[59]"Understanding the American Small Business Owner," OnDeck, 2015, www.ondeck.com/american-dream/.

[60]Ross Levine and Yona Rubenstein, "Does Entrepreneurship Pay? The Michael Bloombergs, the Hot Dog Vendors, and the Return to Self-employment," Haas School of Business, University of California, Berkeley, p. 37; Mirjam Praag, Arjen van Witteloostuijn, and Justin van der Sluis, "Returns for Entrepreneurs vs. Employees: The Effect of Education and Personal Control on the Relative Performance of Entrepreneurs vs. Wage Employees," The Institute for the Study of Labor, December 2009, p. 21.

[61]Luisa Kroll and Kerry A. Dolan, "The Faces of Wealth in America," *Forbes*, September 16, 2013, www.forbes.com/forbes-400/.

[62]Luisa Kroll, "The 40 Richest Entrepreneurs Under 40," *Forbes*, December 12, 2016, https://www.forbes.com/sites/luisakroll/2016/12/12/americas-richest-entrepreneurs-under-40-2016/#42c0d2c267c3.

[63]"Most Middle Class Millionaires Are Entrepreneurs," *Small Business Labs*, May 13, 2008, http://genylabs.typepad.com/small_biz_labs/2008/05/most-middle-cla.html; Thomas Kostigen, "The 'Middle Class Millionaire,'" *MarketWatch*, March 5, 2008, www.marketwatch.com/story/rise-of-the-middle-class-millionaire-is-reshaping-us-culture.

[64]"Picture Perfect," *Forbes*, September 29, 2014, p. 20; Maya Kosoff, "Why Snapchat's New Valuation Is Better Than It Looks," *Vanity Fair*, March 4, 2016, www.vanityfair.com/news/2016/03/why-snapchats-valuation-is-better-than-it-looks; Jordan Crook and Anna Escher, "A Brief History of Snapchat," *TechCrunch*, October 15, 2015, http://techcrunch.com/gallery/a-brief-history-of-snapchat/.

[65]Jeffrey M. Jones, "Confidence in U.S. Institutions Still Below Historical Norms," Gallup, July 6, 2015, www.gallup.com/poll/183593/confidence-institutions-below-historical-norms.aspx?utm_source=institutions&utm_medium=search&utm_campaign=tiles.

[66]*2012 Public Affairs Pulse Survey: What Do Americans Expect from Business?* Public Affairs Council, 2013, p. 18.

[67]Sean Cunniff, "Tapping into Small Business Owners," *Closer Look Series*, Deloitte, June 18, 2013, www.deloitte.com/view/en_US/us/Industries/Banking-Securities-Financial-Services/center-for-financial-services/financial-services-quicklook/e14764b10f24f310VgnVCM2000003356f70aRCRD.htm.

[68]Donna Fenn, "Tony Hsieh: How to Find the Perfect Business Opportunity," *BNET*, April 1, 2011, www.bnet.com/blog/entrepreneurs/tony-hsieh-how-to-find-the-perfect-business-opportunity/1735.

[69]Amy Clarke Burns, "Creating a Brand," *Greenville News*, April 27, 2014, pp. 1E–2E.

[70]Gayle Sato-Stodder, "Never Say Die," *Entrepreneur*, December 1990, p. 95.

[71]"Percentage of U.S. Small Business Owners Reporting Positive Business Conditions Nearly Doubles Since 2010," *Business Wire*, June 6, 2012, www.businesswire.com/news/home/20120606005835/en/Percentage-U.S.-Small-Business-Owners-Reporting-Positive.

[72]Based on data from "Survival Rates of Establishments, by Year Started and Number of Years Since Starting, 1994–2015, in Percent," U.S. Bureau of Labor Statistics, 2016, http://data.bls.gov/cgi-bin/print.pl/bdm/entrepreneurship/bdm_chart3.htm.

[73]Donna J. Kelley, Abdul Ali, Candida Bush, Andrew C. Corbett, Caroline Daniels, Phillip H. Kim, Thomas S. Lyons, Madi Majbouri, and Edward G. Rogoff, *Global Entrepreneurship Monitor 2014 United States Report*, Babson College and Baruch College, 2014, p. 36.

[74]Jason Ankeny, "Do Not Fear the Fear," *Entrepreneur*, March 2016, pp. 29–34.

[75]Ibid.

[76]"Employment Situation Summary," Bureau of Labor Statistics, August 2, 2013, www.bls.gov/news.release/empsit.t18.htm; Mashoka Maimona, "Small Business Owners Work Long Hours Without Complaint: Survey," *Financial Post*, June 17, 2013, http://business.financialpost.com/2013/06/14/small-business-owners-work-long-hours-without-complaint-survey/.

[77]"Understanding the American Small Business Owner," OnDeck, 2015, www.ondeck.com/american-dream/.

[78]Kelly Kearsley, "I Work 70 Hours a Week," *CNN Money*, May 13, 2013, http://money.cnn.com/gallery/smallbusiness/2013/03/06/70-hour-workweek/index.html.

[79]"Small Business Entrepreneurs Go Mobile for Business Success," Manta, July 21, 2015, www.manta.com/resources/press/small-business-entrepreneurs-go-mobile-for-business-success/.

[80]Anne Fisher, "Make Sleep Work for You," *FSB*, September 2008, pp. 85–90.

[81]Geoff Williams, "Guiding Light," *Entrepreneur B.Y.O.B.*, August 2003, p. 84.

[82]"Small Business Owner Report," Bank of America, Spring 2014, p. 5.

[83]Jessica Bruder, "The Affair," *Inc.*, June 2014, pp. 115–118, 130.

[84]Jessica Bruder, "The Psychological Price of Entrepreneurship," *Inc.*, September 2013, www.inc.com/magazine/201309/jessica-bruder/psychological-price-of-entrepreneurship.html.

[85]Frank Newport, "Most U.S. Small Business Owners Would Do It All Over Again," Gallup, May 20, 2014, www.gallup.com/poll/169592/small-business-owners-again.aspx?version=print.

[86]*The State of Small Business Owners and Retirement*, The Guardian Life Small Business Research Institute, 2014, www.guardianlife.com/small-business-owners-retirement-readiness-study.

[87]http://wearegen.co/gew/global-highlights-gew-celebrations. "Global Entrepreneurship Week 2017," Global Entrepreneurship Week, 2017, http://gew.co/.

[88]*Entrepreneurship Education Comes of Age on Campus*, Kauffman Foundation, 2013, p. 1; "List of Colleges with Majors in Entrepreneurship or Small Business," Saint Louis University, 2014, www.slu.edu/x17964.xml; "Major: Entrepreneurial Studies," *BigFuture*, College Board, June 10, 2016; https://bigfuture.collegeboard.org/college-search?major=1751_Entrepreneurial%20Studies.

[89]Whitney Ricketts, "Inaugural Creative Jobs Report Reveals New American Dream," *Creative Live Blog*, March 27, 2014, http://blog.creativelive.com/creative-jobs-report/.

[90]Denali Tietjen, "Sharing That Song in Your Head," *Forbes*, August 17, 2015, pp. 94–96.

[91]"Employment by Major Industry Sector," Bureau of Labor Statistics, December 2015, www.bls.gov/emp/ep_table_201.htm; "U.S. GDP," Trading Economics, 2016, www.tradingeconomics.com/united-states/gdp; "GDP Composition by Sector," *World Fact Book*, Central Intelligence Agency, www.cia.gov/library/publications/the-world-factbook/geos/us.html.

[92]Zack O'Malley Greenburg, "Invent Your Own Profits," *Forbes*, June 25, 2012, p. 140.

[93]Robert Safian, "15 Lessons of Innovation for 2016," *Fast Company*, March 2016, pp. 16–18.

[94]Allison Enright, "U.S. Online Retail Sales Will Grow 57% by 2018; Projected Growth," Internet Retailer, May 12, 2014, www.internetretailer.com/2014/05/12/us-online-retail-sales-will-grow-57-2018.

[95]"Most Popular Online Shopping Categories Worldwide 2015, *Statista*, 2016, www.statista.com/statistics/276846/reach-of-top-online-retail-categories-worldwide/.

[96]Brittney Helmrich, "11 Unique Business Ideas to Inspire You in 2016," *Business News Daily*, January 5, 2016, www.businessnewsdaily.com/4753-unique-business-ideas.html.

[97]Amanda Soderlund, "Small Business Web Sites in 2016: A Survey," *Clutch*, February 17, 2016, https://clutch.co/web-designers/resources/small-business-websites-2016-survey.

[98]Ibid.

[99]Robit Arora, "It's 2016, So Why Do Almost Half of Small Businesses Not Have a Web Site?" *Inc.*, February 19, 2016, www.inc.com/replacemeplease1455908726.html; Amanda Soderlund, "Small Business Web Sites in 2016: A Survey," *Clutch*, February 17, 2016, https://clutch.co/web-designers/resources/small-business-websites-2016-survey.

[100]Mark Brohan, "Mobile Commerce Is Now 30% of All U.S. E-Commerce," *Internet Retailer*, August 18, 2015, www.internetretailer.com/2015/08/18/mobile-commerce-now-30-all-us-e-commerce.

[101]Robit Arora, "It's 2016, So Why Do Almost Half of Small Businesses Not Have a Web Site?" *Inc.*, February 19, 2016, www.inc.com/replacemeplease1455908726.html.

[102]"Statistics and Facts on the Food Delivery Industry in the U.S.," *Statista*, 2016, www.statista.com/topics/1986/food-delivery-industry-in-the-us/.

[103]"Pizza Patrón Updates Web Site with Responsive Design," *Pizza Marketplace*, April 12, 2016, http://pizzapatron.com/pizza-patron-updates-website-with-responsive-design/.

[104]"Exporting Is Good for Your Bottom Line," International Trade Administration, U.S. Department of Commerce, 2016, www.trade.gov/cs/factsheet.asp.

[105]Patrick Delahanty, "Small Businesses Key Players in International Trade," U.S. Small Business Administration Office of Advocacy, December 1, 2015, p. 2.

[106]"Blue Orange Pottery," International Trade Center, University of Texas at San Antonio, 2016, https://texastrade.org/blue-orange-pottery/.

[107]*EY Megatrends 2015*, Ernst and Young, 2015, www.ey.com/GL/en/Issues/Business-environment/ey-megatrends-that-will-shape-our-future-3-entrepreneurship-rising.

[108]Robin Myers and Preety Sidhu, "Minority, Young Students More Entrepreneurially Inclined," *Gallup*, January 1, 2014, www.gallup.com/poll/166808/minority-young-students-entrepreneurially-inclined.aspx.

[109]Sarah Whitten, "8 Young Entrepreneurs Making Serious Money," *CNBC*, July 27, 2015, www.cnbc.com/2015/07/27/8-young-entrepreneurs-making-serious.html.

[110]Amy Haimerl, "The Fastest-Growing Group of Entrepreneurs in America," *Forbes*, June 29, 2015, http://fortune.com/2015/06/29/black-women-entrepreneurs/.

[111]*The 2015 State of Women-Owned Businesses Report*, American Express OPEN, 2015, p. 1.

[112]Kris Frieswick and Kristin Lenz, "The New Startup Math," *Inc.*, October 2014, pp. 20–21; *National Women's Business Council 2012 Annual Report*, Washington, DC: 2012, pp. 2–3; Renee Martin, "Women Entrepreneurs Close the Gap and Dream Big," *Forbes*, June 7, 2010, www.forbes.com/2010/06/07/small-business-loans-funding-forbes-woman-entrepreneurs-great-ideas.html.

[113]*The 2016 State of Women-Owned Businesses Report*, American Express OPEN, 2016, p. 3.

[114]Heather McCarthy, "UV Couture—Fashionable and Sexy Sun Protective Clothing," *Balance My Life*, April 29, 2015, www.uvcouture.com/blogs/press/20554113-balancemylife; Deirdre Kelly, "Made-in-Canada Clothing Line Gives UV Rays the Cold Shoulder," *The Globe and Mail*, June 8, 2016, www.theglobeandmail.com/report-on-business/small-business/sb-growth/the-challenge/made-in-canada-clothing-line-gives-uv-rays-the-cold-shoulder/article30331893/.

[115]"Los Angeles County a Microcosm of Nation's Diverse Collection of Business Owners, Census Bureau Reports," United States Census Bureau, December 15, 2015, www.census.gov/newsroom/press-releases/2015/cb15-209.html.

[116]Kris Frieswick and Kristin Lenz, "The New Startup Math," *Inc.*, October 2014, pp. 20–21.

[117]"Number of Hispanic-Owned Businesses Nearly Doubled over Last Decade," *Huffington Post*, September 13, 2013, www.huffingtonpost.com/2013/09/13/hispanic-owned-businesses_n_3919930.html; Erin McDermott, "Why Hispanic Businesses Are Thriving," Bank of America, *Small Business Community*, October 16, 2013, https://smallbusinessonlinecommunity.bankofamerica.com/community/running-your-business/general-business/blog/2013/10/16/why-hispanic-owned-businesses-are-thriving.

[118]Robert W. Fairlie, *Kauffman Index of Entrepreneurial Activity*, 1996–2013, April 2014, Kauffman Foundation, p. 9.

[119]*Minority Biz Fast Facts*, U.S. Department of Commerce, Minority Business Development Agency, www.mbda.gov/node/562.

[120]"2014 Hispanic Business Fastest Growing 100 Companies: Fru-Veg Distributors Inc.," *Hispanic Business*, 2014, www.hispanicbusiness.com/research/100fastestgrowing/view.asp?companyid=202; "Fru-Veg Marketing," *Retail Business Review*, 2014, www.retail-business-review.com/companies/fru-veg-marketing-inc; "Conchita Espinosa," *LinkedIn*, 2014, www.linkedin.com/in/conchitaespinosa.

[121]Ann Garcia, "The Facts on Immigration Today," *American Progress*, April 3, 2013, www.americanprogress.org/issues/immigration/report/2013/04/03/59040/the-facts-on-immigration-today-3/#population; "A Portrait of U.S. Immigrants," Pew Research Hispanic Trends Project, January 29, 2013, www.pewhispanic.org/2013/02/15/u-s-immigration-trends/ph_13-01-23_ss_immigration_08_mexico-map/.

[122]Yatin Mundkur, "Immigrant Entrepreneurs: Vital for American Innovation," *Forbes*, January 23, 2014, www.forbes.com/sites/techonomy/2014/01/23/immigrant-entrepreneurs-vital-for-american-innovation/; Thomas K. McCraw, "Innovative Immigrants," *New York Times*, November 1, 2012, www.nytimes.com/2012/11/02/opinion/immigrants-as-entrepreneurs.html?pagewanted=all&_r=0; "Andrew Carnegie," *History Channel*, 2014, www.history.com/topics/andrew-carnegie.

[123]"A Nation of Immigrants," *Pew Research Hispanic Trends Project*, January 29, 2013, www.pewhispanic.org/2013/01/29/a-nation-of-immigrants/.

[124]Adam Bluestein, "The Most Entrepreneurial Group in America Wasn't Born in America," *Inc.*, February 2015, pp. 44–50, 100–101; David Dyssegaard Kallick, "Report Breaks New Ground on Immigrant Businesses," Fiscal Policy Institute, June 14, 2012, p. 1.

[125]Mundkur, "Immigrant Entrepreneurs: Vital for American Innovation," *Forbes*, January 23, 2014, www.forbes.com/sites/techonomy/2014/01/23/immigrant-entrepreneurs-vital-for-american-innovation/.

[126]*2015 Kauffman Index of Startup Activity*, Kauffman Foundation, 2015, p. 32.

[127]Adam Bluestein, "The Most Entrepreneurial Group in America Wasn't Born in America," *Inc.*, February 2015, pp. 44–50, 100–101.

[128]Chris Goodfellow, "The Part-Time Social Enterprise That Sold 80,000 Bottles of Beer in Its First Year," *Business Zone*, July 6, 2015, www.businesszone.co.uk/deep-dive/leadership/the-social-enterprise-that-sold-80000-bottles-of-beer-in-its-first-year; Dominic Jones, "People on Purpose: Matt Sandler and the Story of Two Fingers Brewing Company," *On Purpose*, June 8, 2014, http://onpurpose.uk.com/people-purpose-conversation-matt-sadler-co-founder-two-fingers-brewing-co/.

[129]"Home-Based Businesses: The Numbers Are Through the Roof," Service Corps of Retired Executives, 2013, www.score.org/resources/home-based-business-infographic.

[130]"Frequently Asked Questions," Small Business Administration Office of Advocacy, March 2014, p. 2; "Frequently Asked Questions: Advocacy Small Business Statistics and Research," Small Business Administration, 2011; "Frequently Asked Questions," Small Business Administration Office of Advocacy, September 2012, p. 1; "Frequently Asked Questions: Advocacy Small Business Statistics and Research," Small Business Administration, 2011, https://www.sba.gov/sites/default/files/advocacy/SB-FAQ-2016_WEB.pdf.

[131]"Home-Based Businesses: The Numbers Are Through the Roof," Service Corps of Retired Executives, 2013, www.score.org/resources/home-based-business-infographic.

[132]"Starting and Managing: Home-Based Businesses," U.S. Small Business Administration, May 19, 2016, www.sba.gov/starting-business/how-start-business/business-types/home-based-businesses.

[133]"Home-Based Businesses: The Numbers Are Through the Roof," Service Corps of Retired Executives, 2013, www.score.org/resources/home-based-business-infographic.

[134]Ibid.

[135]Ibid.

[136]Jenna Schnuer, "Shaking Things Up," *Entrepreneur*, March 2015, p. 66; "About," Preppi, https://preppi.co/.

[137]"10 Surprising Facts About Family Businesses," Family Firm Institute, 2014, http://familybusinessinstitute.com/blog/10-surprising-facts-about-family-businesses/; "Family Business Facts," University of Vermont, School of Business Administration, 2014, www.uvm.edu/business/vfbi/?Page=facts.html; "Facts About Family Business," S. Dale High Center for Family Business at Elizabethtown College," 2014, http://familybizcenter.user-feedback.com/facts.cfm; Veronica Dagher, "Who Will Run the Family Business?" *Wall Street Journal*, March 12, 2012, p. R6; *Annual Family Business Survey General Results and Conclusions*, Family Enterprise USA, March 2011, p. 1; Karen E. Klein, "Fathers and Daughters: Passing on the Family Business," *Bloomberg Businessweek*, December 27, 2011, www.businessweek.com/small-business/fathers-and-daughters-passing-on-the-family-business-12272011.html.

[138]Chris Arnold, "Wiffle Ball: Born and Still Made in the USA," *National Public Radio*, September 5, 2011, www.npr.org/2011/09/05/140145711/wiffle-ball-born-and-still-made-in-the-usa.

[139]Erick Calonius, "Blood and Money," *Newsweek: Special Issue*, p. 82.

[140]"Family Business Facts," University of St. Francis, Fort Wayne, Indiana, www.sfc.edu/business/fbc_facts.shtml.

[141]*Up Close and Professional: The Family Factor, Global Family Business Survey*, PriceWaterhouseCoopers, 2014, p. 23.

[142]*The MassMutual FamilyPreneurship Study*, MassMutual, March 2010, p. 10.

[143]Michael B. Dougherty, "Bobby Schlesinger Is Just Like Us," *Ocean Drive*, Issue 6, Summer 2014, http://oceandrive.com/living/articles/haute-meets-hip?page=1.

[144]Pia Chatterjee, "Making Beautiful Start-ups Together," *Business 2.0*, September 2007, p. 43.

[145]Echo M. Garrett, "And Business Makes Three," *Small Business Reports*, September 1993, pp. 27–31.

[146]Geoff Weiss, "Husband and Wife Team Named Small Business Persons of the Year," *Entrepreneur*, May 16, 2014; "Founder's Story," Pacifica, 2016, www.pacificabeauty.com/founders-story; Madeline Buxton, "Self-Made Couple Who Inspires: Brook and Billy Taylor," *Self*, January 27, 2015, www.self.com/work/selfmade/2015/01/self-made-couple-pacifica-beauty-brook-billy-taylor/; Will Yakowicz, "From Surfing Vacation Dream to $24 Million Business," *Inc.*, May 16, 2014, www.inc.com/will-yakowicz/sba-national-small-business-persons-of-year-pacifica.html.

[147]*Challenger, Gray and Christmas Job-Cut Announcement Report*, Challenger, Gray and Christmas, March 2016, www.challengergray.com/press/press-releases/2016-april-job-cut-report-job-cuts-jump-65k; "2017 April Job Cut Report: Cuts Fall to 36,602, Retail Leads," Challenger, Gray and Christmas, May 4, 2017, www.challengergray.com/press/press-releases/2017-april-job-cut-report-cuts-fall-36602-retail-leads.

[148]Alison Myers, "Laid-Off Workers in Calgary Turn to Entrepreneurship," *The Globe and Mail*, February 2, 2016, www.theglobeandmail.com/report-on-business/small-business/startups/laid-off-workers-in-calgary-turn-to-entrepreneurship/article28489684/.

[149]Whitney Ricketts, "Inaugural Creative Jobs Report Reveals New American Dream," *Creative Live Blog*, March 27, 2014, http://blog.creativelive.com/creative-jobs-report/.

[150]Adam Herscher, "Why I Left My $254,895 PM Role at Microsoft to Start a Seattle Tech Startup," *LinkedIn Pulse*, October 27, 2014, www.linkedin.com/pulse/20141027200232-1485298-why-i-left-my-254-895-pm-role-at-microsoft-to-start-a-seattle-tech-startup; Taylor Soper, "Why This Microsoft Veteran Left a Nice Paycheck and Made the Startup Leap," *Geekwire*, October 29, 2014, www.geekwire.com/2014/hasmetrics/.

[151]Jules Lichtenstein, "Demographic Characteristics of Business Owners," Small Business Administration Office of Advocacy, Issue Brief Number 2, January 16, 2014, p. 3.

[152]Robert W. Fairlie, *Kauffman Index of Entrepreneurial Activity, 1996–2013*, April 2014, Kauffman Foundation, p. 13.

[153]*Work in Retirement: Myths and Motivations*, Merrill Lynch, 2014, p. 7.

[154]Ibid., p. 1.

[155]"Frequently Asked Questions," U.S. Small Business Administration Office of Advocacy, March 2014, p. 1; "Small Business Profile," U.S. Small Business Administration Office of Advocacy, January 2012, p. 1; *The Small Business Economy: A Report to the President*, Washington, DC, 2010, p. 114.

[156]Ben Casselman, "Risk-Averse Culture Infects U.S. Workers, Entrepreneurs," *Wall Street Journal*, June 3, 2013, pp. A1, A14.

[157]Dane Stangler, *High Growth Firms and the Future of the American Economy*, Kauffman Foundation, March 2010, p. 5.

[158]Erik Hurst and Benjamin Wild Pugsley, "What Do Small Businesses Do?" Brookings Papers on Economic Activity, August 2011, p. 24.

[159]"Frequently Asked Questions," U.S. Small Business Administration Office of Advocacy, March 2014, p. 1; Kathryn Kobe, *Small Business GDP: Update 2002–2010*, Small Business Research Summary, Small Business Administration, Office of Advocacy, January 2012, p. 1.

[160]"Small Business Profile," U.S. Small Business Administration Office of Advocacy, 2014, p. 2.

[161]Jason Daley, "The Entrepreneur Economy," *Entrepreneur*, December 2009, p. 54.

[162]"Frequently Asked Questions," U.S. Small Business Administration, September 2012, p. 3.

[163]Based on data from "Survival Rates of Establishments, by Year Started and Number of Years Since Starting, 1994–2015, in Percent," U.S. Bureau of Labor Statistics, 2016, http://data.bls.gov/cgi-bin/print.pl/bdm/entrepreneurship/bdm_chart3.htm.

[164]Michael Warsaw, "Great Comebacks," *Success*, July/August, 1995, p. 43.

[165]Megan Korn, "From Failure to Success: What Steve Jobs, J. K. Rowling, and Jack Bogle All Have in Common," *The Daily Ticker*, May 10, 2012, http://finance.yahoo.com/blogs/daily-ticker/failure-success-steve-jobs-j-k-rowling-jack-134815058.html; "Famous Rejections #7: Harry Potter Was, Yup, Rejected Too," One Hundred Famous Rejections, July 21, 2010, www.onehundredrejections.com/2010/07/harry-potter-was-yup-rejected-too.html.

[166]Paige Arnof-Fenn, "Failing Your Way to Success," *Entrepreneur*, November 21, 2005, www.entrepreneur.com/worklife/worklifebalanceadvice/theentrepreneurslifecolumnistpaigearnoffenn/article81130.html.

[167]J. K. Rowling, "The Fringe Benefits of Failure, and the Importance of Imagination," *Harvard Magazine*, June 5, 2008, http://harvardmagazine.com/2008/06/the-fringe-benefits-failure-the-importance-imagination.

[168]Marc Gunther, "They All Want a Piece of Bill Gross," *Fortune*, November 11, 2002, p. 140.

[169]Chuck Salter, "Failure Doesn't Suck," *Fast Company*, May 2007, p. 44.

[170]Christopher Hann, "Epic Fail," *Entrepreneur*, January 2013, p. 35.

[171]Ibid.

[172]Ryan Mac, "From Doghouse to Penthouse," *Forbes*, September 28, 2015, pp. 64-66; Lydia Dishman, "Former Pets.com CEO on Starting Over and Finding Success After Spectacular Disappointments," *Fast Company*, June 26, 2014, www.fastcompany.com/3032067/hit-the-ground-running-former-petscom-ceo-on-starting-over-and-finding-success-after-spectac.

[173]Jeff Wilkinson, "USC Students Find Perfect Fit Launching Tux Delivery Service," *Greenville News*, April 24, 2016, p. 9A.

[174]Paula Andruss, "Have You Reached Your Pivot Point?" *Entrepreneur*, November 2013, pp. 83–86; "Next Big Sound," *CrunchBase*, 2014, www.crunchbase.com/organization/next-big-sound; Zack O'Malley Greenberg, "Moneyball for Books? Next Big Sound and Macmillan to Try," *Forbes*, May 27, 2014, www.forbes.com/sites/zackomalleygreenburg/2014/05/27/moneyball-for-books-next-big-sound-and-macmillan-to-try/.

[175]"2015 State of the Startup," Sage, 2015, www.sage.com/na/~/media/site/sagena/responsive/docs/startup/report, p. 4.

[176]Rieva Lesonsky, "A Business Plan Doubles Your Chances of Success, Says a New Survey," *Small Business Trends*, June 20, 2010, http://smallbiztrends.com/2010/06/business-plan-success-twice-as-likely.html.

[177]Lillia Callum-Penso, "Backup Strategy: Frank Mobley's Immedion Aims to Keep Web Sites Humming," *Greenville News*, January 6, 2013, pp. 1E—2E; "Immedion Expands Footprint into Midwest with Acquisition of Appica," Charleston Digital Corridor, December 1, 2015, www.charlestondigitalcorridor.com/news/1448984002157-immedion-expands-footprint-midwest-acquisition-appica/.

[178]Dinah Eng, "Jake Burton: My Life as a Pioneer," *Fortune*, December 8, 2010, p. 72.

[179]Jason Schwartz, "End Game," *Boston Magazine*, August 2012, www.bostonmagazine.com/2012/07/38-studios-end-game/; Dan Primack, "Lessons from the Great Curt Schilling Fiasco," *Fortune*, July 2, 2012, p. 40.

[180]"2015 State of the Startup," Sage, 2015, www.sage.com/na/~/media/site/sagena/responsive/docs/startup/report, p. 4.

[181]Colleen Taylor, "For Startups Pitching VCs, Three Is the Magic Number," Gigaom, May 13, 2011, https://gigaom.com/2011/05/13/multiple-founder-startups/.

[182]"2016/17 Talent Shortage Survey," 2017, Manpower Group, 2017, p. 1; "2016/17 Talent Shortage Survey: The United States Results," Manpower Group, 2017, p. 1.

[183]Aja Frost, "10 Companies That Promote from Within (and Are Hiring Now)," *The Muse*, www.themuse.com/advice/10-companies-that-promote-from-within-and-are-hiring-now; Amanda Augustine, "C-Suite Talk with The Muse's Kathryn Minshew," *Ladders*, http://info.theladders.com/blog/bid/179329/A-Q-A-with-The-Muse-s-Kathryn-Minshew.

[184]Rhonda Abrams, "Building Blocks of Business: Great Faith, Great Doubt, Great Effort," *Business*, March 4, 2001, p. 2.

2

Ethics and Social Responsibility: Doing the Right Thing

Camila Paez/Shutterstock

Learning Objectives

On completion of this chapter, you will be able to:

1. Define business ethics and describe the three levels of ethical standards.

2. Determine who is responsible for ethical behavior and why ethical lapses occur.

3. Explain how to establish and maintain high ethical standards.

4. Explain the difference between social entrepreneurs and traditional entrepreneurs.

5. Define social responsibility.

6. Understand the nature of business's responsibility to the environment.

7. Describe business's responsibility to employees.

8. Explain business's responsibility to customers.

9. Discuss business's responsibility to investors.

10. Describe business's responsibility to the community.

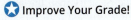
MyLab Entrepreneurship
⭐ **Improve Your Grade!**

If your instructor is using MyLab Entrepreneurship, visit **www.pearson.com/mylab/entrepreneurship** for videos, simulations, and writing exercises.

Business ethics involves the moral values and behavioral standards that businesspeople draw on as they make decisions and solve problems. It originates in a commitment to do what is right. Ethical behavior—doing what is "right" as opposed to what is "wrong"—starts with the entrepreneur. The entrepreneur's personal values begin to shape the business from day one. Entrepreneurs' personal values and beliefs influence the way they lead their companies and are apparent in every decision they make, every policy they write, and every action they take. In addition, the entrepreneurs' values set the tone for the culture that will guide the ethical actions of every employee they bring into their business. Entrepreneurs who succeed in the long term have a solid base of personal values and beliefs that they articulate to their employees, put into practice in ways that others can observe, and demonstrate throughout the culture of the organization. Values-based leaders do more than merely follow rules and regulations; their consciences dictate that they do what is right.

For many entrepreneurs, the ability to determine the values and ethics that shape how business will be conducted is a major motivation to launching a venture. For example, Blake Jones spent several years working as an engineer in Nepal and Egypt. Jones found the caste system in Nepal and the rigid social structure of Egypt appalling. When he returned to the United States, Jones joined with two partners to form a company, Namasté Solar, built on their shared value of the importance of full participation of all employees in the governance of the business. To bring these values to life, Jones and his partners structured Namasté Solar as an employee-owned cooperative. The company Web site describes its business model as follows: "The cooperative model more closely matches our democratic ideals and more equitably distributes the risk/reward equation of our employee-owners."[1] Namasté Solar designs and installs residential and commercial solar electric systems in Colorado. Seventy percent of the employees are owners of the company, with each owning one share valued at $5,000. Each employee-owner has an equal vote in important issues facing the company. "A 22-year-old recent college grad who is an apprentice installing solar panels on rooftops has the same vote as I have," says Jones. "I regularly don't get my way."[2]

The values and morals that entrepreneurs draw on to guide their ethical behaviors come from a variety of sources, including their family upbringing, their faith traditions, mentors who have shaped their lives, and the communities they grew up in. Bringing their personal values into their decision making and actions in their businesses helps ensure that entrepreneurs will act with integrity. Acting with integrity means that entrepreneurs do what is right no matter what the circumstances.

In some cases, ethical dilemmas are apparent. Entrepreneurs must be keenly aware of the ethical entrapments awaiting them and know that society will hold them accountable for their actions. More often, however, ethical issues are less obvious, cloaked in the garb of mundane decisions and everyday routine. Because they can easily catch entrepreneurs off guard and unprepared, these ethical "sleepers" are most likely to ensnare business owners, soiling their reputations and those of their companies. Repeated enough times, these unethical acts can become habits that shape the moral character of the entrepreneur. To make proper ethical choices, entrepreneurs must first be aware that a situation with ethical implications exists.

Complicating the issue even more is that, in some ethical dilemmas, no clear-cut right or wrong answers exist. There is no direct conflict between good and evil, right and wrong, or truth and falsehood. Instead, there is only the issue of conflicting interests among a company's **stakeholders**, the various groups and individuals who affect and are affected by a business. These conflicts force entrepreneurs to identify their stakeholders and to consider the ways in which entrepreneurs will deal with them (see Figure 2.1). For instance, when the founders of a local coffee shop make business decisions, they must consider the impact of those decisions on many stakeholders, including the team of employees who work there, the farmers and companies that supply the business with raw materials, the union that represents employees in collective bargaining, the government agencies that regulate a multitude of activities, the banks that provide the business with financing, the founding partners and other external investors who helped fund the start-up, the general public the business serves, the community in which the company operates, the customers who buy the company's products, and their families. When making decisions, entrepreneurs often must balance the needs and demands of a company's stakeholders, knowing that whatever the final decision is, not all groups will be satisfied.

stakeholders
the various groups and individuals who affect and are affected by a business.

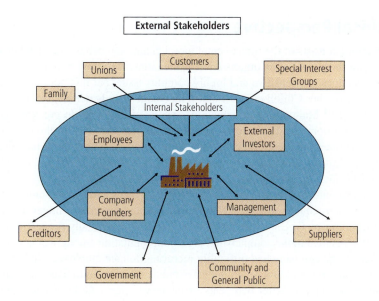

FIGURE 2.1
Key Stakeholders

Ethical leaders approach their organizational responsibilities with added dimensions of thought and action. They link ethical behaviors to organizational outcomes and incorporate social responsibility into daily decisions. They establish ethical behavior and concern for the environment as an integral part of organizational training and eventually as part of company culture. How does a commitment to "doing the right thing" apply to employees, customers, and other stakeholders, and how does it affect an entrepreneur's daily decision making? Large technology companies such as Apple, Google, Yahoo!, Facebook, Microsoft, and Verizon have been facing an ethical dilemma as they attempt to comply with the National Security Administration's request for information. The NSA operates a program known as Prism, which gathers telephone and Internet data to capture information about foreign nationals living in America. The NSA gets this information from technology companies that provide Internet and telephone services to consumers and businesses. Technology companies gain significant revenue from the data they gather from their users. For example, although Google offers many of its products such as Gmail and the Google search engine free to most users, these products generate significant revenue from the information Google amasses from its users' Internet searches and e-mails. Google sells the data to advertisers, which then use it to target ads to specific consumers. Although their customers generally are aware that data mining is commonly a part of having access to technologies at no cost, there is an implied understanding that this data will be protected beyond Google's internal use. However, Google and other large technology companies have a duty to share information from their customers that is tied to national security concerns with the federal government under the Cybersecurity Information Sharing Act.[3] As evidenced by this example, balancing the demands of various stakeholders to make ethical decisions is no easy task.

Business operates as an institution in our often complex and ever-evolving society. Therefore, every entrepreneur is expected to behave in ways that are compatible with the value system of society. It is society that imposes the rules of conduct for all business owners, in the form of ethical standards of behavior and responsibilities to act in ways that benefit the long-term interest of all. Society expects business owners to strive to earn a profit on their investment. Ethics and social responsibility simply set behavioral boundaries for decision makers. **Ethics** is a branch of philosophy that studies and creates theories about the basic nature of right and wrong, duty, obligation, and virtue. **Social responsibility** involves how an organization responds to the needs of the many elements in society, including shareholders, lenders, employees, consumers, governmental agencies, and the environment. Because business is allowed to operate in society, it has an obligation to behave in ways that benefit all of society.

ethics
a branch of philosophy that studies and creates theories about the basic nature of right and wrong, duty, obligation, and virtue.

social responsibility
how an organization responds to the needs of the many elements in society.

LO1

Define business ethics and
describe three levels of
ethical standards.

business ethics
the fundamental moral
values and behavioral standards that form the foun-
dation for the people of an
organization as they make
decisions and interact with
stakeholders.

An Ethical Perspective

Business ethics consists of the fundamental moral values and behavioral standards that form the foundation for the people of an organization as they make decisions and interact with stakeholders. Business ethics is a sensitive and highly complex issue, but it is not a new one. In 560 BC, the Greek philosopher Chilon claimed that a merchant does better to take a loss than to make a dishonest profit.[4] Maintaining an ethical perspective is essential to creating and protecting a company's reputation, but it is no easy task. Ethical dilemmas lurk in the decisions—even the most mundane ones—that entrepreneurs make every day. Succumbing to unethical temptations ultimately can destroy a company's reputation, one of the most precious and most fragile possessions of any business.

Building a reputation for ethical behavior typically takes a long time; unfortunately, destroying that reputation requires practically no time at all, and the effects linger for some time. The Web hosting company GoDaddy became known for running sexually suggestive advertisements, a practice that resulted in the company having a poor reputation among women in the tech industry. As a result, the company had difficultly recruiting female employees and interns. GoDaddy addressed its poor reputation through intensive public relations initiatives and employee training on bias in the workplace. After two years of intensive efforts, GoDaddy was able to triple the number of female workers in the company.[5]

ENTREPRENEURIAL PROFILE: Brian Whitfield, Edwin Todd, and Marsha Whitfield: Sommet Group Brian Whitfield and his father-in-law, Edwin Todd, founded Sommet Group to provide business services, including payroll, human resources, employee benefits, and staffing, to small- and medium-sized companies. Outsourcing these functions allowed its clients to focus on growing their businesses. Marsha Whitfield, Brian's wife and Edwin Todd's daughter, served as vice president of payroll for the company. To help build brand awareness, the Sommet Group entered into a multi-year naming rights agreement in 2007 with the Nashville Predators of the National Hockey League. The company was seeking to become a nationally known provider of outsourced business services. The home arena for the Predators became known as the Sommet Center. However, soon the empire being built by the family-owned business began to unravel. In 2009, just two years after signing the agreement, the Nashville Predators sued the Sommet Group to revoke the naming rights, alleging nonpayment of the agreed-upon naming rights fees. In July 2010 the FBI raided Sommet Group's headquarters, looking for evidence of fraud. In 2011 federal agents also raided the home of Brian and Marsha Whitfield, seeking additional evidence. That same year Marsha filed for divorce. On March 1, 2012, the Whitfields and Todd were indicted in federal court on 15 criminal counts, including wire fraud, conspiracy, theft from an ERISA plan, and money laundering charges. The Whitfields allegedly stole more than $650,000 from an employee pension plan to help pay for the arena naming rights obligations, to buy a houseboat, and to build a pool at their home. The indictment also alleged that the Whitfields failed to report almost $80 million of gross wages paid on behalf of Sommet clients, leading to an underpayment of more than $20 million in income taxes. In July 2013, two former executives of Sommet reached a plea deal with federal prosecutors. Edwin Todd agreed to plead guilty to one count of conspiracy. Marsha Whitfield agreed to testify against her former husband Brian Whitfield and pleaded guilty to one count of conspiracy and one count of wire fraud.[6] ■

Three Levels of Ethical Standards

As displayed in Figure 2.2, there are three levels of ethical standards:

1. *The law*, which defines for society as a whole those actions that are permissible and those that are not. The law is the narrowest level of ethical standards. The law merely establishes the minimum standard of behavior. Actions that are legal, however, may not be ethical. Simply obeying the law is insufficient as a guide for ethical behavior; ethical behavior requires more. Few ethical issues are so simple and one dimensional that the law can serve as the acid test for making a decision.

2. *Organizational policies and procedures*, which serve as specific guidelines for people as they make daily decisions. Policies and procedures include a broader definition of ethical standards that go beyond what is defined by the law. Many colleges and universities

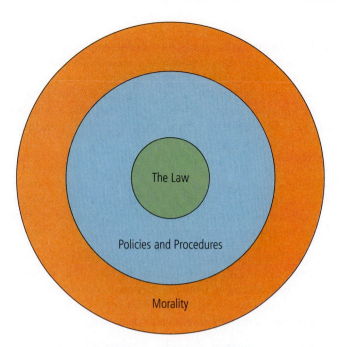

FIGURE 2.2

**Three Levels of
Ethical Standards**

have created honor codes, and companies rely on policies covering everything from sexual harassment and gift giving to hiring and whistle-blowing.

3. *The moral stance* that employees take when they encounter a situation that is not governed by levels 1 and 2. It is the broadest and most fundamental definition of ethical standards. The values people learn early in life at home, from their religious upbringing, in the communities where they were raised, in school, and at work are key ingredients at this level. Morality shapes a person's character. A strong determinant of moral behavior is *training*. As Aristotle said thousands of years ago, you get a good adult by teaching a child to do the right thing. A company's culture can serve either to support or undermine its employees' concepts of what constitutes ethical behavior.

Ethics is something that every businessperson faces daily; most decisions involve some degree of ethical judgment. Over the course of a career, entrepreneurs can be confident that they will face some tough ethical choices. However, that is not necessarily bad! Situations such as these give entrepreneurs the opportunity to flex their ethical muscles and do what is right. Entrepreneurs set the ethical tone for their companies. The ethical stance employees take when faced with difficult decisions often reflects the values that entrepreneurs have used to intentionally shape the culture within their businesses.

ENTREPRENEURIAL PROFILE: Joey Prusak, Dairy Queen Manager Joey Prusak was working at the Dairy Queen franchise where he had been employed for the previous five years. A blind man, who was a regular customer, was standing at the counter paying his bill. While the customer was getting money out of his wallet, he unknowingly dropped a $20 bill. A woman standing behind him in line quickly picked up the $20 bill and put it in her purse. When the woman stepped up to the counter to be served, Prusak asked her to return the money to the man who had dropped it. She refused, claiming it was her money that she had dropped. Prusak refused to serve her, saying that he would not serve her if she was going to be so "disrespectful" to another customer. The woman became belligerent and stormed out of the store. Prusak served the remaining customers in line, apologizing to each one for the incident. Prusak then went over to the blind man, pulled out a $20 bill, and handed him the money, telling him that he had dropped it on the floor when he was paying for his food. A customer who witnessed the entire incident wrote a comment card describing what had happened. The owner of the franchise put the comment card on a bulletin board for all of the employees to see. One of the employees took a picture of the card and posted it on Facebook. The story then went viral. Billionaire Warren Buffet, whose company Berkshire Hathaway owns American Dairy Queen Corporation, heard the story and invited Prusak to be his special guest at the annual shareholder meeting of Berkshire Hathaway.[7] ∎

Moral Management

Although companies may set ethical standards and offer guidelines for employees, the ultimate decision about whether to abide by ethical principles rests with the *individual.* In other words, companies really are not ethical or unethical; individuals are. Managers, however, can greatly influence the behavior of individuals within the company. That influence must start at the *top* of the organization. An entrepreneur who practices ethical behavior establishes the moral tone for the entire organization. Table 2.1 summarizes the characteristics of the three ethical styles of management: immoral, amoral, and moral management.

IMMORAL MANAGEMENT Immoral managers are motivated by selfish reasons such as their own gains or those of the company. The driving force behind immoral management is *greed*: achieving personal or organizational success at any cost. Immoral management is the polar opposite of ethical management; immoral managers do what they can to circumvent laws and moral standards and are not concerned about the impact their actions have on others.

AMORAL MANAGEMENT The principal goal of amoral managers is to earn a profit, but their actions differ from those of immoral managers in one key way: They do not purposely violate laws or ethical standards. Instead, amoral managers neglect to consider the impact their decisions have on others; they use free-rein decision making without reference to ethical standards. Amoral management is not an option for socially responsible businesses.

MORAL MANAGEMENT Moral managers also strive for success but only within the boundaries of legal and ethical standards. Moral managers are not willing to sacrifice their values and violate ethical standards just to make a profit. Managers who operate with this philosophy see the law as a minimum standard for ethical behavior.

TABLE 2.1 Approaches to Business Ethics

Organizational Characteristics	Immoral Management	Amoral Management	Moral Management
Ethical norms	Management decisions, actions, and behavior imply a positive and active opposition to what is moral (ethical). Decisions are discordant with accepted ethical principles. An active negation of what is moral is implicit.	Management is neither moral nor immoral; decisions are not based on moral judgments. Management activity is not related to any moral code. A lack of ethical perception and moral awareness may be implicit.	Management activity conforms to a standard of ethical, or right, behavior. Management activity conforms to accepted professional standards of conduct. Ethical leadership is commonplace.
Motives	Selfish. Management cares only about its or its company's gains.	Well-intentioned but selfish in the sense that impact on others is not considered.	Good. Management wants to succeed but only within the confines of sound ethical precepts such as fairness, justice, and due process.
Goals	Profitability and organizational success at any price.	Profitability. Other goals are not considered.	Profitability within the confines of legal obedience and ethical standards.
Orientation toward law	Legal standards are barriers that management must overcome to accomplish what it wants.	Law is the ethical guide, preferably the letter of the law. The central question is "What we can do legally?"	Obedience toward the letter and spirit of the law. Law is a minimal ethical behavior. Prefer to operate well above what law mandates.
Strategy	Exploit opportunities for corporate gain. Cut corners when it appears useful.	Give managers free rein. Personal ethics may apply but only if managers choose. Respond to legal mandates if caught and required to do so.	Live by sound ethical standards. Assume leadership position when ethical dilemmas arise. Enlightened self-interest.

Source: Archie B. Carroll, "In Search of the Moral Manager," reprinted from *Business Horizons*, March/April, Copyright 1987 by the Foundation for the School of Business at Indiana University. Used with permission.

The Benefits of Moral Management

One of the most common misconceptions about business is that there is a contradiction between earning a profit and maintaining high ethical standards. In reality, companies have learned that these two goals are consistent with one another. Elizabeth Riley, program manager of Impact Engine, a Chicago-based business accelerator that supports for-profit start-ups with strong social missions, says, "Much too often, business leaders are faced with an unnecessary choice between profits and making the world a better place. This is a false construct that has been perpetuated for far too long—profit and purpose should not be mutually exclusive."[8] Many entrepreneurs launch businesses with the idea of making a difference in society. They quickly learn that to "do good," their companies must first "do well." Les Cuistots Migrateurs (The Migrant Cook) is a French catering company started by Louis Jacquot and Sébastien Prunier that employs refugees and immigrants who cook their native foods for its catering clients. The goals of the business include becoming financially successful, providing job opportunities for refugees, and helping improve French people's perceptions of immigrants.[9]

ENTREPRENEURIAL PROFILE: Patrick Woodyard: Nisolo Patrick Woodyard began developing the for-profit social venture he cofounded in 2011, called Nisolo, when he was working on a microfinance project in Peru. Woodyard observed talented craftspeople and artisans who were struggling to find a market for their products. Woodyard launched Nisolo to help Peruvian shoemakers expand the market for their handmade shoes. Nisolo sells high-quality, fashionable men's and women's shoes handmade by artisans in Peru through e-commerce and out of its showroom in Nashville, Tennessee. Nisolo sells shoes that are both fashionable and help support the shoemakers living in impoverished regions. With each purchase, customers receive a business card from the shoemaker who made the shoes purchased. Nisolo's goal is to help Peruvian shoemakers receive a fair price and have steady sales for their shoes. The shoes are high quality and retail for an average price of $160 per pair. Nisolo pays the shoemakers an average of $30 per pair, which is enough to pull them out of poverty and provide a sustainable living for their families. Nisolo purchased Red Earth, a hand-crafted jewelry business, to expand its offer-

Courtesy of Patrick Woodyard, CEO, Nisolo

ing of socially conscious products. Nisolo's business model allows the company to earn a profit and return for its investors while at the same time helping provide economic empowerment for the artisans who supply its handmade shoes and jewelry by offering them a fair price for their products.[10] ∎

Although behaving ethically has value in itself, there are many other benefits to companies that adhere to high ethical standards. First, companies avoid the damaging fallout from unethical behavior on their reputations. Unethical businesses usually gain only short-term advantages; over the long run, unethical decisions don't pay. They are simply not good business.

Second, a solid ethical framework guides managers as they cope with an increasingly complex network of influence from external stakeholders. Dealing with stakeholders is much easier if a company has a solid ethical foundation on which to build.

Third, businesses with solid reputations as ethical companies find it easier to attract and retain quality workers. Mars, a Michigan-based marketing firm, encourages its employees to take a month-long sabbatical to volunteer with the nonprofit of their choice. Debbie Feit, a senior copywriter, worked with the Association for Children's Mental Health and the Depression and Bipolar Support Alliance during her sabbatical. She developed marketing materials and social media campaigns for the nonprofit agency. She wrote a grant to secure $20,000 to update the agency's Web site. As a parent of two young children, Feit would never have had the time to perform that level of volunteerism. She returned from the sabbatical refreshed and fully committed to Mars for giving her the opportunity to volunteer in such a meaningful way.[11]

TABLE 2.2 Reasons to Run a Business Ethically and the Factors That Drive Business Ethics

Top Five Reasons to Run a Business Ethically

1. Protect brand and company reputation
2. It is the right thing to do
3. Maintain customers' trust and loyalty
4. Maintain investors' confidence
5. Earn public acceptance and recognition

Top Five Factors That Drive Business Ethics

1. Corporate scandals
2. Marketplace competition
3. Demands by investors
4. Pressure from customers
5. Globalization

Source: The Ethical Enterprise: A Global Study of Business Ethics, 2005–2015 (American Management Association/Human Resource Institute, 2006), p. 2.

Fourth, ethical behavior has a positive impact on a company's bottom line. Research on the relationship between corporate ethics and financial performance suggests that companies that outperform their competitors ethically also outperform them financially due to the strong employee commitment that an ethical culture creates.[12] However, financial rewards should never become the motivating force behind acting ethically. Entrepreneurs must strive to do the right thing simply because it is the right thing to do!

Finally, a company's ethical philosophy has an impact on its ability to provide value for its customers. The "ethics factor" is difficult to quantify, yet it is something that customers consider when deciding where to shop and which company's products to buy. "Do I want people buying Timberland boots as a result of the firm's volunteer efforts?" asks CEO Jeffrey Swartz. "You bet."[13] Timberland's commitment to "doing good" in addition to "doing well" is expressed in its slogan, "Boots, Brand, Belief." Like other social entrepreneurs, Swartz's goal is to manage the company successfully so that he can use its resources to combat social problems.

Entrepreneurs must recognize that ethical behavior is an investment in the company's future rather than merely a cost of doing business. Table 2.2 shows the results of a comprehensive study that was conducted by the American Management Association of global human resources directors who were asked about the reasons for their companies' engaging in ethical behavior and the factors that drive business ethics today.

Establishing an Ethical Framework

To cope successfully with the many ethical decisions they face, entrepreneurs must develop a workable ethical framework to guide themselves and the organization. Although many frameworks exist, the following five-step process works quite well:

Step 1. *Identify the personal moral and ethical principles that shape all business decisions.* Entrepreneurs build a foundation for making ethical decisions by understanding how their personal values come to life in business situations. This starts with an inventory of the important principles that define one's personal values. The entrepreneur then determines how each of these principles affects each of the major stakeholders of the business. Many entrepreneurs integrate this proactive approach to ethical decision making into their business plans to ensure the integrity of their business actions as they launch and grow their business ventures.

Step 2. *Recognize the ethical dimensions involved in the dilemma or decision.* Before entrepreneurs can make informed ethical decisions, they must recognize that an ethical situation exists. Only then is it possible to define the specific ethical issues involved. Too often, business owners fail to take into account the ethical impact of a particular course of action until it is too late. To avoid ethical quagmires, entrepreneurs must consider the ethical forces at work in a situation—honesty, fairness, respect for the community, concern for the environment, trust, and others—to have a complete view of the decision.

Step 3. *Identify the key stakeholders involved and determine how the decision will affect them.* Every business influences and is influenced by a multitude of stakeholders. Frequently, the demands of these stakeholders conflict with one another, putting a business in the position of having to choose which groups to satisfy and which to alienate. Before making a decision, managers must sort out the conflicting interests of the various stakeholders and determine which ones have important stakes in the situation. Although this analysis may not resolve the conflict, it will prevent the company from inadvertently causing harm to people it may have failed to consider. More companies are measuring their performance using a **triple bottom line (3BL)** that, in addition to the traditional measure of profitability, includes the commitment to ethics and social responsibility and the impact on the environment ("profit, people, and planet").

> **triple bottom line (3BL)**
> measurement of business performance using profitability, its commitment to ethics and social responsibility, and its impact on the environment ("profit, people, and planet").

![ENTREPRENEURIAL PROFILE icon] **ENTREPRENEURIAL PROFILE: Jason Adkins, BrightHouse Luxury Green Home Cleaning** BrightHouse Luxury Green Home Cleaning is a healthy, eco-friendly green home cleaning service, operating out of offices in Jacksonville, Florida, and Nashville, Tennessee. BrightHouse uses all-natural and allergy-reducing products, HEPA filtrations, microfiber, and recyclable packaging. BrightHouse is affiliated with Cleaning for a Reason Foundation, which provides free home cleaning services for women undergoing treatment for cancer. Cleaning for a Reason partners with local cleaning companies such as BrightHouse throughout the United States and Canada. Adkins says that all of BrightHouse's employees can attest to the fact that home cleaning is strenuous work. Providing cleaning for cancer patients enables them to save their strength to tolerate treatment and get well. BrightHouse's nontoxic cleaning solutions do not cause problems for cancer patients whose immune systems are compromised by chemotherapy. Adkins hopes that a clean home can comfort patients during their treatment and recovery.[14] ■

Courtesy of Jason Adkins, BrightHouse Luxury Green Home Cleaning

Step 4. *Generate alternative choices and distinguish between ethical and unethical responses.* When entrepreneurs are generating alternative courses of action and evaluating the consequences of each one, they can use the questions in Table 2.3 for guidance. Asking and answering questions such as these helps ensure that everyone involved is aware of the ethical dimensions of the issue.

Step 5. *Choose the "best" ethical response and implement it.* At this point, there likely will be several ethical choices from which managers can pick. Comparing these choices to the "ideal" ethical outcome may help managers make the final decision. The final choice must be consistent with the company's goals, culture, and value system as well as those of the individual decision makers.

Why Ethical Lapses Occur

> **LO2**
> Determine who is responsible for ethical behavior and why ethical lapses occur.

Although most small business owners run their companies ethically, business scandals involving Enron, WorldCom, Tyco, and other high-profile companies have sullied the reputations of businesses of all sizes. The best way for business owners to combat these negative public perceptions is to run their business ethically. When faced with an ethical dilemma, however, not every entrepreneur or employee will make the right decision. According to the Global Business Ethics Survey, 30 percent of workers in the United States say they have observed ethical lapses in their companies. More than three-fourths (76 percent) of workers reported the violations, and, alarmingly, 53 percent of those who reported violations say they experienced retaliation such

TABLE 2.3 Questions to Help Identify the Ethical Dimensions of a Situation

- Does my decision have ethical implications? If so, what are they?
- Does my decision or action violate the law, relevant standards of behavior, company credo, or ethical principles?
- Will I feel good about myself if I choose this option?
- How would I feel if someone else took this action towards me?
- Would I want my decision or action to become public knowledge?
- Will I be able to justify the rationale for my decision or action if or when my decision or action becomes public knowledge?
- Would an objective bystander consider my decision or action to be justified?
- Does my decision or action deceive or mislead other people?
- Is my decision or action likely to be valid over time? Looking back on this decision or action in 10 years, will others consider it to be reasonable and ethical?
- Can I disclose my decision or action to my family members, my colleagues, my boss, and my friends with no ethical qualms?
- What is my true motivation for making this decision or taking this action? Is my intention honorable? Would the general public consider it the right thing to do?
- How would I feel if my decision or action appeared in the news?
- Whom might my decision or action harm? Have I taken steps to avoid or minimize that harm?
- Is this decision or action consistent with my religious teachings and beliefs?
- Could my decision or action become the foundation for a general principle for others who face the same or similar decision or situation?
- Have I considered the impact of my decision or action on others from their point of view?
- Does my decision or action respect the rights of the people it will affect?

as demotion or firing) as a result. In addition, 22 percent of U.S. workers say that they have felt pressure within their companies to compromise ethical standards."[15] Figure 2.3 shows the results of the KPMG Integrity Survey, which identifies the primary causes of misconduct in businesses. Let's explore some of the causes of ethical lapses in more detail.

An Unethical Employee

Ethical decisions are individual decisions, and some people are corrupt. Try as they might to avoid them, small businesses occasionally find that they have hired a "bad apple." Eliminating unethical behavior requires eliminating these bad apples.

An Unethical Organizational Culture

In some cases, a company's culture has been poisoned with an unethical overtone; in other words, the problem is not the "bad apple" but the "bad barrel." Pressure to prosper produces an environment that creates conditions that reward unethical behavior, and employees act accordingly. Studies show that companies with strong ethical cultures experience fewer ethical violations than those with weak ethical cultures.[16] In fact, an ethical culture positively influences the behaviors of employees *independently* of the degree to which there is a match between employee and organizational values.[17]

Moral Blindness

Sometimes, fundamentally ethical people commit unethical blunders because they are blind to the implications of their conduct. Moral blindness may be the result of failing to realize that an ethical dilemma exists, or it may arise from a variety of mental defense mechanisms. One of the most common mechanisms is rationalization:

"Everybody does it."

"If they were in my place, they'd do it too."

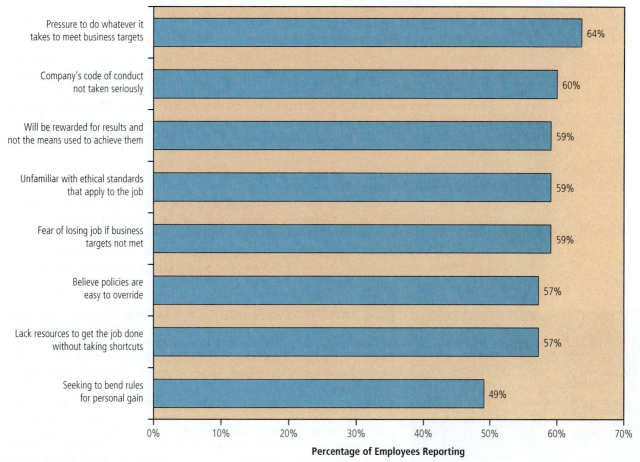

FIGURE 2.3

Causes of Ethical Lapses

Source: Based on KPMG Integrity Survey 2013, p. 12.

"Being ethical is a luxury I cannot afford right now."

"The impact of my decision/action on (whomever or whatever) is not my concern."

"I don't get paid to be ethical; I get paid to produce results."

Conducting ethics training and creating a culture that encourages employees to consider the ethical impact of their decisions reduces the likelihood of moral blindness. Instilling a sense of individual responsibility and encouraging people at all levels of an organization to speak up when they see questionable actions create a company-wide ethical conscience. However, employees are not the only ones who need guidance when facing ethical decisions. Entrepreneurs themselves should also seek out advice and counsel when it comes to ethics. One reason entrepreneurs should establish advisory boards is to serve as sounding boards to help ensure that they understand the moral and ethical dimensions of major decisions.

Competitive Pressures

If competition is so intense that a company's survival is threatened, managers may begin to view what were once unacceptable options as acceptable. Managers and employees are under such pressure to produce that they may sacrifice their ethical standards to reduce the fear of failure or the fear of losing their jobs. Without a positive organizational culture that stresses ethical behavior regardless of the consequences, employees respond to feelings of pressure and compromise their personal ethical standards to ensure that the job gets done.

Opportunity Pressures

When the opportunity to "get ahead" by taking some unethical action presents itself, some people cannot resist the temptation. The greater the reward or the smaller the penalty for unethical acts, the greater is the probability that such behavior will occur. If managers, for example, condone or even encourage unethical behavior, they can be sure it will occur. Those who succumb to opportunity pressures often make one of two mistakes: They overestimate the cost of doing the right thing, or they underestimate the cost of doing the wrong thing. Either error can lead to disaster.

Globalization of Business

The globalization of business has intertwined what once were distinct cultures. This cultural cross-pollination has brought about many positive aspects, but it has created problems as well. Companies have discovered that no single standard of ethical behavior applies to all business decisions in the international arena. Practices that are illegal in one country may be perfectly acceptable, or even expected, in another. Actions that would send a businessperson to jail in Western nations are common ways of working around the system in others.

Courtesy of Robert Grabow, President, Intrepid Sportswear

ENTREPRENEURIAL PROFILE: Rob Grabow: Intrepid Sportswear
Rob Grabow has always loved playing basketball. His experience wearing poor-quality, overpriced uniforms led him to start Intrepid Sportswear from his college dorm room at Gonzaga University. Grabow's business model for Intrepid Sportswear, which is based in Seattle, Washington, focuses on efficiency by shipping product directly from the manufacturer to the customer. The savings from eliminating buyers in international markets, wholesalers, and U.S.-based sales representatives is passed along to its customers. Intrepid customers save as much as 50 percent on uniforms compared to buying from other suppliers. In addition to paying overseas workers above-market wages, Intrepid also gives 5 to 10 percent of its net profits back to these workers. Grabow says he gives back to his employees because it is ethical to share success with those who helped create it. However, the practice also creates positive outcomes for his business. Grabow finds that Intrepid Sportswear's profit sharing has improved employee retention and loyalty. His team is more willing to go above and beyond for the company. Grabow believes doing the right thing and sound business practices are not mutually exclusive. Intrepid sells to teams in all 50 states and to teams in eight countries in Europe. More than 6,400 teams have bought uniforms from Intrepid since Grabow started the business in his dorm room in 2002.[18] ■

Table 2.4 provides a summary of important ethics research concerning the characteristics that are most important to establishing an ethical culture.

TABLE 2.4 Ethics Research Reveals Features of Ethical Cultures

1. Leaders support and model ethical behavior.
2. Consistent communications come from all company leaders.
3. Ethics is integrated into the organization's goals, business processes, and strategies.
4. Ethics is part of the performance management system.
5. Ethics is part of the company's selection criteria and selection process.
6. The needs of the various stakeholders are balanced when making decisions.
7. A strong set of core values supports the vision and mission of the company.
8. The company maintains a long-term perspective on all decisions.

Sources: Based on *The Ethical Enterprise: A Global Study of Business Ethics, 2005–2015* (American Management Association/Human Resource Institute, 2006), pp. 5, 6, 10; Alexandre Ardichvili, James A. Mitchell, and Douglas Jondle, "Characteristics of Ethical Business Cultures," *Journal of Business Ethics*, 2009 (85:4), pp. 445–451.

Establishing and Maintaining Ethical Standards

LO3

Explain how to establish and maintain high ethical standards.

Establishing Ethical Standards

Although they may not have formal ethics programs, entrepreneurs can encourage employees to become familiar with the following ethical tests for judging behavior:

- *The utilitarian principle.* Choose the option that offers the greatest good for the greatest number of people.

- *Kant's categorical imperative.* Act in such a way that the action taken under the circumstances could be a universal law or rule of behavior.

- *The professional ethic.* Take only those actions that a disinterested panel of professional colleagues would view as proper.

- *The Golden Rule.* Treat other people the way you would like them to treat you.

- *The television test.* Would you and your colleagues feel comfortable explaining your actions to a national television audience?

- *The family test.* Would you be comfortable explaining to your children, your spouse, and your parents why you took this action?[19]

Although these tests do not offer universal solutions to ethical dilemmas, they do help employees identify the moral implications of the decisions they face. People must be able to understand the ethical impact of their actions before they can make responsible decisions. Table 2.5 describes

TABLE 2.5 Ten Ethical Principles to Guide Behavior

The study of history, philosophy, and religion reveals a strong consensus about certain universal and timeless values that are central to leading an ethical life.

1. *Honesty.* Be truthful, sincere, forthright, straightforward, frank, and candid; do not cheat, lie, steal, deceive, or act deviously.

2. *Integrity.* Be principled, honorable, upright, and courageous and act on convictions; do not be two-faced or unscrupulous or adopt an ends-justifies-the-means philosophy that ignores principle.

3. *Promise-keeping.* Be worthy of trust, keep promises, fulfill commitments, and abide by the spirit as well as the letter of an agreement; do not interpret agreements in a technical or legalistic manner to rationalize noncompliance or to create excuses for breaking commitments.

4. *Fidelity.* Be faithful and loyal to family, friends, employers, and country; do not use or disclose information earned in confidence; in a professional context, safeguard the ability to make independent professional judgments by scrupulously avoiding undue influences and conflicts of interest.

5. *Fairness.* Be fair and open-minded, be willing to admit error and, when appropriate, change positions and beliefs; demonstrate a commitment to justice, the equal treatment of individuals, and tolerance for diversity; do not overreach or take undue advantage of another's mistakes or adversities.

6. *Caring for others.* Be caring, kind, and compassionate; share, be giving, and serve others; help those in need and avoid harming others.

7. *Respect for others.* Demonstrate respect for human dignity, privacy, and the right to self-determination for all people; be courteous, prompt, and decent; provide others with the information they need to make informed decisions about their own lives; do not patronize, embarrass, or demean.

8. *Responsible citizenship.* Obey just laws (if a law is unjust, openly protest it); exercise all democratic rights and privileges responsibly by participation (voting and expressing informed views), social consciousness, and public service; when in a position of leadership or authority, openly respect and honor democratic processes of decision making, avoid secrecy or concealment of information and ensure that others have the information needed to make intelligent choices and exercise their rights.

9. *Pursuit of excellence.* Pursue excellence in all matters; in meeting personal and professional responsibilities, be diligent, reliable, industrious, and committed; perform all tasks to the best of your ability, develop and maintain a high degree of competence, and be well informed and well prepared; do not be content with mediocrity, but do not seek to win "at any cost."

10. *Accountability.* Be accountable; accept responsibility for decisions, for the foreseeable consequences of actions and inactions, and for setting an example for others. Parents, teachers, employers, many professionals, and public officials have a special obligation to lead by example and to safeguard and advance the integrity and reputation of their families, companies, professions, and the government; avoid even the appearance of impropriety and take whatever actions are necessary to correct or prevent inappropriate conduct by others.

Source: Michael Josephson, "Teaching Ethical Decision Making and Principled Reasoning," *Ethics: Easier Said Than Done*, Winter 1988, pp. 28–29. Copyright © Michael Josephson 2015 josephsoninstitute@jiethics.org reprinted with permission

Courtesy of Christopher Redhage, Co-founder, ProviderTrust Inc.

10 ethical principles that differentiate between right and wrong, thereby offering a guideline for ethical behavior.

ENTREPRENEURIAL PROFILE: Christopher Redhage and Michael Rosen: ProviderTrust Christopher Redhage and Michael Rosen launched ProviderTrust to help healthcare providers ensure that staff and vendors are all fully licensed under Medicare and Medicaid regulations. The 2010 Affordable Care Act expanded the reach of these regulations and increased the penalties for noncompliance. ProviderTrust has experienced high growth from its launch. The founders are committed to building a company that is based on a clear set of core values. Every morning the ProviderTrust employees meet for 10 to 15 minutes. There are two items on the agenda for these daily meetings. The first item on the agenda is to review one of the company's core values or key business practices, which Redhage thinks is important because it helps keep employees' values aligned with the company's core values and keeps everyone focused on a healthy, ethical culture. The second item in the daily meeting allows each member of the team to talk about the one thing he or she will to accomplish that day, which is always shared within the context of the core value or key business practice.[20] ■

Maintaining Ethical Standards

Establishing ethical standards is only the first step in an ethics-enhancing program; implementing and maintaining those standards is the real challenge facing management. What can entrepreneurs do to integrate ethical principles into their companies? To create an environment that encourages ethical behavior, entrepreneurs must make building an intentional culture that is based on a strong ethical foundation a core responsibility as leaders of their businesses.

SET THE TONE "The character of the leader casts a long shadow over the organization and can determine the character of the organization itself," says one business executive.[21] Entrepreneurs must set an impeccable ethical example at all times. Remember that ethics starts at the top. If entrepreneurs and their managers talk about the importance of ethics and then act in an unethical manner, they send mixed signals to employees. Workers believe the *actions* of those in charge more than their words. What you do, how you do it, and what you say set the tone for your employees. The values you profess must be aligned with the behaviors you demonstrate.

company credo

a statement that defines the values underlying the entire company and its ethical responsibilities to its stakeholders.

CREATE A COMPANY CREDO A **company credo** defines the values underlying the entire company and its ethical responsibilities to its stakeholders. It offers general guidance in ethical issues. The most effective credos capture the elusive essence of a company—what it stands for and why it's important—and they can be a key ingredient in a company's competitive edge. A company credo is especially important for a small company, where the entrepreneur's values become the values driving the business. Creating a credo is an excellent way to transform those values into guidelines for employees' ethical behavior. For example, Trustworth, a residential provider of elderly care operating in England, developed the following credo: "Our residents are a mirror of ourselves should we reach old age. They have been entrusted to our care and we have accepted that trust. We resolve to give them the patience, loving care and understanding we would like to receive for ourselves."[22]

ESTABLISH HIGH STANDARDS OF BEHAVIOR It is essential to emphasize to *everyone* in the organization the importance of ethics. All employees must understand that ethics is *not* negotiable. The role that an entrepreneur plays in establishing high ethical standards is critical; no one has more influence over the ethical character of a company than its founder.

INVOLVE EMPLOYEES IN ESTABLISHING ETHICAL STANDARDS Encourage employees to offer feedback on how to establish standards. Involving employees improves the quality of a company's ethical standards and increases the likelihood of employee compliance.

CREATE A CULTURE THAT EMPHASIZES TWO-WAY COMMUNICATION A thriving ethical environment requires two-way communication. Employees must have the opportunity to report any ethical violations they observe. A reliable, confidential reporting system is essential to a whistle-blowing program, in which employees anonymously report breaches of ethical behavior through proper channels. Ethical organizations not only encourage employees to report the ethical violations they witness, but they also protect them from retaliation when they do.

ELIMINATE "UNDISCUSSABLES." One of the most important things entrepreneurs can do to promote ethical behavior is to instill the belief that it is acceptable for employees to question what happens above them. Doing away with undiscussables makes issues transparent and promotes trust both inside and outside the company.[23]

DEVELOP A CODE OF ETHICS A **code of ethics** is a written statement of the standards of behavior and ethical principles a company expects from its employees. A code of ethics spells out what kind of behavior is expected (and what kind will not be tolerated) and offers everyone in the company concrete guidelines for dealing with ethics every day on the job. Although creating a code of ethics does not guarantee 100 percent compliance with ethical standards, it does tend to foster an ethical atmosphere in a company. Workers who will be directly affected by the code should have a hand in developing it.

code of ethics
a written statement of the standards of behavior and ethical principles a company expects from its employees.

ENFORCE THE CODE OF ETHICS THROUGH POLICIES Set appropriate policies for your organization. Communicate them on a regular basis and adhere to them yourself so that others can see. Show zero tolerance for ethical violations and realize that the adage "Don't do as I do; do as I say" does *not* work. Without a demonstration of real consequences and personal accountability from the CEO, organizational policies are meaningless. Managers must take action whenever they discover ethical violations. If employees learn that ethical breaches go unpunished, the code of ethics becomes meaningless. Enforcement of the code of ethics demonstrates to everyone that you believe ethical behavior is mandatory.

RECRUIT AND PROMOTE ETHICAL EMPLOYEES Ultimately, the decision in any ethical situation belongs to the individual. Hiring people with strong moral principles and values is the best insurance against ethical violations.[24] To make ethical decisions, people must have (1) *ethical commitment*—the personal resolve to act ethically and do the right thing; (2) *ethical consciousness*—the ability to perceive the ethical implications of a situation; and (3) *ethical competency*—the ability to engage in sound moral reasoning and develop practical problem-solving strategies.[25] Find colleges and universities that incorporate business ethics into courses and make them prime recruiting sources.

CONDUCT ETHICS TRAINING Instilling ethics in an organization's culture requires more than creating a code of ethics and enforcing it. Managers must show employees that the organization truly is committed to practicing ethical behavior. One of the most effective ways to display that commitment is through ethical training designed to raise employees' consciousness of potential ethical dilemmas. Ethics training programs not only raise employees' awareness of ethical issues but also communicate to employees the core of the company's value system. Rob Kaplan, professor emeritus of management practice at Harvard University, recommends that employees be trained to follow a simple yet powerful three-step process when facing an ethical situation:

1. Slow down.

2. Seek advice and elevate the issue.

3. Don't get bullied into making a quick decision you might later regret.[26]

REWARD ETHICAL CONDUCT The reward system is a large window into the values of an organization. If you reward a behavior, people have a tendency to repeat the behavior.

SEPARATE RELATED JOB DUTIES This is a basic organizational concept. Not allowing the employee who writes checks to reconcile the company bank statement is one example.

PERFORM PERIODIC ETHICAL AUDITS One of the best ways to evaluate the effectiveness of an ethics system is to perform periodic audits. These reviews send a signal to employees that ethics is not just a passing fad.

LO4

Explain the difference
between social
entrepreneurs and
traditional entrepreneurs.

Social Entrepreneurship

Whereas traditional entrepreneurs seek opportunities to create market value, there is a growing trend to use entrepreneurship to pursue opportunities to create social value. These social entrepreneurs, people who start businesses so that they can create innovative solutions to society's most vexing problems, see themselves as change agents for society. Social entrepreneurs are finding the resources to tackle challenging problems confronting the global economy, including pollution, habitat destruction, human rights, AIDS, hunger, poverty, and others. Social entrepreneurship can be characterized by the following:

1. Social entrepreneurs seek solutions for social problems that are met by neither the market nor government.

2. Creating social benefit rather than commercial success motivates social entrepreneurs.

3. Social entrepreneurs tackle social problems by taking full advantage of natural market forces.[27]

Social entrepreneurs use their creativity to develop solutions to social problems that range from cleaning up the environment to improving working conditions for workers around the world; their goal is to use their businesses to make money *and* to make the world a better place to live.

Social entrepreneurship is the fastest-growing type of entrepreneurship in most parts of the world. The Global Entrepreneurship Monitor survey of entrepreneurial activity reports that 8.3 percent of entrepreneurs in the United States are leading social enterprises, and another 7 percent are trying to start one.[28] Bill Drayton, founder of Ashoka, an organization that promotes social entrepreneurship, says, "Social entrepreneurs are not content just to give a fish or teach [someone] how to fish. They will not rest until they have revolutionized the fishing industry."[29]

ENTREPRENEURIAL PROFILE: Katherine Lucey and Neha Misra, Solar Sister Katherine Lucey, cofounder and CEO of Solar Sister, learned about the challenges of energy poverty in Africa while on a visit to Uganda. She met a farmer who had acquired three solar lights for her home. These lights completely transformed the lives of her family. Solar Sister is a nonprofit, women-run direct sales network that distributes solar lights, mobile phone chargers, and clean cook stoves across Africa. Hundreds of millions of rural Africans lack access to electricity. Many rely on kerosene lighting, which often leads to respiratory illness from its smoky fumes. Kerosene also is expensive, taking up as much as 40 percent of household budgets. Solar Sister has helped some 2,000 women become entrepreneurs by offering rural African families an affordable, clean alternative to kerosene.[30] ■

LO5

Define social responsibility.

Social Responsibility

The concept of social responsibility has evolved from that of a nebulous "do-gooder" to one of "social steward," with the expectation that businesses will produce benefits not only for themselves but also for society as a whole. Society is constantly redefining its expectations of business and now holds companies of all sizes to high standards of ethics and social responsibility. Companies must go beyond "doing well"—simply earning a profit—to "doing good"—living up to their social responsibility. They also must recognize the interdependence of business and society. Each influences the other, and both must remain healthy to sustain each other over time. A growing recognition of social responsibility is true not only for large public corporations but also for small businesses. A survey by SurePayroll reports that 55 percent of small businesses' mission statements include a reference to achieving some type of social goal.[31] Another survey by Funding Circle reports that 52 percent of small business owners donate to charity, and nearly half of them say they donate up to $1,000.[32]

Companies that are most successful in meeting their social responsibility select causes that are consistent with their core values and their employees' interests and skill sets. In fact, some entrepreneurs allow employees to provide input into the decision concerning which causes to support. A common strategy is to allow employees to provide pro bono work for the charitable organizations they support.

You Be the Consultant

Funding Social Ventures Through Franchise Businesses

Nonprofits are facing severe funding challenges. Although the number of social ventures is increasing, funding from grants and donations has declined. A recent survey found that 54 percent of nonprofits were not able to generate enough funding to meet demand for their services. As a result, 39 percent of nonprofits surveyed plan to change the main way they raise funding. To meet this challenge, several nonprofits have turned to a creative way to fund their missions. Rather than rely on grants and donations, a growing number are using franchise businesses to generate new revenue streams to fund their causes.

Frozen Yogurt Store Supports Workers with Disabilities

Alan Sims owns three Menchie's frozen yogurt franchises in Knoxville, Tennessee. Christi Rice, a friend of a friend of Sims, approached him about giving her son, Wesley, an after-school job. Wesley has intellectual disabilities that have made it difficult for him to find a part-time job. Although Sims was skeptical, Wesley soon proved to be an enthusiastic employee with a strong work ethic. After observing how positively both coworkers and customers responded to Wesley, Sims decided to donate one of his stores to Open Doors Tennessee, a nonprofit that provides education and training for children with disabilities.

Sims worked with Steve Johnson, Open Doors's founder and director, to legally transfer the store to Open Doors. Six employees with disabilities work alongside several nondisabled employees and volunteers. Employees with disabilities work varied shifts, ranging from two hours to full-time, adjusted to their abilities. Sims and Johnson plan to use the profits from the store to open other businesses that will employ people with disabilities.

Sandwich Shop Helps Build Housing

Affordable Homes of South Texas develops affordable housing for low-income families. In the past, the agency relied on federal grants as its main source of funding. However, this source of funding has declined steadily over the past several years due to government budget cuts, while demand for its services has continued to climb. Bobby Calvillo, the executive director of Affordable Homes of South Texas, had an inspiration when he noticed lines of people waiting for service in a sandwich shop nearby. Calvillo wondered whether Affordable Homes could open its own sandwich shop to help provide badly needed funding for its clients. After getting approval from his board, Calvillo began the process of buying a Blimpie's sandwich franchise. Affordable Homes could not directly own a franchise business because nonprofits are not

allowed to own such investments. Affordable Homes set up an investment corporation as a parent entity and, under it, formed a limited liability company that would own the franchise business. Calvillo projects that the franchise will be able to fund the construction of several homes once it is fully operational.

Clients of Training Center Bake Pizzas to Generate Revenue

Dale Rogers Training Center trains and employs more than 1,100 people with disabilities in Oklahoma City each year. Due to declining private funding, the nonprofit partnered with Papa Murphy's Pizza to open a franchise operation to provide additional funding and offer a place for at least 15 of its clients to work. Dale Rogers Training Center is not new to using social enterprises to support its operating budget. The nonprofit generates 83 percent of its revenue from several social enterprises, including janitorial, cleaning, and delivery services. Dale Rogers Training Center receives 100 percent of the profits from the pizza shop and is able to fill 75 percent of the store's jobs with its clients. Even though this Papa Murphy's restaurant hires people with disabilities, it has the same standards for its employees as every other Papa Murphy's store.

1. What challenges does owning and operating a franchise business create for these nonprofits? Explain.

2. What advantages do franchise businesses offer nonprofits that seek side businesses to generate revenues to support their causes?

3. Select a local nonprofit and work with a team of your classmates to brainstorm ideas for a franchise business that could help create a sustainable cash flow to support the mission of the social venture. What advice can you offer social entrepreneurs on developing alternative revenues to replace declining grants and donations?

Sources: Based on Kristi Nelson, "Yogurt Shop Sweet Opportunity for Nonprofit," *Knoxville News Sentinel,* January 12, 2015, www.knoxnews.com/news/local/yogurt-shop-sweet-opportunity-for-nonprofit-ep-870509701-353686551.html; "Menchie's Frozen Yogurt Franchise Owner Donates Store to Tennessee Nonprofit," *Menchie's Franchise Blog,* November 4, 2014, http://menchiesfranchise.com/2014/11/04/menchies-frozen-yogurt-franchise-owner-donates-store-tennessee-nonprofit/; "Nonprofit Finance Fund Survey of 5900+ Nonprofits: Organizations Innovating and Adapting to New Reality," Nonprofit Finance Fund, March 25, 2013, http://nonprofitfinancefund.org/announcements/2013/state-of-the-nonprofit-sector-survey; Elizabeth Findell, "Nonprofit Starts Sandwich Shop to Gather Revenue to Build Housing," *The Monitor,* May 24, 2013, www.themonitor.com/news/local/article_032f8f20-c367-11e2-b381-001a4bcf6878.html; Hillary McLain, "Oklahoma City Pizza Restaurant to Provide Opportunities for Employees with Disabilities," *The Oklahoman,* July 11, 2013, http://newsok.com/oklahoma-city-pizza-restaurant-to-provide-opportunities-for-employees-with-disabilities/article/3861000.

ENTREPRENEURIAL PROFILE: David Dietz, Modavanti Modavanti is an online fashion retailer that integrates charitable giving into its business model. Modavanti gives 2 percent of each online sale made by its customers to specific charitable causes. For example, Modavanti donates to Nest, which seeks to protect and support the craft of handmade silk in India by donating looms to local artisans. A second charity is Water, which is an NGO that installs systems that provide clean drinking water to impoverished rural communities around the globe.

When customers check out, they are given a choice of the Modavanti-supported charities included in the company's program. Modavanti also offers customers the opportunity to send in their used clothing, which Modavanti then donates to charity. Modavanti gives customers who donate used clothing up to $60 in merchandise credit that can be applied to future online purchases.[33] ■

In a free enterprise system, companies that fail to respond to their customers' needs and demands soon go out of business. Today, customers are increasingly demanding that the companies they buy goods and services from be socially responsible. When customers shop for "value," they no longer consider only the price–performance relationship of the product or service; they also consider the company's stance on social responsibility. Whether a company supports a social or an environmental cause has a significant effect on shoppers' behavior. A study by Penn Schoen Berland, in conjunction with Burson-Marsteller and Landor, reports that more than 75 percent of consumers say social responsibility is important in their purchasing decisions. The survey finds that 55 percent of consumers are more likely to choose a product that supports a certain cause when choosing between otherwise similar products and that 38 percent are willing to pay more for products with added social benefits.[34] Other studies conclude that when price, service, and quality are equal among competitors, customers buy from the company that has the best reputation for social responsibility.

Other studies show a connection between social responsibility and profitability. One team of researchers evaluated 52 studies on corporate social responsibility that were conducted over 30 years and concluded that a positive correlation existed between a company's profitability and its reputation for ethical, socially responsible behavior. The relationship was also self-reinforcing. "It's a virtuous cycle," says Sara Rynes, one of the researchers. "As a company becomes more socially responsible, its reputation and financial performance go up, which causes them to become even more socially responsible."[35] The message is clear: Companies that incorporate social responsibility into their competitive strategies outperform those that fail to do so. Today's socially wired, transparent economy makes ethical and socially responsible behavior highly visible and, conversely, improper behavior more difficult to hide.

One problem businesses face is defining just what socially responsible behavior is. Is it manufacturing environmentally friendly products? Is it donating a portion of profits to charitable organizations? Is it creating jobs in inner cities plagued by high unemployment levels? The nature of a company's social responsibility efforts depends on how its owners, employees, and other stakeholders define what it means to be socially responsible. Typically, businesses have responsibilities to several key stakeholders, including the environment, employees, customers, investors, and the community. Table 2.6 lists simple ways that small businesses can practice social responsibility.

TABLE 2.6 Simple Ways for a Small Business to Be Socially Responsible

1. *Encourage recycling.* Place recycling bins throughout the workplace. If the business sells retail products, encourage customers to bring reusable shopping bags. Use recycled products whenever possible.

2. *Support local fund-raisers.* Provide local fund-raising events with donated products or services. Encourage employees to participate in fund-raising events as a team representing the company.

3. *Join in community service.* Allow employees to participate in community volunteer projects on company time. Designate a day a year for all employees to help with a local charity, such as planting trees on Arbor Day, cleaning up a section of a local highway, helping with a Habitat for Humanity building project, or volunteering at an inner-city school.

4. *Reduce energy usage.* Encourage employees to help find ways to reduce energy consumption in your business. Provide recognition to employees whose ideas help reduce energy usage.

5. *Create a grant program.* Set up a fund that local nonprofits can apply to for small grants. Create a matching program to encourage employee giving to the fund by committing to company matching donations for their gifts.

6. *Support local causes.* Work with employees to identify local causes that the business can support by offering publicity for that cause. Promotion can include flyers in the window, promotion on the company Web site, employee T-shirts supporting the cause, and social media campaigns.

7. *Partner with local schools.* Partner with local schools by providing supplies and encouraging employees to serve as volunteers. Mentor young people through a job shadowing program.

Sources: Based on Lisa Mooney, "Ways for a Small Business to Show Social Responsibility," *AzCentral.com*, n.d., http://yourbusiness.azcentral.com/ways-small-business-show-social-responsibility-2392.html; Lalia Helmer, "7 Ways Small Business Can Embrace Social Responsibility," *Business That Cares*, September 21, 2010, http://businessthatcares.blogspot.com/2010/09/7-ways-small-business-can-embrace.html.

Business's Responsibility to the Environment

LO6

Understand the nature of business's responsibility to the environment.

Due to a strong personal belief in environmental protection, many entrepreneurs seek to start ventures that have a positive impact on the environment or take steps to operate their businesses in ways that help protect the environment. Also driven by their customers' interest in protecting the environment, small businesses have become more sensitive to the impact their products, processes, and packaging have on the planet. Environmentalism has become—and will continue to be—one of the dominant issues for companies worldwide because consumers have added another item to their list of buying criteria: environmental friendliness and safety. Companies have discovered that sound environmental practices make for good business. In addition to lowering their operating costs, environmentally safe products attract environmentally conscious customers and can give a company a competitive edge in the marketplace. Socially responsible business owners focus on the three *R*s:

- *Reduce* the amount of energy and materials used in your company, from the factory floor to the copier room.

- *Reuse* whatever you can.

- *Recycle* the materials that you must dispose of.

ENTREPRENEURIAL PROFILE: Scott Kelly and Jenn Rezeli, Re:Vision Architecture
Scott Kelly and Jenn Rezeli practice their commitment to the environment in every aspect of their business. Re:Vision Architecture, based in Philadelphia, Pennsylvania, specializes in sustainable architecture consulting and offers targeted consulting services to developers, building owners, government agencies, manufacturers, schools, and design professionals. The company offers a full-service staff of architects and planners who can design a sustainable building to conserve natural resources, lower operating costs, and enrich designs. Beyond its design practices, Re:Vision Architecture's business practices reflect its commitment to the environment. More than 75 percent of office supplies come from recycled materials. The company also rewards employees for using public transportation and car-pooling.[36] ∎

Many progressive small companies are taking their environmental policies a step further, creating redesigned, "clean" manufacturing systems that focus on *avoiding* waste and pollution and using resources efficiently. That requires a different manufacturing philosophy. These companies design their products, packaging, and processes from the start with the environment in mind, working to eliminate hazardous materials and by-products and looking for ways to turn what had been scrap into salable products. This approach requires an ecological evaluation of every part of the process, from the raw materials that go into a product to the disposal or reuse of the packaging that contains it.

ENTREPRENEURIAL PROFILE: Russell Bisset, Northern Monk Brew Company
"Wasted" is a new breed of beer being brewed by Northern Monk Brew Company, located in Leeds, England. Northern Monk promotes Wasted as a zero-waste beer. Sugar is critical to the fermentation process when brewing beer. Wasted gets its sugar from recycled overly ripe pears, stale croissants, and other food waste from the local community that would otherwise be destined for the landfill. Northern Monk reuses yeast for the fermentation process from other beers it brews. After brewing Wasted, the brewery donates all the hops used in making the beer to local farmers to use as fertilizer. All the grains used in brewing Wasted are donated to a worm farm, which uses them as worm feed. Finally, Northern Monk sells the beer in bottles made of 100 percent recycled glass. Founder Russell Bisset's goal is to change beer production from a waste-generating business into a zero-waste business.[37] ∎

Business's Responsibility to Employees

LO7

Describe business's responsibility to employees.

Few other stakeholders are as important to a business as its employees. It is common for managers to *say* that their employees are their most valuable resource, but the truly excellent ones actually *treat* them that way. Employees are at the heart of increases in productivity, and they add the personal touch that puts passion in customer service. In short, employees produce the winning competitive advantage for an entrepreneur. Entrepreneurs who understand the value of their employees follow a few simple procedures by doing the following:

- Listening to employees and respecting their opinions

- Asking for their input and involving them in the decision-making process

- Providing regular feedback—positive and negative—to employees

- Telling them the truth—always

- Letting them know exactly what's expected of them

- Rewarding employees for performing their jobs well

- Trusting them; creating an environment of respect and teamwork

 ENTREPRENEURIAL PROFILE: Delight Co. Delight Co. is a Korean company that makes and distributes affordable hearing aid devices to the elderly. To keep its products affordable, Delight manufactures standardized devices and distributes them through company-owned stores located throughout the country. Through its efficient operations, Delight sells its product for $299, which is equivalent to the government subsidy for hearing-impaired people in Korea. Delight employs senior citizens to deliver the products from the headquarters to the branch stores and other hearing-impaired people to work in its manufacturing plant. Delight offers its employees a wide array of benefits, including subsidized meals, transportation, and housing. In addition, Delight employees are eligible for company-sponsored training and tuition reimbursement.[38] ∎

Several important issues face entrepreneurs who are trying to meet their social responsibility to employees, including cultural diversity, drug testing, sexual harassment, and privacy.

Cultural Diversity in the Workplace

The United States has always been a nation of astonishing cultural diversity (see Figure 2.4), a trait that has imbued it with an incredible richness of ideas and creativity. Indeed, this diversity is one of the driving forces behind the greatest entrepreneurial effort in the world, and it continues to grow. The United States, in short, is moving toward a "minority majority," and significant demographic shifts will affect virtually every aspect of business. Nowhere will this be more visible than in the makeup of the nation's workforce (see Figure 2.5). In 2020, members of five different generations will be working side by side in the United States.[39] By 2032, the *majority* of the workforce in the United States will be a member of a minority group.[40] The Hispanic

FIGURE 2.4
Diversity Index by County

Source: Kyle Reese-Cassal, "2015/2020 Esri Diversity Index," Esri, March 2015, p. 4.

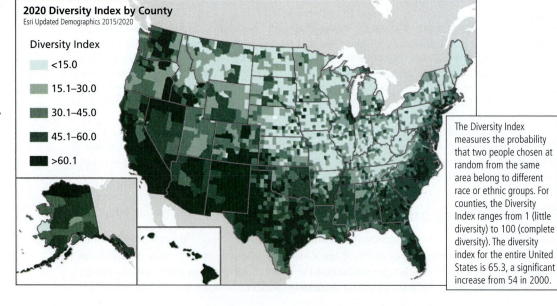

2020 Diversity Index by County
Esri Updated Demographics 2015/2020

Diversity Index

- <15.0
- 15.1–30.0
- 30.1–45.0
- 45.1–60.0
- >60.1

The Diversity Index measures the probability that two people chosen at random from the same area belong to different race or ethnic groups. For counties, the Diversity Index ranges from 1 (little diversity) to 100 (complete diversity). The diversity index for the entire United States is 65.3, a significant increase from 54 in 2000.

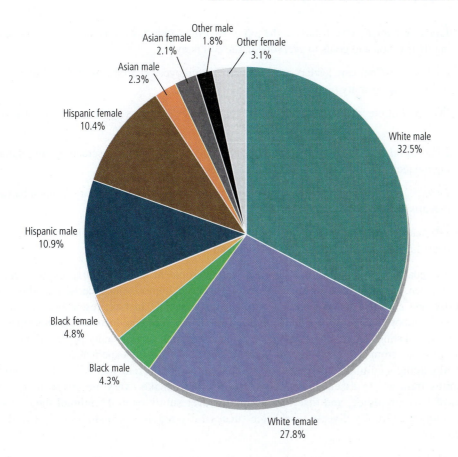

FIGURE 2.5

Projected Composition of the U.S. Workforce in 2020

Source: Based on Mitra Toossi, "Labor Force Projections to 2024: A More Slowly Growing Workforce," *Monthly Labor Review*, January 2015, www.bls.gov/opub/mlr/2015/article/labor-force-projections-to-2024.htm.

population is the fastest-growing sector in the United States, and Hispanics now make up the largest minority population in the nation.

This rich mix of generations, cultures, and backgrounds within the workforce presents both opportunities and challenges to employers. One of the chief benefits of a diverse workforce is the rich blend of perspectives, skills, talents, and ideas employees have to offer. A study by McKinsey and Company suggests that companies that have the greatest racial and ethnic diversity are 35 percent more likely to have financial returns above their industry's norms. The study also found that racial and ethnic diversity in the senior executive team has a direct relationship to overall company performance. For every 10 percent increase in senior executive racial and ethnic diversity, profits increase by 0.8 percent. Results of the study also suggest that companies with the highest gender diversity are 15 percent more likely to have financial returns above their industry's norms.[41]

Managing a culturally diverse workforce presents a real challenge for employers, however. Molding workers with highly varied beliefs, backgrounds, and biases into a unified team takes time and commitment. Stereotypes, biases, and prejudices present barriers workers and managers must constantly overcome. Communication may require more effort because of language differences. In many cases, dealing with diversity causes a degree of discomfort for entrepreneurs because of the natural tendency to associate with people who are similar to us. These reasons and others cause some entrepreneurs to resist the move to a more diverse workforce, a move that threatens their ability to create a competitive edge.

How can entrepreneurs achieve unity through diversity? The only way is by *managing* diversity in the workforce. In its *Best Practices of Private Sector Employers*, an Equal Employment Opportunity Commission task force suggests following a "SPLENDID" approach to diversity:

- *S*tudy. Business owners cannot solve problems they don't know exist. Entrepreneurs must familiarize themselves with issues related to diversity, including relevant laws.

- *P*lan. Recognizing the makeup of the local population, entrepreneurs must set targets for diversity hiring and develop a plan for achieving them.

- *L*ead. A diversity effort starts at the top of the organization, with managers communicating their vision and goals to everyone in the company.

- *E*ncourage. Company leaders must encourage employees at all levels of an organization to embrace the diversity plan.

- *N*otice. Entrepreneurs must monitor their companies' progress toward achieving diversity goals.

- *D*iscussion. Managers must keep diversity on the company's radar screen by communicating the message that diversity is vital to business success.

- *I*nclusion. Involving employees in the push to achieve diversity helps break down barriers that arise.

- *D*edication. Achieving diversity in a business does not happen overnight, but entrepreneurs must be persistent in implementing their plans.[42]

The goal of diversity efforts is to create an environment in which all types of workers—men, women, Hispanic, African American, white, disabled, homosexual, elderly, and others—can flourish and can give top performances to their companies. In fact, researchers at Harvard University report that companies that embrace diversity are more productive than those that shun diversity. A distinguishing factor shared by companies supporting diversity is the willingness of people to learn from their coworkers' different backgrounds and life experiences.[43]

Managing a culturally diverse workforce requires a different way of thinking, and that requires training. In essence, diversity training helps make everyone aware of the dangers of bias, prejudice, and discrimination, however subtle or unintentional they may be. Managing a culturally diverse workforce successfully requires a business owner to do the following:

- *Assess your company's diversity needs.* The starting point for an effective diversity management program is assessing a company's needs. Surveys, interviews, and informal conversations with employees can be valuable tools. Several organizations offer more formal assessment tools—cultural audits, questionnaires, and diagnostic forms—that also are useful. Recently, technology companies have been focusing on diversifying their workforces because only 5 percent of their workers are of Hispanic or African–American heritage even though members of those groups make up 18 percent of computer science and engineering graduates.[44]

- *Learn to recognize and correct your own biases and stereotypes.* One of the best ways to identify your own cultural biases is to get exposure to people who are not like you. By spending time with people who are different from you, you will learn quickly that stereotypes simply don't hold up. Giving employees the opportunity to spend time with one another is an excellent way to eliminate stereotypes. The owner of one small company with a culturally diverse staff provides lunch for his workers every month, with a seating arrangement that encourages employees to mix with one another.

- *Avoid making invalid assumptions.* Decisions that are based on faulty assumptions are bound to be flawed. False assumptions built on inaccurate perceptions or personal bias have kept many qualified minority workers from getting jobs and promotions. Make sure this does not happen in your company.

- *Push for diversity in your management team.* To get maximum benefit from a culturally diverse workforce, a company must promote nontraditional workers into top management. A culturally diverse top management team that can serve as mentors and role models provides visible evidence that nontraditional workers can succeed.

- *Concentrate on communication.* Any organization, especially a culturally diverse one, will stumble if lines of communication break down. Frequent training sessions and regular opportunities for employees to talk with one another in a nonthreatening environment can be extremely helpful.

- *Make diversity a core value in the organization.* For a cultural diversity program to work, top managers must "champion" the program and take active steps to integrate diversity throughout the entire organization.

- *Continue to adjust your company to your workers.* Rather than pressure workers to conform to the company, entrepreneurs with the most successful cultural diversity programs are constantly looking for ways to adjust their businesses to their workers. Flexibility is the key.

As business leaders look to the future, an increasingly diverse workforce stares back. People with varying cultural, racial, gender, and lifestyle perspectives seek opportunity and acceptance from coworkers, managers, and business owners. Currently, women make up 46.8 percent of the U.S. workforce, and minority workers make up more than 35 percent of the labor force. By 2024 women are projected to make up 47.2 percent of the workforce and minorities are projected to grow to 40.4 percent.[45] Businesses that value the diversity of their workers and the perspectives they bring to work enjoy the benefits of higher employee satisfaction, commitment, retention, creativity, and productivity more than do companies that ignore the cultural diversity of their workers. In addition, diverse businesses deepen the loyalty of their existing customers and expand their market share by attracting new customers.

Drug Testing

One of the realities of our society is substance abuse. A related reality, which entrepreneurs now must face head on, is that substance abuse has infiltrated the workplace. In addition to the lives it ruins, substance abuse takes a heavy toll on business and society. Lost productivity due to drug and alcohol abuse cost companies an estimated $437 billion annually.[46] Injury-related absences from work are 2.7 times higher for workers with drinking problems. At least 11 percent of workers killed on the job had alcohol in their systems. Employee turnover is double for active illegal drug users. Alcohol and illegal drugs are commonly used in the workplace. A federal study shows that 24 percent of workers report that they have drunk alcohol during the workday at least once in the past year. Of the 14.8 million Americans using illegal drugs, 70 percent are employed.[47] Small companies bear a disproportionate share of the burden because they are less likely to have drug-testing programs than large companies and are more likely to hire people with substance abuse problems. Abusers who know that they cannot pass a drug test simply apply for work at companies that do not use drug testing. In addition, because the practice of drug testing remains a controversial issue, its random use can lead to a variety of legal woes for employers, including invasion of privacy, discrimination, slander, or defamation of character.

An effective, proactive drug program should include the following five elements:

1. *A written substance abuse policy.* The first step is to create a written policy that spells out the company's position on drugs. The policy should state its purpose, prohibit the use of drugs on the job (or off the job, if it affects job performance), specify the consequences of violating the policy, explain the drug-testing procedures the company will use, and describe the resources available to help troubled employees.

2. *Training for supervisors to detect substance-abusing workers.* Supervisors are in the best position to identify employees with alcohol or drug problems and to encourage them to get help. The supervisor's job, however, is not to play "cop" or "therapist." The supervisor should identify problem employees early and encourage them to seek help. The focal point of the supervisor's role is to track employees' performances against their objectives to identify the employees with performance problems. Vigilant managers look for the following signs:

- Frequent tardiness or absences accompanied by questionable excuses
- Long lunch, coffee, or bathroom breaks
- Frequently missed deadlines
- Withdrawal from or frequent arguments with fellow employees
- Excessive sensitivity to criticism
- Declining or inconsistent productivity
- Inability to concentrate on work
- Disregard for personal safety or the safety of others
- Deterioration of personal appearance

3. *An employee education program.* Business owners should take time to explain the company's substance abuse policy, the reasons behind it, and the help that is available to employees who have substance abuse problems. Every employee should participate in training sessions, and managers should remind employees periodically of the policy, the magnitude of the problem, and the help that is available. Some companies have used inserts in pay envelopes, home mailings, lunch speakers, and short seminars as part of their ongoing educational efforts.

4. *A drug-testing program, when necessary.* Experts recommend that business owners seek the advice of an experienced attorney before establishing a drug-testing program. Preemployment testing of job applicants is a safe policy as long as a company follows it consistently. Testing current employees is a more complex issue, but, again, consistency is the key. If a company tests one employee, it should test them all.

5. *An employee assistance program.* No drug-battling program is complete without a way to help addicted employees. An **employee assistance program (EAP)** is a company-provided benefit designed to help reduce workplace problems such as alcoholism, drug addiction, gambling habit and others and to deal with them when they arise. Although some troubled employees may balk at enrolling in an EAP, the company controls the most powerful weapon in motivating them to seek and accept help: *their jobs.* The greatest fear that substance-abusing employees have is losing their jobs, and the company can use that fear to help workers recover. EAPs, which cost between $12 and $40 per employee each year to operate, are an effective weapon in the battle against workplace substance abuse. Research shows that EAPs can pay for themselves quickly by reducing absenteeism and tardiness by 25 percent and increasing productivity by 25 percent.[48] Numerous studies show that every $1 that companies invest in EAP services produces a return of between $3 and $10.[49] Unfortunately, only 21 percent of small companies (compared to 76 percent of large companies) offer EAPs.[50]

employee assistance program (EAP)
a company-provided benefit designed to help reduce workplace problems such as alcoholism, drug addiction, gambling addiction, and other conflicts and to deal with them when they arise.

ENTREPRENEURIAL PROFILE: Eastern Industries Eastern Industries, a Pennsylvania-based company that produces building supplies, concrete, asphalt, and stone, operates in an industry that traditionally has been plagued by substance abuse problems. A recent study shows that 15.1 percent of workers in the construction industry had substance abuse problems, second only to the food service industry. Initially, Eastern's substance abuse policy was simple: We test for drugs, and if you fail the test, you are fired. The all-or-nothing policy affected the company's ability to keep and retain skilled workers, so managers decided to adopt a new policy that includes prevention, testing, and rehabilitation. Eastern includes educational sessions on substance abuse in its employee orientation program and ongoing programs for all workers. If an employee fails a drug test, he or she can enroll in an employee assistance program including rehabilitation that, once successfully completed, allows the worker to return to his or her job. Managers at Eastern say the program has been a tremendous success, allowing them to keep good workers they would have lost under the old policy and giving employees the opportunity to correct bad decisions and keep their jobs.[51] ■

Sexual Harassment

Sexual harassment is a problem in the workplace. Thousands of workers file sexual harassment charges with the Equal Employment Opportunity Commission (EEOC) against their employers every year. Since awareness of sexual harassment has increased, there has been a steady decline in charges filed over the past decade. Sexual harassment is a violation of Title VII of the Civil Rights Act of 1964 and is considered to be a form of sex discrimination. Studies show that sexual harassment occurs in businesses of all sizes, but small businesses are especially vulnerable because they typically lack the policies, procedures, and training to prevent it.

sexual harassment
any unwelcome sexual advance, request for sexual favors, and other verbal or physical sexual conduct made explicitly or implicitly as a condition of employment.

Sexual harassment is any unwelcome sexual advance, request for sexual favors, and other verbal or physical sexual conduct made explicitly or implicitly as a condition of employment. A recent survey reports that one in three women say that they have been sexually harassed at work.[52] Jury verdicts reaching into the millions of dollars are not uncommon. In 2016, there were 6,758 sexual harassment claims filed with the EEOC (down nearly 1,200 from 2010) that yielded a total of $41.0 million in settlements to the victims.[53] Retaliation, such as demotions and assignments to less attractive work, against employees who file complaints of sexual harassment occurs too often, but the most common form of employer retaliation is termination. Types of behavior that may result in sexual harassment charges include the following.

QUID PRO QUO HARASSMENT The most blatant and most potentially damaging form of sexual harassment is quid pro quo ("this for that"), in which a superior conditions the granting of a benefit such as a promotion or raise on the receipt of sexual favors from a subordinate. Only managers and supervisors, not coworkers, can engage in quid pro quo harassment.

HOSTILE ENVIRONMENT Behavior that creates an abusive, intimidating, offensive, or hostile work environment also constitutes sexual harassment. A hostile environment usually requires a *pattern* of offensive sexual behavior rather than a single, isolated remark or display. When judging whether a hostile environment exists, courts base their decisions on how a "reasonable woman" would perceive the situation. (The previous standard was that of a "reasonable person.") Examples of what creates a hostile work environment might include the following:

- Displaying sexually suggestive pictures or posters
- Engaging in sexually related humor within hearing of someone who takes offense
- Talking about sexual matters where others can hear (as in colorfully relating one's "conquests")
- Making sexual comments to other employees
- Dispensing assignments based on sexual orientation
- Repeatedly asking a coworker for a date after having been refused multiple times[54]

Although not easily defined, a hostile work environment is one in which continuing unwelcome sexual conduct in the workplace interferes with an employee's work performance. Sexual harassment is sexually related behavior that is unwelcome, unwanted, and repeated. Most sexual harassment charges arise from claims of a hostile environment.

HARASSMENT BY NONEMPLOYEES An employer can be held liable for third parties (customers, sales representatives, and others) who engage in sexual harassment if the employer has the ability to stop the improper behavior. For example, one company required a female employee to wear an extremely skimpy, revealing uniform. She complained to her boss that the uniform encouraged members of the public to direct offensive comments and physical contact toward her. The manager ignored her complaints, and later she refused to wear the uniform, which resulted in her dismissal. When she filed a sexual harassment claim, the court held the company accountable for the employee's sexual harassment by nonemployees because it required her to wear the uniform after she complained of harassment.[55]

No business wants to incur the cost of defending itself against charges of sexual harassment, but those costs can be devastating for a small business. Multi-million-dollar jury awards in harassment cases are becoming increasingly common because the Civil Rights Act of 1991 allows victims to collect punitive damages and emotional distress awards. A jury awarded eight former employees of Four Amigos Travel, Inc. and Top Dog Travel, Inc. $20,251,963 after they won a lawsuit claiming daily sexual harassment of women employees in the workplace. The complaint was filed against travel agency owner Ronald Schlom and male managers by employees describing unwanted sexual advances, physical touching, and repeated propositions for sex. The suit described a work environment that was filled with sexual banter, abuse of power, and outright disrespect for women. The company fired the manager who brought forward the victims' complaints. The jury returned a unanimous verdict awarding $3.75 million in compensatory damages, $16 million in punitive damages, and $501,963 in back pay to the former employees. "This was a long journey for these women who were forced to work under unspeakable conditions at this workplace," says Gregory Lee McClinton, the EEOC's lead attorney in the case. "Their testimony about how the sexual harassment occurred and how it affected their lives was very powerful."[56]

The U.S. Supreme Court has expanded the nature of an employer's liability for sexual harassment, rejecting the previous standard that the employer had to be negligent to be liable for a supervisor's improper behavior toward employees. In *Burlington Industries v. Ellerth*, the court ruled that an employer can be held liable *automatically* if a supervisor takes a "tangible employment action," such as failing to promote or firing an employee he has been sexually harassing.

The employer is liable even if he or she was not aware of the supervisor's conduct. If a supervisor takes no tangible employment action against an employee but engages in sexually harassing behavior, such as offensive remarks, inappropriate touching, or sexual advances, the employer is not *automatically* liable for the supervisor's conduct. However, an employer would be liable for such conduct if, for example, he or she knew (or should have known) about the supervisor's behavior and failed to stop it.[57]

A company's best weapons against sexual harassment are education, policy, and procedures.

EDUCATION Preventing sexual harassment is the best solution, and the key to prevention is educating employees about what constitutes sexual harassment. Training programs are designed to raise employees' awareness of what might be offensive to other workers and how to avoid sexual harassment altogether.

POLICY Another essential ingredient is a meaningful policy against sexual harassment that management can enforce. The policy should do the following:

- Clearly define what behaviors constitute sexual harassment
- State in clear language that harassment will not be tolerated in the workplace
- Identify the responsibilities of supervisors and employees in preventing harassment
- Define the sanctions and penalties for engaging in harassment
- Spell out the steps to take in reporting an incident of sexual harassment

In another case, the Supreme Court ruled that an employer was liable for a supervisor's sexually harassing behavior even though the employee never reported it. The company's liability stemmed from its failure to communicate its sexual harassment policy throughout the organization. This ruling makes employers' policies and procedures on sexual harassment the focal point of their defense.

PROCEDURE Socially responsible companies provide a channel for all employees to express their complaints. Choosing a person inside the company (perhaps someone in the human resources area) and one outside the company (a close adviser or attorney) is a good strategy because it gives employees a choice about how to file a complaint. At least one of these people should be a woman. When a complaint arises, managers should do the following:

- Listen to the complaint carefully, without judging. Taking notes is a good idea. Tell the complainant what the process involves. Never treat the complaint as a joke.
- Investigate the complaint *promptly*, preferably within 24 hours. Failure to act quickly is irresponsible and illegal. Table 2.7 offers suggestions for conducting a sexual harassment investigation.
- Interview the accused party and any witnesses who may be aware of a pattern of harassing behavior *privately* and separately.
- Keep findings confidential.
- Decide what action to take, relying on company policy as a guideline.
- Inform both the complaining person and the alleged harasser of the action taken.
- Document the entire investigation.[58]

Privacy

Modern technology has given business owners the ability to monitor workers' performance as they never could before, but where is the line between monitoring productivity and invasion of privacy? With a few mouse clicks, it is possible for managers to view e-mail messages employees send to one another, listen to voice-mail or telephone conversations, and actually see what is on their monitors while they are sitting at their computer terminals. Some employers have begun to demand Facebook usernames and passwords from job applicants, although this is a violation

TABLE 2.7 What to Do When an Employee Files a Sexual Harassment Complaint

When an employee files a sexual harassment complaint, the Equal Employment Opportunity Commission (EEOC) recommends that employers (1) gather detailed information about the complaint from both of the parties involved and (2) seek out other evidence that helps explain what happened. The following list helps ensure that EEOC recommendations are adhered to:

- Carefully assess the victim's statements to ensure that they are consistent throughout and credible.
- Do not weight the accused party's statement of denial too heavily.
- Seek evidence that supports both parties' stories, not just evidence that supports or refutes the accusations, through careful interviews of other employees close to the situation and by talking to those the victim confided in about the events that allegedly occurred, such as coworkers or professionals.
- Ask other employees about any changes in how the two parties interact in the workplace both before and after the alleged incident.
- Examine the background of the victim and the accused for other similar incidences, looking for patterns and making sure to follow up with other employees who may have claimed similar harassment.

To make a just decision on a sexual harassment complaint, gather as much information as possible, not only about the events in question but also about general information about both parties. Ask probing questions of the victim, the accuser, and all witnesses to the alleged incident.

Source: Based on "Questions for Investigations," Women's Studies Database at the University of Maryland, www.mith2.umd.edu/WomensStudies/GenderIssues/SexualHarassment/questions-for-investigations.

The accompanying "Hands On … How To" feature includes a quiz on sexual harassment for both employees and managers.

 ## Hands On . . . How To

How to Avoid Sexual Harassment Charges

The Equal Employment Opportunity Commission handles about 6,800 charges of sexual harassment each year from both women and men. Not surprisingly, women file 84 percent of the charges. Experts say that many other employees are sexually harassed but never file charges because of the stigma associated with doing so. What can you do to ensure that you provide your employees a safe work environment that is free of sexual harassment? Consider the following case and then take the accompanying quizzes on sexual harassment.

Theresa Waldo was the only woman working in the Transmission Lines Department, a traditionally male-dominated job in which workers maintain and repair high-voltage power lines, sometimes at heights up to 250 feet, for Consumers Energy (CE). Her supervisor told her the company did not "have women in this department" and had never had them there and that "they are not strong enough" to do the job. Despite resistance from her supervisor and coworkers, Waldo, who started her career with CE as a meter reader, was participating in a four-year Line Apprentice Training Program that would entitle her to a higher-paying job. On several occasions, Waldo's supervisor told her that he would "wash her out" of the apprenticeship program.

During her time in the apprenticeship program, Waldo alleges that she faced an "abusive and dysfunctional environment" in which she was constantly "bombarded with sexually abusive and derogatory language and conduct." Male coworkers subjected her to magazines, calendars, playing cards, and other items that contained photographs of nude women. They also referred to Waldo using derogatory, sexually offensive names and on one 90-degree day intentionally locked her in a port-a-potty for 20 minutes. On another occasion, her supervisor ordered her to clean up the tobacco spit of the male workers; when she refused, her coworkers locked her in a trailer. Waldo complained

to the company's management about the sexual harassment on several occasions, but managers failed to take any meaningful action to stop the behavior.

After Waldo had successfully completed three years of the apprenticeship program, CE removed her from it and transferred her to the Sub Metro Department, where her pay was $4 less per hour. She filed a sexual harassment charge, alleging that the company had created a hostile work environment, committed sexual harassment, and engaged in gender discrimination and retaliation.

1. Does Waldo have a legitimate sexual harassment complaint? Explain.

One of the primary causes of sexual harassment in the workplace is the lack of education concerning what constitutes harassment. The following quizzes ask you to assume the roles of an employee and of a manager when answering the questions. Learning from these quizzes can help your company avoid problems with sexual harassment.

Answer: 1. Yes. Although the jury in the trial ruled in favor of the *employer* on all claims, the judge granted Waldo's motion for a new trial, acknowledging that the jury's verdict on the hostile work environment and sexual harassment should be set aside because of the "clear evidence presented" in the case. The court ruled that the evidence "demonstrated egregious actions and sexually offensive and demeaning language" directed at Waldo. The court concluded that the harassment created "an intimidating, hostile, and offensive work environment" and that CE "knew of the harassment and failed to implement proper and appropriate corrective action." At the second trial, a jury ruled in Waldo's favor and granted her $400,000 in compensatory damages and $7.5 million in punitive damages.

(continued)

Hands On . . . How To *(continued)*

A Test for Employees

Answer the following true/false questions:

1. If I just ignore unwanted sexual attention, it will usually stop.

2. If I don't mean to sexually harass another employee, he or she cannot perceive my behavior as sexually harassing.

3. Some employees don't complain about unwanted sexual attention from another worker because they don't want to get that person in trouble.

4. If I make sexual comments to someone and that person doesn't ask me to stop, I can assume that my behavior is welcome.

5. To avoid sexually harassing a woman who comes to work in a traditionally male workplace, men simply should not haze her.

6. A sexual harasser may be told by a court to pay part of a judgment to the employee he or she harassed.

7. A sexually harassed man does not have the same legal rights as a woman who is sexually harassed.

8. About 84 percent of all sexual harassment in today's workplace is male to female harassment.

9. Sexually suggestive pictures or objects in a workplace don't create a liability unless someone complains.

10. Displaying nude pictures can constitute a hostile work environment even though most employees in the workplace think they are harmless.

11. Telling someone to stop his or her unwanted sexual behavior usually doesn't do any good.

Answers: (1) False, (2) False, (3) True, (4) False, (5) False, (6) True, (7) False, (8) True, (9) False, (10) True, (11) False

A Test for Managers

Answer the following true/false questions:

1. Men in male-dominated workplaces usually have to change their behavior when a woman begins working there.

2. Employers are not liable for the sexual harassment of one of their employees unless that employee loses specific job benefits or is fired.

3. Supervisors can be liable for sexual harassment committed by one of their employees against another.

4. Employers can be liable for the sexually harassing behavior of management personnel even if they are unaware of that behavior and have a policy forbidding it.

5. It is appropriate for a supervisor, when initially receiving a sexual harassment complaint, to determine if the alleged recipient overreacted or misunderstood the alleged harasser.

6. When a supervisor is to tell an employee that an allegation of sexual harassment has been made against him or her by another employee, it is best for the supervisor to ease into the allegation instead of being direct.

7. Sexually suggestive visuals or objects in a workplace don't create a liability unless an employee complains about them and management allows them to remain.

8. The lack of sexual harassment complaints is a good indication that sexual harassment is not occurring.

9. It is appropriate for supervisors to tell an employee to handle unwelcome sexual behavior if they think the employee is misunderstanding the behavior.

10. The *intent* behind employee A's sexual behavior is more important than the *impact* of that behavior on employee B when determining whether sexual harassment has occurred.

11. If a sexual harassment problem is common knowledge in a workplace, courts assume that the employer has knowledge of it.

Answers: (1) False, (2) False, (3) True, (4) True, (5) False, (6) False, (7) False, (8) False, (9) False, (10) False, (11) True

Sources: Based on *Industry Week*, November 18, 1991, p. 40. Copyright Penton Publishing, Cleveland, Ohio; *Sexual Harassment Manual for Managers and Supervisors* (Chicago: Commerce Clearing House), 1992, p. 22; Andrea P. Brandon and David R. Eyler, *Working Together* (New York: McGraw-Hill), 1994; *Theresa Waldo v. Consumers Energy Company*, 2010 U.S. District Lexus 55068; 109 Fair Employment Practices Case (BNA) 11348, June 4, 2010; John Agar, "Consumers Energy Ordered to Pay $8 Million in Sexual Harassment Lawsuit Verdict," *Mlive*, October 8, 2010, www.mlive.com/news/grand-rapids/index.ssf/2010/10/consumers_energy_ordered_to_pa.html.

of the Facebook terms of use, has been made illegal in several states, and is considered by many experts to be a violation of employee privacy. Employers have established policies that prohibit employees from stating negative information—or in some cases *any* information—about the company in any social media (including Facebook, Twitter, Snapchat, blogs, and so forth). Employers can monitor all activities, including Web usage and text messages that employees send on their employer-issued smart phones. Managers use electronic monitoring to track customer service representatives, word-processing clerks, data entry technicians, and other workers for speed, accuracy, and productivity. Even truck drivers, the "lone rangers of the road," are not immune to electronic tracking. Most trucking companies outfit their trucks with GPS devices they use to monitor drivers' exact locations at all times, regulate their speed, make sure they stop only at approved fueling points, and ensure that they take the legally required hours of rest.

Although many drivers support the use of these devices, others worry about their tendency to create George Orwell's "Big Brother" syndrome.

E-mail also poses an ethical problem for employers. There are more than 2.8 billion e-mail users utilizing 4.9 billion e-mail accounts worldwide. People send more than 120 billion *business* e-mails per day.[59] Most workers do not realize that, in most states, employers legally can monitor their e-mail and voice-mail messages without notification. However, this is limited to company e-mail accounts; employers cannot monitor personal e-mail accounts. Only two states (Connecticut and Delaware) require companies to notify employees that they are monitoring e-mail.

To avoid ethical and legal problems, business owners should follow these guidelines:

- ***Establish a clear policy for monitoring employees' communications.*** Employees should know that the company is monitoring their e-mails and other forms of communication, and the best way to make sure they do is to create an unambiguous policy. Once you create a policy, be sure to follow it. Some managers ask employees to sign a consent form acknowledging that they have read and understand the company's monitoring policy.

- ***Create guidelines for the proper use of the company's communication technology and communicate them to everyone.*** A company's policies and guidelines should be reasonable and should reflect employees' reasonable expectations of privacy.

- ***Monitor in moderation.*** Employees resent monitoring that is unnecessarily invasive. In addition, excessively draconian monitoring may land a company in a legal battle.

Business's Responsibility to Customers

LO8

Explain business's responsibility to customers.

One of the most important groups of stakeholders that a business must satisfy is its *customers.* Building and maintaining a base of loyal customers is no easy task because it requires more than just selling a product or a service. The key is to build long-term relationships with customers. Socially responsible companies recognize their duty to abide by the Consumer Bill of Rights, first put forth by President John Kennedy. This document gives consumers the following rights.

Right to Safety

The right to safety is the most basic consumer right. Companies have the responsibility to provide their customers with safe, quality products and services. The greatest breach of trust occurs when businesses produce products that, when properly used, injure customers.

Product liability cases can be controversial, such as the McDonald's coffee lawsuit, in which a jury found that the fast-food giant's coffee was too hot when served and caused a serious injury when a customer at a drive-through window spilled coffee in her lap. In other situations, the evidence is clear that a product suffers from fundamental flaws in either design or construction and caused an injury to its user when used properly.

Many companies have responded by placing detailed warning labels on their products that sometimes insult customers' intelligence. Consider the following actual examples from product warning labels:

- "Does not supply oxygen" on a dust mask

- "Caution: Do not swallow" on a clothes hanger

- "Wash hands after using" on a common extension cord

- "Not for human consumption," a warning on a package of plastic fishing worms

- "Combustion of this manufactured product results in the emissions of carbon monoxide, soot and other combustion by-products which are known by the State of California to cause cancer, birth defects, or reproductive harm" on a box of matches

- "Do not use while sleeping," a product warning for a Vidal Sassoon hair dryer

- "This product is not intended for use as a dental drill" on a Dremel rotary power tool[60]

You Be the Consultant

Think Before You Tweet

Increasing attention has been given to employee posts on social media sites such as Facebook and Twitter. The National Labor Relations Board (NLRB) and several judges have begun to define what is protected, private speech when it is posted on a personal Facebook or Twitter account. Several cases have helped bring this issue into focus.

Employee Complains About Tip

The owner of a New York City food truck called the Milk Truck fired an employee, Brendan O'Connor, when he tweeted from his personal Twitter account about not receiving a tip. Glass, Lewis & Co. employees ordered $170 worth of grilled cheese sandwiches and milkshakes. After not receiving any tip, O'Conner tweeted, "Shout out to the good people of Glass, Lewis & Co. for placing a $170 order and not leaving a tip. @glasslewis." After Glass, Lewis & Co. employees found the tweets, the company expressed its displeasure to the owner of Milk Truck, who promptly fired O'Connor, saying that O'Conner had embarrassed the company. The owner of Milk Truck apologized to Glass, Lewis & Co., via Twitter. The apology was accepted. However, O'Connor has more than 300 followers on his Twitter account. Most of the discussion on Twitter about O'Connor's firing blasted both Milk Truck and Glass, Lewis & Co.

Tweet About Work Conditions

James Kennedy, a 38-year-old employee of Chipotle, was fired for criticizing his employer on Twitter. Kennedy posted the following tweet: "@ChipotleTweets, nothing is free, only cheap #labor. Crew members make only $8.50hr how much is that steak bowl really?" Kennedy deleted the post after his supervisor showed him a company social media policy that banned "disparaging, false" statements about Chipotle. Two weeks later Kennedy was fired after he circulated a petition among coworkers, complaining about the inability of employees to take breaks.

The National Labor Relations Board ruled that Chipotle had treated Kennedy unfairly. The judge hearing the case ruled that Chipotle's social media rules violated the law. She ordered Chipotle to post signs stating that its social media rules were illegal. In addition, the judge ordered the company to rehire Kennedy and pay him for lost wages.

New Hire Loses Offer

Connor Riley had just gotten a job offer from Cisco Systems, which is based in San Jose, California. Riley was pursuing a master's degree in information systems and management at the University of California, Berkeley. After receiving her offer, Riley tweeted, "Cisco just offered me a job! Now I have to weigh the utility of a fatty paycheck against the daily commute to San Jose and hating the work." It was not too long before Riley received a reply tweet from someone who claimed to be a Cisco employee. It read, "Who is the hiring manager? I'm sure they would love to know that you will hate the work. We here at Cisco are versed in the Web." Riley is not working at Cisco, after all.

Although the National Labor Relations Board (NLRB) protects the use of Facebook and Twitter as equivalent to the modern-day water cooler, there are limits on what speech is protected in social media. Employees can use social media to communicate with each other about work conditions, for example. However, there are clear limits on social media posts that are abusive, target individuals, give away company secrets, and so forth. The boundaries between protected speech and posts that might leave employees subject to disciplinary action remain a gray area of employment law. Employees should be careful when they tweet, and employers should have clear policies that fall within the emerging guidelines established by the courts and the NLRB.

1. If you were the judge reviewing the O'Connor case, how would you rule? Explain your reasoning.

2. If you were the judge in the Riley case, how would you rule? Explain your reasoning.

3. What policies would you put in place as a business owner about employee comments on social media sites like Facebook and Twitter? Explain your policies based on the cases discussed here.

Sources: Based on Hillary Dixer, "Food Truck Employee Fired for Tip-Shaming on Twitter," *Eater*, July 30, 2013, http://eater.com/archives/2013/07/30/food-truck-employee-fired-for-tipshaming-on-twitter.php; Rachel Tepper, "Brendan O'Connor, Former Milk Truck Employee, Fired for Tip-Shaming Customers on Twitter," *Huffington Post*, July 31, 2013; Rachel Quigley, "Food Truck Employee Fired After He Calls Company Out on Twitter for Not Leaving a Tip on a $170 Order—Prompting an Angry Online Backlash," *Daily Mail*, July 31, 2013, www.dailymail.co.uk/news/article2381982/Milk-Truck-employee-Brendan-OConnor-fired-calls-company-Twitter-leaving-tip.html; "Chipotle Must Rehire Worker Fired for Calling Company 'Cheap' on Twitter," *New York Post*, March 16, 2016, http://nypost.com/2016/03/16/chipotle-must-rehire-worker-fired-for-criticizing-company-on-twitter/; "Mr. Lube Employee Fired After Asking for Pot via Twitter," *The Province*, August 15, 2013, www.theprovince.com/business/Tweet+seeking+greases+skids+under+Lube+employee+Toronto+suburb/8788823/story.html; Helen A. S. Popkin, "Twitter Gets You Fired in 140 Characters or Less," *NBC News*, March 23, 2009, www.nbcnews.com/id/29796962/ns/technology_and_science-tech_and_gadgets/#.UkSIEBb3B-V; Helen A. S. Popkin, "Getting the Skinny on Twitter's 'Cisco Fatty,'" *NBC News*, March 29, 2013, www.nbcnews.com/id/29901380/ns/technology_and_science-tech_and_gadgets/t/getting-skinny-twitters-cisco-fatty/#.UkSZDRb3B-U; Catharine Smith and Bianca Bosker, "Fired Over Twitter: 13 Tweets That Got People CANNED," *Huffington Post*, July 14, 2010, www.huffingtonpost.com/2010/07/15/fired-over-twitter-tweets_n_645884.html#s112801title=Cisco_Fatty_Loses.

Right to Know

Consumers have the right to honest communication about the products and services they buy and the companies that sell them. In a free market economy, information is one of the most valuable commodities available. Customers often depend on companies for the information they need to make decisions about price, quality, features, and other factors. As a result, companies have a responsibility to customers to be truthful in their advertising.

Unfortunately, not every business recognizes its social responsibility to be truthful in advertising. The Federal Trade Commission imposed a $2 million fine on Lumos Labs, the maker of the Lumosity app, saying that the company deceived customers with "unfounded" advertising claims. The company made false claims about being able to help prevent memory loss caused by dementia and Alzheimer's. The company also claimed that its games would help children perform better in school. The FTC found that Lumosity simply did not have scientific support for any of its claims.[61]

Right to Be Heard

The right to be heard suggests that the channels of communication between companies and their customers run in both directions. Socially responsible businesses provide customers with a mechanism for resolving complaints about products and services. Some companies have established a consumer ombudsman to address customer questions and complaints. Others have created customer hotlines, toll-free numbers designed to serve customers more effectively. Today, many businesses actively monitor social media, watching for customer complaints or negative comments that customers make about the company or its products and services and then addressing them promptly.

Another effective technique for encouraging two-way communication between customers and companies is the customer report card. The Granite Rock Company, a business that supplies a variety of building materials to construction companies, relies on an annual report card from its customers to learn how to serve them better. Although the knowledge an entrepreneur gets from customer feedback is immeasurable for making improvements, only 1 in 12 small companies regularly schedules customer satisfaction surveys such as Granite Rock's. This tool can boost a company's profitability significantly.

Right to Education

Socially responsible companies give customers access to educational material about their products and services and how to use them properly. The goal is to give customers enough information to make informed purchase decisions. A product that is the wrong solution to a customer's needs may lead to a disappointed customer blaming the manufacturer or retailer for the mistake. Consumer education is an inexpensive investment in customer satisfaction (especially when done online) and increased probability that a satisfied customer will be a repeat buyer.

Right to Choice

Inherent in the free enterprise system is the consumer's right to choose among competing products and services. Socially responsible companies do not restrict competition, and they abide by U.S. antitrust policy, which promotes free trade and competition in the market. The foundation of this policy is the Sherman Antitrust Act of 1890, which forbids agreements among sellers that restrain trade or commerce and outlaws any attempts to monopolize markets.

Business's Responsibility to Investors

LO9

Discuss business's responsibility to investors.

Companies have the responsibility to provide investors with an attractive return on their investments. Although earning a profit may be a company's *first* responsibility, it is not its *only* responsibility; meeting its ethical and social responsibility goals is also a key to success. Investors today want to know that entrepreneurs are making ethical decisions and acting in a socially responsible manner. Those who invest in entrepreneurial ventures are a small community (see Chapter 15). Reputation can mean everything for an entrepreneur because most investors invest more on the basis of the entrepreneur's track record than on the entrepreneur's idea. Maintaining

You Be the Consultant

But Is It Safe?

Kali Hardig, a 12-year-old from Arkansas, spent a day swimming and enjoying the attractions at Willow Springs Water Park. Willow Springs was a popular local attraction that offered a lake for swimming, a water slide, water trampolines, concessions, and a picnic area. A day after her visit to Willow Springs, Kali's mother rushed her to the hospital. She had a high fever, was vomiting, and had an excruciating headache. The Centers for Disease Control and Prevention and the Arkansas Department of Public Health determined that Kali had contracted parasitic meningitis caused by a brain-eating amoeba.

The amoeba, called *Naegleria fowleri*, enters through the noses of people who come into contact with contaminated water or soil. Most cases occur in the summer because the amoeba is most often found in water that is 115 degrees Fahrenheit. The amoeba can enter a human victim only through the nose. Drinking contaminated water cannot lead to infection. The amoeba moves from the nose into the brain, causing the brain to swell (meningitis), and in 99 percent of cases leads to the death of the infected person. Naegleria is very rare, with only 128 cases ever reported in the United States. However, only 2 people have survived this infection. Doctors put Kali into a drug-induced coma to help her fight the infection.

This was the second case of naegleria linked to Willow Springs. Authorities believe that another person was infected at the water park in 2010. However, the owners of the park said they had not been informed about the first infection until Kali's case was diagnosed. Authorities admit that the exact source of the strain is not traceable to a specific location, but they were convinced that the chronology of events and other evidence strongly linked both cases to the lake at Willow Springs. The Arkansas Department of Public Health asked the owners of the water park to voluntarily close the park to protect public health. David and Lou Ann Ratliff, owners of Willow Springs Water Park, say in a statement:

> We, David and Lou Ann Ratliff, as general management of Willow Springs Water Park, have received new information regarding *Naegleria fowleri*, and have elected to close the park as of July 25 at the request of the Arkansas Department of Health. Though the odds of contracting Naegleria are extremely low, they are just not good enough to allow our friends or family to swim. For the thousands of people who love Willow Springs, we will be taking this time to determine the feasibility of installing a solid bottom to the lake. We will not ever reopen as a sand bottom lake. We covet your prayers and our Willow Springs family will continue to be in our thoughts and prayers.

The owners of Willow Springs are not sure about the future of their business or what else they might do with the property. Willow Springs first opened as a water park in 1928. David Ratliff explored the possibility of building a hard surface for the lake bottom, but the cost was prohibitive and the park never reopened for swimming.

By August, Kali was showing signs of recovery. She woke up and spoke briefly to her mother. By early September Kali was able to leave the hospital for short trips with her mother to go to the movies and eat at local restaurants. On September 11, 2013, against all odds, Kali was released to go home from the hospital. She had become only the third person to recover from the naegleria infection.

1. How could the owners of Willow Springs have ensured the safety of their customers and prevented the infections from occurring? Explain.

2. Would it have been ethical for Willow Springs to remain open after Kali's case came to light, even though there could never be definitive evidence linking the infection to its lake? Explain.

3. What do you think the owners of Willow Springs should do with their property? Should they reopen the water park if they can ensure that the water is safe for swimming? Explain.

4. Create a detailed diagram of all the stakeholders of Willow Springs. How is each of the stakeholders affected by the water park's actions? What conclusions can you draw from this analysis? Explain.

Sources: Based on "Girl Contracts Brain Eating Amoeba After Swimming at Arkansas Water Park," *Fox News*, July 29, 2013, www.foxnews.com/health/2013/07/29/girl-contracts-brain-eating-amoeba-after-swimming-at-arkansas-water-park/; "*Naegleria fowleri*—Primary Amebic Meningoencephalitis (PAM)," Centers for Disease Control and Prevention, August 23, 2013, www.cdc.gov/parasites/naegleria/treatment.html; "ADH Confirms Case of Parasitic Meningitis," Arkansas Department of Health, July 26, 2013, www.arkansas.gov/health/newsroom/index.php?do:newsDetail=1&news_id=921; Mark Johanson, "Willow Springs Water Park in Little Rock Closed After Second Child Contracts Rare Brain-Eating Amoeba," *International Business Times*, July 29, 2013, www.ibtimes.com/willow-springs-water-park-little-rock-closed-after-second-child-contracts-rare-brain-eating-amoeba; Katie Moisse, "Brain-Eating Amoeba Victim Shows Signs of Recovery," *ABC News*, August 21, 2013; http://abcnews.go.com/blogs/health/2013/08/21/brain-eating-amoeba-victim-shows-signs-of-recovery/; David Harten, "Willow Springs Shuts for Season After Parasite Discovered," *Arkansas Online*, July 26, 2013, www.arkansasonline.com/news/2013/jul/26/willow-springs-shuts-down-season-after-parasite-di/; "Prayers for Kali Le Ann," Facebook, n.d., www.facebook.com/pages/PrayersFor-Kali-Le-Ann/279567398852251.

high standards of ethics and social responsibility translates into a business culture that sets the stage for future equity investments and in more profitable business operations.

Companies also have the responsibility to report their financial performance in an accurate and timely fashion to their investors. Businesses that misrepresent or falsify their financial and operating records are guilty of violating the fiduciary relationship with their investors.

ENTREPRENEURIAL PROFILE: Chris Faulkner, Breitling Energy Corp. Chris Faulkner, known as the "Frack Master," used frequent media appearances on CNBC, CNN, Fox Business News, and Bloomberg Television to position himself as an energy industry expert. Faulkner used his notoriety to convince investors to back his company, Breitling Energy, with more than $80 million in investments. Faulkner claimed that the investments in his company would be used to drill oil wells. The Securities and Exchange Commission filed a lawsuit, alleging that rather than invest in new oil wells, Faulkner spent much of the money on international travel, jewelry, expensive automobiles, gentlemen's clubs, and prostitutes. The SEC also accused Faulkner and his associates of exaggerating potential earnings and booking fictional drilling costs. Faulkner allegedly used investors' money from other companies he founded to buy stock in Breitling Energy to create the appearance of higher interest in the company and inflate its trading price.[62] ■

Business's Responsibility to the Community

LO10

Discuss business's responsibility to the community.

As corporate citizens, businesses have a responsibility to the communities in which they operate. In addition to providing jobs and creating wealth, companies contribute to the local community in many different ways. Socially responsible businesses are aware of their duty to put back into the community some of what they take out as they generate profits; their goal is to become a neighbor of choice.

Consumers expect companies to be socially responsible and to be good corporate citizens. A survey by Cone Communications finds that 91 percent of consumers expect companies to operate responsibly regarding social and environmental issues and that 84 percent seek out products from socially responsible companies whenever possible.[63] The following are just a few examples of ways small businesses have found to give back to their communities:

- Act as volunteers for community groups such as the American Red Cross, United Way, literacy programs, and community food banks.

- Participate in projects that aid the elderly or economically disadvantaged.

- Adopt a highway near the business to promote a clean community.

- Volunteer in school programs, such as the Network for Teaching Entrepreneurship or Junior Achievement.

Even small companies that may be short on funding can support causes by choosing them strategically and discovering creative ways to help them. The key to choosing the "right" cause is finding one that makes an impact and whose purpose resonates with customers, employees, and owners. Small companies can commit their employees' talent and know-how, not just dollars, to carefully chosen social causes and then tell the world about their cause and their dedication to serving it. By forging meaningful partnerships, both the businesses and the causes benefit in unique ways. Over the years, companies have helped social causes enjoy financial rewards and unprecedented support. In addition to doing good, companies have been able to enhance their reputations, deepen employee loyalty, strengthen ties with business partners, and sell more products or services.

ENTREPRENEURIAL PROFILE: Diana Charabin and Jeff House, Cole+Parker Cole+Parker, cofounded in London, Ontario, Canada, by Diana Charabin and Jeff House, sells brightly colored premium socks through its online retail site and high-end brick and mortar retailers throughout the United States and Canada. The entrepreneurs funded their business in part through a crowdfunding campaign with Indiegogo. The crowdfunding campaign highlighted Charabin and House's intent to donate 20 percent of the revenues of their company to help fund microlending through the company's 1 For Many program. "Ultimately, we want to expand the public's knowledge about micro finance, the powers of sustainability and how to help people living in poverty," says House.[64] ■

Entrepreneurs such as Diana Charabin and Jeff House who demonstrate their sense of social responsibility not only make their communities better places to live and work but also stand out from their competitors. Their efforts to operate ethical, socially responsible businesses create a strong sense of loyalty among their customers and their employees.

Conclusion

Businesses must do more than merely earn profits; they must act ethically and in a socially responsible manner. Establishing and maintaining high ethical and socially responsible standards must be a top concern of every business owner. Managing in an ethical and socially responsible manner presents a tremendous challenge, however. There is no universal definition of ethical behavior, and what is considered ethical may change over time and may be different in other cultures.

Finally, business owners and managers must recognize the key role they play in influencing their employees' ethical and socially responsible behavior. What owners and managers *say* is important, but what they *do* is even more important! Employees in a small company look to the owners and managers as models; therefore, owners and managers must commit themselves to following the highest ethical standards if they expect their employees to do so.

MyLab Entrepreneurship

If your instructor is using MyLab Entrepreneurship, go to **www.pearson.com/mylab/ entrepreneurship** to complete the problems marked with this icon ⭐.

Chapter Summary by Learning Objective

1. **Define business ethics and describe the three levels of ethical standards.**

   - Business ethics involves the fundamental moral values and behavioral standards that form the foundation for the people of an organization as they make decisions and interact with organizational stakeholders. Small business managers must consider the ethical and social as well as the economic implications of their decisions.

   - The three levels of ethical standards are (1) the law, (2) the policies and procedures of the company, and (3) the moral stance of the individual.

2. **Determine who is responsible for ethical behavior and why ethical lapses occur.**

   - Managers set the moral tone for an organization. There are three ethical styles of management: immoral, amoral, and moral. Although moral management has value in itself, companies that operate with this philosophy discover other benefits, including a positive reputation among customers and employees.

   - Ethical lapses occur for a variety of reasons:
     - Some people are corrupt ("the bad apple").
     - The company culture has been poisoned ("the bad barrel").
     - Competitive pressures push managers to compromise.
     - Managers are tempted by an opportunity to "get ahead."
     - Managers in different cultures have different views of what is ethical.

3. **Explain how to establish and maintain high ethical standards.**

   - Philosophers throughout history have developed various tests of ethical behavior: the utilitarian principle, Kant's categorical imperative, the professional ethic, the Golden Rule, the television test, and the family test.

   - A small business manager can maintain high ethical standards in the following ways:
     - Create a company credo.
     - Develop a code of ethics.
     - Enforce the code fairly and consistently.
     - Hire the right people.
     - Conduct ethical training.
     - Perform periodic ethical audits.
     - Establish high standards of behavior, not just rules.
     - Set an impeccable ethical example at all times.
     - Create a culture that emphasizes two-way communication.
     - Involve employees in establishing ethical standards.

4. **Explain the difference between social entrepreneurs and traditional entrepreneurs.**

   - Traditional entrepreneurs seek opportunities to create market value and profit.

   - Social entrepreneurs use entrepreneurship to pursue opportunities to create social value by creating innovative solutions to society's most vexing problems.

5. Define social responsibility.

- Social responsibility is the awareness of a company's managers of the social, environmental, political, human, and financial consequences of their actions.

6. Understand the nature of business's responsibility to the environment.

- Environmentally responsible business owners focus on the three *R*s: *reduce* the amount of materials used in the company from the factory floor to the copier room, *reuse* whatever you can, and *recycle* the materials you must dispose of.

7. Describe business's responsibility to employees.

- Companies have a duty to act responsibly toward some of their most important stakeholders: their employees. Businesses must recognize and manage the cultural diversity that exists in the workplace, establish a responsible strategy for combating substance abuse in the workplace (including drug testing), prevent sexual harassment, and respect employees' right to privacy.

8. Explain business's responsibility to customers.

- Every company's customers have a right to safe products and services; to honest, accurate information; to be heard; to education about products and services; and to choices in the marketplace.

9. Discuss business's responsibility to investors.

- Companies have the responsibility to provide investors with an attractive return on their investments and to report their financial performances in an accurate and timely fashion to their investors.

10. Describe business's responsibility to the community.

- Increasingly, companies are seeing a need to go beyond "doing well" to "doing good"—being socially responsible community citizens. In addition to providing jobs and creating wealth, companies contribute to the local community in many different ways.

MyLab Entrepreneurship

If your instructor is using MyLab Entrepreneurship, go to **www.pearson.com/mylab/entrepreneurship** for Auto-graded writing questions as well as the following Assisted-graded writing questions:

1. Why do ethical lapses occur in businesses?
2. Work with a team of your classmates to identify an unmet social need in your community. Identify alternative approaches you can develop to address this social need. Describe the social venture you would establish to meet the social need.

Discussion Questions

2-1. What is ethics?

⭐ 2-2. Discuss the three levels of ethical standards.

2-3. List the core personal values you intend to bring to your business (e.g., treating people fairly, giving something back to the community).

2-4. Where does each of your core values come from (e.g., religious faith, family, personal philosophy)?

2-5. Why is each of your core values important to you?

2-6. In any organization, who determines ethical behavior?

2-7. Briefly describe the three ethical styles of management.

2-8. What are the benefits of moral management?

⭐ 2-9. Describe the various methods for establishing ethical standards.

2-10. Which method for establishing ethical standards is most meaningful to you?

2-11. Why is it the most meaningful method for establishing ethical standards?

2-12. What can business owners do to maintain high ethical standards in their companies?

2-13. What is a social entrepreneur?

2-14. How do social entrepreneurs differ from traditional entrepreneurs?

2-15. What are some social problems you think could be tackled by social entrepreneurs?

2-16. What is social responsibility?

2-17. Describe business's social responsibility to the environment.

2-18. Describe business's social responsibility to employees.

2-19. Describe business's social responsibility to customers.

2-20. Describe business's social responsibility to investors.

2-21. Describe business's social responsibility to the community.

2-22. What can businesses do to improve the quality of our environment?

2-23. Explain your stance on whether companies should be allowed to test employees for drugs.

2-24. How should a socially responsible drug-testing program operate?

2-25. Many owners of trucking companies use electronic communications equipment to monitor their drivers on the road. They say the devices allow them to remain competitive and to serve their customers better by delivering shipments of vital materials exactly when their customers need them. They also point out that the equipment can improve road safety by ensuring that drivers get the hours of rest the law requires. Opponents argue that the surveillance devices work against safety. "The drivers know they're being watched," says one trucker. "There's an obvious temptation to push." What do you think about this practice?

2-26. What ethical issues do trucking companies create when they use electronic communications equipment to monitor their drivers on the road?

2-27. How should a small trucking company considering the use of electronic communications equipment to monitor its drivers handle the ethical issues created by this practice?

2-28. What rights do customers have under the Consumer Bill of Rights?

2-29. How can businesses ensure consumers' rights?

Beyond the Classroom . . .

2-30. Interview a social entrepreneur in your community to determine the social need addressed by the entrepreneur and the solution applied to that social need.

2-31. Was the social venture established as a nonprofit or a for-profit social enterprise?

2-32. If the firm is a nonprofit, what are its primary sources of funding?

2-33. If the firm is a for-profit social enterprise, what is the primary source of revenues, and how are the profits used to address the social need the company has as its primary focus?

2-34. A key concern with any social enterprise is sustainability of funding. What recommendations can you make to the social entrepreneur to ensure the sustainability of the venture over the long term?

2-35. What are the various ways you could generate the funding you would need to operate your social venture?

Endnotes

[1] "Business Model," Namasté Solar, www.namastesolar.com/about-us/employee-owned-cooperative.

[2] Leigh Buchanan, "Where the CEO Is Just Another Guy with a Vote," *Inc.*, June 21, 2011, www.inc.com/winning-workplaces/magazine/201106/where-the-ceo-is-just-another-guy-with-a-vote.html.

[3] Jason R. Edgecombe, "Interim Guidelines to the Cybersecurity Information Sharing Act," *TechCrunch*, April 13, 2016, https://techcrunch.com/2016/04/13/interim-guidelines-to-the-cybersecurity-information-sharing-act/.

[4] Vernon R. Loucks Jr., "A CEO Looks at Ethics," *Business Horizons*, March/April 1987, p. 2.

[5] Wade Burgess, "A Bad Reputation Costs a Company at Least 10% More per Hire," *Harvard Business Review*, March 29, 2016, https://hbr.org/2016/03/a-bad-reputation-costs-company-at-least-10-more-per-hire.

[6] "Nashville's Sommet Center Renamed in Dispute," *USAToday*, December 3, 2009, http://usatoday30.usatoday.com/sports/hockey/nhl/2009-12-03-3300713859_x.htm; Pierce Greenberg, "Sommet Leaders Indicted," *Nashville Post*, March 1, 2012, http://nashvillepost.com/news/2012/3/1/sommet_leaders_indicted; Bobby Allyn, "Former Sommet Group Executive Plead Guilty in $20M Fraud," *Tennessean*, July 18, 2013, www.tennessean.com/article/20130718/BUSINESS01/307180057/Former-Sommet-Group-executives-plead-guilty-20M-fraud.

[7] Edgar Linares, "Hopkins Dairy Queen Manager's Act of Kindness Goes Viral," *CBS Minnesota*, September 18, 2013, http://minnesota.cbslocal.com/2013/09/18/hopkins-dairy-queen-workers-act-of-kindess-goes-viral/; Oliver Darcy, "This Story of a Nineteen-Year-Old Dairy Queen Employee Standing Up for a Blind Man Will Touch Your Heart," *The Blaze*, September 18, 2013, www.theblaze.com/stories/2013/09/18/this-story-of-a-19-year-old-dairy-queen-employee-standing-up-for-a-blind-man-will-touch-your-heart/; "Warren Buffett Invites Joey Prusak, Good Samaritan Dairy Queen Employee, to Shareholders Meeting," *Huffington Post*, September 23, 2013, www.huffingtonpost.com/2013/09/23/joey-prusak-warren-buffet-_n_3977043.html.

[8] Elizabeth Riley, "Doing Well—And Turning a Profit—By Doing Good," *Crain's Chicago Business*, August 7, 2013, www.chicagobusiness.com/article/20130807/OPINION/130809861/doing-well-and-turning-a-profit-by-doing-good.

[9] Sarah Grossman, "French Catering Company Employs Refugees to Cook Their Native Foods," *Huffington Post*, July 6, 2016, www.huffingtonpost.com/entry/les-cuistots-migrateurs-migrant-cooks-france-paris-refugees-catering_us_577d42e6e4b0a629c1ab8aaa?utm_hp_ref=purpose--profit.

[10] Jamie McGee, "Nisolo Shoe Brand Buys Red Earth Jewelry Company," *Tennessean*, June 9, 2015, www.tennessean.com/story/money/2015/06/09/nisolo-shoe-brand-buys-red-earth-jewelry-company/28742683/; Nevin Batiwalla, "Nashville's Social Entrepreneurs Mix Business, Charity," *Nashville Business Journal*, September 14, 2012, www.bizjournals.com/nashville/print-edition/2012/09/14/nashvilles-social-entrepreneurs-mix.html?page=all; "Nisolo," *Back Down*

South, October 1, 2012, www.backdownsouth.com/2012/10/nisolo/.

[11]Stephanie Vozza, "Why Every Company Should Pay Employees to Volunteer," *Fast Company*, March 11, 2014, www.fastcompany.com/3027465/dialed/why-every-company-should-pay-employees-to-volunteer; "Mars Agency: About 65% of Employees Volunteer as Part of Start Small Initiative," *Crain's Detroit Business*, October 26, 2014, www.crainsdetroit.com/article/20141026/NEWS/310269987/mars-agency-about-65-of-employees-volunteer-as-part-of-start-small.

[12]Jinseok S. Chun, Yuhyung Shin, Jin Nam Choi, and Min Soo Kim, "How Does Corporate Ethics Contribute to Firm Financial Performance? The Mediating Role of Collective Organizational Commitment and Organizational Citizenship Behavior," *Journal of Management*, 2013 (39:4), pp. 853–877.

[13]Joseph Pereira, "Doing Good and Doing Well at Timberland," *Wall Street Journal*, September 9, 2003, pp. B1–B10.

[14]Jason Adkins, personal communication, September 26, 2013; "We Support," n.d., http://brighthousegreencleaning.com/we-support.

[15]*2016 Global Business Ethics Survey: Measuring Risk and Promoting Workplace Integrity*, Ethics Research Center, Ethics and Compliance Initiative, 2016, pp. 9, 18.

[16]Jinseok S. Chun, Yuhyung Shin, Jin Nam Choi, and Min Soo Kim, "How Does Corporate Ethics Contribute to Firm Financial Performance? The Mediating Role of Collective Organizational Commitment and Organizational Citizenship Behavior," *Journal of Management*, 2013 (39:4), pp. 853–877.

[17]Pablo Ruiz-Palomino, Ricardo Martínez-Cañas, and Joan Fontrodona, "Ethical Culture and Employee Outcomes: The Mediating Role of Person-Organization Fit," *Journal of Business Ethics*, August 2012, http://link.springer.com/article/10.1007/s10551-012-1453-9/fulltext.html.

[18]Mason Kelley, "Little Seattle Uniform Maker Takes on Sportswear Giants," *Seattle Times*, April 30, 2012, http://seattletimes.com/html/highschoolsports/2018109113_mason01.html; "About Us," Intrepid Sportswear, n.d., www.intrepidsportswear.com/about-us.php; "Meet Intrepid," Intrepid Sportswear, n.d., www.intrepidsportswear.com/meet-intrepid.php.

[19]Gene Laczniak, "Business Ethics: A Manager's Primer," *Business*, January–March 1983, pp. 23–29.

[20]Christopher Redhage, personal communication, September 10, 2013; "The ProviderTrust Way Playbook," ProviderTrust, n.d.

[21]Patricia Wallington, "Honestly?!" *CIO*, March 15, 2003, p. 42.

[22]"Our Credo," Trustworth, n.d., www.trustworth.co.uk/AboutUs/OurCredo/.

[23]"Don't Mention It: How 'Undiscussables' Can Undermine an Organization," *Knowledge@Wharton*, December 20, 2011, http://knowledge.wharton.upenn.edu/article/dont-mention-it-how-undiscussables-can-undermine-an-organization/.

[24]Adrian Furnham, "Can You Really Test Someone for Integrity?" *Fortune*, August 1, 2015, http://fortune.com/2015/08/11/hiring-integrity-test/.

[25]Michael Josephson, "Teaching Ethical Decision Making and Its Principled Reasoning," *Ethics: Easier Said Than Done*, Winter 1988, p. 28.

[26]Robert S. Kaplan, "On Ethics, You Set the Tone," *Inc.*, February 21, 2012, www.inc.com/robert-kaplan/on-ethics-you-set-the-tone.html.

[27]Arthur C. Brooks, *Social Entrepreneurship* (Upper Saddle River, NJ: Prentice Hall, 2009).

[28]Donna J. Kelley, Abdul Ali, Candida Brush, Andrew C. Corbett, Caroline Daniels, Phillip H. Kim, Thomas S. Lyons, Mahdi Majbouri, Edward G. Rogo, *Global Entrepreneurship Monitor: 2015 United States Report*, Global Entrepreneurship Monitor, 2015, p. 21.

[29]"What Is a Social Entrepreneur?" Ashoka, www.ashoka.org/social_entrepreneur.

[30]Katharine Earley, "From Basket Weavers to Salt Farmers: The Women Leading a Renewables Revolution," *The Guardian*, July 9, 2016, www.theguardian.com/sustainable-business/2016/jul/09/women-leading-clean-energy-revolution; Lyndsey Gilpin, "How Solar Sister Is Fueling a Women-Led Clean Energy Revolution in Africa," *TechRepublic*, July 2, 2015, www.techrepublic.com/article/how-solar-sister-is-fueling-a-women-led-clean-energy-revolution-in-africa/.

[31]"The Big Impact of Small Business," SurePayroll report, June 19, 2012, http://blog.surepayroll.com/the-big-impact-of-small-business.

[32]Joshua Sophy, "42 Percent of Small Businesses Give Up to $1,000 to Charity and Prefer to Donate Cash," Small Business Trends, December 21, 2016, https://smallbiztrends.com/2016/12/small-business-donations.html.

[33]Louise Lee, "How Small Companies Should Give to Charities," *Wall Street Journal*, November 3, 2014, www.wsj.com/articles/how-small-companies-should-give-to-charities-1414965286; Cassandra Postema, "Meet the Cutting-Edge Fashion Designers Doing Good," *The Guardian*, February 12, 2015, www.theguardian.com/sustainable-business/sustainable-fashion-blog/2015/feb/12/meet-the-cutting-edge-fashion-designers-doing-good; "Our Charity Partners," Modavanti, n.d., http://modavanti.com/charity-partners/.

[34]Survey conducted by Penn Schoen Berland, in conjunction with Burson-Marsteller and Landor, from interviews conducted February 10–12, 2010, www.slideshare.net/BMGlobalNews/csr-branding-survey-2010-final.

[35]Edward Iwata, "Businesses Grow More Socially Conscious," *USA Today*, February 14, 2007, www.usatoday.com/money/companies/2007-02-14-high-purpose-usat_x.htm.

[36]"Re:Vision Architecture," B Corporation, n.d., www.bcorporation.net/community/revision-architecture; Catherine Clifford, "Small Companies, Big Hearts: Leading Social Entrepreneurs," *Entrepreneur*, April 17, 2013; www.entrepreneur.com/article/226437.

[37]Elyse Wanshel, "Brewery Taps into the Environment and Creates Zero-Waste Beer," *Huffington Post*, June 30, 2016, www.huffingtonpost.com/entry/northern-monk-brew-co-wasted-zero-waste-beer_us_5774136ee4b0cc0fa1363da1?utm_hp_ref=purpose--profit; Nikkie Sutton, "Zero Waste Beer Made from Croissants and Brioche Is Launched," *Morning Advertiser*, June 7, 2016, www.morningadvertiser.co.uk/Drinks/Beer/Zero-waste-beer-made-from-croissants-and-brioche-is-launched; Harry Readhead, "Would You Drink This 'Landfill Beer' Made from Food Destined for Waste?" *Metro*, May 27, 2016, http://metro.co.uk/2016/05/27/would-you-drink-this-landfill-beer-made-from-food-destined-for-waste-5908419/#top.

[38]"Delight Co., Ltd," B Corporation, n.d., www.bcorporation.net/community/delight-co-ltd; Catherine Clifford, "Small Companies, Big Hearts: Leading Social Entrepreneurs," *Entrepreneur*, April 17, 2013; www.entrepreneur.com/article/226437.

[39]Jennifer J. Salopek, "The 2020 Workplace," *Workforce Management*, June 2010, pp. 36–40.

[40]Valerie Wilson, "People of Color Will Be a Majority of the American Working Class in 2032," *Economic Policy Institute*, June 9, 2016, www.epi.org/publication/the-changing-demographics-of-americas-working-class/.

[41]Vivian Hunt, Dennis Layton, and Sara Prince, "Why Diversity Matters," McKinsey & Company, January 2015,

www.mckinsey.com/business-functions/organization/
our-insights/why-diversity-matters.

[42]Equal Employment Opportunity Commission, "Best
Practices of Private Sector Employers," 2003, www.eeoc.gov/
eeoc/task_reports/best_practices.cfm.

[43]Martha Lagace, "Racial Diversity Pays Off," Harvard
Business School*: Working Knowledge*, June 21, 2004,
http://hbsworkingknowledge.hbs.edu/item.jhtml?id=
4207&t=organizations.

[44]Michael Conner, "Tech Still Doesn't Get Diversity. Here's How
to Fix It," Wired, February 8, 2017, https://www.wired
.com/2017/02/tech-still-doesnt-get-diversity-heres-fix/.

[45]Mitra Toossi, "Labor Force Projections to 2020: A More Slowly
Growing Workforce," *Monthly Labor Review*, December
2015, www.bls.gov/opub/mlr/2015/article/labor-force-
projections-to-2024.htm.

[46]Constance Brinkley-Badgett, "Drug and Alcohol Addiction
Cost Americans $276 Billion a Year," *AOL*, September 30,
2016, https://www.aol.com/article/finance/2016/09/30/
drug-and-alcohol-addiction-costs-americans-276-billion-a-
year/21483951/.

[47]"Drugs and Alcohol in the Workplace," National Council
on Alcoholism and Drug Dependence, Inc., April 26,
2015, www.ncadd.org/about-addiction/addiction-update/
drugs-and-alcohol-in-the-workplace.

[48]Matt Dunning, "Employee Assistance Programs Underuti-
lized by Employees," *Business Insurance*, January 5,
2014, www.businessinsurance.com/article/20140105/
NEWS03/301059979; Gina Ruiz, "Expanded EAPs Lend a
Hand to Employer's Bottom Line," *Workforce Management*,
January 16, 2006, pp. 46–47.

[49]Mark J. Sagor, "Calculating the Value of an Employee
Assistance Program (EAP) from a CFO Perspective,"
CompEap, May 7, 2014, http://compeap.com/calculating-
the-value-of-an-employee-assistance-program-eap-from-a-
cfo-perspective/.

[50]"EAP Facts," Northeast Georgia Employee Assistance
Program, 2013, http://negeap.com/facts.htm.

[51]*The President's National Drug Control Strategy*, February
2007, www.whitehousedrugpolicy.gov/publications/policy/
ndcs07, pp. 14–15; "Nationwide Survey Shows Most Illicit
Drug Users and Heavy Alcohol Users Are in the Workplace
and May Pose Special Problems," Substance Abuse and
Mental Health Services Administration, U.S. Department of
Health and Human Services, July 17, 2007, http://oas.
samhsa.gov/work2k7/press.htm.

[52]Michelle Ruiz and Lauren Ahn, "Survey: 1 in 3 Women
Has Been Sexually Harassed at Work," *Cosmopolitan*,
February 16, 2015, www.cosmopolitan.com/career/news/
a36453/cosmopolitan-sexual-harassment-survey/?dom=
fb_hp&src=social&mag=cos.

[53]Equal Employment Opportunity Commission, "Charges
Alleging Sexual Harassment FY 2010–FY 2016," 2017,
www.eeoc.gov/eeoc/statistics/enforcement/sexual_
harassment_new.cfm.

[54]National Federation of Independent Business, "Sexual
Harassment 101 for Small Business," www.nfib.com/
business-resources/business-resources-item?cmsid=49311.

[55]Sexual Harassment Manual for Managers and Supervisors
(Chicago: Commerce Clearing House, 1992), pp. 25–26.

[56]"EEOC Wins Jury Verdict of More Than $20 Million for
Sexual Harassment and Retaliation," EEOC, May 1, 2013,

www.eeoc.gov/eeoc/newsroom/release/5-1-13a.cfm; Jodie
Tillman, "Jury Rules Against Largo Company in Sexual
Harassment Case," *Tampa Bay Times*, May 1, 2013,
www.tampabay.com/news/courts/civil/jury-rules-against-
largo-company-in-sexual-harassment-case/2118607.

[57]*Burlington Industries v. Ellerth* (97-569) 123 F.3d 490;
"Employer Liability for Harassment," Equal Employment
Opportunity Commission, www.eeoc.gov/types/
harassment.html.

[58]Nicole P. Cantey, "High Court Rules Same Sex Harassment
Is Against the Law," *South Carolina Business Journal*,
August 1998, p. 3; Jack Corcoran, "Of Nice and Men,"
Success, June 1998, pp. 64–67.

[59]Sarah Radicati, "E-mail Statistics Report, 2015–2019,"
Radicati Group, March 2015, p.4.

[60]Brett Nelson and Katy Finneran, "Dumbest Warning Labels,"
Forbes, February 23, 2011, www.forbes.com/2011/02/23/
dumbest-warning-labels-entrepreneurs-sales-marketing-
warning-labels.html; Bob Dorigo Jones, "Baby Strollers
and Legal Reform," *Let's Be Fair*, December 16, 2009,
www.bobdorigojones.com/2009/12/16/baby-strollers-
and-legal-reform/; "16th Annual Wacky Warning Labels
Contest: 2013 Finalists Selected," Wacky Warning Labels,
June 10, 2013, www.prnewswire.com/news-releases/16th-
annual-wacky-warning-labels-contest-2013-finalists-
selected-210831291.html; "17 Utterly Ridiculous Warning
Labels," *MSN Now*, October 17, 2012, http://now.msn.com/
ridiculous-product-warning-labels.

[61]"Lumosity to Pay $2 Million to Settle FTC Deceptive
Advertising Charges for Its 'Brain Training' Program,"
Federal Trade Commission, January 5, 2016, www.ftc
.gov/news-events/press-releases/2016/01/lumosity-
pay-2-million-settle-ftc-deceptive-advertising-charges;
Austen Hufford, "Lumos Labs Fined by FTC over
Brain-Game Claims," *Wall Street Journal*, January 5,
2016, www.wsj.com/articles/lumos-labs-fined-by-ftc-
over-brain-game-claims-1452024646.

[62]"SEC Charges Breitling Energy, Chris Faulkner with Defraud-
ing Investors out of $80 Million," *Oil & Gas 360*, June
27, 2016, www.oilandgas360.com/sec-charges-breitling-
energy-chris-faulkner-with-defrauding-investors-out-of-
80-million/; Matt Robinson and Asjylyn Loder, "SEC Sues
'Frack Master' for Spending Investor Cash on Strippers,"
Pittsburg Post-Gazette, June 27, 2016, http://powersource.
post-gazette.com/powersource/companies/2016/06/27/
SEC-sues-Frack-Master-for-spending-investor-cash-
on-strippers-Breitling-shale/stories/201606250035;
"U.S. SEC accuses Breitling CEO, others of oil-and-gas
fraud," *Reuters*, June 24, 2016, www.reuters.com/article/
breitling-energy-fraud-idUSL1N19G1DD.

[63]"2015 Cone Communications/Ebiquity Global CSR Study,"
Cone Communications, 2015, p. 7.

[64]Mike Donachie, "Londoners Sock It to 'em with Socktober,"
Metro Toronto, October 25, 2013, www.metronews.ca/
news/london/2013/10/25/londoners-sock-it-to-em-with-
socktober.html; John Matisz, "London Entrepreneurs to
Pitch Trendy, Philanthropic Socks on Dragon's Den,"
Metro Toronto, April 2, 2013, www.metronews.ca/news/
london/2013/04/02/london-entrepreneurs-to-pitch-
trendy-philanthropic-socks-on-dragons-den.html; "Our
Story," Cole+Parker, n.d., http://coleandparker.co/pages/
about-cole-and-parker.

3

Creativity and Innovation: Keys to Entrepreneurial Success

Peshkova/Shutterstock

Learning Objectives

On completion of this chapter, you will be able to:

1. Explain the differences among creativity, innovation, and entrepreneurship.

2. Describe why creativity and innovation are such integral parts of entrepreneurship.

3. Explain the 10 "mental locks" that limit individual creativity.

4. Understand how entrepreneurs can enhance the creativity of their employees as well as their own creativity.

5. Describe the steps in the creative process.

6. Discuss techniques for improving the creative process.

7. Describe the protection of intellectual property through patents, trademarks, and copyrights.

MyLab Entrepreneurship

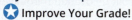 **Improve Your Grade!**

If your instructor is using MyLab Entrepreneurship, visit **www.pearson.com/mylab/entrepreneurship** for videos, simulations, and writing exercises.

One of the tenets of entrepreneurship is the ability to create new and useful ideas that solve the problems and challenges people face every day. Entrepreneurs achieve success by creating value in the marketplace when they combine resources in new and different ways to gain a competitive edge over rivals. From Alexander Fleming's pioneering work that resulted in a cure for infections (penicillin) and the founders of the Rocket Chemical Company's fortieth try to create an industrial lubricant (WD-40) to Jeff Bezos's innovative use of the Internet in retailing (Amazon.com) and Ted Turner's around-the-clock approach to the availability of television news (CNN), entrepreneurs' ideas have transformed the world.

As you learned in Chapter 1, entrepreneurs can create value in a number of ways—inventing new products and services, developing new technology, creating new business models, discovering new knowledge, improving existing products or services, finding different ways of providing more goods and services with fewer resources, and many others. Indeed, finding new ways of satisfying customers' needs, inventing new products and services, putting together existing ideas in new and different ways, and creating new twists on existing products and services are hallmarks of the entrepreneur! "At the heart of any successful business is a great idea," says one business writer. "Some seem so simple we wonder why nobody thought of them before. Others are so revolutionary that we wonder how anybody could have thought of them at all."[1]

ENTREPRENEURIAL PROFILE: Juan Murdoch: Smart PJs In a business meeting, Juan Murdoch, a sales agent for a real estate firm, heard about the benefits of using quick response (QR) codes on the "for sale" signs posted in front of houses. A father of six children, Murdoch began to think about how QR codes could enliven the story time he spent while putting his young children to bed. His idea was to combine two commonplace concepts, pajamas and bedtime stories, and give them a technology update, printing QR codes on children's pajamas that link to a library of classic illustrated bedtime stories accessible from any smart phone or tablet. After Murdoch's built-in focus group (his children) gave his idea a ringing endorsement, he began working with a computer science graduate from Brigham Young University to make it a reality. He invested $50,000 of his own money, but creating QR codes on fabric that were device-readable proved to be difficult until he and his technical expert came up with the idea of a simplified version of a QR code that consisted of a pattern of colorful dots that were easy to scan. Murdoch found a clothing manufacturer, ordered 3,000 pairs of Smart PJs, and began selling them from the back of his pickup truck and on his company's Web site. Stories about "the world's only interactive pajamas" sent shoppers flocking to the site, and Murdoch's Smart PJs recently landed in Brookstone retail stores. Each pair of pajamas includes 47 simplified QR codes that link to different bedtime stories, including "Cinderella," "Humpty Dumpty," "The Gingerbread Man," and many others. Because the words appear on the screen with the narrator's voice, the bedtime stories help children learn to read. Murdoch sees many applications for his ideas beyond pajamas and is developing other apps and negotiating new licensing agreements.[2] ∎

Like many other innovators, Murdoch created a successful business by taking two ordinary common items—pajamas and bedtime stories—that have existed for many years, looked at them in a different way, and combined them in a creative fashion.

Creativity, Innovation, and Entrepreneurship

LO1

Explain the differences among creativity, innovation, and entrepreneurship.

At the macroeconomic level, innovation, economic growth, and prosperity walk in lockstep. According to Battelle and *R&D Magazine*, U.S. companies, government agencies, and universities invest $527 billion annually (a healthy 2.8 percent of GDP) in research and development (R&D), more than 25 percent of the $2.07 trillion global expenditure on R&D.[3] Small companies are an important part of the total R&D picture. One study by the Small Business Administration reports that small companies that receive patents produce 16 times more patents per employee than their larger rivals that receive patents.[4] Small companies are less likely than their larger counterparts to experience creative constraints. According to GE's Global Innovation Barometer, a survey of more than 2,700 executives in 23 countries, 81 percent of executives say that the "start-up ethos" that exists in entrepreneurial companies is becoming the norm for creating a culture of innovation within companies of *all* sizes. The survey also reports that the biggest obstacle to innovation in large companies is the difficulty of generating radical, disruptive ideas, perhaps because nearly two-thirds of executives say that their companies rely on incremental innovation as a way to mitigate the risk of failure.[5] "Small businesses have an inherent innovative advantage over large businesses," explains one writer. "They are less likely to have an interest in maintaining the status quo, and they are more responsive and quicker to change. As a result, they have a disproportionate impact on 'disruptive' innovation—change that creates an entirely new market—as opposed to large firms, which tend to engage in incremental innovation."[6] The danger for companies that fail to innovate—and innovate boldly and quickly—is commercial Darwinism: becoming obsolete as more creative competitors pass them by.

What is the entrepreneurial "secret" for creating value in the marketplace? In reality, the "secret" is no secret at all: It is applying creativity and innovation to solve problems and to exploit opportunities that people face every day. **Creativity** is the ability to develop new ideas and to discover new ways of looking at problems and opportunities. **Innovation** is the ability to apply creative solutions to those problems and opportunities to enhance or to enrich people's lives. Harvard's Ted Levitt says that creativity is *thinking* new things and that innovation is *doing* new things. In short, entrepreneurs succeed by *thinking and doing* new things or old things in new ways. Simply having a great new idea is not enough; transforming the idea into a tangible product, service, or business venture is the essential next step. As management legend Peter Drucker said, "Innovation is the specific instrument of entrepreneurs, the act that endows resources with a new capacity to create wealth."[7] The wealth that innovation creates can be great. A study by PriceWaterhouseCoopers of the world's self-made billionaires reveals that no market is immune to innovation; more than 80 percent of the world's self-made billionaires made their fortunes by disrupting highly competitive markets with established players, such as consumer products, retail, technology, and business services.[8]

Software maker Intuit published a study about how small businesses would compete in 2020 and identified six "enablers" of small business innovation:[9]

1. *Passion.* Entrepreneurs typically start businesses using ideas about which they are passionate. Their passion and enthusiasm make them willing to test new business models and invent new products and services.

2. *Customer connection.* Entrepreneurs are close to their customers, and they listen to their customers, understand their needs and problems, and develop creative solutions for meeting and solving them.

3. *Agility and adaptation.* One hallmark of successful entrepreneurs is their ability to adapt and adjust, making the necessary pivots when their business models do not work the way they anticipated.

4. *Experimentation and improvisation.* Successful entrepreneurs understand that creativity and innovation produce big payoffs but also carry a high probability of failure. They accept that failure is merely a stepping-stone on the pathway to success.

5. *Resource limitations.* Because small companies usually operate with limited resources, they are accustomed to doing more with less. Entrepreneurs' resource limitations often require them to be highly innovative.

6. *Information sharing and collaboration.* Entrepreneurs rely on a strong network of people—customers, friends, suppliers, family members, and social networks—from whom they get useful feedback on their ideas, giving them the ability to discard quickly ideas that do not work and improve those that do.

Successful entrepreneurs introduce new ideas, products, services, and business models that solve a problem or fill a need. In a world that is changing faster than most of us ever could have imagined, creativity and innovation are vital to a company's success—and ultimate survival. That's true for businesses in every industry—from automakers to tea growers—and for companies of all sizes.

Innovation is vital for success in more than just a company's products or services. Companies that continue to do business as usual may find that their business models lose their relevance in the marketplace, putting them at a competitive disadvantage. In other words, to be successful, business leaders must develop innovations in their business models as well as in their product and service lines. Table 3.1 summarizes the results of a study by Hal Gregersen, professor of

creativity
the ability to develop new ideas and to discover new ways of looking at problems and opportunities.

innovation
the ability to apply creative solutions to problems and opportunities to enhance or enrich people's lives.

TABLE 3.1 The Five Dimensions of Discovery-Driven Leadership

Hal Gregersen's research suggests the leaders engage in two types of leadership: delivery driven and discovery driven. Delivery-driven leadership includes the traditional management roles of analyzing, controlling, planning, and directing and often leads to only incremental innovations. Recognizing that many consumers misused Nyquil cold medicine to induce sleep even when they did not have colds, consumer products giant Procter & Gamble introduced an incremental "innovation" with Zzzquil, which is nothing more than its NyQuil cold relief medicine without the cold medication. Incremental innovations produce profitable products, but can companies that become content with incremental innovation succeed in the long run, or will they be eclipsed by companies that create disruptive innovations?

Discovery-driven leadership, which innovative entrepreneurs exhibit, produces disruptive innovations and includes the following five dimensions:

1. *Associating* involves drawing connections among ideas, questions, processes, or problems from diverse and unrelated fields.

2. *Questioning* involves posing questions that challenge conventional thinking and common wisdom. Entrepreneurs recognize that using well-established processes may not be the best way to accomplish a task.

3. *Networking* involves entrepreneurs engaging people from different backgrounds who have different ideas and perspectives from their own. Their goal is to learn from people who are different from themselves.

4. *Observing* the behavior of customers, suppliers, and competitors gives entrepreneurs insight into how they can develop new products, services, processes, and business models.

5. *Experimenting* involves constructing interactive experiences (often with customers or potential customers) to see whether their ideas are successful, to gauge customers' reactions, and to gather meaningful insights.

The following table shows the percentile rankings on the five dimensions of discovery-driven leadership for different types of leaders:

Percentile Rankings for Various Types of Leaders on the Five Dimensions

Type of Leader	Dimension				
	Associating	**Questioning**	**Observing**	**Networking**	**Experimenting**
Non-innovators	48%	49%	48%	47%	39%
Process innovators	70%	65%	68%	61%	68%
Product innovators	78%	77%	79%	72%	74%
Corporate entrepreneurs	76%	67%	75%	77%	69%
Start-up entrepreneurs	78%	72%	75%	74%	73%

Doron Shafrir and Sayre Swarztrauber, who cofounded Quadlogic Controls Corporation in New York City in 1984, demonstrated discovery-driven leadership in their company, which provides products that track energy usage for tenants living in the same building. Their business had just posted its best year ever, with $15 million in annual sales, when the housing market collapsed and Quadlogic's sales plummeted. A few years before, a conversation with a business associate about how energy theft was a major problem in many developing countries had led Shafrir and Swarztrauber to begin tinkering with a new product designed to prevent utility metering systems from being breached by energy thieves. However, the product was incomplete, and the entrepreneurs had not yet identified any potential customers.

They decided that the best strategy for their company was to introduce the new antitheft product and launch it with a big marketing blast. "We saw our survival threatened and that gave us the incentive to make it happen," says Swarztrauber. Their risk-taking strategy paid off; within five months, Quadlogic had signed a multi-million-dollar deal with a utility company in Jamaica. Since then, hundreds of customers in Mexico, Ecuador, Costa Rica, and other countries have purchased the antitheft device, and Quadlogic recently achieved a new sales record, generating $20 million in annual sales. Shafrir and Swarztrauber's discovery-driven leadership style, their ability to spot new business opportunities, and their willingness to take risks probably saved their company.

Sources: Based on Hal Gregersen, "The Entrepreneur's DNA," *Wall Street Journal*, February 26, 2013, p. B13; John Bussey, "The Innovator's Enigma," *Wall Street Journal*, October 4, 2012, http://online.wsj.com/article/SB10000872396390443493304578036753351798378.html; Sarah Needleman, Vanessa O'Connell, Emily Maltby, and Angus Loten, "And the Most Innovative Entrepreneur Is ... " *Wall Street Journal*, November 14, 2011, pp. R1, R4.

innovation and leadership at INSEAD, that explains the difference between delivery-driven and discovery-driven leadership.

Although big businesses develop many new ideas, creativity and innovation are the signatures of small, entrepreneurial businesses. Creative thinking has become a core business skill, and entrepreneurs lead the way in developing and applying that skill. In fact, creativity and innovation often lie at the heart of small companies' ability to compete successfully with their larger rivals. Even though they cannot outspend their larger rivals, small companies can create powerful, effective competitive advantages over big companies by "out-creating" and "out-innovating" them! If they fail to do so, entrepreneurs don't stay in business very long. Leadership expert Warren Bennis says, "Today's successful companies live and die according to the quality of their ideas."[10]

Some small businesses create innovations *reactively* in response to customer feedback or changing market conditions, and others create innovations *proactively*, spotting opportunities on which to capitalize. Sometimes innovation is *revolutionary*, creating market-changing, transformational, disruptive breakthroughs that are the result of generating something from nothing. More often, innovation is *evolutionary*, developing market-sustaining ideas that elaborate on existing products, services, and processes that result from putting old things together in new ways or from taking something away to create something simpler or better. Spencer Silver, a chemist at 3M, was working to improve the adhesive on tape, but his experiments resulted in a glue that hardly stuck at all. Most people would have considered the experiment a total failure and scrapped it, but Silver continued to search for a practical use for his discovery. A few years later, Silver met another 3M chemist, Art Fry, who was also a church organist and was having trouble keeping the paper markers in his hymnal. The two inventors came up with a clever answer to a simple, creative question: What can you do with a glue when you take away most of its stickiness? Their answer led to the invention of one of the most popular office products of all time, the Post-It Note, a product that now includes more than 4,000 variations and accounts for sales of 50 billion units annually.[11] Although both types of innovation produce useful results, revolutionary innovation that produces disruptive changes is momentous—and usually highly profitable.

Some entrepreneurs discover their ideas in the most mundane situations but are clever enough to spot the business opportunities they offer.

ENTREPRENEURIAL PROFILE: Paul Tasner and Elena Olivari: PulpWorks
Paul Tasner spent 35 years in supply chain management, where much of his work focused on packaging. Tasner and his wife often complained about the difficulty that they (and many other people) had opening the plastic packaging (two common versions are known as "clam shells" and "blister packs") used for many products today. His wife purchased a special set of shears designed specifically to open clam shells and blister packs, but, ironically, the shears were packaged in a blister pack. Tasner realized that both shoppers and businesses would benefit from easier-to-open, environmentally friendly packaging and worked with business partner Elena Olivari to launch a company, PulpWorks Inc., in San Rafael, California, to capitalize on the opportunity. They designed a package made of two materials, molded recycled pulp (the same material egg cartons are made from) and recycled cardboard, that includes an open window so that shoppers can easily see the product it contains. The patent-pending packaging, called Karta-Pack, accepts printing just as readily as more traditional, less environmentally friendly packaging does. Originally, Tasner and Olivari intended to manufacture the packages themselves, but after considering the capital investment (and subsequent fund-raising) required, they outsourced production of the packages to manufacturing experts. PulpWorks has won numerous awards for the sustainability of its Karta-Pack packaging and has attracted the attention of major consumer product companies.[12] ■

© Dave Lauridsen

More often, creative ideas arise when entrepreneurs look at something old and think something new or different. Legendary Notre Dame football coach Knute Rockne, whose teams dominated college football in the 1920s, got the idea for his constantly shifting backfields while watching a burlesque chorus routine! Rockne's innovations in the backfield (which included the legendary "Four Horsemen") and his emphasis on the forward pass (a legal but largely unused tactic in that era) so befuddled opposing defenses that his teams compiled an impressive 105–12–5 record.[13]

Entrepreneurship is the result of a disciplined, systematic process of applying creativity and innovation to needs and opportunities in the marketplace. It involves applying focused strategies to new ideas and new insights to create a product or service that satisfies customers' needs or solves their problems. It is much more than random, disjointed tinkering with a new gadget. Millions of people come up with creative ideas for new or different products and services; most of them, however, never do anything with them. Entrepreneurs are people who connect their creative ideas with the purposeful action and structure of a business. "Great ideas are abundant," says Samer Kurdi, head of Entrepreneurs' Organization, "but it is what we decide to do with them that counts."[14] Successful entrepreneurship is a constant process that relies on creativity, innovation, and application in the marketplace.

Innovation must be a constant process because most ideas don't work and most innovations fail. One writer explains, "Trial—and lots of error—is embedded in entrepreneurship."[15] For every 5,000 to 10,000 new drug discoveries, only about 250 get to preclinical trials, and only 5 of those make it to clinical trials. Just 1 or 2 drugs emerge from clinical trials for review by the U.S. Food and Drug Administration, and only 1 typically gets to the market in a process that typically takes 10 to 15 years.[16] New products are crucial to companies' success, however. According to Robert Cooper, a researcher who has analyzed thousands of new product launches, new products (those launched within the previous three years) account for an impressive 38 percent of sales at top-performing companies.[17] Still, successful entrepreneurs recognize that many failures will accompany innovations, and they are willing to accept their share of failures because they know that failure is merely part of the creative process. Rather than quit when they fail, entrepreneurs keep trying. While working as a textbook editor, James Michener had an idea for a book based on his experiences in the Solomon Islands during World War II. He sent the manuscript to a publisher and received the following note: "You are a good editor. Don't throw it all away trying to be a writer. I read your book. Frankly, it's not really that good." Michener persisted and went on to publish *South Pacific*, which earned him a Pulitzer Prize and became the basis for one of Broadway's most successful musicals of all time.[18]

Entrepreneurship requires business owners to be bold enough to try their new ideas, flexible enough to throw aside those that do not work, and wise enough to learn about what will work based on their observations of what did not. We now turn our attention to creativity, the creative process, and methods for enhancing creativity.

LO2

Describe why creativity and innovation are such integral parts of entrepreneurship.

Creativity—Essential to Survival

In this fiercely competitive, fast-faced, global economy, creativity is not only an important source for building a competitive advantage but also a necessity for survival. When developing creative solutions to modern problems, entrepreneurs must go beyond merely relying on what has worked in the past. "A company that's doing all the things that used to guarantee success—providing quality products backed by great service, marketing with flair, holding down costs, and managing cash flow—is at risk of being flattened if it fails to become an engine of innovation," says one business writer.[19] Transforming their organizations into engines of innovation requires entrepreneurs to cast off limiting assumptions, beliefs, and behaviors and develop new insights into the relationship among resources, needs, and value. In other words, they must change their perspectives, looking at the world in new and different ways.

Entrepreneurs must always be on guard against traditional assumptions and perspectives about how things ought to be because they are certain killers of creativity. These self-imposed mental constraints that people tend to build over time push creativity right out the door. These ideas become so deeply rooted in our minds that they become immovable blocks to creative thinking—even though they may be outdated, obsolete, and no longer relevant. In short, they act as logjams to creativity. Children are creative and curious about new possibilities because society has not yet brainwashed them into an attitude of conformity, nor have they have learned to accept *traditional* solutions as the *only* solutions. By retaining their creative "inner child," entrepreneurs are able to throw off the shackles on creativity and see opportunities for creating viable businesses where most people see what they've always seen (or, worse yet, see nothing). Creative exercises such as the one in Figure 3.1 can help adults reconnect with the creativity they exhibited so readily as children.

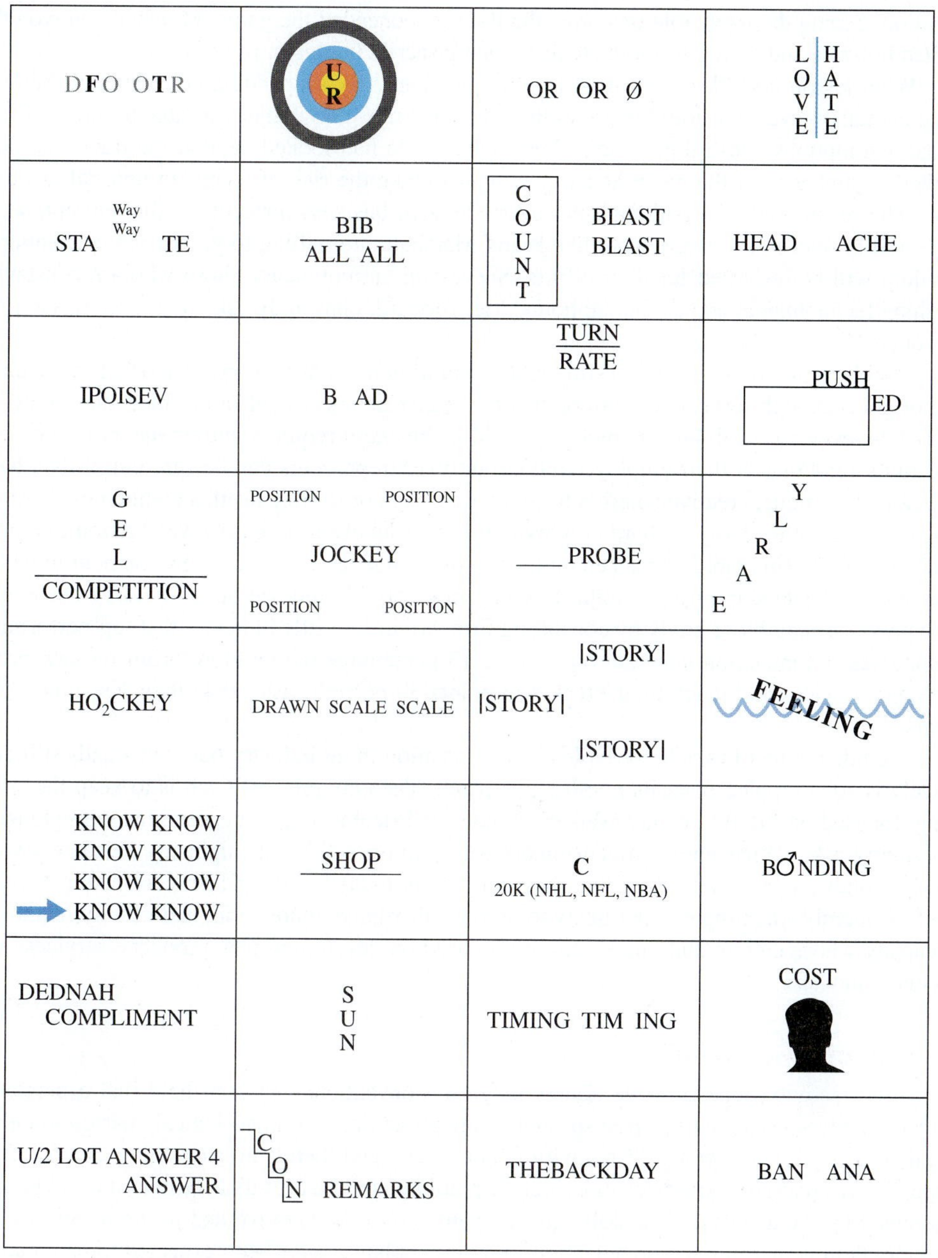

D F O OTR	(target with U/R)	OR OR Ø	L H O A V T E E
STA ^{Way} ^{Way} TE	BIB ——— ALL ALL	C O U BLAST N BLAST T	HEAD ACHE
IPOISEV	B AD	TURN ——— RATE	PUSH ☐ ED
G E L ——— COMPETITION	POSITION POSITION JOCKEY POSITION POSITION	___ PROBE	Y L R A E
HO₂CKEY	DRAWN SCALE SCALE	|STORY| |STORY| |STORY|	FEELING
KNOW KNOW KNOW KNOW KNOW KNOW → KNOW KNOW	SHOP ———	C 20K (NHL, NFL, NBA)	BO♥NDING
DEDNAH COMPLIMENT	S U N	TIMING TIM ING	COST (silhouette)
U/2 LOT ANSWER 4 ANSWER	C O N REMARKS	THEBACKDAY	BAN ANA

FIGURE 3.1

How Creative Are You? Can You Recognize the Well-Known Phrases These Symbols Represent?

Sources: Based on Terry Stickels, "Frame Games," *USA Weekend*, April 26–28, 2013, p. 14; August 10–12, 2007, p. 20; June 8–10, 2012, p. 14; October 19–21, p. 14; November 11–13, 2011, p. 18; September 14–16, 2012, p. 14; November 22–25, 2011, p. 22; May 17–19, 2013, p. 14; July 22–24, 2011, p. 14; July 15–17, 2011, p. 14; January 13–15, 2012, p. 15; August 26–28; 2011, p.14; September 2–4, 2011, p. 14; March 16–18, 2012, p. 15; December 7–9, 2012, p. 22; April 12–14, 2013, p. 14; February 10–12, 2012, p. 14; September 7–9, 2012, p. 14; October 28–30, 2011, p. 14; December 9–11, 2011, p. 19; January 11–13, 2013, p. 14; April 5–7, 2013, p. 14; December 21–23, 2012, p. 14; February 1–3, 2013, p. 14; August 19–21, 2011, p. 18.

Many years ago, during an international chess competition, Frank Marshall made what has become known as one of the most beautiful—and one of the most creative—moves ever made on a chess board. In a crucial game in which he was evenly matched with a Russian master player, Marshall found his queen under serious attack. Marshall had several avenues of escape for his queen. Knowing that the queen is one of the most important offensive players on the chessboard, spectators assumed that Marshall would make a conventional move and push his queen to safety.

Using all of the time available to him to consider his options, Marshall picked up his queen—and paused—and put it down on the most *illogical* square of all—a square from which the queen could easily be captured by any one of three hostile pieces. Marshall had done the unthinkable! He had sacrificed his queen, a move typically made only under the most desperate of circumstances. All of the spectators—even Marshall's opponent—groaned in dismay. Then the Russian—and finally the crowd—realized that Marshall's move was, in reality, a brilliant one. No matter how the Russian opponent took the queen, he would eventually be in a losing position. Seeing the inevitable outcome, the Russian conceded the game. Marshall had won the match in a rare and daring fashion: He had won by sacrificing his queen![20]

What lesson does this story hold for entrepreneurs? By suspending conventional thinking long enough to even consider the possibility of such a move, Marshall was able to throw off the usual assumptions constraining most chess players. He had looked beyond the traditional and orthodox strategies of the game and was willing to take the risk of trying an unusual tactic to win. The result: He won. Although not every creative business opportunity that entrepreneurs take will be successful, many who, like Frank Marshall, are willing to go beyond conventional wisdom will be rewarded for their efforts. Successful entrepreneurs, those who are constantly pushing technological and economic boundaries forward, constantly ask, "Is it time to sacrifice the queen?"

Merely generating one successful creative solution to address a problem or a need usually is not good enough to keep an entrepreneurial enterprise successful in the long run, however. Success—even survival—in the modern world of business requires entrepreneurs to tap their creativity (and that of their employees) constantly. Entrepreneurs can be sure that if they have developed a unique, creative solution to solve a problem or to fill a need, a competitor (perhaps one six times zones away) is hard at work developing an even more creative solution to render theirs obsolete. This rapid and accelerating rate of change has created an environment in which staying in a leadership position requires constant creativity, innovation, and entrepreneurship. The payoff is tangible; a study by consulting firm Arthur D. Little indicates that top-performing companies in innovation generate on average 13 percentage points more profit on new products and services and reach their breakeven points 30 percent faster than their less innovative peers.[21]

A company that has achieved a leadership position in an industry but then stands still creatively is soon toppled from its number-one perch. The entrepreneur's job is to keep the company focused on the future. Jay Walker, founder of Priceline.com, suggests that entrepreneurs constantly ask, "What might my customers want tomorrow? What might my customers want in six months, a year, two years, that they don't want today?"[22] As valuable as customer feedback is, merely soliciting it is not likely to produce disruptive innovation; that usually requires a company whose culture and employees are focused on developing new products, services, and business models.

Can Creativity Be Taught?

Because creativity appears to be almost magical, conventional wisdom held that a person is either creative—imaginative, free-spirited, entrepreneurial—or not—logical, narrow-minded, rigid. Today, we know better. "Creativity is not magic, and there's no such thing as a 'creative type,'" says creativity expert Jonah Lehrer. "Creativity is not a trait that we inherit or a blessing bestowed by the angels. It is a skill. Anyone can learn to be creative and to get better at it."[23] The problem is that in most organizations, employees have never been expected to be creative. In addition, many businesses fail to foster an environment that encourages creativity among employees. Restricted by their traditional thinking patterns, most people never tap into their pools of innate creativity, and the company becomes stagnant. "The direct benefit of employee innovation is a competitive advantage," says creativity expert David Silverstein, "but the secondary benefits are greater employee empowerment and satisfaction."[24]

Not only can entrepreneurs and the people who work for them learn to think creatively, but they must for their companies' sake! "Innovation and creativity are not just for artists," says Joyce Wycoff, author of several books on creativity. "These are skills with a direct, bottom-line payoff."[25]

How can entrepreneurs learn to become more creative thinkers? Creative thinkers tend to model the following types of behavior:

- Always ask the question "Is there a better way?"

- Challenge custom, routine, and tradition, which also is a characteristic of the entrepreneurial personality.

- Are reflective, often staring out windows, deep in thought. (How many traditional managers would stifle creativity by snapping these people out of their "daydreams," chastise them for "loafing," and admonish them to "get back to work"?) Great ideas need time to percolate, and smart entrepreneurs give employees (and themselves) some downtime during the day to think and reflect.

- Are prolific thinkers. They know that generating lots of ideas increases the likelihood of coming up with a few highly creative ideas. Nobel Laureate Paul Berg, recalling his friend Francis Crick, who also won a Nobel Prize as codiscoverer of the structure of DNA, says, "He had 10 ideas for every one that was truly brilliant."[26]

- Ask "What if … ?" John Zimmer, who cofounded Lyft (known for its pink-mustachioed cars) with Logan Green, came up with the idea for the ride-sharing company that offers an alternative to car ownership after hearing a lecture on "green" cities in college and asking a classmate over beers, "What if people could summon a car to their doorsteps whenever they needed one to go wherever they wanted to go?" The privately owned company recently crossed the $1 billion mark in annual sales and is valued at $5.5 billion.[27]

- Play mental games, trying to see an issue from different perspectives.

- Realize that there may be more than one "right answer."

- See mistakes as mere "pit stops" on the way to success.

- See problems as springboards for new ideas. While Cristy Clarke was on her way to a holiday party, she began to think of questions to serve as starters for meaningful, interesting conversations because she did not want to endure yet another dull evening of meaningless small talk. Her experiment was a success, and the next morning Clarke began developing the questions that would become part of the successful party game TableTopics, which Clarke markets along with 29 other products through her company, Ruby Mine Inc.[28]

- Understand that failure is a natural part of the creative process. James Dyson spent 15 years and nearly his entire savings before he succeeded in developing the bagless vacuum cleaner that made him rich and famous. "If you want to discover something that other people haven't," he says, "you need to do things the wrong way. You don't learn from success."[29]

- Have "helicopter skills," the ability to rise above the daily routine to see an issue from a broader perspective and then swoop back down to focus on an area in need of change.

- Relate seemingly unrelated ideas to a problem to generate innovative solutions.

ENTREPRENEURIAL PROFILE: Charles Kaman: Kaman Aircraft Company and Ovation Instruments After graduating from college, Charles Kaman worked in the helicopter division of United Aircraft Corporation, where he helped design helicopters for the military. Using a homemade calculator he called the Aeronalyzer, Kaman developed several innovations in rotor and wing designs, but his employer showed no interest in any of them. In 1945, with $2,000 and his idea for a new dual rotor system that made helicopters more stable and safer to fly, 26-year-old Kaman, also an accomplished guitarist, turned down an offer to join Tommy Dorsey's famous swing band and decided to pursue his innovative designs for helicopters and start the Kaman Aircraft Company in his mother's garage. Over the next 50 years, Kaman built his company into a billion-dollar aviation business, creating many important innovations along the way, including turbine engines; blades made of lightweight, sturdy composite materials; and remote-controlled helicopters. Kaman also maintained an avid interest in guitars and in 1964 began working with a small team of aerospace engineers to build a better acoustic guitar. Drawing on their experience of removing vibrations from helicopters, the team reverse-engineered a guitar with a bowl-shaped body made of composite materials that incorporated more vibration into the instrument, giving it a bolder, richer sound. "In helicopters, engineers spend all of their time trying to figure out how to remove vibration," Kaman said. "To build a guitar, you spend your time trying to figure out how to put vibration in." Kaman founded Ovation Instruments in 1966 and began selling the Balladeer, an acoustical guitar that immediately attracted attention for its superior tone and volume among musicians, including famous artists such as John Lennon, Glen Campbell, Bob Marley, Carly Simon, Jimmy Page, and Melissa Etheridge.[30] ■

The need to enhance creative thinking means that exploring inner space (the space within our brains)—not outer space—becomes the challenge of the century. Successful entrepreneurship requires both *divergent reasoning*, which is the ability to create a multitude of original, diverse ideas, and *convergent reasoning*, which is the ability to evaluate multiple ideas and choose the best solution to a given problem. How can entrepreneurs learn to tap their innate creativity more readily? The first step is to break down the barriers to creativity that most of us have erected over the years. We now turn our attention to these barriers and some suggested techniques for tearing them down.

LO3

Explain the 10 "mental locks" that limit individual creativity.

Barriers to Creativity

The number of potential barriers to creativity is virtually limitless—time pressures, unsupportive management, pessimistic coworkers, overly rigid company policies, and countless others. Perhaps the most difficult hurdles to overcome, however, are those that individuals impose on themselves. In his book *A Whack on the Side of the Head*, Roger von Oech identifies 10 "mental locks" that limit individual creativity:[31]

1. *Searching for the one "right" answer.* The typical education system may teach useful skills but tends to squash creativity and innovation out of children. Although children today are scoring higher on IQ tests than in the past, their level of creativity is deteriorating.[32] Recent research by Kyung Hee Kim, a professor at the College of William and Mary, shows that creativity (as measured by the Torrance Test of Creative Thinking) among both children and adults in the United States has declined markedly since 1990. The decline, which Kim says is "very significant," is particularly acute among the youngest segment of the population, children from kindergarten to sixth grade.[33] Part of the problem is that deeply ingrained in most educational systems is the assumption that there is one "right" answer to a problem. In reality, however, most problems are ambiguous. The average student who has completed four years of college has taken more than 2,600 tests; therefore, it is not unusual for this one-correct-answer syndrome to become an inherent part of our thinking. Depending on the questions one asks, there may be (and usually are) several "right" answers.

ENTREPRENEURIAL PROFILE: ThyssenKrupp North America: Multi Elisha Graves Otis invented the elevator in 1852, and the first elevator was installed in a New York City department store on Broadway in 1857. Graves's invention transformed city skylines across the globe, making the construction of skyscrapers practical. For more than 160 years, elevators moved only vertically. Then engineers at ThyssenKrupp North America asked, "What if an elevator could move horizontally (or in any direction)?" Rather than rely on traditional cables, the creative engineers used magnetic levitation technology (the same technology that drives the world's fastest trains) that allows elevators to move horizontally as well as vertically. Their willingness to search for more than one "right" answer means that tall buildings can take on almost any shape, multiple elevator cars can operate in the same shaft, elevators can take up less building space and use less energy, and elevator banks can occupy a smaller footprint.[34] ■

2. *Focusing on "being logical."* Logic is a valuable part of the creative process, especially when evaluating and implementing ideas. However, in the early imaginative phases of the process, logical thinking can restrict creativity. Focusing too much effort on being logical also discourages the use of one of the mind's most powerful creations: intuition. von Oech advises us to "think something different" and to use nonlogical thinking freely, especially in the imaginative phase of the creative process. Intuition, which is based on the accumulated knowledge and experiences a person encounters over the course of a lifetime and resides in the subconscious, can be unlocked. It is a crucial part of the creative process because using it often requires one to tear down long-standing assumptions that limit creativity and innovation.

You Be the Consultant

10 Keys to Business Innovation

Creativity expert Teresa Amabile identifies three components of creativity: (1) **Expertise.** One must have the technical, procedural, and conceptual knowledge to generate potential solutions to a problem. (2) **Creative thinking skills.** A person must possess the willingness to take risks and to see problems or situations from different perspectives, using many of the techniques described in this chapter. (3) **Motivation.** One must have the internal desire to develop creative solutions. This motivation often comes from the challenge that the work itself presents.

Entrepreneurs and their employees can transform their companies into engines of innovation by combining these three components of creativity with what management consultant The Doblin Group calls the 10 types of innovation:

1. **Business model.** How does your company make money? These are innovations in the value proposition that a company provides its target customers and in the way it delivers value to its customers.

2. **Networks and alliances.** Can you join forces with another company or entity for mutual benefit? A company may forge a synergistic relationship with another organization in which each company's strengths complement the other.

3. **Organizational structure.** How do you support and encourage your employees' creative efforts? The most effective organizations use an appropriate structure and culture to align their talent to spark innovation.

4. **Core process.** How does your company create and add value for customers? These innovations in a company's internal processes result in superior business systems and work methods that result in benefits for customers.

5. **Product or service performance.** What are the most important features and functions of your company's products or services? Innovations in functions and features can give a company's product or service a significant edge over those of competitors.

6. **Product system.** Can you link multiple products into a system or a platform? Bundling products can add value for customers.

7. **Service.** How do you provide value-added service beyond your company's products for customers? Some of the most successful businesses set themselves apart from their competition by providing unparalleled customer service.

8. **Channel.** How do you get your products or services into customers' hands? Some companies provide extra value to their customers by making their products and services available in many venues.

9. **Brand.** What is your company's "identity" in the marketplace? Successful companies use creative advertising, promotion, and marketing techniques to build a desirable brand identity with customers.

10. **Customer experience.** Does your company engage customers and give them reasons to come back to make future purchases? Innovative companies find ways to connect with their customers, creating a loyal base of "fansumers," customers who not only purchase but act like fans who promote the company to their friends and family members.

Roadie

When Marc Golin, cofounder of Kabbage, a small business lender, had to get tile from his home in Atlanta, Georgia, to a renovation project at his condominium in Florida, he did not have the time to make the drive himself. "Someone from Atlanta probably would be driving to Florida and could deliver the materials for him," he thought to himself. Then a grander realization hit him: With 250 million cars on the road every day, someone is going somewhere all the time and could deliver packages to a destination to which they were already headed. That revelation led Golin to launch Roadie, an app-based peer-to-peer business that allows customers to ship items (and now pets) in the vehicles of people who happen to be going to a particular destination. Depending on distance and the size of the item, prices range from $8 to $200. Drivers get 80 percent of the fee, and Roadie collects the remainder, minus a nominal fee to cover insurance. In its first year, Roadies' app has been downloaded 260,000 times, and 20,000 drivers in all 50 states have signed on. Annual sales at Roadie, which is competing with established shipping giants such as UPS and the U.S. Postal Service, are approaching $1 million.

Lee Company

Lee Company, a building maintenance company in Nashville, Tennessee, was steadily losing a major asset—its base of experienced, highly knowledgeable mechanics, electricians, plumbers, and engineers—to retirement. Like many other industrial companies, Lee was having difficulty finding skilled young people to replace them, and CEO Richard Perko realized that the "brain drain" was a serious threat to the business. Adding to the problem is that fact that older workers often cannot get to machinery and equipment that requires servicing because it is in high, hard-to-reach, or dangerous places. Perko came up with a clever solution to the problem that enables older experienced workers to pass

(continued)

You Be the Consultant (continued)

along their knowledge and experience to younger workers with the aid of technology. Lee Company conducted a pilot study that provided young, inexperienced workers with smart safety glasses equipped with a tiny camera, microphone, speaker, detachable flash drive, and wireless antenna. While the young workers begin to repair or service a piece of equipment in the field, older, experienced workers sit in a central command center, where they watch and listen to a live feed of the repair. The experienced workers are able to talk their younger counterparts through any problems and difficulties they may encounter, teaching and coaching them along the way and building their knowledge and confidence. The pilot program proved to be so successful that Perko plans to issue the smart safety glasses to all 300 of his company's employees who work in the field.

Monsieur

When Barry Givens was a student in mechanical engineering at Georgia Tech University, he and his roommate arrived at a bar early so they could get a good seat to watch the NBA Finals. Because the bar was so crowded, their drinks did not show up for two hours, during which time the two came up with an idea for a machine that could dispense simple drinks quickly so that patrons would not have to wait for bartenders to fill their orders. After Givens graduated, he worked for brief stints at large corporations but decided to focus on the idea of a robotic bartender. He sold his house and car to raise capital, and he and his buddy built a prototype of a tabletop box they named Monsieur that holds eight liquor bottles and is capable of mixing up to 300 different drinks. Givens loaned the prototype to a friend for a party; not only was it a huge hit, but it also attracted the attention of one of the guests, an angel investor who provided $40,000 in equity capital for the fledgling business. To fuel the company's growth, Givens then raised $140,000 in a Kickstarter campaign, which led to a $2 million investment from venture capital funds.

Monsieur can dispense a typical drink in only 20 seconds. Patrons can enter their orders from a touchscreen on Monsieur or from their smart phones. Givens has developed a larger, freestanding version of Monsieur, priced at $10,000, that is designed for commercial use and includes proprietary software that manages inventory, provides real-time analytics, allows customers to customize their drinks, and handles payments via a convenient app. The Monsieur app also includes a "responsibility" feature that allows a customer to enter his or her gender and weight; the app tracks how much alcohol the customer has had and sends him or her a notice when his or her estimated blood alcohol content approaches the legal limit and even opens the Uber app to order a driver. Givens has negotiated deals with Marriott Hotels, Regal Cinemas, sports arenas, and many bars and restaurants to use Monsieur, which now generates more than $3 million in annual sales.

Raymond McCrea Jones/Redux

1. Select one of these businesses and explain which of the 10 types of innovation the company used to bolster its success.

2. Explain how the company you selected in question 1 could use at least one of the remaining types of innovation to increase its sales and profitability.

Sources: Based on Laura Stevens, Michael Austin, "Tending Machines," *Entrepreneur*, June 2015, p. 78; John Biggs, "Monsieur, the Drink Robot, Raises $2 Million, *TechCrunch*, October 10, 2014, https://techcrunch.com/2014/10/10/monsieur-the-drink-robot-raises-2-million/; "Technology Bubble? Ask Waffle House," *Wall Street Journal*, February 24, 2015, pp. B1–B2; Elaine Pofeldt, "The Startup Taking on FedEx, UberRUSH, and Postmates," *Forbes*, March 31, 2016, www.forbes.com/sites/elainepofeldt/2016/03/31/can-this-on-demand-app-take-on-fedex/#3bc1f91c7210; Kristen Hall-Geisler, "Roadies Is Like Uber for Shipping," *TechCrunch*, May 16, 2016, https://techcrunch.com/2016/05/16/roadie-is-like-uber-for-shipping/; Teresa M. Amabile, "Componential Theory of Creativity," Harvard Business School, Working Paper 12-096, April 26, 2012, pp. 2–3; Robert F. Brands, "Stay Inspired This Holiday Season: The 12 Days of Innovation," *Huffington Post*, December 20, 2012, www.huffingtonpost.com/robert-f-brands/stay-inspired-holiday-season_b_2334305.html; Paul Davis, "Innovation White Paper," Scanlon Leadership Network, January 2008, p. 3; Sarah E. Needleman, Vanessa O'Connell, Emily Maltby, and Angus Loten, "And the Most Innovative Entrepreneur Is …" *Wall Street Journal*, November 14, 2011, pp. R1, R4; April Joyner, "Unequal Technologies," *Inc.*, February 2013, p. 26; Suzanne Barlyn, "New and Improved," *Wall Street Journal*, April 23, 2009, http://online.wsj.com/article/SB124025160159735869.html; Kelly Spors, "Tough Times Call for New Ideas," *Wall Street Journal*, February 15, 2009, http://online.wsj.com/article/SB123466563957289181.html; and Gene Marks, "Why Most Small Businesses Will Beat the Recession," *Bloomberg Businessweek*, January 8, 2009, www.businessweek.com/smallbiz/content/jan2009/sb2009015_212410.htm.

ENTREPRENEURIAL PROFILE: Entrepreneurial Profile: Joe Landolina and Isaac Miller: Cresilon (formerly known as Suneris) In 2010, Joe Landolina and Isaac Miller founded Cresilon (formerly Suneris), now a privately-held medical devices company that focuses on trauma and wound care treatments, while they were undergraduates at New York University. The young entrepreneurs developed a plant-based gel they named VETIGEL that imitates the structure of the living tissue on which it is placed, which means that it not only stops bleeding, even traumatic bleeding that often results in death, in seconds, but it also acts as a scaffold on which skin can grow and heal a wound. VETIGEL will be available for use by veterinarians in late 2017, and Cresilon currently is seeking approval from the Food and Drug Administration for human use. Cresilon has raised several million in capital from angel investors and has expanded its staff to more than 25 employees. Because they were willing to consider ideas to stop bleeding other than the traditional methods of direct pressure, stitches, and cauterization, Landolina and Miller's creative solution is revolutionizing trauma care and saving lives.[35] ∎

Courtesy of Cresilon.Inc

3. *Blindly following the rules.* We learn at a very early age not to "color outside the lines," and we spend the rest of our lives blindly obeying such rules. Sometimes, creativity depends on our ability to break the existing rules so that we can see new ways of doing things. "Most people's minds are not wired to go against what everybody else is doing," observes neuroscientist Gregory Berns. "When you look at problems, you tend to perceive them in well-worn paths in ways that you've perceived them before. That's the first roadblock in innovating: overcoming your perceptual biases."[36]

ENTREPRENEURIAL PROFILE: King Gillette: Gillette Safety Razor Company In 1895, King Gillette, a traveling salesman who aspired to be an entrepreneur, was shaving with a straight razor, the standard technology of the day, when a creative idea struck him: a "safety razor" that consisted of a small, thin square of sheet steel held in place by a holder equipped with a handle. When a blade became dull, the user would simply replace it. "I saw it all in a moment," Gillette said. "The way the blade would be held in a holder. Then came the idea of sharpening the two opposite edges of a thin piece of steel, and then came the clamping plates for the blades, with a handle centered between the edges. I stood there in a trance of joy." Gillette visited metallurgists at the nearby Massachusetts Institute of Technology, who assured him that it would be *impossible* to produce steel that was thin enough, sharp enough, and inexpensive enough to produce blades for his safety razor. After six years of work, however, two business associates introduced the determined Gillette to William Nickerson, an MIT graduate who produced the blade that Gillette had designed. Gillette received patent number 775,134 for his safety razor from the U.S. Patent and Trademark Office in 1904. The American Safety Razor Company, which later became Gillette Safety Razor Company, began producing blades in Boston in 1903, and the world of shaving was transformed forever because Gillette was willing to question the established "rules" of shaving. Procter & Gamble purchased Gillette in 2005 for $57 billion.[37] ∎

4. *Constantly being practical.* Imagining impractical answers to "what if" questions can be a powerful stepping-stone to creative ideas. Suspending practicality for a while frees the mind to consider creative solutions that otherwise might never arise. Whenever Thomas Edison hired an assistant to work in his creative laboratory, he would tell the new employee, "Walk through town and list 20 things that interest you." When the worker returned, Edison would ask him to split the list into two columns. Then he would say, "Randomly combine objects from column A and column B and come up with as many inventions as you can." Edison's methods for stimulating creativity in his lab proved to be successful; he holds the distinction of being the only person to have earned a patent every year for 65 consecutive years![38]

Periodically setting aside practicality allows entrepreneurs to consider taking knowledge or a concept from one area and placing it in a totally different application. Researchers in Australia have developed a retinal prosthesis based on the eyes of the dragonfly that serves as the foundation of a bionic eye that may allow many blind people to see. To be successful predators, dragonflies, which are capable of chasing prey at speeds up to 37 miles per hour, must have a wide field of vision and the ability to detect fast movements of their prey, even in a swarm of insects. Scientists have created a retinal implant that mimics a dragonfly's vision, and they say that the technology also can make driverless cars safer by enabling them to identify and avoid objects, such as pedestrians and other cars, around them.[39]

5. *Viewing laughter and play as frivolous.* A playful attitude is fundamental to creative thinking. There is a close relationship between the "haha" of humor and the "aha" of discovery. Laughter tends to help people relax, which in turn allows them to be more creative. Researchers have discovered that exposing people to short video clips of stand-up comedy or humorous comedy scenes increases their creativity.[40]

   Play gives us the opportunity to reinvent reality and to rethink established ways of doing things. Play at work causes people to remove idea filters that can be barriers to creativity and sends a signal to employees that they "work in a permissive and playful environment," says Tim Brown, CEO of global design company IDEO. "We need to be able to trust to play and be creative."[41] Children learn when they play, and so can entrepreneurs. Watch children playing, and you will see them invent new games, create new ways of looking at old things, and learn what works (and what doesn't) in their games. Entrepreneurs can benefit from playing in the same way that children do. They, too, can learn to try new approaches and discover what works and what doesn't. Creativity results when entrepreneurs take what they have learned at play, evaluate it, corroborate it with other knowledge, and put it into practice. Encourage employees to have fun when solving problems; they are more likely to push the boundaries and come up with genuinely creative solutions if they do. What kind of invention would Wile E. Coyote, who seems to have an inexhaustible supply of ideas for catching Roadrunner in those cartoons, create in this situation? How might the Three Stooges approach this problem? What would Seinfeld's Kramer suggest? What solution would Si from *Duck Dynasty* offer? What would a 6-year-old do? The idea is to look at a problem or situation from different perspectives.

   ENTREPRENEURIAL PROFILE: Kim Vandenbroucke: Brainy Chick For Kim Vandenbroucke, owner of Brainy Chick and a game inventor with a track record of hits such as Cranium Party Playoff, Barbie Mini Kingdom, and Scattergories Categories (part of which she came up with on her honeymoon), playing is an important part of the creative process. Vandenbroucke, who says she grew up in a household of game players, says she still plays at least one game a day, often drawing on the experience for inspiration. Although she keeps many sources of creative inspiration near her desk, one of her favorites is a copy of *Meet Mr. Product*, a book that features classic characters from the world of advertising. It's "a great place to get ideas," she says. "I love old advertising characters—the styles, the names, the nostalgia." Vandenbroucke also carries a small notebook in which she writes down game ideas, "seeds," she calls them, as they come to her.[42] ∎

myopic thinking
a type of thinking that destroys creativity because it is narrowly focused and limited by the status quo.

6. *Becoming overly specialized.* A common killer of creativity is **myopic thinking**, which is narrowly focused and limited by the status quo. Because experts are so immersed in what they know, they often are victims of myopic thinking. That's why creative companies include *nonexperts* in creative problem solving or idea generation sessions; they are free to ask questions and offer ideas that challenge the status quo and traditional solutions that experts "know" cannot work but often do. "The real disruptors will be those individuals who are not steeped in one industry of choice but individuals who approach challenges with a clean lens, bringing together diverse experiences, knowledge, and opportunities," says serial entrepreneur and philanthropist Naveen Jain.[43]

   Creative thinkers tend to be "explorers," searching for ideas outside their areas of specialty. The idea for the roll-on deodorant stick came from the ballpoint pen. The famous Mr. Potato Head toy was invented by a father sitting with his family at the dinner table who noted how much fun his children had playing with their food. Velcro (a combination of "velvet" and "crochet") was invented by Swiss engineer Georges de Mestral, who, while hiking one day in 1941 to take a break from work, had to stop to peel sticky cockleburs from his clothing. As he picked them off, he noticed how their hooked spines caught on and held tightly to the cloth. When he resumed his hike, he began to think about the possibilities of using a similar design to fasten objects together. After eight years of research and work, Mestral perfected his design for Velcro, which he patented in 1955.[44]

7. *Avoiding ambiguity.* Ambiguity can be a powerful creative stimulus; it encourages us to "think something different." Being excessively detailed in an imaginative situation tends to stifle creativity. Ambiguity, however, requires us to consider at least two different, often contradictory, notions at the same time, which is a direct channel to creativity. Ambiguous situations force us to stretch our minds beyond their normal boundaries and to consider creative options we might otherwise ignore. Although ambiguity is not a desired element when entrepreneurs are evaluating and implementing ideas, it is a valuable tool when they are searching for creative ideas and solutions. Entrepreneurs are famous for asking a question and then going beyond the first answer to explore other possible answers. The result is that they often find business opportunities by creating ambiguous situations.

8. *Fearing looking foolish.* Creative thinking is no place for conformity! New ideas rarely are born in a conforming environment. People tend toward conformity because they don't want to look foolish. The fool's job is to whack at the habits and rules that keep us thinking in the same old ways. In that sense, entrepreneurs are top-notch "fools." They are constantly questioning and challenging accepted ways of doing things and the assumptions that go with them. The noted entrepreneurship theorist Joseph Schumpeter wrote that entrepreneurs perform a vital function—"creative destruction"—in which they rethink conventional assumptions and discard those that are no longer useful. According to Schumpeter, "The function of entrepreneurs is to reform or revolutionize the pattern of production by exploiting an invention or, more generally, an untried technological possibility for producing a new commodity or producing an old one in a new way, by opening up a new source or supply of materials or a new outlet for products, by reorganizing an industry or so on."[45] In short, entrepreneurs look at old ways of doing things and ask, "Is there a better way?" By destroying the old, they create the new.

Stocksnapper/Alamy Stock Photo

ENTREPRENEURIAL PROFILE: Rich Able and Christoph Mack: X2 Biosystems After Rich Able's son sustained a concussion during a high school football game, Able and his business partner Christoph Mack took a new look at an old technology: athletic mouth guards. Able and Mack designed a new mouth guard, the BTX2 Impact Intelligence System, which uses accelerometers and gyroscopes to measure the force and the direction of the blows that an athlete receives. A radio system inside the mouth guard transmits the information to an app that runs on a smart phone or tablet on the sidelines. The app also contains numerous tests to help trainers and medical professionals assess the severity of an athlete's injuries as a result of a blow. Since their high-tech mouth guard passed live tests with several sports teams, Able and Mack's company, X2 Biosystems, has been selling the BTX2 Impact Intelligence System to teams across the United States for about $100 each. The entrepreneurs also have introduced the X-Patch Pro, a small patch that can be attached either to a helmet or directly to the skin that records head impacts and transmits data about them via Bluetooth to portable devices.[46] ■

9. *Fearing mistakes and failure.* Creative people realize that trying something new often leads to failure; however, they do not see failure as an end. It represents a learning experience on the way to success. As you learned in Chapter 1, failure is an important part of the creative process; it signals entrepreneurs when to change their course of action. Entrepreneurship is all about the opportunity to fail! Many entrepreneurs failed numerous times before finally succeeding. Despite their initial setbacks, they were able to set aside the fear of failure and keep trying. Arianna Huffington, author of a dozen books and founder of the news and blog Web site *Huffington Post*, says, "I love talking about my failures more than my successes. Think of failure as a stepping stone to success. I was rejected by 35 publishers before getting to yes." The highly successful *Huffington Post*, which Huffington launched in 2005, attracts more than 35 million unique visitors per month, more than the Web sites of any major newspaper in the United States.[47]

The key is to see failure for what it really is: a chance to learn how to succeed. Entrepreneurs who willingly risk failure and learn from it when it occurs have the best chance of succeeding. Charles F. Kettering, a famous inventor (he invented the lighting and ignition systems in automobiles, among other things), explains, "You fail because your ideas aren't right, but you should learn to fail intelligently. When you fail, find out *why* you failed and each time it will bring you nearer to the goal."[48] Successful entrepreneurs equate failure with innovation rather than with defeat.

Thanks to technology, the cost of failed attempts at innovation has never been lower. Entrepreneurs and companies can test new ideas at speeds and costs that were unimaginable only a few years ago. Building prototypes, getting them into potential customers' hands, and getting useful feedback on them has never been easier and less expensive. Entrepreneurs use the Internet and social media to determine whether customers are interested in purchasing their product and service innovations and to generate ideas for improving them.

10. *Believing "I'm not creative."* Some people limit themselves because they believe creativity belongs only to the Einsteins, Beethovens, and da Vincis of the world. Unfortunately, this belief often becomes a self-fulfilling prophecy. A person who believes he is not creative will, in all likelihood, behave that way and will make that belief come true. Some people who are considered geniuses, visionaries, and inventors actually are no smarter and have no more innate creative ability than the average person; however, they have learned how to think creatively and are persistent enough to keep trying until they succeed.

Successful entrepreneurs recognize that "I'm not creative" is merely an excuse for inaction. *Everyone* has within him or her the potential to be creative; not everyone will tap that potential, however. Innovation expert Hal Gregersen says that his research suggests that "one-third of our creative capacity is in our DNA. The other two-thirds [originates in] the world we grow up and work in."[49] Successful entrepreneurs find a way to unleash their creative powers on problems and opportunities.

By avoiding these 10 mental locks, entrepreneurs can unleash their own creativity and the creativity of those around them as well. Successful entrepreneurs are willing to take some risks, explore new ideas, play a little, ask "what if" questions, and learn to appreciate ambiguity. By doing so, they develop the skills, attitudes, and motivation that make them much more creative—one of the keys to entrepreneurial success. Table 3.2 includes questions designed to spur the imagination.

How to Enhance Creativity

LO4

Understand how entrepreneurs can enhance the creativity of their employees as well as their own creativity.

Enhancing Organizational Creativity

Creativity doesn't just happen in organizations; entrepreneurs must establish an environment in which creativity can flourish—for themselves and for their workers. "Everyone has a creative spark, but many factors can inhibit its ignition," says one writer. "Part of an [entrepreneur's] role is to see the spark in his or her people, encourage its ignition, and champion its success."[50] New ideas are fragile creations, but the right company culture can encourage people to develop and cultivate them. Ensuring that workers have the freedom and the incentive to be creative is one of the best ways to achieve innovation. Entrepreneurs can stimulate their own creativity and encourage it among workers by following the suggestions outlined in the following section; these suggestions are designed to create a culture of innovation.

INCLUDE CREATIVITY AS A CORE COMPANY VALUE AND MAKE IT AN INTEGRAL PART OF THE COMPANY'S CULTURE Innovative companies do not take a passive approach to creativity; they are proactive in their search for new ideas. Smart entrepreneurs establish a culture that encourages employees to share their creative ideas and rewards them for doing so. No one should expect the founder to come up with all the creative ideas simply because he or she started the company. One of the best ways to set a creative tone throughout an organization begins with the company's mission statement. Entrepreneurs should incorporate creativity and innovation into their companies' mission statements and affirm their commitment to them in internal communications. Innovation allows a company to shape, transform, and direct its future, and the natural place to define that future is in the mission statement. If creativity and innovation

TABLE 3.2 Questions to Spur the Imagination

We learn at an early age to pursue answers to questions. Creative people, however, understand that *good questions* are extremely valuable in the quest for creativity. Some of the greatest breakthroughs in history came as a result of creative people asking thought-provoking questions. Bill Bowerman, contemplating a design for the soles of running shoes over a breakfast of waffles, asked, "What would happen if I poured rubber into my waffle iron?" He did, and that's how Nike shoes came to be. (Bowerman's rubber-coated waffle iron is on display in the Nike Town superstore and museum in Chicago.) Albert Einstein, creator of the theory of relativity, asked, "What would a light wave look like to someone keeping pace with it?"

To jump-start creativity, Steve Gillman suggests writing a short list of adjectives, such as *light, cheap, fast, big, short, small, fun,* and others, and use them to ask "what if" questions. What if this product could be lighter? What if this process could be faster? What if this service could be cheaper? Don Wetzel, vice president of product planning at Docutel, a company that developed automated baggage-handling equipment, was standing in a long teller line at a bank in Dallas, Texas, in 1968, when he asked, "What if banks could offer banking services *without* a big, expensive building and bank tellers?" Wetzel pitched his idea to the management of Docutel, and by 1969, the company had a working prototype of an automated teller machine (ATM). Later that year, Chemical Bank in New York City became the first bank to install an ATM and promoted its convenience with an ad campaign that said, "On September 3, 1969, our branch will open its doors at 9:00 A.M. and we'll never close again!" The banking industry would never be the same.

Asking the following questions will help spur your imagination:

1. Is there a new way to do it?
2. Can you borrow or adapt it?
3. Can you give it a new twist?
4. Do you merely need more of the same?
5. Less of the same?
6. Is there a substitute?
7. Can you rearrange the parts?
8. What if you do just the opposite?
9. Can you combine ideas?
10. Are customers using your product or service in ways you never expected or intended?
11. Which customers are you not serving? What changes to your product or service are necessary to reach them?
12. Can you put it to other uses?
13. What else could we make from this?
14. Are there other markets for it?
15. Can you reverse it?
16. Can you rearrange it?
17. Can you put it to another use?
18. What idea seems impossible but, if executed, would revolutionize your business?

Courtesy of Stowaway Cosmetics

After corporate stints with mainstream companies such as Pop Sugar, Ann Taylor and Equinox, Julie Frederickson saw a need in the cosmetics industry for smaller sized beauty products that fit into slim purses and clutches or the pockets of skinny jeans for busy women on the go. Research showed that 10 large corporations control 70 percent of the $60 billion a year cosmetics market and that, due to their cost structures and profit margins, the large companies had no incentive to sell make-up in compact sizes at lower price points. Coupled with the learning that most women never use all of a typical makeup product before it reaches its expiration date, the idea of Stowaway Cosmetics was born. The brand has raised $1.5 million from angel investors and a micro-venture capital firm, lined up top manufacturers, most of whom also supply the major cosmetics companies, and introduced a line of "right-sized" makeup in simple, matte-grey packaging they sell directly to consumers. Stowaway's line meets European Union consumer safety standards, which are far more stringent than those in the United States. By asking, "do you need less?," the Stowaway team came up with a creative idea for a successful business.

Sources: Based on "How to Come Up with a Great Idea," *Wall Street Journal*, April 29, 2013, p. R1; Carren Jao, "Pared Down and Perfect," *Entrepreneur*, October 2015, p. 20; Chuck Frey, "How to Develop a Powerful Arsenal of Creative Questions," *Innovation Tools*, March 1, 2011, www.innovationtools.com/weblog/innovationblog-detail.asp?ArticleID=1570; David Lidsky, "Brain Calisthenics," *Fast Company*, December 2004, p. 95; Thea Singer, Christopher Caggiano, Ilan Mochari, and Tahl Raz, "If You Come, They Will Build It," *Inc.*, August 2002, p. 70; Creativity Web, "Question Summary," www.ozemail.com/au/~caveman/Creative/Techniques/osb_quest.html; *Bits & Pieces*, February 1990, p. 20; *Bits & Pieces*, April 29, 1993, "Creativity Quiz," *In Business*, November/December 1991, p. 18; Doug Hall, *Jump Start Your Brain* (New York: Warner Books, 1995), pp. 86–87; Christine Canabou, "Imagine That," *Fast Company*, January 2001, p. 56; Steve Gillman, "Step Out of Business Mode to Solve Problems," *Regan's Manager's eBulletin*, May 22, 2008, p. 1; Tim McKeough, " The Shape-Shifting Car," *Fast Company*, November 2008, p. 84.

are vital to a company's success (and they are!), they also should be a natural part of its culture. Integrating an attitude of innovation into a company's culture is much easier in small companies than in large ones.

Innovation can be a particularly powerful competitive weapon in industries that are resistant to change and are populated by companies that cling to the same old ways of doing business. Even small companies that are willing to innovate can have a significant impact on entire industries by shaking up the status quo with their creative approaches. The result often is growing market share and impressive profits for the innovator.

HIRE FOR CREATIVITY Research published in the *Sloan Management Review* concludes that the most effective way for companies to achieve continuous innovation over the long term is by hiring and cultivating talented people.[51] Often the most creative people also tend to be somewhat different, even eccentric. Two researchers call these employees "the odd clever people every organization needs" because they use their creativity to create disproportionate amounts of value for their companies.[52] A survey by *Inc.* asked the CEOs of the 500 fastest-growing private companies in the United States about the main contributors to their companies' ability to innovate. Their most common response: Recruiting talent (41 percent), which was cited far more often than the next two most important factors, asking customers which problems they need solved (18 percent) and creating an environment in which failure is acceptable (17 percent).[53]

EMBRACE DIVERSITY One of the best ways to cultivate a culture of creativity is to hire a diverse workforce. When people solve problems or come up with ideas, they do so within the framework of their own experience. Hiring people from different backgrounds with different cultural experiences, hobbies, and interests provides a company with a crucial raw material needed for creativity. Smart entrepreneurs enhance their organization's creativity by hiring beyond their comfort zones, bringing in capable people of diverse backgrounds, different personalities, and varied work experience, confident that this eclectic mix of people will produce creative results for their businesses.

Focusing the talent and creativity of a diverse group of employees on a problem or challenge is one of the best ways to generate creative solutions. Research by Harvard Business School professor Karim Lakhani concludes that the experiences, viewpoints, and thought processes of diverse groups of people are powerful tools for solving problems creatively. "It's very counterintuitive," says Lakhani, "but not only did the odds of a [problem] solver's success actually increase in fields outside his expertise, but also the further a challenge was from his specialty, the greater was the likelihood of success."[54] The lesson for entrepreneurs: To increase the odds of a successful creative solution to a problem, involve in the process people whose background and experience lies *outside* the particular problem area. One manager compares the input of these people to the grit that stimulates an oyster to produce a pearl.[55]

ESTABLISH AN ORGANIZATIONAL STRUCTURE THAT NOURISHES CREATIVITY John Kao, an economist whose nickname is "Mr. Creativity," says that innovative companies are structured like spaghetti rather than like a traditional pyramid. In a spaghetti-style organization, employees are encouraged to mix and mingle constantly so that creative ideas flow freely throughout the company.[56] At innovative companies, managers create organizational structures and cultures that emphasize the importance of creativity. At Taco Bell, managers recognize that innovation is one key to the 55-year-old company's success. The company's headquarters in Newport Beach, California, houses a complex of test kitchens from which most of the company's new product ideas originate. In one kitchen, a small group of employees huddle with outside consultants at a recurring event called Creationeers, where the consultants cook and serve new product ideas. In one recent session, a diverse collection of employees from various departments were tasting dishes that Creationeers were targeting at the company's younger, Generation Z customers. Liz Matthews, Taco Bell's chief food innovation officer, says that the company's strategy is to put people of different backgrounds together to have meaningful conversations and have food present. The result often is clever new ideas to add to the Taco Bell menu.[57]

EXPECT CREATIVITY Employees tend to rise—or fall—to the level of expectations entrepreneurs have of them. One of the best ways to communicate the expectation of creativity is to encourage them to be creative.

ENTREPRENEURIAL PROFILE: West Paw Design West Paw Design, a company based in Bozeman, Montana, that produces eco-friendly pet toys, sponsors a creativity contest in which its 36 employees, from president to seamstresses, form small teams to develop prototypes of new product ideas. The winning team receives the coveted Golden Hairball Award, a statue reminiscent of the Oscar but with one of the company's cat toys perched atop its head. Employees develop ideas and sketches, scrounge through bins of discarded materials, and assemble prototypes in less than two hours. The entire staff votes on a winner by secret ballot, and in addition to the Golden Hairball Award, the winning team members receive $100 gift cards. The winning team in a recent contest was composed of a sales representative, a seamstress, and a shipping department worker. Their idea: the Eco Bed, a stuffed dog bed made completely from recycled materials. West Paw included the bed in its product line, and it became an instant hit among customers.[58] ■

EXPECT FAILURE AND LEARN FROM IT Creative ideas produce failures as well as successes. People who never fail are not being creative. Creativity requires taking chances, and managers must remove employees' fear of failure. The surest way to quash creativity throughout an organization is to punish employees who try something new and fail. Failure is a natural part of the creative process; therefore, entrepreneurs must give employees the freedom to fail early and often by encouraging them to test their new ideas against the lens of reality. The key is not to attempt to avoid failures (which are inevitable) but to learn from them. Inspired by Google's well-known 20 percent policy, in which employees spend 20 percent of their time working on "pet projects" that they find interesting and believe have potential, National Public Radio (NPR) gives employees two or three days off once a quarter during the company's "Serendipity Days" to team up with people from other departments with whom they normally do not work to come up with creative ideas and projects. One purpose of the sessions is to "work with groups you wouldn't ordinarily work with through the course of your week," says Lars Schmidt, NPR's director of talent acquisition and innovation, whose team recently developed a new social media training program for the NPR staff. The goal is to "tap the creative ideas of the team and create a vehicle for getting small, cool projects and research explored," says one NPR employee. "There are some failures," he admits, which led managers to introduce a special award for these pioneers: the Penguin Award, named to honor the first bird in the flock bold enough to jump off the ice floe, knowing that he risks being eaten by a leopard seal. NPR employees have incorporated several of the ideas spawned at Serendipity Days into the company.[59]

INCORPORATE FUN INTO THE WORK ENVIRONMENT Smart entrepreneurs know that work should be fun, and although they expect employees to work hard, they create a company culture that allows employees to have fun. "If you want creative workers, give them enough time to play," says actor John Cleese. At Radio Flyer, the Chicago-based company that makes the classic little red wagon for children, employees routinely participate in fun activities at work that include karaoke, tricycle races, pumpkin-carving contests, and a Hollywood Squares game. CEO Robert Pasin has intentionally made fun events a part of the company's culture. "There's method to the madness," says the company's "chief wagon officer," pointing out that the company's success depends on creative employees who are motivated and engaged in their work.[60]

ENCOURAGE CURIOSITY Curiosity is an important ingredient in creativity. Children are innately curious, which is one reason they are so creative. Entrepreneurs and their employees should constantly ask "what if" questions and take a "maybe we could" attitude. Challenging standing assumptions about how something should be done ("We've always done it that way.") is an excellent springboard for creativity. Doing so allows people to break out of assumptions that limit creativity. Supporting employees' extracurricular activities also can spur creativity on the job. For instance, Clay Carley, owner of a real estate development company in Boise, Idaho, recently hired a local dance troupe, Trey McIntyre Project, to help him and his employees brainstorm ideas for creating a new mixed-use project in Old Boise, a historic downtown district. Carley says that the dance troupe has helped his team imagine the space in nontraditional ways. Watching the dancers perform and learning about their creative process allows him and his staff to challenge the same way they have always done things so that they can design better solutions and solve clients' problems.[61]

Encouraging employees to "think big" also helps. "Incremental innovation is not a winner's game," says creativity expert John Kao. "The opportunity these days is to become a disruptive inventor," striving for major changes that can revolutionize an entire industry and give the company creating it a significant competitive advantage.[62]

ENTREPRENEURIAL PROFILE: Joshua Silver: Adaptive Eyecare Ltd. In the 1980s, Joshua Silver, an atomic physicist at Oxford University and a lifelong tinkerer, began working to develop adjustable eyeglasses whose focusing power users could change themselves. Over time, Silver created a system of two flexible, transparent membranes with a clear silicone fluid between them. Changing the volume of fluid changes the curvature and the power of the lenses. "I did it because I was curious," says Silver of his invention. The adjustable glasses, called Adspecs, are ideal for people in developing nations, where only 5 percent of people wear eyeglasses, primarily because they live in rural areas and have no access to eye care professionals or lack the money to afford glasses. Silver's glasses come with plastic syringes filled with silicone fluid; users add or remove fluid by turning a dial that controls a small pump until the focus is right. Then they remove the syringes, and the adjustable glasses are ready to use. "All users have to do is look at a reading chart and adjust the glasses until they can see the letters clearly," says Silver, who hopes to eventually distribute a billion pairs of the glasses. "It's as simple as that."[63] ∎

DESIGN A WORKSPACE THAT ENCOURAGES CREATIVITY The physical environment in which people work has an impact on their level of creativity. The cubicles made so famous in the "Dilbert" cartoon strip can suck the creativity right out of a workspace. Transforming a typical office space—even one with cubicles—into a haven of creativity does not have to be difficult or expensive. Covering bland walls with funny posters, photographs, murals, or other artwork; adding splashes of color; and incorporating live plants enliven a work space and enhance creativity. Designs that foster employee interaction, especially informal interaction, enhance an organization's creative power. A study by the Massachusetts Institute of Technology reports that 80 percent of breakthrough innovations in products and services at companies came as a result of informal (sometimes chance) encounters among people.[64]

Many leading companies, including Google, Salesforce, and Zappos, have intentionally designed office layouts that encourage interaction among employees—informal employee "collisions." At Google, these informal encounters led to collaborations among employees that resulted in both Gmail and Street View. "We want Googlers to bump into each other and collaborate," says a company spokesperson. At Pixar, Steve Jobs insisted on placing bathrooms in the center of the building so that people working in different parts of the company would encounter one another. Salesforce has installed "lunch button" kiosks that employees can use to find other employees in the company with similar interests with whom to have lunch. Employees also can converse over meals with colleagues in other locations around the world, using a "conversation portal," a videoconferencing system set up in the dining area.[65]

VIEW PROBLEMS AS OPPORTUNITIES Every problem offers the opportunity for innovation. One of the best ways to channel a company's innovative energy productively is to address questions that focus employees' attention on customers' problems and how to solve them.

ENTREPRENEURIAL PROFILE: Kripa K. Varanski and David Smith: LiquiGlide Kripa Varanski, a professor of mechanical engineering at MIT, and David Smith, a graduate student, used their expertise to address one of life's annoying little complications: the inability to get that last bit of product out of a bottle. Research shows that 15 to 25 percent of products in plastic bottles, such as skin lotion, laundry detergents, ketchup, and mayonnaise, is wasted because it sticks to the sides of the container. Varanski and Smith developed a safe, inert coating derived from edible materials that makes the inside of containers permanently slippery so that their contents slide out easily. After winning the Audience Choice Award in a $100,000 business plan competition, the entrepreneurs launched a company, LiquiGlide, to market the coating. The company, which has attracted a $7 million venture capital investment, has acquired three patents (with a dozen more pending), employs 20 workers, and has clients in a wide variety of industries, ranging from paint companies and oil producers to food companies and glue manufacturers.[66] ∎

PROVIDE CREATIVITY TRAINING Almost everyone has the capacity to be creative, but developing that capacity requires training. One writer claims, "What separates the average person from Edison, Picasso, or even Shakespeare isn't creative capacity—it's the ability to tap that capacity by encouraging creative impulses and then acting upon them."[67] Training accomplished through books, seminars, workshops, and professional meetings can help everyone learn to tap their creative capacity. Research shows that even a single creativity training session can enhance employees' creative ability.[68]

ELIMINATE BUREAUCRATIC OBSTACLES AND PROVIDE THE SUPPORT NECESSARY FOR INNOVATION Just as a good carpenter needs the right tools to do his or her job, employees need the right resources and support to be creative, including freedom from bureaucracy to pursue their ideas. Do employees need hardware, software, certain physical spaces, time to collaborate, or other resources? Entrepreneurs also must remember that creativity often requires nonwork phases, and giving employees time to "daydream" is an important part of the creative process. The creativity that employees display when they know that managers value innovation can be amazing—and profitable. These **intrapreneurs**, entrepreneurs who operate within the framework of an existing business, sometimes can transform a company's future or advance its competitive edge. W. L. Gore, which makes more than 1,000 products but is best known for its Gore-Tex breathable, waterproof fabric, gives its employees "dabble time," allowing workers to invest 10 percent of their time working on projects in which they are interested and they believe have potential. One employee, Dave Myers, enjoyed mountain biking and was looking for a way to make his bike's gears shift more smoothly. He coated the gear cables with a Gore-Tex coating, which worked so well that Gore used the idea to introduce its line of Ride-On bicycle gear cables. That success led Myers to look for a way to improve the cables that control the animatronic figures used at venues such as Disney World and Chuck E. Cheese's. He bought some guitar strings and applied the same coating and realized that the result was superb guitar strings that lasted longer than traditional strings and kept a truer tone. Gore began selling the guitar strings under the ELIXIR brand, now the leading string in the acoustic market and the preferred string for famous artists such as Miranda Lambert and Eric Church.[69]

intrapreneurs
entrepreneurs who work within the framework of an existing business.

DEVELOP A PROCEDURE FOR CAPTURING IDEAS Small companies that are outstanding innovators do not earn that mantle by accident; they have a process in place to solicit and then collect new ideas. When workers come up with creative ideas, however, not every organization is prepared to capture them. The unfortunate result is that ideas that might have vaulted a company ahead of its competition or made people's lives better simply evaporate. Without a structured approach for collecting employees' creative concepts, a business leaves its future to chance. Clever entrepreneurs establish processes within their companies that are designed to harvest the results of employees' creativity. At Lark Technologies, a Mountain View, California–based consumer electronics company that makes wearable wellness monitors and a vibrating silent alarm clock, most of the walls are made of whiteboards on which employees write out and draw sketches of new product ideas and post problems that they have not been able to solve. Company founder and CEO Julia Hu says that employees constantly add to each other's ideas on the walls, creating an ongoing brainstorming session that has helped the young company expand its product line beyond its original vibrating silent alarm clock that links to an iPhone or iPod and that awakens only the person wearing it to include a diet, exercise, and sleep monitoring and feedback system. *Fast Company* magazine recently named Lark Technologies one of the 10 most innovative consumer electronics companies in the United States.[70]

LISTEN TO CUSTOMERS—OR, BETTER YET, USE THE WISDOM OF THE CROWD Sometimes the best ideas for new products and services or new applications of existing products and services come from a company's customers. Innovative companies take the time to get feedback about how customers use the companies' products or services, listening for new ideas. The voice of the customer can be an important source of creative ideas, and the Internet allows entrepreneurs to hear their customers' voices quickly and inexpensively. Some companies engage their customers in social media conversations (or at least read what customers are writing about their products in social media); others observe their customers actually using their products or services to glean ideas that may lead to improvements and new features. Others encourage customers to contribute ideas and designs through crowdsourcing.

ENTREPRENEURIAL PROFILE: Chris Lindland and Enrique Landa: BetaBrand Beta-Brand, an apparel maker based in San Francisco that is famous for its unique clothing, offers a crowdsourcing section on its Web site that features clothing designs and ideas on which visitors vote. The company makes prototypes of crowd favorites that it then posts in a "crowd-funding" process. If a sufficient number of customers place orders for an item, BetaBrand manufactures it. Fewer than one-third of the items that people propose advance to the prototype stage, and, of those, about 60 percent survive the gauntlet of crowdfunding and make it into production. Some of BetaBrand's most successful crowdsourced items have included a quilted travel blazer, black travel yoga pants, chef jeans (loaded with many kitchen-friendly features), an ultra-slim laptop backpack that fits beneath a jacket, and a low-profile "wholester" that can carry almost everything that a busy young professional might need.[71] ∎

MONITOR EMERGING TRENDS AND IDENTIFY WAYS YOUR COMPANY CAN CAPITALIZE ON THEM

Detecting meaningful trends in their earliest phases enables a company to capitalize on them with creative solutions. Taco Bell, the quick-service Tex-Mex restaurant chain with more than 6,400 locations, invests resources in monitoring demographic and social trends that influence customers' dining habits. Two trends that the company recently identified among its young post-Millennial Generation Z customers are their preference for natural, healthy food and their penchant for spicy foods. To capitalize on these trends, Taco Bell is testing a variety of new items, including a Yellowbird Queso Quesalupa with Kimchi fried rice, a roasted veggie quinoa taco, and a vegetarian, gluten-free mushroom raja taco. Taco Bell also constantly works on innovations in its processes, including packaging, marketing, and restaurant design. One team is working on a new layout for its stores that includes an open kitchen that allows customers to see ingredients and watch cooks prepare them.[72]

LOOK FOR USES FOR YOUR COMPANY'S PRODUCTS OR SERVICES IN OTHER MARKETS

Focusing on the "traditional" uses of a product or service limits creativity—and a company's sales. Entrepreneurs can boost sales by finding new applications, often in unexpected places, for their products and services.

ENTREPRENEURIAL PROFILE: Charles Yost: Dynamic Systems Inc. Charles Yost led a team of NASA engineers who developed a unique pressure-absorbing material called viscoelastic polyurethane foam to protect astronauts during reentry. Later, Yost started a company, Dynamic Systems Inc., to develop commercial applications of the "temper foam," ultimately finding uses for it in sports helmets, ejection seats, and ski boots. A Swedish company, Fagerdala World Foams, licensed the foam and used it to make Tempur-Pedic mattresses, one of the most popular lines of mattresses in the world.[73] ∎

REWARD CREATIVITY Entrepreneurs can encourage creativity by rewarding it when it occurs. Financial rewards can be effective motivators of creative behavior, but nonmonetary rewards, such as praise, recognition, and celebration, usually offer more powerful incentives for creativity.

ENTREPRENEURIAL PROFILE: Mike Tattersfield: Caribou Coffee At Caribou Coffee, a chain of coffee shops with nearly 500 locations in the United States and abroad, CEO Mike Tattersfield, whose desk doubles as a foosball table, celebrates employees' creative contributions to the company at an awards banquet, where winners receive watermelons as prizes. "You get it for using your melon," explains Tattersfield. The company also awards winners with a pair of custom Converse Chuck Taylor tennis shoes that they themselves design and that Tattersfield inscribes with a personal note of thanks. "All I ask is that they send me a photo of them wearing the sneakers," he says.[74] ∎

MODEL CREATIVE BEHAVIOR Creativity is "caught" as much as it is "taught." Companies that excel at innovation find that the passion for creativity starts at the top. Entrepreneurs who set examples of creative behavior, taking chances, and challenging the status quo will soon find their employees doing the same. "Innovative companies are led by innovative chief executives," says creativity expert Hal Gregersen. "They spend their time asking provocative questions, observing the world, and networking with people who don't think, act, or talk like them. They are willing to experiment and try new things. It's the CEO who sets the stage for innovation."[75]

ENTREPRENEURIAL PROFILE: Jason Fried: 37signals Jason Fried, cofounder of 37signals, a Chicago-based software company, compares his company's product line to the apple trees on his farm. Fried routinely prunes his apple trees to give them a stronger foundation for future growth. Fried applies that same logic to his company, regularly pruning the company's software products. Observers were stunned when Fried sold to another business a service that generated $17,000 per month in profit for 37signals. A few months later, however, at a company meeting, the staff came up with ideas for two new products, one a variation of an existing product, and the other a totally new product. Fried says that the ideas never would have emerged without the decision to cut the company's existing products. Like a tree, a company cannot produce strong new limbs unless someone prunes the old ones.[76] ∎

DON'T FORGET ABOUT BUSINESS MODEL INNOVATION As Jason Fried's experience suggests, creating new products and services is the lifeblood of a company's long-term success; however, business model innovations can produce significant impact on a business as well. A study by the consulting firm Doblin Group reveals that although companies focus most of their creative resources on developing new products and product extensions, those investments are least likely to produce a positive return. In fact, the success rate for new products and product extensions is just 4.5 percent. Innovations in a company's business model, customer service process, distribution system, customer value stream, and internal processes produce higher rates of return.[77] Amazon's Kindle e-reader tablet has proved to be a valuable business model innovation. Although the company generates only a small profit on sales of its Kindle tablet reader, its real profit engine is the content it sells to Kindle users, including books, apps, movies, music, and more. Kindle owners spend an average of $1,233 per year on Amazon purchases compared to $790 per year for non-Kindle owners. Experts estimate that to achieve an impressive 20 percent profit margin on a Kindle unit, Amazon must sell just $10 per month in content sales.[78]

Enhancing Individual Creativity

Just as entrepreneurs can cultivate an environment of creativity in their organizations by using the techniques described above, they can enhance their own creativity by using the techniques discussed in the following section.

ALLOW YOURSELF TO BE CREATIVE As we have seen, one of the biggest obstacles to creativity occurs when a person believes that he or she is not creative. One recent survey reports that 73 percent of U.S. workers believe they are creative, but only 42 percent of them believe their jobs allow them to be creative.[79] Giving yourself the permission to be creative is the first step toward establishing a pattern of creative thinking. Refuse to give in to the temptation to ignore ideas simply because you fear that someone else may consider them "stupid." When it comes to creativity, there are no stupid ideas!

FORGET THE "RULES" Creative individuals take a cue from Captain Jack Sparrow in the *Pirates of the Caribbean* series of movies. When faced with a difficult (sometimes impossible) situation, Sparrow (played by Johnny Depp) usually operates outside the rules and, as a result, comes up with innovative solutions. Sparrow's unwillingness to be encumbered by rules frees him to develop innovative, often unusual, solutions to the problems he encounters.

GIVE YOUR MIND FRESH INPUT EVERY DAY To be creative, your mind needs stimulation. Imagination is the fuel that drives creativity. Do something different each day—listen to a new radio station, take a walk through a park or a shopping center, or pick up a magazine you've never read—to stimulate your imagination. Jay Walker, founder of Priceline.com, says that imagination is a prerequisite for innovation.[80]

ENTREPRENEURIAL PROFILE: New York Police Department The New York City Police Department recently began an innovative training program to improve its officers' visual acuity when approaching a crime scene or an incident. By taking tours of the classic works of art in the Metropolitan Museum of Art, officers enhance their observation and interpretation skills while viewing the details of paintings such as Vermeer's "Mistress and a Maid" and explaining their perception of what is taking place in the scene: Who has done what to whom? Who is the perpetrator?[81] ■

TAKE UP A HOBBY Hobbies provide an avenue to escape your regular routine, and they also give your mind fresh input that can be a source of creative ideas. One study concludes that employees who have creative hobbies are more likely to be creative and collaborative.[82]

TRAVEL—AND OBSERVE Visiting other countries (even other states) is a creativity stimulant. Travelers see new concepts and engage in new experiences that can spark creative ideas.

Sam Hodgson/The New York Times/Redux

ENTREPRENEURIAL PROFILE: Arianne and Scott Bennett: Amsterdam Falafelshop
After Arianne and Scott Bennett discovered falafel, a dish of ancient origin from the Middle East made from chickpeas, on a trip to Amsterdam, the Netherlands, they decided to open their own falafel shop with a do-it-yourself toppings bar similar to the one they encountered on their travels. They opened Amsterdam Falafelshop in Washington, DC's Adams Morgan neighborhood, and it soon became a popular destination for residents and tourists alike. With its expansive list of toppings, the menu, which is all vegetarian, offers nearly 4.2 million variations of falafel and a popular side item, Dutch-style fries with flavorful dipping sauces; everything is made in-house. Amsterdam Falafelshop is growing fast, and the Bennetts now have six franchised locations in Washington, DC, Virginia, and Boston.[83] ∎

COLLABORATE WITH OTHER PEOPLE Working with other people, particularly people from different backgrounds, is an excellent way to stimulate creativity. When he invented the lightbulb, Thomas Edison's team included chemists, mathematicians, and glassblowers.[84] "You need a group composed of individuals who bring different perspectives to the table, who respect different working styles, and who resolve conflicts along the way," says Tina Seelig, an expert in creativity. "Great teams also have a healthy dose of playfulness," she adds.[85]

OBSERVE THE PRODUCTS AND SERVICES OF OTHER COMPANIES, ESPECIALLY THOSE IN COMPLETELY DIFFERENT MARKETS Creative entrepreneurs often borrow ideas from companies that are in businesses totally unrelated to their own and then apply those ideas to their own companies and industries. Angela Benton, founder of NewME Accelerator, advises business owners to look outside their industries to see how other companies are solving problems, pointing out that standard practices in other industries may inspire innovative ideas.[86]

ENTREPRENEURIAL PROFILE: Jerry Barber: Barber Wind Turbines In 1971, Jerry Barber started Venture Ride Manufacturing, a company that produced amusement rides in Greenville, South Carolina. Over the course of the next 18 years, his small business grew to employ 70 people and earned many patents for its amusement ride designs. He sold the company in 1989 and became interested in wind turbines after having a conversation with an old friend who was delivering an SUV-sized gearbox assembly for a wind turbine. Drawing from his years of designing amusement rides, Barber came up with a design for a wind turbine that does not require a gearbox, which costs $250,000 and lasts only 20 years. Barber's turbines have five blades (rather than the traditional three blades) inside a ring, and wheels on the edge of the ring, which are similar to those on a Ferris wheel, turn the generator to produce electricity.[87] ∎

RECOGNIZE THE CREATIVE POWER OF MISTAKES AND ACCIDENTS Innovations sometimes are the result of serendipity, finding something while looking for something else, and sometimes they arise as a result of mistakes or accidents. Creative people recognize that even their errors may lead to new ideas, products, and services. "I would love to get to a place in my life where I can laugh at my failures," says one successful song writer, "because for every failed creative attempt, I'm closer to a successful one."[88] Louis Daguerre, a scene painter for the Paris Opera, was fascinated with lighting and in 1822 began conducting experiments with the effect of light on translucent screens. In 1829, Daguerre formed a partnership with Joseph Niépce, who had invented a primitive version of photography called the heliograph the same year. (The exposure time for Niépce's first photograph was a mere eight hours!) The two men worked for years trying to capture photographic images on metal plates treated with silver iodide, but they made little progress before Niépce died in 1833. One evening in 1835, Daguerre placed one of his treated plates in his chemical cupboard, intending to recoat it for other experiments. When he removed it later, he was surprised to see a photographic image with brilliant highlights. Excited but puzzled by the outcome, Daguerre finally discovered that mercury vapors from a broken thermometer in the cupboard had caused the photographic image to appear on the treated metal plate. Daguerre refined the process he found by accident, named it Daguerreotype after himself, and the world of modern photography was born.[89]

BE POSITIVE A negative outlook drains creative capacity and undermines the brain's ability to generate creative solutions. Research shows that positive emotions increase creativity and high-performance behavior. Barbara Fredrickson, a pioneer in this area of research, says that positive emotions expand one's awareness and attention.[90] The good news: Entrepreneurs tend to be optimistic and resilient.

NOTICE WHAT IS MISSING Sometimes entrepreneurs spot viable business opportunities by noticing something, often very practical and simple, that is *missing*. The first step is to determine whether a market for the missing product or service actually exists (perhaps the reason it does not exist is that there is no market potential), which is one of the objectives of building a business plan.

ENTREPRENEURIAL PROFILE: Shawn Boyer: Snagajob Shawn Boyer was trying to help a friend who was finishing her doctorate in an obscure liberal arts field land an internship and noticed that existing job search sites focused on salaried jobs but offered no listings for people seeking internships or hourly jobs. As entrepreneurs are wont to do, Boyer decided to capitalize on the opportunity he spotted and launched Snagajob, a Web site that lists available full-time and part-time hourly jobs. He quit his job, cashed out his retirement account, and borrowed a significant chunk of money from his parents to start his business. Today, Snagajob has more than 70 million registered job seekers and 45,000 registered employers of all sizes, and it helps nearly 1 million people find hourly jobs each year.[91] ■

PERIODICALLY ASK YOURSELF, "AM I ASKING THE RIGHT QUESTIONS?" Sometimes creative flashes come when we change our perspective and ask questions that frame a problem or situation in a different light.

ENTREPRENEURIAL PROFILE: Yuri Malina and Mert Iseri: SwipeSense While Yuri Malina was a student at Northwestern University, he cofounded Design for America, an organization that helps students create solutions for various social problems, with fellow student Mert Iseri and a faculty member. Malina discovered that hospital-acquired infections, most of which originate because of improper hand washing among healthcare professionals, cause more than 100,000 deaths each year in the United States. Although hospitals provide plenty of hand-sanitizing stations, healthcare professionals do not always use them. To solve the vexing problem, Malina and his team observed doctors and nurses at a local hospital and realized that they were so busy helping patients that they were constantly on the move. Malina realized that hospitals were asking the wrong question: "How can we convince healthcare professionals to comply with handwashing requirements?" Malina and his team posed a different question: "How can we provide a nonintrusive solution to hand sanitizing that meshes with healthcare professionals' work habits and busy schedules?" That led Malina's team to develop SwipeSense, a smart phone-sized hand-sanitizing device that attaches to a healthcare professional's belt or waistband and allows busy doctors and nurses to clean their hands as they move from one patient to the next. Malina and his team have a patent for their device and have raised $12.1 million in equity capital across six rounds of fund-raising.[92] ■

Coutesy of Yuri Malina and Mert Iseri, SwipeSense

KEEP A JOURNAL HANDY TO RECORD YOUR THOUGHTS AND IDEAS Creative ideas are too valuable to waste, so always keep a journal nearby to record them as soon as you get them. Leonardo da Vinci was famous for writing down ideas as they struck him. Patrick McNaughton invented the neon blackboards that restaurants use to advertise their specials. In addition to the neon blackboard, McNaughton has invented more than 30 new products, many of which are sold through the company that he and his sister, Jamie, own. McNaughton credits much of his creative success to the fact that he writes down every idea he gets and keeps it in a special folder. "There's no such thing as a crazy idea," he insists.[93]

LISTEN TO OTHER PEOPLE No rule of creativity says that an idea has to be your own! Sometimes the best business ideas come from someone else, but entrepreneurs are the ones to act on them.

ENTREPRENEURIAL PROFILE: James N. P. O'Brien, Casey Perkal, and Tim Jeon: ShaveFace After a friend told James N. P. O'Brien that disposable razor blades could be sharpened on denim and reused, O'Brien, a musician, began experimenting with the idea. His experiments with an old pair of jeans were successful, so O'Brien asked a friend who was a tailor to transform the jeans into a denim strop, like the leather straps that barbers once used to sharpen their straight razors, with leather trip and brass fittings for hanging on a towel rack. While attending a wedding, he met Casey Perkal, a recent law school graduate who was interested in start-ups, and Tim Jeon, a financial consultant, and showed them photos of his denim strop. The trio invested $10,000 of their own money to start a company, ShaveFace, and fund a small production run of denim strops, build a Web site, and create a series of videos to post online. Sales began to grow, and the young entrepreneurs used Kickstarter to raise $60,000, well above their $24,000 goal, to ramp up production of their denim strops. O'Brien, Perkal, and Jeon say that their strop can extend the life of any disposable razor, saving the user up to $100 per year on razors. Today, ShaveFace, based in Nashville, Tennessee, is adding other shaving items to its product line and lining up independent retail outlets as part of its strategy to increase sales.[94] ∎

GET ADEQUATE SLEEP Sleep restores both our bodies and our brains. A study by the Mental Health Foundation shows a correlation between sound sleep and a person's ability to produce creative ideas and new insights.[95]

WATCH A MOVIE Great business ideas come from the strangest places, even the movies. As a child, Stanley Yang was fascinated by sci-fi movies such as *Star Wars*. That fascination led him to become an engineer so that he could transform his ideas into reality. Yang's company, NeuroSky, has developed headsets that allow people to control video games with their minds, using biosensor technology, a concept used by an advanced alien race in the movie *Battle Los Angeles*. Yang, who still dreams of building a functional light saber, says that watching a movie can spark a creative idea.[96]

GO FOR A WALK Research at Stanford University suggests that taking a walk, even a short one, boosts a person's creative capacity. Although researchers do not fully understand the process, their work shows that creative thinking improves while a person is walking and for a short time afterward. Steve Jobs, the late cofounder and visionary of Apple, was famous for conducting walking meetings, and many other entrepreneurs, including Mark Zuckerberg, founder of Facebook, follow the practice.[97]

TALK TO A CHILD As we grow older, we learn to conform to society's expectations about many things, including creative solutions to problems. Children place very few limitations on their thinking; as a result, their creativity is practically boundless. (Remember all the games you and your friends invented when you were young?)

DO SOMETHING ORDINARY IN AN UNUSUAL WAY Experts say that simply doing something out of the ordinary can stimulate creativity. To stimulate his own creativity, Scott Jones, an entrepreneur who is known as "the guy who invented voice mail" (and many other items as well), often engages in what other people might consider bizarre behavior—eating without utensils, watching television sitting one foot away from the screen, or taking a shower with his eyes closed. "Anything I normally do, I'll do differently just to see what happens," says Jones.[98]

KEEP A TOY BOX IN YOUR OFFICE Your box might include silly objects such as wax lips, a yo-yo, a Slinky, fortune cookie sayings, feathers, a top, a compass, or a host of other items. When you are stumped, pick an item at random from the toy box and think about how it relates to your problem.

TAKE NOTE OF YOUR "PAIN POINTS": DO OTHER PEOPLE EXPERIENCE THEM AS WELL? Entrepreneurs often create innovations to solve problems they themselves face. Observing "pain points" that result from missing products or services or flaws in existing products or services can be an excellent source of business ideas.

ENTREPRENEURIAL PROFILE: Michael Tunney: KeySmart Michael Tunney, a robotics engineer in the auto industry, was annoyed by the bulky key ring he carried in his pocket because the keys jabbed his leg. One evening, while sitting at a bar, he looked down and saw a long line of keys sitting on the bar and realized that he was not the only person with the same problem. His pain point led him to invent the KeySmart, a streamlined device made of aircraft-grade aluminum, titanium, and stainless steel that stacks between 4 and 100 keys neatly and conveniently. At a friend's suggestion, Tunney launched a Kickstarter campaign seeking to raise $6,000 to build a prototype and ended up raising $330,000. Tunney quit his engineering job to focus on KeySmart, which he now sells through the company's Web site (www.getkeysmart.com) and through major retail outlets. Tunney also has introduced a USB drive and a bottle opener using the same materials and design.[99] ∎

DO NOT THROW AWAY SEEMINGLY "BAD" IDEAS Some creative ideas prove to be impractical, too costly, or too silly to work. Creative entrepreneurs, however, do not discard these seemingly bad ideas. Instead, they ask, "What part of this idea can I build on?" and "What could I change about this idea to make it work?" They realize that seemingly bad ideas can be the nucleus of a really good idea. Spencer Williams, president of West Paw Design, the company that encourages creativity with its creativity contest featuring the Golden Hairball Award, says that many of the great ideas for new products come from ideas that don't win the contest. The company's R&D team meets after each contest to review *all* of the ideas that employees submit. "We look for one piece of a new idea," he says.[100]

Courtesy of KeySmart Corporation

COLLABORATE WITH OTHERS Working with other people to solve a problem or to generate ideas brings a fresh perspective to the situation. Two or more people usually are more creative than one person working alone.

READ BOOKS ON STIMULATING CREATIVITY OR TAKE A CLASS ON CREATIVITY Creative thinking is a technique that anyone can learn. Understanding and applying the principles of creativity can improve dramatically the ability to develop new and innovative ideas.

DOODLE Research shows that engaging in artistic activities, even as simple as doodling, stimulates creativity.[101] Doodling keeps a person's brain engaged even when he or she is not focused on a particular task.

TAKE SOME TIME OFF Relaxation is vital to the creative process. Getting away from a problem gives the mind time to reflect on it. It is often while the subconscious works on a problem that the mind generates many creative solutions. One study reports that 35 percent of entrepreneurs say that they come up with their best ideas during downtime, when they are away from work.[102] One creativity expert claims that fishing is the ideal activity for stimulating creativity. "Your brain is on high alert in case a fish is around," he says, "but your brain is completely relaxed. This combination is the time when you have the 'Aha!' moment."[103]

BE PERSISTENT Entrepreneurs know that one secret to success is persistence—a "don't quit" attitude. A dozen publishers rejected J. K. Rowling's manuscript about the adventures of a boy wizard and his friends, which she started writing at age 25 when she was a single mother trying to raise her children on welfare, before Bloomsbury, a small London publishing house, agreed to publish 1,000 copies of *Harry Potter and the Philosopher's Stone*. Rowling's seven-part Harry Potter book series went on to sell more than 450 million copies worldwide, making Rowling the first billionaire author.[104]

The Creative Process

Although creative ideas may appear to strike as suddenly as a bolt of lightning, they are actually the result of the creative process, which involves seven steps:

LO5

Describe the steps in the creative process.

    Step 1. Preparation

    Step 2. Investigation

    Step 3. Transformation

    Step 4. Incubation

    Step 5. Illumination

    Step 6. Verification

    Step 7. Implementation

Hands On . . . How To

Create a Culture of Creativity and Innovation

Creativity and innovation are important drivers of the global economy, allowing companies that use them well to prosper and providing consumers with products and services that make their lives better. A recent study by marketing communications firm MDC Partners reports that 98 percent of top executives say that creativity is critical to economic success; in addition, 76 percent of the managers believe that the world has entered an "imagination economy," in which companies' ability to harness the power of creativity determines their success. How can a company create a culture that promotes creativity among its employees and allows it to use innovation to gain a competitive advantage over its rivals? The following seven tips can help.

Ignite Passion

The philosopher Denis Diderot said, "Only passions, great passions, can elevate the soul to great things." So it is with creativity. The most basic ingredient for building a creative company culture is a passion to discover something new, to contribute to the betterment of society, and to make a difference. That passion starts at the top of an organization with the entrepreneur. Steve Jobs, cofounder of Apple Inc., often said that he wanted "to put a ding in the universe," an attitude that led his company to introduce many innovative products. When Jobs died in 2011, many observers noted how in his brief career he truly had changed the world. Your job as leader is to make sure that your passion for creativity spreads to everyone in your company.

Celebrate Creative Ideas

In some companies, people who come up with new ideas learn quickly that the organization does not value creativity and risk taking and shies away from ideas that might fail. Smart entrepreneurs, however, recognize that the only way to move their companies forward is to take measured risks by implementing creative ideas that have potential. In fact, these entrepreneurs reward employees (and not just financially, although that helps) who develop creative ideas and innovative solutions to problems even if they fail. They understand that even though one idea fails, the next idea might be "the big one." Celebrating creative ideas with praise (both public and private), promotions, and cash sends a clear signal to employees that a company values creativity.

Foster Autonomy

"The act of creativity is one of self-expression," says serial entrepreneur Josh Linkner. To be creative, employees must have the freedom to make decisions and call their own shots. Micromanaging saps creativity out of any organization. Smart entrepreneurs know that their job is to focus employees' efforts on the problems to solve and then to get out of their way and let them do it. "We challenge our employees to be their own CEOs," says Dan Satterwaithe, director of human resources at DreamWorks Animation,

the animated filmmaker. Delegating authority and responsibility requires an atmosphere of trust, which increases the likelihood that employees are engaged in their work and buy into the company's mission. The key is letting employees know that you value their ideas, creativity, and judgment.

Encourage Courage

Some companies actually discourage creativity and innovation by punishing those who dare to take chances and fail. Businesses that succeed over time have cultures that encourage employees to be bold enough to take creative chances without fear of repercussions. At DreamWorks Animation, managers regularly solicit ideas from every employee—and not just those in the creative side of the business. Accountants, administrative assistants, lawyers—anyone—can (and do) submit ideas for everything from story lines for new movies to improving a business system.

Fail Forward

The most creative companies have built cultures that encourage people to try new ideas and recognize that many (perhaps most) of them will fail. Companies that punish failure end up with a cadre of employees who simply keep their heads down, never step out of line, and produce only mediocre results. "Failing forward means taking risks and increasing the rate of experimentation," says Josh Linkner. The key is to fail quickly, learn from the failure, make necessary adjustments, and try again.

Ensure Interaction

Creative managers know that one of the best ways to stimulate creativity is to ensure that employees interact with one another. At DreamWorks Animation, employees use cloud computing technology to collaborate on projects, but managers also insist on face-to-face interactions, both formal and informal, because they know that's where many creative ideas originate. Many companies that cultivate creativity establish work spaces that encourage employees to interact with one another and talk about new ideas.

Maximize Diversity

Companies have discovered that hiring workers from different cultures, with varied backgrounds, and with diverse work experience enhances creativity. The 120 employees at Ziba, an innovation consulting firm in Portland, Oregon, come from 18 different countries and speak 26 different languages. "Genetic diversity breeds creativity, much like it does with biology," says Sohrab Vossoughi, the company's founder and CEO. To encourage creativity, Ziba implemented an "Ambassador Program," in which employees spend three months working in other areas of the company, which are known as tribes. "This helps create an understanding of another world," says Vossoughi.

(continued)

Hands On . . . How To

1. Do you agree with the top managers in the MDC Partners survey who say that we have entered an "imagination economy"? Explain.

2. List and describe two additional steps that a company can take to create a culture of creativity and innovation.

Sources: Based on Josh Linkner, "7 Steps to a Culture of Innovation," *Inc.*, June 16, 2011, www.inc.com/articles/201106/josh-linkner-7-steps-to-a-culture-of-innovation.html; Anita Bruzzese, "DreamWorks Is Believer in Every Employee's Creativity," *USA Today*, http://usatoday30.usatoday.com/money/jobcenter/workplace/bruzzese/story/2012-07-22/dreamworks-values-innovation-in-all-workers/56376470/1; "MDC Partners and Allison and Partners Study Reveals Leading CEOs and CMOs View Creativity as a Critical Driver of the Global Economy," *Business Wire*, October 4, 2011, www.businesswire.com/news/home/20111004005439/en/MDC-Partners-Allison-Partners-Study-Reveals-Leading.

Step 1. Preparation

This step involves getting the mind ready for creative thinking. Preparation might include a formal education, on-the-job training, work experience, and taking advantage of other learning opportunities. This training provides a foundation on which to build creativity and innovation. As one writer explains, "Creativity favors the prepared mind."[105] For example, Dr. Hamel Navia, a scientist at tiny Vertex Pharmaceuticals, was working on a promising new drug to fight the AIDS virus. His preparation included earning an advanced degree in the field of medicine and learning to use computers to create 3-D images of the protein molecules he was studying.[106] How can you prepare your mind for creative thinking?

- Adopt the attitude of a lifelong student. Realize that educating yourself is a never-ending process. Look at every situation you encounter as an opportunity to learn.

ENTREPRENEURIAL PROFILE: Scientific Anglers: Sharkwave Fly Line To develop a new fly line that reduces drag and allows anglers to cast flies more easily, researchers at Scientific Anglers studied how some insects can walk on the surface of the water, the leaves of the lotus plant can clean themselves, and geckos can easily cling to almost any surface. Their research led them to develop a process that embosses the fly line, which they named Sharkwave, with a repeating geometric micropattern that mimics those found in nature and minimizes the line's contact with the rod's guides, greatly reducing friction and allowing the fisherman to cast more easily and to make longer casts. The line, which has a texture like sharkskin, is a radical departure from the traditional smooth-surface fly line that fly fishers have used for decades.[107] ■

- Read—a lot—and not just in your field of expertise. Many innovations come from blending ideas and concepts from different fields in science, engineering, business, and the arts. Reading books, magazines, and papers covering a variety of subject matter is a great way to stimulate your creativity.

- Clip articles that interest you and create a file for them. Over time, you will build a customized encyclopedia of information from which to draw ideas and inspiration.

- Take time to discuss your ideas with other people, including those who know little about it as well as experts in the field. Sometimes, the apparently simple questions an "unknowledgeable" person asks lead to new discoveries and to new approaches to an old problem. At Fahrenheit 212, an innovation consulting firm based in New York City, founder Mark Payne encourages employees to interact with one another to come up with new ideas and solutions to clients' problems. Almost every wall in the creative offices is made of glass, and markers are placed everywhere, allowing employees to sketch ideas as they discover them and to talk about them with coworkers. The work space follows an open design that encourages wandering around, which leads to a spontaneous combustion of ideas, says Payne.[108]

- Join professional or trade associations and attend their meetings. There you have the chance to interact with others who have similar interests. Learning how other people have solved a particular problem may give you fresh insight into solving it.

- Develop listening skills. It's amazing what you can learn if you take the time to listen to other people—especially those who are older and have more experience. Try to learn something from everyone you meet.

- Eliminate creative distractions. Interruptions from telephone calls, e-mails, social media, and visitors can crush creativity. Allowing employees to escape to a quiet, interruption-free environment enhances their ability to be creative.

Step 2. Investigation

This step involves developing a solid understanding of the problem, situation, or decision at hand. To create new ideas and concepts in a particular field, an individual first must study the problem and understand its basic components. Creative thinking comes about when people make careful observations of the world around them and then investigate the way things work (or fail to work). For example, Dr. Navia and another scientist at Vertex had spent several years conducting research on viruses and on a protein that blocks a virus enzyme called protease. His exploration of the various ways to block this enzyme paved the way for his discovery.

ENTREPRENEURIAL PROFILE: Christopher Leamon: Endocyte After earning a PhD in chemistry, Christopher Leamon began researching targeted anticancer therapy using molecules that tumors absorb as "Trojan horses" to deliver drugs that are lethal to them. Initially, Leamon had focused on the vitamin biotin, but after nine months of research and hard work, his experiment was a failure. One morning while sitting at the breakfast table with his wife, Leamon, a longtime cereal lover, was reading the ingredients on the nutrition panel of his box of Kellogg's Frosted Flakes. One of the items, folic acid, caught his attention. Leamon dashed off to the library and found a research paper on how folic acid enters a human cell and realized that this was the breakthrough he had been seeking. Before long, Leamon had developed a technique for attaching cancer drugs to folic acid so that they would be absorbed and enable the cells to fight the disease in much the same way they battle infections. Leamon has licensed the promising therapy to a company called Endocyte, which plans to have drugs on the market within a few years. Leamon says that although he had experienced "Eureka!" moments in the lab, none was as significant as his folic acid breakthrough.[109] ■

Step 3. Transformation

Transformation involves viewing the similarities and differences in the information collected. This phase requires two types of thinking: convergent and divergent. **Convergent thinking** is the ability to see the *similarities* and the connections among various and often diverse data and events. "So much of innovation comes from connecting things where other people don't make connections," says Mark Rice, professor of technology entrepreneurship at Olin College.[110] Johannes Gutenberg made a connection between a common device of his day, the wine press, and a machine he invented that relied on the same principle to print books cheaply and efficiently using movable blocks of letters and graphics. His printing press is often cited as one of the most important inventions in the history of the world.

Divergent thinking is the ability to see the *differences* among various data and events. While developing his AIDS-fighting drug, Dr. Navia studied the work of other scientists whose attempts at developing an enzyme-blocking drug had failed. He was able to see the similarities and the differences in his research and theirs and to build on their successes while avoiding their failures.

How can you increase your ability to transform the information collected into a purposeful idea?

- Evaluate the parts of the situation several times, trying to grasp the big picture. Getting bogged down in the details of a situation too early in the creative process can diminish creativity. Look for patterns that emerge and for connections among things that on the surface do not appear to be connected, a process known as global processing.

- Rearrange the elements of the situation. By looking at the components of an issue in a different order or from a different perspective, you may be able to see the similarities and the differences among them more readily. Rearranging them also may help uncover a familiar

convergent thinking
the ability to see the similarities and the connections among various and often diverse data and events.

divergent thinking
the ability to see the differences among various data and events.

pattern that had been masked by an unfamiliar structure. Engineers at Windtronics, a company in Muskegon, Michigan, rearranged the elements of a traditional power-generating wind turbine, moving them from the center to the outside of the blades. As a result, the blades of Windtronics turbines turn faster, operate more quietly and efficiently, and can generate electricity at wind speeds as low as 2 miles per hour, compared to 6 to 8 miles per hour for traditional turbines. At just 6 feet in diameter, Windtronics turbines are suitable for industrial, commercial, and residential use.[111]

- Try using synectics (a term derived from the Greek words for "to bring together" and "diversity"), taking two seemingly nonsensical ideas and combining them. For example, why not launch a bookstore with no physical storefront and no books—an accurate description of what Jeff Bezos did when he came up with the original idea for Amazon.com.[112]

- Before locking into one particular approach to a situation, remember that several approaches might be successful. If one approach produces a dead end, don't hesitate to jump quickly to another. Considering several approaches to a problem or an opportunity simultaneously would be like rolling a bowling ball down each of several lanes in quick succession. The more balls you roll down the lanes, the greater the probability of hitting at least one strike. Resist the temptation to make snap judgments on how to tackle a problem or an opportunity. The first approach may not be the best one.

Step 4. Incubation

Often, ideas require a gestation period. The subconscious needs time to reflect on the information collected. To an observer, this phase of the creative process would be quite boring; it looks as though nothing is happening! In fact, during this phase, it may appear that the creative person is *loafing*. Incubation occurs while the individual is away from the problem, often engaging in some totally unrelated activity. Research shows that walking away from a problem to engage in routine tasks sparks creativity.[113] Dr. Navia's creative powers were working at a subconscious level even when he was away from his work, not even thinking about his research on AIDS-fighting drugs.

How can you enhance the incubation phase of the creative process, letting ideas marinate in your mind?

- Walk away from the situation. Time away from a problem is vital to enhancing creativity. A study by Wilson Brill, an expert on creativity, of how 350 great ideas became successful products shows that two-thirds of the ideas came to people while they were *away* from work—in the shower, in their cars, in bed, on a walk, and in other nonwork situations.[114] Doing something totally unrelated to the problem gives your subconscious mind the chance to work on the problem or opportunity.

ENTREPRENEURIAL PROFILE: Amy Baxter: Buzzy For years, Amy Baxter, a physician and pain researcher, had been searching for a way to use cold to relieve the pain of children's vaccinations. While driving home from an all-night shift in the emergency room, she noticed that the steering wheel on her car was vibrating (her tires were badly misaligned). When she got out of her car, her hands were numb from the vibration. That's when the idea hit her: Combining vibration and cold temperatures could desensitize a vaccination site. To test her idea, she applied a frozen bag of peas and a vibrating massager to her son's arm and then rolled a small metal wheel used by neurologists over the area, and he could feel nothing. Baxter went on to invent Buzzy, a bee-shaped cold pack outfitted with a vibrating device that more than 500 hospitals and doctors' offices now use before administering vaccinations.[115] ∎

- Take the time to daydream. Creative people build time into their schedules to allow their minds to wander. Although it may *look* as if you're doing nothing, daydreaming is an important part of the creative process. That's when your mind is most free from self-imposed restrictions on creativity. Research shows a connection between daydreaming and creativity; people who daydream are better at generating new ideas.[116] Feel free to let your mind wander, and it may just stumble onto a creative solution.

ENTREPRENEURIAL PROFILE: John Stapleton: 22squared John Stapleton, an ad executive at 22squared in Atlanta, Georgia, had worked without success for weeks to come up with a campaign to encourage people to visit Costa Rica. Only when he left his office, traveled to Costa Rica, and began to relax on the patio at a resort in the midst of a rain forest did he come up with a creative idea. As a rainstorm approached, Stapleton says that the rain forest came to life with an amazing array of sounds from howler monkeys, tropical birds, and other wildlife. He created a successful ad based only on sound and built it around an app that allows people to create their own music, syncing the jungle sounds of rain, howler monkeys, frogs, and flowing streams—all designed to pique people's interest in Costa Rica's lush and beautiful biodiversity. Stapleton says that a key factor in his creative moment was stepping away from his work and the distractions it created.[117] ∎

- Relax—and play—regularly. Perhaps the worst thing you can do for creativity is to work on a problem or an opportunity constantly. Soon enough, fatigue walks in, and creativity walks out! Great ideas often are incubated on the golf course, on the basketball court, on a hiking trail, or in the hammock.

ENTREPRENEURIAL PROFILE: Aaron Lemieux: Tremont Electric Aaron Lemieux was carrying a backpack while hiking the 2,000-plus-mile Appalachian Trail when the idea for his business struck. Lemieux, trained as a mechanical and biomedical engineer, grew tired of purchasing disposable batteries along the way to power his portable devices and began to think about ways to capture the wasted kinetic energy generated by the movement of his backpack. Lemieux's hiking experience led him to launch Tremont Electric, a company that produces the nPower Personal Energy Generator, a small, lightweight electrical generator that produces enough energy to power personal electronic devices by simply harvesting kinetic energy from normal human movement, such as walking.[118] ∎

- Dream about the problem or opportunity. "Dreams have been responsible for two Nobel prizes, the invention of a couple of major drugs, other scientific discoveries, several important political events, and innumerable novels, films, and works of visual art," says Harvard Medical School psychologist Dierdre Barrett.[119] Although you may not be able to dream on command, thinking about an issue just before you drift off to sleep can be an effective way to encourage your mind to work on it while you sleep, a process called lucid dreaming. Barrett's research suggests that about 50 percent of people can focus their dreams by contemplating a particular problem before they go to sleep, in essence "seeding" the subconscious to influence their dreams.[120] Arianna Huffington, founder of the *Huffington Post*, says that when she needs a creative solution, she goes to sleep. "There are many great ideas locked inside us," she says. "We just need to close our eyes to see them." To encourage creativity among her staff, Huffington has set up three "nap rooms" in the company's offices.[121]

- Work on the problem or opportunity in a different environment—somewhere other than the office. Take your work outside on a beautiful fall day or sit on a bench in a mall. The change of scenery will likely stimulate your creativity.

Step 5. Illumination

This phase of the creative process is kicked off at some point during the incubation stage, when a spontaneous breakthrough causes "the lightbulb to go on." It occurs spontaneously and may take place after five minutes or five years. Ben Baldwin, cofounder of ClearFit, a company that helps small companies find the best job candidates and predict their success, says that the idea for the company's business model hatched in his mind while he was driving 80 miles an hour and not thinking about work at all. Baldwin had been working on similar ideas for seven years before ClearFit's business model crystallized in his mind. Baldwin points out that ClearFit is not the first company to help businesses find employees, nor the first to predict job fit, nor the first company to make software that's easy for small businesses to use. However, it is the first to combine these functions to make it easy to find employees who fit.[122]

In the illumination stage, all the previous stages come together to produce the "Eureka!" factor—the creation of the innovative idea. In one study of 200 scientists, 80 percent said that at least once a solution to a problem had "just popped into their heads"—usually when they were away from the problem.[123] For Dr. Navia, the illumination stage occurred one day while he was reading a scientific journal. As he read, Dr. Navia says he was struck with a "hallucination" of a novel way to block protease.

Although the creative process itself may last months or even years, the suddenness with which the illumination step occurs can be deceiving, making the process appear to occur much faster than it actually does. One night, Kent Murphy, an electrical engineer, began dreaming about what it would be like to be a photon of light. "I was riding a ray of light moving through the fiber," he recalls about his dream. Murphy, who holds 30 patents, used the insight from his dream to invent a fiber-optic gauge that monitors on a real-time basis the structural wear in airplanes.[124]

Step 6. Verification

For entrepreneurs, validating an idea as being realistic and useful may include conducting experiments, running simulations, test marketing a product or service, establishing small-scale pilot programs, building prototypes, and many other activities designed to verify that the new idea will work and is practical to implement. The goal is to subject the innovative idea to the test of cold, hard reality. At this phase, appropriate questions to ask include the following:

- Is it *really* a better solution to a particular problem or opportunity? Sometimes an idea that appears to have a bright future in the lab or on paper dims considerably when put to the test of reality.

- Will it work?

- Is there a need for it?

- What is the best application of this idea in the marketplace?

- Does this product or service idea fit into our core competencies?

- How much will it cost to produce or to provide?

- Can we sell it at a reasonable price that will produce adequate sales, profit, and return on investment for our business?

- Will people buy it?

To test the value of his new drug formulation, Dr. Navia used powerful computers at Vertex Pharmaceuticals to build 3-D Tinkertoy-like models of the HIV virus and then simulated his new drug's ability to block the protease enzyme. Subsequent testing of the drug verified its safety. Dr. Navia was convinced that he had an insight into solving the AIDS puzzle that no one else had discovered.[125]

Step 7. Implementation

The focus of this step is to transform the idea into reality. Plenty of people come up with creative ideas for promising new products or services, but most never take them beyond the idea stage. What sets entrepreneurs apart is that they *act* on their ideas. An entrepreneur's philosophy is "Ready, aim, fire," not "Ready, aim, aim, aim, aim." Innowattech, a company based in Ra'anana, Israel, has developed a variety of piezoelectric (PE) crystals that possess the ability to transform vibrations, motion, and temperature changes into clean energy. Like minigenerators, the pressure-sensitive ceramic crystals give off small electrical charges when "squeezed, squashed, bent, or slapped," says Markys Cain, a materials scientist. In a recent test, Innowattech placed PE generators 2 inches beneath a small section of Israel's busy Highway 4, where passing cars compressed the road, activated the tiny generators, and produced energy. The company estimates that placing the PE crystals under a half-mile stretch of highway generates enough energy to supply 250 homes. Innowattech also has developed crystals for collecting clean energy from railways, airport runways, and pedestrian walkways.[126] The key to Innowattech's success is its ability to take a creative idea for a useful new product and turn it into a reality. As one creativity expert explains, "Becoming more creative is really just a matter of paying attention to that endless flow of ideas you generate, and learning to capture and act upon the new that's within you."[127]

For Dr. Navia and Vertex Pharmaceuticals, the implementation phase required testing the drug's ability to fight the deadly virus in humans. If it proved to be effective, Vertex would complete the process by bringing the drug to market. In this final phase of testing, Dr. Navia was so certain that he was on the verge of a major breakthrough in fighting AIDS that he couldn't sleep at night. Unfortunately, the final critical series of tests proved that Dr. Navia's flash of creativity was, as he now says, "completely, totally, and absolutely incorrect." Although his intuition proved to be wrong this time, Dr. Navia's research into fighting AIDS continues. Much of the current work at Vertex is based on Dr. Navia's original idea. Although it proved to be incorrect, his idea has served a valuable purpose: generating new ideas. "We are now applying a powerful technology in HIV research that wasn't used before, one inspired by a hunch," he says.[128]

LO6

Discuss techniques for improving the creative process.

Techniques for Improving the Creative Process

Teams of people working together usually can generate more and more creative ideas. Five techniques that are especially useful for improving the quality of creative ideas from teams are brainstorming, mind mapping, force-field analysis, TRIZ, and rapid prototyping.

Brainstorming

brainstorming

a process in which a small group of people interact with very little structure, with the goal of producing a large quantity of novel and imaginative ideas.

Brainstorming is a process in which a small group of people interact with very little structure, with the goal of producing a large *quantity* of novel and imaginative ideas. The goal is to create an open, uninhibited atmosphere that allows members of the group to "freewheel" ideas. Participants should suggest any ideas that come to mind *without evaluating or criticizing them*. As group members interact, each idea sparks the thinking of others, and the spawning of ideas becomes contagious. The free-flowing energy generated by the team becomes the genesis of a multitude of ideas, some of which may be impractical; however, those impractical ideas may lead to one idea that results in a breakthrough product or service for a company. For a brainstorming session to be successful, entrepreneurs should follow these guidelines:

- Keep the group small—just five to eight members. Amazon founder Jeff Bezos uses the "two-pizza rule"—if a brainstorming group can eat two pizzas, it's too big.[129]

- Make the group as diverse as possible. Include people with different backgrounds, disciplines, and perspectives. At Joe Design Inc., every employee in the small firm takes part in brainstorming sessions. "We bring in everybody from the bookkeeper to the office manager because they see things completely differently than we do," says cofounder Joe Raia.[130]

- Encourage participants to engage in some type of aerobic exercise before the session. One study found that people who exercise—walking, bicycling, swimming, or running—before brainstorming sessions were more creative than those who did not exercise.[131]

- Make company rank and department affiliation irrelevant. Every member of the brainstorming team should be on equal ground.

- Give the group a well-defined problem. Stating the problem in the form of a "why," "how," or "what" question often helps.

- Rather than waste precious group meeting time getting participants up to speed, provide everyone involved in the session with relevant background material about the problem to be solved beforehand. Invite participants to submit at least three ideas by e-mail before the brainstorming session takes place. This gets people's minds focused on the issue.

- Limit the session to 40 to 60 minutes. Beyond that, participants grow weary, and creativity flags because brainstorming is an intense activity.

- Take a field trip. Visit the scene of the problem, if possible. Research shows that brainstorming teams that go "onsite" actually come up with more and better ideas.[132]

- Appoint someone (preferably not a brainstorming participant) as recorder. The recorder should write every idea on a flip chart or board so that everyone can see it.

- Use a seating pattern that encourages communication and interaction (e.g., circular or U-shaped arrangements).

- Throw logic out the window. The best brainstorming sessions are playful and anything but logical.

- Encourage *all* ideas from the team, even wild and extreme ones. Discourage participants from editing their ideas. Not only can ideas that initially seem crazy get the group's creative juices flowing, but they also can spread creativity like wildfire. In addition, the group may be able to polish some of these wild ideas into practical, creative solutions!

- Establish a goal of *quantity* of ideas over *quality* of ideas. There will be plenty of time later to evaluate the ideas generated. At Ideo Inc., a Silicon Valley design firm, brainstorming teams shoot for at least 150 ideas in a 30- to 45-minute session.[133] When chemist Linus Pauling received his second Nobel Prize, someone asked him how he came up with so many great ideas. Pauling replied simply, "I come up with lots of ideas."[134]

- *Forbid* evaluation or criticism of any idea during the brainstorming session. No idea is a bad idea. Criticism slams the brakes on the creative process!

- Encourage participants to use "idea hitchhiking," building new ideas on those already suggested. Often, some of the best solutions are those that are piggybacked on others.

- Dare to imagine the unreasonable. Creative ideas often arise when people suspend conventional thinking to consider far-fetched solutions.

ENTREPRENEURIAL PROFILE: John Nottingham: Nottingham Spirk At Nottingham Spirk, an industrial design firm whose success depends on the creativity of its people, employees routinely use brainstorming to come up with new product ideas and designs. The focus of these sessions is to generate a large quantity of ideas, "from mild to wild," says cofounder John Nottingham, rather than to emphasize the quality of the ideas. By the end of the session, the walls are covered with pieces of paper containing scribbles, sketches, and notes, representing 100 or more ideas. Only after the brainstorming session do employees begin to focus on the quality of the ideas generated. In these meetings, employees judge each idea using a simple scale. Each person can display one of three cards: "Who Cares?" "Nice," and "Wow!" (All participants display their cards simultaneously.) A consensus of "Who Cares?" cards means that the group discards the idea, but a strong showing of "Wow!" cards means the idea moves forward for refinement. A vote of "Nice" usually means that the idea goes back for more brainstorming, hopefully transforming into a "Wow!" idea. An idea for a Christmas tree stand that uses a swivel joint and a locking pedal initially received a "Nice" rating from the group. The idea's champion kept tinkering with it, ultimately adding a self-regulating automatic watering device and other features before returning to the group. In its second pass, the idea went from "Nice" to "Wow!" In the first five years it was sold, the SwivelStraight tree stand sold 1 million units.[135] ∎

Mind Mapping

Another useful tool for jump-starting creativity is **mind mapping**, an extension of brainstorming. One strength of mind mapping is that it reflects the way the brain actually works. Rather than throw out ideas in a linear fashion, the brain jumps from one idea to another. In many creative sessions, ideas are rushing out so fast that many are lost if a person attempts to shove them into a linear outline. Creativity suffers. Mind mapping is a graphical technique that encourages creative thinking by visually displaying the various relationships among ideas and improving the ability to view a problem from many sides.

The mind-mapping process works this way:

1. Start by writing down or sketching a picture symbolizing the problem or area of focus in the center of a large blank page. Tony Buzan, originator of the mind-mapping technique, suggests using ledger paper or covering an entire wall with butcher paper to establish a wide-open attitude toward creativity.

2. Write down *every* idea that comes into your mind, connecting each idea to the central picture or words with a line. Use key words and symbols to record ideas in shorthand. Work as quickly as possible for no more than 20 minutes, doing your best to capture the tide of ideas that flows from your brain. Just as in brainstorming, do not judge the quality of your ideas; just get them onto the paper. Build new ideas on the backs of existing ones. If you see a

mind mapping
a graphical technique that encourages creative thinking by visually displaying the various relationships among ideas and improving the ability to view a problem from many sides.

connection between a new idea and one already on the paper, connect them with a line. If not, simply connect the idea to the center symbol. You will organize your ideas later in the process.

3. When the flow of ideas slows to a trickle, stop! Don't try to force creativity.

4. Allow your mind to rest for a few minutes and then begin to integrate the ideas on the page into a mind map. Use colored pens and markers to connect ideas with similar themes or to group ideas into related clusters. As you organize your thoughts, look for new connections among your ideas. Sometimes the brain needs time to process the ideas in a mind map. (Recall the incubation stage of the creative process.) Walking away from the mind map and the problem for a few minutes or a few hours may lead to several new ideas or to new relationships among ideas. One entrepreneur created the format for his company's business plan with a mind map rather than with a traditional linear outline. When he finished, he not only knew what he should include in his plan but also had a clear picture of the order in which to sequence the elements.

Force-Field Analysis

Force-field analysis is a useful technique for evaluating the forces that support and oppose a proposed change. It allows entrepreneurs to weigh both the advantages and the disadvantages of a particular decision and work to maximize the variables that support it and minimize those that work against it. The process, which, like brainstorming, works well with a group, begins by making three columns and listing the problem to be addressed in the center column. In the column on the left, the group should list driving forces, those that support the issue and move it forward. In the column on the right, the group should list the restraining forces, those that hold back the company from implementing the idea. The specific forces that the group may come up with are almost limitless, but some of the factors the team should consider include people, values, costs, trends, traditions, politics, costs, revenues, environmental impact, regulations, and attitudes.

Once the group has identified a reasonable number of driving and restraining forces (4 to 10 is typical), the next task is to assign a numerical value that reflects the strength of that particular force. For the driving forces column, scores range from 1 (weak) to 4 (strong), and in the restraining forces column, scores range from −1 (weak) to −4 (strong). Adding the scores for the driving forces column and the restraining forces column shows which set of forces dominates the issue. The higher the total score, the more feasible is the idea. If the decision is a "go," the group can focus on ideas to create new driving forces, strengthen existing driving forces, and minimize the impact of restraining forces.

Force-field analysis produces many benefits, particularly when it is combined with other creativity-enhancing techniques. It helps entrepreneurs judge the practicality of a new idea, identify resources the company can use to bring the idea to market, recognize obstacles the company must overcome to implement the idea, and suggest ways to conquer those obstacles.

TRIZ

Developed in 1946 by Genrich Altshuller, a 22-year-old naval officer in the former Soviet Union, TRIZ (pronounced "trees") is a systematic approach designed to help solve any technical problem, whatever its source. The name is derived from the acronym for a Russian phrase that translates as "theory of inventive problem solving." Unlike brainstorming and mind mapping, which are right-brain activities, TRIZ is a scientific, step-by-step process that is based on the study of hundreds of the most innovative patents around the globe. Altshuller claimed that these innovations followed a particular set of patterns. Unlocking the principles behind those patterns allows one not only to solve seemingly insurmountable problems but also to predict where the next challenges will arise.

Altshuller and his colleagues developed 40 principles underlying these innovative patents and then developed the "TRIZ contradiction matrix," a tool that combines these principles to solve a problem. They recognized that innovations come about when someone is able to overcome the inherent contradictions in a process. For instance, in the packaging industry, a contradiction exists between the effectiveness of childproof safety caps for medicine containers and making those containers easy for authorized users to open. Manufacturers of mattresses face the contradiction of making mattresses that are both hard and soft. Too often, companies rely on a very unimaginative solution to contradictions such as these: they compromise. Rather than settle for a mediocre compromise, the TRIZ contradiction matrix is designed to *resolve* these conflicts, using the 40 principles that Altshuller developed. One axis of the matrix displays the characteristic of the process to be improved, and the other axis displays the conflicting characteristic that is becoming worse.

For example, suppose that a candy maker wants to make syrup-filled, bottle-shaped chocolates by molding the chocolate bottles and then pouring syrup into the mold. To speed production of the finished product to meet demand, the business owner tries heating the syrup to allow for faster pouring, but the heated syrup melts the molded chocolate bottles and distorts their shape (the contradiction; see Figure 3.2). Using the TRIZ contradiction matrix, the candy maker recognizes the problem as a conflict between speed and shape. Speed is the characteristic to be improved, and shape is the characteristic that is getting worse. The principles that the matrix suggests for solving this problem include (1) changing the dynamics of the object or the environment (e.g., making a rigid part flexible), (2) discarding or recovering parts of an object (e.g., dissolving a protective case when it is no longer needed), (3) causing an object to vibrate or oscillate (e.g., transforming a standard knife into an electric knife by introducing oscillating blades), and (4) changing the properties of the object (e.g., freezing the chocolate syrup and then molding the bottles around the syrup).

		Characteristic that is getting worse				
		Volume of stationary object	**Speed**	**Force**	**Stress or pressure**	**Shape**	**Stability of the object**
Characteristic to be improved	**Volume of stationary object**	—	*	Taking out Mechanical vibration Thermal expansion	Intermediary Parameter changes	Nested doll Taking out Parameter changes	Discarding and recovering Mechanics substitution Parameter changes Composite materials
	Speed	*	—	The other way around Mechanics substitution Dynamics Periodic action	Universality Mechanical vibration Strong oxidants Composite materials	Dynamics Discarding and recovering Mechanical vibration Parameter changes	Mechanics substitution Homogeneity Segmentation Mechanical vibration
	Force	Taking out Phase transitions Mechanical vibration Thermal expansion	The other way round Mechanics substitution Dynamics Equipotentiality	—	Mechanical vibration Skipping Beforehand cushioning	Preliminary action Parameter changes Composite materials Discarding and recovering	Parameter changes Preliminary action Skipping
	Stress or pressure	Parameter changes Intermediary	Universality Parameter changes Phase transitions	Phase transitions Parameter changes Skipping	—	Parameter changes Asymmetry Dynamics Preliminary action	Parameter changes Homogeneity Taking out Composite materials
	Shape	Nested doll Taking out Parameter changes	Parameter changes Discarding and recovering Mechanical vibration	Parameter changes Preliminary action Thermal expansion Composite materials	Discarding and recovering Dynamics Preliminary action Spheroidality and curvature	—	Homogeneity Segmentation Mechanical vibration Asymmetry

FIGURE 3.2

TRIZ Contradiction Matrix

Source: Based on G. Altshuller, TRIZ 40, http://www.triz40.com/aff_Matrix_TRIZ.php.

Choosing principle 4, the candy maker decides to change the properties of the chocolate syrup by adding a compound that causes it to solidify when exposed to air, making it easier and faster to coat with chocolate. Once enclosed inside the chocolate, the syrup once again becomes a liquid. Problem solved![136]

Rapid Prototyping

Generating creative ideas is a critical step in the process of taking an idea for a product or a service successfully to the market. However, recall that many (perhaps most) ideas that entrepreneurs come up with fail. Inventor and serial entrepreneur Scott Jones says that his kids still enjoy teasing him about one of his offbeat ideas that flopped: a pair of microturbines embedded in the soles of shoes that would propel the wearer forward. (Jones abandoned the idea after seeing a similar concept fail flamboyantly in the movie *Jackass*.)[137] Rapid prototyping plays an important part in the creative process because it serves as a way to screen ideas that are not practical or just won't work so that entrepreneurs can focus their creative energy on other ideas. The premise behind **rapid prototyping** is that transforming an idea into an actual model highlights flaws in the original idea and leads to improvements in its design. "If a picture is worth a thousand words, a prototype is worth ten thousand," says Steve Vassallo of Ideo Inc.[138]

The three principles of rapid prototyping are the three *R*s: *rough*, *rapid*, and *right*. Models do not have to be perfect; in fact, in the early phases of developing an idea, perfecting a model usually is a waste of time. The key is to make the model good enough to determine what works and what does not. Doing so allows an entrepreneur to develop prototypes rapidly, moving closer to a successful design with each iteration. The final *R*, *right*, means building lots of small models that focus on solving particular problems with an idea. "You're not trying to build a complete model," says Vassallo. "You're just focusing on a small section of it."[139]

> **rapid prototyping**
> the process of creating a model of an idea, which enables an entrepreneur to discover flaws in the idea and to quickly make improvements in the design.

> **LO7**
> Describe the protection of intellectual property through patents, trademarks, and copyrights.

Intellectual Property: Protecting Your Ideas

Once entrepreneurs come up with innovative ideas for a product or service that has market potential, their immediate concern should be to protect it from unauthorized use. Counterfeit goods pose a real threat to businesses that have created intellectual property and their customers who use the products based on that intellectual property. Counterfeit goods account for 2.5 percent of all goods traded globally, costing legitimate businesses $461 billion in lost sales annually.[140] Table 3.3 lists the top 10 counterfeit goods seized by U.S. Customs agents.

TABLE 3.3 Top 10 Counterfeit Products Seized by U.S. Customs Agents

In a typical year, U.S. customs agents make about 30,000 seizures of counterfeit goods coming into the United States. These seizures represent only a portion of the total traffic in pirated goods. Which items are most often pirated?

Rank	Product	Percentage of Counterfeit Goods Seized
1	Wearing apparel and accessories	20%
2	Consumer electronics	16%
3	Footwear	12%
4	Watches and jewelry	11%
5	Handbags and wallets	10%
6	Pharmaceuticals and personal care	8%
7	Optical media	3%
8	Computers and accessories	2%
9	Labels and tags	2%
10	Automotive and aerospace	2%

Source: Based on *Intellectual Property Rights: Fiscal Year 2016 Seizure Statistics*, U.S. Customs and Border Protection, Office of International Trade, 2017, p. 8.

China and Hong Kong are the origin of 87 percent of the counterfeit goods seized in the United States.[141]

For many businesses, the value of their intellectual property exceeds the value of their tangible assets. Entrepreneurs must understand how to protect their intellectual property using three common tools—patents, trademarks, and copyrights.

Patents

A **patent** is a grant from the U.S. Patent and Trademark Office (PTO) to the inventor of a product, giving the exclusive right to make, use, license, or sell the invention (and to prevent others from making, using, or selling it) in this country for 20 years from the date of filing the patent application. The purpose of giving an inventor a 20-year exclusive right to a product is to stimulate creativity and innovation. After 20 years, the patent expires and cannot be renewed, and the invention becomes part of the public domain. The popular Keurig single-cup coffee machine is protected by 37 patents, but two of its most crucial patents expired in 2012, opening the door for competitors to introduce their own versions of the device.[142]

Most patents are granted for new product inventions (called *utility patents*), but *design patents*, extending for 14 years beyond the date the patent is issued, are given to inventors who make new, original, and ornamental changes in the design of existing products that enhance their sales. Inventors who develop a new plant can obtain a *plant patent*, provided that they can reproduce the plant asexually (e.g., by grafting or crossbreeding rather than planting seeds). To be patented, a device must be new (but not necessarily better!), not obvious to a person of ordinary skill or knowledge in the related field, and useful. A device *cannot* be patented if it has been publicized in print anywhere in the world or if it has been used or offered for sale in this country prior to the date of the patent application. A U.S. patent is granted only to the true inventor, not a person who discovers another's invention, and is effective *only* in the United States and its territories. (In 2011, Congress passed the America Invents Act, which changed the "first to invent" rule formerly in place to "first to file," which means that a patent goes to the first person to *file* a patent application.) Inventors who want to sell their inventions abroad must file for patents in each country in which they plan to do business. Once a product is patented, no one can copy or sell it without getting a license from its creator. A patent does not give one the right to make, use, or sell an invention but rather the right to exclude others from making, using, or selling it.

Although inventors are never assured of getting a patent, they can enhance their chances by following the basic steps suggested by the PTO. Before beginning the often lengthy and involved procedure, inventors should obtain professional assistance from a patent practitioner—a patent attorney or a patent agent—who is registered with the PTO. Only attorneys and agents who are officially registered may represent an inventor seeking a patent. A list of registered attorneys and agents is available at the PTO's Web site. Approximately 98 percent of all inventors rely on these patent experts to steer them through the convoluted process. Although the filing fees for patents are a few hundred dollars (and are discounted for small businesses and individual inventors), legal fees for filing a patent application range from $4,000 to $25,000, depending on the complexity of the product.

THE PATENT PROCESS Since George Washington signed the first patent law in 1790, the PTO (www.uspto.gov) has issued patents on everything imaginable (and some unimaginable items, too), including mouse traps (of course!), Robert Fulton's steamboat, animals (genetically engineered mice), Thomas Edison's lightbulb, golf tees (764 different patents), games, and various fishing devices. The J. M. Smucker Company even holds a patent issued in 1999 on a "sealed, crustless sandwich," a peanut butter and jelly sandwich it markets very successfully under the name "Uncrustables."[143] The PTO also has issued patents on business processes—methods of doing business—including Amazon.com's controversial patent on its "1-Click" technology, which allows users to store their customer information in a file and then recall it with one mouse click at checkout. Google received a patent for a system of "advertising based on environmental conditions." The patent gives Google the exclusive right to use the technology to send targeted ads to users depending on the weather, for example (e.g., ads for winter coats when the temperature dips into the 30s or rain gear when it rains).[144] To date, the PTO has issued nearly 10 million patents, and it receives more than 620,000 new applications and grants

patent
a grant from the federal government's Patent and Trademark Office to the inventor of a product, giving the exclusive right to make, use, license, or sell the invention in this country for 20 years from the date of the patent application.

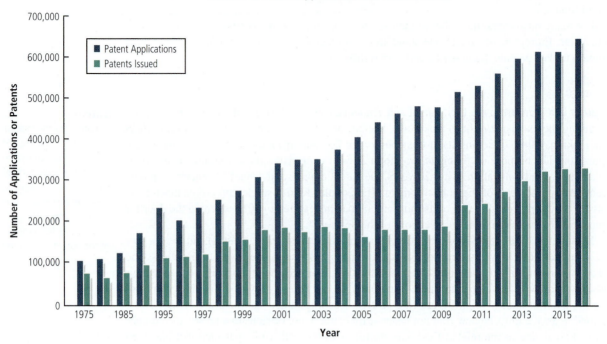

FIGURE 3.3

Patent Applications and Patents Issued

Source: Based on data from the U.S. Patent and Trademark Office, 2016.

about 325,000 patents each year (see Figure 3.3)![145] To receive a patent, an inventor must follow these steps:

1. *Establish the invention's novelty.* An invention is not patentable if it is known or has been used in the United States or has been described in a printed publication in this or a foreign country.

2. *Document the device.* To protect their patent claims, inventors should be able to verify the date on which they first conceived the idea for their inventions. Inventors should document a device by keeping dated records (including drawings) of their progress on the invention and by having knowledgeable friends witness these records.

3. *Search existing patents.* To verify that the invention truly is new, not obvious, and useful, an inventor must conduct a search of existing patents on similar products. The purpose of the search is to determine whether the inventor has a chance of getting a patent. Most inventors hire professionals trained in conducting patent searches to perform the research. Inventors themselves can conduct an online search of all patents granted by the PTO since 1976 from the office's Web site. An online search of these patents does not include sketches; however, subscribers to Delphion's Research Intellectual Property Network can access patents, including sketches, as far back as 1971 at www.delphion.com. Search engine Google also enables entrepreneurs to search patents at www.google.com/patents.

4. *Study search results.* Once the patent search is finished, inventors must study the results to determine their chances of getting a patent. To be patentable, a device must be sufficiently different from what has been used or described before and must not be obvious to a person who has ordinary skill in the area of technology related to the invention.

5. *Complete a patent application.* If an inventor decides to seek a patent, he or she must file an application describing the invention with the PTO. The patent application must include specific *claims*, which describe the invention, what it does, and how it works and any drawings that are necessary to support the claims. The typical patent application runs 20 to 40

US006932368B1

FIGURE 3.4

A Sample (and Unusual) Patent for a Wind Sail for a Bicycle

Source: Based on The U.S. Patent and Trademark Office, Washington, DC.

(12) **United States Patent**
     Zam

(54) **APPARATUS FOR HARNESSING WIND TO DRIVE A BICYCLE**

(76) Inventor: **Vladimir Zam,** 150 Beach 137 st., Rockaway Park, NY (US) 11694

(*) Notice: Subject to any disclaimer, the term of this patent is extended or adjusted under 35 U.S.C. 154(b) by 17 days.

(21) Appl. No.: **10/816,446**

(22) Filed: **Mar. 31, 2004**

(51) Int. Cl.^{7} B62J 11/00
(52) U.S. Cl. **280/213**
(58) Field of Search 280/213, 214, 280/810, 212, 288.4; 114/43, 102, 103, 102.1, 114/102.16, 102.29

(56)   **References Cited**
            U.S. PATENT DOCUMENTS

639,107	A	* 12/1899	Sorensen	280/213
947,731	A	* 1/1910	Couder	280/213
2,038,166	A	* 4/1936	Deal	280/213
2,443,565	A	* 6/1948	Land	280/213

(10) **Patent No.:**   **US 6,932,368 B1**
(45) **Date of Patent:**   **Aug. 23, 2005**

3,982,766	A	* 9/1976	Budge	280/1
3,986,722	A	* 10/1976	Patterson	280/16
4,332,395	A	* 6/1982	Zech	280/213
4,441,728	A	* 4/1984	Schroeder	280/213
4,735,429	A	* 4/1988	Beck	280/213
5,911,427	A	* 6/1999	Lenz, Jr.	280/213

            FOREIGN PATENT DOCUMENTS

FR	2622524	* 10/1957	

*cited by examiner

Primary Examiner— Anne Marie Boehler

(57)   **ABSTRACT**

A sail attachment which when connected to the bicycle harnesses wind to drive the bicycle forward. The attachment is adapted to fit on the rear of the bicycle above its rear wheel and is securable to the bicycle seat. The attachment is provided with a wind receiving sail which when attached to the bicycle can harness wind 45 degrees from either the left or right side of the bicycle, 90 degrees from either the side of the bicycle and at the rear of the bicycle to power the bicycle.

4 Claims, 2 Drawing Sheets

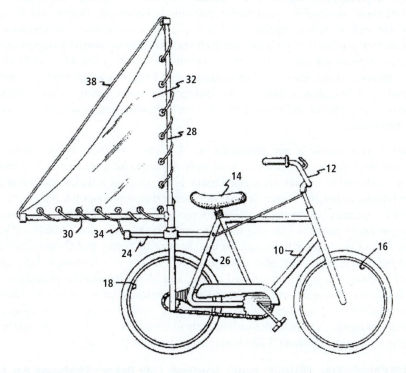

pages, although some, especially those for biotech or high-tech products, are tens of thousands of pages long. The longest patent application to date is one for a gene patent that was 6 million pages long![146] Most inventors hire patent attorneys or agents to help them complete their patent applications. Figure 3.4 shows a portion of the application for a rather unusual patent.

Inventors also can file a provisional application for a patent for a small fee. Filing for a provisional patent does not require the inventor to file any claims but does give him or her the right to use the phrase "patent pending" on the device. After filing for a provisional patent, an inventor has one year to file a standard patent application.

6. *File the patent application.* Before the PTO will issue a patent, one of its examiners studies the application to determine whether the invention warrants a patent. Approval of a patent takes an average of 24.8 months from the date of filing.[147] If the PTO rejects the application, the inventor can amend his or her application and resubmit it to the PTO.

Defending a patent against "copycat producers" can be expensive and time-consuming but often is necessary to protect an entrepreneur's interest. The number of patent infringement lawsuits has increased sharply. In 2009, patent holders filed 2,800 infringement suits; today, courts see nearly 5,600 patent suits per year. The median time for a patent infringement case to get to trial is 2.5 years. The median cost of a patent infringement lawsuit when the amount in dispute is between $1 million and $10 million is about $2 million if the case goes to trial (about 95 percent of patent infringement lawsuits are settled out of court), but the odds of winning are in the patent holder's favor. About two-thirds of patent holders win their infringement suits, and since 2012, the median award has been $5.8 million, which is most often based on the royalties lost to the infringer.[148] Jeff Sasaki founded Element Case, a company that markets high-quality cases for iPhones, in his San Carlos, California, garage in 2007. Within a few years, sales took off, and in 2012, Sasaki was attending a technology exposition in Hong Kong, where he discovered three companies selling counterfeit Element Case products. Furious, Sasaki demanded that the counterfeiters stop selling the knockoffs, but within a matter of weeks, all three companies were selling fake Element Case products online. Sasaki realized that he was in a cat-and-mouse game with counterfeiters and hired a full-time brand protection manager to protect his company's intellectual property—and its sales and profits.[149]

With its global reach and speedy convenience, the Internet compounds the problem of counterfeit sales. Entrepreneurs should set up Google alerts for their companies' and brands' names and be diligent about monitoring social media, particularly Facebook, Twitter, and Instagram, for hashtags that include their companies' and brands' names. Companies also should include a "report counterfeit products" feature on their Web sites to allow customers to report incidents easily. Counterfeit goods are such a problem in consumer electronics that Monster Products, a maker of headphones, shares the cost of investigators and lawyers who go after counterfeiters with other makers of headphones. Monster also incorporates secret features, such as packaging stamps printed in invisible ink and microscopic dots on its headphones, to differentiate its products from counterfeits.[150]

trademark

any distinctive word, phrase, symbol, design, name, logo, slogan, or trade dress that a company uses to identify the origin of a product or to distinguish it from other goods on the market.

service mark

a mark that offers the same protection as a trademark but identifies and distinguishes the source of a service rather than a product.

TRADEMARKS A **trademark** is any distinctive word, phrase, symbol, design, name, logo, slogan, or trade dress that a company uses to identify the origin of a product or to distinguish it from other goods on the market. (A **service mark** is the same as a trademark except that it identifies and distinguishes the source of a service rather than a product.) A trademark serves as a company's "signature" in the marketplace. A trademark can be more than just a company's logo, slogan, or brand name; it can also include symbols, shapes, colors, smells, or sounds. For instance, Coca-Cola holds a trademark on the shape of its bottle, and Owens-Corning has trademarked the unique pink color of its insulation. NBC owns a "sound mark," the auditory equivalent of a trademark, on its three-toned chime, and MGM has similar protection on the roar of the lion (whose name is Leo) that appears at the beginning of its movies.[151] *Trademark infringement* involves using another company's trademark without permission or using a mark that is so similar to another's trademark that it is likely to create confusion about the origin of the goods. Trademark owners file about 3,200 infringement lawsuits per year.[152]

ENTREPRENEURIAL PROFILE: Heath Scurfield: Calli Baker's Firehouse Bar & Grill
Firehouse Subs, a chain of fast-food submarine sandwich shops with more than 450 locations across the United States, filed a trademark infringement suit against Heath Scurfield, a retired firefighter who owns Calli Baker's Firehouse Bar & Grill, claiming that his use of the word "firehouse" in his company's name was likely to confuse customers into believing that his restaurant was affiliated with the national chain. Scurfield argued that the only similarities between his independent, full-service restaurant, which features lunch and dinner entrees, a bar, and a catering service, and the Firehouse Subs chain are the inclusion of the word "firehouse" in their names and the firehouse decor. After three years of legal wrangling, a jury ruled in Scurfield's favor and invalidated Firehouse Subs's trademark because it filed a fraudulent trademark application in 2003, claiming that at the time no other restaurants were using the word "firehouse" in their

You Be the Consultant

How Would You Rule in These Intellectual Property Cases?

Companies in the fashion industry typically defend their trademarks aggressively but traditionally have not relied on patents to protect their intellectual property because few legal protections exist for clothing designs. Fashion designers constantly come up with new designs for garments but find that protecting, say, the shape of a lapel or the cut of a cuff is difficult because clothing is functional and not "novel, useful, and not obvious" in light of current technology, which receiving a patent requires. Fashion companies usually look to trademarks to protect their brands.

Christian Louboutin SA v. Yves Saint Laurent SA

French luxury shoemaker Christian Louboutin (CL) filed a trademark infringement lawsuit against Yves Saint Laurent (YSL), claiming that CL had the right to trademark protection for the "China red" soles the company uses on all of its high heel shoes and that YSL had violated its trademark by introducing a line of "monochrome" high heel shoes in which the red shoes had red soles. CL's attorney argued that Louboutin's use of the red soles had transformed an everyday item, the sole of a shoe, into a work of art and created a well-recognized trademark. "The red sole has become synonymous with Christian Louboutin and high fashion," the company pointed out in its complaint. "Louboutin turned a pedestrian item into a thing of beauty." Celebrities such as Scarlett Johansson, Oprah Winfrey, Gwyneth Paltrow, Halle Berry, Beyoncé, Christina Aguilera, and many others often sport "Loubs." CL also pointed out that other companies have trademark protection for certain colors, such as Tiffany and Company's robin's-egg blue boxes, United Parcel Service's brown trucks and uniforms, and Owens-Corning's pink insulation.

Winning a trademark for color has proven to be more difficult in the fashion industry, where color is a fundamental part of almost any design. That principle became the foundation of YSL's argument. YSL's attorney countered by citing a judge's ruling in a similar case that said, "Granting a producer the exclusive use of a basic element of design (shape, material, color, and so forth) impoverishes other designers' palettes." YSL went on to argue that "allowing Louboutin to claim a monopoly on the use of red on a part of the shoe would have an unprecedented, anti-competitive effect in limiting the design options available to all other designers."

After hearing the parties' arguments, Judge Victor Marrero, a district court judge in New York, ruled in favor of Yves Saint Laurent. "Louboutin's claim would cast a red cloud over the whole industry, cramping what other designers could do while allowing Louboutin to paint with a full palette," he wrote. "Color constitutes a critical attribute of the goods." His ruling meant that Christian Louboutin could not claim trademark protection for its red-soled shoes. Attorneys for Christian Louboutin filed an appeal with the Second Circuit U.S. Court of Appeals with the intent of having the appeals court reverse the trial court's decision.

Lululemon Athletica Inc. v. Calvin Klein Inc.

Lululemon, a maker of yoga apparel based in Vancouver, British Columbia, filed a complaint in a district court in Delaware, claiming that Calvin Klein Inc. (CKI) was selling yoga pants that infringed on three of the company's design patents, including one that included a distinctive waistband made of three overlapping panels of fabric that the company received in 2011. Unlike a utility patent, a design patent protects an item's nonfunctional, ornamental features. To receive a design patent, a product must include the following five elements:

1. The item must be an "article of manufacture."

2. The design must be original.

3. The design must be novel.

4. The design must be non-obvious.

5. The design must be ornamental.

With its three overlapping pieces of Lululemon's trademarked Luon compression fabric, the waistband on the company's Astro yoga pants, which retail for $98, is designed to make the waist look slimmer and, because they can be rolled down to sit lower on the waist, enhance the wearer's athletic performance. Lululemon claimed that the waistband on CKI's yoga pants, which sell for as little as $20, is substantially similar to the waistband on its Astro yoga pants. According to a decision in 2008 by the U.S. Court of Appeals for the Federal Circuit, owners of design patents must prove that to the average observer the alleged infringer's design appears to be substantially the same as its own design (known as the "ordinary observer test").

1. What does a trademark protect? What does a patent protect? What is a design patent?

2. Assume the role of a judge in these two cases. How would you rule? Explain your reasoning. (In the *Lululemon Athletica v. Calvin Klein* case, you may want to search online for images of the two companies' yoga pants and apply the ordinary observer test before making your decision.)

3. Use a search engine to research the outcomes of these two cases. How were the cases resolved? If a judge rendered a decision, summarize his or her reasoning. Do you agree with the judge's decision?

Sources: Based on Tim Sablik, "Can Creativity and Copying Coexist?" *Region Focus*, Fourth Quarter, 2011, p. 24; Ashby Jones, "The Red Sole Case," *Wall Street Journal*, January 25, 2012, pp. B1–B2; Ray A. Smith and Ashby Jones, "Color Wars: Luxury Makers Battle Over Red-Soled Shoes," *Wall Street Journal*, August 11, 2011, pp. B1, B8; Chad Bray, "Red-Soled Shoes Win Appeal," *Wall Street Journal*, September 6, 2012, p. B10; Ashby Jones, "Downward Docket: The Yoga Pants War," *Wall Street Journal*, September 12, 2012, pp. B1, B5; "Lululemon Settles Yoga Pants Lawsuit with Calvin Klein," *CBC News*, November 21, 2012, www.cbc.ca/news/business/lululemon-settles-yoga-pants-patent-lawsuit-with-calvin-klein-1.1183253; Cory Howard, "Lululemon's Yoga-Pant Waistband Stretches the Limits of Design Patent Protection," *Jurist*, October 25, 2012, www.cbc.ca/news/business/lululemon-settles-yoga-pants-patent-lawsuit-with-calvin-klein-1.1183253; "Lululemon Settles Patent Dispute with Calvin Klein," *Jurist*, November 22, 2012, http://jurist.org/paperchase/2012/11/lululemon-settles-patent-dispute-with-calvin-klein.php; Complaint at page 9, *Christian Louboutin v. Yves Saint Laurent*, No. 11-cv-2381, United States District Court, Southern District Court of New York, April 7, 2011; Complaint at page 2, *Defendants/Counterclaim Plaintiffs' Memorandum of Law in Opposition to Motion for Preliminary Injunction*, No. 11-cv-2381, United States District Court of New York, July 12, 2011.

FIGURE 3.5

Trademark Applications and Trademarks and Renewals Issued

Source: Based on data from the U.S. Patent and Trademark Office, 2016.

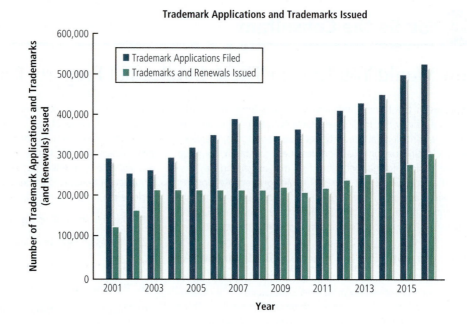

Trademark Applications and Trademarks Issued

names when, in reality, the company knew that many restaurants included "firehouse" in their names. Firehouse Subs appealed the ruling, and the parties ultimately entered into a court-approved settlement under which Scurfield would continue to use his company's name and Firehouse Subs would not renew its trademark and would pay all of Scurfield's legal fees, which amounted to hundreds of thousands of dollars.[153] ■

trade dress

the unique combination of elements that a company uses to create a product's image and to promote it.

Components of a product's identity such as these are part of its **trade dress**, the unique combination of elements that a company uses to create a product's image and to promote it. For instance, a Mexican restaurant chain's particular decor, color schemes, design, and overall look and feel constitute its trade dress. To be eligible for trademark protection, trade dress must be inherently unique and distinctive to a company, and another company's use of that trade dress must be likely to confuse customers.

There are more than 2.2 million trademarks registered and in active use in the United States (see Figure 3.5).[154] Federal law permits a company to register a trademark, which prevents other companies from employing a similar mark to identify their goods. Before 1989, a business could not reserve a trademark in advance of use. Today, the first party who either uses a trademark in commerce or files an application with the PTO has the ultimate right to register that trademark. Before attempting to register a trademark, an entrepreneur must conduct a search to verify that it is not already in use and is not too similar to an existing mark. BizFilings's Trademark Explorer is a handy, low-cost tool for conducting trademark searches. Registering a trademark takes an average of 10.1 months from the time an entrepreneur submits the application.[155] Unlike patents and copyrights, which are issued for limited amounts of time, a trademark lasts indefinitely, as long as the holder continues to use it. However, between 5 and 6 years after a trademark's registration date (and again between 9 and 10 years after the registration date and every 10 years after that), an entrepreneur must file an affidavit of use with the PTO. A trademark does not keep competitors from producing the same product or selling it under a different name; it merely prevents others from using the same or confusingly similar trademark for the same or similar products.

Many business owners are confused by the use of the symbols ™ and ®. Anyone who claims the right to a particular trademark (or service mark) or has filed a trademark application can use the ™ (or ᴴᴹ) symbol. The claim to that trademark or service mark may or may not be valid, however. Only those businesses that have *registered* their marks with the PTO can use the ® symbol. Entrepreneurs do not have to register trademarks or service marks to establish their rights to those marks; however, registering a mark with the PTO does give entrepreneurs greater power to protect their marks. Filing an application to register a trademark or service mark costs from $275 to $375 and is relatively easy, but it does require a search of existing names.

🌐 Hands On . . . How To

Protect Your Company's Intellectual Property— Both at Home and Abroad

In 2004, Thomas Dempsey started a company, SylvanSport, in Brevard, North Carolina, to sell a unique recreational camper trailer he invented and patented. SylvanSport marketed the trailer as "more versatile than a Swiss army knife" because it folds into a trailer that can carry boats, bikes, and other gear and, once onsite, convert in minutes into a camper with a self-inflating mattress and tent. By 2011, the company's annual sales had reached $3 million, 15 percent of which came from outside the United States, particularly South Korea, Japan, and Australia. With international sales growth outpacing domestic sales growth, Dempsey saw a bright future for his company.

Then he received an e-mail from a customer that included a link to the Web site of a Chinese company, Wuyi Tiandi Motion Apparatus, that was selling a camper trailer almost identical to the one he had designed. "We were shocked," says Dempsey. "We thought at first that what we saw was our product, but we realized that [their product] was created from scratch."

Since then, several of Dempsey's international distributors in Asia have dropped SylvanSport's camper and are selling the Chinese company's product. A Japanese distributor mistakenly purchased the Chinese company's camper, thinking it was buying one of SylvanSport's products. Thomas Tang, sales manager for Wuyi Tiandi, admits that SylvanSport was the first company "to make this type of trailer, and we followed them to make a similar product." Although Wuyi Tiandi cannot sell its camper in the United States because of SylvanSport's patent, "we can still sell our trailer everywhere else [in the world]," says Tang. Dempsey is concerned about the sales his company has lost to its Chinese competitor. "There's a very real chance that the Chinese company could be the survivor here and we could go out of business," he says matter-of-factly.

Thomas Dempsey took the proper steps to protect his intellectual property by securing a utility patent for his unique camper trailer in the United States. Like many other entrepreneurs in today's global economy, Dempsey is conducting business internationally, and his U.S. patent offers no protection outside the United States. What lessons can entrepreneurs learn from Dempsey's experience about protecting their intellectual property?

1. ***Recognize that intellectual property, the rights that result when a person uses his or her knowledge and creativity to produce something of value, can be a business's most valuable asset, even for small companies.*** Often intellectual property is the source of a company's competitive advantage. Experts estimate that in the United States alone, 30 to 40 percent of all gains in productivity over the course of the twentieth century originated with intellectual property. A recent study reports that 81 out of 313 (26 percent) industries in the United States are "intellectual property-intensive." These IP-intensive industries are responsible for 27.9 million jobs and account for an impressive 38.2 percent of U.S. GDP.

2. ***Use the appropriate tool to file for protection of your intellectual property and do so promptly.*** The processes of filing for a patent, a trademark, and a copyright are different; make sure you know what each tool protects, which one is right for you, and how to get maximum protection from it for your intellectual property. You may be able to apply for more than one type of protection. For instance, an entrepreneur may be able to trademark a company logo and, if it is a form of artistic expression, copyright it as well.

3. ***Use qualified, experienced intellectual property attorneys to gain the proper protection.*** The time to involve attorneys in protecting the product of your knowledge and creativity is *before* you have to bring them in to take action against someone who has stolen your intellectual property. Filing for patents, trademarks, and copyrights can be intimidating if you have never done it before, and doing it incorrectly may mean that you have no protection at all. Attorneys, consultants, examiners, and other professionals specialize in the various types of intellectual property protection. Use their expertise! They can refer you to patent draftspeople (who create the sketches required for a patent application), design engineers, manufacturers, and others.

4. ***If you do business globally, register your company's patents, trademarks, and copyrights in the countries in which you do business or that are a strategic part of your business.*** Once an entrepreneur has made the proper filings to protect his or her intellectual property in the United States, the next step is to file for protection in the countries in which the company does business and in countries that are strategically important to the business. Only 15 percent of companies that do business internationally realize that U.S. patents and trademarks do *not* protect their intellectual property outside the borders of the United States. Although enforcing intellectual property laws in some countries can be difficult, the chances that you will be successful rise significantly if you have registered your IP with the proper offices in those nations. Most nations grant patents and trademarks to the first person or business to file. Inventors file about 2.9 million patent applications globally each year, and 2011 marked the first time that businesses and entrepreneurs filed more patents in China than in any other country in the world. Today, 38.1 percent of global patent applications are filed in China, compared to 20.4 percent that are filed in the United States. Businesses also file about 8.5 million applications for trademarks globally each year.

Filing to protect intellectual property rights in many individual countries can be expensive and time-consuming.

(continued)

Hands On . . . How To *(continued)*

Fortunately, when applying for trademarks, entrepreneurs benefit from important shortcuts: international registration and a community trademark. Entrepreneurs can file an international registration in all 98 nations that participate in the Madrid Protocol with an application in their home nations that they extend to the other 97 nations (although they must pay a registration fee in each country). Entrepreneurs who register a community trademark file a single application and pay a single fee that grants trademark protection in all 27 countries that belong to the European Union. In 2007, the patent offices in the United States, the European Union, and Japan created a common patent application that allows entrepreneurs to streamline the patent process by filing a single application for each country's patent office.

5. ***Select your company's business affiliates, especially suppliers, carefully.*** Companies in some countries have little concern for others' intellectual property. Some suppliers in foreign countries see no problem manufacturing goods for a business and then running an extra shift to produce the same goods that they themselves sell. In China, which is famous for its copycat culture, the term *shanzai* describes companies' tendency to copy the successful products of other businesses. Entrepreneurs should take extra precautions to ensure that they secure proper protection for their intellectual property before forging relationships with foreign manufacturers, especially those in Asia.

6. ***Protect your rights vigorously.*** If you discover that someone is using your intellectual property without permission, pursue your rights vigorously. Recognize that the costs of taking legal action, especially in foreign lands, may outweigh the benefits, at least in the short run. Entrepreneurs must decide whether pursuing costly legal action to protect their intellectual property rights will yield long-term benefits. A "head-in-the-sand" approach never works. After registering their trademarks and filing for patents in foreign countries, entrepreneurs must monitor them carefully and avidly prosecute violators of their intellectual property rights.

Sources: Based on Justin Antonipillai, Michelle K. Lee, Robert Rubinovitz, David Langdon, Fenwick Yu, William Hawk, Alan C. Marco, Anrew A. Toole, and Asrat Tesfayesus, *Intellectual Property and the U.S. Economy: 2016 Update*, Economics and Statistics Administration and the U.S. Patent and Trademark Office, 2016, p. ii; WIPO Facts and Figures 2016, World Intellectual Property Organization, pp. 11, 21; *World Intellectual Property Indicators*, World Intellectual Property Organization, 2012, p. 3; Kathy Chu, "Chinese Copycats Challenge U.S. Small Businesses," *USA Today*, March 18, 2012, http://usatoday30.usatoday.com/money/smallbusiness/story/2012-03-15/china-copycats-patents/53614902/1; Carolyn Surh, "Staying Ahead of Copy Cats," *QSR*, March 2012, www.qsrmagazine.com/reports/staying-ahead-copy-cats; "How to Protect Your Trademark Internationally," *Business News Daily*, July 13, 2012, www.businessnewsdaily.com/2838-how-to-protect-your-trademark-internationally.html; David Hirschmann, "Intellectual Property Theft: Big Problem, Real Solutions, *The ChamberPost*, March 2008, www.chamberpost.com/2008/03/intellectual-pr.html; Merrill Matthews Jr. and Tom Giovanetti, "Why Intellectual Property Is Important," *Ideas*, Institute for Policy Innovation, July 8, 2002, p. 1; and Nichole L. Torres, "Getting Intellectual," *Entrepreneur*, December 2007, p. 110.

An entrepreneur may lose the exclusive right to a trademark if it loses its unique character and becomes a generic name. Aspirin, escalator, thermos, brassiere, super glue, corn flakes, yo-yo, and cellophane all were once enforceable trademarks that have become common words in the English language. These generic terms can no longer be licensed as trademarks.

Copyrights

copyright

an exclusive right that protects the creators of original works of authorship, such as literary, dramatic, musical, and artistic works (e.g., art, sculptures, literature, software, music, videos, video games, choreography, motion pictures, recordings, and others).

A **copyright** is an exclusive right that protects the creators of original works of authorship, such as literary, dramatic, musical, and artistic works (e.g., art, sculptures, literature, software, music, videos, video games, choreography, motion pictures, recordings, and others). The internationally recognized symbol © denotes a copyrighted work. A copyright protects only the form in which an idea is expressed, not the idea itself. A copyright on a creative work comes into existence the moment its creator puts that work into a tangible form. Just as with a trademark, obtaining basic copyright protection does *not* require registering the creative work with the U.S. Copyright Office (www.copyright.gov).

Registering a copyright does give creators greater protection over their work, however. Entrepreneurs must file copyright applications with the Copyright Office in the Library of Congress for a fee of $35 to $85 per application (plus recording fees). The typical processing time for a copyright application ranges from 8 months (electronic filings) to 13 months (paper filings).[156] A valid copyright on a work lasts for the life of the creator plus 70 years after his or her death. When a copyright expires, the work enters the public domain and can be used by anyone free of charge.

Because they are so easy to duplicate, computer software programs, CDs, and DVDs are among the items most often pirated by copyright infringers. The Business Software Alliance estimates that the global software piracy rate is 39 percent and that the software industry loses $52.2 billion each year to pirates who illegally copy programs.[157]

Table 3.4 provides a summary of the characteristics of patents, trademarks, and copyrights.

TABLE 3.4 **Characteristics of Patents, Trademarks, and Copyrights**

Protection	What It Protects	Who Is Eligible	Length of Protection	Approximate Total Cost
Utility patent	Exclusive right to make, use, and sell an invention	First person to file for a patent	20 years	$4,000 to $25,000, depending on complexity
Design patent	New, original changes in the design of existing products that enhance their sales	First person to file for a patent	14 years	$4,000 to $25,000, depending on complexity
Trademark	Any distinctive word, phrase, symbol, design, name, logo, slogan, or trade dress that a company uses to identify the origin of a product or to distinguish it from other goods on the market	Entity currently using the mark in commerce or one who intends to use it within six months	Renewable between fifth and sixth years and ninth and tenth years and every 10 years afterward	$1,000 to $2,500
Service mark	Same protection as a trademark except that it identifies and distinguishes the source of a service rather than a product	Entity currently using the mark in commerce or one who intends to use it within six months	Renewable between fifth and sixth years and ninth and tenth years and every 10 years afterward	$1,000 to $2,500
Copyright	Original works of authorship, such as literary, dramatic, musical, and artistic works	Author or creator	Life of the author or creator plus 70 years	$140 to $200

Protecting Intellectual Property

Acquiring the protection of patents, trademarks, and copyrights is useless unless an entrepreneur takes action to protect those rights in the marketplace. Unfortunately, not every businessperson respects others' rights of ownership to products, processes, names, and works, and some infringe on those rights with impunity. In other cases, the infringing behavior simply is the result of a lack of knowledge about others' rights of ownership. After acquiring the proper legal protection through patents, copyrights, or trademarks, entrepreneurs must monitor the market (and the Internet in particular) for unauthorized copycat users. If an entrepreneur has a valid patent, trademark, or copyright, stopping an infringer usually requires nothing more than a stern "cease-and-desist" letter from an attorney. Often, offenders don't want to get into expensive legal battles and agree to stop their illegal behavior. If that tactic fails, the entrepreneur may have no choice but to bring an infringement lawsuit, most of which end up being settled out of court.

The primary weapon an entrepreneur has to protect patents, trademarks, and copyrights is the legal system. The major problem with relying on the legal system to enforce ownership rights, however, is the cost and time of infringement lawsuits, which can quickly exceed the budget of most small businesses and occupy huge blocks of managers' time. Lawsuits always involve costs. Before pursuing what could become an expensive and drawn-out legal battle, an entrepreneur must consider the following issues:

- Can the opponent afford to pay if you win?

- Do you expect to get enough from the suit to cover the costs of hiring an attorney and preparing a case?

- Can you afford the loss of time, money, and privacy from the ensuing lawsuit?

Conclusion

As you have seen, creativity and innovation are vital components to entrepreneurial success. Successful entrepreneurs constantly push themselves and the people in their businesses to think bold new thoughts, come up with fresh new ideas, and question the status quo. The results of their efforts are innovative new products, services, and business models that benefit all of us and improve the quality of our lives.

Chapter Summary by Learning Objective

1. Explain the differences among creativity, innovation, and entrepreneurship.

- The entrepreneur's "secret" for creating value in the marketplace is applying creativity and innovation to solve problems and to exploit opportunities that people face every day. Creativity is the ability to develop new ideas and to discover new ways of looking at problems and opportunities. Innovation is the ability to apply creative solutions to those problems and opportunities to enhance or enrich people's lives. Entrepreneurship is the result of a disciplined, systematic process of applying creativity and innovation to needs and opportunities in the marketplace.

2. Describe why creativity and innovation are such integral parts of entrepreneurship.

- Entrepreneurs must always be on guard against paradigms—preconceived ideas of what the world is, what it should be like, and how it should operate—because they are logjams to creativity. Successful entrepreneurs often go beyond conventional wisdom as they ask "Why not?"

- Success—even survival—in this fiercely competitive, global environment requires entrepreneurs to tap their creativity (and that of their employees) constantly.

3. Explain the 10 "mental locks" that limit individual creativity.

- The number of potential barriers to creativity is limitless, but entrepreneurs commonly face 10 "mental locks" on creativity: searching for the one "right" answer, focusing on "being logical," blindly following the rules, constantly being practical, viewing play as frivolous, becoming overly specialized, avoiding ambiguity, fearing looking foolish, fearing mistakes and failure, and believing "I'm not creative."

4. Understand how entrepreneurs can enhance the creativity of their employees as well as their own creativity.

- Entrepreneurs can stimulate creativity in their companies by expecting creativity, expecting and tolerating failure, encouraging curiosity, viewing problems as challenges, providing creativity training, providing support, rewarding creativity, and modeling creativity.

- Entrepreneurs can enhance their own creativity by using the following techniques: allowing themselves to be creative, giving their minds fresh input every day, keeping a journal handy to record their thoughts and ideas, reading books on stimulating creativity or taking a class on creativity, and taking some time off to relax.

5. Describe the steps in the creative process.

- The creative process consists of seven steps. Step 1, preparation, involves getting the mind ready for creative thinking. Step 2, investigation, requires the individual to develop a solid understanding of the problem or decision. Step 3, transformation, involves viewing the similarities and differences in the information collected. Step 4, incubation, allows the subconscious mind to reflect on the information collected. Step 5, illumination, kicks off at some point during the incubation stage, when a spontaneous breakthrough causes "the lightbulb to go on." Step 6, verification, involves validating the idea as being accurate and useful. Step 7, implementation, involves transforming the idea into a business reality.

6. Discuss techniques for improving the creative process.

- Five techniques are especially useful for improving the creative process:

  - Brainstorming is a process in which a small group of people interact with very little structure, with the goal of producing a large *quantity* of novel and imaginative ideas.

  - Mind mapping is a graphical technique that encourages thinking on both sides of the brain, visually displays the various relationships among ideas, and improves the ability to view a problem from many sides.

  - Force-field analysis allows entrepreneurs to weigh both the advantages and the disadvantages of a particular decision and work to maximize the variables that support it and minimize those that work against it.

  - TRIZ is a systematic approach designed to help solve any technical problem, whatever its source. Unlike brainstorming and mind mapping, which are right-brain activities, TRIZ is a left-brain, scientific, step-by-step process that is based on the study of hundreds of the most innovative patents across the globe.

- Rapid prototyping is based on the premise that transforming an idea into an actual model will point out flaws in the original idea and will lead to improvements in its design.

7. Describe the protection of intellectual property through patents, trademarks, and copyrights.

- A patent is a grant from the federal government that gives an inventor exclusive rights to an invention for 20 years.

- A trademark is any distinctive word, symbol, or trade dress that a company uses to identify its product and to distinguish it from other goods. It serves as a company's "signature" in the marketplace.

- A copyright protects original works of authorship. It covers only the form in which an idea is expressed and not the idea itself and lasts for 70 years beyond the creator's death.

MyLab Entrepreneurship

If your instructor is using MyLab Entrepreneurship, go to **www.pearson.com/mylab/entrepreneurship** for Auto-graded writing questions as well as the following Assisted-graded writing questions:

1. One entrepreneur claims, "Creativity unrelated to a business plan has no value." What does he mean? Do you agree?
2. Explain the steps of the creative process. What can an entrepreneur do to enhance each step?

Discussion Questions

⭐ 3-1. Explain the differences among creativity, innovation, and entrepreneurship.

3-2. How are creativity, innovation, and entrepreneurship related?

⭐ 3-3. Why are creativity and innovation so important to the survival and success of a business?

3-4. Can creativity be taught, or is it an inherent trait? Explain.

3-5. Briefly outline the 10 "mental locks" that can limit individual creativity. Give an example of a situation in which you subjected yourself to one of these mental locks.

3-6. What can entrepreneurs do to stimulate their own creativity and to encourage it among workers?

3-7. Interview at least two entrepreneurs about their experiences as business owners. Where did their business ideas originate? How important are creativity and innovation to their success? How do they encourage an environment of creativity in their businesses?

3-8. Explain the differences between a patent, a trademark, and a copyright.

3-9. What forms of intellectual property do patents, trademarks, and copyrights protect?

Beyond the Classroom . . .

3-10. Your dinner guests are to arrive in five minutes, and you've just discovered that you forgot to chill the wine!! Wanting to maintain your reputation as the perfect host/hostess, you must tackle this problem with maximum creativity. What could you do? Generate as many solutions as you can in five minutes working alone and then work with two or three students in a small group to brainstorm the problem.

3-11. Work with a group of your classmates to think of as many alternative uses for the commercial lubricant WD-40 as you can. Remember to think *fluidly* (generating a quantity of ideas) and *flexibly* (generating unconventional ideas).

3-12. A Facebook group of more than 25,000 people is trying to convince Cadbury, the venerable British

confectioner (now owned by Kraft Foods), to produce a giant chocolate Cadbury Crème Egg that contains a filling made from fondant that resembles the yolk and white of a real egg. (Currently, giant Cadbury chocolate eggs, which are about the size of an ostrich egg, are hollow, a great disappointment to fans of the company's smaller chocolate eggs that are filled with creamy white and yolk-colored fondant.) A Cadbury spokesperson says that "creating a [chocolate] shell that is strong enough to contain the sheer weight of the fondant is technically challenging." Use the creativity-enhancing techniques described in this chapter to develop potential solutions that would allow Cadbury to manufacture a giant Crème Egg.

3-13. A major maker of breakfast cereals was about to introduce a new multigrain cereal. Its principal selling point is that it features "three great tastes" in every bowl: corn, rice, and wheat. Because a cereal's name is an integral part of its marketing campaign, the company hired a very expensive consulting firm to come up with the right name for the new product. The consulting firm tackled the job using "a combination of structural linguistics and personal creativity." One year and many dollars later, the consulting firm gave its recommendation. Take 20 minutes to list names that you think would be appropriate for this cereal. Make brief notes about why you think each name is appropriate. Your professor may choose to prepare a list of names from all the members of your class and then take a vote to determine the "winner."

3-14. Every quarter, Inventables, a creative design company in Chicago, sends its clients a package called a DesignAid that contains 20 items, each with "unexpected properties," as a way to stimulate innovation and ideas for new products or services. One recent DesignAid package at Inventables included the following items:

- Translucent concrete—Concrete that contains thin layers of fiber optics, which create semi-transparent stripes in the concrete.

- Sound-recording paper—A piece of cardboard-like paper that records and plays sounds with the help of ultrathin electronics embedded in the page.

- Impact-absorbing silicon—Silicon that, despite being only 1 inch thick, absorbs impact, including microvibrations. If you drop an egg on it, the egg won't break.

- Wireless battery-free speakers—Solar-powered speakers that receive sound via infrared waves rather than radio frequencies and are capable of producing directional sound. In other words, only the person at whom the speakers are aimed can hear the sound coming from them.

Select one of these items and work with a small group of your classmates to brainstorm as many alternative uses for the item as you can in 15 minutes. Remember to abide by the rules of brainstorming!

3-15. Interview at least two entrepreneurs about their experiences as business owners. Where did their business ideas originate?

3-16. How important are creativity and innovation to these entrepreneurs' success?

3-17. How do these entrepreneurs encourage an environment of creativity in their businesses?

Endnotes

[1] "How to Come Up with a Great Idea," *Wall Street Journal*, April 29, 2013, p. R1.

[2] Jodi Helmer, "Sleep Smarts," *Entrepreneur*, November 2013, p. 80; Neil Augenstein, "No Fable: Smart PJs Read Bedtime Stories to Kids," *WTOP Tech News*, January 8, 2014, www.wtop.com/256/3537293/No-fable-Smart-PJs-read-bedtime-stories-to-kids.

[3] *2017 Global R&D Funding Forecast*, Industrial Research Institute and *R&D Magazine*, Winter 2017, pp. 3, 5.

[4] "Frequently Asked Questions," U.S. Small Business Administration, Office of Advocacy, September 2012, p. 3.

[5] *GE Global Innovation Barometer: 2016 Edition*, General Electric, 2016, pp. 25, 32.

[6] Jessie Romero, "What We Don't Know About Innovation," *Region Focus*, First Quarter 2012, p. 13.

[7] "Innovation Quotes," Think Exist, http:/thinkexist.com/quotations/innovation.

[8] Josef Stadler, John Mathews, Michael Spellacy, and Marcel Widrig, *Billionaires Insights: The Changing Faces of Billionaires*, PriceWaterhouseCoopers, 2015, pp. 20–21.

[9] *Intuit Future of Small Business Report: Defining Small Business Innovation*, Intuit, March 2009, pp. 4–5.

[10] Warren Bennis, "Cultivating Creative Collaboration," *Industry Week*, August 18, 1997, p. 86.

[11] Nick Glass and Tim Hume, "The 'Hallelujah Moment' Behind the Invention of the Post-It Note," *CNN*, April 4, 2013, www.cnn.com/2013/04/04/tech/post-it-note-history/.

[12] Amy Westervelt, "Thinking Inside the Box Works, Too," *Wall Street Journal*, February 3, 2014, p. R3; "PulpWorks: Molding a Better World," PulpWorks, www.pulpworksinc.com/.

[13] Roger von Oech, *A Whack on the Side of the Head* (New York: Warner Books, 1990), p. 108.

[14] "How to Come Up with a Great Idea," *Wall Street Journal*, April 29, 2013, p. R1.

[15] Michael Maiello, "They Almost Changed the World," *Forbes*, December 23, 2002, p. 217.

[16] John Bussey, "Expensive Pipeline: Developing New Drugs," *Wall Street Journal*, February 26, 2013, p. B12.

[17] Kevin McGourty, "What Percentage of Sales Should New Product Launches from the Last Three Years Represent?" *INPD Center*, September 10, 2012, http://inpdcenter.com/blog/percentage-sales-product-launches-3-years-represent.

[18] Charlie Farrell, "A Penny for Your Thoughts," *Business & Economic Review*, October–December 2006, p. 25.

[19] David H. Freedman, "Freeing Your Inner Think Tank," *Inc.*, May 2005, pp. 65–66.

[20] Robert Fulghum, "Time to Sacrifice the Queen," *Reader's Digest*, August 1993, pp. 136–138.

[21] *Getting a Better Return on Your Innovation Investment: Results of the 8th Arthur D. Little Global Innovation Excellence Study*, Arthur D. Little, 2013, p.3.

[22] Jay Walker, "The Power of Imagination," *Wall Street Journal*, February 26, 2013, p. B11.

[23]Jonah Lehrer, "How to Be Creative," *Wall Street Journal*, March 10–11, 2012, p. C1.

[24]Nichole L. Torres, "Sparking Bright Ideas," *Entrepreneur*, August 2006, www.entrepreneur.com/article/159896.

[25]Carla Goodman, "Sparking Your Imagination," *Entrepreneur*, September 1997, p. 32.

[26]Holly Finn, "The Slow Road to Invention," *Wall Street Journal*, November 2, 2012, http://online.wsj.com/article/SB10001424052970203880704578089233956502680.html.

[27]Rick Tetzeli, "The Race Is On," *Fast Company*, April 2016, pp. 87–91, 102–103; Heather Somerville, "Lyft Executive Says on Track to Hit $1 Billion in Gross Revenue," *Reuters*, November 17, 2015, www.reuters.com/article/us-lyft-runrate-exclusive-idUSKCN0T621K20151117; Douglas MacMillan, "Lyft Hails Deal Makers," *Wall Street Journal*, June 28, 2016, pp. B1–B2.

[28]"A Passion for Great Conversation," Table Topics, 2013, www.tabletopics.com.

[29]Chuck Salter, "Failure Doesn't Suck," *Fast Company*, May 2007, p. 44; James Dyson, "Cleaning Up in His Industry," *Fortune*, January 22, 2007, p. 33.

[30]Kasey Wehrun, "Twice Blessed," *Inc.*, April 2011, p. 120; Stephen Miller, "Helicopter Designer and Guitar Hero," *Wall Street Journal*, February 2, 2011, p. A6.

[31]Roger von Oech, *A Whack on the Side of the Head* (New York: Warner Books, 1990), pp. 21–167; "Obstacles to Creativity," Creativity Web, www.ozemail.com.au/~caveman/Creative/Basics/obstacles.htm.

[32]Sherri Kuhn, "Kids Are Getting Smarter but Less Creative," *SheKnows*, January 2, 2014, www.sheknows.com/parenting/articles/1024783/kids-are-getting-smarter-but-less-creative.

[33]Erin Zagursky, "Professor Discusses America's Creativity Crisis in *Newsweek*," William and Mary News and Events, July 14, 2010, www.wm.edu/news/stories/2010/professor-discusses-americas-creativity-crisis-in-newsweek-123.php; Po Bronson and Ashley Merryman, "The Creativity Crisis," *Newsweek*, July 10, 2010, www.newsweek.com/2010/07/10/the-creativity-crisis.html.

[34]Richard Morgan, "Cable-less Elevators," *Fortune*, January 1, 2015, p. 45.

[35]Brady Dale, "A Liquid Bandage for Every Pocket," *Fortune*, January 1, 2015, p. 42.

[36]Joe Robinson, "Rebel Yell," *Entrepreneur*, March 2013, p. 30.

[37]Alfred Lief, "King Gillette's Safety Razor," *Modern Mechanix*, January 1954, pp. 99, 211; "Inventor of the Week: King C. Gillette," June 2000, Lemelson MIT Program, http://web.mit.edu/invent/iow/gillette.html; "Patent for Safety Razor Issued November 15, 1904," U.S. Patent and Trademark Office, November 14, 2001, www.uspto.gov/news/pr/2001/01-53.jsp.

[38]Karen Axelton, "Imagine That," *Entrepreneur*, April 1998, p. 96; "Thomas Edison Biography," http://edison-ford-estate.com/ed_bio.htm.

[39]Rachel Pannett, "Dragonfly Vision Helps to Build Bionic Eye," *Wall Street Journal*, October 6, 2015, p. D4.

[40]Jonah Lehrer, "How to Be Creative," *Wall Street Journal*, March 10–11, 2012, pp. C1–C2.

[41]Laurie Tarkan, "Work Hard, Play Harder," *Fox News*, September 15, 2012, www.foxnews.com/health/2012/09/13/work-hard-play-harder-fun-at-work-boosts-creativity-productivity.

[42]Tim McKeough, "Toy Factory," *Fast Company*, December 2011/January 2012, p. 84; Mary Timmins, "Rules of the Game," *Illinois Alumni Magazine*, November 20, 2012, www.uiaa.org/illinois/news/blog/index.asp?id=491.

[43]Naveen Jain, "Rethinking the Concept of 'Outliers': Why Non-Experts Are Better at Disruptive Innovation," *Forbes*, July 12, 2012, www.forbes.com/sites/singularity/2012/07/12/rethinking-the-concept-of-outliers-why-non-experts-are-better-at-disruptive-innovation.

[44]Claire Suddath, "A Brief History of Velcro," *Time*, June 15, 2010, http://content.time.com/time/nation/article/0,8599,1996883,00.html.

[45]Joseph Schumpeter, "The Creative Response in Economic History," *Journal of Economic History*, November 1947, pp. 149–159.

[46]"X2 Biosystems Introduces Their Next Generation X-Patch Pro Head Impact Monitor," *Sport Techie*, March 3, 2016, www.sporttechie.com/2016/03/03/x2-biosystems-introduces-their-next-generation-x-patch-pro-head-impact-monitor/; J. J. McCorvey, "Innovation: Companies on the Cutting Edge," *Inc.*, February 2012, pp. 42–43.

[47]Laurie McCabe, "Seven Daily Inspirations from Dell's Women Entrepreneur Network Event," *Laurie McCabe's Blog*, June 10, 2011, http://lauriemccabe.wordpress.com/2011/06/10/seven-daily-inspirations-from-dell%E2%80%99s-women-entrepreneur-network-event; Daniel McGinn, "How I Did It: Arianna Huffington," *Inc.*, February 1, 2010, www.inc.com/magazine/20100201/how-i-did-it-arianna-huffington.html; Jay Yarow, "*Huffington Post* Traffic Zooms Past the *New York Times*," *Business Insider*, June 9, 2011, www.businessinsider.com/chart-of-the-day-huffpo-nyt-unique-visitors-2011-6?utm_source=twbutton&utm_medium=social&utm_term=&utm_content=&utm_campaign=sai.

[48]*The Best of Bits & Pieces* by Arthur F. Lenehan. Published by Economics Press, 1994, p. 6.

[49]Hal Gregersen, "The Entrepreneur's DNA," *Wall Street Journal*, February 26, 2013, p. B13.

[50]"Harnessing Your Team's Creativity," *BNET*, June 7, 2007, www.bnet.com/2403-13059_23-52990.html.

[51]Frank T. Rothaermel and Andrew M. Hess, "Innovation Strategies Combined," *Sloan Management Review* 51, no. 3 (Spring 2010), pp. 13–15.

[52]Rob Goffee and Gareth Jones, "The Odd Clever People Every Organization Needs," *Forbes*, August 13, 2009, www.forbes.com/2009/08/13/clever-employees-talent-leadership-managing-recruiting.html.

[53]"How the Top CEOs Really Think," *Inc.*, September 2014, www.inc.com/magazine/201409/inc.500-2014-inc-500-ceo-survey-results.html.

[54]Anya Kamenetz, "The Power of the Prize," *Fast Company*, May 2008, pp. 43–45.

[55]John Bessant, Kathrin Möslein, and Bettina Von Stamm, "In Search of Innovation," *Wall Street Journal*, June 22, 2009, p. R4.

[56]Carol Tice, "Fueling Change," *Entrepreneur*, November 2007, p. 47.

[57]Jonathan Ringen, "Most Innovative Companies—Taco Bell: For Combining Corn Beans, Meat, and Cheese into Genius," *Fast Company*, March 2016, pp. 46–49, 116.

[58]Nadine Heintz, "Employee Creativity Unleashed," *Inc.*, June 2009, pp. 101–102.

[59]Rachel Emma Silverman, "The Science of Serendipity in the Workplace," *Wall Street Journal*, May 1, 2013, p. B6; Zach Brand and David Gorsline, "Happy Accidents: The Joy of Serendipity Days," *Inside NPR*, October 14, 2011, www.npr.org/blogs/inside/2011/10/14/141312774/happy-accidents-the-joy-of-serendipity-days.

[60]Matthew Carmichael, "Best Places to Work No. 1: Radio Flyer," *Crain's Chicago Business*, March 29, 2010, www.radioflyer.com/skin/frontend/blank/radioflyer/docs/media/crains_best_il.pdf; Amelia Forczak, "Rolling Down the Path Toward Success," *HR Solutions eNews*, www.hrsolutionsinc.com/enews_1010/RadioFlyer_1010.html.

[61]Cheryl Strauss Einhorn, "Dance Troupe Markets Creativity to Cube-Dwellers," *CNN Money*, April 25, 2013, http://money

.cnn.com/2013/04/23/technology/innovation/trey-mcintyre-project-hewlett-packard/index.html.

[62]Carol Tice, "Fueling Change," *Entrepreneur*, November 2007, p. 47.

[63]Nicholas Bakalar, "Self-Adjustable Eyeglass Lenses," *New York Times*, September 26, 2011, www.nytimes.com/2011/09/27/health/27glasses.html; Mary Jordan, "From a Visionary English Physicist, Self-Adjusting Lenses for the Poor," *Washington Post*, January 10, 2009, http://articles.washingtonpost.com/2009-01-10/world/36786562_1_glasses-plastic-lenses-syringes; Robin McKie, "British Inventor's Spectacles Revolution for Africa," *The Guardian*, May 21, 2011, www.guardian.co.uk/global-development/2011/may/22/joshua-silver-glasses-self-adjusting.

[64]Carol Kinsey Goman, "Want Innovation? Stop Trying So Hard," *Forbes*, February 21, 2012, www.forbes.com/sites/carolkinseygoman/2012/02/21/what-innovation-stop-trying-so-hard/#5f69aa0273d4.

[65]Rachel Emma Silverman, "The Science of Serendipity in the Workplace," *Wall Street Journal*, May 1, 2013, p. B6.

[66]Kenneth Chang, "Solving a Sticky Problem," *New York Times*, March 24, 2015, p. D4.

[67]Robert Epstein, "How to Get a Great Idea," *Reader's Digest*, December 1992, p. 102.

[68]James E. Burroughs, Darren W. Dahl, C. Page Moreau, Amitava Chattopadhyay, and Gerald R. Gorn, "A One-Two Punch to Foster Creativity," *Strategy+Business*, November 4, 2011, www.strategy-business.com/article/re00166?gko=4b582.

[69]Richard Neece, "10 Inspiring Examples of Intrapreneurship," *Wired*, September 17, 2014, http://insights.wired.com/profiles/blogs/10-inspiring-examples-of-successful-intrapreneurship; Alan Deutchsman, "The Fabric of Creativity," *Fast Company*, December 1, 2004, www.fastcompany.com/51733/fabric-creativity.

[70]Sarah E. Needleman and Angus Loten, "3 Ways Small Firms Can Drive Innovation," *Wall Street Journal*, August 30, 2011, http://blogs.wsj.com/in-charge/2011/08/30/how-small-firms-can-drive-innovation.

[71]Christina Binkley, "Fashion Brands Turn to Crowdsourcing for Designs," *Wall Street Journal*, April 28, 2016, p. D3; "Crowdfunding Hits, BetaBrands, www.betabrand.com/collections/crowdfunded-hits.html.

[72]Jonathan Ringen, "Most Innovative Companies—Taco Bell: For Combining Corn Beans, Meat, and Cheese into Genius," *Fast Company*, March 2016, pp. 46–49, 116.

[73]William Harris, "10 New Uses for Old Inventions," How Stuff Works: Science, http://science.howstuffworks.com/innovation/repurposed-inventions/10-new-uses-for-old-inventions5.htm.

[74]Lydia Dishman, "Watermelons, Chuck Taylors, and How Caribou Encourages a Culture of Innovation," *Fast Company*, July 24, 2012, www.fastcompany.com/1843448/watermelons-chuck-taylors-and-how-caribou-coffee-encourages-culture-innovation.

[75]Hal Gregersen, "The Entrepreneur's DNA," *Wall Street Journal*, February 26, 2013, p. B13.

[76]Jason Fried, "When Good Ideas Bear Fruit," *Inc.*, February 2013, p. 33.

[77]Adam Bluestein, "You're Not That Innovative (and That's OK)," *Inc.*, September 2013, pp. 109–114.

[78]Jacob Kleinman, "Kindle Owners Spend Way More Than Non-Kindle Owners on Amazon, Report Shows," *TechnoBuffalo*, December 15, 2013, www.technobuffalo.com/2013/12/15/kindle-owners-spend-way-more-than-non-kindle-owners-on-amazon-report-shows/; Kevin C. Tofel, "Here's How Much in Content Sales Turn Kindle Fire into a Money Maker," *Gigaom*, January 24, 2013, http://gigaom.com/2013/01/24/heres-how-much-in-content-sales-turn-kindle-file-into-a-money-maker/.

[79]Alan Fogg, "National Survey Commissioned by FCEDA Points to 'Creativity Gap' in the U.S. Workplace," Fairfax County Economic Development Authority, December 19, 2014, www.fairfaxcountyeda.org/pressrelease/national-survey-commissioned-fceda-points-%E2%80%9Ccreativity-gap%E2%80%9D-us-workplace.

[80]Jay Walker, "The Power of Imagination," *Wall Street Journal*, February 26, 2013, p. B11.

[81]Sarah Lyall, "Is There a Perp in the Painting?" *New York Times*, April 27, 2016, pp. C1, C5.

[82]Kevan Lee, "How Creative Hobbies Make Us Better at Basically Everything," *Fast Company*, July 16, 2014, www.fastcompany.com/3033028/work-smart/how-creative-hobbies-make-us-better-at-basically-everything.

[83]Judy Kneiszel, "One to Watch: Amsterdam Falafelshop," *QSR*, June 2015, www.qsrmagazine.com/emerging-concepts/one-watch-amsterdam-falafelshop.

[84]"The Keys to Making History," *Fast Company*, December 2012/January 2013, p. 30.

[85]McKenna Grant, "Spark Your Creativity!" *USA Weekend*, June 29–July 1, 2012, p. 4.

[86]"How to Come Up with a Great Idea," *Wall Street Journal*, April 29, 2013, p. R1.

[87]Rudolph Bell, "Local Inventor Puts Finger to the Wind," *Greenville News*, November 13, 2011, pp. 1E, 3E.

[88]Matthew Smith, "The Pressure's Off," *Stand Firm*, April 2012, p. 29.

[89]"Louis-Jacque Mande Daguerre," The Robinson Library, www.robinsonlibrary.com/technology/photography/biography/daguerre.htm; Mary Bellis, "Daguerreotype," www.robinsonlibrary.com/technology/photography/biography/daguerre.htm.

[90]Joe Robinson, "How Positive Thinking Can Make You a Better Problem Solver," *Entrepreneur*, December 18, 2012, www.entrepreneur.com/article/225170.

[91]Robert J. Toth, "Help Wanted? Eureka!" *Wall Street Journal*, April 29, 2013, p. R5.

[92]Jonah Comstock, "SwipeSense Gets $9.6 Million for Hand Hygiene Tracking System," *Mobile Health News*, June 11, 2015, Navi Radjou, http://mobihealthnews.com/44333/swipesense-gets-9-6m-for-hand-hygiene-tracking-system; Jaideep Prabhu, and Simone Ahuja, "Millennials Are the McGyvers of Business," *Harvard Business Review*, March 13, 2012, http://blogs.hbr.org/cs/2012/03/millennials_are_the_macgyvers.html; Peter Frost, "Swipe-Sense Gets a Hand with $50,000 in Seed Capital, Guidance from HealthBox, a Healthcare Technology Accelerator Program," *Chicago Tribune*, April 4, 2012, http://articles.chicagotribune.com/2012-04-04/business/ct-biz-0405-health-pitch-20120404_1_hospital-acquired-infections-angel-investors-wellness-program.

[93]Don Debelak, "Ideas Unlimited," *Business Start-ups*, May 1999, pp. 57–58.

[94]Judy Sutton Taylor, "The Cutting Edge," *Entrepreneur*, December 2015, pp. 99–100.

[95]Katherine Duncan, "Sweet Dreams," *Entrepreneur*, August 2012, p. 43.

[96]Michael White, "Neurosky Headset Reads Minds, Picks Film Twists," *San Francisco Gate*, October 2, 2010, www.sfgate.com/business/article/NeuroSky-headset-reads-minds-picks-film-twists-3172473.php.

[97]Julia Savacool, "Walking Boosts Creativity, So Think on Your Feet," *Greenville News*, June 1, 2014, p. 3U; Margaret Talev

and Carol Hymowitz, "Zuckerberg, Obama Channel Jobs in Search for Alone Time," *Bloomberg*, April 30, 2014, www.bloomberg.com/news/2014-04-30/walking-is-the-new-sitting-for-decision-makers.html; May Wong, "Stanford Study Finds Walking Improves Creativity," *Stanford News*, April 24, 2014, http://news.stanford.edu/news/2014/april/walking-vs-sitting-042414.html.

[98]Julie Sloane, "Inside the Mind of a (Rich) Inventor," *FSB*, November 2007, pp. 90–102.

[99]Danielle Burteaux, "Popping the Lock," *Entrepreneur*, February 2016, pp. 59–60; "About Us," KeySmart, www.getkeysmart.com/pages/about-us.

[100]Nadine Heintz, "Employee Creativity Unleashed," *Inc.*, June 2009, pp. 101–102.

[101]Gwen Moran, "Want More Creative and Productive Employees? Let Them Goof Off," *Entrepreneur*, June 19, 2013, www.entrepreneur.com/article/226919.

[102]Rosa Alphonso, "Small Business Optimism Is on an Upswing, According to the OPEN from American Express Small Business Monitor," American Express, May 24, 2007, http://home3.americanexpress.com/corp/pc/2007/monitor.asp.

[103]Geoff Williams, "Innovative Model," *Entrepreneur*, September 2002, p. 66.

[104]Aaron Pressman, "J.K. Rowling's Magic Touch Sends 'Harry Potter' Sales Booming," *Yahoo! Finance*, January 25, 2016, http://finance.yahoo.com/news/j-k-rowling-s-magic-touch-sends-harry-potter-sales-booming-180159853.html; Diana Lodderhose and Marc Graser, "J. K. Rowling Unveils 'Pottermore,'" *Variety*, June 23, 2011, www.variety.com/article/VR1118039008?refcatid=1009.

[105]Roy Rowan, "Those Hunches Are More Than Blind Faith," *Fortune*, April 23, 1979, p. 112.

[106]Michael Waldholz, "A Hallucination Inspires a Vision for AIDS Drug," *Wall Street Journal*, September 29, 1993, pp. B1, B5.

[107]"Sharkwave," *Scientific Angler*, www.scientificanglers.com/sharkwave/; "Fly Goes Hi-Tech with New S. A. Sharkskin Lines and Sage Targets Bassers," *Tackle Tour*, January 20, 2008, www.tackletour.com/reviewise08flycoverage.html.

[108]Alison Overholt, "From Idea to Innovation," *Fast Company*, February 2013, pp. 49–50.

[109]Siri Schubert, "Folate Is Gr-r-reat!" *Business 2.0*, November 2004, p. 72.

[110]Josh Dean, "Saul's House of Cool Ideas," *Inc.*, February 2010, p. 71.

[111]Nicole Marie Richardson, "The Answer Is Blowing in the (Very Gentle) Wind," *Inc.*, October 2009, pp. 38–39.

[112]Nick D'Alto, "Think Big," *Business Start-ups*, January 2000, pp. 61–65.

[113]Sue Shellenbarger, "Tactics to Spark Creativity," *Wall Street Journal*, April 3, 2013, pp. B1–B2.

[114]Brian Nadel, "The Art of Innovation," Advertising Insert, *Fortune*, December 13, 2004, pp. S1–S22.

[115]Sue Shellenbarger, "Tactics to Spark Creativity," *Wall Street Journal*, April 3, 2013, pp. B1–B2.

[116]Jonah Lehrer, "Bother Me, I'm Thinking," *Wall Street Journal*, February 19, 2011, http://online.wsj.com/article/SB10001424052748703584804576144192132144506.html.

[117]Sue Shellenbarger, "Tactics to Spark Creativity," *Wall Street Journal*, April 3, 2013, pp. B1–B2.

[118]Sarah Kessler, "Walk, Talk, Ride, Recharge," *Inc.*, May 2010, p. 26; "About Us," nPower PEG, www.npowerpeg.com/index.php/our-story.

[119]"What Are Dreams?" *Nova*, PBS, June 29, 2011, www.pbs.org/wgbh/nova/body/what-are-dreams.html.

[120]Thea Singer, "Your Brain on Innovation," *Inc.*, September 2002, pp. 86–88.

[121]"The 100 Most Creative People in Business," *Fast Company*, June 2011, p. 88.

[122]Ben Baldwin, "Ben Baldwin: Stop and Smell the Flowers," *Wall Street Journal Blogs*, May 1, 2013, http://blogs.wsj.com/accelerators/2013/05/01/ben-baldwin-stop-and-smell-the-flowers; "How to Come Up with a Great Idea," *Wall Street Journal*, April 29, 2013, p. R1.

[123]Paul Bagne, "When to Follow a Hunch," *Reader's Digest*, May 1994, p. 77.

[124]Susan Hansen, "The Action Hero," *Inc.*, September 2002, pp. 82–84.

[125]Michael Waldholz, "A Hallucination Inspires a Vision for AIDS Drug," *Wall Street Journal*, September 29, 1993, pp. B1, B5.

[126]Theunis Bates, "Supertiny Power Plants," *Fast Company*, June 2010, p. 38; "Technology," Innowattech, www.innowattech.co.il/technology.aspx.

[127]Robert Epstein, "How to Get a Great Idea," *Reader's Digest*, December 1992, p. 104.

[128]Michael Waldholz, "A Hallucination Inspires a Vision for AIDS Drug," *Wall Street Journal*, September 29, 1993, pp. B1, B5.

[129]Bridget Finn, "Brainstorming for Better Brainstorming," *Business 2.0*, April 2005, pp. 109–114.

[130]Chun, "Theory of Creativity," *Entrepreneur*, pp. 130–131.

[131]Amantha Imber, "Finding Inspiration on the Treadmill," *Get to the Point: Small Business* (Marketing Profs), May 12, 2008, pp. 1–2.

[132]Bridget Finn, "Brainstorming for Better Brainstorming," *Business 2.0*, April 2005, pp. 109–114.

[133]Ed Brown, "A Day at Innovation U," *Fortune*, April 12, 1999, pp. 163–165.

[134]The Hall of Science and Exploration, "Academy of Achievement: Linus Pauling, PhD," www.achievement.org/autodoc/page/pau0pro-1.

[135]Anne Fisher, "Ideas Made Here," *Fortune*, June 11, 2007, pp. 35–41.

[136]Andy Raskin, "A Higher Plane of Problem-Solving," *Business 2.0*, June 2003, pp. 54–56; "TRIZ 40," Triz 40 Principles, www.triz40.com/aff_Principles.htm.

[137]Sloane, "Inside the Mind of a (Rich) Inventor," *FSB*, November 2007, pp. 90–102.

[138]Ed Brown, "A Day at Innovation U," *Fortune*, April 12, 1999, p. 165.

[139]Ibid.

[140]"Trade in Fake Goods Has Worsened to Almost Half a Trillion Dollars: OECD," *Reuters*, April 18, 2016, www.reuters.com/article/us-oecd-fake-idUSKCN0XF127.

[141]*Intellectual Property Rights: Fiscal Year 2015 Seizure Statistics*, Department of Homeland Security, U.S. Customs and Border Protection, Office of International Trade, 2016, p. 11.

[142]Carl De Torres, "The Cups Are All Right," *Fast Company*, September 2012, p. 21; Venessa Wong, Rival K-Cup Makers Are Climbing Green Mountain, *Bloomberg Businessweek*, August 9, 2013, www.businessweek.com/articles/2013-08-09/rival-k-cup-makers-are-climbing-green-mountain.

[143]Sara Schaefer Muñoz, "Patent No. 6,004,596: Peanut Butter and Jelly Sandwich," *Wall Street Journal*, April 5, 2005, pp. B1, B9; Malia Rulon, "Smucker Can't Patent PBJ, Court Says," *Greenville News*, April 9, 2005, pp. 18A, 21A.

[144]L. Gordon Crovitz, "Could Morse Have Patented the Web?" *Wall Street Journal*, March 26, 2012, p. A15; John P. Mello, Jr., "Google Gets Patent for Using Background Noise to Target Ads," *Tech Hive*, March 20, 2012, www.techhive.com/article/252259/google_gets_patent_for_using_background_noise_to_target_ads.html.

[145]"U.S. Patent Statistics," U.S. Patent and Trademark Office, www.uspto.gov/web/offices/ac/ido/oeip/taf/us_stat.pdf.

[146]Michael S. Malone, "The Smother of Invention," *Forbes ASAP*, June 24, 2002, pp. 32–40.

[147]"Data Visualization Center," U.S. Patent and Trademark Office, www.uspto.gov/dashboards/patents/main.dashxml.

[148]Chris Barry, Ronen Arad, Landan Ansell, Meredith Cartier, and HyeYun Lee, *2017 Patent Litigation Study: Change on the Horizon?* PriceWaterhouseCoopers, May 2017, pp. 2–11; Richard W. Goldstein and Donika P. Pentcheva, *Report of the Economic Survey*, American Intellectual Property Association, June 2016, p. 37.

[149]Jennifer Alsever, "Counterfeit Combat," *Inc.*, March 2015, pp. 68–69.

[150]Ibid.

[151]Michael B. Sapherstein, "The Registrability of the Harley-Davidson Roar: A Multimedia Analysis," www.bc.edu/bc_org/avp/law/st_org/iptf/articles/content/1998101101.html; Tomima Edmark, "How Much Is Too Much?" *Entrepreneur*, February 1998, pp. 93–95.

[152]"Judicial Facts and Figures: Copyright, Patent, and Trademark Cases Filed," United States Courts, 2015, www.uscourts.gov/statistics-reports/judicial-facts-and-figures-2015.

[153]David Wren, "Trademark Expiration a Symbolic End to Firehouse Subs Lawsuit Against Myrtle Beach Area Eatery, *MyrtleBeachOnline*, November 21, 2012, www.myrtlebeachonline.com/2012/11/21/3182930/trademark-expiration-a-symbolic.html; David Wren, "Firehouse Restaurant Lawsuit Could Be Headed Back to Court," *Restaurant News*, August 30, 2011, www.restaurantnews.com/firehouse-restaurant-lawsuit-could-be-headed-back-to-court/; David Wren, "S.C. Firefighter Wins Firehouse Subs Trademark Lawsuit," *Star News*, August 24, 2011, www.starnewsonline.com/article/20110824/wire/110829876.

[154]"Trademark Dashboard," U.S. Patent and Trademark Office, www.uspto.gov/dashboards/trademarks/main.dashxml.

[155]Ibid.

[156]"FAQ," U.S. Copyright Office, www.copyright.gov/help/faq/faq-what.html#certificate.

[157]*Seizing Opportunity Through License Compliance: 2016 BSA Global Software Piracy Study,* Business Software Alliance, May 2016, p. 5.

4

Conducting a Feasibility Analysis and Designing a Business Model

Dusit Panyakhom/123RF

Learning Objectives

On completion of this chapter, you will be able to:

1. Describe the process of conducting an idea assessment.

2. Explain the elements of a feasibility analysis.

3. Describe the six forces in the macro environment of an industry.

4. Understand how Porter's Five Forces Model assesses the competitive environment.

5. Describe the various methods of conducting primary and secondary market research.

6. Understand the four major elements of a financial feasibility analysis.

7. Describe the process of assessing entrepreneur feasibility.

8. Describe the nine elements of a business model in the Business Model Canvas.

MyLab Entrepreneurship

⭐ Improve Your Grade!

If your instructor is using MyLab Entrepreneurship, visit **www.pearson.com/mylab/entrepreneurship** for videos, simulations, and writing exercises.

For many entrepreneurs, the easiest part of launching a business is coming up with an idea for a new business concept or approach. Business success, however, requires much more than just a great new idea. In addition to coming up with a business idea and launching a business, five critical steps guide the process of going from idea generation to growing a successful business: idea assessment, feasibility study, business modeling, business planning, and strategic planning. Together these steps make up the new business planning process. Following these steps increases the entrepreneur's chances of launching a successful and sustainable business.

idea assessment
the process of examining a need in the market, developing a solution for that need, and determining the entrepreneur's ability to successfully turn the idea into a business.

Once entrepreneurs develop ideas for new businesses, the next step is to assess these ideas. An **idea assessment** is the process of examining a need in the market, developing a solution for that need, and determining the entrepreneur's ability to successfully turn the idea into a business. The best business ideas start with a group of customers with a common problem or need. Successful entrepreneurs learn to apply the creative processes discussed in Chapter 3 to find solutions for these customers. Entrepreneurs often identify multiple possible business ideas for any given market need. The idea assessment process helps an entrepreneur more efficiently and effectively examine multiple ideas to identify the solution with the most potential. Examining multiple business ideas ensures that the entrepreneur does not lock in on a single idea and overlook others that have even greater chances for success.

After identifying the most promising idea using the idea assessment process, the entrepreneur subjects it to a feasibility analysis to determine whether he or she can transform the idea into a viable business. A *feasibility analysis* is the process of determining whether an entrepreneur's idea is a viable foundation for creating a successful business. Its purpose is to determine whether a business idea is worth pursuing. A feasibility study answers the question "Should we proceed with this business idea?" Its role is to serve as a filter, screening out ideas that lack the potential for building a successful business, before an entrepreneur commits resources to developing and testing a business model or building a business plan. A feasibility study is primarily an investigative tool. It is designed to give an entrepreneur a picture of the market and the sales and profit potential of a particular business idea. Will a ski resort located here attract enough customers to be successful? Will customers in this community support a sandwich shop with a retro rock-n-roll theme? Can we build the product at a reasonable cost and sell it at a price customers are willing and able to pay? Does this entrepreneurial team have the ability to implement the idea successfully?

If the idea passes the feasibility analysis, the entrepreneur moves on to the next steps of the new business planning process. If the idea fails to pass muster, the entrepreneur drops it and moves on to the next idea. He or she has not wasted valuable time, money, energy, and other resources building a plan for launching a business that is destined to fail because it is based on a flawed concept. Although it is impossible for a feasibility study to guarantee an idea's success, conducting a study reduces the likelihood that entrepreneurs will waste their time pursuing fruitless business ventures.

The business model answers the question "How will we proceed with this business idea?" Developing a business model, which is the third step in planning a new business, helps the entrepreneur fully understand all that will be required to launch and build the business. Business modeling is another step that determines the potential for success for the new venture. It is a visual process that examines how all the moving parts of the business must work together to build a successful venture. It is the step in the planning process in which the entrepreneur tests the concept and uses what he or she learns from real customers to refine the business model before commiting the resources to grow the business to its full potential.

The idea assessment, feasibility study, business model, business plan, and strategic plan all play important but separate roles in the start-up and growth of an entrepreneurial venture (see Figure 4.1). This chapter describes the idea assessment, feasibility study, and business model development. Chapter 5 examines how to craft a business plan to guide the start-up of a new business, as well as the strategic planning process that helps navigate the growth of the business.

Idea Assessment

Successful entrepreneurs understand that the process of going from ideas to the launch of a new business venture is like a funnel. When the entrepreneur observes a need in the market, using the creative process generates many business ideas that might address this need. Each step in

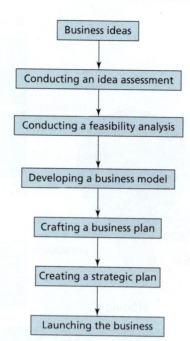

FIGURE 4.1

New Business Planning Process

the new business planning process narrows the number of ideas until the entrepreneur is ready to launch a business that he or she has carefully researched and tested. An idea assessment helps the entrepreneur efficiently evaluate the numerous ideas that come out of the creative process before committing the time and effort to craft a business plan, design a business model, or even conduct a feasibility analysis. One effective tool used to help assess ideas is an idea sketch pad.[1]

Entrepreneurs too often jump ahead and begin modeling or planning their business ideas before they conduct an honest assessment of them. They get excited about the potential they imagine if they launched a business based on the idea. However, most ideas do not become successful businesses. Alex Bruton, developer of The Really Big Idea Sketch Pad, says it is human nature to misjudge how unlikely it is for a new business idea to actually become a successful business.[2] Rather than act on a hunch, successful entrepreneurs are disciplined in evaluating each new idea. Because it takes so many ideas to come up with a viable business concept, entrepreneurs must become adept at quickly sorting through all of them.

An idea sketch pad helps an entrepreneur assess ideas in a relatively short period of time. When using a sketch pad, the entrepreneur asks a series of key questions addressing five key parameters (see Figure 4.2):

1. *Customers.* Start with a group of customers who have a clear need that is not being addressed. This may be a need that no business is currently addressing, or it may be a need that no business is fully or adequately meeting for these customers. The entrepreneur assesses the customers by answering basic questions about the potential users of the product or service and the potential buyers if they are different than the users. For instance, for sugary cereals, children are the users, and their parents are the buyers. Specifically, who would be the users of the offering? How would they use the offering? How many potential customers are there?

2. *Offering.* Describe your idea for a product or service to offer the customers. Are you offering a product, a service, an experience, or a combination of one or more of these? What are its key features? Describe it in detail and sketch out an image of it if you can.

3. *Value proposition.* Explain why your product or service will be important to the customers. Why would your offering be valuable to the user and/or buyer? How does it address the need these customers currently have that is not being met?

4. *Core competencies.* Does your offering include any technologies or unique features that will help differentiate it from competitors? Is it based on intellectual property that you can protect with patents, trademarks, or copyrights?

The Really Big Idea Sketch Pad

These are the parameters to change when creating or refining a venture or project idea. Think of it as sketching your idea.

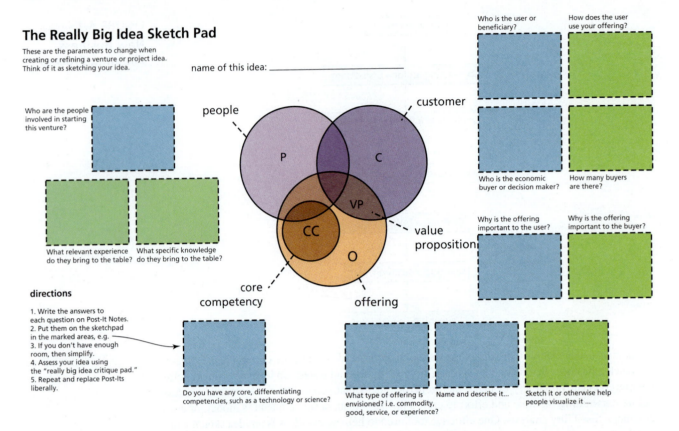

directions

1. Write the answers to each question on Post-It Notes.
2. Put them on the sketchpad in the marked areas, e.g.
3. If you don't have enough room, then simplify.
4. Assess your idea using the "really big idea critique pad."
5. Repeat and replace Post-Its liberally.

FIGURE 4.2

Idea Sketch Pad

Source: Dr. Alex Bruton, The Innographer, Ltd., theinnographer.com/toolkit/idea-modeling.

5. *People.* Identify the key people on the team who will launch this business. Who are the founding entrepreneurs of this venture? Do they have the skills and knowledge necessary to successfully turn the idea into a start-up venture? Can they attract key team members who will fill in any gaps in knowledge, skills, and experience?

By placing the answers to these questions on a sketch pad, entrepreneurs can clearly visualize gaps or weaknesses in their ideas. Rather than use the tool to make minor changes in an idea, they can find ways to fundamentally change the idea to improve its chances for success in the market before they move ahead and launch a new business.[3] Successful entrepreneurs do not become emotionally attached to their ideas. If an idea shows promise based on the idea sketch pad, they move ahead to the next step of conducting a feasibility analysis. If entrepreneurs cannot resolve the gaps or weaknesses that the idea sketch pad reveals in an idea, they turn to the next idea and assess it using the sketch pad process.

LO2

Explain the elements of a feasibility analysis.

feasibility analysis

an analysis of the viability of a business idea that includes four interrelated components: an industry and market analysis, the product or service analysis, a financial analysis, and an entrepreneur analysis.

Feasibility Analysis

After conducting the idea assessment, an entrepreneur scrutinizes the idea further through a **feasibility analysis**. A feasibility analysis consists of four interrelated components: an industry and market feasibility analysis, a product or service feasibility analysis, a financial feasibility analysis, and an entrepreneur feasibility analysis (see Figure 4.3). Rhonda Abrams, nationally syndicated columnist, author, and successful entrepreneur, says that feasibility analysis is an opportunity to take a hard look at your idea to see whether it needs minor or major pivots or, if warranted, whether you should abandon it completely and move on to another idea.[4]

When evaluating the feasibility of a business idea, an analysis of the industry and targeted market segments serves as the starting point for the remaining three components of a feasibility analysis. The focus in this phase is twofold: (1) to determine how attractive an industry is overall as a "home" for a new business and (2) to evaluate possible niches in the industry a small business can occupy profitably. When examining an industry, an entrepreneur should examine both the macro environment that can have an impact across many industries and the specific competitive environment of the industry of interest (see Figure 4.4).

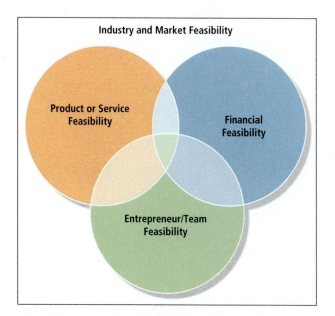

FIGURE 4.3
Elements of a Feasibility Analysis

Industry and Market Feasibility

LO3
Describe the six forces in the macro environment of an industry.

The first step in assessing industry attractiveness is to paint a picture of the industry in broad strokes, assessing it from a "macro" level. Most opportunities for new businesses in an industry are due to changes taking place in it. Foundational macro forces shape industries and the markets they serve. Changes in any of these macro forces can dramatically change the competitive nature of an industry and fundamentally change the needs and wants in its target market. Entrepreneurs must be vigilant when monitoring macro forces. Changes in macro forces may have created the initial opportunity the entrepreneur pursued when launching the business, and change will likely continue. If the entrepreneur does not adapt the business to meet the changes these macro forces create in the industry and market, even the most innovative new business may become outdated and may be left behind in the competitive landscape.

Six foundational macro forces create change in industries and the markets they serve:

1. *Sociocultural.* Social and cultural change can lead to dramatic changes that can create whole new industries and fundamentally transform existing industries. For example, in the 1970s and 1980s women began entering the workforce at much higher rates than had been the case previously. This change was a result of the women's movement of the 1960s.

FIGURE 4.4
Environmental Forces and New Ventures

FIGURE 4.5

American Labor Force Participation Rate

Source: Labor Force Statistics from *Current Population Survey*, U.S. Department of Labor, July 19, 2016, http://data.bls.gov/timeseries/LNS11300000.

Figure 4.5 displays the dramatic increase in the size of the American workforce that resulted from this cultural change. Not only did more women enter the workforce, but they also had career aspirations to compete for jobs that previously had been dominated by male workers. This cultural change led to the birth of the daycare industry. It also resulted in a new segment within the women's fashion industry for women's business attire. It led to rapid growth in the restaurant industry as families began eating in restaurants much more frequently, spending a greater amount on food away from home than previous generations (see Figure 4.6). Finally, as more women entered the workforce, the percentage of families with two cars doubled between 1960 and 2013.[5]

2. *Technological.* Technological breakthroughs lead to the development of new products and entirely new industries. For example, the Internet is a technology that has had a profound impact on many industries. Before the Internet age, a few large companies dominated the music industry. The Internet led to the creation of many new businesses within

FIGURE 4.6

Food Expenditure Away from Home as a Percentage of Total Food Budget

Source: Food Expenditures, U.S. Department of Agriculture, March 2, 2016, www.ers.usda.gov/data-products/food-expenditures.aspx#26636.

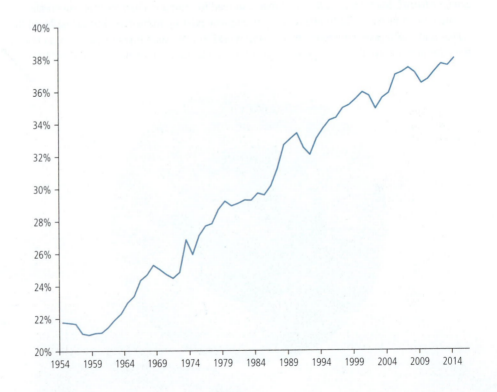

the music industry, including Pandora, Spotify, and Apple's iTunes, which changed how customers buy and listen to music. The Internet also changed how people consume information. As news became available online, there was a dramatic decrease in the number of people reading print newspapers. As result, advertising revenues have plummeted for print newspapers, while online newspapers have experienced steady growth in advertising.

ENTREPRENEURIAL PROFILE: Shawn Glinter: Nanoferix

Nanotechnology develops functional engineered systems at the molecular scale. Applications of nanotechnology innovation range from materials science to biomedical applications. Within medicine, nanotechnology includes the invention of particles that aid in the prevention, diagnosis, and treatment of diseases. Drug delivery using nanotechnology offers the potential benefit of reducing the doses necessary to achieve the same therapeutic benefit as with traditional intravenous and oral delivery of medication. As a result, nanotechnology could reduce the cost of treatment and reduce side effects associated with many drugs. Shawn Glinter, a serial entrepreneur, licensed a promising nanotechnology from Vanderbilt University and assembled a team of scientists in his start-up, Nanoferix, to find commercial applications for the technology. Glinter's focus is on fund-raising with angel investors and venture capitalists. The goal is to develop a commercial application that could lead to a sale of Nanoferix or licensing of its nanotechnology to a large healthcare company. If successful, Nanoferix might allow patients to take a pill monthly rather than once a day.[6] ∎

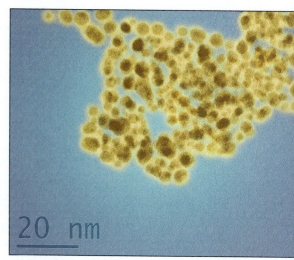

Greenshoots Communications/NCP Images/Alamy Stock Photo

3. *Demographic.* Changing demographics create opportunities for entrepreneurs. For example, as Generation Y, or Millennials, (those born between 1977 and 1995) reaches adulthood, businesses will begin to pay attention to the next generation, Generation Z. Although Generation Y is optimistic and idealistic, those who are part of Generation Z (those born between 1996 and 2010) are much more realistic. School violence and the Great Recession (which began in 2008) have shaped their lives. Generation Z is more realistic in how they view the world and more cynical about the future. Because they watched their parents' generation struggle with prolonged unemployment and economic uncertainty, they intend to be careful with their money. Those in Generation Z will seek products and services that offer value. In a survey of members of Generation Z conducted by the Intelligence Group, 57 percent said they would rather save money than spend it![7]

ENTREPRENEURIAL PROFILE: Sherwin Sheik, CareLinx Members of the Baby Boom Generation are now entering their retirement years. By the year 2050, 20.7 percent of the population will be 65 years or older. However, unlike previous generations, Baby Boomers have no intention of spending their sunset years in a senior care facility; they intend to spend the rest of their lives within the comfort of their own homes. Even though the Baby Boomers will be the largest senior generation ever in the United States, the number of nursing homes is projected to decline by 20 percent by 2021. Medicare and Medicaid are beginning to recognize that home care is a cost-effective alternative to senior living facilities such as nursing homes. Sherwin Sheik noticed this trend and founded CareLinx with the goal of helping the elderly remain safely in their homes by bringing caregivers directly to them. Sheik's interest in providing in-home care comes from his own experience with a sister, who has multiple sclerosis, and an uncle, who suffered from Lou Gehrig's disease. Both family members required 24-hour care. His family tried to arrange in-home care but had little success due to the unreliability of many of the caregivers they contracted with to provide assistance. CareLinx matches families seeking help with more than 150,000 professional caregivers, including nurse assistants, registered nurses, and nurse practitioners. By connecting clients and caregivers online, Sheik says CareLinx saves families about 50 percent compared to traditional home care agencies, while offering caregivers 25 percent higher wages.[8] ∎

Courtesy of Sherwin Sheik, CEO, CareLinx

4. *Economic.* Most business's financial fortunes are tied to the performance of the overall economy. Although most companies struggle during economic downturns, some businesses are able to grow. For example, businesses in the e-learning industry thrived during the Great Recession. Web-based learning provides customers with opportunities to improve their education and skills at an affordable price. Given the highly competitive job market during a recession, additional knowledge and skills offer job seekers a competitive advantage when applying for a new position. However, those who were unemployed or afraid of becoming unemployed were unwilling to pay the growing cost of tuition for traditional educational programs. Companies that provide high-quality Web-based e-learning at a fraction of the cost of traditional university-based education filled this gap in the market.

5. *Political and legal.* The enactment of new legislation creates opportunities for entrepreneurs. For example, when the Patient Protection and Affordable Care Act (also known as Obamacare) was passed in 2010, entrepreneurs recognized that the legislation created a complex array of new requirements for healthcare companies. Because of this legislation, payment for healthcare is shifting from fee-for-service (where healthcare providers are paid a set amount for each procedure or service they provide) to a system based on pay-for-performance. In a pay-for-performance system, insurance companies and government agencies reward healthcare providers and hospitals for initiatives that improve the quality, efficiency, and overall value of healthcare. Because pay-for-performance is new to healthcare, savvy entrepreneurs are creating new companies that help healthcare providers and hospitals track and report performance-related metrics based on the value of the healthcare they provide, measure and improve quality of healthcare outcomes, and enhance efficiency in their healthcare delivery systems.

6. *Global.* Global trends create opportunities for even the smallest of companies. More open global markets allow businesses to seek customers and suppliers from all corners of the world.

Courtesy of Ethan Siegl, Orb Audio LLC

ENTREPRENEURIAL PROFILE: Ethan Siegel, Orb Audio Orb Audio, headquartered in New York City, manufactures high-end speakers for home theater systems from its factory in Sherman Oaks, California. Rather than sell through traditional retail outlets, Orb Audio sells directly to customers through its Web site. When the dollar weakened against other currencies in 2008, cofounder Ethan Siegel noticed a sharp increase in orders from international markets. The weak dollar made American-made goods more attractive to international customers whose buying power improved with the declining dollar. Siegel started running Internet advertisements aimed at consumers in the markets where most of the increase in international sales were coming from, including Great Britain, Canada, Finland, and Australia. Global sales for Orb Audio now account for 35 percent of revenue. Finland alone accounts for 10 percent of total sales for Orb Audio. Although domestic sales for Orb Audio have declined since 2008, total revenue continues to grow due to the expansion of international sales for this small manufacturer.[9] ■

While evaluating the six foundational macro trends, entrepreneurs should answer the following questions to help further evaluate the attractiveness of that industry in light of the impact of the macro forces for change:

- How large is the industry?

- How fast is it growing?

- Is the industry as a whole profitable?

- Is the industry characterized by high profit margins or razor-thin margins?

- How essential are its products or services to customers?

- What trends are shaping the industry's future?

- What threats does the industry face?

- What opportunities does the industry face?

- How crowded is the industry?

- How intense is the level of competition in the industry?

- Is the industry young, mature, or somewhere in between?

Addressing these questions helps entrepreneurs determine whether the potential exists for sufficient demand for their products and services.

Porter's Five Forces Model

LO4

Understand how Porter's Five Forces Model assesses the competitive environment.

After evaluating the broader macro environment, an entrepreneur changes focus to the more immediate competitive environment. A useful tool for analyzing a specific industry's attractiveness within the competitive environment is the Five Forces Model, developed by Michael Porter of the Harvard Business School (see Figure 4.7). Five forces interact with one another to determine the setting in which companies compete and hence the attractiveness of the industry: (1) the rivalry among competing firms, (2) the bargaining power of suppliers, (3) the bargaining power of buyers, (4) the threat of new entrants, and (5) the threat of substitute products or services.

Rivalry Among Companies Competing in the Industry

The strongest of the five forces in most industries is the rivalry that exists among the businesses competing in a particular market. Much like the horses running in the Kentucky Derby, businesses in a market are jockeying for position in an attempt to gain a competitive advantage. When a company creates an innovation or develops a unique strategy that transforms the market, competing companies must adapt or run the risk of being forced out of business.

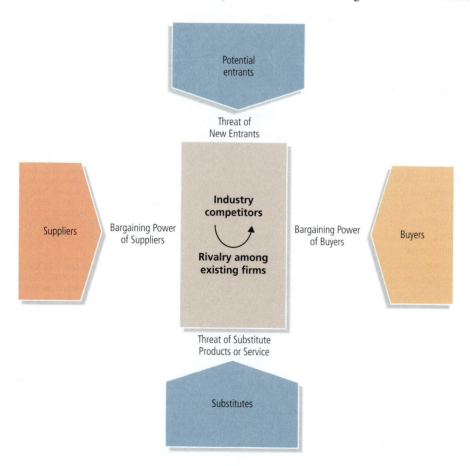

FIGURE 4.7

Five Forces Model of Competition

Source: Adapted from Michael E. Porter, "How Competitive Forces Shape Strategy," *Harvard Business Review* 57, no. 2 (March–April 1979): 137–145.

Hands On . . . How To

Forces Shaping Innovation: The Driverless Car

Driverless cars have been the stuff of science fiction for several decades. As a result of several recent technological breakthroughs, a fully functional driverless car may soon become possible. According to technology consulting firm PTOLEMUS, by 2030, around 380 million vehicles on the roads will have some level of self-driving technology. The firm predicts that this technology could reduce the number of road accidents by 30 percent. However, all of the macro forces shaping the automobile industry must come into alignment for the driverless car to become a true market opportunity:

Sociocultural environment. For generations, the automobile has been enmeshed within the American culture. While other countries developed advanced mass transit systems, Americans stayed loyal to their cars and the freedom they offered to allow them to drive when, where, and how they wanted to. A survey of 1,800 drivers by the American Automobile Association suggests that although 60 percent of respondents would pay for self-driving features, such as automatic braking or self-parking, when purchasing their next car, 80 percent do not trust a fully self-driving automobile. A survey by Pew Research Center found that only 50 percent of Americans would even consider riding in a self-driving car. Some experts believe that the technology for the driverless car may be ready well before consumers are ready to accept the product. However, others believe that the dramatic rise in the use of Uber and other ridesharing services may be softening consumer resistance, as more people are becoming willing to hand over the driving to someone else.

Technological environment. Due to advances in sensors, microcontrollers, GPS, radar, lasers, and cameras, the technological feasibility for a driverless car has advanced quickly in recent years. Traditional automobile companies, including Nissan, General Motors, and Lexus, all have driverless car technologies under development. Google and Tesla are leaders in the development of technology to enable driverless cars. Google has logged hundreds of thousands of miles of testing for its driverless technology with no reported safety issues. However, Tesla's autopilot system (not a fully self-driving car) had a major setback after a fatal accident occurred while a Tesla was in autopilot mode. The car's sensors failed to identify a truck that was turning left in front of it as an obstacle and crashed broadside into the truck. Although the technology for a driverless car is advancing, safety experts caution about rushing autonomous cars to market too quickly.

Demographic environment. As Baby Boomers age, driverless car technologies offer this generation the promise of continued autonomy even after they reach the point when it is no longer safe for them to drive. Google is already targeting the elderly market for self-driving cars.

Economic environment. With continuing concerns about the cost and supply of energy, driverless cars may offer significant fuel savings. Computers in driverless cars will be able to determine the most direct route with the least traffic congestion and will drive at controlled speeds, all of which will improve fuel consumption for every car on the road.

Political/legal environment. Although the other macro forces all seem to favor the emergence of a market for driverless cars, the political and legal environment is not all favorable. Currently, the law assumes that a person is in the driver's seat when an accident or another legal problem arises. This is why Google and Tesla still stress that "drivers" of autonomous automobiles should keep their hands near the wheel and their eyes on the road at all times. That makes the vehicles street legal for now, but it doesn't help speed the rollout of fully autonomous vehicles. Clearly, legislators and the courts must address liability issues for incidents involving autonomous cars before widespread use of driverless cars can become a reality. In addition, regulations and government policies require significant revision to address the drastic changes driverless cars will bring to the roads.

1. What changes in macro environmental forces are shaping the feasibility of the driverless car?

2. If you were an executive at an automobile company, would you pursue creating your own model of a driverless car? Why or why not?

3. What other opportunities for new businesses can you envision that may result from the introduction of the driverless car into the market?

Sources: Based on Michelle Fox, "Driverless Cars Aren't Ready for the Road, Expert Warns," *CNBC*, July 10, 2016, www.cnbc.com/2016/07/10/driverless-cars-arent-ready-for-the-road-expert-warns.html; Chris Isidore, "AAA Says 75% of Drivers Are Scared of Self-driving Cars," *CNN Money*, March 1, 2016, http://money.cnn.com/2016/03/01/autos/aaa-self-driving-cars/; Aaron Smith, "U.S. Views of Technology and the Future," Pew Research Center, April 17, 2014, www.pewinternet.org/2014/04/17/us-views-of-technology-and-the-future/; Christina DesMarais, "Driverless Cars: Tesla, Google, Nissan and Others Shift Gears," *GreenBiz.com*, November 19, 2013, www.greenbiz.com/blog/2013/11/19/driverless-cars-tesla-google-nissan-shift-gear?mkt_tok=3RkMMJWWfF9wsRoluK7NZKXonjHpfsX56u4rUa631MI%2F0ER3fOvrPUfGjI4CTMtqI%2BSLDwEYGJIv6SgFSLHEMa5qw7gMXRQ%3D; Dana Hull, "Google Thinks Self-Driving Cars Will Be Great for Stranded Seniors," *Bloomberg Businessweek*, March 2, 2016, www.bloomberg.com/news/articles/2016-03-02/google-thinks-self-driving-cars-will-be-great-for-stranded-seniors; Mike Spector and Mike Ramsey, "U.S. Proposes Spending $4 Billion to Encourage Driverless Cars," *Wall Street Journal*, January 14, 2016, www.wsj.com/articles/obama-administration-proposes-spending-4-billion-on-driverless-car-guidelines-1452798787; Holman W. Jenkins Jr., "Will Tort Law Kill Driverless Cars?" *Wall Street Journal*, December 17, 2013, http://online.wsj.com/news/articles/SB10001424052702304403804579264261779925166.

the business concept. An overly optimistic entrepreneur may overlook important information about the true feasibility of the business if he or she searches only for information that affirms starting the business. It also is important to search for information that does not support the concept. Depending on the nature and severity of any negative evidence, an entrepreneur can either adapt the concept if it is possible to do so or, if necessary, abandon the idea entirely.

Customer Surveys and Questionnaires

Keep customer surveys and questionnaires short. Word your questions carefully so that you do not bias the results and use a simple ranking system (e.g., a 1-to-5 scale, with 1 representing "definitely would not buy" and 5 representing "definitely would buy"). Test a survey for problems on a small number of people before putting it to use. Web surveys are inexpensive and easy to conduct, and they provide feedback fast. Do not survey only people you know or people who are convenient to reach. Survey people who represent the target market of the business. One word of caution about surveys: They are not generally considered to be highly reliable predictors of customer behaviors. Although they provide useful information, they do not provide definitive insight into market feasibility.

Focus Groups

Conducting a focus group involves enlisting a small number of potential customers (usually 8 to 12) to give you feedback on specific issues about your product or service (or the business idea itself). Listen carefully for what focus group members like and don't like about your product or service as they tell you what is on their minds. The founders of one small snack food company that produced apple chips conducted several focus groups to gauge customers' acceptance of the product and to guide many key business decisions, ranging from the product's name to its packaging. Once again, consider creating virtual focus groups on the Web. One small bicycle retailer conducts 10 online focus groups each year at virtually no cost and gains valuable marketing information from them. Feedback from online customers is fast, convenient, and real-time.

Prototypes

An effective way to gauge the viability of a product is to build a prototype of it. A prototype is an original, functional model of a new product that entrepreneurs can put into the hands of potential customers so that they can see it, test it, and use it. Prototypes usually point out potential problems in a product's design, giving inventors the opportunity to fix them even before they put the prototype into customers' hands. The feedback that customers give entrepreneurs based on prototypes often leads to design improvements and new features, some of which the entrepreneurs might never have discovered on their own. Makers of computer software frequently test prototypes of new products with customers as they develop new products or improve existing ones. Known as beta tests, these trials result in an iterative design process in which software designers collect feedback from users and then incorporate their ideas into the product for the next round of tests. Three-dimensional printing creates a less expensive way for entrepreneurs to develop a basic prototype of a product based on drawings. Although the output of a three-dimensional printer is not a fully functional product, it is a model to test and to use to source manufacturing of component parts.

Workers making prototype products at Arciplex.
Coutesy of Tom Haarlander, CEO, Arciplex

ENTREPRENEURIAL PROFILE: Tom Haarlander: Arciplex Arciplex provides engineering and prototype support to entrepreneurs who have ideas for new products. Arciplex originally developed and marketed its own products. Over time, founder Tom Haarlander recognized that a bigger opportunity existed in helping other entrepreneurs transform their ideas into tangible products. Although design and engineering is the core of Arciplex's business model, many of its customers also need help with manufacturing after their prototypes demonstrate the feasibility of new business ideas. In response, Arciplex added 35 employees and invested $500,000 to add the capability to not only design and engineer ideas but also to help entrepreneurs manufacture them and get them to market. Because many of its customers have ideas for medical products, part of this expansion allows the company to meet FDA standards for designing, engineering, and manufacturing some classes of medical products. Arciplex attracts entrepreneurs from all across the United States.[16] ■

In-Home Trials

in-home trial
a market research technique that involves sending researchers into customers' homes to observe them as they use a company's product or service.

One technique that reveals some of the most insightful information into how customers actually use a product or service is also the most challenging to coordinate: in-home trials. An **in-home trial** involves sending researchers into customers' homes to observe them as they use the company's product or service. However, in-home trials can be expensive to conduct and therefore may not be affordable for most entrepreneurs.

"Windshield" Research

A good source of information is to observe customers interacting with existing businesses within an industry. Windshield research involves driving around and observing customers interacting with similar kinds of businesses and learning what customers like and don't like about those businesses. For example, before one potential investor was willing to commit funding for a new coffee shop, he required that the entrepreneur get traffic counts at local competitors' outlets. He observed heavy demand and often long lines, which helped provide support for the need for a new coffee shop.

Secondary Research

Secondary research should be used to support, not replace, primary research. Secondary research, which is usually less expensive to collect than primary data, includes the following sources.

TRADE ASSOCIATIONS AND BUSINESS DIRECTORIES To locate a trade association, use *Business Information Sources* (University of California Press) or the *Encyclopedia of Associations* (Gale Research). To find suppliers, use *The Thomas Register of American Manufacturers* (Thomas Publishing Company) or *Standard and Poor's Register of Corporations, Executives, and Industries* (Standard and Poor Corporation). *The American Wholesalers and Distributors Directory* includes details on more than 18,000 wholesalers and distributors.

INDUSTRY DATABASES Several online business databases are available through university libraries, such as BizMiner, *Encyclopedia of American Industries*, *Encyclopedia of Emerging Industries*, *Encyclopedia of Global Industries*, *Encyclopedia of Products & Industries—Manufacturing*, *IBISWorld*, *Manufacturing & Distribution USA: Industry Analyses, Statistics and Leading Companies*, and *Market Share Reporter*. These databases offer a rich variety of information on specific industries, including statistical analyses, geographic reports, trend analyses, and profiles.

DEMOGRAPHIC DATA To learn more about the demographic characteristics of customers in general, use *The State and Metropolitan Data Book* (Government Printing Office) and *The Sourcebook of Zip Code Demographics* (CACI, Inc.), which provides detailed breakdowns of the population in every zip code in the country. *Sales and Marketing Management's Survey of Buying Power* (Bill Communications) has statistics on consumer, retail, and industrial buying.

CENSUS DATA The Bureau of the Census publishes a wide variety of reports that summarize the wealth of data found in its census database, which is available at most libraries and at the Census Bureau's Web site, at www.census.gov.

FORECASTS *The U.S. Industry & Trade Outlook* published by the Department of Commerce, International Trade Administration traces the growth of 200 industries and gives a five-year forecast for each one. Many government agencies, including the U.S. Department of Commerce (www.commerce.gov), offer forecasts on everything from interest rates to the number of housing starts. A government research librarian can help you find what you need.

MARKET RESEARCH Someone may already have compiled the market research you need. The *FINDex Worldwide Directory of Market Research Reports, Studies, and Surveys* (Cambridge Information Group) lists more than 10,600 studies available for purchase. Other directories of business research include *Simmons Study of Media and Markets* (Simmons Market Research Bureau Inc.) and the *A.C. Nielsen Retail Index* (A.C. Nielsen Company).

ARTICLES Magazine and journal articles pertinent to your business are a great source of information. Use the *Reader's Guide to Periodical Literature*, the *Business Periodicals Index* (similar to the *Reader's Guide* but focusing on business periodicals), and *Ulrich's Guide to International Periodicals* to locate the ones you need.

🌐 Hands On . . . How To

Do You Want Fries with Those Crickets?

Insects are a common source of food protein for people in many parts of the world. One study suggests that 80 percent of the world population regularly includes insects in their diets. However, in much of the Western world, the thought of eating bugs is less than appetizing! This may soon be changing. With continued global population growth, concerns about the sustainability of Western agricultural practices, and rising meat and grain prices, Western cultures are beginning to entertain the notion of edible insects as a good source of protein. Entrepreneurs have taken note of these changes in attitudes and are beginning to develop business models that will benefit from the growing acceptance of worms and crickets and other bugs as a food source.

Insects in Energy Bars

Patrick Crowley introduced his energy bars, called Chapul, as a means to offer an environmentally friendly source of protein to customers. Through his research, Crowley discovered that crickets are 10 times more efficient than cows or pigs at turning vegetable matter into protein. Crowley partnered with a friend who is a chef to develop a recipe for energy bars using cricket flour and had the bars approved by the Food and Drug Administration. Crowley ran a Kickstarter campaign that raised enough money to make 2,000 bars, which sold quickly through online and retail sales. Based on his early success, Crowley contracted with a company to make larger batches of the bars. In 2014 Crowley appeared on *Shark Tank*. Mark Cuban invested $50,000 for 15 percent of the company. Chain retail grocers such as Natural Grocers, Sprouts, and Publix stock Chapul energy bars, as do many health food stores and gyms.

Suppliers of Bugs

Brothers Jarrod, Ryan, and Darren Goldin are cofounders of Entomo Farms (formerly known as Next Millennium Farms). The company, located in Ontario, Canada, supplies mealworms and crickets, mostly in the form of flour, to processors across North America, Australia, and Europe that make consumer food products out of insects. Entomo Farms has a 60,000-square-foot insect farm that houses more than 100 million crickets and a 3,500-square-foot processing plant that produces 1,500 pounds of flour a week. The company plans to expand to a new 100,000-square-foot space to meet growing demand for its insect-based flour.

Insect Food Cart

Monica Martinez loved snacking on bugs when she was a young child growing up in Mexico. She decided to find a way to share her taste for insects with residents of her new home,

Courtesy of Monica Martinez, Owner, Don Bugito

San Francisco, California. Martinez's food cart, Don Bugito, offers menu items such as wax moth larvae tacos, chocolate covered salted crickets, toffee mealworms over vanilla ice cream, and a snack mix made with crunchy roasted crickets and spiced pepitas. Martinez also offers in-home catering services, featuring a full five-course meal of edible insects, and has begun to sell prepackaged versions of some of her creations.

1. What macro trends support businesses selling edible insects to American consumers?

2. What are the risks that come with being an early entrant into the edible insect market?

3. Do you believe an edible insect business would be successful where you live? Why or why not?

Sources: Based on Kevin Hardy, "Crickets Raised as 'Miniature Livestock,'" *Des Moines Register*, August 1, 2016, www.postbulletin.com/business/crickets-raised-as-miniature-livestock/article_33232720-ecbf-5f1b-a81a-62cb6f7da700.html; Alicia Clegg, "Edible Insects: Grub Pioneers Aim to Make Bugs Palatable," *Financial Times*, February 17, 2015, https://next.ft.com/content/bc0e4526-ab8d-11e4-b05a-00144feab7de#slide0; Parija Kavilanz, "This Energy Bar Gets Its Kick From . . . Crickets," *CNNMoney*, July 23, 2013, http://money.cnn.com/2013/07/23/smallbusiness/cricket-bar/index.html; Kieron Monks, "Centipede Vodka and Fried Crickets: Is This the Future of Food?" *CNN*, July 27, 2015, www.cnn.com/2015/07/24/world/edible-insect-food-business/; Matt Simon, "I've Been to the Future and It Tastes Like Crickets," *Wired*, July 8, 2016, www.wired.com/2016/07/ive-future-tastes-like-crickets/; Amanda Gold, "Bay Area Firms Look Forward with Insect-based Foods, *San Francisco Chronicle*, February 1, 2016, www.sfchronicle.com/green/article/Bay-Area-firms-look-forward-with-insect-based-6798907.php; Katharine Schwab, "Don Bugito Introducing Insects to American Diet," *SF Gate*, September 3, 2013, www.sfgate.com/food/article/Don-Bugito-introducing-insects-to-American-diet-4784046.php; Spencer Michels, "Bugs for Dinner?" *PBS News Hour*, May 7, 2012, www.pbs.org/newshour/rundown/2012/05/bugs-for-dinner.html.

LOCAL DATA Your state department of commerce and your local chamber of commerce will very likely have useful data on the local market of interest to you. Call to find out what is available.

THE INTERNET Entrepreneurs can benefit from the vast amount of market research information available on the Internet. This is an efficient resource with up-to-date information, and much of it is free. Entrepreneurs must use caution, however, to ensure the credibility of online sources.

LO6

Understand the four major
elements of a financial
feasibility analysis.

Financial Feasibility Analysis: Is There Enough Margin?

The third component of a feasibility analysis involves assessing the financial feasibility of a proposed business venture. At this stage of the process, a broad financial analysis that examines the basic economic feasibility is sufficient. This component of the feasibility analysis answers the question "Can this business generate adequate profits?" If the business concept passes the overall feasibility analysis, an entrepreneur should conduct a more thorough financial analysis when developing the business model and creating a full-blown business plan. The four major elements to be included in a financial feasibility analysis are the initial capital requirement, estimated earnings, time out of cash, and resulting return on investment.

Capital Requirements

Just as a Boy Scout needs fuel to start a fire, an entrepreneur needs capital to start a business. Some businesses require large amounts of capital, but others do not. Typically, service businesses require less capital to launch than do manufacturing or retail businesses. Start-up companies often need capital to purchase equipment, buildings, technology, and other tangible assets as well as to hire and train employees, promote their products and services, and establish a presence in the market. A good feasibility analysis provides an estimate of the amount of start-up capital an entrepreneur will need to get the business up and running.

When preparing to launch his Florida-based microbrewery, Cigar City Brewing, Joey Redner needed $585,000 to purchase the brewing system, other equipment, and inventory and to cover initial operating expenses. Redner was able to secure a bank loan after his father agreed to pledge business property as collateral. To help bootstrap his operations, Redner was able to get a large contingent of volunteers to help staff the business, who all agreed to work for free beer. He also set up distribution agreements with two beer distributors before he began brewing his craft beers. However, Redner's brewery was not able to scale with the financing it had available and eventually sold to a stronger brewery out of Colorado.[17]

The typical start-up in the United States can successfully launch with an average of approximately $30,000.[18] However, the actual start-up cost for a specific new business can range from $1,000 to millions of dollars, depending on the type of business. One in five start-ups is launched with no funding at all.[19] How do entrepreneurs get started with so little funding? Most entrepreneurs employ a variety of techniques called *bootstrapping*. Bootstrapping is the process of finding creative ways to exploit opportunities to launch and grow businesses with the limited resources available for most start-up ventures. It includes a variety of strategies and techniques that cover all of the functions of running a business: marketing, staffing, inventory and production management, cash flow management, and administrative processes required to keep a business operating.[20] You will learn more about bootstrapping in Chapter 8 and more about finding sources of business funding, both debt and equity, in Chapter 15.

Estimated Earnings

In addition to producing an estimate of the start-up company's capital requirements, an entrepreneur also should forecast the earning potential of the proposed business. Industry trade associations and publications such as the *RMA Annual Statement Studies* and BizMiner offer guidelines on preparing sales and earnings estimates for specific types of businesses. From these, entrepreneurs can estimate the financial results they and their investors can expect to see from the business venture if the start-up is executed according to plan.

Time Out of Cash

A prominent venture capitalist describes a start-up as a race against time. The cash available to the new business will only last so long. If the entrepreneur cannot reach the point of positive cash flow before running out of available start-up capital, the business dies. In other words, a common cause of business failure is running out of cash before the business breaks even and can support itself through the cash flow from operations. According to a study by accounting software provider CCH and consulting firm Wolters Kluwer, 49 percent of start-ups fail due to insufficient capital—that is, not enough start-up cash.[21] During the planning stage, an entrepreneur should estimate the total cash it will take to sustain the business until it achieves positive cash flow. This estimate should be based on a less-than-optimistic scenario because there are almost always unexpected costs and delays in the start-up and growth of a new business. To calculate the number of months until an operating business runs out of cash, simply divide the amount of available cash remaining in the business by the negative cash flowing from the business each month (its "burn rate"). The result is the number of months the business can survive at its current rate of negative cash flow ("time out of cash"). Ideally, the business will be able to grow quickly enough to avoid reaching the point of no more cash.

Return on Investment

The final aspect of the financial feasibility analysis involves combining the estimated earnings and the capital requirements to determine the rate of return the venture is expected to produce. One simple measure is the rate of return on the capital invested, which is calculated by dividing the estimated earnings the business yields by the amount of capital invested in the business. This aspect of financial feasibility is generally of most concern to investors. Although financial estimates at the feasibility analysis stage typically are rough, they are an important part of the entrepreneur's ultimate "go" or "no go" decision about the business venture. A venture must produce an attractive rate of return relative to the level of risk it requires. This risk–return trade-off means that the higher the level of risk a prospective business involves, the higher the rate of return it must provide to the entrepreneur and investors. Why should an entrepreneur take on all the risks of starting and running a business that produces a mere 3 or 4 percent rate of return when he or she could earn that much in a risk-free investment at a bank or another financial institution? Although entrepreneurs should pay more attention to this calculation, many do not because they tend to get wrapped up in the emotion and excitement of their business ideas. You will learn more about developing detailed financial forecasts for a business start-up in Chapter 12.

Wise entrepreneurs take the time to subject their ideas to a feasibility analysis like the one described here, whatever outcome it produces. If the analysis suggests that transforming the idea into a viable business is not feasible, the entrepreneur can move on to the next idea, confident that he or she has not wasted valuable resources launching a business that is destined to fail.

If the analysis so far finds that there is a market for the idea and that it has real potential as a profitable business, the entrepreneur can move to the final component of the feasibility analysis.

Entrepreneur Feasibility: Is This Idea Right for Me?

LO7

Describe the process of assessing entrepreneur feasibility.

Suppose that a feasibility analysis thus far has established that the industry and market are favorable, there is strong evidence of demand for the product or service in the market, and the concept appears financially feasible. There is one last component of feasibility to examine: the readiness of the entrepreneur (and, if applicable, the entrepreneur's team) to launch the venture successfully. Many new businesses require that an entrepreneur have a certain set of knowledge, experiences, and skills to have any chance of being successful. This is called *entrepreneurial readiness*. Some of these can be simple skills. For example, starting a landscaping business requires knowing how to operate a lawnmower and other equipment. Being successful in a landscaping business also depends on some level of knowledge about plants and grasses. Other new businesses may require a higher level of knowledge and skills. For example, starting an accounting firm requires a high level of knowledge and experience in the laws and practice of accounting. Entrepreneurs may have gained the knowledge and skills they need from previous jobs, from formal education, or from interests or hobbies. They can also acquire knowledge as part of what they work on during the planning process. Entrepreneurial readiness also involves issues such as temperament, work ethic, and so forth. Performing an entrepreneurial self-assessment can help evaluate entrepreneurial readiness (see Table 4.2).

Another way to ensure that the necessary knowledge and skills are in place is to build a start-up team. For example, an aspiring entrepreneur may have an idea for a new app for smart phones but may not have any programming or design skills. He or she would be best served by

TABLE 4.2

Entrepreneurial Self-Assessment

Source: This self-assessment is adapted from J. Cornwall and N. Carter, *University of St. Thomas Entrepreneurial Self-Assessment: Start-Up*, monograph published by the John M. Morrison Center for Entrepreneurship, University of St. Thomas, St. Paul, Minnesota, 1999. Used with permission.

Personal Aspirations and Priorities
- What gets you excited, gives you energy, and motivates you to excel?
- What do you like to do with your time?
- What drains energy from you?
  In the work you do:
  In personal relationships:
- How do you measure success in your personal life?
  Family:
  Friends and relationships:
  Personal interests and hobbies:
  Contributions to community and society:
- What do you consider success in your business and career?
  Short-term:
  Long-term:
- What are your specific goals for your personal life?
  Family:
  Friends and relationships:
  Personal interests and hobbies:
  Contributions to community and society:
- What are your goals for your business and career?
  Income and lifestyle:
  Wealth:
  Free time:
  Recognition and fame:
  Impact on community:
  Other:
- What do you want to be doing:
  In one year:
  In five years:
  In ten years:
  At retirement:

Core Values
- List the core personal values that you intend to bring to your business (e.g., treating people fairly, giving something back to the community).
- Where does each of these core values come from (religious faith, family, etc.)?
- Why is each of them important to you?

Personal Entrepreneurial Readiness
- What are the major reasons you want to start a business?
- How many hours are you willing and able to put into your new venture?
- How would you describe your tolerance for uncertainty and risk?
- Do you easily trust other people working with you on a common activity? Why or why not?
- How much financial risk are you willing to take with your new venture (personal assets, personal debt, etc.)?
- Assume you decide not to start your business. A short time later, you see that someone has started the same business and is doing well. How would you feel? Why?
- What are the nonfinancial risks for you in starting a new business?
- How do you react to failure? Give examples.
- How do you react in times of personal stress? How do you deal with stress in your life?
- How much income do you need to support your current lifestyle?
- How long could you survive without a paycheck?
- How much money do you have available to start your business?
- Which of your personal assets would you be willing to borrow against, or sell, to start your business?
- Whose support (nonfinancial) is important for you to have before starting your business (family, spouse, etc.)?

exploring the possibility of adding to the team people who have those skills. If more than one entrepreneur a is starting a business, they all should complete assessments and use the information gleaned as a launching point to examine their collective entrepreneurial readiness.

When an entrepreneur is ready to start a business, the second step in determining entrepreneurial feasibility is to assess whether the business can meet the financial and nonfinancial needs of the entrepreneur and the team. Will the business be able to generate enough profit to support everyone's income needs? If it is successful, will it also meet the wealth goals of the founding team? Just because a business is profitable does not mean that it is profitable enough to support the entrepreneur and his or her team. This can vary from entrepreneur to entrepreneur. A 22-year-old single entrepreneur fresh out of college has very different financial needs than a 42-year-old married entrepreneur who has a mortgage, car payments, and tuition for private schools for his or her children! But making money is not the only thing that matters for most people. Does the business fit with goals and aspirations the entrepreneur has outside work? A business that demands extensive travel may not work for an entrepreneur who has a goal of being highly involved with his or her family. A restaurant, which often demands that the entrepreneur be involved 6 or 7 days a week, 52 weeks a year, may not provide a good business model for an entrepreneur who wants to travel and take extended vacations.

Once an entrepreneur tests his or her business idea using the four components of a feasibility assessment, the next stage of the new business planning process is to develop a business model.

Developing and Testing a Business Model

LO8

Describe the nine elements of a business model.

In their groundbreaking study of how successful entrepreneurs develop business models, Osterwalder and Pigneur identified the common elements that successful entrepreneurs and investors use when developing and evaluating a business model. They found that most entrepreneurs use a visual process, such as diagraming their business on a whiteboard, when developing their business ideas.[22] They don't just start writing the text of a business plan. Rather, entrepreneurs map out the key components required to make their businesses successful. A business model adds more detail to the evaluation of a new business begun during the feasibility analysis by graphically depicting the "moving parts" of the business and ensuring that they are all working together.

When building a business model, an entrepreneur addresses a series of key questions that explain how the business will become successful. What value does the business offer customers? Who is my target market? What do they, as my customers, expect of me? How do I get information to them, and how do they want to get the product? What are the key activities to make all this come together, and what will they cost? What resources do I need to make this happen, including money? Who are key partners I will need to attract to be successful?

In their study, Osterwalder and Pigneur found a pattern of how entrepreneurs use a visual representation of their business model to answer these questions. They used these findings to develop the Business Model Canvas, which provides entrepreneurs with a dynamic framework to guide them through the process of developing, testing, and refining their business models (see Figure 4.8). The canvas is composed of nine elements:

1. *Customer segments.* A good business model always starts with the customer. The entrepreneur's first step is to identify a segment of customers who have a clearly defined need. In the previous steps outlined in this chapter, the entrepreneur begins to define the market for the new business. For most entrepreneurs, the initial market is defined much too broadly. The entrepreneur uses demographic, geographic, socioeconomic, and other characteristics that add specificity to defining the target market. Narrowing the target market enables a small company to focus its limited resources on serving the needs of a specific group of customers rather than attempting to satisfy the desires of the mass market. Creating a successful business depends on an entrepreneur's ability to attract real customers who are willing and able to spend real money to buy its products or services. Perhaps the biggest marketing error an entrepreneur can commit is failing to define a target market and trying to make the business "everything to everybody." Small companies usually are much more successful at focusing on a specific market niche or niches where they can excel at meeting customers' special

FIGURE 4.8

The Business Model Canvas

Source: Business Model Generation: A Handbook for Visionaries, Game Changers, and Challengers by Osterwalder, Alexander; Pigneur, Yves Reproduced with permission of Wiley in the format Book via Copyright ClearanceCenter.

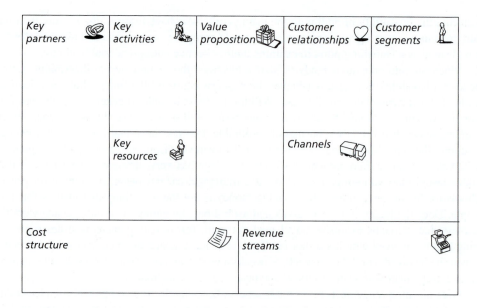

needs or wants. Who is it, specifically, that has the needs the new business will target with its products and/or services? It may be a market niche. It may be a mass market. Or it may be a market segmented based on age, gender, geography, or socioeconomic grouping.

2. *Value proposition.* A compelling value proposition is at the heart of every successful business. The value proposition is the collection of products and/or services the business will offer to meet the needs of the customers. It is all the things that will set the business apart from its competitors, such as convenience, service, speed, pricing, quality, features, and product availability. Most value propositions for new businesses come from fundamental macro trends within the economy, demographics, technology, or society and culture, discussed earlier in the chapter. Trends lead to changes within industries. These trends are first uncovered in the industry and market feasibility analysis. A fundamental role of being an entrepreneur is to find solutions for the problems and needs customers have that result from the change that follows disruptive trends such as these. It could be something about the product itself, such as its price and value, features, performance, durability, or design, or it might be something emanating from the personnel of the company, including their expertise, responsiveness, or reliability.

It is best to identify and focus on one or two benefits that will make the new business stand out to customers and motivate them to purchase from the new business. The best way to develop the key benefits that are at the heart of a strong value proposition is to listen to customers. Although entrepreneurs may think they know what their customers want, most of the time they do not have it quite right. The entrepreneur may have to adjust the product or service to fit with what the customer actually wants or needs.

ENTREPRENEURIAL PROFILE: George Bukhov, Burger & Lobster George Bukhov discovered success in the restaurant business with a highly focused menu and simple business concept that provides a compelling value proposition. Burger & Lobster customers choose from a hamburger, a 1.5-pound lobster, or a lobster roll sandwich, served with a salad and French fries. Every entrée is the same price—about $20, depending on the location. Less than five years after opening his first location, George Bukhov expanded his Burger & Lobster restaurants to multiple locations across Europe, North America, and the Middle East. Burger & Lobster's business model offers a meal that feels like an indulgence at a price point that most people can afford. It is not unusual for a Burger & Lobster restaurant to serve 1,000 customers per day on weekends. Even on weeknights, the wait to get into a Burger & Lobster can reach two hours. To keep customers engaged while waiting for their tables, Burger & Lobster offers a large bar area that plays classic Motown music in a fun and lively atmosphere. Once seated, patrons choose from the limited menu, which helps control quality and costs. By finding a winning value proposition, Bukhov created a business with high quality, high sales volume, and high profit margins.[23] ∎

3. *Customer relationships.* *Customer relationships* describe the type of relationship and the level of service that a business provides to its customers. Not every business provides the same type and same level of customer service. For example, several effective business models provide meals to consumers. Customers may choose to buy food from a vending machine, a fast-food restaurant, a fast casual sit-down restaurant, or an exclusive fine dining establishment. Each of these business models has a very different approach to define the relationship with customers. The vending business offers quick, convenient, and impersonal service. At the other extreme, the fine dining restaurant works closely and personally with customers to ensure that they get exactly what they want. Each approach is effective and appropriate for its particular target market. When developing this segment of the business model, the entrepreneur must answer several questions. How do customers want to interact with the business? Do they want intensive personal service, or would they rather have limited engagement or even automated interaction? There is no one best approach to customer relationship for all businesses, but there usually is one best approach for each particular business model.

4. *Channels.* In the Business Model Canvas, *channels* refer to both communication channels (promotion) and distribution channels (product placement). Communication channels define how customers seek out information about this type of product. Where do potential customers go when they want to get information about products and services? It could be Web sites, social networks, blogs, advertisements, experts, and so forth. Again, there is no one best way to communicate for all businesses, but the specific target market for a given business model will have one or more that are most effective. The distribution channel defines the most effective way to get products to the customers for this type of business. For some business models, it may be best to use direct-to-consumer sales through a Web site or a store on Amazon because customers may prefer to order online from the comfort of home. For other business models, the customer may want to see the merchandise, touch it, and interact with it in an exciting new retail location. The entrepreneur must determine where the customer wants to make the purchase and then determine the most effective way to get it to the customer at that location.

5. *Key activities.* What important things must the entrepreneur do to ensure a successful launch and to sustain the growth of the business? In the business model, the goal is to build a basic checklist of what an entrepreneur must do to open the business and what activities are necessary to ensure its long-term success. The development of the business plan will then expand this list into much greater detail. We will explore creating a business plan in detail in Chapter 5.

6. *Key resources.* What human, capital, and intellectual resources does the business require to be successful? Again, this list will serve as an initial checklist to ensure that the entrepreneur has identified all key resources necessary to support a successful launch and to sustain the business as it grows. The business plan provides the opportunity to explain these in much greater detail and develop all necessary cost estimates for the financial forecasts.

7. *Key partners.* Entrepreneurs cannot expect to become successful all by themselves. The key partner segment of the business model includes key suppliers, key outsourcing partners, investors, industry partners, advisers, and all other external businesses or entities that are critical to make the business model work. Entrepreneurs must build a network of relationships when launching and growing their businesses.

8. *Revenue streams.* How will the value proposition generate revenue? Will it be a one-time sale, ongoing fees, subscriptions, advertising, or some other source of cash? The entrepreneur should answer these questions, using the information discovered in the value proposition, customer segments, customer relationship, and channel components of the business model (the right side of the Business Model Canvas). The revenue streams information serves as the framework for the more detailed revenue forecasts that the entrepreneur will develop later for the business plan.

FIGURE 4.9

**The Business
Modeling Process**

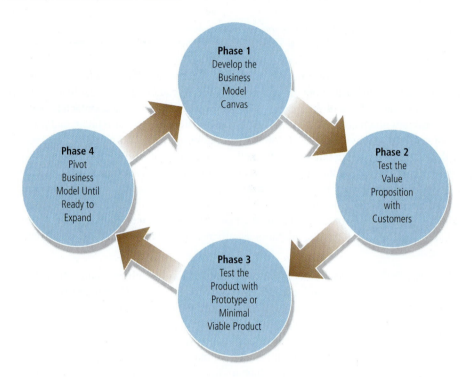

9. *Cost structure.* What fixed and variable costs are necessary to make the business model work? The key activities, key resources, and key partners components of the plan (the left side of the Business Model Canvas) identify the basic types of costs and give some estimate of their scope. Just like the revenue streams, the cost structure of the business model becomes the framework for developing more detailed costs that the entrepreneur will incorporate into the financial forecasts of the business plan. Chapter 12 examines the financial plan in more detail.

Developing a business model is a four-phase process[24] (see Figure 4.9). The first phase is to create an initial Business Model Canvas, as outlined previously. It is best to do this on a white board, on the wall using sticky notes, or using free business model software such as Business Model Fiddle (www.bmfiddle.com). As the entrepreneur goes through the next three phases, the business model will change. At this point in the process, much of the information in the business model is only a series of hypotheses to be tested. The entrepreneur will update the business model as he or she learns more about the customers and the resources it will take to launch and grow the business. The Business Model Canvas allows all the team members involved in the start-up to work from a common framework. The team documents all of the hypotheses about the business model that require further investigation and keeps track of changes in the model that result from testing the hypotheses. The entrepreneurial team also estimates the total market size and the size of the specific target market that would be feasible to attract to the new business when it launches.

The second phase in designing the business model is to test the problem that the team thinks the business solves through its core value proposition. This is best done with primary research data. That means the entrepreneurial team must "get out of the office" and test the model with real customers. By engaging potential customers early in the development of a new business and listening to what they have to say, the team has a much better chance of developing a business model that will attract customers. When engaging with real customers, the entrepreneurial team asks the following questions:[25]

- Do we really understand the customer problem the business model is trying to address?

- Do these customers care enough about this problem to spend their hard-earned money on our product?

- Do these customers care enough about our product to help us by telling others through word-of-mouth?

By answering these questions, the entrepreneur assesses the actual need for the product and the intensity of that need.

The third phase is to test the solution to the problem in the market. One technique to test the solution offered by the business model involves **business prototyping**, in which entrepreneurs test their business models on a small scale before committing significant resources to launch a business that might not work. Business prototyping recognizes that every business idea is a hypothesis that must be tested before an entrepreneur takes it to full scale. If the test supports the hypothesis and its accompanying assumptions, the entrepreneur takes the next step of building a business plan. If the prototype flops, the entrepreneur scraps the business idea with only minimal losses and turns to the next idea.

ENTREPRENEURIAL PROFILE: Chris Fitzgerald: Neoteric Hovercraft Golf Cart Chris Fitzgerald launched Neoteric Hovercraft to offer affordable, small hovercraft vehicles for a variety of applications. The advantage of a hovercraft is that it can easily and smoothly travel on a cushion of air at speeds of up to 50 miles per hour over a variety of terrain, including water. Neoteric's primary customers for its hovercrafts are police and fire departments, the U.S. Air Force, and Disney World. One model developed by Neoteric is a hovercraft golf cart, which can hold up to four people and two sets of golf clubs. Windy Knoll Golf Club in Springfield, Ohio, bought two hovercraft golf carts to assess the feasibility of everyday use of the devices on a golf course and customer interest in paying the significant cost difference of a hovercraft versus a traditional golf cart. The hovercraft golf cart costs about 10 times the cost of a gas or electric cart.[26] ■

The Internet is a valuable business prototyping tool because it gives entrepreneurs easy and inexpensive access to real live potential customers. Entrepreneurs can test their ideas by selling their products on established sites such as eBay or by setting up their own Web sites to gauge customers' response. A process that can guide testing early versions of a product or service is known as *lean start-up*, defined as a process of rapidly developing simple prototypes to test key assumptions by engaging real customers.[27]

To launch a business using the lean start-up process, entrepreneurs begin with what is called a **minimal viable product**, which is the simplest version of a product or service with which an entrepreneur can create a sustainable business. Brian Chesky and Joe Gebbia needed a way to help pay the rent on their San Francisco apartment. They built a simple Web site to post pictures of their apartment and promoted it to people coming to town for conferences. They quickly learned that what they had was the making of a viable business. With their minimal viable product, they learned about the type of customer who would use such a service, how much they would pay, and what features customers wanted as part of the Web site. This minimal viable product soon became a business called Airbnb. Since its launch in 2008, Airbnb has raised more than $3.2 billion in nine rounds of funding.[28]

The fourth phase of designing a business model is to make changes and adjustments in the business, called **pivots**, based on what the entrepreneur learns from engaging the market about the problem and the solution that the new business intends to pursue. Some pivots may be subtle adjustments to the business model, while others may be fundamental changes to key parts of the model, including in the value proposition, markets served, or ideal revenue streams. There are three major types of pivots:

- *Product pivot.* The features that make up a product may not match what the customer really wants or needs. Sometimes the entrepreneur adds features that are not really important to the customer. Although customers may be willing to accept these features as part of the product, they are not willing to pay extra for them. This results in creating a product that is not clearly focused on the market need: It costs more than it should due to the extra features. For example, when Paul Orfalea founded his first Kinko's store (now FedEx Office), he sold a variety of school and office supplies to his fellow University of Southern California students. He also had a copy machine in the back of the store. Students did not buy many supplies, but they were constantly using the copy machine. He narrowed his offering to become primarily a copy shop and grew the

business prototyping
the process by which entrepreneurs test their business models on a small scale before committing significant resources to launch a business that might not work.

minimal viable product
the simplest version of a product or service with which an entrepreneur can create a sustainable business.

pivots
changes and adjustments in a business model that are made on the basis of the feedback a company receives from customers.

You Be the Consultant

RendezWoof: Creating a Minimal Viable Product for a Mobile App

Entrepreneurs create minimal viable products so that they can test a product with real customers as quickly as possible. Testing a product this way helps determine whether consumers really want the product, provides feedback from these customers to help improve the product, and gathers hard data that demonstrates the proof of concept many investors want before they fund an emerging business.

Judson Aikens wanted to start a business but had a good-paying job and was concerned about taking on too much risk. While brainstorming about possible businesses he could launch, Aikens came up with an idea for a new dating app. He had observed that it is easy to meet new people at places like dog parks.

Aikens's idea was to develop an app called RendezWoof (www.rendezwoof.com) that created a virtual dog park. "The app would not only connect dog owners with each other, it would connect them with dog-friendly resources around them," says Aikens. "Using GPS, the app's map would populate restaurants with patios and parks convenient to users interested in meeting up to grab a beer or throw a Frisbee."

Aikens reached out to an entrepreneur, Ben Dolgoff, who had spoken to one of the entrepreneurship classes he had taken in graduate school. Ben was an experienced app developer who had developed and launched several successful apps. After asking Ben to sign a nondisclosure agreement, Aikens shared his idea. Ben said he thought the app had promise as a commercially viable product. He suggested that Aikens develop some designs for his idea and then get back with him. If the idea had promise, Ben said he might be willing to develop the app in exchange for some equity in the new business.

Aikens shared his app idea with a friend who was a graphic designer. She was eager to help him with the designs and was willing to provide ongoing graphic design services in exchange for equity.

The next step was for Aikens to work with the graphic designer to develop a wireframe of the app. A wireframe is a drawing of the various screens that make up an app; it includes the kinds of information displayed, the functions of the app, and the basic flow from screen to screen.

Aikens took the wireframe designs to Ben, who was eager to move forward.

"This arrangement was very acceptable to me," says Aikens. "It simultaneously removed the financial burden of development and provided an experienced go-to consultant I could work with through the life of the app."

Aikens formed an LLC and secured the RendezWoof name on all social platforms and for the Web domain. He opened an Apple developer account and applied for copyrights and trademarks. Because he is still working his day job, Aikens spends

Courtesy of Judson Aikens, RendezWoof, LLC

many late nights working with the developers to improve the app's user interface and user experience.

Because the goal of the initial version of the app is to gain users and prove the concept, RendezWoof initially offered the app for free through the Apple Store. Future versions of the app will have more features, and the company will charge a small fee for the app.

1. Why would you recommend that an entrepreneur develop a minimal viable product or a prototype?

2. Can you think of additional market research that Aikens could have done before developing his product?

3. What are the advantages and disadvantages of offering equity in exchange for work done on a new product?

Sources: Based on Judson Aikens, personal communication, December 17, 2013; Jamie McGee, "App Helps Dog Owners Find Love on the Leash," *USA Today,* May 14, 2014, www.usatoday.com/story/tech/2014/05/14/rendezwoof-dog-owners-app/9089725/.

business to a multinational company with more than 1,200 locations. On the other hand, sometimes the entrepreneur does not offer enough features to fully address the customers' problem. In this situation, the entrepreneur must add the features the customer expects.

- *Customer pivot.* Although a product might solve a real market problem or need, sometimes the initial business model targets the wrong customer segment or even the wrong market. For example, PayPal targeted the handheld device market, which included the PalmPilot, for its electronic payment system. However, the founders of PayPal soon realized by listening to customer feedback that there was a much larger market for its product. Businesses were beginning to engage in commerce on their Web sites. PayPal pivoted its business model and as a result rapidly grew to become a $1.6 billion company facilitating Internet commerce.

- *Revenue model pivot.* There are many ways the revenue model may pivot. One of the most basic revenue decisions is whether to use a high margin/low volume model or low margin/high volume model. For example, Best Buy began as a single-location stereo equipment store called the Sound of Music back in the 1960s. Like all of its competitors, it had a high margin/low volume revenue model. The owners would mark up inventory two to three times what the product cost them to purchase. As a result, the store would turn over its inventory about once a year. After a tornado destroyed the building but left the inventory undamaged, Sound of Music owners rented a large tent and ran a drastic sale. The demand was so overwhelming that when they reopened, they changed their revenue model to low margin/high volume and within a short time renamed the business Best Buy. The low prices created so much demand that the stores would sell their entire inventory about once a month rather than once a year. Other revenue model pivots change the type of payment received. The model may change from a single payment to recurring revenue, or it may shift from hourly billing to charging a fixed price per service. Social entrepreneurs can pivot from a revenue model based on a nonprofit that raises money through grants and donations to a social enterprise that generates revenues from a product or service.

Several minor pivots may also be necessary for a business model around operational aspects of the business, including promotion, distribution, staffing, or outsourcing.

ENTREPRENEURIAL PROFILE: Aayush Phumbhra: Chegg The original business model of Chegg was to establish a site like Craigslist that specialized in connecting college students with each other to offer items they wanted to buy and sell. Company cofounder Aayush Phumbhra noticed that most of the traffic at the site was buying and selling textbooks. Phumbhra wondered whether students would just rather rent their books and avoid the hassle of buying and selling their textbooks every semester. To test the hypothesis, Chegg purchased 2,000 used textbooks online and sent out e-mails to customers about the new service. Within a short time, Chegg's customers clearly demonstrated their preference for renting over buying and selling. Based on the success of the market experiment, Phumbhra pivoted the business model to one that focuses on renting textbooks to college students. Chegg quickly became one of the top sources for textbook rental. However, as the market moved away from print to digital texts, Chegg pivoted its business model once again. In just five years, Chegg grew its digital offerings from only 13 percent of total revenues to 100 percent.[29] ∎

If pivots to the existing business model are not enough, occasionally a company may completely change its business model. For example, when IBM was facing possible failure in the 1990s, the company drastically shifted its business model from a company that manufactured and sold computer and other office hardware to focus primarily on software and information technology consulting. It is now one of the largest and most profitable information technology companies in the world.

You Be the Consultant

When to Call It Quits on a New Business

Jake Jorgovan had become a successful entrepreneur while he was in college. Jorgovan and a classmate started a video production company. They began by making videos of senior recitals for music students at their school. By the time they graduated, their company had hired several employees and was booked up with a combination of music industry work and shoots for corporate clients needing videos. Jorgovan won several local and national business plan competitions based on the plans he developed for the company. Shortly after graduation, Jorgovan was recognized as the Youth Entrepreneur of the Year in Nashville, Tennessee, where the business was headquartered.

Not long after that, Jorgovan made the decision to move away from the video industry and start a new business. After extensive research, Jorgovan identified an opportunity in the telemedicine growth sector of the healthcare industry. Jorgovan started his new company, Telehealth PT, to develop a telemedicine application for physical therapists. Telehealth's business model was to provide a framework that would allow physical therapists to provide care through live video conferencing sessions on patients' mobile devices or computers.

Jorgovan began developing the basic technology he could use to demonstrate that his concept could work. His goal was to offer a simple version of the product and test it with a few physical therapy clinics. However, not long after beginning work on the basic product, Jorgovan began to have doubts about his ability to launch the business. He persevered, trying to overcome the many technical hurdles and personal challenges the new business kept throwing in his path.

Even though it soon became clear that his new business was not going to work, Jorgovan had a hard time accepting this failure, mainly because he had known so much success with his previous business. He continued to try to uncover ways to salvage the venture, but eventually he had to admit he had failed.

One of the possible outcomes of conducting feasibility analyses and developing business models is that, like Jake Jorgovan, the entrepreneur may discover that the business just won't work. Entrepreneurs should consider this a positive outcome because they are able to discover fatal flaws in a business concept early, saving time and money. It can be difficult for entrepreneurs to

admit failure and walk away from an idea even when it becomes clear that it is doomed to fail. Why? What clouds their judgment?

- **Pride and ego.** It is easy for entrepreneurs to let their egos get too wrapped up in their businesses, even very early in the life of their new ventures. They receive affirmation and encouragement from family members and friends for taking the risk to start a business. Soon, their pride in being an entrepreneur can get in the way of making a sound business decision and closing a failing venture.

- **Their "baby."** Many long and lonely hours go into getting a business started. Entrepreneurs can quickly become emotionally attached to a new venture. They can reach a point where they could not even imagine thinking about giving up on it.

- **Getting stuck on sunk costs.** It can be difficult for entrepreneurs to look at the time, money, and reputation they have put into a failing concept as a *sunk cost*. That is, entrepreneurs can never recover the resources they have already committed to the venture. Continuing to pour money into a failing venture simply because one has already invested so much into it is not wise.

The purpose of feasibility analysis is to answer the question "Can this business work?" Sometimes the answer will be "no." The entrepreneur must be ready to accept this answer and move on to the next opportunity.

1. Why was it hard for Jake to admit his newest venture was not going to work?

2. What would you recommend that entrepreneurs do to ensure that they don't hang on too long to a failed business concept?

3. A failed business concept does not mean the entrepreneur has failed. How would you explain this to an entrepreneur facing a failed business concept?

Sources: Based on Jeff Cornwall, "Why Entrepreneurs Never Say Die, but Maybe Should," *Inc.*, December 18, 2013, www.inc.com/jeff-cornwall/why-entrepreneurs-never-say-die-but-maybe-should.html; Jake Jorgovan, personal communication, December 6, 2013; Jake Jorgovan, "Accepting Failure," December 2, 2013, http://jake-jorgovan.com/blog/2013/12/1/accepting-failure.

Conclusion

Entrepreneurs can follow five steps to guide the process of turning a great new idea into a successful business. This chapter examines the first three steps in this process.

The best business ideas start with a group of customers with a common problem or need. Once entrepreneurs develop ideas for new businesses, they can take the first step: assess these ideas by examining a need in the market, developing a solution for that need, and determining the entrepreneur's ability to successfully turn the idea into a business. The idea assessment process helps an entrepreneur more efficiently and effectively examine multiple ideas to identify the solution that has the most potential.

The second step is to conduct a feasibility analysis to determine whether the entrepreneur can transform the idea into a viable business. The role of a feasibility analysis is to serve as a filter, screening out ideas that lack the potential for building a successful business, before an entrepreneur commits the necessary resources to develop and test a business model or to build a business plan.

The third step in the process of evaluating ideas is to develop and test the business model. Developing a business model helps the entrepreneur better understand all that will be required to launch and build the business. In this step in the planning process, the entrepreneur tests the concept and uses what he or she learned from real customers to refine the business model before committing the resources to grow the business to its full potential.

Once the entrepreneur completes the idea assessment, feasibility study, and business model steps, he or she is ready to develop a business plan. As the business becomes more successful, the strategic plan becomes an essential management tool. The business plan and strategic plan are covered in Chapter 5.

MyLab Entrepreneurship

If your instructor is using MyLab Entrepreneurship, go to **www.pearson.com/mylab/entrepreneurship** to complete the problems marked with this icon ⭐.

Chapter Summary by Learning Objective

1. **Describe the process of conducting an idea assessment.**

   - The Idea Sketch Pad is a tool that helps entrepreneurs assess ideas. It has five parameters:

     Customers. Start with a group of customers who have a clear need that is not being addressed.

     Offering. Describe your idea for a product or service to offer to customers.

     Value proposition. Explain why your product or service will be important to customers.

     Core competencies. Determine whether your offering has any technologies or unique features that will help differentiate it from competitors.

     People. Identify the key people on the team who will launch this business.

2. **Explain the elements of a feasibility analysis.**

   - Determine how attractive an industry is overall as a "home" for a new business.

   - Evaluate possible niches a small business can occupy profitably.

3. **Describe the six forces in the macro environment of an industry.**

   - Sociocultural trends can lead to dramatic changes, creating whole new industries and fundamentally transforming existing industries.

   - Technological breakthroughs lead to the development of new products and entirely new industries.

   - Changing demographics create opportunities for entrepreneurs.

   - Economic trends, both positive and negative, create opportunities.

   - Political and legal change, such as new laws and regulations, create opportunities for entrepreneurs.

   - Global trends that open global markets allow businesses to seek customers and suppliers from all areas of the world and can help in even the smallest business.

4. **Understand how Porter's Five Forces Model assesses the competitive environment.**

   - Entrepreneurs should assess five forces that shape the competitive environment for every business:

     The rivalry among competing firms

     The bargaining power of suppliers

     The bargaining power of buyers

     The threat of new entrants

     The threat of substitute products or services

5. **Describe the various methods of conducting primary and secondary market research.**

   - Primary research tools include customer surveys, focus groups, prototypes, in-home trials, and "windshield" research (driving around and observing the competition).

   - Secondary research involves gathering existing data from trade associations and business directories, industry databases, demographic data, census data, forecasts compiled by government agencies, market research reports, articles in magazines and journals, local data, and the Internet.

6. **Understand the four major elements of a financial feasibility analysis.**

   - *Capital requirements.* Start-up companies often need capital to purchase equipment, buildings, technology, and other tangible assets and to hire and train employees, promote their products and services, and establish a presence in the market.

- *Estimated earnings.* In addition to producing an estimate of the start-up company's capital requirements, an entrepreneur should forecast the earning potential of the proposed business.

- *Time out of cash.* To estimate time out of cash, divide the available cash left in the business by the negative cash flow from the business each month. This tells you the number of months the business can survive at its current rate of negative cash flow.

- *Return on investment.* A venture must produce an attractive rate of return relative to the level of risk it requires. This risk–return trade-off means that the higher the level of risk a prospective business involves, the higher the rate of return it must provide to the entrepreneur and investors.

7. Describe the process of assessing entrepreneur feasibility.

- Many new businesses require that an entrepreneur possess certain knowledge, experiences, and skills to have a chance of being successful.

- Entrepreneurial readiness also involves issues such as temperament and work ethic.

8. Describe the nine elements of a business model in the Business Model Canvas.

- *Customer segments.* A good business model always starts with the customer. The entrepreneur's first step is to identify a segment of customers who have a clearly defined need.

- *Value proposition.* The value proposition is the collection of products and/or services the business will offer to meet customers' needs.

- *Customer relationships.* Not every business provides the same type and same level of customer service.

- *Channels.* Channels refer to both communication channels (promotion) and distribution channels (product placement). Communication channels define how the customers seek out information about this type of product. The distribution channel defines the most effective way to get products to the customers for this type of business.

- *Key activities.* The goal is to build a basic checklist of what needs to be done to open the business and what activities are necessary to ensure its long-term success.

- *Key resources.* An entrepreneur needs to build an initial checklist to ensure that all key resources have been identified that will support a successful launch and sustain the business as it grows.

- *Key partners.* This segment of the business model includes important suppliers, outsourcing partners, investors, industry partners, advisers, and all other external businesses or entities that are critical to make the business model work.

- *Revenue streams.* How will the value proposition generate revenue?

- *Cost structure.* The key activities, key resources, and key partners components of the plan help identify the basic types of costs and give some estimate of their scope.

MyLab Entrepreneurship

If your instructor is using MyLab Entrepreneurship, go to **www.pearson.com/mylab/entrepreneurship** for Auto-graded writing questions as well as the following Assisted-graded writing questions:

1. List and describe the six foundational forces that shape the macro environment of a business venture.
2. Explain the steps of the creative process. What can an entrepreneur do to enhance each step?
3. Explain this statement: A sound business model should always begin with a market need.

Discussion Questions

4-1. Describe the new business planning process.

4-2. Explain the parameters of an idea sketch pad.

4-3. What are the risks for an entrepreneur who becomes emotionally attached to an idea for a new business?

⭐ 4-4. Describe the four components of a feasibility analysis.

4-5. Why is it important for an entrepreneur to be aware of the macro forces that shape a new business venture?

4-6. Describe in detail Porter's Five Forces Model.

4-7. What is a market niche?

4-8. Explain the advantages an entrepreneur gains by pursuing a niche market.

4-9. List and describe the various tools for conducting primary market research.

4-10. What are the four elements of a financial feasibility analysis?

4-11. Explain why even a business that passes a market and a financial feasibility analysis may not be a good business for an entrepreneur to launch.

4-12. Why is it essential to develop a sound business model before writing a business plan?

⭐ 4-13. List and describe the nine elements of the Business Model Canvas.

4-14. Describe the four phases involved in developing a business model.

4-15. What is a pivot in a business model?

4-16. Explain the various types of pivots an entrepreneur may need to consider for a business model.

Beyond the Classroom . . .

4-17. Identify an idea for a new business in an industry that interests you.

4-18. Evaluate the idea using an idea sketch pad.

4-19. Assess how the six macro forces are creating change within this industry.

4-20. Examine the idea using Porter's Five Forces Model.

4-21. Develop a plan to conduct market research on your idea using both primary and secondary methods of research.

4-22. Complete an entrepreneurial self-assessment.

4-23. What do you take away from this self-assessment about your entrepreneurial readiness?

4-24. Discuss your findings with someone who knows you well.

4-25. Did that person offer any insights about your entrepreneurial readiness that you may have overlooked?

Endnotes

[1] Alex Bruton, "The Really Big Idea Sketch Pad," The Innographer Ltd., n.d., https://theinnographer.com/toolkit/really-big-idea.

[2] Alex Bruton, *The Big Idea Code* (Calgary, Alberta, Canada: The Innographer, Ltd., 2013), p. 4.

[3] Ibid., p. 8.

[4] Rhonda Abrams, "Before Jumping into a New Venture, Do a Feasibility Study," *USA Today*, April 15, 2010, www.usatoday.com/money/smallbusiness/columnist/abrams/2010-04-15-new-venture_N.htm.

[5] S. C. Davis, S. W. Diegel, and R. G. Boundy, *Transportation Energy Data Book: Edition 34* (Oak Ridge, TN: Oak Ridge National Laboratory, August 2015), p. 190.

[6] Suwussa Bamrungsap, Zilong Zhao, Tao Chen, Lin Wang, Chunmei Li, Ting Fu, and Weihong Tan, "Nanotechnology in Therapeutics," *Nanomedicine*, 2012;7(8), pp. 1253–1271; E. J. Boyer, "What happens when a startup mentor needs mentoring? At NanoFerix, call in the scientists," *Nashville Business Journal*, March 22, 2013, www.bizjournals.com/nashville/blog/2013/03/biotech-start-up-seeks-2-million-to.html.

[7] Emily Anatole, "Generation Z: Rebels with a Cause," *Forbes*, May 28, 2013, www.forbes.com/sites/onmarketing/2013/05/28/generation-z-rebels-with-a-cause/.

[8] Kerry Hannon, "Finding the Right Caregiver, eHarmony Style," *Money*, July 11, 2016, http://time.com/money/4393368/finding-caregivers-on-the-web/; Sherwin Sheik, "The Inevitable Decline of the Nursing Home Industry," *Huffington Post*, July 5, 2016, www.huffingtonpost.com/sherwin-sheik/the-inevitable-decline-of_b_10806604.html.

[9] Ian Mount, "Tips for Increasing Sales in International Markets," *New York Times*, April 21, 2010, www.nytimes.com/2010/04/22/business/smallbusiness/22sbiz.html?_r=2&.

[10] Chad Brooks, "Porter's Five Forces: Analyzing the Competition," *Business News Daily*, November 12, 2013, www.businessnewsdaily.com/5446-porters-five-forces.html.

[11] Nathan Layne, "Wal-Mart puts the squeeze on suppliers to share its pain as earnings sag," *Reuters*, October 19, 2015, www.reuters.com/article/us-wal-mart-suppliers-insight-idUSKCN0SD0CZ20151019.

[12] "Aspire Beverage Company $10.50 Million Financing. Jesse Parker Published Oct 6 Form D," Octafinance, October 8, 2015, www.octafinance.com/aspire-beverage-company-10-50-million-financing-jesse-parker-published-oct-6-form-d/; Elizabeth Crawford, "Aspire Beverage Co. Fuels Growth with Unique Grassroots Marketing That Taps Student Athletes," *Food Navigator USA*, December 21, 2015, www.foodnavigator-usa.com/Manufacturers/ASPIRE-Beverage-Co.-grows-with-student-athlete-grassroots-marketing; "The Latest and Greatest," Aspire Beverage Company, n.d., http://aspirebeverages.com/news/; Sam Black, "Hockey Dads Start Up Sports Drink Line," *Minneapolis/St. Paul Business Journal*, May 10, 2013, http://upstart.bizjournals.com/entrepreneurs/hot-shots/2013/05/10/sports-drink-startup-aspire-aiming-at.html?page=all; Jason DeRusha, "New All-Natural MN Sports Drink Better Than Gatorade?" *CBS Minnesota*, May 15, 2013, http://minnesota.cbslocal.com/2013/05/15/new-mn-sports-drink-healthier-than-gatorade/.

[13] Alan Morrell, "Small Business Spotlight: Passero Associates," *Democrat and Chronicle*, July 16, 2016, www.democratandchronicle.com/story/money/business/2016/07/16/passero-associates-ceo-wayne-wegman-developers-site-plans-architects-planners-engineers-alan-morrell-top-workplace-business-spotlight/87058410/.

[14] Andrew Soergel, "Crafting a Future," *U.S. News & World Report*, April 7, 2016, https://www.usnews.com/news/articles/2016-04-07/in-behemoth-world-of-beer-microbreweries-are-crafting-the-future.

[15] Dan Ozzi, "How Do Festival Apps Monitor Behavior?" *Noisy*, January 29, 2016, http://noisey.vice.com/blog/how-do-festival-apps-monitor-your-behavior; John Patrick Pullen, "The Creative Ways Small Businesses Are Using Beacon Technology," *Entrepreneur*, October 31, 2015, www.entrepreneur.com/article/251645; Jeff Cornwall, "Business Model Demands Patience," *Entrepreneurial Mind*, March 28, 2011, www.drjeffcornwall.com/2011/03/28/business_model_demands_patienc/.

[16] Jamie McGee, "Arciplex to Expand in Nashville," *Tennessean*, February 25, 2016, www.tennessean.com/story/money/2016/02/25/arciplex-expand-nashville/80924016/; "Meet Arciplex Where Nashville Ideas Come to Life," *Forward Beat*, April 4, 2016, http://forwardbeat.com/meet-arciplex-where-nashvilles-ideas-come-to-life/.

[17]Justine Griffin, "Tampa's Cigar City Brewing Sold to Oskar Blues Brewery in Colorado," *Tampa Bay Times*, March 14, 2016, www.tampabay.com/news/business/tampas-cigar-city-brewing-selling-controlling-interest-to-bostons-fireman/2269280; David Kesmodel, "In Lean Times, a Stout Dream," *Wall Street Journal*, March 18, 2009, www.wsj.com/news/articles/SB123733628873664181.

[18]Caron Beesley, "How to Estimate the Cost of Starting a Business from Scratch," U.S. Small Business Adminstration, January 26, 2015, www.sba.gov/blogs/how-estimate-cost-starting-business-scratch.

[19]"2007 Survey of Business Owners." U.S. Census Bureau, www.census.gov/econ/sbo/methodology.html.

[20]J. Cornwall, *Bootstrapping* (Englewood Cliffs, NJ: Pearson/Prentice-Hall, 2009), p. 2.

[21]Cara Waters, "Top Reasons for Small Business Failure: Study," *SmartCompany*, April 12, 2013, www.smartcompany.com.au/growth/31229-top-reasons-for-small-business-failure-study/.

[22]A. Osterwalder and Y. Pigneur, *Business Model Generation* (Hoboken, New Jersey: Wiley, 2010).

[23]Brett Thorn, "Burger & Lobster Finds Success with Narrow Focus," *Restaurant News*, June 24, 2016, http://nrn.com/casual-dining/burger-lobster-finds-success-narrow-focus; Alan Phillips, "The Perfect Restaurant Model," *QSR Magazine*, August 2013, www.qsrmagazine.com/alanphilips-trends-watch/perfect-restaurant-model?utm_campaign=20130816&utm_ source=jolt&utm_medium=email; "The Low-Down," Burger and Lobster, n.d., www.burgerandlobster.com/home/the-low-down/.

[24]Steve Blank and Bob Dorf, *The Startup Owner's Manual* (Pescadero, California: K&S Ranch, 2012).

[25]Ibid.

[26]Scooby Axson, "Hovercraft Golf Carts to Debut This Week at Ohio Course," *Golf.com*, July 26, 2013, http://blogs.golf.com/presstent/2013/07/hovercraft-golfcarts-bubba-watson-to-make-debut.html?sct=hp12; John M. Chang, "First Hovercraft Golf Carts Are Ready to Fly," *ABC News*, July 11, 2013, http://abcnews.go.com/Technology/hovercraft-golf-cartsready-fly/story?id=19629975.

[27]Eric Ries, *The Lean Startup: How Today's Entrepreneurs Use Continuous Innovation to Create Radically Successful Businesses* (New York: Crown Business, 2011).

[28]"Airbnb," *CrunchBase*, August 8, 2016, www.crunchbase.com/organization/airbnb#/entity; Chris Bank, "10 Massively Successful Minimum Viable Products," *Speckyboy*, October 1, 2014, https://speckyboy.com/2014/10/01/successful-minimum-viable-products/.

[29]Jeffrey Feng, "Why Amazon Should Acquire Chegg," *Seeking Alpha*, August 4, 2016, http://seekingalpha.com/article/3995936-amazon-acquire-chegg; Jason Del Rey, "The Art of the Pivot," *Inc.*, February 1, 2011, www.inc.com/magazine/20110201/the-art-ofthe-pivot.html/1.

5

Crafting a Business Plan and Building a Solid Strategic Plan

Galina Peshkova/123RF

Learning Objectives

On completion of this chapter, you will be able to:

1. Explain the benefits of an effective business plan.
2. Describe the elements of a solid business plan.
3. Explain the "five Cs of credit" and why they are important to potential lenders and investors reviewing business plans.
4. Understand the keys to making an effective business plan presentation.
5. Understand the importance of strategic management to a small business.
6. Explain why and how a small business must create a competitive advantage in the market.
7. Develop a strategic plan for a business using the nine steps in the strategic management process.

MyLab Entrepreneurship
⭐ **Improve Your Grade!**

If your instructor is using MyLab Entrepreneurship, visit **www.pearson.com/mylab/entrepreneurship** for videos, simulations, and writing exercises.

A business plan is a planning tool that builds on the foundation of the idea assessment, feasibility analysis, and business model discussed in Chapter 4. A business plan provides a more comprehensive and detailed analysis than the first three steps in the new business planning process. Together with a well-developed business model, it functions primarily as a planning tool, describing in greater detail how to turn the model into a successful business. The primary goals of the business plan are to guide entrepreneurs as they launch their businesses and to help them acquire the necessary financing to launch. Research suggests that, whatever their size, companies that engage in business planning outperform those that do not. A business plan offers:

- A systematic, realistic evaluation of a venture's chances for success in the market
- A way to determine the principal risks facing the venture
- A "game plan" for managing the business successfully during its start-up
- A tool for comparing actual results against targeted performance
- An important tool for attracting capital in the challenging hunt for money

Few activities in the life of a business are as vital—or as overlooked—as developing a strategy for success that guides a business beyond the start-up detailed in the business plan. Companies without clear strategies may achieve some success in the short run, but as soon as competitive conditions stiffen or an unanticipated threat arises, they usually "hit the wall" and fold. Without a basis for differentiating itself from a pack of similar competitors, at best a company can hope for mediocrity in the marketplace.

In today's global competitive environment, any business, large or small, that is not thinking and acting strategically is extremely vulnerable. Every business is exposed to the forces of a rapidly changing competitive environment, and in the future, small business executives can expect even greater change and uncertainty. From sweeping political changes around the planet and rapid technology advances to more intense competition and newly emerging global markets, the business environment has become more turbulent and challenging to business owners. Although this market turbulence creates many challenges for small businesses, it also creates opportunities for companies that have in place strategies to capitalize on them. Entrepreneurs' willingness to adapt, to create change, to experiment with new business models, and to break traditional rules has become more important than ever. "The nature of being an entrepreneur means that you fully embrace ambiguity and are comfortable with being challenged regularly," says Tanya Prive, CEO and cofounder of CoFoundersLab.[1] This chapter explains how to create both a business plan and a strategic plan for a start-up company.

LO1

Explain the benefits of an effective business plan.

The Benefits of Creating a Business Plan

When based on the foundation of a fully developed and tested business model, a well-conceived and factually based business plan increases the likelihood of success of a new business. For decades, research has proved that companies that engage in business planning outperform those that do not. One study by the Small Business Administration reports that entrepreneurs who write business plans early on are two-and-a-half times more likely to actually start their businesses than those who do not.[2] There is currently debate about the need to develop a formal business plan. Some argue that a business plan is a document used only to seek financing from investors and bankers. However, even if an entrepreneur never develops a formal written plan, the implications of the lack of planning are all too evident in the high failure rates that small companies experience.

business plan

a written summary of an entrepreneur's proposed business venture, its operational and financial details, its marketing opportunities and strategy, and its managers' skills and abilities.

A **business plan** is a written summary of an entrepreneur's proposed business venture, its operational and financial details, its marketing opportunities and strategy, and its managers' skills and abilities. Most potential investors and lenders insist on a business plan as an essential step when considering funding an entrepreneurial venture. A business plan describes the direction the company is taking, what its goals are, where it wants to be, and how it intends to get there. It captures a full picture of the business model and all of the planning and preparation an entrepreneur undertakes when starting a business. The plan is written proof that an entrepreneur has performed the necessary research, has studied the business opportunity adequately, and is prepared to capitalize on it with a sound business model.

A business plan serves two essential functions. First, it provides a battery of tools—a mission statement, goals, objectives, budgets, financial forecasts, marketing plans, and entry strategies—to help entrepreneurs subject their ideas to one last test of reality before launching a business and serve as benchmarks to evaluate the progress of the business as it grows. A good business plan also helps an entrepreneur lead the company successfully through the challenging start-up phase.

The second function of a business plan is to attract lenders and investors. A business plan must demonstrate to potential lenders and investors that a venture will be able to repay loans and produce an attractive rate of return. They want proof that an entrepreneur has evaluated the risk involved in the new venture realistically and has a strategy for addressing it. Unfortunately, many small business owners approach potential lenders and investors without having prepared to sell their business concepts. Tim Williamson, cofounder of The Idea Village, an incubator for entrepreneurs, says that of the thousands of entrepreneurs seeking funding, only about 1 percent are ready to get the money.[3] A collection of figures scribbled on a note pad to support a loan application or an investment request is not enough. Applying for loans or attempting to attract investors without a solid business plan rarely lands needed capital. The best way to secure the necessary capital is to prepare a sound business plan. The quality of an entrepreneur's business plan weighs heavily in the final decision to lend or invest funds. It is also potential lenders' and investors' first impression of the company and its managers. Therefore, the finished product should be highly polished and professional in both form and content.

Three Tests of a Business Plan

To get external financing, an entrepreneur's plan must pass three tests with potential lenders and investors: (1) the reality test, (2) the competitive test, and (3) the value test. The first two tests have both external and internal components.

REALITY TEST The external component of the reality test involves proving that a market for the product or service really does exist. It focuses on industry attractiveness, market niches, potential customers, market size, degree of competition, and similar factors. Entrepreneurs who pass this part of the reality test prove in the marketing portion of their business plans that there is strong demand for their business idea. Evidence the entrepreneur gathers while testing the business model is an integral part of the marketing plan and bolsters the proof for the viability of the idea using feedback from real customers.

The internal component of the reality test focuses on the product or service itself. Can the company really build it for the cost estimates in the business plan? Is it truly different from what competitors are already selling? Does it offer customers something of value?

COMPETITIVE TEST The external part of the competitive test evaluates the company's relative position to its key competitors. How do the company's strengths and weaknesses match up with those of the competition? Do these reactions threaten the new company's success and survival? Recall from Chapter 4 that a compelling value proposition must clearly define the problem the target market is facing. Are current choices to address the problem for the target market unworkable? Is some sort of solution for the problem facing the target market inevitable? Is the problem urgent, critical, and clear for the target market? Is the target market underserved? Successful entrepreneurs carefully and honestly evaluate the strength of their product ideas. Do we offer a solution that looks at the problem differently than competitors? Can we protect our intellectual property (if applicable) and/or create a protectable niche? Do we disrupt the market but not so much that the "cost" of changing to us is too high? A value proposition that is properly constructed answers the following questions:[4]

- Who is our target market?

- What options currently exist for this target market?

- What do/will we offer the target market?

- What is the key problem it solves?

- Why is it better than other options from which customers can choose?

A strong and compelling value proposition guides everything entrepreneurs and their employees do while starting and growing their businesses.[5]

The internal competitive test focuses on management's ability to create a company that will gain an edge over existing rivals. To pass this part of the competitive test, a plan must prove the quality, skill, and experience of the venture's management team. What other resources does the company have that can give it a competitive edge in the market?

VALUE TEST To convince lenders and investors to put their money into the venture, a business plan must prove to them that it offers a high probability of repayment or an attractive rate of return. Entrepreneurs usually see their businesses as good investments because they consider the intangibles of owning a business, such as gaining control over their own destinies and freedom to do what they enjoy. Lenders and investors, however, look at a venture in colder terms: dollar-for-dollar returns. A plan must convince lenders that they will be repaid the money they lend to the business, and it must convince investors that they will earn an attractive return on their money.

Even after completing a feasibility analysis and building a business model, entrepreneurs sometimes do not come to the realization that "this business just won't work" until they build a business plan. Have they wasted valuable time? Not at all! The time to find out that a business idea will not succeed is in the planning stages, before committing significant money, time, and effort to the venture. It is much less expensive to make mistakes on paper than in reality. In other cases, a business plan reveals important problems to overcome before launching a company. Exposing these flaws and then addressing them enhances the chances of a venture's success.

The *real* value in preparing a plan is not as much in the plan itself as it is in the process the entrepreneur goes through to create the plan—from the idea assessment, to the feasibility analysis, through developing and testing the business model, and finally with crafting the written business plan. Although the finished product is extremely useful, the process of building the plan requires entrepreneurs to explore all areas of the business and subject their ideas to an objective, critical evaluation from many different angles. What entrepreneurs learn about their industry, target customers, financial requirements, competition, and other factors is essential to making their ventures successful. Building a business plan is one controllable factor that can reduce the risk and uncertainty of launching a company.

The Elements of a Business Plan

LO2

Describe the elements of a solid business plan.

Wise entrepreneurs recognize that every business plan is unique and must be tailor-made. They avoid the off-the-shelf, "cookie-cutter" approach that produces a look-alike business plan. The elements of a business plan may be standard, but the way entrepreneurs tell their stories should be unique and reflect the specific strengths of their business model, the experience of their team, their personality and how it will shape the culture of the business, and their enthusiasm for the new venture. In fact, the best business plans usually are those that tell a compelling story in addition to the facts. For those making a first attempt at writing a business plan, seeking the advice of individuals with experience in this process often proves helpful. Community-based entrepreneurship centers, accelerators, business professors, advisers working with local chapters of the Service Corps of Retired Executives (SCORE), consultants with Small Business Development Centers (SBDCs), accountants, and attorneys are excellent sources of guidance when creating and refining a plan. (For a list of SBDCs, go to the Small Business Administration Web site and see its SBDC Web page [https://www.sba.gov/tools/local-assistance/sbdc]; for a list of SCORE chapters, go to the SCORE Web site [https://www.score.org/find-location].) Remember, however, that you should be the author of your business plan, not someone else. A sample outline of a business plan is displayed in the appendix at the end of this book.

Initially, the prospect of planning a new business may appear to be overwhelming. Many entrepreneurs would rather launch their companies and "see what happens" than invest the time and energy needed to assess the idea, build a business model, define and research their target markets, define their strategies, and map out their finances. After all, planning is hard work; it requires time, effort, and thought. However, in reality, the entrepreneur should do both—*create a plan and see what happens when they engage real customers in the market*. By getting started (at least with a prototype) and seeing what happens, an entrepreneur can test and improve the basic business model. However, planning is essential as the entrepreneur gets ready to build the business and scale its growth. Entrepreneurs who invest their time and energy building plans are better prepared to face the hostile environment in which their companies will compete than those who do not.

Entrepreneurs can use business planning software available from several companies to create their plans. Some of the most popular programs are Business Plan Pro, LivePlan, and Business PlanMaker. These packages help entrepreneurs organize the material they have researched and gathered, and they provide helpful tips on plan writing, with templates for creating financial statements. Business planning software may help to produce professional-looking business plans, but they have a potential drawback: The plans they produce look as if they came from the same mold. That can be a turn-off for professional investors who review hundreds of business plans each year. Entrepreneurs benefit by making the content and appearance of their plans look professional and unique.

In the past, conventional wisdom was that business plans should be 20 to 40 pages in length, depending on the complexity of the business. More recently, experts have begun to recommend that plans should be shorter, typically suggesting that they be limited to 10 to 20 pages. There is mixed opinion on how complex the financial forecasts should be. If the forecasts are based on evidence that is substantiated by testing the business model, more detail will strengthen your case. If the numbers appear to be unsubstantiated or even fabricated, more detail can actually hurt the presentation. In many ways, having to write shorter business plans makes writing them even more challenging. A shorter business plan does not mean that any of the elements of the plan should be omitted. Instead, the entrepreneur must work hard to communicate all of the key aspects of the plan as succinctly as possible. Although entrepreneurs find it difficult to communicate all the important elements of their story within the shorter page length recommendations, plans run the risk of never getting used or read if they get too long.

This section explains the most common elements of a business plan. However, entrepreneurs must recognize that, like every business venture, every business plan is unique. An entrepreneur should use the elements described here as a starting point for building a plan and should modify them as needed to better tell the story of his or her new venture.

TITLE PAGE AND TABLE OF CONTENTS A business plan should contain a title page with the company's name, logo, and address as well as the names and contact information of the company founders. Many entrepreneurs also include the copy number of the plan and the date on which it was issued on the title page. Business plan readers appreciate a table of contents that includes page numbers so that they can locate the particular sections of the plan in which they are most interested.

THE EXECUTIVE SUMMARY To summarize the presentation to each potential financial institution or investors, the entrepreneur should write an executive summary. It should be concise—a maximum of one page—and should summarize all of the relevant points of the proposed deal. After reading the executive summary, anyone should be able to understand the entire business concept, the attributes that differentiate the company from the competition, and the financing that is being requested. The executive summary is a synopsis of the entire plan, capturing its essence in a capsulized form. It should explain the basic business model and the problem the business will solve for customers, and it should briefly describe the owners and key employees, target market(s), financial highlights (e.g., sales and earnings projections, the loan or investment requested, plans for using the funds, and projections for repaying any loans or cashing out investments), and the company's competitive advantage. The executive summary is a written version of what is known as "the elevator pitch." Imagine yourself on an elevator with a potential lender or investor. Only the two of you are on the elevator, and you have that person's undivided attention for the duration of the ride, but the building is not very tall! To convince the investor that your business idea is a great investment, you must condense your message down to its essential elements—key points that you can communicate in a matter of no more than two minutes. In the Pitch George Elevator Competition at George Washington University, students actually make their pitches to judges in an elevator, where they have the opportunity to pitch their business ideas in just three minutes. Winners receive small cash prizes and earn the opportunity to present at the GW Business Plan Competition, where they compete to earn more significant cash prizes.

The following five-part framework helps entrepreneurs develop a meaningful elevator pitch:

1. *Context.* What does your company do, in easy-to-understand words?

2. *Benefit.* What benefit or advantage does your company offer customers? (Recall the value proposition that lies at the heart of Business Model Canvas from Chapter 4.)

3. *Target customers.* For whom does your company provide the benefit?

4. *Point of differentiation.* How is your company different from other companies that provide similar products, services, or solutions?

5. *Clincher.* Can you leave the listener or reader with a memorable, bottom-line sound bite about your company?[6]

Like a good movie trailer, an executive summary is designed to capture readers' attention and draw them into the plan. If it misses, the chances of the remainder of the plan being read are minimal. What is different between an executive summary and a movie trailer is that the executive summary should give away the ending! If it does not, potential funders will never read the full plan. A coherent, well-developed summary of the full plan establishes a favorable first impression of the business and the entrepreneur behind it and can go a long way toward obtaining financing. A good executive summary should allow the reader to understand the business concept and how it will make money, and it should answer the ultimate question from investors or lenders: "What's in it for me?" An effective executive summary is a one-page version of the *entire* business plan. Although the executive summary is the first part of the business plan, it should be the last section written to ensure that it truly captures all of the important points as they appear in the full plan.

MISSION AND VISION STATEMENT A mission statement expresses an entrepreneur's vision for what his or her company is and what it is to become. It is the broadest expression of a company's purpose and defines the direction in which it will move. It anchors a company in reality and serves as the thesis statement for the entire business plan by answering the question "What business are we in?" Every good plan captures an entrepreneur's passion and vision for the business, and the mission statement is the ideal place to express them. Avoid the use of too much business jargon and too many business clichés. The statement should clearly state the product or service the business sells, its target market, and the basic nature of the business (e.g., manufacturing, consulting, service, outsourcing). A mission statement should be limited to no more than 25 words.

DESCRIPTION OF THE FIRM'S PRODUCT OR SERVICE An entrepreneur should describe the company's overall product line, giving an overview of how customers will use its goods or services. Drawings, diagrams, and illustrations may be required if the product is highly technical. It is best to write product and service descriptions so that laypeople can understand them. A statement of a product's position in the product life cycle might also be helpful. An entrepreneur should include a summary of any patents, trademarks, or copyrights that protect the product or service from infringement by competitors.

One danger entrepreneurs must avoid in this part of the plan is the tendency to dwell on the *features* of their products or services. This problem is the result of the "fall-in-love-with-your-product" syndrome, which often afflicts inventors. Customers, lenders, and investors care less about how much work, genius, and creativity went into a product or service than about what it will do for them. This part of the plan builds on the value proposition developed in the business model. The emphasis of this section should be on defining the benefits customers get by purchasing the company's products or services rather than on just a "nuts and bolts" description of the features of those products or services. A **feature** is a descriptive fact about a product or service (e.g., "an ergonomically designed, more comfortable handle"). A **benefit** is what the customer gains from the product or service feature (e.g., "fewer problems with carpal tunnel syndrome and increased productivity"). Benefits are at the core of the value proposition of the business model. This part of the plan must describe how a business will transform tangible product or service features into important but often intangible customer benefits—for example, lower energy bills, faster access to the Internet, less time writing checks to pay monthly bills, greater flexibility in building floating structures, or shorter time required to learn a foreign language. Remember: Customers buy benefits, not product or service features.

feature
a descriptive fact about a product or service.

benefit
what a customer gains from a product or service.

ENTREPRENEURIAL PROFILE: Ami Kassar, Multifunding Ami Kassar came up with the idea for his Philadelphia-based business, Multifunding, from his experience in the small business credit industry. He had seen the difficulty small businesses had when trying to find financing, yet he knew that there was financing available for many of these businesses if they could just get connected to the right sources. Although the value of the service was apparent from the beginning, it took Kassar several pivots of his business model to finally offer small business customers what they wanted, in the way they wanted it. "There is a fundamental difference between a vision and a business model," said Kassar. "While the core model of how we make our money has not changed from day one, we are constantly testing it, and looking for ways to improve it, evolve it, and grow it. Every few months an entrepreneur should take a cold shower, and take the time to look in the rear view mirror, and come up with some new things to test." After getting a profile of a small business client and an assessment of its financing needs, Multifunding puts together a report that gives the small business owner various financing options. Multifunding gets paid only when the financing is completed, taking a small percentage of the approved amount of financing. Multifunding funded 7 small businesses in its first year and 48 in its second. As part of the process of testing and refining its business model, the company began looking into new sources of revenue streams during its third year. With careful business modeling and planning, Multifunding's revenues now exceed $10 million.[7] ∎

Courtesy of Ami Kassar, Founder and CEO of MultiFunding LLC.

BUSINESS AND INDUSTRY PROFILE If one goal of creating a plan is to raise funding, the entrepreneur should include a section that acquaints lenders and investors with the industry in which the company competes. This section should provide readers with an overview of the industry or market segment in which the new venture will operate. Industry data such as key trends or emerging developments within the industry, market size and its growth or decline, and the relative economic and competitive strength of the major firms in the industry set the stage for a better understanding of the viability of a new business. Strategic issues such as ease of market entry and exit, the ability to achieve economies of scale or scope, and the existence of cyclical or seasonal economic trends further help readers evaluate the new venture. This part of the plan also should describe significant industry trends and key success factors as well as an overall outlook for its future. Information about the evolution of the industry helps the reader comprehend its competitive dynamics. *The U.S. Industrial Outlook Handbook* is an excellent reference that profiles a variety of industries and offers projections for future trends. Another useful resource of industry and economic information is the *Summary of Commentary on Current Economic Conditions*, more commonly known as the *Beige Book*. Published eight times a year by the Federal Reserve, the *Beige Book* provides detailed statistics and trends in key business sectors and in the overall economy. It offers valuable information on topics ranging from tourism and housing starts to consumer spending and wage rates. Entrepreneurs can find this wealth of information at their fingertips on the Web site of the Minneapolis Federal Reserve Bank. Industry trade associations are another treasure trove of information about the industries they represent. For example, an entrepreneur who is planning to launch a coffee shop can find valuable information at the National Retail Coffee Association and the Specialty Coffee Association. The business and industry profile section of a business plan should cover all of the relevant information the entrepreneur uncovered during the market and industry feasibility analysis. Data from secondary sources serves as background information. It does not replace the need for primary research that gathers data from real customers.

COMPETITOR ANALYSIS An entrepreneur should describe the new venture's competition and the ways in which its business strategy will position it effectively against key competitors. Failing to assess competitors realistically makes entrepreneurs appear to be poorly prepared, naive, or dishonest, especially to potential lenders and investors. The plan should include an analysis of each significant competitor and how well the competing business is meeting the important criteria that target customers use to make their purchase decisions among the various companies. Entrepreneurs who believe they have no competitors are only fooling themselves and are raising a huge red flag to potential lenders and investors. Gathering information on competitors' market shares, products, and strategies is usually not difficult. Trade associations, customers, industry journals, marketing representatives, and sales literature are valuable sources of data. This section of the plan should focus on demonstrating that the entrepreneur's company has an advantage over its competitors and address these questions:

- Who are the company's key competitors?

- What are their strengths and weaknesses?

- What are their strategies?

- What images do they have in the marketplace?

- How successful are they?

- What distinguishes the entrepreneur's product or service from others already on the market, and how will these differences produce a competitive edge?

Entrepreneurs gain invaluable insights through engaging in firsthand competitive research.

MARKET ENTRY STRATEGY This section of a business plan addresses the question of how to attract customers. By laying out a market entry strategy, an entrepreneur explains how he or she plans to enter the market and gain a competitive edge and how his or her value proposition sets the business apart from the competition. A key component of this section is defining what makes the company unique in the eyes of its customers. One of the quickest routes to business failure is trying to sell "me-too" products or services that offer customers nothing newer, better, bigger (or smaller), faster, or different.

MARKETING STRATEGY One of the most important tasks a business plan must fulfill is proving that a viable market exists for a company's goods or services. The business modeling process (refer to Chapter 4) identifies and describes a company's target customers and their characteristics and habits. Defining the target audience and its potential is one of the most important—and most challenging—parts of the business planning process.

Proving that a profitable market exists involves two steps: showing customer interest and documenting market claims. Both of these steps are part of the business modeling process and should be part of the business plan.

Showing Customer Interest An important element of any business plan is showing how a company's product or service provides a customer benefit or solves a customer problem. Entrepreneurs must be able to prove that their target customers actually need or want their goods or services and are willing to pay for them. This is why using customers to validate the business model is so important. Validation from real customers provides the proof of concept that investors look for in a business plan.

Proving that a viable market exists for a product or service is relatively straightforward for a company already in business but can be quite difficult for an entrepreneur with only an idea. In this case, the key is to find a way to get primary customer data. The feasibility analysis and the process of validating the value proposition during the development of the business model provide this type of real data from real customers. During the development of the business model, an entrepreneur might build a prototype and offer it to several potential customers to get written testimonials and evaluations to show to investors. The entrepreneur also could sell the product to several customers, perhaps at a discount on the condition that they provide evaluations. Doing so proves that there are potential customers for the product and allows customers to experience the product in operation. Getting a product into customers' hands is also an excellent way to get valuable feedback that can lead to significant design improvements and increased sales down the road. Integrating this type of primary data into the actual business plan demonstrates that the plan has a stronger chance of success.

ENTREPRENEURIAL PROFILE: Matt Cooper, Canoe and Kayak Rental Matt Cooper quit his job as an investment banker in New York to start Soggy Bottom Canoe and Kayak Rental in the backwoods of Mississippi. Cooper was tired of the corporate grind and ready for a change of pace. When Cooper arrived in Mississippi, he went full steam ahead, buying the land, building the facilities, and buying canoes, kayaks, trailers, and vans. He did no market research, such as talking to any prospective customers, before investing in the business. In the seven years the business operated, it never reached even half of the revenues it needed to be successful. As a result, Cooper used up all of his savings and much of his parents' savings trying to keep the business afloat. In the end, Cooper closed the business and moved to California to take a job in Silicon Valley. Cooper attributes his business failure to spending his money on buildings and equipment rather than basic market research and marketing.[8] ∎

Documenting Market Claims Too many business plans rely on vague generalizations such as "This market is so huge that if we get just 1 percent of it, we will break even in eight months." Such statements usually reflect nothing more than an entrepreneur's unbridled optimism; in most cases, they are quite unrealistic. In *The Art of the Start*, entrepreneur and venture capitalist Guy Kawasaki calls this the Chinese Soda Lie: "If just 1 percent of the people in China drink our soda, we will be more successful than any company in the history of mankind."[9] The problems with this reasoning are (1) few markets, especially the niche markets that small businesses often pursue, are as large as that, and (2) capturing 1 percent of a big market is extremely difficult to do, especially for a small company. Capturing a large share of a small, well-defined niche market is much more realistic for a small company than is winning a small share of a huge market.

Entrepreneurs must support claims of market size and growth rates with facts, and that requires market research. Results of market surveys, customer questionnaires, and demographic studies developed in the feasibility analyses and business modeling steps in the business planning process lend credibility to an entrepreneur's frequently optimistic sales projections contained within the formal business plan. (Refer to the market research techniques and resources in Chapter 9.) Quantitative market data is important because it forms the basis for all of the company's financial projections in the business plan. Fortunately, entrepreneurs who follow the business planning process will already have this type of data from their feasibility analyses and from building and testing their business models.

As you learned in Chapter 4 on conducting a feasibility analysis and business models, one effective documentation technique involves business prototyping, in which entrepreneurs test their business models on a small scale before committing serious resources to a business that might not work. Business prototyping recognizes that every business idea is a hypothesis that should be tested before an entrepreneur takes it to full scale. If the test supports the hypothesis and its accompanying assumptions, it is time to launch a company. If the prototype flops, the entrepreneur scraps the business idea with only minimal losses and turns to the next idea.

One of the main purposes of the marketing section of the plan is to lay the foundation for financial forecasts that follow. Sales, profit, and cash forecasts must be founded on more than wishful thinking. An effective market analysis should address the following items in detail, based on the framework developed in the business model.

Target Market Who are the company's target customers? How many of them are in the company's trading area? What are their characteristics (e.g., age, gender, educational level, income)? What do they buy? Why do they buy? When do they buy? What expectations do they have about the product or service? Will the business focus on a niche? How does the company seek to position itself in the market(s) it will pursue? Knowing my customers' needs, wants, and habits, what should be the basis for differentiating my business in their minds?

Advertising and Promotion Only after entrepreneurs understand their companies' target markets can they design a promotion and advertising campaign to reach those customers most effectively and efficiently. When developing an advertising and promotion strategy, an entrepreneur should keep in mind what he or she learned when defining the communication channel in the business modeling process. Which media are most effective in reaching the target market? How will they be used? How much will the promotional campaign cost? How will the promotional campaign position the company's products or services? How can the company benefit from publicity? How large is the company's promotional budget?

Market Size and Trends Assessing the size of the market is a critical step. How large is the potential market? Is it growing or shrinking? Why? Are customers' needs changing? Are sales seasonal? Is demand tied to another product or service?

ENTREPRENEURIAL PROFILE: James Park and Eric Friedman, Fitbit James Park faced the same problem as 146 million other working adults in the United States. After several years of focusing on his work and not himself, he had gotten out of shape and had put on weight. Park and his cofounder, Eric Friedman, launched Fitbit as a solution for this problem. They had initially raised $400,000 but were facing growing skepticism among investors they talked with about their new start-up. To demonstrate demand, the partners went to the annual TechCrunch 50 conference with plans to secure 50 preorders for their new device. They left the conference with 2,000 preorders and a story they could sell to potential investors. Five years after their launch, Fitbit's revenues were more than $2 billion, and its initial public offering raised more than $4 billion.[10] ∎

Location   For many businesses, choosing the right location is a key success factor. For retailers, wholesalers, and service companies, the best location usually is one that is most convenient to their target customers. Using census data and other market research, entrepreneurs can determine the sites with the greatest concentrations of their customers and locate there. Which sites put the company in the path of its target customers? Maps that show customer concentrations (available from census maps and other sources), traffic counts, the number of customers using a particular train station and when, and other similar types of information provide evidence that a solid and sizable customer base exists. Do zoning regulations restrict the use of a site? For manufacturers, the location issue often centers on finding a site near their key raw materials or near their primary customers. Using demographic reports and market research to screen potential sites takes the guesswork out of choosing the "right" location for a business.

Pricing   How much does it cost to produce or deliver the product or service? Before opening a restaurant, for example, an entrepreneur should know exactly what it will cost to produce each item on the menu. Failing to know the total cost (including the cost of the food, as well as labor, rent, advertising, and other indirect costs) of putting a plate in front of a customer is a recipe for failure. As we will discuss in Chapter 11, cost is just one part of the pricing equation. Another significant factor to consider is the image a company is trying to create in the market. Pricing helps communicate and reinforce key elements of the value proposition, such as quality and value.

Other pricing issues that a plan should address include: What is the company's overall pricing strategy? Will the planned price support the company's strategy and desired image? Given the company's cost structure, will the price produce a profit? How does the planned price compare to those of similar products or services? Are customers willing to pay it? What price tiers exist in the market? How sensitive are customers to price changes? Will the business sell to customers on credit? Will it accept credit cards? Will the company offer discounts? All of these questions help develop the revenue forecasts in the business plan. Remember that revenues are calculated with a simple formula: Price × Quantity. Therefore, understanding the proper pricing strategy is half the battle in developing accurate revenue forecasts.

Distribution   Developed from the distribution channel component of the business model, this portion of the plan should describe the specific channels of distribution the business will use (e.g., the Internet, direct mail, in-house sales force, sales agents, retailers) to distribute its products and services. Will distribution be extensive, selective, or exclusive? What is the average sale? How large will the sales staff be? How will the company compensate its sales force? What are the incentives for salespeople? How many sales calls does it take to close a sale? What can the company do to make it as easy as possible for customers to buy?

ENTREPRENEURS' AND MANAGERS' RÉSUMÉS The most important factor in the success of a business venture is its management, and financial officers and investors weight heavily the ability and experience of a company's managers in financing decisions. Investors will never invest in just a good idea: There must be a strong team in place to ensure that the idea will be implemented successfully. A common saying among investors is, "I would rather invest in an A team in charge of a C idea than an A idea run by a C team." A plan should include the résumés of business officers, key directors, and any person with at least 20 percent ownership in the company. This is the section of the plan in which entrepreneurs have the chance to sell the qualifications and the experience of their management team. Lenders and investors prefer experienced managers. Ideally, they look for managers with at least two years of operating experience in the industry they are targeting. In a technology business, investors are looking for partners that have both management and technology expertise.

A résumé should summarize each individual's education, work history (emphasizing managerial responsibilities and duties), and relevant business experience. Lenders and investors look for the experience, talent, and integrity of the people who will breathe life into the plan. This portion of the plan should show that the company has the right people organized in the right fashion for success. An entrepreneur can enhance the strength of the management team with a capable, qualified board of advisers. A board of directors or advisers consisting of industry experts lends credibility and can complement the skills of the management team.

PLAN OF OPERATION To complete the description of the business, an entrepreneur should construct an organization chart that identifies the business's key positions and the people who occupy them. Assembling a management team with the right stuff is difficult, but keeping it together until the company is established can be even harder. Most small companies cannot match the salaries that employees can earn at larger competitors, but offering stock options, profit sharing, shares of ownership, and other perks helps retain and motivate key employees. A plan of operation should also describe how the business operates, including space requirements, inventory management (if applicable), staffing plans, and accounting processes and policies.

Finally, this section should contain descriptions of the form of ownership (e.g., sole proprietorship, partnership, joint venture, C corporation, S corporation, LLC) and of any leases, contracts, and other relevant agreements pertaining to the operation.

PRO FORMA (PROJECTED) FINANCIAL STATEMENTS One of the most important sections of a business plan is an outline of the proposed company's financial statements—the "dollars and cents" of the proposed venture. An entrepreneur should carefully prepare projected (pro forma) financial statements for the operation for the next year using past operating data (if available), published statistics, and research to derive forecasts of the income statement, balance sheet, cash forecast (always!), and a schedule of planned capital expenditures. (You will learn more about creating projected financial statements in Chapter 12 and cash flow forecasts in Chapter 13.) Although including only most likely forecasts in the business plan is acceptable, entrepreneurs also should develop forecasts for pessimistic and optimistic conditions that reflect the uncertainty of the future in case potential lenders and investors ask for them.

It is essential that financial forecasts be realistic. Entrepreneurs must avoid the tendency to "fudge the numbers" to make their businesses look good. Experienced lenders and investors can detect unrealistic forecasts easily. In fact, some venture capitalists automatically discount an entrepreneur's financial projections by as much as 50 percent. One experienced angel investor says that when looking at the financial forecasts compiled by an entrepreneur, he always doubles the start-up costs and triples the time it will take to launch.

After completing these forecasts, an entrepreneur should perform a breakeven analysis for the business. The breakeven point is critical for an entrepreneurial venture because it signals the point at which the business is able to sustain itself through cash generated by operations and should not need any additional start-up capital. It also is the point at which the entrepreneur is able to get paid by the business!

It is important to include a statement of the assumptions on which the financial projections are based. Potential lenders and investors want to know how an entrepreneur derived forecasts for sales, cost of goods sold, operating expenses, accounts receivable, collections, accounts payable, inventory, taxes, and other items. Spelling out realistic assumptions gives a plan more credibility and reduces the tendency to include overly optimistic estimates of sales growth and profit margins. Greg Martin, a partner in the venture capital company Redpoint Ventures, says, "I have problems with start-ups making unrealistic assumptions—how much money they need or how quickly they can ramp up revenue. Those can really kill a deal for me."[11]

In addition to providing valuable information to potential lenders and investors, projected financial statements help entrepreneurs run their businesses more effectively and more efficiently after start-up. They establish important targets for financial performance and make it easier for an entrepreneur to maintain control over routine expenses and capital expenditures. An entrepreneur also should construct a financial dashboard that he or she can use to track the progress of the business and assess how well the actual outcomes match the key assumptions made in the business plan.

THE LOAN OR INVESTMENT PROPOSAL The loan or investment proposal section of a business plan should state the purpose of the financing, the amount requested, and the plans for repayment or, in the case of investors, an attractive exit strategy. When describing the purpose of the loan or investment, an entrepreneur must specify the planned use of the funds. An entrepreneur should state the precise amount requested and include relevant backup data, such as vendor estimates of costs or past production levels. The proposal should include all sources of funding for the business, including money the entrepreneur is investing in the business. Most bankers and investors will want to see evidence that the entrepreneur is willing to "put skin in the game"— that is, put some of his or her own money at risk in the venture.

Another important element of the proposal is the repayment schedule for a loan or the exit strategy for an investment. A lender's main consideration when granting a loan is the reassurance that the applicant will repay, whereas an investor's major concern is earning a satisfactory rate of return. Financial projections must reflect a company's ability to repay loans and produce adequate returns. Without this proof, a request for funding stands little chance of being approved. It is necessary for the entrepreneur to produce tangible evidence that shows the ability to repay loans or to generate attractive returns. Developing an exit strategy for investors, such as the opportunity to cash out through an acquisition or a public offering, is essential. This section of a business plan should include specific examples of other firms in the same industry that have already exited to increase the confidence that there is a viable path for the investors to exit the business and realize a return on their investments.

Finally, an entrepreneur should include a realistic timetable for implementing the proposed plan. This should include a schedule showing the estimated start-up date for the project and noting all significant milestones along the way. This most likely will be tied to installments of funding from equity investors or release of funds to the borrower from a loan.

A business plan must present an honest assessment of the risks facing the new venture. Evaluating risk in a business plan requires an entrepreneur to walk a fine line, however. Dwelling too much on everything that can go wrong discourages potential lenders and investors from financing the venture. Ignoring the project's risks makes those who evaluate the plan see the entrepreneur as naive, dishonest, or unprepared. The best strategy is to identify the most significant risks the venture faces and then to describe the plans the entrepreneur has developed to avoid them altogether or to overcome the negative outcome if the event does occur. Figure 5.1 explains how two simple diagrams communicate effectively to investors both the risks and the rewards of a business venture.

FIGURE 5.1

Visualizing a Venture's Risks and Rewards

Source: Based on William A. Sahlman, "How to Write a Great Business Plan," *Harvard Business Review,* July/August 1997, pp. 98–108.

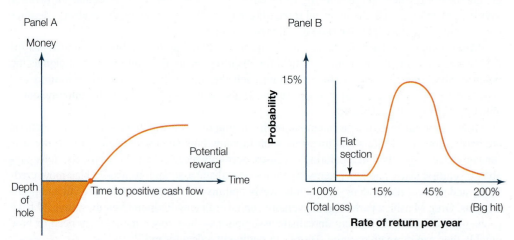

In panel A, the depth of the hole shows lenders and investors how much money it will take to start the business. The length of the chasm shows how long it will take to reach positive cash flow.

Panel B shows investors the range of possible returns and the probability of achieving them. In this example, investors see that there is a 15 percent chance of a total loss and an equal chance that they will earn between 15 and 45 percent on their investment. There is also a small chance that their initial investment will yield a 200 percent return.

There is a difference between a working business plan (the one the entrepreneur is using to guide the business) and a presentation business plan (the one he or she is using to attract capital). Although coffee rings and penciled-in changes in a working plan don't matter (in fact, they're a good sign that the entrepreneur is actually using the plan), they have no place on a plan going to someone outside the company. A plan is usually the tool an entrepreneur uses to make a first impression on potential lenders and investors. To make sure that impression is a favorable one, an entrepreneur should keep in mind these tips:

- Realize that first impressions are crucial. Make sure the plan has an attractive (but not expensive) cover.

- Make sure the plan is free of spelling and grammatical errors and typos. It is a professional document and should look like one.

- Make it visually appealing. Use color charts, figures, and diagrams to illustrate key points. Don't get carried away, however, because you don't want to end up with a "comic book" plan.

- Include a table of contents with page numbers to allow readers to navigate the plan easily. Reviewers should be able to look through a plan and quickly locate the sections they want to see.

- Make it interesting. Boring plans seldom get read; a good plan tells an interesting story.

- Make the case that the business will make money. Start-ups do not necessarily have to be profitable immediately, but sooner or later (preferably sooner), they must make money.

- Use computer spreadsheets to generate a set of realistic financial forecasts. They allow entrepreneurs to perform valuable "what if" (sensitivity) analysis in just seconds.

- Always include cash flow projections. Entrepreneurs sometimes focus excessively on their proposed venture's profit forecasts and ignore cash flow projections. Although profitability is important, lenders and investors are much more interested in cash flow because they know that's where the money to pay them back or to cash them out comes from.

- Keep the plan "crisp." It should be long enough to say what it should but not so long that it is a chore to read.

- Tell the truth. Absolute honesty is critical when preparing a business plan.

Business plans are forecasts about the future that an entrepreneur plans to create. As uncertain and difficult to predict as the future may be, an entrepreneur who launches a business without a plan, arguing that "trying to forecast the future is pointless," is misguided. In the *Harvard Business Review*, William Sahlman says, "the best business plans . . . are like movies of the future. They show the people, the opportunity, and the context from multiple angles. They offer a plausible, coherent story of what lies ahead. They unfold the possibilities of action and reaction."[12] That's the kind of "movie" an entrepreneur should strive to create in a plan.

What Lenders Look for in a Business Plan

To increase their chances of success when using their business plans to attract capital, entrepreneurs must be aware of the criteria lenders use to evaluate the creditworthiness of businesses seeking financing. Lenders and investors refer to these criteria as the *five Cs of credit*: capital, capacity, collateral, character, and conditions.

Capital

A small business must have a stable capital base before any lender will grant a loan. Otherwise, the lender would be making, in effect, a capital investment in the business. Most lenders refuse to make loans that are capital investments because the potential for return on the investment is limited strictly to the interest on the loan, and the potential loss would probably exceed

LO3

Explain the "five Cs of credit" and why they are important to potential lenders and investors receiving business plans.

the reward. In fact, the most common reasons banks give for rejecting small business loan applications are undercapitalization and too much debt. Investors also want to make sure entrepreneurs have invested enough of their own money into the business to survive the tenuous start-up period.

Capacity

Capacity is another word for cash flow. Lenders must be convinced of a company's ability to meet its regular financial obligations and to repay the bank loan, and that takes cash. In Chapter 13, you will see that more small businesses fail from lack of cash than from lack of profit. It is possible for a company to be earning a profit and still run out of cash. Lenders expect a business to pass the test of liquidity; they study closely a small company's cash flow position to decide whether it has the capacity required to succeed. Since the financial crisis of 2008, most lenders have been extremely cautious when evaluating cash flow.

Collateral

Collateral includes any assets an entrepreneur pledges to a lender as security for repayment of the loan. If an entrepreneur defaults on the loan, the bank has the right to sell the collateral and use the proceeds to satisfy the loan. Typically, lenders make very few unsecured loans (those not backed by collateral) to business start-ups. Bankers view an entrepreneur's willingness to pledge collateral (personal or business assets) as an indication of dedication to making the venture a success. Bankers always look first at the personal assets of the entrepreneur because they represent the easiest way to get repaid on a loan if the business fails. Entrepreneurs must be ready to sign personal guarantees for all business loans, stating that they will be personally liable for all bank loans to the business if the business fails. Business assets are lenders' last resort because selling inventory, equipment, and buildings owned by the business to repay loans is not an easy or effective means of repayment for the bank.

Character

Before putting money into a small business, lenders must be satisfied with the owner's character. An evaluation of character frequently is based on intangible factors such as honesty, competence, polish, determination, knowledge, experience, and ability. Although the qualities judged are abstract, this evaluation plays a critical role in a lender's or investor's decision. Banks have also begun to use what potential clients post on social networking sites such as Facebook, LinkedIn, and Twitter to assess character. If the entrepreneur is closely tied to successful businesspeople, this can help bolster the bank's assessment of character. On the other hand, posts and links that are unprofessional damage the lender's impression of the entrepreneur's character.

Lenders and investors know that most small businesses fail because of poor management, and they try to avoid extending loans to high-risk entrepreneurs. Preparing a solid business plan and a polished presentation can go far in convincing potential lenders and investors of an entrepreneur's ability to manage a company successfully.

Conditions

The conditions surrounding a loan request also affect the owner's chance of receiving funds. Banks consider factors relating to the business operation such as potential growth in the market, competition, location, form of ownership, and loan purpose. Again, the owner should provide this relevant information in an organized format in the business plan. Another important condition influencing the banker's decision is the shape of the overall economy, including interest rate levels, the inflation rate, and demand for money. Although these factors are beyond an entrepreneur's control, they are important components in a lender's decision. Conditions have not been as favorable for bank loans since the financial crisis in 2008, which has made getting business loans more difficult for all small businesses.

The higher a small business scores on these five *C*s, the greater its chance of receiving a loan. Wise entrepreneurs keep this in mind when preparing their business plans and presentations.

The Pitch: Making the Business Plan Presentation

LO4

Understand the keys to making an effective business plan presentation.

Entrepreneurs who are informed and prepared when requesting a loan or an investment impress lenders and investors. When entrepreneurs try to secure funding from lenders or investors, the written business plan most often precedes the opportunity to meet face-to-face. In recent years, some investors have moved away from requiring the submission of a formal business plan and instead have based their interest on the entrepreneur's presentation of the business model. However, even in these situations, sound planning is required.

The written plan must first pass muster before an entrepreneur gets the opportunity to present the plan in person. The time for presenting a business opportunity is often short, typically no more than just a few minutes. (When presenting a plan to a venture capital forum, the allotted time is usually less than 20 minutes and rarely more than 30.) When the opportunity arises, an entrepreneur must be well prepared. It is important to rehearse, rehearse, and then rehearse some more. An entrepreneur shouldn't make the mistake of beginning with a long-winded explanation about the technology on which the product or service is based. Within minutes, most of the audience will be lost, and so is any chance the entrepreneur had of obtaining the necessary financing for the new venture. A business plan presentation should cover five basic areas:

- Your company and its products and services. The presentation should answer in simple terms the first question of every potential lender and investor: What does your company do?

- The problem to be solved, preferably told in a personal way through a compelling story. Is it eliminating the time, expense, and anxiety of waiting for the results of medical tests with a device that instantly reads blood samples? Or making hearing aids more effective at filtering out background noise while enhancing the dominant sound for the user?

- A description (again in simple terms) of your company's solution to the problem. Ideally, the solution your company has developed is unique and serves as the foundation of your company's competitive edge in the marketplace.

- Your company's business model. This part of the presentation explains how your company makes money and includes figures such as revenue per sale, expected gross profit and net profit margins, and other relevant statistics. This is your opportunity to show lenders and investors how your company will produce an attractive payback or payoff.

- Your company's competitive edge. Your presentation should identify clearly the factors that set your company apart from the competition.

- A clear exit plan. Investors rarely make long-term investments in entrepreneurial businesses. Your presentation should include evidence that the business model supports robust growth and that there are large companies in the industry interested in acquisitions.

No matter how good a written business plan is, entrepreneurs who stumble through the presentation will lose the deal. Entrepreneurs who are successful at raising the capital their companies need to grow have solid business plans and make convincing presentations of them. Some helpful tips for making a business plan presentation to potential lenders and investors include:

- Prepare. Good presenters invest in preparing their presentations and knowing the points they want to get across to their audiences.

- Practice your delivery and then practice some more.

- Demonstrate enthusiasm about the business but don't be overly emotional. Be genuine and be yourself.

- Focus on communicating the dynamic opportunity your idea offers and how you plan to capitalize on it. Fight the temptation to launch immediately into a lengthy discourse about the details of your product or service or how much work it took to develop it. Otherwise, you'll never have the chance to describe the details to lenders and investors.

- Hook investors quickly with an up-front explanation of the new venture, its opportunities, and the anticipated benefits to them. For some businesses, a story of its impact can be a good hook to start a presentation.

- Use visual aids. They make it easier for people to follow your presentation. Don't make the mistake of making the visuals the star of the presentation, however. Visual aids should punctuate your spoken message and focus the audience's attention on the key points.

- Follow Guy Kawasaki's 10/20/30 rule for PowerPoint presentations. Use 10 slides that you can cover in 20 minutes, and use 30-point font to ensure that you do not try to put too many words on each slide.[13]

- Explain how your company's products or services solve some problem and emphasize the factors that make your company unique.

- Offer proof. Integrate relevant facts into your presentation to prove your plan's claims, customers' satisfaction with your company's products or services, and its profit potential.

- Hit the highlights. Specific questions will bring out the details later. Don't get caught up in too much detail in early meetings with lenders and investors.

- Keep the presentation "crisp," just like your business plan.

- Avoid the use of technical terms that will likely be above most of the audience. Do at least one rehearsal before someone who has no special technical training. Tell him or her to stop you anytime he or she does not understand what you are talking about. When this occurs (and it likely will), rewrite that portion of your presentation.

- Remember that every potential lender and investor you talk to is thinking "What's in it for me?" Be sure to answer that question in your presentation, particularly as it relates to a path to an exit.

- Close by reinforcing the potential of the opportunity. Be sure you have sold the benefits the investors will realize when the business succeeds.

- Be prepared for questions. There is not likely time for a long "Q&A" session, but interested investors may want to get you aside to discuss the details of the plan.

- Anticipate the questions the audience is most likely to ask and prepare for them in advance.

- Be sensitive to the issues that are most important to lenders and investors by reading the pattern of their questions. Focus your answers accordingly. For instance, some investors may be interested in the quality of the management team, whereas others may be more interested in marketing strategies. Be prepared to offer details on either.

- Follow up with every investor to whom you make a presentation. Don't sit back and wait; be proactive. They have what you need: investment capital. Demonstrate that you have confidence in your plan and have the initiative necessary to run a business successfully.

Building a Strategic Plan

LO5

Understand the importance of strategic management to a small business.

The rules of the competitive game are constantly changing. To be successful, entrepreneurs must adapt to changes in the marketplace. Fortunately, entrepreneurs have at their disposal a powerful weapon to cope with an often-hostile, ever-changing environment: the process of

You Be the Consultant

The Battle of the Plans

The Richards Barrentine Values and Ventures Business Plan Competition, run by the Neeley Entrepreneurship Center at Texas Christian University, focuses on for-profit enterprises owned by current undergraduate students that specifically impact society in meaningful ways. Plans must demonstrate a societal or environmental need, such as contributions to sustainability, innovations in the health and life sciences, innovations in energy, or opportunities for underrepresented groups in business. Business plans submitted for the competition must be for-profit values-centered enterprises. The competition defines a values-centered enterprise as one that assures sustainable prosperity while also supporting the needs of company owners and shareholders, employees and their families, suppliers, customers, communities, and the environment. This is not a competition for nonprofit social enterprises.

Values and Ventures is a two-day event. During the first day, teams present in concurrent sessions. The teams are grouped into flights. The first-place team in each flight automatically advances to the finals. The second-place teams compete with each other in a "lightning round," and the top two teams from the lightening round also make the finals. In the second day of competition, each finalist presents again to the judges. Each team gets 12 minutes to present and 10 minutes to respond to questions from the judges.

Teams that do not make the finals compete in an elevator pitch competition: One member from each non-finalist team is invited to participate in a 90-second elevator pitch on the second day of the competition.

One recent competition fielded teams from 49 universities. The third-place team, winner of $10,000, was Separatec from John Hopkins University. Separatec is developing a patent-pending ultrasonic tip that separates scar tissue in the spinal cord during surgery to minimize side effects and improve recovery. The second-place team, winner of $15,000, was The Rooftop Tea Company from George Washington University. The Rooftop Tea Company seeks to create more "green roofs" by empowering women in underserved communities to transform rooftops into profitable tea gardens. The first-place team, winner of $25,000, was InterWallet from Loyola Marymount University. InterWallet provides a low-cost way for lower-income people to pay bills and transfer money. It seeks to disrupt the ATM, bill payment, cash checking, and money transfer markets. InterWallet has developed software that can collect bills for any major service provider through its easy-to-use kiosks.

1. What benefits do entrepreneurs gain by competing in business plan competitions such as the one at Texas Christian University?

2. Work with a team of your classmates to brainstorm ideas for establishing a business plan competition on your campus. How would you locate judges? What criteria would you use to judge the plans? What prizes would you offer the winners, and how would you raise the money to give those prizes? Who would you allow to compete in your competition?

3. Using the ideas you generated in question 2, create a two-page proposal for establishing a business plan competition at your school.

Sources: Based on "Neeley Entrepreneurship Center, Values and Ventures Business Plan Competition," Neeley School of Business, Texas Christian University, n.d., www .neeley.tcu.edu/vandv/; "Hopkins Student Team Takes Third Place in National Business Plan Competition," *The Hub*, Johns Hopkins University, April 13, 2016, http:// hub.jhu.edu/2016/04/13/values-ventures-competition-separatec/; "InterWallet from Loyola Marymount Wins TCU's 2016 Richards Barrentine Values and Ventures," Texas Christian University, April 11, 2016, http://neeley.tcu.edu/News_and_Events/ Top_Stories/Articles/2016/VandV_Winners.aspx.

strategic planning. Strategic planning involves developing a game plan to guide a company as it strives to accomplish its vision, mission, goals, and objectives and to keep it from straying off course.

Working together to create and update a solid strategic plan provides managers and employees a sense of direction. As more team members become committed to making the plan work, it takes on special meaning. The plan gives everyone targets to shoot for, and it provides a yardstick for measuring actual performance against those targets, especially in the crucial and chaotic start-up phase of the business.

Clate Mask, cofounder and CEO of Infusionsoft, says that strategic planning helped his company grow successfully from a small start-up to a 650-employee company, funded with venture capital. Infusionsoft's strategic planning is built from a bold three- to five-year vision of what the business can become and what it can achieve. From there, the company develops three to five annual priorities to ensure progress toward the vision. Finally, managers develop the quarterly priorities and operational tactics necessary to reach their annual goals. "Strategic planning isn't a one-time event," says Mask. "Once you've laid out your strategy, it's crucial to stay focused over the long-term. I've found that it's vital to schedule a steady rhythm of productive meetings—annually, quarterly, monthly, weekly, and daily."[14]

ENTREPRENEURIAL PROFILE: David and Jewel Abt: Abt Electronics Abt Electronics is a family-owned business founded by David and Jewel Abt in Chicago in 1936. To compete with large national chains, such as Best Buy, Abt has pursued several successful strategies. Abt installed several activity and play stations throughout its 350,000-square-foot store, including a flight simulator, a giant granite ball that floats on water, and aquariums teeming with sharks and other fish. Abt employees treat their customers well, offering them coffee and fresh-baked cookies. Abt offers extensive training for its employees and empowers them to offer customers discounts without the need for a supervisor's approval. Abt ties part of employee bonuses to customer service rather than only to sales targets. Abt offers more than just electronics. Customers can buy watches, gourmet food, exercise equipment, furniture, and many other specialty products. Abt was an early entrant into online retailing, beginning Internet sales in 1998. Jon Abt, co-president of the company, says Best Buy's advertising helps build awareness of the products Abt sells in its store. Abt offers more than just its products; it offers an enjoyable experience for the entire family. Although there have been rumors that Abt would open additional locations now that another generation has taken over the family business, the company is sticking to its long-term strategic plan of having one store that is a destination retail establishment.[15] ∎

Perhaps the biggest change that entrepreneurs face is unfolding now: the shift in the world's economy from a base of *financial to intellectual* capital. "Knowledge is no longer just a factor of production," says futurist Alvin Toffler. "It is the *critical* factor of production."[16] Today, a company's intellectual capital is likely to be the source of its competitive advantage in the marketplace.[17] **Intellectual capital** has three components:[18]

intellectual capital
one source of a company's competitive advantage, which consists of human, structural, and customer capital.

1. *Human capital* consists of the talents, creativity, skills, and abilities of a company's workforce and shows up in the innovative strategies, plans, and processes the people in an organization develop and then passionately pursue.

2. *Structural capital* is the accumulated knowledge and experience that a company possesses. It can take many forms, including processes, software, patents, copyrights, and, perhaps most important, the knowledge and experience of the people in the company.

3. *Customer capital* is the established customer base, positive reputation, ongoing relationships, and goodwill that a company builds up over time with its customers.

Increasingly, entrepreneurs are recognizing that the capital stored in these three areas forms the foundation of their ability to compete effectively and that they must manage this intangible capital base carefully. Every business uses all three components in its strategy, but the emphasis on each one varies from company to company.

This knowledge shift is creating as much change in the world's business systems as the Industrial Revolution did in the agriculture-based economies of the 1800s. The Knowledge Revolution threatens the existence of companies that are not prepared for it, but it is spawning tremendous opportunities for entrepreneurs who are equipped with the strategies to exploit these opportunities. Geoff Colvin, senior editor at *Fortune*, says, "The 21st-century corporation will increasingly be an idea-based business, operating not just in infotech but also in media, finance, pharmaceuticals, and other industries that consume lots of brainpower."[19] According to Gary Hamel, author of *Inside the Revolution*, "If you want to find a few ideas with the power to enthrall customers, foil competitors, and thrill investors, you must first generate hundreds and potentially thousands of unconventional strategic ideas. Put simply, you have to crush a lot of rock to find a diamond."[20] In other words, small companies must use the creativity-stimulating techniques discussed in Chapter 3 as one source of competitive advantage over their rivals.

Building a Competitive Advantage

The goal of developing a strategic plan is to create a **competitive advantage**—the value proposition that sets a small business apart from its competitors and gives it a unique position in the market that makes it superior to its rivals. It is the differentiating factor that makes customers want to buy from your business rather than from your competitors. From a strategic perspective, the key to business success is to develop a sustainable competitive advantage—one that is durable, creates value for customers, and is difficult for competitors to duplicate. For example, Whole Foods competes successfully with giant chains such as Wal-Mart and Kroger not on price but by emphasizing superior customer service, higher-quality products, a more extensive inventory of local and organic products, and a commitment to fair-trade suppliers. Its stores are well organized, attractive, and entertaining. However, competitors react to a new entrant's success. Organic food has gone mainstream, forcing Whole Foods to redefine its competitive position in the market. Whole Foods recently introduced its "365 by Whole Foods," which is designed to offer value that will make it a true everyday grocery store for its customers. Whole Foods caters to young shoppers by making shopping there an experience rather than just a place to buy groceries.[21] Companies that fail to define their competitive advantage fall into "me-too" strategies that never set them apart from their competitors and do not allow them to become market leaders or to achieve above-average profits.

Entrepreneurs should examine five aspects of their businesses to define their companies' competitive advantages:

1. *Products they sell.* What is unique about the products the company sells? Do they save customers time or money? Are they more reliable and more dependable than those that competitors sell? Do they save energy, protect the environment, or provide more convenience for customers? By identifying the unique customer benefits of their companies' products, entrepreneurs can differentiate their businesses. Krispian Lawrence and Anirudh Sharma recognized that those who are visually impaired have a challenge when using most navigational apps, which rely primarily on audio instructions. The visually impaired rely heavily on their sense of hearing, so the audio feedback can be distracting. Lawrence and Sharma invented Lechal shoes as a solution. Lechal shoes use vibrations to indicate direction. If you should turn left, the left shoe vibrates. If you should turn right, the right one vibrates. If you are going the wrong way, they both vibrate.[22]

2. *Service they provide.* Many entrepreneurs find that the service they provide their customers is an excellent way to differentiate their companies. Because they are small, friendly, and close to their customers, small businesses can provide customer service that is superior to that which their larger competitors can provide. What services does the company provide (or which ones can it provide) to deliver added value and a superior shopping experience for customers?

3. *Pricing they offer.* As we will see later in this chapter, some small businesses differentiate themselves by using price. Price can be a powerful point of differentiation; offering the lowest price gives some customers a great incentive to buy. However, offering the lowest price is not always the best way to create a unique image. Small companies that do not offer the lowest prices must emphasize the value their products offer.

4. *Way they sell.* Customers today expect to be able to conduct business when they want to, meaning that companies that offer extended hours—even 24-hour service seven days a week (perhaps via the Internet)—have the basis for an important competitive advantage. Zoots, a small chain of dry-cleaning stores in the Northeast, offers customers extended hours seven days a week and allows a secure 24-hour pickup and drop-off service. The company also offers a home pickup and delivery service that customers can book online and an environmentally friendly cleaning process, all of which maximize customers' convenience and set the company apart from its competition.[23]

5. *Values to which they are committed.* The most successful companies exist for reasons that involve far more than merely making money. The entrepreneurs behind these companies understand that one way to connect with customers and establish a competitive edge is to

LO6

Explain why and how a small business must create a competitive advantage in the market.

competitive advantage
the value proposition that sets a small business apart from its competitors and gives it a unique position in the market that makes it superior to its competition.

manage their companies from a values-based perspective and operate them in an ethical and socially responsible fashion. In other words, they recognize that there is no inherent conflict between earning a profit and creating good for society and the environment.

Building a competitive advantage alone is not enough; the key to success over time is building a *sustainable* competitive advantage. In the long run, a company gains a sustainable competitive advantage through its ability to develop a set of core competencies that enable it to serve its selected target customers better than its rivals. **Core competencies** are a unique set of capabilities that a company develops in key areas, such as superior quality, customer service, innovation, team building, flexibility, and responsiveness, that allow it to vault past competitors. As the phrase suggests, they are central to a company's ability to compete successfully and are usually the result of important skills and lessons that a business has learned over time.

core competencies
a unique set of capabilities that a company develops in key areas that allow it to vault past competitors.

Typically, a company develops core competencies in no more than five or six (often fewer) areas. These core competencies become the nucleus of the company's competitive advantage and are usually quite enduring over time. Markets, customers, and competitors may change, but a company's core competencies are more durable, forming the building blocks for everything a company does. To be effective strategically, these competencies should be difficult for competitors to duplicate, and they must provide customers with an important perceived benefit. Small companies' core competencies often have to do with the advantages of their size, such as agility, speed, closeness to their customers, superior service, or the ability to innovate. Smart entrepreneurs use their companies' size to their advantage, recognizing that it allows them to do things that their larger rivals cannot do. The key to success is building the company's strategy on its core competencies and concentrating on providing value for target customers (see Figure 5.2).

Successful small companies are able to build strategies that exploit all the competitive advantages that their size gives them by doing the following:

- Responding quickly to customers' needs
- Providing the precise desired level of customer service
- Remaining flexible and willing to change
- Constantly searching for new, emerging market segments
- Building and defending small market niches
- Erecting "switching costs," the costs a customer incurs by switching to a competitor's product or service, through personal service and loyalty
- Remaining entrepreneurial and willing to take risks and act with lightning speed
- Constantly innovating

ENTREPRENEURIAL PROFILE: Kevin Reddy: Noodles & Company Noodles & Company is a restaurant chain that has grown to more than 500 U.S. locations since it opened its first store in 1996. The company has achieved this growth even after moving away from a franchising model, which is the most common strategic approach for growing restaurant chains. Its strategy is to build a solid base by staying close to customers and offering a simple menu, built on noodles and pasta. Although the company has faced some pressure to grow more quickly since its IPO in 2013, it has continued to focus at least 90 percent of new store growth on company-owned stores and only

FIGURE 5.2

Building a Sustainable Competitive Advantage

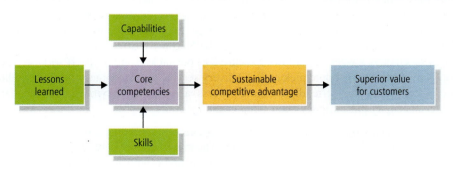

10 percent on franchises. Noodles & Company continues to use feedback from its customers to adapt its business model and strategies. It views its core competency as operational excellence in its restaurants that it uses to build a strong brand. By owning most of the stores, the company focuses on growing its customer base rather than adding a certain number of franchises.[24] ■

Investors use the phrase "trying to boil the ocean" to refer to a business that tries to be everything to everyone; no company can—or should—do this. In fact, one of the biggest pitfalls many entrepreneurs stumble into is failing to differentiate their companies from the crowd of competitors. Entrepreneurs often face the challenge of setting their companies apart from their larger, more powerful competitors (who can easily outspend them) by using their creativity and the special abilities their businesses offer customers. Developing core competencies does *not* necessarily require a company to spend a great deal of money. It does, however, require an entrepreneur to use creativity, imagination, and vision to identify the things that the company does best and that are most important to its target customers. Businesses have an infinite number of ways to create a competitive edge, but building a strategy around a company's core competencies allows it to gain a sustainable competitive advantage based on its strengths.

Strategic management enhances a small company's effectiveness, but entrepreneurs first must have a process designed to meet their needs and their business's special characteristics. It is a mistake to attempt to apply a big business's strategic development techniques to a small business because a small business is not merely "a little big business." Because of their size and their particular characteristics—small resource base, flexible managerial style, informal organizational structure, and adaptability to change—small businesses need a different approach to the strategic management process. The strategic management procedure for a small business should include the following features:

- Use a relatively short planning horizon—two years or less for most small companies.

- Be informal and not overly structured; a shirtsleeve approach is ideal.

- Encourage the participation of employees and outside parties to improve the reliability and creativity of the resulting plan.

- Do not begin with setting objectives because extensive objective setting early on may interfere with the creative process of strategic management.

- Maintain flexibility; competitive conditions change too rapidly for any plan to be considered permanent.

- Focus on strategic *thinking*, not just planning, by linking long-range goals to day-to-day operations.

- Be an ongoing process because businesses and the competitive environment in which they operate constantly change.

The Strategic Management Process

Strategic management is a continuous process that consists of nine steps:

LO7

Develop a strategic plan for a business using the nine steps in the strategic management process.

Step 1. Develop a clear vision and translate it into a meaningful mission statement.

Step 2. Assess the company's strengths and weaknesses.

Step 3. Scan the environment for significant opportunities and threats facing the business.

Step 4. Identify the key factors for success in the business.

Step 5. Analyze the competition.

Step 6. Create company goals and objectives.

Step 7. Formulate strategic options and select the appropriate strategies.

Step 8. Translate strategic plans into action plans.

Step 9. Establish accurate controls.

Step 1. Develop a Clear Vision and Translate It into a Meaningful Mission Statement

VISION Throughout history, the greatest political and business leaders have been visionaries. Whether the vision is as grand as Martin Luther King, Jr.'s "I have a dream" speech or as simple as Ray Kroc's devotion to quality, service, cleanliness, and value at McDonald's, the purpose is the same: to focus everyone's attention on the same target and to inspire them to reach it. The vision is future oriented and touches everyone associated with the company—its employees, investors, lenders, customers, and the community. It is an expression of what an entrepreneur stands for and believes in. Highly successful entrepreneurs communicate their vision and their enthusiasm about that vision to those around them.

ENTREPRENEURIAL PROFILE: Nicolas Jammet, Jonathan Neman, and Nathaniel Ru: Sweetgreen When Nicolas Jammet, Jonathan Neman, and Nathaniel Ru were undergraduate students at Georgetown University, they were often frustrated by the lack of healthy fast-food restaurants near campus. With funding from 40 friends and family members, they launched Sweetgreen to address this gap in the market. Shortly after launch, the initial location routinely had lines of customers out the door. Sweetgreen, a farm-to-table salad chain, has opened more than 60 locations with the help of more than $95 million in venture capital financing. Sweetgreen's vision is to be a "destination for delicious food that's both healthy for you and aligned with your values. We source local and organic ingredients from farmers we know and partners we trust, supporting our communities and creating meaningful relationships with those around us. We exist to create experiences where passion and purpose come together." Its mission is "to build healthier communities by connecting people to real food."[25] ■

A vision is the result of an entrepreneur's dream of something successful that does not exist yet and the ability to paint a compelling picture of that dream for everyone to see. It answers the question "Where are we going?" A strong vision helps a company in four ways:

1. *Vision provides direction.* Entrepreneurs who spell out the vision for their company focus everyone's attention on the future and determine the path the business will take to get there.

2. *Vision determines decisions.* The vision influences the decisions, no matter how big or how small, that owners, managers, and employees make every day in a business. This influence can be positive or negative, depending on how well defined the vision is.

3. *Vision inspires people.* A clear vision excites and ignites people to action. People want to work for a company that sets its sights high.

4. *Vision allows for perseverance in the face of adversity.* Young companies, their founders, and their employees often face many hardships from a multitude of sources. Having a vision that serves as a company's "guiding star" enables people to overcome imposing obstacles.

Vision is based on an entrepreneur's values. Explaining that an entrepreneur's values are the nucleus around which a company grows, author and consultant Ken Blanchard says, "Winning companies first emphasize values—the beliefs that you, as the business owner, have about your employees, customers, quality, ethics, integrity, social responsibility, growth, stability, innovation, and flexibility. Managing by values—not by profits—is a powerful process."[26] Successful entrepreneurs build their businesses around a set of three to seven core values that might range from respect for the individual and innovation to creating satisfied customers and making the world a better place. Indeed, truly visionary entrepreneurs see their companies' primary purpose as more than just "making money," and surveys of business owners suggest that this is a common view among entrepreneurs. Table 5.1 offers useful tips for creating a vision for your company.

The best way to put values into action is to create a written mission statement that communicates those values to everyone the company touches.

mission statement

an enduring declaration of a company's purpose that addresses the first question of any business venture: What business are we in?

MISSION The **mission statement** addresses another basic question of any business venture: "What business are we in?" Establishing the purpose of the business in writing gives a company a sense of direction. As an enduring declaration of a company's purpose, a mission statement

TABLE 5.1 Creating a Vision for Your Company

Ari Weinzweig, cofounder of Zingerman's Community of Businesses, emphasizes the importance of creating a vision to achieve entrepreneurial success. A vision is a picture of what success will look like in a business at a particular time in the future. "The power that comes out of visioning is huge," he says. "Effective visioning allows us to move toward the future we want, not just react to a present-day reality we don't like."

How does an entrepreneur start the visioning process? First, select the time frame, ideally 3 to 10 years out. The next step is to write the first draft of your vision, remembering to shoot for something *great*, even for things that other people have told you repeatedly were unachievable. As you proceed, write as if your vision already has happened. The following questions will help you get started:

1. What are the core values that define how your business operates?
2. What problems will your business model solve in the market over the next 10 years?
3. Who is your target market?
4. How does your business model solve target customers' problem?
5. What has your business achieved that you are most proud of?
    a. Relative rank in your industry
    b. Financial success
    c. Product or service quality
    d. Contribution to the community
    e. Awards and recognitions
6. What are your most important product lines or services?
7. What products or services do you refuse to offer?
8. What is a customer's shopping experience like at your business? What makes that experience different from the experience with your competition?
9. How do you describe your management style?
10. What kind of people do you hire as employees and managers?
11. What kind of relationship do you have with your employees? What do they say about their jobs?
12. How does the community view your business?
13. What do suppliers say about your business?
14. What do industry experts say about your business?

You will probably write several drafts of your vision before sharing it with others, especially with the people who will be involved in making it a reality. Ask for their feedback and input but remember: It's *your* vision. When people ask (and they inevitably will) "How will we achieve that?" remember that vision is about the "*what*"; strategy—the "*how*"—comes later.

Sources: Based on Ari Weinzweig, "Creating a Company Vision," *Inc.*, February 1, 2011, www.inc.com/magazine/20110201/creating-a-company-vision.html/2; Paula Fernandes, "What Is a Vision Statement?" *Business News Daily*, April 20, 2016, www.businessnewsdaily.com/3882-vision-statement.html.

is the mechanism for making it clear to everyone the company touches "why we are here" and "where we are going."

Without a concise, meaningful mission statement, a small business risks wandering aimlessly in the marketplace, with no idea of where to go or how to get there. A great mission statement sets the tone for the entire company and focuses its attention in the right direction.

Elements of a Mission Statement A sound mission statement need not be lengthy to be effective. In fact, shorter usually is better. Entrepreneurs and their employees should address four key questions as they develop a mission statement for their businesses:

- What are we in business to accomplish?
- Who are we in business to serve?
- How are we going to accomplish that purpose?
- What principles and beliefs form the foundation of the way we do business?

A company's mission statement may be the most essential and basic communication that it puts forward. It should inspire and motivate employees by communicating the company's overarching values. If the people on the plant, shop, retail, or warehouse floor don't know what the company's mission is, then, for all practical purposes, it does not have one! The mission statement expresses a company's character, identity, and scope of operations, but writing it is only half the battle, at best. The most difficult and important part is *living* that mission every day. *That's* how employees decide what really matters. To be effective, a mission statement must become a natural part of the organization, embodied in the minds, habits, attitudes, and decisions of everyone in the company every day. In other words, a good mission statement is translated into positive performance in an organization. When Jim Brett became president of West Elm, a company that sells furniture and home decor and accessories, its mission statement was about having customers buy its designers' definition of style. He realized that this was no longer working because customers were making it clear that they wanted to express their own definition of style. As a result, West End changed its mission. The company now to promises its customers to "inspire you to express your personal style at home." The new mission statement refocused all West Elm employees on a new, common purpose that is fully aligned with what its customers really want.[27]

A well-used mission statement serves as a strategic compass for a small company, guiding both managers and employees as they make decisions in the face of uncertainty. Some companies use short, one- or two-sentence mission statements that are easy to remember and understand, and others create longer mission statements with multiple components. Consider the following examples:

- Bongo World is the parent company of five coffee shops in Nashville, Tennessee, all committed to serving organic, fair-trade coffee. Bongo World's mission: "Bongo World supports communities by expanding the definition of quality to include how stuff is produced, purchased, and served."[28]

- Ministry of Supply offers clothing for young professionals. Ministry of Supply's mission: "We've set out to solve long-standing problems around fit, function, and simplicity, using the human body as our guide."[29]

- Putney, Inc., located in Portland, Maine, manufactures generic prescription drugs for pets. Its mission is to "partner with veterinary practices to provide high-quality medicines that meet pet medical needs and offer cost-effective medicines for pet owners."[30]

- Nisolo Shoes is a social enterprise that supports artisans in developing countries by creating distribution and branding for their products. Cofounder Patrick Woodyard says its mission is as follows: "Nisolo is a socially conscious brand dedicated to offering a unique product that fuses quality and fashion with a vision to spur sustainable development throughout impoverished regions of the world."[31]

- PKClean turns waste plastic into oil. Its mission is to "end landfilled waste forever."[32]

A company may have a powerful competitive advantage, but it is wasted unless (1) the owner has communicated that advantage to workers, who, in turn, work hard to communicate it to customers and potential customers and (2) customers recommend the company to their friends because they understand the benefits they are getting from it that they cannot get elsewhere. *That's* the real power of a mission statement. Table 5.2 offers some useful tips on writing a mission statement.

Step 2. Assess the Company's Strengths and Weaknesses

strengths
positive internal factors that a company can use to accomplish its mission, goals, and objectives.

Having defined the vision they have for their company and translated that vision into a meaningful mission statement, entrepreneurs can turn their attention to assessing company strengths and weaknesses. Building a successful competitive strategy requires a business to magnify its strengths and overcome or compensate for its weaknesses. **Strengths** are positive internal factors that a company can draw on to accomplish its mission, goals, and objectives. They might include special skills or knowledge, a superior proprietary product or process, a positive public image, an experienced sales force, an established base of loyal customers, and many other factors. For instance, *The Huffington Post* rated Kitchen 67 as having the best sandwich in the

TABLE 5.2 Tips for Writing a Powerful Mission Statement

A mission statement is a useful tool for getting everyone fired up and heading in the same direction, but writing one is not as easy as it may first appear. Here are some tips for writing a powerful mission statement:

- *Keep it short.* The best mission statements are just a few sentences long. If they are short, people tend to remember them better.
- *Keep it simple.* Avoid using fancy jargon to impress outsiders such as customers or suppliers. The first and most important use of a mission statement is inside a company.
- *Focus on your value proposition.* Your competitors are trying to reach the same customers that you are trying to reach. A mission statement should address the unique value offered by your company and what sets it apart from the competition.
- *Get everyone involved.* If the boss writes the company mission statement, who is going to criticize it? Although the entrepreneur has to be the driving force behind the mission statement, everyone in the company needs the opportunity to have a voice in creating it. Expect to write several drafts before you arrive at a finished product.
- *Keep it current.* Mission statements can get stale over time. As business and competitive conditions change, so should your mission statement. Make a habit of evaluating your mission periodically so that it stays fresh.
- *Make sure your mission statement reflects the values and beliefs you hold dear.* They are the foundation on which your company is built.
- *A mission statement should inspire.* One entrepreneur says a mission statement should "send a message to employees, suppliers, and customers as to what the purpose of the company is aside from just making profits."
- *Make sure your statement reflects a concern for the future.* Business owners can get so focused on the present that they forget about the future. A mission statement should be the first link to the company's future.
- *Keep the tone of the statement positive and upbeat.* No one wants to work for a business with a pessimistic outlook on the world.
- *Use your mission statement to lay an ethical foundation for your company.* This is the ideal time to let employees know what your company stands for—and what it won't stand for.
- *Make sure your mission statement reflects your company's culture.* Although you should look at other companies' mission statements, do not make the mistake of trying to copy them. Your company's mission is unique.
- *Revise it when necessary.* No business is static, and your company's mission statement should change as your company changes. Work with a team of employees on a regular basis to review and revise your company's mission statement.
- *Use it.* Don't go to all the trouble of writing a mission statement just to let it collect dust. Post it on bulletin boards, print it on buttons and business cards, stuff it into employees' pay envelopes. Talk about your mission often and use it to develop your company's strategic plan. That's what it's for!

Sources: Based on Larry Kim, "30 Inspiring Billion-Dollar Startup Company Mission Statements," *Inc.*, November 5, 2015, www.inc.com/larry-kim/30-inspiring-billion-dollar-startup-company-mission-statements.html; Dave Smith, "5 Tips for a Useful Mission Statement," *Inc.*, March 22, 2011, www.inc.com/ss/5-tips-on-developing-an-effective-mission-statement; Ken Blanchard, "The New Bottom Line," *Entrepreneur*, February 1998, pp. 127–131; Alan Farnham, Brushing Up Your Vision Thing," *Fortune*, May 1, 1995, p. 129; Sharon Nelton, "Put Your Purpose in Writing," *Nation's Business*, February 1994, pp. 61–64; Jacquelyn Lynn, "Single-Minded," *Entrepreneur*, January 1996, p. 97.

country. However, owner Johnny Brann, Jr., is not willing to rest on that notoriety alone. He is committed to having the most technologically sophisticated customer service system in the industry. Kitchen 67's customers place orders through a touchscreen system developed by Apple for Brann's restaurant. He also partnered with cell phone providers to ensure the highest-speed Internet. At Kitchen 67, customers can charge their phones simply by placing them on the surface of the table while they dine.[33] **Weaknesses** are negative internal factors that inhibit a company's ability to accomplish its mission, goals, and objectives. Examples of weaknesses include lack of capital, a shortage of skilled workers, the inability to master technology, and an inferior location.

Identifying strengths and weaknesses helps owners understand their businesses as they exist (or that, for start-ups, will exist). An organization's strengths should originate in the core competencies that are essential to gaining an edge in each of the market segments in which the

weaknesses
negative internal factors that inhibit the accomplishment of a company's mission, goals, and objectives.

TABLE 5.3 Identifying Company Strengths and Weaknesses

Strengths (Positive Internal Factors)	Weaknesses (Negative Internal Factors)

firm competes. The key to building a successful strategy is using the company's underlying strengths as its foundation and matching those strengths against competitors' weaknesses.

One technique for taking this strategic inventory is to prepare a "balance sheet" of the company's strengths and weaknesses (see Table 5.3). The left side should reflect important skills, knowledge, or resources that contribute to the firm's success. The right side should record honestly any limitations that detract from the company's ability to compete. This balance sheet should analyze all key performance areas of the business—human resources, finance, production, marketing, product development, organization, and others. This analysis should give owners a realistic perspective of their businesses, pointing out foundations on which they can build future strengths and obstacles that they must remove for the business to progress. This exercise can help entrepreneurs determine the best way to move from their current position to a desired one.

Step 3. Scan the Environment for Significant Opportunities and Threats Facing the Business

OPPORTUNITIES Once entrepreneurs have taken an internal inventory of company strengths and weaknesses, they must turn to the external environment to identify any opportunities and threats that might have a significant impact on the business. **Opportunities** are positive external options that a firm can exploit to accomplish its mission, goals, and objectives. The number of potential opportunities is limitless; therefore, entrepreneurs should analyze only those that are most significant to the business (probably two or three at most). The key is to focus on the most promising opportunities that fit most closely with the company's strengths and core competencies. That requires entrepreneurs to say "no" to opportunities—even promising ones—that do not fit their companies' strategic vision.

When identifying opportunities, an entrepreneur must pay close attention to new potential markets and product offerings. Are competitors overlooking a niche in the market we could easily exploit? Is there a better way to reach our customers, such as a greater focus on online sales? Are there new markets we can expand into with our existing business? Can we develop new products that offer customers better value? What opportunities are trends in the industry creating?

ENTREPRENEURIAL PROFILE: World Wrestling Entertainment The rapid growth in online streaming of video content led World Wrestling Entertainment (WWE) to shift away from relying on cable television distribution of its shows to launching its own 24/7 online streaming network. WWE Network airs all of the WWE live pay-per-view events, original programming, reality shows, documentaries, classic matches from its archives, and more than 1,500 hours of video on demand. Customers pay a flat monthly subscription fee to gain access to all WWE Network content through its Web site and through apps that are compatible with most tablets and smart phones. Viewership of pay-per-view over cable and satellite television has been declining, while online streaming has continued to grow as a new medium for video content. WWE's subscription base has experienced strong growth since launching the online streaming network. In its first two years of operation, subscriptions to its $9.99-per-month service have grown from fewer than 200,000 initial subscribers to more than 1.5 million subscribers, generating more than $15 million per month in subscription revenues.[34] ∎

opportunities

positive external options that a company can exploit to accomplish is mission, goals, and objectives.

As WWE Network's experience illustrates, opportunities arise as a result of factors that are beyond entrepreneurs' control. Constantly scanning for the opportunities that best match their companies' strengths and core competences and pouncing on them ahead of competitors is the key to success.

Threats are negative external forces that inhibit a company's ability to achieve its mission, goals, and objectives. Threats to the business can take a variety of forms, such as new competitors entering the local market, a government mandate regulating a business activity, an economic recession, rising interest rates, mounting energy prices, or technology advances making a company's product obsolete. For instance, the growing reach of cellular phone networks and advances in smart phone technology pose a threat to companies that provide traditional landline phone service and equipment. Landline phones reached their peak in 2001, when there were 57 fixed landlines (business and residential) for every 100 people. Just a decade later, more than half of all American households did not have or use a landline phone. A survey of chief information officers reports that 65 percent believed landline phones would likely disappear from everyday use within five years. AT&T plans to end all landline service by 2020. Businesses that based their business models on the traditional landline phone system, such as companies manufacturing copper wire and telephone switching systems, face the ultimate threat to their future survival.[35]

Many small businesses face a threat from larger rivals who offer lower prices because of their high-volume purchasing power, huge advertising budgets, and megastores that attract customers for miles around. However, small businesses with the proper strategies in place do *not* have to fold in the face of intense competition. The accompanying "Hands On . . . How To" feature explains that, with the proper strategy, small companies can not only survive but also thrive in the shadow of larger, more powerful rivals.

threats
negative external forces that inhibit a company's ability to achieve its mission, goals, and objectives.

 ## Hands On . . . How To

Beat the Big Guys

It's the news that sends shivers down the spines of small business owners everywhere: Wal-Mart (or any other "big-box" retailer) is coming to town. "How can my small business compete against the largest retailer in the world?" they wonder. "Can my business survive?"

Although no business owner welcomes a threat of this magnitude from a giant competitor with greater buying power, more name recognition, and a reputation for driving small companies out of business, it is no reason to fold up the tent and go home. Smart entrepreneurs know that by formulating and executing the proper strategy, they can not only survive in the face of larger competitors but also *thrive* in their presence.

Rule 1. Don't Play Their Game

A fundamental concept in strategy is to avoid matching your company's weaknesses against a competitor's strengths. For instance, because Wal-Mart buys in such huge volume from its suppliers, it can extract the lowest prices from them. Small companies purchasing from those same suppliers cannot; therefore, it makes little sense for small companies to try to compete with Wal-Mart and other giant retailers on price. Unless your small company has another more significant cost advantage, competing on the basis of price is a recipe for disaster. Entrepreneurs who compete successfully emphasize features that giant discounters cannot provide, such as extensive product knowledge, better selection, superior customer service, a hassle-free buying experience, or higher quality. "Not everyone wants the lowest quality at the lowest price," says one expert.

Rule 2. Emphasize the Unique Aspects of Your Company and How They Benefit Your Customers

Joe Runyan, founder of Hangers Cleaners of Kansas City, Missouri, was faced with the challenge of competing with Procter & Gamble's entry into the dry cleaning market with its national rollout of Tide Dry Cleaners. Hangers Cleaners had been able to differentiate its service by offering an environmentally safe dry cleaning process. Hangers Cleaners uses liquid carbon dioxide instead of the harsh chemicals traditionally used by dry cleaners. However, Tide Dry Cleaning also offered eco-friendly dry cleaning services. To compete with a large national brand, Runyan pursued several strategies. Hangers focused on its offbeat image. The company sent out entertaining promotional e-mails, gave away T-shirts bearing the invitation to "Sniff Me," put funny messages on its hangers, and held a St. Patrick's Day tailgate party in the parking lot. The company also pays close attention to customer service. Hangers has several programs to help with fund-raising for local nonprofits and schools. The company offers van service for pick-up and delivery to affluent neighborhoods willing to pay a premium for the extra service. Although many of the other local dry cleaners suffered after the entry of Tide Dry Cleaners, Runyan's business has continued to experience growth in revenues and profits.

Rule 3. Hit 'em Where They Ain't

Big companies usually aim at big markets and often ignore small but profitable niche markets, which are ideal targets for small companies. Ashley Rosebrook and Stefan Peters entered a crowded personalized photo printing industry with their Web

(continued)

Hands On . . . How To *(continued)*

site Pinhole Press. When researching the industry, they found that most of the competition offered too many choices for the most common customer—new grandparents and parents. By creating a simple site that is easy to use, Pinhole found a niche in the market. The founders recently sold Pinhole for $33 million to a large software company.

Rule 4. Hire the Best—And Train Them

Small companies usually cannot afford to pay the highest wages in an area; however, because their companies are small, entrepreneurs have the opportunity to create a work environment in which employees can thrive. For instance, one small company attracts and retains quality workers by allowing them to use flexible work schedules that make it easier for them to manage their busy lives. The owner also invests heavily in training workers so that they can move up the organization—and the pay scale—faster. The training pays off in the form of greater productivity, lower turnover, increased customer satisfaction, and higher sales per employee. Paying attention to seemingly small details, such as more communication, frequent recognition for jobs well done, less bureaucracy, and flexible benefits, enables small companies to build a loyal, motivated workforce that can outperform those at larger companies.

Rule 5. Bring Back What the Big Boys Have Eliminated

Ron Samuels founded Avenue Bank in Nashville, Tennessee, in 2007, not long before the financial crisis rocked the banking industry. However, Avenue Bank not only survived one of the most difficult times in banking since the Great Depression, but the company's old-fashioned approach to banking resulted in strong and steady growth that led to its acquisition less than 10 years after it was founded. Avenue focuses on highly personalized service, which is no longer available in many national bank chains. Avenue Bank offers the same personalized service to small businesses and entrepreneurs. The bank supports start-ups by offering concierge services, working to meet their unique needs from start-up through growth.

Rule 6. Use the Cost Advantages of the Internet to Gain an Edge

Ernesto Perez-Carrillo, Jr., and his family launched EPC Cigar as a premium cigar company. The traditional promotional channels for cigars include taxi-top advertising in large cities, commercials on cable channels, radio ads in large markets, and print ads in national business magazines and specialty publications that cater to the wealthy. This type of advertising is quite costly and not always highly effective. One ad might cost up to half of EPC Cigar's total marketing budget. Because the company could not afford a traditional advertising campaign, Perez-Carrillo invested his marketing budget in the Internet, social media initiatives, trade shows, and special events. EPC Cigar's sales grew to more than $1.5 million in revenue within the first year.

Rule 7. Be *Great* at Something Customers Value, Such as Service and Personal Attention

Do not make the mistake of choosing a "middle-of-the-road" strategy where, one writer says, there "are yellow lines, dead armadillos, and once-great companies that are slowly going out of business." Successful small companies differentiate themselves from their larger, more powerful rivals by emphasizing superior, friendly, personal service, something their size makes them uniquely capable of doing. Successful small companies also treat their customers like VIPs. Many small business owners know their customers by name, something that large companies cannot achieve. One of the best ways to determine exactly how to provide superior service and personal attention is to identify your top five customers and periodically ask them, "How can we serve you better?"

Rule 8. Get Involved in the Community

Entrepreneurs can make their small companies stand out from the crowd by supporting events in their local communities. A big budget is not a prerequisite. For instance, Pizza Ranch franchises host "community impact" nights. Family members and friends of employees bus tables to help with fund-raising for local causes. Pizza Ranch donates all of the evening's tips plus a matching share of the profits. The events generally draw additional donations from the community. The events help the franchises build relationships in the community and make genuine and enduring relationships with customers.

1. Why do many small businesses fail when a big discount retailer such as Wal-Mart enters their market?

2. Work with a team of your classmates to identify a local small business that competes with a bigger competitor. Which of the strategies described here has the small company employed to become a stronger competitor? What other strategies would you recommend to the owner of this business?

3. Based on your work in question 2, develop a one-page report summarizing your strategic suggestions.

Sources: Based on Chad Brooks, "10 Ways You Can Beat Wal-Mart," *Business News Daily*, April 20, 2011, www.businessnewsdaily.com/walmart-small-stores-1201; Norm Brodsky, "How Independents Can Hold Their Ground," *Inc.*, August 2007, pp. 65–66; Thomas M. Box, Kent Byus, Chris Fogliasso, and Warren D. Miller, "Hardball and OODA Loops: Strategy for Small Firms," *Proceedings of the Academy of Strategic Management* 6, no. 1 (2007): 5–10; Matthew Maier, "How to Beat Wal-Mart," *Business 2.0*, May 2005, pp. 108–114; Rhonda Abrams, "Small Businesses Can Compete with the Big Guys," *Business*, September 26, 2004, p. 8; Barry Cotton and Jean-Charles Cachon, "Resisting the Giants: Small Retail Entrepreneurs Against Mega-Retailers—An Empirical Study," paper presented at the International Council for Small Business 2005 World Conference, June 2005; Amy Merrick, Gary McWilliams, Ellen Byron, and Kortney Stringer, "Targeting Wal-Mart," *Wall Street Journal*, December 1, 2004, pp. B1, B2; William C. Taylor, "The Fallacy of the 'Middle of the Road' Strategy," *BNET*, February 23, 2011,www.bnet.com/blog/innovator/the-fallacy-of-the-8220mid-dle-of-the-road-8221-strategy/195; Jessica Shambora, "David vs. Goliath," *Fortune*, November 15, 2010, p. 55; Pamela Ryckman, "A Local Dry Cleaner Tries to Compete Against P.&G.," *New York Times*, April 14, 2010, www.nytimes.com/2010/04/15/business/smallbusiness/15sbiz.html?_r=1&; Judith Ohikuare, "How Pinhole Press Cut the Complexity and Got Noticed," *Inc.*, April 11, 2013, www.inc.com/best-industries-2013/judith-ohikuare/pinhole-press-cuts-the-complexity.html; "Avenue Bank Adds Four to the Team," *Nashville.com*, September 3, 2013, www.nashville.com/news/nashville-business-news/avenue-bank-adds-four-to-the-team; Scott Harrison, "Why Ron Samuels Sold His 10-Year-Old Avenue Bank to Pinnacle," *Nashville Business Journal*, January 29, 2016, www.bizjournals.com/nashville/blog/2016/01/why-ron-samuels-sold-his-10-yearold-avenue-bank-to.html; Jane Levere, "Choosing a Marketing Plan: Traditional or Social Media," *New York Times*, February 24, 2010, www.nytimes.com/2010/02/25/business/smallbusiness/25sbiz.html?ref=casestudies.

TABLE 5.4 Identifying and Managing Threats

Every business faces threats, but entrepreneurs cannot afford to be paranoid or paralyzed by fear when it comes to dealing with them. At the same time, they cannot afford to ignore threats that have the potential to destroy their businesses. The most productive approach to dealing with threats is to identify those that would have the most severe impact on a small company and those that have the highest probability of occurrence.

Research by Greg Hackett, president of management think tank MergerShop, has identified 12 major sources of risk that can wreak havoc on a company's future. Filling out this table helps entrepreneurs determine the threats on which they should focus their attention.

Source	Specific Threat	Severity (1 = Low, 10 = High)	Probability of Occurrence (0 to 1)	Threat Score (Severity × Probability, Max = 10)
1. Channels of distribution				
2. Competition				
3. Demographic changes				
4. Globalization				
5. Innovation				
6. Waning customer or supplier loyalty				
7. Offshoring or outsourcing				
8. Stage in product life cycle				
9. Government regulation				
10. Influence of special interest groups				
11. Influence of stakeholders				
12. Changes in technology				

Once entrepreneurs have identified specific threats facing their companies in some or all of the 12 areas, they rate the severity of the impact of each one on their company on a scale of 1 to 10. Then they assign a probability (between 0 and 1) to each threat. To calculate the threat score, entrepreneurs simply multiply the severity of each threat by its probability. (The maximum threat score is 10.) The higher a threat's score, the more attention it demands. Typically, one or two threats stand out above all the others, and entrepreneurs should focus on those.

Source: Based on Edward Teach, "Apocalypse Soon," *CFO*, September 2005, pp. 31–32.

Opportunities and threats are products of the interactions of forces, trends, and events outside the direct control of the business. These external forces have a direct impact on the behavior of the markets in which the business operates, the behavior of competitors, and the behavior of customers. The number of potential threats facing a business is huge, but entrepreneurs should focus on the three or four most significant threats confronting their companies. Table 5.4 provides a simple analytical tool to help entrepreneurs identify the threats that pose the greatest danger to their companies.

The interactions of strengths, weaknesses, opportunities, and threats can be the most revealing aspects of using a SWOT analysis as part of a strategic plan. This analysis also requires entrepreneurs to take an objective look at their businesses and the environment in which they operate, as they address many issues fundamental to their companies' success in the future.

Step 4. Identify the Key Factors for Success in the Business

KEY SUCCESS FACTORS Every business is characterized by controllable variables that determine the relative success of market participants. By focusing efforts to maximize their companies' performance on these key success factors, entrepreneurs can achieve dramatic market advantages over their competitors. Companies that understand these key success factors tend to be leaders of the pack, whereas those that fail to recognize them become also-rans.

key success factors (KSFs)

the factors that determine a company's ability to compete successfully in an industry.

Key success factors (KSFs), also called *key performance indicators*, come in a variety of patterns, depending on the industry. Simply stated, these factors determine a company's ability to compete successfully in an industry. Every company in an industry must understand the KSFs that drive the industry; otherwise, they are likely to become the industry also-rans like the horses trailing the pack in the Kentucky Derby. Many of these sources of competitive advantages are based on cost factors, such as manufacturing cost per unit, distribution cost per unit, or development cost per unit. Some are less tangible and less obvious but are just as important, such as superior product quality, solid relationships with dependable suppliers, superior customer service, a highly trained and knowledgeable sales force, prime store locations, and readily available customer credit. For example, one restaurant owner identified the following KSFs:

- Experience in the industry

- Sufficient start-up capital

- Tight cost control (15 to 18 percent of sales for labor costs, and 35 to 40 percent of sales for food costs)

- Accurate sales forecasting, which minimizes wasted food

- Proper inventory control

- Meticulous cash management

- Choosing locations that maximize customer convenience

- Cleanliness

- High food quality

- Friendly and attentive service from a well-trained wait staff

- Consistency in quality and service over time

- Speed, particularly at lunch, when the restaurant attracts businesspeople who must dine quickly and get back to work

- A clear definition of the restaurant's distinctive concept—its food, decor, service, and ambiance

These controllable variables determine the ability of any restaurant in this market segment to compete. Restaurants lacking these KSFs are not likely to survive, but those that build their strategies with these factors in mind will prosper. However, before entrepreneurs can build a strategy around the industry's KSFs, they must identify them. Table 5.5 presents a form to help owners identify the most important success factors in the industry and their implications for their companies.

Identifying the KSFs in an industry allows entrepreneurs to determine where they should focus their companies' resources strategically. It is unlikely that a company, even a large one, can excel on every KSF it identifies. Therefore, as they begin to develop their strategies, successful entrepreneurs focus on surpassing their rivals on one or two KSFs to build a sustainable competitive edge. As a result, KSFs become the cornerstones of a company's strategy. The most recent recession took a heavy toll on the casual dining sector of the restaurant industry, forcing many restaurants to refocus their attention on the KSFs in their respective market segments. At Chili's and Cracker Barrel, managers targeted lunch customers by making changes designed to reduce food preparation and service times. Recognizing that shaving even a few minutes from a lunch visit makes a huge difference for the lunch crowd, managers simplified lunch menus, streamlined their service procedures, retrained wait staff, and redesigned their kitchen layouts for maximum efficiency.[36]

In the hotly competitive gourmet burger segment of the industry, entrepreneurs behind chains such as Five Guys Burgers and Fries, Blazing Onion Burger Company, and In-N-Out are emphasizing KSFs to fuel their growth: high-quality burgers made from fresh ingredients, clean restaurants, superior service, and prices that offer good value. Because customers wait

TABLE 5.5 Identifying Key Success Factors

List the specific skills, characteristics, and core competences your business must possess if it is to be successful in its market segment.

Key Success Factor	How Your Company Rates . . .
1	Low 1 2 3 4 5 6 7 8 9 10 High
2	Low 1 2 3 4 5 6 7 8 9 10 High
3	Low 1 2 3 4 5 6 7 8 9 10 High
4	Low 1 2 3 4 5 6 7 8 9 10 High
5	Low 1 2 3 4 5 6 7 8 9 10 High
Conclusions:	

10 minutes and pay anywhere from $7 to more than $10 for a burger at fast-growing chains such as these, managers make sure that customers understand that "this is not a typical fast-food burger joint." At Five Guys, which was founded in 1986 by CEO Jerry Murrell, his wife, and three sons, customers enjoy French fries that are hand cut daily and burgers made from fresh beef. Five Guys, now with more than 1,500 locations, is the fastest-growing restaurant chain in the United States. The Blazing Onion Burger Company, a small chain based in Mill Creek, Washington, offers customers 25 gourmet burgers made from fresh beef as well as a turkey burger, a veggie burger, a meatloaf burger, and an assortment of homemade desserts. Service at Blazing Onion, founded by David Jones in 2007, is paramount. Each table has a "Service Alert" card that resembles a stop sign; when customers post it, "we'll be there in 30 seconds," says Jones, who plans to open a new location every 10 months and recently began franchising.[37]

Step 5. Analyze the Competition

Ask small business owners to identify the greatest challenge their companies face, and the most common response is *competition*. The Internet and e-commerce have increased the ferocity and the scope of the competition entrepreneurs face and have forced many business owners to completely change the ways in which they do business.

ENTREPRENEURIAL PROFILE: PJ's Coffee PJ's Coffee of New Orleans was founded seven years after Starbucks. While Starbucks grew to become the dominant global brand, PJ's Coffee has focused on establishing a strong local brand in New Orleans and growing locations in the Gulf Coast region. PJ's Coffee's strong regional brand has made it difficult for Starbucks to penetrate this region. PJ's Coffee follows a strategy that has been successful for many other regional brands competing against strong national brands. PJ's measures its success based on quality rather than quantity. Whereas Starbucks measures its success by the growth in number of retail outlets and market share, PJ's has developed strong relationships with its farmers and local roasters. PJ's knows its customers and has developed niche products in response. Its growth strategy is based on organic growth and expanding distribution into regional grocery outlets.[38] ∎

Keeping tabs on rivals' movements through competitive intelligence programs is a vital strategic activity. "Business is like any battlefield. If you want to win the war, you have to know who you're up against," says one small business consultant.[39] Unfortunately, most businesses are not very good at competitive intelligence: 97 percent of U.S. businesses do not systematically track the progress of their key competitors.[40] A study of business executives around the world by McKinsey and Company reports that just 23 percent of companies discovered a major competitive innovation by a competitor in time to be able to plan a response before the innovation hit the market.[41] The primary goals of a competitive intelligence program include the following:

- Conducting continuous rather than periodic analysis of competition
- Avoiding surprises from existing competitors' new strategies and tactics
- Identifying potential new competitors
- Improving reaction time to competitors' actions
- Anticipating rivals' next strategic moves

COMPETITOR ANALYSIS Sizing up the competition gives a business owner a realistic view of the market and his or her company's position in it. Yet not every competitor warrants the same level of attention in the strategic plan. *Direct competitors* offer the same products and services, and customers often compare prices, features, and deals from these competitors as they shop. *Significant competitors* offer some of the same products and services. Although their product or service lines may be somewhat different, there is competition with them in several key areas. *Indirect competitors* offer the same or similar products or services only in a small number of areas, and their target customers seldom overlap yours. Entrepreneurs should monitor closely the actions of their direct competitors, maintain a solid grasp of where their significant competitors are heading, and spend only minimal resources tracking their indirect competitors.

Collecting competitive intelligence enables entrepreneurs to update their knowledge of top competitors by answering the following questions:

- What are the primary criteria customers used to choose among competitive businesses in your industry?
- Who are your primary competitors? Where are they located?
- What distinctive competencies have they developed?
- How do their cost structures compare to yours? How do their financial resources compare to yours?
- How do they promote their products and services?
- What do customers say about them? How do customers describe their products or services, their way of doing business, and any additional services they supply?
- What are their key strategies?
- What are their strengths? How can your company counteract them?
- What are their major weaknesses? How can your company capitalize on them?
- Are new competitors entering the business?

According to the Society of Competitive Intelligence, 95 percent of competitive intelligence information is available from public sources that anyone can access—if they know how.[42] Gathering competitive intelligence does not require entrepreneurs to engage in activities that are unethical, illegal, or unsavory (such as dumpster diving). One expert says competitive intelligence involves "taking information from the public domain, adding it to what you know about your company and your industry, and looking for patterns."[43] By collecting many nuggets of information about their competitors, entrepreneurs can assemble the pieces to make reliable inferences about their rivals' overall strategies. Entrepreneurs can use the following low-cost competitive intelligence methods to collect information about their rivals:

- Read industry trade publications for announcements and news stories about competitors.
- Ask questions of customers and suppliers about what they hear competitors may be doing. In many cases, this information is easy to gather because some people love to gossip.

You Be the Consultant

The Escape Game Seeks to Expand Nationwide

When Jonathan and James Murrell were in college, Jonathan at Belmont University and James at nearby Lipscomb University, they launched a success online candy store and distribution business. Although they had success with the candy business, they both wanted to start a venture that had more growth potential. A family friend, Mark Flint, approached them about a new experiential game that was sweeping Europe and Asia, known as an escape room game. In this type of game, participants are locked in a room with clues on how to escape. After visiting several games around the globe, the three decided to become partners and launch their own version of escape games. The Murrells sold their interest in the candy business to their partners and joined with Flint to launch The Escape Game.

In 2014, The Escape Game built its first location in Nashville, Tennessee, in a part of town that was not known for tourism. Despite its out-of-the-way location, The Escape Game became a top attraction on TripAdvisor within a few months of opening. The first location was soon booked up days in advance, from early morning through late at night, drawing a mix of tourists, locals, and businesses looking for team-building experiences.

The Escape Game offers customers several games to choose from at each location, giving them one hour to escape. Jonathan Murrell designs each game with a specific theme, such as Mission to Mars, Prison Break, Gold Rush, and The Heist. The Escape Game is positioned in the escape room market as high quality, with construction budgets that far exceed those of most competitors. The Escape Game carefully trains its staff to ensure the ultimate customer experience. Employees serving as "game guides" observe the games on flat-screen TVs and offer assistance if a team gets stuck. Even with help, a number of groups do not make it out in time.

Seeing the opportunity to grow into other markets, the founding partners of The Escape Game created a corporate team to support growth into other cities. In 2015, The Escape Game added additional stores in Orlando, Florida; Pigeon Forge, Tennessee; downtown Nashville; and Austin, Texas. The company was able to fund much of this growth with the cash flow from the operation of existing units. Each new store quickly filled its schedule with customers, enabling each store to reach its breakeven point within the first month of opening. The rest of the funding came from a venture loan.

The company's recent growth came mainly in the form of adding games to each of The Escape Game's five locations. The new games generated significant revenue with only modest additional expenses. In addition, the company added a new location in Chicago that year.

Future plans include the addition of two or three more locations and expansion of additional games in some of the current locations. Although the popularity of escape room games continues to grow, so does the competition. The Escape Game intends to take advantage of the growth in popularity through continued market expansion over the coming years. It will meet the growth in competition by focusing on high-quality games run by well-trained employees.

1. Visit The Escape Game's Web site, at https://nashvilleescapegame .com, to learn more about the company. Work with a team

Courtesy of The Escape Game

of your classmates to identify the company's strengths and weaknesses.

2. What opportunities and threats does The Escape Game face?

3. Identify The Escape Game's major competitors. What are their strengths and weaknesses?

4. Write a short memo (two pages maximum) to The Escape Game partners and their management team, describing your strategic recommendations for helping The Escape Game gain and maintain a competitive advantage in their industry and realize their goals to grow the company to become a national industry leader.

Sources: Based on Jonathan Murrell, personal communication, August 22, 2016; Lizzy Alfs, "The Escape Game Coming to Downtown Nashville," *Tennessean,* June 17, 2015, www.tennessean.com/story/money/2015/06/17/escape-game-coming-downtown-nashville/28868945/; Stuart Miller, "The Art of the Escape Room," *Newsweek,* May 1, 2015, www.newsweek.com/2015/05/01/art-escape-room-323150.html; Paige Pfleger, "Nashville's Escape Game Locks in Adventure," *Tennessean,* August 14, 2014, www.tennessean.com/story/life/2014/08/14/nashvilles-escape-game-locks-adventure/14027507/; Jonathan Berr, "There's No Escaping the Growing Popularity of These Games," *CBS News,* September 5, 2014, www.cbsnews.com/news/theres-no-escaping-the-growing-popularity-of-these-games/.

- Regularly debrief employees, especially sales representatives and purchasing agents. Experts estimate that 70 to 90 percent of the competitive information a company needs already resides with employees who collect it in their routine dealings with suppliers, customers, and other industry contacts.[44]

- Attend industry "meet-ups" in your local community.

- Attend trade shows and collect competitors' sales literature.

- Monitor social media for insights into your direct competitors.

- Watch for employment ads and job postings from competitors; knowing what types of workers they are hiring can tell you a great deal about their future plans.

- Conduct patent searches for patents competitors have filed. This can yield important clues about new products they are developing.

- Learn about the kinds and amounts of equipment and raw materials that competitors are importing by studying the *Journal of Commerce Port Import Export Reporting Service* (*PIERS*) database. These clues can alert an entrepreneur to new products that a competitor is about to launch.

- If appropriate, buy competitors' products and assess their quality and features. Benchmark their products against yours.

- Obtain credit reports on each of your major competitors to evaluate their financial condition. For less than $200, Dun & Bradstreet and other research firms provide detailed credit reports of competitors that can be helpful in strategic analyses.

- Publicly held companies must periodically file reports with the Securities and Exchange Commission, including quarterly 10-Q and annual 10-K reports. Information on publicly held companies is available at the Securities and Exchange Commission Web site.

- Investigate Uniform Commercial Code reports. Banks file these with the state whenever they make loans to businesses. These reports often include the amount of the loan and what it is for.

- Check out resources at your local library, including articles, computerized databases, and online searches. Press releases, which often announce important company news, can be an important source of competitive intelligence. Many companies supply press releases through PR Newswire. For local competitors, review back issues of the area newspaper for articles on and advertisements by competitors.

- Visit competitors' Web sites periodically to see what news is contained there. The Web enables small companies to uncover valuable competitive information at little or no cost.

- Sign up for competitors' social media feeds to get current news about their businesses.

- Visit competing businesses periodically to observe their operations. Tom Stemberg, CEO of Staples, a chain of office supply superstores, says, "I've never visited a store where I didn't learn something."[45]

- Don't resort to unethical or illegal practices.

competitive profile matrix
a tool that allows business owners to evaluate their companies against major competitors using the key success factors for that market segment.

Entrepreneurs can use the results of their competitive intelligence efforts to construct a competitive profile matrix for the most important competitors. A **competitive profile matrix** allows owners to evaluate their firms against the major competitor by using the KSFs for that market segment. The first step is to list the KSFs identified in step 4 of the strategic planning process (refer to Table 5.5) and to attach weights to them based on their relative importance. (For simplicity, the weights in this matrix add up to 1.00.) In this example, notice that product quality is weighted twice as heavily as (that is, it is twice as important as) price competitiveness.

TABLE 5.6 Sample Competitive Profile Matrix

Key Success Factors (from Step 4)	Weight	Your Business		Competitor 1		Competitor 2	
		Rating	Weighted Score	Rating	Weighted Score	Rating	Weighted Score
Quality	0.25	4	1.00	2	0.50	2	0.50
Customer retention	0.20	3	0.60	3	0.60	3	0.60
Location	0.15	4	0.60	3	0.45	4	0.60
Perception of value	0.20	4	0.80	2	0.40	3	0.60
Cost control	0.20	3	0.60	1	0.20	4	0.80
Total	1.00		3.60		2.15		3.10

The next step is to identify the company's major competitors and to rate each one (and your company) on each of the KSFs:

If Factor Is a . . .	Rating Is . . .
Major weakness	1
Minor weakness	2
Minor strength	3
Major strength	4

Once the rating is completed, the owner simply multiplies the weight by the rating for each factor to get a weighted score and then adds up each competitor's weighted scores to get a total weighted score. Table 5.6 shows a sample competitive profile matrix for a small company. The results show which company is strongest, which is weakest, and which of the KSFs each one is best and worst at meeting. By carefully studying and interpreting the results, an entrepreneur can begin to envision the ideal strategy for building a competitive edge in his or her corner of the market. Notice that the small company profiled in Table 5.6 should emphasize the competitive advantages it holds over its rivals in quality and perception of value in its business strategy.

Step 6. Create Company Goals and Objectives

Before entrepreneurs can build a comprehensive set of strategies, they must first establish business goals and objectives, which give them targets to aim for and provide a basis for evaluating their companies' performance. Without them, it is impossible to know where a business is going or how well it is performing. The following conversation between Alice and the Cheshire Cat, taken from Lewis Carroll's *Alice in Wonderland*, illustrates the importance of creating meaningful goals and objectives as part of the strategic management process:[46]

"Would you tell me please, which way I ought to go from here?" asked Alice.

"That depends a good deal on where you want to get to," said the Cat.

"I don't much care where . . .," said Alice.

"Then it doesn't matter which way you go," said the Cat.

A small business that "doesn't much care where" it wants to go (i.e., one that has no goals and objectives) will find that "it really doesn't matter which way" it chooses to go (i.e., its strategy is irrelevant). However, even with clear goals and strategies in place, entrepreneurs must always be ready to pivot and adjust their plans to unexpected changes in the market.

GOALS The broad, long-range attributes that a business seeks to accomplish are its **goals**; they tend to be general and sometimes even abstract. Goals are not intended to be specific enough for a manager to act on but simply state the general level of accomplishment sought. Do you want to boost your market share? Does your cash balance need to be strengthened? Would you like to enter a new market or increase sales in a current one? Do you want to develop new products

goals
broad, long-range attributes that a business seeks to accomplish; they tend to be general and sometimes abstract.

You Be the Consultant

Finding a Niche with a Subscription Business Model

In his book *Break from the Pack*, Oren Harari explains how business owners can escape the problems of the "Copycat Economy, where everyone has access to the same resources and talent, where the Web is the great equalizer, and where the market's twin foundations are imitation and commoditization." He argues that too many businesses are stuck in the pack with "me-too" products and services that customers see as commodities. The danger of being stuck in the pack (or relying on a "middle-of-the-road strategy") is becoming what entrepreneur Terry Brock calls "disgustingly generic." What can small companies, which often lack the resources that large companies have, do to break from the pack strategically? Consider the lessons we can learn from the following small businesses that all rely on subscription services.

Dollar Shave Club

Michael Dubin, CEO of Dollar Shave Club, effectively uses social media to successfully compete with well-established national brands Schick and Gillette. Dollar Shave Club sends out to its subscribers razors that cost $1, $6, or $9 per month. The products are simple in design but are made of high-quality materials. Dollar Shave Club partners with an overseas manufacturer. The 38 employees who work for Dollar Shave Club focus on marketing, order fulfillment, and product development. The company has a YouTube video that features Dubin, who uses humor and passion to try to convince people to buy shaving goods by mail rather than from the grocery store. This commercial, viewed more than 13 million times in just two years, attracted hundreds of thousands of subscribers.

Graze.com

Graze.com is a subscription-based snack service offering boxes of healthy snacks delivered to customers' doorsteps. Graze.com was founded by seven former corporate managers who wanted to create a healthy alternative for family snacking. Graze.com allows its customers in the United States and United Kingdom to customize their boxes with more than 90 snack options. Each box also includes helpful information on fitness ideas and nutritional information, sent to them in a personal letter from their "in-house nutritionist." Graze.com has experienced steady year-over-year growth in individual subscribers, and the company plans to expand into corporate gift boxes in the coming years. The company claims that it is outselling its competitors that offer chocolate snack subscriptions.

Trunk Club

Trunk Club sells stylish men's attire through a subscription model. The company offers free shipping and free returns to encourage its customers to try new clothing just as they would in a retail store. If something does not look right, is the wrong size, or just is not what the customer is looking for, he can send it back at no charge. Trunk Club ships a box of apparel and accessories based on a profile created by the customer. Trunk Club complements its subscription business with retail locations in several large cities, including Chicago, Washington, DC, Dallas, New York, and Los Angeles. The stores offer a personal stylist and a full bar. Trunk Club recently expanded into women's attire.

1. Which of the strategies discussed in this chapter are these companies using? Explain.

2. What competitive advantages does the successful execution of subscription-based strategies produce for these businesses?

3. What are the risks associated with these companies' strategies?

Sources: Based on Erica Swallow, "Ten Internet Startups That Thrive by Mail," *Forbes*, April 26, 2012, www.forbes.com/sites/ericaswallow/2012/04/26/internet-startups-by-mail/; Daniel Gross, "After 100 Years, the Shaving Industry Is Finally Being Disrupted," *Daily Beast*, January 24, 2014, www.thedailybeast.com/articles/2014/01/24/after-100-years-the-shaving-industry-is-finally-being-disrupted.html; Douglas A. McIntyre, "The Next Dollar Shave Club," *24/7 Wall Street*, August 23, 2016, http://247wallst.com/consumer-products/2016/08/23/the-next-dollar-shave-club/; Fiona Briggs, "Healthy Snacks Brand, Graze, Says It Is Outselling Chocolate Competitors," *Retail Times*, April 8, 2016, www.retailtimes.co.uk/healthy-snacks-brand-graze-says-outselling-chocolate-competitors/; Amanda Lauren, "5 of the Best Men's Personal Stylist Services," *CheatSheet*, August 17, 2016, www.cheatsheet.com/gear-style/best-mens-personal-stylist-services.html/?a=viewall; Fiorella Valdesolo, "What Do You Subscribe To?" *New York*, May 13, 2012, http://nymag.com/shopping/features/subscriptions-2012-5/.

objectives

more specific targets of performance, commonly addressing areas such as profitability, productivity, growth, and other key aspects of a business.

or services? Researchers Jim Collins and Jerry Porras studied a large group of businesses for their book *Good to Great* and determined that one of the factors that set successful companies apart from unsuccessful ones was the formulation of ambitious, clear, and inspiring long-term goals. Collins and Porras called them BHAGs (pronounced "bee-hags," for "Big Hairy Audacious Goals") and suggest that their main benefit is to inspire and focus a company on important actions that are consistent with its overall mission.[47] Figure 5.3 shows that effective BHAGs originate at the intersection of a company's mission, vision, and values; its distinctive competencies; and its KSFs. Addressing these broad issues will help entrepreneurs focus on the next phase—developing specific, realistic objectives.

OBJECTIVES **Objectives** are more specific targets of performance. Common objectives concern profitability, productivity, growth, efficiency, sales, financial resources, physical facilities, organizational structure, employee welfare, and social responsibility. Because some of these

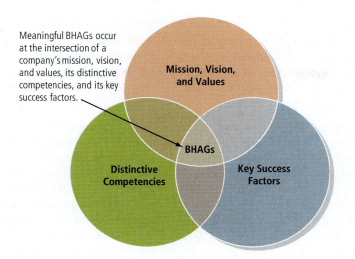

Meaningful BHAGs occur at the intersection of a company's mission, vision, and values, its distinctive competencies, and its key success factors.

FIGURE 5.3

What Makes an Effective BHAG?

objectives might conflict with one another, it is important to establish priorities. Which objectives are most important? Which are least important? Arranging objectives in a hierarchy according to their priority can help an entrepreneur resolve conflicts when they arise. Well-written objectives have the following characteristics:

They are specific. Objectives should be quantifiable and precise. For example, "to achieve a healthy growth in sales" is not a meaningful objective; however, "to increase retail sales by 12 percent and wholesale by 10 percent in the next fiscal year" is precise and spells out exactly what management wants to accomplish.

They are measurable. Managers should be able to plot the organization's progress toward its objectives; this requires a well-defined reference point from which to start and a scale for measuring progress.

They are action commitments. Objectives are linked to specific actions. Ideally, managers and employees should be able to see how their jobs lead to the company achieving its objectives. ProviderTrust is a healthcare software company that is backed by venture capital, which means the management team has specific revenue growth objectives investors expect the company to reach. At the start of every day, all 11 employees meet for 10 to 15 minutes to talk about what they are working on to help the company achieve its revenue objectives.[48]

They are assignable. Unless an entrepreneur assigns responsibility for an objective to an individual, it is unlikely that the company will ever achieve it. Creating objectives without giving someone responsibility for accomplishing them is futile. Accountability is the key.

They are realistic yet challenging. Objectives must be within the reach of the organization, or motivation will disappear. In any case, managerial expectations must remain high. In other words, the more challenging an objective is (within realistic limits), the higher the performance will be. Objectives should challenge a business and its employees.

They are timely. Objectives must specify not only what is to be accomplished but also when it is to be accomplished. A time frame for achievement is important.

They are written down. Setting objectives does not have to be complex; in fact, an entrepreneur should keep the number of objectives relatively small (from 5 to 10). Writing down objectives makes them more concrete and makes it easy to communicate them to everyone in the company.

The strategic planning process works best when managers and employees work together to set goals and objectives. Developing a plan is top management's responsibility, but executing it falls to managers and employees; therefore, encouraging them to participate broadens the plan's perspective and increases the motivation to make the plan work.

Step 7. Formulate Strategic Options and Select the Appropriate Strategies

By this point in the strategic management process, entrepreneurs should have a clear picture of what their businesses do best and what their competitive advantages are. They also should understand their firms' weaknesses and limitations, as well as those of their competitors. The next step is to evaluate strategic options and then prepare a game plan to achieve the stated mission, goals, and objectives.

strategy

a road map of the actions an entrepreneur draws up to fulfill the company's mission, goals, and objectives.

STRATEGY A **strategy** is a road map of the actions an entrepreneur draws up to accomplish a company's mission, goals, and objectives. In other words, the mission, goals, and objectives spell out the ends, and the strategy defines the means for reaching them. A strategy is the master plan that covers all the major parts of the organization and ties them together into a unified whole. The plan must be action oriented; it should breathe life into the entire planning process. An entrepreneur must build a sound strategy based on the preceding steps that uses the company's core competencies and strengths as the springboard to success. Joseph Picken and Gregory Dess, authors of *Mission Critical: The 7 Strategic Traps That Derail Even the Smartest Companies*, write, "A flawed strategy—no matter how brilliant the leadership, no matter how effective the implementation—is doomed to fail. A sound strategy, implemented without error, wins every time."[49]

ENTREPRENEURIAL PROFILE: Zina and Jason Santos: August Kitchen August Kitchen offers a meal starter for hamburgers, called J-BURGER, which was born in the kitchen of Zina and Jason Santos. Their friends kept wanting to take home some of the meal starter the couple used to zest up their burgers. In 2009, they invested about $100,000 of their own funds to commercialize their product. Their first product was J-BURGER (the "J" is for Jason). To ensure that its product is fresh, which is a big selling point, August Kitchen partnered with a packager that could produce small batches tied to grocery store orders. Getting shelf space and building consumer awareness of J-BURGER have been challenging. The Santoses spent many hours cooking mini-burgers to entice shoppers to take J-BURGER home with them. By working with stores that support local products and by listening to what consumers want, the company is gaining market acceptance. More than 60 retailers in 11 states now carry August Kitchen products. August Kitchen has added J-CHILI and J-MEATLOAF meal starters to its product line.[50] ■

A successful strategy is comprehensive and well integrated, focusing on establishing the KSFs that the entrepreneur identified in step 4. For instance, if maximum shelf space is a KSF for a small manufacturer's product, the strategy must identify techniques for gaining more in-store shelf space (e.g., offering higher margins to distributors and brokers than competitors do, assisting retailers with in-store displays, or redesigning a wider, more attractive package).

THREE STRATEGIC OPTIONS Obviously, the number of strategies from which a small business owner can choose is infinite. When all the glitter is stripped away, however, three basic strategies remain. In his classic book *Competitive Strategy*, Michael Porter identifies these strategies as (1) cost leadership, (2) differentiation, and (3) focus (see Figure 5.4).[51]

cost leadership strategy

a strategy in which a company strives to be the low-cost producer relative to its competitors in the industry.

Cost Leadership A company pursuing a **cost leadership strategy** strives to be the lowest-cost producer relative to its competitors in the industry. Many companies attempt to compete by offering low prices, but low costs are a prerequisite for success. Low-cost leaders have a competitive advantage in reaching buyers whose primary purchase criterion is price, and

FIGURE 5.4

Three Strategic Options

Source: Based on Michael E. Porter, *Competitive Strategy* (New York: Free Press, 1980), Chapter 2.

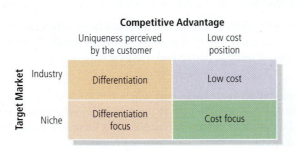

they have the power to set the industry's price floor. This strategy works well when buyers are sensitive to price changes, when competing firms sell the same commodity products and compete on the basis of price, and when companies can benefit from economies of scale. Not only is a low-cost leader in the best position to defend itself in a price war, but it also can use its power to attack competitors with the lowest price in the industry.

There are many ways to build a low-cost strategy, but the most successful cost leaders know where they have cost advantages over their competitors, and they use these areas as the foundation for their strategies. Successful cost leaders often find low-cost suppliers (or use a vertical integration strategy to produce their own products), eliminate the inefficiencies in their channels of distribution, use the Internet to cut costs, and operate more efficiently than their competitors. They are committed to squeezing every unnecessary cost out of their operations.

ENTREPRENEURIAL PROFILE: Eric Casaburi: Retro Fitness Eric Casaburi, founder and CEO of Retro Fitness, pursues a low-cost strategy in a highly competitive industry. Retro Fitness offers gym memberships at a rock-bottom price of $19.99 per month in its more than 100 fitness centers in 13 states. Featuring a 1980s theme, Retro Fitness offers quality equipment and service with no additional frills. Casaburi keeps costs down by negotiating deals with suppliers and by carefully selecting low-cost sites. Instead of building 30,000-square-foot gyms, Retro Fitness is able to fit everything its customers need into a space one-third that size, which saves a significant amount of rent expense each month. Retro Fitness also offers additional products its customers want, such as smoothies, training sessions, and clothing, which adds to the monthly revenue per customer. The company offers an app as part of membership that allows customers to track their workouts, measure progress toward goals, make an appointment with a trainer, and order a smoothie from the smoothie bar. Recently, Retro Fitness noticed that many of its customers had two fitness club memberships. In addition to the $19.99 monthly membership at Retro Fitness, many customers had a second membership at a club that offered boutique individualized personal training. Retro Fitness added a new option of multi-level personalized training at several price points to encourage its customers to meet all of their training needs in one location. Retro Fitness now has 145 locations in 16 states and plans to add at least 20 new franchises each year.[52] ∎

Of course, there are dangers in following a cost leadership strategy. Sometimes a company focuses exclusively on lower manufacturing costs, without considering the impact of purchasing, distribution, or overhead costs. Another danger is incorrectly identifying the company's true cost drivers. Although their approach to managing is characterized by frugality, companies that understand cost leadership are willing to invest in activities that drive costs out of doing business, whether it is technology, preventive maintenance, or some other factor. In addition, over time, competitors may erode a company's cost advantage by finding ways to lower their own costs. Finally, a firm may pursue a low-cost leadership strategy so zealously that, in its drive to push costs downward, it eliminates product or service features that customers consider essential.

Under the right conditions, a cost leadership strategy executed properly can be an incredibly powerful strategic weapon. Small discount retailers that live in the shadows of Wal-Mart and thrive even when the economy slows succeed by relentlessly pursuing low-cost strategies. Small chains, such as Fred's, Dollar General, Family Dollar, 99 Cents Only, and Dollar Tree, cater to low- and middle-income customers who live in inner cities or rural areas. They offer inexpensive products such as food, health and beauty products, cleaning supplies, clothing, and seasonal merchandise, and many of the items they stock are closeout buys (purchases made as low as 10 cents on the dollar) on brand-name merchandise. These companies also strive to keep their overhead costs as low as possible. For instance, 99 Cents Only, whose name describes its merchandising strategy, is housed in a no-frills warehouse in an older section of City of Commerce, California.[53] By keeping their costs low, these retailers offer customers prices that are within 1 to 2 percent of those at Wal-Mart, even though they do not benefit from the same quantity discounts as the low-cost giant. The success of these stores proves that companies pursuing a cost leadership strategy must emphasize cost containment in *every* decision, from where to locate the company headquarters to which items to stock, especially when demand softens due to a stronger economy.[54]

differentiation strategy

a strategy in which a company seeks to build customer loyalty by positioning its goods or services in a unique or different fashion.

Differentiation   A company following a **differentiation strategy** seeks to build customer loyalty by selling goods or services that provide unique attributes and that customers perceive to be superior to competing products. That, in turn, enables the business to command higher prices for its products or services than competitors. There are many ways to create a differentiation strategy, but the key is to be unique at something that is important to the customer. In other words, a business pursuing a differentiation strategy strives to be better than its competitors at something customers value.

Courtesy of Phillip Tompkins, Tompkins Venture LLC, DBA Rent the Chicken

ENTREPRENEURIAL PROFILE: Jenn and Phillip Tompkins, RentTheChicken.com   Jenn and Phillip Tompkins started RentTheChicken.com in Freeport, Pennsylvania, to take advantage of the growing interest in suburban backyard farms. RentTheChicken.com takes the risk out of backyard farming for first-time urban farmers. Every spring, the company provides two egg-laying chickens and all the necessary supplies to its customers. Although it started as a local business serving customers within about an hour of its headquarters, RentTheChicken now serves customers in 18 states. The Tompkins offer lessons to clients to help ensure their success at raising chickens. The chicken rental and supplies costs about $350 to $500 a season. Then, in the fall, RentTheChicken.com picks up the chickens to keep them safe and warm over the winter. If predators eat any of the rented chickens, the company replaces the chickens at no cost. However, if a chicken dies from neglect, RentTheChicken.com picks up the equipment and charges the customer a fee. Environmentalists praise the business model because it reduces the number of chickens that end up in animal shelters after would-be urban farmers find raising chickens to be more work than they had assumed.[55] ∎

If a small company can improve a product's (or service's) performance, reduce the customer's cost and risk of purchasing it, or provide intangible benefits that customers value (such as status, prestige, exclusivity, or a sense of safety), it has the potential to be a successful differentiator. Companies that execute a differentiation strategy successfully can charge premium prices for their products and services, increase their market share, and reap the benefits of customer loyalty and retention. To be successful, a business must make its product or service truly different, at least in the eyes of its customers.

Although few businesses are innately as unique as RentTheChicken.com, the goal for a company pursuing a differentiation strategy is to create that kind of uniqueness in the minds of its customers. The key to a successful differentiation strategy is to build it on a core competency—something a small company is uniquely good at doing in comparison to its competitors. Common bases for differentiation include superior customer service, special product features, complete product lines, instantaneous parts availability, absolute product reliability, supreme product quality, and extensive product knowledge. To be successful, a differentiation strategy must create the perception of value in the customer's eyes. No customer purchases a good or service that fails to produce its perceived value, no matter how real that value may be. One business consultant advises, "Make sure you tell your customers and prospects what it is about your business that makes you different. Make sure that difference is in the form of a true benefit to the customer."[56]

Small companies encounter risks when pursuing a differentiation strategy. One danger is trying to differentiate a product or service on the basis of something that does not boost its performance or lower its cost to customers. Another pitfall is trying to differentiate on the basis of something customers do not see as important. Business owners also must consider how long they can sustain a product's or service's differentiation; changing customer tastes may make the basis for differentiation temporary. Imitations and "knockoffs" from competitors also pose a threat to a successful differentiation strategy. For instance, designers of high-priced original clothing see much cheaper knockoff products on the market shortly after their designs hit the market. Another pitfall is over-differentiating and charging so much that the company prices

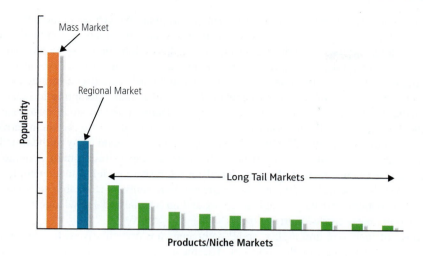

FIGURE 5.5

Long Tail Markets

Source: Based on Chris Anderson, *The Long Tail: Why the Future of Business Is Selling Less of More* (New York: Hyperion Books, 2008).

its products out of the market. The final risk is focusing only on the physical characteristics of a product or service and ignoring important psychological factors, such as status, prestige, and image, which can be powerful sources of differentiation.

Focus   A **focus strategy** recognizes that not all markets are homogeneous. In fact, in any given market, there are many different customer segments, each having different needs, wants, and characteristics. Businesses with a focus strategy sell to these specific segments rather than trying to sell to the mass market. In his book *The Long Tail*, Chris Anderson, editor-in-chief of *Wired Magazine*, explains that the digital age has opened up smaller niche market segments to smaller businesses, creating a long tail of niche markets (see Figure 5.5). Three drivers create the long tail of the market:[57]

focus strategy
a strategy in which a company selects one or more market segments; identifies customers' special needs, wants, and interests; and approaches them with a good or service designed to excel in meeting those needs, wants, and interests.

1. *The tools of production are more affordable.* Software and hardware are now much cheaper to buy and easier to use. For instance, in the past, musical artists recorded their work in a studio at a cost of thousands of dollars per song. Today, musicians no longer have to rely on large record companies to produce their music. With affordable software such as Pro Tools, artists can record and edit music with a personal computer or laptop almost anywhere. The quality of these recordings is so high that it is almost impossible to tell the difference between a recording made in a professional recording studio and one made in an artist's living room.

2. *The Internet has created better access to niche markets.* Internet aggregators, such as Amazon, can pull together all of the products consumers may possibly want. E-commerce sites, such as Symphony Commerce, SquareSpace, and Shopify, offer cloud-based service that allows retailers to increase their product offering and brand awareness through their merchandising and fulfillment platforms.[58] In addition, a small company's own Web site is now a tool to reach consumers directly through digital advertising and social media.

3. *Search tools make it easier to reach specific consumers.* Search engines and recommendations available through Web sites and social media drive consumers to specific products and services on the Internet to meet their particular needs. For example, a consumer who traveled to the Czech Republic and wanted to buy some Czech crystal after returning home can easily search for Czech crystal manufacturers that ship abroad.

The principal idea of a focus strategy is to select one (or more) segment(s); identify customers' special needs, wants, and interests; and provide them with goods or services designed to excel in meeting these needs, wants, and interests. By focusing on small market niches, focus strategies build on *differences* among market segments. Because they are small, flexible, and attentive to their customers' particular needs, small companies can be successful in niches that are too narrow for their larger competitors to enter profitably. These companies focus on a narrow segment of the overall market and set themselves apart either by becoming cost leaders in the segment or by differentiating themselves from competitors.

Focus strategies will become more prevalent among small businesses in the future, as industries increasingly become dumbbell shaped, with a few large companies dominating one end, a relatively small number of midsized businesses in the middle, and a large number of small businesses operating at the other end. Fragmented markets offer small businesses an opportunity because these markets have become easier to identify and reach with digital strategies.

In fact, serving specific target segments or niches rather than attempting to reach the total market is the essence of a focus strategy, making it ideally suited to small businesses, which often lack the resources to reach the overall market. Their goal is to serve their narrow target markets more effectively and efficiently than competitors that pound away at the broad market. Common bases for building a focus strategy include zeroing in on a small geographic area, targeting a group of customers with similar needs or interests (e.g., left-handed people), specializing in a specific product or service (e.g., Batteries Plus Bulbs, a store that sells and services every kind of battery and bulb imaginable), or selling specialized knowledge (e.g., restoring valuable and priceless works of art).

Because of their size and agility, small companies are particularly well suited for serving niche markets that are part of the long tail. The most successful focusers build a competitive edge by concentrating on specific market niches and serving them better than competitors—even powerful giants—can. Small companies are better able to establish personal relationships with their customers. Knowing their customers enables these businesses to adjust more quickly to changes in customers' preferences and needs.

A focus strategy depends on creating value for customers either by being the lowest-cost producer or by differentiating the product or service in a unique fashion but doing it in a narrow target segment. To be worth targeting, a niche must be large enough to be profitable, reachable with marketing media, and capable of sustaining a business over time (i.e., not a passing fad). Many small companies operate quite successfully in small, yet profitable, niches.

Market niches do not have to be glamorous to be profitable. Joshua Opperman lost a fiancée but discovered a market need and a simple business model to exploit it. When his fiancée called off their engagement, he tried to sell the engagement ring he had purchased back to the jeweler. When the store offered him just $3,500 for a ring he paid $10,000 for just a few months earlier, he started his company, I Do Now I Don't, to help people to sell engagement rings and other jewelry with a system that works like Craigslist. The company, which takes a 15 percent commission on all successful sales through its Web site, has seen revenue grow to more than $15 million.[59]

Although it can be a highly profitable strategy, pursuing a focus strategy is not without risks. Companies sometimes struggle to capture a large enough share of a small market to be profitable. If a small company is successful in a niche, there is also the danger of larger competitors entering the market and eroding it. Many entrepreneurs following this strategy face a constant struggle to keep costs down; the small volume of business that some niches support pushes production costs upward, making a company vulnerable to lower-cost competitors as their prices spiral higher. Sometimes a company with a successful niche strategy gets distracted by its success and tries to branch out into other areas. As it drifts farther away from its core strategy, it loses its competitive edge and runs the risk of confusing or alienating its customers. Muddying its image with customers puts a company in danger of losing its identity.

Joshua Opperman, Founder and CEO of I Do Now I Don't

Step 8. Translate Strategic Plans into Action Plans

No strategic plan is complete until it is put into action; planning a company's strategy and implementing it go hand in hand. Entrepreneurs must convert strategic plans into operating plans that guide their companies on a daily basis and become a visible, active part of the business. No small business can benefit from a strategic plan sitting on a shelf collecting dust. Unfortunately, failure to implement a strategy effectively is a common problem. The lesson is that even sound strategies, unless properly implemented, will fail.

EXECUTING THE STRATEGY Implementing a strategy successfully requires both a process that fits a company's culture and the right people committed to making that process work. Getting the right people in place starts with the selection process and includes every other aspect of the human resources function—including hiring, job design, training, motivational methods, and compensation.

To make their strategic plans workable, entrepreneurs should divide them into projects, carefully defining each one by the following:

Purpose. What is the project designed to accomplish?

Scope. Which areas of the company will be involved in the project?

Contribution. How does the project relate to other projects and to the overall strategic plan?

Resource requirements. What human and financial resources are needed to complete the project successfully?

Timing. Which schedules and deadlines will ensure project completion?

Once entrepreneurs assign priorities to projects, they can begin to implement the strategic plan. Involving employees and delegating adequate authority to them is essential because these projects affect them most directly. If an organization's people have been involved in the strategic planning process to this point, they will have a better grasp of the steps they must take to achieve the organization's goals as well as their own professional goals. Early involvement of all employees in the implementation of strategy is a luxury that larger businesses cannot achieve. Commitment to reaching the company's objectives is a powerful force, but involvement is a prerequisite for achieving total employee commitment. The greater the level of involvement of those who will implement a company's strategy in the process of creating the strategy, the more likely the strategy is to be successful. Without a team of committed, dedicated employees, a company's strategy, no matter how precisely planned, usually fails.

Step 9. Establish Accurate Controls

So far, the planning process has created company objectives and has developed a strategy for reaching them, but rarely, if ever, will the company's actual performance match stated objectives. Entrepreneurs quickly realize the need to control actual results that deviate from plans.

CONTROLLING THE STRATEGY Planning without control has little operational value; therefore, a sound planning program requires a practical control process. The plans and objectives created in the strategic planning process become the standards against which actual performance is measured. It is important for everyone in the organization to understand—and to be involved in— the planning and controlling process. Unless entrepreneurs measure progress against the goals and objectives established in step 6, their companies make little progress toward accomplishing them.

Controlling plans and projects and keeping them on schedule means that an entrepreneur must identify and track key success factors. The source of these indicators is the operating data from the company's normal business activity. Financial, production, sales, inventory, quality, customer service and satisfaction, and other operating records are primary sources of data managers can use to control activities. For example, on a customer service project, performance indicators might include the number of customer complaints, the number of orders returned, the percentage of on-time shipments, and a measure of order accuracy.

The most commonly used indicators of a company's performance are financial measures; however, judging a company's performance solely on the basis of financial measures can lead to strategic myopia. To judge the effectiveness of their strategies, many companies use **dashboards**, a set of measurements that incorporate both financial and operational measures to give entrepreneurs and leadership teams a quick yet comprehensive picture of the company's overall performance.

Rather than stick solely to the traditional financial measures of a company's performance, a dashboard gives an entrepreneurial team a comprehensive view from *both* financial and operational perspectives. The premise behind a dashboard is that relying on any single measure of company performance is dangerous. Just as a pilot in command of a jet cannot fly safely by focusing on a single instrument, an entrepreneur cannot manage a company by concentrating on

dashboard
a set of measurements that incorporate both financial and operational measures to give entrepreneurs and their leadership teams a quick but comprehensive picture of a company's performance.

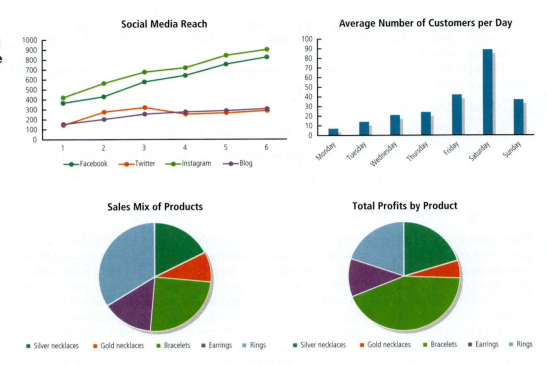

FIGURE 5.6

Sample Dashboard for a Jewelry Store

a single measurement, such as net profits or revenues. The complexity of managing a business demands that an entrepreneur be able to see performance measures in several areas simultaneously. "Knowing whether an enterprise is viable or not doesn't mean looking at just the bottom line," says one manager.[60] Dashboards that combine relevant results from all aspects of the operation allow everyone in the organization to see how his or her job performance connects to a company's mission, goals, and objectives. Specifically, a small business dashboard enables entrepreneurs and their leadership teams to visually track trends related to sales, accounts receivable, customer satisfaction, social media reach, profit margins, customer acquisition, customer retention, Web site traffic, advertising effectiveness, and key competitive and industry trends. Figure 5.6 shows a sample dashboard for a small jewelry store. From the data in this dashboard, the entrepreneur can see the impact of the business's social media activities, the days of the week when it gets the most traffic through the door, which products contribute most to sales, and which products contribute most to profits. From this information, the entrepreneur may decide that it is not worth being open on Mondays, Instagram and Facebook are the most effective social media, and that although silver necklaces contribute the most to sales, bracelets yield the most profits.

When creating dashboards for their companies, entrepreneurs should consider the following:

- Include graphics for strategic objectives and key success factors.

- Display data in such a way that the conclusions are clear for decision making.

- Help identify opportunities to improve profit margins.

- Allow for quick and definitive decisions.

- Offer an overall picture of the business that focuses everyone on the team on a common set of facts.

It is best to start with only the most important objectives and success factors. Three to five indicators are enough at first. Over time, entrepreneurs can add indicators if necessary and, similarly, can delete those indicators that prove to be no longer critical. Too much information can confuse decision making.

If used properly, a dashboard serves as a call to action. When a key success factor is out of control, everyone in the company knows it and can work together to do something about it quickly. The key to using dashboards successfully is making sure the measures included are tied to the company's strategy.

ENTREPRENEURIAL PROFILE: David Abrahamovitch and Kaz James: Grind Grind, cofounded by David Abrahamovitch and Kaz James, is a trendy chain of coffee shops based in London. The chain brings together coffee, live music, a recording studio, local entrepreneurs, food, and craft cocktails in its hipster-inspired coffee shops. Grind's sales have been nearly doubling each year as it has expanded the number of locations and brought in more customers. Its busiest stores have revenues of over $1 million a year, selling about 800 cups of coffee every day. As the business has grown, Abrahamovitch has been concerned about tracking key metrics. He created a dashboard that tracks sales, store operating performance, social media engagement, and the loyalty card program. Sales metrics on the dashboard display overall sales trends, sales per category (coffee, food, alcohol), customer count, and average spend by each customer. A key metric for operating performance is wait time from ordering to delivery of the finished coffee drink. The goal is no more than four minutes. The real-time dashboard is available to everyone in the company on iPads and smart phones, which has led to friendly competition among the six locations and a common focus on growing the company.[61] ∎

Ideally, a balanced scorecard looks at a business from five important perspectives: customer, internal, innovation and learning, financial, and corporate citizenship.

CUSTOMER PERSPECTIVE How do customers see us? Customers judge companies by at least four standards: time (how long it takes the company to deliver a good or service), quality (how well a company's product or service performs in terms of reliability, durability, and accuracy), performance (the extent to which a good or service performs as expected), and service (how well a company meets or exceeds customers' expectations of value). Because customer-related goals are external, managers must translate them into measures of what the company must do to meet customers' expectations.

INTERNAL BUSINESS PERSPECTIVE At what must we excel? The internal factors on which managers should focus are those that have the greatest impact on customer satisfaction and retention and on company effectiveness and efficiency. It is essential to develop goals and measures for factors such as quality, cycle time, productivity, cost control, and others that employees directly influence.

INNOVATION AND LEARNING PERSPECTIVE Can we continue to improve and create value? This view of a company recognizes that the targets required for success are never static but are constantly changing. If a company wants to continue its pattern of success, it cannot stand still; it must continuously innovate and improve. Employee training and development are essential ingredients in this component. A company's ability to innovate, learn, and improve determines its future. These goals and measures emphasize the importance of continuous improvement in customer satisfaction and internal business operations.

FINANCIAL PERSPECTIVE How do we look to shareholders? The most traditional performance measures, financial standards, tell how much the company's overall strategy and its execution are contributing to the bottom line. These measures focus on factors such as profitability, growth, and shareholder value. On balanced scorecards, companies often break their financial goals into three categories: survival, success, and growth.

CORPORATE CITIZENSHIP How well are we meeting our responsibility to society as a whole, the environment, the community, and other external stakeholders? Even small companies must recognize that they must be good business citizens.

Although a dashboard is a vital tool that helps entrepreneurs keep their companies on track, it is also an important tool for changing behavior in a business and for keeping everyone focused on what really matters. Used properly, dashboards allow entrepreneurs and their teams to see how actions in each of the five dimensions of performance influence actions in the others. As competitive conditions and results change, entrepreneurs can use a dashboard to make corrections in plans, policies, strategies, and objectives to get performance back on track. A practical control system is also economical to operate. Most small businesses have no need for a sophisticated, expensive control system. The system should be so practical that it becomes a natural part of the management process.

Conclusion

A solid business plan is essential to raising the capital needed to start a business; lenders and investors demand it. "There may be no easier way for an entrepreneur to sabotage his or her request for capital than by failing to produce a comprehensive, well-researched, and, above all, credible business plan," says one small business expert.[62] Creating a successful business requires entrepreneurs to put the plan into action and then manage the company's growth with a sound strategic plan.

The strategic planning process does *not* end with the nine steps outlined here; it is an ongoing procedure entrepreneurs must repeat. With each round, managers and employees gain experience, and the steps become easier. The planning process described here is designed to be simple. No small business should be burdened with an elaborate, detailed formal planning process it cannot easily use. Some planning processes require excessive amounts of time to operate and generate a sea of paperwork. Entrepreneurs need neither.

What does this strategic planning process lead to? It teaches business owners a degree of discipline that is important to business survival. It helps them learn about their businesses, their core competencies, their competitors, and, most importantly, their customers. Although strategic planning cannot guarantee success, it dramatically increases a small company's chances of survival in a hostile business environment.

Sample Business Plan Outline

Although every company's business plan will be unique, reflecting its individual circumstances, certain elements are universal. The following outline summarizes these components.

   I. Executive Summary (not to exceed one page)
     A. Company name, address, and phone number
     B. Name(s), addresses, and phone number(s) of all key people
     C. Brief description of the business, its products and services, the customer problems they solve, and the company's competitive advantage
     D. Brief overview of the market for your products and services
     E. Brief overview of the strategies that will make your company successful
     F. Brief description of the managerial and technical experience of key people
     G. Brief statement of the financial request and how the money will be used
     H. Charts or tables showing highlights of financial forecasts

  II. Vision and Mission Statement
     A. Entrepreneur's vision for the company
     B. "What business are we in?"
     C. Values and principles on which the business stands
     D. What makes the business unique? What is the source of its competitive advantage?

 III. Company History (for existing businesses only)
     A. Company founding
     B. Financial and operational highlights
     C. Significant achievements

 IV. Company Products and Services
     A. Description
       1. Product or service features
       2. Customer benefits
       3. Warranties and guarantees
       4. Unique selling proposition (USP)

B. Patent or trademark protection
C. Description of production process (if applicable)
  1. Raw materials
  2. Costs
  3. Key suppliers
  4. Lead times
D. Future product or service offerings

V. Industry Profile and Overview
  A. Industry analysis
    1. Industry background and overview
    2. Significant trends
    3. Growth rate
    4. Barriers to entry and exit
    5. Key success factors in the industry
  B. Outlook for the future
  C. Stage of growth (start-up, growth, maturity)

VI. Competitor Analysis
  A. Existing competitors
    1. Who are they? Create a competitive profile matrix.
    2. Strengths
    3. Weaknesses
  B. Potential competitors: Companies that might enter the market
    1. Who are they?
    2. Impact on your business if they enter

VII. Business Strategy
  A. Desired image and position in market
  B. Company goals and objectives
    1. Operational
    2. Financial
    3. Other
  C. SWOT analysis
    1. Strengths
    2. Weaknesses
    3. Opportunities
    4. Threats
  D. Competitive strategy
    1. Cost leadership
    2. Differentiation
    3. Focus

VIII. Marketing Strategy
  A. Target market
    1. Problem to be solved or benefit to be offered
    2. Demographic profile
    3. Other significant customer characteristics
  B. Customers' motivation to buy
  C. Market size and trends
    1. How large is the market?
    2. Is it growing or shrinking? How fast?
  D. Personal selling efforts
    1. Sales force size, recruitment, and training
    2. Sales force compensation
    3. Number of calls per sale
    4. Amount of average sale

E. Advertising and promotion
1. Media used (reader, viewer, listener profiles)
2. Media costs
3. Frequency of usage
4. Plans for generating publicity
F. Pricing
1. Cost structure
   a. Fixed
   b. Variable
2. Desired image in market
3. Comparison against competitors' prices
4. Discounts
5. Gross profit margin
G. Distribution strategy (if applicable)
1. Channels of distribution used
2. Sales techniques and incentives for intermediaries
H. Test market results
1. Surveys
2. Customer feedback on prototypes
3. Focus groups

IX. Location and Layout
A. Location
1. Demographic analysis of location vs. target customer profile
2. Traffic count
3. Lease/rental rates
4. Labor needs and supply
5. Wage rates
B. Layout
1. Size requirements
2. Americans with Disabilities Act compliance
3. Ergonomic issues
4. Layout plan (suitable for an appendix)

X. Description of management team
A. Key managers and employees
1. Their backgrounds
2. Experience, skills, and know-how they bring to the company
B. Résumés of key managers and employees (suitable for an appendix)
C. Future additions to management team
D. Board of directors or advisers

XI. Plan of Operation
A. Form of ownership chosen and reasoning
B. Company structure (organization chart)
C. Decision-making authority
D. Compensation and benefits packages
E. Staffing plans

XII. Financial Forecasts (suitable for an appendix)
A. Key assumptions
B. Financial statements (year 1 by month, years 2 and 3 by quarter)
1. Income statement
2. Balance sheet
3. Cash flow statement
C. Breakeven analysis
D. Ratio analysis with comparison to industry standards (most applicable to existing businesses)

XIII. Loan or Investment Proposal
- A. Amount requested
- B. Purpose and uses of funds
- C. Repayment or "cash out" schedule (exit strategy)
- D. Timetable for implementing plan and launching the business

XIV. Appendices (Supporting documentation, including market research, financial statements, organization charts, résumés, and other items)

MyLab Entrepreneurship

If your instructor is using MyLab Entrepreneurship, go to **www.pearson.com/mylab/ entrepreneurship** to complete the problems marked with this icon ⭐.

Chapter Summary by Learning Objective

1. Explain the benefits of an effective business plan.

- A business plan, which builds on information from the feasibility analysis and business model, serves two essential functions. First and more importantly, it guides the company's operations by charting its future course and devising a strategy for following it. The second function of the business plan is to attract lenders and investors. Applying for loans or attempting to attract investors without a solid business plan rarely attracts needed capital. Rather, the best way to secure the necessary capital is to prepare a sound business plan.

- An effective business plan should pass these three tests:
  - *Reality test.* The external component of the reality test involves proving that a market for the product or service really exists. The internal component of the reality test focuses on the product or service itself.
  - *Competitive test.* The external part of the competitive test evaluates the company's relative position to its key competitors. The internal competitive test focuses on the management team's ability to create a company that will gain an edge over existing rivals.
  - *Value test.* To convince lenders and investors to put their money into the venture, a business plan must prove to them that it offers a high probability of repayment or an attractive rate of return.

2. Describe the elements of a solid business plan.

- Although a business plan should be unique and tailored to suit the particular needs of a small company, it should include these basic elements: executive summary, mission statement, company history, business and industry profile, description of the company's business strategy, profile of its products or services, statement explaining its marketing strategy, competitor analysis, owners' and officers' résumés, plan of operation, financial data, and loan or investment proposal.

3. Explain the "five Cs of credit" and why they are important to potential lenders and investors reviewing business plans.

- Small business owners need to be aware of the criteria bankers use in evaluating the creditworthiness of loan applicants, known as the *five Cs of credit*:
  - *Capital.* Lenders expect small businesses to have an equity base of investment by the owner(s) that will help support the venture during times of financial strain.
  - *Capacity.* Capacity is a synonym for cash flow. The bank must be convinced of the firm's ability to meet its regular financial obligations and to repay the bank loan—and that takes cash.
  - *Collateral.* Collateral includes any assets the owner pledges to the bank as security for repayment of the loan.
  - *Character.* Before approving a loan to a small business, the banker must be satisfied with the owner's character.
  - *Conditions.* The conditions—interest rates, the health of the nation's economy, industry growth rates, and so on—surrounding a loan request affect the owner's chance of receiving funds.

4. Understand the keys to making an effective business plan presentation.

- Entrepreneurs who are informed and prepared when requesting a loan or investment favorably impress lenders and investors.

- Tips include: Demonstrate enthusiasm about the venture but don't be overly emotional; "hook" investors quickly with an up-front explanation of the new venture, its opportunities, and the anticipated benefits to them; use visual aids; hit the highlights of your venture; don't get caught up in too much detail in early meetings with lenders and investors; avoid the use of technological terms that will likely be above the heads of most of the audience; rehearse your presentation before giving it; close by reinforcing the nature of the opportunity; and be prepared for questions.

5. Understand the importance of strategic management to a small business.

- Companies without clear strategies may achieve some success in the short run, but as soon as a competitive threat arises, they often fail.

6. Explain why and how a small business must create a competitive advantage in the market.

- The goal of developing a strategic plan is to create for the small company a competitive advantage— the combination of factors that sets the small business apart from its competitors and gives it a unique position in the market.

- Every small firm must establish a plan for creating a unique image in the minds of its potential customers.

- A company builds a competitive edge on its core competencies, which are a unique set of capabilities that a company develops in key operational areas—such as quality, service, innovation, team building, flexibility, and responsiveness—that allow it to vault past competitors. They are what the company does best and help focus the strategy. This step involves identifying target market segments and determining how to position the firm in those markets.

- Entrepreneurs must identify some way to differentiate their companies from competitors.

7. Develop a strategic plan for a business by using the nine steps in the strategic management process.

- Small businesses need a strategic planning process designed to suit their particular needs. It should be relatively short, it should be informal and not structured, it should encourage the participation of employees, and it should not begin with extensive objective setting.

- Linking the purposeful action of strategic planning to an entrepreneur's ideas can produce results that shape the future.

Step 1. Develop a clear vision and translate it into a meaningful mission statement. Highly successful entrepreneurs communicate their vision to those around them. The firm's mission statement answers the first question of any venture: What business am I in? It sets the tone for the entire company.

Step 2. Assess the company's strengths and weaknesses. Strengths are positive internal factors; weaknesses are negative internal factors.

Step 3. Scan the environment for significant opportunities and threats facing the business. Opportunities are positive external options; threats are negative external forces.

Step 4. Identify the key factors for success in the business. In every business, key factors determine the success of the firms in it, so they must be an integral part of a company's strategy. KSFs are relationships between a controllable variable and a critical factor influencing the firm's ability to compete in the market.

Step 5. Analyze the competition. Business owners should know their competitors almost as well as they know their own companies. A competitive profile matrix is a helpful tool for analyzing competitors' strengths and weaknesses.

Step 6. Create company goals and objectives. Goals are the broad, long-range attributes that the firm seeks to accomplish. Objectives are quantifiable and more precise; they should be specific, measurable, assignable, realistic, timely, and written down. The process works best when managers and employees are actively involved.

Step 7. Formulate strategic options and select the appropriate strategies. A strategy is the game plan the firm plans to use to achieve its objectives and mission. It must focus on establishing for the firm the KSFs identified earlier.

Step 8. Translate strategic plans into action plans. No strategic plan is complete until the owner puts it into action.

Step 9. Establish accurate controls. Actual performance rarely, if ever, matches plans exactly. Operating data from the business assembled into a comprehensive scorecard serves as an important guidepost for determining the effectiveness of a company's strategy. This information is especially helpful when plotting future strategies.

- The strategic planning process does not end with these nine steps; rather, it is an ongoing process that an entrepreneur repeats.

- The three basic strategies a business can pursue are low cost, differentiation, and focus.
- Controls are essential for the effective implementation of a strategic plan. A dashboard is a set of measurements unique to a company that includes both financial and operational measures and gives managers a quick and comprehensive picture of the company's total performance.

MyLab Entrepreneurship

If your instructor is using MyLab Entrepreneurship, go to **www.pearson.com/mylab/entrepreneurship** for Auto-graded writing questions as well as the following Assisted-graded writing questions:

1. What are the five *C*s of credit?
2. Why is it important for a small business to establish a competitive advantage?

Discussion Questions

⭐ 5-1. Why should an entrepreneur develop a business plan?

5-2. Why do entrepreneurs who are not seeking external financing need to prepare business plans?

5-3. Describe the major components of a business plan.

5-4. How can an entrepreneur seeking funds to launch a business convince potential lenders and investors that a market for the product or service really does exist?

5-5. How do lenders and investors use the five *C*s of credit when evaluating a request for financing?

5-6. How would you prepare to make a formal presentation of your business plan to a venture capital forum?

5-7. Why is strategic planning important to a small company?

5-8. What is a competitive advantage?

5-9. What are the steps in the strategic management process?

5-10. A common criticism of mission statements is that entrepreneurs spend too much time crafting them and not enough time implementing them in the business. What is meant by this criticism?

5-11. Discuss the importance of what you do with a mission statement.

5-12. What are strengths, weaknesses, opportunities, and threats?

5-13. Give examples of strengths, weaknesses, opportunities, and threats.

5-14. Explain the characteristics of effective objectives.

5-15. Why is setting objectives important?

5-16. What are business strategies?

⭐ 5-17. Describe the three basic strategies available to small companies.

5-18. Under what conditions is each of the three basic strategies most successful?

5-19. Explain how a company can gain a competitive advantage using each of the three strategies described in this chapter: cost leadership, differentiation, and focus.

5-20. Give an example of a company that is using each of the three strategies.

5-21. How is the controlling process related to the planning process?

5-22. What is a dashboard?

5-23. What value does a dashboard offer entrepreneurs who are evaluating the success of their current strategies?

Beyond the Classroom . . .

5-24. Contact the owner of a small business that competes directly with an industry giant, such as Home Depot, Wal-Mart, or Target.

5-25. What does the owner see as his or her competitive advantage?

5-26. How does the business communicate this competitive advantage to its customers?

5-27. What competitive strategy is the owner using?

5-28. How successful is the competitive strategy?

5-29. What changes would you suggest that the owner make?

5-30. In his book *The HP Way*, Dave Packard, cofounder of Hewlett-Packard, describes the seven commitments of the HP Way:

- Profit—the ultimate source of corporate strength
- Customers—constant improvement in the value of the products and services the company offers them
- Field of interest—seeking new opportunities but limiting them to complementary products and services based on company core competencies
- Growth—a measure of strength and a requirement for survival

- Employees—provide opportunities for advancement, share in their success, and offer job security based on performance
- Organization—foster individual motivation, initiative, and creativity by giving employees the freedom to work toward established goals and objectives
- Citizenship—contribute in a positive way toward the community and society at large

In what ways do these values help HP define its vision?

5-31. In what ways do these values help HP define its competitive edge?

5-32. How important is it for entrepreneurs to define a system of values to guide their companies?

5-33. Contact a local entrepreneur and help him or her devise a dashboard for his or her company.

5-34. What goals did you and the owner establish in each of the four perspectives?

5-35. What measures did you use to judge the company's progress toward those goals?

5-36. Use the strategic tools provided in this chapter to help a local small business owner discover his or her firm's strengths, weaknesses, opportunities, and threats.

5-37. Use the strategic tools provided in this chapter to help identify the relevant KSFs.

5-38. Use the strategic tools provided in this chapter to help analyze its competitors.

5-39. Help the owner devise a strategy for success for his or her business.

5-40. Choose an entrepreneur in your community and interview him or her.

5-41. Does the company have a strategic plan?

5-42. Does the company have a mission statement?

5-43. Explain why the company does or does not have a mission statement.

5-44. What does the owner consider the company's strengths and weaknesses to be?

5-45. What opportunities and threats does the owner perceive?

5-46. What image is the owner trying to create for the business?

5-47. Has the effort been successful?

5-48. Do you agree with the owner's assessment of its effectiveness?

5-49. Which of the generic competitive strategies is the company following?

5-50. Who are the company's primary competitors?

5-51. How does the owner rate his or her chances for success in the future, using a scale of 1 (low) to 10 (high)?

5-52. Compare your evaluation with those of your classmates.

5-53. What, if any, generalizations can you draw from the interview?

Endnotes

[1] Tanya Prine, "Top 32 Quotes Every Entrepreneur Should Live By," *Forbes*, May 2, 2013, www.forbes.com/sites/tanyaprive/2013/05/02/top-32-quotes-every-entrepreneur-should-live-by/#6fad33f921da.

[2] Jianwen Liao and William B. Gartner, "Are Planners Doers? Pre-Venture Planning and the Start-Up Behaviors of Entrepreneurs," *SBA Office of Advocacy*, February 2009, http://archive.sba.gov/advo/research/rs339tot.pdf.

[3] Donna Fenn, "6 Tips for Raising Money During the Recovery," *Inc.*, March 9, 2012, www.inc.com/donna-fenn/6-tips-for-raising-money-in-a-recovering-economy.html.

[4] Michael Skok, "4 Steps to Building a Compelling Value Proposition," *Forbes*, June 14, 2013, www.forbes.com/sites/michaelskok/2013/06/14/4-steps-to-building-a-compelling-value-proposition/#62c83e651f2c/.

[5] Jeff Cornwall, "Following the Value Proposition to Entrepreneurial Success," *Christian Science Monitor*, May 29, 2012, www.csmonitor.com/Business/The-Entrepreneurial-Mind/2012/0529/Following-the-value-proposition-to-entrepreneurial-success.

[6] Bill Reichert, "Part II: A Framework for Building Your WOW Statement," *Open Forum*, November 1, 2010, www.americanexpress.com/us/small-business/openforum/articles/part-ii-a-framework-for-building-your-wow-statement-bob-reichert/.

[7] Russell Grantham, "Online Upstarts Alter Lending Landscape," *Atlanta Journal Constitution*, March 4, 2016, www.myajc.com/news/business/online-upstarts-alter-lending-landscape/nqcjK/; Ami Kassar, personal communication, May 23, 2012.

[8] Matt Cooper, "Bootstrapping Lessons from a Startup Disaster," *Inc.*, November 26, 2013, www.inc.com/matt-cooper/what-my-startup-disaster-taught-me-about-bootstrapping.html.

[9] Guy Kawasaki, *The Art of the Start* (New York: Penguin, 2004), p. 130.

[10] Gary Marshall, "The Story of Fitbit: How a Wooden Box Became a $4 Billion Company," *Wearable*, December 30, 2015, www.wareable.com/fitbit/youre-fitbit-and-you-know-it-how-a-wooden-box-became-a-dollar-4-billion-company; Jennifer Wang, "How Fitbit Is Cashing in on the High-Tech Fitness Trend," *Entrepreneur*, July 27, 2012, www.entrepreneur.com/article/223780.

[11] Michael V. Copeland, "How to Make Your Business Plan the Perfect Pitch," *Business 2.0*, September 2005, p. 88.

[12] William Sahlman, "How to Write a Great Business Plan," *Harvard Business Review*, July 1997, p. 105.

[13] Guy Kawasaki, "The 10/20/30 Rule of PowerPoint," *How to Change the World*, December 20, 2005, http://blog.guykawasaki.com/2005/12/the_102030_rule.html#axzz1vnw0foX3.

[14] Paul Chaney, "For SVP, Painful Business Lessons Lead to Entrepreneurial Success," *Small Business Trends*, June 2, 2016, http://smallbiztrends.com/2016/06/scott-martineau.html; Clate Mask, "Invest in Your Success: Strategic Planning for Small Business," *Small Business Trends*, August 9, 2013, https://smallbiztrends.com/2013/08/strategic-planning-small-business.html.

[15] Laura Heller, "Abt Electronics Defies Odds to Succeed and Be a Best Place to Work," *Forbes*, January 27, 2016, www.forbes

.com/sites/lauraheller/2016/01/27/abt-electronics-defies-odds-to-succeed-and-be-a-best-place-to-work/#57a21adb79f3; Stephanie Clifford, "Retailers Scramble to Adapt to Changing Market," *New York Times*, June 18, 2012, www.nytimes.com/2012/06/19/business/electronics-stores-struggle-to-adapt-to-changing-market.html.

[16]Alvin Toffler, "Shocking Truths About the Future," *Journal of Business Strategy*, July/August 1996, p. 6.

[17]Eduardo Bueno, Carlos Merino, and Cecilia Murcia, "Intellectual Capital as a Strategic Model to Create Innovation in New Technology Based Firms." In *Competitive Strategies for Small and Medium Enterprises* (New York: Springer International Publishing, 2016), pp. 93–105.

[18]Thomas A. Stewart, "You Think Your Company's So Smart? Prove It," *Fortune*, April 30, 2001, p. 188.

[19]Geoff Colvin, "Why Every Aspect of Your Business Is About to Change," *Fortune*, October 22, 2015, http://fortune.com/2015/10/22/the-21st-century-corporation-new-business-models/.

[20]Gary Hamel, "Innovation's New Math," *Fortune*, July 9, 2001, p. 130.

[21]Lou Carlozo, "It's the Moment of Truth for Fitbit, Whole Foods and Twitter (FIT WFM TWTR)," *US News*, August 11, 2016, http://money.usnews.com/investing/articles/2016-08-11/its-the-moment-of-truth-for-fitbit-whole-foods-and-twitter-fit-wfm-twtr.

[22]Carly Okyle, "5 Amazing Inventions That Are Helping the Visually Impaired," *Inc.*, April 27, 2015, www.entrepreneur.com/slideshow/245443; Deepali Gupta, "Indian duo Krispian Lawrence and Anirudh Sharma Launch Smart Shoes with Bluetooth Connectivity," *Economic Times*, March 20, 2014, http://articles.economictimes.indiatimes.com/2014-03-20/news/48401898_1_shoe-device-5-crore.

[23]"Who Are We?" Zoots, www.zoots.com/aboutWhoWeAre.aspx.

[24]Lisa Jennings, "Noodles & Company to Streamline Menu, Slow Unit Growth," *Restaurant News*, August 5, 2016, http://nrn.com/fast-casual/noodles-company-plans-streamline-menu-slow-unit-growth; Austin Wentzlaff, "Noodles & Company: Proven Leadership, Track Record of Growth, and Accelerating Expansion," *Seeking Alpha*, December, 30, 2013, http://seekingalpha.com/article/1920841-noodles-andcompany-proven-leadership-track-record-of-growthand-accelerating-expansion; Jeff Haden, "The Key to Noodles & Company's Explosive Growth," *Inc.*, September 19, 2012, www.inc.com/jeff-haden/noodles-and-company-bucksfranchise-model-for-growth.html.

[25]Anahad O'Connor, "Sweetgreen Makes Healthful Fast Food—But Can You Afford It?" *New York Times*, July 26, 2016, http://well.blogs.nytimes.com/2016/07/26/sweetgreen-makes-healthful-fast-food-but-can-you-afford-it/?_r=0; Peter Elliot, "How Three Grads Turned Sweetgreen into a $95 Million VC Darling," *Bloomberg*, October 12, 2015, www.bloomberg.com/news/articles/2015-10-12/how-salad-chain-sweetgreen-became-a-95-million-vc-success; "Our Story," Sweetgreen, n.d., www.sweetgreen.com/our-story/.

[26]Ken Blanchard, "The New Bottom Line," *Entrepreneur*, February 1998, p. 127.

[27]Jim Brett, "How to Write a Million-Dollar Mission Statement," *Inc.*, May 27, 2016, www.inc.com/magazine/201606/jim-brett/finding-your-companys-vision.html.

[28]"About Us," Bongo World, n.d., www.bongojava.com/about-bongo/.

[29]"Our Story: About Us," Ministry of Supply, n.d., www.ministryofsupply.com/pages/new-our-story.

[30]"Our Story and Mission," Putney, Inc., n.d., http://putneyvet.com/about/mission.

[31]"Nisolo," Back Down South, October 2012, www.backdownsouth.com/2012/10/nisolo/.

[32]"Home," PKClean, n.d., www.pkclean.com.

[33]Molly Reynolds, "Sandwiches with a Side of Technology," *Inc.*, July 16, 2016, www.inc.com/molly-reynolds/sandwiches-with-a-side-of-technology.html.

[34]Brooke Fox, "WWE Gets Streaming Boost as Wrestling Fans Subscribe," *Bloomberg*, July 28, 2016, www.bloomberg.com/news/articles/2016-07-28/wwe-gets-boost-from-streaming-as-more-wrestling-fans-subscribe; Jonathan Keane, "WWE Network to Launch Online with Surprising New Business Model," *Motley Fool*, January 9, 2014, www.fool.com/investing/general/2014/01/09/wwe-network-to-launch-online-withsurprising-new-b.aspx; "Groundbreaking WWE Network to Launch Feb. 24," *Miami Herald*, January 9, 2014, www.miamiherald.com/2014/01/08/3859962/groundbreaking-wwe-network-to.html.

[35]Joe Carmichael, "Landlines Will Disappear Before 2030 Because Economics," *Inverse*, December 29, 2015, www.inverse.com/article/9682-landlines-will-disappear-before-2030-because-economics; Will Dalton, "New Tech Could Bring Demise of Landline Telephones Within 5 Years," *IT Pro Portal*, August 30, 2012, www.itproportal.com/2012/08/30/new-tech-could-bring-demise-of-landline-telephoneswithin-5-years/; Stacey Higginbotham, "Over Half of American Homes Don't Have or Use Their Landline," *Gigaom*, December 26, 2012, http://gigaom.com/2012/12/26/over-half-of-american-homes-dont-haveor-use-their-landline/; "Wireless and Landline Phones," ACA International, 2012, www.acainternational.org/products-wireless-and-landline-phones-6488.aspx.

[36]Jason Daley, "Waiter, Bring Me a Fresh Idea," *Entrepreneur*, March 2010, pp. 89–95.

[37]Monte Burke, "Five Guys Burgers: America's Fastest Growing Restaurant Chain," *Forbes*, July 18, 2012, www.forbes.com/sites/monteburke/2012/07/18/five-guys-burgers-americas-fastest-growing-restaurant-chain/; Rob Sachs, "High-End Burger Joints Raise the Stakes," *National Public Radio*, April 21, 2011, www.npr.org/2011/04/21/135569985/high-end-burger-joints-raise-the-stakes; Judy Kneiszel, "Blazing Onion," *QSR Magazine*, October 22, 2010, www.qsrmagazine.com/new-concepts/blazing-onion.

[38]Adriana Lopez, "How Regional Coffee Chains Are Competing with National Heavy Hitters Like Starbucks," *Forbes*, October 21, 2013, www.forbes.com/sites/adrianalopez/2013/10/21/how-regional-coffee-chains-are-competing-with-national-heavy-hitters-like-starbucks/#b95aad40d064.

[39]Carolyn Z. Lawrence, "Know Your Competition," *Business Start-ups*, April 1997, p. 51.

[40]Beth Kwon, "Toolbox: Staying Competitive," *FSB*, December 2002/January 2003, p. 89.

[41]Kevin Coyne and John Horne, "How Companies Respond to Competitors: A McKinsey Global Survey," *McKinsey Quarterly*, May 2008, www.mckinsey.com/business-functions/strategy-and-corporate-finance/our-insights/how-companies-can-understand-competitors-moves-mckinsey-global-survey-results.

[42]Kirsten Osound, "Secret Agent Plan," *Entrepreneur*, June 2005, p. 98.

[43]Brian Caulfield, "Know Your Enemy," *Business 2.0*, June 2004, pp. 89–90.

[44]Shari Caudron, "I Spy, You Spy," *IndustryWeek*, October 3, 1994, p. 36.

[45]Stephanie Gruner, "Spies Like Us," *Inc.*, August 1998, p. 45.

[46]Lewis Carroll, *Alice in Wonderland* (Mount Vernon, NY: Peter Pauper Press, 1937), pp. 78–79.

[47]Rhonda Abrams, "Set Sights on One Big New Goal for '05," *Business*, October 10, 2004, p. 7; Mark Henricks, "In the BHAG," *Entrepreneur*, August 1999, pp. 65–67.

[48]Christopher Redhage, personal communication, September 10, 2013.

[49]Joseph C. Picken and Gregory Dess, "The Seven Traps of Strategic Planning," *Inc.*, November 1996, p. 99.

[50]Meghan Casserly, "The Burger Business: How August Kitchen Is Carving a Niche in the Condiment Aisle," *Forbes*, July 3, 2013, www.forbes.com/sites/meghancasserly/2013/07/03/the-burger-businessshow-august-kitchen-is-carving-a-niche-in-thecondiment-aisle/.

[51]Michael E. Porter, *Competitive Strategy* (New York: Free Press, 1980), Chapter 2.

[52]Eric Stromgren, "New Retro Fitness Training Program Targets Boutique Consumers," *Club Industry*, June 14, 2016, http://clubindustry.com/profits/new-retro-fitness-training-program-targets-boutique-consumers; Beth Fitzgerald, "Retro Fitness and Its Frozen Yogurt Franchise Get New VP," *NJ Biz*, January 20, 2014, www.njbiz.com/article/20140120/NJBIZ01/140129979/Retro-Fitness-and-its-frozen-yogurt-franchise-getnew-real-estate-VP; "Popular New Jersey Fitness Chain Opens Its First Chicagoland Location," *Chicago Tribune*, January 26, 2014, www.chicagotribune.com/news/local/suburbs/lombard_villa_park/community/chi-ugc-article-popular-new-jersey-fitness-chainopens-its-fi-4-2014-01-16,0,5302477.story; Jeff Haden, "How Retro Prices Can Deliver Cutting-Edge Profits," *Inc.*, August 23, 2012, www.inc.com/jeff-haden/howretro-pricing-can-deliver-cutting-edge-profits.html.

[53]Brendan Coffey, "Every Penny Counts," *Forbes*, September 30, 2002, pp. 68–70; Pratik Thacker, "What Does Dollar General Have in Store for 2014?" *Motley Fool*, December 27, 2013, www.fool.com/investing/general/2013/12/27/what-does-dollar-general-havein-store-for-2014.aspx#.Usbb7Xk6LwJ; Naman Shukla, "Why You Should Sell Family Dollar and Dollar Tree to Buy This Dollar Store," *Seeking Alpha*, January 1, 2014, http://seekingalpha.com/article/1924051-whyyou-should-sell-family-dollar-and-dollar-tree-to-buythis-dollar-store?source=google_news; Mukesh Baghel, "Dollar General, Family Dollar Stores, and Dollar Tree Stores: Which One Should Be in Your Portfolio?" *Motley Fool*, December 28, 2013, www.fool.com/investing/general/2013/12/28/dollar-general-familydollar-stores-and-dollar-tre.aspx#.Usbe4nk6LwI; Ann Zimmerman, "Dollar General Lays Bet on Opening New Stores," *Wall Street Journal*, May 14, 2010, p. B8.

[54]Matt Thalman, "Dollar General and Dollar Tree Under Pressure as Economy Strengthens," *The Street*, August 26, 2016, www.thestreet.com/story/13686202/1/dollar-general-and-dollar-tree-under-pressure-as-economy-strengthens.html.

[55]Kate Silver, "Finally You Can Rent a Farm Animal," *Bloomberg*, August 17, 2016, www.bloomberg.com/news/articles/2016-08-17/finally-you-can-rent-a-farm-animal; Kate Silver, "Which came first? Rent-A-Chicken or the eggs?" *Crains*, May 26, 2016, www.chicagobusiness.com/article/20160526/NEWS07/160529877/which-came-first-rent-a-chicken-or-the-eggs; Kathleen Davis, "From Chickens to Caskets—8 Unique Rental Businesses: Chickens," *Entrepreneur*, October 25, 2013, www.entrepreneur.com/slideshow/229509; Katherine Martinko, "Abandoned Animals Find Solace and Comfort in This NY Sanctuary," *Treehugger*, January 3, 2014, www.treehugger.com/culture/abandoned-animals-find-solace-and-comfort-nysanctuary.html.

[56]Debra Phillips, "Leaders of the Pack," *Entrepreneur*, September 1996, p. 127.

[57]Anderson, Chris. *The Long Tail: Why the Future of Business Is Selling Less of More* (New York: Hyperion Books, 2008).

[58]Himanshu Sareen, "The 6 Best Ecommerce Platforms for Small Businesses," *Entrepreneur*, January 18, 2016, www.entrepreneur.com/article/254103.

[59]Jennifer Neufeld, "I Do Now I Don't, a Website Sprouted from Heartbreak Expands," *Observer*, January 19, 2015, http://observer.com/2015/01/i-do-now-i-dont-a-website-sprouted-from-heartbreak-expands/; "Small to Big: I Do Now I Don't," *Bloomberg*, February 5, 2015, www.bloomberg.com/news/articles/2015-02-05/small-to-big-i-do-now-i-don-t; "Couldn't Believe My Eyes," I Do Now I Don't, n.d., www.idonowidont.com/I-do-founder-josh-oppermanstory; Michelle Juergen, "How a Breakup Led to an Online Marketplace for Used Engagement Rings," *Entrepreneur*, April 13, 2013, www.entrepreneur.com/article/225750.

[60]Michelle Bitoun, "Show Them the Data," *Trustee*, September 2002, p. 35.

[61]Oscar Williams-Grut, "One of London's trendiest coffee chains wants customers to give it £1.5 million," *Business Insider*, June 14, 2015, www.businessinsider.com/hip-london-coffee-chain-grind-launches-15-million-crowdfunding-drive-2015-6?r=UK&IR=T; "Geckoboard Helps Shoreditch Grind Monitor Business Health to Determine Direction of Growth," Geckoboard, n.d., www.geckoboard.com/learn/case-studies/shoreditch-grind/#.V8M5fZMrI_U.

[62]Jill Andresky Fraser, "Who Can Help Out with a Business Plan?" *Inc.*, June 1999, p. 115.

6 Forms of Business Ownership

Monkey Business Images/Shutterstock

Learning Objectives

On completion of this chapter, you will be able to:

1. Explain the advantages and disadvantages of sole proprietorships and partnerships.

2. Describe the similarities and differences between C corporations and S corporations.

3. Understand the characteristics of a limited liability company.

4. Explain the process of creating a legal entity for a business.

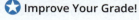

MyLab Entrepreneurship

⭐ **Improve Your Grade!**

If your instructor is using MyLab Entrepreneurship, visit **www.pearson.com/mylab/entrepreneurship** for videos, simulations, and writing exercises.

When an entrepreneur makes the decision to launch a business, one of the first issues he or she faces is choosing a form of ownership. Too often, entrepreneurs invest insufficient time and effort in evaluating the impact that the various forms of ownership will have on them and on their businesses. They simply select a form of ownership by default or choose the form that appears to be most popular at the time. Choosing a form of ownership is a decision that has far-reaching effects for both the entrepreneur and the business. Although the decision is not irreversible, changing from one ownership form to another can be difficult, time-consuming, complicated, and expensive. In many instances, switching an existing business from one form of ownership to another can trigger onerous tax consequences for the owners. Therefore, it is important for entrepreneurs to get it right the first time.

There is no one "best" form of ownership. The form of ownership that is best for one entrepreneur may not be suitable for another. Choosing the "right" form of ownership means that entrepreneurs must understand the characteristics of each form and how well those characteristics match their business and personal circumstances. Only then can they make an informed decision about a form of ownership. One attorney advises that entrepreneurs choose a structure that offers them protection, while being only as complex as their business really needs.[1] The following are some of the most important issues entrepreneurs should consider when they are evaluating the various forms of ownership:

Tax considerations. The amount of net income an entrepreneur expects the business to generate and the tax bill the owner incurs are important factors when choosing a form of ownership. The graduated tax rates that apply to each form of ownership, the government's constant tinkering with the tax code, and the year-to-year fluctuations in a company's income make some forms of ownership more attractive than others.

Liability exposure. Certain forms of ownership offer business owners greater protection from personal liability that might result from financial problems, faulty products, lawsuits, and a host of other difficulties. Entrepreneurs must decide the extent to which they are willing to assume personal responsibility for their companies' financial obligations. Two entrepreneurs who started a company with a portable climbing wall formed a limited liability company to limit their personal liability exposure because of the high-risk nature of their business.

Start-up and future capital requirements. Forms of ownership differ in their ability to raise start-up capital. Depending on how much capital an entrepreneur needs and where he or she plans to get it, some forms are superior to others. In addition, as a business grows, so does its appetite for capital, and some forms of ownership make it easier to attract external growth capital than others.

Control. By choosing certain forms of ownership, an entrepreneur automatically gives up some control over the company. Entrepreneurs must decide early on how much control they are willing to sacrifice in exchange for help from other people to build a successful business.

Managerial ability. Entrepreneurs must assess their skills and abilities to manage a business effectively. If they lack ability or experience in key areas, they may need a form of ownership that allows them to bring in other owners who can provide the necessary skills for the company to succeed.

Business goals. How big and how profitable an entrepreneur plans for the business to become influences the form of ownership chosen. Businesses often switch forms of ownership as they grow, but moving from some formats to others can be extremely complex and expensive.

Management succession plans. When choosing a form of ownership, business owners must look ahead to the day when they will pass their companies on to the next generation or to a buyer. Some forms of ownership make this transition much easier than others.

Cost of formation. Creating some forms of ownership is much more costly and involved than creating other forms. Entrepreneurs must carefully weigh the benefits and the costs of the particular form they choose.

When it comes to organizing their businesses, entrepreneurs have a wide choice of forms of ownership, including sole proprietorship, general partnership, limited partnership, corporation, S corporation, and limited liability company. Figure 6.1 provides a breakdown of these forms of

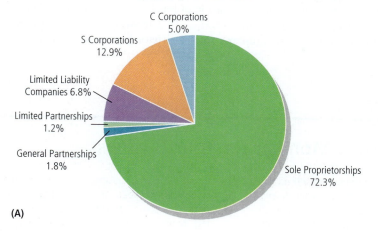

Percentage of Businesses

(A)

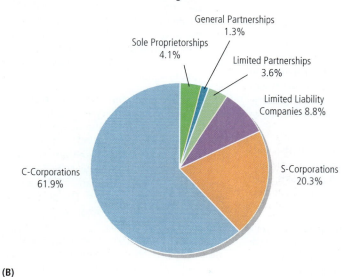

Percentage of Sales

(B)

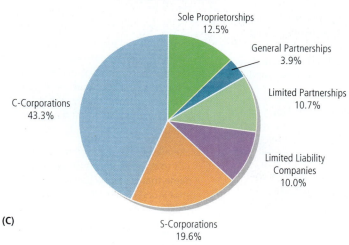

Percentage of Net Income

(C)

FIGURE 6.1

Forms of Business Ownership: (a) Percentage of Businesses, (B) Percentage of Sales, and (c) Percentage of Net Income

Source: Based on data from *Sources of Income*, Internal Revenue Service.

ownership. Notice that sole proprietorships account for the greatest percentage of businesses, but corporations generate the largest portion of business sales and net income. This chapter discusses the key features of these various forms of ownership, beginning with the three most basic forms (from simplest to most complex): sole proprietorship, partnership, and corporation.

 Hands On . . . How To

Come Up with the Perfect Moniker for Your Business

Lorde is best known as a singer and songwriter, but would she still sell out concerts if she performed under the name Ella Marija Lani Yelich-O'Conner, her real name? Perhaps. However, Lorde's stage name is an important part of her brand and her marketing success. Similarly, choosing the right name for a company can enhance its success by creating the proper image and telling customers what it does. A good business name should do the following:

- Reinforce the company's brand positioning. A good name communicates to potential customers something about the brand's personality. For example, Twitter conjures up images of a flock of birds twittering in a tree or excitement over some event ("all atwitter"), both of which reinforce the company's purpose: allowing users to share short bursts of information.

- Resonate with the company's target audience. PayPal puts a warm and friendly image on a product that simply aids financial transactions on the web. This image helps build trust and confidence among the businesses and customers who make payments over the Internet.

- Suggest to customers what your company does. The name Under Armour suggests that the company's sportswear products protect the person wearing them and conveys an image of strength, which is very appealing to its target market of people who are active and physically fit.

- Be clever and differentiate your company from its competitors. For example, Cash 22 (pawn broker), Sherlock Homes (locksmith), Planet of the Grapes (wine store), Florist Gump (flower shop), Curl Up & Dye (hair salon), Character Eyes (optometrist), and The Cod Father (seafood restaurant) are examples of small business names that are clever and memorable.

- Be short, fun, attention getting, and memorable. Not only is Google fun to say, it is also quite memorable. Naming experts say a great name has "emotional hang time," a football metaphor to describe a name that stays in your mind.

- Be easy to spell and pronounce. This is especially important for companies that operate solely online because their names often serve as the URLs for their Web sites. "Wikipedia" works, but "Eefoof," a failed video-sharing site, did not.

- Grow with your business. When choosing a name, it is a good idea to keep an eye on the future. Many entrepreneurs select names for their businesses that can be limiting as their companies grow beyond their existing product lines, geographic areas, and target markets. CompUSA and Best Buy both competed in the same basic market—home electronics. Unfortunately for CompUSA, its brand communicated that it sold only computers (which it did not), while the Best Buy brand communicated its basic value proposition. CompUSA went out of business in 2007, and Best Buy has become the largest consumer electronics retailer in the United States.

Choosing a memorable name can be one of the most fun—and most challenging—aspects of starting a business. It also is an extremely important task because it has long-term implications; the name is the single most visible attribute of a company, and it has the capacity to either engage or repel customers. The business name is the first connection that many customers will have with a company, and it should create an appropriate image in their minds. The president of one small design firm specializing in branding says a company name is the cornerstone for branding. If done properly, a company's name portrays the business's personality, stands out in a crowd, and sticks in the minds of consumers. Large companies may spend hundreds of thousands of dollars in their search for just the right name. Although entrepreneurs don't have the resources to enable them to spend that kind of money finding the ideal name, they can use the following process to come up with the perfect name for a business:

1. Decide on the image you want your company to project to customers, suppliers, bankers, the press, the community, and others. Do you want to create an air of sophistication, the suggestion of a bargain, a sense of adventure, the implication of trustworthiness and dependability, or a spirit of fun and whimsy? The right name can go a long way toward communicating the desired image for a company.

2. Make a list of your competitors' business names. The idea is *not* to borrow from their ideas but to try to come up with a name that is unique. Do you notice any trends among competitors' names? What are the similarities? What are the differences?

3. Work with a group of the most creative people you know to brainstorm potential names for your business. One

(continued)

Hands On . . . How To

entrepreneur called on 10 customers and 10 vendors to help him come up with a business name. Don't worry about quality at this point; the goal is to generate a large quantity of names—at least 100 potential names, if possible. Having a dictionary, a thesaurus, a rhyming dictionary, and samples (or graphics) of your company's products and services help stimulate creativity. Consider names from unrelated sources that might be meaningful.

4. After allowing them to percolate for a few days, evaluate the names generated in the brainstorming session. Narrow the list of choices to 10 or so names with the greatest potential. Print each name in a large font on a single page and look at them all. Which ones are visually appealing? Which ones lend themselves to being paired with a clever logo?

5. Reassemble your creative group, present each name you have printed, and discuss its merits and challenges. Having a designated person to record the group's comments helps. The group may come to a consensus on a preferred name; if not, you can use a round-by-round voting process to move the group toward a consensus.

6. Conduct a search at the U.S. Patent and Trademark Office Web site (www.uspto.gov) to see whether the leading names on your list are already registered trademarks for existing businesses. Remember, however, that the same name can be registered as a trademark as long as there is no overlap in the companies' products, services, or businesses.

7. Conduct searches with domain name companies, such as GoDaddy.com, to see whether other businesses are using your desired business name as a domain name. When the founders of Emma, an e-mail marketing firm, searched for the availability of emma.com, they found that the name was already taken. They chose, instead, the domain myemma.com but kept the name Emma for the business. Several years later, this resulted in a legal dispute with the company that owned the emma.com domain name.

8. Conduct an online search to see whether other businesses conducting business within your intended market have the same or very similar names.

9. Make your choice. Including input from others is useful when selecting a business name, but the final choice is yours.

10. Register your company name with the U.S. Patent and Trademark Office. Doing so gives you maximum protection against others using the name you worked so hard to create. Diane Dassow thought she had the ideal name for her personal history and memoir service business in Lombard, Illinois: Bridging Generations. However, Dassow soon discovered a funeral home in Pennsylvania that was using

that name. She checked with the U.S. Patent and Trademark Office and learned that the funeral home had already registered "Bridging Generations." She changed the name of her company to Binding Legacies and registered it as a trademark to protect her business.

Other helpful tips for creating the ideal business name include the following:

- Look at your name from your potential customer's perspective. Do customers need reassurance (Gentle Dentistry), or do they prefer a bit of humor (Barking Lot Dog Grooming)? Other options include using a name that conveys to your customers an image that expresses your business strategy, such as Tires Now, Quality Muffler, or Pay-Less Auto Detailing.

- Decide the most appropriate quality of your business that you want to convey and incorporate it into your business name. Avoid sending a mixed or inappropriate message. Avoid business names that might leave potential customers confused about what your business does. Remember that the company name will be displayed on all your advertising, packaging, and printed materials.

There are millions of names in the marketplace. Coming up with the one that is just right for your business can help greatly in creating a brand image for your business. Choosing a name that is distinctive, memorable, and positive can go a long way toward helping you achieve success in your business venture. Naming experts at Landor, an international branding firm, say a name "acts as the primary handle for a brand; it's a recall and recognition device, it communicates desired attributes or specific benefits, and, through time and consistent use, it becomes a valuable asset and intellectual property." What's in a name? Everything!

Sources: Based on Mark Henricks, "Choosing the Right Name for Your Business," *Business News Daily*, March 2, 2016, www.businessnewsdaily.com/8829-choosing-business-name.html; Denise Lee Yohn, "How to Name Your Concept (and Do It Right)," *QSR*, March 10, 2011, www.qsrmagazine.com/denise-lee-yohn/how-name-your-concept-and-do-it-right; Emily Maltby, "And Now, the Tricky Part: Naming Your Business," *Wall Street Journal*, http://online.wsj.com/article/SB10001424052748704103904575336942902327092.html; Jeff Wysaki, "22 Extremely Clever Business Names," *Pleated Jeans*, January 30, 2015, www.pleated-jeans.com/2015/01/30/clever-business-names/; Laurel Sutton, "10 Best and Worst Internet Company Names of the Decade," *Marketing Profs*, December 29, 2009, www.marketingprofs.com/articles/2009/3278/10-best-and-worst-internet-company-names-of-the-decade; Scott Trimble, "18 Strategies and Tools for Naming Your Business or Product," *Marketing Profs*, January 24, 2008, www.marketingprofs.com/login/join.asp?adref=rdblk&source=%2F8%2Fhow%2Dto%2Dname%2Dproducts%2Dcompanies%2Dtrimble%2Easp; Alex Frankel, "The New Science of Naming," *Business 2.0*, December 2004, pp. 53–55; Jeff Wuorio, "'Oedipus Wrecks' and Other Business Names to Avoid," *bCentral*, www.bCentral.com/articles/wuorio/153.asp; Suzanne Barlyn, "Name That Firm," *Wall Street Journal*, March 17, 2008, p. R7; "14 Clever Business Names You Just Want to Take Your Money," *WildAmmo*, October 12, 2013, http://wildammo.com/2013/10/12/14-clever-business-names-you-just-want-to-take-your-money/; "The Worst (and Best) Company Name Changes," *CNNMoney*, December 6, 2013, http://money.cnn.com/gallery/leadership/2013/12/06/worst-best-corporate-name-changes.fortune/2.html; Darren Dahl, "The Best (and Worst) Business Names," *AOL Small Business*, May 5, 2010, http://smallbusiness.aol.com/2010/05/10/the-best-and-worst-business-names/.

LO1

Explain the advantages and disadvantages of sole proprietorships and partnerships.

sole proprietorship
a business owned and managed by one individual.

Sole Proprietorships and Partnerships

Sole Proprietorships

The simplest and most popular form of ownership remains the **sole proprietorship**. A sole proprietorship, as its name implies, is a business owned and managed by one individual. Sole proprietorships make up 72 percent of all businesses in the United States.[2]

Advantages of Sole Proprietorships

SIMPLE TO CREATE One of the most attractive features of a proprietorship is how fast and simple it is to begin. If an entrepreneur wants to operate a business under his or her own name (e.g., Strossner's Bakery), he or she simply obtains the necessary licenses from state, county, and/or local governments and begins operation. Entrepreneurs who operate a business under a trade name usually must file a certificate of trade name (or fictitious business name statement) with the secretary of state. Filing this statement notifies the public of the identity of the person behind the business. For most entrepreneurs, it is possible to start a proprietorship in a single day.

LEAST COSTLY FORM OF OWNERSHIP TO BEGIN In addition to being easy to begin, a proprietorship is generally the least expensive form of ownership to establish. There is no need to create and file legal documents that are recommended for partnerships and required for corporations. An entrepreneur simply goes to the city or county government, states the nature of the business he or she will start, and purchases the necessary business licenses. Businesses with employees (including sole proprietorships) must obtain from the Internal Revenue Service (IRS) (at no charge) an employer identification number, a nine-digit number that serves as the equivalent of a business Social Security number. In addition, companies that have employees may be required to register with the state labor department that administers the unemployment insurance and the workers' compensation programs. Businesses that sell goods or services must obtain a state sales tax license from the state tax office that allows them to collect sales tax from their customers and pass it on to the state department of revenue.

PROFIT INCENTIVE One major advantage of proprietorships is that once owners pay all of their companies' expenses, they can keep the remaining profits (less taxes, of course). The profit incentive is a powerful one, and profits represent an excellent way of "keeping score" in the game of business. Sole proprietors report the net income of their businesses within their personal tax form on Schedule C of IRS Form 1040, and the amount is taxed at the entrepreneur's personal tax rate. Because they are self-employed, sole proprietors' income from their business activities also is subject to the self-employment tax, which currently stands at 15.3 percent (12.4 percent for Social Security plus 2.9 percent for Medicare) of the proprietor's income. A ceiling on the Social Security portion of the self-employment tax does apply.

TOTAL DECISION-MAKING AUTHORITY Because the sole proprietor is in total control of operations, he or she can respond quickly to changes, which is an asset in a rapidly shifting market. The freedom to set the company's course of action is a major motivational force. For those who thrive on the challenge of seeking new opportunities in business, the freedom of fast, flexible decision making is vital. Many sole proprietors relish the feeling of control they have over their personal financial futures and the recognition they earn as the owners of their businesses.

NO SPECIAL LEGAL RESTRICTIONS The proprietorship is the least-regulated form of business ownership. In a time when government regulation seems never-ending, this feature has much merit.

EASY TO DISCONTINUE If an entrepreneur decides to discontinue operations, he or she can terminate the business quickly even though he or she will still be personally liable for any outstanding debts and obligations the business cannot pay.

Disadvantages of Sole Proprietorships

Entrepreneurs considering the sole proprietorship as a form of ownership must be aware of its disadvantages.

UNLIMITED PERSONAL LIABILITY Probably the greatest disadvantage of a sole proprietorship is the **unlimited personal liability** of the owner, meaning that the sole proprietor is personally liable for all of the business's debts. In a proprietorship, the owner *is* the business. He or she owns all of the business's assets, and if the business fails, creditors can force the sale of these assets to cover its debts. If unpaid business debts remain, creditors can also force the sale of the proprietor's *personal* assets to recover payment. In short, the *company's* debts are the *owner's* debts. Laws vary from one state to another, but most states require creditors to leave the failed business owner a minimum amount of equity in a home, a car, and some personal items. The reality is that failure of a business can ruin a sole proprietor financially.

unlimited personal liability
a situation in which the owner of a business is personally liable for all of the business's debts.

Courtesy of Larry Kim, WordStream Inc.

ENTREPRENEURIAL PROFILE: Larry Kim: WordStream Larry Kim launched WordStream, a keyword software development tool for Web-based marketing, in 2007 as a sole proprietorship. Kim said that early on, he treated the business as if it were his own personal bank account. After paying for business expenses, Kim kept the rest of the money he made for his own personal expenses. He eventually realized that to grow his business, he needed to leave some funds in the business and pay himself a lower salary. He changed WordStream from a sole proprietorship into a corporation, which allowed him both to invest profits back into the company and to bring on growth investment capital. As a corporation, WordStream raised $28 million in equity financing from venture capital firms and more than $400,000 in debt financing. The investments into the business began to pay off as the company grew. *Inc.* magazine recognized WordStream as one of the fastest-growing small businesses for four consecutive years. WordStream has evolved from a sole proprietorship into a full-service paid search marketing corporation with more than 100 employees.[3] ∎

LIMITED SKILLS AND CAPABILITIES A sole proprietor has total decision-making authority, but that does not mean that he or she has the range of skills that running a successful business requires. Each of us has areas in which our education, training, and work experiences have taught us a great deal, yet there are other areas in which our decision-making ability is weak. Many business failures occur because owners lack the skills, knowledge, and experience in areas that are vital to business success. Owners tend to push aside problems they don't understand or don't feel comfortable with in favor of those they can solve more easily. Unfortunately, the problems they set aside seldom solve themselves. By the time an owner decides to ask for help in addressing these problems, it may be too late to save the company.

FEELINGS OF ISOLATION Running a business alone allows an entrepreneur maximum flexibility, but it also creates feelings of isolation; there is no one else to turn to for help when solving problems or getting feedback on a new idea. Most sole proprietors admit that there are times when they feel the pressure of being alone and completely responsible for every major business decision.

LIMITED ACCESS TO CAPITAL If a business is to grow and expand, a sole proprietor often needs additional financial resources. However, many proprietors have already put all of the resources they have into their businesses and have used their personal assets as collateral to acquire loans, making it difficult to borrow additional funds. A sole proprietorship is limited to whatever capital the owner can contribute and whatever money he or she can borrow. In short, proprietors find it difficult to raise additional money and maintain sole ownership. Most banks and other lending institutions have well-defined formulas for determining borrowers' eligibility. Unfortunately, many sole proprietors cannot meet those borrowing requirements, especially in the early days of the business.

LACK OF CONTINUITY OF THE BUSINESS Lack of continuity is inherent in a sole proprietorship. If the proprietor dies, retires, or becomes incapacitated, the business automatically terminates. Unless a family member or an employee can take over (which means that person is now a sole proprietor), the business will disappear. Because people look for secure employment and an opportunity for advancement, proprietorships often have trouble recruiting and retaining good employees. If no one is willing to step in to run the business in the founder's absence, creditors can petition the courts to liquidate the assets of the dissolved business to pay outstanding debts.

Some entrepreneurs find that forming partnerships is one way to overcome the disadvantages of the sole proprietorship. For instance, when one person lacks specific managerial skills or has insufficient access to needed capital, he or she can compensate for these weaknesses by forming a partnership with someone with complementary management skills or money to invest. In fact, businesses that have multiple owners (not necessarily partners) are more likely to be larger and to survive longer than sole proprietorships.[4]

Partnerships

partnership

an association of two or more people who co-own a business for the purpose of making a profit.

A **partnership** is an association of two or more people who co-own a business for the purpose of making a profit. In a partnership, the co-owners (partners) share the business's assets, liabilities, and profits according to the terms of a previously established partnership agreement (if one exists).

Courtesy of Wichcraft

ENTREPRENEURIAL PROFILE: Tom Colicchio, Jeffrey Zurofsky, and Sisha Ortuzar: 'wichcraft Tom Colicchio, Jeffrey Zurofsky, and Sisha Ortuzar cofounded the first 'wichcraft sandwich shop in New York City in 2003. Colicchio, chef/owner of Craft restaurant, celebrity chef, documentary producer, and former chef/partner of Gramercy Tavern in New York, has also been head judge on the reality television show *Top Chef*. Before going into business together to launch 'wichcraft, the three partners had worked together in several fine-dining restaurants, which formed the basis for 'wichcraft's culinary roots in sourcing, production, and service. 'wichcraft sources seasonal ingredients from local farms and was an early practitioner of the farm-to-table movement. At its peak, 'wichcraft grew to 15 locations in New York, San Francisco, and Las Vegas. However, the company's rapid growth resulted in several underperforming stores. After closing the underperforming stores and upgrading the design of the remaining stores, the company's performance improved significantly.[5] ∎

The law does not require a partnership agreement (also known as the articles of partnership), but it is wise for partners to work with an attorney to develop an agreement that spells out exactly the status and responsibility of each partner. All too often, the parties *think* they know what they are agreeing to, only to find later that no real meeting of the minds took place. This can lead to everything from dysfunctional conflict that gets in the way of the partnership's day-to-day operations all the way to litigation that rips apart the partnership. A **partnership agreement** is a document that states in writing the terms under which the partners agree to operate the partnership and that protects each partner's interest in the business. Every partnership should be based on a written agreement. A partnership agreement helps focus the entrepreneurial energy of business partners on growing their business rather than squabbling about how to manage the partnership. A sound written agreement helps guide the partners through inevitable bumps in the road that every business partnership experiences from time to time. The best time to write a partnership agreement is *before* the business

partnership agreement

a document that states in writing the terms under which partners agree to operate a partnership and that protects each partner's interest in the business.

begins operations, while everyone is still friendly, and there is nothing tangible to argue over. If partners wait until the business is fully operational to create a partnership agreement, it is more likely to lead to conflict and disagreements between the partners. Partnership agreements should be updated from time to time to reflect changes in the business and in the partners' roles, responsibilities, and contributions to the business.

When no partnership agreement exists, the Revised Uniform Partnership Act (RUPA) governs a partnership. If a partnership agreement contains gaps in its coverage, the act fills them. The RUPA codifies the body of law dealing with partnerships in the United States. Under the RUPA, the three key elements of any partnership are common ownership interest in a business, agreement on how the business's profits and losses will be shared, and the right to participate in managing the operation of the partnership. Under the act, each partner has the *right* to do the following:

- Participate in the management and operations of the business
- Share in any profits the business might earn from operations

- Receive interest on loans made to the business

- Be compensated for expenses incurred in the name of the partnership

- Receive his or her original capital contributions if the partnership terminates

- Have access to the business's books and records

- Receive a formal accounting of the partnership's business affairs

The RUPA also sets forth the partners' general obligations. Each partner is *obligated* to do the following:

- Share in any losses sustained by the business

- Work for the partnership without salary

- Submit differences that may arise in the conduct of the business to majority vote or arbitration

- Give the other partners complete information about all business affairs

- Give a formal accounting of the partnership's business affairs

- Live up to a fiduciary responsibility of the partnership and place the interest of the partnership above his or her personal interests

However, the provisions of RUPA may not be as favorable as a specific agreement hammered out among the partners. Creating a partnership agreement is not necessarily costly. In most cases, the partners can discuss their preferences for each of the provisions in advance. Once they have reached an agreement, an attorney can draft the formal document. Bankers often want to see a copy of a partnership agreement before lending money to a partnership. Perhaps the most important feature of the partnership agreement is that it resolves potential sources of conflict that, if not addressed in advance, could later result in partnership battles and the dissolution of an otherwise successful business. Spelling out details—especially sticky ones such as profit splits, contributions, workloads, decision-making authority, dispute resolution, dissolution, and others—in a written agreement at the outset helps avoid damaging tension in a partnership that could lead to a business "divorce." Business divorces, like marital ones, are almost always costly and unpleasant for everyone involved.

David Gage, a partnership mediator, suggests that partners also create a "partnership charter," a document that serves as a guide for running the partnership and dealing with each other as business partners. Whereas a partnership agreement addresses the legal and business issues of running a business, a partnership charter covers the interpersonal aspects of the partners' relationships and serves as a helpful tool in managing the complexity of partnership relations.[6] Even with a partnership charter and a partnership agreement, a partnership must have three more essential elements above all others: mutual trust, respect, and open communication. Any partnership missing even one of these elements is destined to fail.

Advantages of Partnerships

EASY TO ESTABLISH Like a proprietorship, a partnership is easy and inexpensive to establish. The owners must obtain the necessary business licenses and submit a minimal number of forms. In most states, partners must file a certificate for conducting business as partners if the business is run under a trade name.

COMPLEMENTARY SKILLS In a sole proprietorship, the owner must wear lots of different hats, and not all of them will fit well. In successful partnerships, the parties' skills and abilities usually complement one another, strengthening the company's managerial foundation. A common need for many entrepreneurs today is the need for partners with technical skills. Many new businesses have strong Web-based components or are app-based business models. If an entrepreneur lacks the requisite technical skills, bringing in a "tech partner" who can handle the technical elements of the business may be necessary.

DIVISION OF PROFITS There are no restrictions on how partners distribute the company's profits, as long as they are consistent with the partnership agreement and do not violate the rights of any partner. The partnership agreement should articulate each partner's contribution to the business and his or her share of the profits. If the partners fail to create an agreement, the RUPA says the partners share equally in the partnership's profits, even if their original capital contributions were unequal.

LARGER POOL OF CAPITAL The partnership form of ownership can significantly broaden the pool of capital available to a business. Each partner's asset base enhances the business's pool of capital and improves its ability to borrow needed funds; together, partners' personal assets provide a larger capital base and support greater borrowing capacity.

ABILITY TO ATTRACT LIMITED PARTNERS When partners share in owning, operating, and managing a business, they are **general partners**. General partners have unlimited liability for the partnership's debts and usually take an active role in managing the business. Every partnership must have at least one general partner, although there is no limit on the number of general partners a business can have.

Limited partners are financial investors in a partnership, cannot participate in the day-to-day management of a company, and have limited liability for the partnership's debts. If the business fails, they lose only what they have invested in it and no more. A limited partnership can attract investors by offering them limited liability and the potential to realize a substantial return on their investments if the business is successful. Many individuals find it very profitable to invest in high-potential small businesses—but only if they avoid the disadvantages of unlimited liability while doing so. If limited partners are "materially and actively" engaged in a business (defined as spending more than 500 hours per year in the company) or if they hold themselves out as general partners, they will be treated as general partners and will lose their limited liability protection. Two types of limited partners are silent partners and dormant partners. **Silent partners** are not active in a business but generally are known to be members of the partnership. **Dormant partners** are neither active nor generally known to be associated with the business.

A **limited partnership** is composed of at least one general partner and at least one limited partner. There is no limit on the total number of limited partners. In a limited partnership, the general partner is treated, under the law, the same as in a general partnership. Limited partners are treated as investors in the business venture, and they have limited liability for the partnership's debts. They can lose only the amount they have invested in the business. Because of this advantage, limited partnerships own many professional sports teams, including the Miami Heat, Chicago Bulls, and Minnesota Timberwolves of the National Basketball Association (NBA).

Forming a limited partnership requires its founders to file a certificate of limited partnership with the secretary of state's office. A limited partnership must include "limited partnership," "L.P.," or "LP" in its business name.

The limited partner does not have the right to engage actively in managing the business. In fact, limited partners who take an active part in managing the business (more than 500 hours per year) forfeit their limited liability status and are treated just like general partners. Limited partners can, however, make management suggestions to the general partners, inspect the business, and make copies of business records. A limited partner is, of course, entitled to a share of the business's profits, as specified in the certificate of limited partnership. The primary disadvantage of limited partnerships is the complexity and cost of establishing and maintaining them.

ENTREPRENEURIAL PROFILE: Casey Carter, Taylor Hunt, and James Dean: CryptPro Casey Carter, an Internet programmer, wanted to share some code with Taylor Hunt, with whom he was collaborating on a project. However, Carter wanted to protect the code and ensure that it not be shared with anyone else. Carter and Hunt joined with James Dean, an art director at a logo development company, to form a limited partnership called CryptPro to develop the code into a marketable product. Through the limited partnership, the partners developed the code into a secure messaging system that allows two parties to exchange messages over a secure network. Their plan was to allow users to send a small number of secure messages for free but to charge heavier users a monthly subscription fee.[7] ∎

general partners
partners who have unlimited liability for the partnership's debts and usually take an active role in managing the business.

limited partners
partners who are financial investors in a partnership, cannot participate in the day-to-day management of a company, and have limited liability for the partnership's debts.

silent partners
partners who are not active in a business but generally are known to be members of the partnership.

dormant partners
partners who are neither active nor generally known to be members of the partnership.

limited partnership
a partnership composed of at least one general partner and at least one limited partner.

Courtesy of US Logo, Inc and CryptPro, LLC

MINIMAL GOVERNMENT REGULATION Like sole proprietorships, partnerships are not burdened with excessive red tape.

FLEXIBILITY Although not as flexible as a sole proprietorship, a partnership can generally react quickly to changing market conditions because the partners can respond quickly and creatively to new opportunities. In large partnerships, however, getting partners' approval can slow a company's strategic actions. Unless the partnership agreement states otherwise, each partner has a single vote in the management of the company, no matter how large his or her contribution to the partnership.

TAXATION A partnership itself is not subject to federal taxation. It serves as a conduit for the profit or losses it earns or incurs; its net income or loss is passed through to the partners as personal income, and the partners pay income tax on their distributive shares at their individual tax rates. The partnership files an informational return, Form 1065, with the IRS that reports its net income for the tax year and the percentages of the business that each partner owns. The partnership provides each partner with a Schedule K-1, which shows his or her share of the partnership's net income (or loss). Partners must pay taxes on their respective shares of the partnership's net income, even if none of that income actually is distributed to them. A partnership, like a sole proprietorship, avoids the "double-taxation" disadvantage associated with the corporate form of ownership.

Disadvantages of Partnerships

Before entering into a partnership, every entrepreneur should double-check the decision to be sure that the prospective business partner will add value to the business. A partnership is like a business marriage, and before entering into one, an entrepreneur should be aware of the disadvantages.

UNLIMITED LIABILITY OF AT LEAST ONE PARTNER At least one member of every partnership must be a general partner. The general partner has unlimited personal liability for any debts that remain after the partnership's assets are exhausted. In addition, general partners' liability is *joint and several*, which means that creditors can hold all general partners equally responsible for the partnership's debts or can collect the entire debt from just one partner.

ENTREPRENEURIAL PROFILE: AmyLynn Keimach and Kenneth Tran: Border7 Studios
AmyLynn Keimach and Kenneth Tran launched their Web services firm, Border7 Studios, based in Simi Valley, California, as a general partnership. Even though they recognized the liability risks in choosing to operate as a partnership, Keimach and Tran, who started the company after they were laid off from their jobs without severance pay, said they could not afford to form an S corporation, their desired form of ownership. Keimach was concerned that if one of Border7's clients sued the company, it could conceivably take everything the two partners owned. However, as the firm grew, the founders did choose to form an LLC, which now protects them from personal liability in their business.[8] ∎

CAPITAL ACCUMULATION Although the partnership form of ownership is superior to the proprietorship in its ability to attract capital, it is generally not as effective as the corporate form of ownership, which can raise capital by selling shares of ownership to outside investors.

DIFFICULTY IN DISPOSING OF PARTNERSHIP INTEREST Most partnership agreements restrict how partners can dispose of their shares of the business. Usually, an agreement requires a partner to sell his or her interest to the remaining partner(s). Even if the original agreement contains such a requirement and clearly delineates how the value of each partner's ownership will be determined, there is no guarantee that the other partner(s) will have the financial resources to buy the seller's interest. When the money is not available to purchase a partner's interest, the other partner(s) may be forced to accept a new partner or dissolve the partnership, distribute the remaining assets, or begin again. Under prior versions of the RUPA, when a partner withdrew from a partnership (an act called *dissociation*), the partnership automatically dissolved, requiring the remaining partners to form a new partnership. Current provisions of the RUPA, however, do not require dissolution and allow the remaining partners to continue to operate the business without the dissociated partner through a continuation agreement. The dissociated partner no longer has the authority to represent the business or to take part in managing it.

A similar problem arises when a partner dies. The deceased partner's interest in the partnership passes to his or her heirs, in which case the partnership is dissolved and the heirs receive the value of the deceased partner's share of the business. However, the partnership agreement may provide for the partnership to continue to operate, with the remaining partner(s) purchasing the deceased partner's share of the business from his or her estate. To ensure that sufficient funds are available to purchase a deceased partner's interest in the business, the partnership should purchase life insurance policies on each partner, naming the remaining partner(s) as beneficiaries, and use the proceeds to purchase the deceased partner's share of the business for the surviving partner(s).

POTENTIAL FOR PERSONALITY AND AUTHORITY CONFLICTS Being in a partnership is much like being in a marriage. Making sure that partners' work habits, goals, ethics, and general business philosophy are compatible is an important step in avoiding a nasty business divorce. Engaging in serious discussions with potential partners before launching a business together is a valuable and revealing exercise. A better way to "test-drive" a potential partnership is to work with a prospective partner on a joint project to get a sense of how compatible your work styles, business philosophies, and personalities really are. That project might be a small business venture or working together to create a business plan for the proposed partnership. The idea is to work together before committing to a partnership to determine the compatibility of the potential partners' values, goals, personalities, views, and ethics.

Courtesy of Rene Shimada Siegel, President, High Tech Connect, LLC

ENTREPRENEURIAL PROFILE: René Siegel: High Tech Connect René Siegel and her partner launched their business, High Tech Connect, based on a need they discovered among their colleagues in Silicon Valley. Companies required the skills of specialized marketing consultants to work on specific projects, some of which might last for years. High Tech Connect built a strong network of highly skilled, experienced freelancers to provide those marketing services. However, after a few years in business, the partnership became quite contentious. The partners had established High Tech Connect as a 50/50 partnership with no exit clause in their agreement. The dissolution of the partnership included many accounting and legal disputes, which led to litigation before Siegel eventually took full ownership of the business. She credits finding the right attorney, keeping employees focused on moving the business ahead, being able to rely on strong support from her family, and building a strong advisory team with getting through the transition to sole ownership. High Tech Connect now manages a network of more than 1,300 consultants who assist clients with content development, editing, communications, speechwriting, public relations, and marketing through social media. Its consultants serve more than 700 clients, including companies such as Cisco Systems, Intuit, Visa, and Intel.[9] ■

No matter how compatible partners are, friction among them is inevitable. The key is to have a mechanism such as a partnership agreement and open lines of communication for managing conflict. The demise of many partnerships can be traced to interpersonal conflicts and the lack of a process to resolve those conflicts.

PARTNERS ARE BOUND BY THE LAW OF AGENCY Each partner is an agent for the business and can legally bind the partnership and, hence, the other partners, to contracts—even without the remaining partners' knowledge or consent. Because of this agency power, all partners must exercise good faith and reasonable care when performing their responsibilities. For example, if a partner signs a three-year lease for a business jet, a move that only worsens the small company's cash flow struggles, the partnership is legally bound by the agreement even though the remaining partners may not be in favor of the decision.

Some partnerships survive a lifetime, but others struggle because they suffer from many of the problems described here. Conflicts between or among partners can force an otherwise thriving business to close. Too many partners never put into place a mutually agreed-on method of conflict resolution such as a partnership agreement. Without such a mechanism, disagreements can escalate to the point where the partnership dissolves and the business ceases to operate.

You Be the Consultant

Making a Partnership Work

Structured properly, a partnership can be very successful and quite rewarding for its founders. Nick Friedman and Omar Soliman met in tenth grade and became best friends. In his senior year at the University of Miami in Coral Gables, Florida, Soliman enrolled in an entrepreneurship class, where he created a business plan for College Hunks Hauling Junk, the moving and junk-hauling company that he and Friedman operated during their summer breaks from college. He submitted his plan to the Leigh Rothschild Entrepreneurship Competition, where it won first prize and $10,000. After graduating from Pomona College, Friedman accepted a job at a Washington, DC, consulting firm but quickly became disenchanted with his corporate career. At age 22, he and Soliman decided to launch College Hunks Hauling Junk and became the youngest franchisors in the United States.

Today their company, which recycles 50 percent of the material it processes, has grown into a $50 million junk removal business with more than 200 franchisees in 35 states. Friedman and Soliman are best friends, something that has strengthened their business partnership and made their company a success. However, that is not always the outcome when best friends go into business together. Friedman and Soliman offer the following lessons for making a business partnership work:

- *Make certain that you have a common vision before you start.* Friedman says the key to their successful partnership is that they share a common vision and common values. Before they officially launched College Hunks Hauling Junk, each of them wrote separately about where they expected their business to be in five years. They were amazed at how strong their visions for the company matched with each other. Although they have day-to-day disagreements, as is common in any partnership, the two partners never disagree on the direction of the business or the values that underpin how they conduct their business.

- *The ideal partner is one whose skills, experience, talents, and abilities complement yours rather than mirror them.* While their company has grown, Friedman and Soliman have developed distinctive roles that support one another. Soliman is more of the strategic thinker, while Friedman is stronger with business operations and implementation of strategy.

- *Create a partnership agreement—always.* No matter how strong a friendship is, partners should create a partnership agreement. Discussing and then putting in writing how partners will handle sensitive issues, such as financing, daily decision making, deadlocks in decisions, compensation, and withdrawal from the partnership, not only helps resolve disputes down the road but also allows the partners to avoid disputes.

- *Create an advisory board.* Friedman and Soliman are equal owners of College Hunks Hauling Junk. What happens when they disagree on an important decision? In the early stages of the business, they simply "duked it out." (Friedman laughingly concedes that actual punches have been involved on occasion.) Today, the business partners consult with the advisory board they created, which includes professors, executives from large companies, and other entrepreneurs who can offer valuable insight.

In other cases, forming a partnership can be the beginning of an extended nightmare. Three entrepreneurs formed a partnership to sell male enhancement products but never created a partnership agreement. The partner who controlled the company's finances and operations distributed more than $11 million to himself from the partnership but less than $1 million to his partners. The two partners became suspicious and demanded a full accounting of the partnership's records. The managing partner refused, prompting the two partners to file an arbitration claim against him. During the arbitration hearing, the managing partner claimed that because there was no partnership agreement, no partnership existed. The two partners argued that the parties' original intent was to create a partnership and that they should receive equal shares of the partnership's profits. A panel of arbitrators agreed with the two partners and ordered the managing partner to pay them $4.5 million. Of course, the business did not survive the dispute.

Avoiding ugly and costly business divorces that too often bring an end to businesses requires ongoing and active effort. Experts suggest that partners follow these guidelines to keep their partnerships going strong:

- Ask yourself, "Do I really need a partner?" You should take on a partner only if doing so is essential to your company's success. A potential partner should bring to the business skills, contacts, financing, knowledge, or something else you don't have.

- Take a close look at what you're getting. How well do you really know your potential partner? One of the best ways to test your compatibility is to work on small projects together before you decide to go into business with one another. Doing so allows you to judge the compatibility of your management styles, business philosophies, and values.

- Invest in the relationship, not just the deal making. Partners must constantly work to strengthen their relationships. You cannot delegate or ignore this role; otherwise, the partnership is destined to fail.

- Respect your differences but expect to work out conflicts. When potential sources of conflict exist, address them immediately. Festering wounds seldom heal themselves.

(continued)

You Be the Consultant (continued)

- Divide business responsibilities and duties according to each partner's skills, interests, and abilities.

- Be prepared to change. Be open to new opportunities and share with your partners what you see. Partnerships must evolve to survive.

- Help your partners succeed. Work hard to see that every partner plays a role in the business that affords him or her the opportunity to be successful.

- Make sure your partners are people you admire, respect, and enjoy being around.

1. Research relationships between partners and add at least three guidelines to those listed here.

2. Develop a list of the behaviors that are almost certain to destroy a partnership.

3. Suppose that two of your friends are about to launch a business together, with nothing but a handshake. "We've been best friends since grammar school," they say. What advice would you give them?

Sources: Based on Thomas Heath, "Duo Behind College Hunks Moving Company Ditch a Digital Path for Old-School Success," *Chicago Tribune*, August 1, 2016, www.chicagotribune.com/business/ct-college-hunks-moving-company-success-heath-20160801-story.html; Donna Fenn, "Advice from College Hunks: How to Start a Company with Your Best Friend," *BNET*, September 7, 2010, www.bnet.com/blog/entrepreneurs/advice-from-college-hunks-how-to-start-a-company-with-your-best-friend/1213; Laura Petrecca, "A Partner Can Give Your Business Shelter or a Storm," *USA Today*, October 9, 2009, www.usatoday.com/money/smallbusiness/startup/week4partnerships.htm; Patricia Laya, "This Guy Quit His Consulting Job to Haul People's Junk, and Is Making Millions," *Business Insider*, August 8, 2011, www.businessinsider.com/business-tips-nick-friedman-college-hunks-hauling-junk-08-2011?op=1; "$4.5 Million Judgment for Aiken Schenk Clients in Partnership Dispute," Aiken Schenk, 2011, www.ashrlaw.com/news/oral-partnership.htm; "Our Company," Benham Real Estate Group, n.d., http://benhamrealestate.com/our-company/; John Jessup, "Twin Brothers Boost Business Through 'Missioneering,'" *CBN News*, September 23, 2012, www.cbn.com/cbnnews/us/2012/September/Twin-Brothers-Boost-Business-through-Missioneering/.

Limited Liability Partnerships

limited liability partnership (LLP)

a partnership in which all partners in the business are limited partners, giving them the advantage of limited liability for the partnership's debts.

Many states now recognize **limited liability partnerships (LLPs)**, in which *all* partners in a business are limited partners, giving them the advantage of limited liability for all of the partnership's debts. Most states restrict LLPs to certain types of professionals, such as attorneys, physicians, dentists, and accountants. Many states also restrict the limited liability advantage of LLPs to the results of actions taken by other partners. For instance, if an LLP sells a defective product that injures a customer, the injured customer could sue the business *and* the partners as individuals. The partners' unlimited personal liability exposure means that their personal assets would be at risk.

Just as with any limited partnership, the partners must file a certificate of limited partnership in the state in which the partnership will conduct business, and the partnership must identify itself as an LLP to those with whom it does business. In addition, like every other partnership, an LLP does not pay taxes; its income is passed through to the limited partners, who pay taxes on their shares of the company's income.

LO2

Describe the similarities and differences of C corporations and S corporations.

corporation

a separate legal entity apart from its owners that receives the right to exist from the state in which it is incorporated.

Corporations

The corporation is the most complex of the three major forms of business ownership. It is a separate entity apart from its owners and may engage in business, make contracts, sue and be sued, own property, and pay taxes. The Supreme Court has defined a **corporation** as "an artificial being, invisible, intangible, and existing only in contemplation of the law."[10] Because the life of the corporation is independent of its owners, the shareholders can sell their interests in the business without affecting its continuation. Corporations are creations of the states. When a corporation is founded, it accepts the regulations and restrictions of the state in which it is incorporated and any other state in which it chooses to do business.

Because it is a separate legal entity, a corporation allows investors to limit their liability to the total amount of their investment in the business. In other words, creditors of the corporation cannot lay claim to shareholders' personal assets to satisfy the company's unpaid debts. The legal protection of personal assets from business creditors is of critical concern to many potential investors. Autumn Adeigbo chose the corporate form of ownership for her fashion business because she wanted to protect herself from personal liability while raising funding from investors. It also helped present her company as a reputable business that is ready to form investment relationships.[11]

The shield of limited liability may not be impenetrable, however. Because start-up companies are risky, lenders and other creditors often require the founders of corporations to personally guarantee loans made to the business. Experts estimate that 95 percent of small business owners have to sign personal guarantees to get the debt financing they need. Banks, landlords, and vendors may all require personal guarantees from small business owners. By making these guarantees, owners put their personal assets at risk (just as in a proprietorship) despite choosing the corporate form of ownership.

The corporate form of ownership also does not protect its owners from being held personally liable for fraudulent or illegal acts. Court decisions have extended the personal liability of the owners of small corporations beyond the financial guarantees that banks and other lenders require, "piercing the corporate veil" much more than ever before. Courts increasingly are holding entrepreneurs *personally* liable for environmental, pension, and legal claims against their corporations. Courts will pierce the corporate veil and hold entrepreneurs liable for the company's debts and obligations if the owners deliberately commit criminal or negligent acts when handling corporate business. Courts ignore the limited liability shield the corporate form of ownership provides when an entrepreneur:

- Uses corporate assets for personal reasons or commingles them with his or her personal assets

- Fails to act in a responsible manner and creates an unwarranted level of financial risk for the stockholders

- Makes financial misrepresentations, such as operating with more than one set of books

- Takes actions in the name of the corporation that were not authorized by the board of directors

Liability problems associated with piercing the corporate veil almost always originate from actions and decisions that fail to maintain the integrity of a corporation. The most common cause of these problems, especially in closely held corporations, is corporate owners and officers failing to keep their personal funds and assets separate from those of the corporation. Table 6.1 offers some useful suggestions for avoiding legal tangles in a corporation. Corporations have the power to raise large amounts of capital by selling shares of ownership to outside investors, but many corporations have only a handful of shareholders. A **closely held corporation** has shares that are controlled by a relatively small number of people, often family members, friends, or employees. Its stock is not traded on any stock exchange but instead is passed from one generation to the next. Most small corporations are closely held. A **publicly held corporation** has a large number of shareholders, and its stock usually is traded on one of the large stock exchanges.

In general, a publicly-held corporation must report annually its financial operations to its home state's secretary of state and to the Securities and Exchange Commission (SEC). These financial reports become public record. If a corporation's stock is sold in more than one state, it must comply with federal regulations governing the sale of corporate securities. There are substantially more reporting requirements for a corporation than for the other forms of ownership.

Unless a corporation fails to pay its taxes or is limited to a specific length of life by its charter, it can continue indefinitely. The corporation's existence does not depend on the fate of any single individual. Unlike a proprietorship or partnership, in which the death of a founder ends the business, a corporation lives beyond the lives of those who gave it life. This perpetual life gives rise to another major advantage—transferable ownership. However, with most small businesses, the ability of any individual shareholder to sell shares is limited and must follow the processes agreed on by the company founders when they incorporated.

closely held corporation
a corporation whose shares are controlled by a relatively small number of people, often family members, friends, or employees.

publicly held corporation
a corporation that has a large number of shareholders and whose stock usually is traded on one of the large stock exchanges.

TABLE 6.1 **Avoiding Legal Tangles in a Corporation**

Entrepreneurs should take these steps to avoid legal problems if they own a corporation:

- *Identify the company as a corporation by using "Inc." or "Corporation" in the business name.* This alerts all who do business with a company that it is a corporation.

- *File all reports and pay all necessary fees required by the state in a timely manner.* Most states require corporations to file reports with the secretary of state on an annual basis. Failing to do so jeopardizes the validity of a corporation and opens the door for personal liability problems for its shareholders.

- *Hold annual meetings to elect officers and directors.* In a closely held corporation, the officers elected may *be* the shareholders, but that does not matter. Corporations formed by an individual are not required to hold meetings, but the sole shareholder must file a written consent form.

- *Keep minutes of every meeting of the officers and directors, even if it takes place in the living room of the founders.* It is a good idea to elect a secretary who is responsible for recording the minutes.

- *Make sure the corporation's board of directors makes all major decisions.* Problems arise in closely held corporations when one owner makes key decisions alone, without consulting the elected board.

- *Make it clear that the business is a corporation by having all officers sign contracts, loan agreements, purchase orders, and other legal documents in the corporation's name rather than their own names.* Failing to designate their status as agents of the corporation can result in the officers being held personally liable for agreements they think they are signing on the corporation's behalf.

- *Keep corporate assets and the personal assets of the owners separate.* Few things make courts more willing to hold shareholders personally liable for a corporation's debts than commingling corporate and personal assets. In some closely held corporations, owners have been known to use corporate assets to pay their personal expenses (or vice versa) or to mix their personal funds with corporate funds into a single bank account. Protect the corporation's identity by keeping it completely separate from the owner's personal identities.

- *Never sign or negotiate corporate documents, such as contracts and other agreements, or sign official corporate correspondence, as an owner or shareholder.* Maintaining liability protection for the corporation's owners requires that the owners act within only a narrow band of actions, primarily limited to electing the board of directors, approving changes to the corporate charter and by-laws, approving sale of the company or its major holdings, approving outside auditors, and creating or modifying shareholder agreements.

Source: U.S. Small Business Administration, 2010.

C Corporations

C corporations are the traditional form of incorporation. All large publicly traded companies and some small businesses are C corporations. C corporations are separate legal entities and therefore must pay taxes on their net income at the federal level, in most states, and to some local governments as well. Before stockholders receive a penny of its net income as dividends, a C corporation must pay taxes at the *corporate* tax rate, a graduated tax on corporate profits. Then, stockholders must pay taxes on the dividends they receive from these same profits at their *individual* tax rates. Thus, a corporation's profits are taxed twice. This **double taxation** is a distinct disadvantage of the C corporation form of ownership. If a company plans to seek investment from venture capital or other forms of private equity, it should be established as a C corporation. (Sources of financing are discussed in Chapter 15.) A C corporation provides the appropriate structure for investments by corporations, an eventual acquisition, and a future public stock offering.

S Corporations

In 1954, the IRS Code created the Subchapter S corporation, more commonly known as *S corporation* or *S Corp*. Unlike C corporations, S corporations do not pay taxes on corporate income. Income earned by S corporations is passed through to the owners, just as it is in a sole proprietorship or a partnership. The **S corporation** was established specifically for small, closely held businesses to free the owners from the double taxation that occurs with a C corporation. Table 6.2 shows a comparison of the tax bill for a small company organized as a C corporation and the tax liability of the same company organized as an S corporation (or a limited liability company, which shares the same tax treatment as an S corporation). An S corporation is a distinction that is made

double taxation
a disadvantage of the corporate form of ownership in which the corporation's profits are taxed twice, once at the corporate rate and again at the individual rate on the portion of profits distributed to shareholders as dividends.

S corporation
a corporation that retains the legal characteristics of a regular C corporation but has the advantage of being taxed as a partnership if it meets certain criteria.

TABLE 6.2 Tax Rate Comparison: C Corporation and S Corporation or Limited Liability Company

Entrepreneurs must consider the tax bills that their companies incur under the various forms of ownership. For example, S corporations do not pay taxes on their net income. Instead, that income passes through to the owners, who pay taxes on it at their individual tax rates. C corporations, on the other hand, pay a corporate tax on their net income. If a C corporation pays out some or all of its net income as dividends to shareholders, the dividends are taxed a second time, at the shareholders' individual tax rates. Therefore, the tax obligations for an owner of an S corporation may be considerably lower than for an owner of a C corporation.

The following example illustrates the effect of these tax rate differentials. This somewhat simplified example assumes that a small company generates net income of $500,000 and that all after-tax income is distributed to the owner.

	C Corporation	S Corporation or LLC
Corporate or limited liability company net income	$500,000	$500,000
Maximum corporate tax	35%	0%
Corporate tax	**$175,000**	**0**
After-tax income	$325,000	$500,000
Maximum shareholder tax rate	39.6%	39.6%
Shareholder tax	**$65,000***	**$198,000****
Total tax paid	**$240,000**	**$198,000**
(Corporate tax plus shareholder tax)		

Total tax savings by choosing an S corporation or limited liability company = $42,000

*Using the marginal 20% tax rate on dividends: $325,000 × 20% = $65,000.
**Using the marginal 39.6% tax rate on ordinary income: $500,000 × 39.6% = $198,000.
Source: U.S. Small Business Administration, 2010.

only for federal income tax purposes and is, in terms of all other legal characteristics, no different from any other corporation.

A corporation seeking S status must meet the following criteria:

- It must be a domestic corporation.

- It can have only allowable shareholders, including individuals, certain trusts, and estates.

- It cannot include partnerships, corporations, or nonresident aliens as shareholders.

- It cannot have more than 100 shareholders.

- It can issue only one class of stock. However, S corporations can issue shares of stock with different voting rights.

- It cannot be an ineligible corporation, such as certain financial institutions, insurance companies, and domestic international sales corporations.

If a corporation meets the criteria of an S corporation, its shareholders must elect to be treated as one. Shareholders may file for S corporation status at any time during the 12 months that precede the taxable year for which the election is to be effective. (The corporation must have been eligible for S status for the entire year.) To make the election of S status effective for the current tax year, entrepreneurs must file Form 2553 with the IRS within the first 75 days of the corporation's fiscal year. *All* shareholders must consent to have the corporation treated as an S corporation. Jennifer Chu launched Chu Shu, a company that makes odor-absorbing liners for women's shoes, after she was laid off from her investment banking job. Chu incorporated her business and intended to transform it into an S corporation but missed the filing deadline the first year, causing her to forgo several thousands of dollars in tax savings.[12]

An S corporation files an informational return (1120-S) with the IRS and provides its shareholders with Schedule K-1, which reports their proportionate shares of the company's profits. The shareholders report their portions of the S corporation's earnings on their individual income tax returns (Form 1040) and pay taxes on those profits at the individual tax rates (even if they never take the money out of the business). This tax treatment can cause problems for individual shareholders, however. If an S corporation earns a profit but managers choose to plow that income back into the business in the form of retained earnings to fuel its growth and expansion, shareholders still must pay taxes on their share of the company's net income. In that case, shareholders end up paying taxes on "phantom income" they never actually received. S corporations should always distribute enough cash to ensure that shareholders have the funds they need to pay taxes on the income that is passed through from the corporation. S corporations (and other pass-through entities, such as partnerships) should follow the **1/3, 1/3, 1/3 rule of thumb**: Distribute one-third of earnings to the shareholders to cover the taxes they will owe (most often done quarterly), retain one-third of earnings to fund its growth, and earmark the final one-third to pay down debt, add to funding for growth, or distribute to the owners as a return on their investment.

1/3, 1/3, 1/3 rule of thumb

a guideline that calls for an S corporation (and other pass-through entities) to distribute one-third of its earnings to shareholders to cover the taxes they will owe, retain one-third to fund its growth, and earmark one-third to pay down debt, add to funding for growth, or distribute to shareholders as a return on their investment.

S corporations' earnings are not subject to the self-employment tax that sole proprietors and general partners must pay; however, they are responsible for payroll taxes (for Social Security and Medicare) on the wages and salaries the S corporation pays its employees. Therefore, owners of S corporations must be sure that the salaries they draw are reasonable; salaries that are too low or too high draw scrutiny from the IRS.

Before 1998, if an entrepreneur owned separate but affiliated companies, he or she had to maintain each one as a distinct S corporation, with its own accounting records and tax return. Under current law, business owners can set up all of these affiliated companies as qualified S corporation subsidiaries ("Q subs") under the umbrella of a single company, each with its own separate legal identity, and still file a single tax return for the parent company. For entrepreneurs with several lines of businesses, this change means greatly simplified tax filing. Owners also can use losses from one subsidiary company to offset profits from another to minimize their tax bills.

ENTREPRENEURIAL PROFILE: Joseph Rotella: Spencer Organ Company Joseph Rotella is the owner of Spencer Organ Company, an organ maintenance and restoration business based in Waltham, Massachusetts. Spencer Organ Company is an S corporation, and Rotella is the only shareholder. Therefore, all of the company's profits flow through to Rotella as personal income. In a typical year, Spencer Organ Company's profits are about $250,000. Rotella only draws a salary of about one-half that amount. Therefore, he owes income taxes on his salary and also personal income tax on the profits his company earns.[13] ∎

LO3

Understand the characteristics of a limited liability company.

limited liability company (LLC)

a form of ownership that, like an S corporation, is a cross between a partnership and a corporation; it is not subject to the restrictions imposed on S corporations.

Limited Liability Companies

A **limited liability company (LLC)**, like an S corporation, offers its owners limited personal liability for the debts of the business, providing a significant advantage over sole proprietorships and partnerships. LLCs, however, are not subject to many of the restrictions currently imposed on S corporations and offer more flexibility than S corporations. For example, S corporations cannot have more than 100 shareholders, and none of the shareholders can be foreigners or corporations. S corporations are also limited to only one class of stock. LLCs eliminate those restrictions. Although an LLC can have just one owner, most have multiple owners (called "members"). LLCs offer their owners limited liability without imposing any requirements on their characteristics or any ceiling on their numbers. LLC members can include non-U.S. citizens, partnerships, and corporations. Unlike a limited partnership, which prohibits limited partners from participating in the day-to-day management of the business, an LLC does not restrict its members' ability to become involved in managing the company. Today most entrepreneurs form LLCs for their new businesses.

In addition to offering its members the advantage of limited liability, LLCs also avoid the double taxation imposed on C corporations. Like an S corporation, an LLC does not pay income taxes; its income passes through to the members, who are responsible for paying income taxes on their shares of the LLC's net income. Because they are not subject to the many restrictions imposed on other forms of ownership, LLCs offer entrepreneurs another significant advantage: flexibility. An LLC permits its members to divide income (and thus tax liability) as they see fit, including allocations that differ from their percentages of ownership. As in an S corporation, the members' shares of an LLC's earnings are not subject to the self-employment tax. However, the managing member's share of the LLC's earnings is subject to the self-employment tax (15.3 percent), just as a sole proprietor's or a general partner's earned income is.

These advantages make the LLC an ideal form of ownership for many small companies across many industries—retail, wholesale, manufacturing, real estate, and service. Because it offers the tax advantage of a partnership, the legal protection of a corporation, and maximum operating flexibility, the LLC is the fastest-growing form of business ownership.

Creating an LLC is much like creating a corporation. Forming an LLC requires an entrepreneur to create two documents: the articles of organization (which must be filed with the secretary of state) and the operating agreement. The LLC's **articles of organization**, similar to the corporation's articles of incorporation, actually creates the LLC by establishing its name and address, its method of management (board managed or member managed), its duration, and the names and addresses of each organizer. In most states, the company's name must contain the words "limited liability company" or "limited company" or the letters "LLC," "L.L.C.," or "L.C."

Once the members form an LLC, they must adopt an operating agreement. The **operating agreement**, much like a corporation's bylaws, outlines the provisions that govern the way the LLC will conduct business, such as members' capital contributions to the LLC; members' rights, roles, and responsibilities; the admission or withdrawal of members; distributions from the business; and the way the LLC will be managed. To ensure that their LLCs are classified as a partnership for tax purposes, entrepreneurs must draft the operating agreement carefully. The operating agreement must create an LLC that has more characteristics of a partnership than of a corporation to maintain this favorable tax treatment.

Despite their universal appeal to entrepreneurs, LLCs suffer some disadvantages. They can be expensive to create, often costing between $1,500 and $5,000. The costs associated with forming an LLC include legal fees for establishing the LLC and developing the membership agreement and fees charged by the state. Some states also impose annual fees on LLCs. Unlike corporations, which can operate "for perpetuity," LLCs have limited life spans. Entrepreneurs who want to provide attractive benefits to themselves and their employees will not find this form of ownership appealing because the cost of those benefits is not tax deductible in an LLC. Because there is no stock involved, this form of ownership also is not suitable for companies whose owners plan to raise money through an IPO or who want to use stock options or an Employee Stock Ownership Plan (ESOP) as incentives for employees. Venture capitalists also do not prefer to invest in LLCs due to the tax complications of the "pass-through" treatment of the LLC's income to its members. If an entrepreneur plans to raise venture capital or make an IPO, a C corporation is the best choice.

Although an LLC may be ideally suited for an entrepreneur launching a new company, it may pose problems for business owners considering converting an existing business to an LLC. Switching to an LLC from a general partnership, a limited partnership, or a sole proprietorship to bring in new owners is usually not a problem. However, owners of corporations and S corporations may incur large tax obligations if they convert their companies to LLCs.

articles of organization
a document that creates an LLC by establishing its name and address, method of management, duration, and other details.

operating agreement
a document that establishes for an LLC the provisions governing the way it will conduct business.

How to Create a Legal Business Entity

LO4

Explain the process of creating a legal entity for a business.

Establishing and maintaining C corporations, S corporations, and LLCs can be costly and time-consuming. The owners are giving birth to an artificial legal entity, and the gestation period can be prolonged, especially for a novice. Many entrepreneurs hire attorneys to handle the process, but in most states, entrepreneurs can complete all of the required forms, most of which are online, themselves. However, entrepreneurs must exercise great caution when proceeding without the help of an attorney. Incorporating a business requires a variety of fees that are not applicable to proprietorships or partnerships. The average cost to create a legal business entity is around $1,000, but, depending on the complexity of the organization and the type of entity the entrepreneur chooses for the business, fees can range from $500 to $5,000.

Most states allow entrepreneurs to establish a legal business entity without the assistance of an attorney. Some states even provide kits to help in the process. Many entrepreneurs use Web sites such as MyCorporation, BizFilings, and LegalZoom to create legal business entities because they can incorporate for as little as $100.

ENTREPRENEURIAL PROFILE: James O'Leary and Ansar Khan: Refulgent Software James O'Leary and Ansar Khan are cofounders of Refulgent Software, located in Amherst, New York. The company develops point-of-sale software, called Ambur, for restaurants. The partners relied on family support and bootstrapping to launch their new business. To keep their start-up costs down, O'Leary and Khan ran their business out of their apartment and set up their company using LegalZoom. "I would advise folks using services like LegalZoom to do some additional research to make sure they are meeting all the requirements," suggests Khan. "We incorporated in August of 2010 and started selling our product in April of 2011. We had a few hundred dollars in expenses in 2010 and no revenue. We did not realize that we still had to file a tax return for the company for 2010. We did not end up doing that until late 2011 shortly after receiving a letter from the IRS stating that we owed them about $10,000 in fines for not filing a return in 2010. Luckily, we were able to talk to them and the fine was waived. Surprisingly, we figured out pretty much everything else on our own and avoided any other major mistakes!" Refulgent Software grew quickly. Within the first year, it grew to 400 customers and earned six-figure revenues. In 2015, the founders of Refulgent Software negotiated a successful exit through the sale of their company to ShopKeep.[14] ∎

Although it is cheaper for entrepreneurs to complete the process of creating a legal business entity themselves, it is not always the best idea. In some states, the application process is complex, and the required forms are confusing. The price for filing incorrectly can be high. If an entrepreneur completes the process of forming a legal business entity improperly, it is generally invalid. In addition, if there are multiple founders, it is important to get assistance from an attorney to develop shareholder or member agreements. These agreements set the ground rules and expectations for shareholders or members, guide the process for major decisions, and mitigate any possible future shareholder or member disputes.

Once entrepreneurs decide to form a legal business entity, they must choose a state in which to establish the entity. If the business will operate within a single state, it is most logical to form the business entity in that state. States differ—sometimes dramatically—in the requirements they place on the legal business entities they charter and how they treat the entities created within their borders. Some states, such as Delaware, Vermont, and Nevada, offer low business formation fees, favorable laws concerning the sale of securities, low taxes, and minimal legal requirements; many *Fortune* 500 corporations are chartered in these states. However, for most entrepreneurs, creating the legal business entity in the state from which they intend to operate the business usually is best because they are not likely to reap any significant benefits by forming the business out of state.

Table 6.3 provides a summary of the key features of the major forms of ownership discussed in this chapter.

Conclusion

An entrepreneur must decide among several forms of business ownership when launching a new business. Each form of ownership offers both advantages and disadvantages. To choose the best form of ownership, entrepreneurs must understand the characteristics of each form and how well those characteristics match their business and personal circumstances. The most important issues entrepreneurs should consider when they are evaluating the various forms of ownership include tax considerations, liability exposure, start-up and future capital requirements, amount of control over the company, managerial ability, business goals, management succession plans, and cost of formation. The forms of business ownership include sole proprietorship, general partnership, limited partnership, C corporation, S corporation, and limited liability company.

TABLE 6.3 Characteristics of the Major Forms of Ownership

Characteristic	Sole Proprietorship	General Partnership	Limited Partnership	C Corporation	S Corporation	LLC
Definition	A for-profit business owned and operated by one person	A for-profit business jointly owned and operated by two or more people	One general partner and one or more partners with limited liability and no rights of management	An artificial legal entity separate from its owners and formed under state and federal laws	An artificial legal entity that is structured like a C corporation but taxed by the federal government like a partnership	A business entity that provides limited liability like a corporation but is taxed like a partnership; owners are referred to as *members*
Ease of formation	Easiest form of business to set up; acquire licenses and permits, register fictitious name, and obtain taxpayer identification	Easy to set up and operate; a written partnership agreement is highly recommended; must acquire an employer ID number; if necessary, register fictitious name	File a certificate of limited partnership with the secretary of state; name must show that business is a limited partnership; must have written agreement and must keep certain records	File articles of incorporation and other required reports with the secretary of state; prepare bylaws and follow corporate formalities	Must meet all criteria to file as an S corporation; must file timely election with the IRS (within two and a half months of the first taxable year)	File articles of organization with the secretary of state; adopt operating agreement and file necessary reports with secretary of state; the name must show that it is an LLC
Owner's personal liability	Unlimited	Unlimited for general partners; limited for limited partners	Limited	Limited	Limited	Limited
Number of owners	One	Two or more	At least one general partner and any number of limited partners	Any number	Maximum of 100 with restrictions as to who they are	One (a few states require two or more)
Tax liability	Single tax: personal tax rate	Single tax: partners pay on their proportional shares at their individual rate	Single tax: partners pay on their proportional shares at their individual rate	Double tax: corporation pays tax, and shareholders pay tax on dividends distributed	Single tax: owners pay on their proportional shares at individual rate	Single tax: members pay on their proportional shares at individual rate
Current maximum tax rate	39.6%	39.6%	39.6%	35% corporate plus applicable state corporate income tax plus up to 39.6% of dividends to shareholders	39.6%	39.6%
Transferability of ownership	Fully transferable through sale or transfer of company assets	May require consent of all partners	May require consent of all partners	Fully transferable	Transferable (but transfer may affect S status)	Usually requires consent of all members
Continuity of the business	Ends on death or insanity of proprietor or on termination by proprietor	Dissolves on death, insanity, or retirement of a general partner (business may continue)	Dissolves on death, insanity, or retirement of a general partner (business may continue)	Perpetual life	Perpetual life	Perpetual life
Cost of formation	Low	Moderate	Moderate	High	High	High
Liquidity of the owner's investment in the business	Poor to average	Poor to average	Poor to average	High	High	High
Ability to raise capital	Low	Moderate	Moderate to high	Very high	High	High
Formation procedure	No special steps required other than buying necessary licenses	No written partnership agreement required (but highly advisable)	Must comply with state laws regarding limited partnership	Must meet formal requirements specified by state law	Must follow same procedures as C corporation and then elect S status with the IRS	Must meet formal requirements specified by state law

Chapter Summary by Learning Objective

1. **Explain the advantages and disadvantages of sole proprietorships and partnerships.**

   - A sole proprietorship is a business owned and managed by one individual. This is the most popular form of ownership.

   - Sole proprietorships offer these *advantages*: They are simple to create, they are the least costly form to begin, the owner has total decision-making authority, there are no special legal restrictions, and they are easy to discontinue.

   - Sole proprietorships have several *disadvantages*: unlimited personal liability of the owner, limited managerial skills and capabilities, limited access to capital, and lack of continuity.

   - A partnership is an association of two or more people who co-own a business for the purpose of making a profit.

   - Partnerships offer these *advantages*: ease of establishing, complementary skills of partners, division of profits, larger pool of capital available, ability to attract limited partners, little government regulation, flexibility, and tax advantages.

   - Partnerships have several *disadvantages*: unlimited liability of at least one partner, difficulty disposing of partnership, lack of continuity, potential for personality and authority conflicts, and partners bound by the law of agency.

2. **Describe the similarities and differences of C corporations and S corporations.**

   - Both C corporations and S corporations are separate legal entities. To form a corporation, an entrepreneur must file articles of incorporation with the state in which the company will incorporate.

   - Both types of corporations offer these *advantages*: limited liability of stockholders, ability to attract capital, ability to continue indefinitely, and transferable ownership.

   - C corporations have several *disadvantages*: double taxation, potential for diminished managerial incentives, legal requirements and regulatory red tape, and potential loss of control by the founder(s).

   - S corporations are pass-through entities and do not have taxation of profits at the corporate level.

3. **Understand the characteristics of a limited liability company.**

   - An LLC is not a corporation but offers the advantage of limited liability to its owners.

   - An LLC is a cross between a partnership and a corporation yet operates without the restrictions imposed on an S corporation. To create an LLC, an entrepreneur must file the articles of organization with the secretary of state and create an operating agreement.

4. **Explain the process of creating a legal entity for a business.**

   - Establish and maintaining C corporations, S corporations, and LLCs can be costly and time-consuming.

   - Many entrepreneurs hire attorneys to handle the process, but in most states entrepreneurs can complete all the required forms, most of which are online, themselves.

Discussion Questions

⭐ 6-1. What factors should an entrepreneur consider before choosing a form of ownership?

6-2. Why are sole proprietorships so popular as a form of ownership?

6-3. What issues should the articles of partnership address?

6-4. Why are the articles important to a successful partnership?

6-5. Explain why one partner can commit another to a business deal without the other's consent.

6-6. What issues should the certificate of incorporation cover?

⭐ 6-7. How does an S corporation differ from a regular corporation?

6-8. What role do limited partners play in a partnership?

6-9. What happens if a limited partner takes an active role in managing the business?

6-10. What advantages does an LLC offer over an S corporation?

6-11. What advantages does an LLC offer over a partnership?

6-12. How is an LLC created?

Beyond the Classroom . . .

6-13. Interview four local small business owners.

6-14. What form of ownership did each of the business owners choose?

6-15. Why did the business owners you interviewed choose the forms of ownership they did?

6-16. Prepare a brief report summarizing your findings and explaining the advantages and disadvantages those owners face because of their choices.

6-17. Explain why you think these business owners have or have not chosen the form of ownership that is best for their particular situations.

6-18. Invite entrepreneurs who operate as partners to your classroom.

6-19. Do they have a written partnership agreement?

6-20. Are their skills complementary?

6-21. How do they divide responsibility for running their company?

6-22. How do they handle decision making?

6-23. What do they do when disputes and disagreements arise?

Endnotes

[1] Virginia Munger Kahn, "Room to Grow," *Bloomberg*, September 3, 2007, www.bloomberg.com/news/articles/2007-09-02/room-to-grow.

[2] "Sources of Income," Internal Revenue Service, 2016.

[3] "WordStream," *Inc.*, 2016, www.inc.com/profile/wordstream; "WordStream," *CrunchBase*, June 29, 2016, www.crunchbase.com/organization/wordstream#/entity; Larry Kim, "3 Hang-ups That Get in the Way of Growing Your Business," *Inc.*, November 22, 2013, www.inc.com/larry-kim/3-ways-your-hang-ups-get-in-the-wayof-growing-your-business.html; "Learn More About WordStream," WordStream, n.d., www.wordstream.com/company.

[4] *State of Small Business Report: Wave 2 of the Small Business Success Index*, Network Solutions, August 2009, p. 2; Laura Petrecca, "A Partner Can Give Your Business Shelter or a Storm," *USA Today*, October 9, 2009, www.usatoday.com/money/smallbusiness/startup/week4-partnerships.htm.

[5] Bret Thorn, "'wichcraft Gets a Makeover," *Restaurant News*, August 23, 2016, http://nrn.com/fast-casual/wichcraft-gets-makeover.

[6] Amy Joyce, "Getting It Together," *Washington Post*, June 12, 2005, www.washingtonpost.com/wp-dyn/content/article/2005/06/10/AR2005061001353.html.

[7] Emily Behlmann, "New Encrypted Messaging Service CryptPro Would Protect Data from Prying Eyes," *Wichita Business Journal*, July 24, 2013, www.bizjournals.com/wichita/blog/techflash/2013/07/newencrypted-messaging-service.html.

[8] Sarah E. Needleman, "Setting Up a Business Structure," *Wall Street Journal*, September 26, 2010, http://online.wsj.com/article/SB10001424052748703905604575514562263291610.html; "About Border7," Border7 Studios, n.d., www.border7.com/about/.

[9] "Who We Are," High Tech Connect, n.d., www.htconnect.com/whoweare/; "What We Do," High Tech Connect, n.d., www.htconnect.com/work-category/what-we-do/; Rene Shimada Siegel, "How I Survived a Legal Battle with My Business Partner," *Inc.*, April 4, 2013, www.inc.com/rene-siegel/how-to-survive-a-legal-nightmare.html; Ian Griffin, "Interview: René Siegel, High Tech Connect," *Professionally Speaking*, December 10, 2012, www.exec-comms.com/blog/2012/12/10/interviewrene-siegel-high-tech-connect/.

[10] *Dartmouth College v. Woodward*, 4 Wheat. 518, 636, 4L.Ed. 629, 659, 1819.

[11] Autumn Adeigbo, "Why I Changed My Fashion Business from an S-Corp to a C-Corp but Want to Be a B-Corp," *Forbes*, March 20, 2016, www.forbes.com/sites/autumnadeigbo/2016/03/20/how-i-incorporated-my-fashion-business/#362ad6844f4d.

[12] Sarah E. Needleman, "Setting Up a Business Structure," *Wall Street Journal*, September 26, 2010, http://online.wsj.com/article/SB10001424052748703905604575514562263291610.html.

[13] Julie M. Donnelly, "Small-Business Sympathies for the Occupiers," *Boston Business Journal*, November 11, 2011, www.bizjournals.com/boston/print-edition/2011/11/11/small-business-sympathies-for-the.html.

[14] Dan Miner, "Buffalo Startup Refulgent Software Acquired by Manhattan Competitor," *Buffalo Business First*, December 9, 2015, www.bizjournals.com/buffalo/blog/morning_roundup/2015/12/buffalo-startup-refulgent-software-acquired-by.html; Ansar Khan, personal communication, February 25, 2014; Dan Miner, "Taking Orders Launched This Biz Idea," *Buffalo Business First*, March 7, 2013, www.bizjournals.com/buffalo/news/2013/02/13/takingorders-launched-this-biz-idea.html.

7

Buying an Existing Business

Gajus/123RF

Learning Objectives

On completion of this chapter, you will be able to:

1. Describe the advantages and disadvantages of buying an existing business.

2. Explain the five stages in acquiring a business: search, due diligence, valuation, deal, and transition.

3. Explain the three steps in the search stage of buying a business.

4. Describe the four areas involved in conducting due diligence on a business: the seller's motivation, asset valuation, legal issues, and financial condition.

5. Explain the various methods used to estimate the value of a business.

6. Describe the basic principles of negotiating a deal to buy a business and structuring the deal.

7. Understand how to manage the transition stage when a deal is done.

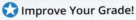
MyLab Entrepreneurship

⭐ **Improve Your Grade!**

If your instructor is using MyLab Entrepreneurship, visit **www.pearson.com/mylab/entrepreneurship** for videos, simulations, and writing exercises.

The entrepreneurial experience always involves risk. Buying a franchise, which we will discuss in Chapter 8, is one approach that can help reduce the risk for an entrepreneur. Another way to reduce the risk associated with entrepreneurship is to purchase an existing business rather than start a new venture. Purchasing an existing business can be a good approach, particularly as the entrepreneurs in the Baby Boom Generation are now reaching retirement age and seeking to sell their businesses. Over the course of the next 30 years, members of the Baby Boom Generation will transfer an amazing $30 trillion in wealth to their Generation X and Millennial heirs, much of it in the form of business assets.[1] Some Baby Boomers will hand over the reins of their businesses to the next generation of family members, but for others, passing their businesses to family members is not an option. These business owners will be looking to sell their companies, which creates a tremendous opportunity for young, aspiring entrepreneurs to purchase established, profitable businesses at reasonable prices. The primary motivation for business buyers purchasing an existing business is the same as it is for entrepreneurs: the desire to be their own bosses.[2]

ENTREPRENEURIAL PROFILE: Robert Santos: Bimac Corporation Roberto Santos was working as a mechanical engineer for a business in the oil industry in Houston, Texas, when he decided that he wanted to pursue the path of entrepreneurship. During a seven-month search for the ideal business to purchase, Santos reviewed 10 different businesses and visited 2 of them before negotiating a contract to purchase Bimac Corporation, a castings manufacturer in Dayton, Ohio, with 40 employees and annual sales of $5.5 million. The purchase price was $2.5 million for the business and its assets, including its real estate. Santos invested $325,000 of his own money. The owners, Dan Bizzarro, Bill Jordan, and Roger Reedy, provided $300,000 in seller financing, and Santos borrowed the remaining $1.875 million from a bank with the help of a loan guaranteed by the Small Business Administration. Bizzarro and Jordan agreed to stay on with Bimac to help Santos make the transition from employee to business owner. Santos says that the previous owners are wonderful teachers and that he plans to keep them around as long as possible. Although Santos has not made any drastic changes, he has plans to automate more of Bimac's manufacturing process and expand its export business.[3] ∎

Maddie McGarvey/The New York Times/Redux

Buying an existing business requires a great deal of analysis and evaluation to ensure that entrepreneurs actually are getting what they *think* they are buying and that the business meets their needs and expectations. Exercising patience and taking the necessary time to research a business before buying it are essential to getting a good deal. Research conducted by Pepperdine University's Graziadio School of Business and Management shows that 85 percent of the purchases of small to medium-size businesses take less than one year to complete, with most taking 9 to 10 months.[4] In too many cases, the excitement of being able to implement a "fast entry" into the market causes an entrepreneur to rush into a deal and make unnecessary mistakes in judgment.

Before buying any business, an entrepreneur must conduct a thorough analysis of the business and the opportunity it presents. Analyzing a target company's history and track record of sales and earnings helps a business buyer assess its likelihood of success in the future. If vital information such as audited financial statements and legal clearances are not available, an entrepreneur must be especially diligent before buying a business. Wise entrepreneurs conduct thorough research before purchasing a business. Answering the following questions provides a good starting point:

- Is this the type of business that you would like to operate?

- Does this business match your experience, knowledge, and talents?

- Will this business offer a lifestyle you find attractive?

- What are the negative aspects of owning this type of business?

- Are there any skeletons in the company closet that might come back to haunt you?

- Is this the best market and the best location for this business?

- Are there important demographic, population, or political changes in the community where the business is located that could affect future sales favorably or unfavorably?

- Do you know the critical factors that must exist for this business to be successful?

- Do you have the experience required to operate this type of business? If not, will the current owner be willing to stay on for a time to teach you the "ropes"?

- Does the present building meet all state and federal accessibility guidelines? If not, what will it take to bring the facility up to code?

- If the business is profitable, why does the current owner(s) want to sell? Can you verify the current owner's reason for selling?

- Does the business have a good reputation with its customers and in the community?

- If the business is currently in decline, do you have a plan to return the business to profitability? How confident are you that your turnaround plan will work?

- Have you examined other similar businesses that are currently for sale or that have sold recently to determine a fair market price for the company?

The time and energy invested in the evaluation of an existing business will earn significant dividends by allowing an entrepreneur to acquire a business that will continue to be successful or to avoid purchasing a business that is heading for failure.

Buying an Existing Business

LO1

Describe the advantages and disadvantages of buying an existing business.

Rather than launch their own businesses, some entrepreneurs opt for a more direct route to business ownership: they buy an existing business. Each circumstance of buying an existing business is unique, but the process of evaluating a potential business acquisition is not. The due diligence process that involves analyzing and evaluating an existing business for possible purchase is no less time-consuming than the process of developing a comprehensive business plan for a start-up. Done correctly, this due diligence process reveals both the negative and positive aspects of an existing business. Glossing over or skipping altogether the due diligence process is a mistake because a business that looks good on the surface may have serious flaws hidden at its core. Investigating a business to discover its real condition and value requires time, dedication, and, as the name implies, diligence, but the process is worthwhile because it can prevent an entrepreneur from purchasing a business destined for failure.

When considering purchasing a business, the first rule is, "Do not rush into a deal." Taking shortcuts when investigating a potential business acquisition almost always leads to nasty—and expensive—surprises. Prospective buyers must be sure they discover the answers to the following fundamental questions:

- Is the right type of business for sale in a market in which you want to operate?

- What experience do you have in this particular business and the industry in which it operates? How critical to your ultimate success is experience in the business?

- What is the company's potential for success?

- What changes will you have to make—and how extensive will they be—to realize the business's full potential?

- What price and payment method are reasonable for you and acceptable to the seller?

- Is the seller willing to finance part of the purchase price?

- Will the company generate sufficient cash to pay for itself and leave you with a suitable rate of return on your investment?

- Should you be starting a business and building it from the ground up rather than buying an existing one?

Figure 7.1 shows a profile of the four major categories of buyers and their characteristics that business brokers have identified.

The Advantages of Buying an Existing Business

A survey by Securian Financial Services reports that 60 percent of small business owners plan to exit their businesses by 2024 and that their most likely exit strategy is selling the business to someone.[5] Over the next decade, as these small business owners decide to retire and sell, entrepreneurs looking to buy existing businesses will have ample opportunities to consider. Those who purchase an existing business may reap the benefits discussed in the following sections.

SUCCESSFUL EXISTING BUSINESSES OFTEN CONTINUE TO BE SUCCESSFUL Purchasing a thriving business at a reasonable price increases the likelihood of success. Although buying an existing business brings certain risks, it tends to be less risky than starting a company from scratch. The previous management team already established a customer base, built supplier relationships, and set up a business system. The customer base inherited in a business purchase can carry an entrepreneur while he or she learns how to build on the company's success.

SUPERIOR LOCATION When the location of the business is critical to its success (as is often the case in retailing), purchasing a business that is already in the right place may be the best choice. Opening in a second-choice location and hoping to draw customers usually proves fruitless.

EMPLOYEES AND SUPPLIERS ARE IN PLACE An existing business already has experienced employees who can help the new owner through the transition phase. Experienced employees enable a company to continue to earn money while a new owner learns the business. Many new owners solicit ideas from employees about methods for increasing sales or reducing costs. Few people know a job better than the people who perform it every day.

In addition, an existing business has an established set of suppliers with a history of business dealings. Those vendors can continue to supply the business while the new owner investigates the products and services of other suppliers.

Main Street Buyers

Want: A business that is manageable and easy to run alone or with a small group of employees.

Revenue Range: Up to $1 million.

Risk Tolerance: Low

Focus: Current and past earnings; often want seller to stay on to assist with transition.

Examples: Car wash, dry cleaners, cafés.

Corporate Refugees

Want: Service businesses with commercial clients and existing contract revenue.

Revenue Range: Less than $5 million.

Risk Tolerance: Low to medium

Focus: Ability to build on his or her corporate experience.

Examples: consulting firms, landscaping, advertising, manufacturing.

Serial Entrepreneurs

Want: Profitable companies with sound management in place.

Revenue Range: Less than $10 million.

Risk Tolerance: Medium to high.

Focus: Building a portfolio of companies in different industries, sectors, or markets; want businesses they can run themselves.

Examples: computer services, rental properties.

Financial Buyers

Want: Profitable companies that offer "hot" products or services and are ready to grow rapidly.

Revenue Range: $10 million to $100 million (or more).

Risk Tolerance: Medium to high (often are VCs or angels).

Focus: Highly profitable exit within five to seven years. Goal is to add capital to the company to turbocharge its growth.

Examples: health care, communications, energy.

FIGURE 7.1

Types of Business Buyers

Source: "Meet the Buyers," by Darren Dahl, *Inc.*, April 1, 2008, pp. 98–99. © 2008 by *Inc. Magazine*. Reprinted with permission.

INSTALLED EQUIPMENT WITH KNOWN PRODUCTION CAPACITY Acquiring and installing new equipment exerts a tremendous strain on a fledgling company's financial resources. A buyer of an existing business can determine the condition of the plant and equipment and its capacity before making the purchase. In many cases, entrepreneurs can purchase physical facilities and equipment at prices significantly below their replacement costs.

INVENTORY IN PLACE The proper amount of inventory is essential to both controlling costs and generating adequate sales volume. Carrying too little inventory means that a business will not have the quantity and variety of products to satisfy customer demand, and holding too much inventory ties up valuable capital unnecessarily, thereby increasing costs, reducing profitability, and putting a strain on cash flow. Owners of successful established businesses have learned the proper balance between these extremes.

TRADE CREDIT IS ESTABLISHED Previous owners have established trade credit relationships with vendors that can benefit the new owner. The business's proven track record gives the new owner leverage in negotiating favorable trade credit terms.

THE TURNKEY BUSINESS Starting a company can be a daunting, time-consuming task, and buying an existing business is one of the fastest pathways to entrepreneurship. When things go well, purchasing an existing business saves the time and energy required to plan and launch a new business. The buyer gets a business that is already generating cash and perhaps profits as well. The day the entrepreneur takes over the ongoing business is the day revenues begin.

THE NEW OWNER CAN USE THE EXPERIENCE OF THE PREVIOUS OWNER In many business sales, the agreement calls for the seller to spend time with a new owner during a transition period, which gives the new manager time to become acclimated to the business and learn about the keys to success. Previous owners also can be extremely helpful in unmasking the unwritten rules of business in the area; these are critically important intangibles, such as how to keep customers happy and who is trustworthy. Hiring the previous owner as a consultant for at least several months can be a valuable investment and increase the probability that the business will continue to be successful.

EASIER ACCESS TO FINANCING Attracting financing to purchase an existing business often is easier than finding the money to launch a company from scratch. Many existing businesses already have established relationships with lenders, which may open the door to financing through traditional sources such as banks. Seller financing also is a common element in business sales.

HIGH VALUE Some existing businesses are real bargains. If the current owner must sell quickly, he or she may have set a bargain price for the company that is below its actual worth. The number of potential buyers may be limited if special skills or training are required to operate the business; therefore, the more specialized the business, the greater the likelihood that a buyer will find a bargain. If the owner wants a substantial down payment or the entire selling price in cash, there may be few qualified buyers, but those who do qualify may be able to negotiate a good deal.

Disadvantages of Buying an Existing Business

CASH REQUIREMENTS One of the most significant challenges to buying a business is acquiring the necessary funds for the initial purchase price. The Small Business Administration advises that because the buyer of a company is purchasing the business concept, existing customers, the company's brands, and other existing elements of the business, the costs of acquiring an existing business usually are greater than the costs of starting one from scratch.[6]

THE BUSINESS IS LOSING MONEY A business may be for sale because it is struggling, and the owner wants out. In these situations, a prospective buyer must be wary. Business owners sometimes attempt to disguise the facts and employ creative accounting techniques to make the company's financial picture appear much brighter than it really is. Few business sellers honestly state "It's losing money" as the reason for putting their companies up for sale. If there is one area of business where the maxim "let the buyer beware" still prevails, it is in the purchase of an existing business. Any buyer unprepared to do a thorough analysis of a business may be stuck with a real money loser. One expert cautions that entrepreneurs who purchase troubled companies in hopes of turning them around face an 85 percent failure rate.[7]

Although buying a money-losing business is risky, it is not necessarily taboo. If a company is poorly managed or suffering from neglect, a new owner may be able to turn it around. However, a prospective buyer who does not have a well-defined plan for improving a struggling business should *not* consider buying it!

ENTREPRENEURIAL PROFILE: Chuck and Alan Bush: Fuzzy's Taco Shop Former restaurateur Chuck Bush was enjoying a meal at Fuzzy's Taco Shop in Fort Worth, Texas, and observing the restaurant's operating system in action. He saw the potential of the restaurant but realized that it suffered from a sloppy operating system. There were no control systems in the business. When Bush asked how many shrimp would be served on a particular dish, each employee gave a different answer. Chuck Bush and his father, Alan, an accountant, put together a group of investors to buy the money-losing restaurant for $80,000. They also assumed $10,000 in liabilities and invested another $15,000 for working capital. Chuck became the onsite manager, and his first step was to close the restaurant for four days, power wash every surface, repaint and redecorate the interior, and retrain the staff. He transcribed all of the recipes, which existed only in one cook's head, and assembled them into a notebook to ensure consistency and cost control. Chuck Bush noted that the food at Fuzzy's was good, which is what stimulated his interest in buying the business; however, its systems needed fine-tuning, and its operations required an overhaul, changes that the Bushes knew how to make. Their changes were successful, and the business became profitable the first year they owned it. They soon opened a second location in Fort Worth and began fielding inquiries about franchises. Today, 95 Fuzzy's Taco Shops operate across Texas and in 10 other states.[8] ∎

Like Fuzzy's, unprofitable businesses often result from at least one of the following problems:

- Inefficient operating systems
- High inventory levels
- Excessively high wage and salary expenses due to excess pay or inefficient use of personnel
- Excessively high compensation for the owner
- Inadequate accounts-receivable collection efforts
- Excessively high rental or lease rates
- High-priced maintenance costs or service contracts
- Poor location or too many locations for the business to support
- Inefficient equipment
- Intense competition from rivals
- Prices that are too low
- Low profit margins
- Losses due to employee theft, shoplifting, and fraud

As Chuck Bush did with Fuzzy's, a potential buyer usually can trace the causes of a company's lack of profitability by analyzing a company and its financial statements. The question is, can the new owner take steps to resolve the problems and return the company to profitability?

PAYING FOR ILL WILL Just as sound business dealings can create goodwill, improper business behavior or unethical practices can create ill will. A business may look great on the surface, but customers, suppliers, creditors, or employees may have negative feelings about their dealings with it. Too many business buyers discover—after the sale—that they have inherited undisclosed credit problems, poor supplier relationships, soon-to-expire leases, lawsuits, mismanaged customer relationships, building code violations, and other problems the previous owner created.

Ill will can permeate a business for years. The only way to avoid these problems is to investigate a prospective purchase target thoroughly *before* moving forward in the negotiation process.

EMPLOYEES INHERITED WITH THE BUSINESS MAY NOT BE SUITABLE The previous owner may have kept marginal employees because they were close friends or because they started with the company. A new owner, therefore, may have to make some very unpopular termination decisions. For this reason, employees often do not welcome a new owner because they feel threatened by change. Some employees may not be able to adapt to the new owner's management style, and a culture clash may result.

UNSATISFACTORY LOCATION What was once an ideal location may have become obsolete as market and demographic trends change. Prospective buyers should evaluate the existing market in the area surrounding an existing business as well as its potential for expansion. Buyers must remember that they are buying the future of a business, not its past. If business success is closely linked to a good location, acquiring a business in a declining area or where demographic trends are moving downward is not a good idea. The value of the business can erode faster than the neighborhood surrounding it.

OBSOLETE OR INEFFICIENT EQUIPMENT AND FACILITIES Potential buyers sometimes neglect to have an expert evaluate a company's facilities and equipment before they purchase it. Only later do they discover that the equipment is obsolete and inefficient and that the business is suffering losses from excessively high operating costs. Modernizing equipment and facilities is seldom inexpensive.

THE CHALLENGE OF IMPLEMENTING CHANGE It is easier to plan for change than it is to implement it. Methods, policies, and procedures the previous owner used in a business may have established precedents that a new owner finds difficult to modify. Employees and customers may resist changes to established procedures.

OBSOLETE INVENTORY Inventory is valuable only if it is salable. Smart buyers know better than to trust the inventory valuation on a firm's balance sheet because inventory depreciates over time. A prospective buyer must judge inventory by its market value, *not* by its book value.

VALUING ACCOUNTS RECEIVABLE Like inventory, accounts receivable rarely are worth their face value. A prospective buyer should age the accounts receivable to determine their collectability. The older the receivables are, the less likely they are to be collected and, consequently, the lower their actual value. Table 7.1 shows a simple but effective method of evaluating accounts receivable when the buyer ages them.

TABLE 7.1 Valuing Accounts Receivable

A prospective buyer asked the current owner of a business about the value of her accounts receivable.

The owner's business records showed $101,000 in accounts receivable. However, when the prospective buyer aged them and then multiplied the resulting totals by his estimated probabilities of collection, he discovered their *real* value.

Age of Accounts (Days)	Amount	Probability of Collection	Value (Amount × Probability of Collection)
0–30	$40,000	95%	$38,000
31–60	$25,000	88%	$22,000
61–90	$14,000	70%	$9,800
91–120	$10,000	40%	$4,000
121–150	$7,000	25%	$1,750
151+	$5,000	10%	$500
Total	**$101,000**		**$76,050**

Had he blindly accepted the "book value" of these accounts receivable, this prospective buyer would have overpaid by nearly $25,000 for them!

THE BUSINESS MAY BE OVERPRICED Most business sales involve the purchase of the company's assets rather than its stock. A buyer must be sure which assets are included in the deal and what their real value is. Many people purchase businesses at prices far in excess of their true value. If a buyer accurately values a business's accounts receivable, inventory, and other assets, he or she will be in a better position to negotiate a price that will allow the business to be profitable. Making payments on an overpriced business is a millstone around the new owner's neck that makes it difficult to keep the business afloat.

The Stages in Acquiring a Business

Roughly 500,000 businesses change ownership each year,[9] although about one-third of all business sales that are initiated fall through. The main reason is an unreasonable demand unrelated to the price of the business by either the buyer or the seller.[10] Figure 7.2 summarizes the steps in the acquisition process.

Purchasing an existing business can be a time-consuming process that requires a great deal of effort, is often difficult to complete, and can be risky if approached haphazardly. Repeated studies report that more than half of all business acquisitions fail to meet the buyer's expectations; therefore, buyers must conduct a systematic and thorough analysis prior to negotiating any deal. The remainder of this chapter examines the five stages that entrepreneurs go through when buying a business: (1) search stage, (2) due diligence stage, (3) valuation stage, (4) deal stage, and (5) transition stage (see Figure 7.3).

LO2

Explain the five stages in acquiring a business: search, due diligence, valuation, deal, and transition.

1. Identify and approach candidate → **2. Sign nondisclosure statement** → **3. Sign letter of intent** → **4. Buyer's due diligence investigation** → **5. Draft the purchase agreement** → **6. Close the final deal** → **7. Begin the transition**

← **Negotiations** →

1. Approach the candidate. If a business is advertised for sale, the proper approach is through the channel defined in the ad. Sometimes buyers will contact business brokers to help them locate potential target companies. If you have targeted a company in the "hidden market," an introduction from a banker, accountant, or lawyer often is the best approach. During this phase, the seller checks out the buyer's qualifications, and the buyer begins to judge the quality of the company.
2. Sign a nondisclosure document. If the buyer and the seller are satisfied with the results of their preliminary research, they are ready to begin serious negotiations. Throughout the negotiation process, the seller expects the buyer to maintain strict confidentiality of all of the records, documents, and information he or she receives during the investigation and negotiation process. The nondisclosure document is a legally binding

contract that ensures the secrecy of the parties' negotiations.
3. Sign a letter of intent. Before a buyer makes a legal offer to buy the company, he or she typically will ask the seller to sign a letter of intent. The letter of intent is a nonbinding document that says that the buyer and the seller have reached a sufficient "meeting of the minds" to justify the time and expense of negotiating a final agreement. The letter should state clearly that it is nonbinding, giving either party the right to walk away from the deal. It should also contain a clause calling for "good faith negotiations" between the parties. A typical letter of intent addresses terms such as price, payment terms, categories of assets to be sold, and a deadline for closing the final deal.
4. Buyer's due diligence. While negotiations are continuing, the buyer is busy studying the business and evaluating its

strengths and weaknesses. In short, the buyer must "do his or her homework" to make sure that the business is a good value.
5. Draft the purchase agreement. The purchase agreement spells out the parties' final deal. It sets forth all of the details of the agreement and is the final product of the negotiation process.
6. Close the final deal. Once the parties have drafted the purchase agreement, all that remains to making the deal "official" is the closing. Both buyer and seller sign the necessary documents to make the sale final. The buyer delivers the required money, and the seller turns the company over to the buyer.
7. Begin the transition. For the buyer, the real challenge now begins: making the transition to a successful business owner!

FIGURE 7.2

The Acquisition Process

Sources: Based on *Buying and Selling: A Company Handbook* (New York: Price Waterhouse, 1993), pp. 38–42; Charles F. Claeys, "The Intent to Buy," *Small Business Reports*, May 1994, pp. 44–47.

FIGURE 7.3
**The Five Stages of
Buying a Business**

1. Search Stage

2. Due Diligence Stage

3. Valuation Stage

4. Deal Stage

5. Transition Stage

LO3

Explain the three steps
in the search stage of
buying a business.

The Search Stage

When buying a business, entrepreneurs must search for a business that fits best with their background and personal aspirations. There are three steps in conducting an effective search for the right business to buy:

1. Conduct a self-inventory, objectively analyzing skills, abilities, and personal interests to determine the type(s) of business that offer the best fit.

2. Develop a list of the criteria that define the "ideal business" for you.

3. Prepare a list of potential candidates that meet your criteria.

Step 1. Self-Inventory: Analyze Your Skills, Abilities, and Interests

The first step in buying a business is *not* searching out potential acquisition candidates. Every entrepreneur who is considering buying a business should begin by conducting a self-audit to determine the ideal business for him or her. The primary focus is to identify the type of business that *you* will be happiest and most successful owning. Answering the following questions can help:

- What business activities do you enjoy most? Least? Why?

- Which industries or markets offer the greatest potential for growth?

- Which industries interest you most? Least? Why?

- What kind of business would you enjoy running?

- What kinds of businesses do you want to *avoid*?

- What do you expect to get out of the business?

- How much time, energy, and money can you put into the business?

- What business skills and experience do you have? Which ones do you lack?

- How easily can you transfer your skills and experience to other types of businesses? In what kinds of businesses would that transfer be easiest?

- How much risk are you willing to take?

- Are you willing and able to turn around a struggling business?

- What size company do you want to buy?

- Is there a particular geographic location you desire?

Answering these and other questions beforehand allows you to develop a list of criteria a company must meet to become a purchase candidate. Addressing these issues early in the process will also save a great deal of time, trouble, and confusion as you wade through a multitude of business opportunities. The better you know yourself and your skills, competencies, and interests, the more likely you will be to find and manage a successful business.

Step 2. Develop a List of Criteria

Based on the answers to the self-inventory questions, the next step is to develop a list of criteria that a potential business acquisition must meet. Investigating every business that you find for sale is a waste of time. The goal is to identify the characteristics of the "ideal business" for you so that you can focus on the most viable candidates as you wade through a multitude of business opportunities. These criteria will provide specific parameters against which you can evaluate potential acquisition candidates.

Step 3. Prepare a List of Potential Candidates

When you know what your goals are for acquiring a business, you can begin your search. Do *not* limit yourself to only businesses that are advertised as being "for sale." In fact, the **hidden market** of companies that might be for sale but are not advertised as such is one of the richest sources of top-quality businesses. Many businesses that can be purchased are not publicly advertised but are available either through the owners themselves or through business brokers and other professionals. Although they maintain a low profile, these hidden businesses represent some of the most attractive purchase targets a prospective buyer may find.

hidden market
low-profile companies that might be for sale but are not advertised as such.

ENTREPRENEURIAL PROFILE: Art and Alan McCraw: B. W. Burdette and Sons When brothers Art and Alan McCraw, two enterprising college graduates, returned to their hometown, they approached the owners of B. W. Burdette and Sons about buying the business. The local hardware store had been founded by the current owners' father 80 years earlier. The company was not listed for sale, but because the McCraws were familiar with the business, they knew that the current owners might be interested in selling. After several months of due diligence and negotiations, the young entrepreneurs closed the deal. They have since expanded the business to include two more locations, expanded its market reach, and increased its profitability many times over. ■

How can you tap into this hidden market of potential acquisitions? Typical sources include the following:

- The Internet, where several sites, such as Bizbuysell.com and Bizquest, include listings of business brokers and companies for sale

- Business brokers, which you can find by visiting the Web site for the International Business Brokers Association at www.ibba.org

- Professionals who provide business services, such as bankers, accountants, attorneys, investment bankers, and others

- Industry contacts—suppliers, distributors, customers, insurance brokers, and others

- Networking—social and business contact with friends and relatives

- Trade associations

- Newspapers' and trade journals' listings of businesses for sale

FIGURE 7.4

Business Purchases by Type of Business

Source: Based on data from "BizBuySell's 2016 Report: Why Buying or Selling a Business Is Becoming a Big Deal," BizBuySell, 2017, http://www.bizbuysell.com/htmlmail/2017/content/BizBuySell-Small-Business-Infographic-2016.pdf?utm_source=bizbuysell&utm_medium=blog&utm_campaign=infographicarticle021417.

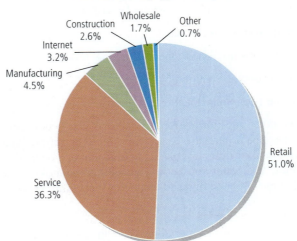

Business Sales by Type of Business

- Construction 2.6%
- Wholesale 1.7%
- Other 0.7%
- Internet 3.2%
- Manufacturing 4.5%
- Retail 51.0%
- Service 36.3%

The more opportunities an entrepreneur has to find and evaluate potential acquisitions, the greater the likelihood of finding a match that meets his or her criteria. Figure 7.4 shows the types of businesses that aspiring entrepreneurs purchase through the Web site BizBuySell, the Internet's largest business-for-sale marketplace.

LO4

Describe the four areas involved in conducting due diligence on a business: the seller's motivation, asset valuation, legal issues, and financial condition.

The Due Diligence Stage

Finding the right company requires patience. Although some buyers find a company after only a few months of looking, the typical search takes much longer, sometimes as much as two or three years. Once you have a list of prospective candidates, it is time to do your homework, learning about the company, analyzing financial statements, making certain that the facilities are structurally sound, and exploring other details by asking questions such as the following:

- What are the company's strengths? Weaknesses?
- Is the company profitable? What is its overall financial condition?
- What is its cash flow cycle? How much cash will the company generate?
- Who are its major competitors?
- How large is the customer base? Is it growing or shrinking?
- Are the current employees suitable? Will they stay?
- What is the physical condition of the business, its equipment, and its inventory?
- What new skills must you learn to be able to manage this business successfully?

Determining the answers to these and other questions presented in this chapter allow a prospective buyer to narrow the list of potential companies to the most attractive ones and to focus on evaluating them.

ENTREPRENEURIAL PROFILE: Randy Shayler: Zeswitz Music Randy Shayler left behind a career as a management consultant for the opportunity to be an entrepreneur, but Shayler decided that buying an existing business rather than starting one was the best route for him. He started with a list of 200 possible businesses, which he winnowed down to just 6 of the most promising companies. His due diligence led him to

Courtesy of Randy Shayler, CEO, Zeswitz Music

settle on Zeswitz Music, a 93-year-old business, for several million dollars. Shayler invested his own money, acquired a bank loan guaranteed by the Small Business Administration, and convinced two former professors (who taught a class on Entrepreneurship Through Acquisition) to become angel investors in the company. Shayler relied on the experience and knowledge of the previous owner during the transition period. Although Shayler has not made any major changes to the company's operations, he has increased marketing efforts in schools, improved the quality of the instruments the company sells, and increased the speed at which repairs are done. The result has been a significant increase in sales.[11] ■

The next section of this chapter explains in more detail the due diligence process.

The Due Diligence Process

Due diligence involves studying, reviewing, and verifying all of the relevant information concerning an acquisition. The goal of the due diligence process is to discover exactly what the buyer is purchasing and avoid any unpleasant surprises *after* the deal is closed. Exploring a company's character and condition through the Better Business Bureau, credit-reporting agencies, its bank, its vendors and suppliers, your accountant, your attorney, and other resources is a vital part of making certain the entrepreneur is going to get a good deal on a business and have the capacity to succeed. It is important to invest in the due diligence process; you can look at it as choosing to pay now or pay later.[12]

due diligence
the process of studying, reviewing, and verifying all the relevant information concerning an acquisition.

ENTREPRENEURIAL PROFILE: Emma Cerulli and Sebastien Barthe: Em and Seb Emma Cerulli and Sebastien Barthe purchased the assets of a failing catering company in Montreal, Quebec. They believed that it had a strong client base and a great deal of potential. Their client base grew to include area hospitals, law firms, and university departments. Barthe, who had been a head chef prior to buying the business, was responsible for the business operations. Cerulli brought her experience from culinary school at the Pacific Institute of Culinary Arts in Vancouver as well as what she had learned working in several well-known Montreal restaurants. However, after they purchased the business, they discovered that their overhead was much higher than they had estimated in their budgets because the financial information they had received from the previous owner was inaccurate. Careful due diligence would have given them a more accurate picture of the real financial situation of the business. In addition, their labor costs were too high. "Although I believe labor cost is the main issue," says Cerulli, "I'm afraid that if we lay people off, we won't have enough staff to meet demand." Despite their best efforts, Cerulli and Barthe ultimately decided to close the business.[13] ■

A thorough analysis of an intended acquisition usually requires an entrepreneur to assemble a team of advisers. Buying a business involves many complex legal, financial, tax, and business issues, and good advice can be a valuable tool. Many entrepreneurs involve an accountant, an attorney, an insurance agent, a banker, and sometimes a business broker to serve as consultants during the due diligence process.

The due diligence process involves investigating four critical areas of the business and the potential deal beyond those already evaluated earlier in the search and deal processes:

- *Motivation.* Why does the owner want to sell?

- *Asset valuation.* What is the real value of the company's assets?

- *Legal issues.* What legal aspects of the business are known or hidden risks?

- *Financial condition.* Is the business financially sound?

MOTIVATION Why does the owner want to sell? The most common reasons business owners give for selling their businesses are planned retirement (40 percent), burnout (21 percent), and the desire to own a bigger business (20 percent).[14] Every prospective business buyer should investigate the *real* reason the business owner wants to sell. Smart business buyers know that the biggest and most unpleasant surprises can crop up outside the company's financial records and may never appear on the spreadsheets designed to analyze a company's financial position. For instance, a business owner might be looking to sell his or her business because a powerful new competitor is about to move into the market, a major highway rerouting will cause customer traffic to evaporate, the lease agreement on the ideal location is about to expire, or the primary customer base is declining. Every prospective buyer should investigate thoroughly any reason a seller gives for wanting to sell a business.

ASSET VALUATION What is the true nature of the firm's assets? A prospective buyer should evaluate the business's assets to determine their true value. The buyer bases the valuation used to negotiate the deal on the financial statements provided by the seller. The buyer and the advising team must verify the actual value of the business through careful inspection of the business and its assets. Questions to ask about assets include the following:

- Are the assets really useful, or are they obsolete?
- Will the assets require replacement soon?
- Do the assets operate efficiently?

A potential buyer should check the condition of all equipment and the building. Even if the building is not part of the sale price, its condition will determine the ability of the business to operate effectively into the future. It may be necessary to hire a professional to evaluate the major components of the building—its structure and its plumbing, electrical, and heating and cooling systems. Renovations are often expensive and time-consuming and can have a negative impact on a buyer's budget.

What is the status of the firm's existing inventory? Can the buyer sell all of it at full price, or is some of it damaged or outdated? How much of it would the buyer have to sell at a loss? Is it consistent with the image the new owner wants to project? A potential buyer may need an independent appraisal to determine the value of the firm's inventory and other assets because the current owner may have priced them far above their actual value. These items typically constitute the largest portion of a business's value, and a potential buyer should not accept the seller's asking price blindly. Remember that *book value is not the same as market value*. Value is determined in the market, not on a balance sheet. A buyer often can purchase equipment and fixtures at substantially lower prices than book value.

Other important factors that the potential buyer should investigate include the status of each of the following:

- *Accounts receivable.* If the sale includes accounts receivable, the buyer must check their quality before purchasing them. How creditworthy are the accounts? What portion of them is past due? By aging the accounts receivable, the buyer can judge their quality and determine their *real* value. (Refer to Table 7.1.)

- *Lease arrangements.* If the seller does not own the building, is the lease included in the sale? When does it expire? What restrictions does it have on renovation or expansion? What is the status of the relationship with the property owner? The buyer should determine beforehand any restrictions the landlord has placed on the lease. Does the lease agreement allow the seller to assign the lease to a buyer? The buyer must negotiate all necessary changes with the landlord and get them in writing prior to buying the business.

- *Business records.* Accurate business records can be a valuable source of information and can tell the story of a company's pattern of success—or lack of it! Unfortunately, many business owners are sloppy record keepers. Consequently, a potential buyer and his or her team may have to reconstruct critical records. It is important to verify as much information about the business as possible. For instance, does the owner have current customer direct mail and e-mail lists? These can be valuable marketing tools for a new business owner.

- *Intangible assets.* As we have seen, determining the value of intangible assets is much more difficult than computing the value of tangible assets, yet intangible assets can be some of the most valuable parts of a business acquisition. Does the sale include intangible assets such as trademarks, patents, copyrights, or goodwill? Edward Karstetter, director of valuation services at USBX, says, "The value placed on intangible assets such as people, knowledge, relationships, and intellectual property is now a greater proportion of the total value of most businesses than is the value of tangible assets such as machinery and equipment."[15]

- *Location and appearance.* The location and appearance of the building are important to most businesses because they send clear messages to potential customers. Every buyer should consider the location's suitability for today and for the near future. Potential buyers also should check local zoning laws to ensure that the changes they want to make are permissible. In some areas, zoning laws are very difficult to change and can restrict a business's growth.

LEGAL ISSUES What legal aspects of the business present risk? Business buyers face myriad legal pitfalls. The most significant legal issues involve liens, contract assignments, covenants not to compete, and ongoing legal liabilities.

Liens The key legal issue in the sale of any asset is typically the proper transfer of good title from seller to buyer. However, because most business sales involve a collection of assorted assets, the transfer of a good title is complex. Some business assets may have **liens** (creditors' claims) against them, and unless those liens are satisfied before the sale, the buyer must assume them and become financially responsible for them. One way to reduce this potential problem is to include a clause in the sales contract that states that any liability not shown on the balance sheet at the time of sale remains the responsibility of the seller. A prospective buyer should have an attorney thoroughly investigate all of the assets for sale and their lien status before buying any business.

liens
claims by creditors against a company's assets.

Contract Assignments A buyer must investigate the rights and obligations he or she would assume under existing contracts with suppliers, customers, employees, lessors, and others. To continue the smooth operation of the business, the buyer must assume the rights of the seller under existing contracts. For example, the current owner may have four years left on a 10-year lease that he or she will assign to the buyer (if the lease allows assignment). A seller can assign most contractual rights unless the contract specifically prohibits the assignment or the contract is personal in nature. For instance, loan contracts sometimes prohibit assignments with **due-on-sale clauses**. These clauses require the buyer to pay the full amount of the remaining loan balance or to finance the balance at prevailing interest rates. Thus, the buyer cannot assume the seller's loan at a lower interest rate. In addition, a seller usually cannot assign his or her credit arrangements with suppliers to the buyer because they are based on the seller's business reputation and are personal in nature. If contracts such as these are crucial to the business's operation and cannot be assigned, the buyer must negotiate new contracts.

due-on-sale clause
a clause that requires the buyer to pay the full amount of the remaining loan balance or to finance the balance at prevailing interest rates, thus preventing the buyer from assuming the seller's loan at a lower interest rate.

The prospective buyer also should evaluate the terms of other contracts the seller has, including the following:

- Patent, trademark, or copyright registrations

- Exclusive agent or distributor contracts

- Insurance contracts

- Financing and loan arrangements

- Union contracts

Covenants Not to Compete One of the most important and most often overlooked legal considerations for a prospective buyer is negotiating a **covenant not to compete** (or a **restrictive covenant**) with the seller. Under a restrictive covenant, the seller agrees not to open a competing business within a specific time period and geographic area of the existing one. (The buyer must negotiate the covenant directly with the owner, not the corporation; if the corporation signs the agreement, the owner may not be bound by it.) However, the covenant must be a part of a business sale and must be reasonable in scope to be enforceable. Without this protection, a buyer may find the new business eroding beneath his or her feet.

covenant not to compete (or restrictive covenant)
an agreement tied to the sale of a business in which the seller agrees not to open a competing business within a specific time period and geographic area of the existing one.

Ongoing Legal Liabilities   Finally, a potential buyer must look for any potential legal liabilities the purchase might expose. These typically arise from three sources:

- Physical premises
- Product liability claims
- Labor relations

Physical Premises   The buyer must first examine the physical premises for safety. Is the employees' health at risk because of asbestos or some other hazardous material? If the business is a manufacturing operation, does it meet Occupational Safety and Health Administration and other regulatory agency requirements?

Product Liability Claims   The buyer must consider whether the product contains defects that could result in **product liability lawsuits**, which claim that a company is liable for damages and injuries caused by the products or services it sells. Existing lawsuits might be an omen of more to follow. In addition, the buyer must explore products that the company has discontinued because he or she might be liable for them if they prove to be defective. The final bargain between the parties should require the seller to guarantee that the company is not involved in any product liability lawsuits.

product liability lawsuit

a lawsuit which claims that a company is liable for damages and injuries caused by the products or services it sells.

Labor Relations   The relationship between management and employees is a key to a successful transition of ownership. Does a union represent employees in a collective bargaining agreement? The time to discover sour management–labor relations is before the purchase, not after.

The existence of liabilities such as these does not necessarily eliminate a business from consideration. Insurance coverage can shift risk from the potential buyer, but the buyer should determine whether the insurance covers lawsuits resulting from actions taken before the purchase. The buyer can also insist on a hold back of a percentage of the purchase price for a period of time to protect against unknown liabilities and other discrepancies. Despite conducting a thorough search, a buyer may purchase a business only to discover later the presence of hidden liabilities, such as unpaid back taxes or delinquent bills, unpaid pension fund contributions, or undisclosed lawsuits. Including a clause in the purchase agreement that imposes the responsibility for such hidden liabilities on the seller can protect a buyer from unpleasant surprises after the sale.

FINANCIAL CONDITION   Is the business financially sound? Any investment in a company should produce a reasonable salary for the owner and a healthy return on the money invested. Otherwise, purchasing the business makes no sense. Therefore, every serious buyer must analyze the records of the business to determine its true financial health. Accounting systems and methods can vary tremendously from one company to another, and buyers usually benefit from enlisting the assistance of an accountant. Some business sellers know all the tricks to make profits appear to be higher than they actually are. For example, a seller might lower costs by gradually eliminating equipment maintenance or might boost sales by selling to marginal customers who will never pay for their purchases. Techniques such as these can artificially inflate a company's earnings, but a well-prepared buyer will be able to see through them. For a buyer, the most dependable financial records are audited statements, those prepared by a certified public accountant in accordance with Generally Accepted Accounting Principles. Unfortunately, most small businesses that are for sale do not have audited financial statements.

A buyer also must remember that he or she is purchasing the future earning potential of an existing business. To evaluate a company's earning potential, a buyer should review past sales, operating expenses, and profits as well as the assets used to generate those profits. The buyer must compare current balance sheets and income statements with previous ones and then develop pro forma statements for the next two or three years. Sales tax records, income tax returns, and financial statements are valuable sources of information.

Earnings trends are another area to analyze. Are profits consistent over time, or have they been erratic? If there are fluctuations, what caused them? Is this earnings pattern typical in the industry, or is it a result of unique circumstances or poor management? If poor management has caused these fluctuations, can a new manager make a difference? Some of the financial records that a potential buyer should examine include the income statement, balance sheet, tax returns, owner's compensation, and cash flow.

Income Statements and Balance Sheets for at Least Three Years It is important to review data from several years because creative accounting techniques can distort financial data in any single year. Even though buyers are purchasing the future earnings of a business, they must remember that many businesses intentionally show low profits to minimize the owners' tax bills. Low profits should prompt a buyer to investigate their causes. Specific entries should be verified using company records for all major categories of expenses and revenues. If the financial statements are not audited, the buyer should take care to validate the financial statements. It is best to seek the assistance of a reputable accountant who has experience in acquisitions.

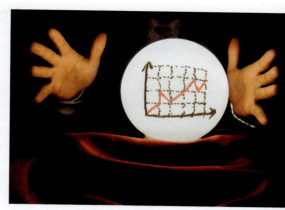

Turk_stock_photographer/Getty Images

Income Tax Returns for at Least Three Years Comparing basic financial statements with tax returns can reveal discrepancies of which the buyer should be aware. Some small business owners "skim" from their businesses; that is, they take money from sales without reporting it as income. Owners who skim will claim their businesses are more profitable than their tax returns show. However, buyers should not pay for "phantom profits."

Cash Flow Most buyers understand the importance of evaluating a company's earnings history, but few recognize the need to analyze its cash flow. They assume that if earnings are adequate, there will be sufficient cash to pay all the bills and to fund an adequate salary for them. *That is not necessarily the case.* Before closing any deal, a buyer should review the information with an accountant and convert the target company's financial statements into a cash flow forecast. This forecast must take into account not only existing debts and obligations but also any modifications the buyer plans to make or additional debts the buyer plans to take on in the business. It should reflect the repayment of financing the buyer arranges to purchase the company. The critical questions are the following: Can the company generate sufficient cash to be self-supporting? How much cash will it generate for the buyer?

A potential buyer must look for suspicious deviations from the average (in either direction) for sales, expenses, profits, assets, and liabilities. Are sales increasing or decreasing? Does the equipment's value on the balance sheet reflect its real value? Are advertising expenses unusually high? How is depreciation reflected in the financial statements?

Finally, a potential buyer should always be wary of purchasing a business if the present owner refuses to disclose the company's financial records. In that case, the buyer's best course of action is to walk away from the deal. Without access to information about the business, a buyer cannot conduct a proper analysis.

 You Be the Consultant

The Power of Seller Financing

After spending several years in the advertising and publishing industries, Janelle Regotti wanted to be her own boss and decided that buying a business would be the best route for her. After spending several months looking for the right business, Regotti found a promising business, Guide Publishing, for sale for $500,000. This northeastern Ohio company distributes a quarterly resource guide aimed at senior adults. However, Regotti had very little in savings and few assets to pledge as collateral, and she knew she would be unlikely to get a bank loan. Working

with the business broker, Regotti convinced the seller to provide financing for 90 percent of the purchase price: Regotti came up with $50,000, and the seller agreed to finance the $450,000 balance over 10 years, with quarterly payments at 6 percent annual interest. Regotti also promised the seller that two years after the purchase, she would apply for a bank loan guaranteed by the Small Business Administration. She promised that if she got the loan at that point, she would pay the loan balance to the seller in full.

(continued)

You Be the Consultant *(continued)*

Like Janelle Regotti, many other potential business buyers, especially young people recently out of college, have not accumulated enough wealth to purchase an existing business, even though it may be the ideal opportunity. That's the position in which Alex Livingston and his business partner, Eddie Santillan, found themselves. The recent college graduates found a facilities maintenance firm for sale by the Baby Boomer founder, who was ready to retire. The company had a long track record of solid financial performance, but there was no way Livingston and Santillan could afford the multi-million-dollar price tag. The enterprising aspiring entrepreneurs approached a private investor group with a business plan for improving and expanding the company and received an equity investment equivalent to 25 percent of the purchase price. With the equity infusion in hand, Livingston and Santillan approached the Exchange Bank in Santa Rosa, California, and received a loan guaranteed by the Small Business Administration for 55 percent of the purchase price. Finally, they convinced the seller to provide financing for the remaining 20 percent of the purchase price. Today, because of their financing creativity, Livingston and Santillan are successful business owners.

Courtesy of Isabel Angell

Finding the financing to make a business purchase can be challenging, but financing the purchase of an existing business usually is easier than financing a business start-up, where the risks are much higher. Many business buyers find that the seller is an ideal source of funding. Although most sellers prefer to finance less than 50 percent of the purchase price, some are willing to finance a greater percentage, especially for the right buyer. Jeremy Bragg had worked at River City Coffee for several years when the owner decided to sell. Bragg and his business partner, Regi Ott, convinced the owner to accept their $10,000 down payment and finance the remaining 86 percent of the $70,000 purchase price.

Buyers who rely on seller financing typically need good credit scores and must be prepared to convince the seller that they will be successful business owners. A realistic business plan showing how the new owner intends to maintain or enhance the company's success and generate sufficient cash flow to keep the business growing while paying the seller's loan is essential. In addition, buyers who rely on seller financing lose some bargaining power when it comes to negotiating a deal.

1. Suppose that you and a friend have recently graduated from college when you discover the ideal business for sale by the founder, who is ready to retire. The asking price is $550,000, but you and your friend have only $15,000. Put together a brief plan for assembling the remaining balance needed to purchase this business.

Sources: Based on Michelle Goodman, "Let's Make a Deal," *Entrepreneur*, May 2015, p. 74; David Ryan, "How to Buy a Business When You Have No Collateral," *Forbes*, December 2, 2014, www.forbes.com/sites/groupthink/2014/12/02/how-to-buy-a-business-when-you-have-no-collateral/#4f28eb292b84; Curtis Kroeker, "4 Things Business Buyers Need to Know About Seller Financing," *The Business Journals*, January 6, 2014, www.bizjournals.com/bizjournals/how-to/buy-a-business/bizbuysell/2014/01/4-things-to-know-about-seller-financing.html; Joyce M. Rosenberg, "Sales of Small Businesses Picking Up," *Greenville News*, November 3, 2013, p. 4E.

LO5

Explain the various methods used to estimate the value of a business.

non-disclosure agreement (NDA)

a legal contract that requires a prospective buyer to maintain the confidentiality of the business, its owner, and any information, financial and otherwise, that the buyer sees as part of the due diligence process.

The Valuation Stage

After conducting due diligence on a target business, an entrepreneur moves into the valuation stage. The valuation stage includes not only a valuation of the business but also signing a non-disclosure agreement.

Non-disclosure Agreement

Prospective business buyers must have access to a company's records and financial information in order to evaluate the opportunity properly. Business sellers must be willing to provide that information to serious, qualified buyers, but because of the sensitive nature of the information, sellers expect prospective buyers to sign a **non-disclosure agreement (NDA)** before giving them access to the information. A non-disclosure agreement is a legal contract, and a buyer who violates its terms is subject to legal action and possibly damages. A typical NDA requires a prospective buyer to maintain the confidentiality of the business, its owner, and any information—financial and otherwise—that the buyer sees. An NDA also requires a prospective buyer to return or destroy any information at the request of the seller. NDAs often contain clauses that prevent prospective buyers from contacting employees, lenders, vendors, and customers of the company without the seller's permission.

Methods for Determining the Value of a Business

Business valuation is partly an art and partly a science. It is important for the prospective buyer to understand that valuation is the point in the process of buying a business at which many deals fail. The sheer number of variables that influence the value of a privately owned business makes establishing a price difficult. These factors include the nature of the business itself, its position in the market or industry, the outlook for the market or industry, the company's financial status and stability, its earning capacity, intangible assets (such as patents, trademarks, and copyrights), and the value of similar companies, among many others. According to BizBuySell, the median asking price for a small company is $250,000, and the median selling price is $237,000, but 8 percent of small businesses sell for more than $1 million.[16] Hip-hop artist Andre "Dr. Dre" Young and music industry veteran Jimmy Iovine recently sold Beats Electronics, the maker of high-end headphones they started in 2008 in Santa Monica, California, to Apple Inc. for an amazing $3 billion. The deal was Apple's largest strategic acquisition to date and included $2.5 million for the Beats Electronics headphone division and $500 million for its music streaming service.[17]

Assessing the value of a company's tangible assets usually is straightforward, but assigning a price to the intangible assets, such as goodwill, almost always creates controversy. The seller expects the value of the goodwill to reflect the hard work and long hours invested in building the business. Valuing goodwill often is an emotional issue for sellers because their businesses are tied closely to their egos. The buyer, however, is willing to pay only for intangible assets that produce extra income. How can a buyer and a seller arrive at a fair price? There are few hard-and-fast rules in establishing the value of a business, but the following guidelines can help:

Hip-hop artist Andre "Dr. Dre" Young and music industry veteran Jimmy Iovine

C Flanigan/Getty Images

- There is no single best method for determining a business's value because each business sale is unique. A practical approach is to estimate a company's value by using several techniques, review those values, and then determine the range in which most of the values converge.

- The deal must be financially feasible for both parties. The seller must be satisfied with the price received for the business, and the buyer cannot pay an excessively high price that requires heavy borrowing that strains cash flow from the outset.

- The buyer should have access to all business records.

- Valuations should be based on facts, not feelings or fiction.

- The two parties should deal with one another openly, honestly, and in good faith.

The main reason that buyers purchase existing businesses is to get their future earning potential. The second-most-common reason is to obtain an established asset base; it is much easier to buy assets than to build them. Although some valuation methods take these goals into consideration, many business sellers and buyers simplify the process by relying on rules of thumb to estimate the value of a business. For instance, one rule for valuing a retail auto parts store is 40 percent of its annual sales plus its inventory.[18] Other rules use multiples of a company's net earnings before interest, depreciation, and amortization (EBITDA) to value the business. Although multipliers vary by industry, most small companies sell for 0.5 to 10 times their EBITDA, with a median selling price of 1.5 to 5.1 times their EBITDA, depending on their size. The median EBITDA multiplier for companies valued at less than $500,000 is 1.5; for companies valued between $1 million and $5 million, the median EBITDA multiplier is 4.0.[19] Factors that increase the value of the multiplier include proprietary products and patents; a strong, diversified base of repeat customers; above-average growth rate; a strong, balanced management team; and dominant market share. Factors that decrease the value of the multiplier include generic, "me-too" products; dependence on a single customer or a small group of customers for a significant portion of sales; reliance on the skills of a single manager (e.g., the founder); declining market share; and dependence on a single product for generating sales.[20] Several companies, including Business Valuation Resources, BizBuySell, and Business Brokerage Press, publish data, including multipliers and prices, that entrepreneurs who are looking to buy (or sell) a business find useful.

This section describes three basic techniques—the balance sheet method, the earnings approach, and the market approach—and several variations on them for determining the value of a hypothetical business, Kuyper Electronics.

net worth (or owner's equity)
Net worth =
Assets – Liabilities

BALANCE SHEET METHOD The balance sheet method establishes the value of a company by computing the book value of its **net worth**, or **owner's equity** (Net worth = Assets − Liabilities. A common criticism of this technique is that it oversimplifies the valuation process. The problem with this technique is that it fails to recognize reality: Most small businesses have market values that exceed their reported book values.

The first step is to determine which assets are included in the sale. In most cases, the owner has some personal assets that he or she does not want to sell. Professional business brokers can help the buyer and the seller arrive at a reasonable value for the collection of assets included in the deal. Remember that net worth on a financial statement will likely differ significantly from actual net worth in the market. Figure 7.5 shows the balance sheet for Kuyper Electronics. This balance sheet shows that the company's net worth is as follows:

$$\$266,091 - \$114,325 = \$151,766$$

Variation: Adjusted Balance Sheet Technique A more realistic method for determining a company's value is to adjust the book value of net worth to reflect the *actual* market value. The values reported on a company's books may either overstate or understate the true value of assets and liabilities. Typical assets in a business sale include notes and accounts receivable, inventory, supplies, and fixtures. If a buyer purchases notes and accounts receivable, he or she should estimate the likelihood of their collection and adjust their value accordingly (refer to Table 7.1).

In manufacturing, wholesale, and retail businesses, inventory is usually the largest single asset in the sale. Taking a physical inventory count is the best way to determine accurately the condition and quantity of goods to be transferred. The sale may include three types of inventory, each having its own method of valuation: raw materials, work in process, and finished goods. Before accepting any inventory value, a buyer should evaluate the condition of the goods to avoid being stuck with inventory that he or she cannot sell.

Fixed assets transferred in a sale might include land, buildings, equipment, and fixtures. Business owners frequently carry real estate and buildings on their books at their original purchase prices, which typically are well below their actual market value. Equipment and fixtures, depending on their condition and usefulness, may increase or decrease the value of the business. Appraisals of these assets on insurance policies are helpful guidelines for establishing market value. In addition, business brokers can be useful in determining the current value of fixed assets. Some brokers use an estimate of what it would cost to replace a company's physical assets (less a reasonable allowance for depreciation) to determine their value. As indicated by the adjusted balance sheet in Figure 7.6, the adjusted net worth for Kuyper Electronics is $279,738 − $114,325 = $165,413, which indicates that some of the entries on its books did not accurately reflect market value.

Business valuations based on any balance sheet methods suffer one major drawback: They do not consider the future earnings potential of the business. These techniques value assets at current prices and do not consider them as tools for creating future profits. An additional omission is that balance sheet methods do not attach value to intangible assets of the business, such as goodwill.

EARNINGS APPROACH The earnings approach is an approach to valuation that finance professionals and experienced entrepreneurs prefer because it considers the future income potential of the business. That is what an entrepreneur really is buying with an existing business—its ability to generate returns on the investment into the future.

ASSETS

Current Assets

Cash		$11,655
Accounts receivable		15,876
Inventory		56,523
Supplies		8,574
Prepaid insurance		5,587
Total current assets		$98,215

Fixed Assets

Land			$24,000
Buildings	$141,000		
less accumulated depreciation	51,500	89,500	
Office equipment	$12,760		
less accumulated depreciation	7,159	5,601	
Factory equipment	$59,085		
less accumulated depreciation	27,850	31,235	
Trucks and autos	$28,730		
less accumulated depreciation	11,190	17,540	
Total fixed assets			$167,876
Total Assets			**$266,091**

LIABILITIES

Current Liabilities

Accounts payable		$19,497
Mortgage payable		5,215
Salaries Payable		3,671
Note Payable		10,000
Total current liabilities		$38,383

Long-Term Liabilities

Mortgage payable		$54,542
Note payable		21,400
Total long-term liabilities		$75,942
Total Liabilities		**$114,325**

OWNER'S EQUITY

Owner's Equity (Net Worth)		$151,766
Total Liabilities + Owner's Equity		**$266,091**

FIGURE 7.5

Balance Sheet for Kuyper Electronics, June 30, 20XX

Variation 1: Adjusted Earnings Method The easiest approach to calculating the value of a business based on its earnings is known as the adjusted earnings method of valuation. Although it does not have the sophistication of the other methods, it is quite commonly used and is accurate enough for many small businesses. This simple method starts with earnings before interest, taxes, depreciation, and amortization (EBITDA) because this is a good measure of the true cash earnings of a business. The buyer deducts interest and taxes because they likely will change with a new owner. Depreciation and amortization will also change because the new owner's accountants will reset the values and time lines that generate these noncash expenses. The buyer normally adjusts the EBITDA reported by the seller to help determine the true value of the business going forward. Because entrepreneurs rarely pay themselves market-based salaries, the buyer replaces the salary of the previous owner with a market-based salary for a typical CEO of a similar-size company. Next, the buyer adds back all personal expenses (such as an auto lease or

FIGURE 7.6

Adjusted Balance Sheet for Kuyper Electronics, June 30, 20XX

ASSETS

Current Assets

Cash	$11,655	
Accounts receivable	10,051	
Inventory	39,261	
Supplies	7,492	
Prepaid insurance	5,587	
Total current assets		$74,046

Fixed Assets

Land		$52,000	
Buildings	$177,000		
less accumulated depreciation	51,500	115,500	
Office equipment	$11,645		
less accumulated depreciation	7,159	4,486	
Factory equipment	$50,196		
less accumulated depreciation	27,850	22,346	
Trucks and autos	$22,550		
less accumulated depreciation	11,190	11,360	
Total fixed assets			$205,692
Total Assets			**$279,738**

LIABILITIES

Current Liabilities

Accounts payable	$19,497	
Mortgage payable	5,215	
Salaries Payable	3,671	
Note Payable	10,000	
Total current liabilities		$38,383

Long-Term Liabilities

Mortgage payable	$54,542	
Note payable	21,400	
Total long-term liabilities		$75,942
Total Liabilities		**$114,325**

OWNER'S EQUITY

Owner's Equity (Net Worth)	$165,413
Total Liabilities + Owner's Equity	**$279,738**

a country club membership) that the current owner runs through the business. Finally, the buyer deducts the costs required to bring inventories up to necessary levels and to update equipment. Suppose that a prospective buyer discovers the following values for Kuyper Electronics:

Reported EBITDA	$200,000
Add: Current owner's salary	50,000
Subtract: Market salary for CEO	(75,000)
Add: Personal expenses	10,000
Subtract: Inventory needed	(25,000)
Subtract: Equipment updates	(40,000)
Adjusted EBITDA	$120,000

Note that the adjusted EBITDA is significantly lower than the EBITDA reported on Kuyper Electronics's income statement. Had the buyer simply used the reported EBITDA, the price paid for buying the business would have been significantly higher!

The buyer then uses the adjusted EBITDA and an *earnings multiple* to project future potential earnings. Recall that the typical multiplier ranges from 0.5 to 10 times EBITDA, with an average multiple between 1.5 and 5.1. Five factors determine the actual multiplier used in a business sale. First, the recent trend of earnings in the business influences the multiple. A business with flat or declining earnings over the three years leading up to the sale will have a much lower multiplier than one that has shown consistently strong growth in recent earnings. Second, the buyer must take into account the growth trends of the overall industry. Third, the buyer must give consideration to market conditions in the industry by looking at multipliers from comparable companies that have sold recently. Fourth, the buyer must consider strategic factors such as unique patents or proprietary processes in determining the earnings multiplier. For example, an engineering firm in Minnesota recently sold for a multiple of *25 times* EBITDA because the company had a proprietary patented technology that several larger firms wanted to control. Finally, the structure of the deal itself has an impact. Buyers who pay with cash typically pay a lower multiple than buyers who rely on owner financing or a stock purchase. Suppose that the buyer's research shows an EBITDA multiplier of 4.0 for electronics companies. Taking into account the factors described earlier, the buyer who is considering Kuyper Electronics uses a multiplier of 4.2. The estimated value of the business is as follows:

$$\$120,000 \times 4.2 = \$504,000$$

Variation 2: Excess Earnings Method This method combines both the value of a company's existing assets (less its liabilities) and an estimate of its future earnings potential to determine the selling price for the business. One advantage of the **excess earnings method** is that it offers an estimate of goodwill. **Goodwill** is the difference between an established, successful business and one that has yet to prove itself. Goodwill is based on the company's reputation and its ability to attract and retain customers. This intangible asset often creates problems in a business sale. A common method of valuing a business is to compute its tangible net worth and then to add an often arbitrary adjustment for goodwill. However, a buyer should not accept blindly the seller's arbitrary adjustment for goodwill because it is likely to be inflated.

The excess earnings method is a reasonable approach for determining the value of goodwill. It measures goodwill by the amount of profit the business earns above that of the average firm in the same industry. It also assumes that the owner is entitled to a reasonable return on the company's adjusted tangible net worth.

Step 1. *Compute adjusted tangible net worth.* The buyer computes the company's adjusted tangible net worth. Total tangible assets (adjusted for market value) minus total liabilities yields adjusted tangible net worth. In the Kuyper Electronics example shown in Figure 7.6, the adjusted tangible net worth is $279,738 – $114,325 = $165,413.

Step 2. *Calculate the opportunity costs of investing in the business.* **Opportunity costs** represent the cost of forgoing a choice. What income does the potential buyer give up by purchasing the business? If the buyer chooses to purchase the assets of a business, he or she cannot invest his or her money elsewhere. Therefore, the opportunity cost of the purchase is the amount that the buyer could have earned by investing the same amount *in an investment with similar risk.*

Three components determine the rate of return used to value a business: (1) the basic, risk-free return, (2) an inflation premium, and (3) the risk allowance for investing in the particular business. The basic, risk-free return and the inflation premium are reflected in investments such as U.S. Treasury bonds. To determine the appropriate rate of return for investing in a business, the buyer must add to this base rate a factor reflecting the risk of purchasing the company. The greater the risk involved, the higher the rate of return. An average-risk business typically indicates a 20 to 25 percent rate of return. Using an average rate of 25 percent for Kuyper Electronics, the opportunity cost of the investment is $165,413 × 25% = $41,353.

excess earnings method
a business valuation method that combines both the value of a company's existing assets (less its liabilities) and an estimate of its future earnings potential to determine the selling price for the business.

goodwill
the difference between an established, successful business and one that has yet to prove itself that is based on the company's reputation and its ability to attract and retain customers.

opportunity cost
the cost of forgoing a choice; the cost of the next best alternative.

The second part of the buyer's opportunity cost is the salary that he or she could have earned working for someone else. For the Kuyper Electronics example, if the buyer purchases the business, he or she must forgo a salary of, say, $75,000 that he or she could have earned working elsewhere. Adding these amounts yields a total opportunity cost of 41,353 + 75,000 = $116,353.

Step 3. *Project net earnings.* The buyer must estimate the company's net earnings for the upcoming year *before* subtracting the owner's salary. Averages can be misleading; therefore, the buyer must be sure to investigate the *trend* of net earnings. Have the earnings risen steadily over the past five years, dropped significantly, remained relatively constant, or fluctuated wildly? Past income statements provide useful guidelines for estimating earnings, but, as you have seen, the buyer often must adjust the earnings. In the Kuyper Electronics example, the buyer and an accountant project the buyer's adjusted net earnings to be $195,000 (earnings of $120,000 plus the buyer's anticipated salary of $75,000).

extra earning power
the difference between a company's forecasted earnings and the total opportunity costs of investing in that company.

Step 4. *Compute extra earning power.* A company's **extra earning power** is the difference between forecasted earnings (step 3) and total opportunity costs of investing (step 2). Many small businesses that are for sale do not have extra earning power (i.e., excess earnings), and they show marginal or no profits. The extra earning power of Kuyper Electronics is $195,000 – $116,353 = $78,647.

Step 5. *Estimate the value of intangibles.* The buyer can use the business's extra earning power to estimate the value of its intangible assets. Multiplying the extra earning power by a years-of-profit figure yields an estimate of the intangible assets' value. The years-of-profit figure ranges from one to seven, but for a normal-risk business typically falls between three and four. A high-risk business may have a years-of-profit figure of one, whereas a well-established firm might use a figure of seven.

Rating the company on a scale of 1 (low) to 7 (high) on the following factors allows an entrepreneur to calculate a reasonable years-of-profit figure to use to estimate the value of the intangibles:[21]

				Score				
Factor	1	2	3	4	5	6	7
1. Risk	More risky					Less risky	
2. Degree of competition	Intense competition					Few competitors	
3. Industry attractiveness	Fading					Attractive	
4. Barriers to entry	Low					High	
5. Growth potential	Low					High	
6. Owner's reason for selling	Poor performance					Retiring	
7. Age of business	Young					10+ years old	
8. Current owner's tenure	Short					10+ years	
9. Profitability	Below average					Above average	
10. Location	Problematic					Desirable	
11. Customer base	Limited and shrinking					Diverse and growing	
12. Image and reputation	Poor					Stellar	

To calculate the years-of-profit figure, the entrepreneur adds the score for each factor and divides by the number of factors (12). For Kuyper Electronics, the scores are as follows:

Risk	3
Degree of competition	2
Industry attractiveness	4
Barriers to entry	2

Growth potential	4
Owner's reason for selling	6
Age of business	6
Owner's tenure	6
Profitability	4
Location	4
Customer base	3
Image and reputation	5
Total	49

Thus, for Kuyper Electronics, the years-of-profit figure is $49 \div 12 = 4.1$, and the value of intangibles is $\$78,647 \times 4.1 = \$322,452$.

Step 6. *Determine the value of the business.* To determine the value of the business, the buyer simply adds together the adjusted tangible net worth (step 1) and the value of the intangibles (step 5). Using this method, the value of Kuyper Electronics is $\$165,413 + \$322,452 = \$487,865$.

Both the buyer and the seller should consider the tax implications of transferring goodwill. Because the *buyer* can amortize both the cost of goodwill and a restrictive covenant over 15 years, the tax treatment of either would be the same. However, the *seller* would prefer to have the amount of the purchase price in excess of the value of the assets allocated to goodwill, which is a capital asset. The gain on the capital asset is at lower capital gains rates. If that same amount were allocated to a restrictive covenant (which is negotiated with the seller personally, not with the business), the seller must treat it as ordinary income, which is taxed at regular rates that currently are higher than the capital gains rates.

Variation 3: Capitalized Earnings Approach Another earnings approach capitalizes expected net earnings to determine the value of a business. The buyer should prepare his own pro forma income statement and should ask the seller to prepare one also. Many appraisers use a five-year weighted average of past sales (with the greatest weights assigned to the most recent years) to estimate sales for the upcoming year.

Once again, the buyer must evaluate the risk of purchasing the business to determine the appropriate rate of return on the investment. The greater the perceived risk, the higher the return the buyer will require. Risk determination is always somewhat subjective but is a necessary consideration for proper evaluation.

The **capitalized earnings approach** divides estimated net earnings (after subtracting a reasonable salary for the owner) by the rate of return that reflects the risk level. For Kuyper Electronics, the capitalized value (assuming a reasonable salary of $75,000) is as follows:

$$\frac{\text{Net earnings (after deducting owner's salary)}}{\text{Rate of return}} = \frac{\$195,000 - \$75,000}{25\%} = \$480,000$$

Companies with lower risk factors offer greater certainty and, therefore, are more valuable. For example, a lower rate of return of 10 percent yields a value of $1,200,000 for Kuyper Electronics, whereas a 50 percent rate of return produces a value of $240,000. Most normal-risk businesses use a rate-of-return factor ranging from 20 to 25 percent. The lowest risk factor that most buyers would accept for any business ranges from 15 to 18 percent.

Variation 4: Discounted Future Earnings Approach The variation of the earnings approach assumes that a dollar earned in the future is worth less than that same dollar today. Using the **discounted future earnings approach**, the buyer estimates the company's net income for several years into the future and then discounts these future earnings back to their present value. The resulting present value is an estimate of the company's worth. The present value represents the cost of the buyers giving up the opportunity to earn a reasonable rate of return by receiving income in the future instead of today.

capitalized earnings approach
a business valuation method that involves dividing a company's estimated net earnings (after subtracting a reasonable salary for the owner) by the rate of return that reflects the risk level of investing in the business.

discounted future earnings approach
a business valuation method that involves estimating a company's net income for several years into the future and then discounts these future earnings back to their present value, which provides an estimate of the company's worth.

To visualize the importance of present value and the time value of money, consider two $1 million sweepstakes winners. Rob wins $1 million in a sweepstakes, and he receives it in $50,000 installments over 20 years. If Rob invests every installment at 8 percent interest, he will have accumulated $2,288,098 at the end of 20 years. Lisa wins $1 million in another sweepstakes, but she collects her winnings in one lump sum. If Lisa invests her $1 million today at 8 percent, she will have accumulated $4,660,957 at the end of 20 years. The dramatic difference in their wealth—Lisa is now worth nearly $2,373,000 more—is the result of the time value of money.

The discounted future earnings approach has five steps:

Step 1. *Project earnings for five years into the future.* One way is to assume that earnings will grow by a constant amount over the next five years. Perhaps a better method is to develop three forecasts—pessimistic, most likely, and optimistic—for each year and find a weighted average by using the following formula:

$$\text{Forecasted earnings for year } i = \frac{\text{Pessimistic earnings for year } i + 4 \times \text{Most Likely earnings for year } i + \text{Optimistic earnings for year } i}{6}$$

The most likely forecast is weighted four times greater than the pessimistic and optimistic forecasts; therefore, the denominator is the sum of the weights $(1 + 4 + 1 = 6)$. For Kuyper Electronics, the buyer's earnings forecasts are as follows:

Year	Pessimistic	Most Likely	Optimistic	Weighted Average
1	$100,000	$120,000	$135,000	**$119,167**
2	108,000	128,000	145,000	**127,500**
3	115,000	140,000	160,000	**139,167**
4	119,000	150,000	170,000	**148,167**
5	125,000	162,000	182,000	**159,167**

The buyer must remember that the further into the future he or she forecasts, the less reliable the estimates will be.

Step 2. *Discount these future earnings by using the appropriate present value factor.* The appropriate present value factor can be found by looking in published present value tables or by solving this equation:

$$1/(1 + k)^t$$

where k = rate of return
and t = time (year 1, 2, 3 ... n).

The rate that the buyer selects should reflect the rate he or she could earn on a similar risk investment. Because Kuyper Electronics is a normal-risk business, the buyer chooses 25 percent.

Year	Income Forecast (Weighted Average)	Present Value Factor (at 25 Percent)	Net Present Value
1	$119,167	.8000	$95,333
2	127,500	.6400	81,600
3	139,167	.5120	71,253
4	148,167	.4096	60,689
5	159,167	.3277	52,156
Total			**$361,031**

Step 3. *Estimate the income stream beyond five years.* One technique suggests multiplying the fifth-year income forecast by 1/(Rate of return). For Kuyper Electronics, the estimate is as follows:

$$\text{Income beyond year 5} = \$159{,}167 \times (1/25\%) = \$636{,}668$$

Step 4. *Discount the income estimate beyond five years using the present value factor for the sixth year.* For Kuyper Electronics,

$$\text{Present value of income beyond year 5: } \$636{,}668 \times 0.2621 = \$166{,}871$$

Step 5. *Compute the total value of the business.*

$$\text{Total value: } \$361{,}031 + \$166{,}871 = \$527{,}902$$

Using the discounted future earnings approach, Kuyper Electronics is worth about $528,000. The primary advantage of this technique is that it values a business solely on the basis of its future earnings potential, but its reliability depends on making accurate forecasts of future earnings and choosing a realistic present value factor. The discounted future earnings approach is especially well suited for valuing service businesses, whose asset bases are often small, and for companies experiencing high growth rates.

MARKET APPROACH The **market (or price/earnings) approach** uses the price/earnings ratios of similar businesses to estimate the value of a company. The buyer must use businesses whose stocks are publicly traded to get a meaningful comparison. A company's price/earnings ratio (P/E ratio) is the price of one share of its common stock in the market divided by its earnings per share (after deducting preferred stock dividends). To get a representative P/E ratio, the buyer should average the P/Es of as many similar businesses as possible.

market (or price/earnings) approach
a business valuation method that involves using the price/earnings ratios of similar publicly traded businesses to estimate the value of a company.

The buyer multiplies the average price/earnings ratio by the private company's estimated earnings (*after* deducting the owner's salary) to compute a company's value. For example, suppose that the buyer found four companies comparable to Kuyper Electronics whose stock is publicly traded. Their price/earnings ratios are as follows:

Company 1	3.9
Company 2	3.8
Company 3	4.3
Company 4	4.1
Average	4.025

This average P/E ratio produces a value of $483,000:

$$\text{Value average P/E ratio} \times \text{Estimated net earnings}$$
$$4.025 \times \$120{,}000 = \$483{,}000$$

The most significant advantage of the market approach is its simplicity. However, the market approach method does have several disadvantages, including the following:

- *Necessary comparisons between publicly traded and privately owned companies.* The stock of privately owned companies is illiquid, and therefore the P/E ratio used is often subjective and lower than that of publicly held companies.

- *Unrepresentative earnings estimates.* The private company's net earnings may not realistically reflect its true earnings potential. To minimize taxes, owners usually attempt to keep profits low and rely on benefits to make up the difference.

- *Finding similar companies for comparison.* Often, it is extremely difficult for a buyer to find comparable publicly held companies when estimating the appropriate P/E ratio.

- *Applying the after-tax earnings of a private company to determine its value.* If a prospective buyer is using an after-tax P/E ratio from a public company, he or she also must use the after-tax earnings from the private company.

Despite its drawbacks, the market approach is useful as a general guideline to establishing a company's value.

FIGURE 7.7

Business Valuation Methods

Source: Based on data from Craig R. Everett, *2017 Private Capital Markets Report*, Pepperdine University, March 15, 2017, p. 55.

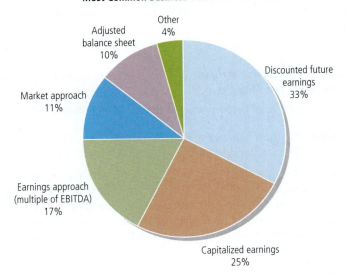

Most Common Business Valuation Methods

- Other 4%
- Adjusted balance sheet 10%
- Market approach 11%
- Discounted future earnings 33%
- Earnings approach (multiple of EBITDA) 17%
- Capitalized earnings 25%

THE BEST METHOD? Figure 7.7 shows the most common valuation methods that business brokers use. Which of these methods is best for determining the value of a small business? Simply stated, there is no single best method. These techniques yield a range of values, but usually several of the values cluster together, giving the buyer useful guidance in determining an offering price. The final price will be based on both the valuation used and the negotiating skills of the parties.

LO6

Describe the basic principles of negotiating a deal to buy a business and structuring the deal.

The Deal Stage

Once an entrepreneur has established a reasonable value for the business, the next step in making a successful purchase is negotiating a suitable deal. Most buyers do not realize that the price they pay for a company often is not as crucial to its continued success as the terms of the purchase. In other words, *the structure of the deal—the terms and conditions of payment—is more important than the price the seller agrees to pay.* A buyer's primary concern is making sure that the terms of the deal do not endanger the company's future financial health and that they preserve the company's cash flow.

On the surface, the negotiation process may appear to be strictly adversarial. Although each party may be trying to accomplish objectives that are at odds with those of the opposing party, the negotiation process does not have to be conflict oriented. The process goes more smoothly and more quickly if the two parties work to establish a cooperative relationship based on honesty and trust from the outset. A successful deal requires both parties to examine and articulate their respective positions while each tries to understand the other party's position. Recognizing that neither of them will benefit without a deal, both parties must work to achieve their objectives while making certain concessions to keep the negotiations alive. To avoid a stalled deal, both buyer and seller should go into the negotiation with a list of objectives, ranked in order of priority. Prioritizing desired outcomes increases the likelihood that both parties will get most of what they want from the bargain. Knowing which terms are most important (and which ones are least important) enables the parties to make concessions without regret and avoid getting bogged down in unnecessary details. If, for instance, the seller insists on a term that the buyer cannot agree to, the seller can explain why he or she cannot concede on that term and then offer to give up something in exchange.

Suhendri/Shutterstock

You Be the Consultant

Would You Buy This Business?

Corbin-Pacific Inc.

Peter Corbin has always loved motorcycles. The founder of Corbin-Pacific Inc., a company based in Hollister, California, still holds the land-speed record, 165 miles per hour, for an electric motorcycle. At 65, Corbin is ready to retire and sell his business, which makes custom seats, saddlebags, fenders, and other motorcycle accessories, preferably to another cycle enthusiast. Listed at $11.5 million, Corbin-Pacific employs 115 workers, including six managers with at least 10 years' experience, in its 82,000-square-foot factory (which also is for sale) and generates annual sales of $14.7 million, down from $16.5 million two years ago. The sales decline occurred after the company had to fire several employees who were undocumented. About 75 percent of the 41-year-old business's sales are direct to end customers, mainly through its Web site, and the remaining 25 percent are to motorcycle dealers.

The company's cash flow declined from $2.73 million two years ago to $722,000 today. Corbin-Pacific incurred losses in each of the last two years but now has returned to profitability.

The purchase price includes 1,500 fiberglass seat molds for every major brand and model of both street and off-road motorbike and intellectual property in the form of 82 patents and copyrights. Corbin is asking $9 million for the patented seat molds, $1.5 million for machinery and equipment, and $719,000 for inventory. Motorcycle sales in the United States have increased 75 percent over the last decade, and Corbin-Pacific is well known to motorcycle enthusiasts from coast to coast and counts celebrities such as Arnold Schwarzenegger and Jay Leno as customers. Corbin says that he is willing to stay on to work with the new owner for up to two years to ensure a smooth transition.

Indiana Machine Shop

This Indiana machine shop is one of approximately 21,000 across the nation that fabricate, press, bend, and drill custom metal products. The sellers, a machinist and his wife, started the company with hand-operated machines, but as the business grew, they invested in computerized numerical control (CNC) equipment that not only increases productivity but also gives them the ability to design custom products and build proto-types quickly and efficiently. The company, which now employs 65 people, generated sales of $8.2 million last year and earned a net income of $625,000, with an EBITDA of $757,150. The company has a diversified customer base and fabricates a variety of products, from wheelchair lifts to livestock feeding systems. Both sales and profits have a strong history of growth. A team of experienced managers is in place and willing to work for the new owner.

An analysis of other machine shop sales shows that the typical price is 5.4 times EBITDA. The owners, both in their mid-40s, are asking $5.3 million for this machine shop, saying that they are ready to move on to other business opportunities. The asking price includes machinery and equipment valued at $2,675,000, real estate at $957,000, and inventory at $750,000.

1. Assume the role of a prospective buyer for these two businesses. How would you conduct the due diligence necessary to determine whether they would be good investments?

2. Do you notice any "red flags" or potential problems in either of these deals? Explain.

3. Which techniques for estimating the value of these businesses would be most useful to a prospective buyer of these companies? Are the owners' asking prices reasonable?

Sources: Based on Darren Dahl, "Business for Sale: A Motorcycle-Seat Manufacturer," *Inc.*, May 1, 2009, www.inc.com/magazine/20090501/business-for-sale-a-motorcycle-seat-manufacturer.html; Joe Delmont, "Seat King Mike Corbin Set to Retire," *Dealer News*, May 4, 2009, www.dealernews.com/dealernews/article/seat-king-mike-corbin-set-retire; Darren Dahl, "Business for Sale: An Indiana Machine Shop," *Inc.*, November 1, 2009, www.inc.com/magazine/20091101/business-for-sale-an-indiana-machine-shop.html.

THE "ART OF THE DEAL" The final deal a buyer strikes depends, in large part, on his or her negotiating skills. The first "rule" of negotiating is to avoid confusing price with value. *Value* is what a business actually is worth; *price* is what the buyer agrees to pay for it. A survey of business brokers found that a gap between the price that the seller wants and the actual valuation of the business is the second-most-common reason deals fall apart.[22] One entrepreneur recalls a negotiation in which he was involved for the potential purchase of a rival's business. The company had $4 million in sales but had incurred losses of more than $1 million in each of the previous two years, owed more than $2.5 million in unpaid bills, and had no machinery that was less than 30 years old. Much to the prospective buyer's amazement, the owner was asking $4 million for the business![23]

FIGURE 7.8

Identifying the Bargaining Zone

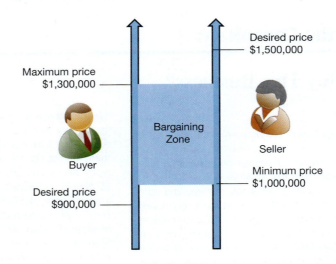

FIGURE 7.8 is not labeled again; the figure shows labels: Maximum price $1,300,000 (Buyer), Desired price $900,000 (Buyer), Bargaining Zone, Desired price $1,500,000 (Seller), Minimum price $1,000,000 (Seller).

Figure 7.8 is an illustration of two individuals prepared to negotiate for the purchase and sale of a business. The buyer and seller both have high and low bargaining points in this example:

- The buyer would like to purchase the business for $900,000 but would not pay more than $1,300,000.

- The seller would like to get $1,500,000 for the business but would not take less than $1,000,000.

- If the seller insists on getting $1,500,000, she will not sell the business to this buyer.

- Likewise, if the buyer stands firm on an offer of $900,000, there will be no deal.

The bargaining process may eventually lead both parties into the *bargaining zone*, the area within which the two parties can reach agreement. It extends from above the lowest price the seller is willing to take to below the maximum price the buyer is willing to pay. The dynamics of this negotiation process and the needs of each party ultimately determine whether the buyer and seller can reach an agreement and for what price.

The following negotiating tips can help parties reach a mutually satisfying deal:

- ***Establish the proper mind-set.*** Successful negotiations are built on a foundation of trust. The first step in any negotiation should be to establish a climate of trust and communication. Too often, buyers and sellers rush into putting their chips on the bargaining table without establishing a rapport with one another.

- ***Know what you want to have when you walk away from the table.*** What will it take to reach your business objectives? What would be the perfect deal? Although it may not be possible to achieve it, defining the perfect deal may help you identify which issues are most important to you.

- ***Develop a negotiating strategy.*** One of the biggest mistakes business buyers can make is entering negotiations with only a vague notion of the strategies they will employ. To be successful, it is necessary to know how to respond to a variety of situations that are likely to arise. Once you know where you want to finish, decide where you will start and remember to leave some room to give. Try not to be the first one to mention price. Let the other party do that and negotiate from there. Every strategy has an upside and a downside, and effective negotiators know what they are.

- ***Recognize the other party's needs.*** For a bargain to occur, both parties must believe that they have met at least some of their goals. Getting answers to open-ended questions can provide insight into the other side's position and enable you to understand why it is important.

- ***Be an empathetic listener.*** To truly understand what the other party's position is, you must listen attentively.

- *Focus on the issue, not on the person.* If the negotiation reaches an impasse, a natural tendency is to attack the other party. Instead, focus on developing a workable solution to accomplish your goals.

- *Avoid seeing the other side as "the enemy."* This attitude reduces the negotiation to an "I win, you lose" mentality that only hinders the process.

- *Educate; don't intimidate.* Rather than try to bully the other party into accepting your point of view, explain the reasoning and the logic behind your proposal.

- *Be creative.* When negotiations stall or come to an impasse, negotiators must seek creative alternatives that benefit both parties or, at a minimum, get the negotiations started again.

- *Keep emotions in check.* A short temper and an important negotiation make ill-suited partners. The surest way to destroy trust and to sabotage a negotiation is to lose one's temper and lash out at the other party. Anger leads to poor decisions.

- *Be patient.* Sound negotiations often take a great deal of time, especially when one is buying a business from the entrepreneur who founded it. The seller's ego is woven throughout the negotiation process, and wise negotiators recognize this. Persistence and patience are the keys to success in any negotiation involving the sale of the business.

- *Don't become a victim.* Well-prepared negotiators are not afraid to walk away from deals that are not right for them.

- *Remember that "no deal" is an option.* What would happen if the negotiations failed to produce a deal? In most negotiations, walking away from the table is an option. In some cases, it may be the best option.

THE BUYER'S GOALS The buyer seeks to realize the following goals:

- Get the business at the lowest price possible.

- Negotiate favorable payment terms, preferably over time.

- Get assurances that he is buying the business he thinks it is.

- Avoid enabling the seller to open a competing business.

- Minimize the amount of cash paid up front.

THE SELLER'S GOALS Entrepreneurs who are most effective at acquiring a business know how important it is to understand the complex emotions that influence the seller's behavior and decisions. For some sellers, this business has been their life and has defined their identity. They may have been the original founder and the person who created the business. For many entrepreneurs, their business defines who they are. They nurtured the business through its infancy and matured it, and now it is time to "let go." Sellers may be asking themselves, What will I do now? Where will I go each morning? Who will I be without "my business"? The negotiation process may bring these questions to light because it requires sellers to, in effect, put a price tag on their life's work. For these reasons, the potential buyer must negotiate in a manner that displays sensitivity and respect.

In general, the seller of the business is looking to accomplish the following goals:

- Get the highest price possible for the company.

- Sever all responsibility for the company's liabilities.

- Avoid unreasonable contract terms that might limit future opportunities.

- Maximize the cash from the deal.

- Minimize the tax burden from the sale.

- Make sure the buyer will make all future payments.

Hands On . . . How To

Be a Successful Negotiator

Buying or selling a business always involves a negotiation, and so do many other business activities, whether an entrepreneur is dealing with a bank, a customer, or a vendor. That's why negotiating skills are among the most important skills that entrepreneurs can learn. How can you become a more successful negotiator? The following advice will help:

1. *Prepare*. Good negotiators know that the formula for a successful negotiation is 90 percent preparation and 10 percent bargaining. What you do—or don't do—*before* the negotiation ever begins is a primary determinant of how successful your negotiation will be. The key is to learn as much as possible about the party with whom you will be negotiating, the issues that are most important to him or her, and his or her likely positions on those issues.

   Your preparation for a negotiation also should include a statement of the outcome you desire from the negotiation. You also should write down what you think your *counterpart's* goals from the negotiation are. This encourages you to look at the negotiation from the other party's perspective and can be a valuable and revealing exercise.

2. *Remember the difference between a "position" and an "interest."* The outcome a person wants from a negotiation is his or her position. What is much more important, however, is his or her interest, the reason behind the position that he or she hopes to achieve. Focusing strictly on their positions usually leads two parties into a win–lose mentality in a negotiation, in which they try to pound one another into submission. When the parties involved in a negotiation focus on their *interests* rather than on their *positions*, however, they usually discover that there are several different solutions that both will consider acceptable and reasonable.

   The parable of the orange provides an excellent lesson on the difference between the two. Two parties each want an orange, but there is only one orange. After much intense negotiating, the two agree to cut the orange in half. As it turns out, however, one party wanted only the rind of the orange to make cookies, and the other party wanted the orange to make orange juice. If the parties involved in the negotiation had focused on their interests rather than their positions and taken a problem-solving approach, both could have gotten exactly what they wanted from the negotiation!

3. *Develop the right mind-set.* Inexperienced negotiators see a negotiation as a zero-sum, win–lose game. "If you win, then I lose." Successful negotiations almost always involve compromise on both sides, which means that *neither* party gets *everything* that he or she wanted. In other words, successful negotiators see a negotiation not just as deal making but also as problem solving. Their goal is to work toward a mutually beneficial agreement that both parties consider to be fair and reasonable.

4. *Always leave yourself an escape hatch.* In any negotiation, you should be prepared to walk away without making a deal. Doing so, however, requires you to define what negotiation experts call a best alternative to a negotiated agreement (BATNA), which is the next best alternative to a negotiated outcome. You cannot determine whether a negotiated agreement is suitable unless you know what your alternatives are, and one alternative (although not always the best one) is to walk away from the negotiation without an agreement—your BATNA.

   Having a BATNA increases your power in a negotiation, but you should use that power judiciously. Do not use your BATNA as a threat to coerce an agreement. In addition, don't kill a deal just because you can. Instead, use your BATNA as the baseline against which you measure your negotiated alternatives.

5. *Keep your emotions in check.* Negotiations can become emotionally charged, especially if those involved allow their egos to enter into the process. It is always best to abide by the golden rule of negotiating: Treat others the way you want to be treated in the negotiation. Be fair but firm. If the other party forgets the golden rule of negotiating, remember that you can always walk away from the negotiation and fall back on your BATNA.

6. *Don't fall into the "rules" trap.* Successful negotiations involve give-and-take by both parties. There are no rules that prohibit either party from making changes to contracts or agreements throughout the process. Nothing is settled until the parties sign the final documents. Until then, the parties can negotiate and change any terms.

7. *Sometimes it's best to remain silent.* A common mistake many people make in the negotiation process is talking too much. Not only does remaining silent allow you to listen to the other party, it also encourages the other party to make the first offer. Some people are disconcerted by prolonged periods of silence and begin talking, only to erode the strength of their negotiation base.

Sources: Based on "How to Negotiate Effectively," *Inc. Guidebook*, vol. 2, no. 7, pp. 1–4; "My Best Negotiation Tips," *Paul's Tips*, June 11, 2006, www.paulstips. com/brainbox/pt/home.nsf/link/10062006-My-eight-best-negotiation-tips; Rhonda Abrams, "Know What You Need Before Starting to Negotiate a Deal," *Greenville News Business*, May 29, 2005, p. 8; "Negotiating to Resolve Conflict," Fed Ex Small Business Center, January 22, 2003, http://www.mysmallbizcenter.com; Scott Smith, "Negotiate from Strength," *Success*, July/August 2000, pp. 74–75; Susan St. John, "Five Steps to Better Negotiating," *E-Merging Business*, Fall–Winter 2000, pp. 212–214; and Rob Walker, "Take It or Leave It: The *Only* Guide to Negotiating You Will Ever Need, *Inc.*, August 2003, pp. 75–82.

The Structure of the Deal

To make a negotiation work, the two sides must structure the deal in a way that is acceptable to both parties. Following are typical ways that parties structure business sales.

STRAIGHT BUSINESS SALE A straight business sale may be best for a seller who wants to step down and turn over the reins of the company to someone else. A study of small business sales in 60 categories found that 94 percent were asset sales. In an asset sale, the seller keeps all liabilities—those that are on the books and any that might emerge in the future due to litigation. That is why buyers favor asset sales. The remaining 6 percent involved the sale of stock. About 22 percent were for cash, and 75 percent included a down payment with a note carried by the seller. The remaining 3 percent relied on a note from the seller with no down payment. When the deal included a down payment, it averaged 33 percent of the purchase price. Only 40 percent of the business sales studied included covenants not to compete.[24]

Although selling a business outright is often the safest exit path for an entrepreneur, it is usually the most expensive. Sellers who want cash and take the money up front may face a significant tax burden. They must pay a capital gains tax on the sale price less their investments in the company. A straight sale is also not an attractive exit strategy for those who want to stay on with the company or for those who want to surrender control of the company gradually rather than all at once. Chris Ludwig recently sold Refrigerant Resources, a refrigerant processing company in Colleyville, Texas, to a division of Japanese conglomerate Sumitomo Corporation. Ludwig insisted on an all-cash deal because he wanted to retire immediately.[25]

Ideally, a buyer has already begun to explore the options available for financing the purchase. (Recall that many entrepreneurs include bankers on their teams of advisers.) If traditional lenders shy away from financing the purchase of an existing business, buyers often find themselves searching for alternative sources of funds. The most common barrier that stands in the way of potential business buyers is raising enough capital to make the purchase.[26] Fortunately, most business buyers discover an important source of financing built into the deal: the seller. Seller financing often is more flexible, faster, and easier to obtain than loans from traditional lenders; in fact, it is currently an essential part of most deals. BizBuySell estimates that in more than 80 percent of business sales, the seller provides at least some portion of the financing.[27] Once a seller finds a suitable buyer, he or she typically accepts a down payment and agrees to finance anywhere from 10 to 75 percent of the purchase price over time, usually 3 to 10 years. The buyer makes regular principal and interest payments over time—perhaps with a larger balloon payment at the end—until the note is paid off.

Sellers must especially be willing to finance a portion of the purchase price, particularly when credit is tight.

ENTREPRENEURIAL PROFILE: Rick Hunt, Risk Removal During a recent recession, Rick Hunt knew that he and his partners would have to accept a note for at least part of the purchase price of their Fort Collins, Colorado–based environmental services company, Risk Removal. With annual sales of $3 million and a good reputation in a lucrative niche market (the company removes asbestos and lead paint from buildings), Risk Removal had attracted attention from several buyers, but none had been able to close a financing deal. Hunt hired a business broker, and within months, he and his partners had accepted an offer from a buyer who had experience in the business and could pay 25 percent of the purchase price in cash. A bank financed 50 percent of the price, and Hunt and his partners accepted a five-year promissory note at 7 percent interest for the remaining 25 percent.[28] ■

The terms of the deal are vital to both buyer and seller. They cannot be so burdensome that they threaten the company's continued existence; that is, the buyer must be able to make the payments to the seller out of the company's cash flow.

TWO-STEP SALE For owners wanting the security of a sales contract now but not wanting to step down from the company's helm for several years, a two-step sale may be ideal. The buyer purchases the business in two phases, getting 20 to 70 percent immediately and agreeing to buy the remainder within a specific time period. Until the final transaction takes place, the original owner retains at least partial control of the company.

FIGURE 7.9

A Typical Employee Stock Ownership Plan

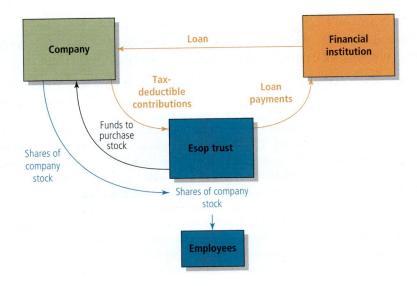

A variation of this strategy is an **earn-out**, in which the seller agrees to accept a percentage of the sales price and stays on to manage the business for a few more years under the new owner. The remaining portion of the price is contingent on the company's performance; the more profit the company generates during the earn-out period, the greater the payout to the seller. By staying on and making sure that the company hits specific performance targets over several years, an entrepreneur can increase his or her payout. Properly structured, earn-outs give sellers an incentive to make sure their companies continue to be successful and prevent buyers from overpaying for a business.

EMPLOYEE STOCK OWNERSHIP PLAN (ESOP) Some owners who want to sell their businesses but keep them intact cash out by selling to their employees through an **employee stock ownership plan (ESOP)**. An ESOP is a type of employee benefit plan in which a trust that is created for employees purchases their employer's stock. Here's how an ESOP works: The company transfers shares of its stock to the ESOP trust, and the trust uses the stock as collateral to borrow enough money to purchase the shares from the company. The company guarantees payment of the loan principal and interest and makes tax-deductible contributions to the trust to repay the loan (see Figure 7.9). As the company repays the loan, it distributes the stock to employees' accounts, based on a predetermined formula. Because of their flexibility, ESOPs permit owners to transfer all or part of a company to employees as gradually or as quickly as they want. More than 9,600 companies in the United States have ESOPs in place, covering 15.1 million employees.[29]

To use an ESOP successfully, a small business should have annual sales of at least $5 million, be profitable (with pre-tax profits exceeding $250,000), and have payroll of at least $1 million a year. Generally, companies with fewer than 30 employees do not find ESOPs beneficial because the cost to set up an ESOP is $40,000 to $50,000, plus a few thousand dollars per year for administration. For companies that prepare properly, ESOPs offer significant benefits for everyone involved. The company gets tax benefits, and employees begin to think and act like business owners, making the business stronger. Company founders receive tax benefits and have the flexibility to determine their retirement schedules. Employees do not make any out-of-pocket payments but over time become owners in the company that employs them, are entitled to share in its profits, and receive sizable retirement benefits. An ESOP also allows an entrepreneur to time the transfer of ownership to meet his or her personal and financial goals.

ENTREPRENEURIAL PROFILE: Bob and Charlee Moore: Bob's Red Mill Natural Foods In 1978, long before people knew about the health benefits of whole-grain products, Bob Moore and his wife, Charlee, salvaged an abandoned 125-year-old flour mill and launched Bob's Red Mill Natural Foods, a company in Portland, Oregon, that produces a variety of products, from grain and flour to hot cereal and baking mixes. In 1993, Moore brought in John Wagner as chief financial officer and co-owner, and the two soon launched a profit-sharing plan for their employees. As Moore passed the normal retirement age, employees began to wonder about the future, especially if Moore and Wagner decided to sell the company to a larger business. Moore and Wagner decided not to sell Bob's Red Mill Natural Foods to a large company; instead, they decided to transfer ownership of the company through the ESOP to the 200 people whom they considered to be instrumental in its success. Moore, who announced the plan on his eighty-first birthday, says that they could have sold the company to outsiders but believed that the employees deserved to have it because they were instrumental in making the business successful.[30] ■

Letter of Intent

Once the buyer and seller have negotiated a deal, they put the details of the structure of the sale into a letter of intent. A **letter of intent** is a firm commitment by both sides that they are ready to move toward closing the sale of the business. The letter clearly states the price and any factors that may affect the actual price paid at closing. It also outlines the terms of the sale, including whether it is an asset sale or a stock sale and the nature of owner financing if it is part of the deal. Any other specific deal points that are important to either side are also included in the letter of intent. Finally, the letter of intent gives specific dates when the deal must close. Although both parties may be committed to closing the sale of the business, only *25 percent* of deals make it from the letter of intent stage to the final closing. The old saying "the devil is in the details" holds true when buying a business. Many deals fall apart during the process of due diligence and during the creation of the closing documents for the sale of the business.

Courtesy of Bob's Red Mill Natural Foods, Inc.

letter of intent
a document that represents a firm commitment by both sides that they are ready to move toward closing the sale of a business.

The Transition Stage

Once the deal stage is completed, the transition stage begins with the actual closing of the purchase. Closing the sale of a business is a complex legal process. Many deals fall apart at the closing table due to unforeseen surprises or last-minute legal maneuvering by either the buyer or seller. Closing documents include the following:

LO7

Understand how to manage the transition stage when a deal is done.

- Asset purchase agreement—the formal agreement of the deal

- Bill of sale—transfers ownership

- Asset list—all assets that are included in the sale, including tangible assets and intellectual property

- Buyer's disclosure statement

- Allocation of purchase price—a formal document that must be filed with the Internal Revenue Service at the end of the tax year that allocates the price among the various assets

- Non-compete agreement

- Consulting/training agreement

- Transfer of subsidiaries associated with the business

- Transfer of utilities

- Transfer of Web sites, social media addresses, and phone numbers

- Documentation of the new entity that will own the business and documentation of the new bank account for that business

- Transfer of merchant accounts

- Notice to creditors

- Lease assignments

- Financing documents, security agreement, promissory note, and UCC financing statement, if seller is financing all or part of the sale

- Sales tax and payroll tax clearance
- Escrow instructions
- Closing adjustments/proration
- Transfer of any third-party contracts
- Corporate resolution authorizing sale of the corporate assets

Once the parties finalize the closing, the challenge of facilitating a smooth transition is next. No matter how well planned a sale, there are always surprises. For instance, the new owner may have ideas for changing the business—perhaps radically—that cause a great deal of stress and anxiety for employees and with the previous owner. Charged with such emotion and uncertainty, the transition phase may be difficult and frustrating—and sometimes painful. To avoid a bumpy transition, a business buyer should do the following:

- Concentrate on communicating with employees. Business sales are fraught with uncertainty and anxiety, and employees need reassurance. Take the time to explain your plans for the company.
- Be honest with employees. Avoid telling them only what they want to hear.
- Listen to employees. They have intimate knowledge of the business and its strengths and weaknesses and usually can offer valuable suggestions. Keep your door and your ears open and come in as somebody who is going to be good for the entire organization.
- Devote time to selling the vision for the company to its key stakeholders, including major customers, suppliers, bankers, and others.
- Consider asking the seller to serve as a consultant until the transition is complete. The previous owner can be a valuable resource.

Conclusion

Rather than start a business "from scratch," some entrepreneurs choose to take a faster, more direct route and purchase an existing business. The process is fraught with pitfalls, but a well-prepared entrepreneur can avoid them. Following the five-stage process described in this chapter increases the odds that an entrepreneur will find an existing business that suits his or her needs and be able to successfully negotiate an outstanding deal to purchase it.

MyLab Entrepreneurship

If your instructor is using MyLab Entrepreneurship, go to **www.pearson.com/mylab/ entrepreneurship** to complete the problems marked with this icon ⭐.

Chapter Summary by Learning Objective

1. Understand the advantages and disadvantages of buying an existing business.

- The *advantages* of buying an existing business include the following: A successful business may continue to be successful, the business may already have the best location, employees and suppliers are already established, equipment is installed and its productive capacity is known, inventory is in place and trade credit is established, the owner hits the ground running, the buyer can use the expertise of the previous owner, and the business may be a bargain.

- The disadvantages of buying an existing business include the following: An existing business may be for sale because it is deteriorating, the previous owner may have created ill will, employees inherited with the business may not be suitable, its location may have become unsuitable, equipment and facilities may be obsolete, change and innovation may be difficult to implement, inventory may be outdated, accounts receivable may be worth less than face value, and the business may be overpriced.

2. **Explain the five stages in acquiring a business: search, due diligence, valuation, deal, and transition.**

- About 500,000 businesses change hands each year. Business buyers go through five stages in acquiring a business: search, due diligence, valuation, deal, and transition.

3. **Explain the three steps in the search stage of buying a business.**

- The three steps in the search stage of buying a business are (1) Take a self-inventory to analyze your skills, abilities, and interests; (2) develop a list of criteria that a potential business acquisition must meet; and (3) prepare a list of potential candidates to research.

4. **Describe the four areas involved in conducting due diligence on a business: the seller's motivation for selling, asset valuation, legal issues, and financial condition.**

- Rushing into a deal is one of the biggest mistakes a business buyer can make. Before negotiating a deal, a buyer should conduct due diligence, exploring four key areas:
    1. Why does the owner want to sell? Look for the *real* reason.
    2. Evaluate the company's assets, both tangible and intangible.
    3. Consider all the legal aspects of buying the business. Have you investigated any potential ongoing legal liabilities? Did you negotiate a covenant not to compete with the seller?

4. Analyze the financial condition of the business, looking at financial statements, income tax returns and, especially, cash flow.

5. **Explain the various methods used to estimate the value of a business.**

- Placing a value on a business is part art and part science. There is no single best method to determine the value of a business. Many buyers rely on multipliers of earnings before interest, taxes, depreciation, and amortization (EBITDA) to estimate a company's value. Other methods include balance sheet techniques, earnings approaches, and the market approach.

6. **Describe the basic principles of negotiating a deal to buy a business and structuring the deal.**

- The first rule of negotiating is to never confuse price with value.
- The best deals result from a cooperative relationship between the parties based on trust.
- Parties may structure a deal in many ways, including a straight business sale, a two-step sale, and an employee stock ownership plan (ESOP).

7. **Understand how to manage the transition when a deal is done.**

- Once the parties finalize the closing, the challenge of facilitating a smooth transition is next. Listening to employees' concerns, communicating with them honestly, and selling them on the buyer's vision are essential.

MyLab Entrepreneurship

If your instructor is using MyLab Entrepreneurship, go to **www.pearson.com/mylab/entrepreneurship** for Auto-graded writing questions as well as the following Assisted-graded writing questions:

1. How should an entrepreneur go about identifying potential business acquisition targets?
2. What tips would you offer a buyer who is about to begin negotiating the purchase of an existing business?

Discussion Questions

7-1. What advantages can an entrepreneur who buys a business gain over one who starts a business "from scratch"?

7-2. How would you go about determining the value of the assets of a business if you were unfamiliar with them?

⭐ 7-3. Why do so many entrepreneurs run into trouble when they buy an existing business?

7-4. Outline the stages involved in buying a business.

7-5. What topics does the due diligence process address?

7-6. Briefly outline the process of valuing a business using the adjusted earnings, the capitalized earnings, and the discounted future earnings approaches.

⭐ 7-7. What determines the bargaining zone between a business seller and a buyer?

7-8. Explain the buyer's position in a typical negotiation for a business.

7-9. Explain the seller's position in a typical negotiation for a business.

7-10. What steps should a business buyer take to ensure a smooth transition after closing the deal to buy a business?

7-11. One entrepreneur who recently purchased a business advises buyers to expect some surprises in the deal, no matter how well prepared they may be. He says potential buyers must build some "wiggle room" into their plans to buy a company. What steps can a buyer take to ensure that he or she has sufficient wiggle room?

Beyond the Classroom . . .

7-12. Interview several new owners who purchased existing businesses.

7-13. How did they determine the value of the business?

7-14. Visit a business broker and ask him or her how he or she brings together a buyer and seller.

7-15. What does the broker do to facilitate the sale?

7-16. What methods does the broker use to determine the value of a business?

7-17. In this broker's experience, what is the most common cause of deals falling through?

7-18. Invite an attorney to speak to your class about the legal aspects of buying a business.

7-19. How does he or she recommend that a business buyer protect himself or herself legally in a business purchase?

Endnotes

[1]Liz Skinner, "The Great Wealth Transfer Is Coming, Putting Advisers at Risk," *Investment News*, July 13, 2015, www.investmentnews.com/article/20150713/FEATURE/150719999/the-great-wealth-transfer-is-coming-putting-advisers-at-risk.

[2]"The Demographics of U.S. Small Business Buyers and Sellers," *BizBuySell*, May 2016, p. 11.

[3]Stacy Cowley, "Baby Boomers Ready to Sell Businesses to Next Generation," *New York Times*, August 19, 2015, www.nytimes.com/2015/08/20/business/smallbusiness/baby-boomers-ready-to-sell-businesses-to-the-next-generation.html; Joe Cogliano, "Exclusive: Local Manufacturer Sold, Plans New Investments to Spur International Growth," *Dayton Business Journal*, April 21, 2015, www.bizjournals.com/dayton/news/2015/04/21/exclusive-local-manufacturer-sold-plans-new.html.

[4]Craig R. Everett, *Capital Markets Report*, Pepperdine Private Capital Markets Project, 2015, p. 61.

[5]"A Graceful Exit? Business Owners at a Loss on Exit Planning," Securian Financial Services, 2014, www.securiannews.com/white-paper/graceful-exit-business-owners-loss-exit-planning.

[6]"Buying a Business," Small Business Administration, https://www.sba.gov/starting-business/how-start-business/business-types/buying-existing-businesses.

[7]Jennifer Wang, "Good Buy," *Entrepreneur*, March 2011, p. 22.

[8]Barry Shlachter, "How Fuzzy's Taco Shop Built a Restaurant Empire," *Star-Telegram*, July 29, 2011, www.star-telegram.com/2011/07/29/3257185/how-fuzzys-taco-shop-built-an.html; "Overview," Fuzzy's Taco Shop, 2016, www.fuzzystacoshop.com/about/overview.

[9]"Survey: Business Owners Spend More Than $35.5 Billion Annually During Ownership Transition," BizBuySell, June 11, 2012, www.bizbuysell.com/news/article084.html.

[10]Craig R. Everett, *Capital Markets Report*, Pepperdine Private Capital Markets Project, 2015, pp. 62–63.

[11]Alina Tugend, "Buying a Business? The Hard Work Is Only Just Beginning," *New York Times*, March 17, 2016, p. B4.

[12]Mark Blayney, *Buying a Business and Making It Work* (London: How To Books, 2007), p. 420.

[13]Donna Nebenzahl, "The Duo: Em & Seb," Urban Expressions, November 26, 2012, www.urbanexpressions.ca/print/story/the-duo-em-seb; Norm Brodsky, "Buying a Business? Expect the Unexpected," *Inc.*, May 1, 2012, www.inc.com/magazine/201205/norm-brodsky/norm-on-buying-a-business.html.

[14]"The Demographics of U.S. Small Business Buyers and Sellers," *BizBuySell*, May 2016, p. 5.

[15]Edward Karstetter, "How Intangible Assets Affect Business Value," *Entrepreneur*, May 6, 2002, http://entrepreneur.com/article/0,4621,299514,00.html.

[16]"Number of Small Business Transactions Jumps in Early 2017 While Median Revenues, Cash Flow Reach Record Levels," *BizBuySell*, April 10, 2017; http://www.bizbuysell.com/news/article123.html; "First Half 2016 Small Business Transactions up Slightly Over 2015; Data Shows Inverse Relationship Between Asking Price and Time on Market," BizBuySell Insight Reports, *BizBuySell*, July 2016, www.bizbuysell.com/news/media_insight.html; Alina Tugend, "Buying a Business? The Hard Work Is Only Just Beginning," *New York Times*, March 17, 2016, p. B4.

[17]Hannah Karp, Ryan Dezember, and Alistair Barr, "Uneven Breakdown in Apple-Beats Deal," *Wall Street Journal*, May 30, 2014, pp. B1, B5; Ethan Smith and Daisuke Wakabayashi, "Apple in Talk for Beats Electronics," *Wall Street Journal*, May 9, 2014, p. B1.

[18]Barbara Taylor, "Determining Your Company's Value: Multiples and Rules of Thumb," *New York Times*, July 15, 2010, http://boss.blogs.nytimes.com/2010/07/15/determining-your-companys-value-multiples-and-rules-of-thumb/?_r=0.

[19]Craig R. Everett, *Capital Markets Report*, Pepperdine Private Capital Markets Project, 2016, p. 64.

[20]James Laabs, "What Is Your Company Worth?" *The Business Sale Center*, www.businesssalecenter.com/new_page_3.htm.

[21]*Business Planning Tools: Buying and Selling a Small Business*, MasterCard Worldwide, www.mastercard.com/us/business/en/smallbiz/businessplanning/businessplanning.html, p. 11.

[22]Craig R. Everett, *Capital Markets Report*, Pepperdine Private Capital Markets Project, 2015, p. 61.

[23]Kevin Kelly, "Look Under the Hood," *FSB*, October 2004, p. 35.

[24]Ryan McCarthy, "A Buyer's Market," *Inc.*, June 2009, p. 85.

[25]Paul Sullivan, "Selling a Business Involves More Than Money," *New York Times*, July 15, 2016, www.nytimes.com/2016/07/16/your-money/selling-a-business-involves-more-than-money.html?_r=0.

[26]"The Demographics of U.S. Small Business Buyers and Sellers," *BizBuySell*, May 2016, p. 11.

[27]Richard Parker, "Buying a Business? Here's How to Do It Right," *BizBuySell*, 2010, www.bizbuysell.com/buyer_resources/buying-a-business-heres-how-to-do-it-right/02/.

[28]Jeanne Lee, "Exit Strategies," *FSB*, April 2009, p. 49.

[29]"A Statistical Profile of Employee Ownership," National Center for Employee Ownership, November 2016, https://www.nceo.org/articles/statistical-profile-employee-ownership.

[30]Karen E. Klein, "ESOPs on the Rise Among Small Businesses," *Bloomberg Businessweek*, March 26, 2010, www.businessweek.com/smallbiz/content/mar2010/sb20100325_591132.htm; Nancy Mann Jackson, "ESOP Plans Let Owners Cash Out and Employees Cash In," *CNNMoney*, June 17, 2010, http://money.cnn.com/2010/06/03/smallbusiness/esop_plans/index.htm; "Meet Bob and Charlee," Bob's Red Mill Natural Foods, 2016, www.bobsredmill.com/bobs-way-meet.

8

Franchising and the Entrepreneur

Zuma Press Inc/Alamy Stock Photo

Learning Objectives

On completion of this chapter, you will be able to:

1. Describe the three types of franchising: trade name, product distribution, and pure.

2-A. Explain the benefits of buying a franchise.

2-B. Explain the drawbacks of buying a franchise.

3. Understand the laws covering franchise purchases.

4. Explain the *right* way to buy a franchise.

5. Describe the major trends shaping franchising.

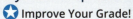

MyLab Entrepreneurship

⭐ **Improve Your Grade!**

If your instructor is using MyLab Entrepreneurship, visit **www.pearson.com/mylab/entrepreneurship** for videos, simulations, and writing exercises.

After graduating from the University of Texas, sisters Emily and Janie Stephens enrolled at Le Cordon Bleu, one of the most prestigious institutions in the world, to study culinary arts. When they graduated from Le Cordon Bleu, the Stephens sisters, both of whom were in their mid-20s, could have gone to work for any of the finest restaurants on the planet; instead, they chose to return to Austin, Texas, and open an Uncle Maddio's Pizza Joint franchise with their cousin, Stewart Geyer, also a University of Texas graduate and an aerospace engineer-turned-entrepreneur. Their Austin location is the first part of an area development deal (more on this later), in which the Stephens sisters and Geyer will open at least four more Uncle Maddio's Pizza Joint franchises in Waco and Dallas within two years. The team of young entrepreneurs was impressed by the franchise's focus on fresh, locally grown vegetables, the pizza dough and sauces that are made fresh in-store every day, and the 50-plus years of experience that the chain's management team has in the fast-casual restaurant business. Company founder Matt Andrew was the president of Moe's Southwest Grill before he left to start Uncle Maddio's Pizza Joint, which now has 375 locations and 200 more under development in the fast-growing create-your-own premium pizza segment. Before opening the first restaurant, Andrew spent a year in a test kitchen, developing the pizza chain's menu, and in the process, he developed proprietary kitchen equipment capable of turning out perfectly cooked pizzas in just seven minutes. Andrew operated that location for two years to perfect the company's business systems before he assembled an experienced management team and began franchising.[1]

Like the Stephens sisters' business, most franchised outlets are small, but as a whole, they have a significant impact on both the U.S. and global economies. Two million franchises employ more than 19 million people around the globe and account for about 4 percent of the typical nation's GDP.[2] In the United States alone, about 3,800 franchisors operate nearly 750,000 franchise outlets (see Figure 8.1), and more are opening constantly.[3] Franchises in the United States generate more than $710 billion in annual sales, account for 2.3 percent of U.S. GDP, and employ more than 7.8 million workers (4.94 percent of the civilian labor force) in more than 300 industries.[4] Much of the popularity of franchising stems from its ability to offer those who lack business experience the chance to own and operate a business with a high probability of success. This booming industry has moved far beyond the traditional boundaries of fast food and hotels into fields as diverse as mosquito spraying, smart phone repair, used clothing, mold detection, pet resorts, and training for kids in the fields of science, technology, engineering, and math (STEM).

ENTREPRENEURIAL PROFILE: Steven and Jason Parker: K-9 Resorts Daycare and Luxury Hotel In 1999, brothers Steven and Jason Parker were just 14 and 12 years old when they started a pet-sitting business to earn extra money. In 2002, the brothers conducted research on the pet industry and learned that people in the United States spent nearly $30 billion annually on their pets, an amount that has more than doubled to $62.75 billion today. In 2005, Steven, 20, and Jason, 18, decided to launch a luxury hotel for dogs and purchased a commercial building in Fanwood, New Jersey, that they converted into one of the most luxurious pet-care facilities in the country. Six years later, the brothers began offering franchises of their business, K-9 Resorts Daycare and Luxury Hotel, which offers amenities such as flooring systems

FIGURE 8.1

Number of Franchised Outlets in the United States

Source: Based on data from *Franchise Business Economic Outlook for 2017,* IHS Economics and the International Franchise Association Educational Foundation, January 2017, p. 2.

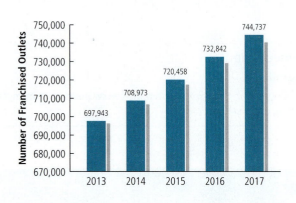

with special antimicrobial properties, premium dog beds, pet-safe courtyards customized for pet play, a specially designed air purification system, and color television tuned to Animal Planet in each pet suite. With more than $4 million in systemwide sales, K-9 Resorts Daycare and Luxury Hotel currently has eight franchisees in the Northeast and is looking to expand nationwide.[5] ■

Figure 8.2 provides a breakdown of the franchise market by industry.

Franchising also has a significant impact on the global economy. Because the United States franchise market is the most mature in the world, U.S. franchisors are expanding globally to reach their growth targets. Currently, 38 percent of the 200 largest U.S.-based franchises have units in other countries. In fact, since 2012, the 200 largest franchisors have added 4 international units for each 1 they have opened domestically.[6] Franchisors based in the United States plan to continue or accelerate the growth of their global franchised units in global markets that have fast-growing populations, rising levels of disposable income, spreading urbanization, and keen interest in American brands. A recent survey by the International Franchise Association reports that 82 percent of its members believe that taking their franchises into international markets is important to the future success of their businesses.[7]

Franchising is a method by which a company (the franchisor) distributes its products or services by selling licenses (the franchise) to its products, its services, and, often, its business systems to business owners (the franchisees), who operate their businesses according to an established business model for an upfront fee and an ongoing royalty fee. In other words, franchisees are semi-independent business owners who pay fees and royalties to a franchisor in return for the right to become identified with its trademark, to sell its products or services, and often to use its business format and system. Franchisees do not establish their own autonomous businesses; instead, they buy a "success package" from the franchisor, who shows them how to use it. Franchisees, unlike independent business owners, don't have the freedom to change the way they run their businesses—for example, shifting advertising strategies or adjusting product lines—but they do have access to a formula for success that the franchisor has worked out. The franchisee's job is to implement the formula and the system that the franchisor has designed. Fundamentally, when franchisees buy franchises, they are purchasing a successful business model. The franchisor provides the business model and the expertise to make it work; the franchisee brings the investment, spirit, and drive necessary to implement the model successfully. Many successful franchisors claim that neglecting to follow the formula is one of the chief reasons some franchisees fail. "If you are overly entrepreneurial and you want to invent your own wheel, or if you are not comfortable with following a system, don't go down [the franchise] path," says Don DeBolt, former head of the International Franchise Association.[8]

franchising

a system of distribution in which semi-independent business owners (franchisees) pay fees and royalties to a parent company (franchisor) in return for the right to become identified with its trademark, to sell its products or services, and often to use its business format and system.

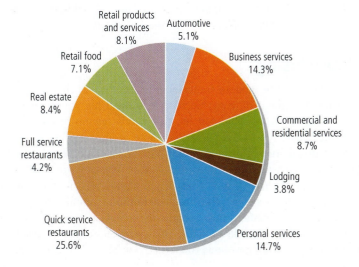

FIGURE 8.2

Franchised Outlets by Industry

Source: Based on data from *Franchise Business Economic Outlook for 2017*, IHS Economics and the International Franchise Association Educational Foundation, January 2017, p. 2.

FIGURE 8.3

The Franchising Relationship

Source: Adapted from *Economic Impact of Franchised Businesses: A Study for the International Franchise Association Educational Foundation*, Copyright 2004 by the International Franchise Association. Reprinted with permission.

Element	The Franchisor	The Franchisee
Site selection	Oversees and approves; may choose site	Chooses site with franchisor's approval
Design	Provides prototype design	Pays for and implements design
Employees	Makes general recommendations and training suggestions	Hires, manages, and fires employees
Products and services	Determines product or service line	Modifies only with franchisor's approval
Prices	Recommends prices but can set maximum prices franchisees can charge	Sets final prices
Purchasing	Establishes quality standards; provides list of approved suppliers; may require franchisees to purchase from the franchisor	Must meet quality standards; must purchase only from approved suppliers; must purchase from supplier if required
Advertising	Develops and coordinates national ad campaign; may require minimum level of spending on local advertising	Pays for national ad campaign; complies with local advertising requirements; gets franchisor approval on local ads
Quality control	Sets quality standards and enforces them with inspections; trains franchisees	Maintains quality standards; trains employees to implement quality systems
Support	Provides support through an established business system	Operates business on a day-to-day basis with franchisor's support

ENTREPRENEURIAL PROFILE: Anita Schlachter: Schlachter's Maaco Auto Painting and Bodyworks Anita Schlachter, co-owner of a highly successful Maaco (automotive services) franchise with her husband and her son, is convinced that the system the franchisor taught them is the key to their company's progress and growth to date. The Schlachters follow the franchisor's plan, using it as a road map to success. Schlachter says franchisees who listen to their franchisors and follow their policies and procedures are likely to be successful. Entrepreneurs who believe they know more about the business than the franchisor should avoid franchising and launch independent businesses.[9] ∎

trade-name franchising
a system of franchising in which a franchisee purchases the right to use the franchisor's trade name without distributing particular products exclusively under the franchisor's name.

LO1
Describe the three types of franchising: trade name, product distribution, and pure.

product distribution franchising
a system of franchising in which a franchisor licenses a franchisee to sell its products under the franchisor's brand name and trademark through a selective, limited distribution network.

Franchising is built on an ongoing relationship between a franchisor and a franchisee (see Figure 8.3). The franchisor provides valuable services, such as a proven business system, training and support, name recognition, and many other forms of assistance; in return, the franchisee pays an initial franchise fee as well as an ongoing percentage of his or her outlet's sales to the franchisor as a royalty and agrees to operate the outlet according to the franchisor's terms. Because franchisors develop the business systems that their franchisees use and direct their distribution methods, they maintain substantial control over their franchisees. Yet this standardization lies at the core of franchising's success as a method of distribution.

Types of Franchising

Many experts trace the roots of modern franchising to the 1850s, when Isaac Singer, founder of the Singer Sewing Machine Company, decided to expand his young business by granting licenses to other businesses that would sell his company's sewing machines in specific geographic areas.[10] Three basic types of franchises operate in almost every industry: trade-name franchising, product distribution franchising, and pure franchising. **Trade-name franchising** involves a brand name, such as True Value Hardware or Western Auto. Here, the franchisee purchases the right to use the franchisor's trade name without distributing particular products exclusively under the franchisor's name. **Product distribution franchising** involves a franchisor licensing a franchisee to sell specific products under the franchisor's brand name and trademark through a selective, limited distribution network. This system is commonly used to market automobiles (Chevrolet, Lexus, Ford), gasoline products (ExxonMobil, Sunoco, Texaco), soft drinks

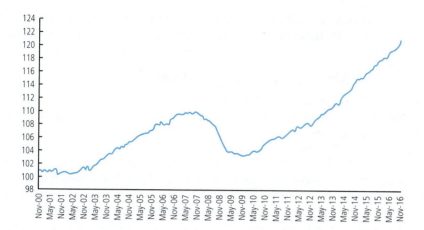

FIGURE 8.4

Franchise Business Index

Source: Franchise Business Economic Outlook for 2017, IHS Economics and International Franchise Association Educational Foundation, January 2017, p. 4.

(Pepsi Cola, Coca-Cola), appliances, cosmetics, and other products. These two methods of franchising allow franchisees to affiliate with the parent company's brand and identity.

Pure franchising (also called *comprehensive* or *business format franchising*) involves providing the franchisee with a complete business format, including a license for a brand name, the products or services to be sold, the store layout, the methods of operation, a marketing plan, a quality control process, a two-way communications system, and the necessary business support services. In short, the franchisee purchases the right to use all of the elements of a fully integrated business operation. Pure franchising is the most common and the fastest growing of the three types of franchising. It is common among quick-service restaurants, hotels, business service firms, car rental agencies, educational institutions, beauty aid retailers, and many other types of businesses.

The franchise industry is not immune to cyclical swings in the economy. Recessions, high unemployment, declining business and consumer confidence and spending, and tight credit conditions lead to failures of both independent and franchised businesses. Figure 8.4 shows the International Franchise Association's Franchise Business Index, a composite measure of the economic health of the franchise industry that includes six different indicators (January $2000 = 100$).

pure franchising
a system of franchising in which a franchisor sells a franchisee a complete business format and system.

The Benefits of Buying a Franchise

LO2A
Explain the benefits of buying a franchise.

A franchisee gets the opportunity to own a small business relatively quickly and, because of the identification with an established product and brand name, often reaches the breakeven point faster than an independent business would. Still, most new franchise outlets don't break even for at least 6 to 18 months.

Franchisees also benefit from the franchisor's business experience. In fact, experience is the essence of what a franchisee is buying from a franchisor. As you learned in Chapter 1, many entrepreneurs go into business by themselves and make costly mistakes. Given the thin margin for error in the typical start-up, a new business owner cannot afford to make many mistakes. In a franchising arrangement, the franchisor already has worked out the kinks in the system by trial and error, and franchisees benefit from that experience. A franchisor has climbed up the learning curve and shares with franchisees the secrets of success it has discovered in the industry. Sean Kelly and Andy Mackensen noticed that almost every vending machine sold food products that were not healthful, and in 2003, the entrepreneurial duo started HUMAN (Helping Unite Mankind and Nutrition) Healthy Markets and began installing vending machines stocked with healthful selections. After investing nearly a decade in learning the details of the industry, refining their business model, and figuring out how to

Andy Mackensen and Sean Kelly
Kirk Mckoy/Los Angeles Times/Getty Images

gain access to ideal locations, Kelly and Mackensen began awarding franchises. Today, HUMAN Healthy Markets has 109 franchisees who stock vending machines with locally sourced sandwiches, salads, smoothies, and snacks, some of which are vegetarian and vegan; they place the vending machines in schools, health clubs, office buildings, corporate headquarters, and other locations.[11] "A great franchisor has developed all of the tools that you need to start a business," says Lori Kiser-Block, president of a franchise consulting firm. "They've developed the marketing system, the training and operation system, the brand, and the marketing tools you need. They've made all of the mistakes for you."[12]

For many first-time entrepreneurs, access to a business model with a proven track record is the safest way to own a business. Still, every potential franchisee must consider one important question: "What can a franchise do for me that I cannot do for myself?" The answer to this question depends on one's particular situation and requires a systematic evaluation of a franchise opportunity. After careful deliberation, one person may conclude that a franchise offers nothing that he or she could not do independently, and another may decide that a franchise is the key to success as a business owner. Franchisees often cite the advantages discussed in the following sections.

A Multitude of Options

Franchises operate in almost every industry, giving potential franchisees an extensive menu of concepts from which to choose. Robert Baruck, aka The Naked Cowboy, a longtime fixture in New York City's Times Square (who actually performs in briefs), has 13 franchisees, 7 of whom are women, who strum guitars, sing, and pose with tourists in public areas in cities such as Los Angeles, Paris, and Nashville.[13] Aspiring franchisees who are more modest can choose businesses in traditional areas such as fast-food restaurants or mobile food truck franchises that sell everything from burgers and grilled cheese sandwiches to lobster and soup and are capable of generating as much in sales in just a few hours as some brick-and-mortar restaurants generate in 24 hours.[14] In the home maintenance and improvement category, franchisees can select from niche businesses such as ScreenMobile, a mobile franchise that sells, repairs, and installs screens for doors, windows, and porches, and Spaulding Decon,

Napa Valley Register/Zuma Press Inc/Alamy Stock Photo

a franchise that specializes in crime scene clean-up, decontamination of illegal drug labs, and decluttering of hoarders' residences. When it comes to franchising, options abound![15]

A Business System

One of the biggest benefits of buying a franchise is gaining access to a business system that has a proven record of success. In many cases, the business system that a franchisor provides allows franchisees to get their businesses up and running faster than if they had tried to launch them on their own. Fran Lubin, who left the corporate office of Goddard School, an early education franchise, to become a Goddard franchisee, recalls, "I understood that the business was mine to run. Goddard was there to help me and to provide multiple resources and a proven system, but it was up to me to take all of those things and to make my business successful."[16]

Using the franchisor's business system as a guide, franchisees can be successful even though they may have little or no experience in the industry. Rather than search for people with industry-specific experience, franchisors prefer to have as franchisees people with business acumen whom they can train to operate successfully multi-million-dollar businesses. In a recent survey by FranchiseDirect, 86 percent of franchisees report that they have management experience.[17] Shirin Behzadi, CEO of Budget Blinds, a mobile franchise that sells and installs blinds, says that in more than 22 years, the company has never been able to define a profile of the "ideal franchisee" because people who are successful franchisees come from diverse backgrounds, such as mechanics, executives, engineers, accountants, repair people, and many others.[18]

ENTREPRENEURIAL PROFILE: Audra De Vera: Chronic Tacos Audra De Vera was an agent for the U.S. Department of Housing and Urban Development when her aunt, a Chronic Tacos franchisee, told her about a Chronic Tacos franchise that was for sale near De Vera's home in Corona, California. Although the outlet was in a great location, it was losing money. De Vera, whose job had trained her to conduct financial investigations for court cases, began studying the franchise's financial statements and discovered that its labor and food costs were out of control. De Vera put together a plan to whip the restaurant into sound financial condition, presented it to the franchisor, and purchased the outlet. Although De Vera had no experience in the restaurant business, her financial acumen, skill at managing teams of people, and work ethic enabled her to turn around the restaurant, increase its sales, and generate a steady profit. De Vera has since opened a second Chronic Tacos location.[19] ■

Management Training and Support

Franchisors want to give their franchisees a greater chance for success than independent businesses and offer management training programs to franchisees prior to opening a new outlet. Many franchisors, especially well-established ones, also provide follow-up training and consulting services. This service is vital because most franchisors do not require franchisees to have experience in the industry. Training programs teach franchisees the fundamentals they need to know for day-to-day operations as well as the nuances of running their businesses successfully.

ENTREPRENEURIAL PROFILE: Cathy Deano and Renee Maloney, Painting with a Twist In 2007, Cathy Deano and Renee Maloney met in their children's kindergarten class. The two entrepreneurial moms eventually started Corks N Canvas, a business based in Mandeville, Louisiana, that combines art instruction and wine to enable customers to relax, have fun with their friends, and create individual works of art. After expanding to four locations, Deano and Maloney began franchising their concept under the name Painting with a Twist in 2009. Today, their company has more than 300 franchisees across the nation, with more under development; to date, only 4 units have closed. The entrepreneurs say that they owe their success to making life as easy as possible for franchisees and providing support to help their franchises succeed. They have assembled a staff of 27 highly responsive consultants whose sole jobs are to help franchisees improve their stores and solve problems when they arise.[20] ■

Training programs often involve both classroom and onsite instruction to teach franchisees the basic operations of the business. CarePatrol, a franchise with 144 franchisees operating in 36 states that helps senior citizens find assisted-living facilities, brings franchisees to its headquarters in Gilbert, Arizona, for a one-week training course, followed by an intensive coaching program in their home territories. Franchise founder Chuck Bongiovanni says that franchisees jokingly refer to the company's extensive training as its "forced success program."[21] McDonald's is famous for Hamburger University, which opened in 1961 and now has seven centers around the world, including the newest one in Shanghai, China. Franchisees and their employees go to one of the Hamburger University centers for five days to learn the proper systems and procedures for operating a restaurant successfully and to hone their leadership and decision-making skills. Training involves classroom instruction from faculty members from around the world, hands-on activities, simulations of events that franchisees are likely to encounter, and computerized e-learning modules. More than 330,000 people have graduated from Hamburger University, earning their degrees in Hamburgerology.[22]

To ensure franchisees' continued success, many franchisors supplement their start-up training programs with ongoing instruction and support, dispensing consultants to resolve franchisees' operating problems. For instance, Ben & Jerry's sends regional trainers to new franchisees' locations for additional training before they open their Scoop Shops. Once they are up and running, franchisees also benefit from ongoing training programs from the Ben & Jerry's field-based support team.[23] Many franchisors now provide special training for multi-unit owners, whose job descriptions change significantly when they move from operating a single outlet to managing multiple outlets. John P. and John C. Crowe, a father-and-son team who opened a Toppers Pizza franchise in Lincoln, Nebraska, took the franchisor's week-long "Above the Store" course, which teaches franchisees how to make the management transition to operating multiple outlets, before they opened their second outlet in nearby Omaha.[24] Franchisors offer these training programs because they realize that their ultimate success depends on their franchisees' success.

Brand-Name Appeal

A franchisee purchases the right to use a nationally known and advertised brand name for a product or service. Thus, the franchisee has the advantage of identifying his or her business with a widely recognized trademark, which provides a great deal of drawing power, particularly for franchisees of established systems. Customers recognize the identifying trademark, the standard symbols, the store design, and the products of an established franchise. Because of the franchise's name recognition, franchisees who have just opened their outlets often discover a ready supply of customers ready to purchase their products or services. Entrepreneurs who launch independent businesses may have to work for years and spend many thousands of dollars in advertising to build a customer base of equivalent size. "One of the reasons I bought an AAMCO [transmission repair] franchise was its name recognition," says Stephen Rogers, who owns a franchise in Lockport, New York.[25]

One of the basic tenets of franchising is cloning the franchisor's success. For example, nearly everyone recognizes the golden arches of McDonald's or the pigtailed little girl on the Wendy's sign (founder Dave Thomas named the company after his daughter) and the standard products and quality offered at each. A customer can be confident that the quality and content of a meal at a Fort Lauderdale McDonald's will be consistent with that of a meal at a San Francisco McDonald's. However, franchisees must be equally aware that negative actions by the franchisor or other franchisees can undermine the value of the brand name and have a negative impact on other stores in the chain. From franchisees' perspective, one of the most important functions that a franchisor performs is promoting and enhancing the company's brand because a stellar brand perception among customers and potential customers translates directly into sales for franchisees. Guillermo Perales, who owns 398 franchises from seven different companies, ranging from Arby's and Burger King to Del Taco and T-Mobile, is one of the most successful franchisees in the United States and understands the necessity of proper brand management. "It's very important for the franchisor to take care of the brand," he says. "[Franchisees] all have a lot riding on this business. Good management of the brand is essential."[26]

Standardized Quality of Goods and Services

Because a franchisee purchases a license to sell the franchisor's product or service and the privilege of using the associated brand name, the quality of the goods or services sold determines the franchisor's reputation. Building a sound reputation in business can take many years, but destroying a good reputation takes no time at all. If some franchisees are allowed to operate at substandard levels, the image of the entire chain suffers irreparable damage; therefore, franchisors normally demand compliance with uniform standards of quality and service throughout the entire chain. In many cases, the franchisor conducts periodic inspections of local facilities to assist in maintaining acceptable levels of performance.

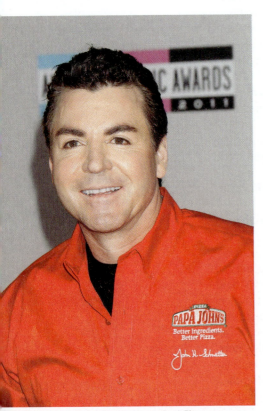

ENTREPRENEURIAL PROFILE: John Schnatter: Papa John's John Schnatter, founder of Papa John's, a fast-growing pizza franchise with more than 4,400 outlets across the United States and 34 global markets, makes personal visits to some of his franchisees' stores four or five times each week to make sure they are performing up to the company's high quality standards. Franchisees say Schnatter, known for his attention to detail, often checks pizzas for air bubbles in the crust and checks tomato sauce for freshness. "Pizza is Schnatter's life, and he takes it very seriously," says one industry analyst.[27] ∎

Maintaining quality is so important that most franchisors retain the right to terminate the franchise contract and repurchase the outlet if the franchisee fails to comply with established standards.

National Advertising Programs and Marketing Assistance

An effective advertising program is essential to the success of every franchise operation. Marketing a brand-name product or service across a wide geographic area requires a far-reaching advertising campaign. A regional or national advertising program benefits all franchisees, and most franchisors have one. About 83 percent of franchisors require franchisees to contribute to a national advertising fund; the average amount is 2 percent of sales.[28] Typically, these advertising campaigns are organized and controlled by the franchisor, but franchisees actually pay for the campaigns. In fact, they are financed by each franchisee's contribution of a percentage of monthly sales, usually 1 to 5 percent, or a flat monthly fee. For example, Five Guys Burgers and Fries franchisees contribute 1 percent of weekly gross sales to the company's national advertising program. Franchisees of sandwich chain Subway, with more than 44,000 restaurants in 112 countries, pay 4.5 percent of weekly gross sales to the company's national advertising program. Franchisors pool these funds and use them for a cooperative advertising program; doing so has more impact than if franchisees spent the same amount of money separately.

Many franchisors also require franchisees to spend a minimum amount on local advertising; once again, the average amount is 2 percent of sales.[29] To supplement the chain's national advertising efforts, to which franchisees contribute 3.5 percent of gross sales, Wendy's requires franchisees to spend at least 0.5 percent of gross sales on local advertising. At Firehouse Subs, franchisees must spend 2 percent of their gross sales on local advertising and contribute 1 percent to the national advertising campaign. Some franchisors assist franchisees in designing and producing local ads. Many companies also help franchisees create marketing plans and provide professionally designed marketing materials, including outdoor advertisements, newspaper inserts, posters, banners, brochures, direct-mail pieces, and platforms for social media and mobile marketing campaigns. Like most other businesses, franchisees are shifting their advertising expenditures to digital and online media; franchisees now invest 43 percent of their advertising budgets in digital media.[30] The pervasiveness of social media and the growing availability of sophisticated analytics and conversion tools for social media platforms are driving the push to digital advertising. The social media tools that franchisees use most often are Facebook (87 percent), LinkedIn (59 percent), Twitter (48 percent), and Pinterest (38 percent).[31] Some franchisors provide a corporate social media presence, with links to franchisees' local pages that allow franchisees to add content that is relevant to their customers. Most franchises, however, allow their franchisees to control their own social media presence and content.[32]

Nearly 55 percent of e-commerce Web traffic now originates from mobile devices such as smart phones and tablets.[33] As mobile marketing becomes more prevalent, franchisors are developing mobile apps that make it easy for customers to purchase from their franchisees. Mobile apps are a natural extension of and complement to franchises' social media marketing efforts. Blaze Fast Fire'd Pizza, a chain of pizza restaurants with 150 locations across the United States and Canada whose special pizza ovens cook its custom-made pizzas in just three minutes, recently launched a mobile app that allows customers to order and pay for their pizzas with their smart phones, find the nearest Blaze Fast Fire'd Pizza outlet, and earn "flame" credits in the company's loyalty program. The app, which is aimed at the company's hundreds of thousands of social media fans, also includes an online order history that enables customers to order their favorite pizzas quickly and easily and a nutrition calculator that allows customers to build virtual pizzas and view their calorie counts and nutritional values.[34]

Financial Assistance

Purchasing a franchise can be just as expensive as (if not more so than) launching an independent business, and some franchisees have difficulty qualifying for bank loans. Fortunately, the Small Business Administration (SBA) has created a program called the Franchise Registry that is designed to provide financing for franchisees through its loan guarantee programs (more on these in Chapter 15). The Franchise Registry streamlines the loan application process for franchisees who pass the screening tests at franchises that are members of the registry. Franchisors submit their franchise agreements and other documents to the registry for preapproval by the SBA, which expedites the loan application process for prospective franchisees. Nearly 1,500 franchises ranging from AAMCO (automotive repair) to Zaxby's (fast-food chicken restaurants) and 7,000 lenders participate in the Franchise Registry program. According to one recent survey, 43 percent of new franchisees and 23 percent of existing franchisees rely on SBA loan guarantees to secure financing.[35] Approximately 11 percent of all SBA loan guarantees go to franchisees. In a recent 10-year period, SBA-guaranteed loans to franchisees experienced a 13 percent charge-off rate (the percentage of the loan amount written off due to nonpayment), which is lower than the overall average charge-off rate of 18 percent for all SBA-guaranteed loans.[36] Franchisees who are interested in the Franchise Registry program should visit its Web site at www.franchiseregistry.com.

ENTREPRENEURIAL PROFILE: Maurice Welton: Edible Arrangements Maurice Welton started his career in the food service industry at age 14, when he began working in a bakery and learned how to bake. After graduating from the College of Culinary Arts at Johnson and Wales and serving a stint in the army as a cook, Welton saw Tariq Farid on a television show. Farid is the cofounder of Edible Arrangements, a franchise that sells floral-inspired arrangements of fresh fruit with nearly 1,200 outlets in the United States and 62 more in international markets. Welton began investigating the franchise and soon opened his first Edible Arrangements franchise in McAllen, Texas, with the help of a loan guaranteed by the SBA's most popular 7(a) program. Today, Welton owns five Edible Arrangements outlets in southern Texas.[37] ■

Although franchisees typically invest a significant amount of their own money in their businesses, most need additional financing. In some cases, the franchisor will provide at least a portion of that additional financing. A basic principle of franchising is to use franchisees' money to grow their businesses, but some franchisors realize that because start-up costs have reached breathtakingly high levels, they must provide financial help for franchisees. In fact, a study by FRANdata, a franchising research company, reports that 20 percent of franchisors offer direct financing to their franchisees.[38] Small franchise systems are more likely to provide direct financial assistance to franchisees than are larger, more established franchisors. Traditionally, franchisors rarely make loans to enable franchisees to pay the initial franchise fee. However, once a franchisor locates a suitable prospective franchisee, it may offer the qualified candidate direct financial assistance in specific areas, such as purchasing equipment, inventory, or even the franchise fee.

In most instances, financial assistance from franchisors takes a form other than direct loans, leases, or short-term credit. Franchisors usually are willing to help qualified franchisees establish relationships with banks, nonbank lenders, and other sources of financing. The support and connections from the franchisor enhance a franchisee's credit standing because lenders recognize the lower failure rate among established franchises. For instance, McDonald's has established relationships with several preferred lenders, including Bank of America, GE Capital, Wells Fargo, PNC, and others, for its franchisees. These lenders provide customized financing so that new franchisees can have sufficient working capital and can purchase furniture, fixtures, and equipment and so existing franchisees can remodel their stores, make lease-hold improvements, and upgrade to the latest technology. McDonald's recently negotiated longer repayment terms with its preferred lenders for its franchisees who construct double-lane drive-through structures or complete major remodeling projects.[39]

In an attempt to reignite their chains' growth, some franchisors are reducing fees, cutting royalties or eliminating them for a specific time period, and extending credit to help franchisees open outlets. Buffalo Wild Wings recently reduced its franchise fee from $35,000 to $5,000 and saw its franchise growth go from 1 new unit the year before to 17 new units after making the reduction. Wine & Design, a franchise that hosts parties in which participants create paintings while sipping wine, began offering an interest-free loan for up to one year to new franchisees to cover the cost of the $25,000 initial franchise fee. Founder Harriet Mills says that the loan allows franchisees to use their money to invest more in marketing and building their customer bases more quickly. Wine & Design also offers existing franchisees a 50 percent reduction in the franchise fee for opening more locations.[40]

Military veterans own one out of seven franchises.[41] In January 2011, the International Franchise Association created the VetFran program to help veterans gain access to franchising opportunities by providing training, financial assistance, and information. More than 650 franchisors participate in the VetFran program, which offers financial incentives, discounts, and mentoring to prospective franchisees. So far, the program has helped more than 6,500 military veterans become new franchise owners.[42]

ENTREPRENEURIAL PROFILE: Andrew Wilson: 1-800-GOT-JUNK and You Move Me After serving tours of duty in Iraq and Afghanistan in the U.S. Army, Andrew Wilson returned home and purchased a 1-800-GOT-JUNK junk removal franchise in Oklahoma. His first foray into franchising proved to be successful, and Wilson invested $166,000 to open two You Move Me moving services franchises in Tulsa and Oklahoma City. Wilson says that his Army experience prepared him well to become a successful franchisee. He points out that success in both the Army and in franchising depends on following established systems and dealing with stressful situations. Wilson's experience, work ethic, and willingness to follow the franchise system enabled him to generate almost $1 million in sales in his first year as a You Move Me franchisee. He is already making plans to open a third You Move Me franchise.[43] ∎

Proven Products, Processes, and Business Formats

As we have seen, franchisees essentially purchase a franchisor's experience in the form of a business system. A franchise owner does not have to build the business from scratch. Instead of being forced to rely solely on personal ability to establish business processes and attract clientele, a franchisee can depend on the methods and techniques of an established business. All Buffalo Wild Wings franchisees use the same point-of-sale systems, which gives them real-time access to detailed sales reports for their own outlets and weekly reports that allow them to compare their performance to that of other stores.[44]

At Papa John's, researchers are constantly looking for ways to improve their pizza and their franchisees' operations. Recent improvements include a simple system for making sauce measurements more precise and an oven calibration process to ensure more even heating throughout franchisees' pizza ovens, thereby producing more consistent pizzas.[45] These standardized procedures, processes, and operations greatly enhance the franchisee's chances of success and prevent the most inefficient type of learning—trial and error.

ENTREPRENEURIAL PROFILE: Ken Morrison and Sam Hance: StoneCoat Ken Morrison wanted to add stone accents to a house he was remodeling to sell but learned that they would be too heavy. He began doing research on stone products and discovered a product called hydraulic limestone that can be ground into a powder, mixed with water, and turned into a slurry that can be sprayed onto almost any surface, interior or exterior, and shaped into practically any pattern—chalk, cast stone, marble, river rock, and more. Morrison spent six years experimenting with various processes and applications of hydraulic limestone. When he had perfected and patented the application process, Morrison launched a company, StoneCoat, to apply the mixture to homes in Dallas, Texas. Five years later, Morrison had perfected his business system and partnered with Sam Hance, a veteran franchise developer, to market StoneCoat as a franchise. StoneCoat currently has 20 franchisees and plans to grow to 150 in the next few years.[46] ∎

Centralized Buying Power

A significant advantage of a franchisee over an independent small business owner is participation in the franchisor's centralized, volume-buying power. If franchisors sell goods and supplies to franchisees (not all do), they may pass on to franchisees cost savings from quantity discounts they earn by buying in volume. Tom Curdes, owner of two Weed Man franchises in Toledo, Ohio, cites the lawn care franchisor's buying power as a major advantage. "The national buying power and the negotiations [with vendors] they do behind the scenes … I couldn't do that myself," says Curdes, whose franchises generate $750,000 in sales and employ 25 people.[47]

Site Selection and Territorial Protection

A proper location is critical to the success of any small business, including franchises. In fact, franchise experts consider the three most important factors in franchising to be *location*, *location*, and *location*. Most franchisors offer franchisees site-selection assistance to increase the probability that their outlets will attract sufficient numbers of customers, reach their breakeven points quickly, and generate consistent profits. Popeyes Louisiana Chicken, a quick-service restaurant with more than 2,000 locations worldwide, recently began using a sophisticated site-selection tool called Birchwood that analyzes the demographics and traffic patterns of potential locations to predict the financial performance of its restaurants. Birchwood is based on a

George Sheldon/Shutterstock

detailed study that the franchisor conducted on the demographic profiles and purchasing patterns of more than 60,000 customers. The system has allowed Popeyes to help its franchisees find not only the best trade areas in which to put restaurants but also the best sites in those trade areas on which to build their restaurants. Restaurants whose sites were selected with Birchwood have average annual sales of $1.5 million, compared to the systemwide average of $1.1 million. Overall, franchisees' profits are higher, and the franchise's share of the chicken market has increased since the company began using Birchwood to select the best sites for its locations.[48]

Sometimes, entrepreneurs discover that becoming affiliated with a franchisor is the best way to get into prime locations. McDonald's, for example, is well known for its ability to obtain prime locations in high-traffic areas. Although choosing a location usually is the franchisee's responsibility, some franchisors control the site-selection process. Stephen Rogers decided to leave a family business to purchase an AAMCO transmission service franchise and relied on the franchisor to select a location for his service center because of the company's experience in selecting prime locations for its outlets. (AAMCO has been selling franchises since 1963.)[49] Even when the franchisee makes the location decision, the franchisor reserves the right to approve the final site. Choosing a suitable location requires a thorough location analysis, including studies of traffic patterns, zoning ordinances, accessibility, population density, and demographics. You will learn more about the location decision in Chapter 14.

Some franchisors offer franchisees territorial protection, which gives franchisees the right to exclusive distribution of brand-name goods or services within a particular geographic area. A clause establishing such a protective zone that bars other outlets from the same franchise from locating there gives franchisees significant protection and security. Even when a franchisor grants territorial protection, the size of a franchisee's territory can vary significantly. The purpose of territorial protection is to prevent an invasion of the existing franchisee's territory and the resulting dilution of sales. One study of successful franchises reports that the failure rate for franchisees is lower in systems that offer exclusive territories than in those that do not.[50]

As existing markets have become increasingly saturated with franchise outlets, the placement of new outlets has become a source of friction between franchisors and franchisees. Existing franchisees complain that franchisors are encroaching on their territories by granting new franchises so close to them that their sales are diluted. Before signing a franchise contract, every prospective franchisee must know exactly the scope of territorial protection, if any, the franchisor guarantees. A fast-growing franchise may be a sign of a healthy business model, but it also may be a precursor to future conflicts between the franchisor and franchisees over encroachment. Why invest years building a successful franchise in a particular location only to have the franchisor allow another franchisee to open nearby, siphoning off sales of the existing outlet?

Greater Chance for Success

Although franchising is built on best practices honed over time, investing in a franchise is not risk free. Between 200 and 300 new franchises enter the market each year, but not all of them survive.[51] One recent study provides an indicator of the failure rate of franchises: Over a recent 16-year period, an average of 13 percent of franchisees who received SBA-guaranteed loans failed to repay them, but the nonpayment rate ranged from 0 to 89 percent, depending on the chain.[52] Despite the fact that franchising offers no guarantees of success, experts contend that franchising is less risky than building a business from the ground up. Max Nguyen reviewed several franchise options but ultimately was attracted to Jimmy John's Gourmet Sandwiches, a sandwich franchise with 2,400 outlets, because it had an overall closure rate of less than 2 percent, and the franchise had had no closures in the previous two years. Nguyen used a loan guarantee from the Small Business Administration to open his first Jimmy John's Gourmet Sandwiches location in Cherry Hill, New Jersey.[53]

The tradition of success for franchises is attributed to the broad range of services, assistance, standard procedures, site-selection assistance, and comprehensive business system that the franchisor provides. Jimmy John Liautaud, who founded Jimmy John's Gourmet Sandwiches in 1983, sees his franchisees as his customers and does everything he can to ensure their success. He says that the key to his company's success is creating a business model and a system that makes money for franchisees, pointing out that the franchise invests a great deal of time in teaching franchisees the system and how to make it work. By providing extensive support and focusing on the small things, Liautaud says, the big things take care of themselves.[54]

A recent study of franchises reports that the success rate of franchisees is higher when a franchise system does the following:

- Requires franchisees to have prior industry experience

- Requires franchisees to actively manage their stores (no "absentee" owners)

- Has built a strong brand name

- Offers training programs designed to improve franchisees' knowledge and skills[55]

The risk involved in purchasing a franchise is two pronged: Success—or failure—depends on the franchisee's managerial skills and motivation and on the franchisor's business experience, system, and support. The franchisor provides the business system, but the franchisee has the responsibility of implementing the system and making the business successful.

Many franchisees are convinced that franchising has been the key to their success in business. Their success is proof of the common sentiment that franchising offers the opportunity to be in business *for* yourself but not *by* yourself. In a recent survey by Franchise Direct, the main reason (cited by 51 percent of respondents) that prospective franchisees give for considering investing in a franchise is that they want to be their own bosses without having to start completely from "scratch."[56] "[Franchising is] the perfect combination of having an independently owned and operated office, but with support," says Olivier Hecht, who left his corporate job to open a Handyman Matters home repair franchise.[57]

 ## You Be the Consultant

Would You Buy This Franchise?

Although opening a franchise is not a "sure thing," franchising's immense popularity is due, in part, to the support, experience, and training that franchisors provide their franchisees. Many would-be entrepreneurs believe that franchising reduces their risk of failure and see it as the key to their success. Large, established franchises have systems in place that have been replicated thousands of times and allow franchisees to follow a formula for success that the franchisor has worked out over many years. Many small franchisors don't have the benefit of learning from the mistakes of setting up thousands of outlets to fine-tune their business systems. Some franchisors build their business models on fads that will fade, while others tap into meaningful trends. Some of these small franchises have the potential to become tomorrow's franchise giants; others will fall by the wayside. What factors increase the probability that a new franchise will succeed?

- **Unique concept.** To be successful, a franchise must offer a unique concept that registers with customers by solving a problem or making their lives better or easier and gives the company a competitive edge in the marketplace.

- **Effective and efficient system.** Successful franchisors have developed a system that enables the business to operate smoothly and efficiently. They also work constantly to improve the system. New franchisors whose goal is to sell franchises rather than to focus on ensuring franchisees'

success by providing them with a well-functioning system are more likely to fail.

- **Replicable system.** Not only must a franchise system be effective and efficient, it also must be replicable. The ideal franchise system is easily teachable to franchisees.

- **Experience.** To be able to provide franchisees with an efficient, effective system, a franchisor must have experience in the industry and must have built a successful operation as an independent business owner before starting to sell franchises.

- **Powerful marketing.** Successful franchisors understand the importance of building recognition for their brands and devote proper resources to protecting their brand names and building recognition for them among customers.

BurgerFi

Nearly half of all consumers eat a hamburger at least once per week, and many "better burger" franchises, such as Five Guys Burgers and Fries, Wayback Burgers, Mooyah, Smashburger, and others, have capitalized on the opportunity to sell premium burgers to hungry customers. In a typical year, Americans eat more than 9 billion burgers. In the United States, hamburger restaurants generate $70 billion in annual sales. In 2010, restaurateur

(continued)

You Be the Consultant (continued)

John Rosatti noticed that one of the best-selling items on his full-service restaurant's menu was its burgers, and in 2010, Rosatti partnered with Lee Goldberg to open two BurgerFi restaurants in southern Florida. BurgerFi features 100 percent pure Angus beef patties with no hormones or antibiotics, made-from-scratch fries, double-battered onion rings, Kobe beef hot dogs, fresh toppings, local craft beers, and wine. Two years later, BurgerFi began selling franchises, and business partners Jim Pagano and Henry Talerico were the company's first franchisees. Pagano had owned several businesses during his career, including an auto dealership, and decided that the time was right to get into the restaurant business. By being the first franchisee in the BurgerFi system, Pagano and Talerico were able to have their choice of territories. They entered into an area development agreement with BurgerFi to open multiple units in Orlando and Gainesville, Florida.

Purchasing a BurgerFi franchise requires an investment of $460,000 to $995,000, including $37,500 for the franchise fee. Prospective franchisees must have a net worth of $1 million, with $500,000 of liquid capital. Franchisees also agree to pay an ongoing royalty of 5.5 percent of their gross sales. BurgerFi requires at least one member of a franchise group to have prior experience operating a restaurant (preferably multiple restaurants). BurgerFi (the name comes from its founders' desire to lead the "Burgerfi-cation" of the United States) plans to have 300 locations across the United States in four years.

The premium burger market is getting crowded, and operating a successful restaurant is extremely challenging. Owners often struggle to keep food and labor costs under control, counteract constant employee turnover, and cope with long hours. Franchisees, however, benefit from affiliating with a recognized brand, relying on an established business system, and leaning on support from an experienced franchisor.

1. What are the advantages and disadvantages of purchasing an outlet from a small franchisor?

2. Suppose that one of your friends is considering purchasing a BurgerFi franchise and asks your opinion. What advice would you offer him or her?

3. Develop a list of questions that a prospective franchisee should ask the franchisor and existing franchisees before deciding to invest in a franchise.

Sources: Based on Jason Daley, "How to Succeed in Franchising Your Business," *Entrepreneur,* ay 2015, pp. 91-97; Julie Bennett, "Hot New Franchise Concepts Offer Rewards, But Not Without Risks," *Wall Street Journal,* September 24, 2015, p. B8; "Exclusive Interview with Nick King, Managing Director of BurgerFi, the World's Fastest Growing All-Natural Burger Franchise," *Franchise Chatter,* June 15, 2012, https://www.franchisechatter.com/2012/06/15/exclusive-interview-with-nick-king-managing-director-of-burgerfi-the-worlds-fastest-growing-all-natural-burger-franchise/; "BurgerFi International LLC," *Entrepreneur,* August 2017, https://www.entrepreneur.com/franchises/burgerfiintlllc/334264.

LO2B

Explain the drawbacks of buying a franchise.

The Drawbacks of Buying a Franchise

The benefits of buying a franchise can mean the difference between success and failure for some entrepreneurs. Prospective franchisees must understand the disadvantages of franchising before choosing this method of doing business. Perhaps the biggest drawback of franchising is that a franchisee must sacrifice some freedom to the franchisor. Other disadvantages are discussed in the following sections.

Franchise Fees and Ongoing Royalties

Virtually every franchisor imposes some type of fees and demands a share of franchisees' sales revenue in return for the use of the franchisor's name, products or services, and business system. The fees and the initial capital requirements vary among the different franchisors. The total investment required for a franchise varies from around $4,000 for some home-based service franchises to $20 million or more for hotel and motel franchises. For example, Jan-Pro, a home-based commercial cleaning service franchise, requires a capital investment that ranges from just $3,935 to $51,605, and Subway, the sandwich and salad chain, estimates that the total cost of opening a franchise ranges from $116,600 for a kiosk location to $263,150 for a traditional restaurant. Culver's, a fast-growing regional chain that sells sandwiches (including the delicious ButterBurger), salads, dinners, and frozen custard, requires an investment of $1.845 million to $4.155 million, depending on land acquisition and building construction costs. Franchisees use many of the same sources to finance franchises that independent entrepreneurs use to finance start-up companies (see Figure 8.5).

Start-up costs for franchises often include a variety of fees. Most franchises impose an initial franchise fee for the right to use the company name. The average up-front fee that franchisors charge is $25,147.[58] Subway's franchise fee is $15,000, but Culver's charges a franchise fee of $55,000. Other franchise start-up costs might include fees for location analysis, site purchase and preparation, construction, signs, fixtures, equipment, management assistance, and training.

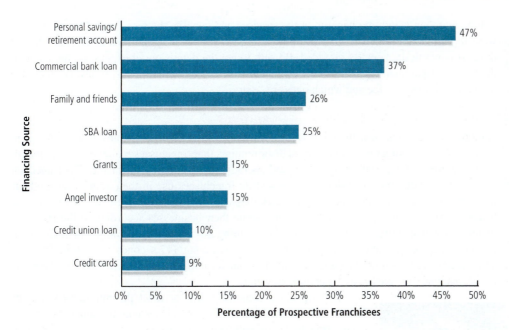

FIGURE 8.5

Planned Sources of Financing for Prospective Franchisees

Note: Percentages sum to more than 100 percent because respondents plan to use more than one method to finance their franchises.

Source: Prospective Franchisee Survey Results, FranchiseDirect, 2016, www.franchisedirect.com/ information/prospectivefra nchiseesurveyresults2016 /?r=5380.

Some franchise fees include these costs, but others do not. Before signing any contract, a prospective franchisee should determine the total cost of a franchise, something that every franchisor is required to disclose in item 7 of its Franchise Disclosure Document (see the section "Franchising and the Law," later in this chapter).

Franchisors also impose continuing royalty fees as revenue-sharing devices. The royalty usually involves a percentage of gross sales, with a required minimum or a flat fee levied on the franchise. More than 95 percent of franchisors charge a royalty based on a percentage of franchisees' sales.[59] Royalty fees range from 1 to 11 percent, and the average royalty rate is 6.7 percent (see Figure 8.6).[60] Culver's charges franchisees a royalty of 4 percent of gross sales, which is payable weekly, and Subway charges a royalty of 8 percent of weekly gross sales. These ongoing royalties increase a franchisee's overhead expenses significantly. Because the franchisor's royalties and fees (the total fees the average franchisor collects amount to 8.4 percent of a franchisee's sales) are calculated as a percentage of a franchisee's sales, the franchisor gets paid even if the franchisee fails to earn a profit.[61] Sometimes, unprepared franchisees discover (too late) that a franchisor's royalties and fees are the equivalent of the normal profit margin for a business. To avoid this problem, prospective franchisees should determine exactly how much fees

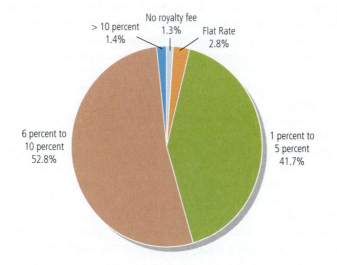

FIGURE 8.6

Franchise Royalty Fees

Source: Based on *2015 Franchise Sales Trends Report,* FranConnect, 2015, p. 6.

will be and then weigh the benefits of the services and benefits the fees cover. One of the best ways to do this is to itemize what you are getting for your money and then determine whether the cost is worth the benefits provided. Be sure to get the details on all expenses—the amount, the timing of payments, and financing arrangements; find out which items, if any, are included in the initial franchise fee and which ones are "extra."

Strict Adherence to Standardized Operations

Although franchisees own their businesses, they do not have the autonomy that independent owners have. To protect its image, a franchisor requires that franchisees maintain certain operating standards. In fact, conformity is standard operating procedure in franchising. The franchisor controls the layout and the color schemes that its franchisees use in their stores, the products they sell, the personnel and operating policies they use, and many other aspects of running the business. At McDonald's, franchisees must operate their businesses according to the franchise manual, which specifies nearly every detail of running a franchise—including how many hamburger patties per pound of beef (10), how long to toast a bun (17 seconds), how long fries can sit before being tossed out (7 minutes), and how much sanitizer to use when cleaning the milkshake machine (one packet to 2.5 gallons of water).

Thomas Padilla/Newscom

If a franchise constantly fails to meet the minimum standards established for the business, the franchisor may terminate its license. Many franchisors determine compliance with standards through periodic inspections and secret shoppers. Secret shoppers work for a survey company and, although they look like any other customer, are trained to observe and then later record on a checklist a franchise's performance on key standards, such as cleanliness, speed of service, employees' appearances and attitudes, and others. At Five Guys Burgers and Fries, founder Jerry Murrell uses secret shoppers to ensure that franchisees comply with the company's strict quality and service standards. Five Guys conducts two independent audits of each store every week. One is a secret shopper who poses as a customer and rates everything from the courtesy of the crew and the appearance of the food to the cleanliness of the bathrooms and the time required for service; the other audit focuses on safety.[62] At times, strict adherence to franchise standards may become a burden to some franchisees.

Restrictions on Purchasing and Prices

In the interest of maintaining quality standards, franchisors may require franchisees to purchase products, special equipment, or other items from the franchisor or from a list of "approved" suppliers. For example, KFC requires that franchisees use only seasonings blended by a particular company because a poor image could result from franchisees using inferior products to cut costs. Under some conditions, these purchase arrangements may be challenged in court as a violation of antitrust laws, but generally franchisors have a legal right to ensure that franchisees maintain acceptable quality standards. Franchisees filed a round of lawsuits against Quiznos, a chain of sandwich shops, in which they allege that the franchisor, based in Denver, Colorado, engaged in fraud and misdealing by requiring franchisees to purchase food and supplies from the franchisor's supply division, making them "captive customers." The complaints contended that Quiznos, whose franchisee count has declined from more than 5,000 in 2007 to 1,500 today, earned millions in profits by using "hidden markups" on items that the contract requires franchisees to purchase from the franchisor, while most franchisees were "losing money or barely breaking even." Quiznos settled the lawsuit for $206 million and, after filing for bankruptcy to eliminate more than $400 million of its debt, reorganized its operations, including eliminating its supply arm. Franchisees now purchase supplies from Sysco, an independent food distributor, and have seen their food costs decline by 3.5 percent as a percentage of gross sales.[63]

For many years, franchisors could legally set the prices they charge for the products they sell to franchisees but could not control the retail prices franchisees charge for products. However, two U.S. Supreme Court decisions (*State Oil Company v. Khan* in 1997 and *Leegin Creative Leather Products v. PSKS, Inc.* in 2007) opened the door for franchisors to establish maximum prices that franchisees can charge. Many franchisors do not impose maximum prices, choosing instead to provide franchisees with suggested prices but allowing them to adjust their final prices to reflect their local markets. Some franchisors do establish price limits, however. "Value menus" have become a source of contention for franchisees of many quick-service restaurants because franchisors impose price limits on items that appear on their value menus. Value menus are an important revenue source for franchises, accounting for 13 to 15 percent of sales, but franchisees complain that making a profit on low-priced items is difficult. To address its franchisees' concerns, McDonald's replaced its Dollar Menu with the Dollar Menu and More, which included 25 items priced between $1 and $5 and was designed to give franchisees more flexibility in pricing and allow them to offset rising commodity and labor costs. McDonald's recently replaced the Dollar Menu and More with McPick, which allows customers to pick two of four items for $2.[64]

Franchisors' right to determine franchisees' retail prices is not unlimited, however. Several Steak 'n Shake franchisees have been locked in a legal battle with the franchisor over the franchisor's insistence that all franchisees comply with its 4 Meals for $4 promotion, claiming that doing so would lead to "financial disaster." The franchisees won an injunction against Steak 'n Shake, effectively blocking the policy that required franchisees to abide by the prices the franchisor sets for its menu items. Stuller, Inc., the chain's oldest franchisee, argued that the policy would cost its five franchises $950,000 per year.[65]

Limited Product Line

In most cases, the franchise agreement stipulates that the franchisee can sell only products approved by the franchisor. Unless they are willing to risk the cancellation of their licenses, franchisees must avoid selling any unapproved products through the franchise. A franchise may be required to carry an unpopular product or may be prevented from introducing a desirable one by the franchise agreement. A franchisee's freedom to adapt a product line to local market conditions is restricted. However, some franchisors actively solicit innovations and product suggestions from their franchisees. Subway's $5 Footlong idea that helped the chain ride out the Great Recession did not come from corporate headquarters but originated with Miami franchisee Stuart Frankel.[66] Some of McDonald's most successful products came not from the corporate kitchen but from franchisees such as Jim Delligatti, who invented the legendary Big Mac in 1967. In 1968, McDonald's put the sandwich on franchisees' menus, where its original price was 49 cents. Today, McDonald's sells 560 million Big Macs each year—an average of more than 17 sandwiches per second![67] Some franchisees are concerned that McDonald's has developed no "home run" products for its menu since the successful introduction of McGriddles, a pancake sandwich, in 2003. Many franchisees also complain that they throw away more of the chain's "healthy" menu items, such as salads, which make up only 2 to 3 percent of sales, than they sell.[68]

When franchisors do introduce new products, franchisees sometimes incur additional costs to provide them. When McDonald's began offering upscale McCafe coffee products, franchisees had to purchase espresso machines that cost between $10,000 and $15,000 per restaurant.[69]

Contract Terms: Termination, Renewal, and Sale or Buyback

Because franchise contracts are written by the franchisor's attorneys, they always are written in favor of the franchisor. Some franchisors are willing to negotiate the terms of their contracts, but many of the well-established franchisors are not because they know they don't have to. The franchise contract is extremely important because it governs the franchisor–franchisee relationship over its life, which may last as long as 20 years. In fact, the average length of a franchise contract is 10.5 years.[70] Still, 18 percent of franchisees say that they did not read the franchise agreement before signing it, and 33 percent of franchisees did not have an attorney review the agreement before signing it.[71]

Although franchise contracts cover everything from initial fees and continuing payments to training programs and territorial protection, three terms cause most franchisor–franchisee disputes: termination of the contract, contract renewal, and transfer and buyback provisions.

TERMINATION One of the most litigated subjects of franchise agreements is the termination of the contract by either party. Most contracts prevent franchisees from terminating the contract but allow franchisors to terminate the agreement if a franchisee fails to abide by the terms of the agreement, including committing violations such as failure to make required payments on time or failure to maintain quality standards or declaring bankruptcy or losing the franchise location. Prospective franchisees should know exactly the circumstances under which the franchisor has the right to terminate the contract. Wendy's recently filed a lawsuit against one of its largest franchisees, DavCo Restaurants, LLC, which operates 152 restaurants, to terminate the franchise relationship because the franchisee refused to incur the expense of remodeling its restaurants and install a new point-of-sale system that facilitates taking orders and payments from mobile devices. DavCo claims that the franchisor's remodeling program offers franchisees little or no chance to earn a return on their investment and estimates that remodeling its restaurants would cost $75 million.[72]

RENEWAL   When the franchise contract expires, the franchisor and the franchisee must negotiate a new agreement. The franchisee must pay a franchise renewal fee (similar to the original one-time franchise fee) and fix any deficiencies in the existing location, including remodeling and updating it to meet current franchise standards. One study by the International Franchise Association and FRANdata reports that the renewal rate of franchise agreements is 94 percent.[73]

TRANSFER AND BUYBACKS   Unlike owners of independent businesses, franchisees typically are not free to sell their franchises to just anyone. Under most franchise contracts, franchisees cannot sell their franchises to a third party without the franchisor's approval. Many franchise contracts also include a right-of-first-refusal clause, which means that franchisees must offer to sell their outlets to the franchisor first. Item 17 of the Franchise Disclosure Document (more on this later) addresses transfers, buybacks, and the right of first refusal.

Unsatisfactory Training Programs

A major benefit of purchasing a franchise is the training that the franchisor provides franchisees so that they are able to run successful operations. The quality of franchise training programs can vary dramatically, however. "Many franchisees think they will get a lot of training but find out it's a one-week crash course," says Marko Grunhagen, a franchising expert at Southern Illinois University.[74] Before signing on with a franchise, it is wise to find out the details of the training program the franchisor provides to avoid unpleasant surprises.

Market Saturation

Franchisees in fast-growing systems reap the benefits of the franchisor's expanding reach, but they also may encounter the downside of a franchisor's aggressive growth strategy: market saturation. As the owners of many fast-food, sandwich, and yogurt franchises have discovered, market saturation is a very real danger. In 2009, 1,022 frozen yogurt stores operated in the United States; five years later, the number had nearly tripled, to 2,910 locations.[75] One researcher has determined that only one place in the contiguous 48 states, a high plain in northwestern South Dakota, is more than 100 miles from a McDonald's restaurant.[76] Subway, which started franchising in 1974, has grown from just 166 outlets in 1981 to more than 44,000 outlets today![77] Any franchise growing that rapidly runs the risk of having outlets so close together that they cannibalize sales from one another, causing them to struggle to reach their breakeven points. Figure 8.7 shows a breakdown of the number of outlets operated by U.S.-based franchises.

As you learned in the previous section, although some franchisors offer franchisees territorial protection, others do not. Territorial encroachment, competition from within the franchise, has become a hotly contested issue in franchising as growth-seeking franchisors have exhausted most of the prime locations and are now setting up new franchises in close proximity to existing ones. Franchisees are upset, claiming that their markets are oversaturated and their sales are suffering. Franchise experts consistently site territorial encroachment as the primary threat to franchisees.

Less Freedom

A basic principle of franchising is repetition of a successful formula; therefore, franchisees give up much of the freedom they would have as independent business owners. This feature of franchising is the source of the system's success, but it also gives many franchisees the feeling that

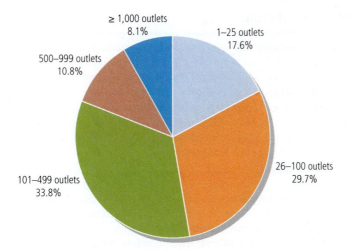

FIGURE 8.7

**Franchise
Breakdown by
Number of Outlets**

Source: Based on *2015 Franchise Sales Trend Report*, FranConnect, 2015, p. 3.

they are reporting to a "boss." "Everything you do in a franchise will be dictated [by the franchisor] from the moment you turn the key in the door in the morning," warns Eric Karp, a Boston attorney who teaches franchising at Babson College.[78]

Franchisees operate their businesses according to the franchisor's policies and standards. Strict uniformity is the rule rather than the exception. For example, a group of franchisees filed a lawsuit against Burger King, claiming that the company had no right to require them to open their stores as early as 6 A.M. and to stay open as late as 2 A.M., but the court dismissed their argument, ruling that the franchise contract, which authorized the extended hours, is unambiguous and enforceable.[79] "There is no independence," says one writer. "Successful franchisees are happy prisoners."[80] As a result, highly independent, "go-my-own-way" entrepreneurs often are frustrated with the basic "go-by-the-rules" philosophy of franchising. Table 8.1 describes 10 myths of franchising.

Franchising and the Law

Franchise Disclosure Document

The franchising boom spearheaded by McDonald's and others in the late 1950s brought with it many prime investment opportunities. However, the explosion of legitimate franchises also ushered in with it numerous fly-by-night franchisors that defrauded their franchisees. By the 1970s, franchising was rife with fraudulent practitioners. David Kaufman, a renowned franchise expert, says, "In the late 1960s and 1970s, the words 'franchise' and 'fraud' had almost become synonymous."[81] Thousands of people lost millions of dollars to criminals and unscrupulous operators who sold flawed business concepts and phantom franchises to unsuspecting investors. In an effort to control the rampant fraud in the industry and the potential for deception inherent in a franchise relationship, California enacted the first Franchise Investment Law in 1971. The law (and those of 14 other states that passed similar laws) required franchisors to register a Uniform Franchise Offering Circular (UFOC) and deliver a copy to prospective franchisees before any offer or sale of a franchise. In October 1979, the Federal Trade Commission (FTC) adopted similar legislation at the national level that established full disclosure guidelines for any company selling franchises and was designed to give potential franchisees the information they needed to protect themselves from unscrupulous franchisors.

In 2008, the FTC replaced the UFOC with a similar document, the **Franchise Disclosure Document (FDD)**, which requires all franchisors to provide detailed information on their operations at least 14 days before a franchisee signs a contract or pays any money. The FDD applies to all franchisors, even those in the 35 states that lack franchise disclosure laws. The purpose of the regulation is to assist potential franchisees' investigations of a franchise deal and to introduce consistency into the franchisor's disclosure statements. The FTC also established a "plain

LO3

Understand the laws covering franchise purchases.

**Franchise Disclosure
Document (FDD)**

a document that every franchisor is required by law to give prospective franchisees before any offer or sale of a franchise; it outlines 23 important pieces of information.

TABLE 8.1 10 Myths of Franchising

Myth #1. Franchising is the safest way to go into business because franchises don't fail. Although the failure rate for franchises is lower than that for independent businesses, there are no guarantees of success. Franchises can—and do—fail. Potential franchisees must exercise the same degree of caution in judging the risk of a franchise as they would any other business.

Myth #2. I'll be able to open my franchise for less money than the franchisor estimates. Launching a business, including a franchise, normally takes more money and more time than entrepreneurs estimate. Be prepared. One franchisee of a retail computer store advises, "If a franchisor tells you you'll need $100,000 to get started, you better have $150,000."

Myth #3. The bigger the franchise organization, the more successful I'll be. Bigger is not always better in the franchise business. Some of the largest franchise operations are struggling to maintain their growth rates because the best locations are already taken, and their markets have become saturated. Market saturation is a significant problem for many large franchises, and smaller franchises are accounting for much of the growth in the industry. Early franchisees in new franchise systems often can negotiate better deals and receive more individual attention from the franchisor than those who purchase units in well-established systems.

Myth #4. I'll use 80 percent of the franchisor's business system, but I'll improve on it by substituting my experience and know-how. When franchisees buy a franchise, they are buying, in essence, the franchisor's experience and knowledge. Why pay all that money if you aren't willing to use the franchisor's system? When franchisors screen potential franchisees, they look for people who are willing to fit into their systems rather than for fiercely independent entrepreneurs. "[Franchisors] have spent years building the company," says Jeff Elgin, founder of FranChoice, a franchise referral consulting firm. "They don't want someone who will come in and try to innovate because that produces chaos." Ideally, franchisors look for franchisees who exhibit a balance between the freewheeling entrepreneurial spirit and a system-focused approach.

Myth #5. All franchises are basically the same. Each franchise has its own unique personality, requirements, procedures, and culture. Naturally, some will suit you better than others. Avoid the tendency to select the franchise that offers the lowest cost. If a franchise does not fit your needs, it is not a bargain, no matter how inexpensive it is. Ask the franchisor and existing franchisees lots of questions to determine how well you will fit into the system. One of the best ways to get a feel for a franchise's personality is to work in a unit for a time.

Myth #6. I don't have to be a hands-on manager. I can be an absentee owner and still be very successful. Most franchisors shy away from absentee owners, and some simply do not allow them in their systems at all. They know that franchise success requires lots of hands-on attention, and the franchise owner is the best person to provide that.

Myth #7. Anyone can be a satisfied, successful franchise owner. With more than 3,000 franchises available, the odds of finding a franchise that appeals to your tastes are high. However, not everyone is cut out to be a franchisee. "If a person is highly entrepreneurial, he or she should not even consider a franchise investment," says Kevin Murphy, a franchise attorney. Those "free spirits" who insist on doing things their way most likely will be miserable in a franchise.

Myth #8. Franchising is the cheapest way to get into business for yourself. Although bargains do exist in franchising, the price tag for buying into some well-established systems is breathtaking, sometimes running more than $1 million. Franchisors look for candidates who are on solid financial footing.

Myth #9. The franchisor will solve my business problems for me; after all, that's why I pay an ongoing royalty. Although franchisors offer franchisees start-up and ongoing training programs, they will not run their franchisees' businesses for them. As a franchisee, your job is to take the formula that the franchisor has developed and make it work in your location. Expect to solve many of your own problems.

Myth #10. Once I open my franchise, I'll be able to run things the way I want to. Franchisees are not free to run their businesses as they see fit. Each franchisee signs a contract that requires him or her to run the business according to the franchisor's requirements. Franchisees who violate the terms of that agreement run the risk of having their franchise relationship terminated.

Sources: Based on Mark Henricks, "Finding the Perfect Fit: How Franchisers Select Franchisees," *Advertising Insert, Inc.*, February 2011, p. 110; April Y. Pennington, "The Right Stuff," *Entrepreneur B.Y.O.B.*, September 2004, pp. 90–100; Andrew A. Caffey, "There's More to a Franchise Than Meets the Eye," *Entrepreneur*, May 1998, www.entrepreneur.com/article/0,4621,228443,00.html; Andrew A. Caffey, "Myth vs. Reality," *Entrepreneur*, October 1998, www.entrepreneur.com/mag/article/0,1539,229435,00.html; Chieh Chieng, "Do You Want to Know a Secret?" *Entrepreneur*, January 1999, pp. 174–178; "Ten Most Common Mistakes Made by Franchise Buyers," Franchise Doctor, www.franchisedoc.com/mistakes.html; and Devlin Smith, "The Sure Thing," *Entrepreneur B.Y.O.B.*, May 2004, p. 100.

English" requirement for the FDD that prohibits legal and technical jargon and makes the document easy to read and understand. The FTC's philosophy is not so much to prosecute abusers as to provide information to prospective franchisees and help them make intelligent decisions. Although the FTC requires each franchisor to provide a potential franchisee with this information, it does not verify the accuracy of this information. Prospective franchisees should use this document only as a starting point for their investigations.

The Trade Regulation Rule requires a franchisor to include 23 major topics in its disclosure statement:

1. Information identifying the franchisor and its affiliates and describing the franchisor's business experience and the franchises being sold.

2. Information identifying and describing the business experience of each of the franchisor's officers, directors, and managers responsible for the franchise program.

3. A description of the lawsuits in which the franchisor and its officers, directors, and managers have been involved. Although most franchisors will have been involved in some type of litigation, an excessive number of lawsuits, particularly if they relate to the same problem, is alarming. Another red flag is an excessive number of lawsuits brought against the franchisor by franchisees. The number and types of lawsuits that a franchisor has faced in the past are good indicators of the nature of the franchisor–franchisee relationship in the future.

4. Information about any bankruptcies in which the franchisor and its officers, directors, and managers have been involved.

5. Information about the initial franchise fee and other payments required to obtain the franchise, the intended use of the fees, and the conditions under which the fees are refundable.

6. A table that describes all of the other fees that franchisees are required to make after start-up, including royalties, service fees, training fees, lease payments, advertising or marketing charges, and others. The table also must include the due dates for the fees.

7. A table that shows the components of a franchisee's total initial investment. The categories included are preopening expenses, the initial franchise fee, training expenses, equipment, opening inventory, initial advertising fee, signs, real estate (purchased or leased), security deposits, business licenses, initial advertising fees, and other expenses, such as legal and accounting fees. Also included is an estimate of the amount of working capital a franchisee should have on hand to sustain the company in its first three months of operation. (Franchisees should be aware that the actual amount of capital required to keep a franchise going until it generates positive cash flow is probably much higher.) These estimates, usually stated as a range, give prospective franchisees an idea of how much their total start-up costs will be. The average initial investment for a franchise is $520,000, but the actual investment that a particular franchisee must make varies greatly around that average, depending on the franchise.[82]

8. Information about quality requirements of goods, services, equipment, supplies, inventory, and other items used in the franchise and where franchisees may purchase them, including required purchases from the franchisor. When interviewing existing franchisees, prospective franchisees should ask whether the prices the franchisees pay for products and services are reasonable.

9. A cross-reference table that shows the location in the FDD and in the franchise contract of the description of the franchisee's obligations under the franchise contract.

10. A description of the financial assistance (if any) available from the franchisor in the purchase of the franchise. Although many franchisors do not offer direct financial assistance to franchisees, they may have special arrangements with lenders who help franchisees find financing.

11. A description of all obligations the franchisor must fulfill to help a franchisee prepare to open and operate a unit, including site selection, advertising, computer systems, pricing, training (a table describing the length and type of training is required), and other forms of assistance provided to franchisees. This usually is the longest section of the FDD.

12. A description of any territorial protection that the franchise receives and a statement about whether the franchisor may locate a company-owned store or other franchised outlet in that territory. The franchisor must specify whether it offers exclusive or nonexclusive territories. Given the controversy in many franchises over market saturation, franchisees should pay close attention to this section. Prospective franchisees should recognize the risk of investing in a franchise that provides no territorial protection or exclusive territories.

13. All relevant information about the franchisor's trademarks, service marks, trade names, logos, and commercial symbols, including where they are registered. Prospective franchisees should look for a strong trademark or service mark that is registered with the U.S. Patent and Trademark Office.

14. Similar information on any patents, copyrights, and proprietary processes that the franchisor owns and the rights that franchisees have to use them.

15. A description of the extent to which franchisees must participate personally in the operation of the franchise. Many franchisors look for hands-on franchisees and discourage or even prohibit absentee owners.

16. A description of any restrictions on the goods or services that franchises are permitted to sell. The agreement usually restricts franchisees to selling only items the franchisor has approved.

17. A table that describes the conditions under which the franchise may be repurchased or refused renewal by the franchisor, transferred to a third party by the franchisee, and terminated or modified by either party. This section also addresses the methods established for resolving disputes, usually either mediation or arbitration, between franchisees and the franchisor. One study reports that 44 percent of franchisors' contracts contain arbitration clauses, which means that if a dispute arises, the parties must submit the dispute to arbitration rather than resolve it in the courts.[83]

18. A description of the involvement of celebrities and public figures in the franchise. Fewer than 1 percent of franchise systems use public figures as part of their promotional strategies.[84]

19. A complete statement of the basis for any earnings claims made to the franchisee, including the percentage of existing franchises that have actually achieved the results that are claimed. Franchisors that make earnings claims must include them in the FDD, and the claims must "have a reasonable basis" at the time they are made. Franchisors are *not* required to make any earnings claims at all, and franchisors' biggest concern about providing them is that statements about averages can be misleading. Still, nearly 70 percent of franchisors provide average financial performance information to prospective franchisees.[85]

20. A table that displays systemwide statistical information about the expansion or contraction of the franchise over the last three years. This section also includes the current number of franchises, the number of franchises projected for the future and the states in which they are to be sold, the number of franchises terminated, the number of agreements the franchisor has not renewed, the number of franchises that have been sold to new owners, the number of outlets the franchisor has repurchased, and a list of the names and addresses (organized by state) of other franchisees in the system and of those who have left the system within the last year. Contacting some of the franchisees who have left the system can alert would-be franchisees to potential problems with the franchise.

21. The franchisor's audited financial statements.

22. A copy of all franchise and other contracts (leases, purchase agreements, and others) that the franchisee will be required to sign.

23. A standardized, detachable receipt to prove that the prospective franchisee received a copy of the FDD. The FTC now allows franchisors to provide the FDD to prospective franchisees electronically.

The FDD is typically 100 to 200 pages long, but every potential franchisee should read and understand it. Unfortunately, many do not, which often results in unpleasant surprises for franchisees. The information contained in the FDD neither fully protects a potential franchise from deception nor guarantees success. The FDD does, however, provide enough information to begin a thorough investigation of the franchisor and the franchise deal, and prospective franchisees should use it to their advantage.

Joint Employer Liability

In a recent decision known as *Browning-Ferris Industries* (*BFI*), the National Labor Relations Board (NLRB) overturned more than 30 years of regulatory practice and franchise law by declaring that franchisors are considered "joint employers" with their franchisees. Even though franchisees make decisions about hiring, paying, scheduling, and firing their employees, the ruling holds franchisors jointly responsible for those decisions. The NLRB decision turns on its head previous law that held that franchisors were jointly responsible for hiring decisions only if the franchisor exercised *direct* control over them. The *BFI* case and a subsequent case the NLRB filed against McDonald's change the standard, making franchisors joint employers with their franchisees even if they have only "indirect" or "potential" control over franchisees' employment decisions. The implications of the decision are significant. A franchisor would be pulled into lawsuits when a single franchisee makes an employment decision that violates some employment law. Employment practices liability insurance rates could skyrocket for all franchisees because they are based on the number of employees a company has; the more employees a business has, the higher its employment liability insurance rates. Systemwide, McDonald's, for example, has 1.9 million employees, 1.5 million of whom work for its franchisees. The ruling also opens the door to forcing franchisors to the bargaining table with labor unions, which could organize employees systemwide. Finally, the decision also puts the nature of the franchisor–franchisee relationship at risk because it will lead to increased control by franchisors over their franchisees' daily business practices, transforming them from semi-independent business owners to mere "store managers."[86] The Browning-Ferris Industries case is under appeal, and 14 states have passed laws to protect franchisors from joint employer liability within their borders.[87]

The *Right* Way to Buy a Franchise

LO4

Explain the *right* way to buy a franchise.

The FDD is a powerful tool designed to help would-be franchisees select the franchise that is right for them and to avoid being duped by dishonest franchisors. Unfortunately, 18 percent of franchisees never read the franchisor's FDD.[88] The best defenses a prospective entrepreneur has against unscrupulous franchisors are preparation, common sense, and patience. By asking the right questions and resisting the urge to rush into an investment decision, potential franchisees can avoid being taken by unscrupulous operators.

Not every franchise "horror story" is a result of dishonest franchisors. More often than not, the problems that arise in franchising have more to do with franchisees buying legitimate franchises without proper research and analysis. They end up in businesses that they don't enjoy and that they are not well suited to operate. Fortunately, most franchisees are happy with their franchise decisions. A recent survey by Franchise Business Review reports that 74 percent of food and beverage franchisees say that if given the chance, they would choose the same franchise again.[89] How can you avoid choosing the wrong franchise? The steps discussed in the following sections will help you to make the right choice.

Evaluate Yourself

Before looking at any franchise, entrepreneurs should study their own traits, goals, experience, likes, dislikes, risk orientation, income requirements, time and family commitments, and other characteristics. Knowing how much money you can invest in a franchise is important, but it is not the only factor to consider. "You not only have to understand simple things such as what kind of investment you're willing to make, but also what kind of risks you are willing to take, how hard you want to work, how many hours you want to work, and what kind of environment you want to work in," advises Lori Kiser-Block, head of franchise consulting service FranChoice.[90] Will you be comfortable working in a structured environment? In what region of the country or world do you want to live and work? What is your ideal job description? Do you want to sell a product or a service? What hours do you expect to work? Do you want to work with people, or do you prefer to work alone? Knowing what you enjoy doing (and what you *don't* want to do) will help you narrow your search. Which franchises are a good match for your strengths, weaknesses, interests, and professional experience? The goal is to find the franchise that is right—for *you*!

Prospective franchisees also must determine how much they can invest in a franchise. Although the FDD shows prospective franchisees the total investment amount required, including working capital, experts recommend that franchisees have an additional cache of capital as a contingency fund to cover the costs of unexpected surprises. Keith Gerson, a top manager for FranConnect, a provider of franchise management software, points out that franchisees start burning through their start-up capital the day they sign their franchise contracts and that the time gap before they begin to generate revenue can be lengthy.[91] Prospective franchisees must realize that despite their best plans, delays in opening a franchise often crop up, pushing back the date when the revenue stream begins. Having a sufficient amount of working capital (experts recommend two to three times the amount the FDD lists) to keep the franchise afloat until it becomes cash flow positive is essential. Gerson notes that insufficient working capital is the number-one cause of franchise failure.[92]

ENTREPRENEURIAL PROFILE: Alex Gashkevich: Aaron's Alex Gashkevich decided to leave behind a career in finance on Wall Street for the opportunity to own a franchise. After months of research, he decided to invest in Aaron's, a franchise that sells furniture, electronics, and appliances under lease-to-own contracts. He invested $400,000 of his own money to renovate and build out a location in Rockaway, New Jersey, and to hire employees. Gashkevich says that the renovations took much longer than he had planned, during which time he paid the employees he had already hired. His franchise reached its breakeven point in just 16 months, but Gashkevich has not yet paid himself a salary, choosing instead to use the profits from his first store to open a second one. He also has signed an area development contract with Aaron's, under which he agrees to open Aaron's stores in seven territories in the New York area. Gashkevich says that he is having an incredible amount of fun as a franchisee.[93] ∎

Table 8.2 is designed to help prospective franchisees evaluate their potential as successful franchisees.

Research Your Market

Before shopping for a franchise, research the market in the area you plan to serve. How fast is the overall area growing? In which areas is that growth occurring fastest? How many competitors already operate in the area? How strong is the competition? Investing some time in developing a profile of the customers in your target area is essential; otherwise, you will be flying blind. Who are your potential customers? How many of them are in your proposed trading area? What are their characteristics? What are their income and education levels? What kinds of products and services do they buy? What gaps exist in the market? These gaps represent potential franchise opportunities for you. Market research also should confirm that a franchise is not merely a fad that will quickly fade. Steering clear of fads and into long-term trends is one way to sustain the success of a franchise. The secret to distinguishing between a fad that will soon fizzle and a meaningful trend that offers genuine opportunity is finding products and services that are consistent with fundamental demographic and lifestyle patterns of the population. Students in the United States have fallen behind the rest of the industrialized world in science (ranked 17th) and math (ranked 25th), and many parents are paying for additional training for their children in STEM (science, technology, engineering, and mathematics). Because job opportunities in STEM fields are growing much faster than in the overall economy and because STEM salaries are much higher than those in non-STEM fields, demand for STEM training for children is growing rapidly. Franchises such as Bricks for Kidz, Professor Egghead, STEM for Kids, and e2

TABLE 8.2 Are You Franchisee Material?

Not everyone is cut out to be a franchisee. What characteristics do successful franchise owners have?

- *Commitment.* Like all other entrepreneurs, successful franchisees must be committed to making their businesses successful. For franchisees, that means learning how the franchisor's system works and how to apply it in their individual markets.

- *Learning attitude.* Franchisees must exhibit a learning attitude and be willing to learn from the franchisor, other franchisees, and other experts. "Franchisors are not necessarily looking for experts in their industry," says one franchise consultant, "but for individuals with a great work ethic, broad business knowledge, and a willingness to follow a proven system."

- *Willingness to work with others.* Franchising success requires a willingness to work with the franchisor in a close, mutually beneficial relationship.

- *Patience.* Franchisees must understand that franchising is *not* a ticket to overnight success; success often requires years of hard work.

- *Positive attitude.* Franchisors look for franchisees who have a positive outlook and are focused on success.

- *General business skills.* Although franchisors usually do not require franchisees to have years of experience in the particular industry in which they operate, they do look for people who have general business experience. Sound leadership and communication skills are important in every industry.

- *Leadership ability.* Getting a franchise up and running successfully requires every ounce of leadership ability that a franchisee has.

- *Coachability.* In addition to being successful leaders, franchisees also must be good followers. Franchisors say that their most successful franchisees are coachable and are willing to learn from the experience of others. Reaping the advantages of the franchisor's experience is one of the primary benefits of franchising, and franchisees should take advantage of it.

- *Perseverance.* Successful franchisees are dedicated to making their franchises successful and work hard to get the job done.

- *Solid people skills.* Whatever field they enter, successful franchisees require good people skills because they will be managing employees and working with customers.

- *Adequate capital.* Franchisors look for franchisees who have adequate financial resources to launch their businesses and to keep them going until they can generate enough cash flow to support themselves.

- *Compatible values.* Successful franchisees have value systems that are compatible with those of the franchisor.

- *Willingness to follow the system.* Some people enter the world of franchising because they have an entrepreneurial streak, which could be a mistake. Although creativity and a fresh approach are valuable assets in any business, franchising boils down to following the system that the franchisor has established. Why pay a franchisor for the benefit of experience if you are not willing to put that experience to work for yourself?

Sources: Based on Jerry Chautin, "Tips to Help Succeed at Owning a Franchise," *Herald Tribune*, September 27, 2010, www.heraldtribune.com/article/20100927/COLUMNIST/9271021; Jeff Elgin, "Are You Franchisee Material?" *Entrepreneur*, April 4, 2005, www.entrepreneur.com/franchises/buyingafranchise/franchisecolumnistjeffelgin/article76896.html; Kim Ellis, "Key Characteristics of Successful Franchise Owners," *Bison*, July 1, 2007, www.bison.com/articles_investigationellis_07012007; Jennifer Openshaw, "Five Keys to Success as a Franchise Owner," *AOL Small Business*, October 8, 2007, http://smallbusiness.aol.com/article/_a/five-keys-to-success-as-a-franchise/2007101217280999000; and Sara Wilson, "Show Me the Way," *Entrepreneur*, September 2006, p. 120.

Young Engineers are tapping into this trend, offering curricula designed to spur children's interest in STEM fields of study and offer them tutoring and instruction.[94]

Consider Your Franchise Options

Magazines (and their Web sites) about entrepreneurship, such as *Entrepreneur* and *Inc.*, devote at least one issue annually to franchising. These guides, which often list hundreds of franchises, can help you find a suitable franchise in your price range. The Internet is another valuable tool for gathering information on franchises. The Web sites of organizations such as the International Franchise Association, the American Association of Franchisees and Dealers, the Canadian Franchise

You Be the Consultant

After the Cheering Stops

Tim Biakabutuka beat the odds. Born in Zaire, Biakabutuka emigrated with his family to Montreal, Canada. He had never played football until his senior year in high school, but once he started, his talent shined, earning him the nickname "Touchdown Tim." Only 6.5 percent of high school football athletes play college football, but Biakabutuka beat the odds and received a scholarship as a running back at the University of Michigan. After a stellar college career, Biakabutuka played for the Carolina Panthers in the National Football League for six years, once again proving his ability to beat the odds because only 1.6 percent of college football players make it to the pros. When Biakabutuka retired from the NFL after six years, he followed the advice of Carolina Panthers owner Jerry Richardson (a former franchisee himself) and became a Bojangles Chicken and Biscuits franchisee. Today, Biakabutuka owns 4 outlets in Augusta, Georgia, and he has plans to open 11 more units in the next few years. Because of franchising, Biakabutuka has beaten the odds once again because one out of six NFL players declare bankruptcy within 12 years of retirement.

Steve Caldeira, president of the International Franchise Association, says athletes are a good fit for franchising because they understand the importance of working as a team and as part of a system to achieve success. Biakabutuka sees many parallels between his football career and his role as a franchisee, including the importance of persistence and hard work, both of which have helped him achieve success in franchising. Michael Stone, who played in the National Football League for seven years, believes that franchising is an ideal fit for professional athletes and worked with the International Franchise Association to form the Professional Athletes Franchise Initiative, an organization that encourages athletes to explore franchising as a post-sports career. Stone points out that athletes are executors, accustomed to following the game plan and plays put together by a coach to win a game. Similarly, franchisees have a game plan and a business model put together by the franchise. Just like an athlete, a franchisee must execute the plan to be successful. Other professional athletes who have found success in franchising include Peyton Manning (Super Bowl winner and Papa John's franchisee), Drew Brees (Super Bowl MVP and Jimmy John's Gourmet Sandwiches franchisee), Keyshawn Johnson (former wide receiver, Super Bowl champion, and Panera Bread franchisee), Reggie Bush (NFL star and Panera Bread franchisee), Venus Williams (tennis professional and Jamba Juice franchisee), and Junior Bridgeman (former NBA player for the Milwaukee Bucks). Bridgeman started his franchising career by purchasing five Wendy's franchises and working in every aspect of the business, including mopping floors and cooking burgers. Bridgeman's business grew steadily, and he owned 195 franchises, including Wendy's, Chili's, and Fannie May Fine Chocolate stores. In 2016, he decided to sell his restaurant franchises to purchase another type of franchise, a bottling and distribution franchise for Coca-Cola in Missouri, Illinois, Kansas, and Nebraska.

1. What benefits does franchising offer professional athletes such as those described here?

2. Do you agree with Michael Stone that franchising is a good fit for athletes? Explain.

Tom Hauck/Getty Images

Jackie Ricciardi/Augusta Chronicle/Zumapress.Com/Newscom

(continued)

You Be the Consultant *(continued)*

3. What steps should prospective franchisees, whether they are athletes or not, take to ensure that franchising is the right path to business ownership for them and that they select the right franchise?

Sources: Based on Kerry Pipes, "Rushing Ahead," *Multi-Unit Franchisee*, Issue III, 2016, pp. 68–70; Ryan Wilson, "Study: 16 Percent of NFL Players Go Bankrupt in 12 Years," *CBS Sports*, April 15, 2015, www.cbssports.com/nfl/news/study-16-percent-of-nfl-players-go-bankrupt-within-12-years/; "Estimated Probability of Competing in Professional Athletics," NCAA, April 25, 2016, www.ncaa.org/about/

resources/research/estimated-probability-competing-professional-athletics; Neil Parmar, "Where Do Athletes Go to Retire?" *Wall Street Journal*, November 3, 2014, p. D5; Andrew Lawrence, "Franchise Player," *Fortune*, July 21, 2014, pp. 18–19; Jason Daley, "Playing for Keeps," *Entrepreneur*, February 2012, pp. 82–87; Jan Norman, "Franchising Courts Pro Athletes," *Orange County Register*, November 10, 2011, www.ocregister.com/articles/franchising-326406-athletes-franchise.html; "The All Franchising Team," *Franchise Help*, October 17, 2011, www.franchisehelp.com/blog/top-professional-athletes-who-own-franchises; Jonathan Maze, "Junior Bridgeman Trades Restaurants for Coca-Cola," Nation's Restaurant News, April 20, 2016, http://nrn.com/people/junior-bridgeman-trades-restaurants-coca-cola.

Association, the National Federation of Independent Businesses, the Small Business Administration, and the Federal Trade Commission offer valuable resources and advice for prospective franchisees. In addition, many cities host franchise trade shows throughout the year, where hundreds of franchisors gather to sell their franchises. Attending one of these franchise showcases is a convenient, efficient way to collect information about a variety of available opportunities.

Many franchisors offer prospective franchisees visits to corporate headquarters, where they have the opportunity to learn more about the franchise, the people who manage it, and its products and services. Known as "discovery days," these visits are an excellent way for prospective franchisees to peek behind the curtain of a franchise operation and for franchisors to size up potential franchisees. Unfortunately, only 46 percent of franchisees attend a discovery day before signing their franchise contract.[95]

ENTREPRENEURIAL PROFILE: Pam Leseman: Pita Pit Pam Leseman had been managing three Subway franchises in Ephrata, Washington, when she learned that the franchisee had decided to sell them and that her job would be eliminated. After three customers suggested that she open her own Pita Pit franchise, Leseman began investigating the franchisor. Impressed with what she read in the FDD, she visited a Pita Pit franchise 70 miles away and talked with the outlet's management team by phone. Her next step was to participate in a Pita Pit discovery day, which convinced her to purchase a franchise. After being named Rookie of the Year, Leseman is now making plans to open a second Pita Pit location in a nearby town.[96] ■

Some franchisors use technology to allow prospective franchisees to make virtual visits to the company's headquarters, watch online videos, participate in webinars, and talk with executives in videoconferences.

Get a Copy of the Franchisor's FDD

Once you narrow your franchise choices, you should contact each franchise (at least two in the industry that you have selected) and get a copy of its FDD. Then read it! This document is an important tool in your search for the right franchise, and you should make the most of it. When Ali Saifi was looking for a franchise, he reviewed disclosure documents from 130 different franchises before selecting Subway. Today, Saifi owns 390 Subway restaurants in South Carolina that employ 4,000 people and generate more than $200 million in annual sales.[97]

When evaluating a franchise opportunity, what should a potential franchisee look for? Although there is never a guarantee of success, the following characteristics make a franchise stand out:

- *A unique concept or marketing approach.* "Me-too" franchises are no more successful than me-too independent businesses. Franchisees of Pizza Fusion, a pizza chain with 21 outlets based in Boca Raton, Florida, are drawn not only to the company's vision and values but to its unique position in the market, which includes a focus on fresh, organic, and natural ingredients and eco-friendly stores and delivery vehicles. Pizza Fusion's slogan is "Saving the earth, one pizza at a time."

- *Profitability.* A franchisor should have a track record of profitability, and so should its franchisees. If a franchisor is not profitable, its franchisees are not likely to be either.

Franchisees who follow the business format should expect to earn a reasonable rate of return. A study of 28,500 franchisees by Franchise Business Review reports that franchisees' median pre-tax net income is $50,000; however, the earnings of franchisees of the top 200 franchises are 15 to 20 percent higher than average. Multi-unit franchisees, of course, generate higher earnings; their median pre-tax net income is $88,000, and 29 percent of multi-unit franchisees earn more than $150,000.[98]

- *A registered trademark.* Name recognition is difficult to achieve without a well-known and protected trademark.

- *A business system that works.* A franchisor should have in place a system that is efficient and is well documented in its manuals and training materials.

- *A solid training program.* One of the most valuable components of a franchise system is the training it offers franchisees. The system should be relatively easy to teach.

- *Affordability.* A franchisee should not have to take on an excessive amount of debt to purchase a franchise. Being forced to borrow too much money to open a franchise outlet can doom a business from the outset. A common cause of failure among franchisees is investing almost all of their equity or taking out large loans to pay up-front fees and build out the unit so that they have insufficient working capital once they are in operation. Respectable franchisors verify prospective franchisees' financial qualifications as part of the screening process rather than hand out franchises to anyone who has the money to buy one.

- *A positive relationship with franchisees.* The most successful franchises see their franchisees as partners—and treat them accordingly. The best franchisors understand that their success depends on their franchisees' success.

The FDD covers the 23 items discussed in the previous section and includes a copy of the company's franchise agreement and any contracts accompanying it. Although the law requires an FDD to be written in plain English rather than "legalese," it is best to have an attorney experienced in franchising review the FDD and discuss its provisions with you. Watch for clauses that give the franchisor absolute control and discretion. Some franchisors are willing to negotiate changes to their standard contracts; others are not. One recent survey reports that 59 percent of franchisees did not propose any changes to the franchisor's contract.[99]

The franchise contract summarizes the details that will govern the franchisor–franchisee relationship over its life. It outlines *exactly* the rights and the obligations of each party and sets the guidelines that govern the franchise relationship. Because franchise contracts typically are long term (more than 70 percent run for 10 years or more), it is extremely important for prospective franchisees to understand their terms *before* they sign them.

franchisee turnover rate

the rate at which franchisees leave a franchise system.

One of the most revealing items in the FDD is the **franchisee turnover rate**, the rate at which franchisees leave the system. If the turnover rate is less than 5 percent, the franchise is probably sound. However, a double-digit franchise turnover rate is cause for concern, and one approaching 20 percent is a sign of serious underlying problems in a franchise. Satisfied franchisees are not inclined to leave a successful system.

Item 3, the description of the lawsuits in which the franchise has been involved, provides valuable insight into the franchisor–franchisee relationship. Although franchise lawsuits are not uncommon, an unusual number of lawsuits relating to the same issue should alert a potential franchisee to problems.

Another important aspect of investigating a potential franchise is judging how well you fit into the company culture. Unfortunately, the FDD isn't much help here. The best way to determine this is to actually work for a unit for a time (even if it's without pay). Doing so not only gives prospective franchisees valuable insight into the company culture but also enables them to determine how much they enjoy the daily activities involved in operating the franchise.

ENTREPRENEURIAL PROFILE: Reynolds Corea: BrightStar After Reynolds Corea was laid off from his executive position at a large consulting firm, he decided that buying a franchise was the best way to realize his entrepreneurial dreams. He went to work at $10 per hour at a local Chick-fil-A restaurant, serving chicken sandwiches, mopping floors, and closing the store to get a better feel for the business. After nine months, Corea decided that owning a restaurant franchise was not for him and worked with a franchise consultant to find a franchise that better suited his interests, goals, and skills. Corea ultimately chose to purchase a franchise from BrightStar, an in-home care service for senior citizens and children. Corea tapped his retirement accounts for the franchise fee and start-up costs, which totaled about $200,000. Corea's franchise is off to a solid start, with 2 full-time employees, 10 part-time caregivers, and plans to hire more.[100] ∎

Talk to Existing Franchisees

As valuable as the FDD is, it is only a starting point for researching a franchise opportunity thoroughly. Perhaps the best way to evaluate the reputation of a franchisor is to visit several franchise owners who have been in business at least one year and interview them about the positive and negative features of the relationship and whether the franchisor delivers on its promises. A recent survey reports that 69 percent of franchisees took the time to visit at least one unit in the system before they invested in it.[101] Questions to ask existing franchisees include: Were their start-up costs consistent with the franchisor's estimates in item 7 of the FDD? Do they get the support the franchisor promised them? Was the training the franchisor provided helpful? How long did it take to reach the breakeven point? Have they incurred any unexpected expenses? What risks are involved in purchasing a franchise? Has the franchise met their expectations concerning sales, profitability, and return on investment? What is involved in operating the franchise on a typical day? How many hours do they work in a typical week? What do they like best (and least) about their work? Knowing what they know now, would they buy the franchise again? When you are onsite, note the volume of customer traffic and the average transaction size and determine whether they are large enough for an outlet to be profitable. How well managed are the franchises you visit?

ENTREPRENEURIAL PROFILE: Tim Huels: Sculpture Hospitality Before leaving his job as a manager with a leading rental car company, Tim Huels decided that, at age 30, he wanted to own his own business but did not want to take on the risk associated with a start-up. Huels began investigating Sculpture Hospitality, a franchise that uses a proprietary inventory management system and training programs to help restaurants and bars operate more efficiently. As part of his due diligence, Huels talked with both current and former franchisees, the franchisor's regional directors and its CEO, and several Sculpture Hospitality clients. Pleased with what his investigation revealed, Huels invested in a Sculpture Hospitality franchise in Dallas and, working with a business partner, purchased two more franchises in Houston that are growing rapidly.[102] ∎

Monitoring franchisees' blogs also enables prospective franchisees to learn the "real story" of running a franchise. Another revealing exercise is to spend an entire day with at least one (preferably more) franchisee to observe firsthand what it is like to operate a franchise unit. Item 20 of the FDD lists all of the company's current franchisees and former franchisees who have left the system within the last year and their contact information, which makes it easy for potential franchisees to contact them. It is wise to interview former franchisees to get their perspectives on the franchisor–franchisee relationship. Why did they leave the system? If their franchises were unsuccessful, what were the causes?

Table 8.3 offers a list of questions prospective franchisees should ask existing franchisees.

Ask the Franchisor Some Tough Questions

Take the time to ask the franchisor questions about the company and its relationship with its franchisees. As a franchisee, you will be in this relationship a long time, and you need to know as much about it as you possibly can beforehand. What is the franchisor's philosophy concerning the relationship? Is there a franchise association made up of franchisees who consult and work with the franchisor's management team? What is the company culture like? How much input do franchisees have into the system? What are the franchise's future expansion plans? How will they affect your franchise? Are you entitled to an exclusive territory? Under what circumstances can either party terminate the franchise agreement? What happens if you decide to sell your franchise in the future? Under what circumstances would you not be entitled to renew the

TABLE 8.3 Questions to Ask Existing Franchisees

One of the most revealing exercises for entrepreneurs who are evaluating potential franchises is to visit and interview franchisees who already are operating outlets for a franchise. This is the chance to get the "inside scoop" from people who know best how a particular franchise system works. One recent survey reports that 87 percent of franchisees interviewed at least one franchisee of the system before investing in it. Vik Patel, owner of 23 Dunkin' Donuts franchises and a Brass Tap franchise in Florida, invested time in talking to many different franchisees he found listed in item 20 of the FDD before he purchased his first unit. Patel says that several franchisees shared their financial statements with him and were quite honest in their assessments of the franchisor–franchisee relationship, pointing out both good and bad features, which enabled him to make an informed decision. Following are some questions to ask:

1. Are you happy with your relationship with the franchisor? Explain.
2. How much control does the franchisor exercise over you and the way you run your franchise?
3. What changes would you make to the franchisor's business system?
4. What did it actually cost you to get your franchise running? How close was the actual amount to the amount the franchisor told you it would cost?
5. Is your franchise profitable? How long did it take for your franchise to break even? How much does your franchise earn? How variable are your franchise's earnings? Are the earnings consistent with your expectations?
6. Did the franchisor estimate accurately the amount of working capital necessary to sustain your business until it began generating positive cash flow?
7. What is the training program like? Were you pleased with the training you received from the franchisor? Did the training prepare you adequately for operating your franchise successfully?
8. Did you encounter any unexpected franchise fees or hidden costs? If so, what were they?
9. Are you pleased with the size of your territory? Is it large enough for you to reach your sales and profitability goals? What kind of territorial protection does the franchisor offer?
10. What restrictions do you face on the products and services you can sell? Are you required to purchase from approved suppliers? Are their prices reasonable?
11. Does the franchisor advertise as much as it said it would? Is the advertising effective in producing sales? Do you receive adequate support from the franchisor now that your outlet is in operation?
12. What kind of education and business experience do you have? How important have they been to your success in the franchise?
13. What is it really like to be a franchisee in this system?
14. If you were considering investing in this franchise again, what would you do differently?
15. Given what you know now, would you purchase this franchise again?

Sources: Based on Bryan Reesman, "Crossing Over," *QSR*, December 2014, www.qsrmagazine.com/franchising/crossing-over; Tracy Stapp Herold, "Words from the Wise," *Entrepreneur*, January 2015, p. 172; *National Survey of Franchisees*, FranchiseGrade, 2015, p. 12; Sara Wilson, "Final Answer," *Entrepreneur*, December 2007, pp. 122–126, and "Ten Questions to Ask Other Franchisees in the Franchise Chain," *AllBusiness*, 2006, www.allbusiness.com/buying-exiting-businesses/franchising-franchises/2188-1.html.

agreement? What kind of earnings can you expect? (If the franchisor made no earnings claims in item 19 of the FDD, why not?) Does the franchisor have a well-formulated strategic plan? What percentage of franchisees own multiple outlets? (A significant percentage of multi-unit franchisees is a good sign that a franchise's brand name and business system are strong.) Has the franchisor terminated any franchisee's contracts? If so, why? How many franchisees have failed? What caused their failure? How are disputes between the franchisor and franchisees settled?

Make Your Choice

The first lesson in franchising is to do your homework *before* you get out your checkbook. Van Jakes played in the National Football League for eight years, and when he retired in 1994, he knew that he wanted to own his own business. He considered opening an independent business, but his research led him to franchising. Jakes evaluated several franchises before settling on McDonald's, and at age 31, he opened his first McDonald's location in Palm Harbor, Florida. Two years later, Jakes decided to move to Atlanta, where he now owns three McDonald's franchises that generate annual revenue of $6.2 million. Jakes recently formed a consulting business,

My 5th Quarter, that offers business and franchise consulting services to current and former athletes as a way of helping others follow his path of success.[103]

Like Jakes, once you have done your research, you can make an informed choice about which franchise is right for you. Then it is time to put together a solid business plan that will serve as your road map to success in the franchise you have selected. The plan is also a valuable tool to use as you arrange the financing for your franchise.

Appendix A at the end of this chapter offers a checklist of questions a potential franchisee should ask before entering into any franchise agreement.

 ## Hands On . . . How To

Select the Ideal Franchise—*For You*!

When Aaron Miller was a student at the University of Vermont, he wrote a business plan for a sports bar as part of an entrepreneurship class he was taking. More than 15 years later, Miller, a former Olympic and professional ice hockey player, and Martti Matheson, close friends since their college days, transformed that business plan into reality when they opened their first Buffalo Wild Wings Grill and Bar franchise in Burlington, Vermont. What lessons can prospective franchisees learn from Miller and Matheson's experience and that of other franchisees?

Lesson 1. Don't be in a rush; start with a self-evaluation to determine whether franchising is right for you. Finding the right franchise can take months—sometimes years. The first step to finding the right franchise is not screening potential franchises; it is to consider whether franchising is the proper route for you. For would-be entrepreneurs who are independent and have definite ideas about how they want their businesses to operate, franchising is not the path they should follow to get into business. Miller and Matheson considered launching their own independent sports bar, but after evaluating their lack of experience in the restaurant business, they decided to go with a franchise because of the support system it offers on everything from establishing the menu and setting up the kitchen to advertising and choosing a location.

Lesson 2. Make sure you understand both the advantages and disadvantages of franchising before making a commitment. The best franchisors offer their franchisees a recipe for success and the support to help them make it work. However, franchisors require that franchisees pay them for the recipe with up-front fees and ongoing royalties and then stick to the recipe as they operate their businesses. Matheson recognizes that operating a franchise can be frustrating because the contract restricts franchisees' decision-making authority on basic business issues. However, pointing out that the benefits that the franchisor provides far outweigh the costs, he says that he does not mind paying the 5 percent (of sales) royalty fee. The average Buffalo Wild Wings Grill and Bar generates $3 million in annual sales, and Matheson knows that getting to that level of sales as an independent restaurateur would take much longer than it would with a franchisor's support.

Lesson 3. Review the FDD with the help of an experienced attorney. The FDD is an extremely valuable resource for anyone who is considering purchasing a franchise. Poring over the document alone can be frustrating, however, because it covers so much. Eric Karp, an attorney who teaches franchising courses at Babson College, says some franchisees are so overwhelmed by the size of the FDD that they make the mistake of not reading it at all.

Lesson 4. Use the FDD to screen potential franchises and don't be shy about asking lots of questions. Rob Parsons worked as the franchise development director for Popeyes Louisiana Kitchen for six years before he decided to switch sides and become one of the company's franchisees. Parsons, who has experienced the FDD from both the franchisor's and the franchisee's perspectives, says that the FDD can be extremely useful to prospective franchisees, particularly item 20, which includes a list of all of the franchisees in a system. Use the list to contact current and past franchisees to discover what it's really like to operate an outlet in the franchisor's system. If they were making the decision today, would they still purchase the franchise?

Lesson 5. Make sure you can afford the franchise without getting in over your head. Some franchises cost millions of dollars; others require only a few thousand dollars. Prospective franchisees should know how much they can afford to spend on a franchise and stay within their budgets. Most franchisors have minimum net worth and minimum liquidity requirements that prospective franchisees must meet.

Lesson 6. Visit your top franchise candidates. After narrowing the list of potential franchises to your top choices, go visit them. Most franchisors sponsor discovery days events, in which they host potential franchisees at their headquarters. Be observant and, once again, ask lots of questions. Ted Dowell says his visit to the operations center of TSS Photography, a franchise that specializes in taking photographs of sports, school, and special events, convinced him to become a franchisee. Dowell was particularly impressed with the franchise's production system, which is a key component in its franchisees' success. He points out that getting a behind-the-scenes, firsthand look at the franchise's system won him over as a franchisee. In addition, recognize that franchisors use these onsite visits to evaluate prospective franchisees.

(continued)

Hands On . . . How To *(continued)*

Lesson 7. Realize that no business, not even a franchise, runs itself. Some new franchisees believe that they can be absentee owners because the business system they purchase from the franchisor will allow their franchises to operate by themselves. It's just not true. Achieving success in franchising, like operating an independent business, requires hard work. Franchisees who expect to sit back and watch the money roll in will be disappointed. Although the franchisor provides franchisees with a formula for success, franchisees must implement the formula and make it work.

Sources: Based on Uri Berliner, "The Roots of Franchising Took Hold in a Hair Salon," *NPR,* October 17, 2013, www.npr.org/2013/10/17/234929759/the-roots-of-franchising-took-hold-in-a-hair-salon-chain; Melissa Pasanen, "Chain Restaurant Model Works for Many Vermont Entrepreneurs," *Burlington Free Press,* June 7, 2010, www.burlgingtonfreepress.com/article/20100607/NEWS01; Dianne Molvig, "Buying a Franchise: Potential and Precautions," Educational Employees Credit Union, January 10, 2011, http://hffo.cuna.org/11270/article/3171/html; Anne Fisher, "Risk Reward," *FSB,* December 2005/January 2006, pp. 45–61; Julie Bennett, "The Road to Discovery," *Entrepreneur,* February 2011, pp. 83–87; Kermit Patterson, "Tight Credit Is Turning Franchisors into Lenders," *New York Times,* June 9, 2010, www.nytimes.com/2010/06/10/business/smallbusiness/10sbiz.html; Jason Daley, "The Cross Over," *Entrepreneur,* March 2011, pp. 101–105; and Emily Maltby, "Want to Buy a Franchise: The Requirements Went Up," *Wall Street Journal,* November 15, 2010, p. R9.

LO5

Describe the major trends shaping franchising.

Trends Shaping Franchising

Franchising has experienced three major growth waves since its beginning. The first wave occurred in the early 1970s, when fast-food restaurants used the concept to grow rapidly. The fast-food industry was one of the first industries to discover the power of franchising, but other businesses soon took notice and adapted the franchising concept to their industries. The second wave took place in the mid-1980s, as the U.S. economy shifted heavily toward the service sector. Franchises followed suit, springing up in every service business. A third wave began in the early 1990s and continues today. It is characterized by new low-cost franchises that focus on specific market niches. In the wake of major corporate downsizing and the burgeoning costs of traditional franchises, these new franchises allow would-be entrepreneurs to get into proven businesses faster and at reasonable costs. These companies feature start-up costs in the range of about $4,000 to $250,000 and span a variety of industries—from leak detection in homes and auto detailing to day care and tile glazing.

Other significant trends affecting franchising are discussed in the following sections.

Changing Face of Franchisees

Franchisees today are a more diverse group than in the past. Minorities own 31.2 percent of all franchises, compared to 14.6 percent of independent businesses.[104] Women now own 26 percent of all franchises. Finding the necessary financing to purchase a franchise is one of the biggest obstacles minorities face. To encourage diversity among their franchisees, some franchisors have established programs that offer special discounts and financing opportunities to members of minority groups. DiversityFran, a program created by the International Franchise Association in 2006 that has the goal of educating minorities about franchising opportunities and recruiting minority franchisees, has nearly 120 franchise members.[105]

ENTREPRENEURIAL PROFILE: Ronald and Ella Avery-Smothers: Burger King and Denny's Growing up, Ronald Smothers dreamed of owning his own business. After graduating from UCLA and a short stint in the business world, Smothers opened his first franchise, a Burger King outlet in the Crenshaw neighborhood of Los Angeles. Over the next several years, Smothers, an African American, opened several more Burger King stores before adding a Denny's restaurant to his multi-unit holdings in 2006. Ronald's wife, Ella, also is a successful franchisee; she owns nine-and-a-half Burger King franchises. (She brought in a long-time, dedicated employee as co-owner of her eighth restaurant.) Ella says that she originally started working in the business to help her husband but then became interested in the restaurant business, which led her to purchase a franchise of her own ... and then another ... and another....[106] ■

Modern franchisees also are better educated, are more sophisticated, have more business acumen, and are more financially secure than those of just 20 years ago. People of all ages and backgrounds are choosing franchising as a way to get into business for themselves (see Figure 8.8). Franchising also is attracting skilled, experienced businesspeople who are opening franchises in their second careers and whose goal is to own multiple outlets that cover entire

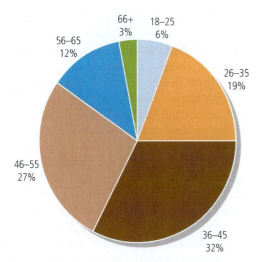

FIGURE 8.8

Age Distribution of Franchisees

Source: Based on "Prospective Franchisees Survey 2016," FranchiseDirect, July 5, 2016, www.franchisedirect .com/information/prospective franchiseesurvey2016/?r=5380.

states or regions. Many of them are former corporate managers—either corporate castoffs or corporate dropouts—looking for a new start on a more meaningful and rewarding career. They have the financial resources, management skills and experience, and motivation to operate their franchises successfully. David Omholt, owner of a franchise brokerage company, says that former executives often make ideal franchisees because they exhibit financial discipline, understand how businesses grow, and are comfortable working within a business system.

ENTREPRENEURIAL PROFILE: Bill Spae: Dairy Queen Bill Spae spent his entire career in the franchise industry but always on the franchisor's side. He began his franchising career working for Burger King before moving on to executive positions with TGI Fridays, Taco Bell, Wendy's, Hollywood Video, and others. When he stepped down as CEO of Mooyah Burgers, Fries, and Shakes, Spae intended to take some time off, but a friend offered him the chance to invest in Vasari LLC and become CEO of the company, which is one of the largest multi-unit Dairy Queen franchisees in the United States. As a franchisee, Spae is at the helm of 76 Dairy Queen franchises and has a goal of owning more than 100 restaurants within three years.[107] ■

International Opportunities

One of the major trends in franchising is the internationalization of American franchise systems. Franchising has become a major export industry for the United States, with franchises focusing on international markets to boost sales and profits as the domestic market has become saturated. Nearly three-fourths of the members of the International Franchise Association say that international markets will be important to the future success of their franchise operations.[108]

McDonald's, which had restaurants in 28 countries in 1980, now operates more than 21,700 outlets in 119 nations outside the United States; international locations account for nearly 67 percent of the company's sales.[109] Only 105 nations in the world, including Bermuda, Cambodia, Montenegro, and North Korea, do not have at least one McDonald's restaurant.[110] International markets are attracting franchisors because they are growing rapidly and offer rising personal incomes, strong demand for consumer goods, growing service economies, and spreading urbanization. Yum! Brands, with more than 14,000 restaurants outside the United States, was an early entrant into China, opening its first KFC store there in 1987. The company now operates more than 5,000 KFC locations in 1,100 cities in China. Yum! Brands launched

Cornelius Kalk/Vario images GmbH & Co.KG/Alamy Stock Photo

its first Pizza Hut in China in 1990, and the brand, which is regarded by Chinese customers as an upscale, trendy restaurant (often requiring reservations), now holds the top position in the pizza market in China, with more than 1,600 locations in 400 cities. Because its China operation is growing so rapidly (opening, on average, 2 restaurants in China each day of the year), the company recently decided to spin off its China division into a separate division, Yum! China.[111]

As they venture into foreign markets, franchisors have learned that adaptation is one key to success. Although a franchise's overall business format may not change in foreign markets, some of the details of operating its local outlets must change. For instance, fast-food chains in other countries often must make adjustments to their menus to please locals' palates. In addition to Original Recipe chicken, KFC restaurants in China also include an extensive menu of beef, seafood, vegetable, and rice dishes (spicy prawn rice and beef rice) as well as soups, breakfast items, and desserts (sugared egg tart) that appeal to Chinese customers' tastes. In Japan, McDonald's (known as "Makudonarudo") outlets sell teriyaki burgers, rice burgers, a bacon potato pie (mashed potatoes and bacon deep fried inside a pastry roll), and katsu burgers (cheese wrapped in a roast pork cutlet topped with katsu sauce and shredded cabbage) in addition to their traditional American fare. To please its Japanese customers' palates, Pizza Hut offers a pizza topped with teriyaki chicken, corn, seaweed, and mayonnaise. Another popular pizza includes prawns, squid, tuna, mayonnaise, broccoli, onions, and tomato sauce. In Japan, both Burger King and McDonald's menus include Kuro ("black") burgers in which the bun, the cheese, and the burger have been dyed with squid ink, turning them black. In Canada, the McDonald's menu includes poutine, a classic comfort dish that consists of French fries topped with cheese curds and gravy. McDonald's has eliminated beef and pork from its menu and has substituted mutton for beef in its burgers in India, a nation that is predominantly Hindu and Muslim.[112] In India, McDonald's sells the Maharaja Mac (two specially seasoned chicken patties with locally flavored condiments and a smoky sauce), the McAloo (a patty made from potatoes, peas, and special spices), and the McSpicy Paneer (a spicy cottage cheese patty made from buffalo milk topped with a tandoori sauce).[113] In many foreign markets, restaurant franchises offer customers a selection of beer and wine.[114]

As China's economy continues to grow and its capital markets expand, increasing numbers of franchisors are opening locations there. In China, Subway, known as Sai Bei Wei (which translates as "tastes better than others" in Mandarin), learned the importance of patience in building a franchise presence in challenging international markets. When the company opened its first outlet in China, managers had to print signs explaining how to order a sandwich. Sales of tuna salad were dismal because residents, accustomed to seeing their fish whole, did not believe that the salad was made from fish at all. In addition, because Chinese diners do not like to touch their food, many of them held their sandwiches vertically, peeled the paper wrapper away gradually, and ate the contents as they would eat a banana![115]

Table 8.4 shows the top 10 countries that present the greatest potential for franchisors, according to a cross-country analysis of five factors, including the availability of business infrastructure and a suitable labor force, sufficient market size, and the government regulatory environment.

TABLE 8.4 Top 10 Franchise Markets

Rank	Country
1	Canada
2	Australia
3	China
4	Indonesia
5	South Africa
6	Mexico
7	India
8	Vietnam
9	Colombia
10	Brazil

Source: 2016 Top Markets Report: Franchising, U.S. Department of Commerce, International Trade Administration, 2016, pp. 2–3.

You Be the Consultant

Franchising in Emerging Markets

U.S. franchises are growing faster abroad than they are in the domestic market. As franchisors have found wringing impressive growth rates from a franchise-saturated domestic market increasingly difficult, they have begun to export their franchises to international markets, including nations with developing economies. In 1990, 1 billion people out of the world's total population of 5 billion were members of the "consuming class," those who had sufficient disposable income to make discretionary purchases. Today, thanks to reduced trade barriers and increased global trade, the size of the consuming class has grown to 2.4 billion people. By 2025, the number will nearly double, to 4.2 billion people out of a global population of 7.9 billion. Correspondingly, by 2025, annual consumption in emerging markets will increase from $12 trillion in 2010, which represents 32 percent of total global consumption, to $30 trillion, or 50 percent of total global consumption. Consulting firm McKinsey and Company calls these growing emerging markets the greatest growth opportunity in the history of capitalism. The largest developing nations, such as China and India, will drive most of that growth. Both China and India appear on the International Trade Administration's list of the world's top 10 franchise markets (see Table 8.4). Franchisors are eager to capitalize on the growth in emerging markets.

Although the growth rate of China's economy is slowing, it is still expected to exceed 6 percent per year for the next several years. India's growth rate is expected to accelerate, exceeding 7 percent per year. With combined populations of 2.7 billion people with rising incomes and growing middle classes, China and India are attracting franchisors from around the globe. In the United States, franchising is built on consistency—the same products offered to customers through the same types of outlets using the same system. In global markets, however, franchisees have learned that adapting their products, services, locations, and business systems is essential to their success. For instance, customers of quick-service restaurants in the United States who travel in some foreign countries might be hard-pressed to find the meals they order so frequently back home. Dunkin' Donuts opened its first outlet in India in 2012. In India, doughnuts are not a popular menu item, so Dunkin' Donuts has expanded its menu and offers as many sandwiches, burgers, and wraps as a typical McDonald's. Like those in McDonald's restaurants in India, the burgers and sandwiches that Dunkin' Donuts sells in India contain no beef. Many of them are vegetarian, made with potato, cheese, or vegetable patties, and others substitute chicken for beef. The doughnuts that the company sells also have taken on a uniquely local flair. Some offer saffron crème or rice pudding fillings, and others reflect common Indian desserts, such as a mango-flavored doughnut, a coconut rasgulla doughnut, a motichoor ladoo doughnut, and a petal gulab jamun doughnut, which are popular during the Diwali holiday.

Because Indian people typically do not start their day with sugary sweets, and breakfast-on-the-go is foreign to Indian culture, Dunkin' Donuts switched its operating hours to later in the day. In the United States, the busiest time for most Dunkin' Donut franchisees is morning; in India, the busiest part of the day is evening. The company even changed the name of its outlets in India to Dunkin' Donuts and More to make it clear to customers that its menu is quite diverse. Sandwich names also might mystify the company's American customers: Naughty Lucy Chicken (the Naughty Lucy Veg is also an option), Big Joy Chicken, Heaven Can Wait, and the Double Mutton Burger.

Domino's Pizza has made similar adaptations to its traditional menu in foreign markets and spent eight months rethinking every ingredient, product, and price point. Customers in India are more likely to see Tandoori Chicken or Peppy Paneer pizzas than they are pepperoni or ground beef. The company's chefs frequently go on "food walks" through local markets, looking for new ingredients and inspiration for product ideas to add to its already diverse menu. On a recent trip, chefs melded together the ingredients from a kebab dish popular in northern India and parathas (flatbread) from southern India to create the Taco Indiana, an herb- and spice-flavored flatbread stuffed with cheese and vegetables or chicken. Domino's Indian menu also includes a burger pizza, a pizza-style, herb-flavored bun filled with spicy melted cheese, vegetables, and chicken. Another recent addition was the locally inspired Cheeseburst pizza, topped with chicken salami, chili peppers, sesame, ginger, garlic, chives, celery, and parsley. The company also sells Pizza Mania Extreme pizzas; customers can select any one of four single-topping personal pizzas for just 95 rupees ($1.42) that are ready in just eight and a half minutes.

Most franchisors entering global markets rely on master franchising relationships with experienced operators who understand local customs, laws, regulations, and business practices. In India, Dunkin' Donuts formed a master franchising contract with Jubilant FoodWorks, Ltd., the same master franchisee that Domino's Pizza relied on in 1996 when it entered the Indian market. With the help of Jubilant Foodworks, Domino's Pizza has grown into the largest foreign-based food chain in India, with more than 800 stores in 170 cities.

1. What steps should U.S.-based franchisors take when establishing outlets in foreign countries?

2. Describe the opportunities and challenges franchisors face when entering emerging markets such as India and China.

3. Use the Internet as a resource to develop a list of at least five suggestions to help new franchisors looking to establish outlets in China or India to be successful.

Sources: Based on "Data: India," World Bank, 2016, http://data.worldbank.org/country/india; "Data: China," World Bank, 2016, http://data.worldbank.org/country/china; Allison Spiegel, "India's Doughnut Flavors Put Ours to Shame," *Huffington Post,* November 5, 2014, www.huffingtonpost.com/2014/11/05/india-doughnuts_n_6100482.html; Yuval Atsmon, Peter Child, Richard Dobbs, and Laxman Narasimhan, "Winning the $30 Trillion Decathlon: Going for Gold in Emerging Markets," McKinsey and Company, August 2012, www.mckinsey.com/business-functions/strategy-and-corporate-finance/our-insights/winning-the-30-trillion-decathlon-going-for-gold-in-emerging-markets; Amrita Nair-Ghaswalla, "Dunkin' to Go Beyond Just Doughnuts," Hindu Business Line, March 22, 2013, www.thehindubusinessline.com/companies/dunkin-to-go-beyond-just-donuts/article4538467.ece; Adam Janofsky, "Fast-Food Franchises Get Creative When They Go Abroad," *Wall Street Journal,* May 26, 2015, www.wsj.com/articles/fast-food-franchises-get-creative-when-they-go-abroad-1432318075; Preetika Rana, "Dipping into India, Dunkin' Donuts Changes Menu," *Wall Street Journal,* November 28, 2014, www.wsj.com/articles/dipping-into-india-dunkin-donuts-changes-menu-1417211158; Sarutha Rai, "How Domino's Won India," *Fast Company,* February 2015, pp. 54–58.

Mobile Franchises

Mobile franchising is one of the fastest-growing segments in the franchise market because mobile franchises typically have lower capital requirements than brick-and-mortar businesses, and they offer a marketing advantage: the ultimate in convenience for customers because the product or service comes to them. Just like creative independent entrepreneurs, franchisors are putting restaurants, bakeries, repair shops, gyms, and other businesses on wheels, and customers are responding. Pressed for time and willing to pay for convenience, customers are embracing mobile franchises. Cycling enthusiasts Chris Guillemet, David Xausa, Boris Martin, and Simon Whitfield spotted a business opportunity in the bicycle repair market and in 2012 launched Velofix, a mobile bike repair business in Vancouver, British Columbia. Two years later, they began franchising Velofix. After paying a $25,000 franchise fee and $50,000 for the mobile build-out (with an 8 percent royalty fee), franchisees get fully equipped, ergonomically designed Mercedes Sprinter vans that enable them to repair any kind of bicycle. All of the tools inside are powered by rechargeable marine batteries, and carefully placed skylights minimize the need for lighting. Each mobile workshop includes a small lounge where customers can sit, enjoy free Wi-Fi, watch cycling events, and talk with the mechanic. Franchisees also benefit from cloud-based software that manages their inventory of parts and accessories, schedules their service routes in the most efficient manner, and allows customers to book service calls online or with an app. Velofix has already sold 25 franchises, and more are under development.[116]

Smaller, Nontraditional Locations

As the high cost of building full-scale locations continues to climb, more franchisors are searching out nontraditional locations in which to build smaller, less expensive outlets. Based on the principle of **intercept marketing**, the idea is to put a franchise's products or services directly in the paths of potential customers, wherever that may be. Locations within locations have become popular. Franchises are putting scaled-down outlets on college campuses; in high school cafeterias, sports arenas, theme parks, churches, hospitals, museums, and zoos; and on airline flights. Maui Wowi, a franchise that sells smoothies and coffee, has made nontraditional outlets part of its strategy, locating outlets, some temporarily, in convention centers, theme parks, racetracks, and rodeos.[117] Subway has more than 8,000 franchises in nontraditional locations that range from airports and military bases to college campuses and convenience stores. The company has restaurants located in a Goodwill store in Greenville, South Carolina, and inside the True Bethel Baptist Church in Buffalo, New York.[118] Perhaps Subway's most unusual location was a temporary restaurant that served only the construction workers building the skyscraper at 1 World Trade Center in New York City. As work progressed on the 105-story building, a hydraulic lift elevated the restaurant, which was housed inside 36 shipping containers welded together.[119]

Many franchisees have discovered that smaller outlets in nontraditional locations often generate more sales per square foot than full-size outlets and at just a fraction of the cost. Locations that emphasize convenience by being close to their customers continue be a key to continued franchise growth in the market.

Conversion Franchising

The recent trend toward **conversion franchising**, in which owners of independent businesses become franchisees to gain the advantage of name recognition, will continue. In a franchise conversion, the franchisor gets immediate entry into new markets and experienced operators; franchisees get increased visibility and often a big sales boost. It is not unusual for entrepreneurs who convert their independent stores into franchises to experience an increase of 20 percent or more in sales because of the instant name recognition the franchise offers.

ENTREPRENEURIAL PROFILE: John Andikian: 7-Eleven John Andikian opened a convenience store in Tustin, California, in 2004 and named it Andy's Market, in memory of his father. He sold typical convenience store fare, including his own version of the Slurpee, the Andy Freeze. After 18 months in business, Andy's Market still had not reached its breakeven point, and Andikian was running out of cash and time. The problem: "Nobody knew what Andy's Market was," he says. To save his business, Andikian decided to convert it into a 7-Eleven franchise and paid a $20,000 franchise fee and $100,000 for inventory and remodeling costs. The transformation required only 48 hours, and Andikian noticed the dramatic difference that adding the franchisor's well-known

intercept marketing
the principle of putting a franchise's products or services directly in the paths of potential customers, wherever they may be.

conversion franchising
a franchising trend in which owners of independent businesses become franchisees to gain the advantage of name recognition.

name made almost immediately. "As soon as they put the 7-Eleven sign outside, my sales doubled," he says. "I was doing about $70,000 a month in sales; now I'm doing about $160,000."[120] ∎

Refranchising

Another trend that has emerged over the last several years is franchises selling their company-owned outlets to franchisees. This process, known as **refranchising**, involves putting outlets into the hands of operators, who tend to run their franchises more efficiently than the franchisor can. Since 2007, McDonald's has reduced the percentage of company-owned stores in the chain from 23 percent to 19 percent and has a target of reducing company-owned outlets to just 5 percent of the system's total over the course of the next several years. Quick-service restaurant franchise Burger King also has pursued refranchising aggressively, selling to franchisees all but about 50 of its 7,400 locations in North America.[121] Refranchising not only increases franchisors' profitability because it generates more royalty income for franchisors but also provides capital to finance international expansion.

refranchising
a technique in which franchisors sell their company-owned outlets to franchisees.

Multi-unit Franchising

Twenty-five years ago, the typical franchisee operated a single outlet. The current generation of franchisees, however, strives to operate multiple franchise units. About 20 percent of franchisees are multiple-unit owners; however, those multi-unit franchisees own 55 percent of all franchise outlets.[122] Although the typical multiple-unit franchise owns five outlets, it is no longer unusual for a single franchisee to own 25, 75, or even 100 units.[123] Planet Fitness, a fitness center franchise, is typical, with 1,000 outlets across the United States operated by 180 franchisees, an average of about six units per franchisee.[124] More than 95 percent of Firehouse Subs franchisees are multi-unit owners, and the typical franchisee owns two restaurants. All of Applebee's franchisees are multi-unit owners, and the average number of outlets that franchisees in its system operates is an impressive 51.[125]

Franchisors are finding that multi-unit franchising is an efficient way to do business. For a franchisor, the time and cost of managing 10 franchisees each owning 10 outlets are much less than managing 100 franchisees each owning 1 outlet. A multi-unit strategy also accelerates a franchise's growth rate. Not only is multiple-unit franchising an efficient way to expand quickly, it also is effective for franchisors who are targeting foreign markets, where having a local representative who knows the territory is essential.

The popularity of multi-unit franchising has paralleled the trend toward increasingly experienced, sophisticated franchisees who set high performance goals that a single outlet cannot meet. For franchisees, owning multiple units offers the opportunity for rapid growth without leaving the safety net of the franchise. Multi-unit franchisees also are less likely to fail, and they earn more than single-unit franchisees.[126] In addition, franchisees may be able to get fast-growing companies for a bargain when franchisors offer discounts off their standard fees for buyers who purchase multiple units.

Although operating multiple units offers advantages for both franchisors and franchisees, there are dangers. Operating multiple units requires franchisors to focus more carefully on selecting the right franchisees—those who are capable of handling the additional requirements of multiple units. The impact of selecting the wrong franchise owners is magnified when they operate multiple units and can create huge headaches for the entire chain. Franchisees must be aware of the dangers of losing their focus and becoming distracted if they take on too many units. In addition, operating multiple units means more complexity because the number of business problems that franchisees face also is multiplied.

Area Development and Master Franchising

Driving the trend toward multiple-unit franchising are area development and master franchising. Under an **area development** franchise, a franchisee earns the exclusive right to open multiple outlets in a specific area within a specified time. In 1973, Steve Kuhnau opened a health food store in New Orleans through which he sold the nutritional fruit smoothies he had developed as a way to combat his own food allergies. Kuhnau's smoothies became so popular that he changed the company's name to Smoothie King. Kuhnau began franchising in 1988, and today Smoothie King, which he sold to franchisee Wan Kim in 2012, has more than 800 locations around the world. To accelerate the company's growth, Smoothie King recently signed 64 area development agreements with new and existing franchisees across the United States that will add 105 outlets to the system. Franchisees Todd and Lorraine Pater are part of that expansion and have agreed to a multi-unit deal in which they will open 12 Smoothie King locations in Orlando, Florida.[127]

area development
a method of franchising in which a franchisee earns the exclusive right to open multiple units in a specific territory within a specified time.

Increasingly, franchisors prefer to deal with area developers because of the economies of scale, increased efficiency, and higher probability of success they offer. Some franchisors now sell franchises only under area development deals.

A **master franchise** (or subfranchise) gives a franchisee the right to create a semi-independent organization in a particular territory to recruit, develop, and support other franchisees. A master franchisee buys the right to develop subfranchises within a territory or sometimes an entire country, takes over many of the duties and responsibilities of the franchisor, and typically earns a portion of the franchise fees and royalties from its subfranchises. Master franchising is particularly common when franchisors open outlets in international markets because the master franchisees understand local laws and the nuances of selling in local markets. Wing Zone, a franchise that specializes in chicken wings started by Matt Friedman and Adam Scott in 1991 at the University of Florida, recently entered into a master franchising deal to enter the Japanese, South American, and Latin American markets. In Japan, Wing Zone partnered with an experienced restaurant operator, Pacific Rim Partners, to open 50 stores of its own or those that Pacific Rim Partners sells to subfranchisees. Wing Zone worked with the U.S. Department of Commerce's Commercial Service department to recruit master franchisees in South America. The company's director of international development says that master franchising makes sense for Wing Zone because its master franchisees in international markets have significant networks of vital contacts, know how to navigate government bureaucracies to receive necessary permits and approvals, and have access to growth capital.[128] Both area development and master franchising "turbocharge" a franchisor's growth.

master franchise
a method of franchising that gives a franchisee the right to create a semi-independent organization in a particular territory to recruit, sell, and support other franchisees.

Cobranding

A growing number of companies are using **cobranding (or piggyback or combination) franchising**—combining two or more distinct franchises under one roof. This "buddy-system" approach works best when the two franchise ideas are compatible and appeal to similar customers. Large franchisors have used the strategy for many years, but many small franchisors are banding together to establish cobranded units that together create synergy and generate more sales and profits than individual, self-standing units. Combining the right brands and products can expand franchisors' customer base and day-part coverage. For example, Bruegger's Bagels and Jamba Juice recently began cobranding their bagel and smoothie franchises to help franchisees increase sales. Fifty-four percent of Breugger's Bagels's sales take place in the morning, while more than half of Jamba Juice's sales occur in the afternoon and evening.[129]

cobranding (or piggyback or combination) franchising
a method of franchising in which two or more franchises team up to sell complementary products or services under one roof.

Cobranded outlets also save their owners money because they lower both real estate and operating costs. The same employees sell both brands, reducing labor costs, and the franchisors share advertising, maintenance, and other costs. Focus Brands, which owns Schlotzsky's (sub sandwiches), Cinnabon (cinnamon buns and other baked treats), and Carvel Ice Cream brands often pairs two and sometimes all three of its franchises in a single location. Both Schlotzsky's and Cinnabon stores bake their products daily, which means that employees of each franchise already have experience with operating ovens, making it easy for them to master baking the other brand's products. The cobranding strategy appears to be working; the owners of more than 200 of Schlotzsky's 350 locations have added a Cinnabon franchise to their stores.[130]

Unless the brands are well-suited complements, cobranding can create more headaches than benefits. Unless it is well planned and managed, cobranding can increase operational complexity and cause product and service quality to decline. To make sure that cobranding works for them, some franchisors, especially small ones, test the concept in a limited number of locations. Dippin' Dots, a flash-frozen ice cream franchise, and Doc Popcorn, which sells gourmet popcorn, recently opened their first cobranded outlet in Battlefield Mall in Springfield, Missouri. The store's success led the companies to partner in other locations around the United States.[131]

Conclusion

Franchising has proved its viability in the U.S. economy and has become a key part of the small business sector because it offers many would-be entrepreneurs the opportunity to own and operate a business with a greater chance for success. Despite its impressive growth rate to date, the franchising industry still has a great deal of room to grow. "Franchising is really small business at its best," says Don DeBolt, former head of the International Franchise Association.[132]

MyLab Entrepreneurship

If your instructor is using MyLab Entrepreneurship, go to **www.pearson.com/mylab/entrepreneurship** to complete the problems marked with this icon ⭐.

Chapter Summary by Learning Objective

1. **Describe the three types of franchising: trade name, product distribution, and pure.**

   - Trade-name franchising involves a franchisee purchasing the right to become affiliated with a franchisor's trade name without distributing its products exclusively.

   - Product distribution franchising involves licensing a franchisee to sell products or services under the franchisor's brand name through a selective, limited distribution network.

   - Pure franchising involves selling a franchisee a complete business format.

2-A. **Explain the benefits of buying a franchise.**

   - Franchises offer many benefits: management training and support, brand-name appeal, standardized quality of goods and services, national advertising programs, financial assistance, proven products and business formats, centralized buying power, territorial protection, and a greater chance of success.

2-B. **Explain the drawbacks of buying a franchise.**

   - Franchising also suffers from certain drawbacks: franchise fees and profit sharing, strict adherence to standardized operations, restrictions on purchasing, limited product lines, unsatisfactory training programs, market saturation, and less freedom.

3. **Understand the laws covering franchise purchases.**

   - The FTC requires all franchisors to disclose detailed information on their operations in a Franchise Disclosure Document at the first personal meeting or at least 14 days before a franchise contract is signed or before any money is paid. The FTC rule covers *all* franchisors and requires franchisors to provide information on 23 topics in their disclosure statements. The FDD is an extremely helpful tool for prospective franchisees.

4. **Explain the *right* way to buy a franchise.**

   - The following steps will help you make the right franchise choice: Evaluate yourself, research your market, consider your franchise options, get a copy of the franchisor's FDD, talk to existing franchisees, ask the franchisor some tough questions, and make your choice.

5. **Describe the major trends shaping franchising.**

   - Key trends shaping franchising today include the changing face of franchisees; international franchise opportunities; smaller, nontraditional locations; conversion franchising; multiple-unit franchising; master franchising; and cobranding (or combination franchising).

MyLab Entrepreneurship

If your instructor is using MyLab Entrepreneurship, go to **www.pearson.com/mylab/entrepreneurship** for Auto-graded writing questions as well as the following Assisted-graded writing questions:

1. Two franchising experts recently debated the issue of whether new college graduates should consider franchising as a pathway to entrepreneurship. Jeff Elgin said recent college graduates are not ready to be franchise owners. "First, most recent college graduates don't have the financial resources to fund a franchise start-up. Second, many lack the life experience and the motivation to run a business effectively and stick with it when times get tough." Jennifer Kushell said franchising is the perfect career choice for many recent college graduates, for several reasons: (1) The support system that franchising provides is ideal for young entrepreneurs, (2) young people have grown up with franchising and understand it well, (3) many college graduates already have launched businesses of their own, and (4) they think big. Which view do you think is correct? Explain.

2. One franchisee says franchising works because the franchisor gets its franchisees going, nurtures them, and, at times, shoves them. However, the franchisor cannot make its franchisees successful. Success depends on how committed one is to finding the right franchise for himself or herself, on what each franchisee brings to the business, and on how hard he or she is prepared to work. Do you agree? Explain.

Discussion Questions

8-1. What is franchising?

8-2. Describe the three types of franchising and give an example of each.

⭐ 8-3. Discuss the advantages and the disadvantages of franchising for the franchisee.

8-4. Why might an independent entrepreneur be dissatisfied with a franchising arrangement?

⭐ 8-5. Fran Lubbs, who after a five-year stint left the corporate office of Goddard School, an early education franchise, to become a franchisee, says, "Follow the system. It's one of the reasons you bought the franchise. Don't try to change it, break it, or fix it." Do you agree with her? Explain.

8-6. What steps should a potential franchisee take before investing in a franchise?

8-7. What is the function of the FDD? Outline the protection the FDD gives prospective franchisees.

8-8. Describe the current trends in franchising.

8-9. Robyn Vescovi, a former financial executive who recently became a Tasti D-Lite franchisee, offers the following advice to first-time franchisees:
- Do your homework. Research the brand (both the long- and short-term business models)
- Know the team behind the brand and understand their vision for that product/business. Know them as franchise experts and know their proven successes.
- Know yourself and your limits. This will help you determine the right business (e.g., new and innovative franchise or well-established franchise).
- Be involved! Don't expect that things "will just happen." You have your own business, but you are part of something bigger, and it is in your best interest to participate in whatever you can in support of that brand/product. Don't be an "absentee franchisee."

Do you agree? Explain. What other advice can you offer first-time franchisees?

Beyond the Classroom . . .

8-10. Visit a local franchise operation and talk to the franchisee. Is it a trade name, product distribution, or pure franchise?

8-11. To what extent did the franchisee investigate before investing?

8-12. What assistance does the franchisor provide the franchisee?

8-13. How does the franchisee feel about the franchise contract he or she signed?

8-14. What would the franchisee do differently now?

8-15. Use the Internet to locate several franchises that interest you. Contact the franchisors and ask for their FDDs and write a report comparing their treatment of the 23 topics the documents cover.

8-16. What are the major differences in the terms of each franchise's contract?

8-17. Are some terms more favorable than others?

8-18. If you were about to invest in a particular franchise, which terms would you want to change?

Appendix A A Franchise Evaluation Checklist

Yourself

1. Are you qualified to operate a franchise successfully? Do you have adequate drive, skills, experience, education, patience, and financial capacity? Are you prepared to work hard?

2. Are you willing to sacrifice some autonomy in operating a business to own a franchise?

3. Can you tolerate the financial risk? Would business failure wipe you out financially?

4. Can you juggle multiple tasks simultaneously and prioritize various projects so that you can accomplish those that are most important?

5. Are you genuinely interested in the product or service you will be selling? Do you enjoy this kind of business? Do you like to sell?

6. Do you enjoy working with and managing people? Are you a "team player"?

7. Will the business generate enough profit to suit you?

8. Has the franchisor investigated your background thoroughly enough to decide whether you are qualified to operate the franchise?

9. What can this franchisor do for you that you cannot do for yourself?

The Franchisor and the Franchise

1. Is the potential market for the product or service adequate to support your franchise? Will the prices you charge be in line with the market?

2. Is the market's population growing, remaining static, or shrinking? Is the demand for your product or service growing, remaining static, or shrinking?

3. Is the product or service safe and reputable?

4. Is the product or service a passing "fad," or is it a durable business idea?

5. What will the competition, direct or indirect, be in your sales territory? Do any other franchisees operate in this general area?

6. Is the franchise international, national, regional, or local in scope? Does it require full- or part-time involvement?

7. How many years has the franchisor been in operation? Does it have a sound reputation for honest dealings with franchisees?

8. How many franchise outlets now exist? How many will there be a year from now? How many outlets are company owned?

9. How many franchises have failed? Why?

10. How many franchisees have left the system within the past year? What were their reasons for leaving?

11. What service and assistance will the franchisor provide? What kind of training program does the franchisor offer? How long does it last? What topics does it cover? Does the franchisor offer ongoing assistance and training?

12. Will the franchise perform a location analysis to help you find a suitable site? If so, is there an extra charge for doing so?

13. Will the franchisor offer you exclusive distribution rights for the length of the agreement, or may it sell to other franchises in this area?

14. What facilities and equipment are required for the franchise? Who pays for construction? Is there a lease agreement?

15. What is the total cost of the franchise? What are the initial capital requirements? Will the franchisor provide financial assistance? Of what nature? What is the interest rate? Is the franchisor financially sound enough to fulfill all its promises?

16. How much is the franchise fee? Exactly what does it cover? Are there any ongoing royalties? What additional fees are there?

17. Does the franchisor provide an estimate of expenses and income? Are they reasonable for your particular area? Are they sufficiently documented?

18. How risky is the franchise opportunity? Is the return on the investment consistent with the risks?

19. Does the franchisor offer a written contract that covers all the details of the agreement? Have your attorney and your accountant studied its terms and approved it? Do you understand the implications of the contract?

20. What is the length of the franchise agreement? Under what circumstances can it be terminated? If you terminate the contract, what are the costs to you? What are the terms and costs of renewal?

21. Are you allowed to sell your franchise to a third party? Does the franchisor reserve the right to approve the buyer?

22. Is there a national advertising program? How is it financed? What media are used? What help is provided for local advertising?

23. Once you open for business, *exactly* what support will the franchisor offer you?

24. How does the franchise handle complaints from and disputes with franchisees? How well has the system worked?

The Franchisees

1. Are you pleased with your investment in this franchise?

2. Has the franchisor lived up to its promises?

3. What was your greatest disappointment after getting into this business?

4. How effective was the training you received in helping you run the franchise?

5. What are your biggest challenges and problems?

6. What is your franchise's cash flow like?

7. How much money are you making on your investment?

8. What do you like most about being a franchisee? Least?

9. Is there a franchisee advisory council that represents franchisees?

10. Knowing what you know now, would you buy this franchise again?

Endnotes

[1]"Millennials Act Their Age: Can Young Operators Succeed as Franchisees?" *Nation's Restaurant News*, April 13, 2015, pp. S8–S9; "Uncle Maddio's Pizza Joint Opens Its First Texas Location; University of Texas Grads Team Up to Open Fast Casual Franchise in Austin," *PRWeb*, December 10, 2014, www.prweb.com/releases/2014/12/prweb12380367 .htm; Judy Kneiszel, "Ones to Watch: Uncle Maddio's Pizza Joint," *QSR*, June 2013, www.qsrmagazine.com/ emerging-concepts/ones-watch-uncle-maddio-s-pizza-joint.

[2]Edith Wiseman and Peter Schwarzer, "Franchising: A Global Engine for Economic Growth," *Franchising World*, July 28, 2015, http://franchisingworld.com/franchising-a-global-engine-for-economic-growth/.

[3]Edith Wiseman and Peter Schwarzer, "Franchising: A Global Engine for Economic Growth," *Franchising World*, July 28, 2015, http://franchisingworld.com/franchising-a-global-engine-for-economic-growth/; *Franchise Business Economic Outlook for 2016*, HIS Economics and the International

Franchise Association Educational Foundation, January 2016, p. 2.

[4] *Franchise Business Economic Outlook for 2017*, HIS Economics and the International Franchise Association Educational Foundation, January 2017, p. 2.

[5] Dan Bukszpan, "Wacky, Oddball Franchises You Won't Believe Exist," *CNBC*, May 11, 2016, www.cnbc.com/2016/05/11/wacky-oddball-franchises-you-wont-believe-exist.html?slide=7; "About the Founders," K-9 Resorts Daycare and Luxury Hotel, August 2016, www.k9resorts.com/k-9-resorts-nj-luxury-pet-hotels/founders/.

[6] *2016 Top Markets Report: Franchising*, U.S. Department of Commerce, International Trade Administration, 2016, p. 5.

[7] "Working with U.S. Commercial Service (USCS) to Succeed in Taking Your U.S. Franchise into New Countries," *GeoWizard*, July 22, 2014, www.geowizard.biz/2014/07/working-with-us-commercial-service-uscs-to-succeed-in-taking-your-us-franchise-into-new-countries/.

[8] Megan Barnett, "Size Up a Ready-Made Business," *U.S. News & World Report*, August 2, 2004, p. 70.

[9] Chieh Chieng, "Do You Want to Know a Secret?" *Entrepreneur*, January 1999, p. 174–178.

[10] Mark Henricks, "Franchise Masters Practice Proven Formulas," *Inc.*, June 2013, pp. 124-128; "History of Franchising," FranChoice, http://www.franchoice.com/franchise-information-guide/what-is-franchise/history-of-franchising.

[11] Jason Daley, "Miracle Grows," *Entrepreneur*, February 2015, pp. 71–75.

[12] Melana Yanos, "Franchise Opportunities for Young People," *NuWire Investor*, May 13, 2008, www.nuwireinvestor.com/articles/franchise-opportunities-for-young-people-51561.aspx.

[13] Jason Daley, "Wacky Franchises," *Entrepreneur*, January 2015, pp. 126–128.

[14] Jason Daley, "Crowding the Roads," *Entrepreneur*, April 2016, pp. 88–93.

[15] Jason Daley, "From Burgers to Screens," *Entrepreneur*, February 2016, pp. 73–74.

[16] Jason Daley, "The Cross Over," *Entrepreneur*, March 2011, pp.101–105.

[17] "Prospective Franchisee Survey Results 2016," FranchiseDirect, July 5, 2016, www.franchisedirect.com/information/prospectivefranchiseesurveyresults2016/?r=5380.

[18] Jason Daley, "What Makes the Difference," *Entrepreneur*, May 2016, pp. 86–95.

[19] Robert Thomas, "Investigative Insights," *QSR*, July 2015, www.qsrmagazine.com/franchising/investigative-insights; Jason Daley, "The Investigator," *Entrepreneur*, March 2015, p. 86.

[20] Jason Daley, "What Makes the Difference," *Entrepreneur*, May 2016, pp. 86–95.

[21] Jason Daley, "Miracle Grows," *Entrepreneur*, February 2015, pp.71–75.

[22] "Hamburger University," McDonald's, www.aboutmcdonalds.com/mcd/corporate_careers/training_and_development/hamburger_university.html; Jessica Wohl, "Hamburger U Grills McDonald's Managers," *Spartanburg Herald Journal*, May 3, 2015, p. A14.

[23] "FAQ," Ben & Jerry's Homemade, Inc., www.benjerry.com/scoop_shops/franchise_info/faqs.cfm.

[24] "Helping Successful Franchisees Grow," *Nation's Restaurant News*, April 13, 2015, pp. S28–S29.

[25] Michele Deluca, "Franchise Owners Pay Price for Success," *Tonawanda News*, April 28, 2008, www.tonawanda-news.com/business/gnnbusiness_story_119141835.html.

[26] Kerry Pipes, "Extreme Growth," *Multi-Unit Franchisee*, Issue III, 2013, p. 36.

[27] "Papa John's Receives Highest Customer Satisfaction Rating for Ninth Consecutive Year," *Reuters*, May 20, 2008, http://www.reuters.com/article/pressRelease/idUS139161+20-May-2008+BW20080520; Anne Field, "Piping Hot Performance," *Success*, March 1999, pp. 76–80.

[28] *2015 Franchise Sales Trends Report*, FranchiseConnect, 2015, p.7; "Navigating the Fees Associated with Running a Franchise," National Federation of Independent Businesses, March 26, 2010, www.nfib.com/content/resources/franchises/navigating-the-fees-associated-with-running-a-franchise-51064/.

[29] *The Profile of Franchising 2006* (Washington, DC: International Franchise Association, 2007), p. 67.

[30] Nicole Spector, "SMB Franchises Rapidly Shift Media Dollars to Digital," *GeoMarketing*, February 24, 2015, www.geomarketing.com/smb-franchises-rapidly-shift-media-dollars-to-digital.

[31] Michael LeConte, "Social Media Marketing for Franchising Brands: Who Does What? Why and How? In 7 Graphics," *LinkedIn*, November 4, 2015, www.linkedin.com/pulse/social-media-marketing-franchising-brands-who-does-7-michel.

[32] Ibid.

[33] 2016 EQ4: Q4 2016 *Monetate Quarterly E-Commerce Report: Quarter 4 2016*, Monetate, 2016, p. 6.

[34] "Blaze Fast-Fire'd Pizza Launches Mobile App," *Yahoo! Finance*, March 16, 2016, http://finance.yahoo.com/news/blaze-fast-fired-pizza-launches-140000743.html.

[35] "General Franchise Stats," FranchiseDirect, March 1, 2016, www.franchisedirect.com/information/usfranchiseindustryinfographic/?r=5238.

[36] Sarah E. Needleman and Coulter Jones, "New Data Reveal Risks of Franchising," *Wall Street Journal*, September 11, 2014, pp. B1, B6.

[37] "Veteran Turned Successful Entrepreneur," U.S. Small Business Administration, www.sba.gov/offices/district/tx/harlingen/success-stories/veteran-turned-successful-entrepreneur; "Featured Owner: Maurice Welton," Edible Arrangements, www.ediblearrangements.com/FranchiseOpportunities/OwnerFullStory.aspx?s_id=86&pageid=4.

[38] *The Profile of Franchising 2006* (Washington, DC: International Franchise Association, 2007), p. 70.

[39] Julie Jargon, "Discontent Simmers Among McDonald's Franchisees," *Wall Street Journal*, June 2, 2015, www.wsj.com/articles/discontent-simmers-among-mcdonalds-franchisees-1433272884.

[40] Elizabeth Garone, "Chains Look to Lure New Buyers," *Wall Street Journal*, January 25, 2016, p. R6.

[41] "General Franchise Stats," FranchiseDirect, March 1, 2016, www.franchisedirect.com/information/usfranchiseindustryinfographic/?r=5238.

[42] "History," VetFran, August 2016, www.vetfran.com/history/.

[43] Kate Taylor, "Franchise Players: How I Turned Military Lessons into a Successful Business," *Entrepreneur*, September 1, 2014, www.entrepreneur.com/article/231816.

[44] "Helping Successful Franchisees Grow," *Nation's Restaurant News*, April 13, 2015, pp. S28–S29.

[45] Brenna Fisher, "Corner Office: Papa John's John Schnatter Is Building a Better Pizza Empire," *Success*, 2011, www.successmagazine.com/papa-johns-john-schnatter/PARAMS/article/947.

[46] Jason Daley, "Franchise the Unexpected," *Entrepreneur*, March 2016, pp. 90–97.

[47] Sheena Harrison, "Franchises Get Head Start on Starting Businesses," *Toledo Blade*, September 23, 2010, www.toledoblade.com/local/2010/09/23/Franchises-get-headstart-on-starting-businesses.html.

[48]Jason Dailey, "Turn, Turn, Turn," *Entrepreneur*, September 2014, pp. 97–101; Bret Thorn, "Popeyes Uses New Site Selection Process to Drive Growth," *Nation's Restaurant News*, March 10, 2012, http://nrn.com/archive/popeyes-uses-new-site-selection-process-drive-growth; Lydia DePillis, "How Popeyes Went Upscale," *Washington Post*, September 27, 2013, www.washingtonpost.com/news/wonk/wp/2013/09/27/how-popeyes-went-upscale/.

[49]Michele Deluca, "Franchise Owners Pay Price for Success," *Tonawanda News*, April 28, 2008, www.tonawanda-news.com/business/gnnbusiness_story_119141835.html.

[50]Steven C. Michael and James G. Combs, "Entrepreneurial Failure: The Case of Franchisees," *Journal of Small Business Management* 46, no. 1 (January 2008): 75–90.

[51]Sarah E. Needleman, "Is Buying a Franchise Riskier Than Ever?" *Wall Street Journal*, August 25, 2014, www.wsj.com/articles/is-buying-a-franchise-riskier-than-ever-1408912041.

[52]Sarah E. Needleman and Coulter Jones, "New Data Reveal Risks of Franchising," *Wall Street Journal*, September 11, 2014, pp. B1, B6; Priyanka Prakesh, "50 Best Franchises and 50 Worst Franchises by SBA Default Rates," *FitSmallBusiness*, May 24, 2016, http://fitsmallbusiness.com/best-franchises-sba-default-rates/.

[53]Julie Bennett, "The New Age of Franchise Financing," *Wall Street Journal*, March 24, 2016, p. B6.

[54]Jason Daley, "Star Power," *Entrepreneur*, January 2016, pp. 90–92.

[55]Steven C. Michael and James G. Combs, "Entrepreneurial Failure: The Case of Franchisees," *Journal of Small Business Management* 46, no. 1 (January 2008): 75–90.

[56]*Prospective Franchise Survey Results 2013*, Franchise Direct, 2013, www.franchisedirect.com/information/trendsfacts/prospectivefranchiseesurveyresults2013introsurveybackground1/8/2383/.

[57]Iris Taylor, "Franchises Can Be Freedom from Corporate America," *WSLS*, July 9, 2008, www.wsls.com/sls/business/consumer/article/franchises_can_be_freedom_from_corporate_america/13747.

[58]*The Profile of Franchising 2006* (Washington, DC: International Franchise Association, 2007), p. 62.

[59]*2015 Franchise Sales Trends Report*, FranConnect, 2015, p. 6.

[60]*The Profile of Franchising 2006* (Washington, DC: International Franchise Association, 2007), p. 66.

[61]Ibid., p. 68.

[62]Jerry Murrell and Liz Welch, "How I Did It: Five Guys Burgers and Fries," *Inc.*, April 2010, p. 80.

[63]Karsten Strauss, "Is Quiznos Toast?" *Forbes*, June 17, 2015, pp. 96–98; Steve Raabe, "Denver-Based Quiznos Hit by New Lawsuits from Disgruntled Franchisees," *Denver Post*, April 30, 2016, www.denverpost.com/2013/03/15/denver-based-quiznos-hit-by-new-lawsuits-from-disgruntled-franchisees/; Lisa Jennings, "Quiznos CEO Aims to Build Trust with Franchisees," *Nation's Restaurant News*, March 24, 2015, http://nrn.com/fast-casual/quiznos-ceo-aims-build-trust-franchisees.

[64]Jessica Wohl, "McDonald's Dollar Menu and More Is No More: Now There's McPick," *Advertising Age*, November 16, 2015, http://adage.com/article/cmo-strategy/mcdonald-s-play-called-mcpick/301385/; Mark Brandau, "McDonald's to Roll Out Dollar Menu and More Nationwide," *Nation's Restaurant News*, October 21, 2013, http://nrn.com/quick-service/mcdonalds-roll-out-dollar-menu-more-nationwide; McDonald's Dollar & More Adds Five Items," *Burger Business*, November 4, 2013, /www.burgerbusiness.com/?p=15963.

[65]Jeff Swiatek, "Steak'n Shake Franchisees Bite Back over $4 Menu," *Indy Star*, November 23, 2013, www.indystar.com/story/money/2013/11/22/steak-n-shake-franchisees-bite-back-over-4-menu/3682149/; Julie Jargon, "Fight Boils Over the $4 Meal," *Wall Street Journal*, August 23, 2013, p. B6; Scott Olson, "More Franchisees Join Revolt Over Steak 'n Shake Menu Pricing, *Indiana Business Journal*, May 1, 2013, www.ibj.com/more-franchisees-join-revolt-over-steak-n-shake-menu-pricing/PARAMS/article/41110.

[66]Matthew Boyle, "The Accidental Hero," *Bloomberg Businessweek*, November 5, 2009, www.businessweek.com/magazine/content/09_46/b4155058815908.htm.

[67]Lauren Saria, "Want to Know How Many Big Macs Are Sold in the United States Every Second? (Hint: It's More Than a Dozen)," *Phoenix New Times*, June 17, 2013, http://blogs.phoenixnewtimes.com/bella/2013/06/fast-food-every-second-video-america-most-popular-businesses.php.

[68]Leslie Patton, "McDonald's Pushing Meat as Salads Fail to Lure Diners," *Bloomberg*, May 29, 2013, www.bloomberg.com/news/2013-05-29/mcdonald-s-pushing-meat-as-salads-fail-to-lure-diners.html; Julie Jargon, "At McDonald's, Salads Just Don't Sell," *Wall Street Journal*, October 19–20, 2013, pp. B1, B4.

[69]"McDonald's Looking to Heat Up U.S. Sales with Breakfast, Coffee," *CNBC*, February 11, 2014, www.cnbc.com/2014/02/11/mcdonalds-looking-to-heat-up-us-sales-with-breakfast-coffee.html.

[70]James A. Brickley, Sanjog Misra, and R. Lawrence Van Horn, "Contract Duration: Evidence from Franchising," *Journal of Law and Economics*, vol. XLIX, April 2006, p. 183.

[71]*National Survey of Franchisees 2015*, FranchiseGrade, 2015, p. 12.

[72]Jonathan Maze, "Wendy's Sues One of Its Largest Franchisees," *Nation's Restaurant News*, January 2, 2015, http://nrn.com/wendys/wendy-s-sues-one-its-largest-franchisees; Beth Ewen, "Wendy's Remodel Offers 'No ROI,' DavCo Counters in Lawsuit," *Franchise Times*, February 2015, www.franchisetimes.com/news/February-2015/Wendys-Remodel-Offers-No-ROI-DavCo-Counters-in-Lawsuit/.

[73]*National Survey of Franchisees 2015*, FranchiseGrade, 2015, p. 24.

[74]Richard Gibson, "Franchise Fever," *Wall Street Journal*, December 15, 2003, p. R1.

[75]"A Snapshot of the Frozen Yogurt Industry," Guidant Financial, June 2, 2015, www.guidantfinancial.com/article/frozen-yogurt-infographic/.

[76]Gus Lubin and Mamta Babkar, "18 Facts About McDonald's That Will Blow Your Mind," *Business Insider*, April 20, 2012, www.businessinsider.com/19-facts-about-mcdonalds-that-will-blow-your-mind-2012-4/#donalds-delivers--in-18-countries-1116.

[77]Kelly K. Spors, "Not So Fast," *Wall Street Journal*, September 19, 2005, p. R11; Joshua Kurlantzick, "Serving Up Success," *Entrepreneur*, November 2003, www.entrepreneur.com/article/print/0,2361,311429,00.html; "History," Subway, www.subway.com/en-us/aboutus/history.

[78]Anne Fisher, "Risk Reward," *FSB*, December 2005/January 2006, p. 58.

[79]"Burger King Late-Night Hours Suit Dismissed," *QSR Online*, November 11, 2008, www.qsrweb.com/article/101069/Burger-King-franchisees-late-night-hours-suit-dismissed.

[80]Gregory Matusky, "What Every Business Can Learn from Franchising," *Inc.*, January 1994, p. 90.

[81]David J. Kaufman, "What a Ride!" *Entrepreneur*, May 2007, p. 111.

[82]Elizabeth Garone, "The New Face of Franchisees," *Wall Street Journal*, August 19, 2013, www.wsj.com/articles/SB10001424127887324021104578553580349491440.

[83]Peter B. Rutledge and Christopher R. Drahozal, "'sticky' Arbitration Clauses?: The Use of Arbitration Clauses After Concepcion and Amex," Social Science Research Network, August 5, 2013, http://ssrn.com/abstract=2306268 or http://dx.doi.org/10.2139/ssrn.2306268.

[84]Julie Bennett, "Deciphering the FDD," Entrepreneur, January 2012, pp. 106–111.

[85]2015 Franchise Sales Trends Report, FranConnect, 2015, p. 8.

[86]Andrea Wells, "How Employer Joint Liability Is Changing," Insurance Journal, February 2016, www.insurancejournal.com/news/national/2016/02/18/398910.htm; Jonathan Maze, "IFA: Franchise Growth Strong, But Headwinds Persist," Nation's Restaurant News, January 7, 2015, http://nrn.com/government/ifa-franchise-growth-strong-headwinds-persist; Alexia Elejalde-Ruiz, "Why Should McDonald's Be a Joint Employer? NLRB Starts to Provide Answers," Chicago Tribune, March 10, 2016, www.chicagotribune.com/business/ct-mcdonalds-labor-case-0311-biz-20160310-story.html; "Franchise Model Under Attack," Nation's Restaurant News, April 13, 2015, pp. S14–S15.

[87]Allison Waterfield, "Joint Employers? NLRB Decision Prompts States to Take Action," Bloomberg BNA, April 6, 2017, https://www.bna.com/joint-employers-nlrb-b57982085985/.

[88]National Survey of Franchisees 2015, FranchiseGrade, 2015, p. 12.

[89]"According to a Recent Study/Survey … " Modern Restaurant Management, July 27, 2016, www.modernrestaurantmanagement.com/according-to-a-recent-studysurvey-end-of-july-2016-edition/.

[90]Douglas MacMillan, "Finding the Perfect Franchise Fit," Bloomberg Businessweek, July 31, 2006, www.bloomberg.com/news/articles/2006-08-30/finding-the-perfect-franchise-fit.

[91]Julie Bennett, "How Much Do You Need to Start a Franchise?" Wall Street Journal, April 29, 2013. p. R8.

[92]Ibid.

[93]Ibid.

[94]Tracy Stapp Herold, "The Fastest-Growing Sectors in the Franchise Industry," Entrepreneur, December 17, 2014, www.entrepreneur.com/article/240720; "What Does the S&E Job Market Look Like for U.S. Graduates?," National Science Foundation, 2014, www.nsf.gov/nsb/sei/edTool/data/workforce-03.html; "7 STEM Career Statistics That Will Surely Surprise You," e2 Young Engineers, July 30, 2015, http://franchise.e2youngengineers.com/2015/07/30/8-stem-career-statistics-that-will-surely-surprise-you/.

[95]National Survey of Franchisees 2015, FranchiseGrade, 2015, p. 12.

[96]Robert Thomas, "Welcome to the Big Leagues," QSR, May 2015, https://www.qsrmagazine.com/franchising/welcome-big-leagues.

[97]Lillia Callum-Penso, "Taking the Subway from Iran," Greenville News, April 29, 2012, pp. 1E, 3E.

[98]Eric Stites, "Real Talk: Is Franchising as Profitable as You Think?" Business.com, April 2, 2015, www.business.com/entrepreneurship/does-franchising-pay/.

[99]National Survey of Franchisees 2015, FranchiseGrade, 2015, p. 13.

[100]Angus Loten, "Finding the Right Franchise," Smart Money, June 2, 2011, www.smartmoney.com/small-business/small-business/finding-the-rightfranchise-1306952100853.

[101]National Survey of Franchisees 2015, FranchiseGrade, 2015, p. 12.

[102]Tracy Stapp Herold, "Master of His Own Destiny," Entrepreneur, April 2016, pp. 98–99.

[103]Kerry Pipes, "The 5th Quarter," Multi-Unit Franchisee, Issue 1, 2016, pp. 20–22.

[104]Jules Lichtenstein, "Demographic Characteristics of Business Owners," Small Business Administration Office of Advocacy, Issue Brief Number 2, January 16, 2014, p. 1; "Franchisee Prospect Insights 2015, FranchiseDirect, May 18, 2015, www.franchisedirect.com/information/prospectivefranchiseesurvey2016/?r=5380.

[105]"DiversityFran," International Franchise Association, 2016, www.franchise.org/diversityfran.

[106]Noel King, "Can Black-Owned Franchises Help Narrow the Wealth Gap?" MarketPlace, May 2, 2013, www.marketplace.org/topics/wealth-poverty/can-black-owned-franchises-help-narrow-wealth-gap; "Ella Avery-Smothers," Los Angeles Local Development Corporation, www.losangelesldc.com/projects/averysmothers.html.

[107]Helen Bond, "Let Your Eagles Fly," Multi-Unit Franchisee, Issue I, 2016, pp. 14–17.

[108]2016 Top Markets Report: Franchising, U.S. Department of Commerce, International Trade Administration, 2016, p. 5.

[109]McDonald's 2016 Annual Report, McDonald's Corporation, 2016, p. 18.

[110]Jessica Naudziunas, "Where in the World Are There No McDonald's?" NPR, August 1, 2013, www.npr.org/sections/thesalt/2013/07/25/205547517/where-in-the-world-are-there-no-mcdonalds.

[111]"Yum China," Yum! Brands, 2016, http://www.yum.com/company/our-brands/china/; Yum! Brands 2015 Annual Report, Yum! Brands, 2015, p. 3.

[112]Adam Janofsky, "Fast-Food Franchises Get Creative When They Go Abroad," Wall Street Journal, May 26, 2015, www.wsj.com/articles/fast-food-franchises-get-creative-when-they-go-abroad-1432318075.

[113]Kushan Mitra, "Paneer Burger for the Indian Palate," Business Today, June 4, 2011, http://businesstoday.intoday.in/story/-paneer-burger-mcspicy-paneer-mccurry-pan/1/15778.html; Dhawal Shah, "India: A Market for the Masses," Franchising World, June 2008, www.franchise.org/india-market-for-the-masses.

[114]Adam Janofsky, "Fast-Food Franchises Get Creative When They Go Abroad," Wall Street Journal, May 26, 2015, www.wsj.com/articles/fast-food-franchises-get-creative-when-they-go-abroad-1432318075.

[115]Franchising Industry in China (Washington, DC: Stat-USA, U.S. Foreign Commercial Service, 2004), www.buyusainfo.net/docs/x_5566195.pdf.

[116]Mary Teresa Bitti, "How a $300,000 Dragon's Den Deal Is Setting Velofix on the Road to Growth," Financial Post, November 30, 2014, http://business.financialpost.com/entrepreneur/deal-with-dragon-sets-mobile-repair-shop-on-road-to-growth-2?__lsa=8c3f-3c9f; Jason Daley, "Curbside Enthusiasm," Entrepreneur, April 2015, pp. 85–91.

[117]Daniel P. Smith, "Uncommon Ground," QSR, August 2014, www.qsrmagazine.com/competition/uncommon-ground.

[118]Venessa Wong and Steph Davidson, "Subway at 40,000: Fast Food's Global King Keeps Growing," Bloomberg Businessweek, August 26, 2013, www.businessweek.com/articles/2013-08-26/subway-at-40-000-fast-foods-global-king-keeps-growing.

[119]Alan J. Liddle, "10 Non-Traditional Subway Restaurants," Nation's Restaurant News, July 26, 2011, www.nrn.com/article/10-non-traditional-subway-restaurants; Geoff Williams, "Subway Opens First Gravity-Defying Restaurant at the Freedom Tower," Daily Finance, January 4, 2010, www.dailyfinance.com/2010/01/04/subway-opens-first-restaurant-at-the-freedom-tower-restaurant.

[120]Tracy Stapp, "Losing the Dream But Saving the Store," Entrepreneur, August 2010, pp. 91–96.

[121]Annie Gasparro, "McDonald's to Speed Refranchising, Cut Costs," *Wall Street Journal*, May 4, 2015, www.wsj.com/articles/mcdonalds-to-speed-refranchising-cut-costs-1430744590.

[122]"Successful Multi-Unit Franchising," Special Report, *Franchise Business Review*, 2015, p. 3; Tracey Stapp Harold, "More Is More," *Entrepreneur*, June 2014, pp. 103–105.

[123]"Potential Franchisees, Take Note: Taco Bell Hopes to Open 2,000 U.S. Restaurants by 2023," *Reuters*, December 2, 2013, www.reuters.com/article/2013/12/02/idUS108638623420131202.

[124]Jason Daley, "How Franchises Grow Fast," *Entrepreneur*, February 2016, pp. 78–83.

[125]"The 2016 Multi-Unit 50: Ranking the Most Multi-Friendly Brands," Multi-Unit Franchisee, Issue III, 2016, p. 58.

[126]*Risky Business: Franchisees' High and Rising Risk of SBA Loan Failure*, We Are Main Street and Service Employees International Union, May 2015, p. 7; Eric Stites, "Real Talk: Is Franchising as Profitable as You Think?" *Business.com*, April 2, 2015, www.business.com/entrepreneurship/does-franchising-pay/.

[127]"Smoothie King Hits 800-Store Mark," *QSR*, July 29, 2016, www.qsrmagazine.com/news/smoothie-king-hits-800-store-mark; "Smoothie King Grows with New Area Development," *QSR*, November 4, 2013, www.qsrmagazine.com/news/smoothie-king-grows-new-area-development.

[128]Jason Daley, "The Benefits of Going South," *Entrepreneur*, July 2016, pp. 69–75; Deborah L. Cohen, "The International Plan," *QSR*, February 2010, www2.qsrmagazine.com/articles/features/138/wing_zone-1.phtml.

[129]Nicole Duncan, "Bruegger's and Jamba Begin Cobranding," *QSR*, July 10, 2015, www.qsrmagazine.com/news/brueggers-and-jamba-begin-cobranding.

[130]Jason Daley, "New Franchises Team Up and Make Cobranding Work," *Entrepreneur*, March 23, 2012, www.entrepreneur.com/article/223144.

[131]"Dippin' Dots and Doc Popcorn to Open Dual Concept," *QSR*, February 13, 2015, www.qsrmagazine.com/news/dippin-dots-and-doc-popcorn-open-dual-concept; "A Sweet and Savory Growth Plan: Doc Popcorn and Dippin' Dots Seek to Open Co-Branded Franchises in Spokane Malls," *Business Wire*, June 24, 2016, www.businesswire.com/news/home/20160614006232/en/Sweet-Savory-Growth-Plan-Doc-Popcorn-Dippin%E2%80%99.

[132]April Y. Pennington, "An American Icon," *Entrepreneur*, January 2005, www.entrepreneur.com/magazine/entrepreneur/2005/january/74992.html.

9

Building a Powerful Bootstrap Marketing Plan

Easy camera/Shutterstock

Learning Objectives

On completion of this chapter, you will be able to:

1. Describe the principles of building a bootstrap marketing plan and explain the benefits of preparing one.

2. Explain how small businesses can pinpoint their target markets.

3. Discuss the role of market research in building a bootstrap marketing plan and outline the market research process.

4. Describe how a small business can build a competitive edge in the marketplace by using bootstrap marketing strategies.

MyLab Entrepreneurship

⭐ **Improve Your Grade!**

If your instructor is using MyLab Entrepreneurship, visit **www.pearson.com/mylab/entrepreneurship** for videos, simulations, and writing exercises.

As you learned in Chapters 4 and 5, creating a solid business model and business plan improves an entrepreneur's odds of building a successful company. The business model and business plan are valuable tools that help define *what* an entrepreneur plans to accomplish in both quantitative and qualitative terms and *how* he or she plans to accomplish it. The plan consolidates many of the topics we have discussed in preceding chapters with those in this section to produce a concise statement of how an entrepreneur plans to achieve success in the marketplace. This section focuses on building two major components of every business plan: the marketing plan and the financial plan.

Many business plans describe in great detail what entrepreneurs intend to accomplish (e.g., "the financials") and pay little, if any, attention to the strategies to achieve those targets. Too often, entrepreneurs squander enormous effort pulling together capital, people, and other resources to sell their products and services because they fail to determine what it will take to attract and keep a profitable customer base. Sometimes they fail to determine whether a profitable customer base even exists! To be effective, a solid business plan must contain both a financial plan *and* a marketing plan. Like the financial plan, an effective marketing plan projects numbers and analyzes them but from a different perspective. Rather than focus on cash flow, net income, and owner's equity, a marketing plan concentrates on the *customer*.

This chapter is devoted to creating an effective marketing plan, which is a subset of a total business plan. Before producing reams of computer-generated spreadsheets of financial projections, an entrepreneur must determine what to sell, to whom and how, and on what terms and at what price, and how to get the product or service to the customer. In short, a marketing plan identifies a company's target customers and describes how the business will attract and keep them. Its primary focus is cultivating and maintaining a competitive edge for a small business. Table 9.1 explains how to build a seven-sentence bootstrap (also sometimes called "guerrilla") marketing strategy.

Building a Bootstrap Marketing Plan

Marketing is the process of creating and delivering desired goods and services to customers and involves all of the activities associated with winning and retaining loyal customers. The "secret" to successful marketing is to understand what your target customers' needs, demands, and wants are before your competitors do; to offer them the products and services that will satisfy those needs, demands, and wants; and to provide customer service, convenience, and value so that they will keep coming back.

The marketing function cuts across the entire company, affecting every aspect of its operation—from finance and production to hiring and purchasing—as well as the company's ultimate success. As competition for customers becomes more intense, entrepreneurs must understand the importance of developing creative marketing strategies. Their success and survival depend on it. Traditional marketing techniques emphasize pushing messages out to potential customers. However, modern technology gives consumers the ability to filter and block many of these messages, limiting the effectiveness of "push" techniques. Successful entrepreneurs recognize that modern marketing strategies also must include techniques such as social media and cause marketing that pull customers into their companies' sphere of influence. The good news is that many of these "pull" strategies are relatively inexpensive and, when infused with a healthy dose of creativity, are extremely effective.

Although they may be small and cannot match their larger rivals' marketing budgets, entrepreneurial companies are not powerless when it comes to developing effective marketing strategies. By using **bootstrap marketing strategies**—unconventional, low-cost, creative techniques—small companies can wring as much or more "bang" from their marketing buck. For instance, facing the power of discount giants such as Amazon, Wal-Mart, Target, and "category killer" superstores such as Best Buy and Home Depot that are determined to increase their market shares, small retail shops are turning to bootstrap marketing tactics to attract new customers and keep existing ones. Jay Conrad Levinson, the late guerrilla and bootstrap marketing guru, said bootstrap marketing is all about maximizing the efficiency of a small company's marketing budget.

An effective bootstrap marketing campaign does *not* require an entrepreneur to spend large amounts of money, but it does demand creativity, ingenuity, and an understanding of customers'

LO1

Describe the principles of building a bootstrap marketing plan and explain the benefits of preparing one.

marketing

the process of creating and delivering desired goods and services to customers; it involves all the activities associated with winning and retaining loyal customers.

bootstrap marketing strategies

unconventional, low-cost, creative marketing strategies designed to give small companies an edge over their larger, richer, more powerful rivals.

TABLE 9.1 A Seven-Sentence Bootstrap (Guerrilla) Marketing Strategy

Building a successful bootstrap marketing plan does not have to be complex. Bootstrap marketing expert Jay Conrad Levinson advised entrepreneurs to create a bootstrap marketing plan with just seven sentences:

1. *What is the purpose of your marketing?* In other words, what action do you want customers or prospective customers to take as a result of your marketing efforts? Should they visit your store? Go to your company's Web site? Buy a subscription from your business? Sign up for additional information by leaving their e-mail?

2. *What primary benefit can you offer customers?* What is your company's competitive advantage, and what does it do for customers? What is your unique selling proposition? Bootstrap marketers express their companies' competitive advantage as a solution to a customer's problem, which is easier to market than just a positive benefit. Successful bootstrap marketing requires an entrepreneur to have a clear understanding of a company's unique selling proposition, a key customer benefit of a product or service that sets it apart from its competition.

3. *Who is your target market?* At whom are you aiming your marketing efforts? Answering this question often requires some basic research about your target customers, their characteristics, their habits, and their preferences. Bootstrap marketers know that broadcasting is old school; they realize that narrowcasting—focusing their marketing efforts on those people who are most interested in and most likely to purchase their goods and services—is much more efficient and effective. Most small companies have more than one target market; be sure to identify all of them.

4. *Which marketing tools will you use to reach your target audience?* This list should include only tools your company understands, knows how to use effectively, and can afford. The good news is that marketing tools do not have to be costly to be effective. Social media has made marketing much more affordable for many smaller companies. However, social media marketing also needs a detailed plan to be effective.

5. *What is your company's niche in the marketplace?* How do you intend to position your company against your competition? Bootstrap marketers understand that their markets are crowded with competitors, some of them much larger and with gigantic marketing budgets that dwarf their own, and that finding a profitable niche to occupy can be highly profitable. Recall from Chapter 5 that many successful entrepreneurs position their companies in profitable niches. It'Sugar, a company founded in 2006 by Jeff Rubin, a veteran of the candy industry, sells many types of candy, ranging from Jelly Belly jelly beans to 5-pound Hershey chocolate bars, through its Web site and its 100 retail stores. Not a typical candy store aimed at children, It'Sugar stores mainly target adults and resemble Victoria's Secret shops, with mannequins dressed in candy, unique displays, and vibrant colors. Like It'Sugar, the key is to carve out a position that allows your company to differentiate itself from all of its competitors.

6. *What is your company's identity in the marketplace?* A company's identity is a reflection of its DNA. Small companies often have an advantage over large businesses when it comes to communicating their identities because of the interesting, unique stories behind their creation and the enthusiasm and passion of their founders. Customers enjoy doing business with small companies that have a clear, meaningful, and compelling identity in the marketplace.

7. *How much money will you spend on your marketing?* What is your marketing budget? The average company in the United States devotes 4 percent of its sales revenue to marketing. Small companies should allocate a portion of their budgets to marketing; after all, it drives sales. The good news is that many of the bootstrap marketing techniques that small companies can use (and that are described in this chapter) are either low cost or no cost. When allocating their budgets, bootstrap marketers recognize the importance of putting their money where they will get the greatest "bang."

Answering these seven questions will give you an outline of your company's marketing plan. *Implementing* a bootstrap marketing plan boils down to two essentials:

1. Having a thorough understanding of your target market, including what customers want and expect from your company and its products and services

2. Identifying the obstacles that stand in your way of satisfying customers (competitors, barriers to entry, processes, outside influences, budgets, knowledge, and others) and eliminating them.

Sources: Based on Jay Conrad Levinson and Jeannie Levinson, "Here's the Plan," *Entrepreneur*, February 2008, pp. 92–97; and Alan Lautenslager, "Write a Creative Marketing Plan in Seven Sentences," *Entrepreneur*, April 24, 2006, www.entrepreneur.com/marketing/marketingideas/guerrillamarketingcolumnistallautenslager/article159486.html; Michael Peterson, "Top Ten Guerrilla Marketing Tactics for Retailers," *Franchise Beacon*, July 29, 2013, http://franchisebeacon.com/top-ten-guerrilla-marketing-tactics-for-retailers/; Ben Morel, "Why Startups Should Throw Away Their Business Plans," *Oxford Launch*, November 13, 2014, http://oxfordlaunch.com/why-startups-should-throw-away-their-business-plans/.

buying habits. Levinson estimates that bootstrap marketers spend between 4 percent and 8 percent of sales on marketing, but they put their money into clever, creative marketing efforts that reach their target customers and raise the profile of their products, services, and companies.[1]

ENTREPRENEURIAL PROFILE: Kimberly Causey: Home Décor Press After spending 10 years working in the wholesale home furnishings industry, Kimberly Causey realized consumers wanted information on home furnishing bargains. She took her knowledge of the industry and set out to self-publish a home furnishings buying guide. Causey could not afford to have her guide professionally printed, so she made her first run of books in her kitchen. She printed the interior pages on her home printer, folded them by hand, and glued them inside professionally printed covers, using a glue gun and a butter knife. She promoted the books by driving all over the Southeast to appear on local morning television shows. Causey used the profits from her homemade books to buy a professionally printed run of books and an RV and began promoting her books across the country. She was able to secure a nationwide contract with Barnes & Noble. Her story eventually caught the attention of the *Today* show. Her appearance on that show pushed her book to a top 10 title on Amazon. Causey continues to promote her books through appearances on both local and national media outlets, as well as through her Web site smartdecorating.com.[2] ∎

A sound bootstrap marketing plan reflects a company's understanding of its customers and acknowledges that satisfying them is the foundation of every business. It recognizes that the customer is the central player in the cast of every business venture. According to marketing expert Ted Levitt, the primary purpose of a business is not to earn a profit; instead, it is to identify and attract customers. If an entrepreneur focuses on this purpose and uses good sense to run the business, profits will follow.[3] In other words, profits are the outcome of creating value for your target customers. Every area of the business must practice putting the customer first, in planning and actions.

A bootstrap marketing plan should accomplish three objectives:

1. It should pinpoint the specific target markets the small company will serve.

2. It should determine customer needs and wants through market research.

3. It should analyze the firm's competitive advantages and build a bootstrap marketing strategy around them to communicate its value proposition to the target market.

This chapter focuses on these three objectives of a small company's marketing plan.

Pinpointing the Target Market

One of the first steps in building a bootstrap marketing plan is to identify a small company's **target market**—the specific group of customers at whom the company aims its goods or services. The more a business knows about its local markets and its customers and their buying habits and preferences, the more precisely it can focus its marketing efforts on the group(s) of customers who are most likely to buy its products or services. Most marketing experts contend that the greatest marketing mistake small businesses make is failing to define clearly the target markets they serve. This is known as "trying to boil the ocean." These entrepreneurs develop new products that do not sell because they are not targeted at a specific audience's needs. They push out their message too broadly through social media or other types of promotion without a specific plan about whom they want to reach. They spend precious time and money trying to reach customers who are not the right market for their product or service. Why, then, do so many small companies make this mistake? Because it is easy and does not require interacting with potential customers and creating a marketing plan. Many entrepreneurs are reluctant to engage real customers as they launch their business, relying instead on their own intuition and encouragement from those around them. Smart entrepreneurs know they do not have the luxury of wasting resources. They must follow a more focused, laserlike approach to marketing. Entrepreneurs must identify a specific market niche that has a specific need or "pain point" and tailor a solution, be it a product or a service, to address this need. As you learned in Chapter 4, an effective value proposition offers a specific solution to a specific

LO2

Explain how small businesses can pinpoint their target markets.

target market
the specific group of customers at whom a company aims its goods or services.

market segment. "It is amazing how many people assume they know what customers want without actually asking customers," says Hunter Phillips, CEO, PRSM Healthcare in Nashville, Tennessee. "Present it as if you are trying to solve a problem for them. Remember, this is about their needs rather than your idea."[4]

To be customer driven, an effective marketing strategy must be based on a clear, comprehensive understanding of a company's target customers and their needs. A customer-driven marketing strategy is a powerful weapon for any company that lacks the financial and physical resources of its competitors. Customers respond when companies take the time to learn about their unique needs and offer products and services designed to satisfy them.

ENTREPRENEURIAL PROFILE: Ron Henry: BlackRapid Ron Henry, a professional photographer for more than 15 years, never was able to find a camera strap that was both comfortable and designed to make quick shots easier. Using parts purchased at a hardware store, Henry constructed a strap that allowed his camera to hang comfortably at his side until he was ready to take a photograph, when it would glide quickly and easily into place. Henry borrowed $5,000 from a friend to launch BlackRapid to produce and sell camera straps based on his new design. At first Henry bought banner ads at wedding Web sites to promote his camera straps. However, that proved to be an expensive strategy that resulted in very few sales. Henry changed his strategy to promoting BlackRapid through photography blogs. He sent each blogger a free strap, hoping that they would spread the word about his product. The strategy worked. After only four years in business, BlackRapid's revenues grew to more than $7 million a year, serving customers in more than 50 countries.[5] ∎

Most successful businesses have well-defined portraits of the customers they are seeking to attract. From market research, they know their customers' income levels, lifestyles, buying patterns, likes and dislikes, and even their psychological profiles—why they buy. These companies offer prices that are appropriate to their target customers' buying power, product lines that appeal to their tastes, and service they expect. The payoff comes in the form of higher sales, profits, and customer loyalty. For entrepreneurs, pinpointing target customers has become more important than ever before as markets in the United States have become increasingly fragmented and diverse. Mass marketing techniques no longer reach customers the way they did 30 years ago because of the splintering of the population and the influence exerted on the nation's purchasing patterns by what were once minority groups such as Hispanic, Asian, and African Americans (see Figure 9.1). Peter Francese, marketing consultant and author of the

FIGURE 9.1

U.S. Population by Race, 2020, 2040, and 2060

Source: Based on data from the U.S. Census Bureau.

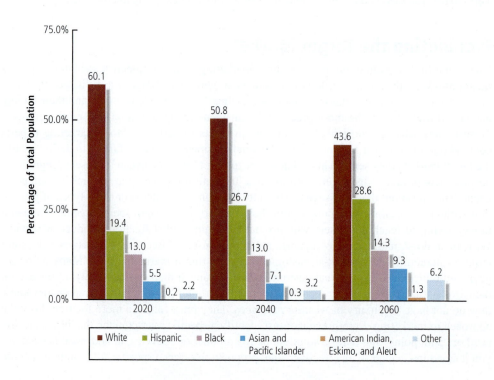

research report *2010 America*, says "the average American" no longer exists.[6] The United States is a multicultural nation in which no race or ethnicity comprises a majority in its two most populous states, California and Texas. The U.S. Census Bureau predicts that whites will no longer constitute the majority in America by 2044, when 50.3 percent of Americans will be members of a minority group. By 2060, the "minority" population in the United States will represent a significant majority—56 percent of the total population.[7] By 2025, multiculturalism will explode, Baby Boomers' spending will be in decline, the most economically disadvantaged market segments will expand, and household spending will grow at a slow pace, all of which will create a very different world for marketers.[8]

When companies follow a customer-driven marketing strategy, they ensure that their target customers permeate the entire business—from the merchandise sold and the music played on the sound system to the location, layout, and decor of the store. These entrepreneurs have an advantage over their larger rivals because the buying experience they create resonates with their target customers. That's why they prosper.

ENTREPRENEURIAL PROFILE: Isy Goldwasser: Thync Thync started out as a typical venture capital–funded business, raising $13 million in Series A funding. The company sells a device that uses ultrasound to raise energy and lower stress. Although Thync caught the attention of some early adopters, it never built a strong base of customers. The company was unable to raise additional capital, and it had to lay off about three-quarters of its employees and auction off most of its hard assets to cut costs and build up some cash. The company changed its target market from anyone who wants to feel calmer and more energized to people who want to cut back on caffeine, alcohol, and sleeping pills. With the more targeted marketing strategy, the company was able to raise additional funding to help it get back on track with more modest growth plans.[9] ■

Determining Customer Needs and Wants Through Market Research

LO3
Discuss the role of market research in building a bootstrap marketing plan and outline the market research process.

demographics
the study of important population characteristics, such as age, income, education, and race.

The changing nature of the U.S. population is a potent force altering the landscape of business. Shifting patterns in age, income, education, race, and other population characteristics (which are the subject of **demographics**) have a major impact on new opportunities in the market and on existing small businesses. Entrepreneurs who ignore demographic trends and fail to adjust their strategies accordingly run the risk of becoming competitively obsolete. Entrepreneurs who stay in tune with demographic, social, and economic trends are able to spot growing and emerging market opportunities.

ENTREPRENEURIAL PROFILE: Enrique Gonzalez, Sr.: Vallarta Supermarkets Enrique Gonzalez, Sr., opened the first Vallarta Supermarkets in Van Nuys, California in 1985 to serve the growing Hispanic community, a target market that major supermarket chains were overlooking at the time. The company has grown to 49 stores, located in communities throughout southern California, and it captures a significant share of the $10.9 billion Hispanic families spend on food each year in that area. The business has remained family owned and is committed to being an inclusive part of the area's diverse Hispanic population by offering products that are part of the classic Hispanic culture, including chorizo made in-house, freshly-prepared tortillas, Latin-style cheeses, and champurrado, a delicious hot chocolate drink. The company's Web site is in both English and Spanish because the stores attract many shoppers who are not part of the Hispanic community.[10] ■

A demographic trend is like a train: A business owner must find out early on where it's going and decide whether to get on board. Waiting until the train is roaring down the tracks and gaining speed means it's too late to get on board. However, by checking the schedule early and planning ahead, an entrepreneur may find himself or herself at the train's controls, wearing the engineer's hat! Similarly, small companies that spot demographic trends early and act on them can gain a distinctive edge in the market. An entrepreneur's goal is to make sure that his or her company's marketing plan is on track with the most significant trends that are shaping the industry. Trend tracking not only keeps a company on the pathway to success but also helps it avoid losing its focus by pursuing opportunities that are out of favor.

Trends are powerful forces and can be an entrepreneur's greatest friend or greatest foe. For entrepreneurs who are observant and position their companies to intercept them, trends can be to their companies what the perfect wave is to a surfer. For entrepreneurs who ignore them or discount their importance, trends can leave their companies stranded like a boat stuck in the mud at low tide.

 ## You Be the Consultant

.CO Internet S.A.S.

Juan Diego Calle was born into an entrepreneurial family in Bogota, Colombia. His parents owned and operated a highly successful wine and beer distribution company. Because of political instability in Colombia, his parents became increasingly worried about the safety of their family. When he was 15 years old, his parents moved Juan and his siblings to Miami. However, his parents chose to stay behind in Colombia to manage the family business.

In 1998, while in college, Calle studied abroad in France. There he became intrigued by the opportunity offered by the Internet. When he returned to Miami, Calle launched an Internet-based business that failed when the Internet bubble burst in 2001. However, Calle continued to pursue Internet-related businesses after the failure of his first endeavor. He had great success with a business that acquired and developed travel domains that matched keywords, such as New York Hotels and London Hotels.

While growing his domain name business, Calle recognized that available domain names ending in .com extensions were becoming scarce. A friend suggested he look into the .co extension, which was the domain name designation for his native country Colombia. After many false starts, Calle was able to convince the government of Colombia to accept his bid to manage the .co extension through his new company called .CO Internet S.A.S.

Calle made the decision to brand the .co extension as a place for start-ups to build their Internet presence. Calle was able to convince trend-setting tech companies to use the .co extension for their Web presence. To achieve his goal, he persuaded executives at Twitter to adopt t.co as its shortened URL address in Colombia. Calle also sold AngelList, the service for connecting entrepreneurs and angel investors, the domain name Angel.co as its Internet address. By associating the .co brand with successful ventures such as these, .CO Internet helped reinforce its branding efforts as the domain of choice for tech start-ups.

The company seeks to position its brand as having more value than just a URL address. .CO Internet offers all businesses that adopt the .co extension "membership," which includes discounts on books and admission to events and forums to connect with other entrepreneurs. To measure the success of its branding efforts, the company conducted a survey after it had been operating for only one year. The results indicated that 80 percent of people thought .co meant "company," while only 3 percent identified it with Colombia.

.CO Internet has more than 1.6 million domain names under management in 200 countries, with revenues of more than $21 million. In 2014, Neustar, a publicly traded company specializing in Internet analytics, agreed to purchase .CO Internet S.A.S. for $109 million.

1. How would you envision the marketing of .CO Internet S.A.S. to change now that it is part of a large corporation? Can large companies effectively take advantage of bootstrap marketing strategies? Explain.

2. What steps can the new owner of .CO Internet S.A.S take to maintain the brand and continue to build customer recognition of it? Refer to Figure 9.2 on page 354 and use the table below to do the following:
   a. List threshold, performance, and excitement attributes for .CO Internet S.A.S.
   b. Identify "proof points" (reasons for customers to believe in the brand) that support each of the attributes you list.
   c. Use the attributes and their proof points to develop a unique selling proposition for .CO Internet.

Threshold Attributes	Performance Attributes	Excitement Attributes
Threshold Proof Points	Performance Proof Points	Excitement Proof Points
Unique selling proposition:		

Sources: Based on Ron Jackson, "The Juan Diego Calle Story: How the .CO CEO Is Turning a Seldom Used ccTLD into a Booming Global Brand," *DN Journal,* December 5, 2010, www.dnjournal.com/cover/2010/november-december.htm; Paul Sloan, ".CO Internet Is a Company Cool Enough for Brooklyn Hipsters," *CNET,* March 13, 2012, www.cnet.com/news/co-internet-is-a-company-cool-enough-for-brooklyn-hipsters/; Nancy Dahlberg, "Miami Tech Company .CO Internet to be Acquired for $109 Million," *Miami Herald,* March 22, 2014, www.miamiherald.com/2014/03/21/4009212/miami-tech-company-co-internet.html.

The Value of Market Research

By performing some basic market research, aspiring entrepreneurs and owners of existing small businesses can detect key demographic and market trends. Marketing consultants argue that information is just as much a business asset as equipment, machinery, and inventory. **Market research** is the process of gathering the information that serves as the foundation for a marketing plan. It involves systematically collecting, analyzing, and interpreting data pertaining to a company's market, customers, and competitors. The objective of market research is to learn how to improve the level of satisfaction for existing customers and to find ways to attract new customers.

Marketing mistakes are extremely costly for small businesses because there is little margin for error when funds are scarce and budgets are tight. Small businesses simply cannot afford to miss their target markets, and market research can help them zero in on the bull's-eye. Market research does *not* have to be time-consuming, complex, or expensive to be useful. By applying the same type of creativity to market research that they display when creating their businesses, entrepreneurs can perform effective market research "on the cheap."

market research
the process of gathering the information that serves as the foundation for a marketing plan; it involves systematically collecting, analyzing, and interpreting data pertaining to a company's market, customers, and competitors.

ENTREPRENEURIAL PROFILE: Shawn O'Connor: Stratus Prep Stratus Prep, founded by Shawn O'Connor in New York City, provides admissions counseling and standardized test preparation for people seeking to enter college, business school, law school, and graduate programs. Before he launched his company, O'Connor held focus groups to determine the market size, the amount that potential customers would be willing to pay for test prep and admissions counseling, and the importance of various specific features. O'Connor then developed a comprehensive expense forecast to determine whether and when his company would become profitable. O'Connor's market research indicated that his company could become quite profitable. Based on this market research, he launched Stratus Prep, which was profitable within the first four months of operations and has remained profitable every month since then.[11] ■

Established companies also can conduct market research on the cheap. For example, Jet-Blue uses Twitter as one of its primary sources for customer feedback. The marketing team monitors Twitter for customer questions, compliments, and complaints and provides quick responses to all tweets.[12] Some entrepreneurs create customer advisory boards (CABs), small groups of customers (the average size is 5) who provide them with useful feedback about a variety of important marketing issues. CABs often alert business owners to customer problems and business opportunities of which the owners are unaware. One study reports that sales at small companies that use CABs are 24 percent higher than comparable companies that do not have CABs.[13] Low-cost market research techniques such as these allow entrepreneurs to get past the barriers that consumers often put up and to uncover their true preferences and hidden thoughts.

Many entrepreneurs are discovering the power, the speed, the convenience, and the low cost of conducting market research over the Internet. Online surveys, customer opinion polls, and other research projects are easy to conduct, cost virtually nothing, and help companies connect with their customers. With online surveys, businesses can get real-time feedback from customers, often using surveys they have designed themselves. Web sites such as Survey Monkey and Zoomerang allow entrepreneurs to conduct low-cost online surveys of existing or prospective customers. Many companies also conduct surveys through Facebook and Twitter. Entrepreneurs can use surveys and social media to gain insight into the market that used to require hiring a marketing research consultant.

ENTREPRENEURIAL PROFILE: Luca Daniel Lavorato and Mario Christian: Joseph Nogucci Joseph Nogucci, an online jewelry store and manufacturer founded by Luca Daniel Lavorato and Mario Christian, uses Facebook to generate customer reactions to new product offerings. The company gauges customer interest in new designs before it puts them into production. The customer feedback also helps the company determine how much inventory to carry and which demographic to target with each of its new product offerings. In addition to promoting and managing inventory for new products, the company posts inspirational stories from customers on its Facebook fan page to build customer loyalty. Joseph Nogucci has more than 250,000 Facebook fans and devotes 80 percent of its marketing budget to Facebook. The company also connects with customers through Twitter, Instagram, and other social media.[14] ■

How to Conduct Market Research

The goal of market research is to reduce the risks associated with making business decisions. For an entrepreneur, there is no bigger decision than the one to start or not start a new business. Market research can replace misinformation and assumptions with facts. Opinion and hearsay are not viable foundations on which to build a solid marketing strategy. Remember, this is a key aspect of developing a sound business model (see Chapter 4). Successful market research consists of four steps: define the objective, collect the data, analyze and interpret the data, and draw conclusions, including how you may need to pivot your business model.

Step 1. *Define the objective.* The first—and most crucial—step in market research is to define the research objective clearly and concisely. For a new business, the objective is to test the assumptions made while developing the business model. For an existing business, the objective is to better understand changes occurring in its business or in its market. A common error at this stage is to confuse a symptom with the true problem. For example, dwindling sales is not a problem; it is a symptom. To get to the heart of the matter, entrepreneurs must list all the possible factors that could have caused it. Do we face new competition? Are our sales representatives impolite or unknowledgeable? Have customer tastes changed? Is our product line too narrow? Do customers have trouble finding what they want? Is our Web site giving customers what they want? Is it easy to navigate?

individualized (one-to-one) marketing
a system based on gathering data on individual customers and developing a marketing program designed to appeal specifically to their needs, tastes, and preferences.

Step 2. *Collect the data.* The marketing approach that dominates today is **individualized (one-to-one) marketing**, which involves gathering data on individual customers and then developing a marketing program designed specifically to appeal to their needs, tastes, and preferences. In a society in which people feel isolated and interactions are impersonal, one-to-one marketing gives a business a competitive edge. Companies following this approach know their customers, understand how to give them the value they want, and, perhaps most important, know how to make them feel special and valued. The idea is to treat each customer as an individual, and the goal is to transform a company's best and most profitable customers into loyal, lifetime customers.

Individualized marketing requires business owners to gather and assimilate detailed information about their customers. Fortunately, owners of even the smallest companies now have access to affordable technology that creates and manages computerized databases, allowing them to develop close, one-to-one relationships with their customers. Much like gold nuggets waiting to be discovered, significant amounts of valuable information about customers and their buying habits are hidden *inside* many small businesses, tucked away in databases. For most business owners, collecting useful information about their customers and potential new products and markets is simply a matter of sorting, organizing, and analyzing data that are already floating around somewhere in their companies. Even small businesses can generate volumes of data about their customers, and business analytics software, such as R, Python, SAS Analytics Pro, Tableau and others, helps entrepreneurs decipher it to detect meaningful patterns and trends that can improve their marketing strategies. Data mining, once available only to large companies with vast computer power and large market research budgets, is now possible for even very small businesses. **Data mining** is a process in which computer software that uses statistical analysis, database technology, and artificial intelligence finds hidden patterns, trends, and connections in data so that business owners can make better marketing decisions and predictions about customers' behavior. By finding relationships among the many components of a data set, identifying clusters of customers with similar buying habits, and predicting customers' buying patterns, data mining gives entrepreneurs incredible marketing power. The key is to mine the data that most companies have at their disposal and turn it into useful information that allows the company to "court" its customers with special products, services, ads, and offers that appeal most to them. How can entrepreneurs gather valuable market and customer information? Two basic methods are available: conducting

data mining
a process in which computer software that uses statistical analysis, database technology, and artificial intelligence finds hidden patterns, trends, and connections in data so that business owners can make better marketing decisions and predictions about customers' behavior.

primary research, data you collect and analyze yourself, and gathering *secondary research*, data that have already been compiled and that are available, often at a reasonable cost or even free. Primary research techniques include the following:

- *Focus groups.* Enlist a small number of customers to give you feedback on specific issues in your business—quality, convenience, hours of operation, service, and so on. Listen carefully for new marketing opportunities as customers or potential customers tell you what is on their minds. Once again, consider using the Internet; one small bicycle company conducts 10 online focus groups each year at virtually no cost and gains valuable marketing information from them.

- *Social media conversations and monitoring.* With social media, companies have the opportunity to engage in direct conversations with their customers. In addition, monitoring social media for comments about a business and its products or services can provide useful feedback from customers. Many companies use the Google Alerts feature of the leading search engine to track and receive e-mail updates whenever someone writes about their brands online. Most social networking sites, including Facebook and Twitter, offer search features that allow users to track what people are saying about a company and its products or services. Shari's Berries ships more than 5 million gourmet berries every Valentine's Day. When the weather forecast showed that a major snow storm would be sweeping across the country on Valentine's Day, the company proactively e-mailed customers and sent messages on Twitter, warning of delivery delays. As the storm hit, the company monitored Facebook and Twitter and responded to every customer who posted a comment. Although there was quite a bit of negative chatter in social media about the company when the storm first hit, within four days, positive comments significantly outnumbered negative comments throughout social media.[15]

- *Test market.* One of the best ways to gauge customer response to a new product or service is to set up a test market. When Smooth Fitness launched its new unobtrusive, low-cost exercise bicycle designed for aging Baby Boomers, the company test-marketed the new product on QVC. The company sold 33,000 bikes in one day on QVC, which convinced its managers that the new product would be successful.[16]

- *Daily transactions.* Sift as much data as possible from existing company records and daily transactions—customer warranty cards, personal checks, frequent-buyer clubs, credit applications, time of day of peak customer activity, peak days of the week, and so on.

- *Customer surveys and questionnaires.* Keep them short. Most experts suggest no more than five questions that address precisely what you want to learn about from your customers. Word your questions carefully so that you do not bias the results and use a simple ranking system (e.g., a 1-to-5 scale, with 1 representing "unacceptable" and 5 representing "excellent"). Test your survey for problems on a small number of people before putting it to use. Online surveys are inexpensive, are easy to conduct, and provide feedback quickly. VerticalResponse, a self-service marketing firm for small businesses, regularly sends out e-mail surveys to its customers. Because the company relies on word of mouth for much of its new business, knowing what its customers like and don't like about how it is doing business and the products it offers is critical to adding new customers.[17]

- *Other ideas.* Set up a suggestion system (for customers and employees) and use it. Talk with suppliers about trends they have spotted in the industry. Contact customers who have not bought anything in a long time and find out why. Contact people who are not customers and find out why. Teach employees to be good listeners and then ask them what they hear.

Collecting secondary research is usually less expensive than collecting primary data. The Internet is the first place most entrepreneurs go to search for marketing data, but it can sometimes be difficult to discern which sources of information are accurate and valid. Many reliable sources are available online, including the following:

- *Business directories.* To locate a trade association, use *Encyclopedia of Associations* (Gale Research). To find suppliers, use the *ThomasNet* (Thomas Publishing Company) or *Standard & Poor's Register of Corporations, Executives, and Industries* (Standard & Poor's Corporation). *The American Wholesalers and Distributors Directory* includes details on thousands of wholesalers and distributors.

- *Demographic data.* Profiles of more specific regions are available in the *State and Metropolitan Area Data Book* (Government Printing Office). The *Sourcebook of ZIP Code Demographics* (CACI, Inc.) provides detailed breakdowns of the population in every ZIP code in the country. *Sales and Marketing Management's Survey of Buying Power* (Bill Communications) has statistics on consumer, retail, and industrial buying.

- *Census data.* The Bureau of the Census publishes a wide variety of reports that summarize the wealth of data found in its census database, which is available at most libraries and at the Census Bureau's Web site (www.census.gov).

- *Forecasts.* The *U.S. Global Outlook* tracks the growth of 200 industries and gives a five-year forecast for each one. Many government agencies, including the U.S. Department of Commerce, offer forecasts on everything from interest rates to the number of housing starts. A government librarian can help you find what you need.

- *Market research.* Someone may already have compiled the market research you need. The *FINDex Worldwide Directory of Market Research Reports, Studies, and Surveys* (Cambridge Information Group) lists more than 10,600 studies available for purchase. Other directories of business research include the *Simmons New Media Study* (Simmons Market Research Bureau Inc.) and the *A. C. Nielsen Retail Index* (A. C. Nielsen Company).

- *Articles.* Magazine and journal articles pertinent to your business are a great source of information. Use the *Reader's Guide to Periodical Literature*, the *Business Periodicals Index* (similar to the *Reader's Guide* but focusing on business periodicals), and *Ulrich's Periodical Directory* to locate the ones you need.

- *Local data.* Your state department of commerce and your local chamber of commerce will very likely have useful data on the local market of interest to you. Call to find out what is available.

Step 3. *Analyze and interpret the data.* The results of market research alone do not provide a solution; business owners must interpret the results. What does the data tell you? Is there a common thread running through the responses? Do the results suggest any changes needed in the way the business operates? Can the entrepreneur can take advantage of new opportunities? There are no hard-and-fast rules for interpreting market research results. Entrepreneurs must use judgment and common sense to determine what the results of their research mean.

Step 4. *Draw conclusions and act.* The market research process is not complete until the business owner acts on the information collected. In many cases, the conclusion is obvious once a small business owner interprets the results of the market research. Based on an understanding of what the facts really mean, the owner must then decide how to use the information in the business. For example, the owner of a small ladies' clothing boutique discovered from a survey that her customers preferred evening shopping hours over early morning hours. She made the schedule adjustment, and sales began to climb.

Plotting a Bootstrap Marketing Strategy: How to Build a Competitive Edge

LO4

Describe how a small business can build a competitive edge in the marketplace by using bootstrap marketing strategies.

To be successful bootstrap marketers, entrepreneurs must be as innovative in creating their marketing strategies as they are in developing new product and service ideas. Table 9.2 describes several low-cost, creative, and highly effective bootstrap marketing tactics small businesses have used to outperform their larger rivals.

Bootstrap Marketing Principles

The following 15 principles can help business owners create powerful, effective bootstrap marketing strategies.

FIND A NICHE AND FILL IT As you learned in Chapter 5, many successful small companies choose their niches carefully and defend them fiercely rather than compete head-to-head with larger rivals. A focus (niche) strategy allows a small company to maximize the advantages of its size and to compete effectively even in industries dominated by giants by serving its target customers better than its competitors. Thriving small companies often find success focusing on niches that are too small to be attractive to large companies.

ENTREPRENEURIAL PROFILE: Craig Rowe: ClearRisk ClearRisk, founded by Craig Rowe, is a company in St. Johns, Newfoundland, that develops risk and claims management apps for government entities and insurance companies around the globe. The company operates in a geographically diverse business-to-business market and relies on social media to reach customers within its narrowly defined niche strategy. The company uses Facebook to connect with its clients and its potential customers and does not use hard-sell tactics with social media. Instead, ClearRisk uses Facebook to disseminate valuable information to its niche market. It uses the contacts it generates on Facebook to make calls on potential customers, which is how the company measures its return on its Facebook marketing budget.[18] ■

USE THE POWER OF PUBLICITY **Publicity** is any commercial news covered by the media that boosts sales but for which a small company does not pay. Publicity has power; because it is from an unbiased source, a news feature about a company or a product that appears in a newspaper or magazine has more impact on people's buying decisions than an advertisement does. Exposure in any medium raises a company's visibility and boosts sales, and, best of all, publicity is free! It does require some creativity and effort, however.

publicity
any commercial news covered by the media that boosts sales but for which a company does not pay.

The following tactics can help entrepreneurs stimulate publicity for their companies:

Write an article that will interest your customers or potential customers. One marketing and advertising consultant writes a twice-monthly column for the local newspaper on useful topics such as "Unlocking the Mysteries of Big Data," "Advertising Strategies for Small Retailers," and "How CEOs Can Use Social Media." Not only do the articles help build his credibility as an expert, but they also have attracted new customers to his business. Do not focus all your writing on traditional media outlets. Outlets such as blogs provide a wide reach to a very targeted market.

Sponsor an event designed to attract attention. Divurgent Healthcare Advisors, located in Dallas, Texas, sponsors local charitable events for children's healthcare. For example, the company raises $5,000 a year for a children's hospital at an annual trade show, and its employees participate in other fundraisers for children's healthcare systems.

Involve celebrities "on the cheap." Few small businesses can afford to hire celebrities as spokespersons for their companies. Some companies have discovered other ways to get celebrities to promote their products, however. For instance, when the founders of Lookout Mobile Security were launching their company, they went to the Academy Awards and set up hardware to extend their Bluetooth signal to more than a mile. Using this technology, they identified all of the celebrities whose mobile devices were vulnerable to being hacked. The stunt got the new company considerable attention in the media. The company has since grown to more than 20 million customers.[19]

TABLE 9.2 Bootstrap Marketing Tactics

- Post on Facebook 5 to 10 times a week.
- Tweet 5 times a day on Twitter.
- Post on LinkedIn once a day.
- Upload photos to Instagram at least once a day.
- Build your own list of e-mails that you capture through your Web site, Facebook, and Twitter and send out e-mail messages once a week.
- Attend events where you are likely to find your customers and build relationships.
- Address all complaints on social media. It is an opportunity to show your brand's customer-service focus.
- Help organize and sponsor a service- or community-oriented project.
- Sponsor offbeat, memorable events. Build a giant banana split or rent a theater for a morning and invite kids for a free movie viewing.
- Offer to speak about your business, industry, product, or service to local organizations.
- Launch a loyalty program that gives customers a reason to return. Be sure to provide loyalty program members with benefits, such as special offers, discounts, shopping previews, and others.
- Reward existing customers for referring new customers to your company. When customers refer business to Choice Translating, a language translation company in Charlotte, North Carolina, they receive a special gift.
- Sell at every opportunity. One brewery includes a minicatalog advertising T-shirts and mugs in every six-pack it sells. Orders for catalog items are climbing fast.
- Develop a sales "script" that asks customers a series of questions to hone in on what they are looking for and what will lead them to the conclusion that your product or service is *it*!
- Sell gift cards. They really boost your cash flow.
- Create samples of your product or let customers try out your service.
- Offer a money-back, no-hassles guarantee. Removing the customer's risk of buying increases your product's attractiveness.
- Create a frequent-buyer program. Remember how valuable existing customers are. Work hard to keep the customers you have! One coffee shop kept its customers coming back with a punch-card promotion in which a customer earned a free pound of coffee after a purchasing nine pounds.
- Test how well your ads "pull" with specific landing pages tied to your Web site to see which ads work. Running an A/B test with different ads on Facebook is a highly effective way to learn what attracts customers.
- Write a blog about your industry—not your company—to reinforce your expertise (e.g., landscape tips on lawn maintenance).
- Find ways to make your product or service irresistible to your customers. One furniture company started e-mailing photos of big-ticket items customers are considering, and sales closing rates climbed 25 percent. This tactic also works on Instagram.
- Create a big event of your own: "January is customer appreciation month. Buy one suit and get a second one at 50 percent off."
- Conduct a contest in the community (e.g., a photographer sponsored a juried photo contest for different age groups). One restaurant that targeted the business crowd for lunch encouraged customers to leave their business cards (which gave the restaurateur the ability to e-mail them daily lunch specials) to enter a drawing for a free $50 iTunes gift card.
- Collect testimonials from satisfied customers and use them on your Web site and in Facebook ads. Testimonials are one of the most effective forms of advertising!
- Get a journalist to help you write a story "pitch" for local media and bloggers.
- Show an interest in your customers' needs. If you spot a seminar that would be of interest to them, e-mail or text them a message about it. Become a valuable resource for them.
- Find unique ways to thank customers, especially first-time buyers, for their business (e.g., a note, a lunch, a gift basket).
- Occasionally give loyal customers a "freebie." You might be surprised at how long they will remember it.
- Create a blog or page on your Web site that features your customers or clients and their businesses (e.g., a photo of a client using your product in his or her business).
- Work with other businesses that sell complementary products and services in marketing efforts and campaigns, a process called *fusion marketing*. Cooperate on e-mail marketing campaigns or work together on a special promotion.
- Use major competitors' coupons against them. The owner of an independent sandwich shop routinely pulled business from a nearby national chain by advertising that he would accept its coupons.
- Market your company's uniqueness. Many customers enjoy buying from small companies that are different and unique. The owners of the only tea plantation in the United States used that fact to their advantage in establishing a customer base.

Sources: Based on Prateek Shah, "10 Affordable Digital Marketing Tips for an Ecommerce Startup," *DigitalDefynd*, January 18, 2016, http://digitaldefynd.com/2016/01/18/how-to-market-a-bootstrapped-ecommerce-startup/; Derek Miller, "8 Digital-Marketing Tips for Bootstrapped Start-ups," *Entrepreneur*, March 10, 2015, www.entrepreneur.com/article/243009; Elisah Harwig, "7 Marketing Tips for Bootstrapped Startups," *Mashable*, June 3, 2013, http://mashable.com/2013/06/03/marketing-startup/#mVkZYzNNhmq1; Mickey Meece, "How to Keep Momentum Going for Customers and Employees," *New York Times*, January 3, 2008, www.nytimes.com/2008/01/03/business/smallbusiness/03tips.html; Jay Conrad Levinson, "Attention Getters," *Entrepreneur*, March 1998, p. 88; Lynn Beresford, Janean Chun, Cynthia E. Griffin, Heather Page, and Debra Phillips, "Marketing 101," *Entrepreneur*, May 1996, pp. 104–114; Guen Sublette, "Marketing 101," *Entrepreneur*, May 1995, pp. 86–98; Denise Osburn, "Bringing Them Back for More," *Nation's Business*, August 1995, p. 31R; Jay Conrad Levinson, "Survival Tactics," *Entrepreneur*, March 1996, p. 84; Tom Stein, "Outselling the Giants," *Success*, May 1996, pp. 38–41; and Gwen Moran, "Get Noticed," *Entrepreneur*, October 2008, pp. 58–61.

Contact local television and radio stations and offer to be interviewed. Many local news or talk shows are looking for guests to talk about topics of interest to their audiences (especially in January and February). Even local shows can reach new customers.

Publish a newsletter. With a personal computer and desktop publishing software, any entrepreneur can publish a professional-looking newsletter. Freelancers can offer design and editing advice. Use the newsletter to provide timely and useful information to existing and potential customers.

Contact local business and civic organizations and offer to speak to them. A powerful, informative presentation can win new business. (Be sure your public speaking skills are up to par first! If they're not, consider joining Toastmasters.)

Offer or sponsor a seminar. Teaching people about a subject you know a great deal about builds confidence and goodwill among potential customers. The owner of a landscaping service and nursery offers a short course in landscape architecture and always sees sales climb afterward.

Write news releases and e-mail them to the media. The key to having a news release picked up and printed is finding a unique angle on your business or industry that would interest an editor. Keep it short, simple, and interesting. E-mail press releases should be shorter than printed ones—typically four or five paragraphs rather than one or two pages—and they should include a link to the company's Web site.

Volunteer to serve on community and industry boards and committees. You can make your town a better place to live and work and raise your company's visibility at the same time.

Sponsor a community project or support a nonprofit organization or charity. Not only will you be giving something back to the community, but you will also gain recognition, goodwill, and, perhaps, customers for your business. The key is to partner with charities that match the company's values and mission, whether that involves rescuing homeless pets or providing back-to-school supplies for underprivileged kids. Sweetwater Brewery in Atlanta, Georgia, sponsors an annual bike ride that raises money for Camp Twin Lake, a camp providing life-changing experiences to children facing serious illnesses, disabilities, and other life challenges.[20]

Courtesy of Sweetwater Brewing Co.

Promote a cause. According to the Cone Communications Social Impact Study, 90 percent of customers (compared to only 66 percent of customers in the study conducted twenty years earlier) say that, other things being equal, they are likely to switch from one brand to another if the other brand is associated with a good cause.[21] By engaging in cause marketing, entrepreneurs can support a worthy cause that is important to them and generate publicity and goodwill for their companies at the same time. The key is choosing a cause that is important to your customers. One marketing expert offers the following formula for selecting the right cause: mission statement + personal passion + customer demographics = ideal cause.[22]

ENTREPRENEURIAL PROFILE: Michael Houlihan and Bonnie Harvey: Barefoot Cellars When Michael Houlihan and Bonnie Harvey launched their San Francisco, California, winemaking company, Barefoot Cellars, they did not have the minimum of $100,000 to commit to advertising that the bigger retail stores require before stocking a new brand. To help gain awareness, Barefoot Cellars began to give away free wine to local nonprofits to support their fundraising events. The strategy worked. People enjoyed the new wine and appreciated the company supporting their favorite causes. As the company expanded into new markets, it continued to use the same strategy. As its primary market entry strategy, Barefoot Cellars hired staff to find nonprofits to support in each new market. After becoming a national brand, the founders sold Barefoot Cellars to E&J Gallo.[23] ■

DON'T JUST SELL; ENTERTAIN Numerous surveys have shown that consumers are bored with shopping and that they are less inclined to spend their scarce leisure time shopping than ever before. Winning customers today requires more than low prices and wide merchandise selection; increasingly, businesses are adopting strategies based on entertailing, the notion of drawing customers into a store by creating a kaleidoscope of sights, sounds, smells, and activities, all designed to entertain—and, of course, sell (think Disney). The primary goal of entertailing is to catch customers' attention and engage them in some kind of entertaining experience so that they shop longer and buy more goods or services. Entertailing involves "making [shopping] more fun, more educational, more interactive," says one retail consultant.[24]

Courtesy of Blendtec

Social media, particularly those that incorporate video, are excellent vehicles for engaging and entertaining a company's online customers. Businesses spend more than $4 billion each year on online video advertising. A video that stands out, is "liked," and is shared with others must be entertaining. For instance, Tom Dickson, CEO and founder of Blendtec, stars in a series of YouTube videos where he sticks a variety of objects into a Blendtec blender to demonstrate its power and durability. Dickson has put an iPhone, glow sticks, a crowbar, golf balls, an iPad, Bic lighters, and a can of Spam in a Blendtec Total Blender to answer the question, "Will it blend?" Many of the videos receive millions of views. The ads have helped grow the company from a start-up to an industry leader employing more than 450 people.[25] When creating online videos, entrepreneurs should employ the following principles:

- *Think "edutainment."* Some of the most successful online videos combine both educational content and entertainment.

- *Be funny.* A common denominator among many successful online videos is humor. For businesses, the key is to link the humor in the video to the company's product or service and its customer benefits.

- *Post videos on multiple social media sites.* Potential customers are more likely to see a video and share it with others when a company makes it available through multiple social media sites, such as Facebook and Twitter.

- *Involve your customers.* Some small businesses have delegated the task of creating videos that promote their companies to their customers. Doing so not only allows them to sidestep the cost and technical issues of creating videos (create a contest!) but also engages their customers and connects them with the company in unique ways.

- *Keep it short.* For a video to produce maximum benefit, it should be between one and three minutes long.

Successful entertailers rely on the following principles:

- *Sponsor events that will attract your target customers.* One goal of entertailing is to get potential customers into the store. An upscale men's clothing store could offer a workshop on personal finance and investing or how to pull off "business casual" dress appropriately.

- *Transform an offbeat holiday into an entertailing event.* Did you know that October 28 is National Chocolate Day or that October 18 is National Chocolate Cupcake Day? Almost every day of the year is designated as a "holiday" to celebrate something unusual, such as National Eat Ice Cream for Breakfast Day, which takes place on the first Saturday in February. Pick one and create a special event around it.

- *Give customers the opportunity to interact with your products.* One golf store has an indoor putting green where customers can try out new putters before buying them.

A sporting goods retailer has a 20-foot rock wall that allows climbing enthusiasts to test climbing gear.

- *Use technology creatively.* A golf equipment retailer uses a simulator that allows customers to "play" some of the world's most famous courses, and a game retailer draws customers into its store by providing a virtual reality game experience for them. A landscape architect uses computer software that allows him to landscape digital photographs of his customers' homes so that they can see exactly how different designs look.

- *Remember that the ultimate goal is to sell.* No matter which entertailing techniques you decide to use, remember to design them with the goal of increasing sales.[26]

STRIVE TO BE UNIQUE One of the most effective bootstrap marketing tactics is to create an image of uniqueness for your business. As you learned in Chapter 5, entrepreneurs can achieve a unique place in the market in a variety of ways, including through the products and services they offer, the marketing and promotional campaigns they use, the store layouts they design, and the business strategies they employ. The goal is to stand out from the crowd. Few things are as uninspiring to customers as a "me-too" business that offers nothing unique. Table 9.3 offers suggestions on ways a retail store can stand out from the competition. Sami Bayrakci started his unique business, the Something Store, in 2008 after a fruitless search for just the right gift for a friend. At the Something Store, customers pay $10 and receive "something" (a randomly selected gift from the company's large inventory) guaranteed to be worth at least $10. Intrigued by the mystique, nearly 300,000 intrepid shoppers have received everything from electronics and toys to wallets and watches.[27]

BUILD A COMMUNITY WITH CUSTOMERS Some of the most successful companies interact with their customers regularly, intentionally, and purposefully to create meaningful, lasting relationships with them. Etsy, an e-commerce Web site that offers handmade or vintage items and art and craft supplies, has fueled growth by connecting its customers into communities referred to as "teams." Etsy has teams that include artists with a common interest (one team of almost 400 is focused on miniature clay foods), customers from a common city (the Des Moines, Iowa, team has 1,689 members), and teams that cross interests and locations (sustainable fashion designers in Seattle, Washington, has 50 members). The teams help each other promote their goods and expand their offerings sold through the Etsy Web site.[28]

Company Web sites and social media also are important tools for building a community with customers. Tyler Rex, owner of Brendan's Irish Pub, used Facebook to build a list of 3,500 fans before the restaurant opened. Rex continues to use Facebook to generate buzz for parties, sell merchandise, and promote various events. Burt's Bees uses Facebook to create new products interactively with its customers. Pacific Bioscience Laboratories, the maker of Clarisonic face brushes, shows customers how to use the product on its Facebook page and conducts a contest to encourage customers to send photos of themselves using a Clarisonic brush. Pacific Bioscience pledged to donate $1 to charity for each new "like" on Facebook, and the effort raised $30,000 to help women with cancer.[29]

CONNECT WITH CUSTOMERS ON AN EMOTIONAL LEVEL Closely linked to building a community with customers is the strategy of creating an emotional attachment with them. Companies that establish a deeper relationship with their customers than one based merely on making a sale have the capacity to be exceptional bootstrap marketers. These businesses win because customers receive an emotional boost every time they buy these companies' products or services. They connect with their customers emotionally by providing captivating products, supporting causes that are important to their customer base, taking exceptional care of their customers, surpassing customers' expectations in quality and service, or making doing business with them an enjoyable experience. Building and nurturing an ongoing relationship with customers establishes a relationship of trust, a vital component of every marketing effort.

The goal is not only to create loyal customers but also to transform customers into passionate brand advocates, people who promote a company's products or services to friends, family members, and others. A recent global poll conducted by The Nielsen Company finds that 84 percent of consumers trust recommendations from family and friends the most when making

TABLE 9.3 Seven Principles That Make Your Shop Pop

Pamela Danziger, president of the marketing consulting firm Unity Marketing, describes seven principles that can transform any store into a shop that "pops."

1. *Offer high levels of customer involvement and interaction.* When customers have the opportunity to interact with a product, they spend more time in the store, which increases the probability that they will buy something. Convenience stores that offer hot food have found that almost 9 out of 10 customers regularly come inside to purchase hot foods, with 44 percent indicating that they're buying hot food more often now than a year ago. Getting them to leave the gas pumps and come inside increases sales per customer and boosts profitability.

2. *Evoke shoppers' curiosity to explore with unique displays, store layout, and selection of merchandise.* One jewelry store captured the attention of passersby with a window display that featured not only unique pieces of jewelry but also a collection of interesting fossils, crystals, geodes, and unusual rock formations. The display increased the number of walk-in shoppers and sales.

3. *Exude a contagious air of excitement, energy, and "electricity."* Warby Parker stores seek to bring together product, lifestyle, and experience. As they browse throughout its retail store, customers are encouraged to download a map of interesting destinations across the United States, along with a customized Spotify playlist of new music, as they look at the latest styles in eyewear.

4. *Create a synergistic convergence of atmosphere, store design, and merchandise that results in a special place for customers.* The goal is to create a "paradox environment," one that offers customers displays and products they expect but also surprises them with something that is unique and unusual, even bizarre. To promote a new loyalty card program called Sprize with the tagline "Turning shopping on its head," a Gap store in London surprised shoppers by displaying 32 mannequins suspended from the ceiling upside down and arranged for three cars and a hot dog stand parked in front of the store to be flipped on their tops.

5. *Provide an authentic values-driven experience.* Godfrey's Welcome to Dogdom, a pet boutique located in Mohnton, Pennsylvania, sees the world from a dog's point of view and stocks a full line of dog-related products, ranging from essentials such as specialty foods, health-related products, and pet care items to luxuries such as hand-cast stone sculptures, cast bronze statues, dog apparel, and healthy fresh-baked dog biscuits in a multitude of flavors. Customers can book their pets for a doggie play group or schedule family time with their pets at one of the store's play parks. Special events such as a Valentine's Day Whine and Dine Brunch, a Pooch Smooch Easter photography session, and a Howl-o-ween Pawrade and Pawty keep customers and their beloved pets coming back to Godfrey's.

6. *Provide a price–value model that customers understand and support.* Businesses that show customers the value their products provide create a good value proposition without having to resort to price cuts. "Our focus is on solutions to our customers' problems and issues with their dogs and is not based on commodity price and product selling," says Barb Emmett of Godfrey's Welcome to Dogdom.

7. *Maintain a friendly, welcoming store that gives customers a reason to return.* In some stores, salespeople act as if they are doing customers a favor by waiting on them. Stores that pop take the opposite approach, welcoming customers and treating them as if they are important (because they are!). At an Arby's franchise in Camp Hill, Pennsylvania, 89-year-old Pearl Weaver greets customers with waving pom-poms, a big smile, and a happy "Welcome to Arby's." The store's manager, Christian Stakes, says not a week goes by without "Miz Pearl," as customers affectionately call her, being mentioned in online and in-store customer satisfaction surveys. "If she's off for a week, people ask about her," he says.

The goal is to create a store with "soul" that engages customers on many different levels; that creates a fun, festive atmosphere; and that has a mission that goes far beyond merely selling products.

Sources: Based on Paula Holewa, "Does Your Shop Pop?" *JCK*, January 13, 2011, www.jckonline.com/blogs/retail-details/2011/01/13/does-your-shop-pop; "Hot Foodservice Boosts Sales, Profits," *CSP Industry News*, September 29, 2016, www.cspdailynews.com/category-news/foodservice/articles/hot-foodservice-boosts-sales-profits; "20 Ideas Worth Stealing in 2016," *National Retail Federation*, January 13, 2016, https://nrf.com/news/20-ideas-worth-stealing-2016; Pam Danzinger, "A Shop That Pops: How Godfrey's, a Pet Boutique, Creates the Ultimate Customer Experience," Unity Marketing, Shops That Pop, www.shopsthatpop.com/cms/Home_Page/White_Papers_Articles.php; Pam Danzinger, "Does Your Shop Pop?" *Shops That Pop*, www.shopsthatpop.com/cms/Home_Page/White_Papers_Articles.php; Glen Stansberry, "10 Examples of Shockingly-Excellent Customer Service," *American Express OPEN Forum*, May 4, 2010, www.openforum.com/idea-hub/topics/managing/article/10-examples-of-shockingly-excellent-customer-service-1; and Lara Brenckle, "Camp Hill Woman, 89, Hands Out Cheers with Sandwiches at Fast-Food Restaurant," *PennLive*, August 10, 2009, www.pennlive.com/midstate/index.ssf/2009/08/camp_hill_woman_89_hands_out_c.html.

unique selling proposition (USP)
a key customer benefit of a product or service that sets it apart from the competition; it answers the critical question every customer asks: "What's in it for me?"

a purchasing decision.[30] Another survey conducted by Word of Mouth Marketing Association and the American Marketing Association (AMA) finds that 64 percent of marketing executives believe word of mouth is the most effective form of marketing.[31] The growth of social media and the growing distrust of the messages in traditional advertising have increased the importance of knowing how to encourage consumers to talk about products through word of mouth.

One important aspect of connecting with customers is defining the company's **unique selling proposition (USP)**, a key customer benefit of a product or service that sets it apart from its competition. To be effective, a USP must actually *be* unique—something the competition does not (or cannot) provide—as well as compelling enough to encourage customers to buy. Unfortunately, many business owners never define their companies' USP, and the result is an uninspiring me-too message that cries out "buy from us" without offering customers any compelling reason to do so.

A successful USP answers the critical question that every customer asks: "What's in it for me?" A USP should express in no more than 10 words what a business can do for its customers. Can your product or service save your customers time or money, make their lives easier or more convenient, improve their self-esteem, or make them feel better? If so, you have the foundation for building a USP. For instance, Toms donates a pair of shoes to an impoverished child for every pair of shoes it sells. Toms also sells eyewear and donates to a charity that helps restore sight to people in developing countries. Toms has a simple but clear USP: "One for one." Saddleback Leather, a maker of high-end leather bags, has a USP that communicates the quality of its products: "They'll Fight Over It When You're Dead." Naomi Dunford, founder of IttyBiz, a marketing consulting firm that helps small companies with no more than five employees create bootstrap marketing strategies, says her company's USP is "Marketing for businesses without marketing departments."[32]

The best way to identify a meaningful USP that connects a company to its target customers is to describe the primary benefit(s) its product or service offers customers. A business is unlikely to have more than three primary benefits, which should be unique and able to set it apart. The fewer the number of primary benefits that a company focuses on, the more intense the connection with those benefits will be. When describing the top benefits the company offers its customers, entrepreneurs must look beyond just the physical characteristics of the product or service. Sometimes the most powerful USP emphasizes the *intangible*, *psychological*, and *emotional* benefits a product or service offers customers—for example, safety, "coolness," security, acceptance, and status. The goal is to use the USP to enable a company to stand out in customers' minds.

It is also important to develop a brief list of facts that support your company's USP, such as 24-hour service, a fully trained staff, awards won, and so on. By focusing the message on these top benefits and the facts supporting them, business owners can communicate their USPs to their target audiences in meaningful, attention-getting ways. Building a firm's marketing message around its core USP spells out for customers the specific benefit they get if they buy that product or service and why they should do business with your company rather than with the competition. Finally, once a small company begins communicating its USP to customers, it has to fulfill the promise! Nothing erodes a company's credibility quite like promising customers a benefit and then failing to deliver on that promise.

Many small companies are finding common ground with their customers on an issue that is becoming increasingly important to many people: the environment. Small companies selling everything from jeans to toothpicks are emphasizing their "green" products and are making an emotional connection with their customers in the process. Companies must be truthful, however, or their marketing pitches can backfire and damage their reputations. Consumers are becoming more vigilant in their search for companies that are guilty of "greenwashing," touting unsubstantiated or misleading claims about the environmental friendliness of their products. Customers feel good about doing business with companies that manufacture products according to green principles, support environmental causes, donate a portion of their pre-tax earnings to philanthropic organizations, and operate with a clear sense of fulfilling their social responsibility.

CREATE AN IDENTITY FOR YOUR BUSINESS THROUGH BRANDING One of the most effective ways for an entrepreneur to differentiate his or her business from the competition is to create a unique identity for it through **branding**. Although most entrepreneurs may not have the resources to build a brand name as well known as Google (Google's brand is estimated to be worth more than $109 billion), they can be successful in building a brand identity for their companies on a smaller scale in the markets they serve.[33] A large budget is not a prerequisite for building a strong brand, but creating one does take a concerted, well-coordinated effort that connects every touch point a company has with its customers with the company's desired image. A strong brand evokes the company's story in customers' minds.[34]

branding
communicating a company's unique selling proposition (USP) to its target customers in a consistent and integrated manner.

FIGURE 9.2

The Connection Between Branding and a USP

Source: Based on Brand-Savvy, Highlands Ranch, Colorado.

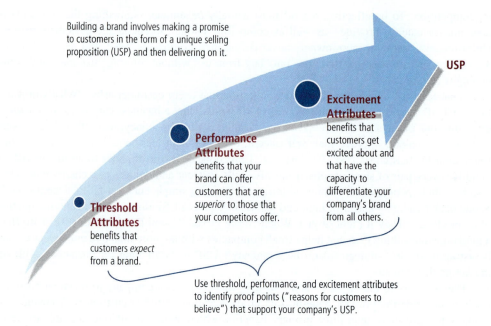

Building a brand involves making a promise to customers in the form of a unique selling proposition (USP) and then delivering on it.

USP

Excitement Attributes
benefits that customers get excited about and that have the capacity to differentiate your company's brand from all others.

Performance Attributes
benefits that your brand can offer customers that are *superior* to those that your competitors offer.

Threshold Attributes
benefits that customers *expect* from a brand.

Use threshold, performance, and excitement attributes to identify proof points ("reasons for customers to believe") that support your company's USP.

Branding involves communicating a company's unique selling proposition to its target customers in a consistent and integrated manner. A brand is a company's "face" in the marketplace, and it is built on a company's promise of providing quality goods or services to satisfy multiple customer needs. A brand sends an important message to customers: It signals that the benefits a company offers (which may be intangible) are worth more than those its competitors can offer. Companies that build brands successfully benefit from increased customer loyalty, the ability to command higher prices, greater visibility, and increased name recognition. Small companies that attempt to lure customers with discounts or constant sales often dilute their brands and cheapen them in the customers' eyes. Figure 9.2 shows the connection between a company's brand and its unique selling proposition.

EMBRACE SOCIAL MARKETING Although social networking sites such as Facebook and Twitter are better known for their personal applications, they also have significant potential as marketing tools. Seventy-six percent of Internet users participate in at least one social networking site, more than double the 34 percent in 2008.[35] Businesses recognize that many of their current and potential customers use social networking sites and are reaching out to them with social marketing efforts. A recent survey of small business owners with 10 or fewer employees finds that 96 percent use social media marketing, and 92 percent of those believe that social media marketing is important for their businesses.[36] Figure 9.3 shows the social media tools most commonly used by entrepreneurs. Most marketers find that social media is not a highly effective means of generating sales. Instead, social media is much more effective as a means of building awareness for a company and its brand, driving traffic to a company's Web site, generating leads, and improving Internet search rankings (see Figure 9.4). Companies still must use marketing tactics such as e-mail marketing and personal selling to generate new customers. Social media helps increase awareness, but in most cases, additional marketing and sales efforts are necessary.

Small companies use a variety of social networking tools to market their companies, including Facebook, Twitter, LinkedIn, and YouTube:

Facebook. Facebook has more than 1.94 billion active users, and the average time these users are active on the site is about 50 minutes each day.[37] Creating a Facebook business page is not the same as creating a personal profile page, however. On Facebook, an entrepreneur should create a welcome page that is designed to create interest in the company's products or services and that encourages visitors to "like" the business. Businesses can generate "likes" by posting the Facebook URL on in-store signs, business cards, shopping

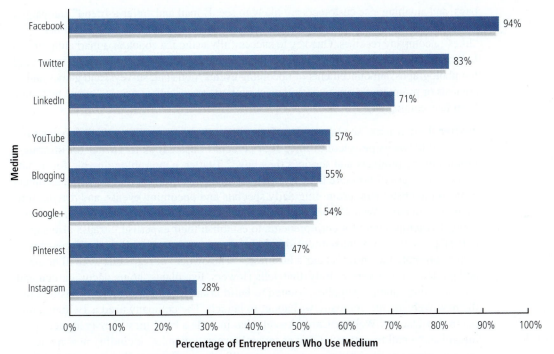

FIGURE 9.3

Social Media Entrepreneurs Use as Marketing Tools

Source: Based on Michael Stelzner, "2016 Social Media Marketing Industry Report," *Social Media Examiner*, May 2016, p. 23.

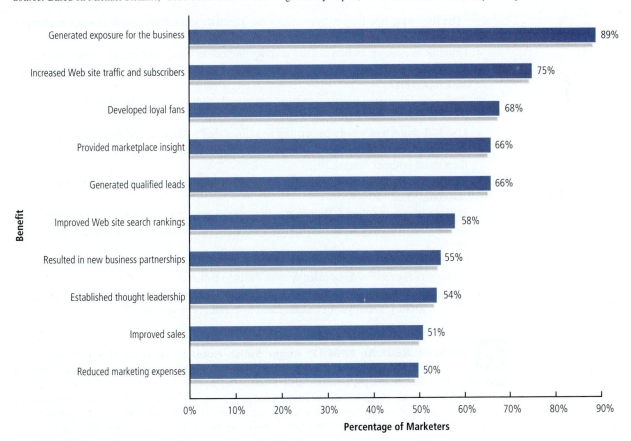

FIGURE 9.4

Benefits of Social Media Marketing

Source: Based on Michael Stelzner, "2016 Social Media Marketing Industry Report," *Social Media Examiner*, May 2016, p. 17.

bags, and anything else customers are likely to see. E-mail and "refer-a-friend" campaigns and links to Facebook from a company's Web site and blog also increase the number of "likes" a company receives. One key to successfully using Facebook as a marketing tool is to keep a company's page fresh, just like the merchandise displays in a physical store. Adding photographs, announcements of upcoming events, polls and surveys, and games and contests or promoting a cause the company supports are excellent ways to create buzz and keep fans coming back.

Twitter. Twitter users send more than 500 million tweets every day, which equates to about 6,000 tweets per second! Fifty-four percent of users look to Twitter for information about the products and services they buy.[38] Twitter, a microblogging platform that allows messages of no more than 140 characters, is ideal for interacting with customers or potential customers, promoting daily specials and upcoming events, and driving traffic to a company's Web site or blog. Small business expert Steve Strauss recommends using Twitter as a way for entrepreneurs to establish their expertise. Strauss also says that 80 percent of content sent out should be about customers, while only 20 percent should promote the entrepreneur's business.[39] The owners of Agricola, a small home and garden shop in Varese, Italy, that sells flowers, live plants, home décor, garden and outdoor items, and pet supplies, wanted to build brand awareness and drive visitors to the new Web site the company was about to launch. The company used a Twitter campaign that featured Website Cards (tweets that include a brief message, an attractive image, and a call to action) aimed at several target audiences, including new homeowners, young online shoppers, women over 40 who are interested in home décor, and men who are interested in gardening and organic food. The eye-catching Twitter campaign was a success, resulting in 210 times more visits to the company's Web site than before.[40]

The following tips help entrepreneurs use Twitter successfully as a bootstrap marketing tool:
- Commit to making Twitter a daily activity, including liking and sharing others' tweets, sending original tweets, posting direct messages, following new accounts, and thanking new followers.
- Although automated tweets using various social media tools can be effective, make sure to include "manual" tweets, as well.
- Use 140 characters wisely by writing headlines that will catch people's attention.
- Include images in your tweets. Tweets with images receive 150 percent more retweets than those without images.[41]
- Connect with others as a person, not as a brand. Twitter users want to talk with people, not companies.
- Engage in conversations. Twitter is a two-way communication tool, not an outlet for sending one-way messages. (That's what press releases and marketing copy are for.)
- Give people a reason to follow you. Reveal the "inside story" of your company, ask customers for feedback, or offer special deals to followers.
- Link Twitter to your company's Web site. Refer followers to your company's Web site, blog, or a video about your company and its products or services.[42]

ENTREPRENEURIAL PROFILE: Roger Smith Hotel Roger Smith Hotel is a boutique property in the heart of Manhattan that offers highly personalized service. Each room is decorated in a different style and features a library of books chosen by hotel employees. The hotel used Twitter to build initial awareness for the property. Hotel management invited key journalists and social media influencers to try out the hotel at no cost and encouraged them to share their experiences via Twitter. The hotel continues to use Twitter as its primary form of promotion. Its Twitter feed includes fun facts and trivia, coupons, and pictures showing the sights of New York City. Roger Smith Hotel offers discounts to customers who reserve a room via Twitter, and the lobby of the hotel features a Twitter kiosk to encourage customers to tweet about their experiences at the hotel.[43] ∎

You Be the Consultant

Auto Repair Goes Social

Victory Auto Service and Glass, founded in 1997 by Jeff Matt, built its base of loyal customers with strong personal relationships. Personal customer service is at the heart of Victory Auto's business model. The company has five locations and a mobile auto glass service in the Minneapolis, Minnesota, metro area.

As the business grew from its first location, Matt found that maintaining the personal relationships with his customers, which was the core of his company's success, became more difficult to maintain. Matt decided to turn to social media to complement face-to-face connections with Victory Auto's customers and sought the help of Stephanie Gutierrez, a communications specialist and loyal customer, to help create a social media strategy for Victory Auto.

Gutierrez experimented with various social media tactics until she found a strategy that supported the personal connection with customers that Matt relied on to build his company. Facebook is the heart of Victory Auto's social media strategy. When Gutierrez developed the company's Facebook page, at first, she posted longer articles with links to articles about cars. However, these posts did not seem to register with the typical customer. Then she took the time to think like the business's average customer: car owners who were not necessarily interested in cars. Customers typically interact with Victory Auto because they have to, not because they want to. Instead of creating a page with information on cars, Gutierrez adds posts related to traffic, commuting, and travel that everyone who owns a car would be interested in reading. She posts much shorter text entries that are written in a personal style with many photos.

The second major aspect of Victory Auto's social media strategy involves YouTube videos. Gutierrez developed several short videos that are geared toward people who do not know much about cars. The videos on Victory Auto's YouTube channel include short how-to videos and tours of its various store locations around Minneapolis. Its most popular video is one that shows how to top off windshield wiper fluid!

Matt believes that success in the auto service business is based on trust and that trust is built by getting to know the people who work at Victory Auto. Many of the social media posts are about employees of Victory Auto, focusing on their birthdays, other celebrations, and day-to-day casual interactions while at work. About 20 percent of Victory Auto employees are active on Facebook. When they become Facebook and sometimes even personal friends with customers, they are encouraged to share photos on Facebook. These photos can then be tagged to help build more traffic at the Victory Auto Facebook page.

Victory Auto Glass uses social media to promote various charities, including Mothers Against Drunk Drivers and Toys for Tots. A local charity that Victory Auto is heavily involved with is Free2Be, which provides auto care and donated cars for economically disadvantaged people in Anoka County, Minnesota. Volunteers with Free2Be can use the repair bays at Victory Auto free of charge to repair donated cars. Victory Auto also gives free or discounted car repairs for people helped by the Free2Be program. Gutierrez posts some of these stories on the company's Facebook page to help promote the charity.

Results

Victory Auto has seen significant returns on its investment in social media:

- The company has opened two of its five locations since implementing its social media strategy.

- Most of the customers of the two newest locations heard about Victory Auto from word of mouth or online.

- More than 60 percent of fans and people "talking about" the company's Facebook page are female.

- Victory Auto became a certified female-friendly auto repair shop with AskPatty, a Web site that provides automotive advice for women.

- The company estimates that 50 to 60 percent of its customers are female, which is far above the industry average.

- Victory Auto has more than 1,200 "likes" on its Facebook page.

1. Identify at least three lessons that entrepreneurs can learn from Victory Auto's use of social media.

2. Work with a team of your classmates to select a local business that has no social media presence and develop a plan to boost its visibility, sales, and profits with a social media strategy.

3. Identify at least three additional bootstrap marketing strategies discussed in this chapter that Victory Auto can use to increase its visibility, sales, and profits. Explain how the company should implement each one.

Sources: Based on Louise Julig, "How an Auto Repair Shop Is Winning Female Customers with Social Media," *Social Media Examiner*, September 25, 2013, www.socialmediaexaminer.com/social-media-case-study-victory-auto/; "About Us," Victory Auto Service and Glass, n.d., www.victoryautoservice.com/AboutUs.html; "Victory Auto Service and Glass," Facebook, n.d., www.facebook.com/VictoryAutoService; "VictoryAutoService," YouTube, n.d., www.youtube.com/channel/UCsBv4zmSqaa4CrLXmN0jMTQ.

LinkedIn. To use LinkedIn as a marketing tool, entrepreneurs should create a personal profile that focuses on their role as owner of a business, send invitations to people with whom they have connections, join (or form) groups that are of interest to customers, and use Answers to demonstrate their expertise. LinkedIn is a good forum for generating leads and advice from like-minded business owners. Entrepreneurs should create a link to their company's Web sites, blog, and Twitter feed. They can also post upcoming events at their businesses and conduct polls among other LinkedIn users. The Updates feature allows users to share blog posts, newsletters, and other timely information.

YouTube. More than one billion people use YouTube, the popular video hosting site. YouTube gives creative entrepreneurs an opportunity to promote their businesses at no cost by creating videos that feature their products and services in action. Unlike running television ads, uploading videos to YouTube costs nothing, and in some cases, the videos reach millions of potential customers. Watching online videos is pervasive; YouTube reports that visitors watch almost 5 billion videos per day. More than half of YouTube visits are from mobile phones, and the average mobile viewing session lasts more than 40 minutes. Online video is highly engaging. Successful online video campaigns don't just educate and inform; they also entertain and engage customers. Although YouTube is still the most commonly used platform for videos, Facebook, Twitter, and Instagram offer alternative outlets for video content as well.

ENTREPRENEURIAL PROFILE: Eric Cook: EricTheCarGuy Eric Cook, who started his career as an Acura service technician, launched EricTheCarGuy in 2009 to help people solve their auto repair issues through the use of instructional videos on YouTube. Eric's YouTube channel includes low-production cost, how-to videos for all kinds of automotive repairs, question-and-answer sessions, and general advice for all car owners. Several of his videos have had millions of views, and his YouTube channel attracts more than 3 million visitors a month. Eric's Web site includes both free and subscription content.[44] ∎

Hands On . . . How To

Make Social Media Work for Your Business

Social media, such as Facebook, Twitter, LinkedIn, Snapchat, and YouTube, can be a vital and productive component of a company's bootstrap marketing strategy. Because a typical customer sees more than 300 advertising and sales messages *each day*, small businesses' marketing efforts, particularly their social media marketing efforts, must be well planned, consistent, and focused. Otherwise, they will become lost in a sea of ads, posts, tweets, and blogs.

The first key to a successful social media marketing strategy is understanding your customers and knowing where they are in the social media universe and what they expect from you. Entrepreneurs can use the following tips and success stories to develop a social media marketing strategy that works for their businesses:

Use social media to build buzz about your business before you launch. Building excitement about a business before it opens helps build sales more quickly once operations actually begin. Magic Leap, which is a start-up developing augmented and virtual reality systems, used social media to build awareness even before its products were ready for market. The company did not talk about the details of the product in the campaign due to concerns about protecting its intellectual property. Instead, the company published thought-provoking content through social media to build awareness of its brand and to build excitement about its launch. Before it began operations, Magic Leap amassed more than 60,000 "likes" on Facebook and more than 32,000 Twitter followers through its interactive and engaging social media content.

Use social media to level the playing field. One of the greatest advantages of using social media is its low cost, which means that large companies have no more of a marketing advantage than small businesses. Houlihan's Restaurants, a small restaurant chain based in Leawood, Kansas, doesn't have the budget to compete with national restaurants when it comes to traditional advertising. However, the company has had great success using social media to gain the attention of consumers and competes effectively in the cities where it operates its restaurants.

Build your brand—and your customer base—with social media. Einstein Bros. Bagels, a bagel, sandwich, and coffee chain with nearly 450 locations across the United States, had amassed 4,700 Facebook fans before launching a social media–based bagel giveaway promotion during the fall. Customers responded and within one week, the number of fans

(continued)

Hands On . . . How To

had increased to 300,000. When Einstein Bros. repeated the promotion on Facebook the following spring, its fan base jumped to more than 600,000. Today, Einstein Bros. boasts more than 750,000 Facebook fans, who ask about new products and upcoming promotions, post photos of themselves (and their pets) enjoying Einstein Bros. bagels, and respond to questions the company posts on its Facebook Wall.

Remember that no matter what media you use to promote your business, no one really cares what you do; potential customers care only about what you can do for them. One of the greatest advantages for small businesses that use social media is the ability to naturally showcase their uniqueness, their informal culture, and their staff's passion for what they do. Once prospects understand the value that a company's products or services hold for them, selling to them becomes much easier. Use social media to showcase the results your company can create for customers.

Be creative in your social media promotions. Using a creative Facebook campaign, California Tortilla, a 26-unit restaurant chain in Rockville, Maryland, increased the number of its Facebook fans by 50 percent and generated a 10 percent increase in same-store sales—and it cost less than $700. The company offered a free order of chips and queso to its Facebook fans but promised to upgrade the offer to a free taco if its fan base reached 13,000 people. The viral nature of social media took over, and California Tortilla ended up with more than 16,000 "likes."

Listen before you talk. Success with social media marketing requires a different approach than traditional advertising, which relies primarily on one-way communication, telling your audience about your business and its products and services. Social media marketing requires that businesses *listen* before they engage their audience in a two-way conversation. Mari Luangrath, owner of Foiled Cupcakes, an upscale cupcake bakery in Chicago, has no physical storefront for her business yet manages to sell 1,000 dozen cupcakes each month at an average price of $38 per dozen. Luangrath says she developed 94 percent of her customer base by using social media marketing tools, especially Twitter. Her strategy is to identify online conversations about food, baking, and cupcakes that she and her employees can join naturally and build trust by providing useful content and comments. She is not concerned with the breadth of her company's marketing reach—she only wants to reach people who are truly interested in her business. Luangrath also has joined groups of Chicago administrative professionals—the people who plan office parties and events—on LinkedIn and posts useful articles for them. By engaging them on LinkedIn, she has developed several new customers for her business.

Use social media to reward loyal customers, fans, followers, and promoters of your brand. Jordan Zweigoron, founder and "chief psycho" of Psycho Donuts, a doughnut shop in Campbell, California, that sells uniquely flavored doughnuts served by employees wearing nurse uniforms, uses Fanminder, a mobile marketing service that allows businesses to send text messages containing special offers and promotions to customers who opt in. The company also uses Twitter to reward its loyal customers, but Zweigoron says Psycho Donuts's Fanminder offers generate a response that is three to four times greater than its Twitter promotions.

Use online video to show off your products and services. Television advertisers have known for decades that video is the ideal way to show people how a product or service works. Social media sites such as YouTube give even the smallest businesses the opportunity to show their products and services in action at minimal cost. Squatty Potty is a device that supports proper posture when using a toilet. More than 28 million people viewed the company's video of a colorful unicorn pooping ice cream. As another example, Kayla Itsines attracted millions of subscribers for her online video workouts through the short sample workout video clips she posts on YouTube.

Give customers a reason to tune in to your business. Create a destination by posting fresh content and promoting upcoming specials, sales, and events. Resist the tendency to let the hectic nature of your schedule drive out the time necessary to make social marketing work for your business. To make social media marketing pay off, entrepreneurs must make social media marketing a regular part of their work schedules.

Use social media to encourage your customers to talk— and then listen. Social media is ideal for engaging customers in two-way conversations.

Use analytics to measure your company's social media results. Entrepreneurs should measure the results of their social media marketing efforts so that they know which ones work best. Social media marketing efforts are always evolving, and entrepreneurs need useful feedback on their results. Many tools are available to measure success, but many of the standards that fit traditional advertising media, such as sales leads, sales, Web site traffic, customer engagement and retention, and profits, apply to social media.

Sources: Based on Jayson Demers, "5 Startups That Are Killing It with Social Media Marketing," *Entrepreneur*, July 21, 2016, www.entrepreneur.com/article/279120; Kristen DeCosta, "5 Entrepreneurs Successfully Selling on YouTube," *Selz Blog*, September 2016, https://selz.com/blog/5-entrepreneurs-successfully-selling-youtube/; Heidi Cohen, "How to Jump into the Social Media Pool Without Drowning," *SmartBlogs*, May 10, 2011, http://smartblogs.com/socialmedia/2011/05/10/how-to-jump-into-the-social-media-pool-without-drowning; Courtney Jeffries, "How 3 Brands Generate Buzz by Employing Social Technologies," *Social Media Club*, August 24, 2011, http://socialmediaclub.org/blogs/from-the-clubhouse/social-business-snapshot-how-3-brands-generate-buzz-employing-social-techno; Jason Ankeny, "Social Climbers," *Entrepreneur*, January 2011, pp. 116–123; Lisa Nicole Bell, "3 Rules for Selling in the New Economy," *Reuters*, January 10, 2011, http://blogs.reuters.com/small-business/2011/01/10/3-rules-for-selling-in-the-new-economy; Mark Brandau, "California Tortilla: Lessons Learned from Facebook Promo," *Nation's Restaurant News*, March 30, 2011, www.nrn.com/article/california-tortilla-lessons-learned-facebook-promo; Brian Quinton, "Baking, Listening, and Selling," *Entrepreneur*, February 2011, pp. 60–61; Jason Ankeny, "Crazy for Mobile Deals," *Entrepreneur*, October 2010, pp. 40–41; Kermit Pattison, "Online Video Offers Low-Cost Marketing for Your Company," *New York Times*, March 16, 2011, www.nytimes.com/2011/03/17/business/smallbusiness/17sbiz.html; and April Joyner, "Social Networking: Who's Talking About You?" *Inc.*, September 2010, pp. 63–64.

BLOG A blog (Web log) is a frequently updated online journal that contains a writer's ideas on a particular topic or area and links to related sites. Business blogging can be an effective part of a bootstrap marketing strategy, enabling small businesses to communicate with large numbers of potential customers economically. One recent survey reports that just 37 percent of the owners of small and medium-sized businesses have created blogs. The main reason business owners cite for not blogging? They lack the time.[45]

Blogs that attract the attention of existing and potential customers boost a company's visibility and sales. Companies post their blogs, promote them on their Web sites and in other social media, and then watch as the viral nature of the Internet takes over, with visitors posting comments and telling their friends about the blog. Many small companies allow customers to contribute to their blogs, offering the potential for one of the most valuable marketing tools: unsolicited endorsements from satisfied users. Blogging's informal dialogue is an ideal match for small companies whose culture and style are also casual. Linked to a company's other social media marketing efforts (such as Facebook, LinkedIn, and Twitter), a blog can serve as the social media hub for the business. Blogs can keep customers updated on new products, enhance customer service, and promote the company. If monitored regularly, blogs also can give entrepreneurs keen insight into their customers' viewpoints and preferences. Creating a blog is not risk free, however. Companies must be prepared to deal with negative feedback from some visitors. Common platforms for creating blogs include WordPress, Ghost, Drupal, Joomla, Medium, SquareSpace, Weebly, TypePad, Blogger, and Tumblr.

The following tips can help entrepreneurs implement a successful blogging strategy:

- *Develop a clear purpose for your blog.* The first step when establishing a new blog is to define the purpose of the blog; it may be industry related or even serve some higher purpose. The entrepreneur should align the purpose with the target market for the business. What are customers interested in? What do they care about?

- *Position the blog with other blogs that already exist.* Once the entrepreneur identifies the blog's purpose, he or she should evaluate other blogs that write about the same general topic or theme. A blog should create a niche that can make it both stand out and complement other blogs already in existence.

- *Focus on key words.* The trick to building awareness of a blog is to identify key words that will drive people to the site through searches. To be effective, the key words must be tied to the business and the industry.

- *Strive to cultivate the image of an expert or a trusted friend on a topic that is important to your customers.* In his blog, the owner of a company that installs water gardens posts tips for maintaining a healthy water garden and answers questions that his readers post.

- *Be patient.* Building up traffic and interest in a blog takes months. To be successful, an entrepreneur must be willing to commit to writing *at least* once a week for a long time before the blog generates traffic and, eventually, new business.

- *Be honest, balanced, and interesting when writing a blog.* High-pressure sales pitches do not work in the blogging world. Telling an interesting "inside story" about the company, its products or services, or some aspect of the business can help attract readers. However, experts recommend the 80–20 rule for posting topics: Keep 80 percent of the posts about more general topics related to your industry or about your customers and only 20 percent of the posts about your company.

- *Ask customers for feedback.* Blogs are powerful tools for collecting real-time market research inexpensively. It is easy to insert instant polls that allow readers to offer quick feedback.

- *Use services such as Google Alerts that scan the Internet for a company's name and send e-mail alerts for posts about a company.* Entrepreneurs must monitor the online "buzz" about their companies; if they discover negative comments, they can address the issues in their blogs.

- *Be cautious.* If you are blogging to promote your business, be careful what you write about. Avoid making negative comments about competitors, addressing controversial topics, or making unsubstantiated claims.

- *Promote the blog via social media and e-mail.* Other bloggers and journalists can help drive traffic to your blog. To encourage inbound traffic like this, bloggers share links to popular blogs that write about similar topics. In addition, successful bloggers push out blog posts via Twitter, Facebook, LinkedIn, and e-mail marketing software, and they include a link to the blog in e-mail signatures.[46]

BE DEDICATED TO SERVICE AND CUSTOMER SATISFACTION Many businesses have lost sight of the most important component of every business: the customer. Entrepreneurs must realize that everything in the business—even the business itself—depends on creating a satisfied customer. The rewards for providing excellent customer service are great, and the penalties for failing to do so are severe. Excellent customer service, as you learned in Chapter 4, is a key component of a company's business model but does not look the same for every business. Excellence in customer service means a company must meet the expectations its business model creates for customers. Excellent customer service may mean quick, efficient service, or it may mean absolute attention to customers' specific wants and needs. A survey by Harris Interactive reports that 55 percent of consumers have become customers of a company just because of the company's reputation for providing outstanding customer service. The study also reveals that 85 percent of customers are willing to pay extra (as much as 25 percent more) for products that are accompanied by excellent customer service.[47] Another Harris Poll reports that 80 percent of customers say they will never return to a business after a negative customer service experience.[48]

When a company delivers poor customer service, lost sales are only the beginning of the company's woes, however. Unhappy customers are likely to tell their poor service stories to family members and friends. The Harris Interactive survey also shows that 79 percent of customers who have negative customer service experiences tell others about them.[49] This negative word of mouth has a detrimental effect on the offending company. A study by the Jay H. Baker Retailing Initiative at University of Pennsylvania reports that 48 percent of shoppers say they will not patronize stores where they know that other customers have had bad service experiences.[50] Most of these customers never complain directly to the store; in fact, for every complaint a company receives, 17 other complaints go unspoken.[51] These disgruntled customers exact revenge over their poor treatment, however. These days, a company that provides poor service may find itself being panned on Yelp, Twitter, Facebook, a YouTube video, a blog, or a Web site. A survey by Lithium Technologies finds that 72 percent of people who make a complaint to a company via Twitter expect a response with one hour—no matter what time of day the tweet is sent. The following tips can help you more effectively address online comments, suggestions, and complaints:[52]

- *Humanize your responses.* On social media, customers prefer to interact with a person rather than just a company. When responding on Twitter to complaints, Virgin Mobile has its representatives include their names in all tweets.

- *Respond quickly.* Acknowledge all social media posts, especially complaints, within one hour. Even if it will take longer to answer a question or resolve a problem, it is important to send an initial response quickly to demonstrate concern about the customer's issue.

- *Respond publicly.* Keep all responses within the public communication channel of the social media to which the complaint is posted. The response may help other customers who have the same concern or problem. Keeping responses public shows all customers that the company is transparent and trustworthy.

- *Avoid a defensive tone when confronted with negative comments.* View the situation from the customer's perspective. Extend a sincere apology and fix the customer's problem. Do not argue with customers.

- *Set up alerts.* Social media monitoring tools, such as Social Mention, Hootsuite, and Topsy, allow a company to keep on top of all comments about its brand across the Internet.

Quick responses can prevent issues from getting out of hand, which can happen quickly, given the viral nature of social media.

- *Create a database of complaints and suggestions.* Smart entrepreneurs recognize that customer complaints and suggestions provide valuable feedback on their businesses. Monitoring them enables business owners to improve their companies over time.

Smart companies are rediscovering that unexpected, innovative, customized service can be a powerful marketing weapon. Perhaps the most effective marketing tool is a satisfied customer who becomes a passionate brand evangelist for a company. Providing incomparable service—not necessarily low prices—is one of the most effective ways to attract and maintain a growing customer base for companies with a business model that includes strong customer service. Smart entrepreneurs create reasonable expectations among their customers and then exceed them, knowing that those customers will generate positive buzz for the companies, which is more valuable and more effective than the most expensive advertising campaign.

Certainly the least expensive—and the most effective—way to achieve customer satisfaction is through friendly, personal service. Numerous surveys of customers in a wide diversity of industries—from manufacturing and services to banking and high tech—conclude that the most important element of service is "the personal touch." Calling customers by name; making attentive, friendly contact; and truly caring about their needs and wants is much more essential than any other factor—even convenience, quality, and speed! In our society, business transactions have become so automated that the typical customer is starved for personal attention. Genuine customer service requires that a business bridge that service gap, treat each customer as an individual, and transform "high-tech" applications into a "high-touch" attitude.

How can a company achieve stellar customer service and satisfaction? Here are some suggestions:

Listen to customers. The best companies constantly listen to their customers and respond to what they hear. This allows them to keep up with customers' changing needs and expectations. The best way to find out what customers really want and value is to ask them. Businesses rely on a number of techniques, including surveys, social media, focus groups, telephone interviews, comment cards, suggestion boxes, toll-free hotlines, and regular one-on-one conversations (perhaps the best technique). As discussed earlier, social media has become an invaluable tool for getting feedback from customers; many companies solicit complaints, suggestions, and ideas.

Keeping customer feedback in its proper perspective is important, however. Although listening to customers produces valuable feedback for business owners in many areas, it is *not* a substitute for an innovative company culture, solid market research, and a well-devised marketing plan. Companies that rely solely on their customers to guide their marketing efforts often find themselves lagging the competition. Customers rarely have the foresight to anticipate market trends and do not always have a clear view of how new products or services could satisfy their needs.

Define customer service expectations. Based on what customers say, entrepreneurs must decide exactly what expectations customers have regarding service. If customer service is important, the company should have a customer service statement that should (1) be a strong statement of intent, (2) differentiate the company from others, and (3) provide value to customers.

Set standards and measure performance. To be able to deliver on its promise of superior service, a business must establish specific standards and measure overall performance against them. Satisfied customers should exhibit at least one of three behaviors: loyalty (increased customer retention rate), increased purchases (rising sales and sales per customer), and resistance to rivals' attempts to lure them away with lower prices (market share and price tolerance).[53] Companies must track their performance on these and other service standards and reward employees accordingly.

Examine your company's service cycle. What steps must a customer go through to purchase your product or service? Business owners often are surprised at the complexity that has seeped into their customer service systems as they have evolved over time. One of the most effective techniques is to work with employees to flowchart each component in the company's service cycle, including *everything* a customer has to do to buy your product or service. The goal is to look for steps, policies, and procedures that are unnecessary, redundant, or unreasonable and then eliminate them.

See customer complaints as a mechanism for improving customer service. Smart entrepreneurs see customer complaints as an important tool for improving their businesses and as a bridge to long-term customer relationships. Ignoring customers leads to disastrous outcomes. Netflix, the movie rental company, made the decision to split its DVD rental business from its online streaming video business, despite negative reactions from customer focus groups. Customers liked the flexibility of being able to get video content from either format. The other negative impact for customers was a 40 percent average increase in the monthly cost of using Netflix services. The result was the loss of 800,000 subscribers during the first three months after the split.[54]

When you create a negative customer experience, apologize and fix it—fast. No customer service system is perfect, but companies can recover from creating a negative customer experience. A recent survey of consumers finds that 82 percent of customers experiencing poor customer service say they are interested in finding a resolution to the problem. However, only one in five from that same survey say that they remained a customer after a poor customer experience. Another survey finds similar results, with 73 percent of customers who changed to a different company after a poor customer experience saying that they would not be willing to switch back to that company in the future.[55]

Hire the right employees. A company's customer service process is important, but the key ingredient in the superior service equation is the *people* who make it work. There is no substitute for friendly, courteous sales and service representatives, and hiring them requires a sound selection process. Business owners must always be on the lookout for employees who emanate a customer service attitude and are empathetic, flexible, articulate, creative, and able to think for themselves. Four Seasons Hotels and Resorts, a company with a business model based on customer service, hires people for their attitudes toward other people. The company's philosophy on hiring is that skills and processes can be taught, but attitude is ingrained in people's character.[56]

Train employees to deliver superior service. Successful businesses train *every* employee who deals directly with customers; they don't leave customer service to chance. Superior service companies devote 1 to 5 percent of their employees' work hours to training, concentrating on how to meet, greet, and serve customers. Apple spends as much time training its technicians who work in its retail stores on communication skills as it does on processes and technical knowledge.[57]

Empower employees to offer superior service. One of the most important variables in determining whether employees deliver superior service is the degree to which they perceive that they have permission to do so. The goal is to push decision making down the organization to the employees who have contact with customers. This includes giving them the latitude to circumvent "company policy" if it means improving customer satisfaction. If frontline workers don't have the power to solve disgruntled customers' problems, they fear being punished for overstepping their boundaries and become frustrated, and the superior service cycle breaks down. Zytec, a manufacturing company in southern Minnesota, authorizes all employees to spend up to $1,000 without any approval to improve their work processes or satisfy a customer. The CEO of Zytec says employees are prudent with these funds and use them responsibly.[58] To be empowered, employees need knowledge and information, adequate resources, and managerial support.

Treat employees with respect and demonstrate to them how valuable they are. Creating a positive work environment, good work–life balance through policies such as flextime and vacation, and meaningful work leads to satisfied workers. Satisfied employees tend to create satisfied customers. In fact, a Gallup survey finds that although work environment is important, creating engaging work is the strongest predictor of satisfaction among employees.[59]

ENTREPRENEURIAL PROFILE: Cindy Lo, Red Velvet Events During weekly Monday morning staff meetings at Red Velvet Events, one employee gives a small plastic troll doll named Pockets to another employee as recognition for his or her help and effort during the previous week. Each recipient of Pockets adds an accessory to the doll (such as clothing or jewelry). Passing along Pockets to a colleague has become an important element of the culture at Red Velvet Events. Cindy Lo, founder and president, says that small rewards like this have a powerful impact on team bonding and employee morale.[60] ∎

Use technology to provide improved service. As the price of technology continues to come down, many technology solutions to improve customer service are now affordable for small businesses. Here are some examples:

- Point-of-sale (POS) software helps businesses automate pricing, analyze revenues, and manage inventories more effectively.
- Entrepreneurs can send personalized e-mails to customers to get quick responses to questions or to address complaints.
- Adding chat features for customer questions to company Web sites is now much more affordable.
- Services such as Freshdesk and Zendesk offer small businesses the ability to include a helpdesk that covers multiple communication channels for a small monthly fee.

Reward superior service. What gets rewarded gets done. Companies that want employees to provide stellar service must offer rewards for doing so. However, pay is not always the most powerful reward for recognizing employees who provide outstanding service. Zendesk uses weeble wobble toys as a reward for truly outstanding customer service. Although the toys have little monetary value, employees are proud of the recognition they get for being able to display weeble wobbles on their desks because everyone in the company knows what they mean.[61]

Get top managers' support. The drive toward superior customer service will fall far short of its target unless top managers support it fully. Success requires more than just a verbal commitment: It calls for managers' involvement and dedication to making service a core company value. Achieving customer satisfaction must become ingrained in the strategic planning process and work its way into every nook and cranny of the organization. Once it does, employees will be able to provide stellar customer service with or without a checklist of dos and don'ts.

Give customers an unexpected surprise. In Louisiana, locals call it a *lagniappe* ("lan-yap"), a small gift that a merchant gives to a customer. When a customer makes a sizable purchase at Wilson Creek Outfitters, a fly-fishing shop in Morganton, North Carolina, the owner includes a dozen flies in the order for free. The cost of giving customers such surprises can be minimal, but the goodwill and loyalty it garners are significant.

View customer service as an investment, not an expense. The companies that lead the way when it comes to retaining their customers view the money they spend on customer service as an investment rather than an expense. One of the most effective ways for entrepreneurs to learn this lesson is to calculate the cost of poor customer service to their companies. Once they calculate it, the cost of lost customers due to poor service is so astonishing to most business owners that they quickly become customer service zealots. For instance, the owner of a small restaurant calculated that if every day he lost to poor service just one customer who spent just $5 per week, his business was losing $94,900 in revenue per year! The restaurateur immediately changed his approach to customer service.

RETAIN EXISTING CUSTOMERS Loyal, long-term customers are the bedrock of every business. High customer retention rates translate into superior financial performance. Earning customers' loyalty requires businesses to take customer focus and service to unprecedented levels, and that means building long-term relationships with customers. Research shows that customers who are satisfied with a company's products and customer service are more likely to be repeat customers and are less sensitive to price increases.[62]

Powell's Books, a Portland, Oregon, landmark known as the "City of Books" for its 68,000-square-foot store (the store takes up an entire city block) and huge inventory, has built a solid base of loyal customers since opening its first location in 1971, enabling the company to compete successfully against industry giants Amazon and Barnes & Noble. Powell's Books has hosted several weddings for customers who met there, and one customer's ashes are interred (at his request) in one of the columns that is made to look like a stack of books at the northwest entrance to the store. Now *that's* customer loyalty![63]

Because about 20 percent of a typical company's customers account for about 80 percent of its sales, focusing resources on keeping the best (and most profitable) customers is a better investment than chasing "fair-weather" customers who will defect to any better deal that comes along. Suppose a company increases its customer base by 10 percent each year but retains only 80 percent of its existing customers. This company actually loses 10 percent of its revenues each year $[10\% - (100\% - 80\%) = -10\%]$. If this same company can raise its customer retention rate to 95 percent, it will actually grow 5 percent per year $[10\% - (100\% - 95\%) = 5\%]$. Therefore, small business owners would be better off answering the question "How can we improve customer value and service to encourage our existing customers to do more business with us?" than "How can we increase our market share by 10 percent?" One way that companies can entice current customers to keep coming back is with a loyalty program, which many companies are linking to their social media presence.

ENTREPRENEURIAL PROFILE: Vanessa Merit Nornberg: Metal Mafia Metal Mafia, a wholesaler of body and costume jewelry, surprises customers when they call to report a problem with defective or damaged goods. Metal Mafia tells customers to throw away the defective item rather than waste their valuable time returning it to the company. Vanessa Merit Nornberg, owner of Metal Mafia, says most customers are surprised when they are told to just throw the item away, and that the company will replace it. Metal Mafia's customers are happy with the company's customer focus, which turns them into repeat customers and makes them eager to tell others about their shopping experience with the company.[64] ■

Courtesy of Vanessa Merit Nornberg, CEO, Metal Mafia

The most successful small businesses have developed a customer focus and have instilled a customer satisfaction attitude *throughout* the company. They understand that winning customers for life requires practicing **customer experience management**, systematically creating the optimum experience for their customers every time they interact with the company. Companies with world-class customer experience management attitudes set themselves apart by paying attention to "little things," such as responding to questions or complaints promptly, remembering a customer's unique product or service preferences, or sending a customer a copy of an article of interest to him or her. Small companies cannot always be leaders in creating product or technology innovations. However, because their size allows them to have more personal contact with their customers than large companies, small companies can develop *experience* innovations that keep customers coming back and create a competitive advantage. Taking care of every small interaction a company has with its customers over time adds up to a positive service experience and can create a strong bond with them.

customer experience management

the process of systematically creating the optimum experience for customers every time they interact with a company.

ENTREPRENEURIAL PROFILE: Joel Fleishman: Drexel Building Supply Joel Fleischman, owner of Drexel Building Supply, routinely hitches a hot dog wagon to his truck and delivers lunch to construction sites where his customers' employees are working. Fleischman brings along other employees, particularly recent hires to the company, to help them learn the art of customer service and to build personal relationships between Drexel employees and construction company customers. Attention to customer service has helped Drexel Building Supply double its workforce over six years. Much of that growth is attributed to referrals from satisfied customers. Drexel Building Supply uses social media to reinforce the message of its attention to customer service. It has 2,664 followers on Facebook, who have made 296 comments. The company is recognized as an industry leader in effective use of social media.[65] ■

Courtesy of Drexel Building Supply

You Be the Consultant

The Impact of Second-Mile Service

The late S. Truett Cathy founded the Chick-fil-A restaurant chain in 1967. When Cathy stayed at a Ritz-Carlton hotel, he was impressed when a person working the front desk replied to Cathy's expression of thanks with the response "My pleasure." Cathy decided then and there that customers of Chick-fil-A should always be greeted the same way. Cathy was so inspired by the customer service of Ritz-Carlton that he formed a partnership with the luxury hotel chain to use its Leadership Institute to train Chick-fil-A's management on creating and sustaining a culture of customer service. The partnership between the two companies remains to this day, with more than 200 Chick-fil-A employees attending Ritz-Carlton's customer service leadership course annually.

The "my pleasure" philosophy adopted by Cathy evolved into a way of conducting business, not just a way to thank its customers. It is known as Chick-fil-A's "second-mile service." For example, managers and employees routinely walk through the fast-food restaurant, asking customers how their meals are and whether they would like their drinks refreshed. Employees have been known to drive to a customer's house to deliver a sandwich that was left out of a bag in a drive-through order. Restaurant staff help families by carrying their overloaded food trays to their table, offer freshly ground pepper to those dining in the restaurant, and accompany customers to their cars with umbrellas when it is raining. Dining at Chick-fil-A is a different experience than customers receive at most other fast-food chains.

Chick-fil-A trains its employees to use at least one of the following six "positive trigger words" in every interaction with a customer: *delighted*, *absolutely*, *pleasure*, *happy*, *sorry*, and *yes*. However, words are never enough! Every interaction with employees must be upbeat and genuine.

Rather than compete on price, Chick-fil-A differentiates itself from its competitors with customer service, high-quality food, cleanliness, and a unique brand. Its competitive strategy has paid off with exceptional financial performance. Chick-fil-A stores average more than $4 million per year in revenues, which is more than $1 million more per store than other top-performing fast-food restaurant chains, such as McDonald's, Jason's Deli, Whataburger, and Panera. Industry experts say that superior customer service is the main contributor to this exceptional performance.

Many of Chick-fil-A's competitors are trying to find ways to improve their customer service. For example, beginning in 2014, Arby's started to require that all of its employees attend intensive training in customer service. Within just the first year, Arby's scored 8 percent higher in independent ratings of customer service and 11.3 percent growth in same-store revenues. KFC also has taken significant steps to improve customer service and as a result has seen renewed growth in same-store revenues. However, even with these improvements, the average Chick-fil-A store still has three times as much revenue as the average KFC store, even though Chick-fil-A is open only six days a week! The successes of Chick-fil-A, Arby's, and KFC comes at a time when only 30 percent of the industry reported increased same-store revenues.

To ensure continued success, Chick-fil-A pays close attention to whom it hires and how new employees are trained. The average employee at Chick-fil-A earns almost 6 percent more per hour than the industry average. This is a significant investment in employees, considering that the average fast-food restaurant spends 25 percent of its total expenses on employee pay. When interviewing prospective hourly employees, Chick-fil-A managers ask many questions about the applicants' career goals and aspirations. Long-term employees are often able to get financial support for furthering their education and training that can lead to management positions. Of course, Chick-fil-A continues to spend much more than competitors to ensure that all of its employees are fully trained to meet its high expectation for customer support.

1. What impact has Chick-fil-A's strategy of providing superior customer service had on the company's success?

2. Chick-fil-A does not compete with its rivals using low prices. What lessons can other small businesses learn from Chick-fil-A about the relationship between prices and customer service?

3. What advice would you give to one of Chick-fil-A's competitors to try to match Chick-fil-A's customer service?

4. Choose a fast-food restaurant that you frequent and identify steps it would need to take to improve its customer service.

Sources: Based on Kate Taylor, "Fast-Food Chains Like KFC and Arby's Are Fixing a Big Customer Service Problem—And It's paying Off," *Business Insider*, October 22, 2016, www.businessinsider.com/chains-double-down-on-customer-service-2016-10; Hayley Peterson, "Why Chick-fil-A's Restaurants Sell 3 Times as Much as KFC's," *Business Insider*, May 10, 2016, www.businessinsider.com/why-chick-fil-a-is-so-successful-2016-5; "The QSR 50," *QSR*, August 2016, www.qsrmagazine.com/reports/qsr50-2016-top-50-chart; Scott Davis, "Chick-fil-A's Raving Fans' Growth Strategy," *Forbes*, December 16, 2013, www.forbes.com/sites/scottdavis/2013/12/16/chick-fil-as-raving-fans-growth-strategy/#7fd007857ce3; Alicia Kelso, "Business Lessons from the Late Founder of Chick-fil-A," *QSR*, September 8, 2014, www.qsrweb.com/articles/business-lessons-from-the-late-founder-of-chick-fil-a/; "Chick-fil-A: Making Fast Service Memorable," The Ritz-Carlton Leadership Center, February 18, 2014, http://ritzcarltonleadershipcenter.com/2014/02/chick-fil-a-making-fast-service-memorable/; Ross Beard, "How Chick-fil-A Creates a Memorable Experience (and Grows Revenue by 13% Annually)," *Client Heartbeat*, November 19, 2014, http://blog.clientheartbeat.com/chick-fil-a-customer-experience/.

The goal is to create a total customer experience that is so positive that customers keep coming back and tell their friends about it. How do these companies manage their customer relationships and stay focused so intently on their customers? They constantly ask customers four basic questions and then act on what they hear:

1. What are we doing right?

2. How can we do that even better?

3. What have we done wrong?

4. What can we do in the future?

Table 9.4 offers some basic strategies for developing and retaining loyal customers.

BE DEVOTED TO QUALITY In this intensely competitive global business environment, quality goods and services are a prerequisite for success. According to one marketing axiom, the worst of all marketing catastrophes is to have great advertising and a poor-quality product. Customers have come to expect and demand quality goods and services, and businesses that provide them consistently have a distinct competitive advantage. Today, quality is more than just a slogan posted on the company bulletin board; world-class companies treat quality as a strategic objective—an integral part of a company's strategy and culture. This philosophy is called **total quality management (TQM)**—quality not just in the product or service itself but also in *every* aspect of the business and its relationship with the customer and *continuous improvement* in the quality delivered to customers.

> **total quality management (TQM)**
> the philosophy of producing a high-quality product or service and achieving quality in every aspect of the business and its relationship with the customer; the focus is on continuous improvement in the quality delivered to customers.

Companies on the cutting edge of the quality movement are developing new ways to measure quality. Manufacturers were the first to apply TQM techniques, but retail, wholesale, and service organizations have seen the benefits of becoming champions of quality. They are tracking customer complaints, contacting "lost" customers, and finding new ways to track the cost of quality and their return on quality (ROQ). ROQ recognizes that, although any improvement in quality may improve a company's competitive ability, only those improvements that produce a reasonable rate of return are worthwhile. In essence, ROQ requires managers to ensure that the quality improvements they implement will more than pay for themselves.

The key to developing a successful TQM philosophy is seeing the world from the customer's point of view. In other words, quality must reflect the needs and wants of the customer. TQM supports the value proposition of the business model. How do customers define quality? According to one survey, Americans rank the quality of a product in this order: reliability (average time between failures), durability (how long it lasts), ease of use, a known or trusted brand name, and, last, low price.[66] When buying services, customers look for similar characteristics: tangibles (equipment, facilities, and people), reliability (doing what you say you will do), responsiveness (promptness in helping customers and in solving problems), and assurance and empathy (conveying a caring attitude).[67] For example, the owner of a very successful pest control company offers his customers a unique, unconditional guarantee: If the company fails to eliminate all insect and rodent breeding and nesting areas on a client's premises, it will refund the customer's last 12 monthly payments and will pay for one year's service by another exterminator. The company has had to honor its guarantee only once in 17 years.

Companies that excel at providing quality products and services discover tangible benefits in the form of increased sales, more repeat customers, higher customer retention, and lower costs. Small businesses that have succeeded in building a reputation for top-quality products and services rely on the following guidelines to "get it right the first time":

- Build quality into the process; don't rely on inspection to obtain quality.

- Foster teamwork and dismantle the barriers that divide disparate departments.

- Establish long-term ties with select suppliers; don't award contracts on low price alone.

- Provide managers and employees the training needed to participate fully in the quality improvement program.

TABLE 9.4 Strategies for Developing and Retaining Loyal Customers

- Believe what your customers tell you. Even though the facts may not back up what customers believe to be true, their belief is all that matters. The customer should be allowed to "win" every argument—no matter what!

- Approach all customers with a feeling of generosity. Put customer happiness ahead of everything else, including company profits. Little things like free refills, offering a little extra help to a customer, and letting "non-customers" use your restrooms can go a long way toward building loyalty with customers.

- Anticipate your customers' needs rather than just waiting for them to ask.

- Identify your best customers and give them incentives to return. Focus resources on the 20 percent of customers who account for 80 percent of sales.

- When you create a dissatisfied customer, fix the problem *fast*. One study finds that, given the chance to complain, 95 percent of customers will buy again *if* a business handles their complaints promptly and effectively. Poor ways to handle a complaint are to ignore it, to pass it off to a subordinate, or to let a lot of time slip by before dealing with it. Shortly after luxury car maker Lexus introduced the new ES350 model, managers discovered that about 700 cars had a small transmission problem that was the result of a factory error. Lexus contacted the affected owners and asked them to take their cars to their local dealers, where they received brand-new Lexus ES350s—with no hassle. Surveys of these customers that were conducted later showed that they were *more* loyal to Lexus than buyers whose cars did not have the problem in the first place.

- Make sure your business system makes it easy for customers to buy from you. Eliminate unnecessary procedures that challenge customers' patience.

- Contact lost customers to find out why they left. You may uncover a problem you never knew existed.

- Ask employees for feedback on improving customer service. A study by Technical Assistance Research Programs, a customer service research firm, finds that frontline service workers can predict nearly 90 percent of the cases that produce customer complaints. Emphasize that *everyone* is part of the customer satisfaction team.

- Allow managers to wait on customers occasionally. It's a great dose of reality. Ron Shaich, founder of Panera Bread, a chain of bakery cafés with 1,185 locations in 40 states, still visits stores regularly, working the cash registers and serving customers so that he can listen to their ideas and concerns.

- Carefully select and train *everyone* who will deal with customers. Never let rude employees work with customers.

- Empower employees to do whatever it takes to satisfy customers. At Ritz-Carlton hotels, employees are authorized to spend up to $2,000 to resolve a customer's complaint. At Zappos, the online shoe retailer, members of the customer loyalty team are authorized to spend as much time as necessary on the phone with customers and to assist with anything customers need, even issues that are unrelated to Zappos.

- Reward employees "caught" providing exceptional service to customers.

- Get in the habit of calling customers by name. It's one of the most meaningful ways of connecting with your customers.

- *Remember*: Customers pay the bills; without them, you have no business. Special treatment wins customers and keeps them coming back.

Sources: Based on Hayley Crum Blanton, "5 Keys to Excellent Customer Service," *Business Journals*, April 5, 2016, www.bizjournals.com/bizjournals/how-to/growth-strategies/2016/04/5-keys-to-excellent-customer-service.html; Jeff Haden, "6 Key Mindsets for Providing Outstanding Customer Service," *Inc.*, October 6, 2014, www.inc.com/jeff-haden/6-key-mindsets-for-providing-outstanding-customer-service.html; Eric Schiffer, "Treat Them Well: 5 Keys to Lasting Customer Service," *Entrepreneur*, February 27, 2014, www.entrepreneur.com/article/231799; Aileron, "The 10 Keys of Excellent Customer Service," *Forbes*, November 15, 2012, www.forbes.com/sites/aileron/2012/11/15/the-10-keys-of-excellent-customer-service/#1e4fd5cc2361; Kasey Wehrum, "How May We Help You?" *Inc.*, March 2011, p. 63; Brandi Stewart, "Able Baker," *FSB*, December 2007/January 2008, pp. 53–58; Jerry Fisher, "The Secret's Out," *Entrepreneur*, May 1998, pp. 1112–1119; and Bill Taylor, "Lessons from Lexus: Why It Pays to Do the Right Thing," *Mavericks at Work*, December 12, 2007, www.mavericksatwork.com/?p=102.

- Empower workers at all levels of the organization; give them authority and responsibility for making decisions that determine quality.

- Get managers' commitment to the quality philosophy. Otherwise, the program is doomed. Employees look to leadership to see if quality is just talked about or actually a part of what the company does.

- Rethink the processes the company uses to get its products or services to its customers.

- Be willing to make changes in processes wherever they may be necessary.

- Reward employees for quality work. Ideally, workers' compensation is linked clearly and directly to key measures of quality and customer satisfaction.

- Develop a companywide strategy for constant improvement of product and service quality.

- Back up the company's quality pledge with a guarantee. For instance, gSchool, a software programming school in Denver, Colorado, guarantees all students a $60,000 job in Colorado as professional Web developers after completing the program. Students who do not land such a job are guaranteed a full refund of their $20,000 tuition![68]

ATTEND TO CONVENIENCE Ask customers what they want from the businesses they deal with, and one of the most common responses is "convenience." In this busy, fast-paced world of dual-career couples and lengthy commutes to and from work, customers increasingly are looking for convenience. Several studies have found that customers rank easy access to goods and services at the top of their purchase criteria. Unfortunately, too few businesses deliver adequate levels of convenience, and they fail to attract and retain customers. One print and framing shop, for instance, alienated many potential customers with its abbreviated business hours—nine to five daily, except for Wednesday afternoons, Saturdays, and Sundays, when the shop was closed! Other companies make it a chore to do business with them. In an effort to defend themselves against unscrupulous customers, these businesses have created elaborate procedures for exchanges, refunds, writing checks, and other basic transactions.

Successful companies go out of their way to make sure that it is easy for customers to do business with them. Retailers and financial institutions are looking to mobile payments with smart phones as a way to making shopping a little easier for their customers. PayPal is partnering with a variety of financial institutions to make mobile payments easier. Customers can load their debit and credit card information into PayPal's app to make in-store payments with mobile phones. Other financial technology companies are working to improve security and to integrate coupons and in-store special offers for customers who want to use mobile payments.[69]

Amazon is making it easier for shoppers by launching "pop-up stores" in shopping malls. The miniature storefronts offer customers some of Amazon's most popular technology devices.[70] Amazon also is developing a checkout-free grocery store called Amazon Go. The stores will use a combination of technology including sensors, cameras, and artificial intelligence to sense what shoppers put into their carts. Once they are done shopping, customers can just walk out of the store without having to check out. The system tracks all purchases and automatically charges the customers for their purchases, eliminating the long lines and slowdowns at the traditional retail checkouts.[71]

How can entrepreneurs boost the convenience level of their businesses? By conducting a "convenience audit" from the customer's point of view to get an idea of its ETDBW ("easy-to-do-business-with") index:

- Is your business located near your customers? Does it provide easy access?

- Are your business hours suitable to your customers? Should you be open evenings and weekends to serve them better?

- Would customers appreciate pickup and delivery service? To enhance customer convenience, more than 30 percent of restaurants, especially those that focus on takeout and delivery, give customers the option of ordering online and have discovered that customer satisfaction, order accuracy, and speed increase.[72] Restaurants also benefit by offering online ordering; the average check at restaurants for online orders is 23 percent larger than the average check for on-site orders.[73]

- Are your employees trained to handle business transactions quickly, efficiently, and politely? Waiting while rude, poorly trained employees fumble through routine transactions destroys customer goodwill.

- Do your employees treat customers with courtesy?

- Does your company provide a sufficient number of checkout stations so that shoppers do not have to stand in long lines to pay for their purchases? Does your company make it easy for customers to make purchases with debit or credit cards?

- Are you using technology to enhance customers' shopping experience? At Sam's Club stores, customers can use a smart phone app, Scan & Go, to scan items as they shop. The app then allows for them to check out on their phones and proceed to the exit, where an employee compares the number of items paid for against the number in the cart.[74]

- Does your company offer "extras" that make customers' lives easier? With a phone call to Hoyt Hanvey Jewelers, a small gift store in Clinton, South Carolina, customers in need of a special gift simply tell how much they want to spend, and the owner takes care of the rest—selecting the gift, wrapping it, and shipping it. All customers have to do is pay the invoice when it arrives in the mail.

- Can you "bundle" some of your existing products or services to make it easier for customers to use them? Whether it involves gardening tools or a spa treatment, assembling products and services into ready-made, all-in-one kits appeals to busy customers and can boost sales.

- Can you adapt existing products to make them more convenient for customers?

- Does your company handle telephone calls quickly, efficiently, and with a real person? Long waits on hold, transfers from one office to another, and too many rings before answering signal to customers that they are not important. New services, such as Ruby Receptionists, give businesses the ability to have a real person answer the phone rather than force customers to struggle through the frustration of navigating an automated answering system.

CONCENTRATE ON INNOVATION As you learned in Chapter 3, innovation is key to a company's future success. Markets change too quickly and competitors move too fast for a small company to remain competitive by standing still. Because they cannot outspend their larger rivals, small companies often turn to superior innovation as a way to gain a competitive edge. Thanks to their organizational and managerial flexibility, small businesses often can detect and act on new opportunities faster than large companies. Innovation is one of the hallmarks of entrepreneurs, and it shows up in the new products, unique techniques, and unusual marketing approaches they introduce. Despite their limited resources, small businesses frequently are leaders in innovation. There is much more to innovation than spending megadollars on research and development. How do small businesses manage to maintain their leadership role in innovating new products and services? They use their size to their advantage, maintaining their speed and flexibility much as a martial arts expert does against a larger opponent. Their closeness to their customers enables them to read subtle shifts in the market and to anticipate trends as they unfold. Their ability to concentrate their efforts and attention in one area also gives small businesses an edge in innovation.

ENTREPRENEURIAL PROFILE: Fair Oaks Farms, LLC Fair Oaks Farms, LLC uses natural gas derived from the manure produced by its 30,000 dairy cows to generate electricity to power its 10 barns, cheese factory, gift store, restaurant, and educational center for children. However, electricity generation uses only half of the 5 million pounds of manure generated by the Fair Oak Farms cows each day. Rather than burn off the excess gas, the farm is now using it to fuel its fleet of 42 tractor-trailer trucks. In addition to saving thousands of dollars in fuel costs, the farm also generates additional revenue from two fueling stations that are open to the general public.[75] ■

EMPHASIZE SPEED Technology, particularly the Internet, has changed the pace of business so dramatically that speed has become a major competitive weapon. Today's customers expect businesses to serve them at the speed of light! Providing a quality product at a reasonable price once was sufficient to keep customers happy, but that is not enough for modern customers who can find dozens of comparable products with a just few mouse clicks. Customers become disgruntled when companies fail to show respect for their busy schedules and corresponding lack of time. At world-class companies, speed reigns. They recognize that reducing the time it takes to develop, design, manufacture, and deliver a product reduces costs, increases quality, improves customer satisfaction, and boosts market share.

This philosophy of speed is based on **time compression management (TCM)**, which involves three principles: (1) speeding new products to market, (2) shortening customer response time in manufacturing and delivery, and (3) reducing the administrative time required to fill an order. Victory in this time-obsessed economy goes to the company that can deliver goods and services the fastest, not necessarily those that are the biggest and most powerful. Businesses that can satisfy their customers' insatiable appetites for speed have a distinct advantage.

Although speeding up the manufacturing process is a common goal, companies using TCM have learned that manufacturing takes only 5 to 10 percent of the total time between an order and getting the product into the customer's hands. The rest is consumed by clerical and administrative tasks. The primary opportunity for TCM to improve speed is in what it can offer to streamline the administrative process. Companies relying on TCM to help them turn speed into a competitive edge should do the following:

> **time compression management (TCM)** a marketing strategy that relies on three principles: (1) speeding products to market, (2) shortening customer response time in manufacturing and delivery, and (3) reducing the administrative time required to fill an order.

- *"Reengineer" the entire process rather than attempt to do the same things in the same way—only faster.* Look for redundant or unnecessary steps in a process to help streamline the work that is truly necessary.

- *Create cross-functional teams of workers and give them the power to attack and solve problems.* In world-class companies, product teams include engineers, manufacturing workers, salespeople, quality experts—and even customers.

- *Set aggressive goals for time reduction and stick to the schedule.* Some companies using TCM have been able to reduce cycle time from several weeks to just a few hours!

- *Rethink your supply chain.* Can you electronically link with your suppliers or your customers to speed up orders and deliveries?

- *Instill speed in the culture.* At Domino's Pizza, kitchen workers watch videos of the fastest pizza makers in the country.

- *Use technology to find shortcuts wherever possible.* Properly integrated into a company's strategy for speed, technology can restructure a company's operating timetable. Rather than build costly, time-consuming prototypes, many time-sensitive businesses use computer-aided design and computer-assisted manufacturing to speed product design and testing.

- *Put the Internet to work.* Perhaps nothing symbolizes speed better than the Internet, and companies that harness its lightning-fast power can become leaders in TCM.

Conclusion

Small companies lack the marketing budgets of their larger rivals, but that does not condemn them to the world of second-class marketers and its resulting anonymity. By using clever, innovative bootstrap marketing strategies such as the ones described in this chapter, entrepreneurs can put their companies in the spotlight and create a special connection with their customers.

MyLab Entrepreneurship

If your instructor is using MyLab Entrepreneurship, go to **www.pearson.com/mylab/ entrepreneurship** to complete the problems marked with this icon ⭐ .

Chapter Summary by Learning Objective

1. **Describe the principles of building a bootstrap marketing plan and explain the benefits of preparing one.**

   A major part of the entrepreneur's business plan is the marketing plan, which focuses on a company's target customers and how best to satisfy their needs and wants. A solid marketing plan should do the following:

   - Determine customer needs and wants through market research.
   - Pinpoint the specific target markets the company will serve.
   - Analyze the firm's competitive advantages and build a bootstrap marketing strategy around them.

2. **Explain how small businesses can pinpoint their target markets.**

   Sound market research helps the owner pinpoint his or her target market. The most successful businesses have well-defined portraits of the customers they are seeking to attract.

3. **Discuss the role of market research in building a bootstrap marketing plan and outline the market research process.**

   Market research is the vehicle for gathering the information that serves as the foundation of the marketing plan. Good research does *not* have to be complex and expensive to be useful. The steps in conducting market research include the following:

   - Defining the objective: "What do you want to know?"

   - Collecting the data from either primary or secondary sources
   - Analyzing and interpreting the data
   - Drawing conclusions and acting on them

4. **Describe how a small business can build a competitive edge in the marketplace by using bootstrap marketing strategies.**

   When plotting a marketing strategy, owners must strive to achieve a competitive advantage—some way to make their companies different from and better than the competition. Successful small businesses rely on 15 sources to develop a competitive edge:

   - Find a niche and fill it.
   - Use the power of publicity.
   - Don't just sell—entertain.
   - Strive to be unique.
   - Build a community with customers.
   - Connect with the customer on an emotional level.
   - Create an identity for your business through branding.
   - Embrace social marketing.
   - Blog
   - Be dedicated to service and customer satisfaction.
   - Retain existing customers.
   - Be devoted to quality.
   - Pay attention to convenience.
   - Concentrate on innovation.
   - Emphasize speed.

MyLab Entrepreneurship

If your instructor is using MyLab Entrepreneurship, go to **www.pearson.com/mylab/entrepreneurship** for Auto-graded writing questions as well as the following Assisted-graded writing questions:

1. How can market research benefit entrepreneurs when starting up?
2. Why is it important for a small business owner to create a plan for establishing a competitive advantage?

Discussion Questions

9-1. Define *marketing plan*. What lies at the center of a marketing plan?

9-2. What objectives should a marketing plan accomplish?

9-3. How can market research benefit entrepreneurs as their businesses grow?

9-4. List some possible sources of market information for an entrepreneur.

⭐ 9-5. Explain why market research does not have to be expensive and sophisticated to be valuable.

9-6. Describe several trends that are driving markets today and their impact on small businesses.

⭐ 9-7. Why is it important for small business owners to define their target markets as part of their marketing strategies?

9-8. What is a competitive advantage?

9-9. Describe how a small business owner could use finding a niche and filling it for a competitive advantage.

9-10. Describe how a small business owner could use the power of publicity for a competitive advantage.

9-11. Describe how a small business owner could use entertaining instead of just selling for a competitive advantage.

9-12. Describe how a small business owner could use striving to be unique for a competitive advantage.

9-13. Describe how a small business owner could use building a community of customers for a competitive advantage.

9-14. Describe how a small business owner could use connecting with customers at an emotional level for a competitive advantage.

9-15. Describe how a small business owner could use creating an identity for the business through branding for a competitive advantage.

9-16. Describe how a small business owner could use social marketing for a competitive advantage.

9-17. Describe how a small business owner could use dedication to service and customer satisfaction for a competitive advantage.

9-18. Describe how a small business owner could use retaining existing customers for a competitive advantage.

9-19. Describe how a small business owner could use devotion to quality for a competitive advantage.

9-20. Describe how a small business owner could use paying attention to convenience for a competitive advantage.

9-21. Describe how a small business owner could use concentrating on innovation for a competitive advantage.

9-22. Describe how a small business owner could use an emphasis on speed for a competitive advantage.

9-23. One experienced entrepreneur says that when a company provides great service, its reputation benefits from a stronger emotional connection with its customers, as well as from increased confidence that it will stand behind its products. Explain why you agree or disagree with this statement.

9-24. Describe a positive service experience you have had with a company and your impressions of that business.

9-25. What are the implications of a company providing poor customer service?

9-26. Describe a negative service experience you have had with a company and your likeliness of doing business with that company again in the future.

9-27. With a 70 percent customer retention rate (the average for most U.S. firms, according to the American Management Association), every $1 million of sales will grow to more than $4 million in 10 years. If you retain 80 percent of your customers, the $1 million will grow to a little over $6 million. If you can keep 90 percent of your customers, that $1 million will grow to more than $9.5 million. What can the typical small business do to increase its customer retention rate?

Beyond the Classroom . . .

9-28. Interview the owner of a local restaurant about its marketing strategy.

9-29. From how large a geographic region does the restaurant owned by the person you interviewed draw its clientele?

9-30. What is the target market of the restaurant?

9-31. What is the demographic profile of the restaurant's target customers?

9-32. Does the restaurant have a competitive edge?

9-33. Visit the Web site for the Small Business Administration's (SBA's) page on marketing. Interview a local business owner, using the resources at the SBA Web site as a guide.

9-34. Based on your interview, what sources for developing a competitive edge did you find?

9-35. Based on your interview, what weaknesses do you see, and how do you recommend overcoming them?

9-36. What recommendations do you have to help the owner make better use of his or her marketing techniques?

9-37. What bootstrap marketing strategies can you suggest to the owner to enhance current marketing efforts?

9-38. Contact two local small business owners and ask them about their marketing strategies.

9-39. Based on your discussions with the two business owners, what bootstrap marketing strategies do their companies use?

9-40. What are the similarities and differences in how the two business owners have achieved a competitive edge?

9-41. Select three local businesses (one large and two small) and play the role of "mystery shopper."

9-42. Based on your mystery shopper experience, how easy was it to do business with each of the three companies?

9-43. How would you rate the service, quality, and convenience of each of the businesses based on your mystery shopper experience?

9-44. Compare and contrast the staff at the three stores based on how helpful, friendly, professional, and courteous they were to you during your mystery shopper visits.

9-45. How would you describe each company's competitive advantage, based on your mystery shopper visits?

9-46. What future do you predict for each company you visited as a mystery shopper?

9-47. Prepare a brief report for your class on your findings and conclusions based on your three mystery shopper visits.

Endnotes

[1] Scott Reeves, "How to Swing with Guerrilla Marketing," *Forbes*, June 8, 2006, www.forbes.com/entrepreneurs/2006/06/08/entrepreneurs-marketingharley-davidson-cx_sr_0608askanexpert.html.

[2] Christina Desmarais, "10 Crazy Bootstrapping Stories," *Inc.*, February 26, 2014, www.inc.com/christina-desmarais/10-crazy-bootstrapping-stories.html.

[3] Howard Dana Shaw, "Customer Care Checklist," *In Business*, September/October, 1987, p. 28.

[4] Hunter Phillips, personal communication, March 22, 2013.

[5] April Joyner, "Case Study: No Marketing Budget? Win Over Bloggers Instead," *Inc.*, October 30, 2012, www.inc.com/april-joyner/bootstrap-how-black-rapid-wonover-bloggers.html.

[6] Karen Talavera, "Do You Really Know Your Customers? Marketing to a Rapidly Diversifying Population," *Marketing Profs*, May 17, 2011, http://www.marketingprofs.com/articles/2011/5057/do-you-really-know-your-customers-marketing-to-a-rapidly-diversifying-population.

[7] "New Census Bureau Report Analyzes U.S. Population Projections," United States Census Bureau, March 3, 2015, https://www.census.gov/newsroom/press-releases/2015/cb15-tps16.html.

[8] "Nielsen: Marketing 'Gravy Train' to Derail by 2020," Marketing Charts, July 30, 2009, http://www.marketingcharts.com/topics/behavioral-marketing/nielsen-marketer-gravy-train-will-derail-by-2020-9978.

[9] Helen Huit, "Brain-Zapping Gadget, Almost Died," *Bloomberg*, May 22, 2016, www.bloomberg.com/news/articles/2016-05-23/how-thync-startup-behind-brain-zapping-gadget-almost-died; "Thync," *Crunchbase*, n.d., www.crunchbase.com/organization/thync/funding-rounds.

[10] Kevin Smith, "Latino Spending Rises, Armstrong's Dtar Fades," *Pasadena Star-News*, March 27, 2016, www.pasadenastarnews.com/business/20160327/latino-spending-rises-armstrongs-star-fades; Ofar Shoshan, "4 Reasons Your Business Should Market to the Hispanic Community," *Entrepreneur*, March 28, 2015; www.entrepreneur.com/article/243475; "Vallarta Supermarkets, INC," *Retail Merchandiser*, June 6, 2012, www.retail-merchandiser.com/reports/retail-reports/710-vallarta-supermarkets-inc.

[11] Shawn O'Connor, "Step 3 for a Successful Startup: The Importance of Market Research," *Forbes*, April 23, 2013, www.forbes.com/sites/shawnoconnor/2013/04/23/step-3-for-a-successful-startup-the-importance-of-market-research/#3b68e57a7596; "About," Stratus Prep, n.d., https://stratusprep.com/about-us/.

[12] Eric Sornoso, "9 Small Business Twitter Marketing Examples to Study," *Social Media Examiner*, March 25, 2014, www.socialmediaexaminer.com/small-businesses-twitter-marketing/.

[13] Natalie Yeadon, "The Power of Customer Advisory Boards for Business Building," Customer Think, April 2, 2016, http://customerthink.com/the-power-of-customer-advisory-boards-for-business-building/.

[14] "Joseph Nogucci," Facebook for Business, n.d., www.facebook.com/business/success/joseph-nogucci.

[15] Abigail Tracy, "How to Use Social Media during a Crisis," *Inc.*, February 26, 2014, www.inc.com/abigailtracy/using-social-media-in-crisis-proflowerssharisberries.html.

[16] John George, "Exercise Company Targets 'Active Sitters,'" *Philadelphia Business Journal*, February 28, 2014, www.bizjournals.com/philadelphia/blog/healthcare/2014/02/fitness-equipment-company-targets.html.

[17] Janine Popick, "How to Get and Cultivate Customer Advocates," *Inc.*, January 4, 2013, www.inc.com/janinepopick/how-to-get-and-cultivate-customer-advocates.html.

[18] Howard Greenstein, "B2B Marketing on Facebook, Simplified," *Inc.*, July 9, 2012, www.inc.com/howardgreenstein/facebook-for-b2b-marketing.html; "About ClearRisk," ClearRisk, n.d., www.clearrisk.com/about-clearrisk/.

[19] J. J. McCorvey, "Keeping Your Mobile Phone Safe from Hackers," *Inc.*, July 2, 2012, www.inc.com/30under30/jj-mccorvey/john-hering-james-burgess-and-kevinmahaffey-founders-of-lookout-mobile-security.html.

[20] "Spin for Kids," Sweetwater Brewing Company, n.d., http://sweetwaterbrew.com/brews/crank-tank/.

[21] *2015 Cone Communications Global CSR Study* (Boston: Cone Communications, 2015), p. 9.

[22] Peggy Linial, "Small Business and Cause Related Marketing: Getting Started," Cause Marketing Forum, http://www.causemarketingforum.com/framemain.asp?ID=189.

[23] Minda Zetlin, "Why Giving Stuff Away Works Better Than Buying Advertising," *Inc.*, March 4, 2014, www.inc.com/minda-zetlin/why-giving-stuff-away-worksbetter-than-buying-ads.html.

[24] Dale D. Buss, "Entertailing," *Nation's Business*, December 1997, p. 18.

[25] Maren Estrada, "Will It Blend? Find Out Yourself with Today's Prime Day Deal on a Blendtec Blender," *BRG*, July 6, 2016, http://bgr.com/2016/07/06/best-blender-2016-prime-day/; Carmen Nobel, "Advertising Symbiosis: The Key to Viral Videos," *Forbes*, June 18, 2013, www.forbes.com/sites/hbsworkingknowledge/2013/06/18/advertising-symbiosis-the-key-to-viral-videos/.

[26] Marty Schultz, "Welcome to Entertailing," *Albany Biz Center*, http://www.bizcenter.org/Article/105/959/1103.

[27] Shannon Gausepohl, "11 Strange Businesses You Didn't Know Existed," *Business News Daily*, March 22, 2017, http://www.businessnewsdaily.com/8755-strange-businesses.html.

[28] "Teams," Etsy, n.d., www.etsy.com/teams.

[29] "20 Best Company Facebook Pages," *Inc.*, March 20, 2011, www.inc.com/ss/20-best-company-facebook-pages.

[30]"Under the Influence: Consumer Trust in Advertising," The Nielsen Company, September 17, 2013, www.nielsen.com/us/en/insights/news/2013/under-the-influence-consumer-trust-in-advertising.html.

[31]Kimberly Whitler, "Why Word of Mouth Marketing Is the Most Important Social Media," *Forbes*, July 17, 2014, www.forbes.com/sites/kimberlywhitler/2014/07/17/why-word-of-mouth-marketing-is-the-most-important-social-media/#ff089907a77c.

[32]"10 Examples of Killer Unique Selling Propositions on the Web," *Fizzle*, August 24, 2010, http://fizzle.co/sparkline/10-examples-of-killer-unique-sellingpropositions-on-the-web.

[33]Madeline Farber, "Google Tops Apple as the World's Most Valuable Brand," *Fortune*, February 2, 2017, http://fortune.com/2017/02/02/google-tops-apple-brand-value/.

[34]Maureen Farrell, "How to Market Your New Idea," *Forbes*, December 21, 2007, www.forbes.com/entrepreneurs/2007/12/21/marketing-branding-identityent-cx_mf_1221brand.html.

[35]"Social Media Usage: 2005–2015," Pew Research Center, October 8, 2015, www.pewinternet.org/2015/10/08/social-networking-usage-2005-2015/.

[36]Suzanne Delzio, "12 Social Media Marketing Trends for Small Business," *Social Media Examiner*, June 9, 2015, www.socialmediaexaminer.com/social-media-marketing-trends-for-small-business/.

[37]"The Top 20 Valuable Facebook Statistics," Zephoria Marketing, May 8, 2017, https://zephoria.com/top-15-valuable-facebook-statistics/; James B. Stewart, "Facebook Has 50 Minutes of Your Time Each Day. It Wants More," *New York Times*, May 6, 2016, www.nytimes.com/2016/05/06/business/facebook-bends-the-rules-of-audience-engagement-to-its-advantage.html?_r=0.

[38]Kit Smith, "44 Twitter Statistics for 2016," *Brandwatch*, May 17, 2016, www.brandwatch.com/2016/05/44-twitter-stats-2016/.

[39]Meghan Casserly, "Making Social Marketing Make Sense for Small Business," *Forbes*, June 7, 2013, www.forbes.com/sites/meghancasserly/2013/06/07/makingsocial-marketing-make-sense-for-small-business/.

[40]"Agricola Success Story," Twitter, 2017, https://business.twitter.com/en/success-stories/agricola.html.

[41]Jesse Mawhinney, "42 Visual Content Marketing Statistics You Should Know in 2017," *Hubspot*, January 3, 2017, https://blog.hubspot.com/marketing/visual-content-marketing-strategy#sm.0000xqcdh7wgeoh10v72lf9jrit7u.

[42]Dominique Jackson, "How to Use Twitter Effectively," *Sprout Social*, December 15, 2015, http://sproutsocial.com/insights/how-to-use-twitter-effectively/; Robert Gourley, "Twitter 101: Seven Tips for Effective Marketing," *Marketing Profs*, June 15, 2010, www.marketingprofs.com/articles/2010/3704/twitter-101-seven-tips-for-effective-marketing.

[43]Mikey Smith, "Have an ice day with a winter trip to New York City," *Mirror*, September 23, 2016, www.mirror.co.uk/lifestyle/travel/usa-long-haul/ice-day-winter-trip-new-8900239; Eric Sornoso, "9 Small Business Twitter Marketing Examples to Study," *Social Media Examiner*, March 25, 2014, www.socialmediaexaminer.com/small-businesses-twitter-marketing/.

[44]Sharon Black, "7 YouTube Marketing Case Studies," *Rival IQ*, January 22, 2016, www.rivaliq.com/blog/7-youtube-marketing-case-studies/; "Eric Cook," LinkedIn, n.d., www.linkedin.com/in/eric-cook-57b67234; "About," EricTheCarGuy, n.d., www.ericthecarguy.com.

[45]Marc Apple, "2017 Small Business Blogging Survey Results," *Forward Push*, December 22, 2016, https://forwardpush.com/2017-small-business-blogging-survey-results/.

[46]Will Blunt, "How to Create a Successful Blog Strategy: A Step-by-Step Guide," *Hubspot*, December 29, 2014, http://blog.hubspot.com/marketing/blog-strategy-guide#sm.0001oa9m7y89ueflxgs13fiyz9wh6; Jeff Cornwall, "Blogging as a Marketing Tool," *The Entrepreneurial Mind*, November 11, 2007, www.drjeffcornwall.com/2007/11/11/blogging_as_a_marketing_tool/; Guy Kawasaki, "Blog-A-Thon," *Entrepreneur*, February 2008, p. 44.

[47]"Consumers Pay More for Great Experience," *Marketing Charts*, October 19, 2010, www.marketingcharts.com/direct/consumers-pay-more-forgreat-experience-14657.

[48]"Debbie Kelly, "Poor Customer Service Paralyzes U.S. Companies," *CRM Daily*, February 8, 2008, www.crm-daily.com/story.xhtml?story_id=103001XXU5EQ.

[49]"Consumers Pay More for Great Experience," *Marketing Charts*, October 19, 2010, www.marketingcharts.com/direct/consumers-pay-more-for-great-experience-14657.

[50]Cathryn Creno, "Retailers Use Customer Satisfaction to Create Loyalty," *Arizona Republic*, December 15, 2007, www.azcentral.com/business/articles/1215biz-three-stores1216.html.

[51]"Beware of Dissatisfied Customers: They Like to Blab," *Knowledge @ Wharton*, March 8, 2006, http://knowledge.wharton.upenn.edu/article.cfm?articleid=1422.

[52]Iris Vermeren, "Marketing: How to Provide Great Customer Service via Social," *Brandwatch*, February 25, 2015, www.brandwatch.com/blog/marketing-provide-great-customer-service-via-social/.

[53]Thomas A. Stewart, "After All You've Done for Your Customers, Why Are They Still NOT HAPPY?" *Fortune*, December 11, 1995, pp. 178–182.

[54]Tom Cheredar, "How Netflix Dropped the Ball by Ignoring Customer Voices," *Venture Beat*, October 27, 2011, http://venturebeat.com/2011/10/27/netflixdropped-the-ball/.

[55]"What Wins Customers Back After A CX Failure?" *MarketingCharts*, May 14, 2015, www.marketingcharts.com/traditional/what-wins-customers-back-after-a-cx-failure-54633/.

[56]Micah Solomon, "The Best Customer Service Training for Your Employees Starts with Their Original Trainers: Mom and Dad," *Forbes*, December 5, 2013, www.forbes.com/sites/micahsolomon/2013/12/05/thebest-customer-service-training-for-your-employees-itcomes-from-their-parents/.

[57]Carmine Gallo, "Apple's Secret Employee Training Manual Reinvents Customer Service in Seven Ways," *Forbes*, August 30, 2012, www.forbes.com/sites/carminegallo/2012/08/30/apples-secret-employeetraining-manual-reinvents-customer-service-in-sevenways/.

[58]Louis Schultz, "Trust Is Key in Developing Empowered Organization," *Inforum*, March 11, 2014, www.inforum.com/event/article/id/429005/.

[59]Jennifer Robinson, "For Employee Wellbeing, Engagement Trumps Time Off," *Gallup Business Journal*, December 18, 2012, http://businessjournal.gallup.com/content/159374/employee-wellbeing-engagementtrumps-time-off.aspx.

[60]Matt Straz, "4 Ways Innovative Companies Are Celebrating Their Employees," *Entrepreneur*, August 17, 2015, www.entrepreneur.com/article/249460; "Creative Ways We Recognize Our Employees for Work Well Done," Red Velvet Events, February 4, 2015, www.redvelvetevents.com/2015/02/creative-ways-we-recognize-our-employees-for-work-well-done/.

[61]Pam Dodrill, "Rewards and Recognition: Happy Employees, Happy Customers," Zendesk, April 18, 2013, www.zendesk.com/blog/rewards-and-recognition.

[62]Charles Gerena, "Hey, a Little Service Here?" *Region Focus*, Summer 2004, p. 52.

[63]Susan Hauser, "Out of Print? Not Walter Powell," *Wall Street Journal*, January 24, 2002, p. A16.

[64]Vanessa Merit Nornberg, "Surprise! You Can Win Customers for Life," *Inc.*, June 14, 2012, www.inc.com/vanessa-merit-nornberg/win-customers-for-lifesurprise.html.

[65]Bradley Hartmann, "The Leery Lumberman's Guide to Social Media," *LBM Journal*, December 2016, www.lbmjournal.com/leery-lumbermans-guide-social-media/; Anni Layne Rodgers, "From Lumberyards to Hot Dogs: How One Growth Company Brings on New Talent," *Inc.*, January 7, 2014, www.inc.com/the-buildnetwork/from-lumberyards-to-hot-dogs.html.

[66]Faye Rice, "How to Deal with Tougher Customers," *Fortune*, December 3, 1990, pp. 39–40.

[67]Valery A. Parasuraman, A. Zeithaml and Leonard L. Berry, "Reassessment of Expectations as a Comparison Standard in Measuring Service Quality: Implications for Future Research," *Journal of Marketing*, January 1994, pp. 111–24.

[68]Greg Avery, "Galvanize Lands $18 Million in Venture Capital to Broaden Its Education Focus," *Denver Post*, August 20, 2014, www.bizjournals.com/denver/blog/boosters_bits/2014/06/galvanize-lands-18-million-in-venture-capital-to.html.

[69]Dan O'Shea, "PayPal Aligns with Citigroup, FIS in Bid to Grow In-store Mobile Payment Opportunities," *Retail Dive*, December 15, 2016, www.retaildive.com/news/paypal-aligns-with-citigroup-fis-in-bid-to-grow-in-store-mobile-payment-op/432507/; Ralph Tkatchuk, "5 Security Concerns with Mobile Payments," *PracticalEcommerce*, December 20, 2016, www.practicalecommerce.com/articles/131983-5-Security-Concerns-with-Mobile-Payments.

[70]Eugene Kim, "Amazon Is Doubling Down on Retail Stores with Plans to Have Up to 100 Pop-up Stores in US Shopping Malls," *Business Insider*, September 9, 2016, www.businessinsider.com/amazon-big-expansion-retail-pop-up-stores-2016-9.

[71]Davey Alba, "Only Amazon Could Make a Check-out Free Grocery Store a Reality," *Wired*, December 6, 2016.

[72]Eric Kim, "A Secular Shift to Online Food Ordering," *TechCrunch*, May 7, 2015, https://techcrunch.com/2015/05/07/a-secular-shift-to-online-food-ordering/.

[73]Ellie Mirman, "Restaurants Using Toast for Online Ordering See 23 Percent Larger Check Size Online Over In-Store Orders," *Toast*, August 24, 2016, https://pos.toasttab.com/press/restaurants-online-ordering-23-percent-larger-check-size.

[74]Lauren Zumbach, "Frustrated by Self-checkout? Retailers Look to Smartphones to Cut the Line," *Chicago Tribune*, September 12, 2016, www.chicagotribune.com/business/ct-self-checkout-amazon-sams-club-1213-biz-20161212-story.html.

[75]Gene Johnston, "Farm Offers Full Transparency in Crop and Livestock Production Practices," *Agriculture.com*, November 23, 2016, www.agriculture.com/family/education/farm-offers-full-transparency-in-crop-and-livestock-production-practices; Steven Yaccino, "Dairy Finds Way to Let Cows Power Trucks," *New York Times*, March 28, 2013, www.nytimes.com/2013/03/28/us/dairy-finds-way-to-letcows-powertrucks.html?_r=2&adxnnl=1&adxnnlx=1370285517-NiWov3%20KQAlIGbvrl4vbkQ&.

10

E-Commerce and the Entrepreneur

Muratkoc/E+/Getty images

Learning Objectives

On completion of this chapter, you will be able to:

1. Understand the factors an entrepreneur should consider before launching into e-commerce.

2. Explain the 11 myths of e-commerce and how to avoid falling victim to them.

3. Explain the basic strategies entrepreneurs should follow to achieve success in their e-commerce efforts.

4. Learn the techniques of designing a killer Web site.

5. Explain how companies track the results from their Web sites.

6. Describe how e-businesses ensure the privacy and security of the information they collect and store from the Web.

MyLab Entrepreneurship
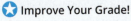 **Improve Your Grade!**

If your instructor is using MyLab Entrepreneurship, visit **www.pearson.com/mylab/entrepreneurship** for videos, simulations, and writing exercises.

The Internet has transformed the way that companies of all sizes do business. It enables entrepreneurs to start businesses faster and more inexpensively than ever before. Are you looking for a supplier to provide a critical part? Using search engines and a host of specialized sites, you can search the globe for potential suppliers in a matter of minutes. Do you want feedback from potential customers about a casual top your company is considering selling? Many crowdsourcing and social media sites allow you to gather comments and tally votes quickly and at very little cost. Do you want to get your business plan into the hands of potential investors? Many sites allow entrepreneurs to reach across the globe to connect with people who are looking for promising start-up ventures in which to invest. Are you searching for a way to analyze your company's financial information more easily and from any location? There are many apps for that!

Advances in technology are reshaping many industries, even those whose methods of operation had changed very little for generations.

Courtesy of Joseph Han-Young Lee, Founder and Chief Product Officer, Coastline Market Inc.

ENTREPRENEURIAL PROFILE: Robert Kirstiuk and Joseph Lee: Coastline Market After starting an organic candle business in high school, Robert Kirstiuk, a theoretical physics major at Western University in Ontario, Canada, and Joseph Lee, a computer science major at the University of British Columbia, launched Coastline Market, a small company that markets an app that allows commercial fishermen to sell their catches directly to restaurants without having to rely on middlemen. The idea came to Kirstiuk one day when he was visiting family along the British Columbia coast and went to the docks to buy fresh fish from local fishermen. He approached Lee with the idea, and the entrepreneurs spent eight months researching the fishing business, prowling the docks talking to fishermen, attending seafood trade shows, and talking to industry executives. Using Coastline Market's app, restaurants place orders for seafood, and local fishermen use the app to fill those orders. Although a Coastline Market truck delivers the fresh catch to the restaurants daily, the company does not store or process the fish; it merely provides a convenient, efficient marketplace through which fishermen and restaurants connect. (In the traditional seafood supply chain, six different middlemen typically handle fish before it reaches its final destination.) Coastline receives 20 percent of each transaction's price, fishermen receive 50 to 200 percent more than if they sold their catches to wholesalers, and by buying directly from the source, restaurants get lower prices than if they purchased from wholesalers. Because the app has traceability features, restaurants can advertise where, how, and when their fish was caught, an important aspect of the industry's farm-to-table (or, in this case, boat-to-table) trend. Kirstiuk and Lee estimate that the seafood market potential in Vancouver alone is $100 million.[1] ∎

Just as in previous revolutions in the business world, some old, established players are being ousted, and new leaders are emerging. The winners are discovering new business opportunities, improved ways of designing work, and better ways of organizing and operating their businesses. Yet one lesson that entrepreneurs engaged in e-commerce have learned is that business basics still apply; companies engaged in e-commerce still have to take care of their customers and earn a profit to stay in business. For an online business to succeed, entrepreneurs must strike a balance and create an e-commerce strategy that capitalizes on the strengths of the Internet while meeting customers' expectations of convenience and service.

In the world of e-commerce, new business models recognize the power that the Internet gives customers, whether they buy online or offline. Online and Internet-influenced sales account for 60 percent of total retail sales, or more than $2.16 trillion, in the United States (see Figure 10.1).[2] The Internet makes pricing more transparent than ever before because with a few mouse clicks or swipes on a smart phone, customers can compare the prices of the same or similar products and services from companies across the globe, often while standing in the aisles of a brick-and-mortar retail store. (A study by Google reports that 82 percent of smart phone owners use their phones to check prices and gather information before they make purchases

FIGURE 10.1

U.S. Online and Web-Influenced Sales

Source: Based on Forrester Data: Web-Influenced Retail Sales Forecast, 2016 to 2021 (US), November 4, 2016. Published by © 2017, Forrester Research, Inc.

at retail stores.[3]) In the connected economy, the balance of power is shifting to customers who comparison shop, a habit they have retained since the Great Recession, and new business models must recognize this fact. Whatever products they may sell—from books and digital cameras to cars and flowers—retailers are dealing with customers who are more informed and aware of the price and feature comparisons of the items for which they are shopping. These informed shoppers are taking price out of the buying equation, and retailers are emphasizing other factors, such as customer service, broad selection, deep product lines, or convenience, to differentiate themselves and build long-term customer relationships.

The connection between online and offline business runs both ways. As a result of offline exposure to a company's ads, shoppers are likely to conduct online searches of the products and services they encounter through traditional media. In addition, customers value other shoppers' opinions about the products they purchase and their shopping experiences with companies. A recent survey of shoppers in North America by BrightLocal, a company that specializes in local search engine optimization strategies, reports that 84 percent of consumers trust online reviews as much as personal recommendations.[4]

Modern shoppers expect to be able to purchase the products and services they want across multiple channels, including the Internet, mobile devices, social media, television shopping channels, catalogs, and brick-and-mortar stores. The multichannel approach that today's shoppers utilize blurs the boundaries between physical stores and the Internet. Multichannel sales now account for 38 percent of all retail purchases (see Figure 10.2).[5] Successful retailers are reimagining their physical stores to provide shoppers with an "endless aisle," using their Web sites to supplement seamlessly the selection of items they have in their stores. They offer shoppers the ability to purchase items from the aisles of their retail

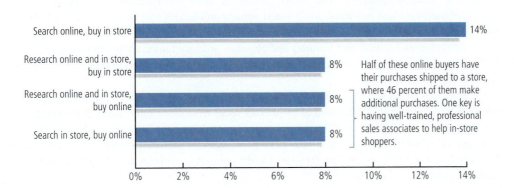

FIGURE 10.2

Multichannel Shopping Methods

Source: Based on *UPS Pulse of the Online Shopper*, UPS, 2016, p. 8.

stores, use in-store pickup for online orders, have their online orders shipped from stores, or simply purchase online. The goal is to meet customers wherever they want to shop by integrating the in-store shopping experience with the convenience of online shopping. Retailers are setting up Wi-Fi access to online customer ratings and reviews in their stores and using geolocation technology to send personalized offers and discounts to in-store shoppers' phones, depending on where they are in the store and which items they are browsing. Others are displaying brand-related hashtags in their stores to encourage shoppers to share their comments and reviews.

Just as brick-and-mortar stores are incorporating Internet-based components into their strategies, companies that once operated only online are building physical stores to overcome the biggest disadvantage of online sales—customers' inability to touch, feel, and try on goods before they make a purchase. Companies such as Bonobos (men's clothing), Warby Parker (eyeglasses), and Blue Nile (jewelry) have discovered that their strategically located retail stores serve as brand promoters for their online shops and allow them to lower the high cost of acquiring online customers. Bonobos operates 20 minimalist stores across the United States that stock only sample garments that customers try on before placing their orders online. Bonobos reports that customers who visit one of their physical stores spend 50 percent more than those who shop online, and their merchandise return rates are lower.[6] Warby Parker revolutionized the market for stylish eyeglasses when it launched an online only business that sells glasses for as little as $95 per pair with free shipping and returns for up to 5 pairs. In 2013, Warby Parker opened its first retail store, and the outlet's sales were significantly higher than the company's founder expected. Today, Warby Parker has more than 50 retail outlets and plans to add more. Cofounder Dave Gilboa says that in a few years, sales at the company's retail stores will equal its online sales.[7] Even online giant Amazon is opening stores in malls across the United States that sell mainly consumer electronics; the company's goal with these stores is to drive more traffic to Amazon's online store.[8]

In the fast-paced world of e-commerce, size doesn't matter as much as speed and flexibility. One of the Internet's greatest strengths is its interactive, social nature and its ability to provide companies with instantaneous customer feedback, giving them the opportunity to learn and to make necessary adjustments. Businesses, whatever their size, that are willing to experiment with different approaches to reaching customers and are quick to learn and adapt will grow and prosper; those that cannot will fall by the wayside. E-commerce is transforming the way businesses in almost every industry operate, including the retail mattress business. For decades, customers bought mattresses in showrooms filled with dozens of styles (traditional springs, pocket springs, memory foam, pillow-top, and more) and a wide range of price points after flopping around on them to test them. Recently, however, several start-up companies, such as Casper Sleep, Leesa Sleep, and Yogabed, have broken into the $14 billion-per-year mattress market in the United States with online-only business models. Primarily targeting tech-savvy Millennials, these companies offer a limited number of foam mattresses (sometimes only one) in various sizes sold only online and shipped free to the customers' door after being compressed into a box the size of a large suitcase. Prices typically range from about $550 to $1,000, and the companies normally offer a 100-night guarantee and free returns. These upstart companies have already captured about 3 percent of the U.S. mattress market.[9]

More than 1.46 billion people, 51.5 percent of the world's online population, use the Internet to make purchases.[10] The items purchased most often online are apparel, books, computer hardware and software, toys, video games, and health and beauty products.[11] However, companies can—and do—sell practically anything over the Web, from antiques and groceries to skeletons (animal and human) and Russian military tanks. eMarketer estimates that 12.8 percent of total global retail sales will occur online in 2019, totaling nearly $3.6 trillion (see Figure 10.3).[12]

Companies of all sizes are busy establishing their presence on the Internet because that's where their customers are. The number of Internet users worldwide now stands at more than 3.7 billion, up from 147 million in 1998.[13] Consumers have adopted the Internet much more quickly than any other major innovations in the past. It reached 50 percent penetration in the United States in just 7 years, compared to 30 years for the computer, 40 years for electricity, and more than 100 years for steam power.[14]

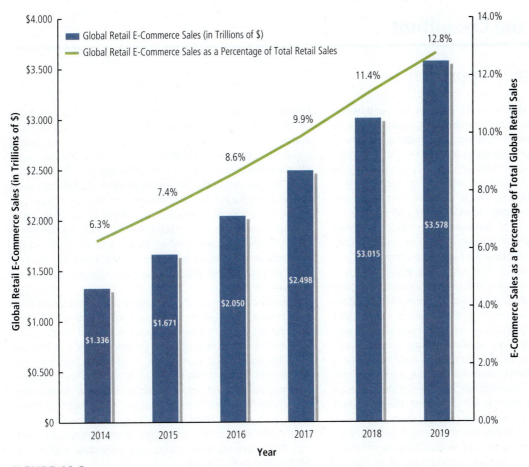

FIGURE 10.3

Global Retail E-Commerce Sales

Source: Based on *Worldwide Retail E-Commerce Sales: EMarketer's Updated Estimates and Forecast Through 2019*, EMarketer, 2015, p. 2.

Factors to Consider Before Launching into E-commerce

The first e-commerce transaction took place on August 11, 1994, when NetMarket, a small company founded by recent college graduate Daniel Kohn, sold a CD by Sting, *Ten Summoner's Tales*, to a student at Swarthmore College for $12.48 plus shipping.[15] From these humble beginnings grew a distribution channel that now accounts for $580 billion in annual retail sales in North America alone.[16] Despite the many benefits the Internet offers, however, not every small business owner is ready to embrace e-commerce. According to a recent study by research firm Clutch, 54 percent of small business owners in the United States have Web sites, more than twice as many as were operating online in 2000. However, 23 percent of small business's Web sites are not mobile-commerce friendly, which puts them at a distinct disadvantage because 58 percent of Web searches take place on mobile devices.[17] The primary reasons that business owners give for not having a Web site is that they believe that a Web site is not relevant to their company (32 percent), creating and maintaining a site is too costly (30 percent), and operating a Web site is not necessary because they use social media instead (12 percent).[18]

Small businesses have been allocating more resources to their e-commerce efforts, investing in developing and updating their Web sites, optimizing their sites to achieve top search engine rankings, making their sites mobile-friendly, and encouraging customers to post reviews of their

LO1

Understand the factors an entrepreneur should consider before launching into e-commerce.

You Be the Consultant

A Multichannel Approach

Although most retail sales still take place in brick-and-mortar stores, e-commerce sales as a percentage of total sales continue to grow. E-commerce continues to disrupt many retail sectors, ranging from florists and fashion to books and bedding. Start-up companies have entered these markets with online strategies that offer the advantages of lower overhead expenses, no cadre of salespeople to hire and train, and minimal operating costs. However, online businesses lack the ability to meet their customers face-to-face and provide them with "hands-on," personalized customer service. Converting browsing shoppers into paying customers continues to be challenging for even the best online companies.

This dilemma is leading many companies, including e-commerce giant Amazon, to take a multichannel approach, coupling a physical presence with brick-and-mortar stores with an extensive e-commerce effort to meet customers wherever they want to shop. In 2010, customers purchased less than 1 percent of all eyewear online, but a team of young entrepreneurs, college friends Neil Blumenthal, Andrew Hunt, Jeffrey Raider, and David Gilboa, quickly changed that. They created Warby Parker, a company that sells chic, retro-style eyeglasses at bargain prices. It stuck with an online-only strategy for years. In 2013, however, the cofounders opened their first retail store in New York City as an experiment. It was so successful that Warby Parker now operates nearly 50 outlets across the United States and Canada. Gilboa says that the stores generate annual sales at an impressive rate of $3,000 per square foot and are profitable. Just as important, however, they drive sales and profits online for Warby Parker by extending its brand in what Gilboa calls a "halo effect."

Other formerly online-only companies are pursuing the same multichannel strategy. Jennifer Fleiss and Jennifer Hyman cofounded Rent the Runway, a company that rents luxury designer fashions such as dresses, accessories, and outerwear, as an e-commerce business. With a 150,000-square-foot fulfillment center, Rent the Runway ships designer dresses in sizes from 0 to 22 that can cost thousands of dollars to its more than 5 million members for four-day rentals that range from $10 to $800. A few years ago, the company launched a subscription service aimed at working women who need to keep their professional wardrobes fresh. After six years of steady online growth, Fleiss and Hyman decided to open a retail outlet in New York City and now have a total of eight stores that support their company's e-commerce strategy. Rent the Runway's annual sales now exceed $800 million.

Other businesses that began as brick-and-mortar retailers have found success with a multichannel strategy. Stephen Gordon launched Restoration Hardware in Eureka, California, in 1979, when he was remodeling a house and had difficulty finding affordable, high-quality hardware, molding, and accessories that fit its classic Victorian style. The company's first retail store was the remodeled home where he and his wife lived. Over time, Restoration Hardware grew to 85 stores, but the pressures of the Great Recession, e-commerce, and big-box competitors forced the company to rescale, close many of its small stores, and open new larger ones in key locations. Today, the company's 69 retail galleries, some of which are as much as 60,000 square feet and are located in renovated historic buildings, serve as ideal showrooms that provide customers with design ideas for their own homes.

Restoration Hardware's Web site is a key component in its sales strategy. CEO Gary Freidman says that the company's vision is to blur the lines between the physical and digital buying experience and to complement its online presence with stores that look more like homes than stores. After experiencing growing pains, Restoration Hardware has simplified its supply chain, improved inventory control, and reduced shipping times for online orders. Like Warby Parker and Rent the Runway, Restoration Hardware's stores support its e-commerce sales. In turn, its e-commerce presence enhances its retail stores' sales. Since launching this strategy, Restoration Hardware's sales have more than tripled, from $600 million to $1.9 billion.

1. What advantages does an "online-only" strategy offer a company? Disadvantages? Why do many start-up companies use this strategy?

2. What advantages do retail stores offer a company? Disadvantages?

3. Why are many companies shifting to a multichannel strategy that involves both physical stores and an online presence?

Sources: Based on Douglas MacMillan, "Online Retailer Conquers a New World: Physical Stores," *Wall Street Journal*, November 18, 2014, pp. B1–B2; Tim Laster, Matt Egol, and Scott Bauer, "Navigating Retail's Last Mile," *Strategy + Business*, November 9, 2015, www.strategy-business.com/article/00369?gko=ad8b1; Rip Empson, "Warby Parker Opens Retail Store in NYC, with Boston Up Next, Beats Google and Amazon to the Punch," *Tech Crunch*, April 13, 2013, https://techcrunch.com/2013/04/13/warby-parker-opens-retail-store-in-nyc-with-boston-up-next-beats-google-amazon-to-the-offline-punch/; Paula Vasan, "Rent the Runway's Designer Closet Tops $800 Million," *CNBC*, July 25, 2015, www.cnbc.com/2015/07/25/rent-the-runways-designer-closet-tops-800-million.html; Dinah Eng, "The Nuts and Bolts of Restoration Hardware," *Fortune*, December 30, 2014, http://fortune.com/2014/12/29/the-nuts-and-bolts-of-restoration-hardware/; "RH Unveils RH Seattle, The Gallery at University Village," Restoration Hardware, November 22, 2016, http://ir.restorationhardware.com/phoenix.zhtml?c=79100&p=irol-newsArticle&ID=2225212.

businesses, products, and services. Before launching an e-commerce effort, entrepreneurs should consider the following important strategic issues:

- The way in which a company exploits the Internet's ability to connect with people anywhere in the world and the opportunities it creates to transform relationships with customers, suppliers and vendors, and other external stakeholders are crucial to its success.

ENTREPRENEURIAL PROFILE: Mary Helen Bowers: Ballet Beautiful After dancing with the prestigious New York City Ballet for a decade, Mary Helen Bowers developed an exercise routine to maintain her fitness. Bowers launched a company, Ballet Beautiful, and began training women, including celebrities and supermodels, in her Upper East Side studio in New York City with targeted exercises and stretches designed to sculpt her clients' bodies into the toned, graceful physique of a ballerina. When Bowers went to California for several months to train Natalie Portman for her Oscar-winning performance in the 2010 film *Black Swan*, she began to move her workouts online so that she could continue to serve her existing clients. Today, Ballet Beautiful's Web site offers workout videos that clients can stream as well as exercise clothing and accessories. Through her company's Web site, Bowers also offers a customized, interactive online workout that her clients can access from anywhere in the world.[19] ■

Nancy Kaszerman/Zuma Press, Inc./Alamy Stock Photo

- Success requires a company to develop a plan for integrating the Internet into its overall business strategy. The plan should address issues such as Web site design and maintenance, brand name creation and management, marketing and promotional strategies, sales, and customer service. *Everything* about a company's Web site—colors, fonts, style, theme, and more—should reflect and reinforce its brand image. A Web site must communicate the company's value proposition consistently.

- Developing deep, lasting relationships with customers takes on even greater importance on the Internet. Attracting online customers costs money, and companies must be able to retain their online customers to make their Web sites profitable. This means that online companies must give their customers good reasons to keep coming back.

- Creating a meaningful presence on the Internet requires an ongoing investment of resources—time, money, energy, and talent. Establishing an attractive Web site brimming with catchy photographs and descriptions of products is only the beginning. Keeping a Web site updated with fresh content and enhancing its performance to create a better customer experience are essential to online success.

- Measuring the success of its Internet-based sales effort is essential if a company is to remain relevant to customers whose tastes, needs, and preferences are always changing. Using Web analytics to continuously improve a Web site is essential.

Doing business on the Internet takes more time and energy than many entrepreneurs expect. The following six factors are essential to achieving e-commerce success:

- *Acquiring customers.* The first e-commerce skill that entrepreneurs must master is acquiring customers, which requires them to drive traffic to their Web sites. Entrepreneurs must develop a strategy for using the many tools that are available, which range from display ads and Google AdWords to social media and search marketing.

- *Optimizing conversions.* Every online entrepreneur's goal is to convert Web site visitors into paying customers. The efficiency with which an online company achieves this goal plays a significant role in determining its profitability. Unfortunately, almost 97 percent of visitors to the typical retail Web site do not purchase anything.

- *Maximizing Web site performance.* Once shoppers find a company's Web site, they should encounter a site that downloads quickly, is easy to navigate, and contains meaningful content that they can find quickly and efficiently. A fast, simple checkout process also is essential. Otherwise, shoppers will abandon the site, never to return.

- *Ensuring a positive user experience.* Achieving customer satisfaction online is just as important as it is offline. Providing top-notch customer service online has far-reaching effects because, as you learned earlier, today's shoppers are likely to engage with a company across multiple channels. Customer satisfaction online influences not just whether shoppers return to the company's Web site but also whether they will buy from its retail store or through a mobile app. An above-average bounce rate (the percentage of single-page visits to a Web site) and shopping cart abandonment rate or a conversion rate that is below average are signs that a company's Web site is not providing a positive customer experience.

- *Retaining customers.* Just as in offline stores, customer retention is essential to the success of online businesses. One study reports that increasing customer retention in a traditional business by 2 percent produces the same financial impact as reducing costs by 10 percent.[20] Another classic study by management consulting firm Bain and Company reports that increasing customer retention by 5 percent increases a company's profits by 25 percent to 95 percent, depending on the industry.[21] The same customer loyalty economics apply to e-commerce companies. Shoppers who return to a company's Web site spend 2.92 times more than one-time shoppers and account for one-third of overall online spending.[22] Customer retention is essential to e-commerce success. To thrive, entrepreneurs must create an online shopping experience that engages customers, offers them value, provides them with convenience, and keeps them coming back.

- *Using Web analytics as part of a cycle of continuous improvement.* Entrepreneurs can use a multitude of Web analytics tools (many of them free) to analyze the performance and the effectiveness of their Web sites. A Web site is never really "finished" but is always a work in progress, and analytics tools provide the data for driving continuous improvement.

We will explain how to achieve these six goals in the "Strategies for E-success" section of this chapter.

LO2

Explain the 11 myths of e-commerce and how to avoid falling victim to them.

Eleven Myths of E-commerce

Although many entrepreneurs have made their fortunes through e-commerce, setting up shop on the Internet is no guarantee of success. Scores of entrepreneurs have plunged unprepared into the world of e-commerce only to discover that there is more to it than merely setting up a Web site and waiting for orders to start pouring in. Make sure you do not fall victim to one of the following e-commerce myths.

Myth 1. If I Launch a Site, Customers Will Flock to It

Some entrepreneurs think that once they set up their Web sites, their expenses end there. Not true! Without promotional support, no Web site will draw enough traffic to support a business. With more than 1.2 billion Web sites in existence (a dramatic increase from fewer than 3,000 in 1994) and 51 million added each year, getting a site noticed in the crowd has become increasingly difficult.[23] Listing a site with popular search engines does not guarantee that online customers will find your company's Web site. Just like traditional retail stores seeking to attract customers, virtual companies have discovered that drawing sufficient traffic to a Web site requires constant promotion—and lots of it! Setting up a Web site and then failing to drive customers to it with adequate promotional support is like setting up a physical store in a back alley; you may be in business, but nobody knows you're there!

Entrepreneurs with both physical and online stores must promote their Web sites at every opportunity by printing their Internet addresses, or uniform resource locators (URLs), on everything related to their physical stores—on signs, in print and broadcast ads, on shopping bags, on merchandise labels, on employees' uniforms, and anything else their customers will see. Successful online entrepreneurs also use social media such as Facebook, Twitter, Linke-dIn, Pinterest, and YouTube to drive traffic to their Web sites and purchase ads on high-traffic sites such as Google (Google AdSense) and Facebook, both of which allow companies to establish maximum expenditures based on the number of people who click on their ads. Using these tools, companies can aim their ads at specific target customers by location, age, and interests.

 ENTREPRENEURIAL PROFILE: Carly Strife, Matt Meeker, and Henrik Werdelin: Bark and Company
Carly Strife, Matt Meeker, and Henrik Werdelin cofounded Bark and Company, a New York City–based business that offers a subscription service for "BarkBoxes," boxes of themed toys and treats shipped to dog owners. The company uses Facebook's Canvas advertising feature to increase its brand recognition, drive new customers to its Web site, and build stronger relationships with its existing customers. Canvas allows businesses to tell their stories and promote their products and services by incorporating still photos, videos, text, and call-to-action buttons into a "canvas" that downloads quickly, especially on mobile devices. With Canvas, Bark and Company targeted specific customers using a profile based on its recent subscribers, high-lifetime-value customers, and people who had clicked on its previous Facebook ads. The company also targeted the ad at other Facebook users who fit this profile. The ad included an introductory video of a happy dog excitedly tearing into his BarkBox, followed by photos of other dogs enjoying their BarkBoxes. Ad copy explained that each BarkBox

Courtesy of Bark and Company

includes all-natural treats and toys built around a unique theme and is carefully curated by experts. The ad also included a clever "Fetch BarkBox" call-to-action button. Using analytics, Bark and Company discovered that its clever Facebook Canvas ad increased its conversion rate 2.6 times, increased its customer acquisition rate 5 percent, and decreased its cost per acquisition by 10 percent.[24] ∎

The keys to promoting a Web site are *networking*, building relationships with other companies, customers, trade associations, online directories, and other Web sites that your company's customers visit; *connecting* with potential customers through an effective search marketing strategy; and *interacting* with existing and potential customers online through social media outlets.

Myth 2. Online Customers Are Easy to Please

Customers who shop online today are experienced Internet users whose expectations of their online shopping experiences are high and continue to rise. Experienced online shoppers tend to be unforgiving, quickly clicking to another site if their shopping experience is subpar or they cannot find the products and information they want. Because Web shoppers are increasingly more discriminating, companies are finding that they must improve their Web sites constantly to attract and keep their customers.

Experts estimate that as many as 24 million e-commerce sites sell goods and services on the Internet; however, only about 650,000 of them generate more than $1,000 in sales annually.[25] To be successful online marketers, small companies must create Web sites with features that appeal to experienced Web shoppers, such as simple navigation; personalized content; customer reviews; an efficient checkout process; multiple payment options; rock-solid security; quick access to product information, videos, and blogs; and the ability to track their shipments online. In addition, when customers have questions about or experience problems with an online shopping experience, companies that provide easy access to customer assistance and support have the advantage. Giving customers easy access to service representatives through multiple options, such as a toll-free telephone number, live chat, click-to-call, live video chat, and texting (for the growing number of customers who shop from their smart phones and other mobile devices), increases the probability that they will complete their transactions and return to shop again. The payoff for creating a positive online experience for shoppers is significant: Customers are more likely to trust the company, complete their purchases, buy from the company again, recommend the company to someone else, and mention it favorably in social media posts. Conversely, a poor online shopping experience translates into shoppers abandoning their shopping carts, having a negative impression of the company, losing trust in the business, and, as a result, purchasing from a competing Web site.[26] Table 10.1 provides useful tips for entrepreneurs to increase the conversion rates for their Web sites.

ENTREPRENEURIAL PROFILE: Johnston & Murphy Founded in 1850, Johnston & Murphy, a maker of quality shoes for men and, since 2008, for women, sold its shoes to generations of customers through traditional retail outlets before launching a Web site in 1996. (The company, based in Nashville, Tennessee, has made shoes for U.S. presidents, starting with Millard Fillmore in the mid-nineteenth century.) Johnston & Murphy recently began using the

TABLE 10.1 Tips for Improving Your Web Site's Conversion Rate

1. *Increase the speed at which your Web site downloads.* Speeding up the rate at which your Web site loads produces higher traffic growth, longer engagement times, lower bounce rates, and higher conversion rates.

2. *Use responsive design in your Web site.* A responsive Web site automatically detects the device a visitor is using and configures the layout and content of the site to fit the screen. Nearly half of Web users say that if a site fails to use responsive design, particularly on mobile devices, they take it as a sign that the business is not customer focused and shop elsewhere.

3. *Use A/B testing to determine which design features produce higher conversion rates.* A/B testing involves generating two versions (A and B) of a Web page, perhaps with a different headline, color scheme, call to action, or some other component, displaying them to two groups of customers simultaneously, and determining which one produces the higher conversion rate.

4. *Be accessible to customers.* One of the best ways to increase sales is to allow customers to contact your business easily. Provide readily visible contact information, including a telephone number and an e-mail address. A live chat option is best. Research shows that 90 percent of online customers consider live chat to be helpful; however, if live chat is not an option for your business, be sure to respond promptly to customers' e-mails and phone calls.

5. *Incorporate clear calls to action using large, easy-to-find buttons.* Including a big call-to-action button that stands out on every page ("Buy now," "Add to cart," and others) will increase your company's conversion rate by 10 to 25 percent.

6. *Build simple navigation into your site's design.* A muddled, poorly planned Web site that is confusing to navigate will send customers scurrying to competitors' Web sites. Smooth, simple navigation improves a site's conversion rate.

7. *Include a search function on your site.* Many online shoppers are accustomed to using a search feature to quickly and easily find the items they seek. Make sure your site includes an easy-to-use search feature located in the upper-right corner of the site. A search feature that provides recommendations of relevant products also helps.

8. *Emphasize your site's security.* Fraud is a top concern for online shoppers, so be sure that your site reassures customers that it meets security standards. Displaying relevant security seals such as Norton, McAfee, Verisign, BBB, and TRUSTe sends an important signal to online shoppers.

9. *Let customers see—really see—the products you are selling.* Clear images of products and a rotate/zoom feature that enables customers to see product details from different angles increase sales. Including videos of a product in use can improve a company's conversion rate by as much as 80 percent.

10. *Include product reviews.* Ninety-two percent of online shoppers read online reviews, and 88 percent of shoppers say that reviews influence their purchase decisions. Including product reviews produces, on average, an 18 percent increase in sales.

11. *Capitalize on the opportunity to cross-sell and upsell.* Including a "Customers who bought this item also bought . . ." feature can increase sales via cross-selling. In addition, showing shoppers a "better" product option than the one they are considering may convince them to upgrade their purchase (upselling).

12. *Design a simple checkout procedure.* When it comes to the checkout process, the fewer steps a site requires, the higher its conversion rate. A study of the top 100 e-commerce site shows that the average number of steps in the checkout process is just five. In addition, offering a guest checkout option is essential because more than one-third of shoppers will abandon their shopping carts if a site requires them to create an account.

Sources: Based on Graham Charlton, "25 E-commerce Conversion Tips," *ClickZ*, May 20, 2016, www.clickz.com/25-ecommerce-conversion-tips-infographic/100433/; Khusbu Shrestha, "50 Stats You Need to Know About Online Reviews," Vendasta, August 29, 2016, www.vendasta.com/blog/50-stats-you-need-to-know-about-online-reviews/; Neil Patel, "5 E-Commerce Stats That Will Make You Change Your Entire Marketing Approach, *Kissmetrics*, January 2015, https://blog.kissmetrics.com/5-ecommerce-stats/; Khalid Saleh, "7 Remarkably Simple Methods to Boost Checkout Conversion Rates," *Usability Geek*, March 9, 2016, http://usabilitygeek.com/7-remarkably-simple-methods-boost-checkout-conversion-rates/; Anis Salvesen, "6 Checkout Optimization Questions: A Q&A with Baymard Institute," MoovWeb, October 15, 2015, www.moovweb.com/blog/6-checkout-optimization-questions-a-qa-with-baymard-institute/.

data it gathers from sales in retail stores to provide a better, more customized experience for online shoppers and to offer them cross-selling promotions, such as discounts on apparel for customers who in the past had purchased only shoes. The responsively designed site also creates personalized content for female visitors, displaying women's shoes and apparel. When a VIP customer logs in, the site provides free two-day shipping on every order. A simple, easy-to-navigate site and streamlined checkout process help close sales. Since redesigning its site, Johnston & Murphy has seen a 16.4 percent increase in revenue per shopping session, a 6.6 percent increase in average order value, and a 23.3 percent increase in its new visitor conversion rate.[27] ∎

Myth 3. Launching an E-Commerce Site Is Free—Or at Least Really Inexpensive

Technology advances have significantly reduced the cost of launching an e-commerce business. Modern e-commerce entrepreneurs can build a basic Web site for next to nothing, outsource the tasks of storing and shipping products, lease space on a server, and rent cloud-computing software to operate their online businesses—all of which lower the cost and complexity of starting an online company. Although e-commerce platform providers advertise low monthly fees (often as low as $30 per month) for a basic Web site, entrepreneurs often must hire Web designers to make their sites look polished and professional, which can cost several thousand dollars. Ensuring the safe transfer of customers' payment data over the Internet requires an e-commerce company to purchase or renew an SSL (Secure Sockets Layer) certificate for between $100 and $1,500 per year. Accepting credit and debit card payments or using payment services such as PayPal, Stripe, and Square requires an online merchant to submit an application and pay monthly fees ranging from $30 to $125 per month, plus transaction fees of 1.8 to 3.5 percent. As companies grow and their Web sites become bigger and more detailed, they often require more bandwidth from their e-commerce providers, which can cost from $50 to $200 or more per month.[28] One experienced e-commerce solutions developer and designer says that most of the Web sites that his company creates cost between $5,000 and $10,000.[29]

Myth 4. Making Money on the Web Is Easy

Promoters who hawk "get-rich-quick" schemes on the Internet lure many entrepreneurs with the promise that making money online is easy. It isn't. The cost of acquiring an online customer continues to climb, which increases the cost of doing business for e-commerce entrepreneurs. Selling products and services online can be very profitable, but making money online requires an up-front investment of time, money, and energy. Success online also requires a sound business strategy that is aimed at the appropriate target audience and that an entrepreneur must implement effectively and efficiently—in other words, the same elements that are required for success *offline*.

Myth 5. Privacy Is Not an Important Issue on the Web

The Internet allows companies to gain access to almost unbelievable amounts of information about their customers' online behavior. Tracking tools monitor customers' behavior while they are on a site, giving Internet-based businesses the information they need to make their Web sites more customer friendly. Many sites also offer visitors "freebies" in exchange for information about themselves. Companies then use this information to learn more about their target customers and how to market to them more effectively. Concern over privacy and the proper use of this information has become a topic of debate by many interested parties, including government agencies, consumer watchdog groups, and customers. The TRUSTe Privacy Index reports that 92 percent of Americans worry about their privacy online, and 74 percent say they have limited their online activity (including making purchases) within the last year because of privacy concerns.[30]

Companies that collect information from their online customers must safeguard their customers' privacy, protect the information they collect against unauthorized use, and use it responsibly. This means that a business should post its privacy policy on its Web site, explaining to customers how it intends to use the information it collects. Then it must be sure to follow it! One of the surest ways to alienate online customers is to abuse the information collected from them by selling it to third parties or by spamming customers with unwanted solicitations.

Many customers don't trust Web sites, especially those of companies they don't know. TRUSTe Privacy Index reports that 44 percent of Americans do not trust businesses with their personal information online.[31] In addition, 28 percent of online shoppers have abandoned their shopping carts because of security concerns.[32] Therefore, a key component of a successful e-commerce effort, especially for small companies that are not well known, is building trust among customers. Posting security icons from certification services assures customers that a site meets security standards. Privacy *does* matter on the Web, and businesses that respect and protect their customers' privacy win their customers' trust. Trust is the foundation on which the long-term customer relationships that are so crucial to Web success are built.

Myth 6. "Strategy? I Don't Need a Strategy to Sell on the Web! Just Give Me a Web Site, and the Rest Will Take Care of Itself"

Building a successful e-business is no different than building a successful brick-and-mortar business; both require well-thought-out strategies. To build a strategy, an entrepreneur must first develop a clear definition of the company's target audience and a thorough understanding of customers' needs, wants, likes, and dislikes. To be successful, a Web site must be appealing to the customers it seeks to attract, just as a traditional store's design and decor must draw foot traffic. If a Web site is to become the foundation for a successful e-business, an entrepreneur must create it with the target audience in mind.

Recall from Chapter 5 that one goal of developing a strategy is to set a business apart from its competition. The same is true for creating a strategy for conducting business online. It is just as important, if not more so, for an online business to differentiate itself from the competition if it is to be successful. Unlike customers in a retail store, who must exert the effort to go to a competitor's store if they cannot find what they want, online customers only have to click or tap a time or two to go to a rival Web site. Therefore, competition online is fierce, and to succeed, a company must differentiate itself from its competitors, often by focusing on a market niche.

ENTREPRENEURIAL PROFILE: Paul Saunders: eLuxurySupply While serving in the Marine Corps in south Texas, Paul Saunders struck a deal with a local golf shop to sell its stagnant inventory online for a percentage of the revenue. His success in that venture and a negative experience buying luxury sheets online (they turned out to be of exceptionally poor quality) led Saunders to start ExceptionalSheets.com, an online business that sells quality luxurious sheets, in his Evansville, Indiana, garage. The business grew quickly, and when his company's expanding product line began taking over the house, Saunders knew it was time to quit his corporate job and focus on his business full-time. After 10 banks refused Saunders's loan application, he received a $250,000 loan from a small local bank that was backed by a guarantee from the Small Business Administration to acquire office and warehouse space. Within a year, Saunders was able to land additional financing, also backed by the SBA, to expand into global markets, including Europe, the United Kingdom, Canada, and Japan. From there, the company grew rapidly, and Saunders has expanded the business to include hundreds of items, ranging from pillows and mattress pads to pet beds and soaps. Today, his company, now called eLuxurySupply, generates $31 million in annual sales and is one of the fastest-growing small businesses in the United States, recording an impressive three-year growth rate of 23,620 percent![33] ∎

Myth 7. The Most Important Part of Any E-Commerce Effort Is Technology

As important as it is to have the right technology to support an e-commerce business, this is *not* the most crucial ingredient in the recipe for success. What matters most is understanding the underlying business and developing a workable business model that offers customers something of value at a reasonable price and produces a profit for the company. The entrepreneurs who are proving to be most successful in e-commerce are those who know how their industries work inside and out and then build an e-business around that knowledge. They know that they can hire Web designers, database experts, and fulfillment companies to handle the technical aspects of their online businesses but that nothing can substitute for a solid understanding of the inner workings of their industry, their target markets, and the strategy needed to pull the various parts together. The key is seeing the Internet for what it really is: another way to reach and serve customers with an effective business model and to minimize the cost of doing business. In other words, the formula for success is business model first, technology to support it second.

Myth 8. Customer Service Is Not as Important Online as It Is in a Traditional Retail Store

The Internet offers the ultimate in shopping convenience. Numerous studies report that convenience and low prices are the primary reasons people shop online. With just a few mouse clicks or taps on the screen of a smart phone or tablet, people can shop for practically anything anywhere in the world and have it delivered to their doorsteps within days. As convenient as online shopping is, customers still expect high levels of service. Unfortunately, some e-commerce companies treat customer service as an afterthought, an attitude that costs businesses in many ways, including lost customers and a diminished public image. The fact is that customer service is just as important (if not more so) online as it is in traditional brick-and-mortar stores.

The average conversion rate for e-commerce sites is just 3.16 percent.[34] In other words, out of 1,000 visitors to the typical company's Web site, only about 32 of them actually make a purchase! Sites that are slow to load, difficult to navigate, suffer from complicated checkout systems, or confuse shoppers turn customers away, many of them never to return. Only 27 percent of e-commerce businesses are satisfied with their conversion rates, and 9 percent are very dissatisfied.[35]

ENTREPRENEURIAL PROFILE: Dan Gerler: OnlineShoes.com Dan Gerler is CEO of OnlineShoes.com, a family-owned chain of retail stores based in Seattle, Washington, that became the first online shoe retailer in 1996. Gerler was determined to increase the company's conversion rate by improving its Web site and making it easier for customers to browse and buy. Web analytics showed Lynn Stetson, the company's director of e-commerce, marketing, and merchandising, that at checkout, many customers had neglected to select a shoe size, and they were forced to backtrack to complete their purchases. Many customers simply abandoned their shopping carts at this point. Stetson added a pop-up reminder that alerted shoppers when they failed to specify a size and included text next to the "add to cart" button that emphasized the company's key selling points: free shipping and exchanges and 365-day-a-year returns. The result was a 20 percent increase in OnlineShoes.com's conversion rate.[36] ∎

There is plenty of room for improvement in customer service on the Web. Shoppers' unmet expectations of superior customer service translate into a high shopping cart abandonment rate. Research shows that 68.6 percent of online shoppers who fill their online shopping carts abandon them without checking out, which costs businesses globally a whopping $4.9 trillion in lost sales.[37] The cart abandonment rate jumps to 97 percent for shoppers who use mobile devices.[38] Figure 10.4 shows the leading causes of shopping cart abandonment.

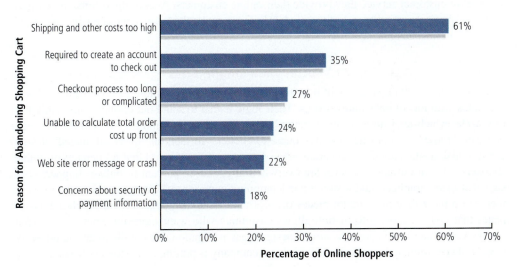

FIGURE 10.4

Reasons Customers Abandon Online Shopping Carts

Source: Based on data from Baymard Institute, 2016.

When customers abandon their shopping carts, companies can close a significant percentage of those "lost" sales (Business Intelligence estimates that retailers can recover 63 percent of them) by sending prompt follow-up "triggered" e-mails designed to convince the customer to complete the purchase.[39] On average, 20 percent of shoppers who abandon their carts and receive follow-up ("re-targeted") e-mails from the company (sooner is better) return to complete their purchases, often spending more than shoppers who completed their purchases without abandoning their carts.[40] These "triggered" e-mails produce an open rate that is 152 percent higher than for the traditional e-mails that companies send.[41] Including an offer for free shipping to customers who abandon their shopping carts is one of the most effective ways to convince them to complete their purchases.[42]

What steps can online entrepreneurs take to provide exceptional customer service? Consider these:

- *Offer live help*. One tool that increases a company's conversion rate and reduces its cart abandonment rate is live help. For reasonable fees, companies can hire virtual assistants, employees who work remotely to answer online shoppers' questions or offer advice (for example, whether an item's sizes tend to run small) in real time by e-mail, social media, or phone. Even small companies that cannot afford to staff a live chat center can offer customer-responsive chat options on their Web sites by using virtual chat agents. Loaded onto a company's site, these avatar-like creations can step in at the appropriate time to interact with customers, answering their questions or giving them the extra nudge they need, such as an offer of free shipping, to close the deal. Seventy-seven percent of online customers say that offering an online chat service positively influences their perception of an online retailer.[43]

- *Provide an easy order-tracking process*. Partnering with delivery services such as UPS and FedEx allows small businesses to offer an order-tracking feature so customers can track the status of their orders at any time.

- *Offer a simple return process*. If customers know up front that they can return items easily, they are more likely to make purchases.

- *Listen—and respond—on social media*. Increasingly, customers are turning to social media for customer service and support. Companies must monitor social media for customers' questions and complaints and address them promptly. Eighty-eight percent of customers say they are less likely to buy from companies that leave social media complaints and questions unanswered.[44]

The lesson for e-commerce entrepreneurs is simple: Devote time, energy, and money to developing an effective system for providing superior customer service. Companies that do will build a sizable base of loyal customers who will keep coming back. Figure 10.5 shows the Customer Experience Maturity Model, which provides a roadmap for online companies to improve the level of customer service they provide their online customers. According to Sitecore, 67 percent of businesses are in Stage 1 of the model (Initiate), and only 4.4 percent of businesses are in Stage 7 (Lifetime customer).[45]

Myth 9. Flashy Web Sites Are Better Than Simple Ones

Some businesses fall into the trap of pouring significant amounts of money into designing flashy Web sites with lots of bells and whistles. Their logic is that to stand out online, a site really has to sparkle, which leads to a "more-is-better" mentality when designing a site. On the Internet, however, "more" does *not* necessarily equate to "better." In fact, an "over-caffeinated" design can diminish a site's ability to generate sales. A recent survey reports that 52 percent of online shoppers say that current Web sites are overwhelming, and 64 percent of online shoppers seek sites that offer simplicity and a streamlined shopping experience.[46] A good rule of thumb is to include no more than three major pieces of information on each page. Providing clear links to pages that contain more information allows customers who want more information to find it easily. A Web site that includes a simple design, easy navigation, clear calls to action on every page, and consistent color schemes shows that a company is putting its customers first.

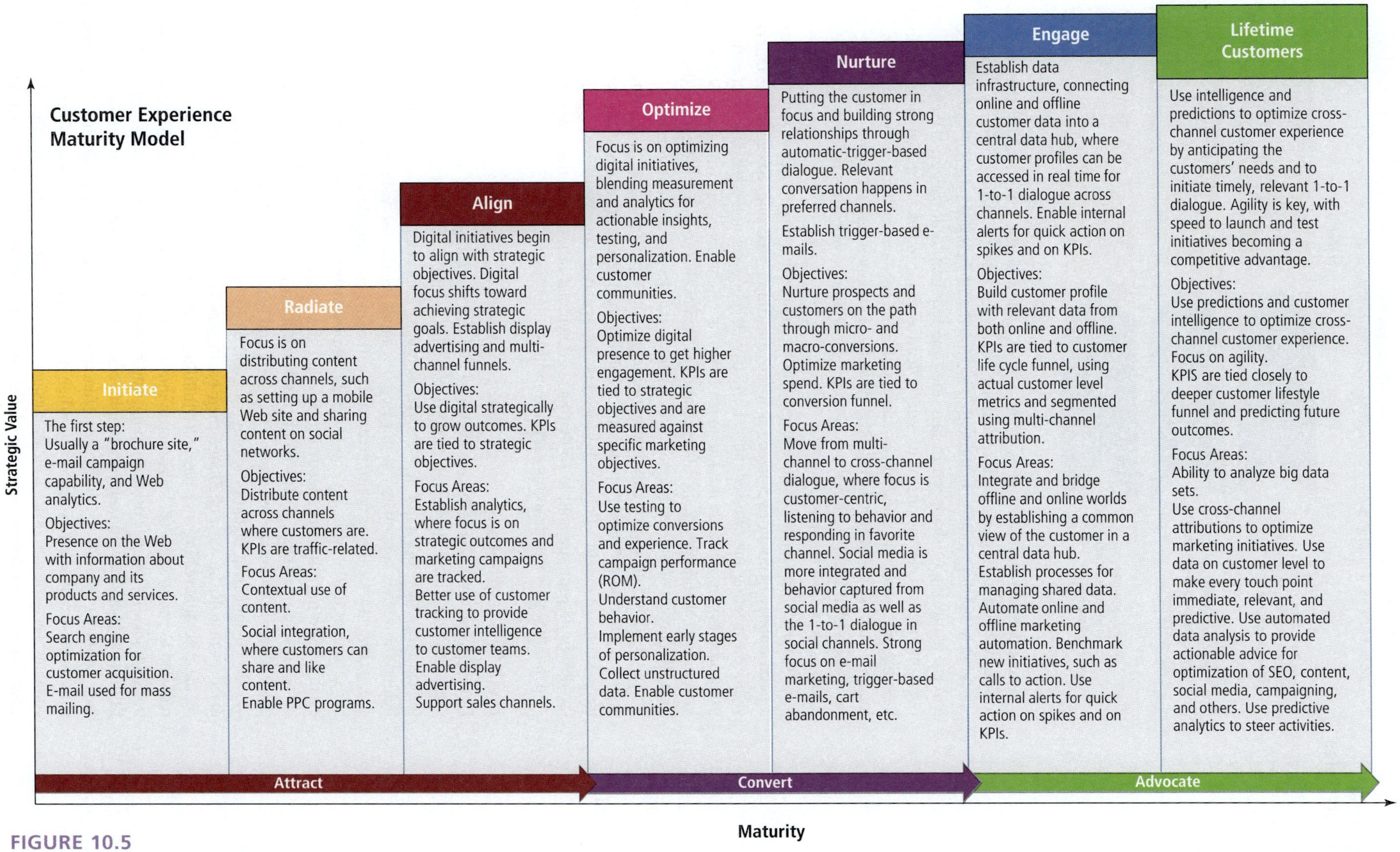

Customer Experience Maturity Model

Strategic Value (vertical axis) — **Maturity** (horizontal axis: Attract → Convert → Advocate)

	Initiate	Radiate	Align	Optimize	Nurture	Engage	Lifetime Customers
Description	The first step: Usually a "brochure site," e-mail campaign capability, and Web analytics.	Focus is on distributing content across channels, such as setting up a mobile Web site and sharing content on social networks.	Digital initiatives begin to align with strategic objectives. Digital focus shifts toward achieving strategic goals. Establish display advertising and multi-channel funnels.	Focus is on optimizing digital initiatives, blending measurement and analytics for actionable insights, testing, and personalization. Enable customer communities.	Putting the customer in focus and building strong relationships through automatic-trigger-based dialogue. Relevant conversation happens in preferred channels. Establish trigger-based e-mails.	Establish data infrastructure, connecting online and offline customer data into a central data hub, where customer profiles can be accessed in real time for 1-to-1 dialogue across channels. Enable internal alerts for quick action on spikes and on KPIs.	Use intelligence and predictions to optimize cross-channel customer experience by anticipating the customers' needs and to initiate timely, relevant 1-to-1 dialogue across channels. Agility is key, with speed to launch and test initiatives becoming a competitive advantage.
Objectives	Presence on the Web with information about company and its products and services.	Distribute content across channels where customers are. KPIs are traffic-related.	Use digital strategically to grow outcomes. KPIs are tied to strategic objectives.	Optimize digital presence to get higher engagement. KPIs are tied to strategic objectives and are measured against specific marketing objectives.	Nurture prospects and customers on the path through micro- and macro-conversions. Optimize marketing spend. KPIs are tied to conversion funnel.	Build customer profile with relevant data from both online and offline. KPIs are tied to customer life cycle funnel, using actual customer level metrics and segmented using multi-channel attribution.	Use predictions and customer intelligence to optimize cross-channel customer experience. Focus on agility. KPIs are tied closely to deeper customer lifestyle funnel and predicting future outcomes.
Focus Areas	Search engine optimization for customer acquisition. E-mail used for mass mailing.	Contextual use of content. Social integration, where customers can share and like content. Enable PPC programs.	Establish analytics, where focus is on strategic outcomes and marketing campaigns are tracked. Better use of customer tracking to provide customer intelligence to customer teams. Enable display advertising. Support sales channels.	Use testing to optimize conversions and experience. Track campaign performance (ROM). Understand customer behavior. Implement early stages of personalization. Collect unstructured data. Enable customer communities.	Move from multi-channel to cross-channel dialogue, where focus is customer-centric, listening to behavior and responding in favorite channel. Social media is more integrated and behavior captured from social media as well as the 1-to-1 dialogue in social channels. Strong focus on e-mail marketing, trigger-based e-mails, cart abandonment, etc.	Integrate and bridge offline and online worlds by establishing a common view of the customer in a central data hub. Establish processes for managing shared data. Automate online and offline marketing automation. Benchmark new initiatives, such as calls to action. Use internal alerts for quick action on spikes and on KPIs.	Ability to analyze big data sets. Use cross-channel attributions to optimize marketing initiatives. Use data on customer level to make every touch point immediate, relevant, and predictive. Use automated data analysis to provide actionable advice for optimization of SEO, content, social media, campaigning, and others. Use predictive analytics to steer activities.

FIGURE 10.5

The Customer Experience Maturity Model

Source: Based on Sitecore, 2015.

FIGURE 10.6

How Page Load Speed Affects Sales

Source: Based on "Why Faster Web Sites Make More Money," *WebpageFX*, July 23, 2014, www.webpagefx.com/blog/internet/website-page-load-time-conversions/.

Research by Kissmetrics shows that every one-second delay in a site's page load time reduces its conversion rate by 7 percent. If your site generates an average of $1,000 per day in sales:

	Per day	Per month	Per year
A 1-second *improvement* in page load speed produces a sales increase of…	$70	$2,130	$25,550
A 2-second *improvement* in page load speed produces a sales increase of…	$140	$4,260	$51,110
A 3-second *improvement* in page load speed produces a sales increase of…	$210	$6,390	$76,650

In e-commerce, milliseconds count. Sites that download slowly usually don't have a chance to sell because customers click to another site. Sites that perform efficiently and load quickly are far better selling tools than those that are filled with "cornea gumbo," are slow to download, and are confusing to shoppers. In fact, the time required to download a Web site is one of the most important determinants of its sales effectiveness. Studies show that sites that load slowly have higher bounce rates and lower conversion rates because customers abandon them for faster-loading sites (see Figure 10.6).[47] Fifty percent of shoppers say that they will not be loyal to a business whose Web site loads too slowly.[48] In addition, Web sites that load faster earn higher rankings on search engines.[49]

To online customers, whose expectations concerning online speed continue to escalate, a good online shopping experience is a fast, uncomplicated one. Successful e-tailers set their sights on meeting the two-second rule: If a Web site does not download within two seconds, users are likely to abandon it. (The mean time that online shoppers wait for a Web site to download before abandoning it is 2.08 seconds.[50]) If a Web site takes more than three seconds to load, 40 percent of online shoppers will abandon it.[51] Proper content, formatting, and design are therefore important ingredients in determining a site's performance. Smart e-tailers frequently test their sites' performance, speed, and reliability in different browsers, using a variety of online tools, such as Google's PageSpeed Insights, Sitespeed.io, and WebPageTest. The lesson: Keep the design of your site simple so that pages download in no more than two seconds and make sure that the site's navigation is easy and intuitive.

Myth 10. It's What's Up Front That Counts

Designing an attractive, efficient Web site and driving traffic to it are important in building a successful e-business. However, designing the back office, the systems that take over once customers place their orders on a Web site, is just as important as designing the site itself. If the behind-the-scenes support is not in place or cannot handle the volume of traffic from the Web site, a company's entire e-commerce effort will come crashing down. The potentially large number of orders that a Web site can generate can overwhelm a small company that has failed to establish the infrastructure needed to support the site. Although e-commerce can lower many costs of doing business, it still requires a basic infrastructure in the channel of distribution to process orders, maintain inventory, fill orders, and handle customer service.

virtual order fulfillment (or drop shipping)
a fulfillment strategy in which a company forwards customers' orders to a wholesaler or distributor, which then ships the product to the customer with the online merchant's label on it.

To customers, a business is only as good as its last order. Web-based entrepreneurs often discover that the greatest challenge their businesses face is not necessarily attracting customers on the Web but creating a viable order fulfillment strategy. Order fulfillment involves everything required to get goods from a warehouse into a customer's hands, such as order processing, warehousing, picking and packing, shipping, and billing. Some entrepreneurs choose to handle order fulfillment in-house with their own employees, and others find it more economical to hire specialized fulfillment houses to handle these functions. **Virtual order fulfillment** (or **drop shipping**) suits many small e-tailers perfectly. When a customer orders a product from its Web site, the company forwards the order to a wholesaler or distributor, which then ships the product to the customer with the online merchant's label on it. This strategy allows a small business to avoid the cost and the risk of carrying inventory.

Although e-tailers that use virtual order fulfillment avoid the major investments in inventory and the problems associated with managing it, they lose control over delivery times and service quality. In addition, finding a fulfillment house willing to handle a relatively small volume of orders at a reasonable price can be difficult for some small businesses. Major fulfillment providers that focus on small companies include Amazon, FedEx, UPS, DHL, ShipWire, and Webgistix.

Some businesses integrate their brick-and-mortar stores into their online order fulfillment strategies. They maximize customer convenience by allowing customers to order online and pick up their items (or return them, if necessary) to a physical store. Other companies use a ship-from-store fulfillment strategy, in which they fill online orders totally or in part from the inventory in their brick-and-mortar stores. Doing so maximizes the selection of merchandise from which customers can choose but requires the company to manage its inventory carefully to avoid starving its physical stores of goods if online demand surges.

ENTREPRENEURIAL PROFILE: Steve Conine and Hiraj Shah: Wayfair Wayfair, an online business founded in 2011 in Boston by Steve Conine and Hiraj Shah, sells thousands of home furnishing items, ranging from tables and lamps to rugs and kitchenware, through its Web site. Wayfair's data mining system enables the company to learn about customers' preferences, interact with them in meaningful ways, and predict the types of items they want to purchase. Managing items from more than 7,000 vendors scattered around the globe is no easy task, but Conine and Shah have developed proprietary software based on sophisticated algorithms to control the entire process. Wayfair relies on virtual order fulfillment and never handles most of the products it sells, eliminating the need to invest in expensive warehouses. When a customer orders a product from Wayfair's Web site, the software notifies the supplier, determines where the item is located, analyzes the best shipping method, and displays an estimated delivery date.[52] ■

Myth 11. My Business Doesn't Need a Web Site

Nearly half of all small businesses do not have Web sites, and many of those that do have sites lack the capability to handle sales online. To online shoppers, especially, these businesses might as well be invisible because doing business online and offline are inextricably connected. Not having a Web site damages a business's image; one survey reveals that 56 percent of shoppers do not trust a business that has no Web site.[53] Today, shoppers' social media interactions are likely to influence their purchases, and the probability that they will make a purchase from a smart phone or some other mobile device is growing rapidly. When they enter a retail store, shoppers still go online to read customer reviews, check prices, or search for similar products. Experienced online shoppers, particularly Millennials and those in Generation Z, expect to do business across multiple channels. Therefore, a multichannel presence is essential for small businesses, even for those that consider themselves completely "local." The key is to meet customers *wherever* they want to do business, with a personalized shopping experience like the ones they encounter in the best brick-and-mortar stores. C. Wonder, a retailer of women's clothing and accessories and home décor, is working hard to build brand recognition and loyalty with customers by surprising and delighting its best online customers with special gifts and handwritten thank-you notes in packages. The young company also relies on social media such as Facebook and Twitter to establish connections and to build a sense of community with its customers. For example, if a customer likes a particular purse on Facebook and later logs into the C. Wonder Web site with her Facebook credentials, the site will display that purse on the home page. The company's Web site also can identify individual customers and, based on their past purchase history, customize the landing pages they encounter to suit their tastes and preferences. "Personalized brand experiences for Web sites, apps, and passbook/wallet concepts using location and customer history and preferences wrapped in insight allow your brand to be more relevant and appealing to the customer," says one e-commerce expert. "Those brands that stand out will win the loyalty battle."[54]

Strategies for E-success

LO3

Explain the basic strategies entrepreneurs should follow to achieve success in their e-commerce efforts.

People now spend more time online than ever before. Today, the average American spends nearly six hours on digital media each day, significantly more than the four hours he or she spends watching television.[55] However, to convert these digital users into online customers, a business must do more than merely set up a Web site and wait for the sales to start rolling in.

How a company integrates the Internet into its overall business strategy determines how successful it will be. Following are some guidelines for building a successful e-commerce strategy for a small company.

Focus on a Niche in the Market

Rather than try to compete head-to-head with the dominant players on the Web that have the resources and the recognition to squash smaller competitors, many entrepreneurs find success serving market niches. Smaller companies' limited resources usually are better spent focusing on niche markets than trying to be everything to everyone. (Recall the discussion of the focus strategy in Chapter 5.) The idea is to concentrate on serving a small corner of the market that the giants have overlooked. Niches exist in every industry and can be highly profitable, given the right strategy. A niche can be defined in many ways, including by geography, customer profile, product, product usage, and many others.

Because of its pervasive reach and ability to tap large numbers of customers with a common interest, the Web provides an ideal mechanism for implementing a focus strategy.

Courtesy of Hearst Connecticut Media

ENTREPRENEURIAL PROFILE: Rishi and Tapasya Bali: YogaSmoga Having grown up in India, the birthplace of yoga, siblings Rishi and Tapasya Bali had practiced yoga since they were children. After moving to the United States to attend college, the Balis launched careers with major firms in the financial industry in New York City and continued their practice of yoga. Soon, the pair began discussing the idea of starting a yoga clothing company. Relying on their backgrounds in finance, they spent four years researching the industry, developing a business plan, and working with textile companies to develop a unique proprietary fabric that provides flexibility, breathability, and durability from which to make their yoga garments. In early 2013, the Balis launched YogaSmoga, an e-commerce site, and began selling their high-quality yoga garments. They knew that they had discovered a profitable niche when their first collection sold out in just three weeks. Following their strategic plan, the entrepreneurial duo opened their first retail store one year later in Greenwich, Connecticut, followed by a second store in Brentwood, California. In addition to its Web site, YogaSmoga sells its yoga garments, which are made in the United States and range from $49 to $165, through 9 retail stores and has plans to expand to 100 stores within a few years. Rishi says that the knowledge that he and his sister gained from the e-commerce side of the business made opening their retail stores much easier because they understood their customers' preferences and characteristics much better.[56] ∎

Build a Community

In an age in which social media dominates, the voice of the customer (VOC) has more power and holds more influence than ever before. Customers who have a bad service experience with a company broadcast it across multiple social media platforms and can bring a company to its knees. Conversely, companies that create brand advocates and champions reap the benefits of positive customer reviews on social media. Social media outlets provide natural avenues for small companies to engage their customers because they give visitors the opportunity to have conversations about products, services, and topics that interest them ("What is your favorite sports drink?"). Small businesses that are most successful at building a community enlist their most passionate customers as company evangelists through social media outlets such as Facebook, Twitter, Pinterest, Instagram, LinkedIn, and YouTube. Companies that successfully create a community with their Web sites serving as the nucleus of the interactions turn their customers into loyal fans who keep coming back and, better yet, invite others to join them. These entrepreneurs intentionally build a social component into their Web sites, with the goal of increasing customers' loyalty by giving them the ability to interact with other like-minded visitors or with experts to discuss and learn more about topics about which they are passionate.

Ideally, a company's Web site provides a mechanism not only for the company to connect with its customers but also for customers to engage one another. Internet users frequent sites of companies that embrace the social aspects of the Internet and give them the opportunity to interact as part of a community with other customers and with company employees. The most successful companies are those that seamlessly blend their Web sites with their social media presence and use one to support the other.

ENTREPRENEURIAL PROFILE: Lauren Pears: Lady Dinah's Cat Emporium After a particularly bad day at work, Lauren Pears decided to leave her corporate job, began writing a business plan, and raised the necessary capital via crowdfunding to launch Lady Dinah's Cat Emporium, a café in London that is home to 13 rescued cats that each week host hundreds of human guests looking for feline companionship at high tea and a 90-minute respite from the hectic pace of life. Pears was confident that her business would succeed, but even she admits to being surprised at the 20,000 reservations the Cat Emporium received in only its first two weeks of operation. Pears drives business to her company's Web site primarily through social media. Every cat has his or her own Twitter handle and regularly tweets photos and comments about his or her activities (or, being cats, lack of activity). The cats and the Cat Emporium have 11,000 followers on Instagram, more than 55,000 likes on Facebook, and 19,000 followers on Twitter. Lady Dinah's Cat Emporium uses social media very effectively to connect with her audience; currently, there is a six-week waiting list for reservations.[57] ∎

Roger Parkes/Alamy Stock Photo

Listen to Your Customers and Act on What You Hear

On social media, customers often talk about the brands they buy and businesses with which they interact. Successful companies make a concerted effort to listen to what their customers are saying about them on social media and respond to the feedback. Because of social media, customer comments, both positive and negative, play a more important role in a company's reputation than ever before. Some negative comments are inevitable, and the worst thing a company can do is ignore them because customers do not. In fact, according to a recent survey by BrightLocal, a search engine optimization company, 88 percent of customers say that they read online reviews to determine local businesses' reputations.[58] Smart entrepreneurs take the time to tune in to social media to hear what customers are saying about their businesses so that they can resolve their customers' problems quickly and improve their companies' reputations. They also solicit ideas and feedback from their customers on social media.

Attract Visitors by Giving Away "Freebies"

One of the most important words on the Internet is "free." Many successful e-merchants have discovered the ability to attract visitors to their sites by giving away something free and then selling them something else. One e-commerce consultant calls this cycle of giving something away and then selling something "the rhythm of the Web."[59] The "freebie" must be something customers value, but it does *not* have to be expensive, nor does it have to be a product. In fact, one of the most common giveaways on the Internet is *information*. Creating a free online or e-mail newsletter with links to your company's site, of course, and to others of interest is one of the most effective ways of driving potential customers to a site. Meaningful content presented in a clear, professional fashion is a must. Experts advise keeping online newsletters short—no more than about 600 words.

ENTREPRENEURIAL PROFILE: Fluent City Fluent City, a business that provides language and culture classes for adults in four major cities in the Northeast, regularly sends themed newsletters to current customers and prospects that provide fun, useful information and, of course, promote upcoming courses. Because the company targets young adults who see learning new languages and cultures as fun, the newsletters usually are quite playful. One recent newsletter that generated lots of interest featured a link to a video of a German professor's impromptu rap that Fluent City also posted on its social media outlets. Mandy Menaker, the company's director of marketing, says that although the goal of the newsletters is to convince people to sign up for classes, Fluent City strives to make the newsletter read like a letter from a friend rather than a sales ad. Every newsletter includes links to Fluent City's Web site and blog posts and buttons linking to its social media sites.[60] ■

Sell the "Experience"

When shoppers enter a retail store, they are courted by an attractive layout, appealing décor, and eye-catching merchandise displays and perhaps are greeted by a salesperson who can offer them information and advice about products and services. Although e-commerce businesses lack this ability to have face-to-face contact with customers, they can still engender loyalty by creating an engaging and enjoyable online shopping experience. Sites that offer shoppers easy navigation, a simple and fast checkout process, and thorough product descriptions with quality images can provide the same positive shopping experience as the best retail stores.

Make Creative Use of E-mail but Avoid Becoming a Spammer

open rate

the percentage of recipients who open an e-mail.

click-through rate

the percentage of recipients who open an e-mail and click through to the company's Web site.

E-mail is still the backbone of online marketing, especially for small businesses. Numerous studies show that e-mail is the most common marketing tool among small businesses. Used properly and creatively, e-mail can be an effective, low-cost way to build traffic on a Web site. Management consulting firm McKinsey and Company reports that the customer acquisition rate for e-mail campaigns is 40 times higher than that of Facebook and Twitter combined.[61] For e-mail marketing messages, the average **open rate** (the percentage of recipients who open an e-mail) is 20.9 percent, and the average **click-through rate** (the percentage of recipients who open an e-mail and click on the link to the company's Web site) is 3.6 percent.[62] One recent survey reports that U.S. marketers rank e-mail as the channel that produces the highest return on investment (122 percent) of their marketing methods, outpacing social media (28 percent), paid search (25 percent), and online display ads (18 percent).[63]

Just as with newsletters, an e-mail's content should offer something of value to recipients, such as useful tips, a link to an informative article, blog, or video ("How to tie a bow tie"), and offers of relevant products or services. Unfortunately, spam, those unsolicited and universally despised e-mail messages (which rank below postal junk mail and telemarketing calls as the worst form of junk advertising), limits the effectiveness of companies' legitimate e-mail marketing efforts. Spam is a persistent problem for online marketers; 57.8 percent of e-mails sent are spam (and nearly 5 percent of e-mails contain links to malicious Web sites).[64] Companies must comply with the CAN-SPAM Act, a law that regulates commercial e-mail and sets standards for commercial e-mail messages. (The penalties can be as much as $16,000 per e-mail for companies that violate the law.)

Globally, people send and receive more than 281 billion e-mails each day.[65] To avoid having their marketing messages become lost in that electronic clutter, companies rely on permission e-mails, collecting customers' and visitors' e-mail addresses (and their permission to send them e-mail messages) when they register on a site to receive a freebie. The most successful online retailers post e-mail opt-in messages prominently throughout their Web sites and on their social media pages as well. When customers sign up to receive permission e-mails, a company should send them "welcome" e-mails immediately. The most successful marketers give new customers a reason to open welcome e-mails, such as including an offer to "enjoy 10 percent off your first order." To be successful at collecting a sufficient number of e-mail addresses, a company must make clear to customers that they will receive messages that are meaningful to them and that the company will not sell e-mail addresses to others (which should be part of its posted privacy policy). Once a business has a customer's permission to send information in additional e-mail messages, it has a meaningful marketing opportunity to create a long-term customer relationship and to build customer loyalty.

Entrepreneurs should design every marketing e-mail to accomplish one purpose—some call to action—and everything in the e-mail, including the subject line, links, photos, and message, should focus tightly on that purpose. Accomplishing that purpose starts with creating the right subject line. A study of the subject lines of more than 3 billion marketing e-mails by

Adestra shows that words such as "thank you," "breaking," "exciting," "essential," "order today," "golden," "launch," and "buy" produce above-average open rates. In contrast, words such as "cheap," "prize," "unforgettable," "good," "get," "$," "fantastic," and "today" result in below-average open rates. How long the subject line should be has been a source of debate for years. One study of more than 2 million e-mails from retailers shows that although the most common subject line length is between 41 and 50 characters, e-mails with subject lines between 61 and 70 characters produce the highest read rates.[66] A subject line that tells recipients exactly what is in the e-mail also helps, and personalized e-mails that include the recipient's name (and city) have higher open rates than generic e-mails. Inside the e-mail, messages that contain no more than three images and 20 lines of text produce the highest click-through rates.[67] When it comes to marketing e-mails, customers welcome well-constructed permission e-mails that direct them to a company's site for information or special deals without resorting to a "hard sell."

E-mail messages must be mobile friendly because 55 percent of e-mails are opened on mobile devices.[68] Mobile users are more likely to read streamlined, single-column e-mails than old-fashioned, bulky, three-column e-mails. Studies show that the best days of the week to send e-mails are (in descending order) Tuesday, Thursday, and Wednesday. The optimum time of day to send e-mails (again in descending order) are 10 A.M., 8 P.M., 2 p.m., and 6 A.M.[69]

ENTREPRENEURIAL PROFILE: Justin Cameron, Lex Pedersen, and Haydn Smith: SurfStitch SurfStitch, Australia's leading online surf, snow, and skate retailer, revamped its e-mail marketing campaign after analyzing its customers' purchasing behavior to predict individual customers' expected order dates. SurfStitch began focusing specialized e-mail campaigns on three groups of inactive customers that it described as At-Risk, Disengaged Subscribers, and Churning Customers. Sending precisely timed "It's been a while," "We miss you," and "We want you back" e-mails, the company was able to reduce its customer churn by 72 percent in just six months. SurfStitch also revised its welcome e-mails for new customers and new newsletter subscribers to include special offers, such as discounts and free shipping and returns; engaged customers with surveys; and included links to its newest products. The changes produced a 40 percent increase in SurfStitch's open rate and a 65 percent increase in its click-through rate.[70] ■

Make Sure Your Web Site Says "Credibility"

Online shoppers are wary, and with the prevalence of online fraud, they have every right to be. Unless a company can build visitors' trust in its Web site, selling to them is virtually impossible. Visitors begin to evaluate the credibility of a site as soon as they arrive. Studies show that shoppers form an impression of a site's credibility within just 50 milliseconds (.005, seconds or about the same amount of time required for a hummingbird to flap its wings 5 times) of arrival.[71] Although quality content is crucial for converting visitors into paying customers, visitors' initial impressions of a site are almost wholly design related, which means entrepreneurs must create sites that are simple, consistent, appealing, and easy to navigate. Does the site look professional? Are there misspelled words and typographical errors? (More than 90 percent of online shoppers say they do not trust Web sites that contain errors.[72]) If the site provides information, does it note the sources of that information? If so, are those sources legitimate and trustworthy? Is the presentation of the information fair and objective, or is it biased? Are there dead links on the site? Does the company have its privacy and merchandise return policies posted in a prominent place?

One of the simplest ways to establish credibility with customers is to use brand names they know and trust. Whether a company sells nationally recognized brands or its own well-known private brand, using those names on its site creates a sense of legitimacy. People buy brand names they trust, and online companies can use this fact to their advantage. Businesses selling lesser-known brands should use customer testimonials and endorsements (with their permission, of course) about a product or service.

An effective way to build customer confidence is by joining an online seal program such as McAfee, TrustWave, TRUSTe, Norton, or BBBOnline. The online equivalent of the Underwriter Laboratories stamp or the Good Housekeeping Seal of Approval, these seals mean that a company meets certain standards concerning the privacy of customers' information and the resolution of customer complaints. Posting a privacy policy (as discussed later in this chapter) is another key ingredient in building trust. Including customer reviews—which Internet users say they believe more than product descriptions from a business—on product Web pages increases customers' trust in an online business. Testimonials, either in writing or on video, from real customers enhance a company's online credibility, especially among first-time customers. Businesses that are the subject of media coverage should include a "media" or "featured in" page with links to articles or videos about the company so that they can magnify the benefits of publicity. Linking to the company's social media accounts using "follow" buttons also lends credibility to an online business. Providing a street address, an e-mail address, and a toll-free telephone number also sends a subtle message to shoppers that a legitimate business is behind a Web site.

Another effective technique is to include an "about us" page on the Web site so that customers can read the company's story—its founders, how they started the business, the challenges they have overcome, and other details. Customers enjoy supporting small businesses with which they feel a connection, and this is a perfect opportunity for a small company to establish that type of connection. Many small companies include photographs of their brick-and-mortar stores and of their employees to combat the anonymity of the Internet and to give shoppers the feeling that they are supporting a friendly small business. One small online retailer includes on his Web site short anecdotes about his dog, Cody, the official company mascot, and Cody's "views" on featured products. The response to the technique has been so strong that Cody has become a celebrity among the company's customers and even has her own e-mail and social media accounts. Table 10.2 offers 12 guidelines for building the credibility of a Web site.

Make the Most of the Web's Global Reach

Despite the Web's reputation as an international marketplace, many entrepreneurs fail to take full advantage of its global reach. More than 3.7 billion people around the world use the Internet, and more than 91 percent of them live outside North America.[73] In addition, more than 74 percent of Web users throughout the world speak a language other than English.[74] Limiting a global market to only a small portion of its potential by ignoring foreign customers makes no sense. E-commerce companies that want to draw significant sales from foreign markets must design their sites with their foreign customers in mind. Global shoppers are much more likely to purchase from sites that are written in their own languages. The most common languages that U.S.-based e-commerce companies translate their content into are French, Spanish, German, Chinese, and Japanese.[75] A common strategy is to include several language buttons on the opening page of a site that take customers to pages in the language of their choice. Experienced e-commerce companies have learned that offering a localized page for every country or region they target pays off in increased sales. Doing so allows entrepreneurs to adapt the terminology they use on their sites and in their search engines to local dialects. For instance, an e-commerce company based in the United States might think it is selling diapers, but its customers in Australia and the United Kingdom are looking for "nappies."

Virtual companies trying to establish a foothold in foreign markets by setting up Web sites dedicated to them run the same risk as brick-and-mortar companies: offending international visitors by using the business conventions and standards the companies are accustomed to using in the United States. Business practices, even those used online, that are acceptable or even expected in the United States may be taboo in other countries. Color schemes can be important, too. Selecting the "wrong" colors and symbols on a site targeting people in a particular country can hurt sales and offend visitors. A little research into the subtleties of a target country's culture and business practices can save a great deal of embarrassment and money. Creating secure, simple, and reliable payment methods for foreign customers also will boost sales. International delivery services offer software that small companies can incorporate into their Web sites to calculate the final "landed cost" (including relevant tariffs and duties) of orders and estimate delivery dates.

When translating the content of their Web sites into other languages, entrepreneurs must use extreme caution. This is *not* the time to pull out their notes from an introductory Spanish course and begin their own translations. Hiring professional translation and localization services to convert a company's Web content into other languages minimizes the likelihood of a company unintentionally offending foreign customers.

Go Mobile

With more than 7.7 billion mobile devices in use around the world, the typical online shopper has expanded his or her reach across multiple screens (and screen sizes) and can shop on the go.[76] In the United States, 72 percent of adults own smart phones, and 45 percent of adults

TABLE 10.2 12 Guidelines for Building the Credibility of a Web Site

Guideline	Tips
1. Allow visitors to verify easily the accuracy of the information on your site.	Include references, which you should cite, from credible third parties to support the information that you present on your site.
2. Show that there are real people behind your site.	List a physical address for your business and post photographs of your store or office or the people who work there. Photos allow shoppers to put faces with the names of the people with whom they are dealing.
3. Emphasize the skills, experience, and knowledge of the people in your company.	Tell visitors about the experts you have on your team, their credentials, and their accomplishments. Is your company or are your employees associated with a well-known, respected national organization? If so, mention it and provide a link to its Web site.
4. Show that honest, trustworthy people stand behind your site.	In addition to posting photographs of the owner and employees, include brief biographical sketches that might include "fun" facts about each person, their hobbies, and links to their blogs, if they have them. Erik Leamon, owner of The Ride, a full-service bicycle store in Conway, Arkansas, markets the charm of his business on The Ride's Web site, which profiles the company's five employees, including Pokey, the shop dog, who serves as the shop's unofficial customer service representative.
5. Make it easy for customers to contact you.	One of the simplest ways to enhance your site's credibility is to include contact information in a highly visible location. Be sure to include a physical address, a telephone number, and e-mail addresses. Always respond promptly to customer communications.
6. Make sure your site has a professional look.	Online shoppers evaluate the quality of a Web site by its appearance within the first few seconds of arriving. Pay careful attention to layout, navigation, search tools, images, grammar, spelling, and other seemingly "minor" details because they *do* make a difference. A professional site does not have to look "corporate" to be professional, however. It should reflect your company's unique personality.
7. Make your site easy to use—and useful.	Sites that are easy for customers to use and that are useful to them score high on credibility. Resist the temptation to dazzle visitors with all the coolest features; instead, focus on keeping your site simple and user friendly. Visitors perceive sites that combine useful information with a purchasing opportunity as more credible than those that merely try to sell them something.
8. Update your site regularly.	Visitors give higher marks to sites that have been updated or reviewed recently than they give to sites that contain outdated or obsolete information.
9. Prominently display your company's privacy policy.	Visitors perceive sites that display a meaningful privacy policy—and follow it—as more credible than those that do not.
10. Be vigilant for errors of all types, no matter how insignificant they may seem.	Typographical errors, misspellings, grammatical mistakes, broken links, and other problems cause a site to lose credibility in customers' eyes. Details matter!
11. Post the seals of approval your company has won.	Seals of approval from third parties such as the Better Business Bureau, TRUSTe, TrustWave, McAfee, and others give shoppers confidence that an online company is reputable and trustworthy.
12. Make sure customers know that their online transactions are secure.	To effectively conduct business online, companies must ensure that customers' credit card transactions are secure. Online retailers typically use SSL technology that is verified as secure by a third party such as Verisign. Be sure to post the secure seal prominently on your Web site.

Sources: Based on J. Walker, "Instilling Credibility into Your Web Site," GNC Web Creations, 2011, www.gnc-web-creations.com/website-credibility .htm; B. J. Fogg, "Stanford Guides for Web Credibility: A Research Summary from the Stanford Persuasive Technology Lab," Stanford University, May 2002, www.webcredibility.org/guidelines; and "The Ride: Your Full Service Bicycle Store," http://therideonline.net/index.php.

own tablets.[77] Research by comScore shows that 67 percent of the time spent online is through a mobile device, most often a smart phone.[78] Mobile users continue to increase the frequency with which they make online purchases from their devices (known as "m-commerce"). More than 52 percent of all traffic to Web sites originates on mobile devices, and mobile customers are willing to spend.[79] Although the average amount per order for desktop computers

Ratchanida Thippayos/123RF

($143.35) currently is greater than for tablets ($114.52) and smart phones ($109.68), mobile commerce sales are growing fastest.[80]

Download speed matters on mobile devices, just as it does on desktops; 85 percent of mobile users expect sites to load as fast as or faster than on a desktop. In addition, 53 percent of mobile users will abandon a Web site that takes more than three seconds to load.[81] Converting visitors on mobile devices into buyers also is more challenging; globally, conversion rates for mobile devices (1.55 percent for smart phones and 3.56 percent for tablets) are lower than those for desktop computers (4.14 percent).[82] Despite the rapid growth of m-commerce (see Figure 10.7), 40 percent of small businesses have Web sites that are not mobile friendly.[83] Companies that fail to develop Web sites that are mobile friendly suffer from lower search engine result rankings and miss out on potential sales because they appear farther down in search engine result pages. However, the payoff for businesses that cater to mobile shoppers is significant: small and medium-size businesses that are not mobile friendly estimate that their sales would increase by $61,000 annually if they upgraded their Web sites.[84]

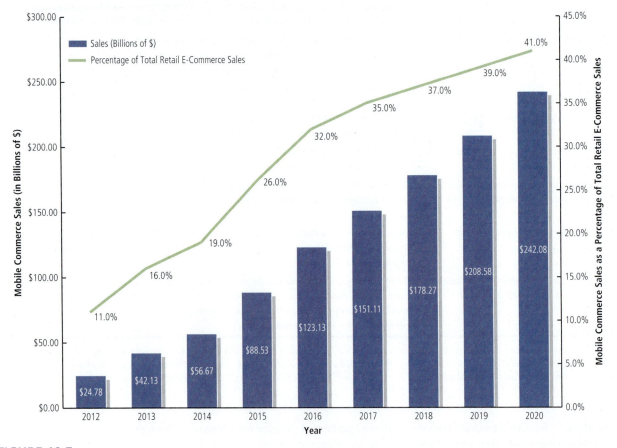

FIGURE 10.7

Mobile Commerce Sales

Source: Based on data from eMarketer, May 4, 2016.

By investing a little more time and money in creating **responsive Web sites**—sites that conform naturally and seamlessly to the size and resolution of the screen on which they are displayed—small companies can accommodate customers on *any* device from which they want to shop. A responsive Web design takes a "one size fits all" approach, eliminates the necessity of creating multiple versions of a Web site for various platforms, and moves a company's Web site higher in Google's all-important search engine rankings. Companies that switch to a responsive design report an average increase of 20 percent in their click-through and conversion rates.[85] Experts say that many businesses make the common mistake of assuming that they must present the same Web content on every screen size. Smart entrepreneurs design their responsive sites to simplify the content that appears on mobile users' screens and making navigation, "call us," and "add to cart" buttons bigger so they are easier to see and touch.

ENTREPRENEURIAL PROFILE: David Adams and Mark Chag: Granite State Growler Tours Friends since childhood, David Adams and Mark Chag decided to capitalize on the growing number of craft microbreweries in their region and launched Granite State Growler Tours, a company that takes guests on four-hour beer tasting excursions and teaches them about beer and the area's rich history of brewing it. Most of the company's bookings come through its Web site, and Adams began to notice that site visits from mobile devices were growing rapidly. Unfortunately, Granite State Growler Tours was losing many of those customers because the company's Web site was not mobile friendly. Adams worked with a Web design company, DudaMobile, to create a new, mobile Web site that allows him to change its content quickly and easily. The new mobile-friendly site reduced the company's bounce rate by 30 percent and produced a significant increase in its click-through rate. After adding a large "Call us" button to the site, Adams says that he immediately noticed a difference in the number of calls from customers.[86] ∎

Consumers' pervasive use of mobile devices, social media, and search engines has led businesses to develop integrated **social-local-mobile (SoLoMo) strategies**. Shoppers use these three tools to enhance their shopping experiences, and smart entrepreneurs can use that tendency to their advantage with an appropriate SoLoMo strategy. Eighty percent of smart phone users access social media sites (Facebook, Instagram, and Twitter are most popular) with their devices, and 94 percent of them use their devices to search for information on local businesses. As a result of their mobile searches, 84 percent take action (often within one hour), either making a purchase or contacting the local business.[87] Ninety percent of all smart phone owners also use their phones to assist them while they are shopping in stores—to compare prices, look up product information, and check online reviews.[88]

What can small companies do to capitalize on the SoLoMo trend? In addition to creating responsive Web sites, entrepreneurs should design their sites to achieve high rankings in local searches by using key words and phrases that allow customers to home in on their business locations. For instance, a jeweler in Birmingham, Alabama, could include location-related terms in the titles, tags, and text of its Web pages and in the key words on which it bids (e.g., Birmingham jewelry, Birmingham diamonds, Birmingham necklaces). The battle for prime space in local search listings has gotten tougher, however, because Google, the largest search engine, changed its AdWords program to display just three local business listings (called the "local pack") instead of seven. Entrepreneurs can use Google My Business (www.google.com/business) to manage how their business information appears in Google searches and on Google maps to include photos (which produce significant increases in click-through rates), directions, contact information, business hours, customer reviews, and a link to the company's Web site.

Even though the information may be available on the search engine results page, every mobile site also should display a small company's address, operating hours, and telephone number (with a click-to-call button) and should include a prominent map. Some business owners offer location-based special offers or discounts to encourage customers to visit the store. Smart phone technology also enables businesses to use geolocation tools to learn about shoppers' behavior and to give them the personalized shopping experiences they seek. With geolocation technology called beacons, business owners can target potential customers within a certain distance of their businesses (even their *competitors'* businesses) or inside their businesses and send these customers/timely promotions, discount coupons, or special sale offers at the critical moment in their purchase decision. Geolocation tools require users' permission, and the average

responsive Web site
a Web site that conforms naturally and seamlessly to the size and resolution of the screen on which it is displayed.

social-local-mobile (SoLoMo) strategies
marketing strategies aimed at capitalizing on shoppers' pervasive use of social media, mobile devices, and search engines to find the products and services they want to purchase and the businesses that sell them.

opt-in rate for "push notifications" is 41 percent.[89] Businesses also can create listings on Yelp, FourSquare, Google+Local, and other apps to encourage mobile users to locate nearby businesses and "check in" when they arrive. Once inside a store, customers expect free Wi-Fi, which allows local stores to offer apps through which shoppers can view product features, prices, and customer reviews—all of which can help close a sale. The owner of a Flip Flop Shop franchise located in a large mall began offering customers free Wi-Fi access and exclusive discount coupons when they log in. In just eight months, the shop added 900 new customers.[90]

Promote Your Web Site Online and Offline

E-commerce entrepreneurs must use every means available—both online and offline—to promote their Web sites and to drive traffic to them. In addition to using traditional online techniques, Web entrepreneurs must promote their sites offline as well. Ads in other media, such as direct mail or newspapers, that mention a site's URL will bring customers to it. It is also a good idea to put the company's Web address on *everything* a company publishes, from its advertisements and letterhead to shopping bags, business cards, and even employees' uniforms. The techniques for generating publicity for an offline business described in Chapter 9 can be just as effective for online businesses that want to make their domain names better known without breaking their budgets. A passive approach to generating Web site traffic is a recipe for failure; entrepreneurs who are as innovative at promoting their e-businesses as they are at creating them can attract impressive numbers of visitors to their sites.

Use Social Media to Attract and Retain Customers

Two-thirds of the world's online users are active on social media.[91] As a result, social media tools such as Facebook, Twitter, LinkedIn, Instagram, Snapchat, and YouTube have become key components of companies' e-commerce efforts. Fifty-eight percent of small business owners use social media in their marketing mix, and 43 percent of them spend at least six hours per week on social media marketing.[92] Figure 10.8 shows the most popular social media networks among marketers, who now spend $13.5 billion annually on social media marketing.[93]

Social media marketing techniques recognize that shoppers, especially young ones, expect to take a proactive role in their shopping experience by writing (and reading) product reviews, asking questions, reading and writing blogs, sharing photographs, watching and creating videos, posting

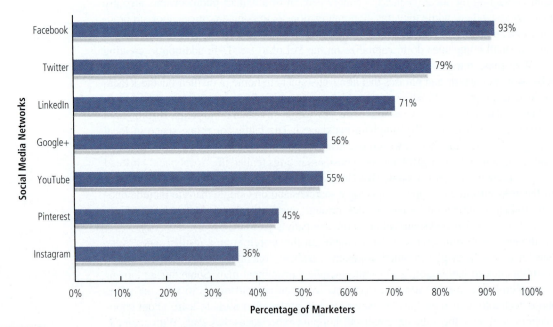

FIGURE 10.8
Most Popular Social Media Networks Marketers Use

Source: Based on data from Ayaz Nanji, "The Most Effective Social Networks for Marketing a Business in 2015," *MarketingProfs*, May 26, 2015, www.marketingprofs.com/charts/2015/27718/the-most-effective-social-networks-for-marketing-a-business-in-2015.

comments, and engaging in other interactive behavior. On individual product pages of their Web sites and at checkout, businesses should include links that allow customers to easily share items on social media. Web sites that include a social sign-in feature, which allows social media users to bypass creating accounts and passwords when they log into a company's Web site, create a seamless integration between a company's Web site and social media. According to business owners, the top benefits of using social media as a marketing tool are gaining increased exposure of their businesses (89 percent), increasing traffic to their Web sites (75 percent), building loyal fans (68 percent), and gaining insight into the markets in which they compete (66 percent).[94]

Small businesses are responding to the opportunity to connect with their customers online by adding the following popular social components to their e-commerce strategies:

- *Social networking.* Many small businesses drive traffic to their Web sites by using their Web sites as a "hub" supported by the "spokes" of social media. Businesses have learned that a successful social media strategy does not focus on making a sale up front but on building connections between customers and potential customers and their brand. The formula that works best is relationships now, sales later. After all, it *is* social media, *not* "sales" media. The goal is to establish your company as a trusted, reliable source of not just products but also information, advice, and assistance. Many small businesses have discovered that the following social media networks provide ideal platforms for engaging and interacting with their customers and listening to what their customers are saying about their businesses, products, and services.

  - *Facebook.* Now with more than 1.94 billion users worldwide, Facebook is the primary marketing tool for many small e-commerce businesses. Nearly 39 percent of the world's online population uses Facebook, and Facebook hosts 50 million small business pages, which enable entrepreneurs to promote their businesses, products, and services to a global audience.[95] Facebook's Page Insights tool provides analytics that allow business owners to track their companies' page performance. Businesses can promote upcoming events and promotions on Facebook's Events apps, gain followers by including a "Like us on Facebook" option in contests, and feature favorite posts on their Web sites. Facebook also offers 12 different advertising options that allow businesses to target specific audiences on Facebook based on geographic location, demographic profile, purchasing history, interests and hobbies, and Facebook connections.

  - *Twitter.* On Twitter, with 320 million active monthly users who send an average of 500 million tweets per day, businesses can engage prospective customers, interact with existing customers, and create ads aimed at a specific target audience.[96] Twitter Cards allows businesses to go beyond the 140-character limit and attach photos and videos to their tweets to help drive traffic to their Web sites. Twitter also offers a "Buy Now" button that allows users to purchase items featured in tweets. Jake Kassan and Kramer LaPlante started MVMT (pronounced "Movement") Watches, a company that markets simple, high-quality watches online, at age 21 with the help of a successful $300,000 crowdfunding campaign on Indiegogo. Because the demographic of MVMT's target customer aligns almost perfectly with the typical Twitter user, Kassan and LaPlante use Twitter to keep their company's followers informed, share content they create about their watches and their business, and drive traffic to MVMT's Web site through a targeted Web site Visits campaign. The company, which has sold more than 100,000 watches (and counting), saw its sales increase 353 percent as a result of a special holiday promotion it conducted on Twitter.[97]

  - *YouTube.* YouTube has more than a billion users worldwide who watch 3.25 billion hours of video each month.[98] Businesses drive millions of customers to their Web sites with clever, humorous videos that include links to their sites. The videos do not have to be of professional quality, but it is important that they

Courtesy of MVMT Watches

tell a compelling story in an engaging way. A small company can use YouTube videos to establish its reputation as a source of reliable information and to build trust with its target customers. Typically, the most successful videos are relatively short, no more than three minutes in length. Like Facebook and Twitter, YouTube also allows businesses to create targeted ads, establish a daily budget, and monitor each ad's performance.

- *LinkedIn.* With more than 500 million registered users, LinkedIn, which operates its professional networking site in 24 languages, is another useful tool for entrepreneurs interested in marketing their businesses or recruiting employees. Small businesses can set up Company Pages on LinkedIn to tell their brand stories, purchase ads aimed at potential customers using a variety of characteristics (geography, industry, job title, age, group status, and many others), and generate sales leads with Sponsored Updates.[99]
- *Pinterest.* Pinterest, the social media site that hosts digital bulletin boards, where users can "pin" content of interest to them, now has more than 150 million active monthly users, 81 percent of whom are women.[100] Two-thirds of pinned content is products from companies' Web sites, and, like Twitter, Pinterest now offers businesses the ability to purchase "Buy it" buttons that enable users to buy pinned items directly without having to leave Pinterest.[101]

Courtesy of Walt Mancini, Pasadena Star-News

ENTREPRENEURIAL PROFILE: Mark Guenther and Mia Mazadiego: Neon Retro Arcade Mark Guenther and his wife Mia Mazadiego launched Neon Retro Arcade in Pasadena, California, with the idea that an old-fashioned arcade featuring more than 50 vintage pinball machines and videogames such as Pac-Man, Donkey Kong, and Mario Brothers would appeal to the Baby Boomers who grew up with them as well as young people who might be curious about the ancestors of modern video games. Rather than feed coins into the machines, customers are Neon Retro Arcade pay an admission fee, which entitles them to play as many games as they want on any of the classic machines. After Guenther and Mazadiego discovered that most of their customers learned about their arcade and the fun events it hosts from their company Facebook page, they created affordable Facebook ads (their first Facebook ad cost just $20) targeting specific types of customers living or working within a few miles of their location. When they reviewed the analytics, the copreneurs discovered that their ad had reached nearly 56,000 prospective customers, "enough people to fill a baseball stadium," says Mazadiego. The couple saw their arcade's sales increase 20 percent in just one month with the help of one Facebook ad.[102] ∎

- *Apps.* Like social media, apps provide a simple way for businesses to stay in their customers' minds and to generate sales. Apps are particularly important for reaching mobile users; 90 percent of the time mobile users spend online is on apps.[103] Kate Burton, owner of Remix Coffee Company, a coffee truck in Cape Girardeau, Missouri, uses a loyalty program app that keeps her customers engaged and informed—and coming back. Not only does Burton's app tell customers where her truck is located, it also keeps her business in front of her customers and encourages them to earn loyalty points toward discounts and free drinks by making repeat purchases. The branded app includes the truck's latest menu and catering packages, notifies customers of upcoming special events, and includes links to all of its social media pages. Since launching the app, Burton has seen a 10 percent increase in the number of repeat customers and an 85 percent increase in sales.[104]

Develop an Effective Search Engine Optimization (SEO) Strategy

Search engine optimization strategies have become an essential part of online companies' marketing strategies. With more than 1.2 billion Web sites (and growing) in existence, it is no surprise that online shoppers' first stop usually is a search engine. As a result, entrepreneurs are devoting more of their marketing budgets to search engine optimization strategies that are focused on landing their Web sites at or near the top of the most popular search engines. For a company engaged in e-commerce, a well-defined search engine optimization strategy is a vital part of its overall marketing strategy. Search engines drive more traffic to e-commerce sites (39.0 percent) than referrals (19.3 percent), social media (3.9 percent), display ads (1.3 percent), or e-mail (0.6 percent).[105] A study by Custora reports that customers who find a company's Web site through a search engine produce a higher lifetime value (54 percent above average) than customers who arrive at a site as a result of e-mail marketing, affiliate ads, banner ads, or social media.[106]

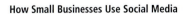

Hands On . . . How To

Use Social Media to Market Your Business

The typical digital consumer now spends an average of 1 hour and 50 minutes each day on social media (and 80 percent of that time is on a mobile device). In addition, 77 percent of online shoppers use social media (Facebook, YouTube, Twitter, and Pinterest are the most popular apps), and more than one-third of online shoppers say that social media has influenced their purchases. Social media apps now offer users "shop now" and "buy now" features that enable them to make purchases directly from the app. In fact, nearly one-fourth of online shoppers have purchased a product on a social media network. Clearly, social media represents a tremendous marketing opportunity for small businesses; however, only 57 percent of small businesses have a social media presence. The accompanying graphic shows how these small businesses put social media tools to work for their companies.

At Sky Zone, an indoor wall-to-wall trampoline park franchise with 127 locations in the United States and 22 outlets in foreign countries, social media marketing emerged organically. CEO Jeff Platt says the company noticed that customers were planning trips to Sky Zone locations on Twitter, so the company joined in the conversations and posted special offers, such as "bring five people to Sky Zone, and we'll give you a free pass." Sky Zone also launched the Twitter campaign #I'dRatherBe@SkyZone to engage customers of all ages and to show people how much fun a Sky Zone adventure can be through posts, photos, and video. Platt was surprised to see how many people posted photos of their Sky Socks, the special socks customers wear on the trampolines, on social media sites. In response, the company created contests and giveaways to encourage more customers to engage with Sky Zone and promote it on social media. Customers can earn credits and discounts at Sky Zone by tagging friends in trampoline photos or posing in their Sky Socks at interesting places. The company also taps into March Madness each year by sponsoring a dunking contest in which customers compete by posting videos of their best slam dunks on social media. Platt says that Sky Zone's social media strategy is to engage customers rather than to advertise to them. The company's social media strategy has been so successful (and trackable) that in just two years, Platt has shifted the company's marketing budget from 80 percent traditional marketing and 20 percent social media marketing to a 50–50 split.

Other small businesses use social media marketing quite effectively as well. Repair Clinic, founded in 1999 by Chris Hall and Larry Beach in Canton, Michigan, sells parts and accessories to customers around the globe so that they can repair their own appliances and tools. The company, which offers more than 3 million parts, uses social media, particularly YouTube and Facebook, to promote the thousands of "how to" repair videos it has created to help customers make repairs. Not only do the videos, which are also available on the Repair Clinic Web site, walk customers through their repair jobs, they also create highly valuable content that places the company's Web site high in search engine rankings.

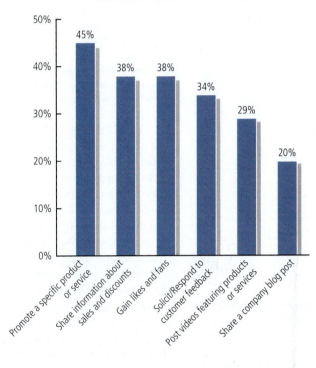

How Small Businesses Use Social Media

Jody Hall, founder of Cupcake Royale, a café in Seattle, Washington, with seven locations that sell fresh cupcakes and homemade ice cream made with farm-fresh ingredients, uses social media to engage and reward her customers. The company posts daily on Facebook, usually including a tempting photo of one of its menu items, and responds promptly to customers' comments and questions. Customers who "like" the company on Facebook receive a coupon that entitles them to a free cupcake on the first of every month. Cupcake Royale also enlists its social media audience when it comes to developing new cupcake and ice cream flavors, asking them for input and feedback. Many of these crowdsourced choices have become best-sellers. Cupcake Royale's social media marketing strategy is designed to raise the company's profile, attract new customers, and engage in a meaningful way with existing customers.

Sources: Based on *UPS Pulse of the Online Shopper*, UPS, 2016, p. 43; Jason Mander, "Social Media Captures 30% of Online Time," *Global Web Index*, June 8, 2016, www.globalwebindex.net/blog/social-media-captures-30-of-online-time; "Learn from Social Media (Without Losing All Your Time)," *Inc.*, November 2014, p. 80; Sarah Patrick, "Small Business Digital Marketing and Social Media Habits: 2016," *Clutch*, March 22, 2016, https://clutch.co/agencies/resources/small-business-digital-marketing-and-social-media-habits-survey-2016; "Infographic: Content Marketing Best Practices for Small Businesses," *SCORE*, September 6, 2016, www.score.org/resource/infographic-content-marketing-best-practices-small-businesses; "Sky Zone Trampoline Park: Getting a Lift from Social Media," *Business Circle*, 2016, https://bizcircle.att.com/small-business-marketing-resources/sky-zone-getting-a-lift-from-social-media/; Andrew Raso, "7 Small Businesses That Showcase Social Media Success on a Budget," InfusionSoft Knowledge Center, July 7, 2016, https://learn.infusionsoft.com/marketing/social-media/7-small-businesses-that-showcase-social-media-success.

TABLE 10.3 **Click-through Rates for E-commerce Sites by Position in Google Organic Search Engine Results Pages (SERPS)**

SERP Position	Average Click-through Rate
1	36.38%
2	10.72%
3	6.90%
4	4.74%
5	3.37%
6–10	1.77%

Source: Alexander Clark, "Search Engine Statistics," *Smart Insights*, August 10, 2016, www.smartinsights.com/ search-engine-marketing/search-engine-statistics/.

One of the biggest challenges facing e-commerce entrepreneurs is maintaining the effectiveness of their search marketing strategies. Because the most popular search engines are constantly updating and refining their algorithms—the secretive formulas and methodology search engines use to find and rank the results of Web searches—entrepreneurs also must evaluate and constantly refine their search strategies. Every time Google, the leading search engine, with 64 percent market share, changes its algorithms, many businesses that had ranked highly in searches find that their listings fall sharply down the search engine results page—and into e-commerce oblivion.

A company's Web search strategy may incorporate the two basic types of search engine results: natural (or organic) listings and paid (or sponsored) listings. Although shoppers are far more likely to click on organic listings (95 percent vs. 5 percent for paid listings), paid listings are still important because on Google's search engine results pages, the number-one organic listing now appears below the top three paid search listings.[107] **Natural (organic) listings** arise as a result of "spiders," powerful programs that search engines use to crawl around the Web and analyze sites for key words, links, and other data. Based on what they find, spiders use complex algorithms to index Web sites so that a search engine can display a list of relevant Web sites when a person enters a key word in the engine to start a search. With natural listings, an entrepreneur's goal is to get his or her Web site displayed at or near the top of the list of search results.

Search engine optimization (SEO) involves managing the content, key words, titles, tags, features, and design of a Web site so that it appears at or near the top of Internet search results. SEO is important because the click-through rate for e-commerce sites is more than 10 times higher for those that are in position one than those in position 5 (see Table 10.3), a difference that can mean thousands or even hundreds of thousands of dollars in revenue for a business.[108] Landing at the top of search results is even more important for searches conducted on the smaller screens of mobile devices, which now account for 58 percent of search volume.[109] A useful resource for entrepreneurs is SEO Book, a search engine optimization site (www.seobook.com) that offers both free tools and more than 100 training modules on a variety of SEO topics.

As you can see, a fierce battle rages among online competitors for spots at or near the top of search results. Companies can use the following tips to improve their search placement results:

- *Create meaningful, relevant content for each Web page, with your customers and their needs in mind.* When it comes to search engine results, content rules. Longer content actually improves a page's ranking. Each page should contain at least 1,000 to 2,000 words that are relevant to the key word used in the title tag. The average Web page that appears on the first page in Google rankings contains about 1,890 words.[110] Organizing the text into well-structured paragraphs using subheadings and bullets and including photographs and illustrations (that have file names that match the key word of that page) and videos also helps. Content that answers typical questions that customers ask increases a site's search ranking. Quality content that includes relevant terms also reduces a site's bounce rate, which increases its SEO ranking. Although key words are important to a page's SEO rankings, entrepreneurs should avoid artificially "stuffing" content (and title tags) with key words because most search engines penalize sites that attempt this maneuver. Providing quality content enables a company to enhance its reputation as an expert in its field, increase its visibility to potential customers (especially by encouraging others to share its

natural (organic) listings

search engine listings that result from "spiders" (powerful programs) crawling around the Web and analyzing sites for key words, links, and other data.

search engine optimization (SEO)

the process of managing the content, key words, titles, tags, features, and design of a Web site so that it appears at or near the top of Internet search results.

content on social media), build an audience of "fansumers," and ensure that customers see it as friendly and approachable.[111]

> **ENTREPRENEURIAL PROFILE: Cesar Milan: Cesarsway.com** Famed dog-whisperer Cesar Milan is at the helm of a multimedia empire, with a television series, 8 million Facebook followers, and a Web site, cesarsway.com, that sells a variety of pet products and provides pet-related information. Analytics showed that the Web site was underperforming, however. Milan began using Searchlight WPM from Conductor Inc. to analyze the site and find ways to increase its conversion rate and sales. The analysis led Milan and his team to focus on optimizing content, including tactics such as refining title tags, repositioning photographs, and adding articles and videos on specific pet-related topics. After revising the site's content, Milan says that in just one year, the number of users increased from 2.2 million to 3.1 million, average visit time increased from 95 seconds to 138 seconds, and sales increased 9 percent. Milan credits the improvements to making the site's content more relevant and useful to customers, which enhanced its reputation as a leading expert in pet care.[112] ∎

- *Develop legitimate links from other related sites.* Links from other Web sites, known as backlinks, tell search engines that a site has credibility and is an "authority" in its field. The links must be legitimate, however; search engines penalize sites that engage in "linkbombing," stuffing a Web site with phony ("black-hat") links in an attempt to improve its search ranking.

- *Conduct brainstorming sessions to develop a list of key words and phrases.* You want to anticipate the words and phrases that searchers are likely to use in a search engine to locate a company's products and services and use those words and phrases on your Web pages. Usually, simple terms are better than industry jargon.

- *Use target key words in the title tags (metatags, which are limited to 140 characters) and headlines of your Web pages.* Some search engines are geared to pick them up. For best results, you should focus each page of your site on one specific key word or phrase that should appear in the page's title. Placing key words in these critical locations can be tedious, but it produces better search results for the companies that take the time to do it.

- *Use Google's AdWords Keyword Tool or Microsoft Bing Ads to determine how many monthly searches users conduct globally and locally for a key word or phrase.* More specific, lower-volume key words and phrases usually produce higher search rankings because they provide potential customers with the focused results they are seeking.

- *Encourage social media shares.* The more shares a site's content gets on social media, the more relevant the site is to search engines.

- *Create unique product descriptions rather than merely copy manufacturer's descriptions.* Search engines penalize sites with duplicate content that appears on other Web sites, a technique known as "scraping."

- *Visit competitors' sites for key word ideas but avoid using exactly the same phrases.* Simply right-clicking on a competitor's Web page and choosing "View Source" will display the key words used in the metatags on the site.

- *Consider using less obvious key words and brand names.* For instance, rather than using simply "bicycles," a small bicycle retailer should consider key words such as "racing bikes" "road racing bike," or "LeMond" to draw customers.

- *Get customer feedback.* Ask customers which words and phrases they use when searching for the products and services the company sells.

- *Use data analytics.* These tools allow entrepreneurs to identify the words and phrases (and the search engines) that brought visitors to the company's Web site.

- *Don't forget about misspellings.* People often misspell the words they type into search engines. Include them in your list.

- *Use services such as Wordtracker or Wordstream to monitor and analyze Web users' search engine tendencies.* These tools analyze billions of online searches and show the monthly volume of searches for more than a billion key words, estimate the degree of competition for them, and offer other key word suggestions, using the same core terms.

- *Block irrelevant results with "negative key words," which are excluded in a search.* Twenty percent of small businesses do not use any negative keywords in their Google AdWords accounts.[113]

- *Include links to other relevant Web sites and land links to your Web site on high-profile Web sites.* Search engines rank sites that have external links to high-volume sites higher than those that do not.

- *Start a blog.* Well-written blogs not only draw potential customers to your site but also tend to attract links from other Web sites. Blogs also allow entrepreneurs to use key words strategically and frequently, moving their sites up in search result rankings.

- *Post videos about your company and its products or services.* In addition to uploading videos to sites such as YouTube and Vimeo, companies should post them to their Web sites because videos improve a site's SEO ranking.

- *Don't forget about download speed.* Recall that search engines rank sites that load quickly higher than sites that are slow to load.

Figure 10.9 shows the four building blocks to a successful organic SEO strategy.

FIGURE 10.9

Four Building Blocks to a Successful Organic SEO Strategy.

Search engines drive more traffic to a company's Web site than any other tool, including referrals, social media, display ads, or e-mail. Because 75 percent of search engine users never scroll past the first page of search engine results, landing a spot at or near the top of the search engine results pages (SERPS) is essential. Entrepreneurs should build their companies' SEO strategies on four blocks:

4. Update. Search engines routinely update the algorithms that drive the rankings of companies' Web sites. Just because your company's Web site receives a top ranking today does not mean that it will occupy that spot tomorrow. Entrepreneurs must constantly track their sites' performance in SERPs and update their strategies to keep their sites highly visible in the rankings. Using Web analytics tools to evaluate a site's performance is the best way to determine how to improve it.

3. Mobile Friendly. Because 75 percent of Internet activity now originates from mobile devices, Web sites that are mobile friendly receive higher rankings in SERPs than those that are not. Currently, 58 percent of Web searches take place on mobile devices, so search engines favor Web sites that use a responsive design, conforming automatically to the size of the screen on which they are displayed. Mobile friendly Web sites are essential because 72 percent of customers who conduct local searches for products or services visit a store within five miles of their location.

2. Backlinks. Another key determinant of a Web site's ranking in SERPs is the number and quality of its backlinks, links to the site from other credible, authoritative Web sites. Modern search engine algorithms are able to differentiate between quality links and phony ones from a link wheel or link pyramid. Three variables determine a site's rating on backlinks:
- Number of backlinks
- Link "authority," the credibility of the linking site
- Diversity of links

Note the role that quality content (building block #1) plays in generating quality backlinks.

1. Content. For most search engines, the most important determinant of a Web site's ranking in SERPs is the quality of its content. Quality content is comprehensive. To land at the top of SERPs, a site's content should:
- Be simple, clear, and coherent
- Be credible
- Be educational
- Be relevant to the user
- Be well organized
- Use titles, headings and bullets to make it easily readable

Source: Based on Aleh Barysevich, "4 Most Important Ranking Factors, According to SEO Industry Studies," *Search Engine Journal,* February 3, 2017, www.searchenginejournal.com/4-important-ranking-factors-according-seo-industry-studies/184619/; Mike McEvoy, "SEO Statistics to Know in 2017," *Web Presence Solutions,* November 29, 2016, http://www.webpresencesolutions.net/seo-statistics-2017-seo-stats/; Nate Dame, "The Complete Guide to Optimizing Content for SEO (with checklist)," *Search Engine Land,* April 12, 2017, searchengineland.com/complete-guide-optimizing-content-seo-checklist-269884; "What Can SEO Do for Your Business?" 1st on the List, 2017, www.1stonthelist.ca/infographics/seo-for-business/.

Ad Rank = Advertiser's Bid Price on Key Word x Advertiser's Quality Score

Example:

Advertiser	Key Word Bid Price	Quality Score	Ad Rank	Ad Position
A	$2.50	10	25	1st
B	$4.00	5	20	2nd
C	$6.00	2	12	3rd
D	$8.00	1	8	4th

> Higher quality scores produce not only higher ad ranks and better ad positions but also result in lower costs per click.

How much does the advertiser pay when a customer clicks on its ad?
Ad Cost = Ad Rank of the Web site below yours ÷ Your Quality Score + $0.01

Example:

Advertiser	Key Word Bid Price	Quality Score	Ad Rank	Ad Cost per Click
A	$2.50	10	25	20 ÷ 10 + $.01 = **$2.01**
B	$4.00	5	20	12 ÷ 5 + $.01 = **$2.41**
C	$6.00	2	12	8 ÷ 2 + $.01 = **$4.01**
D	$8.00	1	8	Highest cost per click

> This is what each advertiser pays when a shopper clicks on its ad that appears on Google's search engine results page.

FIGURE 10.10

How Google Determines a PPC Ad's Position and Cost

Source: Based on "What Is PPC? Learn the Basics of Pay-per-Click (PPC) Marketing, WordStream, January 2, 2017, www.wordstream.com/ppc.

Because organic listings can take months to materialize, many e-commerce companies rely on paid listings to get an immediate presence in search engines. **Paid (sponsored) listings** are short text advertisements with links to the sponsoring company's Web site that appear on the results pages in a search engine when a user types in a key word or phrase. Entrepreneurs use paid search listings to accomplish what natural listings cannot. Fortunately, just three search engines—Google, Microsoft Bing, and Yahoo!—account for nearly 98 percent of the searches conducted in the United States.[114] Google, the most popular search engine, with 64 percent of all searches, displays up to four paid listings at the top and three at the bottom of each results page, and Yahoo! shows "sponsored results" at the top and the bottom of its results pages. Advertisers bid on key words to determine their placement on a search engine's results page. In Google AdWords, an ad's placement in search results is a function of its relevance, which is determined by a quality score of 1 to 10 that Google assigns (higher is better) and the advertiser's bid price on the key word. Three factors determine an ad's quality score: the expected click-through rate (how likely users are to click through to a site when it shows up in Google's paid listings), ad relevance (how closely related the key word is to a company's listing), and landing page experience (an estimate of how useful a site's landing page will be to users, based on its content, organization, and ease of navigation).[115] The ad that gets the most prominent placement (at the top) of the search engine's results page when a user types in that key word on the search engine is the one with the highest combination of quality score and bid price. An advertiser pays only when a shopper clicks through to its Web site from the search engine. For this reason, paid listings also are called pay-per-click (PPC), pay-for-placement, and pay-for-performance ads. The higher an ad's quality score, the lower is its cost per click. Figure 10.10 shows how Google determines a pay-per-click ad's position in the rankings and its cost per click.

The average cost per click on Google AdWords is $2.32, up from 38 cents in 2005.[116] Although paid listings can be expensive, advertisers can evaluate their effectiveness by using the statistical reports the search engine generates. Pay-per-click advertisers can control costs by geotargeting their ads (that is, having them appear only in certain geographic areas) and by setting a spending limit per day. Using generic terms results in large numbers of search results but often produces very small conversion rates and very little in sales; normally, entrepreneurs get better results bidding on more precise, lower-volume ("long-tail") key words. Rather than compete with much larger companies for 5 or 10 common key words, a more effective strategy is to bid on 200 less popular, more specific key words that produce clicks from customers who are more likely to buy.

paid (sponsored) listings
short advertisements with links to the sponsoring company's Web site that appear on the results page of a search engine when the user types in a key word or phrase.

ENTREPRENEURIAL PROFILE: Matt Lauzon: Gemvara Jake Sharpless, marketing specialist at online jeweler Gemvara, a company founded by Babson College student Matt Lauzon, has had success focusing on less expensive, specific words and long-tail phrases because they are not as popular (or expensive) as more common terms. For instance, rather than bidding on the common term "jewelry," Sharpless bids on specific words such as "necklaces," "ruby necklaces," or "fire opal wedding rings." Sharpless says that using long-tail terms produces better conversion rates and lower costs. He also bids on common misspellings of key words and blocks irrelevant results with negative key words.[117] ∎

product listing ads (PLAs)

paid ads on Google that show more information than traditional text ads, including product images, prices, business name, and a short promotional message.

click fraud

a situation that occurs when a company pays for clicks that are generated by someone with no interest in or intent to purchase its products or services.

Google's **product listing ads (PLAs)** show more information, including product images, prices, business name, and a short promotional message, than do traditional text ads. PLAs appear in their own box separate from plain text ads in Google's search results. Businesses set up PLAs through either their AdWords account or through Google's Merchant Center. One study shows that PLAs offer higher click-through rates (21 percent) and lower cost-per-click (26 percent) than text ads.[118] Online magazine *Search Engine Watch* (http://searchenginewatch.com) provides many useful resources for entrepreneurs seeking to optimize their search engine strategies.

One problem facing companies that rely on paid listings and display ads to generate Web traffic is **click fraud**, which occurs when a company pays for clicks that are generated by someone with no interest in or intent to purchase a product or service. "Botnets," programs that hijack computers around the world to generate thousands of phony clicks on a Web site, are a common source of click fraud. Botnets are also a source of digital ad fraud; they generate phony traffic to Web sites on which businesses then pay for advertising space that no one sees. Although the cost of click fraud is difficult to measure, one recent study of nearly 10 billion advertisers reports that botnets account for between 3 and 37 percent of digital advertisers' Web site traffic, and the associated fraud costs an estimated $7.2 billion annually.[119] A botnet known as Methbot involved a network of computers pretending to be humans that generated millions of phony clicks per day that cost online advertisers $3 to $5 million per day.[120] Web analytics software can help online merchants detect click fraud. Large numbers of visitors leaving within seconds of arriving at a site, computer IP addresses that appear from all over the world, and pay-per-click costs that rise without any corresponding increase in sales are clues that a company has fallen victim to click fraud.

LO4

Learn the techniques of designing a killer Web site.

Designing a Killer Web Site

Setting up a shop online has never been easier, but creating a Web site that drives sales requires time and commitment. To be successful, entrepreneurs must pay careful attention to the look, feel, efficiency, and navigability of their Web sites and the impression their sites create with shoppers. A site's look and design determine a visitor's first impression of the company. "Your Web site isn't 'about' your company," says one writer. "It's an extension of your company. If it's unprofessional, you're unprofessional. If it's cluttered, you're cluttered. If it's hard to work with, you're hard to work with. By contrast, if it's well put together, smart, and easy to use, so is your company."[121] Unfortunately, HubSpot Research's grading of more than one million Web sites on a 0- to 100-point scale produced an average score of 59, an F.[122] "A Web site is an engine that runs on remarkable content being pumped into it day after day," says one e-commerce expert. "The goal of a Web site is to attract visitors, convert leads, and delight customers. Your business won't see those benefits unless you turn your Web site into an inbound marketing machine that presents your brand as a thought leader with fresh offers, landing pages, calls-to-action, new media, social conversations, and other content assets."[123]

How can entrepreneurs design Web sites that capture and hold potential customers' attention long enough to make a sale? What can they do to keep customers coming back on a regular basis? There is no surefire formula for providing a best-in-class online shopping experience, but the following suggestions will help.

Start with Your Target Customer

Before launching into the design of their Web sites, entrepreneurs must develop a clear picture of their target customers. Only then will they be ready to design a site that will appeal to their customers. The goal is create a design in which customers see themselves when they visit. Creating a site that is a comfortable fit for customers requires a careful blend of market research, sales know-how, and aesthetics. The challenge for a business on the Web is to create the same image, style, and ambiance in its online presence as in its offline stores. For example, a Web site that sells discount baby clothing will have an entirely different look and feel than one that sells upscale outdoor gear.

Give Customers What They Want

The main reason that people shop online is *convenience*. Online companies that fail to provide a fast, efficient, and flawless shopping experience for their customers will not succeed. A well-designed Web site is intuitive, leading customers to a series of actions that are natural and result in a sale. Sites that provide customers with meaningful content, allow them to find what they are looking for easily, and let them pay for it conveniently and securely keep customers coming back. One way that online companies can achieve these goals is to create a customer journey map that provides a holistic view of the steps a customer takes when using a company's Web site. The idea is to look at the Web site from the customer's perspective, with the goal of creating a stellar customer experience and increasing the site's conversion rate and the company's sales. One company that guides online businesses in creating customer journey maps suggests breaking the map into three sections: (1) the lens through which the customer experiences the Web site; (2) the customer's experience, which includes actions, thought processes, and emotional involvement; and (3) the insights, lessons, and conclusions the company draws from the map.[124]

Including high-quality images of products with alternative views that allow customers to zoom in for detail, rotate them 360 degrees, and see color changes showcases a company's products and increases sales. Unfortunately, fewer than 5 percent of online retailers provide this capability.[125] Product descriptions should be simple, detailed, and jargon free. Videos that show product details or the product in use not only increase customer traffic but also produce higher conversion rates. The goal is to eliminate any element that causes friction—a lengthy registration process, confusing navigation, cluttered pages, and so on—in a customers' shopping experience. Online customers also expect a personalized shopping experience on a Web site that "remembers" their tastes and preferences and recalls information that maximizes the efficiency of their visit. Online retailers can harness big data to understand shoppers' buying habits; detect subtle nuances in their tastes, preferences, and interests; and use that knowledge to recommend the right product at the right time, making the shopping experience easy and convenient.

Select an Intuitive Domain Name

Decide on a domain name that is consistent with the image you want to create for your company and register it. Entrepreneurs should never underestimate the power of the right domain name or URL. It not only tells online shoppers where to find a company but also should suggest something about the company and what it does. Entrepreneurs must recognize that a domain name is part of the brand they are creating and should create the proper image for the company.

The ideal domain name should have the following characteristics:

- *Short.* Short names are easy for people to remember, so the shorter a company's URL, the more likely it is that potential customers will recall it.

- *Memorable.* Not every short domain name is necessarily memorable. Some business owners use their companies' initials as their domain name (e.g., www.sbfo.com for Stanley Brothers Furniture Outlet). The problem with using initials for a domain name is that customers rarely associate the two, making a company virtually invisible on the Web.

- *Indicative of a company's business or business name.* Perhaps the best domain name for a company is one that customers can guess easily if they know the company's name. For instance, mail order catalog company J.Crew's URL is www.jcrew.com, and New Pig, a maker of absorbent materials for a variety of industrial applications, uses www.newpig.com as its domain name. (The company carries this concept over to its toll-free number, which is 1-800-HOT-HOGS.)

- *Easy to spell.* Even though a company's domain name may be easy to spell, it is usually wise to buy several variations of the correct spelling simply because some customers are likely to make mistakes!

Just because entrepreneurs come up with the perfect URL for their companies' Web sites does not necessarily mean that they can use them. With more than 335 million registered domain names (128 million of which are ".com" names), finding the perfect domain name can be challenging, but the Internet Corporation for Assigned Names and Numbers, the organization officially in charge of domain names worldwide, recently authorized the use of generic TLDs such as .app, .autos, .dance, .beauty, .pizza, .bike, and .lawyer, increasing the number of TLDs from about two dozen to thousands.[126] Many new generic TLDs are region or city specific, such as .NYC, .Berlin, and .London, which are beneficial to companies' local marketing efforts.

Domain names are given on a first-come, first-served basis. Before business owners can use a domain name, they must ensure that someone else has not already taken it. The simplest way to do that is to go to a domain name registration service such as Network Solutions (www.networksolutions .com), NetNames (www.netnames.com), or GoDaddy (www.godaddy.com) and conduct a name search. Once entrepreneurs find an unused name that is suitable, they should register it (plus any variations of it)—and the sooner, the better! Registering is quite easy: Simply use one of the registration services cited previously to fill out a form and pay the necessary fees. The next step is to register the domain name with the U.S. Patent and Trademark Office (USPTO) at a cost of $275. The office's Web site (www.uspto.gov) not only allows users to register a trademark online but also offers useful information on trademarks and the protection they offer.

Make Your Web Site Easy to Navigate

Research shows that the primary factor that leads shoppers to choose one Web site over another is ease of navigation and searching.[127] Simplicity reigns supreme at the top-performing Web sites, especially on mobile versions. The design goal is to make a site so intuitive that shoppers do not have to think to use it. If shoppers cannot find what they are looking for in three clicks, they are likely to leave, never to return. The starting point for evaluating a site's navigability is to conduct a user test. Find several willing shoppers, sit them down in front of a computer, and watch them as they cruise through the company's Web site to make a purchase. It is one of the best ways to get meaningful, immediate feedback on the navigability of a site. Watching these test customers as they navigate the site is also useful. Where do they pause? Do they get lost in the site? Are they confused by the choices the site gives them? Is the checkout process too complex? Are the navigation buttons from one page of the site to another clearly marked, and do they make sense? (One popular Web site critic says that sites with vague navigation tools are guilty of "mystery meat navigation.") Web analytics tools (discussed further later in this chapter) also offer insight into how long visitors spend on a company's Web site, where they abandon the site, how they arrived, and lots of other valuable feedback for improving the navigability of a site. The most successful e-commerce companies constantly test various design elements on their sites using A/B tests (e.g., sending visitors to two sites, one with less text and more photos) to see which ones produce the highest conversion rates.

landing pages
the pages on which visitors land after they click on a sponsored link in a search engine, an e-mail ad, or an online ad.

Because many visitors do not start from a Web site's home page, easy navigability involves creating the right **landing pages**, the pages on which visitors land after they click on a sponsored link in a search engine, an e-mail ad, or an online ad. Ideally, each landing page should have the same marketing message as the link that led to it; otherwise, customers are likely to abandon the site immediately (an occurrence that is measured by a site's "bounce rate," the percentage of visits in which customers leave a site from the landing page). In addition to including a clear call to action, a good landing page also allows customers to search or to dig deeper into the company's Web site to the products or services that they are seeking. Unfortunately, 20 percent of small businesses send shoppers who click on paid listings to their sites' home page rather than to a customized landing page.[128]

Successful Web sites recognize that shoppers use different strategies to make purchases. Some shoppers want to use a search tool, others want to browse through product categories, and still others prefer a company to make product recommendations. Effective sites accommodate all three strategies in their design. Two important Web site design features that online companies often get wrong involve the mechanisms by which customers locate products and then get information about them:

Locating products. Customers won't buy what they cannot find! Products should be easy for customers to find, no matter how many pages a Web site includes. Too often, online companies do a poor job of product categorization, listing their product lines in ways that may make sense to them but that befuddle the typical shopper. User tests can be extremely helpful in revealing product categorization problems. After redesigning its landing pages to include less text, a more visible unique selling proposition above the "fold" (the portion of the screen that does not require a user to scroll down), and a more prominent call to action, Kwik-Fit, an insurance company based in the United Kingdom, increased its conversion rate by 78 percent.[129]

In addition to establishing simple product categories that reflect the way customers actually shop (e.g., including categories, such as business dress, business casual, sportswear, outerwear, formal wear, shoes, and accessories for a clothing store), another simple solution is to use an internal search tool. Because 70 percent of online shoppers say that the ability to search, sort, and filter products is important, an easy-to-use internal search tool can pay for itself many times over in higher conversion rates and increased sales.[130] To make the search feature useful, it should appear in the same place on every page in the site (usually the top right). An internal search tool reveals extremely useful information about which items shoppers are looking for and how they search for them, information that online merchants can use in their key word strategies for paid listings. Rather than build their own internal search engines, many online companies use one of Google's Enterprise Search tools, which can cost as little as $100 a year, to power customer searches on their sites. (Google's Custom Search tool is free, but it includes ads.) Managers at Coupon Chief, a directory of online coupons to more than 1,000 e-commerce retailers, replaced the home-grown search function on the company's Web site with a Google search engine and saw the number of successful searches that customers experienced increase by 200 percent.[131]

Getting product information. Once a site is designed to enable shoppers to find products easily, the next task online merchants face is to provide enough product information to convince shoppers to buy. Incomplete product information sends online customers scurrying to competitors' sites. Unlike at brick-and-mortar stores, customers cannot pick up an item, try it on, or engage a salesperson in a face-to-face conversation about its features and merits. Online merchants must walk a fine line because providing too little information may fail to answer the questions customers have, causing them to abandon their shopping carts. On the other hand, providing too much information can overwhelm customers who aren't willing to wade through reams of text just to find answers to some basic questions. The solution is to provide basic product information (no more than three major points per page) in easy-to-understand terms, always including a picture of the item with the option to zoom in on it, and a link to more detailed information (which should be only one click away) that customers can click to if they choose.

Offer Suggestions for Related Products

Many online merchants increase sales with the help of "searchandising" techniques, which combine internal searches with merchandising techniques that are designed to cross sell. For example, a customer who enters the words "French cuff shirt" into a company's search tool might see a link to the company's selection of cufflinks and ties in addition to all of the French cuff shirts that appear. Amazon.com is famous for the success of its searchandising techniques, including its "customers who bought this item also bought …" product suggestions.

Add Wish List Capability

Giving customers the ability to create wish lists of products and services they want and then connecting other people to those lists, often using social media, not only boosts a company's sales but also increases its online visibility.

Create a Gift Idea Center

Online retailers have discovered that one of the most successful tools for improving their conversion rates is to offer a gift idea center—a section of a Web site that shoppers can browse through for ideas based on price, gender, or category. Gift centers can provide a huge boost for e-tailers, particularly around holidays, because they offer creative suggestions for shoppers looking for the perfect gift.

Provide Customer Ratings and Reviews

Customer ratings and reviews are extremely important to online shoppers, exerting the greatest influence on their purchasing decisions.[132] One recent study reports that an overwhelming 95 percent of shoppers consult reviews or ratings before making a purchase and that 92 percent of shoppers trust customer reviews more than any form of advertising.[133] In addition, customers who read reviews are 105 percent more likely to make a purchase and spend 11 percent more than those who do not read reviews.[134] Allowing customers to post product reviews and ratings enhances a site's credibility and leads to increased sales. Online companies that include reviews benefit from conversion rates that are 74 percent higher and customer loyalty rates that are 18 percent higher than those of companies that do not offer reviews.[135] Reviews are especially important in mobile commerce; 70 percent of mobile shoppers are more likely to purchase a product if the mobile site offers customer reviews.[136] Many companies include a review widget that enables customers to post reviews quickly and easily, and some offer incentives for customers to post reviews. Businesses also must monitor their online profiles, being alert to inevitable customer complaints of poor service or product quality problems. Ideally, a company addresses customers' negative reviews and comments quickly, with the goal of resolving their problems. The lesson: Companies must focus on earning and maintaining stellar reputations by providing value and excellent shopping experiences for their customers.

Incorporate Videos

Video has the power to dramatically improve a Web site's performance. Adding video to a Web site increases its conversion rate and improves its search engine ranking. Including video on a Web site landing page increases a company's conversion rate by 80 percent, and including video in e-mails increases recipients' click-through rates between 200 and 300 percent.[137] In addition, shoppers who view videos are 1.68 times more likely to buy than are nonviewing shoppers.[138] Smart online entrepreneurs include more than mere product videos on their Web sites, creating instead videos that offer viewers (i.e., potential customers) something of value—a virtual factory tour that shows the company's dedication to quality, customer testimonials about the company's service, or informational videos that teach customers something.

Courtesy of Jamie Salvatori, Owner, Vat19

ENTREPRENEURIAL PROFILE: Jamie Salvatori: Vat19
Jamie Salvatori is the founder of Vat19, an online gift shop that sells a dazzling array of unique items, ranging from a 5-pound Gummy Bear and a 9-foot-tall beach ball to a mini circus clown bicycle and a 100-pound container of Magnetic Thinking putty. Vat19 has two channels on YouTube, where the company posts more than 400 whimsical videos of its products in action. Vat19's collection of quirky videos has attracted more than 200 million views and landed the company more than 300,000 subscribers. Some of these videos have gone viral, generating a great deal of publicity for the small company. Salvatori says that the videos, all of which the company produces in-house, are an essential part of Vat19's overall marketing strategy because many customers discover the company on YouTube and because they increase the company's conversion rate.[139] ■

Once companies create video content for their Web sites, they can share it (and encourage others to share it) with potential customers by announcing and posting it on social media sites such as Facebook, Twitter, YouTube, Vimeo, and Pinterest. Vat19 uses Facebook and Twitter to announce new product videos that always include links to the company's Web site, which drives traffic to it.[140] YouTube's Analytics gives business owners the ability to determine the effectiveness of the videos they post at reaching potential customers. YouTube's Analytics can show entrepreneurs how many times their videos have been viewed over a period of time, the popularity of their videos compared to other YouTube videos, how viewers discovered their videos, basic demographic profiles of their viewers, and other useful information.

Establish the Appropriate Call to Action on Each Page

Every page of a Web site should have a purpose, steering customers to take a specific action—add to cart, buy now, download for free, continue shopping, review the company's services, learn more, request a consultation, read customer reviews, and so on. A call to action is like a beam that lights the path to the action you want a shopper to take. Make sure that the call to action on every page is highly visible and appropriate; ideally, it is located above the fold, the top part of the screen the customer sees without having to scroll down. Unfortunately, one study reports that 70 percent of small business Web sites had no call to action on their home pages and 72 percent had no call to action on the internal pages of their sites.[141]

Build Loyalty by Giving Online Customers a Reason to Return to Your Web Site

Just as with brick-and-mortar retailers, e-tailers that constantly have to incur the expense of attracting new customers find it difficult to remain profitable because of the extra cost required to acquire customers. One of the most effective ways to encourage customers to return to a site is to establish an incentive program that rewards them for repeat purchases. "Frequent-buyer" programs that offer discounts or points toward future purchases, giveaways such as T-shirts emblazoned with a company's logo, or special services are common components of incentive programs. Incentive programs that are properly designed with a company's target customer in mind really work.

Establish Quality Backlinks with Other Related Businesses, Preferably Those Selling Products or Services That Complement Yours

A backlink is clickable text on a relevant Web site that links back to your site. Listing the Web addresses of complementary businesses on your company's site and having them list its address on their sites offers customers more value, brings traffic to your site that you otherwise would have missed, and improves search engine rankings. For instance, the owner of a site selling upscale kitchen gadgets should consider a cross-listing arrangement with sites that feature gourmet recipes, wines, and kitchen appliances. Recall that search engines penalize sites that contain low-quality, "unnatural" links from unrelated sites, however.

Include an E-mail Option, a Physical Address, and a Telephone Number on Your Site

Customers appreciate the opportunity to communicate with your company, and your Web site should give them many options for doing so. When you include e-mail access on your site, be sure to respond to it promptly. Nothing alienates customers faster than a company that is slow to respond or that fails to respond to e-mail messages. Including a physical address (with an interactive map feature) is important because shoppers frequently use their smart phones to locate businesses. Unfortunately, 60 percent of company Web sites fail to post their physical addresses. In addition, businesses should include a toll-free telephone number for customers who prefer to call with their questions. However, nearly 50 percent of small companies fail to include their telephone numbers on their sites or bury them so deeply within the site's pages that customers never find them.[142]

Give Shoppers the Ability to Track Their Orders Online

Many customers who order items online want to track the progress of their orders. One of the most effective ways to keep customers happy is to send an e-mail confirmation that your company received an order and another e-mail notification when the order ships. The shipment notice should include the shipper's tracking number and instructions on how to track the order from the shipper's site. Order and shipping confirmations instill confidence in even the most Web-wary shoppers.

Offer Online Shoppers a Special All Their Own

Give online customers a special deal that you don't offer in any other advertising piece. Change your specials often (weekly, if possible) and use clever "teasers" to draw attention to the offer. Regular special offers available only on the Internet give customers an incentive to return to a company's site.

Use the Power of Social Media

Make it easy for customers to connect with your company on social media such as Facebook, Pinterest, and Twitter by including social media sharing links and links to your company's social media pages on your Web site.

Follow a Simple Design

Catchy graphics and photographs are important to snaring customers, but designers must choose them carefully. Designs that are overly complex take a long time to download, and customers are likely to move on before they appear. Web Site Garage (http://thewebsitegarage.com), a Web site maintenance company, offers companies a free 21-point inspection of their Web sites and a report that describes problems ranging from slow download speeds to search engine optimization and provides potential solutions.

Following are some specific design tips:

- *Avoid clutter, especially on your site's home page.* The best designs are simple and elegant, with a balance of text and graphics. A minimalist approach usually works best.

- *Use less text on your site's home page, landing pages, and initial product or service pages.* Although including detailed, text-heavy content deeper in your site is acceptable and even desirable, incorporating too much text up front dissuades shoppers. The goal is to make the content easily digestible but allow customers to drill down to more detailed product and service descriptions. Most people skim Web sites in an "F" pattern and rarely read content fully, typically reading only about 20 percent of it. Each paragraph should contain only one idea, and the first two paragraphs are the most important because they are the ones visitors are most likely to read. Catchy headlines that are easily scannable and text that features bullet points and action words are essential components of good design (see Figure 10.11).

- *Avoid huge graphic headers.* These headers typically must download first, prohibiting customers from seeing anything else on your site as they wait (or, more likely, *don't* wait). Use graphics judiciously so that the site loads quickly. Recall that customers abandon Web sites that load slowly. For impatient online shoppers, faster is better.

- *Make the site easy to navigate.* Include navigation buttons at the bottoms of pages to enable customers to return to the top of the page or to the menu bar. This avoids what one expert calls the "pogo effect," when visitors bounce from page to page in a Web site, looking for what they need. Without navigation buttons or a site map page, a company runs the risk of customers getting lost in its site and leaving. An online merchant never knows which page a customer will land on; therefore, it is important for each page to provide a consistent look; relevant, concise content; and easy navigation.

- *Minimize the number of clicks required for a customer to get to any particular page in the site.* Long paths increase the likelihood of customers bailing out before they reach their intended destination.

- *Incorporate meaningful content in the site that is useful to visitors, well organized, easy to read, and current.* The content should be consistent with the message a company sends

FIGURE 10.11

Basic Web Page Design Principles and the Typical "F" Reading Pattern (in blue)

Sources: Based on Brandon Jones, "Web Design Theory: Understanding the F-Layout in Web Design," *Envato*, March 7, 2012, https://webdesign.tutsplus.com/articles/understanding-the-f-layout-in-web-design-webdesign-687; Jerry Cao, "How to Design Web Sites That Mirror How Our Eyes Work," *The Next Web*, April 10, 2015, http://thenextweb.com/dd/2015/04/10/how-to-design-websites-that-mirror-how-our-eyes-work/.

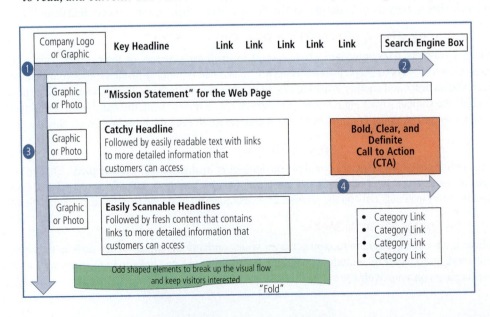

in the other advertising media it uses. Update the site's content frequently. Although a Web site should be designed to sell, providing useful, current information attracts visitors, keeps them coming back, and establishes a company's reputation as an expert in the field.

- *Include a frequently asked questions (FAQ) section.* Adding this section to a site can dramatically reduce the number of telephone calls and e-mails customer service representatives must handle. FAQ sections typically span a wide range of issues—from how to place an order to how to return merchandise—and cover whatever topics customers most often want to know about.

- *Be sure to prominently post privacy and return policies as well as product guarantees the company offers.*

- *Include a search tool that allows visitors to find the product or information they want.* This is especially important if your site is heavy on content—say 100 or more pages—or has more than 100 products for sale. Smaller, simpler sites can get by without a search tool *if* they are organized properly.

- *Avoid fancy typefaces and small fonts because they are too hard to read. Limit font and color choices to two or three to avoid a circus look.*

- *Be vigilant about misspelled words, typographical errors, and formatting mistakes.* Such errors destroy a site's credibility.

- *Avoid using small fonts on "busy" backgrounds; no one will read them!*

- *Choose colors carefully.* The most common color on the top five U.S. Web sites is blue (which is the most common "favorite color" among people), but the sites use contrasting colors to highlight call-to-action buttons and other important features.[143] Color palettes should be limited and simple to prevent a site from falling victim to the "comic book syndrome."

- *Use your Web site to collect information from visitors but don't tie up visitors immediately with a tedious registration process.* Many will simply leave the site, never to return. Allow new customers to complete purchases without registering ("guest checkout") but give them the option of saving their customer information for easy ordering in the future. Be sure to make the registration process short. Offers for a free e-mail newsletter or a contest giveaway can give visitors enough incentive to register with a site.

- *Make sure the overall look of the page is appealing.* Recall that visitors judge the credibility of a Web site in just 50 milliseconds. If it fails to measure up, they will abandon it almost immediately.

- *Remember that simpler is almost always better.*

Create a Fast, Simple Checkout Process

One surefire way to destroy an online company's conversion rate is to impose a lengthy, convoluted checkout process that requires customers to wade through pages of forms just to complete a purchase. When faced with a lengthy checkout process, customers simply abandon a site and make their purchases elsewhere; therefore, businesses should offer a "guest checkout" option but include incentives to encourage shoppers to create accounts, which provides a business more opportunities to send personalized marketing messages based on users' interests and past purchases. The fewer steps required for customers to check out, the more successful a site is at generating sales. (An analysis of the 50 top-grossing Web sites shows that their checkout processes require an average of 5.42 steps, but experts say that the ideal number of steps is 3.[144]) A progress indicator that shows customers where they are in the checkout process also can help, and businesses should avoid asking customers to enter the same information more than once.

Entrepreneurs must make sure that their sites display a prominent "add to cart" button in the same place on every product page and a highly visible "proceed to checkout" button to ensure that customers can make their purchases easily. Once customers put items into a shopping cart, they should be able to review a complete list and thumbnail photographs of the products they have selected and should be able to access more information about them with one click. The cart also should display the price of each item in the shopper's local currency. The cart should allow customers to change product quantities (and, believe it or not, to remove items from the cart) without having to go back to a product page. Every cart should have a "continue shopping" link in it as well.

Provide Customers Multiple Payment Options

Because some customers are skittish about using their credit cards online, online merchants should offer options to pay by PayPal, Google Checkout, or other payment services.

Assure Customers That Their Online Transactions Are Secure

Web-savvy customers are not willing to divulge their credit card information on sites that are not secure. Every e-commerce company must ensure that its site includes the proper security software and encryption devices. Highly visible security certificates and a padlock image tell customers their online transactions are secure and will help close sales. The average amount of an online order is $132, and no business can afford to lose a sale of that magnitude because its Web site lacks proper security![145]

Establish Reasonable Shipping and Handling Charges and Post Them Up Front

The number-one reason that shoppers do not buy more goods online is high shipping costs. A closely related gripe among online shoppers is that some e-tailers reveal their shipping and handling charges too late in the checkout process. Responsible online merchants keep shipping and handling charges reasonable and display them early on in the buying process to avoid customer "cart shock." Merchants have discovered that free shipping (often with a minimum purchase amount) is a powerful tool for boosting online sales because more shoppers have come to expect it. Ninety-three percent of online shoppers say they will purchase more if an online merchant offers free shipping.[146] However, because shipping costs have risen quickly in recent years, online merchants must balance the need to convert browsers into buyers with free or low-cost shipping and keeping costs under control. L.L.Bean, the online and catalog retailer of outdoor clothing and gear, offers free shipping on all orders to its customers—which is tangible evidence of the company's commitment to superior customer service.

Confirm Transactions

When a customer completes an order, a Web site should display a confirmation page. In addition, an order confirmation e-mail, which a company can generate automatically, lets a customer know that the company received the online order; such confirmations can be an important first line of defense against online fraud. If a customer receives a confirmation but did not place an order, the company can cancel it and report the credit card information as suspicious. Confirmation e-mails can contain ads or coupons for future purchases, but they should be short.

Keep Your Site Updated

Customers want to see something new when they visit brick-and-mortar stores, and they expect the same when they visit online stores. Entrepreneurs must be diligent about deleting links that have disappeared and keeping the information on their sites current. Yet, making time to update their companies' Web sites often is crowded out by all of the other demands on entrepreneurs' time; 64 percent of small business owners say that the greatest challenge they face with their Web sites is finding time to update them.[147] One sure way to run off customers on the Web is to continue to advertise your company's "Christmas Special" in August. Fresh information and new specials keep customers coming back.

Test Your Site Often

Smart e-commerce entrepreneurs check their sites frequently to make sure they are running smoothly and not causing customers unexpected problems. A good rule of thumb is to check your site at least monthly—or weekly if its content changes frequently.

Rely on Analytics to Improve Your Site

Web analytics (see the following section) provide a host of useful information ranging from the key words that shoppers use to find your site and how long they stay on it to the number of visitors and their locations. The best way to increase a site's conversion rate is to use analytics to determine which techniques work best and integrate them throughout the site.

Consider Hiring a Professional to Design Your Site

Pros can do it a lot faster and better than you can. However, don't give designers free rein to do whatever they want to with your site. Make sure it meets your criteria for an effective site that can sell.

Entrepreneurs must remember that on the Internet, every company, no matter how big or small, has the same screen size for its site. What matters most is not the size of your company but how you put that screen size to use.

Tracking Web Results

Web sites offer entrepreneurs a treasure trove of valuable information about how well their sites are performing—if they take the time to analyze it. **Web analytics**, tools that measure a Web site's ability to attract customers, generate sales, and keep customers coming back, help entrepreneurs learn what works—and what doesn't—on their sites. Online companies that use Web analytics have an advantage over those that do not. Unfortunately, only 25 percent of small businesses use Web analytics to track traffic patterns on their sites and to strategically refashion them to improve their sites' performance.[148] Owners who use analytics review the data collected from their customers' Web site activity, analyze it, make adjustments to their Web sites, and then start the monitoring process over again to see whether the changes improve the site's performance. In other words, Web analytics give entrepreneurs the ability to apply the principles of continuous improvement to their sites. In addition, the changes these e-business owners make are based on facts (the data from the Web analytics) rather than on mere guesses about how customers interact with a site. Google Analytics is the most popular Web analytics system on the market (and is linked to Google's popular AdWords program), but many other companies also offer Web analytics software packages. The most effective ones offer the following types of information, often in real time:

- *Commerce metrics.* These are basic analytics, such as sales revenue generated, number of items sold, which products are selling best (and which are not), and so on.

- *Visitor segmentation measurements.* These measurements provide entrepreneurs with valuable information about online shoppers and customers, including whether they are return customers or new customers, how they arrived at the site (e.g., via a search engine or a pay-per-click ad), which search terms they used (if they used a search engine), where they are located, what type of device they are using, and so on. The number of repeat visitors to a site is important because it is an indication of customer loyalty. A high percentage of repeat customers benefits a business because selling to an existing customer is much easier than selling to a first-time customer.

- *Content reports.* This information tells entrepreneurs which products customers are looking for and which pages they view most often (and least often), how they navigate through the site, how long they stay, which pages they are on when they exit, and more. Using this information, an entrepreneur can get an idea of the effectiveness of the site's design.

- *Process measurements.* These metrics help entrepreneurs understand how their Web sites attract visitors and convert them into customers. Does the checkout process work smoothly? How often do shoppers abandon their carts? At what point in the process do they abandon them? These measures can lead to higher conversion rates for an online business.

Other common measures of Web site performance include the following:

- The **cost per acquisition** is the cost that a company incurs to generate each purchase (or customer registration):

  Cost per acquisition = Total cost of acquiring a new customer ÷ Number of new customers

  For example, if a company purchases an advertisement in an e-magazine for $200 and the ad yields 15 new customers, then the cost of acquisition is $200 ÷ 15 = $13.33.

- The **bounce rate** is the percentage of visitors to a company's Web site who view a single page and leave without viewing other pages. A high bounce rate indicates that a company's

---

LO5

Explain how companies track the results from their Web sites.

Web analytics
tools that measure a Web site's ability to attract customers, generate sales, and keep customers coming back.

cost per acquisition
the cost that a company incurs to generate each purchase (or customer registration).

bounce rate
a measure of the percentage of visitors to a company's Web site who view a single page and leave without viewing other pages.

Web site lacks credibility or meaningful content that attracts customers' attention or suffers from some other malady. The bounce rate is calculated as follows:

$$\text{Bounce rate} = \text{Number of single-page viewers} \div \text{Total number of visitors}$$

retention rate

a measure of the percentage of customers a company retains over a period of time.

- The **retention rate** measures the percentage of customers a company retains over a period of time. It is an important measure because repeat customers generate the greatest portion of a company's sales, are nine times more likely to make a purchase than a first-time shopper, and generate a higher average order value than first-time buyers.[149] The retention rate is calculated as follows:

$$\text{Retention rate} = (\text{Total number of customers at end of period}$$
$$- \text{Total number of new customers acquired during the period})$$
$$\div \text{Total number of customers at the beginning of the period}$$

lift rate

the percentage change in a company's retention rate from one time period to the next.

For example, if a company had 180 customers at the beginning of the year, added 70 new customers during the year, and had 210 customers at the end of the year, its retention rate is $(210 - 70) \div 180 = 77.8$ percent. An online company's **lift rate** is the percentage change in its retention rate from one time period to the next. For example, suppose that the company in the previous example had a retention rate of 73.5 percent in the previous period. Its lift rate is $(77.8 - 73.5) \div 73.5 = 5.8$ percent.

conversion (browse-to-buy) rate

a measure of the proportion of visitors to a site who actually make a purchase.

- The **conversion (browse-to-buy) rate** is the proportion of visitors to a site who actually make a purchase. It is one of the most important measures of Web success and is calculated as follows:

$$\text{Conversion rate} = \text{Number of customers who make a purchase} \div \text{Number of visitors to the site}$$

Although conversion rates vary dramatically across industries, the average conversion rate is 3.16 percent.[150] In other words, out of every 1,000 people who visit a typical Web site, about 32 of them actually make a purchase. The longer a site's average visit duration and the lower its bounce rate, the higher its conversion rate. The best way for a company to increase its conversion rate is to constantly conduct A/B tests (showing two versions of the same page to visitors) to identify designs, deals, and details that work best.

average order value

the average amount customers purchase per order.

- The **average order value** is the average amount customers purchase per order. Many online companies segment their customers based on the number of times they have made a purchase and calculate the average order value for each group. This information allows them to target each customer segment with a customized e-mail marketing campaign designed to stimulate purchases.

latency

the time between customers' purchases.

- **Latency** is the time between customers' purchases. Shorter is better. Some companies analyze latency to predict the timing of the customer's next order. If it fails to materialize, the company sends a triggered e-mail to encourage a purchase.

customer lifetime value

the total sales that a customer accounts for throughout his or her entire relationship with a business.

- **Customer lifetime value** measures the total sales that a customer accounts for over his or her entire relationship with a business. It is calculated as follows:

$$\text{Customer lifetime value} = \text{Average order value}$$
$$\times \text{Average number of purchases customer had made}$$
$$\times \text{Time (in years) before customer leaves}$$

If a customer's average order value is $132.50, and she makes an average of 6.2 purchases per year and has been a customer for five years, her customer lifetime value is $132.50 \times 6.2 \times 5 = $4,107.50$. Companies can use this information to increase sales by offering special benefits (early access to sales, free shipping, and so on) to their most valuable customers.

cart abandonment rate

the percentage of shoppers who place at least one item in a shopping cart but never complete the transaction.

- The **cart abandonment rate** is the percentage of shoppers who place at least one item in a shopping cart but never complete the transaction:

$$\text{Cart abandonment rate} = 1 - (\text{Number of customers who complete a transaction}$$
$$\div \text{Number of shoppers who place at least one item in a shopping cart})$$

If 500 shoppers place at least one item in a shopping cart but only 175 of them complete their transactions, the company's cart abandonment rate is $1 - (175 \div 500) = 65$ percent.

- The **search engine ranking** shows where a company's Web site ranks in search engines' results pages. Recall that almost 92 percent of search engine users click on a link to a site that appears on the first page of the search results, which means that unless a company's site shows up on that first page of results, it is almost invisible online.

search engine ranking
where a company's Web site ranks in search engines' results pages.

Ensuring Web Privacy and Security

Privacy

The Web's ability to track customers' every move naturally raises concerns about the privacy of the information companies collect. Concerns about privacy and security are two of the greatest obstacles to the growth of e-commerce. E-commerce gives businesses access to tremendous volumes of information about their customers, creating a responsibility to protect that information and to use it wisely. To make sure they are using the information they collect from visitors to their Web sites legally and ethically, companies should take the following steps:

LO6
Describe how e-businesses ensure the privacy and security of the information they collect and store from the Web.

Take an inventory of the customer data collected. The first step in ensuring proper data handling is to assess exactly the type of data the company is collecting and storing. How are you collecting the data? Why are you collecting the data? How are you using it? Do visitors know how you are using the data? Do you need to get their permission to use it in this way? Do you use all of the data you are collecting?

Develop a company privacy policy for the information you collect. A **privacy policy** is a statement explaining the nature of the information a company collects online, what it does with that information, and the recourse customers have if they believe the company is misusing the information. Every online company should have a privacy policy, but many do not. Several online privacy firms, such as TRUSTe (www.truste.org), BBBOnline (www.bbbonline.com), and BetterWeb (www.betterweb.com), offer Web "seal programs," the equivalent of the Good Housekeeping Seal of Approval for privacy. To earn a privacy seal of approval, a company must adopt a privacy policy, implement it, and monitor its effectiveness. Many of these privacy sites also provide online policy wizards, which are automated questionnaires that help e-business owners create comprehensive privacy statements.

privacy policy
a statement that explains the nature of the information a company collects online, what it does with that information, and the recourse customers have if they believe the company is misusing the information.

Post your company's privacy policy prominently on your Web site and follow it. Creating a privacy policy is not sufficient; posting it in a prominent place on the Web site (it should be accessible from *every* page on the Web site) and then abiding by it make a policy meaningful. One of the worst mistakes a company can make is to publish its privacy policy online and then fail to follow it. Not only is this unethical, but it also can lead to serious damage awards if customers take legal action against the company.

Security

Hackers and intruders, whose attacks are growing increasingly sophisticated, have begun targeting small companies, which have limited budgets, few (if any) technical experts on staff, and, as a result, less secure systems. A recent survey reports that only 11 percent of small business owners hire IT professionals (either in-house or outside consultants) to manage their cybersecurity; 83 percent of business owners say that they handle their companies' cybersecurity themselves, and 6 percent say that *no one* handles their cybersecurity.[151] Because small businesses are less likely than large companies to have a full arsenal of cyberprotection in place, they are the easiest targets, and the frequency with which cybercriminals attack them is on the rise. In fact, 43 percent of cyberattacks are aimed at small businesses, an increase from 18 percent in 2011.[152] However, 82 percent of small business owners believe that they are not targets for attacks because they have nothing worth stealing.[153] Yet, 68 percent of small businesses store customers' e-mail addresses, 64 percent store customers' telephone numbers, and 54 percent store billing addresses—all of which are valuable pieces of information to cybercriminals.[154] Nearly one-third of small business owners believe that they will suffer no lost revenue if their businesses' Web sites are down for a day due to a cyberattack.[155] The reality, however, is that a single malware or ransomware attack costs small and medium-size businesses an average of $86,500.[156] The costs associated with a security breach include not only the actual cost of the lost data and the lawsuits that inevitably result but also the long-term impact of the lost trust that customers have for a business whose security has been breached. Cyberattacks threaten the very existence of the typical small business; Google usually "blacklists" companies that suffer cyberattacks, which renders them virtual non-entities online. In addition, nearly 60 percent of companies that are victims of cyberattacks close their doors within six months.[157]

Cybercrime has become big business, to the tune of $575 billion per year.[158] For online merchants, shoppers' concerns over privacy and security translate into lost sales. One recent survey reports that online shoppers abandon 70 percent of their purchases because of security concerns.[159] Most of the data that cybercriminals target involves customer records stolen from companies for the purpose of identity theft, which affects 17.6 million people annually.[160]

Every company that operates online—no matter how small—is a potential target for hackers and other cybercriminals. Experts estimate that 86 percent of all Web sites have at least one "serious vulnerability" that opens the door to cybercriminals seeking to do harm.[161] The following are among the most common types of cyberattacks:

- **Malware.** Malware, an umbrella term for "malicious software," encompasses a wide range of attacks, including viruses that infect and destroy computer systems, spyware that secretly collects users' keystrokes or data, and worms that find their way into a single computer and then crawl through the rest of the network and infect it. Ransomware attacks, in which cybercriminals illegally access a company's network, encrypt its data, and demand a ransom (the average amount demanded is $1,077) to restore access to it, are now the dominant form of malware.[162] Antivirus software detects nearly 1,600 ransomware attempts globally per day.[163]

- **Denial-of-service (DoS) attacks.** In a DoS attack, hackers flood a company's server with an overwhelming number of requests, overloading it, often to the point of causing it to crash, and preventing customers from accessing it.

- **Password attacks.** These attacks use different strategies to determine users' passwords so that hackers can gain access to a network.

- **Phishing.** Phishing involves collecting sensitive information such as passwords, log-in credentials, and so on, often by sending legitimate-looking (but fraudulent) e-mails to unsuspecting users. Forty-three percent of phishing attacks are aimed at small businesses.[164]

Businesses can take advantage of a number of safeguards, but hackers with enough time, talent, and determination usually can beat even the most sophisticated safety measures. If hackers manage to break into a system, they can do irreparable damage, blocking access to data (with ransomware), stealing programs and sensitive customer data, modifying or deleting valuable information, changing the look and content of sites, or crashing sites altogether.

To minimize the likelihood of invasion by hackers, e-companies rely on several tools, including virus detection software, intrusion detection software, and firewalls. At the most basic level of protection is **virus and malware detection software**, which scans computer drives for viruses and malware, nasty programs written by devious hackers and designed to harm computers and the information they contain. This basic protection is essential; on average, cybercriminals around the globe unleash 868,500 new malware, viruses, or ransomware attacks every day![165] Because hackers are *always* writing new viruses to attack computer systems, entrepreneurs must keep their virus detection software up to date and must run it often. An attack by one virus can bring a company's entire e-commerce platform to a screeching halt in no time!

Intrusion detection software is essential for any company doing business on the Web. These packages constantly monitor the activity on a company's network server and alert the

virus and malware detection software
programs that scan computer drives for viruses, or nasty programs written by devious hackers and designed to harm computers and the information they contain.

intrusion detection software
programs that constantly monitor the activity on a company's network server and alert the company if they detect someone breaking into the system or if they detect unusual network activity.

David Evison/Shutterstock

You Be the Consultant

Why Your Small Business Is a Target for Cybercriminals

Paul Eichen, founder of Rokenbok Education, a small company in Solana Beach, California, that sells building blocks and robotic devices to help children learn skills in science, technology, engineering, and math, was looking forward to the sales increase his company would experience during the upcoming holiday season. Then his company's computer system was hacked by cybercriminals in a ransomware scheme, and it created a nightmare for Eichen's seven-person company. The ransomware attack, in which criminals encrypt a company's data, holding it hostage until the business pays a ransom to unlock it, was the second time Eichen's company had experienced a cyberattack. The first one was a denial-of-service attack that shut down the company's Web site for several days, costing it thousands of dollars in lost sales. Rather than pay the ransom to decrypt Rokenbok Education's database files, Eichen used backup files and other records to re-create the stolen data. The process was expensive (but less expensive than the ransom the cybercriminals were demanding) and took four days.

According to computer security firm Symantec, 43 percent of cyberattacks globally are against small businesses. Attacks aimed at small businesses are growing rapidly because cybercriminals see them as easy targets, given that they have fewer resources to spend on computer security than large companies. Cybercrooks who steal data from small businesses empty company bank accounts, file for fraudulent tax refunds, commit health insurance and Medicare fraud, take customers' personal information, and steal companies' intellectual property. Experts estimate that the average cost to a small business to clean up the mess after a cyberattack is a whopping $690,000! Despite the high risk and devastating impact of cyberattacks, nearly 8 out of 10 small companies have no basic cyberattack response plan in place.

Most small businesses can't withstand cyberattacks. In fact, 60 percent of small companies that experience a cyberattack are out of business within six months. That is just what happened to one small online retailer located in the Midwest. One of the company's employees received an e-mail (a common source of the malware that launches a cyberattack) that contained a link to an innocent-looking catalog. One click on the link infected the entire

small company's computer network, which contained everything from sensitive customer account information to the business's accounting software, with ransomware. The cyberthieves soon sent a ransom demand of $50,000. Because the company's backup system had not been working for months, the owner decided to pay the ransom to get a decryption key to access his files; however, the decryption key did not work. The entrepreneur could not afford the cost of rebuilding his company's entire system, and within six months, the company was forced to close its doors, choked by a lack of sales and cash flow.

Cyberattacks on small companies are relentless, and malware is growing rapidly. In just a single year, one computer security firm detected 430 million new pieces of malware, an increase of 36 percent from the previous year. Entrepreneurs who believe that their companies are too small to come under attack are mistaken. Once they face the reality that cybercriminals are targeting small businesses like theirs, entrepreneurs can take many simple, relatively inexpensive steps, such as keeping antivirus software up to date, adding firewalls, and using strong passwords, to strengthen their companies' computer security.

1. Why are cybercriminals increasingly targeting small businesses with their attacks?

2. What are the risks and dangers to a small company that is the victim of a cyberattack?

3. Use the information in this chapter and resources of the Internet to develop a list of at least five suggestions that small business owners can act on to strengthen the computer security in their companies and reduce the threat of a cyberattack.

Sources: Based on Constance Gustkejan, "No Business Too Small to Be Hacked," *New York Times*, January 13, 2016, www.nytimes.com/2016/01/14/business/smallbusiness/no-business-too-small-to-be-hacked.html?_r=0; Elizabeth MacDonald, "Cyber Attacks on Small Businesses on the Rise," *Fox Business*, April 27, 2016, www.foxbusiness.com/features/2016/04/27/cyber-attacks-on-small-businesses-on-rise.html; Gary Miller, "60% of Small Companies That Suffer a Cyber Attack Are out of Business Within Six Months," *Denver Post*, October 23, 2016, www.denverpost.com/2016/10/23/small-companies-cyber-attack-out-of-business/; *2016 Internet Security Threat Report*, vol. 21, Symantec, April 2016, p. 4.

---

company if they detect someone breaking into the company's computer system or if they detect unusual network activity. Intrusion detection software not only can detect attempts by unauthorized users to break into a computer system while they are happening but also can trace the hacker's location. Most packages also have the ability to preserve a record of the attempted break-in that will stand up in court so that companies can take legal action against cyberintruders.

A **firewall** is a combination of hardware and software operating between the Internet and a company's computer network that allows employees to have access to the Internet but keeps unauthorized users from entering a company's network and the programs and data it contains. Establishing a firewall is essential to operating a company on the Web, but entrepreneurs must make sure that their firewalls are set up properly. Otherwise, they are useless! Even with all of these security measures in place, it is best for a company to run its Web site on a separate server from the network that runs the business. If hackers break into the site, they still do not have access to the company's sensitive data and programs. Encryption software, another useful tool, encrypts sensitive data using a special "code" so that if a hacker steals it, the information is meaningless gibberish. Companies also

firewall
a combination of hardware and software that allows employees to have access to the Internet but keeps unauthorized users from entering a company's network and the programs and data it contains.

should back up all of their data in a separate, secure location, or in the cloud, which enables them to recover data from their primary network that may be lost or destroyed.

In e-commerce, just as in traditional retailing, sales do not matter unless a company gets paid! On the Internet, customers demand transactions that they can complete with ease and convenience, and the simplest way to allow customers to pay for e-commerce transactions is with debit or credit cards. From an online customer's perspective, however, one of the most important security issues is the security of his or her debit or credit card information. To ensure the security of their customers' debit or credit card information, online retailers typically use **Secure Sockets Layer (SSL) technology** or its successor, **Transport Layer Security (TLS) technology**, to encrypt customers' transaction information as it travels across the Internet. Web sites that start with "https" (and usually display a padlock icon in the address bar) indicate that they are secured by TLS or SSL technology. Every e-commerce store, no matter how small, must offer its customers secure online transactions.

The ability to process customers' credit and debit cards is essential for an e-commerce business; 78 percent of online shoppers use credit or debit cards to make their purchases.[166] Processing debit and credit card transactions requires a company to obtain a merchant account from a bank or financial intermediary. Setup fees for a merchant account typically range from $500 to $1,000, but companies also pay flat monthly access ("gateway") and statement fees of between $40 and $80 plus transaction fees (for example, "2.00% + 0.10," 2 percent of the transaction amount plus a $0.10 flat fee per transaction) and sometimes address verification service (AVS) fees. Once an online company has a merchant account, it can accept debit and credit cards from online customers.

Online credit card transactions also pose a risk for merchants; online fraud costs companies an estimated $3.5 billion a year, 0.8 percent of their annual revenues.[167] The most common problem is **charge-backs**, online transactions that customers dispute. Unlike credit card transactions in a retail store, those made online ("card-not-present" transactions) involve no signatures, and Internet merchants incur the loss when a customer disputes an online credit card transaction. One way to prevent fraud is to ask customers for their card verification value (CVV or CVV2), the three-digit number above the signature panel on the back of the credit card, as well as their card number and expiration date. Online merchants also can use an address verification system (AVS) that checks the billing address that the customer provides against the customer's address in the credit or debit card company's database. Verifying that the computer's IP address matches the customer's geographic location is another safeguard against charge-backs. Sending confirmation e-mails that include the customer's shipping information after receiving an order also reduce the likelihood of a charge-back. In addition, using a shipper that provides the ability to track shipments enables online merchants to prove that the customer actually received the merchandise and can help minimize the threat of payment fraud. Using these tools, online merchants reject about 2.8 percent of all online orders; small online retailers (those with less than $5 million in sales) reject 2.3 percent of all online orders.[168]

Once a company has proper security technology in place, managers must train employees on proper security measures because people often are the weakest link in a company's security chain. Employees must create unique, secure passwords for all accounts and never reveal them to others. Employees must be vigilant for phishing tactics in which scammers pose as legitimate businesses and attempt to extract sensitive information. In addition, employees should never respond to sketchy e-mails (which often are sources of malware, viruses, and attacks) and must exercise extreme caution on social media. As social media has become more prevalent, attackers have adapted cleverly disguised social media attacks, including fake offerings (inviting users to join a fake group and share sensitive information), "likejacking" (using fake "like" buttons that install viruses and malware on the user's computer), fake apps and plug-ins (convincing users to download apps and plug-ins that contain malicious software), and other malevolent techniques.[169]

With hackers' and cyberthieves' increasing emphasis on small business targets, entrepreneurs should consider purchasing cyber risk insurance, which covers losses due to data breaches and cyberattacks from malware, viruses, and ransomware, including the cost of defending against lawsuits from customers whose data is breached and business interruption. The cost of cyber insurance varies by company size, industry, and the type of services provided, but many small companies can purchase a policy for as little as $650. As part of their cyber risk coverage, insurance companies typically conduct an assessment of a company's IT systems and security practices, identifying potential vulnerabilities and offering solutions to them. Unfortunately, 75 percent of small businesses do not have cyber risk insurance.[170]

Secure Sockets Layer (SSL) technology or Transport Layer Security (TLS) technology
an encryption device that secures customers' transaction information as it travels across the Internet.

charge-backs
online transactions that customers dispute.

Chapter Summary by Learning Objective

E-commerce is creating a new economy, one that is connecting producers, sellers, and customers via technology in ways that have never been possible before. In this fast-paced world of e-commerce, size no longer matters as much as speed and flexibility. The Internet is creating a new industrial order, and companies that fail to adapt to it will soon become extinct.

1. Understand the factors an entrepreneur should consider before launching into e-commerce.

Before launching an e-commerce effort, business owners should consider the following important issues:

- How a company exploits the Web's interconnectivity and the opportunities it creates to transform relationships with its suppliers and vendors, its customers, and other external stakeholders is crucial to its success.

- Web success requires a company to develop a plan for integrating the Web into its overall strategy. The plan should address issues such as site design and maintenance, creating and managing a brand name, marketing and promotional strategies, sales, and customer service.

- Developing deep, lasting relationships with customers takes on even greater importance on the Web. Attracting customers on the Web costs money, and companies must be able to retain their online customers to make their Web sites profitable.

- Creating a meaningful presence on the Web requires an ongoing investment of resources—time, money, energy, and talent. Establishing an attractive Web site brimming with catchy photographs of products is only the beginning.

- Measuring the success of its Web-based sales effort is essential to remaining relevant to customers whose tastes, needs, and preferences are always changing.

2. Explain the 11 myths of e-commerce and how to avoid falling victim to them.

The 11 myths of e-commerce are as follows:
Myth 1. If I launch a site, customers will flock to it.
Myth 2. Online customers are easy to please.
Myth 3. Launching an e-commerce site is free—or at least really inexpensive
Myth 4: Making money on the Web is easy
Myth 5. Privacy is not an important issue on the Web

Myth 6. "Strategy? I don't need a strategy to sell on the Web! Just give me a Web site, and the rest will take care of itself."
Myth 7. The most important part of any e-commerce effort is technology
Myth 8. Customer service is not as important online as it is in a traditional retail store
Myth 9. Flashy Web sites are better than simple ones
Myth 10. It's what's up front that counts
Myth 11. My business doesn't need a Web site

3. Explain the basic strategies entrepreneurs should follow to achieve success in their e-commerce efforts.

Following are some guidelines for building a successful Web strategy for a small e-company:

- Focus on a niche in the market.
- Develop a community of online customers.
- Attract visitors by giving away "freebies."
- Make creative use of e-mail but avoid becoming a spammer.
- Make sure that your Web site says "credibility."
- Make the most of the Web's global reach.
- Go mobile.
- Promote your Web site online and offline.
- Use social media to attract and retain customers.
- Develop an effective search engine optimization strategy.

4. Learn the techniques of designing a killer Web site.

There is no surefire formula for attracting and keeping Web shoppers, but the following suggestions will help:

- Understand your target customer.
- Give customers what they want.
- Select a domain name that is consistent with the image you want to create for your company and register it.
- Make your Web site easy to navigate.
- Offer suggestions for related products.
- Add wish list capability.
- Create a gift idea center.
- Provide customer ratings and reviews.

- Use online videos.
- Establish the appropriate call to action on each page.
- Build loyalty by giving online customers a reason to return to your Web site.
- Establish hyperlinks with other businesses, preferably those selling products or services that complement yours.
- Include an e-mail option and a telephone number on your site.
- Give shoppers the ability to track their orders online.
- Offer Web shoppers a special all their own.
- Follow a simple design for your Web page.
- Create a fast, simple checkout process.
- Provide multiple payment options.
- Assure customers that their online transactions are secure.
- Establish reasonable shipping and handling charges and post them up front.
- Confirm transactions.
- Keep your site updated.
- Test your site often.
- Rely on analytics to improve your site.
- Consider hiring a professional to design your site.

5. Explain how companies track the results from their Web sites.

One option for tracking Web activity is through log-analysis software. Server logs record every page, graphic, audio clip, or photograph that visitors to a site access, and log-analysis software analyzes these logs and generates reports describing how visitors behave when they get to a site. Key metrics for measuring the effectiveness of a site's performance include the cost per acquisition, the bounce rate, the cart abandonment rate, and the conversion rate.

6. Describe how e-businesses ensure the privacy and security of the information they collect and store from the Web.

To make sure that they are using the information they collect from visitors to their Web sites legally and ethically, companies should take the following steps:

- Take an inventory of the customer data collected.
- Develop a company privacy policy for the information collected.
- Post the company's privacy policy prominently on the Web site and follow it.

To ensure the security of the information they collect and store from Web transactions, companies should rely on virus and intrusion detection software and firewalls to ward off attacks from hackers.

MyLab Entrepreneurship

If your instructor is using MyLab Entrepreneurship, go to **www.pearson.com/mylab/entrepreneurship** for Auto-graded writing questions as well as the following Assisted-graded writing questions:

1. Many shoppers use search engines to find the products and services they want to purchase online. Very few shoppers look beyond the first page of the search engine results. Suppose that your company, which once ranked on the first results page, has slipped to a spot many pages down and that sales are declining. What steps can you take to remedy this problem?
2. Describe common metrics that e-companies use to track the effectiveness of their Web sites.

Discussion Questions

10-1. In what ways have the Internet and e-commerce changed how companies do business?

10-2. Discuss the factors entrepreneurs should consider before launching an e-commerce site.

10-3. What are the 11 myths of e-commerce?

10-4. What can an entrepreneur do to avoid falling victim to these 11 myths?

⭐ 10-5. What strategic advice would you offer an entrepreneur who is about to start an e-company?

⭐ 10-6. What design characteristics make for a successful Web page?

10-7. Explain the characteristics of an ideal domain name.

10-8. Give an example of a company with a good domain name and an example of a company with a poor domain name.

10-9. What advantages does each e-commerce metric offer?

10-10. What steps should e-businesses take to ensure the privacy of the information they collect and store from the Web?

10-11. What techniques can e-companies use to protect their banks of information and their customers' transaction data from hackers?

10-12. What challenges does evaluating the effectiveness of a Web site pose for online entrepreneurs?

Beyond the Classroom . . .

10-13. Work with a team of your classmates to come up with an Internet business you would be interested in launching. Come up with several suitable domain names for your hypothetical e-company. Once you have chosen a few names, go to a domain name registration service, such as Network Solutions, at www.networksolutions.com, or NetNames, at www.netnames.com, to conduct a name search. How many of the names your team came up with are already registered to someone else? If an entrepreneur's top choice for a domain name is already registered to someone else, what options does he or she have?

10-14. Select several online companies with which you are familiar and visit their Web sites. What percentage of them have privacy policies posted on their sites? How comprehensive are these policies? What percentage of the sites you visited belonged to a privacy watchdog agency such as TRUSTe or BBBOnline? How important is a posted privacy policy for e-companies? Explain.

10-15. Visit three e-commerce sites on the Web and evaluate them on the basis of the Web site design principles described in this chapter. How well do they measure up? What suggestions can you offer for improving the design of each site? If you were a customer trying to make a purchase from each site, how would you respond to the design?

Endnotes

[1] Rob Gerlsbeck, "Vancouver Startup Helps Fishermen Deliver Directly to Restaurants," *Globe and Mail*, December 2, 2016, www.theglobeandmail.com/report-on-business/small-business/startups/how-a-vancouver-startup-helps-fisherman-deliver-from-dock-to-plate/article33006697/.

[2] Web-Influenced Retail Sales in the United States from 2012 to 2017, by Segment," *Statista*, 2016, www.statista.com/statistics/368309/us-web-influenced-retail-sales/.

[3] Pedro Hernandez, "Think Mobile Commerce for Small Business Success," *Small Business Computing*, January 14, 2016, www.smallbusinesscomputing.com/News/Mobile/think-mobile-commerce-for-small-business-success.html.

[4] "Local Consumer Review Survey," *BrightLocal*, 2016, www.brightlocal.com/learn/local-consumer-review-survey/.

[5] *UPS Pulse of the Online Shopper*, UPS, 2016, p. 8.

[6] Greg Bensinger and Suzanne Kapner, "Amazon Rips Page from Rivals' Offline Playbook," *Wall Street Journal*, February 5, 2016, http://www.wsj.com/articles/amazon-rips-page-from-rivals-offline-playbook-1454708011.

[7] Eliot Brown, "Web Retailers Shift Gears," *Wall Street Journal*, May 17, 2017, p. B4.

[8] Eugene Kim, "Amazon Is Doubling Down on Retail Stores with Plans to have 100 Pop-up Stores in U.S. Shopping Malls," *Business Insider*, September 9, 2016, http://www.businessinsider.com/amazon-big-expansion-retail-pop-up-stores-2016-9.

[9] Sarah Nassauer, "Mattress Makers Unroll New Sales Approach," *Wall Street Journal*, March 8, 2016, pp. B1–B2; "Inbound Marketing: How Influencer Marketing Attracted 100,000 Web Site Clicks to Luxury Mattress Site," MarketingSherpa, March 31, 2016, https://www.marketingsherpa.com/article/case-study/how-influencer-marketing-attracted-website-clicks.

[10] *Worldwide Retail E-Commerce Sales: eMarketer's Updated Estimates and Forecast Through 2019*," eMarketer, 2016, p. 5.

[11] "Rank of Best Selling Internet Products," *Statistic Brain*, January 24, 2016, www.statisticbrain.com/top-selling-internet-items/.

[12] *Worldwide Retail E-Commerce Sales: eMarketer's Updated Estimates and Forecast Through 2019*," eMarketer, 2016, pp. 2, 11.

[13] "Internet Usage Statistics," Internet World Stats, 2017, www.internetworldstats.com/stats.htm.

[14] Jerry Useem, "Our 10 Principles of the New Economy, Slightly Revised," *Business 2.0*, August/September 2001, p. 85.

[15] Susan Kuchinskas, "Where Are We Now? A Decade of E-Commerce," *E-Commerce Guide*, www.ecommerceguide.com/news/trends/article.php/3426371.

[16] Allison Enright, "U.S. E-Commerce Sales Could Top $434 Billion in 2017," *Internet Retailer*, April 25, 2013, www.internetretailer.com/2013/04/25/us-e-commerce-sales-could-top-434-billion-2017.

[17] Amanda Sodurland, "Small Business Web Sites in 2016: A Survey," *Clutch*, February 17, 2016, https://clutch.co/web-designers/resources/small-business-websites-2016-survey; Rohit Arora, "It's 2016, so Why Do Almost Half of Small Businesses Not Have a Web Site?" *Inc.*, February 19, 2016, www.inc.com/replacemeplease1455908726.html.

[18] Amanda Sodurland, "Small Business Web Sites in 2016: A Survey," *Clutch*, February 17, 2016, https://clutch.co/web-designers/resources/small-business-websites-2016-survey.

[19] Sade Strehlke, "Q&A: Mary Helen Bowers," *Wall Street Journal Magazine*, August 11, 2014, p. 98; Pia Catton, "Creating the Body of a Ballerina," *Wall Street Journal*, January 31, 2011, www.wsj.com/articles/SB10001424052748703833204576114361304121324.

[20] "Customer Retention: Keep Customers by Growing Relationships Online," pb Smart for Small Business, Pitney Bowes, www.pbsmartessentials.com/customer-satisfaction/customer-retention-keep-customers-by-growing-relationships-online/.

[21] Frederick F. Reichheld and Phil Schefter, "The Economics of E-Loyalty," *Harvard Business Review*, July 10, 2000, http://hbswk.hbs.edu/archive/1590.html.

[22] *The State of E-Commerce: Yotpo Benchmark Report*, Yotpo, 2016, p. 12.

[23] "Total Number of Web Sites," *Internet Live Stats*, December 18, 2016, www.internetlivestats.com/total-number-of-websites/; Adrienne LaFrance, "How Many Web Sites Are There?" *The Atlantic*, September 30, 2015, www.theatlantic.com/technology/archive/2015/09/how-many-websites-are-there/408151/.

[24]"Success Story: Fetching New Subscribers," Facebook, 2016, www.facebook.com/business/success/barkbox-2; Emmie Martin, "The Company That Wants to Build 'Disney for Dogs' Is Starting with an Office Full of Toys, Treats, and Canine Coworkers," *Business Insider*, August 3, 2016, www.businessinsider.com/bark-and-co-barkbox-office-tour-2016-8.

[25]Ross Paul, "Just How Big Is the E-Commerce Market? You'll Never Guess!" *LemonStand*, June 26, 2015, http://blog.lemonstand.com/just-how-big-is-the-ecommerce-market-youll-never-guess/.

[26]*A Global Study of the Drivers of a Successful Online Experience*, LivePerson, November 2013, pp. 3–5.

[27]Monetate E-Commerce Quarterly Report: 2016 EQ1," *Monetate*, 2016, pp. 7–8; "Johnston and Murphy: Customer Experience Redefined by Data," Monetate Customer Portfolios, 2016, www.customerportfolios.com/wp-content/uploads/2014/01/Costumer-Portfolios-JM-Case-Study-v1c.pdf.

[28]Jordan Lindberg, "The Real Costs of Starting a Web Store," *Practical E-Commerce*, March 30, 2014, www.practicalecommerce.com/articles/94843-The-real-costs-of-starting-a-web-store.

[29]Mark D. Hulett, "How Much Do E-Commerce Web Sites Cost in 2016?" Georgia Web Development, 2016, https://gawebdev.com/much-do-ecommerce-websites-cost-in-2014/.

[30]"The State of Online Privacy 2016," *TRUSTe*, January 28, 2016, www.truste.com/blog/2016/01/28/state-online-privacy-2016/.

[31]Ibid.

[32]Ibid.

[33]"Small Business Owner Finds E-commerce Niche," U.S. Small Business Administration, Indiana District Office, 2014, www.sba.gov/offices/district/in/indianapolis/success-stories/small-business-owner-finds-e-commerce-niche; Helena Ball, "How the 'Worst Idea Ever' Became a $30 Million Business," *Inc.*, August 17, 2016, www.inc.com/helena-ball/2016-inc5000-indiana-ecommerce-manufacturing-fourth-fastest-growing-company-in-america.html.

[34]*Monetate E-Commerce Quarterly Report*: EQI 2016, *Monetate*, Quarter 1, 2016, p. 10.

[35]*Conversion Rate Optimization Report 2015*, EConsultancy and RedEye, 2015, p. 21.

[36]"Success Stories from Customers: OnlineShoes.com," UserTesting, www.usertesting.com/about-us/success-stories#ss-onlineshoes.

[37]Derek Cromwell, "2016 State of E-Commerce: Cart Abandonment and Recapture Statistics," EY Studios, August 12, 2016, www.eystudios.com/2016/08/2016-state-ecommerce/.

[38]Manish Bhalla, "7 Reasons Why Shoppers Are Abandoning Your Mobile Shopping Cart," Ventureburn, January 18, 2016, http://ventureburn.com/2016/01/7-reasons-why-customers-are-abandoning-your-mobile-shopping-cart/.

[39]Cooper Smith, "Shopping Cart Abandonment: Online Retailers' Biggest Headache Is Actually a Huge Opportunity," *Business Intelligence*, March 4, 2015, www.businessinsider.com/heres-how-retailers-can-reduce-shopping-cart-abandonment-and-recoup-billions-of-dollars-in-lost-sales-2014-4.

[40]Ibid.

[41]Peter Presipino, "The Web Is Alive," *Website Magazine*, November 2015, pp. 24–29.

[42]Kasey Wehrum, "Their Carts Are Full. So Why Won't They Buy?" *Inc.*, December 2013/January 2014, p. 28.

[43]"7 Ways to Provide Exceptional Customer Service for E-Commerce," *Website Magazine*, February 16, 2015, http://webmag.co/7-ways-provide-exceptional-customer-service-ecomemrce/.

[44]Ibid.

[45]"Digital Maturity: Most Sites Have a Lot of Growing Up to Do," *Venture Beat*, April 16, 2015, http://venturebeat.com/2015/04/16/digital-maturity-most-brands-have-a-lot-of-growing-up-to-do/.

[46]"New Study Reveals Consumers Are 'Uninspired' by Online Shopping," *Retail Wire*, April 3, 2014, www.retailwire.com/discussion/new-study-reveals-consumers-are-uninspired-by-online-shopping/.

[47]"Why Good Web Design Is So Important," *Website Magazine*, May 5, 2016, http://webmag.co/good-web-design-important/; Allison Howen, "Party of Three," *Website Management*, October 2013, pp. 20-21.

[48]"The Impact of Slow Web Sites," *Website Magazine*, January 12, 2016, http://webmag.co/the-impact-of-slow-websites/.

[49]"The Impact of Slow Web Sites," *Website Magazine*, January 12, 2016, http://webmag.co/the-impact-of-slow-websites/; Allison Howen, "Party of Three," *Website Management*, October 2013, pp. 20-21.

[50]"Why Good Web Design Is So Important," *Website Magazine*, May 5, 2016, http://webmag.co/good-web-design-important/.

[51]"The Impact of Slow Web Sites," *Website Magazine*, January 12, 2016, http://webmag.co/the-impact-of-slow-websites/.

[52]Abram Brown, "The Calculus of Couches," *Forbes*, May 5, 2014, pp. 58-60.

[53]Dan Martin, "Winning on the Web: Why Small Businesses Need to Be Online," *Business Zone*, October 29, 2014, www.businesszone.co.uk/decide/technology/winning-on-the-web-why-small-businesses-need-to-be-online.

[54]Amberly Dressler, "Loyalty for the Modern Digital Buyers," *Website Magazine*, October 2013, pp. 24–30.

[55]"Growth in Time Spent with Media Is Slowing," *eMarketer*, June 6, 2016, www.emarketer.com/Article/Growth-Time-Spent-with-Media-Slowing/1014042.

[56]Hannah Cho, "Small Business Success Story: Online Retailers Get Physical," *Nerdwallet*, May 18, 2015, www.nerdwallet.com/blog/small-business/small-business-online-open-storefront/; Karen Stern, "Starting a Business That Runs in Their Blood," *CNBC*, February 17, 2015, www.cnbc.com/2015/02/17/starting-a-business-that-runs-in-their-blood.html.

[57]Andrew Hutchinson, "5 SMEs That Are Winning at Social Media Marketing and What You Can Learn from Them," *Buildfire*, November 12, 2015, https://buildfire.com/smes-winning-social-media-marketing-learn/; "I Never Predicted We'd Have 20,000 Bookings in the First Two Weeks: Lauren Pears on the Success of London's First Cat Café," *This Is Money*, May 14, 2016, www.thisismoney.co.uk/money/smallbusiness/article-3561871/Lauren-Pears-success-London-s-cat-caf.html.

[58]"Local Consumer Review Survey," *BrightLocal*, 2014, www.brightlocal.com/learn/local-consumer-review-survey-2014/.

[59]Ralph F. Wilson, "The Five Mutable Laws of Web Marketing," *Web Marketing Today*, April 1, 1999, www.wilsonweb.com/wmta/basic-principles.htm, pp. 1–7.

[60]Miranda Paquet, "5 Things Customers Need to Hear You Say in Your E-mail Newsletters," Constant Contact, May 11, 2013, https://blogs.constantcontact.com/what-you-should-say-in-your-email-newsletter/.

[61]E.J. McGowan, "Graduate from E-mail Marketing 101," *Website Magazine*, January 2015, p. 39.

[62]*2016 E-mail Marketing Metrics: Benchmark Study*, IBM Marketing Cloud, 2016, pp. 21–22.

[63]"E-mail Continues to Deliver Strong ROI and Value for Marketers," *EMarketer*, September 12, 2016, www.emarketer.com/Article/Email-Continues-Deliver-Strong-ROI-Value-Marketers/1014461.

64"Global Spam Volume as Percentage of Total E-mail Traffic from January 2014 to September 2016, by Month," *Statista*, December 2016, www.statista.com/statistics/420391/spam-email-traffic-share/; *2016 Global Security Report*, Trustwave, 2016, p. 48.

65*E-mail Statistics Report, 2017–2021*, The Radicati Group (Palo Alto, California: 2017), p. 3.

66Jen Ribble, "The Great Debate: Subject Line Length," *Return Path*, May 27, 2015, https://blog.returnpath.com/the-great-debate-subject-line-length/.

67"The Optimal E-mail Message," *Website Magazine*, April 2015, p. 8.

68Kayla Lewkowicz, "Webmail Increases to 29% for November E-mail Client Market Share," Litmus Software, December 7, 2016, https://litmus.com/blog/webmail-increases-to-29-for-november-email-client-market-share.

69Nathan Ellering, "What Studies Say About the Best Time to Send E-mail," *CoSchedule*, March 23, 2016, http://coschedule.com/blog/best-time-to-send-email/.

70"Windsor Circle Case Study: Automating a Wave of Engagement—SurfStitch.com, Windsor Circle, http://info.windsorcircle.com/surfstitch-case-study-web.

71Katarina Reinecke, Tom Yeh, Luke Miratrix, Rahmatri Mardiko, Yuechen Zhao, Jennu Liu, and Krzysztof Gajos, "Predicting Users' First Impressions of Web Site Aesthetics with a Quantification of Perceived Visual Complexity and Colorfulness," *Proceedings of the SIGCHI Conference on Human Factors in Computing Systems*, 2013, pp. 2049–2058.

72"What Causes Consumers to Lose Trust in Digital Brands?" *Marketing Charts*, September 3, 2015, www.marketingcharts.com/online/what-causes-consumers-to-lose-trust-in-digital-brands-58728/attachment/neustar-consumer-perceptions-trustworthy-websites-sept2015/.

73"Internet Usage Statistics," *Internet World Stats*, 2017, www.internetworldstats.com/stats.htm.

74"Top 10 Languages Used in the Web," *Internet World Stats*, 2017, www.internetworldstats.com/stats7.htm.

75Ayaz Nanji, "Most Global Marketers Lack Multilingual Content Strategy," *MarketingProfs*, October 29, 2013, www.marketingprofs.com/charts/2013/11918/most-global-marketers-lack-multilingual-content-strategy.

76"Responsive Design: The Statistically Superior Mobile Solution," *Website Magazine*, February 26, 2015, http://webmag.co/responsive-design-the-statistically-superior-mobile-solution/.

77Jacob Poushter, "Smartphone Ownership and Internet Usage Continue to Climb in Emerging Economies," Pew Research Center, February 22, 2016, www.pewglobal.org/2016/02/22/smartphone-ownership-and-internet-usage-continues-to-climb-in-emerging-economies/; Monica Anderson, "Technology Device Ownership," Pew Research Center, October 29, 2015, www.pewinternet.org/2015/10/29/technology-device-ownership-2015/.

78*2016 U.S. Mobile App Report*, comScore, 2016, p. 5.

79Marc Hummel, "Just Released EQ3: Mobile Ate the World, and It's Still Hungry," *Monetate*, November 16, 2016, p. 21.

80"Monetate E-Commerce Quarterly Report: 2016 EQ4," *Monetate*, 2016, p. 14.

81Tammy Everts, "Google: 53% of Mobile Users Abandon Sites That Take Longer Than 3 Seconds to Load," *Soasta*, September 14, 2016, www.soasta.com/blog/google-mobile-web-performance-study/.

82"Monetate E-Commerce Quarterly Report: 2016 EQ4," *Monetate*, 2016, p. 8.

83"Some Small Business Web Sites Are Still Not Mobile," *eMarketer*, April 13, 2016, www.emarketer.com/Article/Some-Small-Business-Websites-Still-Not-Mobile/1013824.

84"Stats That Will Shape the New Year," *Website Magazine*, January 2015, p. 9.

85Responsive Design: The Statistically Superior Mobile Solution," *Website Magazine*, February 26, 2015, http://webmag.co/responsive-design-the-statistically-superior-mobile-solution/.

86Jonathan Blum, "Designated Driver," *Entrepreneur*, October 2014, p. 104.

87James Bickers, "Want to Connect with Customers? Think Local First," *Mobile Payments Today*, April 24, 2014, www.mobilepaymentstoday.com/blogs/want-to-connect-with-customers-think-mobile-first-infographic/.

88Greg Sterling, "Survey: 90 Percent of Retail Shoppers Use Smartphones in Stores," *Marketing Land*, July 20, 2015, http://marketingland.com/survey-90-percent-of-retail-shoppers-use-smartphones-in-stores-135759.

89Brandy Shaul, "iOS Push Notifications Have a 41% Opt-in Rate (Infographic)," *Social Times*, June 27, 2016, www.adweek.com/socialtimes/ios-push-notifications-have-a-41-opt-in-rate-infographic/641517.

90Bill McCarthy, "Location-Based Marketing Success Stories: Three Retailers Driving ROI," *ShopperTrak*, June 10, 2016, www.shoppertrak.com/location-based-marketing-success-stories/.

91Dave Chaffey, "Global Social Media Research Summary 2016," *Smart Insights*, August 8, 2016, www.smartinsights.com/social-media-marketing/social-media-strategy/new-global-social-media-research/.

92*2016 Small Business Marketing Trends Report*, Infusionsoft, 2016, p. 3; "How Much Time and Money Do Small Businesses Spend on Social Media?" *Social Media Today*, October 12, 2015, www.socialmediatoday.com/social-business/carianneking/2015-10-12/how-much-time-and-money-do-small-business-spend-social-media.

93"Social Media Marketing Spending in the United States from 2014 to 2019 (in Billions of $)," Statista, 2016, www.statista.com/statistics/276890/social-media-marketing-expenditure-in-the-united-states/.

94Michael Stelzner, "2016 Social Media Marketing Industry Report," *Social Media Examiner*, May 2016, p. 17.

95Josh Constine, "Facebook Hits 100M Hours of Video Watched a Day, 1B Users on Groups, 80M on Fb Lite," *TechCrunch*, January 27, 2016, https://techcrunch.com/2016/01/27/facebook-grows/.

96Antony Maina, "20 Popular Social Media Sites Right Now," *Small Business Trends*, May 6, 2016, http://smallbiztrends.com/2016/05/popular-social-media-sites.html; "Twitter Usage Statistics," Internet Live Stats, December 23, 2016, www.internetlivestats.com/twitter-statistics/.

97"Success Stories: MVMT Watches," Twitter, October 2016, https://business.twitter.com/en/success-stories/mvmtwatches.html; Aimee Milwood, "How Two College Dropouts Sold 100K Watches in 3 Years," *YotPo*, October 2016, www.yotpo.com/blog/two-college-dropouts-launched-coolest-watch-brand-year/.

98"YouTube Company Statistics," Statistic Brain, September 1, 2016, www.statisticbrain.com/youtube-statistics/.

99"Small Business Marketing Playbook," LinkedIn, October 2016, https://smallbusiness.linkedin.com/small-business-marketing/small-business-marketing-tips; Antony Maina, "20 Popular Social Media Sites Right Now," *Small Business Trends*, May 6, 2016, http://smallbiztrends.com/2016/05/popular-social-media-sites.html.

[100] Antony Maina, "20 Popular Social Media Sites Right Now," *Small Business Trends*, May 6, 2016, http://smallbiztrends.com/2016/05/popular-social-media-sites.html; Salman Aslam, "Pinterest by the Numbers: Stats, Demographics, and Fun Facts," OmniCore Digital Marketing Agency, October 26, 2015, www.omnicoreagency.com/pinterest-statistics/.

[101] Salman Aslam, "Pinterest by the Numbers: Stats, Demographics, and Fun Facts," OmniCore Digital Marketing Agency, October 26, 2015, www.omnicoreagency.com/pinterest-statistics/.

[102] "Success Stories: Neon Retro Arcade," Facebook, October 2016, www.facebook.com/business/success/neon-retro-arcade#u_0_3; Kevin Smith, "Neon Retro Arcade Set to Open Friday in Pasadena," *Pasadena Star News*, January 27, 2015, www.pasadenastarnews.com/lifestyle/20150127/neon-retro-arcade-set-to-open-friday-in-pasadena.

[103] Dave Chaffey, "Mobile Marketing Statistics Compilation," *Smart Insights*, October 26, 2016, www.smartinsights.com/mobile-marketing/mobile-marketing-analytics/mobile-marketing-statistics/.

[104] "Case Studies: Remix Coffee Company Success Story," COMO DIY, October 2016, http://diy.como.com/case-studies/remix-coffee-co/.

[105] Joel Zand and Pascal Cohen, *Global Search Marketing Report 2016*, SimilarWeb, March 2016, p. 8.

[106] Joshua Sophy, "Customers via Social Media Are Less Profitable Than Those from Search," *Small Business Trends*, July 11, 2013, http://smallbiztrends.com/2013/07/customers-social-media-less-profitable.html.

[107] Alexander Clark, "Search Engine Statistics," *Smart Insights*, August 10, 2016, www.smartinsights.com/search-engine-marketing/search-engine-statistics/.

[108] Ibid.

[109] Greg Sterling. "Report: Nearly 60 Percent of Searches Now from Mobile Devices," *Search Engine Land*, August 3, 2016, http://searchengineland.com/report-nearly-60-percent-searches-now-mobile-devices-255025; "Top Search Ad Position More Important on Mobiles Than Desktops," *Marketing Charts*, September 25, 2014, www.marketingcharts.com/online/top-search-ad-position-more-important-on-mobiles-than-desktops-46238/.

[110] Dmitry Dragilev, "Six Top SEO Factors in 2016," *MarketingProfs*, May 11, 2016, www.marketingprofs.com/articles/2016/29906/six-top-seo-factors-in-2016.

[111] Eric Enge, "Your First Steps in Content Marketing," *Search Engine Land*, April 27, 2015, http://searchengineland.com/first-steps-content-marketing-219169.

[112] David Port, "Out of the Doghouse," *Entrepreneur*, September 2015, p. 70.

[113] "Extreme PPC Makeover: Small Business Edition," *Wordstream*, 2013, www.wordstream.com/articles/free-advertising.

[114] "comScore Releases October 2013 U.S. Search Engine Rankings," comScore, November 13, 2013, www.comscore.com/Insights/Press_Releases/2013/11/comScore_Releases_October_2013_US_Search_Engine_Rankings.

[115] "About Quality Score," AdWords Help, Google, January 2, 2017, https://support.google.com/adwords/answer/7050591.

[116] "Google AdWords Benchmarks for Your Industry," *Wordstream*, November 20, 2016, www.wordstream.com/blog/ws/2016/02/29/google-adwords-industry-benchmarks.

[117] Bill Briggs, "IRCE 2011 Report: A Retailer's Size Poses No Restrictions for Search Marketing," *Internet Retailer*, June 16, 2011, www.internetretailer.com/2011/06/16/irce-2011-report-size-poses-no-restrictions-paid-search.

[118] Allison Howell, "The Current State of Web Retail," *Website Magazine*, November 2013, pp. 18–19; Natalie Severt, "Retailers Spend More of Paid Search Budgets on Product Listing Ads," *Evigo*, March 9, 2013, http://evigo.com/retailers-spend-paid-search-budgets-product-listing-ads/.

[119] Sarmistha Acharya, "Bot Fraud: Advertisers 'to Lose $7.2 Billion' Globally in 2016," *International Business Times*, January 25, 2016, www.ibtimes.co.uk/bot-fraud-advertisers-lose-7-2bn-globally-2016-1539851.

[120] Matthew Ingram, "The Russian Methbot Scam Is Just the Tip of the Ad Fraud Iceberg," *Fortune*, December 21, 2016, http://fortune.com/2016/12/20/methbot-ad-fraud/.

[121] Steve McKee, "Make Your Web Site Work for You," *Businessweek*, June 2008, www.businessweek.com/smallbiz/content/jun2008/sb2008069_643453.htm.

[122] Mimi An, "Does Your Web Site Make the Grade?" HubSpot Research, August 19, 2016, https://research.hubspot.com/reports/does-your-website-make-the-grade.

[123] Mike Volpe, "Three Deadly Reasons Most Web Sites Fail," *MarketingProfs*, August 26, 2013, www.marketingprofs.com/articles/2013/11495/three-deadly-reasons-most-websites-fail.

[124] Kate Kaplan, "When and How to Create Customer Journey Maps," Nielsen Norman Group, July 31, 2016, www.nngroup.com/articles/customer-journey-mapping/.

[125] "Winning Today's Global Phy-Gital Shoppers," *Mindtree*, 2015, p. 2.

[126] "Domain Name Industry Brief: Q3 2013 Highlights," Verisign, 2013, www.verisigninc.com/en_US/why-verisign/education-resources/domain-name-industry-brief/index.xhtml; Anick Jesdanun, "Businesses Dominate Bids for Internet Suffixes," *Greenville News*, June 17, 2012, p. 3E; Daniel P. Smith, "King of Your Domain," *QSR*, December 2011, www.qsrmagazine.com/exclusives/king-your-domain.

[127] "Online Shoppers Say Ease of Browsing Top Reason for Choosing One Web Site over Another," *Marketing Charts*, November 20, 2013, www.marketingcharts.com/wp/online/online-shoppers-say-ease-of-browsing-top-reason-for-choosing-one-website-over-another-38234/.

[128] "Extreme PPC Makeover: Small Business Edition," *Wordstream*, 2013, www.wordstream.com/articles/free-advertising.

[129] Angela Stringfellow, "5 Businesses That Used A/N Tests to Lift Conversion Rates by Up to 216%," *Unbounce*, http://unbounce.com/a-b-testing/5-businesses-that-used-ab-tests-to-lift-conversion-rates-by-up-to-216/.

[130] "UPS Pulse of the Online Shopper," UPS, 2016, p. 47.

[131] "Customer Success Stories," Google, www.google.com/enterprise/superstars/success.html.

[132] "UPS Pulse of the Online Shopper," UPS, 2016, p. 48.

[133] "The Power of Reviews," Power Reviews, 2014, p. 5; "2016 State of E-Commerce: Cart Abandonment and Recapture Statistics," EY Studios, August 12, 2016, www.eystudios.com/2016/08/2016-state-ecommerce/.

[134] Zac Johnson, "How Important Are Customer Reviews to Your Business?" Yahoo! *Small Business Advisor*, September 16, 2013, http://smallbusiness.yahoo.com/advisor/important-customer-reviews-business-032541175.html; Zac Johnson, "The Importance of Positive Reviews for Your Business," *Brand*, November 14, 2013, www.brand.com/blog/importance-positive-reviews-business/.

[135] Zac Johnson, "The Importance of Positive Reviews for Your Business," *Brand*, November 14, 2013, www.brand.com/blog/importance-positive-reviews-business/.

[136] "The Power of Reviews, Power Reviews," 2014, p. 10.

[137] Lindsay Kolowich, "31 Video Marketing Statistics to Inform Your Strategy," HubSpot, June 14, 2016, http://blog.hubspot.com/marketing/video-marketing-statistics#sm.0001lzeehju0qeajw2325ngzw2o7q.

[138] Ibid.

[139]Richard Lazazzera, "How to Use Video to Increase Conversions and Sales in Your E-Commerce Business," Shopify, May 20, 2015, www.shopify.com/blog/19542212-how-to-use-video-to-increase-conversions-and-sales-in-your-ecommerce-business; Amanda Dhalla, "Why I Hate Boring Video: An Interview with Vat19's Jamie Salvatori," *Video Commerce*, October 2016, http://videocommerce.com/blog/why-i-hate-boring-video-interview-with-vat19s-jamie-salvatori/; Ross Wilson, "Curiously Awesome YouTube Marketing: An Interview with the Creators of Vat19," *Ignite Social Media*, March 28, 2016, www.ignitesocialmedia.com/youtube-marketing/awesome-youtube-marketing-interview-creators-vat19/.

[140]Amanda Dhalla, "Why I Hate Boring Video: An Interview with Vat19's Jamie Salvatori," *Video Commerce*, October 2016, http://videocommerce.com/blog/why-i-hate-boring-video-interview-with-vat19s-jamie-salvatori/.

[141]Karen Axelton, "Study Says Most Small Business Web Sites Miss the Mark," Small Business Forum, September 18, 2013, https://forum.web.com/study-says-most-small-business-websites-miss-the-mark/.

[142]"Small Businesses Devote More Resources to Web Sites, Social," *eMarketer*, March 7, 2013, www.emarketer.com/Article/Small-Businesses-Devote-More-Resources-Websites-Social/1009713.

[143]Pete Prestipino, "Web Design Color Palettes of the Top 5 U.S. Web Sites," *Web Site Magazine*, September 22, 2016, www.websitemagazine.com/content/blogs/infographics/archive/2016/09/22/web-design-color-palettes-of-the-top-5-u-s-websites.aspx.

[144]Christian Holst, "The Average Checkout Flow Has 14.88 Form Fields, Twice as Many as Necessary," Baymard Institute, November 8, 2016, http://baymard.com/blog/checkout-flow-average-form-fields; Derek Cromwell, "2016 State of E-Commerce: Cart Abandonment and Recapture Statistics," EY Studios, August 12, 2016, www.eystudios.com/2016/08/2016-state-ecommerce/.

[145]"Monetate E-Commerce Quarterly Report: 2016 EQ4," *Monetate*, 2016, p. 10.

[146]Derek Cromwell, "2016 State of E-Commerce: Cart Abandonment and Recapture Statistics," EY Studios, August 12, 2016, www.eystudios.com/2016/08/2016-state-ecommerce/.

[147]*2013 Small Business Technology Survey*, National Small Business Association, 2013, p. 8.

[148]"Survey Reveals Small Businesses Struggling to Keep Up with Web Evolution," *Wall Street Journal*, April 23, 2013, http://online.wsj.com/article/PR-CO-20130423-915099.html.

[149]Alex McEachern, "Repeat Customers Are Profitable, and We Can Prove It," Sweet Tooth Rewards, April 2, 2015, www.sweettoothrewards.com/blog/repeat-customers-profitable-stats-to-prove/.

[150]"Monetate E-Commerce Quarterly Report: EQI 2016," *Monetate*, Quarter 1, 2016, p. 10.

[151]"New Survey Finds a Vast Majority of U.S. Small Business Owners Believe Cybersecurity Is a Concern and Lawmakers Should Do More to Combat Attacks, *PR Newswire*, May 4, 2015, www.prnewswire.com/news-releases/new-survey-finds-a-vast-majority-of-us-small-business-owners-believe-cybersecurity-is-a-concern-and-lawmakers-should-do-more-to-combat-cyber-attacks-300076543.html.

[152]*Internet Security Threat Report*, vol. 21, Symantec, April 21, 2016, p. 44.

[153]"SMEs and Cyber Attacks: What You Need to Know," Towergate Insurance, 2015, www.towergateinsurance.co.uk/liability-insurance/smes-and-cyber-attacks.

[154]Joe Ross, "The State of Small Business Security: A 2016 Survey," *Huffington Post*, May 12, 2016, www.huffingtonpost.com/joe-ross/the-state-of-small-busine_b_9911704.html.

[155]"SMEs and Cyber Attacks: What You Need to Know," Towergate Insurance, 2015, www.towergateinsurance.co.uk/liability-insurance/smes-and-cyber-attacks.

[156]Sead Fadilpašić, "Cost of Cyber Attack Will Soon Reach $1 Million for Large Businesses," *Betanews*, September 15, 2016, http://betanews.com/2016/09/15/cyber-attack-cost/.

[157]Graham Winfrey, "Can Your Business Survive a Cyberattack?" *Inc.*, December 5, 2014, www.inc.com/graham-winfrey/how-to-protect-your-company-information-in-the-digital-age.html.

[158]"Internet Security Threat Report 2016," Symantec, 2016, p. 30.

[159]"Trust or Bust: How to Make Summertime Shoppers Feel Safe Online and Boost Your Sales at the Same Time," Symantec, 2015, p. 2.

[160]"Victims of Identity Theft 2014," Bureau of Justice Statistics, U.S. Department of Justice, September 2015, p. 1.

[161]Ashley Carman, "Study: 86 Percent of Websites Contain at Least One 'serious' Vulnerability," *SC Magazine*, May 22, 2015, www.scmagazine.com/whitehat-security-release-website-security-statistics-report/article/416402/.

[162]"Cisco 2016 Midyear Cybersecurity Report," Cisco, 2016, p. 7.

[163]*Internet Security Threat Report*, Symantec, April 2017, p. 56.

[164]"2016 Internet Security Threat Report," Symantec, 2016, p. 46.

[165]Virginia Harrison and Jose Pagliery, "Nearly 1 Million Malware Attacks Released Every Day," *CNN Money*, April 14, 2015, http://money.cnn.com/2015/04/14/technology/security/cyber-attack-hacks-security/.

[166]Tamara E. Holmes, "Payment Method Statistics," June 15, 2015, CreditCards.com, www.creditcards.com/credit-card-news/payment-method-statistics-1276.php.

[167]"Annual Fraud Benchmark Report: A Balancing Act, North America Edition," Cybersource Corporation, 2016, p. 8.

[168]Ibid., p. 10.

[169]"Internet Security Threat Report 2016," Symantec, 2016, p. 30.

[170]Joshua Sophy, "75 Percent of Small Businesses Have No Cyber Risk Insurance," *SmallBizTrends*, July 7, 2016, http://smallbiztrends.com/2016/07/cyber-risk-insurance-small-business.html.

11

Pricing and Credit Strategies

Roman Sigaev/Shutterstock

Learning Objectives

On completion of this chapter, you will be able to:

1. Discuss the relationships among pricing, image, competition, and value.

2. Describe effective pricing techniques for introducing new products or services and for existing ones.

3. Explain the pricing methods and strategies for retailers, manufacturers, and service firms.

4. Explain the impact of credit and debit cards and mobile wallets on pricing.

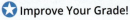

To survive, every business must make a profit. Although many factors determine a company's ability to generate a profit, one of the most important is the prices its sets for its goods and services. Setting prices is a business decision governed by both art and science—with a touch of instinct thrown in for good measure. Setting prices for their products and services requires entrepreneurs to balance a multitude of complex forces, many of them working in opposite directions. Entrepreneurs must determine prices for their goods and services that will draw customers and produce a profit. Unfortunately, many small business owners set prices without enough information about their cost of operations and their customers. Price is an important factor in building long-term relationships with customers, and haphazard pricing techniques confuse and alienate customers and endanger a small company's profitability. Research shows that proper pricing strategies have far greater impact on a company's profits than corresponding increases in unit volume and reductions in fixed or variable costs (see Figure 11.1).[1] For instance, when a company that earns a 10 percent net profit margin raises its prices by just 1 percent, its profits increase by 10 percent (assuming that its unit sales remain the same).

Another complicating factor is a holdover from the Great Recession: Customers have become more price sensitive. As sales slipped during the recession, companies resorted to deals, discounts, and coupons to attract and keep customers. Even though the recession is over, many of those companies have had difficulty weaning customers off of their value-oriented mindset.

Technology poses another pricing challenge. Modern shoppers use their mobile devices to compare prices—often right in the middle of a store's aisles—and they expect consistency in prices across all of a company's channels. One study of shoppers in nine countries reports that nearly 75 percent use a mobile device while in a store. The most common application? Comparing prices with those of competitors.[2] As you learned in Chapter 10, a multichannel shopping approach is quite common, and out-of-store digital activities exert a great deal of influence over shoppers' in-store behavior. In fact, 84 percent of shoppers go online to get price comparisons before they visit a store.[3] The result is a new age of price transparency that entrepreneurs have never before experienced and an environment that makes setting the right prices all the more important—and difficult.

In addition, consumers now prefer a simpler, more convenient (even "automatic") shopping experience. This surging demand for convenience is forcing companies to change their pricing strategies. A survey by *The Economist* reports that 51 percent of global executives are changing the way in which they price and deliver their products and services.[4] The most common change is the introduction of subscription pricing options for shoppers (more on this later in the chapter) pioneered by companies such as Netflix and refined to perfection more recently by companies such as Dollar Shave Club.

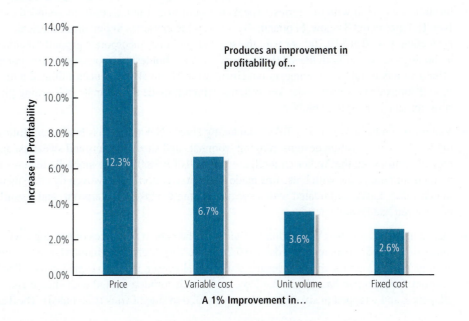

FIGURE 11.1

The Impact of Pricing and Cost Improvements on Profitability

Source: Based on Richard Hayes and Ranjit Singh, "CFO Insights: Pricing for Profitability: What's in Your Pocket," Deloitte, 2013, https://www2 .deloitte.com/content/dam/ Deloitte/us/Documents/ finance-transformation/us-cfo-cfo-insights-pricing-for-profitability-080113.pdf.

Setting prices is not only one of the toughest decisions small business owners face but also one of the most important. Setting prices too high drives customers away and destroys a company's sales. Establishing prices that are too low, a common tendency among first-time entrepreneurs, robs a business of its ability to generate a profit, creates the impression among customers that the company's products and services are of inferior quality, and threatens its long-term success. Improper pricing has destroyed countless businesses whose owners mistakenly thought that their prices were high enough to generate a profit when, in fact, they were not. Inconsistent pricing that confuses customers and sends them mixed signals damages a company's sales and profits.

ENTREPRENEURIAL PROFILE: GNC Holdings After watching sales at its 4,400 retail stores across the United States stagnate, managers at vitamin and nutritional supplement retailer GNC Holdings realized that the company's pricing structure was broken and was confusing potential customers. They decided to perform a complete "reset," shutting down every store, many of which are franchised, and implementing a completely new, simpler pricing system. (Some products featured as many as four different prices on the same label.) About half of the items the company sells saw price decreases, and about one-fourth saw price increases. GNC managers established the new pricing system after an extensive review of competitors' prices on similar products, conducting tests in 10 key markets, consulting with vendors, and gathering feedback from franchise owners and store managers.[5] ∎

Pricing decisions cut across every aspect of a small company, influencing everything from its marketing and sales efforts to its operations and strategy. Price is the monetary value of a product or service in the marketplace; it is a measure of what the customer must give up to obtain various goods and services. Price also is a signal of a product's or service's value to an individual, and different customers assign different values to the same goods and services. From an entrepreneur's viewpoint, price must be compatible with customers' perceptions of value. "Pricing is not just a math problem," says one business writer. "It's a psychology test."[6] The psychology of pricing is an art much more than it is a science. It focuses on creating value in the customer's mind but recognizes that value is what the customer perceives it to be. Customers often look to a product's or service's price for clues about value. Consider the following examples, which illustrate the sometimes puzzling connection between price and perceived value:

- Allen Perkins used his more than 20 years of experience designing high-end audio equipment to launch Spiral Groove, a company based in Berkeley, California, that makes high-performance analog audio products, including its SG1.2 turntable. Spiral Groove makes the SG1.2 from the same case-hardened steel that goes into F1 racing cars' crankshafts and includes vibration-dampening technology and a magnetic levitation system that produces the pure clarity of sound that audiophiles demand. Those who purchase a Spiral Groove turntable can pair it with the Series 5 speaker system from Linn, a company founded by Ivor Tiefenbrun in Glasgow, Scotland, that goes to the extremes in pursuit of musical perfection. Priced at $19,200 per pair, the speakers not only incorporate ground-breaking technology to deliver both the subtlest nuances and the boldest harmonics of music but also offer a variety of fabric coverings to match any room. Linn also produces a limited number of its Klimax distortion-free speaker systems, which provide the ultimate in listening pleasure, for an eye-popping $68,000.[7]

- Visvim, a company founded in Tokyo, Japan, by Hiroki Nakamura, has built a cult following for its unique fashion designs, ranging from hats and shoes to pants and sweaters, and it recently introduced the Atelier Umbrella, which sells for $8,000. The umbrella features ribs made from rattan cane with brass tips made in France; cotton fabric woven by craftsmen in Okayama, Japan, and treated with a special coating to make it waterproof; and a sturdy beechwood handle and shaft.[8]

- Fans at major league baseball stadiums often complain about the prices of hot dogs, which range from just $1 (Cincinnati Reds) to $6.25 (New York Mets and Miami Marlins), with an average of $4.52 across all major league stadiums. However, at the Arizona Diamondbacks' stadium, fans can purchase the D-Bat Dog, an 18-inch corndog stuffed with cheese and jalapeños, and wrapped in six slices of bacon for $26 (a side of fries is included). The Texas

Rangers also sell a $26 hotdog, the Boomstick, a two-foot long, all-beef monster that weighs one pound and is topped with chili, nacho cheese, and grilled onions.[9] Although "regular" hotdogs remain the most popular item on their menus, demand for the premium hotdogs often outstrips the supply at both stadiums.

As you can see, setting higher prices sometimes can *increase* the appeal of a product or service ("If you charge more, you must be worth it"). Value for these products is found not solely in their superior technical performance but also in their scarcity and uniqueness and the resulting image they create for the buyer. Although entrepreneurs must recognize the shallow depth of the market for ultraluxury items such as these, the ego-satisfying ownership of limited-edition watches, pens, cars, jewelry, and other items is the psychological force supporting a premium price strategy.

Three Potent Forces: Image, Competition, and Value

LO1

Discuss the relationships among pricing, image, competition, and value.

Because pricing decisions have such a pervasive influence on all aspects of a small company, one of the most important considerations for entrepreneurs is to take a strategic rather than a piecemeal approach to pricing their companies' products and services. Research by the University of Pennsylvania's Wharton School shows that companies that take a strategic approach to pricing and monitor its results can raise their sales revenue between 1 and 8 percent. After analyzing its existing pricing techniques using price management software, New York City drugstore chain Duane Reade discovered that parents of newborns are less price sensitive than are parents of toddlers. Managers decided to make diaper pricing a function of the child's age, cutting prices to meet those of competitors on toddlers' diapers and raising them on diapers for newborns. A year later, the company's new pricing strategy had produced a 27 percent increase in its baby care revenue.[10]

A company's pricing strategy is a major determinant of its image in the marketplace, is influenced by the pricing strategies of its competitors, and is an important element in the value that customers perceive its products or services provide.

Price Conveys Image

A company's pricing policies communicate important information about its overall image to customers. Pricing sends an important signal to customers about a company, its brand, its position in the market, the quality of its products and services, the image it wants to create, and other important concepts. For example, the prices charged by a posh men's clothing shop reflect a completely different image from those charged by a factory outlet store. Because most people have difficulty judging the quality of many products and services, they typically associate high prices with quality, prestige, and exclusivity. Conversely, they perceive low-priced goods as lower quality and inferior. In a study at Cornell University, an Italian restaurant charged customers either $4 or $8 for the same all-you-can-eat buffet. Customers who paid $8 for the buffet rated the food as tastier and scored the enjoyment of the dining experience much higher than those who paid only $4.[11] As this study suggests, when developing a marketing approach to pricing, entrepreneurs must establish prices that reinforce the image they want to create for their companies and that are compatible with what customers expect and are willing to pay. Too often, entrepreneurs *underprice* their goods and services, believing that low prices are the only way they can achieve a competitive advantage. Doing so merely paints the perception of low quality and exposes the small business to larger competitors that, because of their size, often have lower operating costs and, therefore, the ability to eradicate the small company's competitive advantage.

Prices send a powerful message to customers, and small businesses do not have to charge low prices to be successful. After all, day-old doughnuts are much cheaper than fresh doughnuts, but how many people are willing to eat stale doughnuts just to save a few dollars?

ENTREPRENEURIAL PROFILE: Howard Schultz: Starbucks Reserve Roastery and Tasting Room Howard Schultz, the genius behind the Starbucks coffee chain, was confident that customers would pay more than $1 for a cup of coffee. He was correct; the company, which has more than 25,000 outlets around the globe, sells 4 million coffee drinks per day at an

Jason Redmond/Reuters/Alamy Stock Photo

average price of $3.25 per drink. Having proved that customers are willing to pay for premium coffee products, Schultz's next vision for the company is to open Starbucks Reserve Roastery and Tasting Room outlets that will roast rare, exotic coffee grown in small batches and prepare it onsite using a variety of unique brewing methods. Schultz has stepped down as CEO of Starbucks to focus on opening the high-end shops, which will charge as much as $12 for a 12-ounce cup of exotic coffee. Schultz is confident in Starbucks Reserve's potential because customers' tastes for premium coffee products continues to grow; Millennials, whose disposable income is increasing as they reach their prime earning years, are a primary target audience.[12] ■

Many entrepreneurs make the common pricing mistake of failing to recognize the extra value, convenience, service, and quality they give their customers—all things that many customers are willing to pay for. These companies fall into the trap of trying to compete solely on the basis of price when they lack the sales volume—and, hence, the lower cost structures—of their larger rivals. It is a recipe for failure. "People want quality," says one merchant selling upscale goods at upscale prices. "They want value. But if you lower prices, they think that you are lowering the value and lowering the quality."[13] It is a dangerous cycle that can destroy a business. A study of businesses in multiple industries by Rafi Mohammed, author of *The Art of Pricing*, found that companies that raised prices by 1 percent saw their profits increase 11 percent. Those that raised their prices by 10 percent realized profit increases of 100 percent![14] The study does not imply that businesses have free rein to raise prices to any level, but it does suggest that many companies can raise their prices enough to improve their financial results significantly as long as they convince customers that their products or services offer superior value. One expert explains the relationship between value and price with the following conceptual equation:

$$(S + P)/D > \$ + E$$

where

S = Company's standards of doing business

P = Product or service quality and performance

D = Doubt in customers' minds that detracts from the value of the company's standards and products or services

$ = Product or service price

E = Customers' expectations of a company and its products and services

According to this equation, the value customers gain from doing business with a company and buying its products or services (after being diminished by doubts they have about the company and its products or services) must exceed the price they pay and the expectations they have about the company and its products or services.[15] When guests visit one of the Walt Disney theme parks, all cast members (Disney-speak for employees) know they must measure up to some of the highest expectations of any business in any industry. (After all, the guests are on vacation, and everything should be perfect.) Ticket prices are not cheap (one-day tickets start at about $100, with discounts on multiday tickets), but Disney cast members are highly trained in the art of providing stellar customer service and understand the central role that it plays in the company's culture. Cast members also have the freedom to make decisions on the spot to fix any problems that guests may encounter and always strive not only to meet but also to exceed customers' expectations.

A key ingredient in setting prices properly is to understand a company's target market: the customer groups at which the small company is aiming its goods or services. Rather than ask, "How much should I charge for my product or service?" entrepreneurs should ask, "How much are my target customers willing to pay?" Target market, business image, and pricing strategy are closely related. For example, final prices on T-shirts made in the same factories in Bangladesh for discount retailers and for high-end designer labels often have little connection to their costs but reflect the image the retailer has created for itself. The retail price of a T-shirt made in a Bangladesh factory for Wal-Mart's Asda chain in London is about $6.50. A T-shirt, also made in a Bangladesh factory, from designer brand G-Star Raw sells for $98.50, more than 15 times as much as the Wal-Mart version. Luxury retailers often choose higher-quality fabrics and include small embellishments such as pockets or contrasting piping on seams that add to their costs, but their final prices are more closely related to reinforcing the brands' image than to recovering costs. The manufacturing cost of a basic T-shirt in Bangladesh is about $1.60 to $2.00; the cost of making a typical designer label T-shirt ranges from $5 to $6. In addition to the additional production costs that designer labels incur, their retail prices must cover their higher business costs, such as advertising, rent on boutique shops, and salaries for salespeople.[16] For many of the products upscale brands sell, such as designer bags, their final prices are more a reflection of their desired image than the reality of their costs. The prices of many designer bags start at $850 and escalate quickly to $4,500 or more. One analysis shows that a designer handbag that costs about $81 to make and ship ($33.41 for materials, $30.71 for labor, $11.74 for shipping, and $4.98 for tariffs and duties) typically carries a price of $970, which is a markup of 1,098 percent.[17]

Competition and Prices

Competitors' prices can have a dramatic impact on a small company's sales. Today, small companies face competition from local businesses as well as from online businesses that may be many time zones away. Price transparency due to the Internet, the ease of mobile shopping, and customers' persistent post-recession price sensitivity impose constraints on companies' ability to raise prices (see Figure 11.2). About 60 percent of shoppers in North America report using

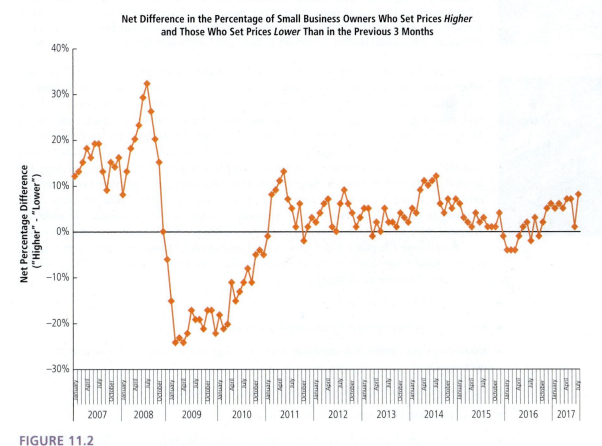

Net Difference in the Percentage of Small Business Owners Who Set Prices *Higher* and Those Who Set Prices *Lower* Than in the Previous 3 Months

FIGURE 11.2

The Reality of Setting Prices

Source: Based on data from William C. Dunkelberg and Holly Wade, "NFIB Small Business Economic Trends," National Federation of Independent Businesses, July 2017, p. 8.

their mobile devices regularly in stores to research prices on items that sell for $100 or more.[18] When setting prices, entrepreneurs must take into account their competitors' prices, but the decision to match or beat them is *not* automatic. A company's pricing policies involve more than covering expenses and generating a profit; they also tell an important story about its position in the marketplace and the extra value it offers customers. However, unless a small company can differentiate itself by creating a distinctive image in customers' minds or by offering superior service, quality, design, convenience, or speed, it must match its competitors' prices or risk losing sales. Before matching any competitor's prices, however, small business owners should consider a rival's motives. A competitor may establish its price structure on the basis of a unique set of criteria and a totally different strategy. Blindly matching competitors' prices can lead a company to financial ruin, and companies that set their prices this way typically do so because they perceive themselves in a position of strategic weakness. Recall from Chapter 5 that companies that execute a successful differentiation strategy can charge prices higher than those of their competitors.

The similarity of competitors' goods and services also influences a company's pricing policies. Entrepreneurs must monitor competitors' prices on products that are identical to or that are close substitutes for those they sell and strive to keep their prices in line with them.

Michael Nagle/Getty Images

Sion Touhig/Getty Images

ENTREPRENEURIAL PROFILE: Sotheby's and Christie's International Auction houses Christie's and Sotheby's International have been in business for a combined 524 years and control 42 percent of the global auction market. Beneath the veneer of quiet professionalism that the two legendary competitors display, a fierce battle rages. The two auction houses hold more than 750 auctions per year in more than 80 categories, ranging from books and jewelry to fine art and watches. Recently, to win the right to auction some of the most sought-after items, both Sotheby's and Christie's have been competing fiercely on price, offering clients guaranteed minimum prices and cutting their commissions to only a fraction of their typical 12 percent fee. For instance, on a recent sale of a silk-screen, "Four Marilyns" by Andy Warhol, Sotheby's provided a minimum guarantee of $45 million and lost money on the auction when the portrait of Marilyn Monroe sold for just $32 million.[19] ■

Generally, entrepreneurs should avoid head-to-head price competition with other firms that can more easily achieve lower prices through lower cost structures. For instance, most locally owned drugstores cannot compete with the prices of large national drug chains that buy in large quantities and negotiate significant discounts. However, many local drugstores operate successfully by using nonprice competition; these stores offer more personalized service, free delivery, credit sales, and other extras that the chains have eliminated. Nonprice competition can be an effective strategy for a small business in the face of larger, more powerful companies because experimenting with price changes can be dangerous for small companies. Price changes cause fluctuations in sales volume that a small company may not be able to tolerate. In addition, frequent price changes may muddle a company's image and damage customer relations.

Recall from Chapter 5 that if a business chooses to offer lower prices than competitors, it must first create a low-cost advantage; otherwise, the strategy is unsustainable. An entrepreneur can create a low-cost advantage by:

- Choosing a low-cost location

- Minimizing operating costs by maximizing efficiency

- Exercising tight control over inventory and restricting product lines to those items that turn over quickly

- Providing customers with no or limited service (e.g., self-service)

- Using low-cost, bootstrap marketing techniques

- Selling basic products but offering customers the option of purchasing additional product or service features that generate higher profit margins

- Achieving high sales volume that allows the business to spread its fixed costs across a large number of units ("economies of scale")

Stuart Wetanson, fourth-generation manager of Dallas BBQ, a chain with 10 locations in New York City that is known for its low-priced, high-quality barbecue, understands that high volume is the key to the company's success, especially given the high costs of its locations. For instance, the company's restaurant in Times Square, which features some of the highest lease rates in the city, can seat 780 people at a time, and on busy nights employees manage to serve 10,000 meals, including catering, takeout, and delivery orders. Dallas BBQ locations are open from 11 A.M. to as late as 1:30 A.M. and offer a simple menu with no desserts, which increases the number of "turns" the restaurants generate each day.[20]

Attempting to undercut competitors' prices is a dangerous strategy, however, and may lead to a price war, one of the deadliest games a small business can play. No business wins a race to the bottom. Price wars can eradicate companies' profit margins and scar an entire industry for years. "Many entrepreneurs cut prices to the point of unprofitability just to compete," says one business writer. "In doing so, they open the door to catastrophe. Less revenue often translates into lower quality, poorer service, sloppier salesmanship, weaker customer loyalty, and financial disaster."[21] Engaging in a price war is like competitors holding guns to each other's heads.

Price wars usually begin when one competitor thinks that he or she can achieve higher volume and take market share from rivals instantaneously by lowering prices. Rather than sticking to their strategic guns, competitors believe they must follow suit. Recently, supermarket chains have been battling to wrest market share from one another, pushing food prices down, and launching a price war. Companies that have survived price wars in the past know that these wars decimate already slim profit margins as rival grocery chains attempt to increase their market share, whatever the cost. Sprouts Farmers Market, a healthy grocery store launched in 2002 in Chandler, Arizona, now with more than 270 stores in 15 states, has tried to stay out of the price war that is ravaging the industry by focusing on offering fresh, often locally grown, healthful organic and natural foods. Sprouts Farmers Market places produce, a typical grocer's lowest-margin product, in the middle of the store, and offers more than 30 promotions annually, in addition to weekly sales. In addition, the chain focuses on selling grocery items that customers cannot find in most supermarkets including attribute-focused products such as gluten free, vegan and non-GMO, and does not stock many products that are standard in other stores, such as Doritos chips, Lucky Charms, or Tide detergent. Staying focused on the needs and preferences of its health-conscious customers, Sprouts Farmers Market emphasizes its "responsible retailing" strategy, which relies on building eco-friendly stores, staying committed to recycling efforts, supporting local health and well-being causes, and assembling a sustainable supply

Courtesy of Sprouts Farmers Market

chain. The company, whose stores include an open central area that is reminiscent of an old-fashioned farmer's market, is on track to achieve its goal of expanding to more than 1,200 stores in many more states over the next 15 years.[22]

Entrepreneurs usually overestimate the power of price cuts. In reality, sales volume rarely increases enough to offset the lower profit margins of a lower price. A business with a 25 percent gross profit margin that cuts its price by 10 percent would have to *triple* its sales volume just to break even—an outcome that is not realistic for most businesses. Discounts also threaten to cheapen a company's image for providing quality products and services. Even when price cuts work, their effects often are temporary. Customers lured by the lowest price usually exhibit little loyalty to a business and leave for the next company offering a lower price. Rather than join in a price war by cutting prices, entrepreneurs can adjust their product and service offerings to appeal to different market segments: offering lower-priced items that use less expensive materials and offer fewer extras for price-sensitive customers and higher-quality, premium products for those who care less about price and more about quality and service. The lesson: The best way to survive a price war is to stay out of it by differentiating your company and emphasizing the unique features, benefits, and value it offers customers.

Focus on Value

Ultimately, the "right" price for a product or service depends on one factor: the value it provides for a customer. There are two aspects of value, however. Entrepreneurs may recognize the *objective* value of their products and services—that is, the price customers would be willing to pay if they understood perfectly the benefits that a product or service delivers for them. Unfortunately, few if any customers can see a product's or a service's true objective value; instead, they see only its *perceived* value, which determines the price they are willing to pay for it. Entrepreneurs can enhance the perceived value of the products and services they sell by emphasizing their unique, desirable attributes. For instance, research shows that restaurant patrons are willing to pay more for items that include longer, more detailed descriptions on menus. Rather than sell "French fries" for $2.95, a restaurant could sell "premium hand-cut, bacon-dusted, artisan fries pre-soaked in a special brine and cooked to perfection so that they are crispy on the outside but fluffy on the inside" for $3.50, which can significantly boost its margins.[23]

"Value" does not necessarily equate to low price, either. Businesses that underprice their products and services or constantly run special discount price promotions may be short-circuiting the value proposition they are trying to build and communicate to their customers. In fact, setting prices too low is one of the most common pricing mistakes that entrepreneurs make. Only 37 percent of shoppers say that finding the lowest price is the primary reason they purchase from a particular retailer (although the percentages of Generation X shoppers, 39 percent, and Generation Y shoppers, 43 percent, are higher).[24] Norm Brodsky, owner of CitiStorage, a document storage company in New York City, says setting prices too low is much more dangerous than setting them too high. The veteran entrepreneur reminds business owners that they can always lower their prices if they initially set them too high. Raising prices that are too low is much more difficult and can create the wrong image for a business.[25]

Customers may respond to price cuts, but companies that rely on them to boost sales risk undermining the perceived value of their products and services. In addition, once customers grow accustomed to buying products and services during special promotions, the habit can be difficult to break. They simply wait for the next sale. The results are extreme swings in sales and diminished value of the brand. In some economic and competitive conditions, however, companies have little choice but to offer lower-priced products. Techniques that companies can use to increase customers' perception of value and, essentially, lower their prices with less risk of diminishing their brands include offering coupons and rebates that are not as closely connected to the product as direct price cuts. Limited-time-only discounts (discussed later in this chapter) used sparingly also increase short-term sales without causing long-term damage to a brand. Another strategy that some companies have used successfully is to launch a **fighter brand**, a less expensive, no-frills version of a company's flagship product that is designed to confront lower-priced competitors head-on, satisfy the appetites of value-conscious customers, and preserve the image of the company's premium product. To combat market share losses to lower-priced supermarkets such as Trader Joe's and Sprouts Farmers Market, Whole Foods started 365 by Whole Foods Market, a chain of smaller stores that feature a larger selection of the company's private label 365 Every Day value brand. The strategy allows Whole Foods to maintain upscale pricing in its branded stores while increasing its sales by appealing to a more price-conscious segment of the market with the 365 fighter brand.[26]

One of the most important determinants of customers' response to a price is whether they perceive the price to be a fair exchange for the value they receive from the product or service. The good news is that, through marketing and other efforts, companies can influence customers' perception of value. Because price is one part of a product's or a service's features, it is another way a company can communicate value to its customers. For most shoppers, three reference points define a fair price: the price they have paid for the product or service in the past, the prices competitors charge for the same or a similar product or service, and the costs a company incurs to provide the product or service. The price customers have paid in the past for an item serves as a baseline reference point, but people often forget that inflation causes a company's costs to rise from year to year. Therefore, it is important for business owners to remind customers periodically that they must raise prices to offset the increased cost of doing business. Norm Brodsky, owner of the successful document storage company, points out that a business's operating costs

fighter brand
a less expensive, no-frills version of a company's flagship product that is designed to confront lower-priced competitors head-on, satisfy the appetites of value-conscious customers, and preserve the image of the company's premium product.

go up over time and that customers respond better to small price increases over time than to big periodic increases.[27] In addition, customers are less likely to notice small, regular price increases that result from rising costs than a single, steep price increase that could send them running to competitors. In the face of rising food and labor costs, McDonald's, the largest restaurant chain in the world, has relied on small, consistent price increases to maintain its profit margins without alienating customers.[28]

As we have seen already, companies often find it necessary to match competitors' prices on the same or similar items unless they can establish a distinctive image in customers' minds. One of the most successful strategies for companies facing direct competition is to differentiate their products or services by adding value for customers and then charging for it. For instance, a company might offer faster delivery, a longer product warranty, premium service, or something else that adds value to an item for its customers and allows the business to charge a higher price.

Perhaps the least understood of the three reference points is a company's cost structure. Customers often underestimate the costs businesses incur to provide products and services, whether it is a simple cotton T-shirt on a shelf in a beachfront shop or a lifesaving drug that may have cost hundreds of millions of dollars and many years to develop. For instance, in a study on pricing conducted by the University of Pennsylvania's Wharton School, shoppers estimated the average grocery store's net profit margin to be 27 percent when, in reality, it is less than 2 percent.[29] Customers forget that business owners must make or buy the products they sell, market them, pay their employees, and cover a host of other operating expenses, ranging from health care to legal fees. Because customers understand so little about a company's cost of producing a product or providing a service, entrepreneurs should focus on setting prices that communicate value to customers and create the desired image for the company.

ENTREPRENEURIAL PROFILE: Ariel Nelson and Lane Gerson: Jack Erwin In 2013, when Ariel Nelson and Lane Gerson started Jack Erwin, a company that sells classic, well-made men's shoes, their goal was to keep costs low so that they could sell their shoe collections at reasonable prices. Their initial strategy was to sell their shoes online only, which enabled them to keep costs low. Nelson and Gerson recently opened a storefront in New York City's trendy Tribeca neighborhood, which allows customers to try on every style of shoe, but the store stocks no other inventory (more cost savings). Customers try on the shoes in the store, place their orders, and the shoes are shipped directly to them from Spain, where the shoes are made, once again to keep costs low. Manufacturing a typical pair of shoes costs less than $100, and Jack Erwin prices them at about $200. The business partners, who have attracted more than $11 million in venture capital financing, sold 3,000 pairs of shoes in their first two months of operation, and their shoes proved to be so popular that they generated a waiting list of 4,000 customer orders, which is an indication that the entrepreneurs could raise their prices.[30] ■

One of the biggest mistakes an entrepreneur can make is underestimating the company's actual total cost of a product or service. Calculating the unit cost of a producing a product or providing a service is just the starting point. Entrepreneurs also must calculate the total cost of the product or service, which includes shipping, labor (wages, salaries, and benefits), and overhead costs (marketing, insurance, rent, utilities, and many others). When setting prices, some entrepreneurs think strictly in terms of product or service costs and fail to consider the total cost of providing the product or service. The result is a price that fails to cover the product's or service's total cost and a company that is never able to produce a profit.

ENTREPRENEURIAL PROFILE: Joshua Henderson: Skillet Street Food Joshua Henderson was a pioneer in the gourmet food truck industry when he launched Skillet Street Food in Seattle, Washington, from a converted Airstream trailer. Because there was no model to follow, Henderson says he had to figure out on his own, often using trial and error, how to price his menu offerings. Getting Skillet's prices right took some time, but Henderson eventually found a sweet spot below the prices of brick-and-mortar restaurants but high enough to cover food costs and generate sustainable profit margins. For instance, the original price of Skillet's popular burger and poutine (hand-cut fries covered in cheese curds and gravy) was $15, but Henderson realized that the company was not making money at that price. Raising the price to $17 produced a profit margin that was in line with the typical restaurant without alienating customers. Skillet Street Food now generates $2 million in annual sales.[31] ■

Entrepreneurs often find themselves squeezed by rising operating and raw material costs but are hesitant to raise prices because they fear losing customers. Businesses facing rapidly rising costs in their businesses should consider the following strategies:

- *Communicate with customers.* Let your customers know why you have to raise prices. Danny O'Neill, owner of The Roasterie, a wholesale coffee business that sells to upscale restaurants, coffeehouses, and supermarkets, operates in a market in which the cost of raw material and supplies can fluctuate wildly because of forces beyond his control. When coffee prices nearly doubled in just three months, O'Neill was able to pass along the rising costs of his company's raw material to customers without losing a single one. He sent his customers a six-page letter and copies of newspaper articles about the increases in coffee prices. The approach gave the Roasterie credibility and helped show customers that the necessary price increases were beyond his control.[32]

- *Rather than raise the price of the good or service, include a surcharge.* Price increases tend to be permanent, but if higher costs are the result of a particular event (e.g., a hurricane that disrupted the nation's ability to process oil and resulted in rapidly rising fuel costs), a company can include a temporary surcharge. If the pressure on its costs subsides, the company can eliminate the surcharge. After a group of restaurateurs in Los Angeles saw the cost of providing healthcare for their employees skyrocket in just a matter of months, they added a 3 percent surcharge to their menu items to help offset their increased cost of operations. The only problem was that the restaurateurs banded together on the price increase, which led to charges of collusion, price-fixing, and violating California's antitrust laws.[33]

- *Eliminate customer discounts, coupons, and promotions.* Eliminating discounts, coupons, and other freebies is an invisible way of raising prices that can add significantly to a small company's profit margin. Entrepreneurs must exercise care, however, because price-conscious shoppers have paid more attention to discounts, coupons, and promotions since the Great Recession. Some entrepreneurs have restructured their discount programs. Although loyal customers still earn discounts, the discounts are smaller and expire faster.

- *Offer products in smaller sizes or quantities.* As food costs have soared, many restaurants have introduced "small plates," reduced-portion items that have enabled them to keep their prices in check. In the quick-service sector, slider-style miniburgers billed as "fun food" and offered in bundles have become a popular item on many menus. Rick Johnson, owner of Lenny's Sub Shop, a chain based in Memphis, Tennessee, with 110 units in 12 states, recently introduced a 5-inch sub sandwich at a lower price point that allows it to compete with the pervasive value menus at quick service restaurants. With four sandwich sizes ranging in price from just $4.45 to $11.49, Johnson says that Lenny's is positioned to appeal to a wide range of customers.[34]

- *Focus on improving efficiency everywhere in the company.* Although raw materials costs may be beyond a business owner's control, other costs within the company are not. One way to cope with the effects of a rapid increase in costs is to find ways to cut costs and to improve efficiency in other areas. These improvements may not totally offset higher raw materials costs, but they can dampen their impact. Blain Supply, founded in 1955 by brothers Claude and Bert Blain in Janesville, Wisconsin, operates 35 discount stores that sell everything from clothing and kitchen appliances to camping gear and tires in Illinois, Iowa, and Wisconsin. To keep its prices low, Blain Supply, now in its second generation of family ownership (with a third generation in training), participated in Wisconsin's Retail Energy Management Challenge, a program that helps companies manage and reduce their energy consumption. Using energy audits and simple energy conservation measures, the company generated savings of $156,000 in just one year.[35]

- *Emphasize the value your company provides to customers.* Unless a company reminds them, customers can forget the unique benefits and value its products offer. Entrepreneurs must recognize that providing exceptional value to their customers insulates their businesses from the negative impact of necessary price increases. Rick Johnson, owner of the Lenny's Sub Shop chain, emphasizes his company's quality ingredients in its marketing rather than focusing on pricing. Johnson says that although value is important to the chain's customers, price is not the primary component in his company's value equation.[36]

- *Raise prices incrementally and consistently rather than rely on large periodic increases.* Companies that raise prices incrementally and consistently are less likely to experience resistance due to customers' sticker shock. Katie McCaskey, co-owner of George Bowers Grocery, a sandwich and burger restaurant in Staunton, Virginia, located in a storefront built in 1881 that housed a grocery store for more than 100 years, anchors the menu with a "pricey" $20 mega-burger whose price remains constant and raises the prices incrementally (typically just once a year) as costs go up on all of the restaurant's other items. Matt Bailey, co-owner of Elm City Social, a restaurant in New Haven, Connecticut, adjusts prices (raising some and, at times, lowering others, depending on costs and competition) at least four times per year, most often as the company debuts its seasonal menus. Bailey says that this pricing strategy minimizes customers' resistance to price increases.[37]

- *Shift to less expensive raw materials, if possible.* Some small businesses combat rising raw materials costs by adding to their lines new products that cost less. When seafood and beef prices increase, many restaurants revamp their menus to include more dishes with less expensive ingredients, such as chicken or turkey.

- *Anticipate rising materials costs and try to lock in prices early.* It pays to keep tabs on raw materials prices and be able to predict cycles of inflation. Entrepreneurs who can anticipate rising prices may be able to make purchases early or lock in long-term contracts before prices take off. In an attempt to smooth the wide swings in the price of raw chicken wings its restaurants were experiencing, Buffalo Wild Wings, a chain of restaurants based in Minneapolis, Minnesota, with more than 1,200 locations around the globe, entered into long-term contracts with suppliers that place limits on the range of prices the company pays per pound for wings. The contract, which covers two-thirds of the company's total supply, protects against the historically high wing prices that had been eroding Buffalo Wild Wings's profits. The company also changed the way it sells wings, selling them by portion size—snack, small, medium, and large—rather than by count, giving the company more flexibility over its pricing and greater control over its costs. The chain also began promoting its fresh, never-frozen wings as a premium product. The changes enabled Buffalo Wild Wings to regain control of its cost of goods sold and preserve its profit margins without experiencing a decline in sales.[38]

- *Consider absorbing cost increases.* When Norm Brodsky, owner of the document storage company mentioned earlier, saw his competitors add a fuel surcharge to their customers' bills to offset steep increases in gas prices, he decided *not* to add a fuel surcharge. Then he used the pricing decision to attract new accounts, telling them that his company had discovered other ways besides imposing a surcharge to deal with rising costs and assuring them that when the company says its contract price is fixed for a set time, customers can count on it. Brodsky also used the fuel surcharge issue to build loyalty among his existing customers, something he is certain will pay off in the future.[39]

- *Modify the product or service to lower its cost.* Taco Bell introduced the first "value menu" in 1988, with items priced at just 59 cents, and Wendy's, Burger King, McDonald's, and other quick-service restaurants soon followed suit. Eventually, restaurants priced their value menu items at $1, and price-sensitive customers responded. Items from the value menu made up about 15 percent of the typical quick-service restaurant's sales. However, rapidly rising food and labor costs began squeezing franchisees' profits on these items, forcing chains to modify the products by eliminating a slice of cheese (which saves 6 cents) or switching to a sandwich with a single beef patty rather than two to maintain the $1 price. Companies using this strategy must exercise caution, taking care not to reduce the quality of their products and services so much that they damage their reputations. Rather than run that risk, McDonald's, Burger King, and other fast-food chains introduced value meals that

FIGURE 11.3

What Determines Price?

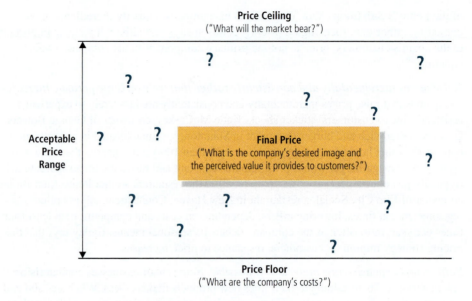

give customers a choice of menu items for a fixed price, which provides their franchisees more price flexibility and allows them to preserve their profit margins.[40]

- *Differentiate your company and its products and services from the competition.* When customers perceive a company's products and services to be superior to those of competitors, they are less sensitive to price increases.

Setting prices with an emphasis on value is more important than trying to choose the ideal price for a product. In fact, for most products, there is an acceptable price range, not a single ideal price. This price range is the area between the price ceiling defined by customers in the market and the price floor established by the company's cost structure. An entrepreneur's goal is to position the company's prices within this acceptable price range. The final price business owners set depends on the desired image they want to create for the business in their customers' minds—discount, middle of the road, or prestige—and the perceived value it provides to customers (see Figure 11.3).

LO2

Describe effective pricing techniques for introducing new products or services and for existing ones.

Pricing Strategies and Tactics

There is no limit to the number of variations in pricing strategies and tactics. This wide variety of options is exactly what allows entrepreneurs to be so creative. Pricing always plays a critical role in a firm's overall strategy; pricing policies must be compatible with a company's total marketing plan and the image it intends to create in the marketplace. This section examines some of the more commonly used tactics.

Introducing a New Product

Most entrepreneurs approach setting the price of a new product with a great deal of apprehension because they have no precedent on which to base their decisions. If the new product's price is excessively high, it is in danger of failing because of low sales volume. However, if its price is too low, the product's sales revenue might not cover costs. In addition, the company runs the risk of establishing the product's value at a low level. Management consulting firm McKinsey and Company claims that 80 to 90 percent of the pricing problems on new products are the result of companies setting prices too low.[41] When pricing any new product, the owner should try to satisfy three objectives:

1. *Get the product accepted.* No matter how unusual a product is, its price must be acceptable to a company's potential customers. The acceptable price range for a new product depends, in part, on the product's position:

   - **Revolutionary products** are so new and unique that they transform existing markets. The acceptable price range for revolutionary products tends to be rather wide, but the

revolutionary products

products that are so new and unique that they transform existing markets.

businesses introducing them must be prepared to make an investment in educating customers about them.

- **Evolutionary products** offer upgrades and enhancements to existing products. The acceptable price range for evolutionary products is not as wide as it is for revolutionary products. Companies that introduce evolutionary products with many new features at prices that are too low may initiate a price war.
- **Me-too products**, as the name suggests, offer the same basic features as existing products on the market. The acceptable price range for these products is quite narrow, and many companies introducing them find themselves left with me-too pricing strategies that are the same as or similar to those of their competitors.

2. *Maintain market share as competition grows.* If a new product is successful, competitors will enter the market, and the small company must work to expand or at least maintain its market share. Continuously reappraising the product's price in conjunction with special advertising and promotion techniques helps to retain market share.

3. *Earn a profit.* A small business must establish a price for a new product that is higher than its total cost. Entrepreneurs should not introduce a new product at a price below cost because it is much easier to lower a price than to increase it once the product is on the market. Pricing their products too low is a common and often fatal mistake for new businesses; entrepreneurs are tempted to underprice their products and services when they enter a new market to ensure their acceptance or to gain market share quickly. Doing so, however, sets customers' value expectations at low levels as well, and that can be a difficult perception to overcome. Steve McKee, president of McKee Wallwork Cleveland Advertising, an advertising agency that targets small companies, says, "It can be odd to feel good about losing customers because of price, but if you're not, you may be backing yourself into a low-margin corner. Don't kid yourself; other than Wal-Mart, very few companies can sustain a low-price position."[42]

Entrepreneurs have three basic strategies to choose from when establishing a new product's price: penetration, skimming, and life cycle pricing.

PENETRATION If a small business introduces a product into a highly competitive market in which a large number of similar products are competing for acceptance, the product must penetrate the market to be successful. To gain quick acceptance and extensive distribution in the mass market, some entrepreneurs introduce the product at a low price. They set the price just above total unit cost to develop a wedge in the market and quickly achieve a high volume of sales. Kensington Publishing Corporation, an independent publishing house started (and still managed) by the Zacharius family in 1974, uses a penetration pricing strategy for many of its books, selling e-books on BookBub, a discount book Web site, for as little as 99 cents, a significant discount from the usual selling price of $12.99 to $14.99. Steven Zacharius, the company's CEO, says that the goal is to entice readers with low prices to introduce them to new authors or book series for which they eventually will pay full price. The low initial prices have stimulated sales, and every promotion that Kensington Publishing has run through BookBub has been profitable. Zacharius admits that the strategy involves certain risks, including making customers accustomed to paying low prices for e-books and purchasing them only when they are on sale.[43]

A penetration pricing strategy is ideal for introducing relatively low-priced goods into a market that has no elite segment and little opportunity for differentiation. The introduction is usually accompanied by heavy advertising and promotional techniques, special sales, and discounts. This strategy works best when customers' "switching cost" (the cost of switching to a lower-priced competitor's product) is high (e.g., video game consoles). Entrepreneurs must recognize that penetration pricing is a long-range strategy; until customers accept the product, profits are likely to be small.

A danger of a penetration pricing strategy is that it attracts customers who know no brand loyalty. Companies that garner customers by offering low introductory prices run the risk of losing their customer bases if they raise their prices or a competitor undercuts their prices. If the strategy works and the product achieves mass-market penetration, sales volume increases, and

evolutionary products
products that offer upgrades and enhancements to existing products.

me-too products
products that offer the same basic features as existing products on the market.

You Be the Consultant

The Psychology of Pricing

Everyone has seen the commercials that advertise a clever new product for "only $19.99," but then the announcer says, "But, wait! If you act right now, we'll *double* your order. All you have to pay is shipping and handling on the second free product." The psychology of doubling customers' orders "for free" helps these companies sell more products. What other techniques do companies use that employ psychological techniques?

- *"No payments until spring."* This pricing technique relies on the principle of pain avoidance. Auto dealers, tire retailers, and many other businesses increase sales of their products by allowing customers to postpone making an initial payment until some point in the future. This "buy now, pay later" principle is powerful because it allows people to avoid "pain," in this case, spending money now.

- *"Try a free sample."* Grocery stores often give shoppers free samples of products, especially on busy shopping days, because they know that sales of the items they allow customers to sample will increase. The psychology behind this strategy relies on the principle of reciprocity: If you give me something (a free sample of the product), I should give you something in return (purchase the product). Price becomes a less important factor in the equation.

- *"Share your purchase on social media."* Businesses, particularly e-commerce companies, encourage customers to share their purchases on social media. Two psychological principles are at work here: positive reinforcement and social acceptance. When friends compliment you on the purchase you just posted on social media, you receive positive reinforcement for making a good decision, a reward that makes future purchases more likely. In addition, promoting your own purchase on social media encourages your friends to do the same because humans strive for social acceptance from family, friends, and even strangers. To achieve that acceptance, people often attempt to act or look like those they admire.

- *"Regular Price $199. Now just $149 but for a limited time only. Hurry!"* Companies often appeal to shoppers' fear of missing out (FOMO) on a good deal by imposing deadlines or stating that only a limited number of items remain. Customers often respond to the urge to "act now" for fear of losing the opportunity to get a bargain.

- *"Sign up for our free newsletter."* By having shoppers sign up for a free newsletter or add their names to a list to receive e-mail updates, companies are using the principle of commitment. Getting shoppers to make a commitment to the business (even a minimal one) increases the likelihood that they will make a purchase in the future. Eyeglass retailer Warby Parker will send up to five pairs

of frames to shoppers, knowing that the probability of making a sale increases because the shopper is already committed.

- *"Our story: We started this company because . . . "* Smart business owners always include an "About us" or "Our story" page on their Web sites. These pages often tell an inspiring story about what drove the entrepreneur to launch the business and what makes it special. After Phil Weiner lost his father to diabetes, he launched UrbnEarth, a small company that sells a compact gardening system that enables people, particularly those who live in crowded urban areas, to grow fresh, healthful food. UrbnEarth's "Our story" page makes an emotional connection with shoppers, who feel good about doing business with a company that strives to accomplish social good.

Michael Dubin, cofounder, Dollar Shave Club

- *"A great shave. Delivered."* That's the tag line for Dollar Shave Club, a company founded by Mark Levine and Michael Dubin. The company uses a subscription pricing model that ships razors to customers based on a schedule the customer defines. By positioning their business in a unique way and emphasizing the value (mainly the convenience of its subscription model versus the inconvenience and cost of buying razors in a store) it offers through its pricing strategy, Dollar Shave Club, which Unilever recently purchased for $1 billion, has disrupted the razor blade business.

- *"Handcrafted Burgers and Fries Since 1986."* At Five Guys Burgers and Fries, a hamburger, French fries, and a drink cost, on average, more than $12, considerably higher than the same bundle cost at a typical fast-food restaurant, but customers do not seem to notice. Why? Because Five Guys's value proposition is quality and freshness, not low price.

1. Use the Internet to find examples of businesses that use these or other psychology-based pricing techniques and

(continued)

You Be the Consultant *(continued)*

write a brief description of the company and its pricing strategy.

2. Why do many entrepreneurs underprice their goods and services, especially when they first get into business? Discuss the connection between the prices a company establishes for its goods and services and the image it creates for the company.

Sources: Based on Laura Forer, "Psych! Five Principles That Explain Why Consumers Take Action (or Don't)," *Marketing Profs*, June 30, 2016, www.marketingprofs .com/chirp/2016/30204/psych-five-principles-that-explain-why-consumers-take-action-or-dont; Beth Morgan, "6 Psychological Triggers That Win Sales and Influence Customers," *Shopify*, www.shopify.com/blog/8920983-6-psychological-triggers-that-win-sales-and-influence-customers; "How the Dollar Shave Club Reinvented Retail," *PYMNTS*, May 18, 2015, www.pymnts.com/exclusive-series/2015/how-the-dollar-shave-club-reinvented-retail/; Bret Thorn, "Menu Economics: Pricing the Plate," *Nation's Restaurant News*, March 7, 2013, http://nrn.com/purchasing/menu-economics-pricing-plate.

the company earns adequate profits. The objectives of the penetration strategy are to break into the market quickly, generate a high sales volume as soon as possible, and build market share. Many consumer products, such as soap, shampoo, and light bulbs, are introduced with penetration pricing strategies.

SKIMMING A skimming pricing strategy often is used when a company introduces a new product into a market with little or no competition or to establish the company and its products or services as unique and superior to those of its competitors. Sometimes a business employs this tactic when introducing a product into a competitive market that contains an elite group that is able to pay a higher price. Companies that use a skimming strategy often achieve success by emphasizing the intangible benefits of their higher-priced goods and services. For instance, one lawn service that targets busy, upscale professionals commands premium prices by emphasizing the time and trouble doing yard work that they save their clients and the ability to have yards that are the envy of the neighborhood. Other companies that use a skimming strategy focus on selling the experience.

ENTREPRENEURIAL PROFILE: The Claus Family: Ultima Thule Lodge The Ultima Thule Lodge (the name comes from the "unknowable realm" that appeared beyond the boundaries of ancient Greek maps), now in its third generation of family ownership, provides adventure-seeking tourists with the ultimate outdoor experience in Alaska's scenic, wild Wrangell-St. Elias Wilderness. Founder John Claus called the lodge "his five acres with a 13-million-acre backyard." The Claus family has spent the last five decades building a homey but luxurious lodge in the middle of nowhere that caters to visitors who want to experience Alaska's rugged beauty first-hand. Because the nearest road is 100 miles away, getting there takes some effort, but once guests arrive, they realize that the six-hour drive from Anchorage to Chitina and the 90-minute flight on a bush plane were well worth the journey. Five well-appointed cabins and a main lodge that include gourmet meals, wrought-iron oil-drip stoves, wood-fired cedar saunas, and outdoor hot tubs await them. The lodge has a fleet of Piper Super Cubs flown by some of the best bush pilots in the state that take guests on customized adventures that include sightseeing, hiking, fishing, rafting, backcountry skiing, or a host of other activities that guests specify. Four-night packages start at $7,900 per person, and five night packages are $9,400 per person.[44] ∎

With a skimming strategy, an entrepreneur uses a higher-than-normal price in an effort to quickly recover the initial developmental and promotional costs of a product or service. The idea is to set a price well above the total unit cost and to promote the product heavily to appeal to the segment of the market that is not sensitive to price. This pricing tactic often reinforces the unique, prestigious image of a business and portrays the product as high quality. Another advantage of this technique is that entrepreneurs can correct pricing mistakes quickly and easily. If a product's price proves to be too low under a penetration strategy, raising the price can be very difficult. If a company using a skimming strategy sets a price too high to generate sufficient sales volume, it can always lower the price. Successful skimming strategies require a company to differentiate its products or services from those of the competition, justifying the above-average price.

LIFE CYCLE PRICING A variation of the skimming price strategy is called life cycle pricing. Using this technique, a small company introduces a product at a high price. Then technological advances enable the firm to lower its costs quickly and to reduce the product's price before its competition can. By beating other businesses in a price decline, the small company discourages competitors and gradually, over time, becomes a high-volume producer. Ultra high-definition television sets are a prime example of a product introduced at a high price that quickly cascaded downward as companies forged important technology advances and took advantage of economies of scale. When ultra high-definition (4K) televisions were first introduced, they sold for $4,000 to $5,000; today, they are priced at $700 or less.

Life cycle pricing is a strategy that assumes competition will emerge over time. Even if no competition arises, however, companies almost always lower the product's price to attract a larger segment of the market. Nonetheless, the initial high price contributes to a rapid return of start-up costs and generates a pool of funds to finance expansion and technological advances.

Pricing Established Goods and Services

Each of the following pricing tactics or techniques are part of the toolbox of pricing tactics entrepreneurs can use to set prices of established goods and services.

odd pricing
a pricing technique that involves setting prices that end in odd numbers to create the psychological impression of lower prices.

ODD PRICING Many entrepreneurs use the technique known as **odd pricing**, in which they establish prices that end in odd numbers, such as 5, 7, or 9, because they believe that merchandise selling for $12.69 appears to be much cheaper than the same item priced at $13.00. Apple establishes prices that end in 9 for most of its products, including its iPhones and iPads. One study of women's clothing items that featured prices from $31 to $39 found that items that end in 9 outsold those whose prices featured all other ending digits by an average 24 percent, even though the other prices were lower.[45] Omitting the $ symbol from prices may help, too. Researchers at Cornell University have discovered that restaurants that list menu prices without the $ symbol (e.g., "21") achieved $5.55 more in sales per check on average than those whose menu prices were written in script or included a $ symbol.[46]

freemium pricing
a pricing strategy that involves providing a basic product or service to customers for free but charging a premium for expanded or upgraded versions of the product or service.

FREEMIUM PRICING Companies that use **freemium pricing** provide a basic product or service to customers for free but charge a premium for expanded or upgraded versions of the product or service. Products or services that customers must use or experience to appreciate their value, such as software, are ideal candidates for a freemium pricing strategy. The goals of a freemium pricing strategy are to gain rapid and extensive adoption of a product or service and to give potential customers a chance to discover the value it offers, particularly in its upgraded versions. The key to a successful freemium strategy is to expose free users to enough product or service features while reserving the most valuable benefits for customers who are willing to pay for the expanded versions. Typically, only about 2 to 4 percent of customers who use the free version of a product actually purchase its upgraded versions; therefore, for a freemium strategy to be successful, the potential market must be sizable.[47] Suppose, for example, that a company's revenue target is $10 million and its average annual revenue per *paying* customer is $120. The company would need 83,333 paying customers ($10 million ÷ $120 per customer) to reach its target. Assuming a conversion rate of 3 percent, the company would have to attract 2,777,778 free users (83,333 customers ÷ 3 percent) to generate $10 million in annual sales. One of the greatest dangers of a freemium pricing strategy is underestimating the cost of providing service and support for free users.

ENTREPRENEURIAL PROFILE: Jesse Volmar and Brad Koch: FarmLogs Jesse Vollmar grew up in rural Michigan and noted that the technology that was changing the rest of the world seemed to have bypassed the typical farming operation. After graduating from Saginaw Valley State University, Vollmar worked with another computer science major, Brad Koch, to launch FarmLogs, a company that provides Web- and mobile-based software that gives farmers real-time access to reports created using sophisticated analytics and big data, such as soil maps, rainfall statistics, heat maps, soil conditions, and yield statistics, to allow them to make their farms more efficient and profitable. The entrepreneurs partnered with a satellite company to gather and analyze key farming data from current and prior growing seasons. Using FarmLogs, farmers can understand the conditions of their fields and know exactly what they must do to maximize their yields. Vollmar and Koch launched FarmLogs with a freemium pricing model and watched their user base grow rapidly; the entrepreneurs report that farmers who grow 25 percent of the row crops acres in the United States now use FarmLogs' software. Farmers can sign up for basic reports included in the standard product package for free, but most upgrade to other reports in additional product packages, which they can purchase for as little as $2.50 per acre.[48] ■

PRICE LINING **Price lining** is a technique that greatly simplifies the pricing decision by pricing different products in a product line at different price points, depending on their quality, features, and cost. Under this system, entrepreneurs sell products in several different price ranges, or price lines. Each category of merchandise contains items that are similar in appearance but that differ in quality, cost, performance, or other features. Many lined products use "the power of three," appearing in sets of three—good (basic), better (upgraded), and best (premium)—at prices designed to satisfy different market segment needs and incomes. Research shows that most customers choose the mid-priced option.[49] Survey Monkey uses a price lining strategy. In addition to its free basic version of its survey platform, the company offers three premium versions, Select ($19 per month), Gold ($25 per month), and Platinum ($85 per month), each with higher levels of performance. Price lining can boost a company's sales because it makes goods available to a wide range of shoppers, simplifies the purchase decision for customers, and allows them to choose products with prices that fit within their budgets. Companies that segment their customer bases and use price lines designed to appeal to each segment can improve their profit margins between 1 and 7 percent.[50]

price lining
a technique that greatly simplifies the pricing function by pricing different products in a product line at different price points, depending on their quality, features, and cost.

PRICE ANCHORING An old adage says, "What's the best way to sell a $2,000 watch? Put it next to a $10,000 watch." The premise behind this concept is **price anchoring**, which is the tendency that people have to rely heavily on the first piece of information they receive (the anchor) when faced with a decision. Shoppers evaluate subsequent information by comparing it to the anchor. Therefore, featuring a $2,000 watch next to a $10,000 watch makes the $2,000 watch look like a bargain. Restaurants often use price anchors, placing a really expensive dish—for example, a $119 lobster dinner—in a prominent spot on the menu, which makes the $30 seafood platter look quite reasonable by comparison.

price anchoring
the tendency that people have to rely heavily on the first piece of information they receive (the anchor) when faced with a decision and to evaluate subsequent information by comparing it to the anchor.

SUBSCRIPTION PRICING A study in *The Economist* reports that 80 percent of global executives say that the way that customers prefer to access goods and services is changing and that 50 percent of companies are changing their pricing strategies as a result.[51] Shoppers increasingly prefer simpler, more convenient shopping experiences. One of the most significant changes companies are making to meet these demands is shifting from pay-per-product pricing models to subscription pricing models. Companies such as Netflix (online streaming of movies, television shows and video games), Birchbox (makeup and beauty products), Surf Air (private air travel on the West coast), and Dollar Shave Club (shaving razor and accessories) have implemented successful subscription pricing models. Subscription pricing provides significant benefits for both businesses and customers. Selling products or services through subscriptions enables businesses to reduce the swings in (and therefore improve the ability to predict) revenue because of the regularly recurring sales, manage inventory more efficiently, and determine the lifetime value of its customers more easily. Subscription models also allow companies to build stronger long-term relationships with customers. Shoppers also experience the benefits of increased convenience and lower transaction costs.

ENTREPRENEURIAL PROFILE: Laura and Doug Zander: Jimmy Beans Wool Laura and Doug Zander, both former software engineers, launched Jimmy Beans Wool, a shop aimed at knitters, in Reno, Nevada, in 2002. In addition to bringing thousands of customers into their storefront, the copreneurs built a successful e-commerce business, selling yarn and knitting accessories around the globe. One of their most successful online promotions was selling yarn samples online, so the Zanders decided to introduce a subscription pricing model; for $10 per month, customers get a pouch containing four different samples of yarn and a few knitting accessories with links to crochet patterns. An e-mail newsletter promoting the subscription offer quickly netted 164 customers, and the Zanders knew that they had hit upon a successful idea. So far, 5,400 customers have purchased Jimmy Beans Wool subscriptions, allowing the Zanders to increase their company's sales by nearly 20 percent.[52] ■

dynamic (customized) pricing

a technique in which a company sets different prices for the same products and services for different customers by using the information collected about the customers.

DYNAMIC PRICING For many businesses, the pricing decision has become more challenging because the Internet gives customers access to real-time pricing information for almost any item, ranging from cars to computers. Increasingly, customers are using the Internet to find the lowest prices available. To maintain their profitability, some companies have responded with **dynamic** (or **customized**) **pricing**, in which they set different prices for the same products and services for different customers using information they have collected about their customers. Rather than sell their products at fixed prices, companies using dynamic pricing rely on fluid prices that may change based on supply and demand and on which customer is buying or when a customer makes a purchase. Movie theaters charge lower admission prices when demand is slow (matinees). Uber, the ride-hailing app, charges customers higher prices when demand for rides surges, for instance, on weekend evenings, after big events such as a concert, and on holidays such as New Year's Eve. One study of Amazon reveals that the online retailer changes the prices of the items it sells more than 2.5 million times each day.[53]

Dynamic pricing is not a new concept. The standard practice in ancient bazaars involved merchants and customers haggling until they came to a mutually agreeable price, meaning that different customers paid different prices for the same goods. Although the modern version of dynamic pricing often involves sophisticated market research, the goal is the same: to charge the right customer the right price at the right time. For example, travelers can purchase last-minute airline tickets at significant discounts, such as a round-trip ticket from New York to Los Angeles for just $250 rather than for the full-fare price of $750. Travelers benefit from lower prices, and the airlines are able to generate revenue from seats that otherwise would have gone unsold.

⚖ Ethics and Entrepreneurship

The Ethics of Dynamic Pricing

In *Casablanca*, the classic romance drama film from 1942, Ilsa, the character played by Ingrid Bergman, is looking at a set of lace napkins in a shopping bazaar when she mentions that she is a friend of Rick, the film's lead character, played by Humphrey Bogart. The merchant quickly replaces the original 700-franc price tag with one bearing a 100-franc price. "For special friends of Rick's, we have special discounts," he explains to Ilsa. The message is clear: Different prices apply to different customers.

Companies now have access to more data on their customers than at any other point in business history, and many of these businesses use that information to serve their customers better, providing them with the goods and services they need just when they need them. One offshoot of this wealth of information is dynamic or customized pricing, a system in which companies charge different prices for the same products and services for different customers using the information they have collected about their customers. The principle is the same as that in *Casablanca*: Different prices apply to different customers. Movie theaters have used a simple version of dynamic pricing for years. Buy a ticket for an afternoon showing, traditionally a slower time for sales of movie tickets, and you get a lower price. Restaurants use the same tactic, offering "early bird" specials at off-peak hours. Airlines have used dynamic pricing for years as well, but their systems are much more complex. Business travelers who fly on short notice on weekdays typically pay higher prices than those who book in advance and travel over weekends. Cities such as London, Singapore, Dallas, San Francisco, and New York use dynamic pricing strategies, charging drivers on toll bridges and roads higher prices at peak commuting times and lower prices during off-peak hours.

Cineclassico/Alamy Stock Photo

Many professional and collegiate sporting events now rely on dynamic pricing, charging higher prices for "high demand" games with arch rivals or stellar matchups between star pitchers and lower prices for games that fans find less appealing or are subject to bad weather. The Center Theater Group in Los Angeles recently introduced dynamic pricing, offering its unsold tickets, which usually are about 10 percent of the total number of tickets, for half-price on the day of the show. By selling seats that otherwise would go unsold, the theater was able to generate $1 million more in sales in just one year.

The practice of dynamic pricing has created controversy, however. Is it ethical for companies to charge different customers

(continued)

Ethics and Entrepreneurship

different prices for the same goods and services? Many surveys report that customers believe dynamic pricing is *not* an acceptable business practice. However, empirical evidence shows that customized pricing benefits not only the companies using it but also customers, making purchases more affordable for many people. Uber, the ride-sharing company, uses dynamic pricing, charging higher prices when demand for rides is high and the supply of cars is low, typically on Friday and Saturday evenings, on certain holidays, and during bad weather. Uber says that its dynamic pricing strategy minimizes customers' wait times and the frequency with which customers experience "no cars available" messages on their phone or tablet screens.

More than 250 ski resorts across the United States now use dynamic pricing. Ragged Mountain, a 49-year-old ski resort in New Hampshire, recently implemented dynamic pricing with the help of Cloud Store, software that gives managers the ability to change prices on lift tickets, equipment rentals, and lessons, depending on weather conditions, holidays, and other factors. A Valentine's Day special, priced at just $14, produced a significant increase in sales of tickets and generated lots of positive buzz for the ski resort. On one occasion, as a big snowstorm approached the area, Ragged Mountain was able to increase its prices gradually each day and still sell out its capacity. Resort managers do not mind reducing prices when demand is low or when conditions are less than ideal because they know that bringing in more customers leads to higher sales of meals, snacks, and beverages.

Dynamic pricing has stood successfully against several legal challenges. Denise Katzman filed a class-action lawsuit against retailer Victoria's Secret when she discovered that a catalog she received listed higher prices than a nearly identical catalog the company sent to a male coworker. She alleged that the company had engaged in illegal price discrimination by charging different prices for identical items to different categories of customers. Because Victoria's Secret had sent the catalogs through the U.S. mail, Katzman claimed that the company's discriminatory pricing structure constituted mail fraud. U.S. District Court Judge Robert W. Sweet upheld the validity of Victoria's Secret's dynamic pricing policies, ruling that "offering different discounts to different catalogue customers does not constitute mail fraud under any reading of the law." On appeal, the U.S. Court of Appeals for the Second Circuit upheld Judge Sweet's decision. This case suggests that businesses can charge different customers different prices as long as the price differences are based on reasonable business practices, such as rewarding loyal customers, and do not discriminate against customers for race, gender, national origin, or some other illegal reason.

Dynamic pricing has emerged as a marketing strategy out of necessity. Entrepreneurs say the Internet has lowered the transaction costs of doing business and moves business along at such a fast pace that the fixed pricing strategies of the past no longer work. To keep up with fluid, fast-changing markets, companies must change their prices quickly, adapting the prices they charge their customers in real-time. Ric Kostick, cofounder of 100% Pure, an online cosmetics company, worked with Freshplum, a company that uses analytics to help companies develop dynamic pricing strategies, to target visitors who are about to leave the site without making a purchase. By offering these shoppers steeper discounts, 100% Pure was able to improve its conversion rate and increase its sales by 13.5 percent.

1. Work with a team of your classmates to define the ethical issues involved in dynamic pricing.

2. What are the advantages and the disadvantages of dynamic pricing to the companies that use it? To the customers of the companies that use it?

3. According to an old proverb, "The value of a thing is what it will bring." Do you agree? Explain. Should companies be allowed to engage in dynamic pricing?

4. If you owned your own business and had the information required to engage in dynamic pricing, would you do so? Explain.

Sources: Based on Adam Tanner, "How Much Did You Pay for That Lipstick?," *Forbes*, April 14, 2014, pp. 46–49; Grant Davis, "Sweet Seats," *Entrepreneur*, April 2014, p. 64, Jack Nicas, "The Price You Pay Depends on Time and Day," *Wall Street Journal*, December 14, 2015, pp. B1, B4; Donna Fenn, "Some Businesses Go Creative on Prices, Applying Technology," *New York Times*, January 22, 2014, www.nytimes .com/2014/01/23/business/smallbusiness/with-new-thinking-and-technology-some-businesses-get-creative-with-pricing.html?_r=1; Grant Davis, "Snow Job," *Entrepreneur*, January 2014, www.entrepreneur.com/article/230219; Bill Gurley, "A Deeper Look at Uber's Dynamic Pricing Model," *Above the Crowd*, March 11, 2014, http://abovethecrowd.com/2014/03/11/a-deeper-look-at-ubers-dynamic-pricing-model/; Patrick Rishe, "Dynamic Pricing: The Future of Ticket Pricing in Sports," *Forbes*, January 6, 2012, www.entrepreneur.com/article/230219; Mark Brown, "Indie Royale Bundle Starts a Price War Between the Stingy and the Wealthy," *Wired*, October 26, 2011, www.wired.co.uk/news/archive/2011-10/26/indie-royale-bundle; Robert M. Weiss and Ajay K. Mehrotra, "Online Dynamic Pricing: Efficiency, Equity, and the Future of E-commerce," *Virginia Journal of Law and Technology*, vol. 6, no. 2 (Summer 2001), p. 7; Matthew Maier, "Finding Riches in a Mine of Credit Data," *Business 2.0*, October 2005, pp. 72–74; and Peter Coffee, "More 'Dynamic Pricing' Is on the Way," *eWeek*, September 2002, www.eweek.com/article2/0,1759,1011178,00.asp.

LEADER PRICING **Leader pricing** is a technique in which a retailer marks down the customary price (i.e., the price consumers are accustomed to paying) of a popular item in an attempt to attract more customers. The company earns a much smaller profit on each unit because the markup is lower, but purchases of other merchandise by customers seeking the leader item often boost sales and profits. In other words, the incidental purchases that consumers make when shopping for the leader item boost sales revenue enough to offset a lower profit margin on the leader. Grocery stores frequently use leader pricing. For instance, during the holiday season, stores often use turkeys as a price leader, knowing that they will earn higher margins on the other items shoppers purchase with their turkeys. To kick off the holiday season, Belk, a regional department store based in Charlotte, North Carolina, offers women's boots that normally sell for

leader pricing
a technique that involves marking down the normal price of a popular item in an attempt to attract more customers who make incidental purchases of other items at regular prices.

$49.99 to $79.99 at a steep discount, just $19.99, as a "door-buster" sale item. Although Belk does not make a profit on the boots at that price, the leader pricing strategy is designed to attract customers who will purchase other items that carry normal markups and generate a profit.[54]

GEOGRAPHIC PRICING Small businesses whose pricing decisions are greatly affected by the costs of shipping merchandise to customers across a wide range of geographic regions frequently employ one of the geographic pricing techniques. For these companies, freight expenses make up a substantial portion of the cost of doing business and may cut deeply into already narrow profit margins. One type of geographic pricing is **zone pricing**, in which a company sells its merchandise at different prices to customers located in different territories. For example, a manufacturer might sell at one price to customers east of the Mississippi and at another to those west of the Mississippi.

Another variation of geographic pricing is uniform **delivered pricing**, a technique in which a firm charges all of its customers the same price regardless of their location, even though the cost of selling or transporting merchandise varies. A company calculates the proper freight charges for each region and combines them into a uniform fee. The result is that local customers subsidize the company's charges for shipping merchandise to distant customers.

A final variation of geographic pricing is **F.O.B. factory**, in which a small company sells its merchandise to customers on the condition that they pay all shipping costs. In this way, the company can set a uniform price for its product and let each customer cover the freight costs.

DISCOUNTS Many small businesses use **discounts** (or **markdowns**)—reductions from normal list prices—to move stale, outdated, damaged, or slow-moving merchandise or to stimulate sales. Among retailers, discounting is the most common pricing strategy; 97 percent of retailers use discounts.[55] A seasonal discount is a price reduction designed to encourage shoppers to purchase merchandise before an upcoming season. For instance, many retail clothiers offer special sales on winter coats in midsummer. Many merchants also offer after-Christmas discounts to make room for their spring merchandise. Some companies grant purchase discounts to special groups of customers, such as senior citizens or college students, to establish a faithful clientele and generate repeat business.

As tempting as discounts are to businesses when sales are slow, they carry risks. Ideally, discounts win loyal customers who make repeat purchases. The reality of discounts, however, is that they often attract customers who are merely seeking bargains and who rarely turn into loyal customers. Cacio e Vino, a Sicilian restaurant in New York City's Manhattan borough, offers a limited number of reservations at a 40 percent discount through Groupon Reserve to draw customers on Sundays, Mondays, and Tuesdays, the restaurant's slowest nights. On Wednesdays and Thursdays, Cacio e Vino offers a limited number of diners 30 percent discounts but only between 5 P.M. and 7 P.M. Manager Christine Ehlert says the discounts are a tool to attract new customers to the restaurant during times that it is operating at less-than-full capacity. Although the discounts have increased sales from an average of $800 to $1,200 to $1,500 on Mondays and Tuesdays, they cut into the restaurant's profit margin, reducing it by 50 percent compared to full-price customers. In addition, fewer than half of Cacio e Vino's discount customers return, and when they do, it almost always is for a discounted meal.[56]

Excessive discounting also diminishes or eradicates altogether a company's profit margin. Perry Schorr, co-owner of Lester's, a 65-year-old retailer that sells clothing for children and teens and targets affluent families, makes limited use of discounts. With four stores in New York, Schorr knows that his customers are more interested in quality products and attentive service than discount prices. During the competitive Black Friday weekend that kicks off the holiday season, which accounts for 15 percent of the company's sales, Lester's offers modest discounts of 20 percent on select items and adds sales staff to ensure that customer service does not suffer. Schorr sees Black Friday as a price-driven event and says small companies such as his cannot build a successful strategy by discounting prices and cheapening their images.[57]

Companies that frequently resort to discounts may ruin their reputation for superior quality and service, thereby diluting the value of their brand and image in the marketplace. Frequent discounting sends customers the message that a company's regular prices are too high and that they should wait for the next sale to make a purchase. As many retailers and restaurants learned from the last recession, weaning customers off of discounts can be difficult; the

---

zone pricing
a technique that involves setting different prices for customers located in different territories because of different transportation costs.

delivered pricing
a technique in which a company charges all customers the same price, regardless of their locations and different transportation costs.

F.O.B. factory
a pricing method in which a company sells merchandise to customers on the condition that they pay all shipping costs.

discounts (markdowns)
reductions from normal list prices.

climb back to "normal" pricing can be long and arduous. Stoney River Steakhouse, an upscale restaurant specializing in hand-cut steaks with 11 locations in seven states, recently eliminated its practice of using discounts as a way to build traffic amid slow sales. After eliminating the discounts, Stoney River Steakhouse saw its average check increase 13.8 percent, but its guest count declined 12.8 percent.[58] One less visible way for companies to offer discounts is to enroll customers in a loyalty program that entitles them to **earned discounts**. Loyalty programs, such as those at supermarkets, pet stores, and bookstores, not only encourage shoppers to return but also provide businesses with meaningful data on customers' buying habits, allowing them to decipher patterns and trends. Belk, a chain of department stores with more than 300 locations in 16 southern states, offers rewards to customers who make purchases on the store-branded credit card. For every $400 customers spend, they receive $10 in Belk Reward Dollars they can use for future purchases.

earned discounts
discounts customers earn by making repeat purchases at a business.

Limited-time offers (LTOs) are discounts that retailers run for a limited amount of time ("Regular price: $150. Sale price $120 *for three days only.*") with the goal of creating a sense of urgency and excitement among customers. Although LTOs are a common pricing tool for many retailers, quick-service restaurants are perhaps the most frequent users of LTOs. To create a successful LTO, retailers should emphasize the end date of the offer and include a distinct call to action in their advertising, promote the offer on social media as well as in traditional advertising channels, and end the offer on the advertised date. Umami Burger, a chain founded in 2009 in Los Angeles by Adam Fleischman that specializes in uniquely flavored burgers and sandwiches, has had great success running periodic LTOs. One of its most successful LTOs is the Artist Series, featuring limited edition burgers designed in collaboration with artists such as Slash, The Black Keys, Andy Samberg, Mindy Kaling, and others. Umami Burger builds excitement for the LTO by promoting it on social media and, because it runs the offer only twice per year, creates a sense of urgency that significantly increases traffic at its 24 locations. The LTO also incorporates a charitable component; the restaurant donates $1 from the sale of each burger to a local charity. Umami Burger has found that its LTO provides a convenient way to test new menu items, such as its highly successful Pizza Burger, with very little risk.[59]

limited-time offers (LTOs)
discounts retailers run for a limited amount of time with the goal of creating a sense of urgency and excitement among customers.

Ringo Chiu/Zuma Press, Inc./Alamy Stock Photo

Recent research suggests that using a **steadily decreasing discount (SDD)**, a limited duration discount that declines over time, is superior to a standard (hi-lo) discount, a common tactic in which a company offers frequent discounts off its standard prices. When one company used a hi-lo discount of 20 percent for three days before returning to the items to full price, sales increased by 75 percent. For the same items, a steadily decreasing discount of 30 percent the first day, 20 percent the second day, and 10 percent the third day (which yielded the same average discount of 20 percent) produced an increase in sales of 200 percent. The researchers conclude that the SDD is more effective because it creates a sense of urgency, especially among wary or indecisive customers.[60] Research also shows that for items other than luxury goods, dollar discounts ("Save $25 now") are more effective at generating sales than percentage discounts ("Save 25% now").[61]

steadily decreasing discount (SDD)
a limited-duration discount that declines over time.

Multiple-unit pricing is a promotional technique that offers customers discounts if they purchase in quantity. Many products, especially those with relatively low unit value, are sold using multiple-unit pricing. For example, instead of selling an item for 50 cents, a small company might offer five for $2. Rob Katz, CEO of Vail Resorts, a company that owns 12 ski resorts in the United States and Australia, recently introduced a version of multiple-unit pricing for its customers. Rather than pay $100 for a daily lift ticket, customers can purchase a Vail Epic Pass for as little as $769 that gives them unlimited access to the slopes at all of Vail's resorts for an entire season. The company now sells 400,000 Epic Passes each year, generating one-seventh of its annual revenue.[62]

multiple-unit pricing
a technique that involves offering customers discounts if they purchase in quantity.

BUNDLING Many small businesses have discovered the marketing benefits of **bundling**, grouping together several products or services or both into a package that offers customers extra value at a special price. Fast-food outlets often bundle items into "meal deals" that customers can purchase at lower prices than if they bought the items separately. Even upscale restaurants use bundled pricing; at New York City's tony Per Se, diners can choose between two nine-course

bundling
grouping together several products or services or both into a package that offers customers extra value at a special price.

prix fixe chef's tasting menus for $310 per person. Bundling is another way for companies to offer customers discounts without damaging their reputations. Sephora, a beauty products company, often uses bundling to encourage customers to buy more products. The company offers limited discounts by bundling related products, such as makeup brushes with blush and bronzers or lipstick and lip glosses, at special prices, always showing the value of the items if they were purchased separately.[63]

optional-product pricing

a technique that involves selling a base product for one price but selling the options or accessories for it at a much higher markup.

OPTIONAL-PRODUCT PRICING Optional-product pricing involves selling the base product for one price but selling the options or accessories for it at a much higher markup. Automobiles are often sold at a base price with each option priced separately. In some cases, the car is sold with some of the options "bundled" together, as explained previously.

ENTREPRENEURIAL PROFILE: Amish Backyard Structures Amish Backyard Structures, a small company in tiny Oxford, Pennsylvania, that makes children's playhouses, sheds, barns, gazebos, and lawn furniture, uses an optional-product pricing strategy. The company's playhouses are handcrafted from top-quality materials, range in size from 6 by 8 feet to 10 by 20 feet, and come in designs that resemble Cape Cod cottages and Victorian mansions. Parents can choose to customize their children's playhouses with a variety of options, such as heart-shaped windows, chimneys, porch swings, fully finished interiors, and playhouse furniture, including wooden sink and stove combinations and refrigerators.[64] ■

captive-product pricing

a technique that involves selling a product for a low price and charging a higher price for the accessories that accompany it.

CAPTIVE-PRODUCT PRICING Captive-product pricing is a pricing strategy in which the base product is not functional without the appropriate accessory. King Gillette, the founder of Gillette, taught the business world that the real money is not in selling the razor (the product) but in selling the blades (the accessory)! Manufacturers of electronic games also rely on captive-product pricing, earning lower margins on the game consoles and substantially higher margins on the games they sell.

by-product pricing

a technique in which a company uses the revenues from the sale of by-products to be more competitive in pricing the main product.

BY-PRODUCT PRICING By-product pricing is a technique in which the revenues from the sale of by-products allow a company to be more competitive in its pricing of the main product. For years, sawmills saw the bark from the trees they processed as a nuisance, something they had to discard. Now it is packaged and sold to gardeners who use the bark chips for ground cover. Zoos around the globe offer one of the most creative examples of by-product pricing, packaging once worthless droppings of exotic animals and marketing it as compost under the clever name "Zoo Doo."

SUGGESTED RETAIL PRICES Many manufacturers print suggested retail prices on their products or include them on invoices or in wholesale catalogs. Small business owners frequently follow these suggested retail prices because doing so eliminates the need to make a pricing decision. Nonetheless, following prices established by a distant manufacturer may create problems for a small company. For example, a men's clothing store may try to create a high-quality, exclusive image through a prestige pricing policy, but manufacturers may suggest prices that are incompatible with the company's image. Another danger of accepting the manufacturer's suggested price is that it does not take into consideration a small company's cost structure or competitive situation. In a U.S. Supreme Court case in 2007, *Leegin Creative Products vs. PSKS*, Leegin, the maker of Brighton brand belts, refused to sell its products to a small Texas boutique when the retailer discounted its prices on Brighton belts below the minimum prices established in an agreement the parties had signed. The court ruled in favor of Leegin, overturning a nearly 100-year-old ruling and allowing manufacturers to set and enforce minimum prices retailers can charge for the manufacturer's products as long as doing so does not reduce competition. Several states are considering passing new antitrust laws in an attempt to preempt the court's decision.[65]

FOLLOW-THE-LEADER PRICING Some small companies make no effort to be price leaders in their immediate geographic areas and simply follow the prices that their competitors establish. Entrepreneurs should monitor their competitors' pricing policies and individual prices by reviewing their advertisements or by hiring part-time or full-time comparison shoppers. However, some retailers use this information to establish me-too pricing policies, which eradicate any opportunity to use pricing to create a unique image for their businesses. Although many retailers must match competitors' prices on identical items, maintaining a follow-the-leader pricing policy may not be healthy for a small business because it robs the company of the opportunity to create a distinctive image in its customers' eyes.

The underlying forces that dictate how a business prices its goods or services vary across industries. The next three sections investigate pricing techniques used in retailing, manufacturing, and service businesses.

Pricing Strategies and Methods for Retailers

LO3A

Explain the pricing methods and strategies for retailers.

As customers have become more price conscious, retailers have changed their pricing strategies to emphasize value. This value–price relationship allows for a wide variety of highly creative pricing and marketing practices. As discussed previously, delivering high levels of recognized value in products and services is one key to retail customer loyalty.

Markup

The basic premise of a successful business operation is selling a good or service for more than it costs to produce or provide. The difference between the cost of a product or service and its selling price is called **markup** (or **markon**). A business's markup must be large enough to produce a reasonable profit. Markup can be expressed in dollars or as a percentage of either cost or selling price:

$$\text{Dollar markup} = \text{Retail price} - \text{Cost of the merchandise}$$

$$\text{Percentage (of retail price) markup} = \frac{\text{Dollar markup}}{\text{Retail price}}$$

$$\text{Percentage (of cost) markup} = \frac{\text{Dollar markup}}{\text{Cost of unit}}$$

markup (markon)
the difference between the cost of a product or service and its selling price.

For example, if a shirt costs $14, and a retailer plans to sell it for $30, the markup would be as follows:

$$\text{Dollar markup} = \$30 - \$14 = \$16$$

$$\text{Percentage (of retail price) markup} = \frac{\$16}{\$30} = 53.3\%$$

$$\text{Percentage (of cost) markup} = \frac{\$16}{\$14} = 114.3\%$$

The cost of merchandise used in computing markup includes not only the wholesale price of the merchandise but also any other costs (e.g., selling or transportation charges) that the retailer incurs and a profit minus any discounts (quantity, cash) that the wholesaler offers. Markups vary across industries, but in the designer clothing business, markups (of cost) of between 150 and 250 percent are common. However, some brands command much higher markups. For instance, a pair of jeans at Kohl's carries a markup of cost of about 100 percent, but True Religion's Phantom jeans generate an impressive 360 percent markup of cost.[66] The markup on a bottle of wine in a retail shop is 50 percent (of cost), but in New York City's fine-dining restaurants, the markup on the same bottles of wine is between 200 and 300 percent.[67] Movie theater popcorn usually carries an even higher markup (of cost) of 1,275 percent.[68] Boll & Branch, an online retailer of luxury sheets, uses a markup (of cost) of 60 percent on its sheets, far below the standard industry markup of 220 percent. Given that the company's cost to make and sell a set of king sheets is about $155, its below average markup produces a retail price of $250 versus $500 if it relied on the industry standard markup.[69] Table 11.1 shows a breakdown of the cost of the components and markup calculations for Samsung's Galaxy S6 Edge and Apple's iPhone 7.

Antonprado/123RF

TABLE 11.1 Costs and Markup Calculations for Samsung's Galaxy S6 Edge and Apple's iPhone 7

Although Apple commands a premium price (without a contract) for its iPhone 7, the company's manufacturing and assembly costs are less than those for Samsung's Galaxy S6 Edge, and that combination produces a very attractive markup for Apple. The following table provides a cost breakdown for each device's components and its markup.

Component	Samsung Galaxy S6 Edge	Apple iPhone 7 (32GB)
Display and touchscreen	$85.00	$43.00
Processors	$29.50	$26.90
Cameras	$21.50	$19.90
User interface and sensors	$14.75	$14.00
Memory	$52.50	$16.40
Modules and processors	$31.50	$43.20
Case and enclosure elements	$12.00	$18.20
Power management device	$5.40	$7.20
Lithium polymer battery	$3.50	$2.50
Mechanical/Electromechanical components	$23.00	$16.70
Box contents	$6.20	$11.80
Assembly and testing cost	$5.60	$5.00
Total Cost	**$290.45**	**$224.80**
Retail price (no contract)	$799.99	$849.99
$ Markup = Price – Cost	**$509.54**	**$625.19**
Percentage (of cost) markup =	**175.4%**	**278.1%**

Source: Based on "iPhone 7 Materials Cost Higher Than Previous Versions, HIS Markit Teardown Reveals," *Business Wire*, September 20, 2016, www.businesswire.com/news/home/20160920006782/en/iPhone-7-Materials-Costs-Higher-Previous-Versions; "Samsung Galaxy S6 Edge Pricier to Build, Cheaper to Buy Than Comparable iPhone 6 Plus, IHS Teardown Reveals," *IHS Markit*, April 14, 2015, http://news.ihsmarkit.com/press-release/technology/samsung-galaxy-s6-edge-pricier-build-cheaper-buy-comparable-apple-iphone-6-.

Once entrepreneurs create a financial plan, including sales estimates and anticipated expenses, they can compute their companies' initial markup. The initial markup is the *average* markup required on all merchandise to cover the cost of the items, all incidental expenses, and a reasonable profit:

$$\text{Initial markup} = \frac{\text{Operating expenses} + \text{Reductions} + \text{Profit}}{\text{Net sales} + \text{Reductions}}$$

where operating expenses include the cost of doing business, such as rent, utilities, and depreciation, and reductions include employee and customer discounts, markdowns, special sales, and the cost of stock-outs. Entrepreneurs must be aware of the impact that discounts have on their markup percentages. Corey Kaplan, owner of NYC Bagel Deli, a bagel shop with three locations in Chicago, recently sold 10,500 coupons on the discount coupon site Groupon that offered $10 worth of food for just $4, an amount that equals the company's cost of goods sold. The result: a markup of zero percent.[70]

Suppose that a small retailer forecasts sales of $980,000, operating expenses of $544,000, and $24,000 in reductions. If the retailer establishes a target profit of $58,000, the initial markup (of retail price) percentage is calculated as follows:

$$\text{Initial markup percentage} = \frac{544{,}000 + 24{,}000 + 58{,}000}{980{,}000 + 24{,}000} = 62\%$$

Any item in the store that carries a markup (of retail price) of at least 62 percent covers costs and meets the owner's profit objective. Any item that has a markup of less than 62 percent reduces the company's net income.

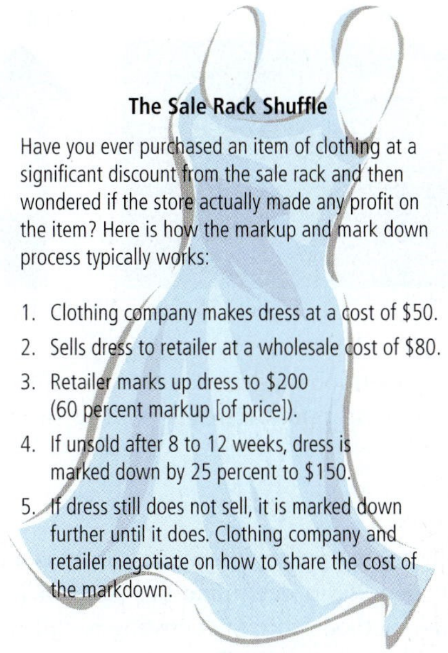

FIGURE 11.4

The Mathematics of Markups and Markdowns

The Sale Rack Shuffle

Have you ever purchased an item of clothing at a significant discount from the sale rack and then wondered if the store actually made any profit on the item? Here is how the markup and mark down process typically works:

1. Clothing company makes dress at a cost of $50.
2. Sells dress to retailer at a wholesale cost of $80.
3. Retailer marks up dress to $200 (60 percent markup [of price]).
4. If unsold after 8 to 12 weeks, dress is marked down by 25 percent to $150.
5. If dress still does not sell, it is marked down further until it does. Clothing company and retailer negotiate on how to share the cost of the markdown.

Once an entrepreneur determines the initial percentage markup, he or she can compute the appropriate retail price using the following formula:

$$\text{Retail Price} = \frac{\text{Dollar cost}}{(1 - \text{Percentage of retail price markup})}$$

For instance, applying the 62 percent markup to an item that cost the retailer $17.00 gives the following result:

$$\text{Retail price} = \frac{\$17.00}{(1 - .62)} = \$44.74$$

The owner establishes a retail price of $44.74 for this item using a 62 percent (of retail price) markup.

Finally, retailers must verify that the retail price they have calculated is consistent with their companies' image. Will it cover costs and generate the desired profit? Is the final price in line with the company's strategy? Is it within an acceptable price range? How does it compare to the prices charged by competitors? And, perhaps most important, are customers willing and able to pay this price? Modern point-of-sale (POS) terminals provide entrepreneurs with valuable information, including sales reports and analytics on real-time sales, inventory levels, and profit margins, concerning the impact of their pricing decisions. Figure 11.4 explains the mathematics of markups—and markdowns—at the retail level.

Pricing Concepts for Manufacturers

LO3B

Explain the pricing strategies and methods for manufacturers.

For manufacturers, the pricing decision requires the support of accurate, timely accounting records. The most commonly used pricing technique for manufacturers is **cost-plus pricing**. Using this method, a manufacturer establishes a price that is composed of direct materials, direct labor, factory overhead, selling and administrative costs, plus a desired profit margin. Figure 11.5 illustrates the cost-plus pricing components.

The main advantage of the cost-plus pricing method is its simplicity. Given the proper cost accounting data, computing a product's final selling price is relatively easy. In addition, because they add a profit onto the top of their companies' costs, manufacturers are likely to achieve their desired profit margins. This process, however, does not encourage the manufacturers to use their resources efficiently. Even if the company fails to employ its resources in the most effective manner, it still earns a profit, and thus there is no motivation to conserve resources in the manufacturing process. Finally, because manufacturers' cost structures vary so greatly, cost-plus

cost-plus pricing
a pricing technique in which a manufacturer establishes a price that covers the cost of direct materials, direct labor, factory overhead, selling and administrative costs, and a desired profit margin.

FIGURE 11.5

Cost-Plus Pricing Components

pricing fails to consider the competition (and market forces) sufficiently. Despite its drawbacks, the cost-plus method of establishing prices remains popular in industries such as restaurants, construction, and printing.

Direct Costing and Pricing

One requisite for a successful pricing policy in manufacturing is a reliable cost accounting system that can generate timely reports to determine the costs of processing raw materials into finished goods. The traditional method of product costing is called **absorption costing** because all manufacturing and overhead costs are absorbed into a finished product's total cost. Absorption costing includes direct materials, direct labor, plus a portion of fixed and variable factory overhead in each unit manufactured. Full absorption financial statements are used in published annual reports and in tax reports and are very useful in performing financial analysis. However, full absorption statements are of little help to manufacturers when determining prices or the impact of price changes.

A more useful technique for managerial decision making is **variable (direct) costing**, in which the cost of the products manufactured includes only those costs that vary directly with the quantity produced. In other words, variable costing encompasses direct materials, direct labor, and factory overhead costs that vary with the level of the company's output of finished goods. Factory overhead costs that are fixed (rent, depreciation, and insurance) are *not* included in the costs of finished items. Instead, they are considered to be expenses of the period.

A manufacturer's goal when establishing prices is to discover the combination of selling price and sales volume that covers the variable costs of producing a product and contributes toward covering fixed costs and earning a profit. Full-absorption costing clouds the true relationships among price, volume, and costs by including fixed expenses in unit cost. Direct costing, however, yields a constant unit cost for the product no matter what volume of production. The result is a clearer picture of the relationship among price, volume, and costs.

The starting point for establishing product prices is the direct cost income statement. As Table 11.2 shows, the direct cost statement yields the same net income as does the full-absorption income statement. The only difference between the two statements is the format. The full-absorption statement allocates costs such as advertising, rent, and utilities according to the activity that caused them, but the direct cost income statement separates expenses into their fixed and variable components. Fixed expenses remain constant regardless of the production level, but variable expenses fluctuate according to production volume.

When variable costs are subtracted from total revenues, the result is the manufacturer's **contribution margin**—the amount remaining that contributes to covering fixed expenses and earning a profit. Expressing this contribution margin as a percentage of total revenue yields the company's contribution percentage. Computing the contribution percentage is a critical step in establishing prices through the direct costing method. This manufacturer's contribution margin percentage is 36.5 percent, which is calculated as follows:

$$\text{Contribution percentage} = 1 - \frac{\text{Variable expenses}}{\text{Revenues}}$$

$$= 1 - \frac{\$502,000}{\$790,000} = 36.5\%$$

absorption costing
the traditional method of product costing, in which all manufacturing and overhead costs are absorbed into the product's total cost.

variable (direct) costing
a method of product costing that includes in the product's cost only those costs that vary directly with the quantity produced.

contribution margin
after variable expenses are paid, the amount left over out of a dollar of sales that contributes to covering fixed expenses and earning a profit.

TABLE 11.2 Full-Absorption Versus Direct-Cost Income Statement

Full-Absorption Income Statement

Sales revenue		$790,000
Cost of goods sold		
Materials	250,500	
Direct labor	190,200	
Factory overhead	120,200	560,900
Gross profit		$229,100
Operating expenses		
General and administrative	66,100	
Selling	112,000	
Other	11,000	
Total operating expenses		189,100
Net income (before taxes)		$ 40,000

Direct-Cost Income Statement

Sales revenue (100%)		$790,000
Variable costs		
Materials	250,500	
Direct labor	190,200	
Variable factory overhead	13,200	
Variable selling expenses	48,100	
Total variable costs (63.5%)		502,000
Contribution margin (36.5%)		288,000
Fixed costs		
Fixed factory overhead	107,000	
Fixed selling expenses	63,900	
General and administrative	66,100	
Other fixed expenses	11,000	
Total fixed expenses (31.4%)		248,000
Net income (before taxes) (5.1%)		$ 40,000

Computing the Break-even Selling Price

The manufacturer's contribution percentage tells what portion of total revenues remains after covering variable costs to contribute toward meeting fixed expenses and earning a profit. This manufacturer's contribution percentage is 36.5 percent, which means that variable costs absorb 63.5 percent of total revenue. In other words, variable costs make up 63.5 percent ($1.00 - 0.365 = 0.635$) of the product's selling price. Suppose that this manufacturer's variable costs per unit include the following:

Material	$2.08/unit
Direct labor	$4.12/unit
Variable factory overhead	$0.78/unit
Total variable cost	$6.98/unit

The minimum price at which the manufacturer would sell the item is $6.98. Any price below this would not cover variable costs. To compute the breakeven selling price for this product, we find the selling price using the following equation:

$$\text{Break-even selling price} = \frac{\text{Profit} + (\text{Variable cost per unit} \times \text{Quantity produced}) + \text{Total fixed cost}}{\text{Quantity produced}}$$

To break even, the manufacturer assumes $0 profit. Suppose that plans are to produce 50,000 units of the product and that fixed costs will be $110,000. The breakeven selling price is as follows:

$$\text{Break-even selling price} = \frac{\$0 + (\$6.98 \times 50,000 \text{ units}) + \$110,000}{50,000 \text{ units}}$$

$$= \frac{\$459,000}{50,000 \text{ units}}$$

$$= \$9.18/\text{unit}$$

Thus, $2.20 ($9.18/unit – $6.98/unit) of the $9.18 breakeven price contributes to meeting fixed production costs. But suppose the manufacturer wants to earn a $50,000 profit. Then the selling price is calculated as follows:

$$\text{Selling price} = \frac{\$50,000 + (\$6.98/\text{unit} \times 50,000 \text{ units}) + \$110,000}{50,000 \text{ units}}$$

$$= \frac{\$509,000}{50,000 \text{ units}}$$

$$= \$10.18/\text{unit}$$

Now the manufacturer must decide whether customers will purchase 50,000 units at $10.18. If not, he or she must decide either to produce a different, more profitable product or to lower the selling price by lowering either its cost or its profit target. Any price above $9.18 will generate some profit, although less than that desired. In the short run, the manufacturer could sell the product for less than $9.18 if competitive factors dictate but *not* below $6.98 because a price below $6.98 would not cover the variable cost of production.

Because the manufacturer's capacity in the short run is fixed, pricing decisions should be aimed at employing these resources most efficiently. The fixed costs of operating the plant cannot be avoided, and the variable costs can be eliminated only if the firm ceases offering the product. Therefore, the selling price must be at least equal to the variable costs (per unit) of making the product. Any price above this amount contributes to covering fixed costs and providing a reasonable profit.

Of course, over the long run, a manufacturer cannot sell below total costs and continue to survive. The final selling price must cover total product cost—both fixed and variable—and generate a reasonable profit.

Pricing Strategies and Methods for Service Firms

LO3C

Explain the pricing strategies and methods for service firms.

Service businesses must establish their prices on the basis of the materials used to provide the service, the labor employed, an allowance for overhead, and profit. As in a manufacturing operation, a service business must have a reliable, accurate accounting system to keep a tally of the total costs of providing the service. Most service firms base their prices on an hourly rate, usually the actual number of hours required to perform the service. Some companies, however, base their fees on a standard number of hours, determined by the average number of hours needed to perform the service. To establish a reasonable, profitable price for service, small business owners must know the cost of materials, direct labor, and overhead for each unit of service they provide. Using these basic cost data and a desired profit margin, an owner of a small service firm can determine the appropriate price for the service.

Consider a simple example for pricing a common service—computer repair. Ned's Computer Repair Shop uses the direct costing method to prepare an income statement for exercising managerial control (see Table 11.3).

Ned estimates that he and his employees spent about 9,250 hours in the actual production of computer repair service. Therefore, total cost per productive hour for Ned's Computer Repair Shop comes to the following:

pocket price

the price a company receives for a product or service after deducting all discounts and purchase incentives.

$$\frac{\$104,000 + \$68,000}{9,250 \text{ hours}} = \$18.59/\text{hour}$$

Calculate Your Company's Pocket Price Band

Pricing decisions have a significant influence on a company's ability to generate a profit. Research by consulting firm Deloitte shows that pricing has four times the impact on profitability as other improvements, such as reducing costs. When entrepreneurs make pricing decisions, they usually look at the retail price or the invoice price they charge. Doing so, however, may be misleading if the company offers significant "off-invoice" discounts, such as cash discounts for paying early, quantity discounts for large purchases, special promotional discounts, and others. These invoice leakages mean that a business is getting less—sometimes far less—than the retail or invoice price listed. In some cases, a company's **pocket price**, the price it receives for a product or a service after deducting all discounts and purchase incentives, is far below the listed retail or invoice price. The impact of these discounts can be significant. Research by the consulting firm McKinsey and Company shows that a decrease of 1 percent in a typical company's average prices reduces its operating profits by 8 percent if all other factors remain constant.

How are discounts affecting your business? To find out, you must estimate your company's pocket price waterfall and its pocket price band. The pocket price waterfall starts with a company's invoice or retail price on the far left of the diagram and then shows how much every discount or incentive the company offers its customers reduces that price. In the example in Figure 1, this small manufacturer offers a cash discount for early payment that shaves 2.0 percent off of the retail price, a 3.5 percent discount for companies whose purchases exceed a particular volume, a cooperative advertising program (in which it splits the cost of advertising its products with retailers) that amounts to 4.4 percent, and periodic promotional discounts to move products that average 10.8 percent. Other discounts the company offered customers further reduced its pocket price. In the end, the company's average pocket price is 77.2 percent of the listed invoice price (see Figure 1).

FIGURE 2

Pocket Price Band

Not every customer qualifies for every discount, however. The type and the amount of the discount vary from one customer to another; the pocket prices they pay can vary a good deal. Therefore, it is important to estimate the width of the company's pocket price band, which shows the percentage of sales that each pocket price (shown as a percentage of the listed invoice or retail price) accounts for (see Figure 2). In this example, pocket prices that are 90 percent or more of the company's invoice price account for just 28.3 percent of its total revenue. Conversely, pocket prices that are 80 percent or less of its invoice price make up 46.2 percent of its total revenue. The final step in the process is to identify the individual customers that make up each segment of the company's pocket price band. When one manufacturer analyzed its pocket price band, managers discovered that sales to 20 percent of its customers had slipped below its breakeven point, causing the company to lose money on sales to those customers. To restore profitability, managers raised prices selectively and lowered their costs by reducing the frequency of deliveries and encouraging customers to place orders online.

A wide pocket price band is not necessarily bad. It simply shows that some customers generate much higher pocket prices than others. When a band is wide, small changes in its shape can produce big results for a company. If an entrepreneur can increase sales at the upper end of the band while reducing or even dropping altogether those at the lower end of the band, the company's revenues and profits will climb. If a company's price band is narrow, an entrepreneur has less room to maneuver prices, changing the shape of the band is more difficult, and any changes the entrepreneur can make tend to have less impact on the company's sales and revenues.

When one lighting company calculated its pocket price band, managers were surprised at its width. Once

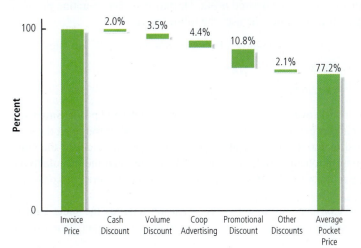

FIGURE 1

Pocket Price Waterfall

(continued)

Hands On ... How To (continued)

managers realized how big a dent discounts were putting in its revenues and profits, they worked with the sales force to realign the company's discount structure. Some of the company's smallest accounts had been getting the largest discounts despite their small volume of purchases. Managers also focused on boosting sales to those accounts that were producing the highest pocket prices. These changes resulted in the company's average pocket price rising by 3.8 percent and its profits climbing 51 percent!

Discounts tend to work their way into a company's pricing structure gradually over time, often one transaction at a time, especially if an entrepreneur gives sales representatives latitude to negotiate prices with customers. Few companies make the effort to track these discounts and, as a result, do not realize the impact that discounts have on their profitability. By monitoring their companies' pocket price waterfall and the resulting pocket price band, entrepreneurs can improve significantly the revenue and the profits they generate.

Sources: Adapted from "Pricing for Profitability: What's in Your Pocket?" *CFO Insights,* Deloitte, 2013, pp. 1–5; Michael V. Marn, Eric V. Roegner, and Craig C. Zawada, "The Power of Pricing," *McKinsey Quarterly,* no. 1, 2003, www .mckinseyquarterly.com; and Cheri N. Eyink, Michael V. Marn, and Stephen C. Moss, "Pricing in an Inflationary Downturn," *McKinsey Quarterly,* September 2008, www.mckinseyquarterly.com/Pricing_in_a_downturn_2189.

TABLE 11.3 Direct-Cost Income Statement, Ned's Computer Repair Shop

Sales revenue		$199,000
Variable expenses		
Labor	52,000	
Materials	40,500	
Variable factory overhead	11,500	
Total variable expenses		104,000
Fixed expenses		
Rent	2,500	
Salaries	38,500	
Fixed overhead	27,000	
Total fixed expenses		68,000
Net income		$ 27,000

Now Ned must add in an amount for his desired profit. He expects a net operating profit of 18 percent on sales. To compute the final price, he uses the following equation:

$$\text{Price Total cost per hour} = \text{productive hour} \div (1 - \text{net profit target as \% of sales})$$

$$= \$18.59 \div (1 - .18)$$

$$= \$22.68/\text{hour}$$

A price of $22.68 per hour will cover Ned's costs and generate the desired profit. Smart service shop owners compute their cost per production hour at regular intervals throughout the year. Rapidly rising labor costs and material prices dictate that an entrepreneur calculate the company's price per hour even more frequently. As in the case of the retailer and the manufacturer, Ned must evaluate the pricing policies of competitors and decide whether his price is consistent with his company's image.

Of course, the price of $22.68 per hour assumes that each job requires the same amount of materials. If this is not a valid assumption, Ned must recalculate the price per hour *without* including the cost of materials:

$$\text{Cost per productive hour} = \frac{\$172,000 - \$40,500}{9,250 \text{ hours}}$$

$$= \$14.22/\text{hour}$$

Adding in the desired 18 percent net operating profit on sales gives the following:

$$\text{Price per hour} = \$14.22/\text{hour} \div (1.00 - 0.18)$$

$$= \$17.34/\text{hour}$$

Under these conditions, Ned would charge $17.34 per hour plus the actual cost of materials used and any markup on the cost of material. A repair job that takes four hours to complete would have the following price, assuming a 60 percent markup (of cost) on materials:

Cost of service (4 hours × $17.34/hour)	$ 69.36
Cost of materials	$ 41.00
Markup on materials (60%)	$ 24.60
Total price	$134.96

Because services are intangible, their pricing offers more flexibility than do tangible products. One danger that entrepreneurs face is pricing their services too low because prospective customers' perceptions of a service are heavily influenced by its price. In other words, establishing a low price for a service may actually harm a service company's sales. For service companies in particular, the right price reflects both the company's cost of providing the service and the customers' perceived value of the service.

The Impact of Credit and Debit Cards and Mobile Wallets on Pricing

LO4

Explain the impact of credit and debit cards and mobile wallets on pricing.

Consumers crave convenience when they shop, and one of the most common conveniences they demand is the ability to purchase goods and services using credit and debit cards or mobile wallets. Small businesses that limit sales to cash-only transactions lose sales to competitors that accept debit and credit cards and mobile wallet payments. A study by Intuit reports that 83 percent of small businesses that had not accepted credit cards but began accepting them saw their sales increase, and 52 percent of the companies reported increases of at least $1,000 per month.[71] However, companies that accept credit and debit cards and mobile payments incur additional expenses for offering this convenience to customers. For most small businesses, however, the benefits outweigh the costs. Customers expect businesses to accept multiple payment methods, including credit and debit cards, and mobile payments. In addition, some small companies offer their customers installment credit and trade credit.

Credit Cards

Consumers in the United States hold nearly 1.9 billion credit cards; in fact, the average credit card holder in the United States has 4 cards.[72] Although customers prefer to use credit cards to make purchases more than any other form of payment (see Figure 11.6), they prefer to use debit cards and cash for smaller daily purchases.[73] Shoppers use credit cards to make 34 billion transactions a year that account for more than $3.16 trillion worth of goods and services annually—more than $100,000 in credit card sales per second.[74] The message is clear: Customers expect to make purchases with credit cards, and small companies that fail to accept credit cards run the risk of losing sales to competitors who do. The average credit card transaction is $93.50.[75]

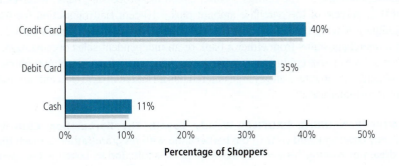

Percentage of Shoppers

FIGURE 11.6

Top Three Payment Preferences Among Shoppers

Source: Based on 2016 U.S. Consumer Payment Study, Total Systems Services, 2016, p. 12.

FIGURE 11.7

How a Typical Credit Card Transaction Works

Sources: Based on "Credit Card Processing," Card Fellow, 2013, www.cardfellow.com/content/credit-card-processing-guide.php#MoneyGo; "Credit Cards," U.S. Government Accounting Office, September 2006, pp. 73–74.

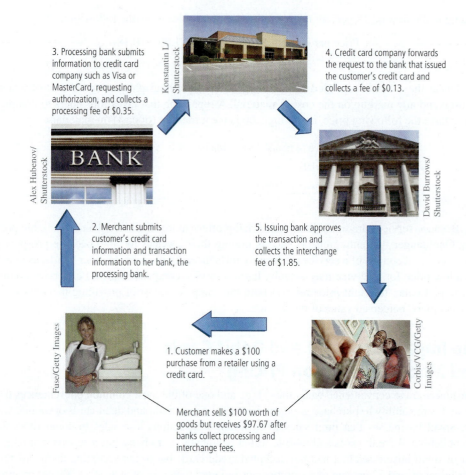

3. Processing bank submits information to credit card company such as Visa or MasterCard, requesting authorization, and collects a processing fee of $0.35.

4. Credit card company forwards the request to the bank that issued the customer's credit card and collects a fee of $0.13.

2. Merchant submits customer's credit card information and transaction information to her bank, the processing bank.

5. Issuing bank approves the transaction and collects the interchange fee of $1.85.

1. Customer makes a $100 purchase from a retailer using a credit card.

Merchant sells $100 worth of goods but receives $97.67 after banks collect processing and interchange fees.

Studies show that customers who use credit cards spend more (typically 12 to 18 percent more) than those who pay with cash.[76] In addition, surveys show that customers rate businesses offering credit options higher on key performance measures such as reputation, reliability, and service.[77] In short, accepting credit cards broadens a small company's customer base and closes sales that it would normally lose if customers had to pay in cash.

Companies that accept credit cards incur additional expenses for offering this convenience, however. Businesses must pay to use the system, typically 1 to 6 percent of the total credit card charge (the average is a little more than 2 percent), which they must factor into the prices of their products or services. They also pay a transaction fee of 5 to 25 cents per charge. (The average fee is 10 cents per transaction.) Given customer expectations, most small businesses cannot afford to drop major cards, even when credit card companies raise the fees merchants must pay. Fees operate on a multistep process (see Figure 11.7). On a typical $100 credit card purchase that a customer makes, the bank that issued the customer's card receives $1.85. This amount

interchange fee
the fee banks collect from retailers whenever customers use a credit or debit card to pay for a purchase.

includes a 1.75 percent processing fee called the **interchange fee**, the fee that banks collect from retailers whenever customers use a credit or a debit card to pay for a purchase, and a 10-cent flat transaction fee. The credit card company takes 0.13 percent (or 13 cents in this example) of the transaction amount. The retailer's bank, called the processing bank, receives a processing fee of 0.25 percent of the purchase amount plus a 10-cent flat transaction fee (or 35 cents in this example), leaving the retailer with $97.67. Before it can accept credit cards, a business must obtain merchant status from either a bank or an independent sales organization. Square, a company that issues a free credit card reader to merchants that attaches to smart phones and tablets, consolidates all three fees and charges merchants a flat fee of 2.75 percent, no matter which credit card a customer uses.

ENTREPRENEURIAL PROFILE: Woody Lovell: The Barbershop Club As a child, Woody Lovell enjoyed visits to the barber shop with his grandfather so much that he realized the dream of owning his own barbershop as an adult. Today, Lovell is the owner of The

Barbershop Club in Los Angeles, where thousands of his loyal customers gather in a relaxed, old-fashioned barbershop atmosphere for superior customer service and the best shaves and haircuts money can buy. Lovell was an early adopter of Square, the credit and debit card reading device used by so many small businesses. In addition to making customers' payments much easier and more convenient (few of Lovell's customers use cash), Square's appointment app saved the Barbershop Club $60,000 in just one year and, coupled with the customer analytics that Square provides, enabled Lovell to double his company's sales.[78] ■

Matthew Simmons/Getty Images

Credit card processing fees, commonly known as "swipe fees," cost merchants more than $40 billion per year, and small businesses typically pay higher credit card processing fees than their larger counterparts.[79] These fees, especially on small purchases, can wipe out any profit the company might have earned. To minimize the fees associated with credit card transactions, some entrepreneurs offer customers incentives to pay with cash or debit cards (on which swipe fees are lower) or establish minimum purchase amounts for credit cards.

Another challenge to merchants, particularly online sellers, is credit card fraud. In the United States, the fraud rate for all credit card transactions is 13 cents per $100, which is much higher than the average of 4 cents per $100 for the rest of the world.[80] About 1.13 percent of *online* credit card transactions are fraudulent, which cost merchants $8.5 billion a year![81] Credit card issuers assume the burden for 62 percent of that loss, and the remaining 38 percent falls on merchants.[82] However, a recent change in merchant liability policies among credit card companies pushes fraud liability onto merchants who have not upgraded to more secure point-of-sale terminals that process chip cards. These more secure EMV terminals that read the chips in credit cards cost retailers between $150 and $600 each.[83] By upgrading to the EMV terminals, however, merchants can avoid liability for fraudulent charges. Unfortunately, only 43 percent of small businesses that accept credit cards have installed chip-enabled payment terminals.[84]

E-COMMERCE AND CREDIT CARDS When it comes to online business transactions, the most common method of payment is the credit card. Internet merchants are constantly challenged by the need to provide secure methods for safe, secure online transactions. As you learned in Chapter 10, many shoppers are suspicious of online transactions for reasons of security and privacy. Therefore, online merchants must ensure their customers' privacy and the security of their credit card transactions by using encryption software.

Because online merchants lack the face-to-face contact with their customers, they face special challenges to avoid credit card fraud. Identity and credit card theft result in customers denying the authenticity of certain purchases and disputing the charges that appear on their bills. Unless merchants are vigilant, they will end up shouldering the burden for these charge-backs. Because small companies are less likely than large businesses to use high-tech online fraud detection tools, they are more likely to be victims of e-commerce fraud. The following steps can help online merchants reduce the probability that they will become victims of credit card fraud:

- Use an address verification system to compare every customer's billing information on the order form with the billing information in the bank or credit card company's records.

- Require customers to provide the CVV2 number from the back of the credit card. Although crooks can get access to this number, it can help screen out some fraudulent orders.

- Check customers' Internet Protocol (IP) addresses. If an order contains a billing address in California but the IP address from which the order is placed is in China, chances are that the order is fraudulent.

- Pay close attention to international orders. The rate of fraud for international orders is 1.5 times that for domestic orders.[85]

- Monitor activity on the Web site with the help of a Web analytics software package. There are many packages available, and analyzing log files helps online entrepreneurs pinpoint the sources of fraud.

- Verify large orders. Large orders are a cause for celebration—but only if they are legitimate. Check the authenticity of large orders, especially if the order is from a first-time customer.

- Post notices on the Web site that your company uses antifraud technology to screen orders. These notices make legitimate customers feel more confident about placing their orders and may deter crooks trying to commit fraud from running their scams.

- Contact the credit card company or the bank that issued the card. If you suspect that an order may be fraudulent, contact the company *before* processing it. Taking this step could save a company thousands of dollars in losses.[86]

Taking these precautions can save a small company thousands of dollars in losses due to fraud. E-commerce companies reject about 2.8 percent of customer orders because of suspicion of fraud.[87]

DEBIT CARDS Consumers in the United States carry more than 5.1 billion debit cards that act as electronic checks, automatically deducting the purchase amount immediately from a customer's checking account.[88] Shoppers conduct nearly 70 billion debit card transactions, totaling $2.6 trillion, each year. The average debit card transaction is $36.83.[89] The equipment that allows businesses to accept debit cards is easy to install and to set up, and the cost to the company is negligible. The payoff can be big, however, in the form of increased sales, improved cash flow, and decreased losses from bad checks. In addition, interchange fees on debit cards are lower than those on credit cards. Credit and debit cards account for 72 percent of all consumer and business payments, and that percentage continues to grow.[90] Small businesses that do not accept credit and debit cards operate at a significant disadvantage compared to their rivals that do.

mobile (electronic) wallets

applications that link a smart phone, watch, or tablet to a credit or debit card, transforming the device into a digital wallet.

MOBILE (ELECTRONIC) WALLETS Modern mobile technology allows shoppers to carry **mobile (electronic) wallets** on their smart phones, watches, or tablets. Mobile payments are growing rapidly, particularly among members of the Millennial generation, 44 percent of whom prefer to pay for goods and services using their phones rather than cash.[91] Shoppers download software that links their mobile devices to a credit or debit card and then wave the devices over a near-field communication (NFC) or similar reader to complete a purchase, verifying it with a fingerprint or PIN. Today, shoppers make more than 50 million mobile purchases valued at $62 billion per year, more than five times the $11.6 billion in 2012.[92] Google offered the first mobile payment system, Google Wallet (now Android Pay), but many companies, including Apple, Samsung, PayPal, Wal-Mart, Softcard, and Square, offer easy-to-use mobile payment platforms that provide superior payment security. To accept payments from customers' mobile wallets, some applications require special NFC hardware (which typically costs between $100 and $200), but others use stores' existing checkout equipment that is updated with software that business owners usually download for free.[93] The technology not only speeds up the checkout process but also allows merchants to recognize customers when they walk into a store; send personalized coupons, incentives, and rewards to them; and generate useful reports, such as how often a shopper buys a particular item or when he or she last shopped. Accepting payments from electronic wallets may help small businesses retain customers; according to one study, 25 percent of shoppers say they are willing to switch to businesses that accept mobile payments.[94] Currito, a chain of 20 Mexican restaurants based in Cincinnati, Ohio, ties its loyalty program directly to customers' mobile wallets. Accepting mobile payments not only allows Currito's customers to make their purchases quickly and easily but the chain also has seen its sales increase, and the money typically shows up in the restaurants' bank accounts the next day.[95]

INSTALLMENT CREDIT Small companies that sell big-ticket consumer durables—such as major appliances, cars, and boats—frequently rely on installment credit to support their sales efforts. Because very few customers can purchase such items in a single lump-sum payment, small businesses finance them over an extended time. The time horizon may range from just a few months up to 30 or more years. Most companies require customers to make an initial down payment for the merchandise and then finance the balance for the life of the loan. The customer repays the loan principal plus interest on the loan. One advantage of installment loans for a small business is that the owner retains a security interest as collateral on the loan. If a customer defaults on the loan, the owner still holds the title to the merchandise. Because installment credit absorbs a small company's cash, many companies rely on financial institutions, such as banks and credit unions, to provide installment credit. When a company has the financial strength to "carry its own paper," the interest income from the installment loan contract often yields more than the initial profit on the sale of the product. For some businesses, such as furniture stores and used car dealerships, this traditionally has been a major source of income.

TRADE CREDIT Companies that sell small-ticket items frequently offer their customers trade credit—that is, they create customer charge accounts. The typical small business bills its credit customers each month. To speed collections, some offer cash discounts if customers pay their balances early; others impose penalties on late payers. Before deciding to use trade credit as a competitive weapon, business owners must make sure that their companies' cash position is strong enough to support the additional pressure credit sales create.

LAYAWAY Although technically not a form of credit, layaway plans, like trade credit, enable customers to purchase goods over time. In the typical layaway plan, a customer selects an item, pays a deposit on it, and makes regular payments on the item until it is paid in full. Unlike trade credit, the retailer keeps the item until the customer has finished paying. Most stores establish minimum payments and maximum payoff dates, and some charge a service fee. Created during the Great Depression as a way to help shoppers purchase goods, layaway has become popular once again, especially around the holiday season, as slow economic growth has kept wages from rising, posing financial challenges for shoppers.

ENTREPRENEURIAL PROFILE: Ama Marfo, Craig Henry, and Emmanuel Buah: Airfordable Most layaway programs focus on the retail sector, but Ama Marfo applied the layaway concept to air travel when she and two cofounders launched Airfordable, a tech start-up based in Chicago that allows customers to purchase airline tickets in advance and pay for them over time. While Marfo was a student at Drexel University, she had to forgo trips home during most school breaks because she could not afford the $2,000 airfare. After graduating, she decided to launch a business that would make air travel accessible to people with modest budgets. After customers submit their itineraries, Airfordable sets up a customized layaway plan that allows them to stretch out the payments on their travel. More than 27,000 people, many of them college students, are using Airfordable's layaway service.[96] ∎

Conclusion

Setting prices is a blend of both art and science. The prices that entrepreneurs set for the products and services they sell are key components in the sales revenue their businesses generate, the profits they earn, and the image they create for their companies.

MyLab Entrepreneurship

If your instructor is using MyLab Entrepreneurship, go to **www.pearson.com/mylab/ entrepreneurship** to complete the problems marked with this icon ⭐.

Chapter Summary by Learning Objective

1. Discuss the relationships among pricing, image, competition, and value.

- Pricing decisions cut across every aspect of a small company, influencing everything from its marketing and sales efforts to its operations and strategy. A company's pricing strategy is a major determinant of its image in the marketplace, is influenced by the pricing strategies of its competitors, and is an important element in the value that customers perceive its products or services provide.

- Ultimately, the "right" price for a product or service depends on one factor: the value it provides for a

customer. For most shoppers, three reference points define a fair price: the price they have paid for the product or service in the past, the prices competitors charge for the same or similar product or service, and the costs a company incurs to provide the product or service.

2. Describe effective pricing techniques for introducing new products or services and for existing ones.

- Pricing a new product is often difficult for business owners, but it should accomplish three objectives: getting the product accepted, maintaining market share as the competition grows, and earning a profit. Generally, three major pricing strategies are used to introduce new products into the market: penetration, skimming, and life cycle.

- Pricing techniques for existing products and services include odd pricing, price lining, dynamic pricing, leader pricing, geographic pricing, discounts, multiple unit pricing, bundling, optional product pricing, captive product pricing, by-product pricing, suggested retail pricing, and follow-the-leader pricing.

3. Explain the pricing methods and strategies for retailers, manufacturers, and service firms.

- Pricing for the retailer means pricing to move merchandise. Markup is the difference between the cost of a product or service and its selling price. Most retailers compute their markup as a percentage of retail price.

- A manufacturer's pricing decision depends on the support of accurate cost accounting records. The most common technique is cost-plus pricing, in which the manufacturer charges a price that covers the cost of producing a product plus a reasonable profit. Every manufacturer should calculate a product's breakeven price, the price that produces neither a profit nor a loss.

- Service firms often suffer from the effects of vague, unfounded pricing procedures and frequently charge the going rate without any idea of their costs. A service firm must set a price on the basis of the cost of materials used, labor involved, overhead, and a profit. The proper price reflects the total cost of providing a unit of service.

4. Describe the impact of credit and debit cards and mobile wallets on pricing.

- Offering consumer credit enhances a small company's reputation and increases the probability, speed, and magnitude of customers' purchases. Small firms offer three types of consumer credit: credit cards, installment credit, and trade credit (charge accounts).

MyLab Entrepreneurship

If your instructor is using MyLab Entrepreneurship, go to **www.pearson.com/mylab/entrepreneurship** for Auto-graded writing questions as well as the following Assisted-graded writing questions:

1. How does pricing affect a small firm's image?
2. Explain the technique for a small service firm setting an hourly price.

Discussion Questions

11-1. What competitive factors must the small firm consider when establishing prices?

⭐ 11-2. Describe the strategies a small business could use in setting the price of a new product.

⭐ 11-3. What objectives should a company's pricing strategy for a new product seek to achieve?

11-4. Define the following pricing techniques: odd pricing, price lining, leader pricing, geographical pricing, and discounts.

11-5. Why do many small businesses use the manufacturer's suggested retail price?

11-6. What are the disadvantages of using the manufacturer's suggested retail price?

11-7. What is a markup?

11-8. How is the markup for a product calculated?

11-9. What is cost-plus pricing?

11-10. Why do so many manufacturers use cost-plus pricing?

11-11. What are the disadvantages of using cost-plus pricing?

11-12. Explain the difference between full-absorption costing and direct costing.

11-13. How does absorption costing help a manufacturer determine a reasonable price?

11-14. What benefits does a small business get by offering customers credit?

11-15. What costs does a business incur by selling on credit?

Beyond the Classroom . . .

11-16. Apple Inc. dominates the market for tablets with its line of iPads, which currently includes the classic iPad, the iPad Mini, and the iPad Air. Because the company constantly introduces new models and features, it also adjusts prices on these popular devices. Use the Web to research the history of the iPad and write a brief summary of Apple's pricing strategy on its tablet. Which products compete with the iPad?

11-17. How do the prices of similar models compare to the iPad?

11-18. Is Apple able to command a premium for its brand?

11-19. If so, what factors allow the company to do so?

11-20. Interview a successful small retailer and ask the following questions: Does he or she seek a specific image through his or her prices?

11-21. What role do competitors play in the business owner's pricing?

11-22. Does the retailer use specific pricing techniques, such as odd pricing, price lining, leader pricing, and geographic pricing?

11-23. How are discounts calculated?

11-24. What markup percentage does the firm use?

11-25. How are prices derived?

11-26. What are his or her cost structures?

11-27. Select an industry that has several competing small firms in your area. Contact these firms and compare their approaches to determining prices. Do prices on identical or similar items differ?

11-28. Why are the companies' prices on identical or similar items different?

Endnotes

[1] Richard Hayes and Ranjit Singh, "CFO Insights: Pricing for Profitability: What's in Your Pocket?" *Deloitte*, 2013, p. 3.

[2] "What's Mobile's Influence In-Store?" Marketing Charts, March 1, 2016, www.marketingcharts.com/online/whats-mobiles-influence-in-store-65972/.

[3] *Second Annual Reality of Retail Report*, InReality, 2016, p. 9.

[4] *Supply on Demand*, Economist Intelligence Unit, 2013, p. 3.

[5] Sara Germano and Khadeeja Safdar, "Setting Prices Stumps Retailers," *Wall Street Journal*, December 28, 2016, pp. B1–B2.

[6] Howard Scott, "The Tricky Art of Raising Prices," *Nation's Business*, February 1999, p. 32.

[7] "Turn Up for What," *Forbes Life*, Holiday 2015, p. 69; "Spiral Groove SG1.2," Spiral Groove, www.spiral-groove.com.

[8] "The $8,000 Umbrella," *Wall Street Journal Magazine*, November 2, 2015, p. 56.

[9] "Price for a Hot Dog in Major League Baseball by Team in 2016," *Statista*, January 10, 2017, www.statista.com/statistics/202743/hot-dog-prices-in-major-league-baseball-by-team/; Kiri Tannenbaum, "Home-Run Hot Dogs: The Best Dogs from America's Baseball Stadiums," *Delish*, February 3, 2016, www.delish.com/food/g1998/baseball-stadium-hot-dogs/?slide=21; Andrew Joseph, "The Arizona Diamondbacks Will Sell a 3,540-Calorie Sundae, and It Looks Amazing," *USA Today*, July 14, 2016, http://ftw.usatoday.com/2016/07/arizona-diamondbacks-triple-play-sundae-mlb; Vanessa Wong, "This Cheese-Stuffed, Bacon-Wrapped Corn Dog Is 3,000 Calories—and Only in Arizona," *Bloomberg News*, April 16, 2014, www.bloomberg.com/news/articles/2014-04-16/this-cheese-stuffed-bacon-wrapped-corn-dog-is-3-000-calories-and-only-in-arizona.

[10] "The Price Is Right, but Maybe It's Not, and How Do You Know?," *Knowledge @ Wharton*, October 3, 2007, http://knowledge.wharton.upenn.edu/article.cfm?articleid=1813; Victoria Murphy Barret, "What the Market Will Bear," *Forbes*, July 3, 2006, www.forbes.com/business/forbes/2006/0703/069.html.

[11] David Just, Özge Siğirci, and Brian Wansink, "Lower Buffet Prices Lead to Less Taste Satisfaction," *Journal of Sensory Studies*, vol. 29, no. 5, 362–370.

[12] Julie Jargon, "Behind Starbuck's Upscale Push," *Wall Street Journal*, December 6, 2016, p. B6.

[13] William Echilkson, "The Return of Luxury," *Fortune*, October 17, 1994, p. 18.

[14] Mark Henricks, "Stop on a Dime," *Entrepreneur*, January 2006, p. 27.

[15] George Swift, "Why You Need to Double Your Prices," *Business Zone*, October 23, 2013, www.businesszone.co.uk/topic/finances/why-you-need-double-your-prices/54251.

[16] Christina Passariello, Tripti Lahiri, and Sean McLain, "Bangladesh's Tale of the T-Shirts," *Wall Street Journal*, July 1, 2013, pp. B1, B8; Zoe Chace and Kaitlin Kenney, "Next Stop Bangladesh as We Follow Planet Money's T-Shirt," WUWM Milwaukee Public Radio, December 4, 2013, wuwm.com/post/next-stop-bangladesh-we-follow-planet-moneys-t-shirt.

[17] "What Would a Luxury Handbag Cost Without the Markup?" *CBS News*, June 3, 2016, www.cbsnews.com/news/what-would-a-luxury-handbag-cost-without-the-markup/; Suzanne Kapner, "Pricey Bags Reaching Their Limit," *Wall Street Journal*, March 5, 2015, p. B8.

[18] "Mobile In-Store Research Frequency Seen Increasing Alongside Price Point," *Marketing Charts*, September 16, 2013, http://www.marketingcharts.com/wp/topics/e-commerce/mobile-in-store-research-frequency-seen-increasing-alongside-price-point-36700/attachment/columbiabizaimia-frequency-mobile-in-store-search-by-price-point-sept2013/.

[19] "House Pride," *The Economist*, January 28, 2016, www.economist.com/news/business/21689614-art-world-changing-faster-sothebys-and-christies-are-adapting-their-business; Stephanie Baker and Katya Kazakina, "Auction Wars: Christie's, Sotheby's, and the Art of Competition," *Bloomberg*, June 21, 2015, www.bloomberg.com/news/articles/2015-06-21/auction-wars-christie-s-sotheby-s-and-the-art-of-competition; Kelly Crow, "Art-Auction Rivals Aim to Hammer Each Other," *Wall Street Journal*, November 4, 2015, pp. A1, A12.

[20] Gary M. Stern, "Small Prices, Big City," *QSR*, October 2013, www.qsrmagazine.com/store/small-prices-big-city.

[21] Gayle Sato Stodder, "Paying the Price," *Entrepreneur*, October 1994, p. 54.

[22] Russ Wiles, "Shoppers Win as Price War Looms in Grocery Business," *Arizona Republic*, September 23, 2016, www.azcentral.com/story/money/business/2016/09/23/sprouts-grocery-store-price-wars-loom/90413794/; "About Sprouts," Sprouts Farmers Market, www.sprouts.com/about-us.

[23] Justin Massa, "The Cost of Outdated Pricing Strategies: Part 2," *QSR*, October 2014, www.qsrmagazine.com/outside-insights/cost-outdated-pricing-strategies-part-2.

[24] Wayne Duggan, "Survey: Gen Y Shoppers Want Low Prices, Boomers and Seniors Want Good Service," *Yahoo! Finance*, September 3, 2015, http://finance.yahoo.com/news/survey-gen-y-shoppers-want-171520023.html.

[25] Norm Brodsky, "Street Smarts," *Inc.*, September 2010, p. 34.

[26] Jeff Turnas, "Introducing Our New Store Concept: 365 by Whole Foods Market," Whole Foods Market, June 10, 2015, www.wholefoodsmarket.com/blog/introducing-our-new-store-concept-365-whole-foods-market; Martin Bishop, "Whole Foods: Launching a Fighter Brand to Take on the Competition," *LinkedIn*, June 29, 2015, www.wholefoodsmarket.com/blog/introducing-our-new-store-concept-365-whole-foods-market.

27Norm Brodsky, "Dealing with Cost Hikes," *Inc.*, August 2005, p. 49.

28Brian Sozzi, "Starbucks and McDonald's Raising Prices—Which Restaurants Are Next?" *The Street*, July 8, 2015, www.thestreet.com/story/13209481/1/starbucks-and-mcdonalds-raising-prices--which-restaurants-are-next.html.

29"Pricing and Fairness: Do Your Customers Assume You Are Gouging Them?" *Knowledge@Wharton*, September 11, 2002, http://knowledge.wharton.upenn.edu/article.cfm?articleid=622#.

30Lauren Sherman, "Neo-Classic Kicks," *Wall Street Journal*, November 8–9, 2014, p. D4.

31Megan Duckett, "Startup Tips from 5 Successful Food Truck Entrepreneurs," *CBS Moneywatch*, May 20, 2011, www.cbsnews.com/8334–505143_162-57235454/startup-tips-from-5-successful-food-truck-entrepreneurs/?pageNum=5.

32Rick Bruns, "Tips for Coping with Rising Costs of Key Commodities," *Fast Company*, December 1997, pp. 27–30.

33Lisa Jennings, "Prominent LA Restaurants Battle Price-Fixing Lawsuit," *Restaurant Hospitality*, September 3, 2015, www.restaurant-hospitality.com/hrlegal/prominent-la-restaurants-battle-price-fixing-lawsuit; Lisa Jennings, "Judge Overrules Attempts to Dismiss Los Angeles Antitrust Case," *Nation's Restaurant News*, August 12, 2016, www.nrn.com/workforce/judge-overrules-attempts-dismiss-los-angeles-antitrust-case.

34Kevin Hardy, "Where We Stand with the Value Wars," *QSR*, March 2016, www.qsrmagazine.com/competition/where-we-stand-value-wars.

35Catalina Lamadrid, "Focus on Energy Recognizes Wisconsin Retailers for Energy Savings Accomplishments," Focus on Energy, October 16, 2012, https://focusonenergy.com/about/news-room/focus-energy-recognizes-wisconsin-retailers-energy-savings-accomplishments; "About Blain's Farm and Fleet," Blain's Farm and Fleet, www.farmandfleet.com/about/.

36Kevin Hardy, "Where We Stand with the Value Wars," *QSR*, March 2016, www.qsrmagazine.com/competition/where-we-stand-value-wars.

37Liz Barrett, "How to Formulate a Strong Menu Pricing Strategy," *Restaurant Hospitality*, February 8, 2016, www.restaurant-hospitality.com/operations/how-formulate-strong-menu-pricing-strategy.

38Jonathan Maze, "Buffalo Wild Wings Wants to Ease Wing Price Swings," *Nation's Restaurant News*, February 6, 2015, www.nrn.com/commodities/buffalo-wild-wings-wants-ease-wing-swings; Mark Brandau, "Buffalo Wild Wings to Implement a New Pricing System," *Nation's Restaurant News*, February 13, 2013, http://nrn.com/latest-headlines/buffalo-wild-wings-implement-new-pricing-system; Mark Brandau, "Buffalo Wild Wings' New Pricing, Service Model Build Brand Confidence," *Nation's Restaurant News*, October 31, 2013, http://nrn.com/corporate/buffalo-wild-wings-new-pricing-service-model-build-brand-confidence.

39Norm Brodsky, "Dealing with Cost Hikes," *Inc.*, August 2005, p. 49.

40Hollis Johnson and Marina Nazario, "We Tried the New Value Menus at McDonald's, Burger King, and Wendy's—And the Winner Is Clear," *Business Insider*, January 6, 2016, www.businessinsider.com/best-value-menu-in-fast-food-2016-1/#the-arena-of-the-fast-food-wars-is-crowded-mcdonalds-burger-king-and-wendys-have-each-recently-debuted-limited-time-value-menus-in-order-to-draw-in-customers-1; Lisa Baertlein, "Beef Price Spike Makes $1 McDouble Harder to Stomach," *Reuters*, February 1, 2013, www.reuters.com/article/2013/02/01/us-mcdonalds-inflation-beef-idUSBRE91008A20130201; Sam Oches,

"The Value Equation," *QSR*, February 2010, www.qsrmagazine.com/competition/value-equation?microsite=9342;microsite=9342; Blair Chancey, "Wendy's Counters McDonald's Struggling $1 Menu," *QSR Magazine*, September 2, 2008, www.qsrmagazine.com/news/wendys-counters-mcdonalds-struggling-1-menu.

41Michael V. Marn, Eric V. Roegner, and Craig C. Zawada, "Pricing New Products," *McKinsey Quarterly*, no. 3, 2003, p. 1.

42Steve McKee, "Low Prices Are Not Always Your Friend," *Businessweek*, April 2008, www.businessweek.com/smallbiz/content/apr2008/sb20080414_027855.htm.

43Jeffrey A. Trachtenberg, "Daily E-book Deals Are Gaining Traction," *Wall Street Journal*, December 29, 2015, pp. B1, B4.

44Ann Abel, "The Next Frontier," *Forbes Life*, June 18, 2015, pp. 30–34; "About Us," Ultima Thule Lodge, www.ultimathulelodge.com/people/claus-family-story.

45Gregory Ciotti, "Pricing Psychology: 10 Timeless Strategies to Increase Sales," *Help Scout*, May 15, 2016, www.helpscout.net/blog/pricing-strategies/.

46Sarah Schmidt, "Diners Spend More if Menu Avoids $ Sign," *Edmonton Journal*, August 14, 2008, www.canada.com/edmontonjournal/news/business/story.html?id=73e86808-da12–4430-acfc-6d64bc3b8efc.

47Uzi Shmilovici, "The Complete Guide to Freemium Business Models," *Tech Crunch*, September 4, 2011, http://techcrunch.com/2011/09/04/complete-guide-freemium/; Tom Tunguz, "Your Start-up's Pricing Strategy," May 25, 2012, http://tomasztunguz.com/2012/05/25/your-startups-pricing-strategy/.

48Jodi Helmer, "Cream of the Crop," *Entrepreneur*, October 2015, p. 74; Dean Takahashi, "How Farmers Are Using Big Data to Grow Better Crops, *Venture Beat*, August 19, 2015, http://venturebeat.com/2015/08/19/how-farmers-are-using-big-data-to-grow-better-crops/; "Pricing," FarmLogs, https://farmlogs.com/pricing.

49Gregory Ciotti, "Pricing Psychology: 10 Timeless Strategies to Increase Sales," *Help Scout*, May 15, 2016, www.helpscout.net/blog/pricing-strategies/.

50Lisa Girard, "10 Questions to Ask When Pricing Your Product," *Entrepreneur*, June 24, 2013, www.entrepreneur.com/article/227083.

51"Supply on Demand: Adapting to Change in Consumption and Delivery Models," *The Economist*, 2013, pp. 5, 7.

52"Subscription-Powered Growth," *Forbes*, November 23, 2015, p. 80.

53Hayley Peterson, "Amazon Changed the Price of a Single Item 8 Times in a Single Day," *Business Insider*, August 1, 2014, www.businessinsider.com/amazon-price-tracking-2014-8.

54Suzanne Kapner, "Stores Find a Perfect 'Door-Buster,'" *Wall Street Journal*, November 25, 2016, pp. B1–B2.

55Justin Guinn, "The Top Retail Pricing Strategy for Your Business," *Software Advice*, 2015, www.softwareadvice.com/resources/retail-pricing-strategies-report-2015/.

56Donna Fenn, "Some Businesses Go Creative on Prices, Applying Technology," *New York Times*, January 22, 2014, www.nytimes.com/2014/01/23/business/smallbusiness/with-new-thinking-and-technology-some-businesses-get-creative-with-pricing.html?_r=0.

57Angus Loten and Ruth Simon, "Shoppers Gobble Up Thursday Deals," *Wall Street Journal*, November 29, 2013, pp. B1–B2.

58Jonathan Maze, "Restaurants Find Kicking Discounting May Hurt Sales, Traffic," *Nation's Restaurant News*, November 7, 2011, www.nrn.com/finance/restaurants-find-kicking-discounting-may-hurt-sales-traffic.

59Liz Barrett, "6 Secrets to Successful LTOs," *Restaurant Hospitality*, March 15, 2016, www.restaurant-hospitality.com/marketing/6-secrets-successful-ltos.

[60]"Don't Let This One Get Away," *Get to the Point: Customer Insight*, January 20, 2010, pp. 1–2.

[61]"New Study on Retail Discounting: What Works for Some Products Might Be a Bust for Others," Kelley School of Business, Indiana University, November 18, 2009, http://info.kelley.iu.edu/news/page/normal/12630.html.

[62]"Vail Resorts," *Fast Company*, March 2016, pp. 94–95.

[63]Bryan Robinson, "Priced to Sell: 5 Pricing Strategies to Grow Your Business," *Business*, February 12, 2016, www.business.com/product-management/5-pricing-strategies-to-grow-your-business/.

[64]"Playhouses," Amish Backyard Structures, www.amishbackyardstructures.com/playhouses.html.

[65]*Leegin Creative Products Inc. v. PSKS*, The Oyez Project, Chicago-Kent College of Law, www.oyez.org/cases/2000-2009/2006/2006_06_480.

[66]Christina Binkley, "Sweater Sticker Shock," *Wall Street Journal*, November 21, 2013, pp. D1–D2; Christina Binkley, "How Can Jeans Cost $300?" *Wall Street Journal*, July 7, 2011, pp. D1–D2.

[67]Lettie Teague, "Highs and (Rare) Lows in Restaurant Wine Prices," *Wall Street Journal*, June 21, 2013, http://online.wsj.com/news/articles/SB10001424127887324520904578551532766601460.

[68]Renee Morad, "20 Products with Giant Markups," *Yahoo! Finance*, September 27, 2012, http://finance.yahoo.com/news/20-products-giant-markups-115730856.html.

[69]Christina Binkly, "What Goes into the Price of Luxury Sheets?" *Wall Street Journal*, March 27, 2014, p. D6.

[70]Christine Blank, "Daily Deals Evolve," *QSR*, September 2013, www.qsrmagazine.com/exclusives/daily-deals-evolve.

[71]Anita Campbell, "Cash Isn't Always King: Accepting Credit Cards Can Increase Your Business," *Small Business Trends*, July 24, 2013, https://smallbiztrends.com/2013/07/accepting-credit-cards-increase-business.html.

[72]"Credit Card Ownership Statistics," *StatisticBrain*, August 24, 2016, www.statisticbrain.com/credit-card-ownership-statistics/.

[73]*2016 U.S. Consumer Payment Study*, Total System Services, 2016, p. 12.

[74]*The Federal Reserve Payments Study 2016*, Federal Reserve, 2017, p. 2.

[75]Ibid.

[76]Utpal Dhulakia, "Does It Matter Whether You Pay with Cash or a Credit Card?" *Psychology Today*, July 11, 2016, www.psychologytoday.com/blog/the-science-behind-behavior/201607/does-it-matter-whether-you-pay-cash-or-credit-card; "Check, Please! Why a Credit Card Merchant Sees Higher Tickets," *Vantiv*, 2017, www.vantiv.com/merchant-services/credit-card-merchants-higher-revenue.

[77]"Top 10 Reasons to Start Accepting Credit Cards Today," *100 Best Merchant Accounts*, www.100best-merchant-accounts.com/articles1.html.

[78]"Square Stories: The Barbershop Club," Square, 2017, https://squareup.com/stories/barber-shop-club.

[79]"Retailers and Issuers Are Still Battling Over Payment Card Fees," *The Economist*, October 15, 2016, www.economist.com/news/finance-and-economics/21708669-five-years-after-crackdown-federal-reserve-credit-card-industry.

[80]Robin Sidel, "Cost of Credit-Card Fraud Is Set to Shift," *Wall Street Journal*, September 29, 2015, www.wsj.com/articles/card-liability-is-set-to-shift-1443567562.

[81]Tony Zarucha, "Online Retail Credit Card Fraud Spikes over Busy Weekend," *Bankless Times*, November 30, 2016, www.banklesstimes.com/2016/11/30/online-retail-credit-card-fraud-spikes-over-busy-weekend/; Kerry Close, "Credit Card Fraud in the U.S. Topped $8 Billion in 2015," *Money*, October 25, 2016, http://time.com/money/4544400/credit-card-fraud-us/.

[82]Sienna Kossman, "7 Merchant Tips to Understanding EMV Fraud Shift Liability," CreditCards.com, December 20, 2016, www.creditcards.com/credit-card-news/understanding-EMV-fraud-liability-shift-1271.php.

[83]Ruth Simon, "Small Firms Slow to Add New Chip-Card System," *Wall Street Journal*, September 3, 2015, pp. B1, B6.

[84]*Small Business Chip Card Payment Survey*, National Federation of Independent Businesses Research Foundation, October 2015, p. 4.

[85]*Annual Fraud Benchmark Report: A Balancing Act, North American Edition*, CyberSource, 2016, p. 11.

[86]Michael Bloch, "Preventing Credit Card Chargebacks-Anti-Fraud Strategies," Taming the Beast, www.tamingthebeast.net/articles2/card-fraud-strategies.htm.

[87]*Annual Fraud Benchmark Report: A Balancing Act, North American Edition*, CyberSource, 2016, p. 10.

[88]"Facts on Debit Cards," Statista, 2017, www.statista.com/topics/1598/debit-cards/.

[89]*The Federal Reserve Payments Study 2016*, Federal Reserve, 2017, p. 2.

[90]Ibid., p. 3.

[91]Greg Burch, "5 Ways to Boost the Fast Casual Mobile Experience," *Pizza Marketplace*, January 14, 2016, www.fastcasual.com/articles/5-ways-to-boost-the-fast-casual-mobile-experience/.

[92]"Mobile Payments Will Triple in the U.S. in 2016," *eMarketer*, October 26, 2015, www.emarketer.com/Article/Mobile-Payments-Will-Triple-US-2016/1013147; "Plastic Will Be Passé," *Inc.*, December 2012/January 2013, pp. 59–60.

[93]Javier Espinoza, "Mobile Wallets: A Primer for Retailers," *Wall Street Journal*, April 29, 2013, p. R4.

[94]"The Best Mobile Wallets of 2017," *Top Ten Reviews*, October 27, 2016, www.toptenreviews.com/business/payment-processing/best-mobile-wallets/.

[95]"How Mobile Payment Processing Can Increase Your Business Revenue," *POS Today*, January 26, 2017, www.postoday.com/blog/mobile-payment-processing.

[96]Dionne Mahaffey, "Black-Owned Startup 'Airfordable' Lets You Pay for Flights on Layaway," WhereUCameFrom, October 11, 2016, https://whereyoucamefrom.biz/article/black-owned-startup-airfordable-lets-you-pay-for-flights-on-layaway-plan.html.

Alexander Raths/123RF

12 Creating a Successful Financial Plan

Learning Objectives

On completion of this chapter, you will be able to:

1. Describe how to prepare the basic financial statements and use them to manage a small business.

2. Create projected (pro forma) financial statements.

3. Understand the basic financial statements through ratio analysis.

4. Explain how to interpret financial ratios.

5. Conduct a breakeven analysis for a small company.

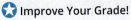

MyLab Entrepreneurship

⭐ **Improve Your Grade!**

If your instructor is using MyLab Entrepreneurship, visit **www.pearson.com/mylab/entrepreneurship** for videos, simulations, and writing exercises.

Fashioning a well-designed financial plan as part of a comprehensive business plan is one of the most important steps in launching a new business venture. Entrepreneurs who fail to develop workable strategies for reaching positive cash flow and earning a profit from the outset eventually suffer the ultimate business penalty: failure. In addition, potential lenders and investors demand a realistic financial plan before putting their money into a start-up company. More important, a financial plan is a vital tool that allows entrepreneurs to manage their businesses more effectively, steering their way around the pitfalls that cause failures. Proper **financial management** requires putting in place a system that provides entrepreneurs with relevant financial information in an easy-to-read and readily understandable format on a timely basis. It allows entrepreneurs to know not only *how* their businesses are doing financially but also *why* their companies are performing that way. The information in a small company's financial records is one resource to which competitors have no access. Smart entrepreneurs recognize this and put their companies' numbers to work for them so that they can make their businesses more successful. Understanding financial statements and other accounting records can alert entrepreneurs to emerging problems in their businesses, help them trim costs, and offer clues on how to improve cash flow and boost profits.

Unfortunately, failure to collect and analyze basic financial data is a common mistake among entrepreneurs. A recent survey by Intuit reports that 40 percent of small business owners consider themselves to be financially illiterate, although 81 percent handle all of their own finances.[1] A study by the National Federation of Independent Business reports that 79 percent of small business owners have no plans to provide their employees with financial training.[2] Both research and anecdotal evidence suggest that a significant percentage of entrepreneurs run their companies without any kind of financial plan and never analyze their companies' financial statements as part of the decision-making process. Bill Hettinger, business consultant and author of *Finance Without Fear*, estimates that 75 percent of business owners do not understand or fail to focus on the financial details of their companies.[3] To reach profit objectives, entrepreneurs must be aware of their companies' overall financial position and the changes in financial status that occur over time. Most accounting experts advise entrepreneurs to use one of the popular computerized small business accounting programs such as QuickBooks, FreshBooks, Xero, and others to manage routine record-keeping tasks. More than three-quarters (77 percent) of small business owners use accounting software to help track revenues and expenses.[4] Working with an accountant to set up the system at the outset and then having an employee or a bookkeeping service enter the transactions is most efficient for most businesses. These programs make preparing reports, analyzing a company's financial statements, and summarizing data a snap. Studies show that business owners who use accounting software are more likely to be financially literate than those who do not.[5]

This chapter focuses on some practical tools that help entrepreneurs develop a workable financial plan, keep them aware of their company's financial performance, and enable them to plan for profit. They can use these tools to anticipate changes and plot an appropriate profit strategy to meet these shifts head-on. These cash flow and profit-planning techniques are not difficult to master, nor are they overly time-consuming. We will discuss the techniques involved in preparing projected (pro forma) financial statements, conducting ratio analysis, and performing breakeven analysis.

Basic Financial Statements

Before we begin building projected financial statements, it would be helpful to review the basic financial reports that measure a company's financial position: the balance sheet, the income statement, and the statement of cash flows. The level of financial sophistication among small business owners may not be high, but the extent of financial reporting among small businesses is. Most small businesses regularly produce summary financial information, almost all of it in the form of these traditional financial statements.

The Balance Sheet

Like a digital camera, the **balance sheet** takes a "snapshot" of a business's financial position, providing owners with an estimate of its worth on a given date. Its two major sections show the assets the business owns and the claims creditors and owners have against those assets. The

---

financial management
a process that provides entrepreneurs with relevant financial information in an easy-to-read format on a timely basis; it allows entrepreneurs to know not only how their businesses are doing financially but also why they are performing that way.

LO1
Describe how to prepare the basic financial statements and use them to manage a small business.

balance sheet
a financial statement that provides a snapshot of a business's financial position, estimating its worth on a given date; it is built on the fundamental accounting equation: Assets = Liabilities + Owner's equity.

FIGURE 12.1

Sam's Appliance Shop, Balance Sheet

Assets		
Current Assets		
Cash		$49,855
Accounts Receivable	$179,225	
Less Allowance for Doubtful Accounts	$6,000	$173,225
Inventory		$455,455
Prepaid Expenses		$8,450
Total Current Assets		$686,985
Fixed Assets		
Land		$59,150
Buildings	$74,650	
Less Accumulated Depreciation	$7,050	$67,600
Equipment	$22,375	
Less Accumulated Depreciation	$1,250	$21,125
Furniture and Fixtures	$10,295	
Less Accumulated Depreciation	$1,000	$9,295
Total Fixed Assets		$1,57,170
Intangibles (Goodwill)		$3,500
Total Assets		$847,655
Liabilities		
Current Liabilities		
Accounts Payable		$152,580
Notes Payable		$83,920
Accrued Wages/Salaries Payable		$38,150
Accrued Interest Payable		$42,380
Accrued Taxes Payable		$50,820
Total Current Liabilities		$367,850
Long-Term Liabilities		
Mortgage		$127,150
Note Payable		$85,000
Total Long-Term Liabilities		$212,150
Owner's Equity		
Sam Lloyd, Capital		$267,655
Total Liabilities and Owner's Equity		$847,655

current assets

assets such as cash and other items to be converted into cash within one year or within the company's normal operating cycle.

fixed assets

assets acquired for long-term use in a business.

liabilities

creditors' claims against a company's assets.

current liabilities

debts that must be paid within one year or within the normal operating cycle of a company.

balance sheet is usually prepared on the last day of the month. Figure 12.1 shows the balance sheet for Sam's Appliance Shop for December 31, 20xx.

The balance sheet is built on the fundamental accounting equation: Assets = Liabilities + Owner's equity. Any increase or decrease on one side of the equation must be offset by an increase or a decrease on the other side, hence the name *balance sheet*. It provides a baseline from which to measure future changes in assets, liabilities, and equity. The first section of the balance sheet lists the company's assets (valued at cost, not actual market value) and shows the total value of everything the business owns. **Current assets** consist of cash and items to be converted into cash within one year or within the normal operating cycle of the company, whichever is longer, such as accounts receivable and inventory. **Fixed assets** are assets acquired for long-term use in the business. Intangible assets include items such as goodwill, copyrights, patents, and licenses that, although valuable, are not tangible.

The second section shows the business's **liabilities**—the creditors' claims against the company's assets. **Current liabilities** are debts that must be paid within one year or within the

Net Sales Revenue		$1,870,841
Credit Sales	$1,309,589	
Cash Sales	$561,252	
Cost of Goods Sold		
Beginning Inventory, 1/1/xx	$805,745	
+ Purchases	$939,827	
Goods Available for Sale	$1,745,572	
– Ending Inventory, 12/31/xx	$455,455	
Cost of Goods Sold		$1,290,117
Gross Profit		$580,724
Operating Expenses		
Advertising	$139,670	
Insurance	$46,125	
Depreciation		
Building	$18,700	
Equipment	$9,000	
Salaries	$224,500	
Travel	$4,000	
Entertainment	$2,500	
Total Operating Expenses		$444,495
General Expenses		
Utilities	$5,300	
Telephone	$2,500	
Postage	$1,200	
Payroll Taxes	$25,000	
Total General Expenses		$34,000
Other Expenses		
Interest Expense	$39,850	
Bad Check Expense	$1,750	
Total Other Expenses		$41,600
Total Expenses		$520,095
Net Income		$60,629

FIGURE 12.2

Sam's Appliance Shop, Income Statement

normal operating cycle of the company, whichever is longer, and **long-term liabilities** are those that come due after one year. This section of the balance sheet also shows the **owner's equity**, the value of the owner's investment in the business. It is the balancing factor on the balance sheet, representing all of the owner's capital contributions to the business plus all accumulated (or retained) earnings not distributed to the owner(s).

long-term liabilities
liabilities that come due after one year.

owner's equity
the value of the owner's investment in the business.

The Income Statement

The **income statement** (also called the profit-and-loss statement) compares expenses against revenue over a certain period of time to show the firm's net income (or loss). Like a digital video recorder, the income statement is a "moving picture" of a company's profitability over time. The annual income statement reports the bottom line of the business over the fiscal or calendar year. Figure 12.2 shows the income statement for Sam's Appliance Shop for the year ended December 31, 20xx.

To calculate net income or loss, an entrepreneur records sales revenues for the year, which includes all income that flows into the business from sales of goods and services. Income from

income statement
a financial statement that represents a moving picture of a business, comparing its expenses against its revenue over a period of time to show its net income (or loss).

cost of goods sold

the total cost, including shipping, of the merchandise sold during the accounting period.

other sources (rent, investments, and interest) also must be included in the revenue section of the income statement. To determine net sales revenue, owners subtract the value of returned items and refunds from gross revenue. **Cost of goods sold** represents the total cost, including shipping, of the merchandise sold during the accounting period. Manufacturers, wholesalers, and retailers calculate cost of goods sold by adding purchases to beginning inventory and subtracting ending inventory. Service-providing companies typically have no cost of goods sold because they do not carry inventory.

Subtracting the cost of goods sold from net sales revenue results in a company's gross profit. Allowing the cost of goods sold to get out of control whittles away a company's gross profit and threatens its ability to generate positive net income because a company must pay all of its operating expenses out of its gross profit. Dividing gross profit by net sales revenue produces the **gross profit margin**, a ratio that every small business owner should watch closely. If a company's gross profit margin slips too low, it is likely that it will operate at a loss (negative net income). A business that operates at a gross profit margin of 50 percent must generate $2 in sales for every $1 of operating expenses just to break even. However, a company with a 10 percent gross profit margin must generate $10 in sales for every $1 of operating expenses to reach its breakeven point.

gross profit margin

gross profit divided by net sales revenue.

Many business owners whose companies are losing money mistakenly believe that the problem is inadequate sales volume; therefore, they focus on pumping up sales at any cost. In many cases, however, the losses their companies are incurring are the result of an inadequate gross profit margin, and pumping up sales only deepens their losses! Repairing a poor gross profit margin requires a company to raise prices, cut manufacturing or purchasing costs, refuse orders with low profit margins, "fire" unprofitable customers (see Figure 12.3), or add new products with more attractive profit margins. *Increasing sales will not resolve the problem.* Monitoring the gross profit margin over time and comparing it to those of other companies in the same industry are important steps to maintaining a company's long-term profitability.

Courtesy of Paul Spiegelman, Chief Culture Officer, Stericycle

ENTREPRENEURIAL PROFILE: Paul Spiegelman: Stericycle Stericycle, a medical waste company headquartered in Lake Forest, Illinois, is a company that relies on a fundamental set of beliefs to drive how its business operates. The core values that guide Stericycle's culture include accountability to its customers, teamwork in pursuit of a common goal, customers first, continuous improvement, and a strong sense of camaraderie and enjoying work. Paul Spiegelman, chief culture officer of Stericycle, says that if the company's clients don't share these values, the result is a significant negative impact on the company's culture. The founders landed a multi-million-dollar client that shared the values on which they founded the business, but over time the client's priorities shifted from customer service to maximizing sales. The client began to provide services its customers did not ask for, adding unwanted items to their monthly bills. Despite the negative impact on the company's profits, Stericycle terminated the contract with the client. Employees were pleased to know that Stericycle delivered on its commitment to the customer and sent letters to management, thanking them for acting with integrity. Spiegelman says that maintaining this culture as the company has experienced significant growth has required commitment from company leadership, consistent application of company values even if financial performance suffers in the short term, transparency in communication about major decisions, and a process to hire and reward employees who fit into Stericycle's culture and its values.[6] ■

operating expenses

costs that contribute directly to the manufacture and distribution of goods.

Operating expenses are costs that contribute directly to the manufacturing and distribution of goods. General expenses are indirect costs incurred in operating the business. "Other expenses" is a catchall category covering all other expenses that don't fit into the other two categories. Subtracting total expenses from total revenue gives the company's net income (or loss) for the accounting period. Reducing expenses increases a company's net income, and even small reductions in expenses can add up to big savings.

ENTREPRENEURIAL PROFILE: Jeff DeVries and Shane Thompson: WestWind Logistics When Jeff DeVries and Shane Thompson bought WestWind Logistics, a pallet recycling company located in Des Moines, Iowa, their goal was to grow the company. After purchasing

A classic study reports that 20 percent of the typical company's customers are unprofitable. Many business owners who take the time to analyze their customer bases are surprised to discover that some of the customers they thought were profitable actually are costing their companies money. The solution: Raise prices or fees, or "fire" the unprofitable customers. The following customer profitability map helps entrepreneurs identify which of their customers are best — and worst — for their businesses.

Methodology: Select your biggest customers and assign each one a "resonance score" from 1 (difficult) to 10 (easy) that reflects how easy they are to serve. Then calculate the profit margin (profit as a percentage of sales) your company makes from each customer. Plot each customer's score on the map as a circle. The size of the circle should be proportionate to the percentage of the company's total sales for which the customer accounts. The result is a map that shows how your company's customers fall into each of the quadrants.

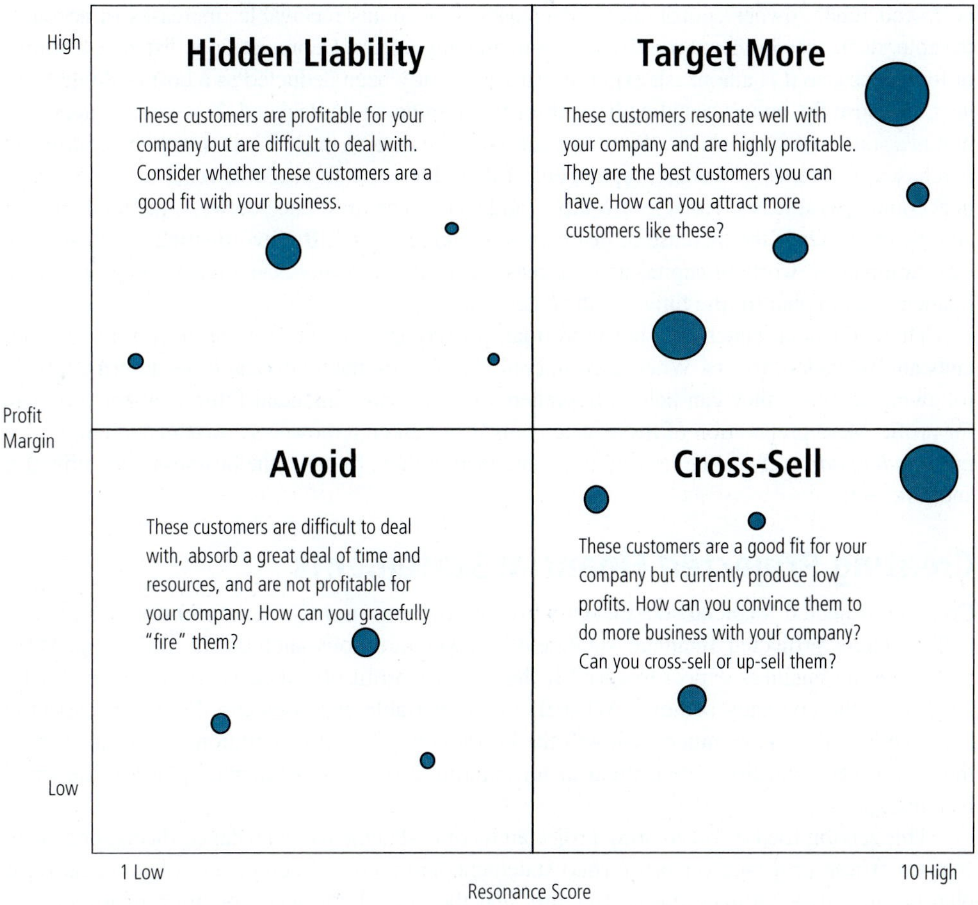

FIGURE 12.3

Customer Profitability Map

Sources: Based on Lawrence Siff, "Your Unprofitable Customers Are Killing You," *Forbes,* May 21, 2012, www.forbes.com/sites/lawrencesiff/2012/05/21/your-unprofitable-customers-are-killing-you/#a0e61685f2ba; Gwen Moran, "Six Weeks to a Better Bottom Line," *Entrepreneur,* January 2010, pp. 47–51; Kashing Woo and Henry K.Y. Fock, "Retaining and Divesting Customers: An Exploratory Study of Right Customers, 'At Risk' Right Customers, and Wrong Customers," *Journal of Services Marketing,* vol. 18, no. 2/3, 2004, pp. 187–197.

Hidden Liability

These customers are profitable for your company but are difficult to deal with. Consider whether these customers are a good fit with your business.

Target More

These customers resonate well with your company and are highly profitable. They are the best customers you can have. How can you attract more customers like these?

Avoid

These customers are difficult to deal with, absorb a great deal of time and resources, and are not profitable for your company. How can you gracefully "fire" them?

Cross-Sell

These customers are a good fit for your company but currently produce low profits. How can you convince them to do more business with your company? Can you cross-sell or up-sell them?

High — Profit Margin — Low

1 Low — Resonance Score — 10 High

the company from its previous owners, DeVries and Thompson committed to investing in infrastructure to support growth. The new owners realized that automated inventory management would be a key area to invest in to ensure good cash flow and profits along with growth. Better inventory management through automation resulted in more efficient operation with less need for company employees to physically manage the inventory. Each pallet has a barcode, which allows the system to track and organize inventory. The company handles 4 million pallets per year due in large part to the automated system, an increase of almost 10 times the number the company handled before it upgraded its inventory and other related systems.[7] ■

Comparing a company's current income statement to those of prior accounting periods often reveals valuable information about key trends and a company's progress toward its financial goals. "Numbers run companies," says Norm Brodsky, serial entrepreneur and founder of CitiStorage, a successful storage company based in New York City. "It's your responsibility as an owner to know and understand not only the income statement but also the balance sheet of your business. You ignore them at your peril."[8]

The Statement of Cash Flows

The **statement of cash flows** show the changes in a company's working capital from the beginning of the accounting period by listing both the sources of funds and the uses of those funds. Many small businesses never need to prepare such a statement; instead, they rely on a cash budget, a less formal managerial tool you will learn about in Chapter 13 that tracks the flow of cash into and out of a company over time. Sometimes, however, creditors, lenders, investors, or business buyers may require this information.

To prepare the statement, owners must assemble the balance sheet and the income statement summarizing the present year's operations. They begin with the company's net income for the period (from the income statement). Then they add the sources of the company's funds: borrowed funds, owner contributions, decreases in accounts receivable, increases in accounts payable, decreases in inventory, depreciation, and any others. Depreciation is listed as a source of funds because it is a noncash expense that has already been deducted as a cost of doing business. Because the owner has already paid for the item being depreciated, however, its depreciation is a source of funds. Next, the owner subtracts the uses of these funds: plant and equipment purchases, dividends to owners, repayment of debt, increases in accounts receivable, decreases in accounts payable, increases in inventory, and so on. The difference between the total sources and the total uses is the increase or decrease in working capital. By investigating the changes in their companies' working capital and the reasons for them, owners can create a more practical financial action plan for the future of the enterprise.

These financial statements are more than just complex documents used only by accountants and financial officers. When used in conjunction with the analytical tools described in the following sections, they can help entrepreneurs map a firm's financial future and actively plan for profit. Mere preparation of these statements is not enough, however; owners and employees must *understand and use* the information contained in them to make the business more effective and efficient.

Creating Projected Financial Statements

Creating projected financial statements helps entrepreneurs transform their business goals into reality. These projected financial statements answer questions such as the following: What profit can the business expect to earn? If the owner's profit objective is x dollars, what sales level must the company achieve? What fixed and variable expenses can the owner expect at that level of sales? How much cash will the business need to stay operational? The answers to these and other questions are critical in formulating a functional financial plan for the small business.

This section focuses on creating projected income statements and balance sheets for a small start-up. These projected (or pro forma) statements are a crucial component of every business plan because they estimate the profitability and the overall financial condition of a company in the future. They are an integral part of convincing potential lenders and investors to provide the financing necessary get the company off the ground (the topic of Chapter 14). In addition, because these statements project a company's financial position through the end of the forecasted period, they help entrepreneurs to plan the route to improved financial strength and healthy business growth. To be useful, however, these forecasts must be *realistic and well researched*! Entrepreneurs typically find that revenues are the most difficult to forecast. However, even though estimating future revenues is challenging, the accuracy of these forecasts can make or break a business as it grows.

Because an established business has a history of operating data from which to construct projected financial statements, the task is not nearly as difficult as it is for a start-up company. When creating pro forma financial statements for a business start-up, entrepreneurs typically rely on published statistics that summarize the operation of similar-size companies in the same industry. These statistics are available from a number of sources (described later), but this section draws on information found in the *Annual Statement Studies*, a compilation of financial data collected from 260,000 companies across 794 industries organized by Standard Industrial Classification (SIC) Code and North American Industry Classification System (NAICS) published by the Risk Management Association (RMA) and in BizMiner, a service that provides financial ratios and analysis for businesses in 5,000 industries. Because conditions and markets change so rapidly, entrepreneurs developing financial forecasts for start-ups should focus on creating projections for two years into the future. Although these sources offer guidelines to gauge how reasonable a company's projections are, entrepreneurs should use values that apply to their own particular circumstances to derive their forecasts. Remember that any published financial data is based on operating businesses. For a start-up company, the key is accurate forecasts that show how the business will get to these industry standards. Investors want to see that entrepreneurs have developed well-researched, realistic expectations about their companies' income and expenses and when they expect to start earning a profit.

Projected Financial Statements for a Small Business

One of the most important tasks confronting an entrepreneur launching a new enterprise is to determine the amount of funding required to begin operation as well as the amount required to keep the company going until it begins to generate positive cash flow. The amount of money needed to begin a business depends on the type of operation, its location, inventory requirements, sales volume, and many other factors. Every new firm must have enough capital to cover all start-up costs, including funds to rent or buy plant, equipment, and tools and to pay for advertising, wages, licenses, utilities, and other expenses. In addition, an entrepreneur must maintain a reserve of capital to carry the company until it begins to generate positive cash flow. Too often, entrepreneurs are overly optimistic in their financial plans and fail to recognize that expenses initially exceed income (and cash outflow exceeds cash inflow) for most small firms. This period of net losses (and negative cash flow) is normal and may last from just a few months to several years. During this time, entrepreneurs have enough cash to pay the company's regular bills, meet payroll, purchase inventory, take advantage of cash discounts, pay the company's regular bills, grant customers credit, and meet their personal financial obligations.

THE PROJECTED INCOME STATEMENT When creating a projected income statement, the first step is to create a sales forecast. An entrepreneur has two options: develop a sales forecast and work down or set a profit target and work up. Developing a realistic sales forecast for a business start-up is not always easy, but with creativity and research, it is possible. Talking with owners of existing businesses in the industry (outside the local trading area, of course) can provide meaningful insight into the sales levels a company can expect to generate during its early years. For a reasonable fee, entrepreneurs can access published aggregated financial statistics that industry trade associations collect on the companies in their industries. Other organizations, such as the Risk Management Association, BizMiner, and Dun & Bradstreet, publish useful financial information for a wide range of industries. Internet searches and trips to the local library will produce the necessary information. Interviews with potential customers and test-marketing an actual product or service also can reveal the number of customers a company can expect to attract. One method for checking the accuracy of a sales estimate is to calculate the revenue other companies in the same industry generate per employee and compare it to your own projected revenue per employee. Also, many companies are willing to share some of their basic financial data with entrepreneurs engaged in a start-up company in their industry. A value that is out of line with industry standards is not likely to be realistic. Experienced investors will expect any sales forecasts to be clearly explained by a sound marketing plan.

Many entrepreneurs prefer the second method of creating a projected income statement, targeting a profit figure and then working up to determine the sales level they must achieve to reach it. This also is known as a reverse income statement, or discovery-driven planning.[9] Of course, it is important to compare this sales target against the results of the marketing plan to determine whether it is realistic. Once an entrepreneur determines a reasonable profit target, the next step is to estimate the expenses the business will incur to generate that profit.

The profit a small company produces must be large enough to provide a reasonable return on the time the owners spend operating the business and a return on their investment in the business. Entrepreneurs who earn less in their own businesses than they could earn working for someone else must weigh carefully the advantages and disadvantages of choosing the path of entrepreneurship. Why be exposed to all of the risks, sacrifices, and hard work of beginning and operating a small business if the rewards are less than those of remaining in the secure employment of another? Although there are many nonfinancial benefits of owning a business, the net income a company generates should be at least as much as an entrepreneur could earn by working for someone else.

An adequate profit must also include a reasonable return on the owner's total investment in the business. (The owner's total investment is the amount contributed to the company plus any retained earnings from previous years that were funneled back into the business.) In other words, an entrepreneur's target income is the sum of a reasonable salary for the time spent running the business and a normal return on the amount invested in the company. Determining this amount is the first step in creating the projected income statement.

An entrepreneur then must translate this target profit into a net sales figure for the forecasted period. To calculate net sales from a target profit, the entrepreneur can use published industry statistics. Suppose an entrepreneur wants to launch a small retail comic book store and has determined that his target net income is $10,000. Statistics gathered from BizMiner show that the typical comic book store's net profit margin (Net profit ÷ Revenues) is 5.44 percent.[10] Using this information, he can compute the sales level required to produce a net profit of $10,000:

$$\text{Net profit margin} = \frac{\text{Net income}}{\text{Sales (annual)}}$$

Solving for net sales produces the following result:

$$\text{Net sales} = \frac{\$10,000}{0.0544}$$

$$= \$183,824$$

Now the entrepreneur knows that to make a net profit of $10,000 (before taxes), he or she must achieve annual sales of $183,824. To complete the projected income statement, the owner simply applies the appropriate statistics from BizMiner to the annual sales figure. Because the statistics for each income statement item are expressed as percentages of net sales, the entrepreneur merely multiplies the proper percentage by the annual sales figure to obtain the desired value. For example, cost of goods sold usually makes up 62.48 percent of net sales for the typical comic book store; therefore, the owner of this new comic book store expects his cost of goods sold to be the following:

$$\text{Cost of goods sold} = \$183,824 \times 0.6248 = \$114,853$$

The comic book store's complete projected income statement is shown as follows:

Net sales	(100%)	$183,824
−Cost of goods sold	(62.48%)	$114,853
Gross profit margin	(37.52%)	$ 68,971
−Operating expenses	(32.08%)	$ 58,971
Net profit (before taxes)	(5.44%)	$10,000

At this point, the business appears to be a viable venture. However, remember that this income statement represents a sales *goal* the owner may not be able to reach. The next step is to determine whether this required sales volume is reasonable. One useful technique is to break down the required annual sales volume into *daily* sales figures. Assuming that the store will be open six days per week for 52 weeks (312 days), we see that the owner must average $589 per day in sales:

$$\text{Average daily sales} = \frac{\$183,824}{312} = \$589/\text{day}$$

This calculation gives the owner a better perspective of the sales required to yield an annual profit of $10,000.

To determine whether the profit expected from the business will meet or exceed the target income, the entrepreneur also should use this same process to create income statements that are built on pessimistic, most likely, and optimistic sales estimates. The previous analysis shows an entrepreneur the sales level required to reach a desired profit. But what happens if sales are lower? Higher? Making these projections requires a reliable sales forecast, using the market research techniques described in Chapter 9.

Suppose, for example, that after conducting research on the industry, a marketing survey of local customers, and discussions with owners of comic book stores in other markets, the prospective entrepreneur projects annual sales for the proposed business's first year of operation to be $210,000. The entrepreneur can take this sales estimate and develop a projected income statement:

Net sales	(100%)	$210,000
−Cost of goods sold	(62.48%)	$131,208
Gross profit margin	(37.52%)	$ 78,792
−Operating expenses	(32.08%)	$ 67,368
Net profit (before taxes)	(5.44%)	$11,424

Based on sales of $210,000, this entrepreneur can expect a net income (before taxes) of $11,424. If this amount is acceptable as a return on the investment of time and money in the business, the entrepreneur should proceed with his or her planning.

At this stage in developing the financial plan, the entrepreneur should create a more detailed picture of the venture's expected operating expenses. In addition to gathering information from industry trade associations about typical operating expenses, an entrepreneur can contact potential vendors, suppliers, and providers to get estimates of the expenses he or she can expect to incur in his or her area of operation. One entrepreneur who was preparing a business plan for the launch of an upscale women's clothing store contacted local utility companies, insurance agencies, Web site-hosting company, radio and television stations, newspapers, and other vendors to get estimates of her utility, insurance, advertising, and other expenses.

To ensure that they have not overlooked any business expenses in preparing the business plan, entrepreneurs should list all of the expenses they will incur and have an accountant review the list. Sometimes in their estimates of expenses, entrepreneurs neglect to include salaries for themselves, which immediately raises a red flag among lenders and investors. Without drawing a salary, how will an entrepreneur pay his or her own bills? At the other extreme, lenders and investors frown on exorbitantly high salaries for owners of business start-ups. Typically, salaries are not the best use of cash in a start-up; one guideline is to draw a salary that is about 25 to 30 percent below the market rate for a similar position (and to make adjustments from there if conditions warrant). In addition, as the company grows, executive salaries should be among the *last* expenses to be increased. Reinvesting the extra money in the company accelerates its growth rate.

THE PROJECTED BALANCE SHEET In addition to projecting a start-up's net profit or loss, an entrepreneur must develop a pro forma balance sheet outlining the fledgling firm's assets and liabilities. Most entrepreneurs' primary concern is profitability because, on the surface, the importance of a business's assets is less obvious. In many cases, small companies begin their lives on weak financial footing because entrepreneurs fail to determine their firms' total asset requirements. To prevent this major oversight, entrepreneurs should prepare a projected balance sheet listing every asset their businesses will need and all the claims against these assets.

ASSETS Cash is one of the most useful assets the business owns; it is highly liquid and can quickly be converted into other tangible assets. But how much cash should a small business have at its inception? Obviously, there is no single dollar figure that fits the needs of every small firm. One practical rule of thumb, however, suggests that a company's cash balance should cover its operating expenses (less depreciation, a noncash expense) for at least one inventory turnover period. Using this guideline, we can calculate the cash balance for the small comic book store as follows:

Operating expenses = $67,368 (from projected income statement)

Less depreciation (0.80% of annual sales[*]) of $1,680 (a noncash expense)

Equals: cash expenses (annual) = $65,688

Annual inventory turnover ratio* = 5.17 times per year

$$\text{Cash requirement} = \frac{\text{Cash expenses}}{\text{Average inventory turnover}}$$

$$= \frac{\$65,688}{5.17}$$

$$= \$12,706$$

*From BizMiner.

Notice the inverse relationship between the small firm's average turnover ratio and its cash requirement. The higher the number of inventory turns a company generates, the lower its cash requirement. For instance, if this comic book store could turn its inventory eight times per year, its cash requirement would be $65,688 ÷ 8 = $8,211, nearly $4,500 less.

Another decision facing the entrepreneur is how much inventory the business should carry. A rough estimate of the inventory requirement can be calculated from the information found on the projected income statement and from published statistics:

Cost of goods sold = $131,208 (from projected income statement)

$$\text{Average inventory turnover} = \frac{\text{Cost of goods sold}}{\text{Average inventory level}} = 5.17 \text{ times per year}$$

Rearranging the equation to solve for inventory level produces the following:

$$\text{Average inventory level} = \frac{\$131,208}{5.17}$$

$$\text{Average inventory level} = \$25,379$$

The entrepreneur also includes $1,800 in miscellaneous current assets. The estimate of fixed assets is as follows:

Fixtures	$14,500
Office equipment	5,250
Computers/cash register	5,125
Signs	7,200
Miscellaneous	1,500
Total	$33,575

LIABILITIES To complete the projected balance sheet, the owner must record all of the small firm's liabilities, the claims that creditors have against its assets. The comic book store owner was able to finance 50 percent of the inventory and fixtures ($19,940) through suppliers and has a short-term note payable in the amount of $3,750. The only other major claim against the firm's assets is a note payable to the entrepreneur's father-in-law for $25,000. The difference between the company's assets ($73,460) and its total liabilities ($48,690) represents the owner's investment in the business (owner's equity) of $24,770.

The final step is to compile all of these items into a projected balance sheet, as shown in Figure 12.4.

Assets		Liabilities	
Current Assets		**Current Liabilities**	
Cash	$12,706	Accounts Payable	$19,940
Inventory	25,379	Note Payable	3,750
Miscellaneous	1,800		
Total Current Assets	$39,885	Total Current Liabilities	$23,690
Fixed Assets		**Long-Term Liabilities**	
Fixtures	$14,500	Note Payable	$25,000
Office Equipment	5,250		
Computer/Cash Register	5,125	Total Liabilities	$48,690
Signs	7,200		
Miscellaneous	1,500		
Total Fixed Assets	$33,575	**Owner's Equity**	$24,770
Total Assets	$73,460	**Total Liabilities and Owner's Equity**	$73,460

FIGURE 12.4

Projected Balance Sheet

Ratio Analysis

LO3

Understand the basic financial statements through ratio analysis.

Would you be willing to drive a car on an extended trip without being able to see the dashboard displays showing fuel level, engine temperature, oil pressure, battery status, or the speed at which you were traveling? Not many people would! Yet many small business owners run their companies exactly that way. They never take the time to check the vital signs of their businesses using financial dashboards that indicate the current status of their businesses and any potential problems that may be developing. The result: Their companies develop engine trouble, fail, and leave them stranded along the road to successful entrepreneurship. To help avoid becoming a failure statistic, entrepreneurs must understand the numbers that drive their businesses. Business owners develop a feel for their financial statements and the specific numbers that they must watch closely to ensure their companies' success. By watching the numbers over time, successful entrepreneurs learn to identify patterns that can signal problems in their businesses.

Smart entrepreneurs know that once they have their businesses up and running with the help of a solid financial plan, the next step is to keep their companies moving in the right direction with the help of proper financial controls. Establishing these controls—and using them consistently—is one of the keys to keeping a business vibrant and healthy. A sound system of financial controls serves as an early warning device for underlying problems that could destroy a young business. A company's financial accounting and reporting systems signal entrepreneurs that their businesses are experiencing declining profits, increasing overhead expenses, and growing inventories or accounts receivable. All of these changes have negative impacts on cash flow, the lifeblood of every business. When cash flow suffers, entrepreneurs may struggle to pay vendors, may not be able to order enough raw materials and hire enough workers, and may not be able to maintain equipment properly. To avoid these problems, entrepreneurs must tune in to the signals that their businesses send about their performance.

What are these signals, and how does an entrepreneur go about tracking and focusing on them? One extremely helpful tool is ratio analysis. **Ratio analysis**, a method of expressing the relationships between any two elements on financial statements, provides a convenient technique for performing financial analysis. When analyzed properly, ratios serve as barometers of a company's financial health. Ratio analysis allows entrepreneurs to determine whether their companies are carrying excessive inventory, experiencing heavy operating expenses, overextending credit, taking on too much debt, and managing to pay their bills on time and to answer other questions relating to the efficient and effective operation of the overall business. Unfortunately, few business owners actually compute financial ratios and use them to manage their businesses.

ratio analysis
a method of expressing the relationship between any two accounting elements that allows business owners to analyze their companies' financial performances.

Smart business owners use financial ratio analysis to identify problems in their businesses while they are still problems and not business-threatening crises. Tracking these ratios over time permits an owner to spot a variety of red flags that are indications of these problem areas. This is critical to business success because business owners cannot solve problems they do not know exist! Business owners also can use ratio analysis to increase the likelihood of obtaining loans. By analyzing their financial statements with ratios, business owners can anticipate potential problems and identify important strengths in advance. Lenders and investors use ratios to analyze the financial statements of companies looking for financing, comparing them against industry averages and looking for trends over time. Business owners should do this same thing!

How many ratios should an entrepreneur monitor to maintain adequate financial control over a business? The number of ratios that an owner could calculate is limited only by the number of accounts on a firm's financial statements. However, tracking too many ratios creates confusion and saps the meaning from an entrepreneur's financial analysis. The secret to successful ratio analysis is *simplicity*, focusing on just enough ratios to provide a clear picture of a company's financial standing. At a minimum, the entrepreneur should track the ratios that his or her lenders and/or investors follow. However, it is wise to track ratios that reflect the overall financial condition of a business.

Twelve Key Ratios

In keeping with the idea of simplicity, we will describe 12 key ratios that enable most business owners to monitor their companies' financial positions without becoming bogged down in financial details. This section presents explanations of these ratios and examples based on the balance sheet and the income statement for Sam's Appliance Shop shown in Figure 12.1 and Figure 12.2. We will group them into four categories: liquidity ratios, leverage ratios, operating ratios, and profitability ratios.

liquidity ratio

a measure of whether a small business will be able to meet its short-term financial obligations as they come due.

LIQUIDITY RATIOS Liquidity ratios tell whether a small business will be able to meet its short-term financial obligations as they come due. These ratios forewarn a business owner of impending cash flow problems. A small company with solid liquidity not only is able to pay its bills on time but also has enough cash to take advantage of attractive business opportunities as they arise. Liquidity ratios measure a company's ability to convert its assets to cash quickly and without a loss of value to pay its short-term liabilities. The primary measures of liquidity are the current ratio and the quick ratio.

current ratio

a measure of a small firm's solvency that indicates the firm's ability to pay current liabilities out of current assets.

1. Current Ratio The **current ratio** measures a small firm's solvency by indicating its ability to pay current liabilities (debts) from current assets. It is calculated in the following manner:

$$\text{Current ratio} = \frac{\text{Current assets}}{\text{Current liabilities}}$$

$$= \frac{\$686,985}{\$367,850}$$

$$= 1.87{:}1$$

Sam's Appliance Shop has $1.87 in current assets for every $1 it has in current liabilities.

Current assets are assets that an owner expects to convert into cash in the ordinary business cycle and normally include cash, notes/accounts receivable, inventory, and any other short-term marketable securities. Current liabilities are short-term obligations that come due within one year and include notes/accounts payable, taxes payable, and accruals.

The current ratio is sometimes called the *working capital ratio* and is the most commonly used measure of short-term solvency. Typically, financial analysts suggest that a small business maintain a current ratio of at least 2:1 (i.e., $2 of current assets for every $1 of current liabilities) to maintain a comfortable cushion of working capital. Generally, the higher a company's current ratio, the stronger its financial position; however, a high current ratio does not guarantee that a company is using its assets in the most profitable manner. For example, a business may have an abundance of accounts receivable (many of which may not even be collectible) or may be overinvesting in inventory.

With its current ratio of 1.87, Sam's Appliance Shop could liquidate its current assets at 53.5 percent (1 ÷ 1.87 = 53.5%) of its book value and still manage to pay its current creditors in full.

2. Quick Ratio The current ratio sometimes can be misleading because it does not reflect the *quality* of a company's current assets. As we have already seen, a company with a large number of past-due receivables and stale inventory could boast an impressive current ratio and still be on the verge of financial collapse. The **quick ratio** (sometimes called the acid test ratio) is a more conservative measure of a company's liquidity because it shows the extent to which its most liquid assets cover its current liabilities. This ratio includes only a company's "quick assets"—assets that a company can convert into cash immediately if needed—and excludes the most illiquid asset of all, inventory. It is calculated as follows:

quick ratio
a conservative measure of a firm's liquidity that indicates the extent to which the firm's most liquid assets cover its current liabilities.

$$\text{Quick ratio} = \frac{\text{Quick assets}}{\text{Current liabilities}}$$

$$= \frac{\$686,985 - \$455,455}{\$376,850}$$

$$= 0.63:1$$

Sam's Appliance Shop has 63 cents in quick assets for every $1 of current liabilities.

The quick ratio is a more rigorous test of a company's liquidity. It measures a company's capacity to pay its current debts if all sales income ceased immediately. Generally, a quick ratio of 1:1 is considered satisfactory. A ratio of less than 1:1, as is the case with Sam's Appliance Shop, indicates that the small firm is dependent on inventory, successful collection of outstanding accounts receivable, and future sales to satisfy short-term debt. A quick ratio of greater than 1:1 indicates a greater degree of financial security.

ENTREPRENEURIAL PROFILE: Alan Knitowski: Phunware Alan Knitowski, chairman and CEO of the mobile apps company Phunware, learned about the importance of managing cash flow and liquidity from his two previous start-ups. He underestimated the time and expense required to develop the software products for his first company but was able to raise more funding and eventually sell the company to Cisco Systems. In his second company, in which he was an investor and a board member, the outcome was not as happy. Two large customers were unable to pay their bills after they were hit hard by the credit crisis of 2008, which forced Knitowski's company into bankruptcy. In his third start-up, Phunware, Knitowski implemented several practices to ensure effective financial and cash management. Every Friday, Phunware's controller e-mails cash on hand, current accounts payable, and the company's quick ratio to the entire management team, which analyzes the financial data to identify any troublesome trends. If the key financial metrics are trending in the wrong direction, managers identify the reason and quickly take corrective actions. The team pays particular attention to accounts receivable to determine whether any customers are paying too slowly and what actions might be necessary as a result of any late payments. Managers monitor cash on hand using a color-coded system. If the company has at least 18 months of cash on hand, managers see a green bar. If cash on hand would cover 12 to 18 months of expenses, the cash on hand figure is coded yellow, and managers immediately begin to evaluate debt and equity funding sources to improve Phunware's cash position. They do not wait until the company's cash on hand drops too low to act. The company has never dropped below 12 months of cash on hand, which would be coded red. In addition to its successful venture capital funding, Phunware has used its strong cash position to help support its rapid growth. Multiple national rankings compiled by business publications have named Phunware as a top performer in its industry.[11] ∎

Courtesy of Alan Knitkowski, CEO, Phunware

LEVERAGE RATIOS **Leverage ratios** measure the financing supplied by a firm's owners against that supplied by its creditors; they are a gauge of the depth of a company's debt. These ratios show the extent to which an entrepreneur relies on debt capital (rather than equity capital) to finance the business. They also provide a measure of the degree of financial risk in a company.

leverage ratio
a measure of the financing supplied by a firm's owners against that supplied by its creditors; it is a gauge of the depth of a company's debt.

Generally, small businesses with low leverage ratios are less affected by economic downturns, but the returns for these firms are lower during economic booms. Conversely, small companies with high leverage ratios are more vulnerable to economic slides because their debt loads demolish cash flow; however, they have greater potential for large profits.

Today, 63 percent of small businesses that have employees rely on some form of debt financing. Young companies carry less debt than their older counterparts. The most common source of debt financing is banks, although some entrepreneurs also rely on debt from family and friends, credit cards, or proceeds from home equity loans.[12] Debt is a powerful financial tool, whatever its source, but companies must handle it carefully. Unfortunately, some companies push their debt loads beyond the safety barrier and threaten their ability to survive. Heavy debt loads can be deadly to a business, particularly when a company's sales or earnings falter, as often happens during economic downturns. Managed carefully, however, debt can boost a company's performance and improve its productivity.

debt ratio

a measure of the percentage of total assets financed by a company's creditors compared to its owners.

3. Debt Ratio A small company's **debt ratio** measures the percentage of total assets financed by its creditors compared to its owners. The debt ratio is calculated as follows:

$$\text{Debt ratio} = \frac{\text{Total debt (or liabilities)}}{\text{Total assets}}$$

$$= \frac{\$367,850 + \$212,150}{\$847,655}$$

$$= 0.68{:}1$$

Creditors have claims of 68 cents against every $1 of assets that Sam's Appliance Shop owns, meaning that creditors have contributed twice as much to the company's asset base as its owners have.

Total debt includes all current liabilities and any outstanding long-term notes and bonds. Total assets represent the sum of the firm's current assets, fixed assets, and intangible assets. A high debt ratio means that creditors provide a large percentage of a company's total financing and, therefore, bear most of its financial risk. Owners generally prefer higher leverage ratios; otherwise, business funds must come either from the owners' personal assets or from taking on new owners, which means giving up more control over the business. In addition, with a greater portion of a firm's assets financed by creditors, the owner is able to generate profits with a smaller personal investment. Creditors, however, typically prefer moderate debt ratios because a lower debt ratio indicates a smaller chance of creditor losses in case of liquidation. To lenders and creditors, high debt ratios mean a higher risk of default.

ENTREPRENEURIAL PROFILE: Rhythm and Hues Rhythm and Hues, a visual-effects company founded in El Segundo, California, in 1987 by John Hughes and Keith Goldfarb, achieved acclaim for many of the films on which it worked, including *Life of Pi*, *Babe*, *Django Unchained*, *The Golden Compass*, and others. The company, which counted on just three movie studios for 97 percent of its revenue, grew to more than $121 million in annual revenue and, at its peak, employed 700 workers. However, when two of its customers cut back on movie production, Rhythm and Hues' sales declined rapidly. Increased competition from low-cost visual-effects companies in foreign countries forced the company to cut its prices, causing it to operate at a loss and throwing it further into a tailspin. Rhythm and Hues took on more debt, including a short-term $17 million loan from Universal Studios that enabled the company to finish work on several movies for Universal, but Rhythm and Hues could not recover and soon filed for bankruptcy. At the time of the filing, the company had assets of $27 million and liabilities of $33.8 million, which gave it a debt ratio of 1.25:1. In other words, Rhythm and Hues owed creditors $1.25 for every $1 it held in assets. Eventually, Prana Studios, an animation and visual effects company based in Los Angeles, purchased what was left of Rhythm and Hues in a bankruptcy sale for $30 million.[13] ∎

debt-to-net-worth (debt-to-equity) ratio

a measure that expresses the relationship between the capital contributions from creditors and those from owners that indicates how highly leveraged a company is.

4. Debt-to-Net-Worth Ratio A small company's **debt-to-net-worth (debt-to-equity) ratio** also expresses the relationship between the capital contributions from creditors and those from owners and measures how highly leveraged a company is. This ratio reveals a company's capital structure by comparing what the business "owes" to "what it is worth." It is a measure of a small company's ability to meet both its creditor and owner obligations in case of liquidation. The debt-to-net-worth ratio is calculated as follows:

$$\text{Debt-to-net worth ratio} = \frac{\text{Total debt (or liabilities)}}{\text{Tangible net worth}}$$

$$= \frac{\$367{,}850 + \$212{,}150}{\$267{,}655 - \$3{,}500}$$

$$= 2.20{:}1$$

Sam's Appliance Shop owes creditors $2.20 for every $1 of equity Sam owns.

Total debt is the sum of current liabilities and long-term liabilities, and tangible net worth represents the owners' investment in the business (Capital + Capital stock + Earned surplus + Retained earnings) less any intangible assets (e.g., goodwill) the firm owns.

The higher this ratio, the more leverage a business is using and the lower the degree of protection afforded creditors if the business fails. A higher debt-to-net-worth ratio also means that the firm has less capacity to borrow; lenders and creditors see the firm as being "borrowed up." Conversely, a low ratio typically is associated with a higher level of financial security, giving the business greater borrowing potential.

 ENTREPRENEURIAL PROFILE: William Porter: E*TRADE Financial Corporation William Porter founded the company that became E*TRADE in 1982 as a back-end system to facilitate online stock trading. The company went public in 1996, the same year it launched its own online trading site, etrade.com. Throughout its history, E*TRADE grew through expansion into new related lines of business, such as its own retail brokerages, and through strategic acquisitions. It has funded most of its growth through cash flow from operations. The company's debt-to-equity ratio is 0.24:1, which is about one-third the average of publicly traded companies. This low debt-to-equity ratio has kept its stock price strong, even during economic downturns. Investors view companies with low debt ratios as being much more able to weather economic ups and downs.[14] ■

You Be the Consultant

The Challenges of Debt

Charles Kuhn's business, Kopp's Cycle, is a part of bicycling history. E. C. Kopp founded Kopp's Cycle in Princeton, New Jersey, in 1891. The Kopp family operated the business until the Kuhn family purchased it. Eventually Charles took over the store from his father in the late 1970s. Celebrities from Albert Einstein to Brooke Shields have purchased bicycles from Kopp's Cycle. Legendary road racing cyclist Greg LeMond was a customer from the time he was a junior racer.

Kopp's Cycle looks like a typical bike shop. The front of the retail store displays high-end bicycles and accessories. In the back of the store is a repair shop that looks the same as it did when Kuhn's father first purchased the business.

Charles Kuhn purchased the building that houses Kopp's Cycle in 2004 for about $800,000, which he financed with a $775,000 loan secured by an SBA guarantee. Kuhn was not happy with SBA financing, however, because it came with significant additional paperwork. In addition, the SBA loan had an adjustable rate, which made him worry about the actual long-term cost of the loan and the uncertainty about payments as the interest rate changed. As a result, Kuhn refinanced the loan through another bank that offered him a conventional fixed-rate

loan for $825,000. This new loan was not an SBA-guaranteed loan, which pleased Kuhn. At the time of the refinancing, the building was appraised at $1.3 million. Although the loan was amortized over 25 years, it had a balloon payment of $775,000 due in three years. Balloon payments are a common feature of loans to small business owners. At the time of the balloon payment, the borrower must refinance, either with the current lender or with a new lender.

The economic downturn in 2008 hit Kopp's Cycle hard—as it did many other small businesses. In addition, online sales of high-end bicycles were increasing significantly. Online retailers were able to offer prices that a small business like Kopp's Cycle could not compete with due to its lower sales volume and higher overhead. Revenues dropped from $498,000 in 2008 to $393,000 in 2009. Kuhn cut prices in 2010 to compete with online retailers, which did bring his sales levels back up. However, the price cuts resulted in profit margins dropping from 10 to 15 percent down to 1 percent. To manage cash flow during this time, Kuhn relied on credit cards as a funding source for the business. He amassed credit card debt of more than $100,000.

(continued)

You Be the Consultant *(continued)*

Ashadhodhomei/Shutterstock

With the growth in online sales, Kopp's Cycle has created an increase in demand for service. To address this change in the industry, Kuhn has doubled the number of employees in the service department and streamlined the process for accessing service in his store. When the focus was more on bicycle sales, customers often waited up to a month to get their bicycles back from service. With the new focus on service as a key part of its business model, Kopp's Cycle now gets service done in less than a week.

Kuhn decided to seek new financing for his business. His plan was to borrow $1 million to pay off the $800,000 balance on the building loan, pay off the credit card balances, and provide $100,000 in working capital to help manage cash flow. Kuhn estimated that his building is now worth about $1.5 million, which he believed should be more than enough equity to support the loan.

The first bank Kuhn contacted about a loan declined to make a loan. After reviewing Kopp's Cycle's financial statements,

the loan officer said Kopp's Cycle's debt coverage ratio, the ratio of monthly net cash flow divided by debt payments, did not meet the bank's minimum of 1.1 to 1.5. With Kopp's Cycle's declining profit margins, it could not meet the required debt coverage ratio. Bankers want to see a significant cushion in a company's monthly cash flow to ensure that even if the company's financial position declines, it can maintain payments on the loan. The second bank Kuhn approached gave him the same answer. A third banker did not even return Kuhn's phone calls.

Kuhn then turned to a loan broker, to whom he paid an upfront fee and who would take 10 percent of the loan amount once a loan was closed. However, the bank the loan broker found for Kuhn to talk with also passed on the loan, citing concerns over the true market value of Kuhn's building.

Although Kuhn did not believe that a new loan was essential for the survival of the business, he had hoped he could secure new financing to bolster Kopp's Cycle's financial position. In addition, Kuhn must address the balloon payment that is part of his current building loan sooner than later. There is no guarantee that his current bank will renew this loan, and he has not had much luck finding alternative financing.

1. What are the benefits to entrepreneurs who use debt capital (leverage) to finance their companies' growth?

2. What are the risks associated with debt financing?

3. Why is using ratio analysis to keep track of their companies' financial performance over time so important for entrepreneurs?

4. What lessons concerning the use of debt financing can entrepreneurs learn from Charles Kuhn's experience?

5. Assume the role of a small business banker. Suppose that Kuhn were to approach you for a bank loan to refinance his debt. Which financial ratios would you be most interested in? Why? What advice would you offer him?

6. Assume the role of a small business counselor. What advice would you offer him to ensure the long-term survival of Kopp's Cycle?

Sources: Based on Rich Fisher, "What's in Store: Find Your Ride at Kopp's," *centraljersey.com*, April 14, 2016, www.centraljersey.com/lifestyle/what-s-in-store-find-your-ride-at-kopp-s/article_ed711630-0275-11e6-8e3c-570dba02aa75.html; Robb Mandelbaum, "A Bicycle Shop Struggles to Get a Loan," *New York Times*, June 2, 2011, p. B5; "Welcome to Kopp's Cycle," Kopp's Cycle, n.d., http://koppscycle.net/articles/kopps-cycle-history-pg59.htm; Linda Arntzenius, "All in a Day's Work: Charles Kuhn," *Town Topics*, n.d., www.towntopics.com/sep1306/other4.html.

As a company's debt-to-net-worth ratio approaches 1:1, the creditors' interest in the business approaches that of the owners. If the ratio is greater than 1:1, creditors' claims exceed those of the owners, and the business may be undercapitalized. In other words, the owner has not supplied an adequate amount of capital, forcing the business to be overextended in terms of debt. Lenders become nervous when a company's debt-to-equity ratio reaches 3:1 or more.

times-interest-earned ratio
a measure of a small firm's ability to make the interest payments on its debt.

5. Times-Interest-Earned Ratio The **times-interest-earned ratio** is a measure of a small company's ability to make the interest payments on its debt. It tells how many times a company's earnings cover the interest payments on the debt it is carrying. This ratio measures the size of the cushion a company has in covering the interest cost of its debt load. The times-interest-earned ratio is calculated as follows:

$$\text{Times interest earned} = \frac{\text{Earnings before interest and taxes (EBIT)}}{\text{Total interest expense}}$$

$$= \frac{\$60,629 + \$39,850}{\$39,850}$$

$$= 2.52:1$$

Sam's Appliance Shop's earnings are 2.5 times greater than its interest expense.

EBIT is the firm's profit *before* deducting interest expense and taxes; the denominator measures the amount the business paid in interest over the accounting period. A high ratio suggests that a company has little difficulty meeting the interest payments on its loans; creditors see this as a sign of safety for future loans. Conversely, a low ratio is an indication that the company is overextended in its debts; earnings will not be able to cover its debt service if this ratio is less than 1. Many banks look for a times-interest-earned ratio of at least 2:1, but some creditors may want to see 4:1 to 6:1 before pronouncing a small company a good credit risk. According to a Pepperdine University survey of bankers, the top reason that business loans are denied is inadequate cash flow and profits.[16] Marston's, which operates a high-growth chain of restaurants and a brewery, faced significant pressure from its investors and bankers when its times-interest-earned ratio slipped to 0.9:1.[15]

Although low to moderate levels of debt can boost a company's financial performance, trouble looms on the horizon for businesses whose debt loads are so heavy that they must starve critical operations, research and development, customer service, and other vital areas just to pay interest on the debt. Because their interest payments are so large, highly leveraged companies find that they are restricted when it comes to spending cash, whether on an acquisition, normal operations, or capital spending. Some entrepreneurs are so averse to debt that they run their companies with little or no borrowing, relying instead on their business's cash flow to finance growth.

ENTREPRENEURIAL PROFILE: Richard and Kate Hanley: Hanley's Foods The inspiration to start Hanley's Foods came to Richard Hanley when he noticed that there were no bottled versions of a local salad dressing known as Sensation. Richard and his wife Kate launched their salad dressing business by selling their own version of Sensation salad dressing at a local farmer's market. Their salad dressing sold out quickly each time they offered it at the market. With that market research, Richard quit his job at an advertising firm and funded the start-up by increasing a car loan by $3,000. Rather than pursue debt or equity financing, the Hanleys have relied on bootstrapping (including temporarily moving in with Richard's parents) and a series of small short-term loans from a friend. After three years, Hanley's Foods sells its salad dressing in more than 400 stores and is able to pay its two founders a modest salary. Although they may eventually secure outside funding, avoiding debt and equity has helped the Hanleys build a lean, successful start-up that is free from debt and its corresponding interest payments.[17] ∎

OPERATING RATIOS **Operating ratios** help an entrepreneur evaluate a small company's overall performance and indicate how effectively the business uses its resources. The more effectively the business uses its resources, the less capital it requires. These five operating ratios are designed to help entrepreneurs spot the areas they must improve to keep their businesses competitive.

operating ratio
a measure that helps an entrepreneur evaluate a small company's overall performance and indicates how effectively the business uses its resources.

6. Average-Inventory-Turnover Ratio A small firm's **average-inventory-turnover ratio** measures the number of times its average inventory is sold out, or turned over, during the accounting period. This ratio tells the owner whether he or she is managing inventory properly. It indicates whether a business's inventory is understocked, overstocked, or obsolete. The average-inventory-turnover ratio is calculated as follows:

average-inventory-turnover ratio
a measure of the number of times a company's average inventory is sold out, or turned over, during an accounting period.

$$\text{Average-inventory-turnover ratio} = \frac{\text{Cost of goods sold}}{\text{Average inventory}}$$

$$= \frac{\$1,290,117}{(\$805,745 + \$455,455) \div 2}$$

$$= 2.05 \text{ times/year}$$

Sam's Appliance Shop turns over its inventory about two times a year, or once every 178 days.

Average inventory is the sum of the value of the firm's inventory at the beginning of the accounting period and its value at the end of the accounting period, divided by 2.

This ratio tells an entrepreneur how fast merchandise is moving through the business and helps him or her balance the company's inventory on the fine line between oversupply and undersupply. To determine the average number of days that the existing inventory will last, the owner can divide the average-inventory-turnover ratio into the number of days in the accounting period (e.g., 365 days ÷ average-inventory-turnover ratio). The result is called *days inventory* (or *average age of inventory*). Auto dealerships often use days of inventory on hand as a measure of their performance and consider 45 to 60 days' worth of new cars to be an adequate inventory. Most used car dealers' goal is to have 35 to 45 days' worth of used cars in inventory. Slow-turning inventory cannibalizes car dealers' profitability because of the interest and other expenses they incur. The National Auto Dealer Association estimates that the cost of holding a new car in inventory can be as high as $90 per day; at the typical used car dealership, the cost is about $21 per day. If a used car dealership sells a car within 20 days, it earns an average gross profit of $2,000. However, if that same car sits on the lot for 80 days before it sells, the average gross profit is just $740 (an occurrence known in the industry as "lot rot"). When auto sales began to slow nationwide, Larry Kull, owner of a Honda dealership in New Jersey, saw his day's inventory of new cars increase to 60 days from the normal 45 days. Not only is lot rot a concern for Kull, but for the first time in 37 years, he also had to rent extra space to store the unsold inventory of new cars.[18]

ENTREPRENEURIAL PROFILE: Jennifer Cattaui: Babesta Jennifer Cattaui, founder of Babesta in New York City, sells children's clothing and furniture online and through two retail stores. Cattaui uses a financial dashboard that helps the Babesta management team monitor the financial health of the business and make decisions based on financial data. The dashboard gives the team metrics to assess the company's cash balance, cash flow, inventory, and revenue. Cattaui uses software that displays key metrics using a gauge. If a gauge is in the red zone, the team digs deeper to find the cause. If it is in the green zone, the team knows that things are going well for that specific financial aspect of the business. For example, when its inventory gauge was in the red, the management team assessed the company's inventory and realized that they had furniture in inventory that was not selling. After cutting back the number of those items in Babesta's inventory, the gauge soon returned to the green zone, telling management that inventory turnover had returned to a satisfactory level.[19] ■

An above-average inventory turnover indicates that the small business has a healthy, salable, and liquid inventory and a supply of quality merchandise that is supported by sound pricing policies. A below-average inventory turnover suggests an illiquid inventory characterized by obsolescence, overstocking, stale merchandise, and poor purchasing procedures. Businesses that turn their inventories more rapidly require a smaller inventory investment to produce a particular sales volume. These companies therefore tie up less cash in inventory that idly sits on shelves. For instance, if Sam's could turn its inventory *four* times each year instead of just *two*, the company would require an average inventory of just $322,529 instead of the current level of $630,600 to generate sales of $1,870,841. Increasing the number of inventory turns would free up more than $308,000 in cash currently tied up in excess inventory! Sam's would benefit from improved cash flow and higher profits.

The inventory turnover ratio can be misleading, however. For example, an excessively high ratio could mean that a company does not have enough inventory on hand and may be losing sales because of stock-outs. Similarly, a low ratio could be the result of planned inventory stockpiling to meet seasonal peak demand. Another problem is that the ratio is based on an inventory balance calculated from two days out of the entire accounting period. Thus, inventory fluctuations due to seasonal demand patterns are ignored, and this may bias the resulting ratio. There is no universal, ideal inventory turnover ratio. Financial analysts suggest that a favorable turnover ratio depends on the type of business, its size, its profitability, its method of inventory valuation, and other relevant factors. The most meaningful benchmark for comparison is other companies of similar size in the same industry. For instance, the typical supermarket turns its inventory on average about 14.0 to 15.1 times a year, but a traditional jewelry store averages just 1.3 to 1.5 inventory turns a year.[20]

7. Average-Collection-Period Ratio A small firm's **average-collection-period ratio** (or days sales outstanding [DSO]) shows the average number of days it takes to collect accounts receivable. To compute the average-collection-period ratio, an entrepreneur must first calculate the company's receivables turnover. Given that Sam's Appliance Shop's *credit* sales for the year were $1,309,589 (out of the total sales of $1,870,841), the company's receivables turnover ratio is as follows:

$$\text{Receivables-turnover-ratio} = \frac{\text{Credit sales}}{\text{Accounts receivable}}$$

$$= \frac{\$1,309,589}{\$179,225}$$

$$= 7.31 \text{ times/year}$$

average-collection-period ratio

a measure of the number of days it takes to collect accounts receivable.

This ratio measures the number of times the firm's accounts receivable turn over during the accounting period. Sam's Appliance Shop turns over its receivables 7.31 times per year. The higher the firm's receivables turnover ratio, the shorter the time lag is between the sale and the cash collection.

Use the following to calculate the firm's average-collection-period ratio:

$$\text{Average-collection-period ratio} = \frac{\text{Days in accounting period}}{\text{Receivables turnover ratio}}$$

$$= \frac{365 \text{ days}}{7.31 \text{ times/year}}$$

$$= 50.0 \text{ days}$$

Sam's Appliance Shop's accounts receivable are outstanding for an average of 50 days. Typically, the higher a firm's average-collection-period ratio, the greater its chance of incurring bad debt losses. Sales don't count unless a company collects the revenue from them.

One of the most useful applications of the collection period ratio is to compare it to the industry average and to the company's credit terms. This comparison indicates the degree of control a small company exercises over its credit sales and collection techniques. A healthy collection period ratio depends on the industry in which a company operates. For instance, the average collection period for companies that manufacture medical equipment is 50 days; for tire retailers, it is just 14 days.[21] Perhaps the most meaningful analysis is comparing the collection period ratio to a company's credit terms. One rule of thumb suggests that a company's collection period ratio should be no more than one-third greater than its credit terms. For example, if a small company's credit terms are net 30 (payment due within 30 days), its average-collection-period ratio should be no more than 40 days (30 + 30 × 1/3). For this company, a ratio greater than 40 days indicates poor collection procedures.

Slow payers represent a great risk to many small businesses. Many entrepreneurs proudly point to rapidly rising sales only to find that they must borrow money to keep their companies going because their credit customers are paying their bills in 45, 60, or even 90 days instead of the desired 30 days. Slow receivables are a real danger because they usually lead to a cash crisis that threatens a company's survival. Table 12.1 shows how to calculate the savings associated with lowering a company's average-collection-period ratio.

8. Average-Payable-Period Ratio The converse of the average-collection-period ratio, the **average-payable-period ratio** (or days payables outstanding [DPO]) indicates the average number of days it takes a company to pay its accounts payable. Like the average collection period, it is measured in days. To compute this ratio, an entrepreneur first calculates the payables turnover ratio. Sam's Appliance Shop's payables turnover ratio is as follows:

average-payable-period ratio

a measure of the number of days it takes a company to pay its accounts payable.

$$\text{Payables turnover ratio} = \frac{\text{Purchases}}{\text{Accounts payable}}$$

$$= \frac{\$939,827}{\$152,580}$$

$$= 6.16 \text{ times/year}$$

TABLE 12.1 How Lowering Your Average Collection Period Can Save You Money

Too often, entrepreneurs fail to recognize the importance of collecting their accounts receivable on time. After all, collecting accounts is not as glamorous or as much fun as generating sales. Lowering a company's average-collection-period ratio, however, *can* produce tangible—and often significant—savings. The following formula shows how to convert an improvement in a company's average-collection-period ratio into dollar savings:

Annual savings

$$= \frac{(\text{Credit sales} \times \text{Annual interest rate} \times \text{Number of days average collection period is lowered})}{365}$$

where

Credit sales = company's annual credit sales in dollars

Annual interest rate = the interest rate at which the company borrows money

Number of days average collection period is lowered = the difference between the previous year's average collection period ratio and the current one

Example

Sam's Appliance Shop's average-collection-period ratio is 50 days. Suppose that the previous year's average-collection-period ratio was 58 days, so this year there has been an eight-day improvement. The company's credit sales for the most recent year were $1,309,589. If Sam borrows money at 8.75%, this eight-day improvement has generated savings for Sam's Appliance Shop of:

$$\text{Savings} = \frac{\$1,309,589 \times 8.75\% \times 8 \text{ days}}{365 \text{ days}} = \$2,512$$

By collecting his accounts receivable just eight days faster, on average, Sam has saved his business more than $2,500! Of course, if a company's average-collection-period ratio rises, the same calculation will tell the owner how much that change costs.

To find the average payable period, use the following computation:

$$\text{Average-payable-period ratio} = \frac{\text{Days in accounting period}}{\text{Payables turnover ratio}}$$

$$= \frac{365 \text{ days}}{6.16 \text{ times per year}}$$

$$= 59.3 \text{ days}$$

Sam's Appliance Shop takes an average of 59 days to pay its accounts with vendors and suppliers.

One of the most meaningful comparisons for this ratio is against the credit terms suppliers offer (or an average of the credit terms offered). If the average payable ratio slips beyond vendors' credit terms, the company probably suffers from a sloppy accounts-payable procedure or from cash shortages, and its credit rating is in danger. An excessively high average-payables-period ratio indicates the presence of a significant amount of past-due accounts payable. Although sound cash management calls for a business owner to keep his or her cash as long as possible, slowing payables too drastically can severely damage the company's credit rating. If this ratio is significantly lower than vendors' credit terms, the company is not using its cash most effectively by paying vendors too quickly.

Comparing a company's average-collection-period ratio (DSO) to its average-payable period ratio (DPO) gives owners meaningful insight into their companies' cash position. Ideally, the average payable period matches (or exceeds) the time it takes to convert inventory into sales and ultimately into cash. In this case, the company's vendors are financing its inventory and its credit sales. Some large companies benefit from this situation. For example, Amazon does not pay its suppliers until 24 days after it collects payments from its customers, and Macy's takes 71 days.[22] Subtracting DSO from DPO yields a company's **float**, the net number of days of cash that flow into or out of a company. Sam's Appliance Shop's float is:

float
the net number of days of cash flowing into or out of a company; Float = Days payables outstanding (DPO) – Days sales outstanding (DSO).

$$\text{Float} = \text{DPO} - \text{DSO} = 59.3 \text{ days} - 50.0 \text{ days} = 9.3 \text{ days}$$

A positive value for float means that cash will accumulate in a company over time, but a negative number means that the company's cash balance will diminish over time. Multiplying float by the company's average daily sales tells Sam how much the company's cash balance will change over the course of the year as a result of its collection and payable processes:

$$\text{Change in cash position} = \$1,870,841 \div 365 \text{ days} \times 9.3 \text{ days} = \$47,668$$

We will see the impact that these three operating ratios—inventory turnover, accounts receivable, and accounts payable—have on a small company's cash flow in the next chapter.

9. Net-Sales-to-Total-Assets Ratio A small company's **net-sales-to-total-assets** (also called the **total-asset-turnover) ratio** is a general measure of its ability to generate sales in relation to its assets. It describes how productively the firm uses its assets to produce sales revenue. The total-assets-turnover ratio is calculated as follows:

$$\text{Total-assets-turnover ratio} = \frac{\text{Net sales}}{\text{Net total assets}}$$

$$= \frac{\$1,870,841}{\$847,655}$$

$$= 2.21:1$$

Sam's Appliance Shop is generating $2.21 in sales for every dollar of assets.

The denominator of this ratio, net total assets, is the sum of all of a company's assets (cash, inventory, land, buildings, equipment, tools, and everything it owns) less depreciation. This ratio is meaningful only when compared to that of similar firms in the same industry category. Monitoring it over time is very helpful for maintaining a sufficient asset base as a small business grows. A total-assets-turnover ratio below the industry average indicates that a small company is not generating an adequate sales volume for its asset size.

A recent study by the National Federation of Independent Businesses of businesses that reported declining earnings shows that the most common reason for their lower earnings is a decrease in sales volume.[23] If a company's sales fall below its breakeven point, it operates at a loss, which is not sustainable.

PROFITABILITY RATIOS **Profitability ratios** indicate how efficiently a small company is being managed. They provide the owner with information about a company's ability to use its resources to generate a profit, its "bottom line."

10. Net-Profit-on-Sales Ratio The **net-profit-on-sales ratio** (also called the profit-margin-on-sales ratio or the net-profit-margin ratio) measures a company's profit per dollar of sales. This ratio (which is expressed as a percentage) shows the portion of each sales dollar remaining after deducting all expenses. The profit margin on sales is calculated as follows:

$$\text{Net-profit-on-sales ratio} = \frac{\text{Net profit}}{\text{Net sales}}$$

$$= \frac{\$60,629}{\$1,870,841}$$

$$= 3.24\%$$

For every dollar in sales Sam's Appliance Shop generates, Sam keeps 3.24 cents in profit.

The average net profit margin for privately held companies varies widely from one industry to another and varies with economic conditions. Some industries have razor-thin net profit margins of less than 1 percent, while others can have average net profit margins that approach 20 percent. Examples of businesses that tend to have lower profit margins include beverage manufacturers, grocery stores, office supply stores, assisted living facilities, and waste collection. Examples of businesses that tend to have higher profit margins include accounting and tax preparation firms, car rental companies, health care practitioners, and electronic maintenance and repair.[24] It is important for a business owner to know industry ratio benchmarks. If a

net-sales-to-total-assets (total-asset-turnover) ratio
a measure of a company's ability to generate sales in relation to its asset base.

profitability ratio
a measure that indicates how efficiently a small company is being managed.

net-profit-on-sales ratio
a measure of a company's profit per dollar of sales.

company's profit margin on sales is below the industry average, it may be a sign that its prices are too low, that its costs are excessively high, or both. A recent survey reports that the members of the general public believe that the average net profit margin for businesses is 36 percent! In reality, the average net profit margin for businesses is about 6.5 percent (in other words, the business earns 6.5 cents in profit out of every \$1 in sales), *5 times lower* than the public's perception.[25]

ENTREPRENEURIAL PROFILE: Bill Riddle: Valle Luna Valle Luna Mexican restaurant is a third-generation family business in Phoenix, Arizona. Bill Riddle is the latest family member to run the business, which has three locations and 277 employees. After the citizens of the state of Arizona passed a proposition that increased the state's minimum wage from \$8.05 to \$10 an hour—an increase of more than 24 percent—Valle Luna immediately increased its menu prices to try to offset the impact of the wage increase on its profit margin. However, Riddle expressed concerns about additional cost increases as suppliers also raise their prices to offset the impact on their profit margins.[26] ■

A natural reaction to low profitability ratios is to embark on a cost-cutting effort. Although minimizing costs does improve profitability, entrepreneurs must be judicious in their cost cutting, taking a strategic approach rather than imposing across-the-board cuts. The key is to reduce costs without diminishing customer service and damaging employee morale. Cutting costs in areas that are vital to operating success—such as a retail jeweler eliminating its advertising expenditures or a restaurant reducing the quality of its ingredients—usually hurts a company's ability to compete and can lead to failure. For instance, choosing to lay off workers, a common reaction of many companies facing financial challenges, often backfires. Not only does a company risk losing talented workers and the knowledge they have built up over time, but research also shows that repeated rounds of layoffs destroy the morale and productivity of the remaining workers.[27] However, sometimes businesses face the dilemma of either cutting costs or going out of business.

If a company's net-profit-on-sales ratio is excessively low, the owner should first check the gross profit margin (net sales minus cost of goods sold expressed as a percentage of net sales). Of course, a reasonable gross profit margin varies from industry to industry. For instance, a service company may have a gross profit margin of 75 percent, while a manufacturer's may be 35 percent. The key is to know what a reasonable gross profit margin is for your particular business. If this margin slips too low, the company's future is in immediate jeopardy. An inadequate gross profit margin cannot cover all of a company's business expenses and also generate a profit.

ENTREPRENEURIAL PROFILE: Elisa Zenari: Zenari's Elisa Zenari, co-owner of Zenari's Italian restaurant in Edmonton, Alberta, is facing challenges due to rising food costs. Zenari's focuses on authentic Italian recipes that include fresh ingredients. The cost of much of its produce has increased up to three times over the last year. For example, a case of sweet peppers that used to cost about \$30 is up to more than \$80. The kitchen staff continue to explore creative ways to change the menu items using less expensive produce options. The staff decided to alter soup recipes to cut back or even eliminate the need for sweet peppers by adding more potatoes, carrots, and leeks, which are all much less expensive. The goal at Zenari's is to find ways to avoid price increases on the menu as much as possible while maintaining its net profit margin.[28] ■

operating leverage
a situation in which increases in operating efficiency mean that expenses as a percentage of sales revenue flatten or even decline.

net-profit-to-assets (return-on-assets) ratio
a measure of how much profit a company generates for each dollar of assets that it owns.

Monitoring the net profit margin is especially important for fast-growing companies in which sales are climbing rapidly. Unbridled growth can cause expenses to rise faster than sales, eroding a company's net profit margin. Success can be deceptive: Sales are rising, but profits are shrinking. Ideally, a company reaches a point at which it achieves **operating leverage**, a situation in which increases in operating efficiency mean that expenses as a percentage of sales revenues flatten or even decline. As a result, the company's net profit margin climbs as it grows.

11. Net-Profit-to-Assets Ratio The **net-profit-to-assets** (or **return-on-assets [ROA]) ratio** tells how much profit a company generates for each dollar of assets it owns. This ratio describes how efficiently a business is putting to work all the assets it owns to generate a profit. It tells how much net income an entrepreneur is squeezing from each dollar's worth of the company's assets. It is calculated as follows:

$$\text{Net-profit-to-assets ratio} = \frac{\text{Net profit}}{\text{Total assets}}$$

$$= \frac{\$60,629}{\$847,655}$$

$$= 7.15\%$$

Sam's Appliance Shop earns a return of 7.15 percent on its asset base. This ratio provides clues about the asset intensity of an industry. Return-on-assets ratios that are below 5 percent are indicative of asset-intense industries that require heavy investments in assets to stay in business (e.g., manufacturing and railroads). Return-on-assets ratios that exceed 20 percent tend to occur in asset-light industries such as business or personal services—for example, advertising agencies and computer services. A net-profit-to-assets ratio that is below the industry average suggests that a company is not using its assets efficiently to produce a profit. Another common application of this ratio is to compare it to the company's cost of borrowed capital. Ideally, a company's return-on-assets ratio should exceed the cost of borrowing money to purchase those assets. Companies that experience significant swings in the value of their assets over the course of a year often use an average value of the asset base over the accounting period to get a more realistic estimate of this ratio.

12. Net-Profit-to-Equity Ratio The **net-profit-to-equity ratio** (or **return on net worth ratio**) measures the owners' rate of return on investment (ROI). Because it reports the percentage of the owners' investment in the business that is being returned through profits annually, it is one of the most important indicators of a firm's profitability or a management's efficiency. The net-profit-to-equity ratio is computed as follows:

net-profit-to-equity ratio
a measure of the owners' rate of return on investment (ROI).

$$\text{Net-profit-to-equity ratio} = \frac{\text{Net profit}}{\text{Owners' equity (or net worth)}}$$

$$= \frac{\$60,629}{\$267,655}$$

$$= 22.65\%$$

Sam is earning 22.65 percent on the money he has invested in this business.

This ratio compares profits earned during the accounting period with the amount the owner has invested in the business at the time. If this interest rate on the owners' investment is excessively low, some of this capital might be better used elsewhere. A business should produce a rate of return that exceeds its cost of capital.

Interpreting Business Ratios

LO4

Explain how to interpret financial ratios.

Ratios are useful yardsticks when measuring a small firm's performance and can point out potential problems before they develop into serious crises. However, calculating these ratios is not enough to ensure proper financial control. In addition to knowing how to calculate these ratios, entrepreneurs must understand how to interpret them and apply them to managing their businesses more effectively and efficiently. Many entrepreneurs use key financial ratios in a performance dashboard that helps them manage by continuously assessing trends in the financial strength of their businesses.

ENTREPRENEURIAL PROFILE: Peter Smith: Golden Spiral The leadership team of Golden Spiral, a business-to-business marketing agency in Nashville, Tennessee, believes in using financial statements and KPIs to help gauge the health of the business. In addition to monitoring its income statement and balance sheet, Peter Smith, president and COO, developed a company scorecard that assesses each of the company's major functions (sales, marketing, finance, and operations). This scorecard includes the bank balance,

Courtesy of Peter Smith, President & COO, Golden Spiral

You Be the Consultant

All Is Not Paradise in Eden's Garden: Part 1

Joe and Kaitlin Eden, co-owners of Eden's Garden, a small nursery, lawn, and garden supply business, have just received their year-end financial statements from their accountant. At their last meeting with their accountant, Shelley Edison, three months ago, the Edens had mentioned that they seemed to be having trouble paying their bills on time. "Some of our suppliers have threatened to put us on 'credit hold,'" said Joe.

Balance Sheet, Eden's Garden

Assets

Current Assets

Cash		$6,457
Accounts Receivable	$29,152	
Less Allowance for Doubtful Accounts	$3,200	$25,952
Inventory		$88,157
Supplies		$7,514
Prepaid Expenses		$1,856
Total Current Assets		$129,936

Fixed Assets

Land		$59,150
Buildings	$51,027	
Less Accumulated Depreciation	$2,061	$48,966
Autos	$24,671	
Less Accumulated Depreciation	$12,300	$12,371
Equipment	$22,375	
Less Accumulated Depreciation	$1,250	$21,125
Furniture and Fixtures	$10,295	
Less Accumulated Depreciation	$1,000	$9,295
Total Fixed Assets		$150,907
Intangibles (Goodwill)		$0
Total Assets		$280,843

Liabilities

Current Liabilities

Accounts Payable	$54,258
Notes Payable	$20,150
Credit Line Payable	$8,118
Accrued Wages/Salaries Payable	$1,344
Accrued Interest Payable	$1,785
Accrued Taxes Payable	$1,967
Total Current Liabilities	$87,622

Long-Term Liabilities

Mortgage	$72,846
Note Payable	$47,000
Total Long-Term Liabilities	$119,846

Owner's Equity

Sam Lloyd, Capital	$73,375
Total Liabilities and Owner's Equity	$280,843

Income Statement, Eden's Garden

Net Sales Revenue*		**$689,247**
Cost of Goods Sold		
Beginning Inventory, 1/1/xx	$78,271	
+ Purchases	$403,569	
Goods Available for Sale	$481,840	
− Ending Inventory, 12,31/xx	$86,157	
Cost of Goods Sold		$395,683
Gross Profit		$293,564
Operating Expenses		
Advertising	$22,150	
Insurance	$9,187	
Depreciation		
Building	$26,705	
Autos	$7,895	
Equipment	$11,200	
Salaries	$116,541	
Uniforms	$4,018	
Repairs and Maintenance	$9,097	
Travel	$2,658	
Entertainment	$2,798	
Total Operating Expenses		$212,249
General Expenses		
Utilities	$7,987	
Telephone	$2,753	
Professional Fees	$3,000	
Postage	$1,892	
Payroll Taxes	$11,589	
Total General Expenses		$27,221
Other Expenses		
Interest Expense	$21,978	
Bad Check Expense	$679	
Miscellaneous Expense	$1,248	
Total Other Expenses		$23,905
Total Expenses		$263,375
Net Income		$30,189

*Credit sales represented $289,484 of this total.

(continued)

You Be the Consultant *(continued)*

"I think you need to sit down with me very soon and let me show you how to analyze your financial statements so you

Kpg_Payless/Shutterstock

can see what's happening in your business," Edison told them at that meeting. Unfortunately, it was the beginning of Eden's Garden's busy season, and the Edens were so busy running the company that they never got around to setting a time to meet with Shelley.

"Now that business has slowed down a little, perhaps we should call Shelley and see what she can do to help us understand what our financial statements are trying to tell us," said Kaitlin.

"Right. Before it's too late to do anything about it," said Joe, pulling out the financial statements presented here.

1. Assume the role of Shelley Edison. Using the financial statements for Eden's Garden, calculate the 12 ratios covered in this chapter.

2. Do you see any ratios that, on the surface, look suspicious? Explain.

weekly revenue, organic Web site sessions, content pieces shared on the company blog or social media, inbound leads, outreach to new leads, and billable hours. If any of these scorecard numbers are off target on any given week, the leadership team discusses the issue in a weekly meeting and creates a plan to address the issue. The scorecard also includes a "people-operations-profit" ratio, which shows each number as a percentage of gross profit. Smith says that these ratios are key to effectively managing the company's costs and hitting the profitability goals. In addition, the company has assigned every employee a performance target to track that is relevant to his or her job function. For designers and developers, this is usually the number of billable hours they must book in a given week. For the head of sales, it is the number of meetings or calls with new or potential clients each week. It is each employee's and his or her supervisor's responsibility to discuss this number monthly to ensure that everything is on track. All of the employee targets are tied to the company's objectives and together ensure that Golden Spiral reaches its targeted sales and profits.[29] ∎

As Peter Smith's experience at Golden Spiral suggests, not every business measures its success with the same ratios. In fact, key performance ratios vary dramatically across industries and even within different segments of the same industry. Entrepreneurs must know and understand which ratios are most crucial to their companies' success and focus on monitoring and controlling those indicators. Sometimes business owners develop ratios and measures that are unique to their own operations to help them achieve success. Known as **critical numbers (or key performance indicators [KPIs])**, these indicators measure key financial and operational aspects of a company's performance. When these critical numbers are headed in the right direction, a business is on track to achieve its objectives. Norm Brodsky, founder of a successful document storage and delivery business in New York City, breaks his business into four categories and tracks critical numbers for each one. Every Monday morning, he receives a report comparing the previous week's critical numbers to those of the previous 28 weeks and the same week for the previous three years. With these figures, he can quickly assess how the business is performing. If there are problems with any KPI, he can seek out more information to identify any problems or concerns.[30] Examples of critical numbers at other companies include the following:

critical numbers (or key performance indicators [KPIs]) indicators that measure key financial and operational aspects of a company's performance.

- Many consumer businesses track customer satisfaction associated with each interaction with the company, including connections through social media, Web sites, and e-mail marketing. Each "touch point" with the customer can be rated meets, does not meet, or exceeds expectations.[31]

- A supermarket may track sales per labor hour.

- A healthcare facility might pay attention to the number of referrals. Managers can use this number to predict the number of new patients they can expect and to identify swings in patient revenue. This information helps with staffing decisions and managing cash flow.

- Businesses engaged in digital marketing track indicators such as the number of people who subscribe to electronic newsletters, e-mail open rates, Facebook "likes" and shares, click-through rates from landing pages, and search engine results.

- An Internet service provider tracks its utilization ratio—billable hours as a percentage of total hours worked.

- Site traffic and sales dollars per transaction are two critical numbers for an e-commerce business to monitor on a daily basis.

- Sell-through rates, which measure the percentage of a given product sold from a retailer's inventory each month, identify which products are meeting sales expectations and which ones are sitting on the shelf too long.

Critical numbers may be different for two companies that compete in the same industry. The key is identifying *your* company's critical numbers, monitoring them, and then driving them in the right direction. This requires communicating the importance of these critical numbers to employees and giving them feedback on how well the business is achieving them.

Another valuable way to use ratios is to compare them with those of similar businesses in the same industry. By comparing their companies' financial statistics to industry averages, entrepreneurs are able to locate problem areas and maintain adequate financial controls. Known as **financial benchmarking**, comparing a company's key financial indicators to averages from many firms of similar size in the same industry can help identify problem areas that the company's own history may not show. Benchmarking also is an effective way to set KPIs to ensure that your business is at least doing as well as others in the industry, if not exceeding their performance.

financial benchmarking
a process in which entrepreneurs compare a company's key financial indicators to averages from many companies of similar size in the same industry to identify problem areas that the company's own history may not show.

The principle behind calculating these ratios and comparing them to industry norms is the same as that of most medical tests in the healthcare profession. Just as a healthy person's blood pressure and cholesterol levels should fall within a range of normal values, so should a financially healthy company's ratios. A company cannot deviate too far from these normal values and remain successful for long. When deviations from "normal" do occur (and they will), a business owner should focus on determining the cause of a deviation. In some cases, deviations result from sound business decisions, such as taking on inventory in preparation for the busy season or investing heavily in new technology. In other instances, however, ratios that are out of the normal range for a particular type of business are indicators of what could become serious problems for a company. When comparing a company's critical numbers to industry standards, entrepreneurs should answer the following questions:

- Is there a significant difference in my company's ratio and the industry average?

- If so, is the difference meaningful?

- Is the difference good or bad?

- What are the possible causes of this difference? What is the most likely cause?

- Does this cause require me to take action?

- If so, what action should I take to correct the problem?

When used properly, critical numbers can help owners identify potential problem areas in their businesses early on—*before* they become crises that threaten their very survival. Several organizations regularly compile and publish operating statistics, including key ratios, that summarize the financial performance of many businesses across a wide range of industries. The local library should subscribe to most of these publications:

Risk Management Association. Founded in 1914, the RMA publishes its *Annual Statement Studies*, showing ratios and other financial data for more than 790 different industrial, wholesale, retail, and service categories that are organized by NAICS and SIC code.

Dun & Bradstreet, Inc. Since 1932, Dun & Bradstreet has published *Industry Norms and Key Business Ratios*, which covers more than 800 business categories. Dun & Bradstreet also publishes *Cost of Doing Business*, a series of operating ratios compiled from the Statistics of Income reports of the Internal Revenue Service (IRS).

BizMiner. Users can segment industry financial data by both company size and geographic location for 5,000 industries.

Almanac of Business and Financial Ratios. Published by CCH, this almanac reports comparative financial data and ratios for nearly 200 industries by company size.

Standard & Poor's Industry Surveys. In addition to providing information on financial ratios and comparative financial analysis, these surveys also contain useful details on industry operations, current industry trends, and key terms in the industry.

Online resources. Many companies publish comparative financial resources online. Some require subscriptions, but others are free:

- BizStats publishes common-size financial statements and ratios for 250 industries.
- Reuters provides an overview of many industries that includes industry trends and news as well as financial ratios.
- A subscription to Lexis/Nexis allows users to view detailed company profiles, including financial reports and analysis, for publicly held companies.

Industry associations. Virtually every type of business is represented by a national trade association that publishes detailed financial data compiled from its membership. For example, owners of small supermarkets could contact the National Association of Retail Grocers or check the *Progressive Grocer*, its trade publication, for financial statistics relevant to their operations.

Government agencies. Several government agencies, including the IRS, the Federal Trade Commission, the Department of Commerce, the Census Bureau, the Department of Agriculture, and the Securities and Exchange Commission, periodically publish reports that provide financial operating data on a variety of industries, although the categories are more general. For instance, the IRS publishes *Statistics of Income*, which includes income statement and balance sheet statistics that are compiled from income tax returns and are arranged by industry, asset size, and annual sales. Every five years (years ending in 2 and 7), the Census Bureau publishes the *Economic Census* (www.census.gov/econ/census), which provides general industry statistics and ratios.

What Do All of These Numbers Mean?

Learning to interpret financial ratios takes little a practice! This section and Table 12.2 show you how it's done by comparing the ratios from the operating data already computed for Sam's Appliance Shop to those taken from current data from BizMiner, using only small firms in the same industry with revenues similar to Sam's ($1 million to $2.5 million). Calculating the variance from the industry average—that is, (Company ratio – Industry average ratio) ÷ Industry average ratio—helps entrepreneurs identify the areas in which the company is out of line with the typical company in the industry.

When comparing ratios for their individual businesses to published statistics, entrepreneurs must remember that the comparison is made against averages. An entrepreneur should strive to achieve ratios that are at least as good as these average figures. The goal should be to manage the business so that its financial performance is above average. As a company compares its financial performance to published statistics, it inevitably will discern differences between them. The company should note items that are substantially out of line from the industry average. However, a ratio that varies from the average does not *necessarily* mean that the small business is in financial jeopardy. Instead of making drastic changes in financial policy, entrepreneurs must explore *why* the figures are out of line.

TABLE 12.2 Ratio Analysis: Sam's Appliance Shop Versus the Industry Median

Sam's Appliance Shop	Industry Median	Variance (%)
Liquidity ratios—Tell whether a small business will be able to meet its maturing obligations as they come due.		
1. Current ratio = 1.87:1	1.60:1	16.7%
Sam's Appliance Shop falls short of the rule of thumb of 2:1, but its current ratio is above the industry median by a significant amount. Sam's should have no problem meeting its short-term debts as they come due. By this measure, the company's liquidity is solid.		
2. Quick ratio = 0.63:1	0.81:1	−22.2%
Sam's is below the rule of thumb of 1:1, and it falls below the industry standard. Sam's relies more heavily on selling inventory to satisfy short-term debt than industry standards. If sales slump, the result could be liquidity problems for Sam's.		
Leverage ratios—Measure the financing supplied by the company's owners against that supplied by its creditors as a gauge of the depth of a company's debt.		
3. Debt ratio = 0.68:1	0.69:1	−1.4%
Creditors provide 68 percent of Sam's total assets, which is slightly below the industry median of 69 percent. Although Sam's does not appear to be overburdened with debt, the company might have difficulty borrowing additional money, especially from conservative lenders.		
4. Debt-to-net-worth ratio = 2.20:1	2.27:1	−3.1%
Sam's Appliance Shop owes $2.20 to creditors for every $1 the owners have invested in the business (compared to $2.27 in debt to every $1 in equity for the typical business). Although this is not an exorbitant amount of debt by industry standards, many lenders and creditors see Sam's as "borrowed up." Borrowing capacity is somewhat limited because creditors' claims against the business are more than twice those of the owners.		
5. Times-interest-earned ratio = 2.52:1	12.55:1	−79.9%
Sam's earnings are high enough to cover the interest payments on its debt by a factor of 2.52. Sam's Appliance Shop has a small cushion when meeting its interest payments when compared to the typical firm in the industry. Its ability to get a loan may depend on how closely the bank looks to industry standards, which in this case are unusually high.		
Operating ratios—Evaluate a company's overall performance and show how effectively it is putting its resources to work.		
6. Average-inventory-turnover ratio = 2.05 times/year	4.1 times/year	−50.0%
Inventory is moving through Sam's at a *very* slow pace. The typical appliance store on average, turns over its inventory about once a quarter, while Sam's turns it over about every six months. The company has a problem with slow-moving items in its inventory and, perhaps, too much inventory. Which items are they, and why are they slow moving? Does Sam need to drop some product lines? Sam's inventory issues require *immediate* attention because they have significant cash flow and profitability ramifications.		
7. Average-collection-period ratio = 50.0 days	14.2 days	252.1%
Sam's Appliance Shop collects the average accounts receivable after 50 days, compared with the industry median of about 14 days, nearly four times longer. A more meaningful comparison is against Sam's credit terms; if credit terms are net 30 (or anywhere close to that), Sam's has a dangerous collection problem, one that drains cash and profits and also demands *immediate* attention!		
8. Average-payable-period ratio = 59.3 days	32.4 days	83.0%
Sam's payables are significantly slower than those of the typical firm in the industry, almost twice as long as the standard. Stretching payables too far could seriously damage the company's credit rating, causing suppliers to cut off future trade credit. This could be a sign of cash flow problems or a sloppy accounts-payable procedure. This problem, which indicates that the company suffers from cash flow problems, also demands *immediate* attention.		

TABLE 12.2 **Ratio Analysis: Sam's Appliance Shop Versus the Industry Median (*continued*)**

Sam's Appliance Shop	Industry Median	Variance (%)
9. Net-sales-to-total-assets ratio = 2.21:1	4.06:1	−45.6%

Sam's Appliance Shop is not generating enough sales, given the size of its asset base. This could be a result of a number of factors—improper inventory, inappropriate pricing, poor location, poorly trained sales personnel, and many others. The key is to find the cause—*fast*!

Profitability ratios—Measure how efficiently a firm is operating and offer information about its bottom line.

	Industry Median	Variance (%)
10. Net-profit-on-sales ratio = 3.24%	7.11%	−54.4%

After deducting all expenses, 3.24 cents of each sales dollar remains as profit for Sam's—more than 50 percent below the industry median. Sam should review his company's gross profit margin and investigate its operating expenses, checking them against industry standards and looking for those that are out of balance.

	Industry Median	Variance (%)
11. Net-profit-to-assets ratio = 7.15%	21.41%	−66.6%

Sam's generates a return of 7.15% for every $1 in assets, which is 67 percent below the industry average and below the company's cost of capital. This is another sign that Sam's business is not as profitable as it should be based on industry standards.

	Industry Median	Variance (%)
12. Net-profit-to-equity ratio = 22.65%	70.04%	−67.7%

Sam's Appliance Shop's owners are earning 22.65 percent on the money they have invested in the business. This yield is well below the industry average, another indication that the company is not as profitable as it should be.

In addition to comparing ratios to industry averages, owners should analyze their firms' financial ratios over time. By themselves, these ratios are "snapshots" of a company's financial position at a single instant; however, by examining these trends over time, an entrepreneur can detect gradual shifts that otherwise might go unnoticed until a financial crisis is looming (see Figure 12.5).

breakeven point
the level of operation (sales dollars or production quantity) at which a company neither earns a profit nor incurs a loss.

LO5

Conduct a breakeven analysis for a small company.

Breakeven Analysis

Another key component of every sound financial plan is a breakeven (or cost-volume-profit) analysis. A small company's **breakeven point** is the level of operation (typically expressed as sales dollars or production quantity) at which it neither earns a profit nor incurs a loss. At this level of activity, sales revenue equals expenses—that is, the firm "breaks even." A business that

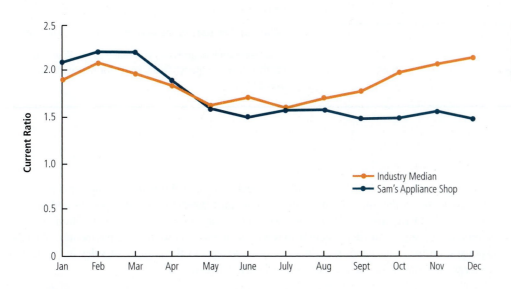

FIGURE 12.5

Trend Analysis of the Current Ratio

generates sales that are greater than its breakeven point will produce a profit, and one that operates below its breakeven point will incur a net loss. Many entrepreneurs leave their own salary out of a breakeven calculation. This is *not* a wise approach. Although the entrepreneur may forgo paychecks during start-up, the business does not truly break even until the entrepreneur is able to earn a market salary from the business. In addition, although reaching the breakeven point is an important milestone for any small business, entrepreneurs should view it as a signpost on the way to reaching profitability goals.

By analyzing costs and expenses, an entrepreneur can calculate the minimum level of activity required to keep a company in operation. These techniques can then be refined to project the sales required generate the desired profit. Most potential lenders and investors expect entrepreneurs to prepare a breakeven analysis to assist them in evaluating the earning potential of the new business. In addition to its being a simple, useful screening device for financial institutions, breakeven analysis can also serve as a planning device for entrepreneurs. It can show an entrepreneur just how unprofitable a poorly planned business venture is likely to be.

You Be the Consultant

All Is Not Paradise in Eden's Garden: Part 2

Remember Joe and Kaitlin Eden, co-owners of Eden's Garden? Assume the role of Shelley Edison, their accountant. Tomorrow, you have scheduled a meeting with them to review their company's financial statements and to make recommendations about how they can improve their company's financial position. Use the following worksheet to summarize the ratios you calculated earlier in this chapter. Then compare them against the industry averages for businesses of a similar size from BizMiner's *Industry Financial Report*.

Ratio Comparison

Ratio	Eden's Garden	Nursery, Garden Center, and Farm Supply Stores Industry Average*
Liquidity Ratios		
Current ratio		1.89
Quick ratio		0.66
Leverage Ratios		
Debt ratio		0.61
Debt-to-net-worth ratio		1.59
Times-interest-earned ratio		3.45

Operating Ratios	
Average-inventory-turnover ratio	7.07
Average-collection-period ratio	9.37 days
Average-payable-period ratio	39.28 days
Net-sales-to-total-assets ratio	3.26
Profitability Ratios	
Net-profit-on-sales ratio	2.90%
Net-profit-to-assets ratio	11.13%
Net-profit-to-equity ratio	28.79%

*BizMiner's *Industry Financial Report*.

1. Analyze the comparisons you have made of Eden's Garden's ratios with those from BizMiner. What red flags do you see?

2. What might be causing the deviations you have observed?

3. What recommendations can you make to the Edens to improve their company's financial performance in the future?

fixed expenses
expenses that do not vary with changes in the volume of sales or production.

variable expenses
expenses that vary directly with changes in the volume of sales or production.

Calculating the Breakeven Point

An entrepreneur can calculate a company's breakeven point by using a simple mathematical formula. To begin the analysis, the entrepreneur must determine fixed expenses and variable expenses. **Fixed expenses** are expenses that do not vary with changes in the volume of sales or production (e.g., rent, depreciation expense, insurance, lease or loan payments). **Variable expenses**, on the other hand, vary directly with changes in the volume of sales or production (e.g., raw material costs, sales commissions, hourly wages).

Some expenses cannot be neatly categorized as fixed or variable because they contain elements of both. These semi-variable expenses change, although not proportionately, with changes in the level of sales or production (electricity is one example). These costs remain constant up to a particular production or sales volume and then climb as that volume is exceeded. To calculate the breakeven point, an entrepreneur must separate these expenses into their fixed and variable components. A number of techniques are available (which are beyond the scope of this text), and a good cost accounting system can provide the desired results.

Here are the steps an entrepreneur must take to compute the breakeven point using an example of a typical small business, the Magic Shop:

Step 1. *Forecast the expenses the business can expect to incur.* With the help of a forecast for a new venture or a budget for an operating small business, an entrepreneur can develop estimates of sales revenue, cost of goods sold, and expenses for the upcoming accounting period. The Magic Shop expects net sales of $950,000 in the upcoming year, with a cost of goods sold of $646,000 and total expenses of $236,500.

Step 2. *Categorize the expenses estimated in step 1 into fixed expenses and variable expenses.* Separate semi-variable expenses into their component parts. From the budget, the owner anticipates variable expenses (including the cost of goods sold) of $705,125 and fixed expenses of $177,375.

Step 3. *Calculate the ratio of variable expenses to net sales.* For the Magic Shop, this percentage is $705,125 ÷ $950,000 = 74 percent. The Magic Shop uses 74 cents out of every sales dollar to cover variable expenses, which leaves 26 cents ($1.00 − 0.74) of each sales dollar as a contribution margin to cover fixed costs and make a profit.

Step 4. *Compute the breakeven point by inserting this information into the following formula:*

$$\text{Break-even sales } (\$) = \frac{\text{Total fixed cost}}{\text{Contribution margin expressed as a percentage of sales}}$$

For the Magic Shop:

$$\text{Breakeven sales} = \frac{\$177,375}{0.26}$$

$$= \$682,212$$

Thus, the Magic Shop will break even with sales of $682,212. At this point, sales revenue generated will just cover total fixed and variable expenses. The Magic Shop will earn no profit and will incur no loss. We can verify this with the following calculations:

Sales at breakeven point	$ 682,212
−Variable expenses (74% of sales)	−504,837
Contribution margin	177,375
−Fixed expenses	−177,375
Net profit (or net loss)	$ 0

Some entrepreneurs find it more meaningful to break down their companies' annual breakeven point into a monthly or even daily sales figure. If the Magic Shop will be open 312 days per year, the average daily sales it must generate just to break even is $682,212 ÷ 312 days = $2,187 per day.

Adding a Profit

The Magic Shop's owner, like all other entrepreneurs, should have a goal beyond just breakeven. Just as a track coach tells runners to run through the finish line and football coaches want their players to run over the goal line into the end zone, an entrepreneur should never be satisfied with simply reaching breakeven. The goal is to move through breakeven into profitability. Breakeven analysis can be adjusted to consider this goal. Suppose the owner expects a reasonable profit (before taxes) of $80,000. What level of sales must the Magic Shop achieve to generate this? The entrepreneur can calculate this by treating the desired profit as if it were a fixed cost, modifying the breakeven formula to include the desired net income:

$$\text{Sales (\$)} = \frac{\text{Total fixed expenses} + \text{Desired net income}}{\text{Contribution margin expressed as a percentage of sales}}$$

$$= \frac{\$177,375 + \$80\,000}{0.26}$$

$$= \$989,904$$

To achieve a net profit of $80,000 (before taxes), the Magic Shop must generate net sales of $989,904. Once again, if we convert this annual sales volume into a daily sales volume, we get $989,904 ÷ 312 days = $3,173 per day.

Breakeven Point in Units

Some small businesses prefer to express the breakeven point in units produced or sold instead of in dollars. Manufacturers often find this approach particularly useful. The following formula computes the breakeven point in units:

$$\text{Breakeven volume} = \frac{\text{Total fixed costs}}{\text{Sales price per unit} - \text{Variable cost per unit}}$$

For example, suppose that Trilex Manufacturing Company estimates its fixed costs for producing its line of small appliances at $390,000. The variable costs (including materials, direct labor, and factory overhead) amount to $12.10 per unit, and the selling price per unit is $17.50. Trilex computes its contribution margin this way:

$$\text{Contribution margin} = \text{Price per unit} - \text{Variable cost per unit}$$

$$= \$17.50 \text{ per unit} - \$12.10 \text{ per unit}$$

$$= \$5.40 \text{ per unit}$$

So, Trilex's breakeven volume is as follows:

$$\text{Breakeven volume (units)} = \frac{\text{Total fixed costs}}{\text{Per-unit contribution margin}}$$

$$= \frac{\$390,000}{\$5.40 \text{ per unit}}$$

$$= 72,222 \text{ units}$$

To convert this number of units to breakeven sales dollars, Trilex simply multiplies it by the selling price per unit:

$$\text{Breakeven sales} = 72,222 \text{ units} \times \$17.50 \text{ per unit} = \$1,263,889$$

Trilex could compute the sales required to produce a desired profit by treating the profit as if it were a fixed cost:

$$\text{Sales (units)} = \frac{\text{Total fixed costs} + \text{Desired net income}}{\text{Per-unit contribution margin}}$$

For example, if Trilex wanted to earn a $60,000 profit, its required sales would be:

$$\text{Sales (units)} = \frac{390,000 + 60,000 = 83,333 \text{ units}}{5.40}$$

which would require 83,333 units × $17.50 per unit = $1,458,328 in sales.

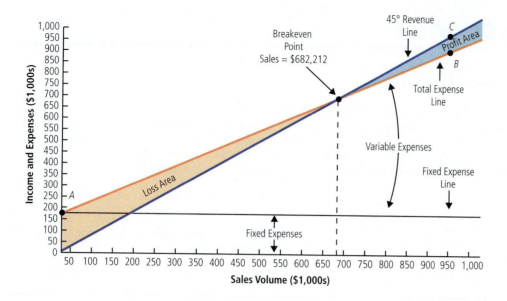

FIGURE 12.6

Breakeven Chart for the Magic Shop

Constructing a Breakeven Chart

The following steps outline the procedure for constructing a graph that visually portrays a company's breakeven point (that point where revenues equal expenses):

Step 1. *On the horizontal axis, mark a scale measuring sales volume in dollars (or in units sold or some other measure of volume).* The breakeven chart for the Magic Shop shown in Figure 12.6 uses sales volume in dollars because it applies to all types of businesses, departments, and products.

Step 2. *On the vertical axis, mark a scale measuring income and expenses in dollars.*

Step 3. *Draw a fixed expense line intersecting the vertical axis at the proper dollar level parallel to the horizontal axis.* The area between this line and the horizontal axis represents the company's fixed expenses. On the breakeven chart for the Magic Shop shown in Figure 12.6, the fixed expense line is drawn horizontally beginning at $177,375 (point A). Because this line is parallel to the horizontal axis, it indicates that fixed expenses remain constant at all levels of activity.

Step 4. *Draw a total expense line that slopes upward beginning at the point where the fixed cost line intersects the vertical axis.* The precise location of the total expense line is determined by plotting the total cost incurred at a particular sales volume. The total cost for a given sales level is found by using the following formula:

Total expenses = Fixed expenses + Variable expenses expressed as a % of sales × Sales level

Arbitrarily choosing a sales level of $950,000, the Magic Shop's total costs would be as follows:

$$\text{Total expenses} = \$177{,}375 + (0.74 \times \$950{,}000)$$
$$= \$880{,}375$$

Thus, the Magic Shop's total cost is $880,375 at a net sales level of $950,000 (point B). The variable cost line is drawn by connecting points A and B. The area between the total cost line and the horizontal axis measures the total costs the Magic Shop incurs at various levels of sales. For example, if the Magic Shop's sales are $850,000, its total costs will be $806,375.

Step 5. *Beginning at the graph's origin, draw a 45-degree revenue line showing where total sales volume equals total income.* For the Magic Shop, point C shows that sales = income = $950,000.

You Be the Consultant

Where Do We Break Even?

Anita Dawson is doing some financial planning for her small gift store. According to her budget for the upcoming year, Anita is expecting sales of $495,000. She estimates that the cost of goods sold will be $337,000, and other variable expenses will total $42,750. Using the previous year as a guide, Anita anticipates fixed expenses of $78,100.

Anita recalls a meeting she had recently with her accountant, who mentioned that her store already had passed its breakeven point eight and a half months into the year. She was pleased but really didn't know how the accountant had come up with that calculation. Now Anita is considering expanding her store into a vacant building next door to her existing location and taking on three new product lines. The company's cost structure would change, adding another $66,000 to fixed costs and $22,400 to variable expenses. Anita believes the expansion could generate additional sales of $102,000 in the first year.

She wonders what she should do.

1. Calculate Anita's breakeven point without the expansion plans. Draw a breakeven chart.

2. Compute the breakeven point, assuming that Anita decides to expand her business.

3. Do you recommend that Anita expand her business? Explain.

Step 6. *Locate the breakeven point by finding the intersection of the total expense line and the revenue line.* If the Magic Shop operates at a sales volume to the left of the breakeven point, it will incur a loss because the expense line is higher than the revenue line over this range. This is shown by the triangular section labeled "Loss Area." On the other hand, if the firm operates at a sales volume to the right of the breakeven point, it will earn a profit because the revenue line lies above the expense line over this range. This is shown by the triangular section labeled "Profit Area."

Using Breakeven Analysis

Breakeven analysis is a useful planning tool for a potential small business owner, especially when approaching lenders and investors for funds. It provides an opportunity for integrated analysis of sales volume, expenses, income, and other relevant factors. Breakeven analysis is a simple, preliminary screening device for an entrepreneur faced with the business start-up decision. It is easy to understand and use. With just a few calculations, an entrepreneur can determine the effects of various financial strategies on the business operation. It is a helpful tool for evaluating the impact of changes in investments and expenditures.

Calculating the breakeven point for a start-up business is important because it tells an entrepreneur the minimum volume of sales required to stay in business in the long run.

ENTREPRENEURIAL PROFILE: Dal LaMagna: IceStone After a successful exit from a beauty supply company, Dal LaMagna took over IceStone, a company that manufactures recycled glass countertops. The company was in financial distress due to the severe recession that had begun in 2008. The company was losing $250,000 a month, falling well short of its $600,000-per-month breakeven sales level. The employees who now had an ownership stake in the company developed a long list of ways to reduce its breakeven point and make the company sustainable. Through their efforts, the company's breakeven point fell from $600,000 a month in sales to $350,000 a month.[32] ■

Breakeven analysis does have certain limitations. It is too simple to use as a final screening device because it ignores the importance of cash flows. In addition, the accuracy of the analysis depends on the accuracy of the revenue and expense estimates. Finally, the assumptions pertaining to breakeven analysis may not be realistic for some businesses. Breakeven calculations assume that fixed expenses remain constant for all levels of sales volume, variable expenses change in direct proportion to changes in sales volume, and changes in sales volume have no effect on unit sales price. Relaxing these assumptions does not render this tool useless, however. For example, the owner could employ nonlinear breakeven analysis to determine a company's breakeven point.

MyLab Entrepreneurship

If your instructor is using MyLab Entrepreneurship, go to **www.pearson.com/mylab/entrepreneurship** to complete the problems marked with this icon ⭐ .

Chapter Summary by Learning Objective

1. Describe how to prepare the basic financial statements and use them to manage a small business.

- Entrepreneurs rely on three basic financial statements to understand the financial conditions of their companies:

  1. *The balance sheet*—Built on the accounting equation, Assets = Liabilities = Owner's equity, the balance sheet provides an estimate of the company's value on a particular date.
  2. *The income statement*—This statement compares a firm's revenues to its expenses to determine its net income (or loss). It provides information about the company's bottom line.
  3. *The statement of cash flows*—This statement shows the change in the company's working capital over the accounting period by listing the sources and the uses of funds.

2. Create projected (pro forma) financial statements.

- Projected financial statements are a basic component of a sound financial plan. They help a manager plot the company's financial future by setting operating objectives and by analyzing the reasons for variations from targeted results. In addition, a small business in search of start-up funds will need these pro forma statements to present to prospective lenders and investors. They also assist in determining the amount of cash, inventory, fixtures, and other assets the business will need to begin operation.

3. Understand the basic financial statements through ratio analysis.

- The 12 key ratios described in this chapter are divided into four major categories: *liquidity ratios*, which show the small firm's ability to meet its current obligations; *leverage ratios*, which tell how much of the company's financing is provided by owners and how much by creditors; *operating ratios*, which show how effectively the firm uses its resources; and *profitability ratios*, which disclose the company's profitability.

- Many agencies and organizations regularly publish such statistics. If there is a discrepancy between a small firm's ratios and those of the typical business, the owner should investigate the reason for the difference. A below-average ratio does not necessarily mean that the business is in trouble.

4. Explain how to interpret financial ratios.

- To benefit from ratio analysis, a small company should compare its ratios to those of other companies in the same line of business and look for trends over time.

- When business owners detect deviations in their companies' ratios from industry standards, they should determine the cause of the deviations. In some cases, such deviations are the result of sound business decisions; in other instances, however, ratios that are out of the normal range for a particular type of business are indicators of what could become serious problems for a company.

5. Conduct a breakeven analysis for a small company.

- Business owners should know their firm's breakeven point, the level of operations at which total revenues equal total costs; it is the point at which companies neither earn a profit nor incur a loss. Although just a simple screening device, breakeven analysis is a useful planning and decision-making tool.

MyLab Entrepreneurship

If your instructor is using MyLab Entrepreneurship, go to **www.pearson.com/mylab/entrepreneurship** for Auto-graded writing questions as well as the following Assisted-graded writing questions:

1. Why is developing a financial plan so important to an entrepreneur about to launch a business?
2. How can breakeven analysis help an entrepreneur planning to launch a business?

Discussion Questions

12-1. How should a small business manager use the 12 ratios discussed in this chapter?

⭐ 12-2. Outline the key points of the 12 ratios discussed in this chapter.

⭐ 12-3. What signals does each of the 12 ratios give a business owner?

12-4. Describe the method for building a projected income statement and a projected balance sheet for a beginning business.

12-5. Why are pro forma financial statements important to the financial planning process?

Beyond the Classroom . . .

12-6. Ask the owner of a small business to provide your class with copies of his or her company's financial statements (current or past).

12-7. Using these statements, compute the 12 key ratios described in this chapter.

12-8. Compare the company's ratios with those of the typical firm in this line of business.

12-9. Interpret the ratios and make suggestions for operating improvements.

12-10. Prepare a breakeven analysis for the owner.

12-11. Find a publicly held company of interest to you that provides its financial statements on the Web. You can conduct a Web search using the company's name, or you can find lists of companies at the Securities and Exchange Commission's

EDGAR database or visit AnnualReports.com to download the annual report of this company.

12-12. Analyze the company's financial statements by calculating the 12 ratios covered in this chapter and compare these ratios to industry averages found in RMA's *Annual Statement Studies*, *BizMiner*, or one of the other financial analysis resources available in your library.

12-13. Do you spot any problem areas in the company's financials?

12-14. What are the financial strengths of the company?

12-15. What recommendations can you make to improve the company's financial position?

12-16. What do you project the company's future to be?

12-17. Explain why you would or would not recommend investing in the company.

Endnotes

[1] "QuickBooks Survey: More Than 40 Percent of Small Business Owners Identify as Financially Illiterate," Intuit, November 13, 2014, http://investors.intuit.com/press-releases/press-release-details/2014/QuickBooks-Survey-More-Than-40-Percent-of-Small-Business-Owners-Identify-as-Financially-Illiterate/default.aspx.

[2] William J. Dennis, Jr., "NFIB National Small Business Poll: Finance Questions," *National Federation of Independent Business*, vol. 7, no. 7, 2007, p. 6.

[3] Karen E. Klein, "Building a Business vs. Making a Living," *Bloomberg*, June 10, 2011, www.bloomberg.com/news/articles/2011-06-10/building-a-business-vs-dot-making-a-living.

[4] "New Survey Finds That Biggest Challenge to Tracking Business Expenses for Entrepreneurs is the 'Time-Intensive Process,'" *American Express OPEN*, April 3, 2014, http://about.americanexpress.com/news/pr/2014/amex-open-intuit-receiptmatch-quickbooks.aspx.

[5] "Sage Canadian Small Business Financial Literacy Survey," Sage North America, November 2012, p. 8.

[6] Paul Spiegelman, "When to Double Down on Culture," *Forbes*, August 29, 2016, www.forbes.com/sites/paulspiegelman/2016/08/29/when-to-double-down-on-culture/#55ef0f334072; Paul Spiegelman, "4 Reasons to Fire a Client," *Inc.*, February 1, 2012, www.inc.com/paul-spiegelman/fourreasons-to-fire-a-client.html; "Our Culture," Stericycle, n.d., www.stericycle.com/our-culture.

[7] Tim Cox, "WestWind Just Keeps Right on Growing: Two AMS Systems Give Iowa Company a Boost," *Pallet Enterprise*, December 1, 2016, www.palletenterprise.com/view_article/4761/WestWind-Just-Keeps-Right-on-Growing:-Two-AMS-Systems-Give-Iowa-Company-a-Boost.

[8] Norm Brodsky, "Balance Sheet Blues," *Inc.*, October 2011, p. 34.

[9] Rita McGrath and Ian MacMillan, "Discovery-Driven Planning," *Harvard Business Review*, July–August 1995, https://hbr.org/1995/07/discovery-driven-planning.

[10] "Industry Financial Report: Comic Book Stores," *BizMiner*, December 2016.

[11] "Phunware Named as a Red Herring Top 100 Company for Third Consecutive Year," prweb, December 5, 2016, www.prweb.com/releases/2016/12/prweb13894152.htm; Jill Hamburg-Coplan, "Don't Run Out of Cash: 3 Growth-Company Case Studies," *Inc.*, February 1, 2014, www.inc.com/magazine/201402/jill-hamburgcoplan/cash-flow-squeeze-growth-companies.html.

[12] "Frequently Asked Questions: Small Business Finance," Office of Advocacy and Small Business Data, U.S. Small Business Administration, July 2016, p. 1.

[13] Eriq Gardner, "Former Rhythm and Hues Owners Sued for Having 'Pillaged' Oscar-Winning VFX House," *Hollywood Reporter*, February 16, 2015, http://www.hollywoodreporter.com/thr-esq/rhythm-hues-owners-sued-having-773839; Richard Verrier, "Judge Approves Interim Loan for Rhythm and Hues," *Los Angeles Times*, February 15, 2013,

http://articles.latimes.com/print/2013/feb/15/entertainment/
la-et-ct-rhythm-hues-20130215; Richard Verrier, "Rhythm
and Hughes Finalized Sale to Prana Studios," *Los Angeles
Times*, March 29, 2013, http://articles.latimes.com/
2013/mar/29/entertainment/la-et-ct-rhythm-hues-prana-
20130329.

[14] "Why E*TRADE (ETFC) Stock Is an Attractive Pick
Right Now," *Zacks*, December 30, 2016, www.zacks.com/
stock/news/243972/why-etrade-etfc-stock-is-an-attractive-
pick-right-now.

[15] Felix Olsen, "Is Marston's PLC's (LSE:MARS) Balance Sheet
a Threat to Its Future?" *Simply Wall St.*, January 3, 2017,
https://simplywall.st/news/2017/01/03/is-marstons-plcs-
lsemars-balance-sheet-a-threat-to-its-future/.

[16] Mary Ellen Biery, "Why Business Loans Get Rejected," *Forbes*,
March 10, 2014, www.forbes.com/sites/sageworks/2014/03/
10/why-business-loans-getrejected/.

[17] Robin D. Schatz, "Secret Sauce: Four Bootstrapping Tips from
a Salad-Dressing Startup in Louisiana," *Forbes*, January
11, 2016, www.forbes.com/sites/robindschatz/2016/01/11/
secret-sauce-four-bootstrapping-tips-from-a-louisiana-salad-
dressing-startuphanleys/2/#7a6dcef01bad.

[18] Gabrielle Coppola, "Car Dealer's First Overflow Lot in 37 Years
Exposes U.S. Pileup," *Bloomberg*, February 28, 2017,
https://www.bloomberg.com/news/articles/2017-02-28/
car-dealer-s-first-overflow-lot-in-37-years-exposes-u-s-
pileup; Cliff Banks, "New Ways to Move Used Cars," *Ward's
Dealer Business*, November 1, 2005, http://
wardsdealer.com/ar/auto_new_ways_move/; Alex Taylor III,
"Survival on Dealer's Row," *Fortune*, March 31, 2008, p. 24.

[19] Issie Lapowsky, "My Favorite Tool for Analyzing Financials,"
Inc., November 2, 2012, www.inc.com/magazine/201211/
issie-lapowsky/favorite-tool-analyzing-financials.html.

[20] "Retail Benchmark Trends," The Retail Owners Institute,
n.d., http://retailowner.com/Benchmarks.

[21] "Industry Financial Report: Medical Equipment and Supplies
Manufacturing," *BizMiner*, December 2016, p. 13;
"Industry Financial Report: Tire Dealers," *BizMiner*,
December 2016, p. 13.

[22] Justin Fox, "Big Companies Don't Pay Their Bills on Time,"
Bloomberg, September 30, 2015, www.bloomberg.com/
view/articles/2015-09-30/big-companies-don-t-pay-
their-bills-on-time.

[23] William C. Dunkelberg and Holly Wade, "NFIB Small Business
Economic Trends," National Federation of Independent
Businesses, May 2017, p. 6.

[24] Mary Ellen Biery, "The State of U.S. Small Business,"
Sageworks Blog, February 10, 2016, www.sageworks.com/
blog/post/2016/02/10/the-state-of-u-s-small-businesses
.aspx; "The Most Profitable Industries in the U.S.," Sageworks, August 28, 2015, www.sageworks.com/datareleases
.aspx?article=329&title=The-Most-Profitable-Industries-
in-the-U.S.&date=August-28-2015.

[25] Mark J. Perry, "The Public Thinks the Average Company
Makes a 36% Profit Margin, Which Is About 5X too High,"
American Enterprise Institute, April 2, 2015, http://www
.aei.org/publication/the-public-thinks-the-average-company-
makes-a-36-profit-margin-which-is-about-5x-too-high/.

[26] Laurie Notaro, "Minimum Wage Increase Complicates Matters
for Phoenix Food Industry," *Phoenix New Times*, January 5,
2017, www.phoenixnewtimes.com/restaurants/minimum-
wage-increase-complicates-matters-for-phoenix-food-
industry-8960917; B. Christopher Agee, "WJ Investigates:
Critics Warn Recent Minimum-Wage Hikes Will Have Wide-
Ranging Impact," *Western Journalism*, January 4, 2017,
www.westernjournalism.com/wj-investigates-critics-warn-
recent-minimum-wage-hikes-will-have-wide-ranging-impact/.

[27] Jon E. Hilsenrath, "Adventures in Cost Cutting," *Wall Street
Journal*, May 10, 2004, pp. R1, R3.

[28] Julia Wong, "Higher Food Costs Hurting Edmonton Restaurants,"
Global News, January 15, 2016, http://globalnews.ca/
news/2456435/higher-food-costs-hurting-edmonton-
restaurants/; "Meet the Family," Zenari's, n.d., http://zenaris
.ca/about.

[29] Peter Smith, personal communication, January 25, 2017.

[30] Bo Burlingham, "*Inc.* Query: What Do Your Customers See?"
Inc., February 1, 2002, www.inc.com/magazine/20020201/
23857.html.

[31] Daniel Newman, "Customer Journey Mapping: What You Must
Know," *Forbes*, December 13, 2016, www.forbes.com/sites/
danielnewman/2016/12/13/customer-journey-mapping-what-
you-must-know/#42d4fd9a502f.

[32] Elaine Pofeldt, "How One Company Survived the Storms,
Together," *Inc.*, May 2014, www.inc.com/magazine/
201405/elain-pofeldt/dal-lamagna-hurricane-sandy-
recovery-empowered-employees.html.

Billion Photos/Shutterstock

13 Managing Cash Flow

Learning Objectives

On completion of this chapter, you will be able to:

1. Explain the importance of cash management to a small company's success.
2. Differentiate between cash and profits.
3. Describe the five steps in creating a cash budget.
4. Describe the fundamental principles involved in managing the "big three" of cash management: accounts receivable, accounts payable, and inventory.
5. Explain the techniques for avoiding a cash crunch in a small company.

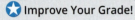 **MyLab Entrepreneurship**

⭐ **Improve Your Grade!**

If your instructor is using MyLab Entrepreneurship, visit **www.pearson.com/mylab/entrepreneurship** for videos, simulations, and writing exercises.

Cash is a four-letter word that has become a curse for many small businesses. Lack of this valuable asset has driven countless small companies into bankruptcy. More small businesses fail for lack of cash than for lack of profit. Unfortunately, many more firms will become failure statistics because their owners have neglected the principles of cash management that can spell the difference between success and failure. "Everything is about cash," says entrepreneur-turned-venture-capitalist Guy Kawasaki, "raising it, conserving it, collecting it."[1] Indeed, developing a cash forecast is essential for new businesses because start-up companies usually do not generate positive cash flow right away. A common cause of business failures, especially in start-up and fast-growth companies, is overemphasis on increasing sales with little concern for collecting the receivables those sales generate. "Your sales figures may be great, but it's cash flow that determines whether you can keep the doors open," says one business writer.[2] Another problem is that entrepreneurs neglect to forecast how much cash their companies will need to get through the **valley of death**, the time period during which start-up companies experience negative cash flow as they ramp up operations, build their customer bases, and (ideally) become self-supporting (see Figure 13.1). Unless a company has enough cash to get through the valley of death to the point of viability—the point at which it generates enough cash to sustain itself—the result is always the same: a cash crisis and, in many cases, business failure. CB Insights, a venture capital database, reports that the second-most-common cause of small business failures (29 percent) is running out of cash. (The most common cause is no need for the product or service the company was selling.)[3]

Serial entrepreneur and small business consultant Norm Brodsky tells the story of a small start-up that sold biodegradable household goods made from renewable materials. The cofounders had raised several hundreds of thousands of dollars from investors, but the young company was not generating enough cash to cover its expenses, much less to pay down the debt it had taken on. With the company's cash balance declining, the cofounders were desperately seeking external cash infusions from investors to keep the company afloat. Potential investors were far too savvy, however, given the company's tenuous position. Facing a dwindling gross profit margin, excessive costs, and limits on the prices they could charge due to intense competition, the company was unable to emerge from the valley of death and closed because it ran out of cash.[4]

As you learned in the previous chapter, controlling the financial aspects of a business using the analysis of basic financial statements with ratios is immensely important; however, by themselves, these techniques are insufficient for achieving business success. Entrepreneurs are prone to focus on their companies' income statements—particularly sales and profits. The income statement, of course, shows only part of a company's financial picture. It is entirely possible for a business to earn a profit and still go out of business by *running out of cash*. In other words, managing a company's total financial performance effectively requires an entrepreneur to look

valley of death
the time period during which start-up companies experience negative cash flow as they ramp up operations, build their customer bases, and become self-supporting.

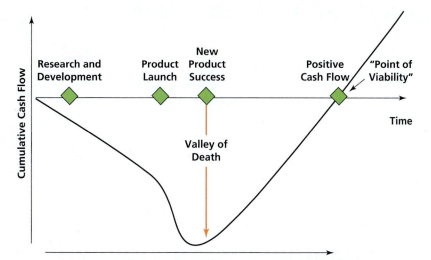

A start-up company must have enough cash to survive the depth and the breadth of the valley of death, or it will become another failure statistic.

FIGURE 13.1

The Valley of Death

Source: Based on Yoshitaka Osawa and Kumiko Miyazaki, "An Empirical Analysis of the Valley of Death: Large Scale R&D Project Performance in a Japanese Diversified Company," *Asian Journal of Technology Innovation,* vol. 14, no. 2, 2006, pp. 93–116.

beyond the "bottom line" and focus on what it takes to keep a company going—cash. "If a company isn't producing cash from its ongoing business, all the rest is smoke and mirrors," says Michael Connellan, a successful entrepreneur and former investment banker.[5]

LO1

Explain the importance of cash management to a small company's success.

Cash Management

Managing cash flow is a universal problem for entrepreneurs. A survey by Wasp Barcode reports that 42 percent of the owners of small businesses with 50 or fewer employees say that managing cash flow is the top business problem they face.[6] Although cash flow is a common concern for almost every business owner, it is a particularly acute problem for start-up companies. According to the Startup Founder Data Survey, 75 percent of start-up founders report cash flow concerns as their top challenge. When asked about the lowest point he experienced in his first year in business, Edward De Valle II, founder of 3A/Worldwide, a full-service marketing and communications firm based in Miami, Florida, said it was the time when he had only $3 left in the bank.[7]

A sluggish recovery from the Great Recession also put excess strain on the cash flow of many companies. Since 2010, the percentage of small business owners who report that their companies' cash flow is either somewhat or very poor has declined, while the percentage of owners who say their companies' cash flow is either somewhat or very good has increased. However, small business's cash positions are just beginning to return to pre-recession levels (see Figure 13.2). The best way to avoid a potentially business-crushing cash crisis is to use the principles of sound cash management. **Cash management** involves forecasting, collecting, disbursing, investing, and planning for the cash a company needs to operate smoothly. Cash management is a vital task because cash is the most important yet least productive asset a small business owns. A business must have enough cash to meet its obligations, or it will be declared bankrupt. Creditors, employees, and lenders expect to be paid on time, and cash is the required medium of exchange. However, some companies retain excessive amounts of cash to meet any unexpected circumstances that might arise. These dormant dollars have an income-earning potential that owners are ignoring; investing this cash, even for a short time, can add to a company's earnings. Proper cash management permits owners to adequately meet the cash demands of their businesses, avoid retaining unnecessarily large cash balances, and stretch the profit-generating power of each dollar their companies own.

cash management

the process of forecasting, collecting, disbursing, investing, and planning for the cash a company needs to operate smoothly.

FIGURE 13.2

Small Business Owners' Ratings of Their Companies' Cash Flow

Source: Based on data from *Wells Fargo Small Business Index, 3rd Quarter, 2017*, pp. 12–13.

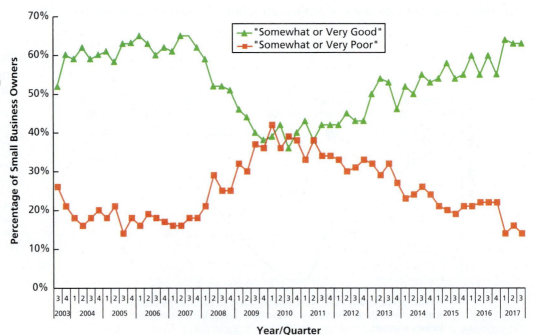

Although cash flow difficulties afflict companies of all sizes and ages, young companies, especially, are cash sponges, soaking up every available dollar and always hungry for more. The reason usually is that their cash-generating "engines" are not operating at full speed yet and cannot provide enough power to generate the cash necessary to cover rapidly climbing operating expenses. Entrepreneurs must manage cash flow from the day they launch their businesses.

ENTREPRENEURIAL PROFILE: H.J. Heinz: H.J. Heinz Company Shortly after H.J. Heinz, who started in the food business at age 14 when he began selling horseradish he grew in his garden, and two partners launched their first food business (which sold bottled horseradish) in 1875, their company's rapidly growing sales outstripped their start-up capital, and the company ran out of cash. A local newspaper called the entrepreneurs a "trio in a pickle." After the company failed, Heinz personally was liable for $20,000, a huge sum in that day (the equivalent of more than $431,000 today). Through much determination, he paid off the entire debt. Undaunted, Heinz learned from his mistakes and launched a second food company the very next year. In this venture, he added the product that would eventually make him famous—ketchup—and with the help of careful cash management, the H.J. Heinz Company grew into one of the largest food companies in the world.[8] ∎

Courtesy of The Kraft Heinz Company

Managing cash flow is also an acute problem for rapidly growing businesses. In fact, fast-track companies are most likely to suffer cash shortages. Many successful, growing, and profitable businesses fail because they become insolvent; they do not have adequate cash to meet the needs of a growing business with a booming sales volume. As a company's sales increase, its owner also must hire more employees, expand plant capacity, increase the sales force, build inventory, and incur other drains on the firm's cash supply. During rapid growth, cash collections typically fall behind, compounding the problem. Cash flows out of these high-growth companies much faster than it comes in. The head of the National Federation of Independent Business says many small business owners "wake up one day to find that the price of success is no cash on hand. They don't understand that if they're successful, inventory and receivables will increase faster than profits can fund them."[9] Table 13.1 shows signs that a company is facing an impending cash flow crisis.

ENTREPRENEURIAL PROFILE: Amanda Albright: All Bright Therapies Trained as a speech and occupational therapist, Amanda Albright had worked with thousands of children in an established therapy practice, but after two years, she decided to strike out on her own and launched All Bright Therapies in Chicago. Her practice grew rapidly, and Albright hired staff members, moved into a larger space, and incurred higher operating expenses. Albright says that although her company's growth was part of her plan, she found managing cash flow to be one of her greatest challenges. Most of her company's revenue comes from insurance companies and state agencies, neither of which are fast payers. By concentrating on controlling expenses, developing cash forecasts, and securing a line of credit at her bank, Albright has avoided the cash crises that destroy so many promising businesses.[10] ∎

Courtesy of Amanda Albright, Owner, All Bright Therapies

Table 13.2 shows how to calculate the additional cash required to support an increase in sales.

The first step in managing cash more effectively is to understand the company's **cash flow cycle**—the time lag between paying suppliers for merchandise or materials and receiving payment from customers after it sells the product or service (see Figure 13.3). The longer this cash flow cycle, the more likely the business owner will encounter a cash crisis. Small companies, especially those that buy from or sell to larger businesses, are finding that their cash flow cycles are growing longer as large companies have stretched their invoice payment times to suppliers and decreased their invoice collection times from customers to improve their cash flow. A recent study by PwC

cash flow cycle
the time lag between paying suppliers for merchandise or materials and receiving payment from customers.

TABLE 13.1 Signs of an Impending Cash Flow Crisis

Following are signs that a company may be on the verge of a cash crisis:

- Excess supplies of inventory
- Large stock of "old" inventory items that never sold
- Significant volume of fixed asset purchases, such as machinery and equipment
- Accounts receivable that are past due and growing
- Failing to take advantage of cash discounts from vendors and suppliers
- Late payments to vendors and suppliers
- Missed quarterly tax payments
- Past-due loan payments
- Above-average interest expense because of excessive business debt
- Average collection period ratio above the industry median
- Missed sales because popular inventory items are out of stock
- Difficulty meeting payroll on time
- Rapid increase in business expenses
- Rapid increase in accounts receivable balance
- Minimal or no financial controls in place to monitor potential theft
- Infrequent preparation and use of financial statements as a managerial tool
- Failure to develop cash flow forecasts

Source: Based on Steve LeFever, "Cash Flow Checklist: How Do You Rate?" *Multi-Unit Franchisee*, no. IV, 2013, p. 76.

TABLE 13.2 How Much Cash Is Required to Support an Increase in Sales?

Too often, entrepreneurs believe that increasing sales is the ideal solution to a cash crunch, only to discover (often after it is too late) that it takes extra cash to support extra sales. The following worksheet demonstrates how to calculate the amount of additional cash required to support an increase in sales.

To make the calculation, a business owner needs the following information:

- The increase in sales planned ($)
- The time frame for adding new sales (days)
- The company's gross profit margin: Gross profit ÷ Net sales (%)
- The estimated additional expenses required to generate additional sales ($)
- The company's average collection period (days)

To calculate the amount of additional cash needed, use the following formula:

Extra cash required = [(New sales − Gross profit + Extra overhead expenses) × (Average collection period × 1.20*)] ÷ (Time frame in days for adding new sales)

Example

The owner of Ardent Company wants to increase sales by $75,000 over the next year. The company's gross profit margin is 30 percent of sales (so its gross profit on these additional sales would be $75,000 × 30% = $22,500), its average collection period is 47 days, and managers estimate that generating the additional sales will require an increase in expenses of $21,300. To calculate the additional cash that Ardent will need to support this higher level of sales, use the above formula:

Extra cash required = [($75,000 − $22,500 + 21,300) × (47 × 1.2)] ÷ 365 = $11,404

Ardent will need $11,404 in extra cash to support the additional sales of $75,000 it plans to bring in over the next year.

*The extra 20 percent is added as a cushion.

Source: Based on Norm Brodsky, "Paying for Growth: How Much Cash You Need to Carry New Sales," *Inc.*, www.inc.com/tools/details/0,6152,CNT61_HOM1_LOC0_NAVhome_TOL11648,00.html.

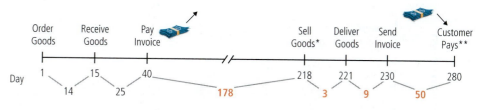

FIGURE 13.3

The Cash Flow Cycle

*Based on Average Inventory Turnover:

$$\frac{365 \text{ days}}{2.05 \text{ times/year}} = 178 \text{ days}$$

Cash Flow Cycle = 240 days

**Based on Average Collection Period:

$$\frac{365 \text{ days}}{7.31 \text{ times/year}} = 50 \text{ days}$$

shows that large companies have an average days sales outstanding (DSO) of 43.0 days but an average days payable outstanding (DPO) of 60.3 days (a difference of −17.3 days). The numbers for small companies show the "cash squeeze" that large companies are putting them in: Their DSO is 74.4 days, and their DPO is 67.8 days (a difference of +6.6 days).[11] In other words, large companies use their customers' cash for an average of 17 days, but small businesses must pay their suppliers, on average, nearly 7 days *before* they receive payments from their customers.

Once entrepreneurs understand their companies' cash flow cycle, the next step in effective cash management is to analyze it, looking for ways to reduce its length. For the company whose cash flow is illustrated in Figure 13.3, reducing the cycle from 240 days to, say, 150 days would free up incredible amounts of cash that this company could use to finance growth and dramatically reduce its borrowing costs. What steps do you suggest the owner of this business take to reduce its cash flow cycle?

Preparing a cash forecast that recognizes this cycle helps avoid a cash crisis. Understanding the cash flow patterns of a business over the course of a year is essential to creating a successful cash management strategy. Business owners should calculate their cash flow cycles whenever they prepare their financial statements (or at least quarterly). On a *daily* basis, business owners should generate a report showing the following items: total cash on hand, bank balance, a summary of the day's sales, a summary of the day's cash receipts, a summary of the day's cash disbursements, and a summary of accounts receivable collections. Compiling these reports into monthly summaries provides the foundation for making reliable cash forecasts and enables entrepreneurs to understand the rhythm of their companies' cash flow.

Cash and Profits Are Not the Same

LO2

Differentiate between cash and profits.

For their companies to survive, entrepreneurs must generate both profits and cash. As important as earning a profit is, a company's survival also depends on its ability to generate positive cash flow. Attempting to discern the status of a small company's cash position by analyzing its profitability is futile; profitability is *not* necessarily highly correlated with cash flow. Entrepreneurs often equate higher sales with better cash flow, but that is usually not the case. In fact, a company can be growing and earning a profit and still be forced to close its doors because it runs out of cash. For instance, say that a company sells $5,000 of merchandise on credit. The sale shows up as revenue on the income statement, but the company's cash balance does not increase until it actually collects (if it ever collects) the account receivable, which may be months later. An income statement does not tell an entrepreneur anything about the condition of the company's cash flow. "The stumbling block is that a lot of organizations have a hard time getting their arms around cash management and understanding it operationally," says John Cummings, a consultant at KPMG who advises companies on cash management strategies. "They're so used to a profit-and-loss statement world and do not understand the implications of cash flow on operations."[12]

In addition, slow sales also spell problems for a company's cash flow, but in a different way. When sales falter, cash flows in more slowly, which means the company has less cash to cover its required payments. The result, however, is still the same: a cash crisis. Jay Goltz, owner of five successful art-related and home décor businesses in Chicago, says, "I am dealing with cash flow issues because sales are off, thanks to record snowfall and subzero temperatures, and because we

FIGURE 13.4

Strategies Small Business Owners Use to Increase Sales

Source: Based on data from *2017 State of Small Business Report*, Wasp Barcode, 2017, www.waspbarcode.com/small-business-report.

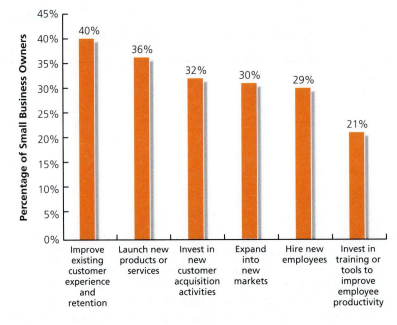

started buying direct from all over the world in bigger quantities—in some cases a year's worth of merchandise. Eventually, this will mean better [profit] margins, a better selection of products, and way more inventory than I had last year at this time, but at the moment, it also means I have way less cash. I am still able to pay the bills, but I have learned that it is always better to have as much cash available as possible."[13] Figure 13.4 shows the most common strategies small business owners use to increase their sales. Note that every strategy requires an investment of cash.

Profit (or net income) is the difference between a company's total revenue and its total expenses. It measures how efficiently a business is operating. Cash is the money that is free and readily available to use in a business. **Cash flow** is a measure of a company's liquidity and represents the balance of cash payments that flow into and out of a company over a particular period of time. Many small business owners soon discover that profitability does not guarantee liquidity. As important as earning a profit is, no business owner can pay suppliers, creditors, employees, government entities, and lenders in profits; that requires *cash*! Many entrepreneurs focus on their company's earnings because they know that a company must earn a profit to stay in business. However, adequate cash flow is also essential because it represents the money that flows through a business in a continuous cycle without being tied up in any other asset. "Businesses fail not because they are making or losing money," warns one financial expert, "but because they simply run out of cash."[14]

Figure 13.5 shows the flow of cash through a typical small business. Cash flow is the volume of cash that comes into and goes out of the business during an accounting period. Decreases in cash occur when a business purchases, on credit or for cash, goods for inventory or materials for use in production. A business sells the resulting inventory either for cash or on credit. When a company takes in cash or collects payments on accounts receivable, its cash balance increases. Notice that purchases for inventory and production *lead* sales; that is, a company typically pays these bills *before* sales are generated. On the other hand, collection of accounts receivable *lags* behind sales; that is, customers who purchase goods on credit do not pay until after the sale, sometimes months later.

cash flow

a method of tracking a company's liquidity and its ability to pay its bills and other financial obligations on time by tracking the flow of cash into and out of the business over a period of time.

LO3

Understand the five steps in creating a cash budget.

The Cash Budget

The need for a cash budget arises because in every business the cash flowing in is rarely in sync with the cash flowing out of the business. This uneven flow of cash creates periodic cash surpluses and shortages, making it necessary for entrepreneurs to track the flow of cash through their businesses so that they can make realistic projections of the cash that will be available throughout the year. Many entrepreneurs operate their businesses without knowing the pattern of their cash flows, believing that the process is too complex or time-consuming. In reality, entrepreneurs simply cannot afford to disregard the process of cash management. They must

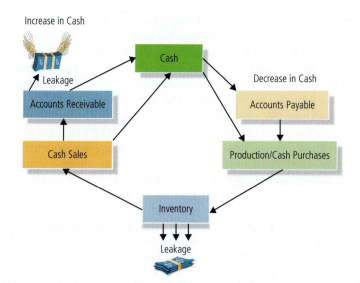

FIGURE 13.5

Cash Flow

ensure that their businesses have on hand an adequate but not excessive supply of cash to meet their operating needs. The goal of cash management is to have enough cash available to meet the company's cash needs at a given time.

How much cash is enough? What is suitable for one business may be totally inadequate for another, depending on each firm's size, nature, seasonal pattern of sales, and particular situation. An entrepreneur should prepare a **cash budget**, which is nothing more than a "cash map" showing the amount and the timing of the cash receipts and the cash disbursements day by day, week by week, or month by month. It is used to predict the amount of cash a company will need to operate smoothly over a specific period of time, and it is a valuable tool in managing a company successfully. A cash budget can illuminate a host of approaching problems, giving entrepreneurs adequate time to handle or, better yet, avoid them. A cash budget reveals important clues about how well a company balances its accounts payable and accounts receivable, controls inventory, finances its growth, and makes use of the cash it has.

Typically, small business owners should prepare a projected monthly cash budget for at least one year into the future and quarterly estimates for another year. The forecast must cover all seasonal sales fluctuations. The more variable a firm's sales pattern, the shorter its planning horizon should be. For example, a company whose sales fluctuate widely over a relatively short time frame might require a weekly cash budget. The key is to track cash flow over time. The timing of a company's cash flow is as important as the amounts. "An alert cash flow manager keeps an eye not on cash receipts or on cash demands as average quantities but on cash as a function of the *calendar*," says one business owner.[15]

Creating a written cash plan is not an excessively time-consuming task and can help entrepreneurs avoid unexpected cash shortages, a situation that often causes businesses to fail. Someone in the company should have the responsibility of forecasting and tracking the company's cash flow. If the entrepreneur delegates the task to an employee, he or she must be sure that the employee is trained to do the job properly. Joanna Norris, a partner in the Ratio Law Firm in Manchester, England, says that although the firm's cash disbursements tend to be predictable, its cash receipts can be quite variable, which makes daily cash management an essential task. She and her partners have trained their office manager to track the practice's cash flow every day to ensure that the law firm always has sufficient cash on hand.[16] Preparing a cash budget helps business owners avoid nasty cash flow surprises. Most entrepreneurs rely on computer spreadsheets such as Microsoft Excel to track their cash flow and to forecast cash receipts and disbursements, but popular small business accounting software includes cash management tools that require very little time and effort and produce reliable results. Many accounting software makers offer cloud-based applications that include cash management modules for less than $20 per month. One study reports that 39 percent of small business owners in Canada do not prepare any cash flow forecasts. In addition, the smaller the company, the less likely the owner is to prepare cash forecasts.[17]

A cash budget is based on the cash method of accounting, meaning that cash receipts and cash disbursements are recorded in the forecast *only when the cash transaction is expected to take place.*

cash budget
a "cash map" showing the amount and the timing of cash receipts and cash disbursements on a daily, weekly, or monthly basis.

For example, credit sales to customers are not reported as cash receipts until the company expects to collect the cash from them. Similarly, purchases made on credit are not recorded until the owner expects to pay them. Because depreciation, bad-debt expense, and other noncash items involve no cash transfers, they are omitted entirely from the cash budget. The typical small business has a median cash inflow of $11,430 per month and a median cash outflow of $11,220 per month, although cash inflows and outflows vary widely by industry.[18] This slim difference (just $210 per month) means that most entrepreneurs have little margin for error when managing their companies' cash flow.

A cash budget is a forecast of the firm's cash inflows and outflows for a specific time period, and it will never be completely accurate. However, it does give an entrepreneur a clear picture of a company's estimated cash balance for the period, pointing out when it may require external cash infusions or when surplus cash balances are available to invest. In addition, by comparing actual cash flows with projections, an entrepreneur can revise the forecast so that future cash budgets will be more accurate.

ENTREPRENEURIAL PROFILE: Andrew Johnson: Powwownow Andrew Johnson, controller of Powwownow, a small company based in Surrey, England, that provides low-cost, easy-to-use telephone conferencing services, understands how deadly running out of cash can be for a small company and does everything he can to make sure that Powwownow avoids that trap. Johnson uses a spreadsheet he updates weekly to produce accurate forecasts of the company's cash flow for one year into the future.[19] ∎

Formats for preparing a cash budget vary depending on the pattern of a company's cash flow. Table 13.3 shows a most likely monthly cash budget for a small retail store over a six-month

TABLE 13.3 Cash Budget for a Small Retail Store

Assumptions:

Cash balance on December 31 is $12,000

Minimum cash balance is $10,000

Sales are 75% credit and 25% cash

Credit sales are collected in the following manner:

60% collected in the first month after the sale

30% collected in the second month after the sale

5% collected in the third month after the sale

5% are never collected

Sales forecasts are as follows:	Pessimistic	Most Likely	Optimistic
October (actual)	—	$ 300,000	—
November (actual)	—	350,000	—
December (actual)	—	400,000	—
January	120,000	150,000	175,000
February	160,000	200,000	250,000
March	160,000	200,000	250,000
April	250,000	300,000	340,000
May	260,000	315,000	360,000
June	265,000	320,000	375,000

Rent is $3,000 per month

Interest payments of $664 and $817 are due in April and May, respectively.

A tax prepayment of $18,000 is due in March.

A capital addition payment of $130,000 is due in February.

A bank note payment of $7,500 is due in March.

Insurance premiums are $475 per month.

TABLE 13.3 **Cash Budget for a Small Retail Store (*continued*)**

Other expense estimates include:	Purchases	Wages and Salaries	Utilities	Advertising	Miscellaneous
January	$ 140,000	$ 30,000	$ 1,450	$ 1,600	$ 500
February	140,000	38,000	1,400	1,600	500
March	210,000	40,000	1,250	1,500	500
April	185,000	42,000	1,250	2,000	550
May	190,000	44,000	1,250	2,000	550
June	180,000	44,000	1,400	2,200	550

	Oct	Nov	Dec	Jan	Feb	Mar	Apr	May	Jun
Cash Receipts									
Sales	$ 300,000	$ 350,000	$ 400,000	$ 150,000	$ 200,000	$ 200,000	$ 300,000	$ 315,000	$ 320,000
Credit Sales	225,000	262,500	300,000	112,500	150,000	150,000	225,000	236,250	240,000
Collections									
60%—First month after sale				180,000	67,500	90,000	90,000	135,000	141,750
30%—Second month after sale				78,750	90,000	33,750	45,000	45,000	67,500
5%—Third month after sale				11,250	13,125	15,000	5,625	7,500	7,500
Cash Sales				37,500	50,000	50,000	75,000	78,750	80,000
Other cash receipts				25	35	50	60	60	65
Total Cash Receipts				307,525	220,660	188,800	215,685	266,310	296,815
Cash Disbursement									
Purchases				140,000	140,000	210,000	185,000	190,000	180,000
Rent				3,000	3,000	3,000	3,000	3,000	3,000
Utilities				1,450	1,400	1,250	1,250	1,250	1,400
Bank Note				—	—	7,500	—	—	—
Tax Prepayment				—	—	18,000	—	—	—
Capital Additions				—	130,000	—	—	—	—
Wages and Salaries				30,000	38,000	40,000	42,000	44,000	44,000
Insurance				475	475	475	475	475	475
Advertising				1,600	1,600	1,500	2,000	2,000	2,200
Interest				—	—	—	664	817	—
Miscellaneous				500	500	500	550	550	550
Total Cash Disbursements				177,025	314,975	282,225	234,939	242,092	231,625
End-of-Month Balance									
Beginning cash balance				12,000	142,500	48,185	10,000	10,000	14,218
+ Cash receipts				307,525	220,660	188,800	215,685	266,310	296,815
− Cash disbursements				177,025	314,975	282,225	234,939	242,092	231,625
Cash (end-of-month)				142,500	48,185	(45,240)	(9,254)	34,218	79,408
Borrowing				—	—	55,240	19,254	—	—
Repayment				—	—	—	—	20,000	54,944
Final Cash Balance				$ 142,500	$ 48,185	$ 10,000	$ 10,000	$ 14,218	$ 24,464
Monthly Surplus/(Deficit)				130,500	(94,315)	(93,425)	(19,254)	24,218	65,190

period. (Creating pessimistic and optimistic cash forecasts is a snap once the most likely cash budget is in place.) Each monthly column should be divided into two sections—estimated and actual (not shown)—so that each succeeding cash forecast can be updated to reflect actual cash flows. (The Service Corps of Retired Executives provides a handy set of templates, including one for forecasting cash flow, on its Web site, at www.score.org/resources/business-plans-financial-statements-template-gallery.) Comparing forecasted amounts to actual cash flows and learning the causes of any significant discrepancies allows entrepreneurs to improve the accuracy of future cash budgets by creating a rolling forecast one year into the future.

Creating a cash budget involves five basic steps:

1. Determining an adequate minimum cash balance

2. Forecasting sales

3. Forecasting cash receipts

4. Forecasting cash disbursements

5. Estimating the end-of-month cash balance

Step 1: Determining an Adequate Minimum Cash Balance

What is considered an excessive cash balance for one small business may be inadequate for another, even though the two companies are in the same industry. Some suggest that a firm's cash balance should equal at least one-fourth of its current liabilities, but this general rule clearly will not work for all small businesses. Many financial experts recommend that businesses build a cash reserve or contingency fund large enough to cover three to six months of operating expenses. Highly seasonal businesses often require an even larger reserve fund, one large enough to cover their expenses for both their busy and "off" seasons. The median cash reserve for small businesses in the United States is $12,100, but there is wide variation both across and within industries. That amount translates into just 27 cash buffer days, the number of days a business can pay its cash outflows out of its cash reserves if its cash inflows ceased. Twenty-five percent of small companies hold less than 13 buffer days of cash, and another 25 percent have enough cash on hand to cover at least 62 days of cash outflows.[20]

The most reliable method of deciding the right minimum cash balance is based on past experience. Past operating records indicate the cash cushion an entrepreneur needs to cover any unexpected expenses after all normal cash outlays are deducted from the month's cash receipts. For example, past records may indicate that it is desirable to maintain a cash balance equal to five days' sales. Seasonal fluctuations may cause a firm's minimum cash balance to change. For example, the minimum cash balance for a retailer may be greater in June than in December.

Step 2: Forecasting Sales

The heart of the cash budget is the sales forecast. It is the central factor in creating an accurate picture of the firm's cash position because sales ultimately are transformed into cash receipts and cash disbursements. For most businesses, sales constitute the primary source of the cash flowing into the business. Similarly, sales of merchandise require that cash be used to replenish inventory. As a result, a cash budget is only as accurate as the sales forecast from which it is derived.

For an established business, a sales forecast is based on past sales, but owners must be careful not to be excessively optimistic in projecting sales. Economic swings, increased competition, fluctuations in demand, normal seasonal variations, weather, and other factors can drastically affect sales patterns and, therefore, a company's cash flow. Most businesses, from retailers and hotels to accounting firms and builders, have sales patterns that are "lumpy" and not evenly distributed throughout the year.

ENTREPRENEURIAL PROFILE: Katherine Hudson: The Arabian Tent Company The Arabian Tent Company, a business that Katherine Hudson launched in 2004 and operates from her home in East Sussex, England, provides luxurious tents and decorations for outdoor

Courtesy of The Arabian Tent Company

weddings, parties, and festivals. Hudson's business is highly seasonal, with almost all of the company's sales occurring between April and September; sales during the remaining six months of the year are lean. To accommodate the seasonality of her business's cash flow, Hudson requires customers to pay a 25 percent deposit when they book an event and a second 25 percent deposit on January 1 of the year of the event. She also has launched a complementary business that provides furniture rental and decorating services for indoor events, particularly during the holiday season. Hudson recently began shipping half of her company's tents to Australia during the winter (which is Australia's summer) to help fill the seasonal gap in her company's cash flow.[21] ■

Many small retailers generate most of their sales and as much as one-third of their profits in the months of November and December. Veera Gaul, co-owner of the Oil & Vinegar shop in Greenville, South Carolina, sees 25 percent of her company's sales in the last six weeks of the year.[22] Forty percent of all toy sales take place in the last six weeks of the year, and companies that make fruitcakes typically generate 50 to 90 percent of their sales during the holiday season.[23] The typical wine and spirits shop makes 15 to 18 percent of its total sales volume for the entire year between December 15 and December 31.[24] Super Bowl Sunday is the busiest day of the year for pizza restaurants (and for the companies that produce pizza take-out boxes), producing revenues that are five times that of a typical Sunday.[25] For fireworks companies, the three weeks before July 4 account for the majority of annual sales, with another smaller peak occurring before New Year's Eve.[26] Costume makers generate almost all of their sales before Halloween but must invest in the raw materials and the labor to make the costumes in the spring and summer months, when their cash balances are at their lowest.[27] For companies with highly seasonal sales patterns, proper cash management is an essential activity.

Dmitry Kalinovsky/Shutterstock

Several quantitative techniques that are beyond the scope of this text (linear regression, multiple regression, time-series analysis, and exponential smoothing) are available to owners of existing businesses with an established sales pattern for forecasting sales. These methods enable the small business owner to extrapolate past and present sales trends to arrive at accurate sales forecasts.

The task of forecasting sales for a start-up is more difficult but not impossible. For example, an entrepreneur might conduct research on similar firms and their sales patterns in the first year of operation to come up with a forecast. The local chamber of commerce and trade associations in various industries also collect such information. Publications such as the *Annual Statement Studies* published by the Risk Management Association (RMA) and BizMiner, which profile financial statements for companies of all sizes in hundreds of industries, are also useful tools. Market research is another source of information that entrepreneurs can use to estimate annual sales for a start-up. Other potential sources that may help predict sales include census reports, newspapers, radio and television customer profiles, polls and surveys, and local government statistics. Talking with owners of similar businesses (outside the local trading area, of course) can provide entrepreneurs with realistic estimates of start-up sales. Table 13.4 provides an example of how one entrepreneur used such marketing information to derive a sales forecast for his first year of operation.

TABLE 13.4 Forecasting Sales for a Business Start-Up

Robert Adler wants to open a repair shop for imported cars. The trade association for automotive garages estimates that the owner of an imported car spends an average of $485 per year on repairs and maintenance. The typical garage attracts its clientele from a trading zone (the area from which a business draws its customers) with a 20-mile radius. Census reports show that the families within a 20-mile radius of Robert's proposed location own 84,000 cars, of which 24 percent are imports. Based on a local consultant's market research, Robert believes he can capture 9.9 percent of the market this year. Robert's estimate of his company's first-year sales are as follows:

Number of cars in trading zone	84,000 autos
× Imports percentage	× 24%
= Number of imported cars in trading zone	20,160 imports
Number of imports in trading zone	20,160 imports
× Average expenditure on repairs and maintenance	× $485
= Total import repair sales potential	$9,777,600
Total import repair sales potential	$9,777,600
× Estimated share of the market	× 9.9%
= Sales estimate	$967,982

Now Robert Adler can convert this annual sales estimate of $967,982 into monthly sales estimates for use in his company's cash budget.

No matter what techniques entrepreneurs use, they must recognize that even the best sales estimates will be wrong. Many financial analysts suggest that an owner create *three* estimates—an optimistic, a pessimistic, and a most likely sales estimate—and then make a separate cash budget for each forecast (a very simple task with a spreadsheet or modern accounting software). This type of dynamic forecast enables the owner to determine the likely range of his or her sales as the year progresses.

Step 3: Forecasting Cash Receipts

As you learned earlier, sales constitute the primary source of cash receipts. When a company sells goods and services on credit, the cash budget must account for the delay between the sale and the collection of the proceeds. Remember that entrepreneurs cannot spend cash they haven't collected! For instance, an appliance store might not collect the cash from a refrigerator sold in February until April or May, and the cash budget must reflect this delay. To accurately project cash receipts, an entrepreneur must analyze accounts receivable to determine the company's collection pattern. For example, past records may indicate that 20 percent of sales are for cash, 50 percent are paid in the month following the sale, 22 percent are paid two months after the sale, 5 percent are paid after three months, and 3 percent are never collected. In addition to cash and credit sales, a small business may receive cash in a number of forms—interest income, rental income, dividends, and so on.

 Hands On . . . How To

Manage Cash Flow in a Highly Seasonal Business

Allen and Jeanne Bell came up with the idea for Sea Turtle Sports, a small leisure sports company that designs, manufactures, and markets creative outdoor games and accessories aimed at beachgoers, while on a family vacation at a Florida beach. Their friends who lived at the beach introduced the couple's two young sons, who seemed to be addicted to video games, to beach bocce ball. The young boys enjoyed playing bocce ball on the beach so much that they put aside their video games, which made a distinct impression on their parents, who were concerned about the decline in offline interaction among family members and friends.

The bocce set the boys played with had been damaged by the salty air and sun, so the Bells set out to create a bocce set that was more durable and portable, featuring bright colors and beach themes and balls made from materials that would not crack or rust. They launched Sea Turtle Sports from their New Orleans home and were surprised at customers' enthusiastic response to their beach bocce ball game. Inspired by their early success, the Bells and their two sons, now old enough to help in the family business, set out to create more games to encourage families and friends to get outside, have fun, and create lifelong memories.

(continued)

Hands On . . . How To *(continued)*

Within a few years, the Bells transformed Sea Turtle Sports into a full-time business and relocated it to Pass Christian, Mississippi.

Because the majority of their sales take place during the warm-weather months but their expenses continue year-round, the Bells face the same challenge that all seasonal business owners face: managing cash flow. For example, the Bells have to begin building up their inventory during the winter months when their cash balance is at its lowest and their fixed costs of operation remain in place. Not only does gearing up for the busy summer season blitz require lots of advance planning, it also demands some clever cash management techniques, particularly for the slower off-season. For instance, the Bells require their wholesale customers to pay a 50 percent deposit for each order so that they have sufficient cash to produce the necessary items. They also have established a line of credit with their bank, which has increased as their company has grown, giving them the equivalent of a cash flow "safety net."

As the Bells have learned, seasonal businesses are far more difficult to manage than those that generate sales and cash year-round. How can business owners whose companies face highly seasonal sales patterns manage the uneven cash flow?

- *Be financially disciplined.* Seasonal business owners must establish a realistic budget, stick to it, and avoid the temptation to spend lavishly when cash flow is plentiful. Teevan McManus, owner of the Coronado Surfing Academy in San Diego, failed to heed this advice in his first year of business. "I burned through everything I made in the summer and was living off of my business line of credit before the next season came around," he recalls. "I barely made it to the next June."

- *Manage your time and your employees' time carefully.* During the busy season, employees may be working overtime to serve the rush of customers; during the off-season, a business owner may cut back to 20-hour workweeks or operate with a skeleton crew.

- *Use permanent employees sparingly.* Many owners of seasonal businesses use a small core of permanent employees and then hire part-time workers or student interns during their busy season. Planning for the right number of seasonal employees and recruiting them early ensures that a business will be able to serve its customers properly.

- *Put aside cash in a separate account that you use only for the lean months of your seasonal business.* The Bells put aside a cash reserve each year to use for emergencies or unexpected opportunities, such as a large order.

- *Maximize your productivity in the off-season.* Use the slow season to conduct market research, perform routine maintenance and repairs, revise your Web site, and stay in touch with customers. Steve Kopelman's company, Haunt-edHouse.com, earns all of its $2.6 million in annual revenue in a six-week period leading up to Halloween. Starting in November, Kopelman surveys his customers so that he can refine his marketing efforts for the next season and solicit suggestions for improvement. He visits trade shows to look for the latest technology and gadgets to keep his haunted houses fresh and exciting for his customers. Kopelman also

negotiates leases on properties for the next season and studies his competition by visiting every haunted house Web site he can find.

- *Keep inventory at minimal levels during the off-season.* As you will learn in this chapter, holding inventory unnecessarily ties up valuable cash uselessly.

- *Negotiate payment terms with vendors that are synchronized with your company's cash flow.* Schedule payments to vendors so that they coincide with your company's cash peaks rather than its cash valleys.

- *Offer off-peak discounts.* Doing so may generate some revenue during slow periods.

- *Consider starting a complementary seasonal business.* The weeks leading up to Halloween are the peak season for Sam Fard, owner of Los Angeles–based Roma Costume, a manufacturer of costumes for women. To reduce the highly seasonal nature of his business, Fard added a line of bikinis and lingerie to his company's product mix.

- *Create a cash flow forecast.* Perhaps one of the most important steps that seasonal business owners can take is to develop a forecast of their companies' cash flow. Doing so allows them to spot patterns and trends and to make plans for covering inevitable cash shortages. Make sure that you include a pessimistic or worst-case scenario in your cash forecast.

- *Establish a bank line of credit.* The line of credit should be large enough to cover at least three months' worth of expenses. Use your cash flow forecast to show the banker how and when your company will be able to repay the loan. A good cash forecast "shows the banker that you know exactly where the peaks and valleys are and what your cash needs are," says one banker.

1. What impact do highly seasonal sales have on a small company's cash flow?

2. What advice can you offer owners of seasonal businesses about coping with the effects of their companies' highly irregular sales patterns? About managing cash flow in general?

Sources: Based on Allen Bell and Allison Goldman, "Secrets to Managing Cash Flow in a Seasonal Small Business," All Business, www.allbusiness.com/managing-cash-flow-seasonal-small-business-106086-1.html; "Our Story," Sea Turtle Sports, https://seaturtlesports.com/pages/our-story-1; Nick Mead, "Seasonal Businesses: Dealing with Quieter Months Is Critical to Cash Flow," *The Guardian*, January 10, 2014, www.theguardian.com/small-business-network/2014/jan/10/seasonal-business-cashflow-income; Rohit Arora, "Winter Brings Seasonal Cash Flow Issues," *Fox Business*, February 5, 2013, http://smallbusiness.foxbusiness.com/marketing-sales/2013/02/05/winter-brings-seasonal-business-cash-flow-issues/; Cindy Vanegas, "Creating a Successful Seasonal Business All Year-Round," *Fox Business*, November 16, 2011, http://smallbusiness.foxbusiness.com/marketing-sales/2011/11/16/creating-successful-seasonal-business-all-year-round; Gwendolyn Bounds, "Preparing for the Big Bang," *Wall Street Journal*, June 29, 2004, pp. B1, B7; Rich Mintzer, "Running a Seasonal Business," *Entrepreneur*, March 16, 2007, www.entrepreneur.com/management/operations/article175954.html; Sarah Pierce, "Surviving a Seasonal Business," *Entrepreneur*, July 15, 2008, www.entrepreneur.com/startingabusiness/businessideas/article195680.html; Dan Kehrer, "10 Steps to Seasonal Success," *Business.com*, May 2006, www.business.com/directory/advice/sales-and-marketing/sales/10-steps-to-seasonalsuccess; Amy Barrett, "Basics for Seasonal Business Owners," *Businessweek*, April 16, 2008, www.businessweek.com/magazine/content/08_64/s0804058908582.htm?chan=smallbiz_smallbiz+index+page_best+of+smallbiz+magazine.

FIGURE 13.6

Probability of Collecting Accounts Receivable

Source: Based on data from the Commercial Agency Section, Commercial Law League of America, 2011.

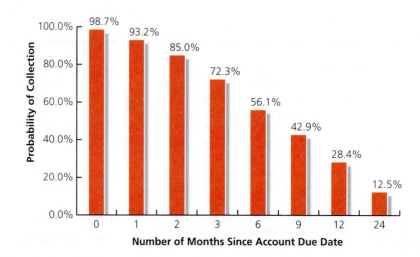

Number of Months Since Account Due Date

Collecting accounts receivable promptly poses problems for many small companies. Figure 13.6 demonstrates the importance of acting promptly when an account becomes past due. Notice how the probability of collecting an outstanding account diminishes the longer the account is delinquent. Table 13.5 illustrates a concept of which many business owners are not aware: the high cost of failing to collect accounts receivable on time.

ENTREPRENEURIAL PROFILE: Ron Box: Joe Money Machinery Ron Box, chief financial officer of Joe Money Machinery, a family-owned reseller of heavy construction equipment in Birmingham, Alabama, has watched as the company's large customers, mainly construction firms and municipal governments, stretch out payment times on their invoices to 60 or more days, a practice that puts pressure on the small company's cash flow. In an attempt to speed up collections, Box recently began offering customers cash discounts for early payments. About 30 percent of Joe Money Machinery's customers have taken advantage of the discounts. The company also has encouraged customers to pay with corporate credit cards, but that option has had limited success.[28] ■

TABLE 13.5 The High Cost of Slow Payers

Are your customers who purchase on credit paying late? If so, these outstanding accounts receivable represent a significant leak in your company's cash flow. Slow-paying customers are, in effect, borrowing money from your business interest free. One experienced business owner says, "Whether you realize it or not, you're sort of a banker, and you need to start thinking like one . . . to assess the quality of your [customers' accounts]." Slow-paying customers are using your money without paying you interest while you forgo opportunities to place it in interest-earning investments or pay interest on money that you must borrow to replace the missing funds. Exactly how much is poor credit control costing your company? The answer may surprise you.

The first step is to calculate your company's average-collection-period ratio (see the section "Operating Ratios" in Chapter 12). The second step is to age your accounts receivable to determine how many accounts are current and how many are overdue. The following example shows how to use these numbers to calculate the cost of past-due accounts for a company whose credit terms are "net 30":

Average collection period	65 days
− Credit terms	− 30 days
Excess in accounts receivable	35 days
Average daily sales of $21,500* × 35 days	$752,500
× Normal rate of return	× 8%
Annual cost of excess	$60,200

Slow-paying customers are costing this company more than $60,000 a year! If your business is highly seasonal, quarterly or monthly figures may be more meaningful than annual ones.

*Average daily sales = Annual sales ÷ 365 days = $7,847,500 ÷ 365 = $21,500 per day

Sources: Based on Norm Brodsky, "What Are You, a Bank?" *Inc.*, November 2007, pp. 81–82, and "Financial Control," *Inc.* Reprinted with permission of the publisher.

Many banks now offer cash management tools designed to speed up the collection of invoices to small companies that once were reserved only for large businesses. Once set up with a bank, **electronic (or Automated Clearing House [ACH]) collections** automatically deduct invoice amounts from customers' accounts and deposit them into the seller's account within 24 hours. Businesses can use electronic collections for single or periodic transactions, but they are ideal for recurring transactions. **Remote deposit**, which allows businesses to scan customers' checks (still the most widely accepted form of payment among small businesses) and deposit them from anywhere by using a smart phone or a tablet, is becoming increasingly popular among small businesses. Scanned checks create an online, digital deposit that eliminates time-consuming runs to the bank and gets customers' payments into the business's account faster. Banks typically charge a monthly fee and a flat amount for each scanned check. Entrepreneurs should compare the benefits and the costs of these services at various banks, which provide a daily list of transactions to allow entrepreneurs to reconcile payments with their accounts-receivable records. Although only 17 percent of small businesses currently use remote deposit, banks expect that percentage to grow rapidly as business owners become more technologically savvy and more banks offer the service.[29]

Ryan J Lane/E+/Getty Images

electronic (Automated Clearing House) collections

a bank service that allows businesses to automatically deduct invoice amounts from customers' accounts and deposit them into the seller's account within 24 hours.

remote deposit

a bank service that allows businesses to scan customers' checks and deposit them from anywhere using a portable scanner, a computer, and an Internet connection.

Step 4: Forecasting Cash Disbursements

Entrepreneurs must have sufficient cash on hand to pay their bills as they come due. Every entrepreneur should know his or her company's monthly "burn rate," the amount of cash it spends each month. Fortunately, most owners of established businesses can easily develop a clear picture of their companies' pattern of cash disbursements. Many cash payments, such as rent, loan repayments, and interest, are fixed amounts due on specified dates; others, such as purchases of goods and services, vary from one month to another. The key factor when forecasting disbursements for a cash budget is to record them in *the month in which the owner will pay them, not when the business incurs the obligation to pay*. Of course, the number of cash disbursements varies with each particular business, but the following disbursement categories are common: purchase of inventory or raw materials, wages and salaries, rent, insurance, utilities, taxes, Web site security and maintenance, loan payments, interest, advertising, fixed-asset purchases, and miscellaneous expenses.

When preparing a cash budget, one of the biggest mistakes an entrepreneur can make is to underestimate cash disbursements, which can result in a cash crisis. To prevent this, wise entrepreneurs cushion their cash disbursement estimates, assuming that they will be higher than expected. This is particularly important for entrepreneurs opening new businesses. In fact, some financial analysts recommend that new owners estimate cash disbursements as best they can and then add another 25 to 50 percent of the total! (Remember Murphy's law?)

Sometimes business owners have difficulty developing initial forecasts of cash receipts and cash disbursements. One of the most effective techniques for overcoming the "I don't know where to begin" hurdle is to make a *daily* list of the items that generated cash (receipts) and those that consumed it (disbursements).

ENTREPRENEURIAL PROFILE: Susan Bowen: Champion Awards Susan Bowen, CEO of Champion Awards, a $9 million T-shirt screen printer, monitors cash flow by tracking the cash that flows into and out of her company every day. Focusing on keeping the process simple, Bowen sets aside a few minutes each morning to track updates from the previous day on four key numbers:

Accounts receivable:

1. What did we bill yesterday?
2. How much did we actually collect?

Accounts payable:

1. What invoices did we receive yesterday?
2. How much in total did we pay out?

If Bowen observes the wrong trend—more new bills than new sales or more money going out than coming in—she makes immediate adjustments to protect her cash flow. The benefits produced (not the least of which is the peace of mind of knowing that no cash crisis is looming) more than outweigh the 10 minutes she invests in the process every day. "I've tried to balance my books every single day since I started my company," says Bowen.[30] ∎

Step 5: Estimating the End-of-Month Cash Balance

To estimate a company's cash balance for each month, entrepreneurs first must determine the cash balance at the beginning of each month. The beginning cash balance includes cash on hand as well as cash in checking and savings accounts. As development of the cash budget progresses, the cash balance at the *end* of one month becomes the *beginning* balance for the following month. Next, the owner adds to the beginning balance the projected total cash receipts and subtracts the projected total cash disbursements to obtain the end-of-month balance before any borrowing takes place. A positive amount indicates that the firm has a cash surplus for the month, but a negative amount shows that a cash shortage will occur unless the owner is able to collect, raise, or borrow additional funds.

Normally, a company's cash balance fluctuates from month to month, reflecting seasonal sales patterns in the business. These fluctuations are normal, but business owners must watch closely for *trends* in the cash balance over time. A trend of increases indicates that a company is solvent; on the other hand, a pattern of cash decreases should alert the owner that the business is approaching a cash crisis. One easy but effective tracking technique is to calculate the company's monthly cash surplus or deficit (cash receipts minus cash disbursements) at the bottom of the cash budget (see Table 13.3). Strings of deficits (and the declining cash balance that results from them) should set off alarms that a company is headed for a cash crisis.

Preparing a cash budget not only illustrates the flow of cash into and out of a small business but also allows the owner to *anticipate* cash shortages and cash surpluses. "Then," explains a small business consultant, "you can go to the bank and get a 'seasonal' line of credit for six months instead of twelve. Right there you can cut your borrowing costs in half."[31] By planning cash needs ahead of time, a small business can achieve the following benefits:

- Increase the amount and the speed of cash flowing into the company

- Reduce the amount and the speed of cash flowing out of the company

- Make the most efficient use of available cash

- Take advantage of money-saving opportunities, such as quantity and cash discounts

- Finance seasonal business needs

- Develop a sound borrowing program

- Develop a workable program of debt repayment

- Impress lenders and investors with its ability to plan and repay financing

- Provide funds for expansion

- Plan for investing surplus cash

"Cash flow spells survival for every business," claims one expert. "Manage cash flow effectively, and your business works. If your cash flow is not well managed, then sooner or later your business goes under. It's that simple."[32] Unfortunately, most small business owners forgo these benefits because they fail to track their company's cash flow consistently. Because cash flow problems usually sneak up on a business over time, improper cash management is often a costly—and fatal—mistake. Entrepreneurs cannot track their companies' cash flow "in their heads." There are too many variables involved, including cash sales, credit sales, collections from credit sales, inventory purchases, invoice due dates, seasonal and cyclical fluctuations, and so on. Trying to manage a company's cash without a system to record and report receipts and disbursements is like a juggler who can juggle three balls but is overwhelmed as the number of balls increases. One way to avoid this pitfall is to establish a *weekly* report that shows the amount of cash on hand, the cash received, and the cash spent. Some entrepreneurs also monitor the status of the company's accounts receivable and accounts payable balances weekly.

You Be the Consultant

In Search of a Cash Flow Forecast

Rowena Rowdy had been in business for slightly more than two years, but she had never taken the time to develop a cash budget for her company. Based on a series of recent events, however, she knew the time had come to start paying more attention to her company's cash flow. The business was growing fast, with sales more than tripling from the previous year, and profits were rising. However, Rowena often found it difficult to pay all of the company's bills on time. She didn't know why exactly, but she knew that the company's fast growth was requiring her to incur higher levels of expenses.

Last night, Rowena attended a workshop on managing cash flow sponsored by the local chamber of commerce. Much of

what the presenter said hit home with Rowena. "This fellow must have looked at my company's financial records before he came here tonight," she said to a friend during a break in the presentation. On her way home from the workshop, Rowena decided that she would take the presenter's advice and develop a cash budget for her business. After all, she was planning to approach her banker about a loan for her company, and she knew that creating a cash budget would be an essential part of her loan request. She started digging for the necessary information, and this is what she came up with:

Current cash balance	$10,685
Sales pattern	63% on credit and 37% in cash
Collections of credit sales	61% in 1 to 30 days;
	27% in 31 to 60 days;
	8% in 61 to 90 days;
	4% never collected (bad debts).

Sales forecasts:

	Pessimistic	Most Likely	Optimistic
January (actual)	—	$24,780	—
February (actual)	—	$20,900	—
March (actual)	—	$21,630	—
April	$19,100	$23,550	$25,750
May	$21,300	$24,900	$27,300
June	$23,300	$29,870	$30,000
July	$23,900	$27,500	$29,100
August	$20,500	$25,800	$28,800
September	$18,500	$21,500	$23,900

Utilities expenses	$950 per month
Rent	$2,250 per month
Truck loan	$427 per month

The company's wages and salaries (including payroll taxes) estimates are:

April	$3,550
May	$4,125
June	$5,450
July	$6,255
August	$6,060
September	$3,525

(continued)

You Be the Consultant (continued)

The company pays 66 percent of the sales price for the inventory it purchases, an amount that it actually pays in the following month. (Rowena has negotiated "net 30" credit terms with her suppliers.)

Other expenses include:

Insurance premiums	$1,200, payable in April and September
Office supplies	$125 per month
Maintenance	$75 per month
Uniforms/cleaning	$80 per month
Office cleaning service	$85 per month
Internet and computer service	$225 per month
Computer supplies	$75 per month
Advertising	$450 per month
Legal and accounting fees	$250 per month
Miscellaneous expenses	$95 per month

A tax payment of $3,140 is due in June.
Rowena has established a minimum cash balance of $1,500.

If Rowena must borrow money, she uses her line of credit at the bank, which charges interest at an annual rate of 10.25 percent. Any money that Rowena borrows must be repaid the next month.

1. Help Rowena put together a cash budget for the six months beginning in April.

2. Does it appear that Rowena's business will remain solvent, or could the company be heading for a cash crisis?

3. What suggestions can you make to help Rowena improve her company's cash flow?

LO4

Describe the fundamental principles involved in managing the "big three" of cash management: accounts receivable, accounts payable, and inventory.

The "Big Three" of Cash Management

Tracing the flow of every dollar through a business is unrealistic and futile. However, by concentrating on the three primary causes of cash flow problems, entrepreneurs can dramatically reduce the likelihood of experiencing a devastating cash crisis. The "big three" of cash management are accounts receivable, accounts payable, and inventory. These three variables are leading indicators of a company's cash flow. If a company's accounts receivable balance is increasing, its cash balance is probably declining. Similarly, accounts payable and inventory balances that are increasing faster than sales are signs of mounting pressure on a company's cash flow. A good cash management "recipe" involves accelerating a company's receivables to collect cash as quickly as possible, paying out cash as slowly as possible (without damaging the company's credit rating), and maintaining an optimal level of inventory. The big three of cash management interact to create a company's **cash conversion cycle**, the length of time required to convert inventory and accounts payable into sales and accounts receivable and finally back into cash. A company's cash conversion cycle equals its days inventory outstanding (DIO) + days sales outstanding (DSO) − days payable outstanding (DPO). Ideally, a company's cash conversion cycle is negative, meaning that it turns over its inventory quickly and collects payments from its customers before it pays its vendors and suppliers. The cash conversion cycle for the typical small business is a lengthy 80 days (see Figure 13.7).[33]

cash conversion cycle
a measure of the length of time required to convert inventory and accounts payable into sales and accounts receivable and finally back into cash. Equals Days inventory outstanding − Days sales outstanding + Days payable outstanding.

Accounts Receivable

Selling merchandise and services on credit is a necessary evil for most small businesses. Many customers expect to buy on credit, and business owners extend it to avoid losing customers to competitors. However, selling to customers on credit is expensive; it requires more paperwork,

FIGURE 13.7

Cash Conversion Cycle for the Typical Small Business

Source: Based on data from "2016 Annual Working Capital Opportunity—Corporation Size," PwC, 2016, www.pwc.com/gx/en/services/advisory/deals/business-recovery-restructuring/working-capital-opportunity/size.html.

*Cash Conversion Cycle = Days Inventory Outstanding + Days Sales Outstanding − Days Payable Outstanding = 75.4 + 66.9 − 62.4 = 79.9 days

more staff, and more cash to service accounts receivable. In addition, because extending credit is, in essence, lending money, the risk involved is higher. Every business owner who sells on credit encounters customers who pay late or, worse, never pay at all. A recent survey by Wasp Barcode Technologies reports that the most common accounting challenge for small business owners (51 percent) is collecting accounts receivable.[34] Caneum, a company based in Newport Beach, California, that provided IT services to businesses and government agencies, experienced a cash crisis when California's legislature failed to pass a budget, which meant that one of the company's major clients, the Los Angeles Unified School District, could not pay the invoice for $660,000 worth of work that Caneum had done. When another client, whom Caneum had billed for $750,000, was late making its payment, Caneum's cash balance could not recover, and the company filed for Chapter 7 bankruptcy (liquidation).[35]

As you have seen, most small companies operate with very thin cash reserves, and many lack reliable access to credit; therefore, a late payment from a major customer can create a cash crisis. Many business owners have noticed that the Great Recession caused a permanent shift to longer payment terms, especially among large businesses. According to Dun & Bradstreet, only 13 percent of large companies in the United States pay invoices by the due date.[36] Before the recession, large companies often paid invoices in 30 to 45 days; now, they routinely take 60 to 100 days to pay them, but small business owners, who lack sufficient bargaining power with large customers, can do little about it. Consumer goods giant Procter & Gamble, which makes $50 billion in purchases annually from 75,000 suppliers, many of them small companies, recently told its vendors that it was extending its payment terms from 45 days to 75 days. Although the move freed up more than $2 billion in cash for P&G, the change has produced a ripple effect on its vendors, creating cash problems for many of them, especially small companies.[37]

Fundbox, a company that helps small businesses manage cash flow, estimates that at any given moment, U.S. small businesses have $825 billion outstanding in unpaid invoices, 81 percent of which are 30 days past due.[38] Slow payments from customers put more pressure on these small companies' cash flow.

ENTREPRENEURIAL PROFILE: David Schier: Jacobus Energy Jacobus Energy, a petroleum distribution company founded in 1919 in Milwaukee, Wisconsin, faced the problem of slowing receivables. The company had outgrown its manual system for tracking past-due accounts receivable, and nearly 9 percent of its accounts were more than 30 days past due. Credit manager David Schier switched to an online credit-checking and collection system, and the percentage of 30-plus-day past-due accounts declined to just 3.3 percent. In addition, the company's average collection period ratio decreased from 27.3 days to 20.2 days, greatly improving its cash flow.[39] ■

Selling on credit is a common practice in business. Experts estimate that 90 percent of industrial and wholesale sales are on credit and that 40 percent of retail sales are on account.[40] Because credit sales are so prevalent, an assertive collection program is essential to managing a company's cash flow. A credit policy that is too lenient can destroy a business's cash flow, attracting too many slow-paying or "deadbeat" customers who never pay. On the other hand, a carefully designed policy can be a powerful selling tool, attracting customers and boosting cash flow. Transforming accounts receivable into cash is essential to staying in business; entrepreneurs must remember that a sale does not count until they collect the cash from it! In other words, a business owner cannot use a $10,000 account receivable to meet the company's payroll or pay its bills.

HOW TO ESTABLISH A CREDIT AND COLLECTION POLICY The first step in establishing a workable credit policy is to screen customers carefully *before* granting them credit. Unfortunately, many small businesses neglect to conduct any kind of credit investigation before selling to a new customer. The first line of defense against bad-debt losses is a detailed credit application. Before selling to any customer on credit, a business owner should have the customer fill out a customized application designed to provide the information needed to judge the potential customer's creditworthiness. At a minimum, this credit profile should include the following information about customers:

- Name, address, tax identification number, and telephone number
- Form of ownership (proprietorship, S corporation, LLC, corporation, and so on) and number of years in business
- Credit references (e.g., other suppliers), including contact names, addresses, and telephone numbers
- Bank and credit card references

After collecting this information, a business owner should use it to check the potential customer's credit references. The savings from lower bad-debt expenses can more than offset the cost of using a credit reporting service. Companies such as Dun & Bradstreet (www.dnb.com), Experian (www.experian.com), Equifax (www.equifax.com), and TransUnion (www.transunion .com) enable entrepreneurs to gather credit information on potential customers. For entrepreneurs who sell to other businesses, these reporting agencies also offer financial stability scores that enable them to evaluate the risk of selling on credit to new businesses. The National Association of Credit Management (www.nacm.org) is another important source of credit information because it collects information on many small businesses that other reporting services ignore. The cost to check a potential customer's credit at reporting services such as these starts at $40, a small price to pay when a small business is considering selling goods or services worth thousands of dollars to a new customer. Unfortunately, few small businesses take the time to conduct a credit check.

ENTREPRENEURIAL PROFILE: Ron Phelps: Boulevard Tire Center Ron Phelps, commercial credit manager at Boulevard Tire Center, a tire retailer with 26 locations in Florida, uses an online business credit reporting service called Cortera Pulse to screen new credit customers and to keep tabs on existing ones. Recently, when Pulse alerted Phelps that the Internal Revenue Service had imposed a large federal tax lien on one of its customers, Phelps immediately cut off the small trucking company's credit and converted it to a "cash only" customer to avoid the risk of writing off a bad debt.[41] ■

The next step involves establishing a firm written credit policy and letting every customer know in advance the company's credit terms. The credit agreement must be in writing and should specify a customer's credit limit (which usually varies from one customer to another, depending on their credit ratings), any required deposits (often stated as a percentage of the purchase price), the terms of any discounts (e.g., a 2 percent discount if the invoice is paid within 10 days), and the number of days before payment is due (immediately, 30 days, 60 days, and so on). A credit agreement should state clearly all of the terms the business will enforce if the account goes bad, including interest, late charges, attorney's fees, and so on. Failure to specify these terms up front in the contract so that the parties have a meeting of the minds means that they *cannot* be added later, after problems arise. One entrepreneur compares credit customers to unruly children; unless entrepreneurs set clear boundaries and enforce them, they can expect problems.[42] To maximize a small company's cash flow, its credit policies should be as tight as possible (within federal and state credit laws). Although the goal is to incur no bad debts, achieving that goal is unrealistic. According to the American Collectors Association, if a business is writing off more than 5 percent of sales as bad debts, the owner should tighten its credit and collection policy.[43]

The third step in an effective credit policy is to send invoices promptly because customers rarely pay *before* they receive their bills. One study reports that 20 percent of British small business owners have forgotten to send an invoice for goods or services at least once. The study estimates the value of the lost revenue from forgotten invoices to be £3.7 billion annually.[44] Remember: The sooner a company sends invoices, the sooner its customers will pay them.

Manufacturers and wholesalers should make sure invoices are en route to customers as soon as the shipments go out the door (if not before). Service companies should keep track of billable hours daily or weekly and bill as often as the contract with the client permits. Some businesses use **cycle billing**, in which a company bills a portion of its credit customers each day or each week of the month, to smooth out the inflow cash receipts.

Online (or electronic) billing makes managing accounts receivable much easier, is less expensive, and produces faster payments than paper invoices. Unfortunately, out of the 25 billion invoices that businesses in the United States send each year, only about 25 percent of them are in electronic form.[45]

cycle billing
a method in which a company bills a portion of its credit customers each day of the month to smooth out uneven cash receipts.

ENTREPRENEURIAL PROFILE: Laura Pendlebury: Decorus Academy Laura Pendlebury, owner of Decorus Academy, a ballet school in Bedfordshire, England, was constantly chasing past-due accounts from her students, which put pressure on her small company's cash flow. Pendlebury could not afford to hire a bookkeeper or an administrative assistant to help her, so she turned to a smart phone app called Zapper Scan-to-Pay. Pendlebury simply attaches to each invoice a QR code that contains each customer's payment information. Customers simply scan the code with their phones, confirm the amount, and pay the invoice in just seconds.[46] ∎

When an account becomes past due, a small business owner must take *immediate* action. The longer an account is past due, the lower the probability of collecting it (refer to Figure 13.6). One of the most effective techniques is to have someone in the company who already has a relationship with the customer, perhaps a salesperson or a customer service representative, call him or her about the past-due account the next day. The best approach is to start with a friendly reminder; getting "tough" too soon can damage the relationship with a good customer. When contacting a delinquent customer, the goal is to get a commitment to pay the full amount of the bill by a specific date (*not* "soon" or "next week"). Following up the personal contact with an e-mail or a letter that summarizes the verbal commitment also helps. If the customer still refuses to pay the bill, collection experts recommend the following:

- Send a letter from the company's attorney.
- Turn the account over to a collection attorney.
- As a last resort, hire a debt collection agency. The Commercial Law League of America (www.clla.org) can provide a list of reputable agencies.

Debt collection agencies collect more than $55 billion for their business clients each year.[47] Although collection agencies and attorneys typically take 25 to 30 percent of any accounts they collect, they are often worth the price. Seventy percent of the accounts turned over to collection agencies are considered "bad debts," which are 90 days or more past due. According to the American Collectors Association, only 5 percent of accounts more than 90 days delinquent will be paid voluntarily.

Business owners must be sure to abide by the provisions of the federal Fair Debt Collection Practices Act, which prohibits any kind of harassment when collecting debts (e.g., telephoning repeatedly, issuing threats of violence, telling third parties about the debt, or using abusive language). The act also prevents collectors from making false statements and from contacting debtors at inconvenient times (e.g., before 8 A.M. or after 9 P.M.) or places. The primary rule when collecting past-due accounts is to *never* lose your cool. Establishing a friendly but firm attitude and treating customers with respect is more likely to produce payment than hostile threats. Table 13.6 outlines 10 collection blunders small business owners typically make and how to avoid them.

TECHNIQUES FOR ACCELERATING ACCOUNTS RECEIVABLE Small business owners can use a variety of other techniques to speed cash inflow from accounts receivable:

- Speed up orders by having customers e-mail them to you.

- Send invoices when goods are shipped or when the job is completed—not a day or a week later; electronic invoices reduce in-transit time to a minimum. Small business accounting software packages allow users to e-mail the invoices they generate.

- Owners of service firms should offer clients retainer packages that provide their clients with a fixed number of hours of work each month that the client pays for in advance. To reduce the variability in her company's cash flow, Yva Yorston, owner of Boost Business Support, a company offering virtual assistance with administration, marketing, and research to small business owners, began offering clients retainer packages. On those accounts, Yorston is paid in advance, and her company's cash flow is much more predictable, giving her peace of mind.[48]

- Ensure that all invoices are clear, accurate, and timely. State clearly a description of the goods or services purchased, a purchase order reference number, and an account number and make sure that the prices and the language on invoices agree with the price quotations on purchase orders or contracts.

- Include a telephone number and a contact person in your organization in case the customer has a question or a dispute.

- Call the customer a few days after sending the invoice to make sure it arrived and to ensure that the customer has no problems with the quality of the product or service.

- Highlight the balance due and the terms of sale (e.g., "net 30") on all invoices. A study by Xerox Corporation found that highlighting with color the "balance due" and "due date" sections of invoices increased the speed of collection by 30 percent.[49] Using phrases such as "Please pay in 21 days" rather than "Terms: net 21" increase the probability of getting paid on time. Including "Thank you for your business" also helps.[50]

- Allow customers to use multiple payment methods such as checks, credit cards, PayPal, money orders, and cash.

- Offer incentives to encourage customers to pay invoices early and impose penalties on customers who pay late.

- Restrict a customer's credit until past-due bills are paid. Make sure salespeople know which of their customers are behind in their payments.

- Deposit cash, checks, and credit card receipts from invoices *daily*.

- Identify the top 20 percent of your customers (by sales volume), create a separate file system for them, and monitor them closely. Twenty percent of the typical company's customers generate 80 percent of all accounts receivable.

- Ask customers to pay at least a portion of the purchase price up front. Chris Carey, owner of Modern Automotive Performance, a 40-employee company based in Cottage Grove, Minnesota, that sells after-market automotive supplies, asks customers to pay for their purchases up front. Doing so allows Carey to have customers' payments in hand before he has to pay his vendors, which improves his company's cash flow dramatically.[51]

- Watch for signs that a customer may be about to declare bankruptcy. If that happens, creditors typically collect only a small fraction, if any, of the debt owed. If a customer does file for bankruptcy, the bankruptcy court notifies all creditors with a "Notice of Filing" document. If an entrepreneur receives one of these notices, he or she should create a file to track

TABLE 13.6 10 Collection Blunders and How to Avoid Them

Business owners often make mistakes when trying to collect the money their customers owe. Checking potential credit customers' credit records and creating a thorough sales contract that spells out exactly what happens if the account becomes past due can help minimize collection problems. Sooner or later, however, even the best system will encounter late payers. What happens then? Business owners should avoid these collection blunders.

Blunder 1: Delaying collection phone calls. Many entrepreneurs waste valuable time and resources sending four or five past-due letters to delinquent customers, usually with limited effectiveness.

Instead: Once a bill becomes past due, call the customer immediately to verify that he or she received the bill and that it is accurate. Ask for payment.

Blunder 2: Failing to ask for payment in clear terms. To avoid angering a customer, some entrepreneurs ask meekly, "Do you think you could take care of this bill soon?"

Instead: Firmly but professionally ask for payment (the full amount) by a specific date.

Blunder 3: Sounding desperate. Some entrepreneurs show weakness by saying that they must have payment or they "can't meet payroll" or "can't pay bills." That gives the customer more leverage to negotiate additional discounts or time.

Instead: Ask for payment simply because the invoice is past due—without any other explanation. Don't apologize for your request; it's *your* money.

Blunder 4: Talking tough. Getting nasty with delinquent customers does not make them pay any faster and may be a violation of the Fair Debt Collections Practices Act.

Instead: Remain polite and professional when dealing with past-due customers, even if you think they don't deserve it. *Never* lose your temper. Don't ruin your reputation by being rude.

Blunder 5: Trying to find out the customer's problem. Some entrepreneurs think it is necessary to find out why a delinquent customer has not paid a bill.

Instead: Don't waste time playing private investigator. Focus on the business at hand: collecting your money.

Blunder 6: Asking customers how much they can pay. When customers claim that they cannot pay the bill in full, inexperienced entrepreneurs ask, "Well, how much can you pay?" They don't realize that they have just turned control of the situation over to the delinquent customer.

Instead: Take charge of negotiations from the outset. Let the customer know that you expect full payment. If you cannot get full payment immediately, suggest a new deadline. Only as a last resort should you offer an extended payment plan.

Blunder 7: Continuing to talk after you get a promise to pay. Some entrepreneurs "blow the deal" by not knowing when to stop talking. They keep interrogating a customer after they have a promise to pay.

Instead: Wrap up the conversation as soon as you have a commitment. Summarize the agreement, thank the customer, and end the conversation on a positive note.

Blunder 8: Calling without being prepared. Some entrepreneurs call customers without knowing exactly which invoices are past due and what amounts are involved. The effort is usually fruitless.

Instead: Have all account details in front of you when you call and be specific in your requests.

Blunder 9: Trusting your memory. Some entrepreneurs think they can remember previous collection calls, conversations, and agreements.

Instead: Keep accurate records of all calls and conversations. Take notes about each customer contact and resulting agreements.

Blunder 10: Letting computer software control your collection efforts. Inexperienced entrepreneurs tend to think that their computer software can manage debt collection for them.

Instead: Recognize that computer software is a valuable tool in collecting accounts but that you are in control. Automated past-due notices generated by software may collect some accounts, but your efforts will produce more results. Getting to know the people who handle the invoices at your customers' businesses can be a major advantage when collecting accounts.

Sources: Based on "Tips for Collecting Cash," *FSB*, May 2002, p. 72; Janine Latus Musick, "Collecting Payments Due," *Nation's Business*, January 1999, pp. 44–46; Bob Weinstein, "Collect Calls," *Entrepreneur*, August 1995, pp. 66–69; and Elaine Pofeldt, "Collect Calls," *Success*, March 1998, pp. 22–24.

the events surrounding the bankruptcy and take action immediately. To have a valid claim against the debtor's assets, a creditor must file a proof-of-claim form with the bankruptcy court within a specified time, often 90 days. If, after paying the debtor's secured creditors, any assets remain, the court will distribute the proceeds to unsecured creditors who have legitimate proof of claim.

- Use technology to manage cash flow. Cloud-based accounting packages also include modules that allow business owners to monitor their cash flow from anywhere on smart phones, tablets, or laptops.

- Track the results of the company's collection efforts. Managers and key employees should receive a weekly report on the status of the company's outstanding accounts receivable.

Another strategy that small companies, particularly those selling high-priced items, can use to protect the cash they have tied up in receivables is to couple a security agreement with a financing statement. This strategy falls under Article 9 of the Uniform Commercial Code (UCC), which governs a wide variety of business transactions, including the sale of goods and security interests. A **security agreement** is a contract in which a business selling an asset, usually a "big ticket" item, on credit gets a security interest in that asset (the collateral), protecting its legal rights in case the buyer fails to pay. To get the protection it seeks in the security agreement, the seller must file a financing statement called a UCC-1 form with the proper state or county office (a process the UCC calls "perfection"). The UCC-1 form gives notice to other creditors and to the general public that the seller holds a secured interest in the collateral named in the security agreement. The UCC-1 form must include the name, address, and signature of the buyer; a description of the collateral; and the name and address of the seller. If the buyer declares bankruptcy, the small business that sells the asset is not guaranteed payment, but the filing puts its claim to the asset ahead of those of unsecured creditors. A small company's degree of safety on a large credit sale is much higher with a security agreement and a properly filed financing statement than it is without a security agreement.

security agreement
a contract in which a business selling an asset on credit gets a security interest in that asset (the collateral), protecting its legal rights in case the buyer fails to pay.

Hands On . . . How To

Avoid Losses from Accounts Receivable

Rob Dube and Joel Pearlman demonstrated their entrepreneurial inclinations early on, selling Blow Pops out of their lockers to other ninth graders. They also learned a valuable business lesson that they would build into future entrepreneurial endeavors: Providing reliable customer service and quality products leads to customer loyalty. After graduating from college, Dube and Pearlman launched Image One, a business that sells printer and toner cartridges. Soon, the young entrepreneurs added business machines to their product line, and their company grew quickly, reaching $1 million in sales within four years. Dube and Pearlman were so focused on growing their business that they paid little attention to the details of its financial statements. They did not yet understand that monitoring a company's financial status, no matter its size, is essential to its success. Four years later, with their company approaching $2.5 million in annual sales, the entrepreneurs realized that they had to get serious about taking control of Image One's finances, particularly its accounts receivable. They implemented a financial tracking system that provides managers with a unique set of "critical numbers" to help them manage the business. Once they defined their company's critical numbers, the system produced a weekly financial dashboard that enabled them to

monitor weekly metrics concerning accounts receivable, accounts payable, inventory, sales, and other measures. The report also showed them the company's progress toward its budget and revenue goals.

Although the importance of taking financial control of their company was a lesson Dube and Pearlman were somewhat slow to learn, they now embrace it. Image One, now with annual sales of more than $15 million, relies on sophisticated financial software that still provides a financial dashboard (but is now real time rather than weekly) and produces reports on key aspects of the company's operations, including basic financial statements, cash flow, and accounts receivable and payable. Managers also use the system to track the profitability and performance of the accounts of the company's 200 largest customers to make sure that none of their accounts payable fall behind.

Small businesses report that their customers, particularly large companies, are stretching their accounts payable longer, paying invoices more slowly now than they were just a few years ago. When faced with 30-day credit terms, it is not uncommon for large companies to delay their payments to 45 to 60 days, sometimes longer. The Small Business Network Monitor, a study

(continued)

Hands On . . . How To *(continued)*

of small businesses by American Express, confirms the challenge this presents for entrepreneurs. More than half of the small business owners surveyed say their companies experience cash flow problems, and one of their primary concerns is collecting accounts receivable. The average small business incurs $5,140 in past-due accounts receivables from its customers each month.

"If the money is coming in the front door at 100 miles per hour," explains Brian Hamilton, CEO of Sageworks, a financial consulting firm, "and going out the back door at 110 miles per hour, that's not a good thing. Businesses don't fail because they are unprofitable; they fail because they get crushed on the accounts receivable side." What steps can entrepreneurs take to avoid a cash crisis caused by accounts receivable that turn slowly? The following steps can help:

- *Evaluate your company's collection process.* How many people are involved in generating an invoice? (Fewer is better.) Where do bottlenecks in the billing process occur? (Setting a time limit on processing paperwork helps.) What percentage of your company's invoices are erroneous? (The higher the percentage of errors, the slower the company's collections will be.)

- *Increase your company's cash reserves.* Smart business owners keep at least three months' worth of expenses on hand so that they aren't caught cash short if receivables slow down more than expected or if sales suddenly decline.

- *Boost your company's line of credit.* Business owners can increase their lines of credit with their banks, but the key is to do so *before* you need the money. Be prepared to use your company's financial statements to prove to your banker why you need—and deserve—an increased line of credit.

- *Monitor accounts receivable closely.* Like the founders of Image One, some entrepreneurs generate weekly (or even daily) summaries of their company's accounts receivable, always on the lookout for disturbing trends. Doing so enables them to spot slow payers who might become nonpayers if the company doesn't take action immediately.

- *Get to know the people responsible for paying invoices at your biggest customers' or clients' companies.* Collections are easier if you know the right person to call.

- *Take immediate action when an account becomes past due.* Resist the tendency to simply sit back and wait for the customer to pay. If a customer has not paid by the invoice due date, contact him or her immediately and ask for payment.

- *Watch for signs that customers may be about to declare bankruptcy.* When a customer declares bankruptcy, the probability of collecting cash that is owed is miniscule. Terri Oyarzun, founder of Goats R Us, a company that owns a herd of goats that provide fire mitigation services by eating shrubs and brush that could fuel blazes, realized that when one customer declared bankruptcy, she would never be able to collect the $53,000 the company owed her business. Oyarzun says she had to postpone purchasing a new truck for the farm and hiring new goat herders.

- *Stick to your credit terms.* Define the credit terms with every client up front. If clients balk when it comes time for payment, remind them that they have a commitment to live up to the terms of the sales contract.

- *Raise prices to cover the extra cost of late payments.* If clients refuse to pay on time, determine how much their slower payments cost your company and raise your rates or your prices enough to cover the cost.

- *Require customers to pay at least part of the total price of a contract up front.* Because the jobs that one small film production company performs require the owner to incur some rather sizable expenses before they are completed, he implemented a policy that requires customers to pay one-third of the cost up front, another one-third at mid-project, and the balance on completion.

- *Offer discounts to encourage early payment.* Cash discounts (such as "2/10, net 30," which means that you offer the client a 2 percent discount if he or she pays within 10 days; otherwise, the full invoice amount is due in 30 days) can reduce a small company's profit margin, but they also provide an incentive for clients to pay early. Remember: More companies fail for lack of cash than for lack of profit.

Sources: Based on Jill Hamburg Coplan, "Don't Run Out of Cash: 3 Growth-Company Case Studies," *Inc.*, February 2014, www.inc.com/magazine/201402/jill-hamburg-coplan/cash-flow-squeeze-growth-companies.html; Jill Hamburg-Coplan, "Nice Growth Company You Got There. So How Come You're Running Out of Cash?" *Inc.*, February 2014, pp. 74–78, 106; Christopher Null, "Growth Spurt Secret," May 17, 2012, *Intuit GoPayment Blog*, http://blog.gopayment.com/money-trends/get-growing-small-businesses-miss-an-estimated-100-billion-in-annual-sales-by-denying-credit-cards-infographic/attachment/intuitpayments-getbusinessgrowing-final/; Shivani Vora, "Need Cash? Try Looking Inward," *Inc.*, May 2008, pp. 43–44; Amy Feldman, "The Cash-Flow Crunch," *Inc.*, December 2005, pp. 50–52; and Michael Corkery and Alex Frangos, "Far Away from Wall Street, a Herd Gets Gored," *Wall Street Journal*, January 24–25, 2009, pp. A1, A12.

Accounts Payable

The second element of the big three of cash management is accounts payable. The timing of payables is just as crucial to proper cash management as the timing of receivables, but the objective is exactly the opposite. Entrepreneurs should strive to stretch out payables as long as possible *without damaging their companies' credit rating*. Otherwise, suppliers may begin demanding prepayment or cash-on-delivery (C.O.D.) terms, which severely impair a company's cash flow, or they may stop doing business with it altogether. When Borders, once the second-largest bookstore chain in the United States, ran into cash flow problems, the company stopped making

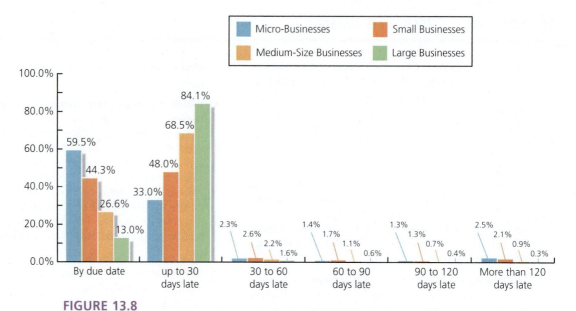

FIGURE 13.8

Accounts Payable Pattern Among Businesses by Size of Company
Source: Based on data from Payment Study 2016, Dun & Bradstreet, 2016, p. 44.

payments to book publishers, many of which halted shipments to the book retailer. In an attempt to survive, Borders downsized to just 400 stores but ultimately succumbed to its cash flow woes, declared bankruptcy, and closed its doors for good.[52] It is perfectly acceptable for a small business owner to regulate payments to his or her company's advantage. Efficient cash managers set up a payment calendar each month that allows them to pay their bills on time and to take advantage of cash discounts for early payment. Figure 13.8 shows the accounts payable pattern for businesses by size.

ENTREPRENEURIAL PROFILE: Nancy Dunis: Dunis & Associates Nancy Dunis, CEO of Dunis & Associates, a Portland, Oregon, marketing firm, recognizes the importance of controlling accounts payable. Dunis says that accounts payable are the key to keeping her company's cash flow running smoothly. She has set up a simple five-point accounts-payable system:

1. *Set scheduling goals.* Dunis strives to pay her company's bills 45 days after receiving them and to collect all her receivables within 30 days. Even though customers do not always pay within 30 days, her goal is to collect her cash as close to 30 days as possible.
2. *Keep paperwork organized.* Dunis dates every invoice she receives and carefully files it according to her payment plan. The system helps remind her when to write checks to pay her company's invoices, which she attempts to stretch out over a period of days or weeks to avoid having to make large cash disbursements at the same time. Proper scheduling of cash disbursement significantly improves the company's cash flow.
3. *Prioritize.* Dunis cannot stretch out all of her company's creditors for 45 days; some demand payment sooner. Those suppliers are at the top of the accounts-payable list.
4. *Be consistent.* Dunis says that companies value customers who pay their bills regularly and consistently. Most companies are willing to extend trade credit for 20 to 30 days as long as they know that the customer will pay the bill in full on time.
5. **Look for warning signs.** Dunis sees her accounts payable as an early warning system for cash flow problems. "The first indication I get that cash flow is in trouble is when I see I'm getting low on cash and could have trouble paying my bills according to my staggered filing system," she says.[53] ■

Other signs that a business is heading for cash flow problems include difficulty making payments on loans and incurring penalties for late payment of routine bills.

Business owners should verify all invoices before paying them. Some unscrupulous vendors send out invoices for goods they never shipped or services they never provided, knowing that many business owners simply pay bills without checking their authenticity. Two common scams aimed at small business owners involve bogus operators sending invoices for office supplies or ads in nonexistent printed or online "yellow pages" directories. In some cases, the directories actually do exist, but their distribution is so limited that ads in them are useless. To avoid falling victim to such scams, someone in the company—for instance, the accounts-payable clerk—should have the responsibility of verifying *every* invoice received.

A clever cash manager also negotiates the best possible credit terms with his or her suppliers. Almost all vendors grant their customers trade credit, and small business owners should take advantage of it. Favorable credit terms can make a tremendous difference in a company's cash flow. Table 13.7 shows the same cash budget from Table 13.2 with one exception: Instead of purchasing on C.O.D. terms as shown in Table 13.3, the owner has negotiated "net 30" payment terms.

TABLE 13.7 Cash Budget—Most Likely Sales Forecast After Negotiating "Net 30" Trade Credit Terms

Cash Receipts	Oct	Nov	Dec	Jan	Feb	Mar	Apr	May	Jun
Sales	$300,000	$350,000	$400,000	$150,000	$200,000	$200,000	$300,000	$315,000	$320,000
Credit sales	225,000	262,500	300,000	112,500	150,000	150,000	225,000	236,250	240,000
Collections	—	—	—	—	—	—	—	—	—
60%—first month after sale				180,000	67,500	90,000	90,000	135,000	141,750
30%—second month after sale				78,750	90,000	33,750	45,000	45,000	67,500
5%—third month after sale				11,250	13,125	15,000	5,625	7,500	7,500
Cash sales				37,500	50,000	50,000	75,000	78,750	80,000
Other cash receipts	—	—	—	25	35	50	60	60	65
Total Cash Receipts				307,525	220,660	188,800	215,685	266,310	296,815
Cash Disbursements									
Purchases*				105,000	140,000	140,000	210,000	185,000	190,000
Rent				3,000	3,000	3,000	3,000	3,000	3,000
Utilities				1,450	1,400	1,250	1,250	1,250	1,400
Banknote				—	—	7,500	—	—	—
Tax prepayment				—	—	18,000	—	—	—
Capital additions				—	130,000	—	—	—	—
Wages and salaries				30,000	38,000	40,000	42,000	44,000	44,000
Insurance				475	475	475	475	475	475
Advertising				1,600	1,600	1,500	2,000	2,000	2,200
Interest				—	—	—	249	—	—
Miscellaneous				500	500	500	550	550	550
Total Cash Disbursements				142,025	314,975	212,225	259,524	236,275	241,625
End-of-Month Balance									
Beginning cash balance				12,000	177,500	83,185	59,760	15,921	45,956
+ Cash receipts				307,525	220,660	188,800	215,685	266,310	296,815
− Cash disbursements	—	—	—	142,025	314,975	212,225	259,524	236,275	241,625
Cash (end of month)				177,500	83,185	59,760	15,921	45,956	101,146
Borrowing				—	—	—	—	—	—
Repayment	—	—	—	—	—	—	—	—	—
Final Cash Balance				$177,500	$83,185	$59,760	$15,921	$45,956	$101,146
Monthly Surplus/(Deficit)				165,500	(94,315)	(23,425)	(43,839)	30,035	55,190

*After negotiating "net 30" trade credit terms.

Notice the drastic improvement in the company's cash flow that results from improved credit terms.

If owners find themselves financially strapped when payment to a vendor is due, they should avoid making empty promises that "the check is in the mail" or sending unsigned checks. Instead, they should discuss the situation honestly with the vendor. Most vendors will work out payment terms for extended credit. One small business owner who was experiencing a cash crisis says:

> One day things got so bad I just called up a supplier and said, "I need your stuff, but I'm going through a tough period and simply can't pay you right now." They said they wanted to keep me as a customer, and they asked if it was okay to bill me in three months. I was dumbfounded: *They didn't even charge me interest.*[54]

Many entrepreneurs use their business credit cards, many of which offer "cash back" rewards, to improve their cash flow. By charging purchases to their credit cards and paying off their balances each month, business owners can generate anywhere from a few hundred dollars to tens of thousands of dollars in cash back rewards. Chris Carey, owner of Modern Automotive Performance, sometimes charges as much as $750,000 per month on his business credit card and receives up to $15,000 in cash back rewards if he pays off the balance each month.[55]

Entrepreneurs also can improve their firms' cash flow by scheduling controllable cash disbursements so that they do not come due at the same time. For example, paying employees every two weeks (or every month) rather than every week reduces administrative costs and gives the business more time to use its cash. Owners of fledgling businesses may be able to conserve cash by hiring part-time employees or by using freelance workers rather than full-time, permanent workers. Scheduling insurance premiums monthly or quarterly rather than annually also can improve cash flows.

Inventory

Offering customers a wider variety of products is one way a business can outshine its competitors, but product proliferation increases the need for tight inventory control to avoid a cash crisis. The typical grocery store now stocks about 39,500 items, nearly three times as many as it did 20 years ago, and many other types of businesses are feeling the pressure to follow suit to attract customers.[56] Although inventory is the largest investment for many businesses, entrepreneurs often manage it haphazardly, creating a severe strain on their companies' cash flow. As a result, the typical small business has not only too much inventory but also too much of the *wrong* kind of inventory! Because inventory is illiquid, it can quickly siphon off a company's pool of available cash. "Small companies need cash to grow," says one consultant. "They've got to be able to turn [cash] over quickly. That's difficult to do if a lot of money is tied up in excess inventory."[57] After being caught in a cash crisis due to excess inventory early in her entrepreneurial career, Laura Zander, founder of Jimmy Beans Wool, a yarn shop in Reno, Nevada, learned from her mistake. Now she ensures that her inventory grows no faster than her business. "We would rather have extra cash than extra inventory," she says.[58] Entrepreneurs cut back on their inventory purchases during the last recession, and have been managing inventory more closely and maintaining leaner inventory levels ever since (see Figure 13.9).

Surplus inventory yields a zero rate of return and unnecessarily ties up a company's cash. "Carrying inventory is expensive," says one small business consultant. "A typical manufacturing company pays 25 percent to 30 percent of the value of the inventory for the cost of borrowed money, warehouse space, materials handling, staff, lift-truck expenses, and fixed costs. This shocks a lot of people. Once they realize it, they look at inventory differently."[59] After Frank Muscarello was forced to close his company Vision Point of Sale, a company that sold point-of-sale terminals to businesses, during the Great Recession, he decided to start a business that carried no inventory. He launched MarkITx, an online marketplace where businesses of all sizes buy and sell refurbished computers, servers, and other technology items. MarkITx takes payments from buyers and arranges for sellers' items to be refurbished and shipped but carries no inventory, greatly reducing the company's cash flow requirements and lowering its risk.[60]

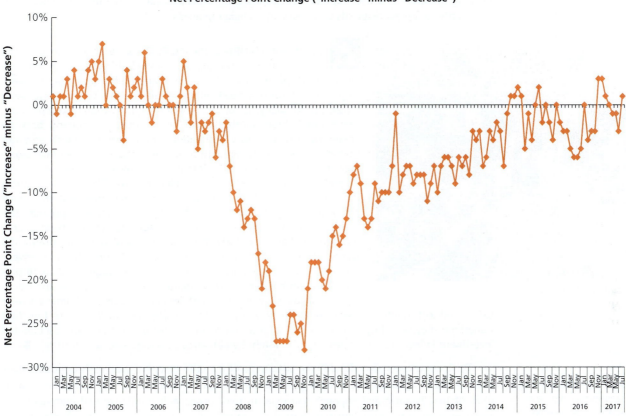

**Changes in Small Business Inventories During the Previous 3 Months
Net Percentage Point Change ("Increase" minus "Decrease")**

FIGURE 13.9

Changes in Small Business Inventories

Source: Based on data from William C. Dunkelberg and Holly Wade, *Small Business Economic Trends*, National Federation of Independent Businesses, July 2017, p. 15.

Even though volume discounts from vendors lower a company's inventory costs, large purchases tie up the company's valuable cash. Wise business owners avoid overbuying inventory, recognizing that excess inventory locks up valuable cash unproductively. In fact, only 20 percent of a typical business's inventory turns over quickly; therefore, owners must watch constantly for stale items. If a small business must pay its suppliers within 30 days of receiving an inventory shipment and the merchandise sits on the shelf for another 30 to 60 days (or more), the pressure on its cash flow intensifies. Increasing a company's inventory turnover ratio frees surprising amounts of cash. For instance, if a company with $2 million in annual sales that turns its inventory twice each year improves its inventory turnover ratio by just two weeks, it will improve its cash flow by nearly $18,900.

Carrying too little inventory is not the ideal solution to cash flow challenges because companies with excessive stock-outs lose sales (and eventually customers, if the problem persists). However, carrying too much inventory usually results in slow-moving inventory and a low inventory turnover ratio. Experienced business owners understand the importance of shedding slow-moving inventory during end-of-season sales, even if they must resort to markdowns.

Carrying too much inventory increases the chances that a business will run out of cash. An entrepreneur's goal is to minimize the company's investment in inventory without sacrificing sales, selection, and customer satisfaction. Inventory should grow no faster than a company's sales. "The cash that pays for goods is channeled into inventory," says one business writer, "where its flow is dead-ended until the inventory is sold and the cash is set free again. The cash flow trick is to commit just enough cash to inventory to meet demand."[61] Scheduling inventory deliveries at the latest possible date prevents premature payment of invoices. In addition, given goods of comparable quality and price, an entrepreneur should purchase goods from the fastest supplier to keep inventory levels as low as possible. All of these tactics require entrepreneurs to manage their supply chains carefully and to treat their suppliers as partners in their businesses. Keeping inventory churning rapidly through a small business requires creating a nimble, adaptive supply chain that responds to a company's changing needs.

Stefan Ember/Alamy Stock Photo

ENTREPRENEURIAL PROFILE: Zara Zara, a chain of retail stores that sells inexpensive, stylish clothing to young, fashion-conscious people, manages its supply chain so efficiently that its inventory turnover ratio is much higher than the industry average. As a result, the company ties up less cash in inventory than its competition. Zara's fast-fashion approach also keeps customers coming back by keeping stores' inventory fresh, adding new items constantly at a rate that leaves most of its competitors in awe. In fact, Zara can take a garment from design to store shelf in just 2 to 3 weeks instead of the 5 to 12 months that most clothing retailers require. The company tracks the latest fashion trends and manufactures small runs of items, which allows it to avoid being stuck with large quantities of unpopular garments it must mark down. Zara manufactures larger quantities of only those items that sell quickly. The result is that Zara's more than 2,100 stores, which are located in 88 countries, sell 85 percent of their inventory at full price, compared to the industry average of 60 to 70 percent. Zara has created an irresistible image of scarcity that appeals to its faithful customers who shop at Zara an average of 17 times per year (compared to 4 to 6 times a year for other clothing retailers) and who know that when they find something they like, they had better buy it, or it may be gone—for good. The result is a minimal investment in inventory that ties up little cash but yields above-average sales and profits.[62] ∎

quantity discounts
discounts that give businesses a price break when they order large quantities of merchandise and supplies. They exist in two forms: cumulative and noncumulative.

Business owners also should take advantage of quantity discounts and cash discounts their suppliers offer. **Quantity discounts** give businesses a price break when they order large quantities of merchandise and supplies and exist in two forms: noncumulative and cumulative. A company earns a noncumulative quantity discount only if it purchases a certain volume of merchandise in a single order. For example, a wholesaler may offer small retailers a 3 percent discount only if they purchase 10 gross of Halloween masks in a single order. Cumulative quantity discounts apply if a company's purchases from a particular vendor exceed a specified quantity or dollar value over a predetermined time period. The time frame varies, but a year is most common. For example, a manufacturer of appliances may offer a small business a 3 percent discount on subsequent orders if its purchases exceed $10,000 per year.

cash discounts
discounts offered to customers as an incentive to pay for merchandise promptly.

Cash discounts are offered to customers as an incentive to pay for merchandise promptly. Many vendors grant cash discounts to avoid being used as an interest-free bank by customers who purchase merchandise and then fail to pay by the invoice due date. To encourage prompt payment of invoices, many vendors allow customers to deduct a percentage of the purchase amount if they pay within a specified time. Cash discount terms "2/10, net 30" are common in many industries. These terms mean that the total amount of the invoice is due in 30 days, but if the bill is paid within 10 days, the buyer may deduct 2 percent from the total. A discount offering "2/10, EOM" (EOM means "end of month") indicates that the buyer may deduct 2 percent if the bill is paid within 10 days of the end of the month after purchase.

In general, it is sound business practice to take advantage of cash discounts because a company incurs an implicit (opportunity) cost by forgoing a cash discount. By failing to take advantage of the cash discount, an entrepreneur is, in effect, paying an annual interest rate to retain the use of the discounted amount for the remainder of the credit period. For example, suppose the Print Shop receives an invoice for $1,000 from a vendor offering a cash discount of 2/10, net 30. Figure 13.10 illustrates this situation and shows how to compute the cost of forgoing the cash discount. Notice that the cost of forgoing this cash discount is 37.25 percent. Table 13.8 summarizes the cost of forgoing cash discounts with different terms.

Monitoring the big three of cash management helps every business owner avoid cash crises while making the best use of available cash. According to one expert, maximizing cash flow involves "getting money from customers sooner; paying bills at the last moment possible; consolidating money in a single bank account; managing accounts payable, accounts receivable, and inventory more effectively; and squeezing every penny out of your daily business."[63]

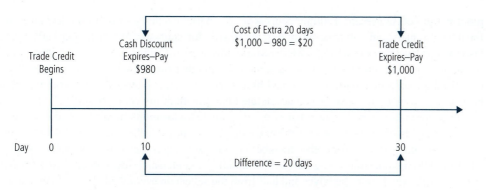

FIGURE 13.10

A Cash Discount

Annual Cost of Foregoing a 2/10, net 30 Cash Discount:

$$Rate = Interest/Principle \times Time$$
$$Rate = \frac{\$20}{\$980 \times 20 \text{ days}/365 \text{ days}}$$
$$Rate = 37.25\%$$

TABLE 13.8 Cost of Forgoing Cash Discounts

Cash Discount Terms	Cost of Forgoing the Cash Discount (Annually)
2/10, net 30	37.25%
2/10, net 40	24.83%
3/10, net 30	56.44%
3/10, net 40	37.63%

Avoiding the Cash Crunch

LO5

Explain the techniques for avoiding a cash crunch in a small company.

Nearly every small business has the potential to improve its cash position with little or no investment. The key is to make an objective evaluation of the company's financial policies, searching for inefficiency in its cash flow. Young firms cannot afford to waste resources, especially one as vital as cash. By using the following techniques, entrepreneurs can get maximum benefit from their companies' pool of available cash.

Barter

bartering
exchanging goods and services for other goods and services rather than for cash.

Bartering, the exchange of goods and services for other goods and services rather than for cash, is an effective way to conserve cash. An ancient concept, bartering has regained popularity in recent years. Bootstrapping entrepreneurs often use bartering to finance the start-up costs of their businesses, and many exchange equity in their companies for essential services such as legal, accounting, and Web design services, enabling them to conserve precious cash in one of the most critical periods of a company's life.

Today, more than 500 barter exchanges operate across the United States (visit the National Association of Trade Exchanges, at www.natebarter.com, to locate them), and they cater primarily to small and medium-size businesses looking to conserve cash. Some 400,000 companies—most of them small—engage in $12 to $14 billion worth of barter each year.[64] Every day, entrepreneurs across the nation use bartering to buy much-needed materials, services, equipment, and supplies—*without* using precious cash.

In addition to conserving cash, companies that use barter also have the opportunity to transform slow-moving inventory into much-needed products and services. Buying goods and services with barter also offers the benefit of a built-in discount. Although a company gets credit for the retail value of the goods or services it offers, the real cost to the company is less and depends on its gross profit margin. For instance, the owner of an Italian restaurant bartered $1,000 worth of meals for some new furniture, but his actual cost of the meals was only $680, given his gross profit margin of 32 percent. Entrepreneurs who join barter exchanges often find new customers for their products and services, an important benefit for start-ups. When Logan Hale opened his video production company, V3 Media Marketing, in Fort Collins, Colorado, he immediately began bartering his services for legal, accounting, and other professional services—even a gym membership. Hale says bartering enabled him to land business clients that he would not have been able to attract otherwise, which accelerated the growth of his young business.[65]

In a typical barter exchange, businesses accumulate trade credits (think barter dollars) when they offer goods or services through the exchange. Then they use their trade credits to purchase other goods and services from other members of the exchange. The typical exchange charges a $400 to $800 membership fee, a $10 to $15 monthly maintenance fee, and an 8 to 10 percent transaction fee (half from the buyer and half from the seller) on every deal. The exchange acts as a barter "bank," tracking the balance in each member's account and typically sending monthly statements summarizing account activity. Before joining a barter exchange, entrepreneurs should investigate its fee structure, the selection and the prices of its goods and services, and its geographic coverage to make sure the fit is a good one. In addition, barter exchanges report their members' barter transactions because they are subject to taxes.

Trim Overhead Costs

High overhead expenses can strain a small company's cash supply to the breaking point, and simple cost-cutting measures can save big money. Operating a business efficiently improves its cash flow. When it began in 1998, RNnetwork, a company that provides travel nurse recruiting and placement services, rented apartments across the United States to house the nurses it recruited and placed with its clients. Many of the apartments sat vacant for significant portions of time. Recently, housing manager Michelle McAndrew decided to outsource its housing operation to Travelers Haven, a company that provides nationwide short-term living accommodations for companies. The move freed up more than $217,000 in cash flow by eliminating security deposits on apartments and saved the company an additional $305,000 in rent.[66]

Frugal small business owners can trim their overhead in a number of ways.

ASK FOR DISCOUNTS AND "FREEBIES" Entrepreneurs can conserve cash by negotiating discounts on the purchases they make and using free services whenever possible. For instance, rather than pay a high-priced consultant to assist him with his business plan, one entrepreneur opted instead to use the free services of his local SBDC. The move not only improved the quality of his business plan, enabling him to get the financing he needed to launch his business, but also conserved valuable cash for the start-up.

ENTREPRENEURIAL PROFILE: Mark Viggiano: Viggiano's BYOB Mark Viggiano, owner of Viggiano's BYOB, a restaurant in Conshohocken, Pennsylvania, that serves family-style Italian meals, recently approached his landlord and was able to negotiate a lower lease payment on the building that houses his restaurant.[67] ∎

CONDUCT PERIODIC EXPENSE AUDITS Business owners should evaluate their operating costs periodically to make sure they have not gotten out of line. Comparing current expenses with past levels is helpful, and so is comparing a company's expenses against industry standards. Useful resources for determining typical expenses in an industry include the RMA's *Annual Statement Studies*, Dun & Bradstreet's *Industry Norms and Key Business Ratios*, Bizminer, and Prentice Hall's *Almanac of Business and Industrial Financial Ratios*.

Matt Rourke/AP Images

ENTREPRENEURIAL PROFILE: Daron Horowitz: Daddies Board Shop Daddies Board Shop, a business in Portland, Oregon, that sells skateboards, snowboards, and accessories, ships products to customers by UPS. Daron Horwitz, president of Daddies Board Shop, says that the company had been using UPS's "signature required" option, which cost the company $3.25 extra on each order. By eliminating the signature requirement, the company saved $65,000 per year, and its customer service ratings improved.[68] ∎

WHEN PRACTICAL, LEASE INSTEAD OF BUY Businesses spend about $1.7 trillion on equipment annually, and they acquire about 39 percent of that equipment through leases rather than purchases.[69] By leasing automobiles, computers, office equipment, machinery, and many other types of assets rather than buying them, entrepreneurs can conserve valuable cash. The value of these assets is not in *owning* them but in *using* them. Leasing is a popular cash management strategy; about 85 percent of companies lease some or all of their equipment.[70] "These companies are long on ideas, short on capital, and in need of flexibility as they grow and change," says Suzanne Jackson of the Equipment Leasing Association of America. "They lease for efficiency and convenience."[71]

Although total lease payments typically are greater than those for a conventional loan, most leases offer 100 percent financing, meaning that the owner avoids the large capital outlays required as down payments on most loans. (Sometimes a lease requires the first and last months' payments to be made up front.) Leasing also protects a business against obsolescence, especially when it comes to equipment such as computer hardware and software, whose technological life is limited to perhaps just two or three years. Furthermore, leasing is an "off-the-balance-sheet" method of financing and requires no collateral. The equipment a company leases does not have to be depreciated because the small business does not actually own it. A lease is considered an operating expense on the income statement, not a liability on the balance sheet. Thus, leasing conserves a company's borrowing capacity. Because lease payments are fixed amounts paid over a particular time period, leasing allows business owners to forecast more accurately their cash flows. Lease agreements also are flexible; entrepreneurs can customize their lease payments to coincide with the seasonal fluctuations in their companies' cash balances. Leasing companies typically allow businesses to stretch payments over a longer time period than do conventional loans.

Entrepreneurs can choose from two basic types of leases: operating leases and capital leases. At the end of an **operating lease**, a business turns the equipment back over to the leasing company with no further obligation. Businesses often lease computer and telecommunications equipment through operating leases because it becomes obsolete so quickly. At the end of a **capital lease**, a business may exercise an option to purchase the equipment, usually for a nominal sum.

operating lease
a lease at the end of which a company turns the equipment back over to the leasing company and has no further obligation.

capital lease
a lease at the end of which a company may exercise an option to purchase the equipment, usually for a nominal sum.

AVOID NONESSENTIAL OUTLAYS By forgoing costly ego indulgences like ostentatious office equipment, first-class travel, and flashy company cars, entrepreneurs can make the most efficient use of a company's cash and put their money where it really counts. Before putting scarce cash into an asset, every business owner should put the decision to the acid test: "Will this purchase improve my company's profits and cash flow or enhance its ability to compete?" The secret to successful cost saving is cutting *nonessential* expenditures. Making across-the-board spending cuts to conserve cash is dangerous because the owner runs the risk of cutting expenditures that drive the business. One common mistake during business slowdowns is cutting marketing and advertising expenditures. Economic slowdowns present a prime opportunity for smart business owners to bring increased attention to their products and services and to gain market share if they hold the line on their marketing and advertising budgets as their competitors cut back.

BUY USED OR RECONDITIONED EQUIPMENT, ESPECIALLY IF IT IS "BEHIND-THE-SCENES" MACHINERY One restaurateur saved thousands of dollars in the start-up phase of his business by buying used equipment from a restaurant equipment broker.

HIRE PART-TIME EMPLOYEES AND FREELANCE SPECIALISTS WHENEVER POSSIBLE Hiring part-time workers and freelancers rather than full-time employees saves on the cost of salaries, vacations, and benefits.

ENTREPRENEURIAL PROFILE: Gina Kleinworth: HireBetter Gina Kleinworth, CEO of HireBetter, a business based in Austin, Texas, that helps small and midsize companies find the talent they need, relies on an entirely part-time workforce of 35 employees. Kleinworth keeps her company's payroll costs under control, and her workers appreciate the flexibility in their schedules. "Employees have time to get their work done, and go to the gym, take their kids to the park, or volunteer in their communities," she says.[72] ■

OUTSOURCE One technique that many entrepreneurs use to conserve valuable cash is to outsource certain activities to businesses that specialize in performing them rather than hiring someone to do them in-house (or doing the activities themselves). In addition to saving cash, outsourcing enables entrepreneurs to focus on the most important aspects of running their businesses. "Stick to what you are good at and outsource everything else," advises one entrepreneur.[73] Outsourcing is one principle of launching a lean start-up.

USE E-MAIL RATHER THAN MAIL Whenever appropriate, entrepreneurs should use e-mail rather than mail to correspond with customers, suppliers, and others to reduce postage costs.

NEGOTIATE FIXED LOAN PAYMENTS TO COINCIDE WITH YOUR COMPANY'S CASH FLOW CYCLE Many lenders allow businesses to structure loans so that they can skip specific payments when their cash flow ebbs to its lowest point. Negotiating such terms gives businesses the opportunity to customize their loan repayments to their cash flow cycles.

ESTABLISH AN INTERNAL SECURITY AND CONTROL SYSTEM Too many owners encourage employee theft by failing to establish a system of controls. Reconciling the bank statement monthly and requiring approval for checks over a specific amount—say, $1,000—helps to minimize losses. Separating record-keeping and check-writing responsibilities, rather than assigning them to a single employee, offers additional protection against fraud.

DEVELOP A SYSTEM TO BATTLE CHECK FRAUD Although the use of checks in the United States continues to decline, customers still write more than 17 billion checks per year that total nearly $27 trillion.[74] Unfortunately, millions of those are bad checks that cost businesses nearly billions of dollars per year. Bad checks and check fraud can wreak havoc on a small company's cash flow. Simple techniques for minimizing losses from bad checks include requesting proper identification (preferably with a photograph) from customers, recording customers' telephone numbers, and training cashiers to watch for forged or counterfeit checks. Perhaps the most effective way to battle bad and fraudulent checks is to subscribe to an electronic check processing service. The service works at the cash register, and approval takes only seconds. The fee a small business pays to use the service depends on the volume of checks. For most small companies, charges amount to 1 to 2 percent of the cleared checks' value.

CHANGE YOUR SHIPPING TERMS Changing a company's shipping terms from "F.O.B. (free on board) buyer," in which the *seller* pays the cost of freight, to "F.O.B. seller," in which the *buyer* absorbs all shipping costs, improves its cash flow.

START SELLING GIFT CARDS Gift cards are a huge business, generating annual sales of $160 billion, and can provide a real boost to a small company's cash flow.[75] Customers pay for the cards up front, but the typical recipient does not redeem the gift card until later, sometimes much later, giving the company the use of the cash during that time. Selling gift cards also increases a company's revenue because studies show that 72 percent of card recipients spend more than the value of the gift card (The typical gift card recipient spends an average of 20 percent more than the value of the card[76]). Selling gift cards is an effective way to increase a small company's customer base; 41 percent of customers say they shopped at a business for the first time because they received a gift card for that business, and 72 percent of them returned to that business to make repeat purchases.[77] E-gift cards, digital gift cards that recipients receive via e-mail and can redeem with their smart phones or other mobile devices, represent one of the fastest-growing sectors in the gift card market.

ENTREPRENEURIAL PROFILE: Colleen Stone: Inspa Corporation Colleen Stone, owner of Inspa Corporation, a fast-growing chain of day spas based in Seattle, Washington, uses gift cards to stretch her company's cash flow. Gift cards account for 25 percent of her company's sales, and Stone has discovered that many of the gift cards she sells are not redeemed for a year, giving her a source of interest-free cash in the interim. "We plow all that cash flow right back into opening new stores," says Stone.[78] ■

SWITCH TO ZERO-BASED BUDGETING Zero-based budgeting (ZBB) primarily is a shift in the philosophy of budgeting. Rather than build the current-year budget on *increases* from the previous year's budget, ZBB starts from a budget of zero and evaluates the necessity of every item. The idea is to start each year's budget with a zero balance and then review each expense category to determine whether it is necessary.

BE ON THE LOOKOUT FOR SHOPLIFTING AND EMPLOYEE THEFT Companies lose an estimated $60 billion each year to shoplifting and employee theft. Although any business can be a victim of shoplifting or employee theft, retailers are particularly vulnerable. Shoplifting is the most common business crime, costing retailers an estimated $13 billion each year. Experts estimate that 27 million shoplifters are at work in the United States. Shoplifting takes an especially heavy toll on small businesses because they usually have the weakest lines of defense against shoplifters. The odds that a shoplifter will be caught are just 1 in 48.[79] If a shoplifter steals just one item that sells for $100 from a small business with an 8 percent net profit margin, the company must sell an additional $1,250 worth of goods to make up for the loss.

Even though shoplifting is more common than employee theft, businesses lose more money each year to employee theft. On average, businesses apprehend 1 out of every 38 employees for theft.[80] Dishonest employees steal 4.6 times more from the businesses for which they work than shoplifters. The Association of Certified Fraud Examiners estimates that companies worldwide lose 5 percent of their annual revenue to fraud or theft by employees.[81] The most common item stolen is, not surprisingly, cash. Because small business owners often rely on informal procedures for managing cash (or have no procedures at all) and often lack proper control procedures, they are most likely to become victims of employee theft, embezzlement, and fraud by their employees. Although 64 percent of small businesses report having experienced employee theft, only 16 percent of business owners reported the theft to police.[82] The median loss suffered by small companies in the United States is a disproportionately large $150,000.[83] The most common types of employee theft in small businesses are corruption (e.g., bribery, kickbacks), fraudulent billing

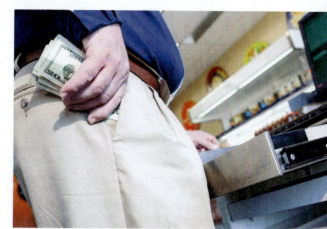

Fertnig/E+/Getty Images

schemes, check tampering, and "skimming" cash transactions. Alarmingly, the typical fraud goes on for 18 months before the owner discovers it, most often after another employee tips off the owner to the theft.[84] Although establishing a totalitarian police state and trusting no one is not conducive to a positive work environment, putting in place adequate financial control systems is essential. Separating among at least two employees key cash management duties, such as writing checks and handling bank statements and conducting regular financial audits, can effectively deter employee theft.

BUILD A CASH CUSHION Entrepreneurs who have experienced a cash crisis keenly understand the need for every business to build a working capital account as an emergency fund. How much should an entrepreneur put aside? Opinions differ, but most experts say that a small business should put aside enough cash to cover three to six months' worth of expenses—more if conditions warrant. A sufficient "rainy-day fund" may save a company from bankruptcy if disaster strikes.

INVEST SURPLUS CASH Because of the uneven flow of receipts and disbursements, a company will often temporarily have more cash than it needs—for a week, month, quarter, or even longer. When this happens, most small business owners simply ignore the surplus because they are not sure how soon they will need it. They believe that relatively small amounts of cash sitting around for just a few days or weeks are not worth investing. However, small business owners who put surplus cash to work *immediately* rather than allowing it to sit idle soon discover that the yield adds up to a significant amount over time. This money can help ease the daily cash crunch during business troughs. Business owners' goal should be to invest every dollar that they are not using to pay their current bills so that they can improve their cash flow.

However, when investing surplus cash, an entrepreneur's primary objective should *not* be to earn the highest yield (which usually carries with it high levels of risk); instead, the focus should

You Be the Consultant

Controlling Employee Theft

Managers at Holt of California, a heavy equipment dealer based in Pleasant Grove, California, noticed some "unusual" accounting transactions and began to investigate them. Gradually, they discovered that over seven years, their controller, "Stan" (not his real name), who had worked for the company for nine years, had stolen $4.8 million from the company. Stan had used company credit cards, some of which had been issued to former employees, to purchase goods and services, including electronics, cars, airline tickets, landscaping for his home, a country club membership, cosmetic surgery, season tickets to professional sporting events, and online games, for his personal use. In an unusual twist, authorities discovered that Stan had spent $1 million of his employer's money playing *Game of Fortune*. To cover his theft, Stan had vendors send bills to his home, where he could alter them, and created a steady stream of false financial reports. Fortunately, Holt was able to survive its employee theft incident, but some entrepreneurs have to close their businesses because employee theft and fraud destroy their cash flow.

Because small businesses often lack the financial and control procedures that large companies impose, they are disproportionately more likely to be victims of employee theft. Small companies are common targets of employee theft because employees, especially long-term employees, know the weaknesses in the company's systems, procedures, and controls and take advantage when the opportunity presents itself. Indeed, the longer the tenure of an employee who steals, the greater the amount stolen. According to a recent study by the Association of Certified Fraud Examiners, the median theft by perpetrators who had been with a company more than 10 years is $250,000; the median theft for those who stole from a company in their first year of employment is $49,000. One expert cites the following "formula" for employee theft:

Pressure + Rationalization + Opportunity = Employee theft

The only factor in the equation that employers can control is opportunity, which is why entrepreneurs' money is better spent *preventing* employee theft than *detecting* it.

As mentioned earlier, although 64 percent of small businesses report being victims of employee theft, only 16 percent reported the theft to the police. Business owners cite four reasons for failing to report theft by employees: (1) They do not perceive the theft as one warranting any more attention than firing the employee, (2) their attorneys often advise them that the cost in time and energy to prosecute the thief would likely outweigh any benefits, (3) the decision to prosecute is charged with emotion because the employee has worked alongside the owner for many years or is a family member, and (4) they see the police and criminal justice system as ineffective. The median amount stolen among small companies is $150,000, an amount significant enough to threaten the existence of many businesses. Oftentimes, such theft leaves the business in a cash bind from which it is unable to recover. In fact, the U.S. Chamber of Commerce estimates that one-third of all small business bankruptcies result from employee theft. In small businesses, the typical fraud

goes on for 18 months before the owner discovers it. Nearly 30 percent of the time, an employee tips off the owner to the theft, twice the percentage of thefts that are discovered by management review (14.5 percent). Seven percent of thefts are discovered by accident.

Many entrepreneurs are shocked to discover that the people who are stealing from their businesses are their most trusted, highly valued employees—the *last* people they would suspect. In the United States, managers are more likely to steal (43.0 percent) than are employees (30.8 percent), and they cause 2.7 times more damage. The median theft by managers is $173,000, compared to $65,000 by employees. Managers' thefts also are more difficult to detect, requiring a median of 18 months to detect, compared to 12 months for those that employees commit. The most common red flags that lead to detection are employees living beyond their means, having financial difficulties, having an unusually close association with a company vendor, and being unwilling to share their job duties (for fear of detection).

The most effective way to deal with employee theft is to prevent it. Entrepreneurs can take the following steps to reduce the threat of employee theft:

- **Screen potential employees thoroughly.** Statistics show that, on average, 1 out of every 38 employees is caught committing employee theft. A business owner's most useful tool against theft is a thorough pre-employment screening. The best time to weed out prospective criminals is before hiring them.

- **Monitor inventory closely.** Business owners who fail to keep up-to-date, accurate inventory records are inviting employee theft. When the co-owners of two ice cream stores realized that their employees were stealing, they began to take inventory of their stock twice each day. Once employees knew that controls were in place, the thefts stopped, and profits went up.

- **Use technology to discourage theft.** A variety of technology tools help business owners minimize losses to employee theft and fraud at very reasonable prices. Simple video camera systems, such as the ones used on the Food Network's show *Restaurant Stakeout*, are responsible for nabbing many employee thieves, especially cameras that are focused on checkout stations and cash registers.

- **Set up a hotline.** One of the most effective tools for minimizing employee theft is to encourage employees to report suspicious activity and give them a mechanism for reporting. Remember that the most common way that managers detect employee theft is by getting tips from other employees.

- **Embrace a zero-tolerance policy.** When business owners catch an employee thief, the best course of action is to fire the perpetrator and to prosecute. Most owners take the attitude "Resign, return the money, and we'll forget it." Letting

You Be the Consultant (continued)

thieves off, however, only encourages them to move on to other businesses where they will steal again.

1. Identify the factors that led Holt of California to become a victim of employee theft and embezzlement. What impact does this crime have on a company's cash flow and survival?

2. Are small businesses more likely than large ones to be victims of employee theft? Explain.

3. List at least five steps, in addition to the ones described here, that entrepreneurs should take to prevent their businesses from becoming victims of employee theft and embezzlement.

Sources: Based on Travis M. Andrews, "A California Man Steals $5 Million, Spends $1 Million on a Cellphone Game," *Washington Post*, December 12, 2016, www .washingtonpost.com/news/morning-mix/wp/2016/12/12/a-calif-man-stole-nearly-5-million-from-his-company-then-spent-1-million-on-a-cellphone-game/?utm_term=

.462a0a0a6671; Mark Anderson, "Caterpillar Dealer Holt Says Former Controller Embezzled $4 Million, Went on Spending Spree," *Sacramento Business Journal*, June 23, 2015, www.bizjournals.com/sacramento/news/2015/06/23/caterpillar-dealer-holt-says-former-controller.html; Mark Doyle, "25th Annual Retail Theft Survey: Shoplifter and Dishonest Employee Apprehensions and Recovery Dollars," Jack L. Hayes International, June 2013, http://hayesinternational.com/wp-content/uploads/2013/06/SURVEY-2013-25th-Annual-Retail-Theft-Survey-Hayes-International-Thoughts-Behind-Numbers-Final.pdf; Kelly Morris, "Techniques for Preventing or Reducing Employee Theft in Your Restaurant Business," *Yahoo! Voices*, January 11, 2014, http://voices.yahoo.com/techniques-preventing-reducing-employee-theft-12475702.html?cat=5; Mary-Bridget Reilly, "Surprising Survey: Most Small Businesses Remain Silent Rather Than Report Employee Theft," University of Cincinnati, February 17, 2014, www.uc.edu/news/NR.aspx?id=19231; Kent Stolt, "How to Guard Against Theft," *Biz Journals*, January 24, 2013, www.bizjournals.com/bizjournals/how-to/human-resources/2013/04/how-to-guard-against-employee-theft.html?page=all; Kathleen Johnston Jarboe, "Employee Theft at Small Business High and Hard to Detect," *The Daily Record*, October 14, 2005, http://findarticles.com/p/articles/miqn4183/is_20051014/ai_n15712876; John Tate, "Little White Thefts," *Small Business Development Center Business Report*, September 5, 2008, p. 2; "Employee Theft Statistics Infographic," *Infographics Showcase*, March 3, 2010, www.infographicsshowcase.com/employee-theft-statistics-infographic; *Report to the Nations on Occupational Fraud and Abuse: 2016 Global Fraud Study*, Association of Certified Fraud Examiners, 2016.

be on the safety and liquidity of the investments. Making high-risk investments with a company's cash cushion makes no sense and could jeopardize its future. The need to minimize risk and to have ready access to the cash restricts an entrepreneur's investment options to just a few such as money market accounts, zero-balance accounts, and sweep accounts. A **money market account** is an interest-bearing account offered by a variety of financial institutions ranging from banks to mutual funds. Money market accounts pay interest while allowing depositors to write checks (most have minimum check amounts) without tying up their money for a specific period of time.

A **zero-balance account (ZBA)** is a checking account that technically never has any funds in it but is tied to a master account. The company keeps its money in the master account, where it earns interest, but it writes checks on the ZBA. At the end of the day, the bank pays all of the checks drawn on the ZBA; then it withdraws enough money from the master account to cover them. A ZBA allows a company to keep more cash working during the float period, the time between a check being issued and its being cashed. A **sweep account** automatically "sweeps" all funds in a company's checking account above a predetermined minimum into an interest-bearing account, enabling it to keep otherwise idle cash invested until it is needed to cover checks.

KEEP YOUR BUSINESS PLAN CURRENT Before approaching any potential lender or investor, a business owner must prepare a solid business plan. Smart owners keep their plans up to date in case an unexpected cash crisis forces them to seek emergency financing. Revising the plan annually also forces the owner to focus on managing the business more effectively.

Conclusion

Successful owners run their businesses "lean and mean." Trimming wasteful expenditures, investing surplus funds, and carefully planning and managing the company's cash flow enable them to compete effectively. The simple but effective techniques covered in this chapter can improve every small company's cash position. One business writer says, "In the day-to-day course of running a company, other people's capital flows past an imaginative CEO as opportunity. By looking forward and keeping an analytical eye on your cash account as events unfold (remembering that if there's no real cash there when you need it, you're history), you can generate leverage as surely as if that capital were yours to keep."[85]

money market account

an interest-bearing account that allows depositors to write checks without tying up their money for a specific period of time.

zero-balance account (ZBA)

a checking account that never has any funds in it. A company keeps its money in an interest-bearing master account tied to the ZBA; when a check is drawn on the ZBA, the bank withdraws enough money from the master account to cover it.

sweep account

a checking account that automatically sweeps all funds in a company's checking account above a predetermined minimum into an interest-bearing account.

Chapter Summary by Learning Objective

1. Explain the importance of cash management to a small company's success.

- Cash is the most important but least productive asset a small business has. An entrepreneur must maintain enough cash to meet the company's normal requirements (plus a reserve for emergencies) without retaining excessively large, unproductive cash balances.
- Without adequate cash, a small business will fail.

2. Differentiate between cash and profits.

- Cash and profits are *not* the same. More businesses fail for lack of cash than for lack of profits.
- Profits, the difference between total revenue and total expenses, are an accounting concept. Cash flow represents the flow of actual cash (the only thing businesses can use to pay bills) through a business in a continuous cycle. A business can be earning a profit and be forced out of business because it runs out of cash.

3. Describe the five steps in creating a cash budget.

- The cash budgeting procedure outlined in this chapter tracks the flow of cash through the business and enables the owner to project cash surpluses and cash deficits at specific intervals.
- The five steps in creating a cash budget are determining a minimum cash balance, forecasting sales, forecasting cash receipts, forecasting cash disbursements, and determining the end-of-month cash balance.

4. Describe fundamental principles involved in managing the "big three" of cash management: accounts receivable, accounts payable, and inventory.

- Controlling accounts receivable requires business owners to establish clear, firm credit and collection policies and to screen customers *before* granting them credit. Sending invoices promptly and acting on past-due accounts quickly also improve cash flow. The goal is to collect cash from receivables as quickly as possible.
- When managing accounts payable, a manager's goal is to stretch out payables as long as possible without damaging the company's credit rating. Other techniques include verifying invoices before paying them, taking advantage of cash discounts, and negotiating the best possible credit terms.
- Inventory frequently causes cash headaches for small business managers. Excess inventory earns a zero rate of return and ties up a company's cash unnecessarily. Owners must watch for stale merchandise.

5. Explain the techniques for avoiding a cash crunch in a small company.

- Key strategies include trimming overhead costs by bartering; leasing assets rather than buying them; avoiding nonessential outlays; buying used equipment; hiring part-time employees; negotiating fixed payments to coincide with a company's cash flow cycle; implementing an internal control system boosts a firm's cash flow position; developing a system to battle check fraud; selling gift cards; using zero-based budgeting; being on the lookout for shoplifting and employee theft; building a cash cushion; and keeping the business plan current.
- In addition, investing surplus cash maximizes the firm's earning power. The primary criteria for investing surplus cash are security and liquidity.

Discussion Questions

⭐ 13-1. Why must entrepreneurs concentrate on effective cash flow management?

⭐ 13-2. Explain the difference between cash and profit.

13-3. Outline the steps involved in developing a cash budget.

13-4. How can an entrepreneur launching a new business forecast sales?

13-5. What are the big three of cash management?

13-6. What effect do the big three of cash management have on a company's cash flow?

13-7. How can bartering improve a company's cash position?

13-8. What should be a small business owner's primary concern when investing surplus cash?

Beyond the Classroom . . .

13-9. Interview several local small business owners about their cash management policies. Do they know how much cash their businesses have during the month? How do they track their cash flows? Do they use some type of cash budget? If not, ask if you can help the owner develop one. Does the owner invest surplus cash? If so, where?

13-10. Volunteer to help a small business owner develop a cash budget for his or her company. What patterns do you detect? What recommendations can you make for improving the company's cash management system?

13-11. Contact the International Reciprocal Trade Association (www.irta.net) and get a list of the barter exchanges in your state. Interview the manager of one of the exchanges and prepare a report on how barter exchanges work and how they benefit small businesses. Ask the manager to refer you to a small business owner who benefits from the barter exchange and interview him or her. How does the owner use the exchange? How much cash has bartering saved? What other benefits has the owner discovered?

13-12. Use the resources of the Internet to research leasing options for small companies. The Equipment Leasing and Financing Association of America (www.elfaonline.org) is a good place to start. What advantages does leasing offer? Disadvantages? Identify and explain the various types of leases.

13-13. Contact a local small business owner who sells on credit. Is collecting accounts receivable on time a problem? What steps does the owner take to manage the company's accounts receivable? Do late payers strain the company's cash flow? How does the owner deal with customers who pay late?

13-14. Conduct an online search for the National Retail Security Survey that the University of Florida Department of Criminology, Law, and Society conducts annually. Summarize the key findings of the survey concerning losses that businesses incur from shoplifting, employee theft, and fraud. What steps can small businesses take to minimize their losses to these problems?

Endnotes

[1]Wendy Taylor and Marty Jerome, "Dead Men Talking," *Smart Business*, December 2001/January 2002, p. 19.

[2]Ilana DeBare, "Tips for Small Businesses to Survive Recession," *San Francisco Chronicle*, March 23, 2008, www.sfgate.com/cgi-bin/article.cgi?f=/c/a/2008/03/22/BUSQVMKH3.DTL.

[3]*The Top 20 Reasons Startups Fail*, CB Insights, 2016, p. 3.

[4]Norm Brodsky, "Ignore the Unicorn," *Inc.*, July/August 2016, p. 64.

[5]Michael Connellan, "'Show Me the Kwan, Jerry!' Cash Is King," *Seeking Alpha*, December 8, 2011, http://seekingalpha.com/article/312705-show-me-the-kwan-jerry-cash-is-king.

[6]*2015 State of Small Business*, Wasp Barcode, 2015, p, 6.

[7]"Inc. 500 CEO Survey," *Inc.*, September 2014, p. 170.

[8]Mike Hofman, "Archive," *Inc.*, January 2002, p. 104; "John Heinz and the Heinz Family," *John Heinz: A Western Pennsylvania Legacy*, www.johnheinzlegacy.org/heinz/heinzfamily.html.

[9]Daniel Kehrer, "Big Ideas for Your Small Business," *Changing Times*, November 1989, p. 58.

[10]"Client Profile: Amanda Albright," *Small Business Owner Report*, Spring 2014, Bank of America, p. 11.

[11]*2016 Annual Working Capital Opportunity—Company Size*, PwC, 2016, www.pwc.com/gx/en/services/advisory/deals/business-recovery-restructuring/working-capital-opportunity/size.html.

[12]Elizabeth Wasserman, "Cash Is King, Again," *American Express Inside Edge*, September 21, 2010, http://corp.americanexpress.com/gcs/insideedge/articles/cash-isking-again-elizabeth-wasserman.aspx.

[13]Jay Goltz, "What I'm Still Learning About Managing Cash Flow," *New York Times*, March 5, 2014, http://boss.blogs.nytimes.com/2014/03/05/what-im-still-learning-about-managing-cash-flow/?_php=true&_type=blogs&_r=0.

[14]Douglas Bartholomew, "4 Common Financial Management Mistakes . . . and How to Avoid Them," *Your Company*, Fall 1991, p. 9.

[15]Robert A. Mamis, "Money in, Money Out," *Inc.*, March 1993, p. 98.

[16]Rosie Niven, "Small Business Tips: 10 Steps to Cash Flow Heaven," *The Guardian*, October 30, 2013, www.theguardian .com/small-business-network/2013/oct/30/cashflow-top-tips-small-business.

[17]"Cash Flow Management," Business Development Bank of Canada, April 2014, p. 9.

[18]"Cash Is King: Flows, Balances, and Buffer Days," JP Morgan Chase & Company, 2016, p. 4.

[19]Rosie Niven, "Small Business Tips: 10 Steps to Cash Flow Heaven," *The Guardian*, October 30, 2013, www.theguardian .com/small-business-network/2013/oct/30/cashflow-top-tips-small-business.

[20]"Cash Is King: Flows, Balances, and Buffer Days," JP Morgan Chase & Company, 2016, pp. 5–6.

[21]Alison Coleman, "Running a Seasonal Small Business from Home," *The Guardian*, February 20, 2014, www.theguardian .com/small-business-network/2014/feb/20/running-seasonal-small-business-home.

[22]Rudolph Bell, "Small Businesses Working Together," *Greenville News*, November 23, 2014, pp. 1A, 7A.

[23]Kortney Stringer, "Neither Anthrax nor the Economy Stops the Fruitcake," *Wall Street Journal*, December 19, 2001, pp. B1, B4; Dirk Smillie, "Signs of Life," *Forbes*, November 11, 2002, p. 160.

[24]Gwendolyn Bounds, "Store's Sales Can Rest on a Moment," *Wall Street Journal*, January 3, 2006, p. A23.

[25]Bob Tita, "It's Crunch Time for Pizza Boxes," *Wall Street Journal*, January 30, 2015, pp. B1, B9; Michelle Lock, "Pie-Makers Aim for Pizza Super Bowl Action," *Washington Post*, January 31, 2011, www.washingtonpost.com/wp-dyn/ content/article/2011/01/31/AR2011013102711.html; Ash-win Verghese, "Rochester-Area Pizza Shops Prepare for Annual Super Bowl Blitz," *Democrat Chronicle*, January 26, 2009, www.democratandchronicle.com/article/20090126/ NEWS01/901260336.

[26]Gwendolyn Bounds, "Preparing for the Big Bang," *Wall Street Journal*, June 29, 2004, pp. B1, B7.

[27]Jenny Munro, "Halloween in July," *Business*, July 25, 2004, pp. 1, 6–7.

[28]Alix Stuart, "Negotiating with Goliath," *CFO*, May 2011, p. 12.

[29]Bob Meara, *Positioning Business Mobile Deposit to Win with SMBs*, Celent and Deluxe Corporation, August 12, 2016, p. 2.

[30]Jill Andresky Fraser, "Monitoring Daily Cash Trends," *Inc.*, October 1992, p. 49.

[31]William G. Shepherd Jr., "Internal Financial Strategies," *Venture*, September 1985, p. 66.

[32]David H. Bangs, *Financial Troubleshooting: An Action Plan for Money Management in the Small Business* (Dover, NH: Upstart Publishing Company, 1992), p. 61.

[33]*2016 Annual Working Capital Opportunity—Corporation Size*, PwC, 2016, http://www.pwc.com/gx/en/services/advisory/ deals/business-recovery-restructuring/working-capital-opportunity/size.html.

[34]"Small Business Report—Accounting," Wasp Barcode Technologies, 2016, www.waspbarcode.com/small-business-report-accounting.

[35]Jill Hamburg-Coplan, "Don't Run Out of Cash: 3 Growth Company Case Studies," *Inc.*, February 2014, www.inc .com/magazine/201402/jill-hamburg-coplan/cash-flow-squeeze-growth-companies.html.

[36]*Payment Study 2016*, Dun & Bradstreet, 2016, p. 44.

[37]Serena Ng, "Firms Pinch Payments to Suppliers," *Wall Street Journal*, April 17, 2013, p. A1.

[38]"The Economic Impact of Unpaid Invoices," Fundbox, 2016, https://fundbox.com/blog/unpaid-invoices/.

[39]"Jacobus Energy Fuels Up with Cortera," Cortera, December 13, 2011, www.cortera.com/customersuccess-stories/ jacobus-energy.

[40]"Cash Flow/Cash Flow Management," *Small Business Reporter*, no. 9, p. 5.

[41]Hannah Seligson, "Learn How to Collect from Slow Payers," *New York Times*, April 6, 2011, www.nytimes.com/ 2011/04/07/business/smallbusiness/07sbiz.html? pagewanted=all.

[42]Peter Czapp, "Proactive Accountant: How to Be Sure Your Business Never Runs Out of Cash," *Business Zone*, March 5, 2014, www.businesszone.co.uk/topic/finances/ how-ensure-your-business-never-runs-out-cash/55913.

[43]American Collectors Association, www.collector.com; Howard Muson, "Collecting Overdue Accounts," *Your Company*, Spring 1993, p. 4.

[44]Rebecca Burn-Callander, "UK Small Business Are Failing to Invoice for Billions," *The Telegraph*, October 7, 2013, www .telegraph.co.uk/finance/yourbusiness/10361901/UK-small-businesses-are-failing-to-invoice-for-billions.html.

[45]*U.S. Adoption of Electronic Invoicing White Paper*, Federal Reserve Bank of Minneapolis, 2016, p. 13.

[46]Daniel Thomas, "Cash Flow Is King for Tech Savvy Small Businesses," *BBC News*, March 31, 2014, www.bbc.com/news/ business-26673698.

[47]Josh Adams, "Third Party Debt Collection in the U.S. Economy," The Association of Credit and Collection Professionals, January 2016, p. 2.

[48]Rosie Niven, "Small Business Tips: 10 Steps to Cash Flow Heaven," *The Guardian*, October 30, 2013, www.theguardian .com/small-business-network/2013/oct/30/cashflow-top-tips-small-business.

[49]Elaine Pofeldt, "Collect Calls," *Success*, March 1998, pp. 22–24.

[50]"The Best Invoice Payment Terms to Get Paid Fast," FreshBooks, March 17, 2016, www.freshbooks.com/blog/invoice-payment-terms.

[51]Elaine Pofeldt, "5 Ways to Tackle the Problem That Kills One of Every Four Small Businesses," *Money*, May 19, 2015, http://time.com/money/3888448/cash-flow-small-business-startups/.

[52]Jeffrey A. Trachtenberg, "Borders to Try Again to Sway Publishers," *Wall Street Journal*, January 13, 2011, p. B3; "Borders Announces Liquidation, Closing 400 Stores," KTLA, July 18, 2011, www.ktla.com/news/landing/ ktla-borders-bankrupt,0,2928708.story.

[53]Jill Andresky Fraser, "How to Get Paid," *Inc.*, March 1992, p. 105.

[54]G. Shepherd Jr., "Internal Financial Strategies," *Venture*, September 1985, p. 68.

[55]Elaine Pofeldt, "5 Ways to Tackle the Problem That Kills One of Every Four Small Businesses," *Money*, May 19, 2015, http://time.com/money/3888448/cash-flow-small-business-startups/.

[56]"Supermarket Facts," Food Marketing Institute, 2016, www.fmi.org/research-resources/supermarket-facts.

[57]Stephanie Barlow, "Frozen Assets," *Entrepreneur*, September 1993, p. 53.

[58]Laura Zander, "This Isn't How You're Supposed to Manage Cash Flow, but It Worked," *Inc.*, October 2013, p. 74.

[59]Roberta Maynard, "Can You Benefit from Barter?" *Nation's Business*, July 1994, p. 6.

[60]Joyce M. Rosenberg, "Owners Glean Lessons from Painful Recession," *Greenville News*, July 6, 2014, p. 3E.

[61] Robert A. Mamis, "Money in, Money Out," *Inc.*, March 1993, p. 102.

[62] "The World's Most Valuable Brands: #53 Zara," *Forbes*, May 2016, www.forbes.com/companies/zara/; Susan Berfield and Manuel Baigorri, "Zara's Fast-Fashion Edge," *Bloomberg Business Week*, November 14, 2013, www.businessweek.com/articles/2013-11-14/2014-outlook-zaras-fashion-supply-chain-edge; Walter Loeb, "Zara's Secret to Success: The New Science of Retailing," *Forbes*, October 14, 2013, www.forbes.com/sites/walterloeb/2013/10/14/zaras-secret-to-success-the-new-science-of-retailing-a-must-read/; Seth Stevenson, "Polka Dots Are In? Polka Dots It Is!" *Slate*, June 21, 2012, www.slate.com/articles/arts/operations/2012/06/zara_s_fast_fashion_how_the_company_gets_new_styles_to_stores_so_quickly_.html; Doug Hardman, Simon Harper, and Ashok Notaney, "Keeping Inventory—and Profits—Off the Discount Rack," Booz, Allen, and Hamilton, www.boozallen.com/media/file/Off_the_Discount_Rack.pdf, pp. 1–2; Rachel Tiplady, "Zara: Taking the Lead in Fast-Fashion," *Businessweek*, April 4, 2006, www.boozallen.com/media/file/Off_the_Discount_Rack.pdf.

[63] Jeffrey Lant, "Cash Is King," *Small Business Reports*, May 1991, p. 49.

[64] "The Barter and Trade Industry," International Reciprocal Trade Association, 2016, www.irta.com/about/the-barter-and-trade-industry/.

[65] Christina Le Beau, "Rules of the Road," *Entrepreneur*, February 2014, pp. 77–81.

[66] Michelle McAndrew and Grant Davis, "How I Saved $522,000," *Entrepreneur*, 2017, www.entrepreneur.com/slideshow/282683#7.

[67] Joyce M. Rosenberg, "Owners Glean Lessons from Painful Recession," *Greenville News*, July 6, 2014, p. 3E.

[68] Dan Horwitz and Margaret Littman, "How I Saved $65,000," *Entrepreneur*, 2017, www.entrepreneur.com/slideshow/282683#9.

[69] "U.S. Equipment Finance Market Study 2016-17 Fact Sheet," Equipment Leasing and Financing Foundation, 2017, p. 1.

[70] "Equipment Leasing: Six Surprising Benefits," GE Capital, 2015, www.americas.gecapital.com/insight-and-ideas/capital-perspectives/equipment-leasing-six-surprising-benefits.

[71] Jill Amadio, "To Lease or Not to Lease?," *Entrepreneur*, February 1998, p. 133.

[72] "Shifting Full-Time Employees to Part-Time," National Federation of Independent Businesses, www.nfib.com/business-resources/business-resources-item?cmsid=55167.

[73] Gerry Blackwell, "Don't Hire, Outsource," *Small Business Computing*, July 5, 2005, www.smallbusinesscomputing.com/news/article.php/3512451.

[74] *The Federal Reserve Payments Study 2016*, U.S. Federal Reserve, 2016, p. 2.

[75] "2015 Gift Card Sales to Reach New Peak of $130 Billion," *PR Newswire*, December 8, 2015, www.prnewswire.com/news-releases/2015-gift-card-sales-to-reach-new-peak-of-130-billion-300189615.html.

[76] "Gift Card Statistics," GiftCards.com, 2015, www.giftcards.com/gift-card-statistics.

[77] "Gift Cards: They're Good for Business," *World Pay*, 2013, www.worldpay.us/merchant-advisor/fall-2013/gift-cards-good-for-business.

[78] David Worrell, "It's in the Cards," *Entrepreneur*, April 2005, p. 57.

[79] "Shoplifting Statistics," StatisticBrain, 2017, www.statisticbrain.com/shoplifting-statistics/.

[80] "Company Shrink Stats and Trends," Jack L. Hayes International, December 12, 2016, http://hayesinternational.com/2016/12/company-shrink-stats-trends/.

[81] *Report to the Nations on Occupational Fraud and Abuse*, 2016 Global Fraud Study, Association of Certified Fraud Examiners, 2016, p. 8.

[82] William Atkinson, "Small Business Employee Theft," Benefits Pro, February 17, 2015, www.benefitspro.com/2015/02/17/small-business-employee-theft.

[83] *Report to the Nations on Occupational Fraud and Abuse*, 2016 Global Fraud Study, Association of Certified Fraud Examiners, 2016, p. 32.

[84] Ibid., pp. 14, 17.

[85] Robert A. Mamis, "Money In, Money Out," *Inc.*, March 1993, p. 103.

14

Choosing the Right Location and Layout

Suphakit73/Shutterstock

Learning Objectives

On completion of this chapter, you will be able to:

1. Explain the stages in the location decision: choosing the region, the state, the city, and the specific site.

2. Describe the location criteria for retail and service businesses.

3. Outline the location options for retail and service businesses: central business districts, neighborhoods, shopping centers and malls, near competitors, shared spaces, inside large retail stores, nontraditional locations, at home, and on the road.

4. Explain the site selection process for manufacturers.

5. Describe the criteria used to analyze the layout and design considerations of a building, including the Americans with Disabilities Act.

6. Explain the principles of effective layouts for retailers, service businesses, and manufacturers.

MyLab Entrepreneurship

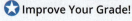 **Improve Your Grade!**

If your instructor is using MyLab Entrepreneurship, visit **www.pearson.com/mylab/entrepreneurship** for videos, simulations, and writing exercises.

Location: A Source of Competitive Advantage

LO1

Explain the stages in the location decision: choosing the region, the state, the city, and the specific site.

Much like choosing a form of ownership and selecting particular sources of financing, the location decision has far-reaching and often long-lasting effects on a small company's future. Entrepreneurs who choose their locations wisely—with their customers' preferences and their companies' needs in mind—establish an important competitive advantage over rivals who choose their locations haphazardly. Because the availability of qualified workers, tax rates, quality of infrastructure, traffic patterns, quality of life, and many other factors vary from one site to another, the location decision is an important one that can influence the growth rate, the cost structure, and the ultimate success of a company. State and local governments levy taxes and fees in different ways, utility and wage rates vary from one area to another, and the cost of acquiring land and buildings differs depending on location, all of which have significant influences on a company's cost structure. Thanks to widespread digital connectivity, mobile computing, extensive cellular coverage, and affordable air travel, entrepreneurs have more flexibility when choosing a business location than ever before.

Every gardener knows that for a particular plant to thrive and grow, it must be in the right location to suit its needs. Too much shade (or sun), the wrong type of soil, or too much (or too little) water will cause the plant to wither. Similarly, a particular business must have the right location to suit its needs if it is to thrive. The conditions that a business requires depend on the type of business involved, but the location decision is important for every business because of its influence on the company's sales. Myriad variables influence an entrepreneur's choice of location, often making for a difficult decision. However, by conducting research and gathering and analyzing information about potential sites, entrepreneurs can find locations that are ideally suited for their businesses. When screening sites for both Disneyland and Disney World, Walt and Roy Disney hired site selection pioneer Buzz Price to conduct exhaustive studies that included demographic analysis, population growth projections, and examination of future highway construction, accessibility, weather patterns, and other relevant factors. The location analysis successfully pinpointed ideal locations for both Disney theme parks; today the two parks host more than 33 million guests each year.

The location decision process resembles an inverted pyramid. The first level of the decision is the broadest, requiring an entrepreneur to select a particular region of the country. (We will address locating a business in a foreign country in Chapter 16.) Then an entrepreneur must choose the right state, the right city, and, finally, the right site within the city. The key to selecting the ideal location lies in knowing the factors that are most important to a company's success and then finding a location that satisfies as many of them as possible, particularly those that are most critical. For instance, one of the most important location factors for high-tech companies is the availability of a skilled labor force. If physically locating near customers is vital to a company's success, an entrepreneur's goal is to find a site that makes it most convenient for his or her target customers to do business with the company.

ENTREPRENEURIAL PROFILE: Tony and John Calamunci, Johnny's Lunch Tony and John Calamunci sell franchises of the family-owned diner that their grandparents, Johnny and Minnie Colera, started in Brooklyn Square in Jamestown, New York, in 1936 (and that their parents still operate). In launching the franchise operation, they realized that opening outlets in areas in which large concentrations of their target customers lived was essential to their success. They hired an experienced franchise veteran, George Goulson, and worked with Pitney-Bowes Software's MapInfo, using geospatial technology to determine the ideal locations for their restaurants, which sell budget-priced meals such as hot dogs, hamburgers, onion rings, and milkshakes. The Calamuncis started by defining their target customers, which they discovered include people in the lower-middle- to upper-middle-income bracket who are between the ages 16 to 24 and over 60. Using the software, they identified 72 types of neighborhoods that best match the demographic and psychographic profile of Johnny's Lunch customers. The next step was to find locations that matched the 72 prototype neighborhoods. Managers identified 4,500 areas across the United States that held large concentrations of potential Johnny's Lunch customers (most of whom lived within 1 mile of the proposed location) and would be good locations for restaurants. "These models increase our ability to pick 'home-run' locations and avoid the site mistakes that can cripple a budding franchise," says Goulson. Johnny's Lunch is launching its franchising effort in and around Toledo, Ohio, which Goulson says is a microcosm of the United States. "Small restaurant owners like us can use location intelligence to prevent mistakes that could cripple franchising plans from the start. We can't afford not to invest in location intelligence."[1] ■

The characteristics that make for an ideal location vary dramatically from one company to another because of the nature of their business. In the early twentieth century, companies looked for ready supplies of water, raw materials, and access to railroads; today, they are more likely to look for sites that are close to universities and offer high-speed Internet access and accessible airports. In fact, one study concludes that the factors that make an area most suitable for starting and growing small companies include access to dynamic universities, an ample supply of skilled workers, a nearby airport, a temperate climate, and a high quality of life.[2] The key to finding a suitable location is identifying the characteristics that can give a company a competitive edge and then searching out potential sites that meet those criteria.

Choosing the Region

The first step in selecting the best location is to focus on selecting the right region. This requires entrepreneurs to look at the location decision from the "30,000-foot level," as if he or she were in an airplane looking down. In fact, in the early days of their companies, Sam Walton, founder of retail giant Wal-Mart, and Ray Kroc, who built McDonald's into a fast-food giant, actually used private planes to survey the countryside for prime locations for their stores.

ENTREPRENEURIAL PROFILE: Walt Disney: Disney World In 1963, Walt Disney flew over central Florida in a private plane (which is now on display at Disney World) to look at a tract of nondescript swampland as a potential site for Disney World. Disney lacked sufficient space to expand Disneyland in California and, with the help of site selection expert Buzz Price and a group of top managers, established several criteria for the company's second theme park, including a place with good weather throughout most of the year, plenty of land at bargain prices, a location near a major city, and access to major highways and infrastructure for the company's second theme park (dubbed "Project X"). When Disney flew over the intersection of Interstate 4 and Route 192 near Orlando, he knew he had found the ideal location for Disney World, which now encompasses 30,000 acres, an area about the size of San Francisco![3] ■

Which region of the country has the characteristics necessary for a new business to succeed? Above all, entrepreneurs must think of their customers first when considering a location. As the experiences of Johnny's Lunch and Disney suggest, facts and statistics, not speculation, lead entrepreneurs to the best locations for their businesses. Common requirements may include rapid growth in the population of a certain age group, rising disposable incomes, the existence of necessary infrastructure, access to an essential raw material, a capable workforce, and low operating costs. At the broadest level of the location decision, entrepreneurs prefer to locate in regions of the country that are experiencing substantial growth. Every year, many popular business publications prepare reports on the various regions of the nation—which ones are growing, which are stagnant, and which are declining. Studying overall trends in population and business growth gives entrepreneurs an idea of where the action is—and isn't. Questions to consider include the following: How large is the population? How fast is it growing? What is the makeup of the overall population? Which segments are growing fastest? Slowest? What is the trend in the population's income? Are other businesses moving into the region? If so, what kind of businesses? Generally, entrepreneurs want to avoid declining regions, which simply cannot support a broad base of potential customers.

One of the first stops entrepreneurs should make when conducting a regional evaluation is the U.S. Census Bureau site (www.census.gov). There entrepreneurs can access specific locations' vital demographic information, such as age, income, educational level, employment level, occupation, ancestry, commuting times, housing data (house value, number of rooms, mortgage or rent status, number of vehicles owned, and so on), and many other characteristics. With a little practice, entrepreneurs can prepare customized reports on the potential sites they are considering. These Web-based resources give entrepreneurs instant access to important site-location information that only a few years ago would have taken many hours of intense research to compile. In 2012, the Census Bureau ceased publication of the *U.S. Statistical Abstract* (published annually since 1878), which contained about 1,400 useful data sets about the United States, ranging from basic population characteristics and leisure activity expenditures to poverty rates and energy consumption. However, ProQuest, an information gateway company founded in 1943, now publishes in both print and online formats the *ProQuest Statistical Abstract of the United States* (http://cisupa.proquest.com/ws_display.asp?filter=Statistical%20Abstract), which closely resembles the discontinued Census Bureau publication.

The Census Bureau's American FactFinder site (http://factfinder.census.gov) provides easily accessible demographic fact sheets and maps on nearly every community in the United States, including small towns. The Census Bureau's American Community Survey provides annual updates on the demographic and economic characteristics of areas with populations of at least 65,000, three-year updates on areas with populations between 20,000 and 65,000, and five-year updates on areas with populations of less than 20,000. Both the American FactFinder and the American Community Survey allow entrepreneurs to produce easy-to-read, customizable maps of the information they generate in their searches.

Entrepreneurs also can use nongovernment sources to research potential locations. Zoom-Prospector (www.zoomprospector.com) is a useful Web site that allows entrepreneurs to search for the ideal location using a multitude of factors, including population size, job growth rate, number of patents issued, venture capital invested, education level, household incomes, and proximity to interstate highways, railroads, and airports. Entrepreneurs who are considering a particular region can display "heat maps" that visually display the areas that have the highest concentrations of people who have a particular characteristic, such as a bachelor's degree or the highest household incomes.

The Population Reference Bureau (www.prb.org/DataFinder.aspx) provides a detailed breakdown of the most relevant data collected from the most recent census reports. The Population Reference Bureau's DataFinder is a database that includes 244 variables for the United States and 133 variables for 220 other nations. The site includes easy-to-generate maps and charts and helpful articles that discuss the implications of the changing demographic and economic profile of the nation's (and the world's) population, such as the impact of aging Baby Boomers on business and the composition of the U.S. workforce.

Other helpful resources merit mention as well. *Lifestyle Market Analyst*, a four-part annual publication, matches population demographics with lifestyle interests. Section 1 provides demographics and lifestyle information for 210 "Designated Market Areas" across the United States. Section 2 gives demographic and geographic profiles of 77 lifestyle interests that range from avid readers and dieters to wine aficionados and pet owners. Section 3 describes the dominant lifestyle interests for each of the 210 market areas. Section 4 provides comparisons of other activities that correspond with each lifestyle interest. Entrepreneurs can use *Lifestyle Market Analyst* to determine, for example, how likely members of a particular market segment are to own a dog, collect antiques, play golf, own a vacation home, engage in extreme sports, invest in stocks or bonds, or participate in a host of other activities.

Another useful source of demographic data is *The American Marketplace: Demographics and Spending Patterns*, which provides useful demographic information in eight areas: education, health, income, labor force, living arrangements, population, race and ethnicity, and spending and wealth. Most of the tables in the book are derived from government statistics, and *The American Marketplace* also includes a discussion of the data in each table as well as a forecast of future trends. Many users say that the primary advantage of *The American Marketplace* is its ease of use.

The U.S. Census Bureau also offers the ZIP Code Tabulation Areas (ZCTA) Web site (www.census.gov/geo/reference/zctas.html), which organizes the wealth of census data by ZIP code. The database of 33,120 ZCTAs across the United States allows users to create tables and plot maps of census data by ZIP code.

Site Selection magazine (www.siteselection.com) is another useful resource that helps entrepreneurs determine the ideal location for their companies. Issues contain articles that summarize the incentive programs that states offer, profiles of each region of the country, and the benefits of locating in different states.

States, counties, and cities now provide geographic information systems (GIS) files online that allow entrepreneurs to identify sites that match the criteria they establish for the ideal location. GIS packages allow users to search through virtually any database containing a wealth of information and plot the results on a map of the country, an individual state, a specific city, or even a single city block. The visual display highlights what otherwise would be indiscernible business trends. For instance, using GIS programs, entrepreneurs can plot their existing customer base on a map, with various colors representing the different population densities. Then they can zoom in on the areas with the greatest concentration of customers, mapping a detailed view of ZIP code borders or even city streets. GIS street files originate in the U.S. Census Department's TIGER (Topographically Integrated Geographic Encoding Referencing) file, which contains map information broken down for every square foot of metropolitan statistical areas (MSAs). TIGER files contain the name and location of every street in the country and detailed block statistics for the 345 largest urban areas. In essence, TIGER is a massive database of geographic features such as roads, railways, and political boundaries across the United States that, when linked with mapping programs and demographic databases, gives entrepreneurs incredible power to pinpoint existing and potential customers on easy-to-read digital maps.

The Small Business Administration's Small Business Development Center (SBDC) program also offers location analysis assistance to entrepreneurs. These centers, numbering more than 900 nationwide, provide training, counseling, research, and other specialized assistance to entrepreneurs and existing business owners on a wide variety of subjects, all at no charge. They are an important resource, especially for entrepreneurs who do not have access to a computer. (To locate the SBDC nearest you, contact the SBA office in your state or go to the SBA's Small Business Development Center locations page, at www.sba.gov/tools/local-assistance/sbdc.)

For entrepreneurs interested in demographic and statistical profiles of international markets, Euromonitor International (www.euromonitor.com) and the Organisation for Economic Co-operation and Development (www.oecd.org) are excellent resources. Several other organizations also publish reports on the top countries and cities around the world, based on their suitability as locations for various types of businesses. For instance, the World Economic Forum annually publishes the *Global Competitiveness Report*, which provides a comprehensive assessment of nearly 140 nations and shows their suitability for doing business. The IMD World Competitiveness Center produces a similar report summarizing the performance of 62 nations using more than 340 business-related criteria.

Once an entrepreneur has identified the best region of the country, the next step is to evaluate the individual states in that region.

Choosing the State

Every state has an economic development office working to recruit new businesses. Even though the publications produced by these offices are biased in favor of locating in that state, they are excellent sources of information and can help entrepreneurs assess the business climate in each state. Some of the key issues to explore include the laws, regulations, and taxes that govern businesses; costs of operation; workforce availability; and incentives or investment credits the state offers to entice businesses to locate there.

ENTREPRENEURIAL PROFILE: Terry Douglas: ProNova Solutions After investing a year looking at potential sites for a new $52 million manufacturing plant, ProNova Solutions, a company that is developing next-generation proton therapy cancer treatment technology, selected a location in Pellissippi Place, a technology research and development park in Maryville, Tennessee. The area, dubbed Innovation Valley because of its proximity to the University of Tennessee and the Oak Ridge National Research Laboratory (ORNL), which is conducting research in the field, is ideally suited for ProNova's needs. Tennessee's pro-business culture and the area's talented workforce and existing infrastructure, including the Pellissippi Parkway, a highway that connects the R&D park with ORNL, sold ProNova's CEO Terry Douglas on the location. Because of ORNL, workers in the area already are familiar with the technology that ProNova uses, including linear accelerators and cyclotrons.[4] ■

Factors that entrepreneurs often consider when choosing a location include proximity to markets, proximity to raw materials, wage rates, quantity and quality of the labor supply, general business climate, tax rates, Internet access, and total operating costs.

PROXIMITY TO MARKETS Locating close to markets they plan to serve is extremely critical for manufacturers, especially when the cost of transporting finished goods is high relative to their value. Locating near customers is necessary to remain competitive. Service firms also often find that proximity to their clients is essential. If a business is involved in repairing equipment used in a specific industry, it should be located where that industry is concentrated. The more specialized a business or the greater the relative cost of transporting the product to the customer, the more likely it is that proximity to the market will be of critical importance in the location decision.

Locating close to potential customers is an important consideration for many other types of businesses as well.

ENTREPRENEURIAL PROFILE: Rahul Marwah: Denny's Rahul Marwah is a multi-unit franchisee for Denny's, a chain with more than 1,700 locations across the United States that bills itself as "America's Diner." When Marwah realized that New York City had no Denny's locations, he applied to open a restaurant in the city. Based in Pasadena, California, Marwah spent a year learning about New York City, its boroughs and neighborhoods, its inhabitants, and its restaurant culture so that he could match as closely as possible a specific location to the company's target customers. After reviewing many potential sites, Marwah selected a location in the first floor of an upscale condominium complex in Manhattan on the edge of the Financial District. Marwah believes his location is ideal because of the high population density in the area (which produces plenty of potential customers, especially in the evenings), its proximity to one of the busiest train stations in Manhattan (which generates lots of commuter traffic during the day), and its location directly across from Pace University, home to nearly 13,000 students.[5] ∎

PROXIMITY TO SUPPLIERS AND RAW MATERIALS For some entrepreneurs, locations near suppliers of essential services or raw materials are vital to success. Fashion designer Trina Turk, whose company produces 11 distinct collections each year, located her business in Alhambra, California, a suburb of Los Angeles, rather than in the bustling city center for several reasons, including safety (she employs a significant number of young women who sometimes work after normal business hours) and low rental rates. However, the location's main draw is its proximity to Los Angeles's garment district, where many of the company's sewing contractors are based. Although Turk says her company's neighborhood is not glamorous or known as a fashion center, the location does give her company a competitive advantage.[6]

If a business uses raw materials that are difficult or expensive to transport, it may require a location near the source of those raw materials. Transporting heavy, low-value raw material over long distances is impractical—and unprofitable. For products in which bulk or weight is not a factor, locating manufacturing operations in close proximity to suppliers facilitates quick deliveries and reduces inventory holding costs. Hamlet Protein, a company based in Horsens, Denmark, originally chose Findlay, Ohio, for the location of a manufacturing plant because it lies in the heart of soybean country, a key ingredient in its animal feed products. Findlay proved to be such a good fit for Hamlet Protein that the company recently doubled its production capacity at the factory there, citing the skilled, highly motivated workforce, proximity to major transportation networks, and high quality of life.[7] The value of raw materials, their cost of transportation, and their unique functions together determine how close a business should be to its suppliers.

WAGE RATES Existing and anticipated wage rates provide another measure for comparison among states. Wages can sometimes vary from one state or region to another, significantly affecting a company's cost of doing business. For instance, according to the Bureau of Labor Statistics, the average hourly compensation for workers (including wages and benefits) ranges from a low of $30.54 in the South to a high of $41.19 in the Northeast.[8] Wage rate differentials within geographic regions can be even more drastic. Saving just $1 per hour on wages translates into significant savings for a company. When reviewing wage rates, entrepreneurs must be sure to measure the wage rates for jobs that relate to their particular industries or companies. In addition to surveys by the Bureau of Labor Statistics (www.bls.gov), local employment ads can give entrepreneurs an idea of the pay scale in an area. Entrepreneurs also can obtain the latest wage and salary surveys with an e-mail or telephone call to the local chambers of commerce for cities in the region under consideration. Entrepreneurs should study not only prevailing wage rates but also *trends* in rates. How does the rate of increase in wages compare to those in other states? Another factor influencing wage rates is the level of union activity in a state. How much union organizing activity has the state seen within the last two years? Which industries have unions targeted in the recent past?

ENTREPRENEURIAL PROFILE: Axiom Inc. Axiom Inc., a maker of fishing rods based in New York City, shifted production of its entry-level line of rods from China to Zacatecas, Mexico. Axiom was attracted by the region's low wage rates, pool of young workers, and ability to ship products to customers in North America much faster. When the company was manufacturing rods in China, meeting customers' orders quickly, managing the supply chain, and controlling inventory proved problematic because shipments would take 30 days to arrive and up to another 30 days to clear customs and travel to the company's factory in Wisconsin, where employees inspected them for quality. In Mexico, the availability of a stable workforce and wages that are 25 to 30 percent lower than those in the United States were driving factors in the company's location decision.[9] ■

SIZE AND QUALITY OF LABOR FORCE The most important criterion for site selection among business executives is the availability of skilled workers.[10] The number of workers available in an area and their levels of education, training, and experience determine a company's ability to fill jobs with qualified workers at reasonable wages. One study finds that the companies that make *Inc.* magazine's list of fastest-growing businesses tend to locate in areas that have highly educated workforces.[11] For example, Utah, home to Brigham Young University, Utah State University, and the University of Utah, hosts a large concentration of technology companies (several with market valuations of more than $1 billion), second only to California's Silicon Valley but without the high costs. (In fact, the crescent of cities along the Rocky Mountains from Ogden to Provo is known as Silicon Slopes.) One reason that software companies find Utah attractive is its above-average concentration of college graduates. In Provo, for example, more than 40 percent of the city's residents have a bachelor's degree or higher (compared to 29.7 percent in the United States as a whole).[12] Other features that attract start-up technology companies to Utah include affordable taxes, inexpensive real estate, a business-friendly environment, high quality of life (especially for young people who love the outdoors), the availability of venture capital, and access to Google Fiber, the super high-speed Internet connection currently available in just a handful of cities.[13]

Courtesy of SimpleCitizen

ENTREPRENEURIAL PROFILE: Brady Stoddard, Adyé Soto, and Sam Stoddard: SimpleCitizen Brady Stoddard was a graduate student at Brigham Young University when he married Eunjoon Yoon, who is from South Korea. When the couple learned that having an attorney handle Yoon's application for a visa (which the attorney said was a "simple" case) would cost $2,000, Stoddard decided to handle the application himself, believing that it would be an easy process. The process ended up being incredibly complicated and took Stoddard four months to complete. That experience led Stoddard to work with fellow BYU students Adyé Soto and Sam Stoddard to launch SimpleCitizen, a company that helps people navigate the complex process of applying for visas, visa renewals, and citizenship for just $249. The SimpleCitizen Web site, which provides a learning center with a library of articles and video tutorials and access to experts to answer immigration-related questions, guides users through the entire process; at the end, the company submits the completed application to an immigration attorney for verification. Although SimpleCitizen landed a coveted spot in the Y Combinator accelerator in Mountain View, California, its founders intend to stay in Provo, Utah, because their company benefits from the area's large pool of well-educated workers, low cost of doing business, and high quality of life.[14] ■

Before selecting a location, entrepreneurs should know how many qualified people are available in the area to perform the work required in their businesses. To evaluate potential locations, businesses can use a tool from LinkedIn, Economic Graph (www.linkedin.com/economic-graph), that provides global maps of workers' skills, companies, colleges and universities, and job openings.[15] Some regions have attempted to attract industry with the promise of cheap labor.

Rather than saving money due to low wages, many companies that locate in those areas experience higher costs because of the unskilled, low-wage workers who are ill suited for performing the work the companies need and are difficult to train. Zeynep Ton, a professor at MIT, cites more than a decade of research that shows a link in the service sector between paying *higher* wages and earning *higher* profits.[16]

Knowing the exact nature of the workforce needed and preparing job descriptions and job specifications in advance help business owners to determine whether there is a good match between their companies' needs and the available labor pool. Reviewing the major industries already operating in an area provides clues about the characteristics of the local workforce as well. Checking educational statistics to determine the number of graduates in relevant fields of study tells entrepreneurs about the available supply of qualified workers. Uber, the ride-sharing company, selected Pittsburgh, Pennsylvania, as the location for its research and development center, which is working on the company's autonomous vehicle project, because the city is home to Carnegie Mellon University, which hosts one of the world's leading centers of autonomous driving technology and is capable of supplying the pool of talent the company demands.[17]

BUSINESS CLIMATE What is the state's overall attitude toward your kind of business? Has it passed laws that impose restrictions on the way a company can operate? Do "blue laws" prohibit certain business activity on Sundays? Does the state offer small business support programs or financial assistance to entrepreneurs?

ENTREPRENEURIAL PROFILE: Eclipse Aerospace Eclipse Aerospace, maker of "the world's most efficient very light jet," selected Albuquerque, New Mexico, as the location for its new 215,000-square-foot manufacturing facility because of the state's business-friendly environment. The state legislature passed legislation that eliminated the sales tax on aircraft parts, services, and finished aircraft. Because the base price of Eclipse Aerospace's newest jet is $2.9 million, the exemption saves the company hundreds of thousands of dollars annually. The company's factory is conveniently located next to Albuquerque's International Sunport Airport, which boasts one of the longest runways in the United States, and access to a railroad spur and to two major interstate highways. In addition, as one CEO points out, Albuquerque treats entrepreneurs like rock stars.[18] ∎

Some states and cities create policies that are more small business friendly than others. In South Carolina, antiquated laws that prohibit small craft breweries from distributing their beers, ales, and lagers beyond their immediate locations and a high tax on beer discourage small breweries from locating there. One national study reports that states that allow craft breweries to self-distribute their products have 75 percent more breweries than states that require breweries to sell only through outside distributors. For example, South Carolina is home to only 36 breweries and brewpubs, while its neighbor, North Carolina, which offers a lower tax on beer and allows brewers to self-distribute up to 25,000 barrels per year, has more than 120, with more opening each year.[19]

The Small Business & Entrepreneurship Council publishes an annual "small-business-friendly" ranking of the states and the District of Columbia that includes a composite measure of 47 factors, ranging from a variety of taxes and regulations to crime rates and energy costs (see Table 14.1).

Jacob Biba/The Washington Post/Getty Images

TAX RATES Another important factor that entrepreneurs must consider when screening states for potential locations is the tax burden they impose on businesses and individuals. Does the state impose a corporate income tax? How heavy are the state's property, income, and sales taxes? Income taxes may be the most obvious tax that states impose on both business and individuals, but entrepreneurs also must evaluate the impact of payroll taxes, sales taxes, property taxes, and specialized taxes on the cost of their operations. Figure 14.1 shows how each state's overall tax burden measured by 114 variables ranks. Currently, seven states (Alaska, Florida, Nevada,

TABLE 14.1 Most and Least Small-Business-Friendly States

States *Most* Friendly to Small Businesses

1. Nevada	6. Washington
2. Texas	7. Indiana
3. South Dakota	8. Arizona
4. Wyoming	9. Alabama
5. Florida	10. Ohio

States *Least* Friendly to Small Businesses

41. Oregon	46. Vermont
42. Iowa	47. Minnesota
43. Connecticut	48. New York
44. Maine	49. New Jersey
45. Hawaii	50. California

Source: Based on Raymond J. Keating, *Small Business Policy Index 2017*, Small Business & Entrepreneurship Council, 21st Annual Edition, February 2017, p. 2.

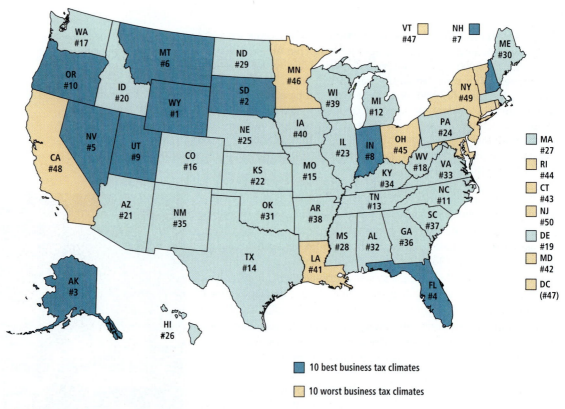

■ 10 best business tax climates

☐ 10 worst business tax climates

FIGURE 14.1

State Business Tax Climate Index

Source: Jared Walczak, Scott Drenkard, and Joseph Henchman, *2017 State Business Tax Climate Index*, Tax Foundation, September 28, 2016, p. 1.

South Dakota, Texas, Washington, and Wyoming) impose no state individual income tax (two others do not tax wage income), and three states (Nevada, Wyoming, and South Dakota) have no corporate income tax, but state governments always impose taxes of some sort on businesses and individuals.[20] In some cases, states offer special tax credits or are willing to negotiate fees in lieu of taxes (FILOTs) for companies that create jobs and stimulate the local economy.

As the battle to attract businesses has intensified, the economic development tax incentives that states and cities offer have tripled since 1990. One study estimates that tax incentives now offset 30 percent of the taxes the companies otherwise would have paid, compared to a 9 percent offset in 1990.[21]

ENTREPRENEURIAL PROFILE: Riddell Inc. Riddell Inc., a maker of football helmets for college and professional players, moved its factory from Elyria, Ohio, to nearby North Ridgeville, Ohio, after North Ridgeville offered a $7 million tax incentive package and lower corporate and individual income tax rates over several years. Although the new location is just two miles away from Riddell's former factory, the company received tax credits for creating jobs and for making a capital investment in North Ridgeville.[22] ∎

HIGH-SPEED INTERNET ACCESS Speedy, reliable Internet access is an increasingly important factor in the location decision (see Figure 14.2). Fast Internet access is essential for high-tech companies, those that rely on cloud computing, and those that engage in e-commerce; however, even companies that may not sell to customers over the Internet find high-speed Internet to be a valuable business tool. Companies that fall behind in high-speed Internet access find themselves at a severe competitive disadvantage. Google Fiber, a high-speed fiber network from Google that runs 100 times faster (1 gigabyte per second) than current broadband, is already in place in Kansas City (Kansas and Missouri), Austin (Texas), Atlanta (Georgia), Charlotte (North Carolina), Salt Lake City (Utah), Nashville (Tennessee), Raleigh-Durham (North Carolina), Provo (Utah), and Orange County (California) and is proving to be an important factor in many entrepreneurs' decisions to locate in these cities. Google currently is working with other cities, such as Phoenix (Arizona), San Antonio (Texas), Louisville (Kentucky), and Huntsville (Alabama), to bring Google Fiber to their businesses and residents. Wherever Google Fiber goes, entrepreneurs tend to follow.

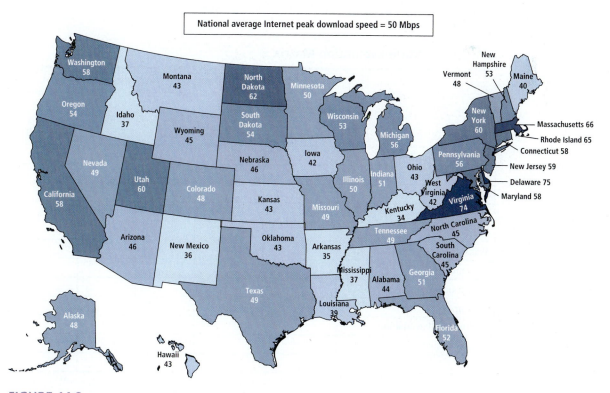

FIGURE 14.2

Average Internet Peak Download Speeds (Mbps) by State

Source: Based on data from "Internet Connection Speed Map," FastMetrics, 2017, www.fastmetrics.com/internet-connection-speed-map-usa.php#average-speeds-by-state.

ENTREPRENEURIAL PROFILE: Vinay Mahadik and Bharath Madhusudan: Securly
Vinay Mahadik and Bharath Madhusudan chose Charlotte, North Carolina, as the home for their start-up, Securly, in part because of the availability of high-speed Google Fiber. The entrepreneurs recognized that access to high speed Internet could provide a competitive advantage for their company, which provides a cloud-based Web filter that is designed to provide parental controls for students around the world using school-issued computers and to protect them from cyberbullying and dangerous online activity.[23] ∎

TOTAL OPERATING COSTS When scouting a state in which to locate a company, entrepreneurs must consider the total cost of operating a business. For instance, a state may offer low utility rates, but its labor costs and tax rates may be among the highest in the nation. To select the ideal location, entrepreneurs must consider the impact of a state's total cost of operation on their business ventures. Loudon County, Virginia, is known as Data Center Alley because it houses 9 million square feet of data centers, massive buildings that house banks of servers that power our online searches, stream our music and movies online, and store our data in the cloud. As much as 70 percent of global Internet traffic flows through Loudon County's data centers each day. One of the largest expenses of operating a data center is the electricity to power the thousands of servers, and Loudon County's affordable electricity rates is one reason that so many data centers have located there. In fact, data centers in Loudon County pay electricity rates that are 28 percent below the national average.[24]

The state evaluation matrix in Table 14.2 provides a handy tool designed to help entrepreneurs determine which states best suit the most important location criteria for their companies. This same matrix can be adapted to analyze individual cities as well. Claremont McKenna College's Kosmont-Rose Institute Cost of Doing Business Survey reports that cities in Texas tend to offer the lowest cost of operation (6 cities among the 20 least expensive), while cities in California are among the most expensive (13 cities among the 20 most expensive).[25]

TABLE 14.2 State Evaluation Matrix

Location Criterion		State Weighted Score (Weight × Score)			
	Weight	Score (Low = 1, High = 5)	State 1	State 2	State 3
Quality of labor force					
Wage rates					
Union activity					
Property/building costs					
Utility costs					
Transportation costs					
Tax burden					
Educational/training assistance					
Start-up incentives					
Raw material availability					
Quality of life					
Other:					
		Total Score			

Assign to each location criterion a weight that reflects its relative importance to your company. Then score each state on a scale of 1 (low) to 5 (high). Calculate the weighted score (Weight × Score) for each state. Finally, add up the total weighted score for each state. The state with the highest total score is the best location for your business.

TABLE 14.3 Best and Worst States for Doing Business

Top 10 States for Doing Business

Overall Rank*	State	Taxes and Regulations	Rank Based on Workforce Quality	Living Environment
1	Texas	#6	#5	#10
2	Florida	7	23	9
3	North Carolina	15	10	3
4	Tennessee	4	8	8
5	Indiana	10	4	17
6	Arizona	12	14	11
7	South Carolina	11	19	6
8	Georgia	14	9	7
9	Nevada	3	22	21
10	Ohio	24	7	23

Bottom 10 States for Doing Business

Rank*	State	Taxes and Regulations	Workforce Quality	Living Environment
41	Rhode Island	#44	#37	#39
42	Mississippi	33	48	50
43	Maryland	45	45	41
44	Hawaii	43	49	4
45	Massachusetts	47	16	38
46	Connecticut	48	36	37
47	New Jersey	42	40	48
48	Illinois	46	44	45
49	New York	49	38	47
50	California	50	35	26

*Rank is the result of a survey by *Chief Executive* magazine that asked 650 business leaders to rank the states on factors such as taxes, regulatory burden, quality of workforce, and quality of life.

Source: Based on "2016 Best and Worst States for Business," *Chief Executive*, May 6, 2016, http://chiefexecutive.net/2016-best-and-worst-states-for-business-full-list/.

Table 14.3 shows the states that CEOs rank as the 10 best states and the 10 worst states on factors such as taxes and regulations, quality of workforce, and living environment.

Choosing the City

POPULATION TRENDS Analyzing over time the lists of "best cities for business" compiled annually by many magazines reveals one consistent trend: Successful small companies in a city tend to track a city's population growth. In other words, more potential customers mean that a small business has a better chance of success. *Forbes* magazine recently ranked the fastest-growing major cities in the United States; Austin, Texas, is at the top of the list, followed by San Francisco, California, and Dallas, Texas.[26] Austin, a thriving university town that is home to many technology-related companies, including Dell, Apple, IBM, and Samsung, is a haven for entrepreneurial start-ups. With its funky culture, progressive music scene, abundant festivals (including the quirky South by Southwest Festival), and temperate climate, the city has become a magnet for young, creative people. The median age of Austin's population is 32.1, well below the national average of 37.6. A highly educated workforce, large concentrations of angel and venture capital, and an entrepreneurial support system that includes business incubators and accelerators such as Capital Factory add to the city's attractiveness for entrepreneurs.

Courtesy of Blake Garrett, CEO, Aceable

ENTREPRENEURIAL PROFILE: Blake Garrett: Aceable Blake Garrett moved from Boston to Austin because he believed the Texas high-tech hot spot would be the ideal place to launch his company, Aceable, which markets a mobile app for driver's education that transforms traditional lecture-based courses into fast-paced, interactive content. Armed with only an idea, Garrett landed a spot in one of the Capital Factory accelerator's first classes, where he interacted with software engineers, other company founders, financial advisors, attorneys, investors, and others. Two early investors, in particular, helped Garrett identify the pivots his start-up needed to make and shaped Aceable's focus. Aceable has raised a total of $8.7 million in three rounds of financing and now has more than 60 employees. (New employees go through a scarfing ceremony, in which Garrett presents each one with an Aceable soccer scarf to a ringing round of applause from coworkers.)[27] ∎

By analyzing population and other demographic data, entrepreneurs can examine a city in detail, and the location decision becomes more than just an educated guess or, worse, a shot in the dark. Studying the trends and the demographics of a city, including population size and density, growth trends, family size, age breakdowns, education, income levels, job categories, gender, religion, race, and nationality, gives entrepreneurs the facts they need to make an informed location decision. Useful information is available from the U.S. Census Bureau for cities of all sizes, including metropolitan and micropolitan areas (those with an urban core of between 10,000 and 50,000 people) and small towns. There are 575 micropolitan areas in the United States, and Table 14.4 shows the states that have the greatest number of micropolitan areas listed in the top 100.

In fact, using only basic census data, entrepreneurs can determine residents' income levels, what home values are in an area, how many rooms they contain, how many bedrooms they contain, what percentage of the population own their homes, and how much residents' monthly rental or mortgage payments are. Imagine how useful that information would be to someone about to launch a bed-and-bath shop!

A company's location should match the market for its products or services, and assembling a demographic profile tells an entrepreneur how well a particular site measures up to his or her target market's profile. For instance, an entrepreneur planning to open a fine art shop would likely want information on a city's household income, size, age, and education level. To succeed, this art shop should be located in an area where people appreciate its products and have the discretionary income to purchase them.

TABLE 14.4 States with the Most Top Micropolitan Areas

State	Number of Top 100 Micropolitan Areas
Ohio	19
Kentucky	9
Indiana	6
North Carolina	6
Georgia	5
Illinois	5
Tennessee	4
Alabama	4
Nebraska	4
Michigan	4

Source: Based on Ron Starner, "The Findlay Formula Effect," *Site Selection*, March 2016, pp. 115–129.

ENTREPRENEURIAL PROFILE: Texas Roadhouse, Anchorage, Alaska Texas Roadhouse, a 410-unit casual dining chain, recently opened its first restaurant in Anchorage, Alaska, the state's largest and wealthiest city. With a per capita income of nearly $55,000 and a population of nearly 300,000 people, Anchorage is capturing the attention of several restaurant chains. Texas Roadhouse executives say that although Anchorage is somewhat remote, the market is underserved and represents a huge growth opportunity. The chain's theme, a steak-oriented menu and country music, fits well with Alaska's culture. The Anchorage restaurant incorporates several modifications that reflect the region's unique characteristics. The restaurant is bigger than those located in the lower 48; it needs more storage space because supply deliveries are less frequent in remote locations. The lights also are brighter to offset the long periods of darkness (an average of nearly 18½ hours per day in January) the region experiences in the winter months. The menu features the chain's signature steaks and ice cold beer but also includes several local items, including salmon and crab legs.[28] ∎

The amount of available data on the population of any city or town is staggering. These statistics allow entrepreneurs to compare a wide variety of cities or towns and to narrow the choices to those few that warrant further investigation. Analyzing all of this data makes it possible to screen out undesirable locations and to narrow the list of suitable locations to a few, but it does not make the final location decision for an entrepreneur. Entrepreneurs must see the potential locations on their "short list" *firsthand*. Only by seeing a potential location can an entrepreneur add the intangible factor of intuition into the decision-making process. Spending time at a potential location tells an entrepreneur not only how many people frequent it but also what they are like, how long they stay, and what they buy. Walking or driving around the area gives an entrepreneur clues about the people who live and work there. What are their houses like? What kinds of cars do they drive? What stage of life are they in? Do they have children? Is the area on the rise, or is it past its prime?

ENTREPRENEURIAL PROFILE: Michael Chernow: Seamore's Before restaurateur Michael Chernow chooses a location for one of his New York City restaurants, he studies the demographics of potential sites but always spends time walking the neighborhoods to get a feel for the location's potential before making a final decision. Chernow, who recently opened Seamore's, a seafood restaurant focusing on sustainably caught fish, in the city's Nolita ("North of Little Italy") neighborhood to rave reviews, says that he is always on the lookout for superior restaurant spaces as he travels around New York City.[29] ∎

Following are other factors that entrepreneurs should consider when evaluating cities as possible business locations.

COMPETITION For some retailers, locating near competitors makes sense because similar businesses located near one another may serve to increase traffic flow to both. This location strategy works well for products for which customers are most likely to comparison shop. For instance, in many cities, auto dealers locate next to one another in a "motor mile," trying to create a shopping magnet for customers. The convenience of being able to shop for dozens of brands of cars all within a few hundred yards of one another draws customers from a sizable trading area. Locating near competitors is a common strategy for restaurants as well. Of course, this strategy has limits. Overcrowding of businesses of the same type in an area can create an undesirable impact on the profitability of all competing firms.

ENTREPRENEURIAL PROFILE: Wesley Wright: Chef Daddy's When Wesley Wright started Chef Daddy's, a food truck and catering business, that specializes in locally sourced, unique tacos and sliders, in Asheville, North Carolina, in 2013, he faced only 10 other food truck operators. In just three years, the number of food truck competitors had grown to 60. Believing that the Asheville market had become saturated, Wright decided to move Chef Daddy's to Greenville, South Carolina, which Livability recently listed as one of the top 10 downtowns in the United States. The citys offers a fast-growing, upscale population and a business-friendly environment but very few food truck competitors.[30] ∎

Studying the size of the market for a product or service and the number of existing competitors helps an entrepreneur determine whether he or she can capture a sufficiently large market share to earn a profit. Again, census reports can be a valuable source of information. *County*

Business Patterns gives a breakdown of businesses in manufacturing, wholesale, retail, and service categories and estimates companies' annual payrolls and number of employees broken down by county. *ZIP Code Business Patterns* provides the same data as *County Business Patterns* except it organizes the data by ZIP code. The *Economic Census*, which is produced for years that end in 2 and 7, gives an overview of the businesses in an area—their sales (or other measure of output), employment, payroll, and form of organization. It covers eight industry categories, including retail, wholesale, service, manufacturing, construction, and others, and gives statistics not only at the national level but also by state, metropolitan statistical area, county, places with 2,500 or more inhabitants, and ZIP code. The *Economic Census* is a useful tool for helping entrepreneurs determine whether the areas they are considering as a location are already saturated with competitors.

clusters

geographic concentrations of interconnected companies, specialized suppliers, and service providers that are present in a region.

CLUSTERS   Some cities have characteristics that attract certain industries, and, as a result, companies tend to cluster there. **Clusters** are geographic concentrations of interconnected companies that share specialized supply chains, resources, labor force, distribution networks, and service providers that are present in a region.[31] Businesses in a cluster build on the same pool of resources and strengthen the entire business ecosystem in the area. According to Harvard professor Michael Porter, clusters allow companies in them to increase their productivity, gain a competitive edge, and increase their likelihood of survival. "Specialization in a region increases the number of patents and business formations and leads to higher wages," adds Harvard's Rich Bryden, who has helped develop a map of business clusters in the United States.[32] Northeastern Ohio is home to dozens of companies, most of them small businesses, in the flexible electronic components (those that can be bent, folded, and stretched) field, many of them inspired by the world-renowned work of Kent State University's Liquid Crystal Institute and the pioneering work in polymer science at the University of Akron and Case Western Reserve University.[33] A cluster of 60 craft breweries has developed in the mountainous region surrounding Asheville, North Carolina, which leads the nation in the number of breweries per capita. Almost all of them are small, family-owned operations that are among the best in the United States. As in most clusters, these brewers have shared both knowledge and best practices, leading to the formation of more breweries, increased productivity and innovation, and the resulting competitive advantages. The area is becoming known as a craft beer destination; Asheville's Convention and Visitor's Bureau reports that more than 25 percent of tourists visit one of the city's 28 breweries (more are on the way) and 14 percent of visitors say that the area's breweries are the primary reason for their visit.[34]

ENTREPRENEURIAL PROFILE: Greig, Brandi, and Brad Hillman: Hillman Beer   Greig, Brandi, and Brad Hillman moved from Brooklyn, New York, to Asheville to start Hillman Beer in a 4,000-square-foot former nightclub. Their brewery offers 15 different beers, including some produced by other local craft breweries. Their carefully selected location is just minutes from the historic Biltmore House, the largest home in the United States, built by George Vanderbilt in 1895, which draws more than 1.1 million visitors annually.[35] ∎

As Asheville's craft brewery cluster demonstrates, once a concentration of companies takes root in a city, other businesses in that industry tend to spring up there as well. Grand Forks, North Dakota, has become a hub for companies making drones (officially known as unmanned aerial systems [UAS]) because of the available resources and infrastructure it offers. Grand Forks is home to the nation's first drone airport, Grand Sky Development Park (a former Air Force base) and the Federal Aviation Administration's Northern Plains UAS Test Site, which, at 45,000 square miles, boasts the largest authorized UAS airspace in the United States. The University of North Dakota offers a major in UAS, and its UAS graduates are an important part of the pipeline of talent that supplies the growing number of drone companies locating in Grand Forks, which also houses the North Dakota Center for Innovation, a business incubator that focuses on UAS companies and currently hosts 26 UAS-related companies, most of them small businesses.[36]

Dave Kolpack/AP Images

ENTREPRENEURIAL PROFILE: Matt Dunlevy: SkySkopes
SkySkopes, a tenant in the North Dakota Center for Innovation

incubator founded by Matt Dunlevy, was one of the first UAS companies approved by the Federal Aviation Administration to fly drones for business purposes. Now with more than 20 drone pilots, most of whom are University of North Dakota graduates, SkySkopes provides its large fleet of drones to companies for conducting industrial inspections, providing security, detecting leaks, managing power, engaging in precision agriculture, and other purposes. The young company already has logged more than 600 successful missions and more than 10,000 hours of unmanned flights.[37] ■

COMPATIBILITY WITH THE COMMUNITY One of the intangibles that can be determined only by a visit to an area is the degree of compatibility a business has with the surrounding community. In other words, a small company's image must fit in with the character of a town and the needs and wants of its residents. For example, Beverly Hills's ritzy Rodeo Drive or Palm Beach's Worth Avenue are home to shops that match the characteristics of the area's wealthy residents. Exclusive shops such as Cartier, Jimmy Choo, Versace, Louis Vuitton, and Tiffany & Company abound, catering to the area's rich and famous residents.

LOCAL LAWS AND REGULATIONS Before settling on a city, entrepreneurs must consider the regulatory burden local government will impose. Government regulations affect many aspects of a small business's operation, from acquiring business licenses and building permits to erecting business signs and dumping trash. The World Bank ranks nations according to the ease of starting a business, and the United States has fallen to 51st out of 190 countries.[38] Some states and cities are regulatory activists, creating so many rules that they discourage business creation; others take a more laissez-faire approach, imposing few restrictions on businesses. According to the World Bank, starting a business takes an average of 6 days in the United States, compared to just 2 days in Canada, 16 days in Sweden, and 76 days in Latin American countries. The global average time required to start a business is 52 days.[39]

ENTREPRENEURIAL PROFILE: Damien Graf and Robyn Semien: Bibber and Bell Wine and Spirits Copreneurs Damien Graf and Robyn Semien found the ideal location for their wine and spirits shop, Bibber & Bell Wine and Spirits, in the Williamsburg neighborhood in Brooklyn, New York. Negotiating a lease for the building, which is located in a high-traffic area just one block away from a busy subway station, took time and patience but was nothing compared to the gyrations the couple had to go through to get a retail liquor license from the State Liquor Authority. The paperwork they were required to submit to the authority took three months to process while Graf and Semien continued to pay rent (about $14,000) and other expenses (about $6,000) so that they would not lose their desired location. The couple persisted and ultimately opened their shop, which they continue to operate successfully.[40] ■

Zoning laws can have a major impact on an entrepreneur's location decision. New York City passed the first comprehensive zoning laws in 1916, and most cities now have **zoning laws** that divide a city or county into cells or districts to control the use of land, buildings, and sites.[41] Their purpose is to contain similar activities in suitable locations. For instance, one section of a city may be zoned residential, whereas the primary retail district may be zoned commercial and another zoned industrial to house manufacturing operations. Before selecting a particular site within a city, entrepreneurs must explore local zoning laws to determine whether there are any ordinances that would place restrictions on business activity or that would prohibit establishing a business altogether. Zoning regulations may make a particular location out of bounds.

In some cases, an entrepreneur may appeal to the local zoning commission to rezone a site or to grant a **variance** (a special exception to a zoning ordinance), but this is risky and could be devastating if the board disallows the variance. Stan Freemon opened his first Eggs Up Grill, a franchise that serves an extensive breakfast menu as well as sandwiches and salads, on a busy road with a high concentration of retail shops in Greenville, South Carolina. Several months later, Freemon opened his second franchise in Greenville's vibrant downtown district, drawn by its youthful population, art galleries, live theaters, and eclectic mix of retail shops. Because zoning laws restricted operating hours of downtown businesses, Freemon had to secure a variance from the city's Board of Zoning Appeals to open his restaurant between midnight and 5 A.M.[42]

zoning laws
laws that divide a city or county into small cells or districts to control the use of land, buildings, and sites.

variance
a special exemption to a zoning ordinance.

As the number of home-based businesses has increased in the last several years, more entrepreneurs have found themselves at odds with city zoning regulations. In Kansas City, entrepreneurs, some of whom came from as far away as Boston and Portland, are launching businesses in the Kansas City Startup Village (KCSV), drawn by the speed of Google Fiber. Start-up companies located in KCSV, a cluster of properties in the Spring Valley neighborhood, which is zoned "residential," have encountered resistance from long-time residents who are concerned about the impact of the businesses on the fabric of their neighborhood.[43]

APPROPRIATE INFRASTRUCTURE AND UTILITIES Business owners must consider the quality of the infrastructure and availability of utilities in a potential location. Is an airport located nearby? Are flights available to the necessary cities, and are the schedules convenient? If a company requires access to a railroad spur, is one available in the city? How convenient is the area's access to major highways? What about travel distances to major customers? How long will it take to deliver shipments to them? Are transportation rates reasonable? In some situations, double or triple handling of merchandise and inventory causes transportation costs to skyrocket. Are sufficient supplies of necessary inputs such as water and natural gas available? Are utility rates reasonable? What impact will utility costs have on the company's operation?

ENTREPRENEURIAL PROFILE: Lawson Products Lawson Products, a distributor of industrial maintenance and repair supplies founded in 1952 by Sydney Port in Chicago, has five strategically located distribution centers across the United States that serve the company's domestic customers. Lawson's customers' expectations for speedy delivery have escalated over the years, which required the company, whose product line includes 300,000 products, to find sites that provide quick access to airports and interstate highways that allow it to provide same- and next-day deliveries while minimizing costs.[44] ∎

INCENTIVES Many states, counties, and cities offer financial and other incentives to encourage businesses that will create jobs to locate within their borders. These incentives range from job training for workers and reduced tax rates to financial grants and loans, but companies have to earn the incentives through capital investments or job creation. QVC, founded by Joseph Segel in 1986, is one of the world's leading multichannel retailers (television and e-commerce) and qualified for $1.4 million in tax credit incentives from California when it selected Ontario, California, as the location for a 1 million-square-foot distribution center that created jobs for 1,000 workers. The center fulfills 20 percent of QVC's customers' orders, most of whom live on the West Coast. When QVC announced its decision, top managers said that the primary factor in their site selection decision was the ability to optimize service to its West Coast customers.[45] Although incentives are not the primary driver of companies' location decisions, they often are the "tie-breaker" between similar sites.

Companies that accept incentives must be aware of "clawback" provisions that require them to repay the state the value of some or all of the incentives if the company fails to create a minimum number of jobs or make a minimum capital investment. State and local government entities approved nearly $270 million in incentives to convince Dell Inc. to build a computer assembly plant in Winston–Salem, North Carolina, on the condition that the company create at least 900 jobs. Four years later, however, in a move to improve its efficiency, Dell decided to close the factory, which required the company to repay $28 million under the contract's clawback provision.[46]

QUALITY OF LIFE A final consideration when selecting a city is the quality of life it offers. For many entrepreneurs, quality of life is one of the key determinants of their choice of locale. Cities that offer comfortable weather, cultural events, colleges and universities, museums, outdoor activities, concerts, unique restaurants, and an interesting nightlife have become magnets for entrepreneurs looking to start companies. Over the last two decades, cities such as Austin, Boston, Seattle, San Francisco, Washington, Dallas, Denver, and Colorado Springs have become incubators for creativity and entrepreneurship as educated young people drawn by the cities' quality of life have moved in.

Not only can a location in a city offering a high quality of life be attractive to an entrepreneur, but it can also make recruiting employees much easier. According to a study of the importance of location on recruiting employees conducted by the Human Capital Institute, the three most important factors in attracting talent are job opportunities, a clean and safe community, and an affordable cost of living.[47]

ENTREPRENEURIAL PROFILE: K.C. Walsh: Simms Fishing Products A few years ago, K.C. Walsh, CEO of Simms Fishing Products, a company launched by entrepreneur and fly fisher John Simms in 1980 that makes fishing waders and accessories, relocated its headquarters to Bozeman, Montana. The quality of life (and superb fly fishing) in and around Bozeman was the primary factor in the decision. Walsh, a lifelong fly fisher, said his dream was to live, work, and play in Montana. Because most of the company's 120 employees are avid fly fishers and outdoor enthusiasts, Bozeman's access to some of the best trout rivers and streams, mountains, and natural beauty make it an ideal location for Simms. Montana is a business-friendly state, and Simms can field-test its products under real-world conditions quite easily.[48] ■

Choosing the Site

The final step in the location selection process is choosing the specific site for the business. Once again, entrepreneurs must let the facts guide them to the best location. Every business has its own unique set of criteria for an ideal location. A manufacturer's prime consideration may be access to raw materials, suppliers, labor, transportation, and customers. Service firms require access to customers but can generally survive in lower-rent properties. A retailer's prime consideration is sufficient customer traffic. For example, an entrepreneur who is planning to launch a convenience store should know that generating a sufficient volume of sales requires a significant population of at least 500 to 1,000 people who live within a one-mile radius of the outlet and choose a location accordingly.[49] The one element common to all three types of businesses is the need to locate where customers want to do business.

Some entrepreneurs test the suitability of potential locations by opening "pop-up" stores, shops that are open for only a few days, weeks, or months before shutting down. These temporary stores open in available spaces, sell their merchandise quickly, close, and move on to the next location; they are low-cost, efficient ways for an entrepreneur to test a location as a potential site for a permanent business.

ENTREPRENEURIAL PROFILE: Kate Welsh and Rachel Bell: The Hat Girls Friends since high school, Kate Welsh and Rachel Bell ended up going their separate ways to work in the world of fashion before returning to Louisville, Kentucky, in 2013 to launch The Hat Girls, a business that creates custom hats for all occasions but with a special focus on creating show-stopping hats for the Kentucky Derby. Known for their one-of-a-kind custom creations, The Hat Girls decided to introduce a line of ready-to-wear hats and to open a pop-up store to test the feasibility of opening a permanent retail store from which to sell their stylish chapeaus. In addition to serving as a test site, the pop-up store, which will be open for just two months around the Kentucky Derby, serves as a showcase for entrepreneurs' unique products and introduces them to customers the company normally would not reach, including tourists attending the famous race.[50] ■

Rental or lease rates are an important factor when choosing a site. Of course, entrepreneurs must be sure that the rent or lease payments for a particular location fit comfortably into their budgets. Although "cheap" rental rates can be indicative of a second-class location (and the resulting poor revenues they generate), entrepreneurs should not agree to exorbitant rental rates that jeopardize their ability to surpass their breakeven points.

ENTREPRENEURIAL PROFILE: Sean Scott: Subculture Coffee Sean Scott, owner of Subculture Coffee, which has locations in West Palm Beach and Delray Beach, Florida, knows the importance of a good location to the success of his business. When choosing the locations for his coffee shops, Scott prefers downtown locations because of the high concentration of customers and sites that are convenient for both walkers and drivers and have plenty of available parking. His shops' are in high-traffic locations, and Scott warns against selecting second-tier locations with lower traffic counts simply because they are less expensive.[51] ■

Many businesses are downsizing their outlets to lower their start-up and operating costs and to allow for a greater number of location options that are not available to full-size stores.

TABLE 14.5 Top 20 Metropolitan Hot Spots for Start-up Companies

1. Austin, Texas	11. Richmond, Virginia
2. Provo, Utah	12. McAllen, Texas
3. Washington, DC	13. Colorado Springs, Colorado
4. Denver, Colorado	14. Raleigh, North Carolina
5. Charlotte, North Carolina	15. Sarasota, Florida
6. Houston, Texas	16. El Paso, Texas
7. Ogden, Utah	17. Atlanta, Georgia
8. Dallas, Texas	18. Salt Lake City, Utah
9. Des Moines, Iowa	19. Las Vegas, Nevada
10. San Antonio, Texas	20. Seattle, Washington

Source: Based on "The Top 20 Metro Areas to Start a Business in America," *CNBC*, August 11, 2016, www.cnbc.com/2016/08/11/the-top-20-metro-areas-to-start-a-business-in-america.html?slide=1.

Franchises such as Smashburger, Subway, Cinnabon, and Burger King are finding success by placing smaller, less expensive outlets in locations that cannot support a full-size store. After experiencing success at Notre Dame University and Texas A&M University, Smashburger is targeting other college campuses as locations for its franchises. Using a compact kitchen design the company developed, the fast-casual chain based in Denver, Colorado, can fit an outlet into locations that are as small as 400 square feet. Despite their size, the sales per square foot at these smaller outlets often exceed those of full-size franchise stores.

Finally, an entrepreneur must be careful to select a site that creates the right impression for a business in the customers' eyes. A company's location speaks volumes about a company's "personality."

 ENTREPRENEURIAL PROFILE: Charlene Dupray and Pascal Siegler: South 'n France
When copreneurs Charlene Dupray and Pascal Siegler saw an old diner in downtown Wilmington, North Carolina, with its salmon pink concrete exterior, 13-foot ceilings, and diner stools, they knew they had found the perfect building to house their chocolate bonbon business, South 'n France. In addition to its unique character, the building came equipped with freezers capable of holding 20,000 bonbons, provided sufficient space for Dupray and Siegler to manufacture their chocolate delicacies, and included rooms they could convert into a retail storefront. Even though their business is on the verge of outgrowing the space, Dupray says, "We love it so much that we're considering adding another story or buying nearby residences because this old luncheonette really is a workhorse for us."[52] ∎

Table 14.5 shows the top 20 metropolitan areas that are "hot spots" for start-up companies due to many factors, including entrepreneurial support systems, educated workforces, low cost of living and of conducting business, business-friendly policies, and superior quality of life.

You Be the Consultant

Temporary Locations Can Be Just Great for Business

Pop-up stores are temporary locations that are open for only a few hours, days, or weeks before shutting down. For entrepreneurs who operate highly seasonal businesses (think Halloween costume stores and Christmas décor shops), pop-up stores are a way of life, but other entrepreneurs use them to test new markets, new business ideas, or potential locations, create brand awareness, clear out excess inventory, and promote their full-time locations.

Danny Bowien had grown tired of working for others in the restaurant business and decided to start his own restaurant. In an attempt to generate the financing he needed and to build brand recognition, Bowien decided to open a pop-up restaurant inside an existing Chinese restaurant in San Francisco's Mission District. Although the location was not ideal, Bowien's Sichuanese restaurant, Mission Chinese Food, drew rave reviews and huge crowds. After *Bon Appetit* and *GQ* magazines named it one of

(continued)

You Be the Consultant

the best new restaurants in the United States, Bowien was able to move to a permanent location in the Mission District. A short time later, he opened a second Mission Chinese Food on busy Broadway in New York City. Inspired by Bowien's success, other restaurateurs around the nation are opening pop-up restaurants. In major metropolitan areas where rents and operating costs can be astronomical, some restaurateurs are making a living by opening "permanent" pop-up restaurants.

Danny Newberg's goal was to open a small, classic seafood restaurant in New York City, but because of high start-up costs, he decided to start by operating pop-up restaurants inside existing restaurants through a company he started called Joint Venture. After running the numbers based on the rent he would have to pay (for example, $12,000 per month for a tiny 450-square-foot space in the East Village where the only access to the restroom was through the kitchen) for a space of his own and the expenses to operate it (including rising minimum wage rates imposed by many cities), he realized that setting up his dream restaurant may be out of reach. Newberg decided that, for now, the best strategy would be to continue to operate pop-up restaurants through Joint Venture. In other words, he would use a permanent pop-up shop strategy but rotate his location to different restaurants in New York City and other cities in the northeast.

Jen Moreau, Lib Ramos, and Erin Godbey, owners of the Makers Collective, a nonprofit organization that supports local entrepreneurs and artists in Greenville, South Carolina, recently opened a pop-up shop during the busy holiday season in a coffee roasting house, Methodical Coffee, that provided retail space. Fifty-five entrepreneurs and artists selling everything from custom-made blue jeans and hand-made jewelry to paintings and sculpture used the space to sell their unique products for 12 days during the holidays, the all-important time during which many of them generate the bulk of their annual sales.

When Laura Bruland, who makes unique laser-cut jewelry from recycled books (she ran a successful Kickstarter campaign to raise the money to purchase her first laser cutter), opened her pop-up shop, Yes & Yes Designs, in a retail space in San Francisco that provides space for five new pop-up shops each month, she realized that she needed a much bigger and bolder display for her innovative designs. Her one-month experience with the physical store gave her the confidence to start selling her jewelry successfully at festivals and craft fairs. Bruland, who operates the online company from her own studio in Oakland, California, with the help of her partner, Julien Shields, and their wonder dog, Toto, also has benefitted from her in-depth conversations with customers, many of whom have given her ideas for new designs and new products. After one customer asked about a gift for her husband, Bruland created a line of cufflinks. Several early participants in the program have gone on to create physical stores to supplement their online sales.

1. What advantages and disadvantages do pop-up stores such as the ones described here offer entrepreneurs?

2. What types of businesses would be successful opening pop-up stores temporarily on your campus or on a nearby campus? What advice would you offer entrepreneurs who are considering opening the store? When should it open and for how long?

3. Would pop-up stores be successful in your community? Explain. Work with a team of your classmates to identify three products or product lines that would be successful in your community if they were sold from a pop-up store.

Sources: Based on Jane Black, "Pop Goes the Business Model," *Wall Street Journal*, February 25–26, 2017, p. D6; Stephanie Burnett, "Handmade for the Holidays," *Greenville News*, November 26, 2016, pp. 1D, 8D; Joshua David Stein, "No Space Too Small, No Lease Too Short," *New York Times*, December 20, 2013, www.nytimes.com/2013/12/22/fashion/Pop-Up-Stores-Storefront.html; Amy Westervelt, "A Shot at the Real World," *Wall Street Journal*, February 3, 2014, p. R5.

Location Criteria for Retail and Service Businesses

LO2

Describe the location criteria for retail and service businesses.

Few decisions are as important for retailers and service firms as the choice of a location. Because their success depends on a steady flow of customers, these businesses must locate their businesses with their target customers' convenience and preferences in mind. The following are important considerations:

Trade Area Size

Every retail and service business should determine the extent of its **trade area**, the region from which a business can expect to draw customers over a reasonable time span. The primary variables that influence the scope of the trading area are the type and size of the business. If a retail store specializes in a particular product line and offers a wide selection and knowledgeable salespeople, it may draw customers from a great distance. In contrast, a convenience store with a general line of merchandise has a small trading area, typically only two miles, because it is unlikely that customers will drive across town to purchase items that are available within blocks of their homes or businesses.[53] As a rule, the larger the store, the greater its selection, and the better its service, the broader is its trading area. "Big box" retailers' trade areas can extend up to 40 miles. Cabela's, the outdoor outfitter, has nearly 80 stores across the United States and

trade area
the region from which a business can expect to draw customers over a reasonable time span.

Canada (with more on the way) that average 127,500 square feet (one store is 247,000 square feet) and carry more than 225,000 SKUs, ranging from outdoor apparel and hunting and fishing gear to boats and home furnishings. With their extensive inventories and unique features (museum-quality wildlife displays and huge aquariums), Cabela's stores are destination stores, often drawing shoppers from 100 or more miles away.[54] Businesses that offer a narrow selection of products and services tend to have smaller trading areas. For instance, the majority of a restaurant's customers live within a radius of 10 miles; therefore, when considering locations, restaurateurs must pay close attention to the number of potential customers who live within that trading area.[55]

ENTREPRENEURIAL PROFILE: Ray Wiley, Matt Curtis, Tim Tefs, and Jim Savakinas: Rapid Fired Pizza Rapid Fired Pizza, a fast-casual restaurant chain that allows customers to select the sauce, cheeses, and fresh toppings for their pizzas, which are then cooked in a special oven in just three minutes, recently opened an outlet in Fairborn, Ohio, directly across the street from Wright State University, home to more than 16,500 students and just five minutes from the state's biggest employer, Wright-Patterson Air Force Base, which employs more than 26,000 airmen, civilians, and contractors. Cofounders Ray Wiley, Matt Curtis, Tim Tefs, and Jim Savakinas chose the location because the high concentration of potential customers in close proximity generates a high volume of sales for the restaurant.[56] ∎

Retail Compatibility

retail compatibility
the benefits a company receives by locating near other businesses that sell complementary products and services or that generate high volumes of traffic.

Shoppers tend to be drawn to clusters of related businesses. That's one reason shopping malls and outlet shopping centers are popular destinations for shoppers and are attractive locations for retailers. The concentration of businesses pulls customers from a larger trading area than a single freestanding business does. **Retail compatibility** describes the benefits a company receives by locating near other businesses that sell complementary products and services or that generate high volumes of foot traffic. Clever business owners choose their locations with an eye on the surrounding mix of businesses. For instance, grocery store operators prefer not to locate in shopping centers with movie theaters, offices, and fitness centers, all businesses whose customers occupy parking spaces for extended time periods. Drugstores, nail salons, and ice cream parlors have proved to be much better shopping center neighbors for grocers.

ENTREPRENEURIAL PROFILE: Carol Buie-Jackson and Jay Jackson: Birdhouse on the Greenway Carol Buie-Jackson and her husband, Jay Jackson, spent months screening potential locations for their wild bird product shop, Birdhouse on the Greenway. They chose a 1,600-square-foot space in The Shops at Piper Glen, a shopping center on the fast-growing south side of Charlotte, North Carolina, that offers two prime advantages. The store is located in the middle of one of the city's most affluent residential areas that contains large numbers of the Jacksons' target customers, people who are in their 50s and 60s with above-average incomes and are environmentally conscious. It also sits at the entrance of Four-Mile Creek Greenway, a popular walking trail that winds through natural habitat and has connectors to local neighborhoods. The other businesses in the shopping center complement Birdhouse on the Greenway because they draw the same customers the Jacksons target. Trader Joe's is just two doors down, and other stores include Starbucks and Great Harvest Bread Company. Because of their wise choice of a location for their shop, the Jacksons say Birdhouse on the Green is thriving.[57] ∎

Degree of Competition

The size, location, and activity of competing businesses also influence the size of a company's trading area. If a business will be the first of its kind in a location, its trading area might be quite extensive. However, if the area already has 8 or 10 nearby stores that directly compete with a business, its trading area might be very small because the market is saturated with competitors. Market saturation is a problem for businesses in many industries, ranging from convenience stores to restaurants. Noodles and Company, a chain of fast-casual restaurants based in Broomfield, Colorado, recently closed 71 of its more than 500 locations because of poor location choices. The company said that most of the underperforming restaurants were in new markets where the company has little brand recognition and faces intense competition.[58]

The Index of Retail Saturation

One of the best measures of the level of saturation in an area is the index of retail saturation (IRS), which takes into account both the number of customers and the intensity of competition in a trading area. The **index of retail saturation** is a measure of the potential sales per square foot of store space for a given product within a specific trading area. It is the ratio of a trading area's sales potential for a particular product or service to its sales capacity:

$$IRS = \frac{C \times RE}{RF}$$

where

C = number of customers in the trading area

RE = retail expenditures, or the average expenditure per person ($) for the product in the trading area

RF = retail facilities, or the total square feet of selling space allocated to the product in the trading area

index of retail saturation
a measure of the potential sales per square foot of store space for a given product within a specific trading area; it is the ratio of a trading area's sales potential for a product or service to its sales capacity.

This computation is an important one for every retailer to make. Locating in an area already saturated with competitors results in dismal sales volume and often leads to failure.

To illustrate the index of retail saturation, suppose an entrepreneur who is looking at two sites for a shoe store finds that he needs sales of $175 per square foot to be profitable. Site 1 has a trading area with 25,875 potential customers who spend an average of $42 on shoes annually; the only competitor in the trading area has 6,000 square feet of selling space. Site 2 has 27,750 potential customers spending an average of $43.50 on shoes annually; two competitors occupy 8,400 square feet of space:

Site 1

$$\text{Index of retail saturation} = \frac{25,875 \times 42}{6,000}$$

$$= \$181.12 \text{ sales potential per square foot}$$

Site 2

$$\text{Index of retail saturation} = \frac{27,750 \times 43.50}{8,400}$$

$$= \$143.71 \text{ sales potential per square foot}$$

Although site 2 appears to be more favorable on the surface, the index shows that site 1 is preferable; site 2 fails to meet the minimum standard of $175 per square foot.

Reilly's Law of Retail Gravitation

Reilly's Law of Retail Gravitation, a classic work in market analysis published in 1931 by William J. Reilly, uses the analogy of gravity to estimate the attractiveness of a particular business to potential customers. A business's ability to draw customers is directly related to the extent to which customers see it as a "destination" and is inversely related to the distance customers must travel to reach it. Reilly's model also provides a way to estimate the trade boundary between two market areas by calculating the "break point" between them. The break point between two primary market areas is the boundary between the two where customers become indifferent about shopping at one or the other. The key factor in determining this point of indifference is the size of the communities. If two nearby cities have the same population sizes, the break point lies halfway between them. The following is the equation for Reilly's Law:[59]

$$BP = \frac{d}{1 + \sqrt{\dfrac{P_b}{P_a}}}$$

where

BP = distance in miles from location A to the break point

d = distance in miles between locations A and B

P_b = population surrounding location B

P_a = population surrounding location A

For example, if city A and city B are 22 miles apart and city A has a population of 25,500 and city B has a population of 42,900, the break point, according to Reilly's law, is:

$$BP = \frac{22}{1 + \sqrt{\dfrac{42,900}{25,500}}} = 9.6 \text{ miles}$$

The outer edge of city A's trading area lies about 9.6 miles between city A and city B. Although only a rough estimate, this simple calculation using readily available data can be useful for screening potential locations.

Transportation Network

For many retail and service businesses, easy customer access from a smoothly flowing network of highways and roads is essential. If a location is inconvenient for customers to reach, a business located there will suffer from a diminished trading area and lower sales. Entrepreneurs should verify that the transportation system works smoothly and is free of barriers that prevent customers from reaching their shopping destinations. Is it easy for customers traveling in the opposite direction to cross traffic? Do traffic signs and lights allow traffic to flow smoothly?

E-commerce companies also must consider accessibility to trucking routes, such as interstate highways, and airports so that they can expedite customers' orders. Zappos, the online shoe retailer, moved its fulfillment center to Louisville, Kentucky, so that the company can ship orders almost anywhere in the United States within one day. The Zappos center is located just 12 miles from the UPS Worldport, the world's largest automated package-sorting facility (which can sort 416,000 packages per hour) in the Louisville International Airport. From this airport, flights can reach 75 percent of the population of the United States in just 2.5 hours and 95 percent of the population in 4 hours. The city also has three interstate highways and two railways. Because of Zappos's location, a package that leaves UPS Worldport by 12:45 A.M. can arrive at the home or business of any customer in the United States that same day, giving the company a competitive edge in customer service.[60]

Physical and Psychological Barriers

Trading area shape and size also are influenced by physical and psychological barriers. Physical barriers may be parks, rivers, lakes, bridges, or any other natural or man-made obstruction that hinders customers' access to the area. Locating on one side of a large park may reduce the number of customers who will drive around it to get to a store. Psychological barriers include areas that have a reputation for crime and illegal activities. If high-crime areas exist near a site, potential customers will not travel through them to reach a business.

Customer Traffic

Perhaps the most important screening criterion for a potential retail location (and often for service locations as well) is the number of potential customers passing by the site during business hours. To be successful, a business must be able to generate sufficient sales to surpass its break-even point, and that requires an ample volume of customer traffic going past its doors. The key success factor for many retail stores is a high-volume location with easy accessibility. Entrepreneurs should use traffic counts (pedestrian and/or auto) and traffic pattern studies (usually available from state highway departments) to confirm that the sites they are considering as potential locations are capable of generating sufficient sales volume.

ENTREPRENEURIAL PROFILE: Mike Mohammed: Chronic Tacos Chronic Tacos, a fast-casual Mexican grill offering a made-to-order menu created from fresh, locally sourced ingredients, operates an outlet at Angel Stadium in Anaheim, California, home of the Los Angeles Angels baseball team. The Angels play only 80 games in the stadium, but the stadium seats more than 45,000 fans, providing Chronic Tacos with plenty of customer traffic and high sales volume. CEO Mike Mohammed says that the exposure the company receives at the ballpark is proving to be valuable as it expands throughout the region. Mohammed is looking at opening outlets in stadiums and concert venues in other cities where Chronic Tacos is expanding.[61] ■

Adequate Parking

If customers cannot find convenient and safe parking, they are not likely to shop in the area. Many downtown areas lose customers because of inadequate parking. Although shopping malls average five parking spaces per 1,000 square feet of shopping space, many central business districts get by with 3.5 spaces (or fewer) per 1,000 square feet. In addition, some central business districts require visitors to feed meters or apps to pay for parking, another deterrent to shoppers. Even when free parking is available, some potential customers may not feel safe on the streets, especially after dark. Some large city downtown business districts become virtual ghost towns at the end of the business day. A location where traffic vanishes after 6 P.M. may not be as valuable as mall or shopping center locations that mark the beginning of the prime sales time at 6 P.M.

ENTREPRENEURIAL PROFILE: Chris Wysocki and Robert Fulbright: Yarnhouse Chris Wysocki and Robert Fulbright opened Yarnhouse, a specialty knitting, crocheting, and fiber art shop in 2008 in a building on North Davidson Street, in the heart of Charlotte, North Carolina's arts district (known as "NoDa"). The arts district location provided significant exposure and attracted a large number of the entrepreneurs' target customers, but customers often complained about the scarcity of available parking. They knew their sales were suffering because many customers were not willing to walk several blocks to shop at their store. Wysocki and Fulbright decided to move their store, but they did not go far—just a half-mile down North Davidson Street, to a building surrounded by ample parking spaces and just three doors away from one of Charlotte's most popular restaurants, Amelie's French Bakery. Their rent is 20 percent lower, customer traffic at Yarnhouse already has increased, and Wysocki says the new location is proving to be "monumental."[62] ■

Reputation

Like people, a site can have a bad reputation. Sites in which businesses have failed repeatedly create negative impressions in customers' minds; many people view the business as just another one that soon will be gone. Sometimes previous failures are indicative of a fundamental problem with the location itself; in other cases, the cause of the previous failure was the result not of a poor location but of a poorly managed business. When entrepreneurs decide to conduct business in a location that has housed previous failures, it is essential that they make many highly visible changes to the site to exorcise the "ghosts" of the failed businesses that came before them and to give customers the perception of a company making a "fresh start."

ENTREPRENEURIAL PROFILE: Mike Hanley and Jerry Dilembo: Burgatory When restaurateurs Mike Hanley and Jerry Dilembo decided to open their fourth location of Burgatory, they chose a high-traffic location near the waterfront in West Homestead, Pennsylvania, situated across the street from a busy 22-screen theater and surrounded by a variety of retail shops, including Ulta, Barnes & Noble, and Victoria's Secret. Despite its attractiveness, they had some misgivings about the location because it had been home to four failed restaurants over the previous 12 years. Dismissing comments that the location was "jinxed" for restaurants, Hanley and Dilembo set about renovating the space to erase the memory of past failures from customers' minds and opened their upscale hamburger shop to rave reviews. The chain has since expanded to eight locations, and its West Homestead location remains a top performer.[63] ■

Visibility

A final characteristic of a good location is visibility. Highly visible locations simply make it easy for customers to find a business and make purchases. A site that lacks visibility puts a company at a major disadvantage before it ever opens its doors for business. Upper-level locations typically do not generate the traffic that street-level locations do because they are not as visible to

You Be the Consultant

Where Should Our Next Retail Store Be Located?

When Fan Bi was a college student at Australia's University of New South Wales, he visited Shanghai and discovered the joy of shopping for custom-made shirts in the city's famous fabric markets. Bi says that he once was satisfied with buying dress shirts "off the rack," but he quickly grew accustomed to going to a fabric market, being measured, selecting the specific fabrics, and designing the details of his shirts. Not only were the shirts Bi purchased of better quality than the off-the-rack shirts he had been purchasing, they also were less expensive, which led Bi to an idea for a Web-based customized shirt company aimed at graduating college students who need professional wardrobes but cannot afford luxury prices. While studying abroad at Babson College in Wellesley, Massachusetts, Bi met Danny Wong, a student at nearby Bentley University. Together, they teamed up with a programmer on the West Coast and launched Blank Label, an online business based in Boston that allows shoppers to design their own custom shirts ("Designed by you, stitched by us"). Customers can select the fabric, collar style and color, placket, cuff, pocket, buttons, monogram, and even a custom label. In less than 18 months, Bi and Wong sold more than 7,000 shirts and used the Internet exclusively to operate their company. Soon, however, Bi recognized the importance to retailers of a multichannel approach, offering customers the ability to purchase items online or in a retail store. Allowing customers to touch and see products is important in a retail setting, especially for companies such as Blank Label that sell custom clothing. That realization led Bi to open the first Blank Label retail store four years later in Fort Pointe, one of Boston's fastest-growing areas, and saw its sales increase significantly. As a result, the company, which now sells custom suits and pants in addition to shirts, opened a second location, this one in downtown Boston. Before long, sales at its physical stores were generating 70 percent of the company's total sales, and Bi began making plans to open other retail stores. The goal is to open four to five retail stores per year initially before unveiling twice that many in three or four years.

The big question, of course, is where to locate them. Bi believes that a city along the East Coast would be ideal because he believes that the custom menswear market there is underserved. Cities he thinks may be best include Washington, DC, and Charlotte, North Carolina. As CEO, Bi recognizes that spending time on an airplane or a train traveling to a distant retail location is not the best use of his time. Bi knows that the next city he chooses for a retail store should match Blank Label's customer base, which is quite different from what he and cofounder Wong initially assumed. Rather than being comprised of twenty-somethings building their professional wardrobes, the majority of the company's 30,000 customers are educated, professional men between the ages of 35 and 45 who appreciate the high quality and custom fit that Blank Label garments offer at reasonable prices. Tailors on London's Savile Row typically charge $275 or more for custom-made shirts, and bespoke suits often start at $1,200 and can quickly reach $4,000 to $5,000; Blank Label's custom shirts start at just $95, and its custom suits start at $750. Bi is considering using temporary pop-up stores in cities that make the short list for potential expansions as a way to test their market potential.

1. What process should Bi use to identify the best cities for Blank Label's retail expansion plans? How might the company use its database of information on its existing online and retail store customers in the location decision?

2. What criteria should Bi use to evaluate prospective cities?

3. Do you agree with Bi's idea of using temporary pop-up shops in certain cities to test their market potential for Blank Label's custom-made clothing line? Explain. What are the advantages and disadvantages of this technique?

4. Use the resources of the Internet to identify cities that Bi should consider for Blank Label's next retail store and explain why you chose them.

Sources: Based on Randy Myers, "Location, Location, Frustration," *Inc.*, October 2014, pp. 120–124; Lauren Zumbac, "Custom Menswear Retailer Blank Label Moving to the Loop," *Chicago Tribune*, July 1, 2016, www.chicagotribune.com/business/ct-blank-label-st-john-0702-biz-20160701-story.html; Krystina Gustafson, "Custom Mens Wear Shop on Expansion Track," *CNBC*, June 29, 2014, www.cnbc.com/2014/06/29/blank-label-custom-mens-wear-shop-starts-expansion.html.

---

shoppers. Attractive window displays draw in passersby at street level, but upper-level locations do not have that advantage. After 59 years of selling furs from street-level locations in downtown Greenville, South Carolina, Stan and May Sedran, owners of Sedran Furs, learned that their landlord would not renew their lease. Believing that a location in the revitalized, bustling central business district was essential, the Sedrans settled for a space located up two flights of stairs. Their business lost its visibility in the new location, however, and three years later, the Sedrans closed their shop after 62 years in business.[64]

LO3

Outline the location options for retail and service businesses: central business districts, neighborhoods, shopping centers and malls, near competitors, shared spaces, inside large retail stores, nontraditional locations, at home, and on the road.

Location Options for Retail and Service Businesses

There are nine basic areas where retail and service business owners can locate: the central business district, neighborhoods, shopping centers and malls, near competitors, shared spaces, inside large retail stores, nontraditional locations, at home, and on the road. The average cost to lease space in a shopping center is about $15 per square foot, and at malls, lease rates average about $41 per square foot. In central business locations, the average cost ranges from $18 to $45 per square foot. Rental rates vary significantly depending on the city, however.[65] Along New York City's ritzy Fifth Avenue, home to high-end retailers such as Fendi, Bergdorf Goodman, and Tiffany, space leases for an incredible $3,500 per square foot![66] Of course, cost is just one factor a business owner must consider when choosing a location.

Central Business District

The central business district (CBD) is the traditional center of town—the downtown concentration of businesses established early in the development of most towns and cities. Entrepreneurs derive several advantages from a downtown location. Because the business is centrally located, it attracts customers from the entire trading area of the city. In addition, a small business usually benefits from the customer traffic generated by the other stores in the district. Many cities have undertaken revitalization efforts in their CBDs and have transformed these areas into thriving, vigorous hubs of economic activity that are proving to be ideal locations for small businesses. However, locating in some CBDs does have certain disadvantages. Many CBDs are characterized by intense competition, high rental rates, traffic congestion, and inadequate parking facilities.

ENTREPRENEURIAL PROFILE: David and Margaret Smith: Blowin' in the Wind David Smith, a fourth-generation carpenter and artist, and his wife, Margaret, moved to Las Vegas, New Mexico (not to be confused with its casino-laden namesake in Nevada) in 2006 to realize David's dream of opening a business. With a population of 14,000, Las Vegas, which was settled in the 1830s while still a part of Mexico, is unique in that its central business district features an uninterrupted avenue of well-preserved commercial buildings from the late nineteenth and early twentieth centuries that reflect a variety of styles, including Victorian, Mission Revival, and Queen Anne. More than 900 of the town's buildings are listed on the National Register of Historic Places, and its main street recently was named one of the top 10 Great American Streets. The unique architecture and intriguing colors of the buildings that line historic Bridge Street reflect Las Vegas's frontier history as an important hub of commercial and transportation activity on the famous Santa Fe Trail. The Smiths considered many different locations in the small town before choosing a 7,500-square-foot building at the foot of historic Bridge Street, which connects the "Old Town" with the "New Town," as the site for their gallery and boutique, Blowin' in the Wind, because of its large windows that allow them to feature their merchandise. The copreneurs have filled the space with an eclectic collection of merchandise ranging from wind sculptures and furniture (all made by David) to jewelry and clothing.[67] ■

Beginning in the 1950s, many cities saw their older downtown business districts begin to decay as residents moved to the suburbs and began shopping at newer, more conveniently located malls. Today, however, many of these CBDs are experiencing rebirth as cities restore them to their former splendor and shoppers return. Many customers find irresistible the charming atmosphere that traditional downtown districts offer with their rich mix of stores, their unique architecture and streetscapes, and their historic character. Cities have begun to reverse the urban decay of their downtown business districts through proactive revitalization programs designed to attract visitors and residents alike to cultural events by locating major theaters and museums in the downtown area. In addition, many cities are providing economic incentives to real estate developers to build apartment and condominium complexes in the heart of the downtown area. Vitality is returning as residents live and shop in the once nearly abandoned downtown areas. The "ghost-town" image is being replaced by both younger and older residents who love the convenience, culture, and excitement of life in the city center.

ENTREPRENEURIAL PROFILE: Peter Agnefjäll: IKEA When Peter Agnefjäll, CEO of Swedish furniture retailer IKEA, discovered that 70 percent of the world's population will live in cities by 2050, he began shifting the company's plans for locating its stores. The company traditionally has built large (325,000 square feet or more), freestanding stores in the suburbs but has begun to open smaller stores in urban areas to cater to city residents who prefer IKEA's furniture and storage products that are geared toward small living spaces.[68] ■

Neighborhood Locations

Small businesses that locate near residential neighborhoods rely heavily on the local trading area for business. Businesses that provide convenience as a major attraction for customers find that locating on a street or road just outside major residential areas provides the needed traffic counts essential for success. Gas stations, convenience stores, and grocery stores thrive in these high-traffic areas. One study of food stores found that the majority of the typical grocer's customers live within a 5-mile radius. The primary advantages of a neighborhood location include relatively low rental rates and close contact with customers.

Courtesy of Smitten Ice Cream

ENTREPRENEURIAL PROFILE: Robyn Sue Fisher: Smitten Ice Cream Robyn Sue Fisher moved from Boston to Oakland, California, and decided to pursue a passion she had developed in her career with a management consulting firm. Using her life's savings, she worked with two engineers to develop a unique ice cream machine she named Brr! that uses liquid nitrogen to churn exceptionally smooth, creamy ice cream made with local, organic ingredients. Fisher then launched Smitten Ice Cream, opening her first store in a converted shipping container in the Hayes Valley neighborhood of San Francisco. Smitten Ice Cream has grown to 10 locations, each one in a carefully planned location in a Bay Area neighborhood. Fisher's choice of locations that are convenient for and near her target customers has played a significant role in her stores' success.[69] ∎

Shopping Centers and Malls

Until the early twentieth century, central business districts were the primary shopping venues in the United States. As cars and transportation networks became more prevalent in the 1920s, shopping centers began popping up outside cities' central business districts. Then in October 1956, the nation's first shopping mall, Southdale, opened in the Minneapolis, Minnesota, suburb of Edina. Designed by Victor Gruen, the fully enclosed mall featured 72 shops anchored by two competing department stores (a radical concept at the time), a garden courtyard with a goldfish pond, an aviary, hanging plants, and artificial trees. With its multilevel layout and parking garage, Southdale was a huge success and forever changed the way Americans would shop.[70] Today, shopping centers and malls are a mainstay of the American landscape. The typical customer in the United States makes a purchase at a mall or shopping center 5 times per month.[71] Approximately 109,500 shopping centers and 1,050 traditional enclosed malls operate in the United States. In a typical three-month period, 184 million adults, 75 percent of the adult population in the United States, visit a mall.[72] Because many different types of stores operate under one roof, shopping centers and malls give meaning to the term "one-stop shopping." There are nine types of shopping centers (see Table 14.6):

- *Strip shopping centers.* Strip shopping centers are made up of attached rows of retail stores or service outlets that provide local shoppers a narrow range of goods and services. Nearly 69,000 strip shopping centers operate across the United States. Although strip shopping centers are the smallest of all shopping centers with an average size of 13,200 square feet of space, they make up 60 percent of the total number of shopping centers and account for 12 percent of the shopping center space available in the United States.[73]

- *Neighborhood shopping centers.* The typical neighborhood shopping center is relatively small, containing from 5 to 20 stores and serving a population of up to 40,000 people who live within a 10-minute drive, with a focus on convenience. The anchor store in these centers is usually a supermarket or a drugstore. Neighborhood shopping centers serve primarily the daily shopping needs of customers in the surrounding area. More than 32,500 neighborhood shopping centers operate across the United States; the average size is nearly 72,000 square feet.[74]

TABLE 14.6 U.S. Shopping-Center Classification and Typical Characteristics*

Type of Shopping Center	Concept	Typical GLA Range (Sq. Ft.)	Acres	# of Anchors	% Anchor GLA	Typical Number of Tenants	Typical Type of Anchors	Trade Area Size
General-Purpose Centers								
Super-Regional Mall	Similar in concept to regional malls, but offering more variety and assortment.	800,000+	60–120	3+	50–70%	N/A	Full-line department store, mass merchant, discount department store, fashion apparel store, minianchor, cineplex or other largescale entertainment attraction, and food-and-beverage service cluster.	5–25 miles
Regional Mall	General merchandise or fashion-oriented offerings. Typically, enclosed with inward-facing stores connected by a common walkway. Parking surrounds the outside perimeter.	400,000–800,000	40–100	2+	50–70%	40–80 stores	Full-line department store, mass merchant, discount department store, fashion apparel store, minianchor, cineplex or other largescale entertainment attraction, and food-and-beverage service cluster.	5–15 miles
Community Center ("Large Neighborhood Center")	General merchandise or convenience-oriented offerings. Wider range of apparel and other soft goods offerings than neighborhood centers. The center is usually configured in a straight line as a strip, or may be laid out in an L or U shape, depending on the site and design.	125,000–400,000	10–40	2+	40–60%	15–40 stores	Discount store, supermarket, drug, large-specialty discount (toys, books, electronics, home improvement/furnishings or sporting goods, etc.)	3–6 miles
Neighborhood Center	Convenience-oriented.	30,000–125,000	3–5	1+	30–50%	5–20 stores	Supermarket	3 miles
Strip/Convenience	Attached row of stores or service outlets managed as a coherent retail entity, with on-site parking usually located in front of the stores. Open canopies may connect the storefronts, but a strip center does not have enclosed walkways linking the stores. A strip center may be configured in a straight line, or have an "L" or "U" shape. A convenience center is among the smallest of the centers, whose tenants provide a narrow mix of goods and personal services to a very limited trade area.	<30,000	<3	Anchor-less or a small convenience-store anchor.	N/A	N/A	Convenience store, such as a minimart.	<1 mile
Specialized-Purpose Centers								
Power Center	Category-dominant anchors, including discount department stores, off-price stores, wholesale clubs, with only a few small tenants.	250,000–600,000	25–80	3+	70–90%	N/A	Category killers, such as home improvement, discount department, warehouse club and off-price stores	5–10 miles
Lifestyle	Upscale national-chain specialty stores with dining and entertainment in an outdoor setting.	150,000–500,000	10–40	0–2	0–50%	N/A	Large-format upscale specialty	8–12 miles
Factory Outlet	Manufacturers' and retailers' outlet stores selling brand-name goods at a discount.	50,000–400,000	10–50	N/A	N/A	N/A	Manufacturers' and retailers' outlets	25–75 miles
Theme/Festival	Leisure, tourist, retail and service-oriented offerings with entertainment as a unifying theme. Often in urban areas, they may be adapted from older—sometimes historic—buildings, and part of a mixed-use project.	80,000–250,000	5–20	Unspecified	N/A	N/A	Restaurants, entertainment	25–75 miles
Limited-Purpose Property								
Airport Retail	Consolidation of retail stores located within a commercial airport	75,000–300,000	N/A	N/A	N/A	N/A	No anchors; retail includes specialty retail and restaurants	N/A

*Disclaimer: While every effort is made to ensure the accuracy and reliability of the information contained in this report, ICSC does not guarantee and is not responsible for the accuracy, completeness or reliability of the information contained in this report. Use of such information is voluntary, and reliance on it should only be undertaken after an independent review of its accuracy, completeness, efficiency, and timeliness. Criteria used in the definitions above are intended to be only typical of general features, rather than covering all situations.

- *Community shopping centers.* A community shopping center contains from 15 to 40 stores and serves a population ranging from 40,000 to 150,000 people. The leading tenant often is a large department or variety store, a super-drugstore, or a supermarket. Community shopping centers sell more clothing and other soft goods than do neighborhood shopping centers. Of the nine types of shopping centers, community shopping centers take on the greatest variety of shapes, designs, and tenants. Nearly 9,800 community shopping centers operate across the United States. Together neighborhood and community shopping centers make up more than 56 percent of the total space available in shopping centers in the United States.[75]

- *Power centers.* A power center combines the drawing strength of a large regional mall with the convenience of a neighborhood shopping center. Anchored by several large specialty retailers, such as warehouse clubs, discount department stores, or large specialty stores, these centers target older, wealthier Baby Boomers who want selection and convenience. In the United States, there are more than 2,250 power centers, where anchor stores usually account for 80 percent of power center space, compared with 50 percent in the typical community shopping center. The average power center contains nearly 439,000 square feet of space.[76] Just as in a shopping mall, small businesses can benefit from the traffic generated by anchor stores, but they must choose their locations carefully so that they are not overshadowed by their larger neighbors. When William James opened the Arms Room gun shop, which includes a shooting range, he selected a former Circuit City store in a power center in Houston, Texas. James spent $5 million to purchase and renovate the 20,000-square-foot building, a bargain compared to what it would have cost to build.[77]

- *Outlet centers.* As their name suggests, outlet centers feature manufacturers' and retailers' outlet stores selling name-brand goods at a discount. Unlike most other types of shopping centers, outlet centers typically have no anchor stores; the discounted merchandise they offer draws sufficient traffic. Most outlet centers are open air and are laid out in strips or in clusters, creating small "villages" of shops. Currently, 367 outlet centers operate in the United States, and they generate sales of $45.6 billion annually, or an average of about $546 in sales per square foot of leasable space.[78]

- *Theme or festival centers.* Festival shopping centers employ a unifying theme that individual stores display in their decor and sometimes in the merchandise they sell. Entertainment is a common theme for these shopping centers, which often target tourists. Many festival shopping centers are located in urban areas and are housed in older, sometimes historic buildings that have been renovated to serve as shopping centers. The 159 theme centers in the United States have an average of about 148,000 square feet of selling space.[79]

- *Lifestyle centers.* Typically located near affluent residential neighborhoods where their target customers live, lifestyle centers are designed to look less like shopping centers and malls and more like the busy streets in the central business districts that existed in towns and cities in their heyday. Occupied by many upscale national chain restaurants such as P. F. Chang's and specialty stores such as Talbots, Coach, Brooks Brothers, and Michael Kors, the 491 lifestyle centers in the United States combine shopping convenience and entertainment ranging from movie theaters and open-air concerts to art galleries and people watching. Lifestyle centers make up only 2.2 percent of the total shopping center space available in the United States, but they generate higher sales per square foot than traditional malls.[80] With 336,000 square feet of selling space, the typical lifestyle center is considerably smaller than a regional mall, which includes nearly 600,000 square feet of space.[81] The first lifestyle center, The Shops of Saddle Creek, opened in Germantown, Tennessee, in 1987.[82]

- *Regional shopping malls.* The regional shopping mall serves a large trading area, usually from 5 to 15 miles or more in all directions. These enclosed malls contain from 40 to 80 stores and serve a population of 150,000 or more living within a 20- to 40-minute drive. The anchor is typically one or more major department stores with smaller specialty stores occupying the spaces between the anchors. In the United States, 600 regional malls currently are in operation.[83] Apparel and accessories are the most popular items sold in regional shopping malls.

- *Superregional shopping malls.* A superregional mall is similar to a regional mall but is bigger, containing more anchor stores and a greater variety of shops that sell deeper lines of merchandise. The typical superregional mall encompasses 1.25 million square feet of space, and its trade area stretches up to 25 miles out. Currently, 620 superregional malls operate in the United States.[84] Canada's West Edmonton Mall, the largest mall in North America, with more than 800 stores and 100 restaurants, is one of the most famous super-regional malls in the world. In addition to its abundance of retail shops, the mall, which draws an average of nearly 31 million visitors a year, contains an ice skating rink, a water park, an amusement park, an aquarium, a bungee tower, miniature golf courses, and a 21-screen movie complex. West Edmonton Mall boasts the world's largest parking lot and occupies space that is equivalent to 48 city blocks.[85]

Major department or mass merchandising stores serve as anchors and attract a significant volume of customer traffic to malls and shopping centers, allowing small businesses with their unique, sometimes quirky product offerings, boutique atmospheres, and marketing approaches to thrive in their shadows. In fact, as mall vacancy rates have climbed, mall owners are eager to rent space to small businesses, tenants that in the past many of them had shunned in favor of large brand-name retailers.

ENTREPRENEURIAL PROFILE: Sam Josi, Stryker Sales, and Nate Valentine: Blue Barn Sam Josi, Stryker Sales, and Nate Valentine, founders of Blue Barn, a neighborhood deli in San Francisco that sells salads, sandwiches, and soups made from local ingredients, decided to open their second location in Town Center Corte Madera, a lifestyle center modeled after an Italian hill town with 65 shops located in nearby Corte Madera. The restaurant's target customers are a good fit with the demographic profile of the upscale shopping center's customers, and since opening in Town Center in 2013, Blue Barn has seen its sales increase an average of 5 percent each year.[86] ∎

When evaluating a mall or shopping center location, an entrepreneur should consider the following questions:

- Is there a good fit with other products and brands sold in the mall or center?

- Who are the other tenants? Which stores are the anchor tenants that will bring people into the mall or center? How financially stable are the anchor tenants?

- Demographically, is the center a good fit for your products or services? What are its customer demographics?

- How much foot traffic does the mall or center generate? How much traffic passes the specific site you are considering?

- What is the mall's average sales per square foot (a common metric for measuring a mall's attractiveness)? The average sales generated per square foot for all malls is $445 per square foot, but 34 percent of malls generate less than $300 per square foot in sales. Only 29 percent of malls generate sales per square foot of $500 or more.[87]

- How much vehicle traffic does the mall or center generate? Check its proximity to major population centers, the volume of tourists it draws, and the volume of drive-by freeway traffic. A mall or center that scores well on all three is more likely to be a winner.

- What is the mall's vacancy rate? What is the turnover rate of its tenants?

- How much is the rent, and how is it calculated? Most mall tenants pay a base amount of rent plus a small percentage of their sales above a specified level.

A mall location is no guarantee of business success, however. Malls have been under pressure lately, especially from online retailers and fast-growing discount stores, and mall foot traffic is declining. Many weaker malls (known as "grayfields") have closed or have been redeveloped. As chains such as Macy's and Sears, which are anchor stores in many malls, shutter some of their stores, more malls will be under pressure. Some real estate and retail experts estimate that between 15 and 33 percent of the malls in operation today will close by 2025.[88] The basic problem is an oversupply of mall space; there is nearly 24 square feet of mall and shopping center retail space for every person in the United States, compared to just 15 square feet per capita in Canada and 5 square feet per capita in the United Kingdom.[89] The last new enclosed shopping mall in the United States opened in 2006.[90] After the Fort Steuben Mall in Steubenville, Ohio, lost two of its anchor tenants, Sears and Macy's, many "in line" stores (the stores between the anchors) saw their sales plummet. The owner of the Scent Shop, a small retail store that sells candles and home accessories, says that her company's sales declined 35 percent after the anchors' closure.[91]

Another problem is that many malls are showing their age, requiring mall owners to remodel them, adding more restaurants, unique small businesses, upscale movie theaters, and supermarkets—experiences that shoppers cannot get online.[92] In addition, the demographic makeup of a mall's shoppers often changes over time, creating a new socioeconomic customer base that may not be compatible with a small company's target customer profile. As a result, many malls have undergone extensive renovations to transform themselves into "entertailing" destinations, adding entertainment features to their existing retail space in an attempt to generate more traffic. For instance, in addition to its 520 retail shops and 60 restaurants, Minneapolis's Mall of America, the second-largest mall in the United States (located only a few miles from Southdale, the nation's first mall), includes a 7-acre Nickelodeon Universe amusement park at its center, the Sea Life Minnesota Aquarium, a LEGOland play area, and a 14-screen movie complex in its 4.2 million square feet of space.[93]

Near Competitors

One of the most important factors in choosing a retail or service location is the compatibility of nearby stores with the retail or service customer. For example, businesses selling cars, antiques, and other shopping goods find it advantageous to locate near competitors to facilitate comparison shopping. Locating near competitors can be a key factor for success in those businesses selling goods that customers shop for and compare on the basis of price, quality, color, and other factors.

Although some business owners avoid locations near direct competitors, others see locating near rivals as an advantage. For instance, restaurateurs know that successful restaurants attract other restaurants, which, in turn, attract more customers. Many cities have at least one "restaurant row," where restaurants cluster together; each restaurant feeds customers to the others.

Locating near competitors has its limits, however. Clustering too many businesses of a single type into a small area ultimately erodes their sales once the market reaches the saturation point. When an area becomes saturated with competitors, the shops cannibalize sales from one another, making it difficult for any of them to be successful.

Shared Spaces (Coworking)

coworking
a situation in which two or more small companies share the same space.

Because outstanding locations can be expensive or hard to find, some small companies are sharing spaces with other small businesses, a trend known as **coworking**. Entrepreneurs can reduce their rent and maintenance costs (and, therefore, their financial risk) by operating in a shared space. Nearly 15,000 coworking spaces housing about 1.6 million people operate across the United States (with forecasts of more than 26,000 such spaces by 2020), usually in renovated historic buildings in the central business districts of cities, and many give entrepreneurs the flexibility of leasing anything from a communal desk (about $200 per month) to a private suite (about $700 per month).[94] Amenities include conference rooms, high-speed Internet access, private "booths" in which to conduct business calls, and free coffee.

Entrepreneurs often find that sharing space with other businesses sparks creativity because their employees have the opportunity to network with people outside of their industries, some of whom become customers, suppliers, or advisors.

Lynne Sladky/AP Images

ENTREPRENEURIAL PROFILE: Adam Boalt: LiveAnswer
Adam Boalt, a serial entrepreneur who recently sold a business, decided to rent a private desk at Pipeline, a coworking space in downtown Miami, Florida, for $500 a month, amidst other entrepreneurs while he developed plans for his next business. Boalt says that by locating in the shared space, he was able to meet attorneys, accountants,

Web developers, and others who helped him launch his latest business, LiveAnswer, a company that allocates the unused time of agents in call centers to small businesses that otherwise could not afford to hire a call center. As LiveAnswer grew, Boalt decided to stay at Pipeline and rent more space to accommodate his rapidly expanding company.[95] ■

Inside Large Retail Stores

Rather than compete against giant retailers, some small business owners are cooperating with them, locating their businesses inside the larger company's stores. These small companies offer products that the large retailers do not and benefit from the large volume of customer traffic the large stores attract. The world's largest retailer, Wal-Mart, is host to several small businesses, including franchisees of national chains Subway, McDonald's, Checkers, Noble Roman's Pizza, Philly Pretzel Factory, and Seattle's Best Coffee. Ben Miller, Brian Krider, and Scott Jones, cofounders of Ben's Soft Pretzels, a retail pretzel chain known for its authentic Amish pretzel recipe with more than 70 outlets in the United States, negotiated lease agreements with Wal-Mart and Meijer to locate franchisees inside the supercenters' stores. The goal is to tap into the high volume of customer traffic that the retail giants attract. Currently, Ben's Soft Pretzel franchisees operate outlets in 24 Wal-Mart and 12 Meijer supercenters, and more in-store locations are on the way.

Nontraditional Locations

Rather than select a location and try to draw customers to it, many small businesses are discovering where their customers already are and setting up locations there. These nontraditional locations include airports, museums, office buildings, churches, casinos, college and university campuses, athletic arenas, and others that offer high concentrations of potential customers. Mark Talarico, a successful Domino's Pizza franchisee, recently set up interactive pizza-ordering kiosks (not vending machines) in high-traffic areas near residence halls on the campuses of the University of California, Santa Barbara and Santa Barbara City College. Students who order pizzas through the kiosks receive a $1 discount.[96] In many cases, nontraditional locations are smaller and less expensive to build but generate much more in sales per square foot than traditional, full-size stores. Tina Flaherty operates a year-round kiosk, Cellairis, that sells smart phone and tablet accessories at Anderson Mall in Anderson, South Carolina. Her kiosk is open whenever the mall is open. Flaherty owns two other kiosks, a 100-square-foot kiosk that sells Christmas ornaments and a 325-square-foot kiosk that sells games, puzzles, and calendars, that are open for only 60 days during the holiday season. One retail analysts says that kiosks are growing in popularity among entrepreneurs because their start-up costs and rental rates are only a fraction of those of businesses that lease permanent space in shopping malls.[97]

Dunkin' Donuts has more than 750 nontraditional locations out of 11,700 outlets in the United States and around the globe, including theme parks, military bases, college and university campuses, mass transit stations, travel centers on interstate highways, entertainment venues, and others.[98] More than 8,000 of Subway's nearly 45,000 restaurants worldwide are in nontraditional locations, including zoos, hotels, casinos, museums, sports arenas, theaters, and others.[99] One Subway outlet is in a high school in Detroit (students actually operate the outlet), and another is located in a church in Buffalo, New York. Subway also has an outlet on the MS *Stolzenfels* riverboat that cruises the Rhine River in Germany. Subway's nontraditional locations account for 20 percent of the chain's total sales.[100]

Home-Based Businesses

For millions of entrepreneurs, home is where the business is, and their numbers are swelling. One recent study from the Small Business Administration reports that nearly 52 percent of all small companies are home based.[101] Although a home-based retail business usually is not a good idea, locating a service business at home is quite common. Many service companies do not have customers come to their places of business, so an expensive office location is unnecessary. For instance, customers typically contact plumbers or exterminators by telephone, and the work is performed in customers' homes.

Entrepreneurs locating their businesses at home reap several benefits. Perhaps the biggest benefit is the low cost of setting up the business. Most often, home-based entrepreneurs set up shop in a spare bedroom or basement, avoiding the cost of renting, leasing, or buying a building. With a few basic pieces of office equipment—a computer or tablet, printer, copier, and smart phone—a lone entrepreneur can perform just like a major corporation.

ENTREPRENEURIAL PROFILE: Eyal and Noa Levy: Yogibo When Eyal Levy's wife, Noa, was pregnant, the couple searched for a product that would allow her to sleep comfortably on her growing belly but could not find one. While traveling overseas, the couple discovered a soft spandex fabric and purchased some of it. Back home, they sewed some of the fabric to form a long pillow and filled it with tiny foam beads. The result was the Yogibo Max, a 6-foot-long modern version of a beanbag that customers can use as a chair, recliner, couch, or bed or body pillow. The Levys launched Yogibo Inc. in the basement of their Nashua, New Hampshire, home, and their early marketing strategy was to demonstrate the versatile product at home shows, craft fairs, and festivals. The Yogibo was a hit with customers, and when the Levys opened their first retail store in 2010, sales exploded. Today, Yogibo, which has expanded its product line to include pillows, cushions, and loungers, operates 27 stores in the Northeast and generates annual sales of nearly $50 million.[102] ■

Choosing a home location has certain disadvantages, however. Interruptions are more frequent, the refrigerator is all too handy, work is always just a few steps away, and isolation can be a problem. Another difficulty facing some home-based entrepreneurs involves zoning laws. As their businesses grow and become more successful, entrepreneurs' neighbors often begin to complain about the increased traffic, noise, and disruptions from deliveries, employees, and customers who drive through their residential neighborhoods to conduct business. Many communities now face the challenge of passing updated zoning laws that reflect the reality of today's home-based businesses while protecting the interests of residential homeowners.

On the Road

Some entrepreneurs are finding that the best location is not a permanent location but a mobile business that takes products and services to customers. Veterinarians, dentists, restaurants, and others are outfitting mobile units and taking their businesses on the road. Although mobile entrepreneurs avoid the costs of building or renovating permanent locations, they must incur the expense of setting up their mobile businesses. They also face other obstacles, such as finding suitable parking spaces in high-traffic areas, getting complaints from owners of nearby businesses, and securing the necessary permits to operate. Some communities welcome mobile businesses, while others restrict them or even forbid them to operate.

ENTREPRENEURIAL PROFILE: Dr. Sara Creighton: Studio Dental Dr. Sara Creighton, a dentist in San Francisco, noticed the popularity of food trucks (restaurants on wheels) and decided to sell her brick-and-mortar practice to launch Studio Dental, a mobile dental practice that takes dental care to her patients. To launch her business, Creighton set up a 38-foot-long trailer equipped with everything in a typical dental office and pitched the idea of partnering with several of the area's high-tech companies, including Google, Airbnb, and Salesforce. Because their employees work long hours and prefer to stay on their employers' campuses during work hours, the companies welcomed Studio Dental. Creighton has since opened her mobile practice to the general public, and after only one year, Studio Dental is running well ahead of Creighton's financial projections.[103] ■

LO4

Explain the site selection process for manufacturers.

The Location Decision for Manufacturers

The criteria for the location decision for manufacturers are very different from those for retailers and service businesses; however, the decision can have just as much impact on the company's success. In some cases, a manufacturer has special needs that influence the choice of location. For instance, when one manufacturer of photographic plates and digital cameras was searching for a location for a new plant, it had to limit its search to sites with a large supply of available fresh water, a necessary part of its process. In other cases, the location decision is controlled by zoning ordinances. If a manufacturer's process creates offensive odors or excessive noise, it may be further restricted in its choices.

The type of transportation network required dictates location of a factory in some cases. Some manufacturers may need to locate on a railroad siding, whereas others may need only reliable trucking service. If raw materials are purchased by the carload for economies of scale, the location must be convenient to a railroad siding. Bulk materials are sometimes shipped by barge and consequently require a facility convenient to a navigable river or lake. The added cost of using multiple shipping methods (e.g., rail to truck or barge to truck) can significantly increase shipping costs and make a location unfeasible for a manufacturer.

As fuel costs escalate, the cost of shipping finished products to customers also influences the location decision for many manufacturers, requiring them to open factories or warehouses in locations that are close to their primary markets to reduce transportation costs. Thermo-Pur Technologies, a small company that has developed a new stainless-steel heat exchanger core that makes automotive radiators lighter, more efficient at transferring heat, and less expensive to manufacture, recently selected the Clemson University International Center for Automotive Research in Greenville, South Carolina, as the location for its headquarters and first North American factory. Company managers considered other locations but selected Greenville because of its growing reputation as a knowledge center for automotive products, excellent transportation network, proximity to potential customers (including BMW, Mercedes Benz, Volvo, and Kia), cost of operation, and overall quality of life.[104]

Foreign Trade Zones

Foreign trade zones can be attractive locations for small manufacturers that engage in global trade and are looking to reduce or eliminate the tariffs, duties, and excise taxes they pay on the materials and the parts they import and the goods they export. A **foreign trade zone** (see Figure 14.3) is a specially designated area in or near a U.S. customs port of entry that allows resident companies to import materials and components from foreign countries; assemble, process, manufacture, or package them; and then ship the finished product back out while either reducing or eliminating completely tariffs and duties. As far as tariffs and duties are concerned, a company located in a foreign trade zone is treated as if it is located outside the United States. For instance, a maker of speakers can import components from around the world and assemble them at its plant located in a foreign trade zone. The company pays no duties on the components it imports or on the speakers it exports to other foreign markets. The only duties the manufacturer pays are on the speakers it sells in the United States; the duty the company pays is either on the finished speakers or the imported component parts, whichever is less. More than 2,900 businesses in the United States ship $660 billion worth of goods into and $85 billion worth of goods out of the 186 foreign trade zones that operate in the United States.[105] Another 4,100 FTZs operate in other countries around the globe.[106]

foreign trade zone
a specially designated area in or near a U.S. customs port of entry that allows resident companies to import materials and components from foreign countries; assemble, process, manufacture, or package them; and then ship the finished product while either reducing or eliminating tariffs and duties.

Business Incubators and Accelerators

For many start-up companies, a business incubator may make the ideal initial location. A **business incubator** is an organization that combines low-cost, flexible rental space with a multitude of support services for its small business residents. The primary reason for establishing an incubator is to enhance economic development by growing new businesses that create jobs and diversify the local economy. An incubator's goal is to nurture young companies during the volatile start-up period and help them survive until they are strong enough to go out on their own.

business incubator
an organization that combines low-cost, flexible rental space with a multitude of support services for its small business residents.

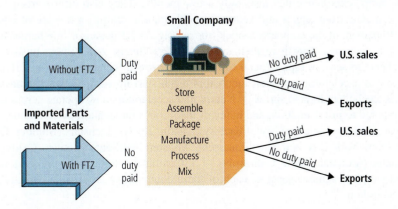

FIGURE 14.3

How a Foreign Trade Zone Works

Common sponsors of incubators include colleges or universities (32 percent), economic development organizations (25 percent), and government entities (16 percent). Most incubators (54 percent) are "mixed use," hosting a variety of start-up companies, followed by incubators that focus on technology companies (37 percent).[107] Some incubators operate virtually, with no physical presence, much like a social network, providing entrepreneurs with mentoring and the opportunity to collaborate with other entrepreneurs.

In addition to discounted lease rates, incubators also offer tenants valuable resources, such as telephone systems, computers and software, high-speed Internet service, meeting and conference rooms, and sometimes management consulting services and financing contacts. Not only do these services save young companies money (reducing a small company's start-up costs in some cases by 40 to 50 percent), they also save them valuable time.[108] Entrepreneurs can focus on getting their products and services to market faster than competitors rather than searching for the resources they need to build their companies. The typical incubator has entry requirements that prospective residents must meet. Incubators also have criteria that establish the conditions a business must maintain to remain in the facility as well as the expectations for "graduation" into the business community (usually within three to five years).

More than 1,500 incubators operate across the United States (and 7,500 incubators worldwide), up from just 12 in 1980; they house an estimated 49,000 start-up companies.[109] Perhaps the greatest advantage of choosing to locate a start-up company in an incubator is a greater chance for success; according to the National Business Incubation Association, graduates from incubators have a reported success rate of between 75 and 87 percent, and 84 percent of the companies that graduate stay in the local community.[110]

Courtesy of Cathy Cheney

ENTREPRENEURIAL PROFILE: Ben Jacobsen: Jacobsen Salt Company Inspired by the food culture in Portland, Oregon, Ben Jacobsen decided to start an artisanal sea salt company and began learning how to harvest salt from the Pacific Ocean. Jacobsen turned to KitchenCru, a 4,800-square-foot incubator aimed at food companies in Portland, where tenants rent space for $23 to $28 per hour in a fully equipped, licensed commercial kitchen. Jacobsen designed his own salt harvesting and processing equipment using 600-gallon stockpots and raised the start-up capital he needed for his business, Jacobsen Salt Company, on Kickstarter ($28,000) and from family members and friends ($100,000). Jacobsen operated his business out of the incubator for 18 months before graduating to his own space. Today, Jacobsen Salt Company, now with 35 employees, harvests 18,000 pounds of salt each month and sells it to food enthusiasts across the nation, including numerous celebrity chefs at some of the finest restaurants.[111] ■

Accelerator

an organization that provides business start-ups a range of valuable support services, such as workshops, seminars, access to vital business networks, mentoring, and access to capital investments from angels and venture capital firms in return for a share of equity, typically 2 to 10 percent of the company's stock, usually in a "boot camp" experience that lasts only a few months.

Like incubators, accelerators are designed to help promising start-up businesses succeed, but their focus is somewhat different. **Accelerators** provide a range of valuable support services, such as workshops, seminars, access to vital business networks, and mentoring, to their clients, usually in a "boot camp" experience that lasts only a few months. They also offer start-ups access to capital investments from angels and venture capital firms in return for a share of equity, typically 2 to 10 percent of the company's stock (the average is 7.3 percent).[112] Whereas incubators foster slower, sustained growth in their small business clients, accelerators push their high-potential clients to achieve rapid, "petal-to-the-metal" growth (hence their name). The director of one business accelerator says that incubators teach start-up companies to stand and walk; accelerators teach them how to sprint.[113] Nearly 580 accelerators now operate across the United States, compared to just 1 in 2005, and many of them focus on technology companies.[114] Some of the top accelerators include, Capital Factory (Austin, Texas), Techstars (Boulder, Colorado), AngelPad (New York City and San Francisco), MuckerLab (Santa Monica, California), and Y Combinator (Mountain View, California).[115] Y Combinator helped the founders of Airbnb, Stripe, and Dropbox achieve success; each of these companies has a market valuation well in excess of $1 billion.[116]

Layout and Design Considerations

Once an entrepreneur chooses the best location for his or her business, the next issue to address is designing the proper layout for the space to maximize sales (retail) or productivity (manufacturing or service). **Layout** is the logical arrangement of the physical facilities in a business that contributes to efficient operations, increased productivity, and higher sales. Planning for the most effective and efficient layout in a business environment can produce dramatic improvements in a company's operating effectiveness, efficiency, and overall performance. Unfortunately, in the United States, 23 percent of workers are dissatisfied with their work environments.[117] An attractive, effective layout can help a company's recruiting efforts, reduce absenteeism, and improve employee productivity, satisfaction, and engagement. A survey by Steelcase, a maker of office furniture, reports that employees who are more satisfied with their workplace design also are more engaged with their work.[118] The comprehensive *U.S. Workplace Survey* by global design firm Gensler reports that top-performing companies have work space designs that are more effective than those of average companies.[119] The changing nature of work demands that work space design also changes. Although many jobs require the ability to focus on "heads-down" individual tasks, other jobs require collaboration with coworkers (sometimes *virtual* collaboration with workers in remote locations). An effective work space must be flexible enough to accommodate and encourage both types of work. Increasingly, work is becoming more complex, team based, technology dependent, and mobile; work spaces must adapt to accommodate these characteristics. The study by Gensler concludes that top-performing employees are five times more likely to work in spaces that support both individual and collaborative work.[120]

The design of a company's work space should reflect its character and culture, which is especially important for start-ups that are trying to recruit employees or attract investors. The "cube farms," rows of impersonal cubicles in expansive open spaces, dominated office designs for decades but are disappearing in favor of smaller work spaces that are more informal and contain workstations and furniture that employees can rearrange quickly and easily (see Figure 14.4). Research shows that open offices, with their distractions and lack of privacy, impede employees' productivity, reduce their creativity, and increase their stress levels.[121] One design expert says that the most effective workplace designs encourage employees to engage in a "kaleidoscope of interactions" with other workers when appropriate and allow them to retreat into private spaces so that they can concentrate and focus on complex tasks when necessary.[122] Modern, flexible work spaces encourage collaboration among employees, look less like a traditional office and more like a comfortable living room, and can be rearranged easily to accommodate different tasks, technology, and types of work.

LO5

Describe the criteria used to analyze the layout and design considerations of a building, including the Americans with Disabilities Act.

layout

the logical arrangement of the physical facilities in a business that contributes to efficient operations, increased productivity, and higher sales.

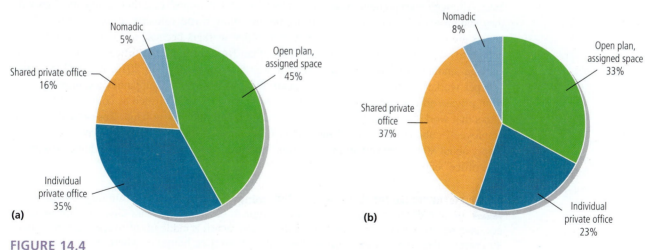

FIGURE 14.4

Work Space Design Characteristics in the United States (part a) and Globally (part b)

Source: Based on *Steelcase Global Report*, 2014, p. 212.

ENTREPRENEURIAL PROFILE: Mark Zuckerberg: Facebook Facebook recently moved into its new headquarters on a 57-acre tract in Menlo Park, California, whose design encourages creativity, productivity, interaction, and collaboration among its more than 4,000 workers. The goal is to create a headquarters that more closely resembles a college campus than a corporate office. Designers took out interior walls, cubicles, and private offices in the existing building to create an open space, covered the walls with whiteboard paint, and sprinkled comfortable sofas and hundreds of small breakout rooms throughout the space, where workers can conduct informal meetings and brainstorming sessions. In a tribute to Facebook's "hacker culture," the design features exposed beams and ductwork and plywood-covered corridors to remind employees that their work is never done. Freestyle artwork throughout the space signals the value of creativity and self-expression. The renovated building features a glass roof that provides plenty of natural light and a central courtyard with cafés, dry cleaners, a fitness center, a medical clinic, and other services to maximize employee convenience—even a giant, outdoor screen on which employees can watch movies after hours. Facebook recently announced the addition of a 494-unit housing community, Anton Menlo, that is within walking distance of its headquarters. Like company headquarters, the community's layout encourages people to interact and share ideas.[123] ■

When creating a layout, managers must consider its impact on the space itself (comfort, flexibility, size, and ergonomics), the people who occupy it (type of work, special requirements, need for interaction, and tasks performed), and the technology they use (communication, Internet access, and equipment).[124] Employee seating patterns also have an impact on employee productivity and performance. One recent study reports that locating weaker-performing employees next to stronger-performing employees improves the weaker employees' performance without diminishing the stronger employees' performance. Grouping employees with complementary strengths creates a symbiotic relationship in which each employee improves by feeding off the other employees' strengths. The study concludes that the "spillover" effect from strong employee performance is much greater than that from poor employee performance and that strategically locating employees can improve their productivity by as much 13 percent and their effectiveness by as much as 17 percent.[125]

The following factors have a significant impact on a space's layout and design.

Size and Adaptability

A building must offer adequate space and be adaptable enough to accommodate a business's daily operations. If it is too small at the outset of operations, efficiency will suffer. A space must have enough room for customers' movement, inventory, displays, storage, work areas, offices, and restrooms. Haphazard layouts undermine employee productivity and create organizational chaos. Businesses that launch in locations that are too small at the outset must make premature and costly moves to larger spaces, interfering with their ability to maintain a loyal customer base. Although entrepreneurs want spaces capable of accommodating their companies' growth, they should avoid spaces that are too big because they waste valuable resources. Many businesses are reducing the space they allocate to office workers because technology allows some people to work from almost anywhere rather than from a traditional office. In the 1970s, the average amount of office space per worker was 600 square feet; in 2010, it was 225 square feet per worker; today, it is only 151 square feet per worker.[126] Companies are moving away from private offices and even cubicles to unassigned work spaces, such as communal tables or desks that workers share and can rearrange easily to suit the task at hand. Research shows that employees' cubicles are unused more than 60 percent of the time and that private offices sit empty about 80 percent of the time.[127] Some entrepreneurs have done away with the concept of "the office" entirely.

ENTREPRENEURIAL PROFILE: Jill Bluming: The Creative Type Although Jill Bluming's graphic design company, The Creative Type, is based in New York City, her eight employees have no office space. Instead, her creative team, which is made up of copywriters, designers, illustrators, and others, work together "virtually," from their homes or wherever they are. When Bluming needs a conference room for a client meeting, she uses a Web-based service to rent one by the hour. Bluming says The Creative Type is driven by flexibility rather than a particular structure, pointing out that her company's low overhead costs give it a competitive advantage.[128] ■

Construction and Appearance

Is the construction of the building sound? Having an expert look it over before buying and leasing the property can pay big dividends. Beyond the soundness of construction, does the building have attractive external and internal appearances? The physical appearance of the building provides customers with their first impression of a business. Retailers and service providers, in particular, must recognize the importance of creating the proper image for their stores and how their shops' layouts and physical facilities influence this image. A store's external appearance contributes significantly to establishing its identity among its target customers. Does the building convey the appropriate signals to potential customers about the type of company it houses? Physical facilities send important messages to customers. Should the building project an upscale image or an economical one? Is the atmosphere informal and relaxed or formal and businesslike?

Lee and Aimee Hill, founders of Elkmont Trading Company, an outdoor outfitter in Clemson, South Carolina, wanted to differentiate their business from all of the "big box" chains that sell outdoor clothing and equipment. The building they built to house their business sends a clear signal to customers that the Hills are passionate about the outdoors (Lee successfully hiked the entire Appalachian Trail several years ago) and that their outdoor outfitting company is quite different from its larger competitors. The structure is made of natural stone and wood reclaimed from old barns (including Lee's grandfather's barn) and other heirloom structures. Lee spent more than a decade collecting the vintage wood from which to build the store. Inside, neatly displayed racks of clothing and outdoor gear are nestled in nooks and alcoves that invite shoppers to explore. The reclaimed wood theme runs throughout the store's interior, and a stone fireplace welcomes guests to pull up a chair and warm themselves on chilly days. Below the main sales floor, the Lees have an extensive display of canoes and kayaks that are available for sale or rent. Out back is a rustic bar featuring wood accents that offers soft drinks, a variety of locally crafted artisan beers, and food items supplied by local small businesses. The building that houses the Elkmont Trading Company goes a long way toward creating the right mood for its target customers, who love the outdoors and enjoy the homey look and feel of the shop.[129]

Courtesy of Katrice Hardy, Greenville News

Communicating the right signals through layout and physical facilities is an important step in attracting a steady stream of customers. Retail consultant Paco Underhill advises merchants to "seduce" passersby with their storefronts. "The seduction process should start a minimum of 10 paces away," he says.[130]

A store's window display and in-store displays can be powerful selling tools if used properly. Often, a store's displays are an afterthought, and many business owners neglect to change their displays often enough. The following tips help entrepreneurs create window displays that sell:

- *Keep displays simple.* Simple, uncluttered, and creative arrangements of merchandise draw the most attention and have the greatest impact on potential customers.

- *Keep displays clean and current.* Dusty, dingy displays or designs that are outdated send a negative message to passersby.

- *Change displays frequently.* Customers do not want to see the same merchandise on display every time they enter a store. Experts recommend changing displays at least quarterly, but stores selling trendy items should change their displays twice a month.

- *Get expert help if necessary.* Not every business owner has a knack for designing displays. Their best bet is to hire a professional or to work with the design department at a local college or university.

Entrances

Entrances to a business should *invite* customers into a store. Wide entryways and attractive merchandise displays that are set back from the doorway draw customers into a business. A store's entrance should catch passing customers' attention and draw them inside. "That's where you want somebody to slam on the brakes and realize they're going someplace new," says Underhill.[131] Retailers with heavy traffic flows, such as supermarkets or drugstores, often install automatic doors to ensure a smooth traffic flow into and out of their stores. Retailers must remove any barriers that interfere with customers' easy access to the storefront. Broken sidewalks, sagging steps, mud puddles, and sticking or heavy doors create not only obstacles that might discourage potential customers but also legal hazards for a business if they cause customers to be injured. The goal is to eliminate anything that creates what one expert calls "threshold resistance."[132]

The Americans with Disabilities Act

Approximately 12.6 percent of people in the United States are disabled.[133] The **Americans with Disabilities Act (ADA)**, enacted in 1990, requires practically all businesses, regardless of their size, to make their facilities available to physically challenged customers and employees. Most states have similar laws, many of them more stringent than the ADA, that apply to small companies as well. The rules of these state laws and the ADA's Title III are designed to ensure that mentally and physically challenged customers have equal access to a firm's goods or services. For instance, the act requires business owners to remove architectural and communication barriers when "readily achievable" (that is, accomplished without unreasonable difficulty or expense). The ADA allows flexibility in how a business achieves this equal access, however. For example, a restaurant could either provide menus in Braille or offer to have a staff member read the menu to blind customers. A small dry cleaner might not be able to add a wheelchair ramp to its storefront without incurring significant expense, but the owner could comply with the ADA by offering curbside pickup and delivery services at no extra charge for disabled customers.

The Department of Justice revised the ADA in 2010, and all newly constructed or renovated buildings that are open to the public and were occupied after March 15, 2012, must comply with the 2010 requirements. For example, in retail stores, checkout aisles must be wide enough—at least 36 inches—to accommodate wheelchairs. Restaurants must have at least 5 percent of their tables accessible to wheelchair-bound patrons. Miniature golf courses must make at least 50 percent of the holes on the course accessible to disabled customers.

Complying with the ADA does not necessarily require businesses to spend large amounts of money. According to a recent study by the U.S. Department of Labor's Job Accommodation Network, 59 percent of employers say that the accommodations they made for disabled employees cost nothing. For employers that did incur expenses making accommodations, the average expenditure is just $500. Only 4 percent of businesses reported ongoing, annual costs to make accommodations for their workers.[134] In addition, companies with $1 million or less in annual sales or with 30 or fewer full-time employees that invest in making their locations more accessible qualify for a tax credit up of to $5,000. The credit is 50 percent of their expenses between $250 and $10,250. Businesses that remove physical, structural, and transportation barriers for disabled employees and customers also qualify for a tax deduction of up to $15,000. Unfortunately, the number of ADA lawsuits filed in federal courts has been increasing, and many of them are aimed at small businesses (see Figure 14.5). Alan Rigerman, who walks with a cane, sued Arbetter's Hot Dogs, a 1,000-square-foot diner that Dave Arbetter's family has owned since 1960, claiming that the 60-year-old building that houses the restaurant violated the ADA. Rigerman's lawsuit

FIGURE 14.5

Number of ADA Lawsuits Filed in U.S. District Courts

Source: Based on data from U.S. District Courts, Judicial Business of the United States Courts, United States Courts, www.uscourts.gov/statistics-reports/analysis-reports/judicial-business-united-states-courts.

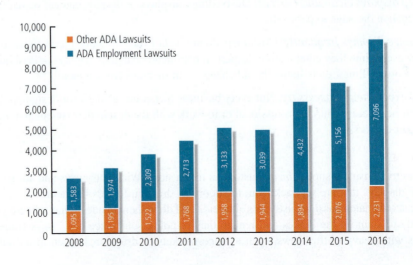

cited 28 ADA violations, including a lack of fixed floor mats and handicap-accessible restrooms. Arbetter spent $10,000 to install a wheelchair ramp and make other modifications to his diner, which generates sales of just $600,000 per year, and $14,000 in legal fees.[135]

Signs

One of the lowest-cost and most effective methods of communicating with customers is a business sign. Signs serve as guideposts for a business, telling potential customers what it does, where it is, and what it is selling. Ideally, a sign conveys a positive image of the company's brand. In a highly mobile society, a well-designed, well-placed sign can be a powerful tool for reaching potential customers. Readability is the top design concern; a sign should be large enough for passersby to read from a distance, taking into consideration the location and speed of surrounding traffic arteries. To be most effective, the message should be short, simple, and clear. Including the company's Web site URL on the sign promotes its e-commerce business. A sign should be legible both in daylight and at night; proper illumination is a must. Contrasting colors and simple typefaces are best, and an eye-catching graphic or company logo helps attract attention. Business signs constructed from quality materials look better and last longer. The most common problems with business signs are that they are illegible, poorly designed (including unattractive color schemes and type that is hard to read), improperly located, and/or poorly maintained.

Before investing in a sign, an entrepreneur should investigate the local community's sign ordinance. In some cities and towns, local regulations impose restrictions on the size, location, height, and construction materials used in business signs.

Building Interiors

Designing a functional, efficient interior layout demands research, planning, and attention to detail. Retailers in particular have known for a long time that their stores' layouts influence their customers' buying behavior. Some retailers, such as Lowe's, Aldi, and Wal-Mart, reinforce their discount images with layouts that communicate to shoppers a warehouse environment, often complete with pallets. Luxury retailers, such as Tiffany and Company, Coach, and Nordstrom, create opulent layouts in which their upscale customers feel comfortable. Retailers such as Cabela's, Barnes & Noble, and Starbucks use layouts that encourage customers to linger and spend more time (and more money), a trend known as "slow shopping." Research shows that shoppers who spend more time in a retail store do spend more money. Origins, a chain of 87 stores located around the world that sells beauty and skincare products, recently began redesigning its stores, incorporating features designed to encourage shoppers to linger. A long communal table with a giant sink encourages shoppers to test various soaps, scrubs, and cleansers. Comfortable seating invites shoppers to relax while beauty consultants give them facials or show them products and explain their benefits. Attractive displays teach customers about the characteristics of the herbs and plants used in the company's lotions and creams and the journey they take from plant to product. One wall of the store has special lighting for taking perfect selfies. Stores that feature the new slow shopping design have experienced sales increases of 20 to 40 percent.[136]

Building interiors send important signals to shoppers about a business's image, and cleanliness and order are essential. In restaurants, for example, dining areas or bathrooms that are dirty send customers scurrying. Studies consistently show that the most common reason that customers refuse to return to a restaurant has nothing to do with food or service; it is dirty bathrooms![137] ("If the bathrooms are this bad, the kitchen must be worse.") Because entrepreneurs are in their buildings every day and are focused on the "big picture," overlooking details in the physical space can happen easily but can be deadly for sales. Is the carpet in need of cleaning or replacement? Are displays and decorations dusty and disheveled? Would a coat of fresh paint brighten the space? Does clutter detract from a good first impression? Cinnabon, a franchise with more than 1,450 locations worldwide that sells delectable cinnamon buns, recently embarked on a remodeling program for its shops that features a cleaner, simpler design (the goal was to "declutter" the layout) with a lighter color palette that reminds customers of a French patisserie. The new look puts the company's high-margin beverages in a prominent place up front and includes larger bakery cases with LED lighting that focuses attention on the company's signature products. The company also moved the ovens toward the front so that customers can see—and smell—employees baking fresh pastries.[138]

ergonomics

the science of adapting work and the work environment to complement employees' strengths and to suit customers' needs.

Coordinating an effective layout is not a haphazard process. **Ergonomics**, the science of adapting work and the work environment to complement employees' strengths and to suit customers' needs, is an integral part of a successful design. For example, chairs, desks, and table heights that allow people to work comfortably can help employees perform their jobs faster and more easily. Design experts claim that improved lighting, better acoustics, and proper climate control benefit the company as well as employees. An ergonomically designed workplace can improve workers' productivity significantly and reduce days lost due to injuries and accidents. A study for the Commission of Architecture and the Built Environment and the British Council for Offices reports that simple features, such as proper lighting, reduce absenteeism by 15 percent and increase productivity between 2.8 and 20 percent.[139]

Unfortunately, many businesses fail to incorporate ergonomic design principles into their layouts, and the result is costly worker's compensation claims, absences from work, and lost productivity. The good news for employers, however, is that preventing injuries, accidents, and lost days does *not* require spending thousands of dollars on ergonomically correct solutions. Most of the solutions actually are quite simple and inexpensive, ranging from installing equipment that eliminates workers' repetitive motions to introducing breaks during which workers engage in exercises designed by occupational therapists to combat injuries.

Drive-Through Windows

For many businesses, a drive-through window adds another dimension to the concept of customer convenience and is a relatively inexpensive way to increase sales. In the quick-service restaurant business, drive-through windows are an essential design component, accounting for between 60 and 70 percent of sales; for some chains, drive-through window sales make up 85 percent of total sales.[140] Although drive-through windows are staples at quick-service restaurants, other businesses, including fast-casual restaurants, drugstores, convenience stores, hardware stores, and even wedding chapels and funeral homes (!), benefit from them. Managers at fast-casual restaurant chain Panera Bread studied and tested drive-through windows for 10 years before introducing them throughout the chain because they did not want to diminish the dining experience for drive-through customers or in-store customers, who might be distracted by the noise of a drive-through window. Panera's strategy includes drive-throughs that are isolated from the dining room, sufficient staff dedicated solely to serving drive-through customers, technology to support fast, accurate orders, and special packaging designed to ensure the integrity of customers' food. Panera says sales at outlets with drive-through windows have experienced double-digit sales increases, and all new outlets include drive-through windows.[141]

Sight, Sound, Scent, and Lighting

Retailers can increase sales by sending important subconscious signals to customers using what design experts call "symbolics." For instance, when shoppers enter many supermarkets, they enter a "decompression zone," featuring displays of fragrant fresh flowers and brightly colored fruits and vegetables. Not only are the flowers', fruits', and vegetables' colors and smells pleasing, but they also send a clear message to customers: "You are embarking on an adventure in freshness in our store—flowers, produce, meats, seafood, *everything*."[142] Layouts that engage all of customers' senses also increase sales. Paco Underhill, founder of Envirosell, a market research company, says most of customers' unplanned purchases come after they touch, taste, smell, or hear something in a store. For example, stores that sell fresh food see sales increase if they offer free samples to customers. One study reports that offering shoppers free samples increases not only sales of the item offered but also sales of other products. Research also shows that customers are willing to pay more for products they can see, touch, taste, or try.[143] "If somebody doesn't try 'em, they're not going to buy 'em," quips Underhill.[144] Sight, sound, scent, and lighting are particularly important aspects of retail layout.

SIGHT A business can use colors and visual cues in its interior designs to support its brand and image in subtle yet effective ways. At the Larder at Tavern, a unique combination of a restaurant, a food market, and a bar, owners Suzanne Goin and Caroline Stine recently remodeled, creating a more relaxed, inviting ambiance for dine-in customers by painting formerly white and neutral walls a deep, rich green that evokes the color of a full bottle of red wine and installing softer, cozier lights that mimic candlelight. They also moved the refrigerated cases containing prepared foods and artisanal cheeses away from the dining space and closer to the entrance so that they are more convenient for to-go customers.[145] At the Vermont Country Deli in Brattleboro, Vermont, wooden bookshelves and odd tables filled with colorful displays of jams, jellies, and desserts greet customers as they enter the store. The mismatched tables and shelves give the store an authentic, down-home look, and signs such as "Life is short. Eat cookies." entice customers to make purchases. At Whole Foods, prices for fresh fruits and vegetables appear to be hand scrawled on fragments of black slate, a tradition in outdoor markets in Europe—as if a farmer had pulled up that morning, unloaded the produce, and posted the price before heading back to the farm. Some of the produce also is sprinkled with water droplets. When customers at the restaurant Tallulah on the Thames in Newport, Rhode Island, are seated, waiters hand them a rustic clipboard with a handwritten list of the daily "farm-to-table menu."[146] The subtle message these symbolics send to customers is *freshness*.[147]

SOUND In an attempt to engage all of their customers' senses, companies are realizing the impact that sound has on shoppers and are incorporating it into their layouts. Research shows that a business's "soundscape" can have an impact on the length of time customers shop and the amount of money they spend. Background music that appeals to a company's target customers can be an effective marketing tool, subtly communicating important messages about its brand to customers. In addition, research shows that 95 percent of people prefer to shop in stores that play background music (but not too loud, which causes people to leave a store, usually without buying anything).[148] The ideal playlist depends on the company's target customers and the mood the business wants to create. Restaurants that want their guests to stay longer should play slow music; those that count on turning tables quickly should play faster music.[149] Quaker State & Lube, a chain of 50 casual dining restaurants in 14 states that feature an automotive theme, hired experts at Ambiance Radio to create playlists for its outlets for different parts of the day (lunch, dinner, and late night). At peak times, Quaker State & Lube plays upbeat, fast-tempo music to encourage faster dining and to speed up the number of table turns.[150] Thomas Pink, an upscale London-based retailer known for its branded shirts and ties with stores in major cities in Europe, Asia, the United States, and the Middle East, plays an eclectic list of songs that is designed to be part of customers' interaction with the brand. The company worked with soundscape specialty company Mood Media to create a customized playlist that is far-reaching, ranging from The Beatles and David Bowie to The Jam and the Mystery Jets, but is decidedly British. The company also launched a Web radio channel that streams its in-store playlists.[151] For most retail soundscapes, one rule is clear: Slow is good. People's biorhythms reflect the sounds around them, and soothing classical music encourages shoppers to relax and slow down, meaning that they will shop longer and spend more. Classical music also makes shoppers feel more affluent and increases sales more than any other type of music.[152] Before incorporating music into a company's soundscape, however, business owners must pay for licenses to use it, typically from BMI (Broadcast Music Inc.), ASCAP (American Society of Composers, Authors, and Publishers), or some other performing rights organization.

David Lyons/Alamy Stock Photo

SCENT The Sense of Smell Institute reports that the average human being can recognize 10,000 different odors and can recall scents with 65 percent accuracy after one year, a much higher recall rate than visual stimuli produce.[153] Research shows that humans' sense of smell is the "most emotional" scent; therefore, scent marketing has a powerful effect in retail stores.[154] When one gas station/convenience store pumped the smell of fresh-brewed coffee at its gas pumps, coffee sales increased by 300 percent.[155] In another experiment, when Eric Spangenberg of Washington State University diffused a subtle scent of vanilla into the women's department of a store and rose maroc into the men's department, he discovered that sales nearly doubled. He also discovered that if he switched the scents, sales in both departments fell well below their normal average.[156] Vanilla connotes warmth and comfort, and citrus scents tend to be energizing and invigorating.

Research shows that scent marketing causes shoppers to linger longer, browse more merchandise, and increase their perception of the quality of the company's goods.[157] More companies—from casinos to convenience stores—are beginning to understand the power of scent marketing. Bakeries use fans to push the smell of fresh-baked breads and sweets into pedestrian traffic lanes, tempting them to sample some of their delectable goodies. Panera Bread, a chain of 2,000 restaurants in 46 states, recently switched bread-baking in its stores from the night shift to the day shift so that customers can smell the enticing aroma of freshly baked bread (and watch the bakers at work). Hamley's, a well-known toy store founded in 1760 in London that holds a royal warrant designating it as a supplier to the British royal family, disperses the scent of piña coladas throughout its stores, which encourages parents to linger with their children longer—and make more purchases.[158] Charles Tyrwhitt, another British company that sells classic menswear, opted for the scent of mahogany in its stores to remind its customers of its classic English heritage.[159] These companies understand the power of adding a scent component to their company's brand.

LIGHTING Lighting has a direct impact on employee productivity, customers' perceptions of a store and its products, and a company's operating costs. Good lighting defines the "mood" of a space and allows employees to work at maximum efficiency. Proper lighting is measured by the amount of light required to do a job properly with the greatest lighting efficiency. Efficiency is essential because lighting consumes more than 17 percent of the total energy used in the typical commercial building.[160] Traditional incandescent lighting, which Congress banned on January 1, 2014, is least efficient. Only 10 percent of the energy it generates is light; the remaining 90 percent is heat. Compact fluorescent lights (CFLs) generate far less heat, use 75 percent less energy, and last 10 times longer than traditional incandescent lights. Technology advances are increasing the popularity of light-emitting-diode (LED) lighting. Although still more expensive to purchase, LEDs use just 20 to 25 percent of the electricity of incandescent lights and 50 percent of the electricity of CFLs. They also last six times longer than CFLs and 25 times longer than incandescent lights. LEDs generate the least amount of heat, reducing business's cooling costs during warm months.[161] Kirk Taylor, president of Nino Salvaggio International Market, a company that sells freshly picked fruits and vegetables from three locations in Michigan, recently replaced more than 3,000 incandescent and halogen bulbs in its stores with highly efficient LED bulbs. In addition to receiving cash incentives from its electric utility for making the switch, the company has seen its lighting, cooling, and refrigeration costs decline significantly.[162]

A common mistake when designing lighting is relying on overhead lights to do most or all of the work, which almost always creates harsh lighting and glare, both of which can reduce employee productivity or diminish the ambiance a retail business is trying to create. Another common lighting mistake is uniformity, often a result of using overhead lighting to bathe the entire environment in the same luminosity. Uniformity affects people's moods negatively, causes fatigue, and creates spaces with no character and charm. Proper lighting design requires the use of five layers of lighting:[163]

1. *General lighting* is the foundation layer for lighting a space and provides lighting for the basic activities that will take place in it.

2. *Ambient lighting* creates a "mood" in a space without directly affecting users' activities. It is designed to invoke emotion by adding color, intensity, and even texture to a space.

3. *Task lighting* is dedicated to helping users perform specific tasks in a space, such as reading, cooking, assembling a small part, and others. Task lighting should minimize both glare and shadows.

4. *Accent lighting* creates interest in a space by highlighting specific components, such as artwork, décor, or architectural features, using contrast.

5. *Decorative lighting* is specialty lighting that adds aesthetic appeal to a space rather than performing a specific function. Often, the light fixture itself is the focal point.

Lighting provides a good return on investment, given its overall impact on a business. Few people seek out businesses that are dimly lit because they convey an image of untrustworthiness. Layouts that use natural light not only are less expensive to operate but also give businesses an open and cheerful look and actually can boost sales. A series of studies by energy research firm Heschong Mahone Group found that work space designs that include natural light can increase employee productivity by 6 to 16 percent. In addition, retail stores that use natural light experience sales that are on average 40 percent higher than those of similar stores that use traditional fluorescent lighting.[164] In a retail environment, proper lighting should highlight featured products and encourage customers to stop and look at them.

Sustainability and Environmentally Friendly Design

Businesses are designing their buildings in more environmentally friendly ways not only because it is the right thing to do but also because it saves money. Companies are using recycled materials; installing high-efficiency lighting, fixtures, and appliances; and using Leadership in Energy and Environmental Design (LEED) principles in construction and renovation. LEED principles cover every phase of construction and include concepts ranging from installing self-contained, solar-powered energy sources and water-conserving plumbing fixtures to collecting rainwater for use in landscape irrigation and using renewable and recycled construction materials. Starbucks, the popular chain of coffee shops, built its latest roasting plant in Sandy Run, South Carolina, to LEED standards and has built several LEED-certified outlets out of old shipping containers that otherwise would have gone to a landfill. Some of these outlets are micro drive-throughs. At just 380 square feet, they are the smallest Starbucks stores in existence, but they allow the company to access high-traffic locations that otherwise would be out of reach and can be operating in just one week. Other outlets are larger, made of several shipping containers connected to or stacked on top of one another. Each "recycled" outlet contains all of the amenities of a "regular" Starbucks store and is decorated to reflect the local character of each location. The company plans to build more "green" outlets in the future.[165] Other companies are transforming what was once "wasted space" into useful functions. The owner of a building in Bethesda, Maryland, that houses multiple restaurants recently converted its rooftop into a garden oasis that, in its first year, supplied more than 7,000 pounds of fresh produce to its restaurant tenants.[166]

Layout: Maximizing Revenues, Increasing Efficiency, or Reducing Costs

LO6

Explain the principles of effective layouts for retailers, service businesses, and manufacturers.

The ideal layout for a building depends on the type of business it houses and on the entrepreneur's strategy for gaining a competitive edge. An effective layout can reinforce a brand and contribute to a company's desired image.

ENTREPRENEURIAL PROFILE: John Kunkel: Lime Fresh Mexican Grill John Kunkel, founder of Lime Fresh Mexican Grill, a small chain of casual burrito restaurants that Ruby Tuesday recently purchased, was repulsed by the hard plastic interiors of other quick-service Mexican restaurants. He contends that the design sends a clear signal to customers: "Finish your food quickly and make room for the next customer." Kunkel wanted to create a comfortable, welcoming environment that supported his company's image. He says he took cues from Starbucks and tried to make Lime Fresh Mexican Grill a social place where people can come to hang out. A large tub filled with ice and bottled beverages sits on a countertop, reminding customers of a friendly backyard cookout. Large windows that diffuse natural light, golden-toned walls, warm hammered-copper and brick accents, and comfortable chairs invite customers to linger inside, and umbrella-covered sidewalk tables beckon hungry customers to sit and relax. Dining room attendants called "fronters" greet customers and provide café-style service, delivering beverage refills, chips, salsas, and desserts.[167] ■

Retailers design their layouts with the goal of maximizing sales revenue and reinforcing the brand; manufacturers see layout as an opportunity to increase efficiency and productivity and to lower costs.

Layout for Retailers

Retail layout is the arrangement of merchandise and displays in a store. For retailers, layout is all about understanding a company's target customers and crafting every element of a store's design to appeal to those customers. Paco Underhill says, "A store's interior architecture is fundamental to the customers' experience—the stage upon which a retail company functions."[168] A retail layout should pull customers into the store and make it easy for them to locate merchandise; compare price, quality, and features; and ultimately make a purchase. This is another area in which small stores may have an advantage over their larger rivals. Small stores allow customers to find the products that they want to purchase more quickly and easily than in giant "big-box" stores, often with the help of a friendly, knowledgeable salesperson. (The typical Wal-Mart Supercenter carries about 120,000 different items.[169])

In addition, a floor plan should take customers past displays of other items they may buy on impulse. Customers make a significant percentage of their buying decisions once they enter a store, meaning that the right layout can boost sales significantly. One of the most comprehensive studies of impulse purchases found that one-third of shoppers made impulse purchases. The median impulse purchase amount was $30 but varied by product category, ranging from $6 for food items to $60 for jewelry and sporting goods. Although the urge to take advantage of discounts was the most common driver of unplanned buying decisions, the location and attractiveness of the display also were important factors.[170]

Retailers have long recognized that some locations within a store are superior to others. Customer traffic patterns give the owner a clue to the best location for the highest gross margin items. Generally, prime selling space should be reserved for products that carry the highest markups. If customers come into the store for specific products and have a tendency to walk directly to those items, placing complementary products in their path boosts sales. Grocery stores typically place their dairy displays at the back of the store because those items are some of the most commonly purchased items; requiring shoppers to walk past hundreds of other items to get to the dairy section increases the chances that they will purchase some of the other items. Displays at the ends of aisles, called end caps, are some of the most valuable space in retail stores. A study by the National Retail Hardware Association reports that a product placed on an end cap display sells eight times faster than the same item placed on an aisle shelf.[171]

Layout in a retail store evolves from a clear understanding of customers' buying habits. Observing customer behavior helps entrepreneurs identify "hot spots" where merchandise sells briskly and "cold spots" where it may languish indefinitely. Hannaford Supermarket, a supermarket chain based in Scarborough, Maine, with 189 stores, recently unveiled a new prototype store in Bedford, New Hampshire, whose design is based on extensive research with shoppers and an evaluation of the best practices of leading competitors. The new design features a colorful, attractive produce display in the primary hot spot, the front section of the store to the right of the front door. Because market research shows that produce is the most important factor in choosing a grocery store and winning customer loyalty, Hannaford located its produce section there and created a more open layout. Produce displays also use wood shelves, carts, and display tables as symbolics to send a message of freshness. Customer feedback led Hannaford to place its meat department adjacent to the produce section. The store also includes an impressive Brew Room that offers more than 230 quality craft beers. The company placed its expanded line of wines (more than 900 types, curated by an award-winning sommelier) on the last aisle of the store, which managers say is usually a "boring" aisle—but not at this location. Because more shoppers want to purchase prepared foods in grocery stores, Hannaford created Hannaford Kitchen, a sit-down café with options such as custom stir-fry, sandwiches, salads, burritos, and fried chicken. The store includes a meeting room that local nonprofit organizations can use for free. The innovative layout creates the image of a series of small specialty shops inside a large supermarket and incorporates an attractive décor that communicates a message of freshness, sophistication, and quality.[172]

Business owners should display merchandise as neatly and attractively as possible. Customers' eyes focus on displays, which tell them the type of merchandise the business sells. It is easier for customers to relate to one display than to a rack or shelf of merchandise. Open displays of merchandise can surround a focal display, creating an attractive selling area. Spacious aisles provide shoppers an open view of merchandise and reduce the likelihood of shoplifting. One study found that shoppers, especially women, are reluctant to enter narrow aisles in a store. Narrow aisles force customers to jostle past one another (experts call this the "butt-brush factor"), making them extremely nervous. The same study also found that placing shopping

Hands On . . . How To

Create the Ideal Layout

As the world shifts to a knowledge-based economy, more workers are engaging in office work, in which measuring productivity sometimes proves difficult. Research shows that a well-designed office is one of the simplest and most cost-effective ways to increase workers' productivity and satisfaction. For instance, if a company builds and operates an office building, the cost of initial construction accounts for just 2 percent of the building's total cost over 30 years. Operating expenses account for 6 percent. The remaining 92 percent of the total cost of operating the building over 30 years goes to paying the salaries and benefits of the people who occupy the space! The implication of this research is that top-performing companies recognize that their employees account for the largest portion of the total cost of a work environment and make adequate investments to ensure that the work space maximizes their efficiency, satisfaction, and productivity. Unfortunately, many other companies remain stuck in the antiquated cubicle culture that provides the fodder for so many Dilbert cartoon strips and that squelches individual expression, collaboration with colleagues, and creativity. Research from international design firm Gensler shows that only one in four employees in the United States is in an optimal work environment; the remaining 75 percent struggle in inefficient, poorly designed work spaces that inhibit their productivity, limit their innovative ability, and minimize their level of engagement with their work.

Vasilyev/Shutterstock

In the early to mid-twentieth century, companies used office layouts that resembled factory layouts with workers sitting in long rows performing repetitive tasks. The layout reflected management's attitude that workers were simply parts in the company machinery. In the 1960s and 1970s, the landscape office emerged, featuring a design in which managers and their staffs sat together so that they could accomplish related tasks efficiently. In the 1980s, as real estate prices escalated, companies used cubicles as an efficient way to pack lots of workers into a limited amount of space, giving cubicles the reputation of housing employees in the same way that a hive houses bees. Today, office designs are more open and reflect the changing nature of work: Small teams of employees collaborate on projects, and creativity improves when employees from different parts of the company exchange ideas as a result of impromptu encounters. Modern offices employ furniture, features, and designs that are more flexible, allowing employees to shift them according to the tasks they need to perform.

At Pandora's, location in New York City, the design includes open spaces punctuated by amenities such as recreation areas for ping-pong tables, centralized kitchen areas with stocked pantries that encourage employees to gather, and a yoga room. Dedicated offices and workstations are few, and work areas incorporate a flexible design that allows employees to interact and collaborate when they need to and retreat into private spaces when they need to concentrate and focus. Employees flow from one work environment to another, depending on which one suits the tasks they are performing at the time. Each of the two floors includes interactive spaces that take the form of smaller "telephone booths," "huddle" areas, plenty of relaxed, comfortable seating spaces, and more traditional conference rooms. According to one expert, the idea is to encourage collaboration, stimulate creativity, and produce a "hotbox for ideas."

What principles make for a good office design and allow a company to get the most out of its investment in designing a work space?

Observe How Employees Use the Existing Space

The nature of employees' work changes over time, and work space needs change as well. A design that was suitable a few years ago may be inappropriate today. Entrepreneurs should take the time to observe employees at work. When do workers use office space? Which spaces are at maximum capacity, and which ones are underutilized? Why? Does the existing design support employees' ability to do their jobs or hinder it? Red flags include the following:

- People whose work requires collaboration do not naturally interact with their colleagues during the course of a day.

- Employees waste a lot of time in transit to meeting rooms, printers, copiers, and other office equipment.

- Workers are competing for the use of certain pieces of office equipment.

- An area is either typically overcrowded or empty.

- Employees schedule meetings at nearby coffee shops or restaurants because these places provide better common space for collaboration.

Involve Employees in the Redesign

One of the biggest mistakes designers make is creating a new layout without the input of the people who will be working in

(continued)

Hands On . . . How To (continued)

the space. Asking employees up front for ideas and suggestions is essential to producing an effective layout. What barriers to their work does the existing design create? How can you eliminate them? One surefire way to alienate employees is to fail to involve them in the redesign of their work space.

Plan the New Design

Redesigning a work space can be a major undertaking. The process goes much more smoothly, and the end result is superior, for companies that invest in significant planning than for those companies that do not. Successful designs usually result when entrepreneurs and their employees define two to five priorities, such as increased collaboration, enhanced productivity, reduced absenteeism and turnover, or improved energy efficiency, for design professionals to achieve.

Creating an effective design does not have to be expensive, but it does demand a good plan. An extensive report, *Innovative Workplace Strategies*, from the General Services Administration, lists the following hallmarks of the productive workplace:

- *Spatial equity.* Do workers have adequate space to accomplish their tasks and have access to privacy, natural light, and aesthetics?

- *Healthfulness.* Is the work space a healthy environment with access to air, light, and water? Is it free of harmful contaminants and excess noise?

- *Flexibility.* Can workers adjust their work environment to respond to important functional changes?

- *Comfort.* Can workers adjust light, temperature, acoustic levels, and furnishings to their individual preferences?

- *Technological connectivity.* Can onsite and offsite workers stay connected with one another and gain access to the information they need? Does technology enhance their ability to collaborate on projects?

- *Reliability.* Does the workplace have dependable mechanical and technological systems that receive proper support?

- *Sense of place.* Does the workplace decor and atmosphere reflect the company's mission and brand? Does the space create a culture that is appropriate for accomplishing the tasks at hand?

When Eventbrite, the company that provides a platform for organizers to promote and sell tickets to events, moved into its new office in downtown San Francisco, it created an open, flexible environment that eliminates dedicated workstations, emphasizing instead a design that enables people to choose the space that best suits the tasks they are performing. Although their work requires a great deal of collaboration, employees also need time to focus and concentrate, and the space gives them the ability to withdraw to private spaces, including a library and hooded chairs. Thirty 60-inch monitors placed strategically throughout the work space give employees real-time feedback on key company metrics and help them to see how their jobs affect the company's performance. The open layout gives employees a visual connection to

one another, sends a message that "we are all in this together," and encourages free-flowing communication and collaboration.

Create a Design That Helps People Get Their Work Done

A work space should *never* impede employees' productivity—although most designs do. A proper layout should *enhance* employees' ability to do their jobs. The best work spaces balance employees' needs for interaction and collaboration with their needs for focus and concentration. Gensler's research shows that workers at companies that give employees choices about where (and when) they work are more innovative and more productive. At animated film company Pixar, the work space is designed to encourage collaboration among employees; it includes large open areas with large couches and high-top tables that encourage impromptu meetings. Even the company's volleyball and basketball courts encourage employee interaction, making Pixar headquarters a haven of creativity. However, recognizing that sometimes employees must work "heads down" without interruption, Pixar also created more private, quiet spaces.

Design for Sustainability

Work spaces today incorporate energy-efficient fixtures, recycled materials, toxin-free substances, and green spaces that incorporate live plants. One study in the United Kingdom reports that incorporating plants into office spaces increased workers' productivity by 15 percent. Modern sustainable designs recognize that work spaces have a significant impact on employees' well-being, motivation, and engagement. Creating spaces that focus on the well-being of workers' bodies and souls improves their work performance. Many companies incorporate outdoor spaces, such as terraces for dining or walking trails, designed to be areas of respite for employees. Gensler includes active furniture, such as standing desks and treadmill desks, in its designs.

Rely on Continuous Improvement

A redesign project is not finished just because the work is complete. Smart entrepreneurs resist the temptation to sit back and admire the finished product and think about how happy they are to be "done." Instead, they recognize that no redesign, however well planned, is perfect. They are willing to tweak the project and to make necessary adjustments to meet employees' changing needs.

Sources: Based on *2013 U.S. Workplace Survey: Key Findings*, Gensler, 2013, pp. 1–12; Julia Hartz, "Design Your Office Around Your Business's Goals," *Inc.*, September 2014, p. 122; Lana Bortolot, "Workers First," *Entrepreneur*, August 2014, pp. 52–55; Shereen Lehman, "Green Offices Make Employees Happier and More Productive: Study," *Reuters*, October 2, 2014, www.reuters.com/article/us-health-psychology-office-plants-idUSKCN0HR2DW20141002; Stephanie Orma, "Branding at Work," *Entrepreneur*, February 2014, p. 20; Lisa Ward, "Design for Working," *Wall Street Journal*, April 28, 2014, p. R6; Ben Kesling and James R. Hagerty, "Say Goodbye to the Office Cubicle," *Wall Street Journal*, April 3, 2013, pp. B1, B6; "How to Design an Office That Makes Everyone Happy," *Inc.*, November 2013, p. 60; Aaron Herrington, "Pixar Is Inspiration for Modea's New Headquarters," *Modea*, September 19, 2011, www.modea.com/blog/pixar-isinspiration-for-modeas-new-headquarters; Jane Hodges, "How to Build a Better Office," *BNET*, 2007, www.bnet.com/2403-13056_23-190221.html; Julie Schlosser, "The Great Escape," *Fortune*, March 20, 2006, pp. 107–110; Michael Lev-Ram, "How to Make Your Workspace Better," *Business 2.0*, November 2006, pp. 58–60; Jeffrey Pfeffer, "Thinking Outside the Cube," *Business 2.0*, April 2007, p. 60; and *Innovative Workplace Strategies*, General Services Administration, Office of Governmentwide Policy, Office of Real Property, 2003, p. 70.

baskets in several areas around a store can increase sales. Seventy-five percent of shoppers who pick up a basket buy something, compared to just 34 percent of customers who do not pick up a basket.[173]

Retailers can also boost sales by displaying together items that complement each other. For example, displaying ties near dress shirts or handbags next to shoes often leads to multiple sales. Placement of items on store shelves is important, too, and store owners must keep their target customers in mind when stocking shelves. For example, putting hearing aid batteries on bottom shelves where elderly shoppers have trouble getting to them or placing popular children's toys on top shelves where little ones cannot reach them hurts sales. Retailers also must avoid wasting prime selling space on nonselling functions (e.g., storage, office, fitting rooms, and so on). For a typical retailer, the ratio of selling to nonselling space is 80/20. Although nonselling activities are necessary for a successful retail operation, they should not occupy a store's most valuable selling space. Shoppers who use fitting rooms to try on garments make purchases 67 percent of the time, compared to a 10 percent purchase rate for shoppers who do not use a fitting room. Clothing retailer Ann Taylor recently revamped its fitting rooms, enhancing their lighting to be more flattering, enlarging them to accommodate shoppers' and their friends, and making them more like a shopper's walk-in closet. The company also added displays of complementary merchandise, such as camisoles, underwear, and shapewear, to its fitting room areas.[174] Some retailers have added wall-mounted tablets to their dressing rooms that give shoppers access to the store's inventory system so that they can find items in other sizes or colors or summon a sales associate. Many retailers place their nonselling departments in the rear of the building, recognizing the value of each foot of space in a retail store and locating their most profitable items in the best-selling areas.

The checkout process is a particularly important ingredient in customer satisfaction and often ranks as a sore spot with shoppers. Research shows that shoppers tend to be impatient, willing to wait only about four minutes in a checkout line before becoming exasperated; after eight minutes, customers are likely to abandon the checkout line and leave the store without making a purchase. In addition, more than 75 percent of customers say long checkout lines make them less likely to return to a store.[175] Retailers are discovering that simplifying and speeding up the checkout process increases customer convenience, lowers shoppers' stress levels, and makes them more likely to come back. Studies conclude that having shoppers form a single line that leads to multiple cashiers results in faster checkout times than having shoppers form multiple lines in front of multiple cashiers.[176] Some retailers have eliminated cash registers altogether, use roving clerks equipped with mobile devices to hasten the checkout process. Burberry's, the iconic British luxury brand that sells men's, women's, and children's clothing and accessories, allows shoppers to check out anywhere in the store with iPad-carrying sales clerks. Recognizing that many customers who shop in retail stores expect the same ease, speed, and convenience of their online shopping experience, designer Rebecca Minkoff gives customers in her retail shops a self-checkout option right in the dressing room or anywhere else in the store by using their phones to scan the QR code on a security tag and paying with a debit or credit card. Like Burberry's, Minkoff's sales representatives carry mobile devices to check out customers anywhere. The goal is to reduce customers' "pain of paying," enhance the convenience of their shopping experience, and encourage them to interact with sales people (unless they choose the self-checkout option).[177] Eliminating cash registers also opens prime store space in which to display more merchandise for sale.

The value of a store's space for generating sales depends on floor location in a multistory building, location with respect to aisles and walkways, and proximity to entrances. Space values decrease as the distance from the main entry-level floor increases. Selling areas on the main level contribute a greater portion to sales than those on other floors in the building because they offer greater exposure to customers than either basement or higher-level locations. Therefore, main-level locations carry a greater share of rent than other levels.

Space values also depend on their position relative to the store entrance. Typically, the farther away an area is from the entrance, the lower is its value. Another consideration is that in North America, most shoppers turn to the right after entering a store and move around it counterclockwise. (This apparently is culturally determined; studies of shoppers in Australia and Great Britain find that they turn *left* on entering a store.) Finally, only about one-fourth of a store's

FIGURE 14.6

Space Values for a Small Store

Source: From Dale M. Lewison, *Retailing*, 6th ed. Copyright © 1997 by Dale M. Lewison. Reprinted with permission.

customers will go more than halfway into the store. Based on these characteristics, Figure 14.6 illustrates space values for a typical small store.

Retail layout is a never-ending experiment in which entrepreneurs learn what works and what doesn't.

Layout for Manufacturers

Manufacturing layout decisions take into consideration the arrangement of departments, workstations, machines, and stock-holding points within a production facility. The objective is to arrange these elements to ensure a smoothly flowing, efficient, and highly productive work flow. Manufacturing facilities have come under increased scrutiny as companies attempt to improve quality, reduce inventory, and increase productivity through layouts that are integrated, flexible, and efficient. Facility layout has a dramatic effect on product processing, material handling, storage, production volume, and quality.

FACTORS IN MANUFACTURING LAYOUT The ideal layout for a manufacturing operation depends on several factors, including the following:

- *Type of product.* Product design and quality standards, whether the product is produced for inventory or for order, and physical properties, such as the size of materials and products, special handling requirements, susceptibility to damage, and perishability, influence the ideal manufacturing layout.

- *Type of production process.* Production process factors include technology used, types of materials handled, means of providing a service, and processing requirements in terms of number of operations involved and amount of interaction between departments and work centers.

- *Ergonomic considerations.* It is important to ensure worker safety, avoid injuries and accidents, and increase productivity.

- *Economic considerations.* Economic considerations include volume of production; costs of materials, machines, workstations, and labor; pattern and variability of demand; and cycle time, the amount of time between receiving a customer's order and delivering the finished product.

- *Space availability within the facility itself.* It is important to ensure that the space will adequately meet current and future manufacturing needs.

TYPES OF MANUFACTURING LAYOUTS Manufacturing layouts are categorized either by the work flow in a plant or by the production system's function. There are three basic types of layouts that manufacturers can use separately or in combination—product, process, and fixed position—and they are differentiated by their applicability to different conditions of manufacturing volume.

Product Layouts In a **product (line) layout**, a manufacturer arranges workers and equipment according to the sequence of operations performed on the product. Conceptually, the flow is an unbroken line from raw material input or customer arrival to finished goods or customer departure. This type of layout is applicable to rigid-flow, high-volume, continuous-process or a mass-production operation or when the service or product is highly standardized. Automobile assembly plants, paper mills, and oil refineries are examples of product layouts. Product layouts offer the advantages of low material handling costs; simplified tasks that can be done with low-cost, lower-skilled labor; small amounts of work-in-process inventory; and relatively simplified production control activities. All units are routed along the same fixed path, and scheduling consists primarily of setting a production rate.

product (line) layout
an arrangement of workers and equipment according to the sequence of operations performed on a product.

Disadvantages of product layouts are their inflexibility, monotony of job tasks, high fixed investment in specialized equipment, and heavy interdependence of all operations. A breakdown in one machine or at one workstation can idle the entire line. This layout also requires business owners to duplicate many pieces of equipment in the manufacturing facility, which for a small firm can be cost prohibitive.

Cellular Layouts In a cellular layout, workers who perform related tasks are organized into a small "cell" so that they can work as a team to move a single item completely through the manufacturing process rather than perform individualized work on multiple batches of items before passing them on to the next station for more processing. The goal is to minimize the time required to move an item through the entire production process. After learning about the principles of lean manufacturing, Jan Erickson, founder of Janska, a manufacturer of lightweight outerwear for women, including jackets, coats, vests, scarves, capes, and other items, based in Colorado Springs, Colorado, recently switched the skilled sewers in her small factory to a cellular layout. Previously, the company's sewers worked on batches of garments before passing them to the next worker in the assembly line in big bundles. In the new one-piece flow system, sewers sit next to each other and work on one garment at a time. On their first test piece using the new system, the workers completed a cape in just five minutes, compared to the normal 10 to 12 minutes required under the old layout. Erickson says that not only has quality improved, but the new one-piece flow also allows the sewers to produce more than 300 garments on many days, a huge increase over the company's previous production rate.[178]

Process Layouts In a **process layout**, a manufacturer groups workers and equipment according to the general functions they perform, without regard to any particular product or customer. Process layouts are appropriate when production runs are short, when demand shows considerable variation and the costs of holding finished goods inventory are high, or when the service or product is customized. Process layouts offer the advantages of being flexible for doing custom work and promoting job satisfaction by offering employees diverse and challenging tasks. Its disadvantages are the higher costs of materials handling, requirement of more skilled labor, lower productivity, and more complex production control.

process layout
an arrangement of workers and equipment according to the general function they perform, without regard to any particular product or customer.

ENTREPRENEURIAL PROFILE: C.C. Filson C.C. Filson, a company that began supplying gold miners with outdoor gear in 1897, recently moved into a new 57,400-square-foot factory in which the company manufactures its line of durable luggage and bags. The new factory uses an efficient process layout that is divided into three departments, each of which focuses on making 10 similar types of products. Workstations are arranged so that products flow smoothly from one to the next without having to double-back (as they did in the old, cramped factory). Quality manager Teresa Whittaker says making this change alone saved the company huge amounts of time and money. In the new factory, workers use rolling carts to move bundles of fabric and leather to their workstations, which are equipped with special chairs designed for a sewing operation, rather than hauling them by hand in the old factory. Managers say that since moving into the new factory, employee productivity has increased by more than 50 percent.[179] ∎

fixed position layout
an arrangement in which materials do not move down a production line but rather, because of their weight, size, or bulk, are assembled on the spot.

Fixed Position Layouts In a **fixed position layout**, materials do not move down a line as in a production layout but rather, because of the weight, size, or bulk of the final product, are assembled in one spot. In other words, workers and equipment go to the material rather than having the material flow down a line to them. Aircraft assembly plants and shipyards typify this kind of layout.

DESIGNING PRODUCTION LAYOUTS Two important criteria for selecting and designing a layout are workers' productivity and material handling costs. An effective layout allows workers to maximize their productivity by providing them the tools and a system for doing their jobs properly. For example, a layout that requires a production worker to step away from the work area in search of the proper tool is inefficient. An effective manufacturing layout avoids what lean manufacturing principles identify as the seven forms of waste:

- *Transportation.* Unnecessary movement of inventory, materials, and information
- *Inventory.* Carrying unnecessary inventory
- *Motion.* Engaging in motion that does not add value to the product or process
- *Waiting.* Periods of inactivity when people, materials, or information are idle
- *Overproduction.* Producing more than customer demand dictates
- *Processing.* Using tools and procedures that are inappropriate for the job
- *Defects.* Producing poor-quality products, which requires scrapping or reworking material

In its newest factory in Miyagi, Japan, Toyota positioned cars on the assembly line side by side rather than tip to tail, reducing the required length of the production line by 35 percent and increasing worker productivity by allowing employees to walk shorter distances between cars.[180]

Manufacturers can lower materials handling costs by using the following principles that are hallmarks of a lean, efficient manufacturing layout:

- Planned materials flow pattern
- Straight-line layout where possible
- Straight, clearly marked aisles
- "Backtracking" of products kept to a minimum
- Related operations located close together
- Minimum amount of in-process inventory on hand
- Easy adjustment to changing conditions
- Minimum materials handling distances
- Minimum of manual handling of materials and products
- Ergonomically designed work centers
- Minimum distances between workstations and processes
- No unnecessary rehandling of material
- Minimum handling between operations
- Minimum storage
- Materials delivered to production employees just in time
- Materials efficiently removed from the work area
- Maximum visibility; maintain clear lines of site to spot problems and improve safety
- Orderly materials handling and storage

- Good housekeeping; minimize clutter

- Maximum flexibility

- Maximum communication

Using the principles of lean manufacturing can improve efficiency, quality, and productivity and lower costs.

ENTREPRENEURIAL PROFILE: Bensonwood Homes Bensonwood Homes, a premier designer and builder of energy-efficient timber frame homes based in Walpole, New Hampshire, applies the 5S principles (sort, shine, simplify, standardize, and sustain) that world-class automaker Toyota uses in its lean manufacturing process. (Bensonwood also added a sixth "S" principle, safety.) As the company's 65 employees began to buy into the process, improvements quickly became apparent. Employees applied lean and 5S principles to processes for both standard and custom products; productivity increased by 40 percent, setup time for several machining processes decreased by 90 percent, and the company experienced dramatic reductions in costs associated with the seven forms of waste.[181] ∎

MyLab Entrepreneurship

If your instructor is using MyLab Entrepreneurship, go to www.pearson.com/mylab/ entrepreneurship to complete the problems marked with this icon ⭐ .

Chapter Summary by Learning Objective

1. **Explain the stages in the location decision: choosing the region, the state, the city, and the specific site.**

   - The location decision is one of the most important decisions an entrepreneur ever makes, given its long-term effects on the company. An entrepreneur should look at the choice as a series of increasingly narrow decisions: Which region of the country? Which state? Which city? Which site? Choosing the right location requires an entrepreneur to evaluate potential sites with his or her target customers in mind. Demographic statistics are available from a wide variety of sources, but government agencies such as the Census Bureau have a wealth of detailed data that can guide an entrepreneur in his or her location decision.

2. **Describe the location criteria for retail and service businesses.**

   - For retailers, the location decision is especially crucial. Retailers must consider the size of the trade area, the compatibility of surrounding businesses, the degree of competition, the suitability of the surrounding transportation network, physical and psychological barriers, volume of customer traffic, adequacy of parking spots, a site's reputation, and the site's visibility.

3. **Outline the location options for retail and service businesses: central business districts,** neighborhoods, shopping centers and malls, near competitors, shared spaces, inside large retail stores, nontraditional locations, at home, and on the road.

   - Retail and service businesses have nine basic location options: central business districts; neighborhoods; shopping centers and malls; near competitors; shared spaces; inside large retail stores; nontraditional locations, such as museums, sports arenas, and college campuses; at home; and on the road.

4. **Explain the site selection process for manufacturers.**

   - A manufacturer's location decision is strongly influenced by local zoning ordinances. Some areas offer industrial parks designed specifically to attract manufacturers. Two crucial factors for most manufacturers are the reliability (and the cost of transporting) raw materials and the quality and quantity of available labor.

   - A foreign trade zone is a specially designated area in or near a U.S. customs port of entry that allows resident companies to import materials and components from foreign countries; assemble, process, manufacture, or package them; and then ship the finished product while either reducing or eliminating tariffs and duties.

- Business incubators are locations that offer flexible, low-cost rental space to their tenants as well as business and consulting services. Their goal is to nurture small companies until they are ready to "graduate" into the business community. Many government agencies and universities sponsor incubator locations.

5. **Describe the criteria used to analyze the layout and design considerations of a building, including the Americans with Disabilities Act.**

- When evaluating the suitability of a particular building, an entrepreneur should consider several factors: size (Is it large enough to accommodate the business with some room for growth?), construction and external appearance (Is the building structurally sound, and does it create the right impression for the business?), entrances (Are they inviting?), legal issues (Does the building comply with the Americans with Disabilities Act? If not, how much will it cost to bring it up to standard?), signs (Are they legible,

well located, and easy to see?), interior (Does the interior design contribute to our ability to make sales? Is it ergonomically designed?), and lights and fixtures (Is the lighting adequate for the tasks workers will be performing? What is the estimated cost of lighting?).

6. **Explain the principles of effective layouts for retailers, service businesses, and manufacturers.**

- Layout for retail stores and service businesses depends on the owner's understanding of his or her customers' buying habits. Some areas of a retail store generate more sales per square foot and therefore are more valuable.

- The goal of a manufacturer's layout is to create a smooth, efficient work flow. Three basic options exist: product layout, process layout, and fixed position layout. Two key considerations are worker productivity and materials handling costs.

MyLab Entrepreneurship

If your instructor is using MyLab Entrepreneurship, go to **www.pearson.com/mylab/entrepreneurship** for Auto-graded writing questions as well as the following Assisted-graded writing questions:

1. Explain the Americans with Disabilities Act. Which businesses does it affect? What is its purpose?
2. According to market research firm NPD Group, in 1985, women purchased 70 percent of all men's clothing; today, women buy just 34 percent of men's apparel. What implications does this have for modern store layouts?

Discussion Questions

✪ 14-1. Buzz Price, the location expert who helped Disney and other entrepreneurs find the ideal locations for their businesses, described the location decision in the following way: "Guessing is dysfunctional. Using valid numbers to project performance is rational." How can entrepreneurs find "valid numbers" to help them project the performance of their businesses in different locations?

14-2. What factors should a manager consider when evaluating a region in which to locate a business? Where are such data available?

14-3. Outline the factors that are important when selecting a state in which to locate a business.

14-4. What factors should a seafood processing plant, a beauty shop, and an exclusive jewelry store consider in choosing a location? List factors for each type of business.

14-5. What intangible factors might enter into the entrepreneur's location decision?

14-6. What are zoning laws? How do they affect the location decision?

14-7. What is the trade area? What determines a small retailer's trade area?

14-8. Why is it important to discover more than just the number of passersby in a traffic count for a potential location?

14-9. What types of information can an entrepreneur collect from census data?

14-10. Why may a "cheap location" not be the "best location"?

14-11. What is a foreign trade zone? A business incubator? What advantages and disadvantages does each one offer a small business locating there?

14-12. Why is it costly for a small firm to choose a location that is too small?

14-13. What function does a small company's sign serve? What are the characteristics of an effective business sign?

14-14. What is ergonomics? Why should entrepreneurs apply the principles of ergonomics in the design of their facilities?

14-15. Explain the statement, "Not every portion of a small store's interior space is of equal value in generating sales revenue." What areas are most valuable?

✪ 14-16. What are some of the features that determine a good manufacturing layout?

Beyond the Classroom . . .

14-17. Select a specific type of business you would like to go into one day and use census data to choose a specific site for the business in the local region. What location factors are critical to the success of this business? Would it be likely to succeed in your hometown?

14-18. Interview a sample of local small business owners. How did they decide on their particular locations? What are the positive and negative features of their existing locations?

14-19. Visit the Web sites for *Entrepreneur* and *Fortune* magazines and find articles about the "best cities for (small) business." (For *Entrepreneur*, it is usually the October issue, and for *Fortune*, it is normally an issue in November.) Which cities are in the top 10? What factors did the magazine use to select these cities? Pick a city and explain what makes it an attractive location for a business.

14-20. Select a manufacturing operation, a wholesale business, or a retail store and evaluate their layouts using the guidelines presented in this chapter. What changes would you recommend? Why? How does the new layout contribute to a more effective operation? How much would the changes you suggest cost?

14-21. Every year, *Site Selection* magazine selects the states with the top business climates. Use the Internet to locate the latest state rankings. Which states top the list? Which states are at the bottom of the list? What factors affect a state's ranking? Why are these factors important to entrepreneurs' location decisions?

14-22. Visit the Web site for the Census Bureau, at www.census.gov. Go to the census data for your town and use it to discuss its suitability as a location for the following types of businesses:

- A new motel with 25 units
- A bookstore
- An exclusive women's clothing shop
- A Mexican restaurant
- A residential plumber
- A day care center
- A high-quality stereo shop
- A family hair care center

14-23. Visit the Census Bureau's Web site and use the American FactFinder section to prepare a demographic profile of your hometown or city or of the town or city in which you attend college. Using the demographic profile as an analytical tool, what kinds of businesses do you think would be successful there? Unsuccessful? Explain.

Endnotes

[1] Dennis Phillips, "Johnny's Lunch Turns 75 Years Old," *Post-Journal*, September 25, 2011, www.post-journal.com/page/content.detail/id/591527/Johnny-s-Lunch-Turns-75-Years-Old.html?nav=5003; Karen E. Klein, "Finding the Perfect Location," *Business Week*, March 24, 2008, www.businessweek.com/smallbiz/content/mar2008/sb20080324_098559.htm?chan=smallbiz_smallbiz+index+page_top+small+business+stories; Nora Parker, "Johnny's Lunch Plans Franchise Expansion with LI," *Directions Magazine*, October 8, 2007, www.directionsmag.com/article.php?article_id=2569&trv=1; Chris Knape, "New Diner Downtown Is Johnny on the Spot," *Grand Rapids Press*, May 12, 2008, p. B4.

[2] Mark Henricks, "Hot Spots," *Entrepreneur*, October 2005, pp. 68–74.

[3] Louis Mongello, "Walt Disney World History 101: How to Buy 27,000 Acres of Land and No One Notice," Gather.com, December 18, 2005, www.gather.com/viewArticle.jsp?articleId=281474976719796.

[4] Adam Bruns, "Looks Like We Have Companies," *Site Selection*, March 2013, www.siteselection.com/LifeSciences/2013/mar/diagnostics.cfm; Mark Arend, "Mountain Air Boosts Longevity," *Site Selection*, July 2013, p. 133.

[5] "Fine Dinering," *Entrepreneur*, April 2015, p. 94.

[6] Liz Welch and Trina Turk, "The Way I Work," *Inc.*, December 2012/January 2013, pp. 111–114.

[7] "Top States," *Site Selection*, March 2016, pp. 115–129.

[8] "Private Industry Workers, by Census Region and Division," U.S. Bureau of Labor Statistics, June 9, 2017, www.bls.gov/news.release/ecec.t07.htm.

[9] Jude Webber, "Modern Mexico: Location and Young Workforce Prove Attractive," *Financial Times*, March 4, 2015, p. 3; Douglas L. Donahue, "Why Manufacturers Are Choosing Mexico Over—and in Addition to—China," Area Development, August 2012, www.areadevelopment.com/BusinessGlobalization/August2012/why-manufacturers-are-nearshoring-to-Mexico-292711.shtml?Page=2; "Case Study Axiom: Manufacturing with Entrada Makes a Reel Difference," Entrada Group, www.entradagroup.com//wp-content/uploads/entrada-case-study-axiom.pdf.

[10] Steve Stackhouse-Kaelble, "Critical Site Selection Factor #1: Availability of Skilled Labor," Area Development, Q4, 2016, www.areadevelopment.com/skilled-workforce-STEM/q4-2016/skilled-labor-availability-site-selection-factor.shtml.

[11] Minghao Li, Stephan J. Goetz, Mark Partridge, and David A. Fleming, "Location Determinants of High-Growth Firms," *Entrepreneurship and Regional Development*, vol. 28, December 2015, pp. 1–29.

[12] "Educational Attainment: Provo, Utah," American FactFinder, U.S. Census Bureau, 2017, https://factfinder.census.gov/faces/tableservices/jsf/pages/productview.xhtml?src=CF.

[13] Andrew Zaleski, "A High-Tech Mecca Rises in Silicon Valley," *CNBC*, July 13, 2016, www.cnbc.com/2016/07/13/a-high-tech-mecca-rises-to-rival-silicon-valley.html; Jefferson

Graham, "Utah's Silicon Slopes," *USA Today*, September 20, 2015, p. 6B.

[14] Andrew Zaleski, "A High-Tech Mecca Rises in Silicon Valley," *CNBC*, July 13, 2016, www.cnbc.com/2016/07/13/a-high-tech-mecca-rises-to-rival-silicon-valley.html; Minna Wang, "SimpleCitizen, Campus Founders Fund's Third Portfolio Company, Is Simplifying Immigration," *Beehive Startups*, July 9, 2016, https://beehivestartups.com/simplecitizen-campus-founders-funds-third-portfolio-company-is-simplifying-immigration-ab8167a0a981#.eirenc1bn; "SimpleCitizen Is TurboTax for Immigration," Y Combinator, June 20, 2016, http://blog.ycombinator.com/simplecitizen/.

[15] "Economic Graph," LinkedIn, March 15, 2017, www.linkedin.com/economic-graph.

[16] Richard Florida, "The Business Case for Paying Workers More," *CityLab*, March 3, 2014, www.citylab.com/work/2014/03/case-paying-service-workers-more/8506/.

[17] James R. Hagerty and Greg Bensinger, "Taking a Ride in Uber's Robo-Taxi," *Wall Street Journal*, September 15, 2016, pp. B1–B2.

[18] "The Taxman Leaveth," *Site Selection*, July 2013, pp. 19–26.

[19] Tony Kiss, "Yes, We Can," *Greenville News*, May 30, 2015, pp. 1A, 4A.

[20] Jared Walczak, Scott Drenkard, and Joseph Henchman "2017 State Business Tax Climate Index," Tax Foundation, September 28, 2016, https://taxfoundation.org/2017-state-business-tax-climate-index/.

[21] Ruth Simon, "U.S. Cities Battle Each Other for Jobs with $45 Billion in Incentives," *Wall Street Journal*, March 16, 2017, www.wsj.com/articles/u-s-cities-battle-each-other-for-jobs-with-45-billion-in-incentives-1489675343.

[22] Ibid.

[23] "Google Fiber Cities and Their Start-Ups," StoryMapJS, 2017, https://uploads.knightlab.com/storymapjs/08a9d8ec65352c3dc1e63a6799849180/google-fiber-cities-and-their-startups/index.html; Securly Inc. Media Kit, Securly Inc., 2017, pp. 2–3.

[24] Patty Rasmussen, "Intrinsic Industry," *Site Selection*, March 2016, pp. 144–145.

[25] "Annual Kosmont-Rose Institute Cost of Doing Business Survey Report," *PR Newswire*, November 21, 2016, www.prnewswire.com/news-releases/annual-kosmont-rose-institute-cost-of-doing-business-survey-report-300366668.html.

[26] Erin Carlyle, "America's Fastest-Growing Cities 2016," *Forbes*, March 8, 2016, www.forbes.com/sites/erincarlyle/2016/03/08/americas-fastest-growing-cities-2016/#55a8b0081aac.

[27] Rachel Lerman, "Nurturing Austin's Tech Start-ups Is a Community Affair," *Seattle Times*, March 4, 2017, www.seattletimes.com/business/technology/nurturing-austins-tech-startups-is-a-community-affair/; "Aceable," *Crunchbase*, March 9, 2017, www.crunchbase.com/organization/aceable#/entity.

[28] Ron Ruggless, "Major Restaurant Chains Make First Moves in Alaska," *Nation's Restaurant News*, February 13, 2014, http://nrn.com/latest-headlines/major-restaurant-chains-make-first-moves-alaska; "Sunlight Hours by Month in Alaska," ABS Alaskan, www.absak.com/library/average-annual-insolation-alaska.

[29] Wil Brawley, "Meatball Shop Creator Shares Tactics for Site Selection, Motivation, More," Restaurant Hospitality, December 6, 2016, www.restaurant-hospitality.com/owner/meatball-shop-creator-shares-tactics-site-selection-motivation-more.

[30] Lillia Callum-Penso, "Taco Truckin' to Greenville," *Greenville News*, December 9, 2016, p. 5.

[31] "Clusters and Cluster Development," Institute for Strategy and Competitiveness, Harvard Business School, www.isc.hbs.edu/econ-clusters.htm.

[32] Emily Maltby, "Where the Action Is," *The Wall Street Journal*, August 23, 2011.

[33] Catherine Clifford, "This Kind of Cluster Could Actually Help Your Business," *Entrepreneur*, July 10, 2013, www.entrepreneur.com/article/227354; "Portman Visit Highlights Northeast Ohio's Liquid Crystal Assets," *The Business Journals*, January 10, 2013, www.bizjournals.com/prnewswire/press_releases/2013/01/10/DC40781; Catherine Clifford, "Ohio Gets Strong on Flexible Electronics Entrepreneurs," *Entrepreneur*, December 17, 2012, www.entrepreneur.com/article/225296.

[34] John Boyle, "Is a Beer Saturation Point Possible?" *Asheville Citizen-Times*, February 20, 2017, www.citizen-times.com/story/news/local/2017/02/19/beer-saturation-point-possible-asheville/97964520/.

[35] Tony Kiss, "New Brewery for South Asheville," *Asheville Citizen-Times*, May 27, 2016, www.citizen-times.com/story/news/local/2016/05/27/new-brewery-south-asheville/85031550/; John Boyle, "Is a Beer Saturation Point Possible?" *Asheville Citizen-Times*, February 20, 2017, www.citizen-times.com/story/news/local/2017/02/19/beer-saturation-point-possible-asheville/97964520/.

[36] Sally French, "There's a New Silicon Valley of Drones, and It Isn't in California," *Market Watch*, June 23, 2015, www.marketwatch.com/story/theres-a-new-silicon-valley-of-drones-and-it-isnt-in-california-2015-06-22; Bruce Gjovig, "Grand Forks UAS Companies Making Great Strides," *Droning On*, January 4, 2017, https://droningon.areavoices.com/2017/01/04/gjovig-grand-forks-uas-companies-making-great-strides/.

[37] Sally French, "There's a New Silicon Valley of Drones, and It Isn't in California," *Market Watch*, June 23, 2015, www.marketwatch.com/story/theres-a-new-silicon-valley-of-drones-and-it-isnt-in-california-2015-06-22; Bruce Gjovig, "Grand Forks UAS Companies Making Great Strides," *Droning On*, January 4, 2017, https://droningon.areavoices.com/2017/01/04/gjovig-grand-forks-uas-companies-making-great-strides/.

[38] "Doing Business: Measuring Business Regulations," World Bank, March 17, 2017, www.doingbusiness.org/rankings.

[39] "Time Required to Start a Business," World Bank, March 10, 2017, http://data.worldbank.org/indicator/IC.REG.DURS?name_desc=false.

[40] Lettie Teague, "Want to Open a Wine Store? Proceed with Caution," *Wall Street Journal*, May 10–11, 2014, p. D8.

[41] Julie V. Iovine, "Zoning Laws Grow Up," *Wall Street Journal*, January 19, 2012, p. D6.

[42] Rudolph Bell, "Eggs Up to Crack Downtown Market," *Greenville News*, May 10, 2014, p. 5B.

[43] Rick Montgomery, "In One KCK Neighborhood, the Present and the Future Collide,' *Kansas City Star*, April 18, 2015, www.kansascity.com/news/business/technology/article18882093.html.

[44] Jack Rosenberg, "Speed Rules," *Site Selection*, September 2015, p. 84.

[45] Ron Starner, "From the Small Screen to the Big Box," *Site Selection*, September 2015, pp. 99–102; Andrew Asch, "QVC: Living Large with First West Coast Distribution Center," *California Apparel News*, September 1, 2016, www.apparelnews.net/news/2016/sep/01/qvc-living-large-first-west-coast-distribution-cen/.

[46] Matt Evans, "Controversy Aside, Incentives Usually Deliver as Promised," *Business Journal*, July 5, 2010, www.bizjournals.com/triad/stories/2010/07/05/story2.html?page=all.

[47] "Worker Relocation Worries," *Inside Training Newsletter*, November 29, 2007, p. 1.

[48] Adam Bruns, "Grow if You Want To," *Site Selection*, July 2013, pp. 120–123.

[49]Starting a Convenience Store," Canada Business: Services for Entrepreneurs, November 25, 2008, www.canadabusiness.ca/servlet/ContentServer?cid=1099483437618&lang=en&pagename=CBSC_FE%2Fdisplay&c=GuideHowto.

[50]Bridget Weaver, "Designer to Open Derby Pop-up Shop in Norton Commons," *Louisville Business First*, March 2, 2017, www.bizjournals.com/louisville/news/2017/03/02/designer-to-open-derby-popup-shop-in-norton.html.

[51]Wil Brawley, "In-House Roasting, Quality Focus Fuel Subculture Coffee," *Restaurant Hospitality*, June 23, 2016, www.restaurant-hospitality.com/owner/house-roasting-quality-focus-fuel-subculture-coffee.

[52]"The Story of South 'n France," South 'n France, http://southnfrance.com/our-story/; Charlene Dupray, "A Trip Inside the Bon-Bon Factory," *Fortune Small Business*, February 14, 2008, http://money.cnn.com/2008/02/13/smbusiness/bon_bons.fsb/index.htm?section=money_topstories&utm_source=feedburner&utm_medium=feed&utm_campaign=Feed%3A+rss%2Fmoney_topstories+%28Top+Stories%29.

[53]*How Convenience Stores Work*, National Association of Convenience Stores, February 2017, p. 8.

[54]Rudolph Bell, "Cabela's to Bring Customers, Congestion to Greenville When It Opens," *The State*, February 18, 2014, www.thestate.com/2014/02/18/3274844/cabelas-to-bring-customers-congestion.html; Steve Van, "Go Big or Small in Sporting Goods?" *The Motley Fool*, December 3, 2012, http://beta.fool.com/readwriter/2012/12/03/go-big-or-small-sporting-goods/17741/; "Investor Relations: Company Profile," Cabela's, http://phx.corporate-ir.net/phoenix.zhtml?c=177739&p=irol-homeprofile.

[55]Dwight Muhlbrandt, "5 Ways to Gauge Impact of Online Promotions," *Restaurant Hospitality*, November 15, 2016, www.restaurant-hospitality.com/marketing/5-ways-gauge-impact-online-promotions.

[56]"Rapid Fired Pizza Opens Near Wright State University," *Pizza Marketplace*, March 24, 2016, www.pizzamarketplace.com/news/rapid-fired-pizza-opens-across-from-wright-state-university/.

[57]Caroline McMillan, "Location Makes a Big Difference for Small Retail Shops," *Charlotte Observer*, April 2, 2013, www.charlotteobserver.com/2013/04/02/v-print/3950725/location.

[58]Mark Harden, "Noodles and Company to Close 55 Restaurants," *Denver Business Journal*, February 9, 2017, www.bizjournals.com/denver/news/2017/02/09/noodles-company-to-close-55-restaurants.html.

[59]Matt Rosenberg, "About Reilly's Law of Retail Gravitation," About.com, http://geography.about.com/cs/citiesurbangeo/a/aa041403a.htm; G. I. Thrall and J. C. del Valle, "The Calculation of Retail Market Areas: The Reilly Model," *GeoInfoSystems* 7, no.4, (1997): 46–49.

[60]Alex Konrad, "Louisville Flies High," *Fortune*, October 18, 2010, pp. 32–33.

[61]Cherryh Cansler, "Restaurants Hitting Home Runs in Baseball Stadiums," *Fast Casual*, May 12, 2015, www.fastcasual.com/articles/restaurants-hitting-home-runs-in-baseball-stadiums/.

[62]Caroline McMillan, "Location Makes a Big Difference for Small Retail Shops," *Charlotte Observer*, April 2, 2013, www.charlotteobserver.com/2013/04/02/v-print/3950725/location.

[63]Melissa McCart, "Dine: 'Jinxed' Locations Can Beat the Odds," *Pittsburgh Post-Gazette*, May 18, 2014, www.post-gazette.com/life/dining/2014/05/18/Dine-Pittsburgh-restaurants-succeed-in-locations-where-others-failed/stories/201405180060.

[64]Eric Conner, "Sedran Furs, Longtime Fixture in Downtown, to Close," *Greenville News*, July 8, 2015, www.greenvilleonline.com/story/news/local/2015/07/08/sedran-furs-longtime-fixture-downtown-close/29856837/.

[65]Jennifer Duel Popvec, "Retail Landlords Keep Pushing Rent Up," *National Real Estate Investor*, October 8, 2015, http://nreionline.com/retail/retail-landlords-keep-pushing-rents; "Retail Outlook: United States," JLL, Q1, 2016, p. 5.

[66]Paul Wahba, "Top 10 Highest-Rent Shopping Strips in the World," *Fortune*, January 25, 2015, http://fortune.com/2015/01/21/10-highest-rent-shopping-strips-in-the-world/.

[67]Sharon Vander Meer, "Blowin' in the Wind New on Bridge Street," *In the Meadows*, July 3, 2013, http://inthemeadowslv.blogspot.com/2013/07/entrepreneur-spotlight-las-vegas-nm.html; *Las Vegas and San Miguel County 2014 Visitor and Relocation Guide*, Las Vegas First Independent Business Alliance, p. 28; Brett Schwartz, "Las Vegas, New Mexico: A Place with a Past (and a Future)," January 9, 2013, National Association of Development Organizations, www.nado.org/las-vegas_nm_vibrant_rural_communities/.

[68]Saabira Chaudhuri, "Retailer to Locate Stores More Centrally," *Wall Street Journal*, December 8, 2016, p. B7.

[69]Amy Johnson, "The Secret Sauce of 3 Beloved Businesses," *TownSquared*, April 29, 2016, https://townsquared.com/ts/bay-area-small-business-success/; Anna Volpacelli, "We Wanna Be Friends with Smitten Ice Cream Founder Robyn Sue Fisher," *7X7*, March 29, 2016, www.7x7.com/we-wanna-be-friends-with-smitten-ice-cream-founder-robyn-sue-fisher-1787326817.html.

[70]Paul Lukas, "Our Malls, Ourselves," *Fortune*, October 18, 2004, pp. 243–256.

[71]"Industry Conditions: Shopping Centers: Where Americans Buy, Socialize, Play, and Work," International Council of Shopping Centers, May 19, 2016, http://www.thecenterofshopping.com/news/industry-conditions-shopping-centers-where-americans-buy-socialize-play-and.

[72]Ibid.

[73]"U.S. Shopping Center Classifications and Characteristics," International Council of Shopping Centers and CoStar Reality, January 2017, p. 1.

[74]Ibid.

[75]Ibid.

[76]Ibid.

[77]Kris Hudson and Miguel Bustillo, "New Tricks for Old Malls," *Wall Street Journal*, October 26, 2011, pp. B1–B2.

[78]"U.S. Shopping Center Classifications and Characteristics," International Council of Shopping Centers and CoStar Reality, January 2017, p. 1; "2015 State of the Outlet Industry," *Value Retail News*, August 2015, p. 10.

[79]"U.S. Shopping Center Classifications and Characteristics," International Council of Shopping Centers and CoStar Reality, January 2017, p. 1.

[80]"U.S. Shopping Center Classifications and Characteristics," International Council of Shopping Centers and CoStar Reality, January 2017, p. 1.

[81]Ibid.

[82]"Saddle Creek Welcomes Three New Tenants," Shops of Saddle Creek, May 20, 2016, www.shopsofsaddlecreek.com/press/saddle-creek-welcomes-three-new-tenants/2130564954/.

[83]"U.S. Shopping Center Classifications and Characteristics," International Council of Shopping Centers and CoStar Reality, January 2017, p. 1.

[84]Ibid.

[85]"Facts," West Edmonton Mall, March 13, 2017, www.wem.ca/about-wem/facts.

[86]Krystina Gustafson, "Small Businesses Shake Up the Mix at Local Malls," *CNBC*, June 21, 2016, www.cnbc.com/2016/06/21/small-businesses-shake-up-the-mix-at-local-malls.html.

[87]"Class A Malls Standing Tall," Chilton Capital Management, July 2016, www.chiltoncapital.com/assets/reit-outlook—july-2016—final.pdf; Suzanne Kapner, "Retailers Bolt Aging Malls for More Luxurious Digs," *Wall Street Journal*, April 21, 2016, pp. B1, B6.

[88]Tom DiChristopher, "1 in 3 American Malls Are Doomed: Retail Consultant Jan Kniffen," *CNBC*, May 12, 2016, www.cnbc.com/2016/05/12/1-in-3-american-malls-are-doomed-retail-consultant-jan-kniffen.html; Hayley Peterson, "America's Shopping Malls Are Dying a Slow, Ugly Death," *Business Insider*, January 31, 2014, www.businessinsider.com/shopping-malls-are-going-extinct-2014-1.

[89]Suzanne Kapner, "Retailers Bolt Aging Malls for More Luxurious Digs," *Wall Street Journal*, April 21, 2016, pp. B1, B6.

[90]Natasha Geiling, "The Death and Rebirth of the American Mall," *Smithsonian*, November 25, 2014, www.smithsonianmag.com/arts-culture/death-and-rebirth-american-mall-180953444/.

[91]Esther Fung, "Mall's Woes Ripple Across Small Town," *Wall Street Journal*, January 20, 2017, p. A3.

[92]Kris Hudson, "Top-Tier Malls Are Getting a Facelift," *Wall Street Journal*, December 19, 2012, pp. C1, C10.

[93]"Mall of America Facts and Figures," Bloomington, March 9, 2017, www.bloomingtonmn.org/General-Landing-Pages/moa-special-offers%20/page/1/mall-of-america-facts.jsp.

[94]"Coworking Forecast: 26,000 Spaces and 3.8 Million Members by 2020," *Small Business Labs*, August 2, 2016, www.smallbizlabs.com/2016/08/coworking-forecast-44-million-members-in-2020.html; Marisol Medina, "Shared Workspaces Are Gaining Ground," *Greenville News*, October 25, 2015, p. 4E.

[95]Marisol Medina, "Shared Workspaces Are Gaining Ground," *Greenville News*, October 25, 2015, p. 4E; Amanda Coyne, "Coworking Spaces Expand," *Greenville News*, October 9, 2016, pp. 1E, 6E.

[96]Natalie Gagliordi, "Domino's Franchisee Using Self-Service Kiosks to Reach College Crowd," *Pizza Marketplace*, May 10, 2013, www.pizzamarketplace.com/articles/dominos-franchisee-using-self-service-kiosks-to-reach-college-crowd/.

[97]Abe Hardesty, "Kiosks Add Spice to Holiday Shopping," *Greenville News*, December 4, 2016, p. 5A.

[98]"Dunkin' Donuts Offers Even More Convenience by Opening New, Non-Traditional Locations from Coast-to-Coast," *PR Newswire*, February 16, 2016, www.prnewswire.com/news-releases/dunkin-donuts-offers-even-more-convenience-by-opening-new-non-traditional-locations-from-coast-to-coast-300219149.html.

[99]"Submit a Location," Subway, March 2017, www.subway.com/en-us/ownafranchise/submitalocation#.

[100]"Subway MS Stolzenfels Koblenz Germany," *WayMarking*, March 2017, www.waymarking.com/waymarks/WMK0JC_Subway_MS_Stolzenfels_Koblenz_Germany; Eno Alfred, "Six Crazy Subway Locations," *CNN Money*, March 10, 2011, http://money.cnn.com/galleries/2011/fortune/1103/gallery.the_6_craziest_subway_locations.fortune/; Alan J. Liddle, "10 Non-Traditional Subway Restaurants," *Nation's Restaurant News*, July 26, 2011, http://nrn.com/article/10-non-traditional-subway-restaurants; Bret Thom, "The New Nontraditional Location," *Nation's Restaurant News*, October 24, 2011, http://nrn.com/article/new-nontraditional-location.

[101]"Frequently Asked Questions," U.S. Small Business Administration Office of Advocacy, June 2016, p. 3.

[102]"Small Business Owners Find Success Despite Odds," *UPS Compass*, August 2016, https://compass.ups.com/inspirational-stories-startups/; Yogibo, BuzzFile, March 10, 2017, http://www.buzzfile.com/business/Yogibo-LLC-603-595-0207.

[103]"Why Sara Creighton Sold Her Brick-and-Mortar Practice to Create the Uber of Dentistry," BizWomen, April 14, 2015, www.bizjournals.com/bizwomen/news/profiles-strategies/2015/04/why-sara-creighton-sold-her-brick-and-mortar.html.

[104]Rudolph Bell, "ICAR Start-up Predicts Growth," *Greenville News*, March 19, 2011, p. 8A.

[105]*The 77th Annual Report of the Foreign Trade Zones Board to the Congress of the United States*, Foreign Trade Zones Board, September 2016, pp. 1, 6.

[106]Adam Bruns, "The FTZ Appeal, *Site Selection*, November 2015, pp. 148–155.

[107]"8 Amazing Facts About Incubators and Accelerators," Center for Entrepreneurial Innovation, August 17, 2015, www.slideshare.net/ceigateway/8-amazing-facts-about-business-incubators-accelerators.

[108]"8 Amazing Facts About Incubators and Accelerators," Center for Entrepreneurial Innovation, August 17, 2015, www.slideshare.net/ceigateway/8-amazing-facts-about-business-incubators-accelerators.

[109]Michelle Goodman, "Laser-Focused Launch Pads," *Entrepreneur*, September 2015, pp. 59–65; "8 Amazing Facts About Incubators and Accelerators," Center for Entrepreneurial Innovation, August 17, 2015, www.slideshare.net/ceigateway/8-amazing-facts-about-business-incubators-accelerators.

[110]"8 Amazing Facts About Incubators and Accelerators," Center for Entrepreneurial Innovation, August 17, 2015, www.slideshare.net/ceigateway/8-amazing-facts-about-business-incubators-accelerators.

[111]Michelle Goodman, "Laser-Focused Launch Pads," *Entrepreneur*, September 2015, pp. 59–65; Matt McCue, "For These Artisan Founders, Cute Small-Batch Goods Were Just the Beginning," *Entrepreneur*, August 2016, www.entrepreneur.com/article/278734.

[112]John Brandon, "The Field Guide to Accelerators," *Inc.*, March 2015, pp. 6–27.

[113]Fernando Sepulveda, "The Difference Between a Business Accelerator and a Business Incubator?" *Inc.*, July 31, 2012, www.inc.com/fernando-sepulveda/the-difference-between-a-business-accelerator-and-a-business-incubator.html.

[114]Scott Shane, "Why Are Business Accelerators Increasing in Number?" *Small Business Trends*, June 20, 2016, https://smallbiztrends.com/2016/06/business-accelerators-increasing.html.

[115]John Brandon, "The Field Guide to Accelerators," *Inc.*, March 2015, pp. 6–27.

[116]Douglas MacMillan, "Incubator Doubles Down on Darlings," *Wall Street Journal*, October 23, 2015, pp. B1, B4.

[117]*Engagement and the Global Workplace*, Steelcase, 2016, p. 214.

[118]"The Privacy Crisis," 360 Magazine, November 12, 2014, www.steelcase.com/insights/articles/privacy-crisis/.

[119]*U.S. Workplace Study 2016*, Gensler Research, 2016, p. 4.

[120]Ibid., p. 3.

[121]Lana Bortolot, "The Un-Office," *Entrepreneur*, March 2014, pp. 20–21.

[122]"The Privacy Crisis," 360 Magazine, November 12, 2014, www.steelcase.com/insights/articles/privacy-crisis/.

[123]Reed Albergotti, "Facebook's Company Town," *Wall Street Journal*, October 3, 2013, pp. B1, B5; Sam Laird, "Facebook Completes Move into New Menlo Park Headquarters," *Mashable Social Media*, December 19, 2011, http://mashable.com/2011/12/19/facebook-completes-move-into-new-menlo-park-headquarters; Moign Khawaja, "Facebook 'Likes' Its New Cool Space Campus," *Arabian Gazette*, December 20, 2011, http://arabiangazette.com/facebook-likes-its-cool-space-campus; Dan Levy, "Facebook's 'Cool Space' Campus Points to Future of Office Growth," *Businessweek*, December 22, 2011, www.businessweek.com/news/2011-12-28/facebook-s-cool-space-campus-points-to-future-of-office-growth

.html; Matt Rosoff, "The 15 Coolest Offices in Tech: Facebook Menlo Park Headquarters Tour," *Business Insider*, December 19, 2011, www.businessinsider.com/15-coolest-offices-in-tech-2012-1.

[124]*The Integrated Workplace*, Office of Governmentwide Policy, Office of Real Property, 2008, pp. 8–9.

[125]"New Study Shows Who Sits Where at Work Can Impact Employee Performance and Company Profits," Cornerstone On Demand, July 27, 2016, http://investors .cornerstoneondemand.com/investors/news-and-events/news/ news-details/2016/New-Study-Shows-Who-Sits-Where-at-Work-Can-Impact-Employee-Performance-and-Company-Profits/default.aspx.

[126]Denis Mehigan, "What Is the Average Square Footage of Office Space per Person?" The Mehigan Company, March 26, 2016, http://mehiganco.com/wordpress/?p=684; Jena McGregor, "Workplace Design Could Help Improve Workers' Focus," *Greenville News*, May 24, 2015, p. 5E.

[127]Ben Kesling and James R. Hagerty, "Say Goodbye to the Office Cubicle," *Wall Street Journal*, April 3, 2013, pp. B1, B6.

[128]Lana Bortolot, "The Un-Office," *Entrepreneur*, March 2014, pp. 20–21.

[129]Ron Barnett, "A Passion for the Outdoors," *Greenville News*, February 1, 2015, pp. 1E, 3E.

[130]Laura Tiffany, "The Rules of … Retail," *Business Start-Ups*, December 1999, p. 106.

[131]Ibid.

[132]A. Alfred Taubman, "Getting over the Threshold," *Inc.*, April 2007, pp. 75–76.

[133]W. Lee Erickson and S. von Schrader, *2014 Disability Status Report: United States*, Cornell University Yang Tan Institute on Employment and Disability, 2016, www.disabilitystatistics .org/reports/2014/English/HTML/report2014.cfm?fips=2000000.

[134]*Workplace Accommodations: Low Cost, High Impact*, Job Accommodation Network, U.S. Department of Labor Office of Disability Employment Policy, September 1, 2016, p.4.

[135]Angus Loten, "Disabled-Access Lawsuits Surge," *Wall Street Journal*, October 16, 2014, p. B4.

[136]Ellen Byron, "If You Spend Longer, You Spend More," *Wall Street Journal*, October 21, 2015, pp. B1–B2.

[137]Ed Zimmerman, "Clean Restaurants Build Customers' Confidence," *Pizza Marketplace*, January 7, 2013, www.pizzamarketplace .com/blogs/clean-restaurants-build-customers-confidence/.

[138]Suzette Parmley, "Cinnabon's Bet on iPad Lets You Tap a Screen to Buy the Pastries," *The Philadelphia Inquirer*, June 26, 2016, www.philly.com/philly/columnists/suzette-parmley/20160626_Cinnabon_s_bet_on_iPad_lets_you_ tap_a_screen_to_buy_the_pastries.html; Bret Thorn, "Cinnabon President Talks Redesign and Software," *Nation's Restaurant News*, June 9, 2016, www.nrn.com/technology/ cinnabon-president-talks-redesign-and-software.

[139]Brian Amble, "Poor Workplace Design Damages Productivity," *Management-Issues*, May 23, 2006, www.management-issues.com/2006/8/24/research/poorworkplace-design-damages-productivity.asp.

[140]Nicole Duncan, "The Drive-Thru Performance Study," *QSR*, October 2015, www.qsrmagazine.com/reports/drive-thru-performance-study-2015; Mary Avant, "Can the Drive Thru Be Saved?" *QSR*, October 2015, www.qsrmagazine.com/ drive-thru/can-drive-thru-be-saved.

[141]Joan M. Lang, "Fast-Casual Restaurants Add Drive-Through Service," *Restaurant Business*, December 31, 2012, www .restaurantbusinessonline.com/improving-operations/ideas/ articles/fast-casual-restaurants-add-drive-thru-service.

[142]Tiffany Craig, "Grocery Store Secrets: Dissecting the Grocery Store Layout to Keep You on Budget," KHOU, May 20,

2016; www.khou.com/news/investigations/watching-out-for-you/grocery-store-secrets-dissecting-the-supermarket-layout-to-keep-you-on-budget/206445378; Amanda MacArthur, "Retail Atmospherics: Can You Really Influence Customer Buying Habits?" *Swipely*, September 19, 2011, http://blog. swipelyworks.com/restaurant-store atmospherics/retail-atmospherics-can-you-really-influence-customer-buying-habits.

[143]Ned Smith, "Consumers Will Pay More for Products They Can Touch," *Business News Daily*, September 13, 2010, www .businessnewsdaily.com/203-consumers-willpay-more-for-products-they-can-touch.html.

[144]"Paco Underhill: Shopping Scientist," *CBC News*, November 7, 2000, www.cbc.ca/consumers/market/files/home/shopping/ index.html.

[145]Tara Fitzpatrick, "Makeover Creates Cozier, Sexier Space for Suzanne Goin's The Larder at Tavern," *Restaurant Hospitality*, October 20, 2016, www.restaurant-hospitality.com/design/ makeover-creates-cozier-sexier-space-suzanne-goins-larder-tavern.

[146]Amanda MacArthur, "Retail Atmospherics: Can You Really Influence Customer Buying Habits?" *Swipely*, September 19, 2011, http://blog.swipelyworks.com/restaurant-store-atmospherics/retail-atmospherics-can-you-really-influence-customer-buying-habits.

[147]Martin Lindstrom, "How Whole Foods 'Primes' You to Shop," *Fast Company*, September 15, 2011, www.fastcompany. com/1779611/priming-whole-foods-derren-brown.

[148]"Why Use Music?" RadioSushi, March 2017, www.audiosushi .com/music-for-business/benefits.html.

[149]Humayun Khan, "How Retailers Manipulate Sight, Smell, and Sound to Trigger Purchase Behavior in Consumers," *Shopify*, April 25, 2016, www.shopify.com/retail/119926083-how-retailers-manipulate-sight-smell-and-sound-to-trigger-purchase-behavior-in-consumers.

[150]David Galic, "How to Choose the Right Music for Your Retail Store," *Humanity*, June 3, 2016, www.humanity.com/blog/ how-to-choose-the-right-music-for-your-retail-store.html; Mark Brandau, "Operators in the Mood for Music," *Nation's Restaurant News*, August 3, 2011, http://nrn.com/article/ operators-music-mood.

[151]Ray A. Smith, "Shop Too Much? Blame the Music," *Wall Street Journal*, December 12, 2013, pp. D1, D3; "Customers: Thomas Pink," Mood Media, 2014, www.moodmedia.hu/ clientsdetail.asp?id=2.

[152]David Galic, "How to Choose the Right Music for Your Retail Store," *Humanity*, June 3, 2016, www.humanity.com/blog/how-to-choose-the-right-music-for-your-retail-store.html; Eric Markowitz, "How Cinnamon Smells Will Save Holiday Sales," *Inc.*, November 3, 2011, www.inc.com/articles/201111/ how-cinnamon-smells-will-save-holiday-sales.html; Michael Morain, "Muzak—It Remains Music to Retailers' Ears," *Greenville News*, December 23, 2007, p. 3F; Theunis Bates, "Volume Control," *Time*, August 2, 2007, www.time.com/ time/printout/0,8816,1649304,00.html.

[153]Hannah Elliott, "Marketing to Your Nose," *Forbes*, November 18, 2013, pp. 164–168.

[154]Humayun Khan, "How Retailers Manipulate Sight, Smell, and Sound to Trigger Purchase Behavior in Consumers," *Shopify*, April 25, 2016, www.shopify.com/retail/119926083-how-retailers-manipulate-sight-smell-and-sound-to-trigger-purchase-behavior-in-consumers.

[155]Guinevere Orvis, "The Science of Smell: How Retailers Can Use Scent Marketing to Influence Shoppers," *Shopify*, August 11, 2016, www.independent.co.uk/news/media/ advertising/the-smell-of-commerce-how-companies-use-scents-to-sell-their-products-2338142.html.

156 Linda Tischler, "Smells Like a Brand Spirit," *Fast Company*, August 2005, pp. 52–59.

157 Guinevere Orvis, "The Science of Smell: How Retailers Can Use Scent Marketing to Influence Shoppers," *Shopify*, August 11, 2016, www.independent.co.uk/news/media/advertising/the-smell-of-commerce-how-companies-use-scents-to-sell-their-products-2338142.html.

158 Christopher White, "The Smell of Commerce: How Companies Are Using Scents to Sell Their Products," *Independent*, August 15, 2011, www.independent.co.uk/news/media/advertising/the-smell-of-commerce-how-companies-use-scents-to-sell-their-products-2338142.html.

159 Lucy Bannerman, "Smells Sell, as Hard Nosed Traders Discover," ScentAir, March 13, 2014, www.scentair.com/why-scentair/news-press/smells-sell-as-hard-nosed-traders-discover.

160 "Commercial Buildings Energy Consumption Survey: Energy Usage Summary," U.S. Energy Information Administration, March 2016, www.eia.gov/consumption/commercial/reports/2012/energyusage/.

161 "Lighting Choices to Save You Money," Energy.gov, March 2017, https://energy.gov/energysaver/lighting-choices-save-you-money.

162 Jay Greene, "More Companies Take a Shine to LED Lighting's Benefits," *Craine's Detroit Business*, August 22, 2013, www.crainsdetroit.com/article/20130822/BLOG010/130829941/more-companies-take-a-shine-to-led-lightings-benefits; Edward Cardenas, "Ninos Sees the Light and Goes Green," *Patch*, September 28, 2011, http://patch.com/michigan/troy/ninos-sees-the-light-and-goes-green-3cb98848.

163 Mark Cloud, "Lighting Design in Layers," Integrated Solutions Group, April 10, 2015, www.isgnow.net/2015/04/lighting-design-in-layers/.

164 Torrin Greathouse, "What Business Benefits Does Natural Lighting Bring?" CiraLight, August 21, 2015, http://www.ciralight.com/blog/what-business-benefits-does-natural-lighting-bring.

165 Beth Kowitt, "Coffee Shop, Contained," *Fortune*, May 20, 2013, p. 24; Anthony Perez, "Sustainable Store Design in Action," Starbucks, February 17, 2012, www.starbucks.com/blog/sustainable-store-design-in-action/1158.

166 Bob Krummert, "Trendinista: Rooftop Gardens Elevate Cuisine, Bottom Line," *Restaurant Hospitality*, March 21, 2016, www.restaurant-hospitality.com/trendinista/trendinista-rooftop-gardens-elevate-cuisine-bottom-line.

167 Jason Daley, "Stay Awhile," *Entrepreneur*, December 2011, p. 118.

168 Paul Keegan, "The Architect of Happy Customers," *Business 2.0*, August 2002, pp. 85–87.

169 Sarah Nassauer, "Wal-Mart Shrinks the Big Box, Vexing Vendors," *Wall Street Journal*, October 25, 2015, www.wsj.com/articles/wal-mart-shrinks-the-big-box-vexing-vendors-1445820469.

170 Annette Elton, "I'll Take That Too: Increasing Impulse Buys," *Gift Shop*, Spring 2008, www.giftshopmag.com/2008/spring/unique_giftware/increasing_impulse_buys.

171 Rebecca Rupp, "Surviving the Sneaky Psychology of Supermarkets," *The Plate*, June 15, 2015, http://theplate.nationalgeographic.com/2015/06/15/surviving-the-sneaky-psychology-of-supermarkets/.

172 Jon Springer, "New Hannaford Prototype Marries Convenience, Innovation," *Supermarket News*, June 20, 2016, www.supermarketnews.com/latest-news/new-hannaford-prototype-marries-convenience-innovation.

173 Kenneth Labich, "This Man Is Watching You," *Fortune*, July 19, 1999, pp. 131–134.

174 Elizabeth Holmes and Day A. Smith, "Why Are Fitting Rooms So Awful?" *Wall Street Journal*, April 6, 2011, pp. D1–D2.

175 Dan Berthiaume, "Study: Long Checkout Lines Impact Customer Return Rates," *Chain Store Age*, February 25, 2014, www.chainstoreage.com/article/study-long-checkout-lines-impact-customer-return-rates.

176 Ray A. Smith, "Find the Best Checkout Line," *Wall Street Journal*, December 8, 2011, pp. D1–D2.

177 Ray A. Smith, "Where Did the Register Go?" *Wall Street Journal*, March 8, 2016, pp. D1, D3.

178 Colleen DeBaise, "A Small Clothing Maker Tries to Keep Sewing in the U.S.," *New York Times*, September 10, 2014, https://boss.blogs.nytimes.com/2014/09/10/a-small-clothing-maker-tries-to-keep-sewing-in-the-u-s/?_r=0.

179 Nadine Heintz, "Inside a Factory Makeover," *Inc.*, November 2013, www.inc.com/magazine/201311/nadine-heintz/inside-a-factory-makeover.html.

180 Chester Dawson, "For Toyota, Patriotism and Profits May Not Mix," *Wall Street Journal*, November 29, 2011, pp. A1, A16.

181 "The Beam Team Gets Lean," Massachusetts Manufacturing Advancement Center, www.massmac.org/newsline/0705/article02.htm.

15

Sources of Financing: Equity and Debt

Timur Arbaev/123RF

Learning Objectives

On completion of this chapter, you will be able to:

1. Describe the differences between equity capital and debt capital.

2. Discuss the various sources of equity capital available to entrepreneurs.

3. Describe the process of "going public."

4. Describe the various sources of debt capital.

5. Describe the various loan programs available from the Small Business Administration.

6. Identify the various federal and state loan programs aimed at small businesses.

7. Explain other methods of financing a business.

MyLab Entrepreneurship

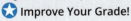 Improve Your Grade!

If your instructor is using MyLab Entrepreneurship, visit **www.pearson.com/mylab/entrepreneurship** for videos, simulations, and writing exercises.

Capital is a crucial element in the process of creating new ventures, yet raising the money to launch a new business venture has always been challenging for entrepreneurs. Capital markets rise and fall with the stock market, overall economic conditions, and investors' fortunes. These swells and troughs in the availability of capital make the search for financing look like a wild roller-coaster ride. Entrepreneurs, especially those in less glamorous industries or those just starting out, face difficulty finding outside sources of financing. Many banks shy away from making loans to start-ups, venture capitalists are looking for ever-larger deals, private investors have grown cautious, and making a public stock offering remains a viable option for only a handful of promising companies with good track records and fast-growth futures. The result has been a credit crunch for entrepreneurs looking for small to moderate amounts of start-up capital. Entrepreneurs and business owners who need between $100,000 and $3 million are especially hard hit because of the vacuum that exists at that level of financing. A recent survey by the National Small Business Association reports that nearly one-third of small business owners say that they are unable to obtain adequate financing to fuel their companies' growth.[1]

Three major factors influence the availability of credit for small businesses. First, businesses of all sizes find that the ease of securing credit is tied to economic conditions. During periods of strong economic growth, credit tends to flow more freely. On the other hand, during economic slowdowns, banks tighten credit to control their risk. Small businesses feel the brunt of this shift more severely than do larger, more well-established corporations. Second, the financial strength of a small business directly impacts its ability to secure credit. Third, the age of a small business is a factor most banks use to determine creditworthiness. Most banks lend only to small firms that have *at least* three years of operating history and at least two years of profitability.

The key to securing credit for any small business is learning to manage capital carefully and knowing the right kind of capital to raise for the right needs in your business. The goal should not be to raise as much capital as you can; you should raise only as much as your business needs.

When searching for the capital to launch their companies, entrepreneurs must remember the following "secrets" to successful financing:

- *Choosing the right sources of capital for a business can be just as important as choosing the right form of ownership or the right location.* It is a decision that can influence a company for a lifetime, and entrepreneurs must weigh their options carefully before committing to a particular funding source. For example, short term loans are generally best for working capital needs, long term loans are generally best for funding the purchase of assets, and equity investments are generally best for funding growth and expansion.

- *The money is out there; the key is knowing where to look.* Entrepreneurs must do their homework *before* they set out to raise money for their ventures. Understanding which sources of funding are best suited for the various stages of a company's growth and then taking the time to learn how those sources work is essential to success.

- *Raising money takes time and effort.* Sometimes entrepreneurs are surprised at the energy and time required to raise the capital needed to feed their cash-hungry, growing businesses. The process usually includes lots of promising leads, most of which turn out to be dead-ends. Meetings with and presentations to lots of potential investors and lenders can crowd out the time needed to manage a growing company. Entrepreneurs also discover that raising capital is an ongoing job that can extend over a significant period of time.

- *Creativity counts.* Although some traditional sources of funds now play a lesser role in small business finance than in the past, other sources—from large corporations and customers to international venture capitalists and state or local programs—are taking up the slack. To find the financing their businesses demand, entrepreneurs must use as much creativity in attracting financing as they did in generating the ideas for their products and services.

- *The Internet puts at entrepreneurs' fingertips vast resources of information that can lead to financing. Use it.* The Internet offers entrepreneurs, especially those looking for relatively small amounts of money, the opportunity to discover sources of funds they otherwise might miss. The Internet also provides a low-cost, convenient way for entrepreneurs to get their business plans into potential investors' hands anywhere in the world.

- *Put social media to work to locate potential investors.* Social media such as Facebook, Twitter, LinkedIn, and others are useful tools for locating potential investors. For example, LinkedIn has several groups that help investors and entrepreneurs connect with each other, such as Angel Investors, Impact Investors, and Angel Investor Group.

- *Be thoroughly prepared before approaching potential lenders and investors.* In the hunt for capital, tracking down leads is tough enough; don't blow a potential deal by failing to be ready to present your business idea to potential lenders and investors in a clear, concise, convincing way. That, of course, requires a solid business plan and a well-rehearsed elevator pitch—one or two minutes on the nature of your business and the source of its competitive edge to win over potential investors and lenders.

- *Entrepreneurs cannot overestimate the importance of making sure that the "chemistry" among themselves, their companies, and their funding sources is a good one.* Too many entrepreneurs get into financial deals because they need the money to keep their businesses growing only to discover that their plans do not match those of their financial partners.

- *Plan an exit strategy.* Although it may seem peculiar for entrepreneurs to plan an exit strategy for investors when they are seeking capital to *start* their businesses, doing so increases their chances of closing a deal. Investors do not put their money into a business with the intent of leaving it there indefinitely. Their goal is to get their money back—along with an attractive return on the investment. Entrepreneurs who fail to define potential exit strategies for their investors reduce the likelihood of getting the capital their companies need to grow.

- *When capital gets tight, remember to bootstrap.* Because capital is tighter for small businesses, don't forget to use some of the clever ways you employed to get your business going when you had limited funds. Bootstrapping is not just for start-ups!

Rather than rely primarily on a single source of funds as they have in the past, entrepreneurs must piece together capital from multiple sources, a method known as **layered financing**. They have discovered that raising capital successfully requires them to cast a wide net to capture the financing they need to launch their businesses.

layered financing
the technique of raising capital from multiple sources.

ENTREPRENEURIAL PROFILE: John and Patrick Collison: Stripe After launching their first company and selling it in just 10 months, brothers John and Patrick Collison launched Stripe, an online payments company, with their own money. While working on several projects, Patrick realized how difficult taking online payments was for merchants and decided that he and his brother could develop a better method. They tested their simple payment solution with online shoppers, made the necessary modifications, and landed a spot (and the seed financing that came with it) in Y Combinator, a prestigious business accelerator in Mountain View, California. Stripe grew quickly, and the Collisons secured investments from several high-profile angel investors, including entrepreneurs Elon Musk and Peter Thiel, and eventually venture capital firms. Just six years after start-up, the Collisons had raised more than $440 million in capital, and Stripe was worth an estimated $9.2 billion.[2] ∎

Becoming a successful entrepreneur requires one to become a skilled fund-raiser, a job that usually requires more time and energy than most business founders realize. In start-up companies, raising capital can easily consume as much as one-half of the entrepreneur's time and can take many months to complete. In addition, many entrepreneurs find it necessary to raise capital constantly to fuel the hefty capital appetites of their young, fast-growing companies. Although the amount an entrepreneur needs to launch a start-up varies significantly by the type of business being launched, the Global Entrepreneurship Monitor reports that new entrepreneurs need on average about $15,000 to $22,000 to start their businesses.[3] However, these "small" amounts of capital can be most difficult to secure.

capital

any form of wealth used to produce more wealth.

Capital is any form of wealth used to produce more wealth. It exists in many forms in a typical business, including cash, inventory, plant, and equipment. Entrepreneurs have access to two different types of capital: equity and debt. This chapter will guide you through the myriad financing options available to entrepreneurs, focusing on both sources of equity (ownership) and debt (borrowed) financing.

LO1

Describe the differences between equity capital and debt capital.

equity capital

capital that represents the personal investment of the owner (or owners) of a company; sometimes called risk capital.

Equity Capital Versus Debt Capital

Equity capital represents the personal investment of the owner (or owners) in a business and is sometimes called *risk capital* because these investors assume the primary risk of losing their funds if the business fails. If a venture succeeds, however, founders and investors share in the benefits, which can be quite substantial. The founders of and early investors in Yahoo!, Sun Microsystems, FedEx, Intel, and Microsoft became multimillionaires when the companies went public and their equity investments finally paid off. Michael Moritz, a partner in the venture capital firm Sequoia Capital, recalls a meeting in 1999 that took place around a Ping-Pong table that doubled as a conference table for Sergey Brin and Larry Page, the founders of a start-up company that had developed a search engine called Google. The young company had just changed its name from Backrub and had only 12 employees when Moritz agreed to invest $12.5 million. When Google made an initial public offering five years later, Moritz's original investment was worth $3 billion![4]

To entrepreneurs, the primary advantage of equity capital is that it does not have to be repaid, like a loan does. Equity investors are entitled to share in the company's earnings (if there are any) and usually to have a voice in the company's future direction. The primary disadvantage of equity capital is that the entrepreneur must give up some—sometimes even *most*—of the ownership in the business to outsiders. Although 50 percent of something is better than 100 percent of nothing, giving up control of a company can be disconcerting and dangerous. Entrepreneurs are most likely to give up significant amounts of equity in their businesses in the start-up phase than in any other. To avoid having to give up control of their companies early on, entrepreneurs should strive to launch their companies with the least amount of money possible.

debt capital

financing that an entrepreneur borrows and must repay with interest.

Debt capital is the financing an entrepreneur borrows and must repay with interest. Very few entrepreneurs have adequate personal savings to finance the total start-up costs of a small business; many of them must rely on some form of debt capital to launch their companies. Lenders of capital are more numerous than investors, but small business loans can be just as difficult (if not more difficult) to obtain. Although borrowed capital allows entrepreneurs to maintain complete ownership of their businesses, it must be carried as a liability on the balance sheet, and it must be repaid with interest in the future. In addition, because lenders consider small businesses to be greater risks than bigger corporate customers, they require higher interest rates on loans to small companies because of the risk–return trade-off: The higher the risk, the greater the return demanded. Most small firms pay the prime rate—the interest rate banks charge their most creditworthy customers—*plus* a few percentage points. Still, the cost of debt financing often is lower than that of equity financing. Because of the higher risks associated with providing equity capital to small companies, investors demand greater returns than lenders. In addition, unlike equity financing, debt financing does not require entrepreneurs to dilute their ownership interest in their companies.

LO2

Discuss the various sources of equity capital available to entrepreneurs.

Sources of Equity Financing

Personal Savings

bootstrapping

a process in which entrepreneurs tap their personal savings and use creative low-cost start-up methods to launch their businesses.

The *first* place entrepreneurs should look for start-up money is in their own pockets. It's the least expensive source of funds available! A start-up has very little if any financial history, and investors view investments in early-stage companies as high risk. Therefore, the earlier in the life of the company that an entrepreneur must raise capital, the more he or she will likely have to give up ownership to secure that financing. Entrepreneurs apparently see the benefits of self-sufficiency; tapping their personal savings and using creative, low-cost start-up methods, a technique known as **bootstrapping**, is one of the most common sources of funds used to start a business. According to a survey by the Kauffman Foundation and LegalZoom, more than 86 percent of U.S. entrepreneurs use personal savings and assets as a primary source of financing for their

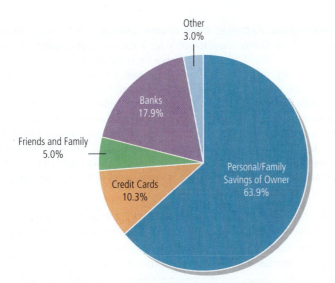

FIGURE 15.1

Sources of Financing for Typical Start-up Businesses

Source: Based on data from Donna J. Kelley, Abdul Ali, Candida Brush, Andrew C. Corbett, Caroline Daniels, Phillip H. Kim, Thomas S. Lyons, Mahdi Majbouri, and Edward G. Rogoff, "2015 United States Report," *Global Entrepreneurship Monitor*, 2016, p. 43.

start-ups.[5] However, it is not just small businesses that rely on personal savings. A recent survey of companies in the *Inc.* 500 list of America's fastest-growing companies finds that 67.2 percent of the entrepreneurs who founded these high-growth ventures also relied on personal savings to help fund their businesses.[6] The Global Entrepreneurship Monitor survey reports that entrepreneurs in the U.S. rely on personal savings for about 64 percent of total funding (see Figure 15.1).[7] Bootstrappers learn quickly to be frugal and stretch the income-generating power of every dollar, especially when most or all of those dollars come from their personal savings.

ENTREPRENEURIAL PROFILE: Eric and Nancy Schneider: Headrush Roasters Coffee & Tea In 2011, Eric Schneider withdrew all of his retirement savings from his 401(k) to launch a new business with his wife, Nancy. Using $250,000 from Eric's retirement account and another $100,000 in savings, the Schneiders opened Headrush Roasters Coffee & Tea in Kansas City, Missouri. Eric had spent 25 years in commercial insurance and had no experience in the coffee industry. Nancy kept her full-time job as a software engineer to ensure that the couple had health insurance coverage and other benefits during the start-up. Eric chose to use the couple's retirement savings rather than take out debt financing. The couple was debt free, and they did not want to risk their personal assets to start the business. They used a Rollovers as Business Start-ups (ROBS), which allowed them to directly invest the funds in their new business. Under this plan, Eric rolled his existing retirement account into a new retirement plan that the couple then invested it in their business. Although it is a complicated process, the Schneiders incurred no debt to launch the business and no penalties or taxes by using a retirement account to launch Headrush Roasters Coffee and Tea.[8] ∎

Lenders and investors *expect* entrepreneurs to put their own money into a business start-up. If an entrepreneur is not willing to risk his or her own money, potential investors are not likely to risk their money in the business either. Furthermore, failing to put up sufficient capital of their own means that entrepreneurs must either borrow an excessive amount of capital or give up a significant portion of ownership to outsiders to fund the business properly. Excessive borrowing in the early days of a business puts intense pressure on its cash flow, and becoming a minority shareholder may dampen a founder's enthusiasm for making a business successful.

Friends and Family Members

Although most entrepreneurs look to their own bank accounts first to finance a business, few have sufficient resources to launch their businesses alone. After emptying their own pockets, where should entrepreneurs turn for capital? The second place most entrepreneurs look is to friends and family members who might be willing to invest in (or lend to) a business venture. Because of their relationships with the founder, these people are most likely to invest. Often, they are more patient than other outside investors and are less meddlesome in a business's affairs (but not always!) than many other types of investors.

ENTREPRENEURIAL PROFILE: Ryan Shank: Mhelpdesk: After graduating from Clemson University, Ryan Shank went to work for a company that sells extended warranties on products. After a few years, Shank decided to leave his cubicle-confining job to start Mhelpdesk, a company based in Sterling, Virginia, that sells cloud-based management software to field-based small businesses. He invested $8,120 of his own money (all he had at the time) and bootstrapped his start-up. As he built Mhelpdesk, Shank turned to his former boss as a mentor, gathering advice on building a customer base, hiring the right people, and other matters. As the company grew, so did its capital needs, and Shank naturally turned to his friend and former boss for a capital investment. Because his friend was already familiar with Mhelpdesk, its market, and its potential, he decided to invest nearly $1 million in the young company. The investment paid off when HomeAdvisor, the leading marketplace for connecting homeowners with local service professionals, purchased Mhelpdesk a few years later.[9] ■

Investments from family members and friends are an important source of capital for entrepreneurs, but the amounts invested typically are small, often no more than a few thousand dollars. According to the Global Entrepreneurship Monitor, 39 percent of entrepreneurs in the United States receive some level of funding from friends and family members.[10]

Investments (or loans) from family members and friends are an excellent source of seed capital and can get a start-up far enough along to attract money from private investors or venture capital companies. Inherent dangers lurk in family business investments and loans, however. One study reports a default rate of 14 percent on business loans from family members and friends, compared to a default rate of 1 percent for bank loans.[11] Unrealistic expectations or misunderstood risks have destroyed many friendships and have ruined many family gatherings. Remember: Thanksgiving comes around every year! To avoid problems, an entrepreneur must honestly present the investment opportunity and the nature of the risks involved to avoid alienating friends and family members if the business fails. Smart entrepreneurs treat family members and friends who invest in their companies in the same way they would treat outside investors. Some investments in start-up companies return more than friends and family members ever could have imagined. In 1995, Mike and Jackie Bezos invested $300,000 in their son Jeff's start-up business, Amazon.com. Today, Mike and Jackie own 6 percent of Amazon.com's stock, and their shares are worth more than $29 billion![12] The accompanying "Hands On . . . How To" feature offers suggestions for structuring successful family or friendship financing deals.

Crowdfunding

Historically, securities laws limited who can invest in small businesses. Investing in entrepreneurial businesses has been the realm of those with the knowledge and financial ability to assume the risks that come with such investments. Known as **accredited investors**, these people must have a sustained net worth (excluding their primary residence) of at least $1 million or annual income of at least $200,000. There are 12.38 million accredited investors in the United States; however, only a small percentage of these accredited investors have made direct investments in entrepreneurial businesses.[13] A few creative entrepreneurs have used a loophole to raise money from investors who do not meet the requirements of accredited investors using a funding technique called **crowdfunding**. Crowdfunding taps the power of the Internet and social networking and allows entrepreneurs to post their elevator pitches and proposed investment terms on specialized Web sites and raise money from ordinary people who invest as little as $100. Crowdfunding primarily has been used to raise money to support social causes, fund aspiring artists, or support local small business start-ups. The money received from crowdfunding had to be considered a contribution or a donation, rather than an investment. In most cases, entrepreneurs offer some nominal benefit in return for financial support. For example, a musician might show appreciation to contributors by giving them a free download of a new song. Likewise, an owner of a new restaurant may offer each contributor a special discount. The contributors are motivated by the desire to help the aspiring musician or restaurateur. The most commonly used Web sites that promote traditional crowdfunding are Kickstarter, Rock the Post, and Indiegogo. AngelList is a crowdfunding site for accredited angel investors looking to make small investments. Kiva and Accion are crowd lending sites that link small businesses with people willing to provide micro loans.

accredited investors
investors who have a sustained net worth (excluding their primary residences) of at least $1 million or annual income of at least $200,000.

crowdfunding
a method of raising capital that taps the power of social networking and allows entrepreneurs to post their elevator pitches and proposed investment terms on specialized Web sites and raise money from ordinary people who invest as little as $100.

🌐 Hands On . . . How To

Structure Family and Friendship Financing Deals

Tapping family members and friends for start-up capital, whether in the form of equity or debt financing, is a popular method of financing business ideas. In a typical year, some 6 million individuals in the United States invest about $100 billion in entrepreneurial ventures. Unfortunately, not all of these deals work to the satisfaction of both parties. The following suggestions can help entrepreneurs avoid needlessly destroying family relationships and friendships:

- **Family should not be your first financing option.** Loans and investments from family members should never be considered the easy option for financing a business. Make sure you have done everything you can to bootstrap your business to minimize the cash you actually will need before turning to family for help.

- **Choose your financier carefully.** One of the first issues to consider is the impact of the investment on everyone involved. Will it cause a hardship for the investor or lender? Is the investor putting up the money because he or she wants to or because he or she feels obligated? Can all parties afford the loan if the business folds? No matter how much capital you may need, accepting more than family members or friends can afford to lose is a recipe for disaster—and perhaps bankruptcy for the investors. Lynn McPhee used $250,000 from family members to launch Xuny, a Web-based clothing store. Her basic rule was that if the investment would cause any financial distress or potential hardship, she would not accept the money. Remember that relationships often suffer if a business fails and friends and family members lose their money.

- **Keep the arrangement strictly business.** The parties should treat all loans and investments in a business-like manner, no matter how close the friendship or family relationship, to avoid problems down the line. If the transaction is a loan exceeding $10,000, it must carry a rate of interest at least as high as the IRS minimum rate; otherwise, the Internal Revenue Service may consider the loan a gift and penalize the lender. Treat family investors just like any other early stage investor in the business.

- **Prepare a business plan.** Treat friends and family members just as you would angel investors, bankers, venture capitalists, and other professionals by doing your research and preparing a business plan. The most important use of a business plan is to communicate the business model to potential investors, so prepare a thoroughly researched business plan and go over it carefully with any potential family members interested in providing funding for the business. Be honest and be clear about the worst-case scenario in your plan.

- **Settle the details up front.** Before any money changes hands, both parties must agree on the details of the deal. How much money is involved? Is it a loan or an investment? How will the investor cash out? How will the loan be paid off? What happens if the business fails?

- **Create a written contract.** Don't make the mistake of closing a financial deal with just a handshake. The probability of misunderstandings skyrockets! Putting an agreement in writing demonstrates the parties' commitment to the deal and minimizes the chances of disputes from faulty memories and misunderstandings.

- **Treat the money as "bridge financing."** Although family members and friends can help you launch your business, it is unlikely that they can provide enough capital to sustain it over the long term. Sooner or later, you will need to establish a relationship with other sources of credit if your company is to survive and thrive. Consider money from family and friends as a bridge to take your company to the next level of financing.

- **Develop a payment schedule that suits both the entrepreneur and the lender or investor.** One of the primary benefits of financing from family members and friends is that the repayment or cash-out schedule usually is flexible. Although lenders and investors may want to get their money back as quickly as possible, a rapid repayment or cash-out schedule can jeopardize a fledgling company's survival. Establish a realistic repayment plan that works for the parties without putting excessive strain on your young company's cash flow. Family members are usually very willing to be patient funders of your business.

- **Have an exit plan.** Every deal should define exactly how investors will "cash out" their investments or loans.

Sources: Based on Tony Armstrong, "Dos and Don'ts of Asking Family and Friends for Startup Funds," *NerdWallet*, January 19, 2015, www.nerdwallet.com/blog/small-business/dos-donts-asking-family-friends-startup-funds/; Luke Landers, "8 Rules for Borrowing Money from Friends and Family," *Consumerism Commentary*, February 26, 2013, www.consumerismcommentary.com/rules-borrowing-money-friends-family/; Caron Beesley, "6 Tips for Borrowing Startup Funds from Friends or Family," *SBA Community*, January 3, 2012, http://community.sba.gov/community/blogs/community-blogs/small-business-cents/6-tips-borrowing-startup-funds-friends-or-family; Rosalind Resnick, "For You, Graduate, Some Start-up Capital," *Wall Street Journal*, June 7, 2011, http://online.wsj.com/article/SB10001424052702304432304576369842747489336.html; Sarah Dougherty, " 'Love Money' Seeds Many Budding Ventures," *Financial Post*, January 30, 2008, www.financialpost.com/small-business/business-solutions/story.html?id=269859; Paulette Thomas, "It's All Relative," *Wall Street Journal*, November 29, 2004, pp. R4, R8; Andrea Coombes, "Retirees as Venture Capitalists," *CBS MarketWatch*, November 2, 2003, http://netscape.marketwatch.com/news/story.asp?dist=feed&siteid=netscape&guid={1E1267CD-32A4-4558-9F7E-40E4B7892D01}; Paul Kvinta, "Frogskins, Shekels, Bucks, Moolah, Cash, Simoleans, Dough, Dinero: Everybody Wants It. Your Business Needs It. Here's How to Get It," *Smart Business*, August 2000, pp. 74–89; Alex Markels, "A Little Help from Their Friends," *Wall Street Journal*, May 22, 1995, p. R10; Heather Chaplin, "Friends and Family," *Your Company*, September 1999, p. 26.

Photo courtesy of Olivia Rae James, Information Courtesy Olivia Management

ENTREPRENEURIAL PROFILE: Erin Anderson: Olivia Management and Secret Sisters Erin Anderson, founder of Olivia Management, is the manager of several recording artists in Nashville, Tennessee, including a relatively new band called The Secret Sisters. The Secret Sisters, from Florence, Alabama, had released two records with a major recording studio (Universal), before the label dropped them. Due to ongoing legal issues with their former manager, the band was forced to declare bankruptcy, and the founders of the band seriously considered ending their musical careers. Under new management with Olivia Management, the band members used crowdfunding to restart their musical careers with the help of loyal fans of their music. Anderson and the band used Pledge Music, a platform that asks fans to buy a record even before it is recorded. The Secret Sisters also offered private concerts, handmade art, signed albums, and exclusive posters and T-shirts to raise badly needed funding. The goal of the campaign was to raise enough to make a new record. The crowdfunding campaign exceeded its goal by 25 percent, and the band donated a percentage of the extra proceeds to a local animal shelter.[14] ∎

The intent of the Jumpstart Our Business Startups (JOBS) Act of 2012 was to significantly expand the use of crowdfunding as a way to raise equity investment for small businesses by making investments possible for a larger group of people who may not be accredited investors. However, when fully implemented, it fell short of the goals that many of its original advocates had envisioned. The original legislation was broadly written, leaving the development of the specific rules and implementation of the program to the Securities and Exchange Commission (SEC). Although the JOBS Act was passed in 2012, the SEC has not yet finalized its equity-based crowdfunding rules, but the agency's proposed rules would allow a small business to raise up to $1 million in a 12-month period. In addition, investors could invest up to 10 percent of their annual income in any 12-month period, depending on the amount of their annual income and their net worth. In addition, the crowdfunding platforms through which entrepreneurs raise money would have to join a national securities association that is recognized by the SEC.

Attracting investors through crowdfunding, particularly traditional crowdfunding Web sites, requires a different approach than an entrepreneur uses when pursuing more sophisticated and experienced investors. Unlike experienced investors who invest more in people than in their ideas, crowdfunding investors tend to be attracted to compelling stories and business ideas they can see themselves using. Crowdfunding works through social media, so the entrepreneur's existing network of contacts must be advocates to lend credibility to the business among the broader network.[15] The accompanying "Hands On ... How To" feature offers some additional cautions when using crowdfunding to finance a small business.

Accelerators

accelerator program
a program, possibly sponsored by a community or university, that provides a small amount of seed capital and a wealth of additional support for start-up companies.

Inexperienced entrepreneurs have difficulty finding early-stage seed funding. A first-time entrepreneur doesn't have the credibility to attract professional investors and typically doesn't have the personal wealth required to launch a business. To help bridge this gap in funding, many communities and universities have established **accelerator programs** that offer new entrepreneurs a small amount of seed capital and a wealth of additional support. Accelerator programs help move entrepreneurs from the idea stage to a point when the business has a proven story and a strong business model that the founder can pitch for more significant funding. Accelerators offer a structured program that lasts from three months to one year. A select group of entrepreneurs, typically 10 to 20, are invited to participate as a group in an accelerator program. The accelerator provides entrepreneurs with about $15,000 to $25,000 in seed capital, gives them temporary space to work on their business models and their elevator pitches and connects them with a team of mentors who each get a small share of equity in the business in return for their guidance. All of this requires the entrepreneur to give up 6 to 10 percent of the ownership in the business. At the end of the program, the accelerator hosts a large pitch event. Local angel investors and venture capitalists are invited to hear all of the pitches of the accelerator participants. Investors who are interested can join the mentor team as investors in businesses that "graduate" from the

Hands On . . . How To

Use Crowdfunding Successfully

Start-ups often turn to crowdfunding Web sites, such as Kickstarter, and portals developed since the JOBS Act passed to get seed funding. Many companies have gotten the start-up capital they needed for a successful launch through a crowdfunding campaign.

Green Sense Farms, a start-up based in Portage, Indiana, is an early market leader in developing indoor farms, which offer a means of raising food that requires much less land and water than traditional farming methods. Crops are grown in vertical racks, using artificial light and no soil. Indoor farming requires up to 95 percent less water than traditional agriculture. Green Sense Farms launched a crowdfunding campaign on startengine.com to raise at least $100,000. The company exceeded its goal in its first day of fundraising.

Nikolaj Hviid, an inventor of several successful technologies, raised seed money to develop a new wireless headphone through Kickstarter. His product, The Dash, is one of the many Bluetooth headphones to enter the market. However, unlike its competitors, it can work autonomously, storing up to 1,000 songs within the earbud itself, and it can monitor the user's activity during workouts. Hviid raised $3.4 million on Kickstarter to launch this new product.

David Toledo and Caleb Light invented a cooking pot, called the PowerPot, that generates power by converting heat into electricity as it cooks food. For example, a camper using the PowerPot to cook an evening meal over the campfire can generate enough power to charge a cell phone or a tablet using its USB connection. Toledo and Light raised $126,204 as seed money for their product through Kickstarter. They then went on the television show *Shark Tank*, where they raised enough money from Mark Cuban to launch the business. The PowerPot is now distributed through most major outdoor retailers.

The Dark Side of Crowdfunding

Not every crowdfunding story has a happy ending, however.

Seth Quest launched a Kickstarter campaign to raise $10,000 in seed money to help launch his iPad stand called Hanfree. He put a photo of a prototype on his Kickstarter fundraising page. The description on the Kickstarter page said that for a minimum pledge of $50, backers could preorder a Hanfree, which would be made in San Francisco, California, out of sustainably forested alder wood. He also promised that each one would be hand-numbered and signed by the designer. The campaign was a success, raising more than $35,000 from 440 backers.

However, the excitement over Quest's fundraising success quickly faded. Quest had no business experience and had never manufactured a product before. As a result, he was unable to fill the preorders as promised. Some of the backers became angry, and soon there were hundreds of negative comments on Hanfree's Kickstarter page. Quest realized that he was not going to be able to fill the orders, so he posted a promise that he planned to refund the money given by the backers. However, after several weeks with no refunds, some of the backers decided to take action against Quest. One of the backers filed a breach of contract lawsuit against Quest, and Quest eventually filed for bankruptcy.

Avoiding a Kickstarter Disaster

Crowdfunding remains a popular tool for entrepreneurs to use to get hard-to-find seed capital. When approached carefully, crowdfunding can be a highly effective means for raising funding. The following suggestions can help entrepreneurs avoid creating disastrous situations when raising money using crowdfunding:

- ***Start with a business plan.*** Although business plans are not required by crowdfunding Web sites, it is always advisable to develop one as part of your preparation. Remember that one of the most important uses of a business plan is to communicate with investors and lenders. Although Kickstarter backers are not technically investors, developing a plan that spells out what you will do with the money and how you will achieve what you promise benefits both investors and the entrepreneur.

- ***Have contracts in place.*** Because crowdfunding usually involves some sort of product, make sure you have contacts in place with suppliers or outsource manufacturers to ensure that you can deliver what you promise at the price you have planned for in your projections and budgets.

- ***Be honest about the risks.*** If risks and challenges may prevent you from delivering a product, be open and honest about all of them in the information you present on the crowdfunding Web site. Doing so avoids nasty surprises if things do not go as planned.

- ***Remember that backers view themselves as customers, not investors.*** When people provide backing for your project, they are assuming that they have placed a preorder with you that you will fulfill. They do not view themselves as investors who may or may not get a return for the money they give you.

Sources: Based on Joseph S. Pete, "Green Sense Farms Reaches Crowdfunding Goal on Day 1," *NWI Times*, September 10, 2016, www.nwitimes.com/business/local/green-sense-farms-reaches-crowdfunding-goal-on-day/article_a9f53c25-94ff-575b-8052-70c42110814d.html; Amy Feldman, "Ten of the Most Successful Companies Built on Kickstarter," *Forbes*, April 14, 2016, www.forbes.com/sites/amyfeldman/2016/04/14/ten-of-the-most-successful-companies-built-on-kickstarter/#38f77da24579; Katie Lally, "PowerPot After Shark Tank Update—PowerPot Now in 2017," *Gazette Review*, June 29, 2016, http://gazettereview.com/2016/06/powerpot-after-shark-tank-update-now/; Karen E. Klein, "How to Get Funded on Kickstarter," *Bloomberg Businessweek*, April 18, 2014, www.businessweek.com/articles/2014-04-18/how-to-get-funded-on-kickstarter; Eric Markowitz, "When Kickstarter Investors Want Their Money Back," *Inc.*, January 10, 2013, www.inc.com/eric-markowitz/when-kickstarter-investors-want-their-money-back.html; James Holloway, "Kickstarter Disaster: When Crowdfunding Backfires," *Gizmag*, July 30, 2013, www.gizmag.com/kickstater-disaster/28514/; "Don't Call Me Ma'am," Fundable, n.d., www.fundable.com/dont-call-me-maam; Todd Hixon, "Is Crowdfunding a Boon or a Disaster?" *Forbes*, April 4, 2012, www.forbes.com/sites/toddhixon/2012/04/04/is-crowdfunding-a002Dboon-or-a-disaster/.

accelerator program. Private accelerators are located in most major cities, and a growing number of universities have accelerator programs to assist student and alumni entrepreneurs.

Three of the most successful accelerator programs are AngelPad, MuckerLab, and Techstars. Although accelerators do provide small investments, the most important contribution they offer is the coaching and mentoring from angel investors and experienced entrepreneurs. Angel investors work alongside the founding entrepreneurs, serving as mentors and advisers. As a result, they shape the business models of the companies in which they invest and improve their chances for success. For example, the Techstars accelerator program reports that almost 80 percent of its participants are still active companies and that the average amount of subsequent funding per company is more than $3.1 million.[16]

Courtesy of Rich Razgaitis,
CEO and Co-fouder, FloWater, Inc.

private investors (angels)

wealthy individuals, often entrepreneurs themselves, who invest in business start-ups in exchange for equity stakes in the companies.

ENTREPRENEURIAL PROFILE: Rich Razgaitis, FloWater Rich Razgaitis, CEO of FloWater, launched his business by using both a crowdfunding platform and an accelerator program. FloWater's water refill stations quickly dispense purified, chilled water through a proprietary filtration system, thus helping to eliminate single water bottle waste that ends up in landfills. After completing the Blue Startups accelerator in Hawaii, FloWater raised more than $7 million from investors. The company has already installed hundreds of dispensers in health clubs, corporations, schools, and hotels.[17] ∎

Angels

After dipping into their own pockets and convincing friends and relatives to invest in their business ventures, many entrepreneurs still find themselves short of the seed capital they need. Frequently, the next stop on the road to business financing is private investors. These **private investors** (or **angels**) are wealthy individuals, often entrepreneurs themselves, who are accredited investors and choose to invest their own money in business start-ups in exchange for equity stakes in the companies. Angel investors have provided much-needed capital to entrepreneurs for many years. Alexander Graham Bell, inventor of the telephone, used angel capital to start Bell Telephone in 1877. More recently, companies such as Google, Apple, Starbucks, Kinko's (now FedEx Office), and the Body Shop relied on angel financing in their early years to finance growth.

In many cases, angels invest in businesses for more than purely economic reasons—for example, because they have a personal interest or experience in a particular industry—and they are willing to put money into companies in the earliest stages, long before venture capital firms and institutional investors jump in. Angel financing, the fastest-growing segment of the small business capital market, is ideal for companies that have outgrown the capacity of investments from friends and family but are still too small to attract the interest of venture capital companies. Angel financing is vital to the nation's small business sector because it fills this capital gap in which small companies need investments ranging from $100,000 or less to perhaps $5 million or more. For instance, after raising the money to launch Amazon.com from family members and friends, Jeff Bezos turned to angels for capital because venture capital firms were not interested in investing in a business start-up. Bezos attracted $1.2 million from a dozen angels before landing $8 million from venture capital firms a year later.[18]

Angels are a primary source of capital for companies in the start-up stage through the growth stage, and their role in financing small businesses is significant. Research at the University of New Hampshire shows that nearly 298,000 angels and angel groups invest $21.3 billion a year in 64,380 small companies, most of them in the start-up phase.[19] In short, angels are one of the largest and most important sources of external equity capital for small businesses. Their investments in young companies nearly match those of professional venture capitalists, providing vital capital to more than 14 times as many entrepreneurial ventures (see Figure 15.2).

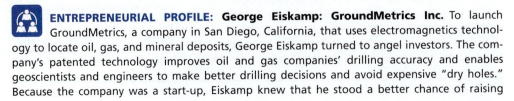

ENTREPRENEURIAL PROFILE: George Eiskamp: GroundMetrics Inc. To launch GroundMetrics, a company in San Diego, California, that uses electromagnetics technology to locate oil, gas, and mineral deposits, George Eiskamp turned to angel investors. The company's patented technology improves oil and gas companies' drilling accuracy and enables geoscientists and engineers to make better drilling decisions and avoid expensive "dry holes." Because the company was a start-up, Eiskamp knew that he stood a better chance of raising

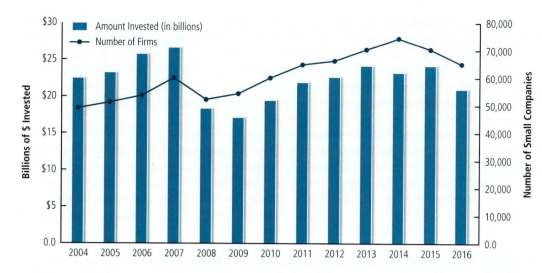

FIGURE 15.2

Angel Financing

Source: Based on data from the Center for Venture Research, Whittemore School of Business, University of New Hampshire, https://paulcollege.unh .edu/research/center-venture-research/ cvr-analysis-reports.

capital from angel investors than from venture capital firms. He pitched the company's business plan to members of the Tech Coast Angels, an angel capital network in San Diego, and 15 angels invested $1.2 million in GroundMetrics. Eiskamp has raised a total of nearly $10 million, all from angel investors, in six subsequent rounds of financing. He says that his success with angel financing is the result of networking to find the angel investors and having a sound business plan and elevator pitch to convince them of his company's competitive advantage.[20] ■

Angels fill a significant gap in the seed capital market. They are most likely to finance start-ups with capital requirements in the $10,000 to $2 million range, well below the $5 million to $10 million minimum investments most professional venture capitalists prefer. Because a $1 million deal requires about as much of a venture capitalist's time to research and evaluate as a $20 million deal, venture capitalists tend to focus on big deals, where their returns are bigger. The average angel investment (including angel funds and networks) in a company is nearly $331,000.[21] Because angels tend to invest in the earliest stages of a business, they incur the highest levels of risk. In fact, although angel investors have an average return of 22 percent on their overall investments, 70 percent of all investments made by angels lose money. However, the potential for investing in big winners exists; 6 percent of angels' investments produce a return of more than 10 times their original investments.[22] Because of the inherent risks in start-up companies, many venture capitalists have shifted their investment portfolios away from start-ups toward more established businesses. That's why angel financing is so important: Angels often finance deals that no venture capitalist will consider.

Most angels are seasoned entrepreneurs themselves; on average, angel investors have founded 2.7 companies and have 14.5 years of entrepreneurial experience. They also are well educated; 99 percent have college degrees. Research also shows that 86 percent of angel investors are men (their average age is 57 years) who have been investing in promising small companies for 9 years. The typical angel invests in one company per year.[23] When evaluating a proposal, angels look for a qualified management team (generally not just an individual entrepreneur) and a business with a clearly defined niche, market potential, and competitive advantage. They also want to see market research that proves the existence of a sizable customer base and a viable exit strategy, the avenue by which they get their investments back, ideally with a handsome return. Angels want a path to a clean exit for their investment rather than a business that might yield dividends over time. Angels seek, on average, about a 20 percent ownership stake in the businesses they invest in.

Entrepreneurs in search of capital quickly learn that the real challenge lies in *finding* angels. Most angels have substantial business and financial experience, and many of them are entrepreneurs or former entrepreneurs. Because most angels frown on "cold calls" from entrepreneurs they don't know, locating them boils down to making the right contacts. Networking is the key. Asking friends, attorneys, bankers, stockbrokers, accountants, other business owners, and consultants for suggestions and introductions is a good way to start. Many angel investors use their attorneys and accountants as gatekeepers for potential deals. Angels almost always invest their money locally, so entrepreneurs should look close to home for them—typically within a 50- to 100-mile radius. In fact, 7 out of 10 angels invest in companies that are within 50 miles of their homes or offices. Angels also look for businesses they know something about, and most expect to invest their knowledge, experience, and energy as well as their money in a company. In fact, the advice and the network of contacts that angels bring to a deal can sometimes be as valuable as their money!

Angel investing has become more organized and professional than it was 20 years ago, with investors pooling their resources to form angel networks and angel capital funds, dubbed "super-angels," that operate like miniature versions of professional venture capital firms and draw on investors' skills, experience, and contacts to help the start-ups in which they invest to succeed. Today more than 300 angel capital networks operate in cities of all sizes across the United States (up from just 10 in 1996). Angel networks make the task of locating angels much easier for entrepreneurs in search of capital.

ENTREPRENEURIAL PROFILE: Crista Freeman: Phin & Phebes Ice Cream Crista Freeman, CEO and cofounder of Phin & Phebes Ice Cream, launched her business with the help of an investment by angel investor William Hines, who was part of the company's $150,000 seed funding round. Phin & Phebes Ice Cream is made with no preservatives, conventional stabilizers, or syrups of any kind. It is made with milk, cream, sugar, and egg yolks. Phin & Phebes has expanded into 39 states and more than 1,800 stores in its first six years in business. Its products are sold in stores such as Whole Foods, Earth Fare, Central Market, Gourmet Garage, Fresh Direct, and Morton Williams. The second round of fundraising was another angel round, this time raising $360,000. Angel investors in the second round included Brad Feld and Joanne Wilson. Feld is part of Foundry Group, which is a venture capital and angel investment group in Boulder, Colorado. Wilson is a businesswoman from New York City who is an active angel investor.[24] ∎

The Internet has greatly expanded the ability of entrepreneurs in search of capital and angels in search of businesses to find one another. Dozens of angel networks have set up shop on the Internet, many of them members of the Angel Capital Association (www.angelcapitalassociation.org). Entrepreneurs can expand the scope of their hunt for financing by including online angel groups and the Angel Capital Association's membership list in their searches. AngelList is another Web site that connects angel investors with high potential deals. AngelList also helps start-ups recruit new employees who have experience working in high growth companies.

Angels are an excellent source of "patient money," often willing to wait seven years or longer to cash out their investments. They earn their returns through the increased value of the business, not through dividends and interest. For example, more than 1,000 early investors in Microsoft Inc. are now multimillionaires. Angels' return-on-investment targets tend to be lower than those of professional venture capitalists. Whereas venture capitalists shoot for 60 to 75 percent returns annually, angel investors usually settle for 20 to 50 percent (depending on the level of risk involved in the venture). A study by the Kauffman Foundation reports that the average return on angels' investments in small companies is 2.5 times the original investment in 4.5 years.[25] Angel investors look for the same exit strategies that venture capital firms look for: either an initial public offering or a buyout by a larger company. The lesson: If an entrepreneur needs relatively small amounts of money to launch or to grow a company, angels are an excellent source.

Venture Capital Companies

venture capital companies
private, for-profit organizations that purchase equity positions in young businesses that they believe have high-growth and high-profit potential.

Venture capital companies are private, for-profit organizations that assemble pools of capital that they use to purchase equity positions in young businesses they believe have high-growth and high-profit potential, producing annual returns of 300 to 500 percent within five to seven years. More than 400 venture capital firms operate across the United States today, investing billions of dollars in promising small companies in a wide variety of industries (see Figure 15.3). Companies in the high-tech hubs San Francisco, San Jose, Boston, New York, Los Angeles, and San Diego account for about 45 percent of all *global* venture capital investments, but "secondary" cities, such as Raleigh (North Carolina), Austin (Texas), Seattle (Washington), Jacksonville (Florida), and Salt Lake City (Utah), offer thriving venture capital sectors that invest significant

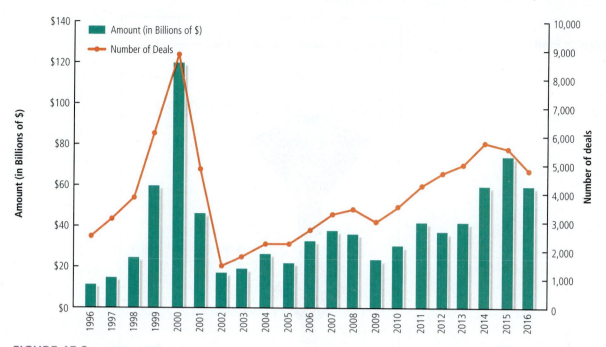

FIGURE 15.3

Venture Capital Funding

Source: Based on PriceWaterhouseCoopers, www.pwcmoneytree.com/MTPublic/ns/nav.jsp?page=historical.

sums of money, especially in local small businesses with high growth potential.[26] Venture capital firms have invested billions of dollars in high-potential small companies over the years, including such notable businesses as Google, Apple, Tesla, Genentech, Bed Bath & Beyond, Starbucks, Whole Foods Market, Costco, and Uber.

ENTREPRENEURIAL PROFILE: Vikas Gupta: Wonder Workshop After his daughter was born, entrepreneur Vikas Gupta began to wonder how early she could begin learning computer programming. His research revealed that children as young as five could learn programming concepts if they could interact with a tangible toy, so Gupta set out to create one. The result was Bo and Yana, two interactive robots designed to help children ages 5 to 12 learn computer programming skills. To bring the programmable robots to market, Gupta worked with Saurabh Gupta and Mikal Greaves to launch Play-i, now called Wonder Workshop. The trio started a crowdfunding campaign on its Web site, and in just 30 days, Wonder Workshop received 11,000 pre-orders that totaled $1.4 million, which enabled Gupta and his cofounders to begin production of the interactive robots, Dash and Dot. With proof that the business could be successful, the entrepreneurs closed a Series A round of venture capital that generated $8 million from Madrona Venture Group in Seattle and Charles River Ventures in Menlo Park, California. They used that growth capital to increase the size of the company's engineering, software development, and design teams, expand production, and develop educational robots designed to help older children learn programming skills. To fuel Wonder Workshop's rapid growth, the cofounders have since closed two more rounds of venture capital, totaling $27 million, which they are using to expand the company into global markets, including Australia, China, South Korea, and nations in both Europe and South America and to sponsor the Wonder League, a network of robotic competitions in which teams of children program Dash and Dot to accomplish particular tasks.[27] ■

POLICIES AND INVESTMENT STRATEGIES Venture capital firms usually establish stringent policies to implement their overall investment strategies.

Investment Size and Screening The average venture capital firm's investment in a small company has ranged over the last several years from about $7.1 million to $13.4 million, depending on the state of the economy and number of attractive venture deals.[28] Depending on the size of the venture capital company, minimum investments range from $100,000 to $5 million, but most

FIGURE 15.4

The Business Plan Funnel

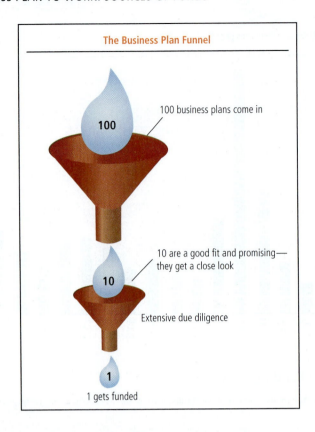

The Business Plan Funnel

100 business plans come in

100

10 are a good fit and promising—
they get a close look

10

Extensive due diligence

1

1 gets funded

venture capital firms seek investments in the $5 million to $25 million range to justify the cost of screening the large number of proposals they receive.

In a typical year, venture capital firms invest in about 3,800 of the nearly *28 million* small businesses in the United States. The venture capital screening process is *extremely* rigorous. According to the Global Entrepreneurship Monitor, only about 0.16 percent of businesses in the United States receive venture capital during their existence.[29] The typical venture capital firm receives about 1,200 business plans each year, although some receive many more. For every 100 business plans the average venture capital firm receives, 90 of them are rejected immediately because they do not match the firm's investment criteria or requirements. The firm conducts a thorough due diligence investigation of the remaining 10 companies and typically invests in only 1 of them (see Figure 15.4). The average time required to close a venture capital deal is 60 to 90 days.

Ownership and Control Most venture capitalists prefer to purchase ownership in a small business through common stock or convertible preferred stock. Although many venture capital firms purchase less than 50 percent of a company's stock, others buy a controlling share of a company, leaving its founders with a minority share of ownership. Most venture capitalists prefer to let the founding team of managers employ its skills to operate a business *if* they are capable of managing its growth. However, it is quite common for venture capitalists to join, and often control, the boards of directors of the companies in which they invest. Sometimes venture investors step in and shake up the management teams in the companies in which they invest. Janet Effland, a partner in the venture capital firm Apax Partners, says her fund changes management in the deals it funds about 40 percent of the time.[30] In other words, entrepreneurs should *not* expect venture capitalists to be passive investors! Some serve only as financial and managerial advisers, but others take an active role in managing the company—recruiting employees, providing sales leads, choosing attorneys and advertising agencies, and making daily decisions. The majority of these active venture capitalists say they are forced to step in because the existing management team lacks the talent and experience to achieve growth targets.

Stage of Investment Most venture capital firms invest in companies that are in the early stages of development (called early-stage investing), in the rapid-growth phase (called expansion-stage investing), or in the later stage of development. About 96 percent of all venture capital

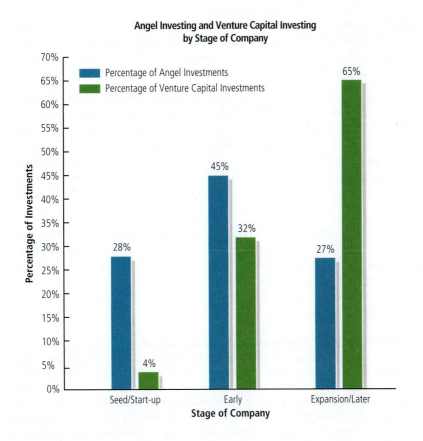

Angel Investing and Venture Capital Investing
by Stage of Company

FIGURE 15.5

Angel Versus VC Investments

Sources: Based on Jeffrey Sohl, "The Angel Investor Market in 2015: A Buyers Market," Center for Venture Research, May 25, 2015, https://paulcollege.unh.edu/sites/paulcollege.unh.edu/files/webform/Full%20Year%202015%20Analysis%20Report.pdf; "Explore the Data," *PwC MoneyTree*, 2016, www.pwc.com/us/en/technology/moneytree/explorer.html#/.

investments go to businesses in these stages; very few invest in small companies that are in the start-up phase.[31] Most venture capital firms do not make just a single investment in a company. Instead, they invest in a company over time across several stages, where their investments often total $10 million to $15 million or more.

Advice and Contacts In addition to the money they invest, more venture capital companies are providing the small companies in their portfolios with management advice and access to valuable networks of contacts of suppliers, employees, customers, and other sources of capital than they did just a few years ago. One of their goals in doing so is to strengthen the companies in which they have invested, thereby increasing their value.

Investment Preferences Venture capital firms now are larger, more professional, and more specialized than they were 25 years ago. As the industry matures, venture capital funds increasingly are focusing their investments in niches—everything from information technology to biotechnology. Some will invest in almost any industry, but most prefer companies in later stages. Traditionally, few companies receiving venture capital financing are in the start-up or seed stage, when entrepreneurs are forming a company or developing a product or service and when angels are most likely to invest (see Figure 15.5). Most of the start-up businesses that attract venture capital are technology companies in "hot" fields such as Internet related start-ups, mobile and telecommunications, healthcare, non-Internet related software, and computer hardware and services.[32]

WHAT VENTURE CAPITALISTS LOOK FOR Entrepreneurs must realize that it is difficult for any small business, especially fledgling or struggling firms, to pass the intense screening process of a venture capital company and qualify for an investment. A great elevator pitch and a sound business plan are essential to convincing venture capital firms to invest in a company. Geeta Vemuri, a principal in a venture capital firm, says investors want to see proof of concept for deals they consider investing in.[33] Two factors make a deal attractive to venture capitalists: high returns and a convenient (and profitable) exit strategy. When evaluating potential investments, venture capitalists look for the following features.

Competent Management The most important ingredient in the success of any business is the ability of the management team, and venture capitalists understand this. To venture capitalists, the ideal management team has experience, managerial skills, commitment, and the ability to expand the team as the business grows.

Competitive Edge Investors are searching for some factor that will enable a small business to set itself apart from its competitors. This distinctive competence may range from an innovative product or service that satisfies unmet customer needs to a unique marketing or research-and-development (R&D) approach. It must be something with the potential to create a sustainable competitive edge, making the company a leader in its industry. Bill Turner, founder of venture capital firm Signature Capital, stresses that he looks for transformational business models, such as his investments in an online music service, a hearing-aid maker, and an HIV-therapy company.[34]

Growth Industry Hot industries attract profits—and venture capital. Most venture capital funds focus their searches for prospects in rapidly growing fields because they believe the profit potential is greater in these areas. Venture capital firms are most interested in young companies that have enough growth potential to become at least $100 million businesses within three to five years. Venture capitalists know that most of the businesses they invest in will flop, so their winners have to be *big* winners.

ENTREPRENEURIAL PROFILE: Chieh Huang, Boxed Chieh Huang, founder and CEO of Boxed, is trying to become a giant killer. Huang founded Boxed with the intent of creating an app to compete with the likes of Amazon, Costco, and Wal-Mart. Boxed is an e-commerce company (like Amazon) that offers discounts on large quantities of bulk items (like Costco). Boxed sells its products online and through a mobile app and ships to customers anywhere in the United States. Huang raised $6.5 million in an A round of funding that was led by venture capital firms Greycroft Ventures, First Round Capital, and Signia Venture Partners. Three other venture capital firms also participated in the company's first round of funding, which Huang used to complete the development of the app and launch the company. In January 2015, Boxed raised $25 million in its B round from 20 investors that included venture capital firms and angel investors. Boxed used the B round of funding to expand its shipping of bulk items to consumers through its Web site and increase its marketing efforts. One year later, Boxed raised $100 million in its C round of funding to fund expansion of its team and further increase its marketing efforts.[35] ∎

Viable Exit Strategy Venture capitalists look for promising companies with the ability to dominate a market, and they also want to see a plan for a feasible exit strategy, typically to be executed within three to five years. Venture capital firms realize the return on their investments when the companies they invest in either make an initial public offering or are acquired by or merged into another business. Since the Sarbanes-Oxley Act passed in 2002, the number of public offerings has dropped significantly. Without as many public offerings, venture capitalists have had to be more patient in their exit strategies. Venture-backed companies that go public now take an average of 11 years from the time of their first venture capital investment to their initial stock offering, up from an average of less than three years in 1998.[36]

Intangible Factors Some other important factors considered in the screening process are not easily measured; they are the intuitive, intangible factors that the venture capitalist detects by gut feeling. This feeling might be the result of the small firm's solid sense of direction, its strategic planning process, the chemistry of its management team, or other factors. Venture capital firms want to know that entrepreneurs will use their money wisely—for investments that provide profitable results and not those that merely feed entrepreneurial egos.

Despite its many benefits, venture capital is not suited for every entrepreneur. Venture capital investments come with many strings attached and can limit entrepreneurs' ability to navigate their companies as they would prefer.

Corporate Venture Capital

Large corporations have gotten into the business of financing small companies and investing in businesses for both strategic and financial reasons. The investment arms of large corporations that are most active in venture capital markets are Google Ventures, Intel Capital, Comcast

Ventures, Salesforce Ventures, Qualcomm Ventures, Samsung Ventures, GE Ventures, and Cisco Investments. Even JetBlue and Campbell Soup Company have formed venture capital divisions to invest in promising young companies. Corporate venture capital is active across all stages of funding, including seed rounds.[37] Today, more than 13.4 percent of all venture capital deals involve corporate venture capital. The average investment that large corporations make in small companies is $28.3 million.[38] Young companies not only get a boost from the capital injections large companies give them but also stand to gain many other benefits from the relationship. The right corporate partner may share technical expertise, distribution channels, and marketing know-how and provide introductions to important customers and suppliers. Another intangible yet highly important advantage an investment from a large corporate partner gives a small company is credibility, often referred to as "market validation." Doors that otherwise would be closed to a small company magically open when the right corporation becomes a strategic partner.

ENTREPRENEURIAL PROFILE: Savioke GV (formerly known as Google Ventures), the corporate venture capital firm owned by the parent company of Google, joined five other venture firms in funding the $2 million seed round for robotics start-up Savioke. Savioke specializes in robots for the service industry, including hotels, hospitals, and restaurants. GV's investment in Savioke follows eight acquisitions of robot companies by its parent company, Alphabet, Inc. Andy Wheeler, a partner in GV, says that the firm invested in Savioke based on the strength of its founding team. The first robot Savioke developed was a delivery robot that was tested in the Aloft Cupertino Hotel in Silicon Valley. The robot delivers items, such as shampoo and toothbrushes, to guest rooms from the front desk. After its early product success, five major international hotel brands purchased Savioke robots for their properties. Based on the success of its early robots, corporate venture capital firm Intel Capital committed to becoming the lead investor of Savioke's $15 million series A financing to support expanded sales of its robots and to develop next-generation products.[39] ■

Public Stock Sale ("Going Public")

In some cases, companies can "go public" by selling shares of stock to outside investors. In an **initial public offering (IPO)**, a company raises capital by selling shares of its stock to the general public for the first time. An IPO is an effective method of raising large amounts of capital, but it can be an expensive and time-consuming process filled with regulatory nightmares. Once a company makes an IPO, *nothing* will ever be the same again. Managers must consider the impact of their decisions not only on the company and its employees but also on shareholders and the value of their stock.

Going public isn't for every business. In fact, most small companies do not meet the criteria for making a successful public stock offering. Since 2001, the average number of companies that make IPOs each year is 108, and the average size of an IPO is $303 million (see Figure 15.6). Only about 20,000 companies in the United States—less than 1 percent of the total—are publicly held. The dramatic decline in the number of IPOs that occurred in the early part of this century was due in large part to the passage of the Sarbanes-Oxley Act, a law that put significant restrictions and requirements on publicly traded companies. An outcome of this law was to make IPOs unaffordable for smaller companies. Since Sarbanes-Oxley became law, few new companies with less than $25 million in annual sales manage to go public successfully. Since 2001, 64 percent of the companies that have completed IPOs have had annual sales of $50 million or more.[40] For instance, LinkedIn, the professional networking Web site, was generating sales of $243 million at the time of its IPO. When Zygna, the creator of popular Facebook games such as Farmville, Cityville, and Words with Friends, filed for its IPO, the company's sales were $597 million.[41]

It is almost impossible for a start-up company with no track record of success to raise money with an IPO. Instead, the investment bankers who underwrite public stock offerings typically look for established companies with the following characteristics:

- *Consistently high growth rates.* In the three years prior to its IPO, Snapchat's revenues grew 11,138 percent![42]

- *Scalability.* Underwriters and institutional investors want proof that a company can maintain or improve its efficiency as it experiences the strain that rapid growth imposes.

LO3

Describe the process of "going public."

initial public offering (IPO)

a method of raising equity capital in which a company sells shares of its stock to the general public for the first time.

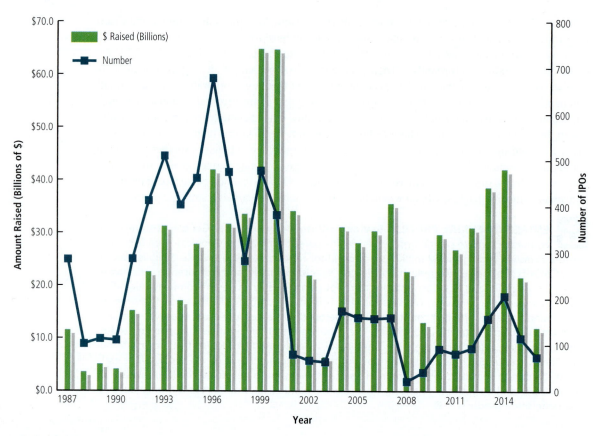

FIGURE 15.6

Initial Public Offerings (IPOs)

Source: Based on data from Jay R. Ritter, "Initial Public Offerings: Updated Statistics," University of Florida, March 8, 2016, http://bear.warrington.ufl.edu/ritter/IPOs2013Statistics.pdf.

- *A strong record of earnings.* Strangely enough, profitability at the time of the IPO is not essential; since 2001, 54 percent of companies making IPOs have had negative earnings.[43]

  - *Three to five years of audited financial statements that meet or exceed Securities and Exchange Commission (SEC) standards.* After the Enron and WorldCom scandals, investors are demanding impeccable financial statements.

  - *A solid position in a rapidly growing industry.* The median age of companies making IPOs since 2001 is 9.7 years, and almost all of them are in fast-growing industries.[44]

  - *A sound management team with experience and a strong board of directors.*

 **ENTREPRENEURIAL PROFILE: Evan Spiegel and Bobby Murphy: Snap** On March 1, 2017, Snap, the parent company of the social media mobile app Shapchat, went public, raising more than $33 billion. Lightspeed Venture partners invested $485,000 in seed funding in 2012. When Snap went public in 2017, Lightspeed's 8.6 percent ownership was worth about $2.064 billion, an increase of more than 4,255 times its initial investment. The venture capital firm Benchmark invested $21 million in Snap's Round A funding in 2013. Benchmark's 13 percent ownership was worth $3.12 billion when Snap's shares went public. Although both venture capital firms made

significant returns on their investments, Snap cofounders Evan Spiegel, 26 years old at the time of the IPO, and Bobby Murphy, 28 years old at the time, had the largest windfalls when Snap went public. Both of the cofounders were able to maintain roughly 22.2 percent ownership in Snap leading up to the IPO. At the time of Snap's IPO, *each* of the cofounders owned stock worth $5.33 billion![45] ■

THE REGISTRATION PROCESS Taking a company public is a complicated, bureaucratic process that usually takes several months to complete. Many experts compare the IPO process to running a corporate marathon, and both the company and its management team must be in shape and up to the grueling task. The typical entrepreneur *cannot* take his or her company public alone. It requires a coordinated effort from a team of professionals, including company executives, an accountant, a securities attorney, a financial printer, and at least one underwriter. The key steps in taking a company public are as follows:

- *Choose the underwriter.* The single most important ingredient in making a successful IPO is selecting a capable **managing underwriter (or investment banker)**. The managing underwriter serves two primary roles: helping to prepare the registration statement for the issue and promoting the company's stock to potential investors. The underwriter works with company managers as an adviser to prepare the registration statement that must be filed with the SEC, promotes the issue, prices the stock (usually in the $10 to $20 per share range), and provides aftermarket support. Once the registration statement is finished, the managing underwriter's primary job is selling the company's stock through an underwriting syndicate of other investment bankers it develops.

- *Negotiate a letter of intent.* To begin an offering, the entrepreneur and the underwriter must negotiate a **letter of intent**, which outlines the details of the deal. The letter of intent covers a variety of important issues, including the type of underwriting, its size and price range, the underwriter's commission, and any warrants and options included. It almost always states that the underwriter is not bound to the offering until it is executed—usually the day before or the day of the offering. However, the letter usually creates a binding obligation for the company to pay any direct expenses the underwriter incurs relating to the offer.

- *Prepare the registration statement.* After a company signs the letter of intent, the next task is to prepare the **registration statement** to be filed with the SEC. This document describes both the company and the stock offering and discloses information about the risks of investing. It includes information on the use of the proceeds, the company's history, its financial position, its capital structure, the risks it faces, its managers' experience, and *many* other details. The statement is extremely comprehensive and may take months to develop. To prepare the statement, entrepreneurs must rely on their team of professionals.

- *File with the SEC.* When the statement is finished (with the exception of pricing the shares, proceeds, and commissions, which cannot be determined until just before the issue goes to market), the company officially files the statement with the SEC and awaits the review of the Division of Corporate Finance, a process that takes 30 to 45 days (or more). The division sends notice of any deficiencies in the registration statement to the company's attorney in a comment letter. The company and its team of professionals must cure all of the deficiencies in the statement noted in the comment letter. Finally, the company files the revised registration statement along with a pricing amendment (giving the price of the shares, the proceeds, and the commissions).

- *Wait to go effective.* While waiting for the SEC's approval, the managers and the underwriters are busy. The underwriters are building a syndicate of other underwriters who will market the company's stock. (No stock sales can be made prior to the effective date of the offering, however.) The SEC also limits the publicity and information a company may release during this quiet period (which officially starts when the company reaches a preliminary agreement with the managing underwriter and ends 25 days after the effective date).

- *Road show.* Securities laws do permit a **road show**, a gathering of potential syndicate members sponsored by the managing underwriter. Its purpose is to promote interest among

managing underwriter (investment banker) a financial company that serves two important roles: helping to prepare the registration statement for an issue and promoting the company's stock to potential investors.

letter of intent an agreement between the underwriter and the company about to go public that outlines the details of the deal.

registration statement the document a company must file with the SEC that describes both the company and its stock offering and discloses information about the risk of investing.

road show a gathering of potential syndicate members sponsored by the managing underwriter for the purpose of promoting a company's IPO.

potential underwriters in the IPO by featuring the company, its management, and the proposed deal. The managing underwriter and key company officials barnstorm major financial centers at a grueling pace.

- *Sign underwriting agreement.* On the last day before the registration statement becomes effective, the company signs the formal underwriting agreement. The final settlement, or closing, takes place a few days after the effective date for the issue. At this meeting, the underwriters receive their shares to sell, and the company receives the proceeds of the offering. Typically, the entire process of going public takes from 120 to 180 days, but it can take much longer if the issuing company is not properly prepared for the process.

- *Meet state requirements.* In addition to satisfying the SEC's requirements, a company also must meet the securities laws in all states in which the issue is sold. These state laws (or "blue-sky" laws) vary drastically from one state to another, and the company must comply with them.

NONPUBLIC REGISTRATIONS AND EXEMPTIONS The IPO process just described, called an *S-1 filing*, requires maximum disclosure in the initial filing and discourages most small businesses from using it. Fortunately, the SEC allows several exemptions from this full-disclosure process for small businesses seeking to sell stock through a limited private stock offering. Entrepreneurs can sell stock through a limited private offering to accredited investors, corporations and trusts, and insiders to the business. The SEC has established simplified registration statements and exemptions from the registration process through what is known as Regulation D (Rules 504, 505, and 506).

Regulation D rules minimize the expense and time required to raise equity capital for small businesses by simplifying or eliminating the requirement for registering the offering with the SEC, which often takes months and costs many thousands of dollars. Under Regulation D, the whole process typically costs less than half of what a traditional public offering costs. The SEC's objective in creating Regulation D was to give small companies the access to equity financing that large companies have via the stock market while bypassing many of the costs and filing requirements. A Regulation D offering requires only minimal notification to the SEC.

Rule 504 is the most popular of the Regulation D exemptions because it is the least restrictive. It allows a company to sell shares of its stock to an unlimited number of investors without regard to their experience or level of sophistication. A business also can make multiple offerings under Rule 504 as long as it waits at least 6 months between them; however, Rule 504 places a cap of $1 million in a 12-month period on the amount of capital a company can raise. One variation of Rule 504 is the Small Company Offering Registration (SCOR), which allows entrepreneurs to file a standard, "plain English" registration form, the U-7, which is recognized by 43 states. The completed U-7 registration statement, which is in a question-and-answer format, does not require a battery of attorneys, accountants, and securities experts to complete and serves as the company's prospectus for soliciting investors.

An offering under Rule 505 has a higher capital ceiling ($5 million in a 12-month period) than Rule 504 but imposes more restrictions (e.g., no more than 35 nonaccredited investors, no advertising of the offer, more stringent disclosure requirements).

Rule 506 imposes no ceiling on the amount that can be raised, but most companies that make Rule 506 offerings raise between $1 million and $50 million in capital. Like a Rule 505 offering, it limits the issue to no more than 35 nonaccredited investors and prohibits advertising the offer to the public. There is no limit on the number of accredited investors, however. Rule 506 also requires detailed disclosure of relevant information, but the extent depends on the size of the offering.

LO4

Describe the various sources of debt capital.

Sources of Debt Financing

Debt financing involves funds that the small business owner borrows and must repay with interest. Debt financing is a popular tool that many entrepreneurs use to acquire capital. In a typical year, small businesses borrow more than $1 trillion, with about half of that amount coming from banks. Debt financing accounts for only about 20 percent of total financing used by small business start-ups, but owners of existing businesses rely more heavily on debt capital.[46] Unfortunately, many entrepreneurs cannot secure the debt financing they need to fuel their companies' growth. One recent study reports that 45 percent of small businesses with employees applied for debt financing, and 75 percent of them requested less than $250,000 (and 55 percent requested less than $100,000). However, only 53 percent of the entrepreneurs say that lenders approved their loan requests in full. Nearly one-fourth of the entrepreneurs say that lenders completely denied their loan requests.[47]

ENTREPRENEURIAL PROFILE: Vicky Vij, Bukhara Grill Vicky Vij, an immigrant from Delhi, India, built a successful restaurant called Bukhara Grill in downtown New York City. The restaurant had sales of more than $2.5 million a year, three straight years of profitability, and excellent credit. However, when Vij decided to buy a catering business to expand the operation, he had no success getting funding from local banks. Vij turned to an online service, Biz2Credit. com, which was able to find a bank in Salt Lake City that was willing to give his business an SBA-guaranteed loan for $3.9 million to purchase a banquet hall and equipment.[48] ■

Although borrowed capital allows entrepreneurs to maintain complete ownership of their businesses, their companies must carry it as a liability on the balance sheet and must repay it with interest at some point in the future. In addition, because lenders consider small businesses to be greater risks than bigger corporate customers, they must pay higher interest rates because of the risk–return trade-off—the higher the risk, the greater is the return demanded. Most small firms pay well above the **prime rate**, the interest rate that banks charge their most creditworthy customers. A study by David Walker, a professor at Georgetown University, reports that small businesses pay two to three times the prime rate, primarily because they rely heavily on credit cards and other high-cost methods of debt financing.[49]

Entrepreneurs seeking debt capital are quickly confronted with an astounding range of credit options, varying greatly in complexity, availability, and flexibility. Not all of these sources of debt capital are equally favorable, however. By understanding the various sources of debt capital and their characteristics, entrepreneurs can greatly increase the chances of obtaining a loan.

Figure 15.7 shows the financing strategies that existing small businesses use. We now turn to the various sources of debt capital.

prime rate
the interest rate that banks charge their most creditworthy customers.

Commercial Banks

Commercial banks are the very heart of the financial market for small businesses, providing the greatest number and variety of loans to small companies. Seventy-one percent of small companies with employees have outstanding debt.[50] Currently, small businesses in the United States have 24.2 million bank loans with a total outstanding balance of $599 billion.[51] For small business owners, banks are lenders of *first* resort. The average microbusiness bank loan (those less than $100,000) is $12,455, and the average small business bank loan (those between $100,000 and $1 million) is $342,500.[52]

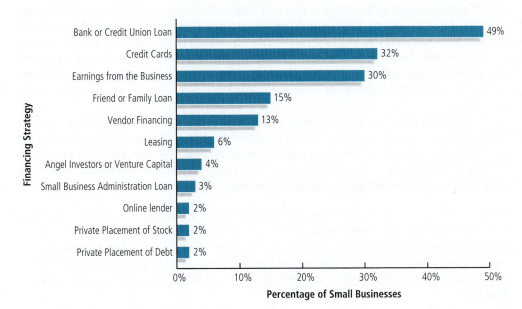

FIGURE 15.7

Small Business Financing Strategies

Sources: Based on National Small Business Association, *2016 Year-End Economic Report*, p.10.

Banks tend to be conservative in their lending practices and prefer to make loans to established small businesses rather than to high-risk start-ups. Unfortunately for entrepreneurs, turbulence in the financial markets has caused banks to tighten their lending standards, making it more difficult for small businesses, even established ones, to qualify for loans.

ENTREPRENEURIAL PROFILE: Georgette Miller: Georgette Miller Law Georgette Miller, an immigrant from Jamaica, decided to leave the large law firm where she had been working since she graduated from law school to start her own law practice. Georgette Miller Law specializes in real estate law and consumer and small business bankruptcies. The firm expanded quickly, opening three additional offices. Miller tried to find a traditional large bank that would provide her practice with a badly needed line of credit, but she had no success. She then contacted a loan broker, Multifunding, which was able to help her secure a loan from a local community bank. With funding in place, she was able to expand her business into two additional locations and add a second attorney and a paralegal.[53] ∎

Bankers prefer to make loans to existing businesses with successful track records. They are concerned with a firm's operating past and will scrutinize its financial reports to project its position in the future. They also want proof of the stability of the company's sales and its ability to generate adequate cash flow to repay the loan. If they do make loans to a start-up venture, banks like to see sufficient cash flow to repay the loan, ample collateral to secure it, or an SBA guarantee to insure it. Small banks are more likely than large banks to extend loans to small businesses. Small banks also tend to be more small business friendly and are more likely than their larger counterparts to customize the terms of their loans to the particular needs of small businesses, offering, for example, flexible payment terms to match the seasonal pattern of a company's cash flow or interest-only payments until a piece of equipment begins generating revenue. Small and midsize banks approve 48.9 percent of small business loan requests, and large banks approve only 23.1 percent of loan requests from small companies.[54]

When evaluating a loan application, especially for a business start-up, banks focus on a company's capacity to create positive cash flow because they know that is where the money to repay their loans will come from. The ability of the business to comfortably repay the loan, both interest and principal, is the first source of payment bankers want to see. The first question in most bankers' minds when reviewing an entrepreneur's business plan is, "Can this business generate sufficient cash to repay the loan?"

Bankers look to business owners as the second source of repayment if a company is not able to repay a small business loan. Banks and other lenders also require entrepreneurs to sign personal guarantees for any loan they make to small businesses. By making a personal loan guarantee, an entrepreneur is pledging that he or she will be liable *personally* for repaying the loan in the event that the business itself cannot repay the loan. Recall from Chapter 6 that in the eyes of the law, a sole proprietor or a general partner and the business are one and the same; therefore, for them, personal loan guarantees are redundant. However, because the owners of S corporations, corporations, and LLCs are separate from their businesses, they are not automatically responsible for the company's debts. Once the owners of these businesses sign a personal loan guarantee, however, they become liable for their companies' loans. It is as if these individuals have "cosigned" the loan with the business, just as many parents cosign loans for their young adult children.

Even though bankers rely on collateral to secure their loans, the last thing banks want is for a borrower to default, forcing them to sell the collateral (often at "fire-sale" prices) and use the proceeds to pay off the loan. Therefore, collateral is actually the third source of repayment bankers look to for repayment of a small business loan. That's why bankers stress cash flow when analyzing loan requests and demand personal guarantees from the entrepreneurs.

SHORT-TERM LOANS Short-term loans, extended for less than one year, are the most common type of commercial loan banks make to small companies. These funds typically are used to replenish the working capital account to finance the purchase of inventory, boost output, finance credit sales to customers, or take advantage of cash discounts. As a result, an entrepreneur repays the loan after converting inventory and receivables into cash. There are several types of short-term loans.

Home Equity Loans Many entrepreneurs use the equity that they have built in their homes to finance their business start-ups. Entrepreneurs borrow from themselves by pledging their homes as collateral for the loans they receive. However, declining real estate values in many parts of the country have reduced or wiped out the equity in many people's homes, making securing home equity loans for their businesses much more difficult than it once was. Brother and sister Russell and Julia Lundstrom funded their start-up Simple Smart Science, which produces cognitive and memory nutritional products, with a $125,000 home equity loan from a community bank.[55]

Commercial Loans (or "Traditional Bank Loans") A basic short-term loan is the commercial bank's specialty. Business owners typically repay the loan, which often is unsecured because secured loans are much more expensive to administer and maintain, as a lump sum within three to six months. In other words, the bank grants a loan to a business owner without requiring him or her to pledge any specific collateral to support the loan in case of default. The owner repays the total amount of the loan at maturity. Sometimes the interest due on the loan is prepaid— deducted from the total amount borrowed. Until business owners can prove their companies' creditworthiness to the bank's satisfaction, they are not likely to qualify for unsecured commercial loans.

Lines of Credit One of the most common requests entrepreneurs make of banks and commercial finance companies is to establish a commercial **line of credit**, a short-term loan with a preset limit that provides much-needed cash flow for day-to-day operations. A recent study reports that 86 percent of owners of small businesses with employees applied for a line of credit, but only 68 percent were approved.[56] A line of credit is ideal for helping business owners smooth out the uneven flow of cash that results from seasonal sales, funding inventory purchases, extending trade credit, and smoothing out fluctuations in a business's working capital. With a commercial line of credit, a business owner can borrow up to the predetermined ceiling at any time during the year by quickly and conveniently drawing down on the line of credit. Bankers often require a company to rest its line of credit during the year, maintaining a zero balance, as proof that the line of credit is not a perpetual crutch. Like commercial loans, lines of credit can be secured or unsecured but normally require a personal guarantee.

line of credit
a short-term bank loan with a preset limit that provides working capital for day-to-day operations.

ENTREPRENEURIAL PROFILE: Jordan Drake When Jordan Drake was approved to open a State Farm Insurance agency in Hendersonville, Tennessee, he knew that he would need additional financing to supplement the personal savings he was using to start his new business. Drake was able to get a $25,000 line of credit through his local bank by securing the loan with his personal pickup truck. State Farm provided an additional $25,000 unsecured line of credit. Fortunately, through careful negotiation of his lease and prudent cash management, Drake was able to open the business without drawing on either line of credit. However, he says he sleeps easier knowing he has access to additional funding if his start-up hits any bumps in the road.[57] ∎

Floor Planning Floor planning is a form of financing frequently employed by retailers of "big-ticket items" that are easily distinguishable from one another (usually by serial number), such as automobiles, boats, and major appliances. For example, a commercial bank finances Auto City's purchase of its inventory of automobiles and maintains a security interest in each car in the order by holding its title as collateral. Auto City pays interest on the loan monthly and repays the principal as it sells the cars. The longer a floor-planned item sits in inventory, the more it costs the business owner in interest expense. Banks and other floor planners often discourage retailers from using their money without authorization by performing spot checks to verify prompt repayment of the principal as items are sold.

INTERMEDIATE- AND LONG-TERM LOANS Although banks are primarily lenders of short-term capital to small businesses, they will make intermediate- and long-term loans. Intermediate- and long-term loans, which are normally secured by collateral, are extended for one year or longer. Commercial banks grant these loans for constructing buildings, purchasing real estate and equipment, expanding a business, and other long-term investments. Matching the amount and the purpose of a loan to the appropriate type and length of loan is important. Loan repayments are normally made monthly or quarterly.

Installment Loans One of the most common types of intermediate-term loans is an installment loan, which banks make to small firms for purchasing equipment, facilities, real estate, and other fixed assets. When financing equipment, a bank usually lends the small business from 60 to 80 percent of the equipment's value in return for a security interest in the equipment. The loan's amortization schedule, which is based on a set number of monthly payments, typically coincides with the length of the equipment's usable life. In financing real estate (commercial mortgages), banks typically lend up to 75 to 80 percent of the property's value and allow a lengthier repayment schedule of 10 to 30 years.

term loan

a bank loan that imposes restrictions (covenants) on the business decisions an entrepreneur makes concerning the company's operations.

Term Loans Another common type of loan banks make to small businesses is a **term loan**. Banks grant these typically unsecured loans to businesses whose past operating history suggests a high probability of repayment. Some banks make only secured term loans, however. Term loans impose restrictions (called *covenants*) on the business decisions an entrepreneur makes concerning the company's operations. For instance, a term loan may set limits on owners' salaries, prohibit further borrowing without the bank's approval, or require maintaining certain financial ratios (recall the discussion of ratio analysis in Chapter 12).

The accompanying "Hands On . . . How To" feature describes the seven most common reasons bankers reject small business loan applications and how to avoid them.

Hands On . . . How To

Get a Bank to Say "Yes" to Your Loan Application

Landing a loan to start or expand a small business is much more difficult today than it was in the past because of stodgy credit markets and upheaval in the banking and financial industries. Entrepreneurs often complain that bankers don't understand the financial needs they face when starting and operating their businesses. In many instances, however, business owners fail to help themselves when they apply for bank loans. Following are the seven most common reasons bankers reject small business loan applications—and how you can avoid them.

Reason 1. "Our bank doesn't make small business loans."

Cure: Select the right bank. Before applying for a bank loan, research banks to find out which ones actively seek the type of loan you need. Some banks don't make loans of less than $500,000, whereas others focus almost exclusively on small company loans. The SBA's reports *Micro-Business-Friendly Banks in the United States* and *Small Business Lending in the United States* are valuable resources for locating the banks in your area that are most likely to make small business loans. Small, local banks tend to be more receptive to small business loan requests than many large banks, which often rely on formulas and templates to make lending decisions. Other factors that influence the types of loans that banks make include the industry in which the company competes, the company's geographic location, and the length of time it has been in business. Establishing a relationship with a bank before you need a loan also increases the probability that your loan request will be successful. Once you find the right bank for your business, open an account there, seek a small line of credit, and repay it consistently.

Reason 2. "I don't know enough about you or your business."

Cure: Although a business plan that explains what your company does (or will do) is a good first step, develop a personal relationship with the banker so he or she gets to know you better and hears about your business from your perspective. If you already have a physical location for your business, try to get the banker to meet with you there. If not, try to find a neutral location that gets the banker out of his or her office. Make sure you have your elevator pitch honed because it creates the first impression of you and your business. You should be able to describe your business—what it does, sells, or makes and its competitive edge—in just one or two minutes. Your business plan should address why there is an opportunity in the market, your company's major competition, what it will take to succeed in the market, and how your business will gain a competitive advantage in the market. Keep your plan focused and concise. Do not fill it up with operational details. In addition, be prepared to supply multiple scenarios of your financial projections, business credit references, and a personal credit history.

Reason 3. "You haven't told me why you need the money."

Cure: A solid business plan with clear financial forecasts and budgets will explain how much money you need and how you plan to use it. Make sure your request is specific; avoid requests for loans "for working capital." Don't make the mistake of answering the question "How much money do you need?" with "How much will you lend me?" Also, don't just throw out a rough number without any rationale or justification. If a banker thinks you are just guessing on your financing needs, the conversation will be

(continued)

Hands On . . . How To

over immediately. Instead, know how much money you need and be able to explain how the money will benefit your business and get it profitable enough to easily repay the loan. Remember that bankers want to make loans (after all, that's how they generate a profit), but they want to make loans only to those people they believe will repay them. Their primary responsibility is to protect the money that all of us entrust with them in our checking and savings accounts.

Reason 4. "Your numbers don't support your loan request."

Cure: Include a cash flow forecast in your business plan. Bankers analyze a company's balance sheet and income statement to judge the quality of its assets and its profitability, but they lend primarily on the basis of cash flow. "Can you repay the loan balance?" is the question that most concerns bankers, and they know that repaying a loan requires adequate cash flow. Collateral that backs up the loan is their last form of repayment, so do not stress collateral in your presentation—stress cash flow! If your business does not generate adequate cash flow, don't expect to get a loan. Prove to the banker that you understand your company's cash flow and how to manage it properly.

As a measure of a company's ability to repay a loan, bankers calculate the company's *cash coverage ratio*, which is its net income plus its noncash expenses (such as depreciation and amortization) divided by the annual payments on the proposed loan. They want to see a cash coverage ratio of at least 1.5:1 before granting a loan. In other words, to support $100,000 of loan payments, a company should have net cash flow of at least $150,000.

Reason 5. "You don't have enough collateral."

Cure: Be prepared to pledge your company's assets—and your personal assets—as collateral for the loan. If a company's cash flow declines to the point that it cannot make loan payments, banks look for other ways to get their money back. To protect themselves in a worst-case scenario (a business that is unable to repay a loan), bankers want the security of collateral before they make a loan. They will look to your personal assets first through your personal guarantee. They also expect more than $1 in collateral for every $1 of money they lend a business. Banks typically lend 50 to 90 percent of the value of real estate, 50 to 80 percent of the value of accounts receivable, and just 10 to 50 percent of the value of inventory and equipment pledged as collateral.

Reason 6. "Your business does not support the loan on its own."

Cure: Be prepared to provide a personal guarantee on the loan. This is a given for most small business loans until the company has a history of strong financial performance. By giving a personal guarantee, you're telling the banker that

if your business cannot repay the loan, you will. Many bankers see their small business clients and their companies as one and the same. Even if you choose a form of ownership that provides you with limited personal liability, bankers will ask you to override that protection by personally guaranteeing the loan. Another way to lower the risk of a bank extending a loan to a small company is to secure a loan guarantee through one of the SBA's programs.

Reason 7: "You don't have enough 'skin' in the game."

Cure: Increase the amount of money you have invested in the project. A few years ago, entrepreneurs were able to get loans for projects by investing as little as 5 to 10 percent of the total amount. Today, depending on the project, bankers expect entrepreneurs to put up at least 20 to 25 percent of the project's cost—and sometimes much more. Be prepared to use your company's retained earnings to pay for a significant portion of the cost of a project.

David Pitts, owner of Classic Graphics, a printing company in Charlotte, North Carolina, knows firsthand how the small business lending environment has changed. In the company's 30-year history, Pitts has relied on many bank loans to finance the company's growth. Recently, however, securing bank loans has been much more difficult despite Classic Graphics's rapid growth (from $39 million in sales to $50 million in sales in just one year) and strong financial performance. Securing several loans that ranged from $200,000 to more than $1 million became much more difficult than in the past, says Pitts. Although Pitts took realistic financial projections and a strong business plan to banks, several bankers rejected his loan requests for Classic Graphics. Pitts decided to merge Classic Graphics with a much larger firm in Minneapolis. This merger was one of many in an industry that has been suffering from declining profit margins.

There's no magic to getting a bank to approve your loan request. The secret is proper preparation and building a solid business plan that helps explain your business model and builds your credibility with the banker as a reliable business owner.

Sources: Based on John Rampton, "8 Reasons Your Business Loan Was Rejected," *Entrepreneur*, November 8, 2016, www.entrepreneur.com/article/284810; Anna Johansson, "5 Tips to Improve Your Odds of Getting a Small Business Loan," *Entrepreneur*, www.entrepreneur.com/article/289979; Jim Hammerand and Sam Black, "Shakopee Printer Acquires North Carolina Company," *Minneapolis/St. Paul Business Journal*, December 2, 2013, www.bizjournals.com/twincities/news/2013/12/02/imagine-printer-classic-merging.html; "Five Tips to Increase Your Chances of Getting a Small Business Bank Loan," American Bankers Association, March 25, 2013, www.aba.com/press/pages/032513TipsForSmallBankLoan.aspx; Marla Tabaka, "4 Tips for Getting a Business Loan," *Inc.*, January 21. 2013, www.inc.com/marla-tabaka/4-ways-to-get-a-business-loan.html; Kirsten Valle Pittman, "Small Businesses Ready for Recovery, Lenders Aren't," *MCT/Joplin Globe*, July 18, 2011, www.joplinglobe.com/dailybusiness/x357284366/Smallbusinesses-ready-for-recovery-but-their-lenders-aren-t; Emily Maltby, "How to Land a Bank Loan, *CNNMoney*, September 17, 2008, http://money.cnn.com/2008/09/16/smallbusiness/land_a_bank_loan.smb/index.htm; Jim Melloan, "Do Not Say 'I Just Want the Money,'" *Inc.*, July 2005, p. 96; Crystal Detamore-Rodman, "Raising Money: Loan Packaging Help," *Entrepreneur*, October 2008, p. 56; Kate Lister, "The Numbers That Matter," *Entrepreneur*, November 2010, pp. 98–99.

LO5

Describe the various loan programs available from the Small Business Administration.

The Small Business Administration (SBA) Loan Guarantee Programs

The SBA works with local lenders (both bank and nonbank) to offer many other loan programs that are designed to help entrepreneurs who cannot get capital from traditional sources gain access to the financing they need to launch and grow their businesses. When they were just small companies, Callaway Golf, Outback Steakhouse, and Intel Corporation borrowed through the SBA's loan programs. The SBA has several programs designed to help finance both start-up and existing small companies that cannot qualify for traditional loans because of their thin asset base and their higher risk of failure. The SBA guarantees an average of more than 95,000 small business loans totaling more than $33 billion each year, which enable many entrepreneurs to get the financing they need for start-up or for growth.[58]

The SBA's $128.5 billion loan portfolio makes it the largest single financial backer of small businesses in the nation.[59] SBA loan programs are aimed at entrepreneurs who do not meet lending standards at conventional lending institutions. About 30 percent of SBA-backed loans go to start-up companies.[60] The SBA does *not* actually lend money to entrepreneurs directly; instead, entrepreneurs borrow money from a traditional lender, and the SBA guarantees repayment of a percentage of the loan (at least 50 percent and sometimes as much as 85 percent) in case the borrower defaults. The loan application process can take from three days to several months, depending on how well prepared the entrepreneur is and which bank or lender is involved.

Qualifying for an SBA loan guarantee requires cooperation among the entrepreneur, the participating lender, and the SBA. The participating lender determines the loan's terms and sets the interest rate within SBA limits. Contrary to popular belief, SBA-guaranteed loans do *not* carry special deals on interest rates. The average interest rate on SBA-guaranteed loans is prime plus 2 percent (compared to prime plus 1 percent on conventional bank loans).

The average duration of an SBA loan is 12 years—far longer than the average commercial small business loan. In fact, longer loan terms are a distinct advantage of SBA loans. At least half of all bank business loans are for less than one year. By contrast, SBA real estate loans can extend for up to 25 years (compared to just 10 to 15 years for a conventional loan), and working capital loans have maturities of 7 years (compared with 2 to 5 years at most banks). These longer terms translate into lower loan payments, which are more suitable for young, fast-growing, cash-strapped companies.

Because SBA-guaranteed loans are riskier than standard commercial loans, they have a higher default rate (3.1 percent) than the commercial and industrial loans that banks make (1.54 percent).[61] Because the SBA assumes most of the credit risk, lenders are more willing to consider riskier deals that they normally would refuse. With the SBA's guarantee, borrowers also have to come up with less collateral than with a traditional bank loan.

The SBA offers several loan programs, which are summarized in the following sections. Table 15.1 displays a summary of the most popular SBA loan programs.

7(a) loan guaranty program

an SBA program in which loans made by private lenders to small businesses are guaranteed up to a ceiling by the SBA.

7(A) LOAN GUARANTY PROGRAM The **7(a) loan guaranty program** is the SBA's flagship loan program (see Figure 15.8 on page 639). More than 2,500 private lenders in the United States make SBA loans to small businesses, but the SBA guarantees them (85 percent of loans up to $150,000 and 75 percent of loans that range from $150,001 up to the loan cap of $3.75 million for 7(a) loans). A 7(a) loan is a term loan that business owners can use for expansion, renovation, new construction, purchasing land or buildings, purchasing equipment, working capital, a seasonal line of credit, inventory, or starting a business.

ENTREPRENEURIAL PROFILE: Dennis Clem: Clem's Service Station Dennis Clem learned about the business of running a service station from his father, and Clem is teaching his own son what he will need to know to run the family business someday. In 2010, Clem decided he would buy out his siblings who also had inherited shares in the business to allow him to pass the business on to his son when he was ready to retire. All of the siblings agreed because Dennis was the only family member who worked in the service station. The Clem family had never used credit to fund the growth of the business; instead, the family funded each new expansion by the company's retained earnings. However, buying out his siblings would require more cash than the business could generate. Clem was able to secure an SBA-guaranteed loan through the 7(a) loan program from his local bank to purchase the business from his siblings.[62] ■

 **You Be the Consultant**

The Never-Ending Hunt for Financing

The Automobile Film Club of America

Ralph Lucci, owner of The Automobile Film Club of America in Stapleton, New York, operates a true niche market business. Lucci's business rents vintage and specialty cars for use in movies and television shows filmed in the New York City area. The Automobile Film Club of America has been operating since 1993. Although the business suffered in the aftermath of 9/11, it survived that setback, and Lucci was able to rebuild the company as film and television production returned to New York.

At its peak, the business grew to 14 full-time employees who helped support the more than 300 cars the company rented for film and television productions. However, over the next few years the business faced more challenges. The company lost the lease on the lot it used to store the cars, and Lucci could not find a lot large enough to keep his entire inventory, forcing him to sell off many of the cars. Revenues declined, and soon the business could support only him and his wife on the payroll. When hurricane Irene hit in 2011, the company took another financial hit due to damage to its property and lost business.

However, the worst was yet to come.

When hurricane Sandy hit in October 2012, the storm surge flooded Lucci's car lot and garage, completely submerging almost all of his cars in saltwater. The cars and much of his equipment were a total loss. The building he used for offices and car maintenance also was severely damaged by the flooding. He estimated that the total loss was more than $400,000. The only insurance he carried on the business was for liability, so there was no coverage for his lost property.

Lucci, who is 60 years old, must decide whether he is willing to use his personal assets, including his home, as collateral and attempt to secure a business loan to restart his company.

Wogies

Aaron Hoffman grew up in the restaurant business. His father, William "Wogie" Hoffman, operated several pizza restaurants in Philadelphia. When Aaron opened his Philly cheesesteak restaurant, he named it Wogies in honor of his father. Aaron and his wife decided to expand their restaurant by opening a small bakery to bake their own rolls in the basement of the cheesesteak shop. They ordered the equipment and began the expansion. However, the bank loan they had assumed would come through never materialized. The couple needed $50,000, and they needed it fast, to pay for the expansion they had already begun. Having no success getting financing through a traditional bank, the couple turned to a merchant cash advance on credit card sales. Although they got the funding they needed, it was at much higher closing costs and interest rate than they would pay for a typical bank loan. A typical merchant cash advance charges 20 to 25 percent of the loan as a closing fee in addition to the equivalent of a 30 to 60 percent annual interest rate.

Although not happy with paying a 20 percent fee on the loan amount at closing, Hoffman says that he had no alternative.

1. Which of the funding sources described in this chapter do you recommend that Ralph Lucci and Aaron Hoffman consider for financing their businesses? Which sources do you recommend they *not* use? Why?

2. What can entrepreneurs do to increase the probability that bankers will approve their loan requests?

3. Work with a team of your classmates to brainstorm ways these entrepreneurs could attract the capital they need for their businesses. What steps do you recommend they take before they approach the potential sources of funding you have identified?

Sources: Based on Phyllis Furman, "As Banks Turn a Cold Shoulder, Small NYC Firms Look Elsewhere to Heat Up Their Businesses," *New York Daily News*, November 4, 2013, www.nydailynews.com/new-york/banks-turn-cold-shoulder-small-nyc-firms-heat-businesses-article-1.1505949; "About Wogies," Wogies, n.d., http://wogies.com/; Suzanne Sataline, "Wiped Out by Sandy, an Owner Sizes Up the Risk in Starting Over," *New York Times*, February 7, 2013, p. B6; "About Auto Film Club," Automobile Film Club of American, n.d., www.autofilmclub.com/aboutus.htm.

SECTION 504 CERTIFIED DEVELOPMENT COMPANY PROGRAM The second-most-popular SBA loan program is the Section 504 program, which is designed to encourage small businesses to purchase fixed assets, expand their facilities, and create jobs. Section 504 loans provide long-term, fixed-asset financing to small companies to purchase land, buildings, or equipment—"brick-and-mortar" loans. Three lenders play a role in every 504 loan: a bank, the SBA, and a **certified development company (CDC)**, which is a nonprofit organization licensed by the SBA and designed to promote economic growth in local communities. Some 270 CDCs operate across the United States and make about 8,000 loans in a typical year. The entrepreneur is required to make a down payment of just 10 percent of the total project cost rather than the typical 20 to 30 percent traditional bank loans require. The CDC provides 40 percent at a long-term fixed rate, supported by an SBA loan guarantee in case the entrepreneur defaults. The bank provides long-term financing for the remaining 50 percent, also supported by an SBA guarantee. The major advantages of Section 504 loans are their fixed rates and terms, their 10- and 20-year maturities, and the low down payment required. The maximum loan amount that the SBA will guarantee is $5 million.

certified development company (CDC)
a nonprofit organization licensed by the SBA and designed to promote growth in local communities by working with commercial banks and the SBA to make long-term loans to small businesses.

TABLE 15.1 SBA Loan Program Overview

Program	Maximum Loan Amount	Guaranty Percentage	Use of Proceeds	Loan Maturity	Maximum Interest Rates
Standard 7(a)	$5 million	85% on loans up to $150,000; 75 percent on loans greater than $151,000 (up to $3.75 million maximum)	Term loan. Expansion/renovation; new construction, purchase land or buildings; purchase equipment, fixtures, lease-hold improvements; working capital; refinance debt for compelling reasons; seasonal line of credit; inventory; or starting a business	Depends on ability to repay. Generally, working capital, machinery, and equipment is up to 10 years; real estate is 25 years.	Loans less than 7 years: $0–$25,000 prime + 4.25%; $25,001–$50,000 prime + 3.25%; more than $50,000 prime + 2.25%. Loans 7 years or longer: 0–$25,000 prime + 4.75%; $25,001–$50,000 prime + 3.75%; more than $50,000 prime + 2.75%
7(a) Small Loan	$350,000	Same as 7(a)	Same as 7(a)	Same as 7(a)	Same as 7(a)
SBA*Express*	$350,000	50%	Revolving line of credit or term loan [same as 7(a)]	Up to 7 years for revolving line of credit; otherwise, same as 7(a)	Loans of $50,000 or less: prime + 6.5%; loans of $50,001 to $350,000: prime + 4.5%
Export *Express*	$500,000	90% on loans of $350,000 or less; 75% on loans greater than $350,000	Same as SBA*Express* plus standby letter of credit	Same as SBA*Express*	Same as SBA*Express*
SBA Veterans Advantage	Same as SBA*Express*	Same as SBA*Express*	Same as SBA*Express*	Same as SBA*Express*	Same as SBA*Express*
CAPLines	$5 million	Same as 7(a)	Seasonal and short-term working capital needs including advances for inventory and accounts receivable	Up to 10 years except Builders CAPLine, which is 5 years	Same as 7(a)
International Trade	$5 million	90% (maximum of $4 million for working capital)	Term loan for working capital, equipment, facilities, land and buildings and debt refinance related to international trade	Up to 25 years	Same as 7(a)
Community Advantage	$250,000	Same as 7(a)	Same as 7(a)	Same as 7(a)	Prime + 6%
Export Working Capital	$5 million	90%	Short-term working capital for exporting	Generally 1 year or less, may go up to 3 years	No cap
Section 504 through Community Development Corporation (CDC)	$5 to $5.5 million, depending on type of business	CDC: up to 40% Lender: 50% Equity: 10%	Long-term, fixed asset projects such as constructing new buildings, purchasing and renovating existing buildings, and purchasing equipment and machinery	Equipment—up to 10 years; real estate—up to 20 years	Fixed rate depends on when SBA's debenture-backed loan is sold. Penalty for early payment.
Microloan	$50,000	N/A	Purchase machinery and equipment, fixtures, leasehold improvements, financing receivables, or working capital. Cannot be used to repay existing debt.	Shortest term possible, up to 6 years	7.75 % or 8.5% above intermediary cost of funds

Sources: "Loan Program Quick Reference Guide," U.S. Small Business Administration, October 2015, www.sba.gov/sites/default/files/files/SBA-Loan-Chart-Quick-Reference-Guide-10_15.pdf.

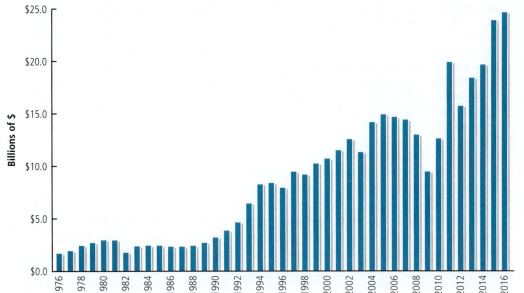

FIGURE 15.8

SBA 7(A) Guaranteed Loans

Source: Based on Small Business Administration Loan Program Performance, U.S. Small Business Administration, https://www.sba.gov/about-sba/sba-performance/performance-budget-finances/small-business-administration-sba-loan-program-performance.

ENTREPRENEURIAL PROFILE: Hazel Chu: Mizati Luxury Alloy Wheels While attending California State University in Los Angeles, Hazel Chu noticed how much Americans love their cars. After graduating with an accounting degree in 2001, Chu launched Mizati Luxury Alloy Wheels to capitalize on the passion drivers have for their cars and the accessories they purchase for them. Several years later, with her company growing rapidly, Chu worked with Zions Bank and a local CDC to apply for a $2.4 million Section 504 loan so that she could purchase a 16,000-square-foot building in Walnut, California, that houses her company's headquarters and warehouse. The larger space has enabled Chu to expand Mizati Luxury Alloy Wheels's inventory, which has resulted in increased sales that now top $4 million annually.[63] ■

MICROLOAN PROGRAM About three-fourths of all entrepreneurs need less than $100,000 to launch their businesses. Indeed, most entrepreneurs require less than $50,000 to start their companies. Unfortunately, loans of that amount can be the most difficult to get. Lending these relatively small amounts to entrepreneurs starting businesses is the purpose of the SBA's Microloan program. Called **microloans** because they range from just $100 to as much as $50,000, these loans have helped thousands of people take their first steps toward entrepreneurship. Banks typically shun loans in such small amounts because they consider them to be risky and unprofitable. In an attempt to fill the void in small loans to start-up companies, the SBA launched the microloan program in 1992, and it has gone on to become the single largest source of funding for microenterprises. Today, more than 200 authorized lenders, all of them non-profit community-based organizations, make SBA-backed microloans. The average size of a microloan is $13,000, with a maturity of three years (the maximum term is six years) and maximum interest rates that typically are between 8 and 13 percent. Microloans do not carry SBA guarantees, but once a lender, which must be a nonprofit organization, makes at least 5 microloans, it qualifies for discounted loans from the SBA. The SBA also requires microlenders to provide training and technical assistance to its small business borrowers. Microlenders' standards are less demanding than those of conventional lenders. A majority of SBA microloans go to women and minority entrepreneurs, and many are used to help fund start-up businesses. A recent survey found that 54 percent of all start-up microbusiness owners rely on another job as their main source of income.[64] Entrepreneurs can find a listing of microloan intermediaries at the SBA's Web site.

microloan
a loan made through an SBA program aimed at entrepreneurs who can borrow amounts of money as small as $100 and up to a maximum of $50,000.

ENTREPRENEURIAL PROFILE: Chelsea Hershey: Down Home Emporium With her husband deployed overseas, Chelsea Hershey returned to her tiny hometown, Arnold, Nebraska, where she studied entrepreneurship. She noticed that the building that had housed a retail shop in which she worked while in high school was for sale. With her husband's encouragement, Hershey rented the building and launched a flower shop from which she also sells gifts, toys, and home décor. By providing floral services to customers in small towns as far away as 75 miles, Down Home Emporium grew quickly. After a very successful holiday season, Hershey wanted to expand her shop's inventory. She also wanted to perform some cosmetic renovations on the building that houses her business and upgrade its lighting and insulation to reduce energy costs. Hershey applied for and received a microloan from the Rural Enterprise Assistance Project, a nonprofit in Lyon, Nebraska, that focuses on providing financing and technical assistance to small companies that cannot secure traditional loans from banks and other lenders. The microloan has spurred Down Home Emporium's growth, and Hershey is planning to expand her wedding and floral service.[65] ∎

Other SBA Loan Programs

SBA*EXPRESS* PROGRAM To reduce the paperwork requirements and processing time involved in its loans, the SBA offers its SBA*Express* program that gives entrepreneurs responses to their loan applications within 36 hours. In the *SBAExpress* program, participating lenders use their own loan procedures and applications to make loans of up to $350,000 to small businesses. Because the SBA guarantees 50 percent of the loan, banks often are willing to make smaller loans to entrepreneurs who might otherwise have difficulty meeting lenders' standards. Entrepreneurs can use these flexible term loans for a variety of business purposes, such as purchasing equipment, fixtures, land, or buildings; renovating existing structures or building new ones; buying inventory; and obtaining a seasonal line of credit. Loan maturities on *SBAExpress* loans typically are between 5 and 10 years, but loan maturities for fixed assets can be up to 25 years. The maximum interest rate is prime + 6.5 percent.

SMALL LOAN ADVANTAGE AND COMMUNITY ADVANTAGE LOAN PROGRAMS In 2011, the SBA introduced two new loan programs, the Small Loan Advantage and Community Advantage programs. The Small Loan Advantage program is designed to encourage existing, experienced SBA lenders, known as preferred lenders, to make smaller loans, which are most likely to benefit disadvantaged borrowers. The Community Advantage Loan program encourages new lenders that operate in economically challenged communities that have had little or no access to SBA loans to enter the SBA's 7(a) loan program. Both programs include SBA guarantees of 85 percent on loans up to $150,000 and 75 percent on loans between $150,001 and the ceiling of $350,000 and use a streamlined application process.

THE CAPLINE PROGRAM In addition to its basic 7(a) loan guarantee program (through which the SBA makes about 75 percent of its loans), the SBA provides guarantees on small business loans for start-up, real estate, machinery and equipment, fixtures, working capital, exporting, and restructuring debt through several other methods. About two-thirds of all of the SBA's loan guarantees are for machinery and equipment or working capital. The **CAPLine program** offers short-term capital to growing companies seeking to finance seasonal buildups in inventory or accounts receivable under five separate programs, each with maturities up to five years: seasonal line of credit (provides advances against inventory and accounts receivable to help businesses weather seasonal sales fluctuations), contract line of credit (finances the cost of direct labor and materials costs associated with performing contracts), builder's line of credit (helps small contractors and builders finance labor and materials costs), standard asset-based line of credit (an asset-based revolving line of credit for financing short-term needs), and small asset-based line of credit. CAPLine helps cash-hungry small businesses by giving them a credit line to draw on when they need it. A line of credit is what many small companies need most because they are flexible, efficient, and, unfortunately, quite difficult for small businesses to get from traditional lenders.

LOANS INVOLVING INTERNATIONAL TRADE For small businesses going global, the SBA has the **Export *Express* program**, which, like its other express programs, offers quick turnaround times on applications for guarantees of 75 to 90 percent on loans up to $500,000 to help small companies develop or expand their export initiatives. Loan maturities range from 5 to 25 years.

The SBA also offers the **Export Working Capital (EWC) program**, which is designed to provide working capital to small exporters. The SBA works in conjunction with the Export-Import Bank to administer this loan guarantee program. Applicants file a one-page loan application, and the response time normally is 10 days or less. The maximum loan is $5 million with a 90 percent guarantee, and proceeds must be used to finance small business exports.

CAPLine program
an SBA program that makes short-term capital loans to growing companies seeking to finance seasonal buildups in inventory or accounts receivable.

Export *Express* program
an SBA loan program that offers quick turnaround times to small companies that are developing or expanding their export initiatives.

Export Working Capital (EWC) program
an SBA loan program that is designed to provide working capital to small exporters.

ENTREPRENEURIAL PROFILE: Brian Coughren and Tom Wittmen: Seattle Safety
Former Boeing engineers Brian Coughren and Tom Wittmen started Seattle Safety, a company with a unique niche: It produces the crash test sleds that automakers around the world use in safety tests for their cars. In addition to selling to auto manufacturers in the United States, the company exports its sleds all over the world, selling to automakers in Japan, Taiwan, South Korea, the United Kingdom, Brazil, France, Germany, India, Italy, and Canada. When Seattle Safety received three large orders for more than $9 million from companies in China and Europe, Coughren and Wittmen needed financing to ramp up production. They applied for and received a $5 million Export Working Capital loan that enabled their company to fill the orders. Seattle Safety now has 45 employees and controls more than 50 percent of the global market for crash test sleds.[66] ■

The **International Trade program** is for small businesses that are engaging in international trade or are adversely affected by competition from imports. The SBA allows global entrepreneurs to combine loans from the Export Working Capital program with those from the International Trade program for up to $5 million with a maximum guarantee of $4.5 million. Loan maturities range from 1 to 25 years.

> **International Trade program**
> an SBA loan program for small businesses that are engaging in international trade or are adversely affected by competition from imports.

DISASTER LOANS As their name implies, **disaster loans** are made to small businesses devastated by some kind of financial or physical losses from hurricanes, floods, earthquakes, tornadoes, and other natural disasters. The maximum disaster loan usually is $2 million, but Congress often raises that ceiling when circumstances warrant. Disaster loans carry below-market interest rates as low as 4 percent and terms as long as 30 years. Loans for physical damage above $14,000 require an entrepreneur to pledge some kind of collateral, usually a lien on the business property. In the aftermath of wildfires in the Smokey Mountains in Tennessee, the SBA approved more than $10 million in disaster loans for the victims of the devastating fires. Loans were made available for small businesses, nonprofit organizations, homeowners and renters for property lost and damaged by the fires.[67]

> **disaster loan**
> an SBA loan to a small business devastated by some kind of financial or physical loss.

Nonbank Sources of Debt Capital

Although they usually are the first stop for entrepreneurs in search of debt capital, banks are not the only lending game in town. We now turn our attention to other sources of debt capital that entrepreneurs can tap to feed their cash-hungry companies.

ASSET-BASED LENDERS Thousands of asset-based lenders across the U.S. allow small businesses to borrow money by pledging otherwise idle assets, such as accounts receivable, inventory, or purchase orders, as collateral. Most asset-based lenders are part of smaller commercial banks, commercial finance companies, specialty lenders, or divisions of bank holding companies. In a typical year, these lenders provide about $85 billion in asset-based financing to businesses.[68] This method of financing works especially well for manufacturers, wholesalers, distributors, and other companies that have significant stocks of inventory or accounts receivable. Asset-based borrowing is an efficient method of borrowing because business owners borrow only the money they need when they need it. Even unprofitable companies whose financial statements cannot convince loan officers to make traditional loans often can get asset-based loans. These cash-poor but asset-rich companies can use normally unproductive assets—accounts receivable, inventory, and purchase orders—to finance rapid growth and the cash crises that often accompany it.

Like banks, asset-based lenders consider a company's cash flow, but they are more interested in the quality of the assets pledged as collateral. The amount a small business can borrow through asset-based lending depends on the **advance rate**, the percentage of an asset's value that a lender will lend. For example, a company pledging $100,000 of accounts receivable might negotiate a 70 percent advance rate and qualify for a $70,000 asset-based loan. Advance rates can vary dramatically depending on the quality of the assets pledged and the lender. Because inventory is an illiquid asset (i.e., hard to sell), the advance rate on inventory-based loans is quite low, usually 10 to 50 percent. A business pledging high-quality accounts receivable as collateral, however, may be able to negotiate up to an 85 percent advance rate. The most common types of asset-based financing are discounting accounts receivable, inventory financing, and purchase order financing.

> **advance rate**
> the percentage of an asset's value that a lender will lend.

Discounting Accounts Receivable The most common form of secured credit is accounts-receivable financing. Under this arrangement, a small business pledges its accounts receivable as collateral; in return, the lender advances a loan against the value of approved accounts receivable. The amount of the loan tendered is not equal to the face value of the accounts receivable, however. Even though the lender screens the firm's accounts and accepts only qualified receivables, it makes an allowance for the risk involved because it will have to write off some of them as uncollectible. A small business usually can borrow an amount equal to 55 to 85 percent of its receivables, depending on their quality. Generally, lenders do not accept receivables that are past due.

Inventory Financing With inventory financing, a small business loan is secured by its inventory of raw materials, work in process, and finished goods. If an owner defaults on the loan, the lender can claim the pledged inventory, sell it, and use the proceeds to satisfy the loan (assuming that the bank's claim is superior to the claims of other creditors). Because inventory usually is not a highly liquid asset and its value can be difficult to determine, lenders are willing to lend only a portion of its worth, usually no more than 50 percent of the inventory's value. Most asset-based lenders avoid inventory-only deals; they prefer to make loans backed by inventory *and* more secure accounts receivable. The key to qualifying for inventory financing is proving that a company has a plan or a process in place to ensure that the inventory securing the loan sells quickly. To ensure the quality of the assets supporting the loans they make, lenders must monitor borrowers' assets, a task that increases the paperwork requirements on these loans.

Purchase Order Financing Small companies that receive orders from large customers can use those purchase orders as collateral for loans. The customer places an order with a small business, which needs financing to fill the order. The small company pledges the future payment from the customer as security for the loan, and the lender verifies the credit rating of the customer (not the small business) before granting the short-term loan, which often carries interest rates of 40 percent or more. Borrowers usually repay the loan within 60 days.

Asset-based loans are more expensive than traditional bank loans because of the cost of originating and maintaining them and the higher risk they involve. Rates usually run from 2 to 7 percent (or more) above the prime rate. Because of this rate differential, small business owners should not use asset-based loans for long-term financing; their goal should be to establish their credit through asset-based financing and then to move up to a line of credit.

VENDOR FINANCING Many small companies borrow money from their vendors and suppliers in the form of trade credit. Because of its ready availability, trade credit is an extremely important source of financing to most entrepreneurs. When banks refuse to lend money to a start-up business because they see it as a high credit risk, an entrepreneur may be able to turn to trade credit for capital. Getting vendors to extend credit in the form of delayed payments (e.g., "net 30" credit terms) usually is much easier for small businesses than obtaining bank financing. Essentially, a company receiving trade credit from a supplier is getting a short-term, interest-free loan for the amount of the goods purchased. Vendors and suppliers often are willing to finance a small business's purchases of goods from 30 to 60 days (sometimes longer), interest free.

EQUIPMENT SUPPLIERS Most equipment vendors encourage business owners to purchase their equipment by offering to finance the purchase. This method of financing is similar to trade credit but with slightly different terms. Equipment vendors offer reasonable credit terms with only a modest down payment, with the balance financed over the life of the equipment (often several years). In some cases, the vendor will repurchase equipment for salvage value at the end of its useful life and offer the business owner another credit agreement on new equipment. Start-up companies often use trade credit from equipment suppliers to purchase equipment and fixtures such as display cases, refrigeration units, and machinery. It pays to scrutinize vendors' credit terms, however, because they may be less attractive than those of other lenders.

COMMERCIAL FINANCE COMPANIES When denied bank loans, small business owners often look to commercial finance companies for the same types of loans. Commercial finance companies are second only to banks in making loans to small businesses, and, unlike their conservative counterparts, they are willing to tolerate more risk in their loan portfolios. Of course, their primary consideration is collecting their loans, but finance companies tend to rely more on obtaining a security interest in some type of collateral, given the higher-risk loans that make up their portfolios. Because commercial finance companies depend on collateral to recover most of their losses, they are able to make loans to small companies with irregular cash flows or to those that are not yet profitable.

Large commercial finance companies, such as AT&T Small Business Lending, GE Capital Small Business Finance, Eastern Funding, and others, make a variety of loans to small companies, ranging from asset-based loans and business leases to construction and SBA loans. Dubbed "the Wal-Marts of finance," commercial finance companies usually offer many of the same credit options that commercial banks do. Because their loans are subject to more risks, finance companies charge a higher interest rate than commercial banks. Their most common methods of providing credit to small businesses are asset-based—accounts-receivable financing and inventory loans. Rates on these loans vary but can be as high as 15 to 30 percent (including fees), depending on the risk a particular business presents and the quality of the assets involved. Because many of the loans they make are secured by collateral (if not accounts receivable or inventory, then the business equipment, vehicles, real estate, or inventory purchased with the loan), finance companies often impose more onerous reporting requirements, sometimes requiring weekly (or even daily) information on a small company's inventory levels or accounts-receivable balances. However, entrepreneurs who cannot secure financing from traditional lenders because of their short track records, less-than-perfect credit ratings, or fluctuating earnings often find the loans they need at commercial finance companies.

SAVINGS-AND-LOAN ASSOCIATIONS Savings-and-loan associations specialize in loans for real property. In addition to their traditional role of providing mortgages for personal residences, savings-and-loan associations offer financing on commercial and industrial property. In the typical commercial or industrial loan, the savings-and-loan association will lend up to 80 percent of the property's value with a repayment schedule of up to 30 years. Most savings-and-loan associations hesitate to lend money for buildings specially designed for a particular customer's needs. They expect the mortgage to be repaid from the company's future earnings.

STOCKBROKERS Households in the United States own $23.8 trillion in stocks and mutual funds and $4.4 trillion in bonds.[69] Some entrepreneurs use their stock and bond portfolios as collateral for loans to finance their business start-ups. Many of the loans stockbrokers make to their customers carry lower interest rates than those from banks. These **margin loans** carry lower rates because the collateral supporting them—the stocks and bonds in the customer's portfolio—is of high quality and is highly liquid. Moreover, brokerage firms make it easy to borrow. Brokers often set up a line of credit for their customers when they open a brokerage account. To tap that line of credit, the customer simply writes a check or uses a debit card. Typically, there is no fixed repayment schedule for a margin loan; the debt can remain outstanding indefinitely as long as the market value of the borrower's portfolio of collateral meets minimum requirements. Aspiring entrepreneurs can borrow up to 50 percent of the value of their stock portfolios, up to 70 percent of their bond portfolios, and up to 90 percent of the value of their government securities.

There is risk involved in using stocks and bonds as collateral on a loan. Brokers typically require a 30 percent cushion on margin loans. If the value of the borrower's portfolio drops, the broker can make a **margin (maintenance) call**; that is, the broker can call the loan and require the borrower to provide more cash and securities as collateral. Recent swings in the stock market have translated into margin calls for many entrepreneurs, requiring them to repay a significant portion of their loan balances within a matter of days—or hours. If an account lacks adequate collateral, the broker can sell off the customer's portfolio to pay off the loan.

CREDIT UNIONS Credit unions are nonprofit financial cooperatives that promote saving and provide loans to their members. More than 5,800 state- and federally-chartered credit unions with more than 109,000 members operate in the United States, and they make about $85 billion in loans annually.[70] Although credit unions are best known for making consumer and car loans, many are also willing to lend money to their members to launch and operate businesses. More than 38 percent of credit unions make business loans to their members.[71] In fact, the Federal Reserve estimates that about 9 percent of small business loans are issued by credit unions.[72] To

margin loan
a loan from a stockbroker that uses the stocks and bonds in the borrower's portfolio as collateral.

margin (maintenance) call
a situation that occurs when the value of a borrower's portfolio drops and the broker calls the loan in, requiring the borrower to put up more cash and securities as collateral.

credit union
a nonprofit financial cooperative that promotes saving and provides loans to its members.

qualify for a loan, an entrepreneur must be a member of the credit union. Lending practices at credit unions are very much like those at banks, but credit unions usually are willing to make smaller loans. Federal law currently limits a credit union's loans to businesses to 12.25 percent of the credit union's assets, although there have been several recent attempts to raise this cap. The SBA also recently opened its 7(a) loan program to credit unions, providing yet another avenue for entrepreneurs in search of financing. Because banks have tightened their lending requirements, many entrepreneurs are turning to credit unions for start-up and operating business loans. However, credit union approval rates of small business loans have been declining over recent years.[73]

ENTREPRENEURIAL PROFILE: Tom Hoebbel: Thomas Hoebbel Photo-Video Tom Hoebbel operates a small video and photography business in Brooktondale, New York. When it came time to purchase new equipment to expand his business's offerings, Hoebbel applied for a business loan from a local credit union, where he had been a member for many years. The credit union helped Hoebbel secure an SBA 7(a) loan for $25,000 to purchase equipment to allow him to expand his business into online video production. Purchasing this new equipment helped Hoebbel establish his business as a producer of online marketing videos, enabling him to diversify his business from traditional photo and video projects. Hoebbel credits this change in his business as the reason he has been able to survive recent economic downturns.[74] ■

Entrepreneurs in search of a credit union near them can use the online database at the Credit Union National Association's Web site (www.cuna.org).

PRIVATE PLACEMENTS Private placements are available for both equity and debt instruments. A private placement involves selling debt to one or a small number of investors, usually insurance companies or pension funds. Private placement debt is a hybrid between a conventional loan and a bond. At its heart, it is a bond, but its terms are tailored to the borrower's individual needs as a loan would be.

In addition to making equity investments in small companies, venture capital firms also provide venture debt financing, often in private placements. Interest rates on venture debt typically vary from prime plus 1 percent to prime plus 5 percent, and the loan terms range from 24 to 48 months. Venture debt deals often include warrants, which give the venture capital firm the right to purchase shares of stock in a company at a fixed price. Venture debt financing is a hybrid between a loan and venture capital. Most venture loans also come with covenants, requirements that a company must meet or incur a penalty, such as paying a higher interest rate or giving up more stock.

Small Business Investment Companies (SBICs)
privately owned financial institutions that are licensed by the SBA and use a combination of private capital and federally guaranteed debt to provide long-term venture capital to small businesses.

SMALL BUSINESS INVESTMENT COMPANIES Small Business Investment Companies (SBICs), created in 1958 when Congress passed the Small Business Investment Act, are privately owned financial institutions that are licensed and regulated by the SBA. The 292 SBICs operating in the United States use a combination of private capital and federally guaranteed debt to provide growing small businesses with long-term venture capital. Like their venture capital counterparts, most SBICs prefer later-round financing over funding start-ups. Funding from SBICs helped launch companies such as Costco, Tesla, Apple, Intel, Gymboree, Cutter and Buck, Build-a-Bear Workshop, FedEx, Staples, Sun Microsystems, and Callaway Golf.

Since 1958, SBICs have provided more than $73.3 billion in long-term debt and equity financing to some 118,000 small businesses, adding millions of jobs to the U.S. economy.[75] SBICs must be capitalized privately with a minimum of $5 million, at which point they qualify for up to $3 (but most often $2) in long-term SBA loans for every $1 of private capital invested in small businesses up to a maximum of $150 million. As a general rule, SBICs may provide financial assistance only to small businesses with a net worth of less than $18 million and average after-tax earnings of $6 million during their last two years. However, employment and total annual sales standards vary from industry to industry. SBICs are limited to a maximum investment or loan amount of 20 percent of their private capital to a single client.

SBICs provide both debt and equity financing to small businesses. Most SBIC financing is in the much-needed range of $250,000 to $5 million. When they make equity investments, SBICs are prohibited from obtaining a controlling interest in the companies in which they invest (no more than 49 percent ownership).

ENTREPRENEURIAL PROFILE: Rand Capital SBIC: Gemcor II, LLC Tom Speller, founder of Gemcor II, LLC, developed the automated riveting machine used worldwide by aircraft manufacturers during World War II. For decades, the company was a major player in the aircraft industry, but when the aircraft manufacturing industry went through a prolonged slump in the early 2000s, Gemcor received an investment from Rand Capital SBIC, Inc., to reengineer its supply chain and implement a variable cost supply model. In the seven years after Rand Capital SBIC's investment and the changes it helped fund, Gemcor's revenues grew from $8 million to $19 million. During that same period, the number of employees at Gemcor nearly doubled, from 31 to 61. In 2016, Ascent Aerospace, a California-based aerospace manufacturer, acquired Gemcor for $45 million.[76] ■

Other Federal and State Programs

LO6
Identify the various federal and state loan programs aimed at small businesses.

Federally sponsored lending programs have experienced budget fluctuations over the last several years, but some entrepreneurs have been able to acquire financing from the following programs.

Economic Development Administration

The Economic Development Administration (EDA), a branch of the Commerce Department, offers loan guarantees to create new businesses and to expand existing businesses in areas with below-average incomes and high unemployment rates. Focusing on economically distressed communities, the EDA often works with local governments to finance long-term investment projects needed to stimulate economic growth and to create jobs by making loan guarantees. The EDA guarantees up to 80 percent of business loans between $750,000 and $10 million. Entrepreneurs apply for loans through private lenders, for whom an EDA loan guarantee significantly reduces the risk of lending. Start-ups and existing businesses must make equity investments of at least 15 percent of the guaranteed amount. Small businesses can use the loan proceeds in a variety of ways, from supplementing working capital and purchasing equipment to buying land and renovating buildings.

EDA business loans are designed to help revitalize economically distressed areas by creating or expanding small businesses that provide employment opportunities in local communities. To qualify for a loan, a business must be located in a disadvantaged area, and its presence must directly benefit local residents. Some communities experiencing high unemployment or suffering from the effects of devastating natural disasters have received EDA Revolving Loan Fund Grants to create loan pools for local small businesses.

ENTREPRENEURIAL PROFILE: Russ Maier: Russ Maier Hay Grinding Russ Maier launched his hay grinding business in 2003. Grinding hay makes it a more efficient means of feeding ruminant animals, such as cattle, sheep, and goats. Maier purchased a new grinder for his business in 2012 with a loan from the Northeast Council of Government Development Corporation (NECOG DC), a development corporation formed by an association of city and county governments in South Dakota supported by EDA funding. Maier went back to the NECOG DC four years later for a second loan to buy a second grinder to expand his business operations. Maier also was able to add a full-time seasonal employee due to the growth of his business.[77] ■

Department of Housing and Urban Development

Although the Department of Housing and Urban Development (HUD) does not extend loans or grants directly to entrepreneurs for launching businesses, it does sponsor several programs that can help qualified entrepreneurs to raise the capital they need. Community Development Block Grants (CDBGs) are extended to cities and counties that, in turn, lend or grant money to entrepreneurs to start or expand small businesses, thereby strengthening the local economy. Grants are aimed at cities and towns that need revitalization and economic stimulation. Some grants are used to construct buildings and factories to be leased to entrepreneurs, sometimes with an option to buy. Others are earmarked for revitalizing a crime-ridden area or making start-up loans to entrepreneurs or expansion loans to existing business owners. No ceilings or geographic limitations are placed on CDBG loans and grants, but projects must benefit low- and moderate-income families.

ENTREPRENEURIAL PROFILE: Cheryl and Stephen Kraus: Upcountry Provisions Bakery & Bistro When Cheryl and Stephen Kraus were renovating a building in downtown Traveler's Rest, South Carolina, to house their retail bakery, the copreneurs received a $5,750 Façade Improvement Grant from a grant funded by HUD's CDBG program. The 1,664-square-foot building on Main Street that serves as the home for the Upcountry Provisions Bakery & Bistro had once housed a drugstore but had stood vacant for 20 years. Cheryl and Stephen Kraus wanted a location with more foot traffic, and the Main Street location offered that. This grant allowed them to secure the property. Cheryl and Stephen Kraus received a second grant of $5,000 five years later to expand their outdoor eating space.[78] ■

HUD also makes loan guarantees through its Section 108 provision of the CBDG program. These loan guarantees allow a community to transform a portion of CDBG funds into federally guaranteed loans large enough to pursue economic revitalization projects that can lead to the renewal of entire towns.

U.S. Department of Agriculture's Business Programs and Loans

The U.S. Department of Agriculture provides financial assistance to certain small businesses through partnerships with the private sector and the community-based organizations. The various programs fund projects that create or preserve quality jobs and/or promote a clean rural environment in underserved rural communities. For example, through its Business and Industry Guaranteed Loan program, the Rural Development Rural Business Services (RBS) will guarantee as much as 80 percent of a commercial lender's loan up to $5 million, 70 percent for loans between $5 million and $10 million, and 60 percent for loans in excess of $10 million. Entrepreneurs apply for loans through private lenders, who view applicants with loan guarantees much more favorably than those without guarantees. The guarantee reduces a lender's risk dramatically because the guarantee means that the government agency would pay off the loan balance (up to the ceiling) if the entrepreneur defaults on the loan.

ENTREPRENEURIAL PROFILE: Jim Bouhachem: Sibley Mart Jim Bouhachem had a successful career as a design engineer in the auto industry. However, his work led to chronic back pain, and his physician recommended he find another line of work. Bouhachem found a business owner in his hometown of Strasburg, Ohio, who was trying to sell his convenience store. Bouhachem purchased the business and, after several years of successful growth, decided to open a new location near Kent State University. To finance his company's expansion, Bouhachem obtained a $2.4 million USDA Business and Industry loan through a local bank with an 80 percent guarantee from the USDA.[79] ■

Small Business Innovation Research Program

Started as a pilot program by the National Science Foundation in the 1970s, the Small Business Innovation Research (SBIR) program has expanded to 11 federal agencies, ranging from NASA to the Department of Defense. The total SBIR budget across all 11 agencies is more than $2 billion annually. These agencies award cash grants or long-term contracts to small companies that want to initiate or to expand their R&D efforts. SBIR grants give innovative small companies the opportunity to attract early-stage capital investments *without* having to give up significant equity stakes or taking on burdensome levels of debt.

The SBIR process involves three phases. Phase I (proof of concept) grants, which determine the feasibility and commercial potential of a technology or product, last for up to six months and have a ceiling of $150,000. Phase II (prototype development) grants, designed to develop the concept into a specific technology or product, run for up to 24 months and have a ceiling of $1 million. Approximately one-third of all Phase II applicants receive funding. Phase III is the commercialization phase, in which the company pursues commercial applications of the R&D conducted in Phase I and Phase II and must use private or non-SBIR federal funding to bring a product to market.

Small Business Technology Transfer Program

The Small Business Technology Transfer (STTR) program complements the SBIR program. Whereas the SBIR program focuses on commercially promising ideas that originate in small businesses, the STTR program helps companies to use the vast reservoir of commercially promising ideas that originate in universities, federally funded R&D centers, and nonprofit research institutions. Researchers at these institutions can join forces with small businesses and can spin off commercially promising ideas while remaining employed at their research institutions. Five federal agencies award grants of up to $750,000 in three phases to these research partnerships.

ENTREPRENEURIAL PROFILE: Kent Murphy: Luna Innovations Luna Innovations, a company based in Roanoke, Virginia, has received numerous Phase I and Phase II grants from the SBIR and STTR programs. The company, founded in 1990 by Kent Murphy, developed coating technology that the Army has used to treat uniforms so that they stay clean longer and provide protection against harmful chemicals. The Air Force has used Luna Innovations' technology to treat the cowlings on its jets to make landing on aircraft carriers safer, especially in foul weather. With the help of the SBIR/STTR programs, Luna Innovations has been able to commercialize many of the products it has developed for its government customers.[80] ■

State and Local Loan Development Programs

Many states have created their own loan and economic development programs to provide funds for business start-ups and expansions. They have decided that their funds are better spent encouraging small business growth rather than "chasing smokestacks"—trying to entice large businesses to locate within their boundaries. These programs come in many forms, but they all tend to focus on developing small businesses that create the greatest number of jobs and economic benefits. Entrepreneurs who apply for state and local funding must have patience and be willing to slog through some paperwork, however.

Although each state's approach to economic development is somewhat special, one common element is some kind of small business financing program: loans, loan guarantees, development grants, venture capital pools, and others. One approach many states have had success with is **capital access programs (CAPs)**, first introduced in Michigan in 1986. Many states now offer CAPs that are designed to encourage lending institutions to make loans to businesses that do not qualify for traditional financing because of their higher risk. Under a CAP, a bank and a borrower each pay an upfront fee (a portion of the loan amount) into a loan-loss reserve fund at the participating bank, and the state matches this amount. The reserve fund, which normally ranges from 6 to 14 percent of the loan amount, acts as an insurance policy against the potential loss a bank might experience on a loan and frees the bank to make loans that it otherwise might refuse.

> **capital access program (CAP)**
> a state lending program that encourages lending institutions to make loans to businesses that do not qualify for traditional financing because of their higher risk.

Even cities and small towns have joined in the effort to develop small businesses and help them grow. Many communities across the United States operate **revolving loan funds** that combine private and public funds to make loans to small businesses, often at favorable interest rates, for the purpose of starting or expanding businesses that create jobs and contribute to economic development. As money is repaid into the funds, it is loaned back out to other entrepreneurs.

> **revolving loan funds**
> community programs that combine private and public funds to make loans to small businesses, often at below-market interest rates.

ENTREPRENEURIAL PROFILE: Oregon Business Development Fund: Krauss Craft, Inc. Krauss Craft, Inc., located in Merlin, Oregon, manufactures commercial playground equipment under the trademark Playcraft Systems and sells its products nationwide to cities, school districts, and park districts. Krauss Craft secured a $500,000 loan through the Oregon Business Development Fund (OBDF) to build a 30,000-square-foot building and to purchase two rotational molding machines and related equipment. Krauss Craft added 40 new jobs as a result of the expansion project.[81] ■

In addition to revolving loan funds, nearly 1,000 communities across the United States have created **community development financial institutions (CDFIs)** that designate at least some of their loan portfolios to supporting entrepreneurs and small businesses. CDFIs operate through a variety of institutions, including microenterprise loan funds, community development loan funds, and others, to provide capital and credit to otherwise "unbankable" business owners and aspiring entrepreneurs in low-income communities across the United States. Because the loans that they make are higher risk, the interest rates that CDFIs charge are higher than those charged by traditional lenders.

> **community development financial institutions (CDFIs)**
> community-based financial institutions that designate at least a portion of their loan portfolios to otherwise "unbankable" business owners and aspiring entrepreneurs.

ENTREPRENEURIAL PROFILE: Tina Ferguson-Riffe: Smoke Berkeley Tina Ferguson-Riffe had been unemployed for three years before she started her restaurant, Smoke Berkeley, in Berkeley, California. Ferguson-Riffe needed to buy new equipment to support the growth of her business. Unable to secure a traditional business loan, a program called the Opportunity Fund offered Tina a $20,000 EasyPay loan. Instead of making a fixed monthly payment, Smoke Berkeley repays its loan based on daily credit and debit card sales. Ferguson-Riffe says being able to pay the loan back based on sales helps when seasonal slowdowns occur during the rainy season.[82] ∎

LO7

Explain other methods of financing a business.

Other Methods of Financing

Small business owners do not have to rely solely on financial institutions and government agencies for capital; their businesses have the capacity to generate capital. Other common methods of financing, including factoring, leasing rather than purchasing equipment, and using credit cards, are available to almost every small business.

Factoring Accounts Receivable

factor

a financial institution that buys a business's accounts receivable at a discount.

Instead of carrying credit sales on its own books (some of which may never be collected), a small business can sell outright its accounts receivable to a factor. A **factor** buys a company's accounts receivable and pays for them in two parts. The first payment, which the factor makes immediately, is for 50 to 80 percent of the accounts' agreed-on (and usually discounted) value. The factor makes the second payment of 15 to 18 percent, which makes up the balance less the factor's service fees, when the original customer pays the invoice. High interest rates (often 36 percent or more) make factoring a more expensive type of financing than loans from either banks or commercial finance companies, but for businesses that cannot qualify for those loans, it may be the only choice. Factoring volume totals more than $98.8 billion per year.[83]

Factoring deals are either with recourse or without recourse. Under deals arranged with recourse, a small business owner retains the responsibility for customers who fail to pay their accounts. The business owner must take back these uncollectible invoices. Under deals arranged without recourse, however, the owner is relieved of the responsibility for collecting them. If customers fail to pay their accounts, the factor bears the loss. About 73 percent of factoring deals are without recourse.[84] Because the factor assumes the risk of collecting the accounts, it screens a company's credit customers, accepts those judged to be creditworthy, and advances the small business owner a portion of the value of the accounts receivable. Factors discount anywhere from 2 to 40 percent of the face value of a company's accounts receivable, depending on the following factors related to a small company:

- Customers' financial strength and credit ratings

- The industry and its customers' industries, because some industries have a reputation for slow payments

- History and financial strength, especially in deals arranged with recourse

- Credit policies[85]

The discount rate on deals without recourse usually is higher than on those with recourse because of the higher level of risk they carry for the factor.

Although factoring is more expensive than traditional bank loans (a 2 percent discount from the face value of an invoice due in 30 days amounts to an annual interest rate of 24.8 percent), it is a source of quick cash and is ideally suited for fast-growing companies, especially start-ups that cannot qualify for bank loans. Small companies that sell to government agencies and large corporations, both famous for stretching out their payments for 60 to 90 days or more, also find factoring attractive because they collect the money from the sale (less the factor's discount) much faster.

Leasing

Leasing is another common bootstrap financing technique. Today, small businesses can lease virtually any kind of asset, including office space, telephones, computers, and heavy equipment. By leasing expensive assets, the small business owner is able to use them without locking in valuable capital for an extended period of time. In other words, entrepreneurs can reduce the long-term capital requirements of their businesses by leasing equipment and facilities and are not investing their capital in depreciating assets. In addition, because no down payment is required and because the cost of the asset is spread over a longer time (lowering monthly payments), a company's cash flow improves.

ROBS

Thousands of aspiring entrepreneurs, particularly Baby Boomers, are tapping into their retirement accounts to fund business start-ups or acquisitions of existing small businesses. Many of them are turning to **Rollovers as Business Startups (ROBS)** as a means of using their retirement savings to fund their businesses. By using a 401(k) rollover, entrepreneurs are able to move existing retirement funds into a start-up. The tax laws governing ROBS are complex, and if not set up properly, this form of funding can lead to significant penalties by the IRS. Recent IRS cases show increased scrutiny of these funding plans, so entrepreneurs should exercise extreme care when using a retirement account rollover to fund a business. Once established, ROBS require entrepreneurs to meet certain reporting and fiduciary responsibilities.[86]

Rollovers as Business Startups (ROBS)
a method of financing that allows entrepreneurs to use their retirement savings to fund their business start-ups.

ENTREPRENEURIAL PROFILE: Suzie and Todd Ford: NoDa Brewing Company Suzie Ford, a former banker, and her husband Todd, a former airline pilot, used all of their retirement accounts to launch NoDa Bewing Company in Charlotte, North Carolina. The couple recognized the risk of using their retirement accounts as seed money for starting a business, but they did everything they could to minimize the risk, including developing a business plan, conducting market research, and hiring top-notch employees. Two years after launching NoDa Brewing Company, the Fords say that 325 restaurants, bars, and sports arenas now serve their beer. NoDa Brewing recently received international acclaim when its Hop, Drop, 'N Roll IPA won a gold medal at the highly competitive World Beer Cup.[87] ■

Merchant Cash Advance

A **merchant cash advance** is used by small businesses to help finance working capital needs. The provider of the merchant cash advance prepurchases credit and debit card receivables at a discount. Each time the business makes a sale, it forwards a percentage of the card receivable to the cash advance provider or purchaser until all of the purchased receivables are paid off. Merchant cash advances are most often used for the purchase of new equipment, purchasing inventory, expansion or remodeling, payoff of debt, and emergency funding. Like factoring accounts receivable, merchant cash advances are an expensive source of funding.

merchant cash advance
a method of financing in which a provider prepurchases credit and debit card receivables at a discount.

ENTREPRENEURIAL PROFILE: Ivan and Mayra Rincon: Orchid Boutique Ivan and Mayra Rincon, founders of the online swimwear shop Orchid Boutique, needed help funding the highly seasonal nature of their business. Although the business had solid profit margins on its $3 million in annual sales, the Rincons were always scrambling to find cash to fund the next season's inventory purchases. After several banks rejected their loan requests, they were able to secure a merchant cash advance of $200,000. The company had to pay $55,000 for the advance, however, which meant that the Rincons paid 15 percent of sales to the provider until they paid off the $255,000. The funding cost the company an effective annual interest rate of more than 50 percent![88] ■

Peer-to-peer Lending

New online funding options are emerging to help small businesses with credit. **Peer-to-peer loans** are Web-based vetting platforms, such as Lending Club, Prosper, and Fundation, that create an online community of lenders who provide funding to creditworthy small businesses. Globally, peer-to-peer lending is a $180 billion business.[89] Lending Club, one of the leading peer-to-peer platforms, reports that it is making more than $120 million in loans to small businesses *each month*! Interest rates can range from less than 7 percent to more than 25 percent. Lending Club has a maximum loan limit of $35,000. Lydia Aguinaldo, owner of Pines Home Health Care Services, in Broward County, Florida, secured a $250,000 loan from Fundation at a 19 percent interest rate payable over three years.[90]

peer-to-peer loans
loans made via Web-based platforms that create online communities of lenders who provide funding to creditworthy small businesses.

Loan Brokers

loan broker

a business that specializes in helping small companies find loans by tapping into a wide network of lenders.

Loan brokers specialize in helping small businesses find loans by tapping into a wide network of lenders that include SBA lenders, working capital financing, real estate loans, bridge financing, franchise financing, merchant cash advances, and asset-based lending. Most loan brokers do not charge a fee for the initial evaluation and consulting on financing options for a small business. Loan brokers take a small percentage of the total loan amount, usually 1 to 2.5 percent, once the business is successfully financed. MultiFunding, Biz-2Credit, and Loan Finder are a few of the larger companies offering these services to small business clients.

ENTREPRENEURIAL PROFILE: Patricia and Jim McGrath, Branches Atelier Patricia and Jim McGrath, owners of Branches Atelier, a preschool in Santa Monica, California, wanted to find a larger location to house their growing business. They found a perfect location to buy. The mortgage would cost them no more each month than their current rent, so they were confident that getting a loan would not be difficult. However, when they went to their bank—where they had done business for 20 years—to apply for a loan to buy the building, the bank turned down their loan request. They were shocked because they had enough cash for a down payment and a long waiting list of new students. The McGraths went to a loan brokerage firm, Multifunding, which was able to find a bank willing to give them the loan they needed to buy the building.[91] ■

Credit Cards

Unable to find financing elsewhere, many entrepreneurs launch their companies using the fastest and most convenient source of debt capital available: credit cards. A recent study finds that about 67 percent of small businesses have business credit cards.[92] The SBA estimates that 11 percent of financing for small businesses comes from credit cards (both personal and business cards).[93] Putting business start-up costs on credit cards charging 20 percent or more in annual interest is expensive, risky, and can lead to severe financial woes. A study by Robert Scott of Monmouth University and the Kauffman Foundation reports that taking on credit card debt *reduces* the likelihood that a start-up company will survive its first three years of operation. Every $1,000 increase in credit card debt results in a 2.2 percent increase in the probability that a company will fail.[94] Putting business start-up costs on credit cards is expensive and risky, especially if sales fail to materialize as quickly as planned, but some entrepreneurs have no other choice. Prudent entrepreneurs rely on credit cards only for making monthly purchases that they are certain can be paid off when the credit card bill comes due.

MyLab Entrepreneurship

If your instructor is using MyLab Entrepreneurship, go to **www.pearson.com/mylab/ entrepreneurship** to complete the problems marked with this icon ⭐.

Chapter Summary by Learning Objective

1. Describe the differences between equity capital and debt capital.

- Capital is any form of wealth employed to produce more wealth. Entrepreneurs have access to two different types of capital:
  - Equity financing represents the personal investment of the owner (or owners), and it offers the advantage of not having to be repaid with interest.

- Debt capital is the financing a small business owner has borrowed and must repay with interest. It does not require entrepreneurs to give up ownership in their companies.

2. Discuss the various sources of equity capital available to entrepreneurs.

- The most common source of financing for a business is the owner's personal savings. After emptying their own pockets, the next place entrepreneurs turn for capital is family members and friends. Crowdfunding taps the power of social networking and allows entrepreneurs to post their elevator pitches and proposed investment terms on crowd-funding Web sites and raise money to fund their ventures from ordinary people who invest as little as $100. Angels are private investors who not only invest their money in small companies but also offer valuable advice and counsel to them. Some business owners have success financing their companies by taking on limited partners as investors or by forming an alliance with a corporation, often a customer or a supplier. Venture capital companies are for-profit, professional investors looking for fast-growing companies in "hot" industries. When screening prospects, venture capital firms look for competent management, a competitive edge, a growth industry, and important intangibles that will make a business successful. Some owners choose to attract capital by taking their companies public, which requires registering the public offering with the SEC.

3. Describe the process of "going public."

- Going public involves (1) choosing the underwriter, (2) negotiating a letter of intent, (3) preparing the registration statement, (4) filing with the SEC, and (5) meeting state requirements.

4. Describe the various sources of debt capital.

- Commercial banks offer the greatest variety of loans, although they are conservative lenders. Typical short-term bank loans include commercial loans, lines of credit, discounting accounts receivable, inventory financing, and floor planning.

- Trade credit is used extensively by small businesses as a source of financing. Vendors and suppliers commonly finance sales to businesses for 30, 60, or even 90 days.

- Equipment suppliers offer small businesses financing similar to trade credit but with slightly different terms.

- Commercial finance companies offer many of the same types of loans that banks do, but they are more risk oriented in their lending practices. They emphasize accounts-receivable financing and inventory loans.

- Savings-and-loan associations specialize in loans to purchase real property—commercial and industrial mortgages—for up to 30 years.

- Stock brokerage houses offer loans to prospective entrepreneurs at lower interest rates than banks because they have high-quality, liquid collateral—stocks and bonds in the borrower's portfolio.

- Small Business Investment Companies are privately owned companies licensed and regulated by the SBA that qualify for SBA loans to be invested in or loaned to small businesses.

- Small Business Lending Companies make only intermediate- and long-term loans that are guaranteed by the SBA.

5. Describe the various loan programs available from the Small Business Administration.

- Almost all SBA loan activity is in the form of loan guarantees rather than direct loans. Popular SBA programs include the SBA*Express* program, the 7(a) loan guaranty program, the Section 504 Certified Development Company program, the Microloan program, the CAPLine program, the Export Working Capital program, and the Disaster Loan program.

6. Identify the various federal and state loan programs aimed at small businesses.

- The Economic Development Administration, a branch of the Commerce Department, makes loan guarantees to create and expand small businesses in economically depressed areas.

- The Department of Housing and Urban Development extends grants (such as Community Development Block Grants) to cities that, in turn, lend and grant money to small businesses in an attempt to strengthen the local economy.

- The Department of Agriculture's Rural Business Cooperative Service loan program is designed to create nonfarm employment opportunities in rural areas through loans and loan guarantees.

- The Small Business Innovation Research program involves 11 federal agencies that award cash grants or long-term contracts to small companies wanting to initiate or to expand their R&D efforts.

- The Small Business Technology Transfer program allows researchers at universities, federally funded R&D centers, and nonprofit research institutions to join forces with small businesses and develop commercially promising ideas.

- Many state and local loan and development programs, such as capital access programs, revolving loan funds, and community development financial institutions, complement those sponsored by federal agencies.

7. Explain other methods of financing a business.

- Business owners can get the capital they need by factoring accounts receivable, leasing equipment instead of buying it, borrowing against their retirement accounts, borrowing against future credit card sales, borrowing from peers, using a loan broker, or even using credit cards.

MyLab Entrepreneurship

If your instructor is using MyLab Entrepreneurship, go to **www.pearson.com/mylab/entrepreneurship** for Auto-graded writing questions as well as the following Assisted-graded writing questions:

1. What is the most common source of equity funds in a typical small business?
2. What advice would you offer an entrepreneur about to strike a deal with a private investor to avoid problems?

Discussion Questions

⭐ 15-1. Why is it difficult for most small business owners to raise the capital needed to start, operate, or expand their ventures?

15-2. What is capital?

15-3. Define *equity financing*.

15-4. What advantage does equity financing offer over debt financing?

15-5. If an owner lacks sufficient equity capital to invest in the firm, what options are available for raising it?

⭐ 15-6. What guidelines should an entrepreneur follow if friends and relatives choose to invest in her business?

15-7. What is an angel investor?

15-8. Assemble a brief profile of the typical private investor.

15-9. How can entrepreneurs locate potential angels to invest in their businesses?

15-10. What types of businesses are most likely to attract venture capital?

15-11. What investment criteria do venture capitalists use when screening potential businesses?

15-12. How do venture capitalist criteria for investing compare to the typical angel's criteria?

15-13. How do venture capital firms operate?

15-14. Describe a venture capitalist procedure for screening investment proposals.

15-15. Summarize the major exemptions and simplified registrations available to small companies wanting to make public offerings of their stock.

15-16. What role do commercial banks play in providing debt financing to small businesses?

15-17. Outline and briefly describe the major types of short-, intermediate-, and long-term loans commercial banks offer.

15-18. What is trade credit?

15-19. How important is trade credit as a source of debt financing to small firms?

15-20. What function do SBICs serve?

15-21. How does an SBIC operate?

15-22. What methods of financing do SBICs rely on most heavily?

15-23. Explain the advantages and disadvantages of using crowdfunding.

15-24. Briefly describe the loan programs offered by the Economic Development Administration.

15-25. Briefly describe the loan programs offered by the Department of Housing and Urban Development.

15-26. Briefly describe the loan programs offered by the Department of Agriculture.

15-27. Explain the purpose and the methods of operation of the Small Business Innovation Research program and the Small Business Technology Transfer program.

15-28. What is a factor?

15-29. How does the typical factor operate?

15-30. Explain the advantages and the disadvantages of using factors as a source of funding.

15-31. Explain how an entrepreneur can use retirement funding to start a business using Rollovers as Business Startups (ROBS).

15-32. How do merchant cash advances work as a source of financing a small business?

15-33. What is peer-to-peer lending?

15-34. What is the role and function of loan brokers?

15-35. What role do credit cards play in financing small business?

15-36. Explain the dangers of using credit cards to finance the start-up costs of a small business.

Beyond the Classroom . . .

15-37. Interview several local business owners about how they financed their businesses.

15-38. Where did the initial capital come from for the small business owners you interviewed?

15-39. Ask the small business owners how much money they needed to launch their businesses.

15-40. Ask the small business owners how much of their own money they used to start their businesses.

15-41. Ask the small business owners how they raised the additional capital they needed to start their businesses.

15-42. Ask the small business owners what percentage of the money they raised to start their businesses was debt capital and what percentage was equity capital.

15-43. Ask the small business owners about which of the sources of funds described in this chapter they used.

15-44. Ask the small business owners about any advice they might offer others seeking capital.

15-45. Contact a local private investor and ask him or her to address your class.

15-46. Ask the investor about the kinds of businesses he or she prefers to invest in.

15-47. Ask the investor about the screening criteria he or she uses to select investments.

15-48. Ask the investor about how the deals in which he or she invests are typically structured.

15-49. Contact a local venture capitalist and ask him or her to address your class.

15-50. Ask the venture capitalist about the kinds of businesses his or her company invests in.

15-51. Ask the venture capitalist about the screening criteria used by his or her firm.

15-52. Ask the venture capitalist about how the deals are typically structured when his or her firm invests in an entrepreneurial venture.

15-53. Why are bankers so cautious when making business loans?

15-54. What are the consequences when banks make too many bad business loans?

15-55. How does the cautious attitude of bankers affect entrepreneurs' access to bank financing?

15-56. Contact a local banker who works with small businesses and ask him or her how the small business lending market has changed over the past five years.

15-57. What steps can entrepreneurs take to increase the likelihood that a bank will approve their loan requests?

15-58. Interview the administrator of a financial institution program offering a method of financing with which you are unfamiliar and prepare a short report on its method of operation.

15-59. Contact your state's economic development board and prepare a report on the financial assistance programs it offers small businesses.

15-60. Go to the "IPO Home" section of the Web site for Renaissance Capital, explore the details of a company that is involved in making an initial public offering, and view some of the documents the company has filed with the SEC, especially the IPO filing.

15-61. Prepare a brief report on the company you reviewed at the "IPO Home" section of the Web site for Renaissance Capital, addressing the type of business, its competitors, growth in its industry, risk factors, the money it plans to raise in its IPO, its anticipated stock price, and the number of shares it intends to sell.

15-62. Explain why you would or would not invest in the company you reviewed at the "IPO Home" section of the Web site for Renaissance Capital.

15-63. With a team of classmates, develop a detailed plan for a Kickstarter campaign for a new business that one of the group members is interested in launching.

Endnotes

[1]"2016 Year-End Economic Report," National Small Business Association, 2017, p. 9.

[2]Rolfe Winkler and Telis Demos, "Stripe's Valuation Nearly Doubles to $9.2 Billion," Wall Street Journal, November 25, 2016, www.wsj.com/articles/stripes-valuation-nearly-doubles-to-9-2-billion-1480075201; Douglas MacMillan, "Payments Start-Up Stripe Gets Boost, Value Hits $1.75 Billion," Wall Street Journal, January 23, 2014, p. B4; "Stripe," CrunchBase, 2017, www.crunchbase.com/organization/stripe#/entity; Derek Andersen, "The Story Behind Payment Disrupter Stripe.com and Its Founder Patrick Collison," TechCrunch, May 20, 2012, http://techcrunch.com/2012/05/20/thestory-behind-payment-disruptor-stripe-com-and-itsfounder-patrick-collison/.

[3]Donna J. Kelley, Abdul Ali, Candida Brush, Andrew C. Corbett, Caroline Daniels, Phillip H. Kim, Thomas S. Lyons, Mahdi Majbouri, and Edward G. Rogoff, "2015 United States Report," Global Entrepreneurship Monitor, 2016, p. 43.

[4]Douglas MacMillan, "Google's Historic IPO Run: Beatable," Bloomberg, August 16, 2007, www.bloomberg.com/news/articles/2007-08-16/googles-historic-ipo-run-beatablebusinessweek-business-news-stock-market-and-financial-advice; Catherine Elsworth, "The Man Who Googled Himself $1 Billion," The Telegraph, October 5, 2004, www.telegraph.co.uk/culture/3624998/The-man-who-Googled-himself-1-billion.html.

[5]"Who Started New Businesses in 2013," Kauffman Foundation, January 22, 2014, p. 8.

[6]Jason Weis and Jordan Bell-Masterson, "How Entrepreneurs Access Capital and Get Funded," Entrepreneurship Policy Digest, Kauffman Foundation, June 2, 2015, p. 1.

[7]Alicia Robb and Arnobio Morelix, "Startup Financing Trends by Race: How Access to Capital Impacts Profitability," Kauffman Foundation, October 2016, p. 3.

[8]Tammy Ljungblad, "Modern Era Mom and Pop Businesses Make it Work Out," Kansas City Star, May 27, 2014, www.kansascity.com/news/business/article415785/Modern-era-Mom-and-Pop-businesses-make-it-work-out.html; Parija Kavilanz, "Should You Drain Your 401(k) to Start a Business?" CNN Money, June 23, 2014, http://money.cnn.com/2014/06/23/smallbusiness/startup-funding-401k/.

[9]Michelle Goodman, "Playing with the Boss's Money," Entrepreneur, May 2014, p. 68; Ryan Shank, "Going All In: Here Is How I Rented Out My Bedroom to Join Mhelpdesk Full Time," Mhelpdesk, February 19, 2015, https://www.mhelpdesk.com/going-all-in-heres-how-i-rented-my-bedroom-to-

join-mhelpdesk-full-time/; "HomeAdvisor Acquires a Majority Stake in Field Service Management Software, Mhelpdesk," IAC, September 3, 2014, http://iac.com/media-room/press-releases/homeadvisor-acquires-majority-stake-field-service-management-software-mhelpdesk.

[10] Donna J. Kelley, Abdul Ali, Candida Brush, Andrew C. Corbett, Caroline Daniels, Phillip H. Kim, Thomas S. Lyons, Mahdi Majbouri, and Edward G. Rogoff, "2015 United States Report," *Global Entrepreneurship Monitor*, 2016, p. 41.

[11] Rachel Gotbaum, "Avoiding the Pitfalls of Family Borrowing," *NPR*, October 6, 2006, www.npr.org/templates/story/story.php?storyId=6208227.

[12] Paul Kvinta, "Frogskins, Shekels, Bucks, Moolah, Cash, Simoleans, Dough, Dinero: Everybody Wants It. Your Business Needs It. Here's How to Get It," *Smart Business*, August 2000, pp. 74–89.

[13] "Report on the Review of the Definition of 'Accredited Investor,'" U.S. Securities and Exchange Commission, December 18, 2015, p. 48.

[14] Erin Anderson, personal communication, February 7, 2017.

[15] Catherine Clifford, "3 Rules for Successful Crowdfunding," *Entrepreneur*, May 23, 2012, www.entrepreneur.com/article/223608.

[16] "Companies," Techstars, 2016, www.techstars.com/companies/.

[17] "FloWater," CrunchBase, 2017, www.crunchbase.com/organization/flo-water#/entity.

[18] Pamela Sherrid, "Angels of Capitalism," *U.S. News & World Report*, October 13, 1997, pp. 43–45.

[19] Jeffrey Sohl, "The Angel Investor Market in 2015: A Buyers Market," Center for Venture Research, University of New Hampshire, May 25, 2015, p. 1.

[20] Eliot Peper, "A Founder's Guide to Working with Angel Investors," *Medium*, January 10, 2017, https://medium.com/swlh/a-founders-guide-to-working-with-angel-investors-dec8619b50b6; Mike Freeman, "GroundMetrics Nets $2.73 Million from Investors," *San Diego Union Tribune*, April 23, 2014, http://www.sandiegouniontribune.com/business/technology/sdut-Groundmetrics-Quasar-Cowboy-Technology-Angels-2014apr23-story.html.

[21] Jeffrey Sohl, "The Angel Investor Market in 2015: A Buyers Market," Center for Venture Research, University of New Hampshire, May 25, 2016, p. 1.

[22] Robert Wiltbank and Wade Brooks, "Tracking Angel Returns 2016," Kauffman Foundation and NASDAQ OMX Foundation, May 8, 2016, p. 2.

[23] Robert E. Wiltbank and Warren Boeker, "Angel Performance Project," Angel Capital Education Foundation, November 2007, www.angelcapitalassociation.org/dir_downloads/resources/RSCH_-_ACEF_-_Returns_to_Angel_Investors_PPT.pdf.

[24] Adrianne Pasquarelli, "Why the Business of Artesian Ice Cream Is Harder Than It Looks," *Crain's*, June 8, 2015, www.crainsnewyork.com/article/20150608/RETAIL_APPAREL/150609903/new-york-is-hankering-for-homemade-ice-cream-from-van-leeuwen-others; "Phin and Phebes Ice Cream," AngelList, n.d., https://angel.co/phin-phebes-ice-cream.

[25] Robert Wiltbank and Wade Brooks, "Tracking Angel Returns 2016," Kauffman Foundation and NASDAQ OMX Foundation, May 8, 2016, p.3.

[26] Richard Florida, "The Global Cities Where Tech Venture Capital Is Concentrated," *The Atlantic*, January 26, 2016, www.theatlantic.com/technology/archive/2016/01/global-startup-cities-venture-capital/429255/.

[27] Michelle Goodman, "Play Pals," *Entrepreneur*, October 2014, p. 122; "Wonder Workshop," Crunchbase, June 20, 2017, https://www.crunchbase.com/organization/play-i/

funding-rounds; Blake Montgomery, "Robot Maker Wonder Workshop Raises a $20 Million Series B to Expand Internationally," *EdSurge*, July 28, 2016, https://www.edsurge.com/news/2016-07-28-robot-maker-wonder-workshop-raises-a-20m-series-b-to-expand-internationally.

[28] "Explore the Data," *PwC MoneyTree*, 2016, www.pwc.com/us/en/technology/moneytree/explorer.html#/.

[29] Caroline Daniels, Mike Herrington, and Penny Kew, *Special Topic Report 2015–2016: Entrepreneurial Finance*, Global Entrepreneurship Research Association, 2016, p. 11.

[30] Janet Effland, "How to Bet on the Next Big Thing," *Business 2.0*, December 2002/January 2003, p. 90.

[31] "Explore the Data," *PwC MoneyTree*, 2016, www.pwc.com/us/en/technology/moneytree/explorer.html#/.

[32] "MoneyTree Report Q4 and Full-Year 2016," PwC, January 9, 2017, p. 18.

[33] Kate O'Sullivan, "Not-So-Easy Money, *CFO*, October 2005, p. 20.

[34] Andrea Poe, "Venturing Out," *Entrepreneur*, September 2008, p. 31.

[35] Biz Carson, "A Costco-Killer Just Raked in Another $100 Million to Convert the Next Generation of Bulk Buyers," *Business Insider*, January 20, 2016, www.businessinsider.com/boxed-wholesale-raises-100-million-2016-1; "GGV Capital, Digital Sky Technologies, Founder's Fund and AME Cloud Ventures Invest in Mobile Commerce Innovator Boxed Wholesale," *BusinessWire*, January 14, 2015, www.businesswire.com/news/home/20150114005761/en/Boxed-Closes-25-Million-Series-Funding; Ryan Lawler, "Wholesale Shopping App Boxed Raises $6.5M from Greycroft, First Round, and Signia," *TechCrunch*, May 13, 2014, https://techcrunch.com/2014/05/13/boxed-6-5m/; Holly Slade, "'Costco of Mobile Apps' Boxed Raises $6.5M to Take on Amazon Prime," *Forbes*, May 13, 2014, www.forbes.com/sites/hollieslade/2014/05/13/costcoof-mobile-apps-boxed-raises-6-5m-to-take-on-amazonprime/?ss=business; Erin Griffith May, "Millennials May Kill Costco, and Mobile App Boxed Is Happy to Speed That Along," CNNMoney, May 13, 2014, http://fortune.com/2014/05/13/millennials-may-kill-costco-and-mobile-app-boxed-is-happy-to-speed-that-along/.

[36] Russell Lange, "But When Will They Go Public? A Profile of the Average Company at IPO," *EquityZen*, August 13, 2015, https://equityzen.com/blog/company-at-ipo/; John Cook, "Venture-Backed IPOs and M&A Deals Decline in 2011, but It's Not All Bad News," *GeekWire*, January 3, 2012, www.geekwire.com/2012/venturebacked-companies-complete-ipos-ma-deals-decline/; Rebecca Buckman, "Baby Sitting for Start-ups," *Wall Street Journal*, March 13, 2006, pp. B1, B3.

[37] "The H1 2016 Corporate Venture Capital Report," *CB Insights*, pp. 28, 34.

[38] "Venture Monitor Q4 2016," National Venture Capital Association, 2017, p. 11.

[39] Cromwell Schubarth, "Andy Wheeler of GV (Google Ventures) on Hardware Investing, Robots and AI Fears," *Silicon Valley Business Journal*, January 19, 2016, www.bizjournals.com/sanjose/blog/techflash/2016/01/andy-wheeler-of-gv-google-ventures-on-hardware.html; "Savioke Announces $15 Million Series A Funding from Intel Capital, EDBI, Northern Light Venture Capital," *Business Wire*, January 13, 2016, www.businesswire.com/news/home/20160113005191/en/Savioke-Announces-15-Million-Series-Funding-Intel; Tim Hornyak, "Google Shows More Love for Robots with Savioke Investment," *PC World*, April 9, 2014, www.pcworld.com/article/2142160/google-shows-more-love-for-robots-with-savioke-investment.html; Beth McKenna, "Backed by

Google Ventures, the First Robot Hotel Butler Just Reported for Duty," *Motley Fool*, August 25, 2014, www.fool.com/investing/general/2014/08/25/backed-by-google-ventures-the-first-robot-hotel-bu.aspx.

[40]Jay R. Ritter, "Initial Public Offerings: Updated Statistics," University of Florida, March 29, 2017, p. 5.

[41]Burt Helm, "So, You Think You're Going Public?" *Inc.*, September 2011, pp. 162–168; Julianne Peppitone, "Zynga Shares Close below IPO Price," *CNN Money*, December 16, 2011, http://money.cnn.com/2011/12/16/technology/zynga_ipo/index.htm.

[42]Julien Rath, "Data Shows Nearly Half of Snapchat's Revenue Comes from Discover Ads," *Business Insider*, January 31, 2017, www.businessinsider.com/data-shows-nearly-half-of-snapchats-revenue-comes-from-discover-ads-2017-1.

[43]Jay R. Ritter, "Initial Public Offerings: Updated Statistics," University of Florida, March 29, 2017, p. 27.

[44]Ibid. p. 13.

[45]Seth Fiegerman, "Snapchat Raises $3.4 Billion in IPO," *CNN Money*, March 1, 2017, http://money.cnn.com/2017/03/01/technology/snap-ipo-final-pricing/; Alex Konrad, "Snap's IPO Means a Huge Windfall for These VC Investors," *Forbes*, February 2, 2017, www.forbes.com/sites/alexkonrad/2017/02/02/snap-ipo-means-big-windfall-for-early-snapchat-investors/#2c980b2231e8; Katie Roof, "CEO Evan Spiegel's Snap Ownership Is Worth About $3.5 Billion," *TechCrunch*, February 2, 2017, https://techcrunch.com/2017/02/02/ceo-evan-spiegels-snap-ownership-is-worth-about-3-5-billion/.

[46]*Frequently Asked Questions About Small Business Finance*, Small Business Administration Office of Advocacy, July 2016, p. 1.

[47]*2016 Small Business Credit Survey: Report on Employer Firms*, Federal Reserve Bank, April 2017, p. iv.

[48]Lori Ioannou, "Small Business Still Reeling from Credit Crunch," *CNBC*, September 5, 2013, www.cnbc.com/id/101009116.

[49]John Tozzi, "Credit Cards Replace Small Business Loans," *Businessweek*, August 20, 2008, www.businessweek.com/smallbiz/content/aug2008/sb20080820_288348.htm?chan=smallbiz_smallbiz+index+page_top+small+business+stories.

[50]*2016 Small Business Credit Survey: Report on Employer Firms*, Federal Reserve Bank, April 2017, p. 7.

[51]*Small Business Lending: Quarterly Lending Bulletin*, U.S. Small Business Administration, Office of Advocacy, Second Quarter 2015, p.1.

[52]Victoria Williams, *Small Business Lending in the United States*, 2013, Small Business Administration, Office of Advocacy, December 2014, p. 26.

[53]Anika Richards, "Jamaican Shakes Things Up in the US," *All Woman*, October 26, 2014, www.jamaicaobserver.com/magazines/allwoman/Jamaican-shakes-things-up-in-the-US_17805566; "Georgette Miller: Success Story," Multifunding, n.d., www.multifunding.com/success_stories/georgette-miller/.

[54]Shubhomita Bose, "Small Business Loan Approval Rates at Big Banks Decline, Biz2Credit Index Finds," *Small Business Trends*, August 31, 2016, https://smallbiztrends.com/2016/08/july-2016-biz2credit-small-business-lending-index.html.

[55]Jeremy Quittner, "Housing Gains Trigger Uneven Small Business Recovery," *Inc.*, June 10, 2013, www.inc.com/jeremy-quittner/small-business-housing-recovery-loans.html.

[56]*2016 Small Business Credit Survey: Report on Employer Firms*, Federal Reserve Bank, April 2017, pp. 13, 15.

[57]Jordan Drake, personal communication, May 6, 2014.

[58]"Small Business Administration Loan Program Performance," U.S. Small Business Administration, March 31, 2017, https://www.sba.gov/about-sba/sba-performance/performance-budget-finances/small-business-administration-sba-loan-program-performance.

[59]Ibid.

[60]"7(a) Gross Loan Approvals," National Association of Government Guaranteed Lenders, September 26, 2014, p.1.

[61]*Small Business Administration Agency Financial Report 2016*, U.S. Small Business Administration, 2017, p. 24; "Delinquency Rate on Commercial and Industrial Loans, All Commercial Banks," Federal Reserve Bank of St. Louis, June 16, 2017, https://fred.stlouisfed.org/series/DRBLACBS.

[62]"Building a Legacy: Clem's Garage," U.S. Small Business Administration, n.d., www.sba.gov/about-offices-content/2/3155/success-stories/45411.

[63]"Wheeling Prosperity," CDC Small Business Finance, https://cdcloans.com/success-stories-featured/success-stories/.

[64]Ben Ryan, "Many U.S. Microbusiness Owners Depend on Second Job," Gallup, April 3, 2014, www.gallup.com/poll/168215/microbusiness-owners-depend-secondjob.aspx.

[65]"Floral Business Booms, Thanks to SBA Microloan," Center for Rural Affairs, February 13, 2014, http://www.cfra.org/news/140213/floral-business-blooms-thanks-sba-microloan.

[66]"Small Business Jobs Act Success Stories," U.S. Senate Committee on Small Business and Entrepreneurship, https://www.sbc.senate.gov/public/_cache/files/9/6/967a2032-0f3a-4918-a31d-652e8fc4fb82/64BB8A6DC2A10E03DCD29E05F702889D.sbja-success-stories.pdf.

[67]Steve Alillen, "Loan Help Center for Sevier County Fire Victims Closing Monday," *Knoxville News Sentinel*, February 23, 2017, www.knoxnews.com/story/news/local/tennessee/gatlinburg/2017/02/23/loan-help-center-sevier-county-fire-victims-closing-monday/98310530/.

[68]Lisa A. Miller, "The World of ABL Lending: Still Flat After All These Years," *ABF Journal*, November/December 2016, http://www.abfjournal.com/%3Fpost_type%3Darticles%26p%3D54795.

[69]"Assets and Liabilities of the Personal Sector," *Financial Accounts of the United States*, Board of Governors of the Federal Reserve System, First Quarter 2017, p. 14.

[70]*U.S. Credit Union Profile*, First Quarter 2017, Credit Union National Association, 2017, p. 2.

[71]Ibid. p. 8.

[72]"2015 Small Business Credit Survey," Federal Reserve Banks, March 2016, p. 11.

[73]"Small Business Lending Index," Biz2Credit, January 2017, www.biz2credit.com/small-business-lending-index.

[74]Daniel Carlsson, "Credit Unions Are Increasingly Business Friendly," *Entrepreneur*, May 27, 2014, www.entrepreneur.com/article/234208; Katie Morell, "5 Ways to Thrive in an Overcrowded Industry," *OPENforum*, September 14, 2011, www.americanexpress.com/us/small-business/openforum/articles/5-ways-to-thrive-in-a-overcrowded-industry/.

[75]"SBIC Program History," Small Business Investor Alliance, n.d., www.sbia.org/?page=sbic_program_history.

[76]David Robinson, "Gemcor Deal Has Incentive to Retain Jobs," *Buffalo News*, January 11, 2016, http://buffalonews.com/2016/01/11/gemcor-deal-has-incentive-to-retain-jobs/; "The Small Business Investment Company (SBIC) Program: Annual Report FY 2012," U.S. Small Business Administration, 2013, p. 23.

[77]"NECOG-DC Revolving Loan Fund Success Stories: Russ Maier Hay Grinding, Bowdle," Northeast Council of Governments Development Corporation, Aberdeen, SD, n.d., http://necog.org/rlf/necog-success-stories.

[78]Lillia Callum-Penso, "TR's Upcountry Provisions Turns over a New Leaf," *Greenville Online*, March 23, 2016, www.greenvilleonline.com/story/entertainment/2016/03/23/trs-upcountry-provisions-turns-over-new-leaf/82133778/; Angelia Davis, "Filling a Need," *Greenville News*, November 6, 2011, pp. 1E–2E.

[79]"Business Loan Brings Jobs, Growth to Appalachian Ohio County," U.S. Department of Agriculture, Rural Development, n.d., www.rd.usda.gov/newsroom/success-stories/business-loan-brings-jobs-growth-appalachian-ohio-county.

[80]"Luna Innovations, Inc.," SBBR-STTR, U.S. Small Business Administration, 2017, https://www.sbir.gov/sbc/luna-innovations-incorporated; "Transition: Equipping the War Fighter," *Air Force SBIR/STTR*, April 2017, pp.1-2.

[81]"Krauss Craft, Inc.," Business Oregon, n.d., www.oregon4biz.com/story.php?storyID=20.

[82]"Previously Laid Off, Tina Today Owns a Thriving Business with the Help of Opportunity Fund," Calvert Foundation, n.d., http://map.calvertfoundation.org/stories/12/37.82/-122.28?sector=business.

[83]"Annual Asset-Based Lending and Factoring Survey Highlights, 2015," Commercial Finance Association, March 22, 2016, p. 7.

[84]Ibid. p. 9.

[85]Roberta Reynes, "A Big Factor in Expansion," *Nation's Business*, January 1999, pp. 31–32; Bruce J. Blechman, "The High Cost of Credit," *Entrepreneur*, January 1993, pp. 22–25.

[86]Charles C. Scott, "A Creative Way to Fund Your Entrepreneurial Passion: Your 401(k)," *Kiplinger*, February 13, 2017, www.kiplinger.com/article/business/T001-C032-S014-a-creative-way-to-fund-a-business-your-401-k.html.

[87]Paul Sullivan, "Financing Start-up Dreams with Retirement Savings," *New York Times*, September 14, 2013, p. B5.

[88]Amy Cortese, "Can't Get a Bank Loan? The Alternatives are Expanding," *New York Times*, March 6, 2014, p. B4.

[89]Oscar Williams-Grut, "Deloitte Just Trashed the Hype Around a $180 Billion Fintech Market," *Business Insider*, May 23, 2016, http://www.businessinsider.com/deloitte-report-marketplace-lending-not-significant-players-peer-to-peer-2016-5.

[90]Amy Cortese, "Can't Get a Bank Loan? The Alternatives are Expanding," *New York Times*, March 6, 2014, p. B4.

[91]Wendy Kaufman, "In Tight Credit Market a Tool for Small Businesses," *NPR*, May 25, 2012, www.npr.org/2012/05/25/153610068/in-tight-credit-market-a-tool-for-small-businesses.

[92]Daniel P. Ray, "Business credit card statistics," CreditCards.com, June 13, 2016, www.creditcards.com/credit-card-news/business-credit-card-statistics.php.

[93]"Small Business Finance: Frequently Asked Questions," SBA Office of Advocacy, February 2014, p. 2.

[94]Robert H. Scott, "The Use of Credit Card Debt by New Firms," Kauffman Foundation, August 2009, p. 4.

16 Global Aspects of Entrepreneurship

Shutter_M/Shutterstock

Learning Objectives

On completion of this chapter, you will be able to:

1. Explain why "going global" has become an integral part of many small companies' marketing strategies.

2. Describe the principal strategies small businesses can use for going global.

3. Discuss the major barriers to international trade and their impact on the global economy.

4. Describe the trade agreements that will have the greatest influence on foreign trade in the twenty-first century.

MyLab Entrepreneurship

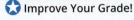 **Improve Your Grade!**

If your instructor is using MyLab Entrepreneurship, visit **www.pearson.com/mylab/entrepreneurship** for videos, simulations, and writing exercises.

Until recently, the world of international business was much like astronomy before Copernicus, who revolutionized the study of the planets and the stars with his theory of planetary motion. In the sixteenth century, the Copernican system replaced the Ptolemaic system, which held that the Earth was the center of the universe, with the Sun and all the other planets revolving around it. The Copernican system, however, placed the Sun at the center of the solar system, with all of the planets revolving around it. Astronomy would never be the same.

In the same sense, business owners around the globe have been guilty of having Ptolemaic tunnel vision when it came to viewing international business opportunities. Like their pre-Copernican counterparts, owners saw an economy that revolved around the nations that served as their home bases. Market opportunities stopped at their homeland's borders, and global trade was only for giant corporations. American small businesses lag behind their counterparts in most countries around the globe when it comes to exporting. Only 5 percent of U.S. small businesses with employees engage in exporting.[1] In contrast, small businesses in the European Union are 4 to 5 times more likely to engage in exporting than their U.S. counterparts. In fact, 27 percent of small businesses (those with 10 to 49 employees) and 20 percent of microbusinesses (those with 1 to 9 employees) in the European Union export goods and services to other nations.[2] The most common reasons that small business owners in the United States cite for not exporting are selling goods and services that are not exportable (39 percent), not knowing how to start exporting (37 percent), concerns about getting paid (24 percent) by foreign customers, and overcoming regulatory barriers to exporting (24 percent). The majority of small businesses in the United States are content to focus on the domestic market. However, 96 percent of the world population lives outside U.S borders! The good news is that a recent study by the National Small Business Association and Small Business Exporting Association suggests that the number of U.S. small businesses engaging in international trade is increasing.[3]

ENTREPRENEURIAL PROFILE: Hampel Corporation Hampel Corporation, based in Germantown, Wisconsin, manufactures large plastic component parts for manufacturers and designs and manufactures products for the agriculture industry. Hampel's revenues have grown significantly since the company increased its focus on international customers. Revenues almost doubled during the 10 years following the company's commitment to expand its international customer base. About 20 percent of its $40 million in revenues comes from exports. Of Hampel's 130 employees, 28 positions in the company are directly dependent on international business. Company executives say that Hampel faces limitations on additional international sales growth due to high import duties designed to protect local producers that are imposed by a growing number of countries. The company also faces infringement on its intellectual property because foreign companies copy its patented products.[4] ■

Today, the global marketplace is as much the territory of small upstart companies as it is the territory of giant multinational corporations. The world market for goods and services continues to grow, fueled by a global economy that welcomes consumers with new wealth. By 2028, more than 5 billion people globally will be classified as middle-class consumers, creating a tremendous opportunity for small businesses.[5] Powerful, affordable technology; the Internet; increased access to information on conducting global business; and the growing interdependence of the world's economies have made it easier for small companies, many of which had never considered going global, to engage in international trade. These micromultinational companies are proving that even the smallest companies can succeed in the global marketplace.

As globalization transforms entire industries, even experienced business owners and managers must rethink the rules of competition on which they have relied for years. To thrive, they must develop new business models and new sources of competitive advantages and be bold enough to seize the opportunities that the global marketplace offers. Opportunities for global trade can come from anywhere. Many small businesses focus on markets that are nearby and/or share a common language, including Canada, the United Kingdom, and Australia. However, entrepreneurs also should pay attention to the top emerging markets, which include Poland, Hungary, Russia, Mexico, Brazil, China, and Thailand.[6]

Entrepreneurs are discovering that the tools of global business are within their reach, the costs of going global are decreasing, and the benefits of conducting global business can be substantial. Nearly 80 percent of the world's purchasing power lies *outside* the borders of the United States![7]

Worldwide, countries trade more than $16.5 trillion in goods and services annually, a dramatic increase from $58 billion in 1948.[8] There has never been a better time for small companies to become players in the global marketplace.

Why Go Global?

LO1

Explain why "going global" has become an integral part of many small companies' marketing strategies.

Failure to cultivate global markets can be a lethal mistake for modern businesses, whatever their size. A few decades ago, small companies had to concern themselves mainly with competitors who were perhaps six blocks away; today, small companies face fierce competition from companies that may be six *time zones* away! As a result, entrepreneurs find themselves under greater pressure to expand into international markets and to build businesses without borders. Today, the potential for doing business globally for companies of all sizes means that where a business's goods and services originate or where its headquarters is located is insignificant. Operating a successful business increasingly requires entrepreneurs to see their companies as global citizens rather than as companies based in a particular geographic region. For small companies around the world, going global is a matter of survival, not preference. To be successful, small companies must take their place in the world market. Unfortunately, most small companies follow a *reactive* approach to going global (engaging in global sales because foreign customers initiate the contact) rather than pursue a *proactive* global sales strategy that involves researching and analyzing foreign markets that represent the best fit for their products and services.[9]

Going global can put a tremendous strain on a small company, but entrepreneurs who take the plunge into global business can reap many benefits, including the ability to offset sales declines in the domestic market, increase sales and profits, improve the quality of their products to meet the stringent demands of foreign customers, lower the manufacturing cost of their products by spreading fixed costs over a larger number of units, and enhance their competitive positions to become stronger businesses. In fact, companies that sell their goods and services in other countries generate more sales revenue, grow faster, are more profitable, have higher levels of productivity, and are less likely to fail than those that limit their sales to the domestic market.[10]

Success in a global economy requires constant innovation; staying nimble enough to use speed as a competitive weapon; maintaining a high level of quality and constantly improving it; being sensitive to foreign customers' unique requirements; adopting a more respectful attitude toward foreign habits and customs; hiring motivated, multilingual employees; and retaining a desire to learn constantly about global markets. In short, business owners must strive to become "insiders" rather than just "exporters."

Becoming a global entrepreneur requires a different mindset. To be successful, entrepreneurs must see their companies from a global perspective and must instill a global culture throughout their companies that permeates everything the business does. To these entrepreneurs and their companies, national boundaries are irrelevant; they see the world as a market opportunity. An absence of global thinking is one of the barriers that most often limit entrepreneurs' ability to move beyond the domestic market. Indeed, learning to *think globally* may be the first—and most challenging—obstacle an entrepreneur must overcome on the way to creating a truly global business. Global thinking is the ability to appreciate, understand, and respect the different beliefs, values, behavior, and business practices of companies and people in different cultures and countries. This requires entrepreneurs to "do their homework" to learn about the people, places, business techniques, potential customers, and culture of the countries in which they intend to do business. Several U.S. government agencies, including the Department of Commerce, offer vast amounts of information about all nations, including economic data that can be useful to entrepreneurs searching for market opportunities. Doing business globally presents extraordinary opportunities only to those who are prepared.

Strategies for Going Global

LO2

Describe the principal strategies small businesses can use for going global.

Small companies pursuing a global presence have 10 principal strategies from which to choose: creating a presence on the Web, relying on trade intermediaries, establishing joint ventures, engaging in foreign licensing arrangements, franchising, using countertrading and bartering,

FIGURE 16.1

Ten Strategies for Going Global

exporting products or services, establishing international locations, importing and outsourcing, and becoming an expat entrepreneur (see Figure 16.1).

Creating a Web Site

In our technology-rich global environment, the fastest, least expensive, and lowest-cost strategic option to establish a global business presence is to create a Web site. As you saw in Chapter 10 on e-commerce, the Internet gives even the smallest business the ability to sell its goods and services all over the globe. By establishing a presence online, a local candy maker or a home-based luxury boat broker gains immediate access to customers around the world. With a well-designed Web site, an entrepreneur can extend his or her reach to customers anywhere in the world—without breaking the budget! A company's Web site is available to potential customers everywhere and provides exposure to its products or services 24 hours a day seven days a week. For many small companies, the Internet has become a tool that is as essential to doing business as the telephone. Unfortunately, 62 percent of small business owners say that their Web sites are unable to process international orders.[11]

Establishing an Internet presence has become an important part of many small companies' strategies for reaching customers outside the United States. Internet World Stats estimates the number of Internet users worldwide to be almost 4 billion. Just 320 million of them live in the North America, leaving more than 3.6 *billion* potential Internet customers in the rest of the world (see Figure 16.2)![12] A study by eMarketer, a market research firm, estimates that global ecommerce retail sales will reach $4 trillion by 2020.[13]

FIGURE 16.2

Internet Users Worldwide

Source: Based on "Internet Users in the World, by Regions, 2017 Q1," Internet World Stats, March 31, 2017, www.internetworldstats .com/stats.htm.

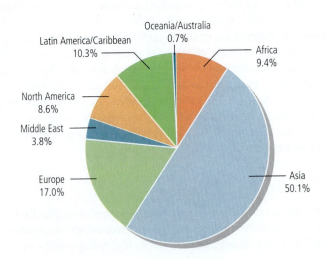

Just as business owners who conduct international business in person must be sensitive to the cultural nuances and differences in the business practices of other countries, entrepreneurs who conduct business online must take these same factors into account when they design their companies' Web sites. Entrepreneurs must "think local" when they create Web sites that target customers in other countries. Although having a single domain name with separate "language" buttons for translations is simpler and less expensive, e-commerce experts say having separate domain names for each targeted country produces better sales results. The designs of Web sites that target foreign customers must reflect the local culture, customs, and language. For instance, not all cultures read from left to right, and colors that may be appropriate in one culture may be offensive to customers in another. A U.S. entrepreneur won't have much luck listing "soccer cleats" for sale on a Web site aimed at customers in the United Kingdom, where customers would search for "football boots." Although there are online tools to help translate keywords and Web site content into multiple languages, the subtleties of language and culture require getting help from people with specific expertise in a new market.

Before the advent of the Internet, small businesses usually took incremental steps toward becoming global businesses. They began selling locally and then, after establishing a reputation, expanded regionally and perhaps nationally. Only after establishing themselves domestically did small businesses begin to think about selling their products or services internationally. The Internet makes that business model obsolete because it provides entrepreneurs with a low-cost global distribution channel that they can use from the day they launch their businesses.

TRADE INTERMEDIARIES Although many small businesses handle their foreign sales efforts in-house, another alternative for getting into international markets with a minimum of cost and effort is to use a trade intermediary. **Trade intermediaries** are domestic agencies that serve as distributors in foreign countries for domestic companies of all sizes. They rely on their networks of contacts, their extensive knowledge of local customs and markets, and their experience in international trade to market products effectively and efficiently all across the globe. These trade intermediaries serve as the export departments for small businesses, enabling the small companies to focus on what they do best and delegate the responsibility for coordinating foreign sales efforts to the intermediaries. They are especially valuable to small companies that are getting started in the global arena, often producing benefits that far outweigh their costs. Lawrence Harding, president of High Street Partners, a trade intermediary that manages foreign sales for small companies, points to the example of a company that imported telecommunications equipment into the United Kingdom to sell to its customers there. The deal triggered a hefty 17.5 percent duty that Harding says the company could have avoided paying if it had imported the equipment in a different way.[14]

Although a broad array of trade intermediaries is available, the following are ideally suited for small businesses.

Export Management Companies **Export management companies (EMCs)** are an important channel of foreign distribution for small companies just getting started in international trade or for those that lack the resources to assign their own people to foreign markets. Most EMCs are merchant intermediaries, working on a buy-and-sell arrangement with domestic small companies, taking title to the goods and then reselling them in foreign markets; others work on commission. More than 1,000 EMCs operate across the United States, and many of them specialize in particular industries, products, or product lines as well as in the foreign countries they target. For instance, Dorian Drake International, an EMC started in 1947, specializes in selling equipment around the world for U.S.-based companies in four industries—automotive, food service, lawn and garden, and environmental. For more than 40 years, Dorian Drake has managed global sales for American Lawn, the leading U.S. maker of manual reel lawn mowers, a family-owned business founded in Shelbyville, Indiana, in 1895.[15]

EMCs provide small businesses with a low-cost, efficient, independent international marketing and export department, offering services that range from conducting market research and giving advice on patent protection to arranging financing and handling shipping. The greatest benefits that EMCs offer small companies are ready access to global markets and an extensive knowledge base on foreign trade, both of which are vital for entrepreneurs who are inexperienced in conducting global business. In return for their services, EMCs usually earn an extra

trade intermediary
a domestic agency that serves as a distributor in foreign countries for domestic companies of all sizes.

export management company (EMC)
a merchant intermediary that provides small businesses with a low-cost, efficient, offsite international marketing department.

You Be the Consultant

Going Global from the Outset

Entrepreneurs are discovering that doing business globally is not just for large corporations. Some entrepreneurs take their companies global from the outset, and their micro-multinational companies are reaping the benefits. Entrepreneurs who launch businesses and target international markets at the outset should rely on the following principles:

- *Grow one country at a time.* Although it might feel like the world is your market, it is best to tackle one new country at a time. Keep in mind the old saying that the way to eat an elephant is one bite at a time.

- *Give it a local feel.* Securing URLs that are specific to the countries you are marketing in gives your business a more local feel to potential customers. If you do business by phone, secure a local phone number, as well.

- *Find local partners.* A digital educational content company based in the United States established local content platforms with partners in Canada, Australia, and Ireland to help it launch as an international company.

- *Build a global brand.* Use social media, content creation, and Google to establish the brand of your company as a global brand.

DesignCrowd

Alec Lynch, founder and CEO of global crowdsourcing start-up DesignCrowd, launched his company with the intent of pursuing international customers from the beginning. DesignCrowd connects its network of more than 500,000 freelance designers located around the world to create logos, simple Web sites, T-shirts, and other marketing materials for its international clients.

DesignCrowd is based in Australia, and 75 percent of the company's customers come from outside its home country. To support customers in all different time zones, DesignCrowd opened a satellite office in San Francisco. DesignCrowd has local phone numbers for all of its major markets, including the United States, Great Britain, Australia, New Zealand, Canada, Brazil, and Singapore. Lynch recommends going global from the start if internationalization is at the heart of your business model.

Zkipster

David Becker and Daniel Dessauges launched their company, Zkipster, in their home country of Switzerland. Zkipster is a guest list app that creates cloud-based guest lists that eliminate the need for paper guest lists. After launch, the partners recognized that focusing only on events in Zurich would not allow them to scale the business: They needed to go global. They believed that New York City would be the ideal market to relaunch their company as a global brand, so they moved across the Atlantic to establish Zkipster as an international product.

Because the founders had raised no money for the start-up, Becker and Dessauges bootstrapped the company, running their business out of coworking spaces and coffee shops until they had enough cash flow to support an office. Zkipster quickly gained new customers throughout New York City. The next step was to move into the major global markets that fit Zkipster's business model of a large, concentrated business community. They opened operations first in Hong Kong, followed closely by London and São Paulo, Brazil. In each market, Zkipster established strong sales teams, which are supported by the corporate offices in New York. Becker and Dessauges spend about 30 percent of their time traveling to work with their local teams.

Zee Wines USA

Roy Goslin and his wife, Dianne Ferrandi, grew up in South Africa, where both had connections to that country's wine industry. Ferrandi's parents owned vineyards and sold grapes to local vintners, and Goslin worked in materials and process management for one of South Africa's largest wineries. Both Goslin and Ferrandi grew up with wine as an integral part of meals. In 1998, recruited by a large information technology consulting firm, the couple moved to Minneapolis, Minnesota, but they never lost their passion for the fine wines of South Africa. Because few people in the United States knew about the storied winemaking tradition and superb vineyards of South Africa, Goslin and Ferrandi had difficulty finding wines from their homeland in Minnesota. Their solution: Start their own wine import business that specializes in wines from South Africa. They announced their decision at a dinner with friends, where one friend suggested that they name their company "Z Wines." ("You've got zee food, and we have zee wine," he joked.)

In 2006, Goslin and Ferrandi started Zee Wines USA as a home-based business with the goal of importing from South Africa wines that they knew were the best the country had to offer and wholesaling them to retail stores. Many of the wineries the company buys from have been operating for hundreds of years. With its diverse climate, rich soil, amazing biodiversity, and rich winemaking tradition, South Africa produces some of the world's finest, most distinctive wines. The couple knew they could import wines from South Africa and sell them for just $10 to $15 per bottle in the United States.

In addition to the South African wines they import, Goslin and Ferrandi also sell domestic wines from Washington, Oregon, and California. With $500,000 in annual sales, their total portfolio of wines numbers only about 100. Although the owners could have pursued a more aggressive growth strategy, they chose to focus on wines that fit their business model of providing high value for their customers. The company accepts only 1 to 2 percent of the wines its owners evaluate.

1. As the global market grows, more small businesses are expanding into other markets. What are the implications for small companies that have the potential to conduct business globally?

(continued)

You Be the Consultant

2. What advice can you offer the founders of Zee Wines USA about selling their products globally?

3. Notice that the founders of Zkipster used a direct, localized sales approach to enter new markets. What are the advantages and disadvantages of setting up local sales operations? Why do most small companies that sell internationally use trade intermediaries rather than open local offices?

Sources: Based on Alec Lynch, "How to Take Your Startup Global on a Shoestring Budget," *The Next Web*, October 11, 2014, https://thenextweb.com/entrepreneur/2014/10/11/take-startup-global-shoestring-budget/#.tnw_lJ2N6CKo#.tnw_8Hwqxkca; David Becker, "How to Take Your Startup Global, Without Going Bust," *The Guardian*, August 5, 2014, www.theguardian.com/media-network/media-network-blog/2014/aug/05/how-to-startup-global-costs-tips; John Garland, "Roy Goslin and Dianne Ferrandi of Z Wines," *Heavy Table*, March 2, 2011, http://heavytable.com/roy-goslin-and-dianne-ferrandi-of-z-wines; Phil Bolsta, "Small Business Success Stories: Z Wines USA," *Twin Cities Business*, December 2008, www.tcbmag.com/superstars/smallbusinesssuccessstories/106542p1.aspx.

discount on the goods they buy from their clients or, if they operate on a commission rate, a higher commission than domestic distributors earn on what they sell. EMCs charge commission rates of about 10 percent on consumer goods and 15 percent on industrial products. Although EMCs rarely advertise their services, finding one is not difficult. The Federation of International Trade Associations provides useful information for small companies about global business and trade intermediaries on its Web site (www.fita.org/), including a listing of EMCs. Industry trade associations and publications and the U.S. Department of Commerce's Export Assistance Centers also can help entrepreneurs locate EMCs and other trade intermediaries.

Export Trading Companies Another tactic for getting into international markets with a minimum of cost and effort is through export trading companies. **Export trading companies (ETCs)** are businesses that buy and sell products in a number of countries, and they typically offer a wide range of services, such as exporting, importing, shipping, storing, and distributing, to their clients. Unlike EMCs, which tend to focus on exporting, ETCs usually perform both import and export trades across many countries' borders. Although EMCs usually create exclusive contracts with companies for a particular product line, ETCs often represent several companies selling the same product line. However, like EMCs, ETCs lower the risk of exporting for small businesses. Some of the largest ETCs in the world are based in the United States and Japan. In fact, many businesses that have successfully navigated Japan's complex system of distribution have done so with the help of ETCs.

> **export trading company (ETC)**
> a business that buys and sells products in a number of countries and offers a wide variety of import and export services to its clients.

In 1982, Congress passed the Export Trading Company Act to allow producers of similar products to form ETC cooperatives without the fear of violating antitrust laws. The goal was to encourage U.S. companies to export more goods by allowing businesses in the same industry to band together to form ETCs.

Manufacturer's Export Agents **Manufacturer's export agents (MEAs)** act as international sales representatives in a limited number of markets for various noncompeting domestic companies. Unlike the close, partnering relationship formed with most EMCs, the relationship between an MEA and a small company is a short-term one, and the MEA typically operates on a commission basis.

> **manufacturer's export agent (MEA)**
> a business that acts as an international sales representative in a limited number of markets for noncompeting domestic companies.

Export Merchants **Export merchants** are domestic wholesalers that do business in foreign markets. They buy goods from many domestic manufacturers and then market them in foreign markets. Unlike MEAs, export merchants often carry competing lines, meaning that they have little loyalty to suppliers. Most export merchants specialize in particular industries, such as office equipment, computers, and industrial supplies.

> **export merchant**
> a domestic wholesaler that does business in foreign markets.

Resident Buying Offices Another approach to exporting is to sell to a **resident buying office**, a government- or privately-owned operation of one country established in another country for the purpose of buying goods made there. Many foreign governments and businesses have set up buying offices in the United States. Selling to them is just like selling to domestic customers because the buying office handles all the details of exporting.

> **resident buying office**
> a government- or privately owned operation of one country established in another country for the purpose of buying goods made there.

Foreign Distributors Some small businesses work through foreign distributors to reach international markets. Domestic small companies export their products to these distributors, who handle all of the marketing, distribution, support, and service functions in the foreign country.

The key to success is screening potential distributors to find ones that are reliable, financially sound, and customer focused.

ENTREPRENEURIAL PROFILE: Dick Sams: NuStep Before cofounding NuStep, CEO Dick Sams, CEO, designed the first heart–lung machine for cardiac surgery in the 1960s. Based on his career-long interest in cardiac health, Sams designed an exercise machine for recovering heart patients and cofounded NuStep in Ann Arbor, Michigan, to manufacture and distribute his latest product. Unfortunately, Sams launched NuStep as a severe recession took hold of the economy. Sams decided that he would expand his market internationally to help offset the weak sales in the U.S. market. Sams hired Elena Stegemann, a native of Ukraine who speaks several languages, as an international sales manager. With the help of the U.S. Commercial Service, Stegemann traveled abroad and recruited foreign distributors in many countries. NuStep's international sales rapidly grew to be nearly 20 percent of total revenues. NuStep, which exports to 25 countries around the world, recently won the President's "E" Star Award, the highest national recognition any U.S. entity can receive for making a significant contribution to the expansion of U.S. exports.[16] ∎

The Value of Using Trade Intermediaries Using trade intermediaries such as the ones discussed in this section is becoming increasingly popular among small businesses attempting to branch out into world markets because they make that transition much faster and easier. Most small business owners simply do not have the knowledge, resources, or confidence to go global alone. Intermediaries' global networks of buyers and sellers allow their small business customers to build their international sales much faster and with fewer hassles and mistakes. Entrepreneurs who are inexperienced in global sales and attempt to crack certain foreign markets alone quickly discover just how difficult the challenge can be. However, with their know-how, experience, and contacts, trade intermediaries can get small companies' products into foreign markets quickly and efficiently. The primary disadvantage of using trade intermediaries is that doing so requires entrepreneurs to surrender control over their foreign sales. However, by maintaining close contact with intermediaries and evaluating their performance regularly, entrepreneurs can avoid major problems.

The key to establishing a successful relationship with a trade intermediary is conducting a thorough screening to determine which type of intermediary—and which one in particular—will best serve a small company's needs. Entrepreneurs should look for intermediaries that specialize in the products their companies sell and that have experience and established contacts in the countries they have targeted. An entrepreneur looking for an intermediary should compile a list of potential candidates using some of the sources listed in Table 16.1. After compiling the list, entrepreneurs should evaluate each one by using a list of criteria to narrow the field to the most promising ones. Interviewing a principal from each intermediary on the final list should tell entrepreneurs which ones are best able to meet their companies' needs. Finally, before signing any agreement with a trade intermediary, it is wise to conduct thorough background and credit checks. Entrepreneurs with experience in global trade also suggest entering short-term agreements of about a year with new trade intermediaries to allow time to test their ability and willingness to live up to their promises. Many entrepreneurs begin their global business initiatives with trade intermediaries and then venture into international business on their own as their skill and comfort levels increase.

JOINT VENTURES Joint ventures, both domestic and foreign, lower the risk of entering global markets for small businesses. They also give small companies more clout in foreign lands. In a **domestic joint venture**, two or more U.S. small businesses form an alliance for the purpose of exporting their goods and services. For export ventures, participating companies get antitrust immunity, allowing them to cooperate freely. The businesses share the responsibility and the costs of getting export licenses and permits, and they split the venture's profits. Establishing a joint venture with the right partner has become an essential part of maintaining a competitive position in global markets for a growing number of industries.

In a **foreign joint venture**, a domestic small business forms an alliance with a company in the target nation. The host partner brings to the joint venture valuable knowledge of the local market and its method of operation as well as of the customs and the tastes of local customers, making it much easier to conduct business in the foreign country. Sometimes foreign countries place certain limitations on joint ventures, such as requiring host companies to hold a majority stake in the venture.

domestic joint venture
an alliance of two or more U.S. small companies that band together for the purpose of exporting their goods and services abroad.

foreign joint venture
an alliance between a U.S. small business and a company in the target nation.

TABLE 16.1 Resources for Locating a Trade Intermediary

Trade intermediaries make doing business around the world much easier for small companies, but finding the right one can be challenging. Fortunately, several government agencies offer a wealth of information to businesses interested in reaching into global markets with the help of trade intermediaries. Entrepreneurs looking for help in breaking into global markets should contact the International Trade Administration, the U.S. Commerce Department, and the Small Business Administration to take advantage of the following services:

- *Agent/Distributor Service (ADS).* This service provides customized searches to locate interested and qualified foreign distributors for a product or service. The search cost is $250 per country.

- *Commercial Service International Contacts (CSIC) List.* This list provides contact and product information for more than 82,000 foreign agents, distributors, and importers interested in doing business with U.S. companies.

- *Country Directories of International Contacts (CDIC) List.* This list provides the same kind of information as the CSIC List but is organized by country.

- *Industry Sector Analyses (ISAs).* This service offers in-depth reports on industries in foreign countries, including information on distribution practices, end users, and top sales prospects.

- *International Market Insights (IMIs).* This service provides reports on specific foreign market conditions, upcoming opportunities for U.S. companies, trade contacts, trade show schedules, and other information.

- *Trade Opportunity Program (TOP).* This program provides up-to-the-minute, prescreened sales leads around the world for U.S. businesses, including joint venture and licensing partners, direct sales leads, and representation offers.

- *International Company Profiles (ICPs).* Commercial specialists investigate potential partners, agents, distributors, or customers for U.S. companies and issue profiles on them.

- *Commercial News USA.* This government-published magazine promotes U.S. companies' products and services to 400,000 business readers in 176 countries at a fraction of the cost of commercial advertising. Small companies can use *Commercial News USA* to reach new customers around the world for as little as $499.

- *Gold Key Service.* For a small fee, business owners wanting to target a specific country can use the U.S. Commercial Service's Gold Key Service, in which experienced trade professionals arrange meetings with prescreened contacts whose interests match their own.

- *Platinum Key Service.* The U.S. Commercial Service's Platinum Key Service is more comprehensive than its Gold Key Service, offering business owners long-term consulting services on topics such as building a global marketing strategy, deciding which countries to target, and serving the needs of customers in foreign markets.

- *Matchmaker Trade Delegations Program.* This program helps small U.S. companies establish business relationships in major markets abroad by introducing them to the right contacts.

- *Multi-State/Catalog Exhibition Program.* The Department of Commerce presents companies' product and sales literature to hundreds of interested business prospects in foreign countries for as little as $450.

- *Trade Fair Certification Program.* This service promotes U.S. companies' participation in foreign trade shows that represent the best marketing opportunities for them.

- *Globus and National Trade Data Bank (NTDB).* Most of the information listed above is available on the NTDB, the U.S. government's most comprehensive database of world trade data. With the NTDB, small companies have access to information that once only Fortune 500 companies could afford for an annual subscription rate of just $200.

- *Economic Bulletin Board (EBB).* This service provides online trade leads and valuable market research on foreign countries compiled from a variety of federal agencies.

- *U.S. Export Assistance Centers.* The Department of Commerce has established 19 export centers (USEACs) in major metropolitan cities around the country to serve as one-stop shops for entrepreneurs who need export help.

- *Trade Information Center.* The center helps locate federal export assistance, provides export assistance, and offers a 24-hour automated fax retrieval system that gives entrepreneurs free information on export promotion programs, regional market information, and international trade agreements. Call USA-TRADE.

- *Office of International Trade.* Through the Office of International Trade, the Small Business Administration works with other government and private agencies to provide export development assistance, how-to publications, online courses, and information on foreign markets.

- *Export-U2.com.* This Web site offers free export webinars to business owners on topics that range from the basics, "Exporting 101," to more advanced topics such as export financing arrangements. The site also provides links to many useful international trade Web sites.

- *U.S. Commercial Service.* The U.S. Commercial Service, a division of the International Trade Administration, provides many of the services listed in this table. Its Web site is an excellent starting point for entrepreneurs who are interested in exporting.

- *Export.gov.* This Web site from the U.S. Commercial Service is an excellent gateway to myriad resources for entrepreneurs who are interested in learning more about exporting, including market research, trade events, and trade leads.

- *Federation of International Trade Associations (FITA).* The FITA Global Trade Portal is an excellent source for international import and export trade leads and events and provides links to about 8,000 Web sites related to international trade.

ENTREPRENEURIAL PROFILE: Sean "Diddy" Combs and Diageo Beverages: DeLeon Tequila Sean "Diddy" Combs, a successful entertainer and entrepreneur, formed a joint venture with the British beverage company Diageo Beverages to purchase the Mexican tequila brand DeLeon. DeLeon tequila sells at prices that range from $120 to more than $1,000 a bottle. Both parties contributed cash to the transaction and are equal owners in the joint venture. In addition to the cash he invested, Combs offers strong marketing skills and connections to the entertainment industry. In addition to its cash contribution, Diageo brings its industry leadership in the adult beverage market.[17] ■

The most important ingredient in the recipe for a successful joint venture is choosing the right partner. The following tips will help an entrepreneur avoid problems:

- Select a partner that shares the company's values and standards of conduct.
- Define at the outset important issues such as each party's contributions and responsibilities, the distribution of earnings, the expected life of the relationship, and the circumstances under which the parties can terminate the relationship.
- Understand the partner's reasons and objectives for joining the venture.
- Spell out in writing exactly how the venture will work and where decision-making authority lies.
- Select a partner whose skills are different from but compatible with those of the company's.
- Prepare a "prenuptial agreement" that spells out what will happen in case of a "business divorce."

FOREIGN LICENSING Rather than sell their products or services directly to customers overseas, some small companies enter foreign markets by licensing businesses in other nations to use their patents, trademarks, copyrights, technology, processes, or products. In return for licensing these assets, a small company collects royalties from the sales of its foreign licenses. Licensing is a relatively simple way for even the most inexperienced business owner to extend his or her reach into global markets. Licensing is ideal for companies whose value lies in its intellectual property, unique products or services, recognized name, or proprietary technology. Although many businesses consider licensing only their products to foreign companies, the licensing potential for intangibles, such as processes, technology, copyrights, and trademarks, often is greater. Some entrepreneurs earn more money from licensing their know-how for product design, manufacturing, or quality control than they do from actually selling their finished goods in a highly competitive foreign market with which they are not familiar. Foreign licensing enables a small business to enter foreign markets quickly and easily and with virtually no capital investment. Risks to the company include the potential loss of control over its manufacturing and marketing processes and creating a competitor if the licensee gains too much knowledge and control. Securing proper patent, trademark, and copyright protection beforehand can minimize those risks.

INTERNATIONAL FRANCHISING As you learned in Chapter 8, franchising has become a major export industry for the United States. Over the last several decades, a growing number of franchises have been attracted to international markets to boost sales and profits as the domestic market has become increasingly saturated with outlets and much tougher to wring growth from. Franchisors should consider expanding into global markets when foreign markets present an important growth opportunity for the franchise. At a time when some restaurant brands, such as McDonald's and KFC, are moving out of China, Starbucks is increasing its presence there, through both company-owned and franchised locations. Almost 10 percent of all Starbucks stores are in China, second in number only to its U.S. stores. Starbucks has captured about 75 percent of retail coffee sales in China.[18]

To be successful in global markets, a franchisor should have the following characteristics:

- Sufficient managerial and financial resources to devote to globalization
- A solid track record of success in the United States
- Adequate trademark protection for the franchise's brand
- Time-tested training, support, and reporting procedures that help franchisees succeed[19]

Franchisors that decide to expand internationally should take these steps:

1. *Identify the country or countries that are best suited to the franchisor's business concept.* Factors to consider include a country's business climate, demographic profile, level of economic development, rate of economic growth, degree of legal protection, language and cultural barriers, and market potential. Franchisors making their first forays into global markets should consider focusing on a single nation or a small group of similar nations.

2. *Generate leads for potential franchisees.* Franchisors looking for prospective franchisees in foreign markets have many tools available to them, including international franchise trade shows, their own Web sites, trade missions, and brokers. Many franchisors have had success with trade missions, such as those sponsored by trade groups like the International Franchise Association or the U.S. Department of Commerce's Gold Key Program. These trade missions are designed to introduce franchisors to qualified franchise candidates in target countries. Others rely on brokers who have extensive business contacts in specific countries.

3. *Select quality candidates.* Just as in any other franchise relationship, the real key to success is choosing the right franchisee. Because of the complexity and cost of international franchising, selecting quality franchisees is essential to success. Establishing an intranet allows franchisors to stay in contact with their international franchisees across time zones.

4. *Structure the franchise deal.* Franchisors can structure international franchise arrangements in a variety of ways, but three techniques are most popular:

   - *Direct franchising.* Direct franchising, common in domestic franchise deals, involves selling single-unit franchises to individual operators in foreign countries. Although dealing with individual franchisees makes it easier for the franchisor to maintain control, it also requires more of the franchisor's time and resources.
   - *Area development.* Area development is similar to direct franchising except that the franchisor allows the franchisee to develop multiple units in a particular territory, perhaps a province, a county, or even an entire nation. A successful area development strategy depends on a franchisor selecting and then supporting quality franchisees. In 2001, brothers Manpreet and Gurpreet Gulri entered into an area development agreement with Subway to expand the sandwich chain's presence in India; they now operate more than 600 stores there.[20]
   - *Master franchising.* Master franchising is the most popular strategy for companies entering international markets. In a master franchising arrangement, a franchisor grants an experienced master franchisee the right to sell outlets to subfranchisees in a broad geographic area or sometimes in an entire country. Franchisors use this method to expand into international markets quickly and efficiently because their master franchisees understand local laws and customs and the nuances of selling in local markets. Although master franchising simplifies a franchisor's expansion into global markets, it generates less revenue for franchisers than direct franchising and gives them the least amount of control over their international franchisees. Domino's Pizza, with more than 13,800 outlets in 85 countries outside the United States, relies on master franchises, especially in emerging markets such as India, China, Malaysia, and Turkey. More than 50 percent of Domino's sales now come from franchise stores outside the United States. Jubilant FoodWorks Limited, Domino's Pizza's master franchisee in India, operates more than 1,100 outlets.[21]

Just as they do in the United States, franchisors in international markets sell virtually every kind of product or service imaginable—from fast food to daycare for children. In some cases, the products and services sold in international markets are identical to those sold in the United States. However, most franchisors have learned that adaptation is the key to making sure their goods and services suit local tastes and customs. Traveling the world, one discovers that American fast-food giants such as Domino's, KFC, and McDonald's make significant modifications in their menus to remain attractive to the demands of local customers.

ENTREPRENEURIAL PROFILE: Jay Yim: Creamistry While on a trip to South Korea, Jay Yim saw a street vendor making ice cream from fresh ingredients using liquid nitrogen, which is so cold that it freezes the ingredients instantly. When he returned to the United States,

Yim decided to leave the family-owned chain of bakeries his father had started to launch Creamistry, a business based in Irvine, California, that uses high quality, fresh ingredients and liquid nitrogen to make delicious ice cream in a multitude of flavors. With 41 franchises operating in the United States, Yim saw the potential for taking Creamistry into global markets and sold franchises to operators in India and Saudi Arabia. Yim recently expanded Creamistry into Kuwait and signed a master franchising deal with a company in China to open 100 outlets in just one year. Although Yim will continue to open more outlets in the United States, he sees great potential in international markets and plans to focus his company's franchise development efforts there.[22] ■

countertrade

a transaction in which a company selling goods in a foreign country agrees to promote investment and trade in that country.

COUNTERTRADING AND BARTERING A **countertrade** is a transaction in which a company selling goods in a foreign country agrees to promote investment and trade in that country. The goal of the transaction is to help offset the capital drain from the foreign country's purchases. As entrepreneurs enter more and more developing countries, they will need to develop skills at implementing this strategy. In some cases, small and medium-size businesses find it advantageous to work together with large corporations that have experience in the implementation of this marketing strategy.

Countertrading suffers numerous drawbacks. Countertrade transactions can be complicated, cumbersome, and time-consuming. They also increase the chance that a company will get stuck with merchandise that it cannot move. They can lead to unpleasant surprises concerning the quantity and quality of products required in the countertrade. Still, countertrading offers one major advantage: Sometimes it's the only way to make a sale!

Entrepreneurs must weigh the advantages against the disadvantages for their company before committing to a countertrade deal. Because of its complexity and the risks involved, countertrading is not the best choice for a novice entrepreneur looking to break into the global marketplace.

bartering

the exchange of goods and services for other goods and services.

Bartering, the exchange of goods and services for other goods and services, is another way of trading with countries lacking convertible currency. In a barter exchange, a company that manufactures electronics components might trade its products for the coffee that a business in a foreign country processes, which it then sells to a third company for cash. Barter transactions require finding a business with complementary needs, but they are much simpler than countertrade transactions.

EXPORTING For many years, small businesses in the United States focused solely on the domestic market, never venturing beyond its borders. However, growing numbers of small companies, realizing the growth and profit potential that exporting offers, are making globalization part of their marketing plans. Although small and medium-size companies account for nearly 98 percent of the more than 304,000 U.S. businesses that export goods and services, they generate just one-third of the nation's export sales. Owners of small companies that export say that two of the main benefits their companies reap are increased sales and profits and larger, more diversified customer bases.[23]

Many more small companies have the potential to export but are not doing so. The biggest barrier facing companies that have never exported is not knowing where or how to start, but entrepreneurs have a treasure trove of resources, training, and consulting on which they can draw. The International Trade Administration's *Export Programs Guide* provides entrepreneurs with a comprehensive list of 100 federal programs in 20 agencies designed to help U.S. exporters. The U.S. Commercial Service Web site is an excellent starting point for entrepreneurs who are looking for international business partners to help their companies expand into global markets. Many entrepreneurs also find the U.S. Small Business Administration's Export Business Planner, a comprehensive set of worksheets that guides users through the process of building an export business plan, to be a valuable resource.

Another source of useful information is the U.S. Export Assistance Centers, which serve as single contact points for information on the multitude of federal export programs that are designed to help entrepreneurs who want to start exporting. The U.S. government's Export.gov Web site gives entrepreneurs access to valuable information about exporting in general (finance, shipping, documentation, and so on) as well as details on individual nations (market research, trade agreements, statistics, and more). Learning more about exporting and realizing that it is within the realm of possibility for small companies—even *very* small companies—is the first and often most difficult step in breaking the psychological barrier to exporting. The next challenge is to create a sound export strategy, which involves the following steps:

Step 1. *Recognize that even the tiniest companies and least experienced entrepreneurs have the potential to export.* Many entrepreneurs never consider exporting

You Be the Consultant

Selling a Simple Product to a Global Market

Courtesy of John Aron, President, The Pasta Shoppe, LLC

The Pasta Shoppe, located in Nashville, Tennessee, manufactures and distributes pasta. John Aron and his wife Carey, cofounders of The Pasta Shoppe, first came up with the idea for a pasta business while on their honeymoon in Italy. They were inspired by the many shapes of pasta they discovered as they traveled throughout the many regions of Italy. What differentiates The Pasta Shoppe from its competitors is that it makes pasta in a variety of fun shapes that are tied to people's favorite college sports teams and to various holidays, such as Christmas, St Patrick's Day, Halloween, and Thanksgiving. The Arons found a way to Americanize the variety of pasta shapes that had caught their imaginations while on their honeymoon.

Rather than compete with other mass-production pasta businesses, the Arons chose to build the company by focusing on small batch production using high-quality ingredients and a carefully designed manufacturing process. The company buys all of its wheat from the Dakotas and uses specially designed bronze tools to cut the pasta into the various shapes. The Pasta Shoppe dries the pasta overnight in carts rather than using the speed-drying machines favored by large manufacturers. The company sells its products online, through specialty retailers, and as fund-raising products for schools and youth programs. The Pasta Shoppe is able to favorably price its products by avoiding selling through mass retailers, which typically demand discounts. Since it was founded in 1994, the company has experienced strong growth in the U.S. market, even during economic downturns.

In 1998, The Pasta Shoppe entered its first international market, Japan, which remains its largest market outside the United States. Its success in Japan is due to Japanese interest in Western celebrations and holidays. John Aron recognized that international markets would extend the company's season for its holiday products due to the earlier production needed to move its product to Japanese distributors. The company quickly learned that to be successful, it had to customize its products and packaging to fit the Japanese consumer market.

The Pasta Shoppe's first entry into Japan had to be cut short due to the outbreak of Asian flu. Because the two years it sold in Japan were highly successful, the company reentered the Japanese market three years later, after the Asian flu scare had passed.

Based on its success in Japan, The Pasta Shoppe now exports to Canada, Australia, the United Kingdom, Mexico, Chile, and Guam. The company is currently attempting to develop distribution channels in the Philippines and South Korea. However, although the Arons have tried, they have made no headway into exporting to China.

When considering a move into a new international market, the Arons use specific criteria to assess its attractiveness. In addition to the quality of the foreign distributor and projected cash flow, timing is everything. The company looks for international sales that do not conflict with sales in the domestic market, which peak from September through December, because the U.S. market remains its most profitable market.

Pricing is key to success in international markets for The Pasta Shoppe. Aron says that international sales channels are the toughest to price.

1. Identify the risks and the benefits The Pasta Shoppe faces by operating as a global business.

2. Identify some of the barriers that companies such as The Pasta Shoppe encounter as they expand internationally. What steps can entrepreneurs take to overcome these obstacles?

3. What steps do you recommend that entrepreneurs such as John Aron take before they make the decision to take their companies global?

Sources: Based on John Aron, personal communication, May 20, 2014; "John Aron: The Pasta Shoppe," *Talkapolis: Entrepreneurial Mind*, January 9, 2014, https://talkapolis.com/show/entrepreneurial-mind/john-aron; Brian Reisinger, "Pasta Shoppe elbows in on international markets," *Nashville Business Journal*, November 12, 2010, www.bizjournals.com/nashville/print-edition/2010/11/12/pasta-shoppe-elbows.html?page=all; Carey Aron, "Why Fun Pasta—The Pasta Shoppe," *Readable*, n.d., www.allreadable.com/vid/why-fun-pasta-the-pasta-shoppe%2C-nashville-tn-489722.html.

because they think their companies are too small; however, a business's size has nothing to do with the global potential of its products. In fact, 67 percent of the small companies that are exporters have fewer than 20 employees.[24] If a company's products meet the needs of global customers, it has the potential to export. Studies suggest that small companies that export are stronger and grow markedly faster than those that do not. Table 16.2 provides nine questions designed to help entrepreneurs assess the export potential of their companies.

TABLE 16.2 Assessing Your Company's Export Potential

1. *Does your company have a product or service that it sells successfully in the domestic market?* A product's or service's success in the domestic market is a good indicator of its potential success in markets abroad. However, because selling domestically and internationally are entirely different ventures, entrepreneurs should read *A Basic Guide to Exporting* (www.export.gov/article2?id=Why-Companies-should-export) to learn what to expect when selling internationally.

2. *Does your company have or is your company preparing an international marketing plan with defined goals and strategies?* Many companies begin export activities haphazardly, without carefully screening markets or options for market entry. A marketing plan allows your company to find and focus on the best export opportunities. Formulating an export strategy based on good information and proper assessment increases the chances that you will choose the best options, that you will use your company's resources effectively, and, therefore, that your efforts will be successful. To find valuable market research on the countries you are interested in selling to, visit the Export.gov Web site's Market Intelligence page (https://www.export.gov/Market-Intelligence).

3. *Does your company have sufficient production capacity to commit to the export market?* To export successfully, your company must meet the demand that it creates in foreign markets. You may need more space and equipment to manufacture for the specific countries you are selling to (and you must understand their particular product standards and regulations). Expanding into the international marketplace will result in a higher number of units to manufacture, and you do not want this increase in production to reduce your company's quality of output.

4. *Does your company have the financial resources to actively support the marketing of your products in the targeted overseas markets?* Developing foreign markets requires financial resources. This is a big hurdle for many small companies because it involves activities such as international travel, participation in trade shows, market research, and international business training. However, many government programs can help finance companies' export sales, including the Export-Import Bank (Ex-Im Bank) (www.exim.gov), the U.S. Small Business Administration (www.sba.gov/content/export-loan-programs), the U.S. Department of Agriculture (www.fas.usda.gov), and the Overseas Private Investment Corporation (www.opic.gov).

5. *Is your company's management committed to developing export markets and willing and able to dedicate staff, time, and resources to the process?* Management commitment is the number-one determining factor for export success. Developing an export market takes time and effort, and managers must be certain they can afford to allocate sufficient time to exporting. Whether managers are willing to invest the time to build an export business plan is a good indicator of their commitment to an export initiative.

6. *Is your company committed to providing the same level of service to foreign customers that it gives to domestic customers?* This is a commitment every business must make before it begins selling in foreign markets. Successful exporters treat their foreign customers with the same commitment and service as their domestic customers. They are responsive to inquiries from international customers, work hard to build positive relationships with them, and establish systems to provide the same top-notch service they provide to their domestic customers.

7. *Does your company have adequate knowledge in modifying product packaging and ingredients to meet foreign import regulations and cultural preferences?* Selecting and preparing your product for export requires not only product knowledge but also knowledge of the unique characteristics of each market your company is targeting. Sound market research and input from foreign representatives tell a company about the potential to sell its products or services in specific target countries. Before the sale can occur, however, a company may have to modify its products and services to satisfy customers' tastes, needs, or preferences and legal requirements in foreign markets. Entrepreneurs can learn about product and packaging regulations both in the United States and in foreign countries at Export.gov's Product Preparation Overview page (https://www.export.gov/Product-Preparation).

8. *Does your company have adequate knowledge about shipping its product overseas, such as identifying and selecting international freight forwarders and freight costing?* When shipping a product overseas, entrepreneurs must be aware of packaging, labeling, documentation, and insurance requirements. Violating these requirements often leads to severe and expensive penalties. This is where international freight forwarders can help. These agents understand the export regulations of the U.S. government, the import rules and regulations of foreign countries, appropriate methods of shipping, and the documents related to foreign trade. Freight forwarders assist exporters in preparing price quotations by advising on freight costs, port charges, consular fees, costs of special documentation, insurance costs, and handling fees. To find a freight forwarder, entrepreneurs can visit the National Customs Brokers and Forwarders Association of America, at www.ncbfaa.org.

9. *Does your company have adequate knowledge of export payment mechanisms, such as developing and negotiating letters of credit?* Experienced exporters have extensive knowledge of export payment mechanisms and extend credit cautiously. They evaluate new customers with care and continuously monitor existing customers' accounts. For general information on ways to receive payments, methods of payment, and currency issues and payment problems, see *A Basic Guide to Exporting* and other resources described in this chapter. Conducting a credit check of potential buyers is essential because collecting delinquent accounts receivable from foreign customers is more difficult than collecting them from domestic customers. Exporters can conduct background checks on potential export partners by using the International Company Profiles (ICPs) at the Export.gov Web site (https://www.export.gov/International-Company-Profile). ICPs contain financial profiles of foreign companies and information on their size, capitalization, and number of years in business.

Source: Adapted from "Begin Exporting," BusinessUSA, https://business.usa.gov/begin-exporting?_hstc=120003415.f01b03575992d8234484c dff0c7fcc2c.1489257839152.1489257839152.1489257839152.1&_hssc=120003415.1.1491146615232&_hsfp=3706891617&hsCtaTracking= 4b810d1f-1b0e-4979-a056-dcd5668d05e6%7Cb5d53f62-bb71-4731-8726-58a1ba32db8f#wizard-step-id-1.

ENTREPRENEURIAL PROFILE: Bryan Trussel: Glympse Glympse, based in Seattle, Washington, offers its customers an app that lets them privately share their location via a smart phone with only those individuals they select for as short as a few seconds to as long as a few hours. Parents keeping track of their teenagers, carpoolers getting up-to-the-minute updates on arrival times, and coworkers tracking each other down at a conference are just a few examples of the uses people have found for this app. After a successful launch of the app in the United States, Glympse sought help from the U.S. Small Business Administration's State Trade Expansion Program (STEP) to expand sales to Europe. After a successful round of venture capital fundraising, Glympse added several corporate customers in Europe, and it reached agreements with several European communication companies.[25] ∎

Step 2. *Analyze your product or service.* Is it special? New? Unique? High quality? Priced favorably because of lower costs or favorable exchange rates? Does it fit well with the culture and traditions of a country or region? Process Barron, owned by Cliff Moss and Ken Nolen, manufactures large fans used to clean air in factories. The company, located in Pelham, Alabama, struggled when first attempting to sell its products internationally. Moss and Nolen realized they lacked the knowledge necessary be successful exporters. After sending members of the management team to export seminars at a local university, the company had success negotiating financing and payment terms with international customers. Its international accounts helped the company to grow even in the midst of the Great Recession, which was not the case for many companies operating in the industrial sector.[26]

In many foreign countries, products from the United States are in demand because they have an air of mystery about them. In some cases, entrepreneurs find that they must make slight modifications to their products to accommodate local tastes, customs, and preferences. For instance, when Joseph Zaritski, owner of an Australian juice company, began marketing his company's products in Russia, he met with limited success until he realized that package size was the problem. Willing customers simply could not afford to purchase the 2-liter bottles in which the juice was packaged. Zaritski switched to 1-liter bottles and saw sales climb by 80 percent within six months![27]

Step 3. *Analyze your commitment.* Are you willing to devote time and energy to developing export markets? Does your company have the necessary resources? Patience is essential, but entering foreign markets isn't as tough as most entrepreneurs think. More than two-thirds (68 percent) of owners of small businesses that export report that they spent less than 5 percent of their companies' annual revenue to launch their export initiatives.[28] Thanks to export assistance programs from many sources, starting an exporting initiative does not require a huge investment of time up front, even for the smallest of businesses (see Figure 16.3).

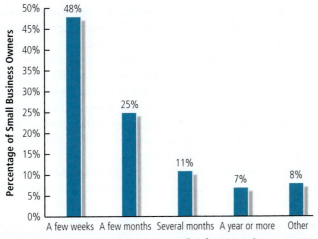

FIGURE 16.3

Length of Time Small Business Owners Invest Before Exporting

Source: Based on data from "Infographic: Small Business, Big Trade," Service Corps of Retired Executives, March 7, 2017, https://www.score.org/resource/infographic-small-business-big-trade.

FIGURE 16.4

Number of Countries to Which U.S. Small Businesses Export

Source: Based on data from "2016 Small Business Exporting Survey," National Small Business Association and Small Business Exporters Association, p. 6.

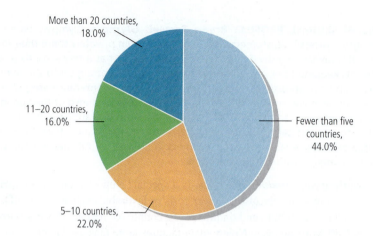

More than 20 countries, 18.0%

11–20 countries, 16.0%

5–10 countries, 22.0%

Fewer than five countries, 44.0%

Step 4. *Research markets and pick your target.* Forty-four percent of small businesses that export sell to fewer than five countries (see Figure 16.4). Before investing in a costly sales trip abroad, however, entrepreneurs should search the Internet or make a trip to the local library or the nearest branch of the Department of Commerce. Exporters can use a multitude of Web sites, guides, manuals, books, newsletters, videos, and other resources to help them research potential markets. Market research must include more than just the size of the potential market; it should include a detailed analysis of the demographic and buying habits of the customers in it as well as the cultural nuances of selling there.

ENTREPRENEURIAL PROFILE: Jonathan Mercado: Blue Orange Pottery Blue Orange Pottery, located in Laredo, Texas, designs, manufactures, and distributes home and garden décor products, including clay pottery, ceramics, wooden décor, and recycled metal art. Jonathan Mercado, president of Blue Orange Pottery, sought assistance from the University of Texas at San Antonio International Trade Center to expand his company's exports by gathering and analyzing data, ongoing market intelligence, and market research on countries including Canada, the Netherlands, Switzerland, the United Kingdom, Australia, Germany, Austria, and New Zealand. Blue Orange Pottery increased its sales by 30 percent by using distributors in Canada, Switzerland, Australia, and Germany.[29] ∎

Armed with research, entrepreneurs can avoid wasting time and money on markets with limited potential for their products and can concentrate on those with the greatest promise. The nations that account for the greatest export volume for U.S. businesses are Canada, Mexico, the United Kingdom, China, and Australia.[30] Some of the most helpful tools for researching foreign markets are the Country and Industry Market Reports available at the Export.gov Web site (www.export.gov/Market-Intelligence); these reports provide detailed information on the economic, political, regulatory, and investment environment for countries ranging from Afghanistan to Zimbabwe. Research can help entrepreneurs determine whether they need to modify their existing products and services to suit the tastes and preferences of their foreign target customers. Sometimes, foreign customers' lifestyles, housing needs, body size, and cultures require exporters to make alterations in their product lines. Making just slight modifications to adapt products and services to local tastes can sometimes spell the difference between success and failure in the global market. Entrepreneurs also should consider traveling to trade shows in the countries they are targeting to witness firsthand customers' responses to their products and services.

Step 5. *Develop a distribution strategy.* Should you use a trade intermediary or sell directly to foreign customers? As you learned earlier in this chapter, many small companies just entering international markets prefer to rely on trade intermediaries to break new ground. Using intermediaries often makes sense until an entrepreneur has the chance to gain experience in exporting and to learn the ground rules of selling in foreign lands.

ENTREPRENEURIAL PROFILE: Joe Moran: Western New York Food Products, Inc.
Joe Moran, whose New York company produces Jake's Grillin' Coffee Rubs and Barbeque sauces, secured a South Korean buyer through a regional food show that attracted international buyers. The South Korean food distributor asked Moran to send sample products and to provide details on its production process, ingredients, shelf life, and specific labeling requirements. Moran complied and soon received his company's first international order for $13,500. Western New York Food Products now has a regular customer in South Korea to whom it sells barbeque sauces and coffee-ground barbeque rubs made in the U.S.[31] ■

Step 6. *Find your customer.* According to a study by the U.S. International Trade Commission, one of the most common problems among small business exporters is finding prospective customers.[32] After all, establishing a network of business contacts takes time and resources. Small businesses can rely on a host of export specialists to help track down foreign customers. The U.S. Department of Commerce and the International Trade Administration should be the first stops on any entrepreneur's agenda for going global. These agencies have the market research available to help locate the best target markets for a particular company and specific customers in those markets. Industry Sector Analyses, International Market Insights, and Customized Market Analyses are just some of the reports and services global entrepreneurs find useful. These agencies also have knowledgeable staff specialists experienced in the details of global trade and in the intricacies of foreign cultures. GlobalEDGE (http://globaledge.msu.edu), an international trade information Web site, also offers useful information on doing business in more than 200 countries, including directories, tutorials, online courses, and diagnostic tools designed to help companies determine their potential for conducting global business. The World Bank Group's Enterprise Surveys give entrepreneurs useful profiles of the business environments in 139 countries, ranging from overviews of basic infrastructure and business regulations to corruption and business obstacles. Through its Gold and Platinum Key services, the U.S. Commercial Service provides entrepreneurs who want to take their companies global with a list of prescreened distributors and potential customers and arranges face-to-face meetings with them.

One of the most efficient and least expensive ways for entrepreneurs to locate potential customers for their companies' products and services is to participate in a trade mission. These missions usually are sponsored by either a federal or state economic development agency or an industry trade association for the purpose of cultivating international trade by connecting domestic companies with potential trading partners overseas. A trade mission may focus on a particular industry or may cover several industries but target a particular country. Dave Shogren, president of U.S. International Foods, a small company with just 4 employees based in St. Louis, Missouri, that sells high quality food and grocery products around the world under its Kirksville Farms brand, recognized Vietnam as a potentially lucrative market. Although the company generates 100 percent of its sales from exports, it had no experience and no contacts in Vietnam. Shogren participated in a trade mission to Vietnam sponsored by the U.S. Department of Agriculture for makers of food products that resulted in nearly $50,000 in orders but, more importantly, relationships with two food distributors in Vietnam that he believes will generate future sales.[33]

Step 7. *Find financing.* One of the biggest barriers to small business exports is lack of financing. Access to adequate financing is a crucial ingredient in a successful export program because the cost of generating foreign sales often is higher and collection cycles are longer than in domestic markets. The trouble is that bankers and other providers of capital don't always understand the intricacies of international sales and view financing them as excessively risky. In addition, among major industrialized nations, the U.S. government spends the least per capita to promote exports.

Several federal, state, and private programs are operating to fill this export financing void, however. Loan programs from the Small Business Administration include its Export Working Capital program (90 percent loan guarantees up to $5 million), International Trade Loan program (90 percent loan guarantees up to $5 million), and Export Express program (75 to 90 percent loan guarantees up to $500,000). In addition, the Ex-Im Bank, the Overseas Private Investment Corporation, and a variety of state-sponsored programs offer export-minded entrepreneurs both direct loans and loan guarantees. The Ex-Im Bank, which has been financing the sale of U.S. exports since 1934, provides small exporters with export credit insurance and loans through its working capital line of credit and a variety of preexport loan programs. The Overseas Private Investment Corporation provides loans and loan guarantees up to $250 million to support foreign investments by small and medium-size companies and offers businesses discounted political risk insurance. The Bankers Association for Foreign Trade is an association of banks around the world that matches exporters in need of foreign trade financing with interested banks.

ENTREPRENEURIAL PROFILE: Brian Yeazel: Frigid Fluid Company Frigid Fluid Company, located in Northlake, Illinois, manufactures and distributes embalming fluids and cemetery supplies. The company made its first international sale in 1968 to a company in South Africa. The company continued to engage in limited international trade for the next four decades. After the recession eased in 2012, Brian Yeazel, who is the fifth-generation leader of this family business, decided to expand Frigid Fluid's international sales efforts. The company secured an SBA International Trade loan to add new capacity to increase production, and through the SBAExpress loan program secured a working capital loan to better manage the business's cash flow position as it expanded international trade. Since increasing its international sales and marketing efforts with trade visits to Italy, the United Kingdom, Poland, Australia, and New Zealand, the company has grown 25 percent and added four new employees.[34] ■

Step 8. *Ship your goods.* Export novices usually rely on international freight forwarders and customs brokers—experienced specialists in overseas shipping—for help in navigating the bureaucratic morass of packaging and regulatory requirements, tariffs, and paperwork demanded by customs. These specialists, also known as transport architects, are to exporters what travel agents are to travelers and normally charge relatively small fees for a valuable service. They not only move shipments of all sizes to destinations all over the world efficiently, saving entrepreneurs many headaches, but they are also well versed in the regulations that govern exported products and services. For example, packaging for Ganong Brothers, Canada's oldest candy maker, must read "5 mg" (with a space between the number and unit of measurement) for products sold in Canada. To sell the same product in the United States, just across the border from its factory, the company's packaging must read "5mg" (with no space between the number and unit of measurement).[35] Exporters can find local freight forwarders and customs brokers at the National Customs Brokers and Forwarders Association of America's Web site (www.ncbfaa.org).

Shipping terms, always important for determining which party in a transaction pays the cost of shipping and bears the risk of loss or damage to the goods while they are in transit, take on heightened importance in international transactions.

Step 9. *Collect your money.* A survey by the National Small Business Association and the Small Business Exporters Association reports that the top concern shared by 44 percent of companies that export is collecting payment for the goods and services they sell.[36] Collecting foreign accounts can be more complex than collecting

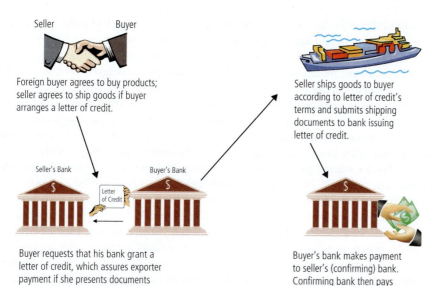

Seller   Buyer

Foreign buyer agrees to buy products; seller agrees to ship goods if buyer arranges a letter of credit.

Seller ships goods to buyer according to letter of credit's terms and submits shipping documents to bank issuing letter of credit.

Seller's Bank   Buyer's Bank

Letter of Credit

Buyer requests that his bank grant a letter of credit, which assures exporter payment if she presents documents proving goods were actually shipped. Bank makes out letter of credit to seller and sends it to seller's bank (called the confirming bank).

Buyer's bank makes payment to seller's (confirming) bank. Confirming bank then pays seller amount specified in letter of credit.

FIGURE 16.5

How a Letter of Credit Works

Source: A Basic Guide to Exporting, 10th ed. (Washington DC: U.S. Department of Commerce, International Trade Administration, 2008), p. 5.

domestic ones; however, by picking their customers carefully and checking their credit references closely, entrepreneurs can minimize bad-debt losses. Businesses that engage in international sales use four primary payment methods (ranked from least risky to most risky): cash in advance, a letter of credit, a bank (or documentary) draft, and an open account. The safest method of selling to foreign customers is to collect cash in advance of the sale because it eliminates the risk of collection problems and provides immediate cash flow. However, requiring cash payments up front severely limits a small company's base of foreign customers.

A **letter of credit** is an agreement between an exporter's bank and the foreign buyer's bank that guarantees payment to the exporter for a specific shipment of goods. In essence, a letter of credit reduces the financial risk for the exporter by substituting a bank's creditworthiness for that of the purchaser (see Figure 16.5). A **bank draft** is a document the seller draws on the buyer, requiring the buyer to pay the face amount (the purchase price of the goods) either on sight (a sight draft) or on a specified date (a time draft) once the goods have been shipped. With either letters of credit or bank drafts, small exporters must be sure that all of the required documentation is present and accurate; otherwise, they may experience delays in the payments due to them from the buyer or the participating banks. Rather than use letters of credit or drafts, some exporters simply sell to foreign customers on open account. In other words, they ship the goods to a foreign customer without any guarantee of payment. This method is riskiest because collecting a delinquent account from a foreign customer is even more difficult than collecting past-due payments from a domestic customer. One way that small exporters can minimize the risk of bad-debt losses on foreign credit sales is to purchase export credit insurance, which protects a company against the nonpayment of its foreign customers' open accounts. The cost of export credit insurance typically is a small percentage of the amount of the foreign sale a company is insuring. Private insurers and the Ex-Im Bank offer export credit insurance.

letter of credit
an agreement between an exporter's bank and a foreign buyer's bank that guarantees payment to the exporter for a specific shipment of goods.

bank draft
a document that a seller draws on a buyer, requiring the buyer to pay the face amount either on sight or on a specified date.

ESTABLISHING INTERNATIONAL LOCATIONS Once established in international markets, some small businesses set up permanent locations there. Establishing an office or a factory in a foreign land can require a substantial investment that may be beyond the budget of a small company. In addition, setting up an international office can be an incredibly frustrating experience in some countries, where business infrastructure is in disrepair or is nonexistent. Hayden Hamilton, founder of GreenPrint Technologies, a company that sells software that reduces printing costs by eliminating unnecessary pages, opened an office in India, where he can get bargain rates on quality software programming. He was frustrated when it took three hours to apply for a telephone line—and one month to get it installed. Because power outages in India are common, GreenPrint also had to purchase expensive backup generators.[37]

In some countries, securing necessary licenses and permits from bureaucrats takes more than filing the necessary paperwork; in some nations, bureaucrats expect payments to "grease the wheels" of commerce. American entrepreneurs consider payments to reduce the amount of red tape involved in an international transaction to be bribery, and many simply avoid doing business in countries where "grease payments" are standard procedure. In fact, the Foreign Corrupt Practice Act, passed in 1977, considers bribing foreign officials to be a criminal act. One study by the World Bank of grease payments for the purpose of minimizing the red tape imposed by foreign regulations concludes that the payments do not work; in fact, companies that actually used them experienced greater government scrutiny and red tape in their international transactions. If an American company gets caught making even small payments that are considered a bribe, it can end up facing huge penalties that can run into the millions of dollars.[38] Finally, finding the right person to manage an international office is crucial to success; it also is a major challenge, especially for small businesses. Small companies usually have lean management staffs and cannot afford to send key people abroad without running the risk of losing their focus.

Small companies that establish international locations can reap significant benefits. Start-up costs are lower in some foreign countries (but not all!), and lower labor costs can produce significant savings. In addition, by locating in a country, a business gains a firsthand understanding of local customers' preferences, tastes, and habits and the nuances of how culture influences business practices. In essence, the business becomes a local corporate citizen.

Courtesy of Peter Marcum, Co-founder, DevDigital, LLC

ENTREPRENEURIAL PROFILE: Peter Marcum: DevDigital
DevDigital has offices in Nashville, Tennessee, and Baroda, India. DevDigital began as company that bought used Internet network assets, such as routers and switches, from distressed companies at a steep discount. The company would refurbish the hardware and resell it to small independent network companies. Eventually the company expanded into operating digital networks. As profit margins for network operators became razor thin, the company made another major strategic shift. DevDigital purchased a small Web site programming shop in India that was being sold by one of its customers. Peter Marcum, cofounder of DevDigital, believed that if larger companies—Google, IBM, and Apple—found success in diversifying globally in their software production, so could his small business. DevDigital made the move into Web site development for small companies. It took about four years to fully integrate the two locations. Due to its cost advantage and stable employment, the company has been able to grow in the highly competitive market of Web site development. DevDigital does about 80 percent work for hire, and for the remainder of its work, it takes equity in exchange for Web site development. Marcum says that the key to success is to focus as much on building a strong team for your foreign office as you do for your U.S. operations.[39] ■

IMPORTING AND OUTSOURCING In addition to selling their goods in foreign markets, small companies also buy goods from distributors and manufacturers in foreign markets. In the United States alone, companies import more than $2.7 trillion worth of goods and services annually.[40] The intensity of price competition in many industries—from textiles and handbags to industrial machinery and computers—means that more companies now shop the world market, looking for the best deals they can find. Because labor costs in countries such as Mexico, Taiwan, and India are far below those in other nations, businesses there offer goods and services at very low prices. Increasingly, these nations are home to well-educated, skilled workers who are paid far less than comparable workers in the United States or Western Europe. For instance, a computer programmer in the United States might earn about $80,000 a year, but in India, a computer programmer doing the same work earns $7,000 a year or less. As a result, many companies either import goods or outsource work directly to manufacturers in countries where costs are far lower than they would be domestically.

Courtesy of Nuvar, Inc.

ENTREPRENEURIAL PROFILE: Mark Kuyper: Nuvar Nuvar Inc., located in Holland, Michigan, develops and designs office furniture and healthcare products. Nuvar's in-house engineering assists its customers with product development and design. Mark Kuyper, president of Nuvar, says that the company utilizes a global network of manufacturing suppliers. Nuvar sources component parts for its manufacturing from Europe (France, Germany, and Italy), Asia (China, Taiwan, and Malaysia), and North America (Mexico and Canada). Parts are then shipped to its facilities in Michigan, where they are assembled, packaged, and shipped to the final customer. Scott Kuyper, international supply chain lead at Nuvar, says that different markets have different requirements for testing, standards, and so forth. Thanks to its international relationships, Nuvar has learned the importance of being open-minded and flexible when it comes to differences in the cultures, strategies, and economies of its various global partners.[41] ■

Entrepreneurs who are considering importing goods and service or outsourcing their manufacturing to foreign countries should consider the following:

- *Make sure that importing or outsourcing is right for your business.* Even though foreign manufacturers often can provide items at significant cost savings, using them may not always be the best business decision. Some foreign manufacturers require sizable minimum orders, sometimes hundreds of thousands of dollars' worth, before they will produce a product. Entrepreneurs sometimes discover that achieving the lowest price may require trade-offs of other important factors, such as quality and speed of delivery.

- *Establish a target cost for your product.* Before setting off on a global shopping spree, entrepreneurs should determine exactly what they can afford to spend on manufacturing a product and make a profit on it. Given the low labor costs of many foreign manufacturers, products that are the most labor intensive make good candidates.

ENTREPRENEURIAL PROFILE: Tom Haarlander: Arciplex Arciplex, headquartered in Nashville, Tennessee, is a medical manufacturing company. Arciplex works with entrepreneurs and established companies to invent, design, develop, and produce health and wellness products. Tom Haarlander, president and cofounder, made the strategic decision to move Arciplex's manufacturing from China to Mexico in early 2014. The company had been using a Chinese manufacturer for a little over a year but found a lack of consistency in the products from China, which resulted in warranty issues after the products were delivered to customers. Haarlander sent team members to live in China to monitor quality control, but the problems persisted. In an effort to improve its product quality and its team's quality of life, Haarlander decided to move manufacturing back to North America. Haarlander was able to find manufacturers in the United States and sourced some work to a company in Mexico, which has allowed his company to cut travel and various other overhead costs. Although its manufacturing cost per unit has increased, the costs of testing, quality control, and rework have dropped dramatically, cutting the company's overall cost. In the long run, Haarlander says that he made the best strategic decision for building a strong foundation for his company that can support its anticipated growth.[42] ■

- *Do your research before you leave home.* Before setting foot on foreign soil, it is essential to invest time in basic research about the industry and potential suppliers in foreign lands. Useful resources are plentiful, and entrepreneurs should take advantage of them, including the Internet (e.g., Export.gov), the Federation of International Trade Associations, industry trade associations, government agencies (e.g., the U.S. Commercial Service's Gold Key Matching Service), and consultants.

- *Be sensitive to cultural differences.* When making contacts, setting up business appointments, or calling on prospective manufacturers in foreign lands, make sure you understand what constitutes accepted business behavior and what does not. This is where your research pays off; be sure to study the cultural nuances of doing business in the countries you will visit.

- *Do your groundwork.* Once you locate potential manufacturers, contact them to set up appointments and go visit them. Preliminary research is essential to finding reliable sources of supply, but "face time" with representatives from various companies allows entrepreneurs to judge the intangible factors that can make or break a relationship. Entrepreneurs who visit foreign suppliers often find that they receive better service because their suppliers know them personally.

- *Protect your company's intellectual property.* A common problem that many entrepreneurs have encountered with outsourcing is knockoffs. Some foreign manufacturers see nothing wrong with agreeing to manufacture a product for a company and then selling their own knockoff version of it that they manufacture in a "ghost shift." Securing a nondisclosure agreement and a contract that prohibits such behavior helps, but experts say that securing a patent for the item in the source country itself (not just the United States) is a good idea.

- *Select a manufacturer.* Using quality, speed of delivery, level of trust, degree of legal protection, cost, and other factors, select the manufacturer that can do the job for your company.

- *Provide an exact model of the product you want manufactured.* Providing a manufacturer with an actual model of the item to be manufactured will save lots of time, mistakes, and problems.

- *Stay in constant contact with the manufacturer and try to build a long-term relationship.* Communication is a key to building and maintaining a successful relationship with a foreign manufacturer. Weekly teleconferences, e-mails, and periodic visits are essential to making sure that your company gets the performance you expect from a foreign manufacturer.

Courtesy of David English, Study Abroad Mendoze, LLC

expat entrepreneur
an entrepreneur who keeps citizenship in his or her home country but lives and runs his or her business on foreign soil.

EXPAT ENTREPRENEURS   Some entrepreneurs take advantage of opportunities in foreign markets by actually moving to a country and starting a new business. People who take up residence and work in a foreign country are known as expatriates or, more commonly, expats. **Expat entrepreneurs** are entrepreneurs who keep their citizenship in their home country but live and run their businesses on foreign soil. American expat entrepreneurs can be found living in countries on every continent. Expats from the same home country often form social groups to offer each other support and keep a little bit of their homeland's culture active in their lives. American expats use social networking sites such as Facebook to help build community and share common challenges faced by expat entrepreneurs. Some countries have been making it easier to become an expat entrepreneur to encourage economic development. For example, Spain recently cut the red tape associated with expats starting businesses to help ease its chronic unemployment and low rate of entrepreneurial activity. Although being an expat entrepreneur creates unique hurdles and problems, those with an adventurous spirit can find amazing experiences starting and growing companies in other countries. The accompanying "You Be the Consultant" feature highlights three expat entrepreneurs who started businesses in Argentina, as told in David English's book *Expat Entrepreneurs in Argentina.*

LO3

Discuss the major barriers to international trade and their impact on the global economy.

Barriers to International Trade

Governments traditionally have used a variety of barriers to block free trade among nations in an attempt to protect businesses within their own borders. The benefit of protecting their own companies, however, comes at the expense of foreign businesses, which face limited access to

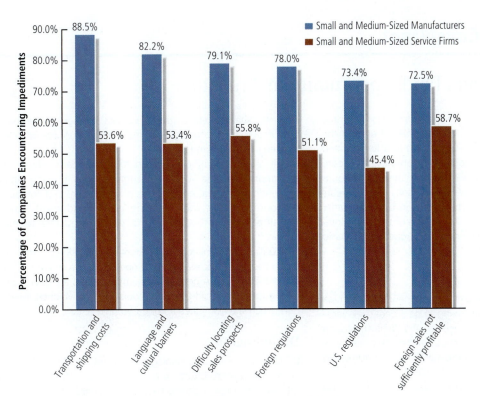

FIGURE 16.6

Most Frequently Encountered Impediments to International Trade

Source: U.S. International Trade Commission, *Small and Medium-Sized Enterprises: Characteristics and Performance*, Publication 4189, November 2010, pp. 6–8.

Impediment to International Trade

global markets. Numerous trade barriers—domestic and international—restrict the freedom of businesses in global trading (see Figure 16.6). Even with these barriers, global trade of goods and services has grown to nearly $17 trillion.[43]

Domestic Barriers

Sometimes the biggest barriers potential exporters face are those at home. Three major domestic roadblocks are common: attitude, information, and financing. Perhaps the biggest barrier to small businesses exporting is the attitude that "My company is too small to export. That's just for big corporations." The first lesson of exporting is to take nothing for granted about who can export and what you can and cannot export (see Table 16.3). The first step to building an export program is recognizing that the opportunity to export exists.

Another reason entrepreneurs neglect international markets is a lack of information about how to get started. The keys to success in international markets are choosing the correct target market and designing the appropriate strategy to reach it. This requires access to information and research. Although a variety of government and private organizations make volumes of exporting and international marketing information available, many small business owners never use it. A successful global marketing strategy also recognizes that not all international markets are the same. Companies must be flexible and willing to make adjustments to their products and services, promotional campaigns, packaging, and sales techniques.

An additional obstacle is the inability of small firms to obtain adequate export financing. Financial institutions that serve small companies often are not experienced in financing international sales and are unwilling to accept the perceived higher levels of risk they create for the lender.

International Barriers

Domestic barriers aren't the only barriers that export-minded entrepreneurs must overcome. Trading nations also erect obstacles to free trade. Two types of international barriers are common: tariff and nontariff.

You Be the Consultant

Expat Entrepreneurs Find Opportunity in Argentina

Entrepreneurs who start new businesses in a foreign country, expat entrepreneurs, can be found in countries all around the globe. Expat entrepreneurs start new ventures in a foreign land for many different reasons—the specific opportunity, the desire to live in a different country, the wish to leave their home country, or life circumstances. Whatever the reason, entrepreneurs face unique challenges operating businesses in countries other than their homeland. What follows are profiles of three entrepreneurs from a book, *Expat Entrepreneurs in Argentina*, by David English, who is an expat himself.

Michael Evans

Michael Evans's career as an expat entrepreneur in Argentina began with what he thought was going to be a one-week vacation in Mendoza, in the heart of wine country. What he found was that Mendoza had none of the amenities of other wine destinations he had visited. Argentina felt like a new frontier to Evans.

Evans decided to stay in Mendoza for six months to do research with a potential partner he had met, Pablo Giménez Riili, whose family had been in the wine business for several decades. In addition to having skills, knowledge, and local credibility that Evans needed for this business, Giménez Riili's approach to business meshed well with Evans's business philosophies.

The two developed a business plan for a start-up to serve the emerging wine industry and its associated tourism. The concepts of a small hotel, a wine tasting room, and a direct wine sales business emerged from their work together.

The business, The Vines of Mendoza, was successful beyond any of their plans. The Vines of Mendoza has grown to include operating a wine store in the Park Hyatt Mendoza, managing more than 100 private vineyard estates, overseeing a direct wine sales business that exports Argentinian wine to the United States, and operating their own winery. They also have opened their own five-star resort for wine tourists.

Carolyn Gallagher

Carolyn Gallagher grew up in Sacramento, California. While she was in high school, she became close friends with an exchange student from Argentina. Gallagher went to visit her friend in Argentina after finishing school, fell in love with the country, and envisioned moving there someday to settle down. Gallagher went to college at the University of California at Santa Barbara, where she studied geography and linguistics. After college, she went to work as a river guide, winery worker, and English tutor for construction companies to save money for her move to Argentina.

In 1998, Gallagher bought a one-way ticket to Mendoza. She had no definitive plans, but she was confident she could find a niche for herself in Argentina. For two years, she taught English.

However, she wanted to start a business. Gallagher returned to California to study cooking, wine making, and business, while she worked in the wine industry.

In 2004, Gallagher returned to Argentina, ready to find an opportunity. She noticed that tourism was growing rapidly in Mendoza and that nobody was offering tours that combined outdoor adventure with cooking classes and great wine— the three things that make the region attractive to most visitors.

Gallagher launched her business, Uncorking Argentina, which has been successful since it opened. In the meantime, Gallagher married her Argentine boyfriend. The two are now happily raising their two children in the country she envisioned living in back when she first visited it right after high school.

David English

David English was a technology consultant for Qwest Communication in New York City on his way to meet with executives of CitiGroup to close a contract for a new project. On that sunny morning, everything changed. It was September 11, 2001. As he left his offices on the way to the meeting, ashes began to fall. People were saying that someone had flown a plane into one of the towers of the World Trade Center. English did not think much about it. He hopped on the subway to go to his meeting. When he emerged from the subway, the city was in chaos from the attack on the World Trade Center's Twin Towers. Although it was several more years before English left America to start his new life in Argentina, he sees the events of that day as the turning point in his life that led him down the path to eventually becoming an expat entrepreneur.

After graduating from college, English traveled to Argentina in 1997 through an exchange program run by the Rotary Club. English spent six weeks in Argentina visiting Rotarians in Argentina and touring their businesses. He fell in love with the country and began to look for an opportunity to return.

He got that opportunity in 2003. He discovered a niche helping American businesses by serving as their connection with local Argentines. He launched English & Associates with a single client who was developing a wine business in Argentina. English enrolled in an MBA program in Argentina that he credits with teaching him about doing business within the culture of Argentina and honing his Spanish communication skills.

The scope of his business broadened over time. English & Associates provides due diligence for foreigners buying real estate in Argentina, prepares and files tax returns for nonresident investors, consults with entrepreneurs looking to start a business in Argentina, and develops study-abroad programs in Mendoza for leading universities around the world.

English says that becoming a successful expat entrepreneur involves not just knowing how to run a business. Successful

(continued)

You Be the Consultant

expats play active roles in their new communities and find ways to make a positive impact beyond just the economic impact from their business venture.

1. How are expat entrepreneurs' assumptions about conducting business internationally different from those of entrepreneurs pursuing more traditional international strategies? Explain.

2. What advice would you give to someone who wants to become an expat entrepreneur? Explain.

3. What lessons did each of these expat entrepreneurs learn that would be useful for others interested in this type of lifestyle? Explain.

Source: Based on David English, *Expat Entrepreneurs in Argentina* (Mendoza, Argentina: Expat Books, 2013).

TABLE 16.3 Global Business Assumptions

Old Assumption	New Assumption
Exporting is too risky for my small company.	Exporting to "easy" markets such as Canada is no more risky than selling to companies in the United States. Each international market has its own level of risk. Entrepreneurs can identify the most significant risks their companies face and reduce them by using the extensive amount of affordable export assistance that is available now.
Getting paid is cumbersome, and I'll lose my shirt.	Trade finance and global banking have evolved to the point where buying and selling goods and services internationally is routine, safe, and efficient. Reliable collection methods, including credit cards, online payments, and letters of credit, are readily available. Some delivery firms will collect payment from customers at the time of delivery.
Exporting is too complicated.	Most exporting requires minimal paperwork. Often, entrepreneurs can research markets and find buyers from their computers using free or low-cost information.
My domestic market is secure. I don't need to export.	Globalization has made buying and selling goods in multiple markets easy. Few markets remain static, and new markets are constantly opening. Most U.S. businesses are involved in or affected by international markets, whether they realize it or not. More small and medium-size companies have the potential to benefit from going global, but doing so requires an international marketing strategy.
I'm too small to go global.	No company is too small to go global. In fact, 67 percent of U.S. exporters have fewer than 20 employees.
My product or service probably won't sell outside the United States.	If your product or service sells well in the United States, there is a good chance you can find a foreign market in which it will sell. In addition, help is available for entrepreneurs who want to test the appeal of their products and services in more than 100 countries around the globe. In some markets, entrepreneurs must make modifications to their products and services because of cultural, regulatory, or other differences. However, most modifications are small and simple to make. In addition, by learning to sell successfully in other markets, small companies become stronger and better able to compete in all of their markets.
I won't be successful because I don't speak another language and have never been abroad.	Cultural knowledge and business etiquette are important, but you can learn as you go. English is the language of business in many countries, but you can easily hire translators and interpreters when necessary. Researching cultural differences before engaging in foreign transactions helps prevents embarrassing faux pas, but a friendly disposition, a sense of humor, and a willingness to learn can make up for many unintended mistakes.

Sources: Based on "Table 1.1: Global Business Assumptions," *A Basic Guide to Exporting*, 10th ed. (Washington, DC: U.S. Department of Commerce, International Trade Administration, 2008), p. 7; "U.S. Export Loan Programs," U.S. Small Business Administration, www.sba.gov/content/export-loan-programs.

TARIFF BARRIERS A **tariff** is a tax, or duty, that a government imposes on goods and services imported into that country. Tariffs raise the prices of the imported goods—making them less attractive to consumers—and protect the domestic makers of comparable product and services. Established in the United States in 1790 by Alexander Hamilton, the tariff system generated the majority of federal revenues for about 100 years. Currently, the *Harmonized Tariff Schedule*, which sets tariffs for products imported into the United States, includes 37,000 categories

tariff
a tax, or duty, that a government imposes on goods and services imported into that country.

Hands On . . . How To

Build a Successful Global Company

Brothers Jeff and Tony Logosz grew up enjoying water sports in the Columbia River Gorge in the state of Washington. They ultimately found a way to turn their passion into a business, launching Slingshot Sports to design and manufacture kiteboards.

Slingshot Sports helped to create a market for kiteboards, which were the focus of a relatively new sport at the time. Slingshot Sports soon began to find success promoting kiteboarding and selling its products to a growing market.

One day, a distributor from the United Kingdom showed up at the Slingshot Sports offices in North Bonneville, Washington, wanting to import its products. Like many other small business owners, the Logosz brothers had no idea how exporting worked. However, the request prompted them to learn how to export their products. When they did, they found strong growth in demand for kiteboards around the globe. Distributors from around the world came clamoring for contracts to sell Slingshot Sports kiteboards.

The company eventually expanded its product line by adding wakeboards. Unlike kiteboards, wakeboards were a well-established product in a market with many competitors. Rather than having global distributors seeking out Slingshot Sports at the national trade show, the company had to develop a sales strategy in which the founders traveled to markets around the globe to pitch their new wakeboards. The strategy was successful, and sales of Slingshot Sports wakeboards soon exceeded all of the brothers' projections. Following are some of the lessons the Logosz brothers and other entrepreneurs have learned about operating a global small business.

Don't assume that your company has to be big to be an international player. As the Logosz brothers learned, even very small companies have the opportunity to be successful in the global arena. Success in international markets does not require size, but it does require commitment and a sound strategy.

Know what you don't know. Perhaps the most important item in a global entrepreneur's briefcase is *knowledge*. Before embarking on any international business initiative, entrepreneurs should take the time to educate themselves and their employees. This chapter is filled with useful resources, many of which are free, that are designed to help business owners get their global business efforts off to a good start. The starting point for successfully conducting international business is learning about best practices for key issues such as identifying target markets, developing distribution strategies, complying with regulations, adapting products when necessary, collecting payments, and providing customer service.

Build a network of connections. Having a contact in a foreign country who can open doors to potential suppliers and customers greatly reduces the risk involved in international business. Mia Abbruzzese, founder of Morgan & Milo, a children's shoe company, had launched several shoe lines during her days as an executive for three large global shoe companies and knew that success in the shoe business requires an extensive network of connections in all corners of the globe. Using her industry contacts, Abbruzzese found a Taiwanese investor who provided start-up capital for Morgan & Milo and introduced Abbruzzese to the owner of the factory in southern China that makes many of the shoes that Morgan & Milo designs. Two other advisers on whom Abbruzzese relies are industry veterans who have an extensive network of contacts in the shoe industry and have proved to be extremely valuable to her company.

Learn about the cultural aspects of conducting business in the countries in which your company operates. Business dealings are a reflection of a country's culture, and entrepreneurs should educate themselves about the nuances of doing business in the host country to avoid committing embarrassing cultural blunders. In the United States, businesspeople are transaction oriented. They want to set up an appointment, negotiate a deal quickly and efficiently, sign a contract, and leave. In many other countries, landing a deal takes much longer because businesspeople expect to get to know their potential partners first. Particularly in Asia, businesspeople tend to be relationship oriented, doing business only with people they know, like, and respect. Developing relationships can take time, making a network of connections all the more important. When doing business in Asia, entrepreneurs quickly learn that formal contracts, which are the foundation of business deals in the United States, are not as important. They also learn to adjust the speed at which they close deals and take more time to build relationships with reliable suppliers.

Go there. As Slingshot Sports learned when it expanded into wakeboards, building a global business usually requires entrepreneurs to travel to the countries in which they plan to do business. It's an excellent way to build a network of contacts. Participating in international trade missions, attending international trade shows, and using matching services such as the U.S. Department of Commerce's Gold Key and Platinum Key services are ideal methods for connecting with potential customers, distributors, and suppliers.

Recognize that foreign sales often put additional demands on a company's cash flow. Expanding a company's sales efforts into international markets can strain a company's cash flow, and many traditional lenders are hesitant to extend loans to cover foreign credit sales because they perceive the risk to be too great. Help is available for small companies, however. The Small Business Administration and the Ex-Im Bank offer loan and loan guarantee programs to finance small companies' foreign credit sales. CellAntenna Corporation, a maker of cell phone jamming and control technology in Coral Springs, Florida, secured a $250,000 line

(continued)

Hands On . . . How To

of credit through the Small Business Administration's Export Working Capital loan guaranty program to finance its export sales. The company recently landed a $100,000 order from a prison in Australia.

Make sure you collect payments from foreign sales.
Collecting payments on delinquent foreign sales is more involved than collecting payments on delinquent domestic sales. The best way to avoid this problem is to sell to customers who pay their bills on time. Conducting credit checks before selling to international customers is just as important as it is before selling to domestic customers. In addition, small companies can reduce the risk of foreign credit sales by purchasing export credit insurance from either private insurers or the Ex-Im Bank. CellAntenna Corporation routinely sells to foreign customers on open account but purchases export credit insurance from the Ex-Im Bank to mitigate the risk of nonpayment.

Sources: Based on "Slingshot Sports," *Export Washington*, n.d., www.exportwashington .com/why-export/success-stories/Pages/Slingshot-Sports.aspx; "How SMEs Can Internationalize," *Forbes*, April 20, 2015, www.forbes.com/sites/iese/2015/04/20/how-smes-can-internationalize/#734225551eb8; Diana Ransom, "Five Tips for Getting Started in Exporting," *Entrepreneur*, May 17, 2011, www.entrepreneur .com/article/219650; Ian Mount, "Tips for Increasing Sales in International Markets," *New York Times*, April 21, 2010, www.nytimes.com/2010/04/22/business/smallbusiness/22sbiz.html; John Jantsch, "Around the Block or Around the World," Duct Tape Marketing, September 21, 2010, www.ducttapemarketing.com/blog/2010/09/21/around-the-block-or-around-the-world; Anita Campbell, "Preparing Your Business to Go Global," *Small Business Trends*, November 19, 2010, http://smallbiztrends.com/2010/11/preparing-your-business-to-go-global.html; Allessandra Bianchi, "Small & Global: The World as a Factory," *FSB*, June 2004, pp. 40–42; Sheri Qualters, "Operating on a Shoestring," *Boston Business Journal*, June 10, 2005, http://boston.bizjournals.com/boston/stories/2005/06/13/smallb1.html; *2011 National Export Strategy: Powering the National Export Initiative*, Trade Promotion Coordinating Committee, June 2011, p. 23.

of goods. The average U.S. tariff on imported goods is 1.64 percent (compared to the global average of 2.88 percent).[44] American tariffs vary greatly and depend on the particular type of good. For instance, inexpensive men's acrylic sweaters imported into the United States carry a 16 percent tariff, but the tariff on cashmere sweaters is 4 percent; cheap sneakers are taxed at 48 percent, but golf shoes carry a 6 percent tariff.[45] Tariff rates also vary among nations. Singapore, Switzerland, and Hong Kong impose no tariffs at all on imported goods, but Bermuda's is 15.3 percent.[46]

NONTARIFF BARRIERS Many nations have lowered the tariffs they impose on products and services brought across their borders, but they rely on other nontariff structures as protectionist trade barriers.

Quotas Rather than impose a direct tariff on certain imported products, nations often use quotas to protect their industries. A **quota** is a limit on the amount of a product imported into a country. Those who favor quotas argue that they protect domestic industries and the jobs they create. Those who oppose quotas say that they artificially raise prices on the restricted goods, imposing a hidden tax on customers who purchase them. China imposes a quota on foreign films, allowing only 34 foreign films to be released each year. Before 2012, the quota was 20 foreign films per year. China's total box office sales are $3.8 billion annually. China has more than 39,000 movie screens, which is just slightly fewer than the United States has. Despite pressure from the World Trade Organization (WTO) to eliminate the film quota, Chinese officials have refused, expressing concern that removing the barrier would unleash a flood of foreign films that might wipe out the local film industry. However, industry insiders argue that allowing more foreign films into China will push Chinese filmmakers to improve their product.[47]

quota
a limit on the amount of a product imported into a country.

Embargoes An **embargo** is a total ban on imports of certain products. The motivation for embargoes is not always economic; it also can involve political differences, environmental disputes, war, terrorism, and other issues. For instance, the United States imposes embargoes on products from nations it considers to be adversarial, including Cuba, Iran, Iraq, and North Korea, among others. An embargo on trade with Cuba, started in 1962 when Fidel Castro nationalized all U.S. businesses on the island nation and formed an alliance with the Soviet Union, still exists today, although the U.S. government has relaxed some of its provisions. In 1994, the United States lifted a total trade embargo on Vietnam that had stood since 1975, when Saigon fell into communist hands at the end of the Vietnam War. Today, the United States imports $42.1 billion worth of goods from Vietnam and exports goods worth $10.2 billion.[48]

embargo
a total ban on imports of certain products into a country.

Embargoes also originate from cultural differences. For instance, the United States, the European Union, and the World Trade Organization all impose embargoes on any harp seal products from Norway under the Marine Mammal Protection Act. Norway, where seal products make up a multi-million-dollar industry, has pushed for the elimination of the embargo, arguing that harp seals are not an endangered species.[49]

dumping

selling large quantities of goods at prices that are below cost in foreign countries in an effort to grab market share quickly.

Dumping In an effort to grab market share quickly, some companies have been guilty of **dumping** products: selling large quantities of them at prices that are below cost in foreign countries. The United States has been a dumping ground for steel, televisions, shoes, and computer chips from other nations in the past. Under the U.S. Antidumping Act, a company must prove that the foreign company's prices are lower here than in the home country and that U.S. companies are directly harmed. Disputes over dumping brought before the WTO have increased significantly over the last five years, and China has been the target of most of the complaints from WTO member nations. The U.S. Department of Commerce, without the involvement of the WTO, recently ruled that government-subsidized makers of solar cells and panels in China were guilty of dumping their products in the United States at prices that average 31 percent below "fair value." SolarWorld Industries America and six other U.S.-based solar cell and panel manufacturers initiated the charge, claiming that artificially low prices on solar products from China are crippling the domestic industry. As part of its ruling, the U.S. Department of Commerce imposed punitive dumping margins (the difference between the fair value of the items and their actual export price) of 31 percent on the Chinese companies. The European Union, Australia, Canada, India, and Turkey also imposed anti-dumping tariffs against Chinese solar panels.[50]

Political Barriers

Entrepreneurs who go global quickly discover a labyrinth of political tangles. Although many U.S. business owners complain of excessive government regulation in the United States, they are often astounded by the onerous web of governmental and legal regulations and barriers they encounter in foreign countries. One entrepreneur who established a business location in Russia says he had to visit more than two dozen agencies to complete the necessary paperwork and get 90 different documents signed.[51]

Companies doing business in politically risky lands face the very real dangers of government takeovers of private property; coups to overthrow ruling parties; kidnapping, bombings, and other violent acts against businesses and their employees; and other threatening events. Their investments of millions of dollars may evaporate overnight in the wake of a government coup or the passage of a law nationalizing an industry (giving control of an entire industry to the government).

ENTREPRENEURIAL PROFILE: Alexey Rashevskiy Alexey Rashevskiy is a successful serial tech entrepreneur in Dublin, Ireland. Rashevskiy, who is originally from Russia, decided to launch a new app company with a friend who still lives in Russia. The company was to be based in Dublin. Incorporating the business in Ireland proved to be simple; the process took only a couple of days. However, the next step in establishing the new company—setting up the checking account—proved to be much more difficult due to Irish banking regulations. Rashevskiy and his Russian cofounder each filled out the required forms. The Russian partner sent them via overnight mail to Rashevskiy in Ireland. Rashevskiy was informed when he brought in the paperwork that all directors of the corporation must show up in person when the paperwork is submitted to the bank with government IDs. Because that would not work with his Russian cofounder, they decided to remove the Russian cofounder as a director of the company and make him a shareholder instead. The bank then informed them that the Russian partner would still have to fill out some of the forms, but he would not need to submit them in person if he had them notarized. When the bank got the notarized forms from Russia, they said that the notary seal was in Russian, but Irish law requires that all official documentation be in English. However, Russian officials will only issue documentation in Russian! Unfortunately, their start-up lost momentum as it struggled with so many regulatory hurdles, and the entrepreneurs never launched it.[52] ■

Business Barriers

American companies doing business internationally quickly learn that business practices and regulations in foreign lands can be quite different from those in the United States. Simply duplicating the practices they have adopted (and have used successfully) in the domestic market and using them in foreign markets is not always a good idea. Perhaps the biggest shock comes in the area of human resources management, in which international managers discover that practices common in the United States, such as overtime and employee benefits, are restricted, disfavored, or forbidden in other cultures. Business owners new to international business sometimes are shocked at the wide range of labor costs they encounter and the accompanying wide range of skilled labor available. In some countries, what appear to be "bargain" labor rates turn out to be excessively high after accounting for the quality of the labor force and the benefits their governments mandate: from company-sponsored housing, meals, and clothing to profit sharing and extended vacations. For instance, laws in many European countries mandate a minimum of 20 days of vacation in addition to paid holidays, giving workers there an average of 35 paid days off per year.[53] Some countries' labor laws make it extremely difficult or even impossible to terminate employees once hired. Hefty taxes, ineffective legal systems, corruption, and shady business associates can make doing business in foreign countries difficult.

Cultural Barriers

Even though travel and communications technology have increased the ease and the frequency with which entrepreneurs engage in global transactions, the potential for cultural blunders has increased. The **culture** of a nation includes the beliefs, values, views, and mores its inhabitants share. Differences in cultures among nations create another barrier to international trade. The diversity of languages, business philosophies, practices, and traditions make international trade more complex than selling to the business down the street. Consider the following examples:

culture
the beliefs, values, views, and mores that a nation's inhabitants share.

- A U.S. entrepreneur, eager to expand into the European Union, arrives at the headquarters of his company's potential business partner in France. Confidently, he strides into the meeting room, enthusiastically pumps his host's hand, slaps him on the back, and says, "Tony, I've heard a great deal about you; please, call me Bill." Eager to explain the benefits of his product, he opens his briefcase and gets right down to business. The French executive politely excuses himself and leaves the room before negotiations ever begin, shocked by the American's rudeness and ill manners. Rudeness and ill manners? Yes—from the French executive's perspective.

- Another American business owner flies to Tokyo to close a deal with a Japanese executive. He is pleased when his host invites him to play a round of golf shortly after he arrives. He plays well and manages to win by a few strokes. The Japanese executive invites him to play again the next day, and again he wins by a few strokes. Invited to play another round the following day, the American asks, "But when are we going to start doing business?" His host, surprised by the question, says, "But we *have* been doing business."

- An American businesswoman in London is invited to a party hosted by an advertising agency. Unsure of her ability to navigate the streets and subways of London alone, she approaches a British colleague who is driving to the party and asks him if she could "get a ride from him." After he turns bright red from embarrassment, he regains his composure and politely informs her that she had inadvertently requested a sexual encounter with him, not a lift to the party![54]

- One pharmaceutical company was about to market a weight loss pill under the name Tegro, which sounds harmless enough in English. However, phonetically, the word sounds identical to the French phrase *t'es gros*, which translates "You are fat." Another global company attempted to market a technology training system whose name sounded exactly like the Korean phrase for "porn movie."[55]

When American businesspeople enter international markets for the first time, they often are amazed at the differences in foreign cultures' habits and customs. In the first scenario above, for instance, had the entrepreneur done his homework, he would have known that the French are very formal (backslapping is *definitely* taboo!) and do not typically use first names in business relationships (even among longtime colleagues). In the second scenario, a global manager would have known that the Japanese place a tremendous importance on developing personal relationships before committing to any business deals. Thus, he would have seen the golf games for what they really were: an integral part of building a business relationship.

Understanding and heeding subtle cultural differences is one of the most important keys to international business success. Conducting a business meeting with a foreign executive in the same manner as one with an American businessperson could doom the deal from the outset. Business customs and behaviors that are acceptable, even expected, in the United States may be taboo in others, and entrepreneurs who fail to learn the differences in the habits and customs of the cultures in which they hope to do business are at a distinct disadvantage.

Courtesy of Tyler Seymour, Co-founder, Aloompa, LLC

ENTREPRENEURIAL PROFILE: Aloompa Aloompa is an app development business located in Nashville, Tennessee, that specializes primarily in apps for music festivals. Its first customer was the Bonnaroo Music and Arts Festival in Manchester, Tennessee. The app includes a map of the festival grounds, including the location of food vendors, bathrooms, retail spaces, and stages. It also includes bios of performers, audio samples of performers' music, and reviews that can be pushed out to Facebook, Instagram, and Twitter. After growing to more than two dozen music festivals in the United States, Aloompa expanded to international festivals. The first was the Playa del Carmen in Mexico. The app for this festival is available in both English and Spanish. Aloompa is quickly adding new festivals for customers in Asia, Europe, and South America. Caleb Jones, part of the business development team for Aloompa, says that as the company has expanded into the international market, it had to learn how to communicate across culture barriers and familiarize itself with a variety of business practices around the globe. For example, as Aloompa expanded into South America, the business development team learned that it is necessary to start negotiations in that region a full month earlier than in other parts of the world due to longer time lines.[56] ∎

Culture, customs, and the norms of behavior differ greatly among nations, and making the correct impression is extremely critical to building a long-term business relationship. Consider the following examples:

- In Chile, punctuality is highly respected, and meetings should therefore start and end on time. At the start of every meeting, everyone exchanges business cards, which should be printed in English on one side and Spanish on the other.[57]

- In New Zealand, business conversation is expected to take place prior to and after eating lunch. Dinners are never a meal where business is discussed because it is considered a social time. However, loud and boisterous behavior is not acceptable during any meal with businesspeople, even if alcohol is part of the meal.[58]

- In Spain, foreigners are expected to be on time for meetings, although Spaniards do not put great emphasis on time themselves. Deadlines are considered a guideline, not an objective that is expected to be met, and most deadlines are not achieved as planned.[59]

- In India, "no" is considered to be an extremely harsh response. Indians use vague, evasive responses such as "I'll try" but rarely come out and reject a request, even if they have no intention of following through.[60]

- When doing business in Greece, U.S. executives must be mindful of their hand gestures; the hand-waving gesture that means "good-bye" in the United States is considered an insult in Greece.[61]

- In Japan and South Korea, exchanging business cards, known in Japan as *meishi*, is an important business function (unlike in Great Britain, where exchanging business cards is less popular). A Western executive who accepts a Japanese companion's card and then slips it into his pocket or scribbles notes on it has committed a major blunder. Tradition there says that a business card must be treated just as its owner would be treated—with respect. Travelers should present their own cards using both hands, with the card positioned so that the recipient can read it. (The flip side should be printed in Japanese, an expected courtesy.)

- Business attire and formality are very important when doing business in the eastern region of Argentina. Business dress is conservative, with men and women generally wearing dark suits. However, in the western cities, business is conducted much more casually, with little attention to formal attire, promptness, and agendas.

- Exercise caution when giving gifts. Although gift giving is standard practice in Japan, businesspeople in other countries, such as Malaysia, may see a gift as a bribe. In many countries, gifts of flowers are considered inappropriate because they connote romantic attention. In South Korea, giving a clock as a gift is considered good luck, but in China, it is considered a bad omen.[62] Avoid giving business associates gifts that are traditional symbols of their own cultures, such as chocolates to the Swiss or tea to the Chinese.

- In China, entrepreneurs need an ample dose of the "three *P*s": patience, patience, and patience. Nothing in China—especially business—happens fast, and entrepreneurs wanting to do business there must be persistent! In conversation and negotiations, periods of silence are common; they are a sign of politeness and contemplation. The Chinese view personal space much differently than Americans; in normal conversation, they stand much closer to their partners. At a business meal, sampling every dish, no matter how exotic, is considered polite. In addition, do not expect to conduct business the week before or after the Chinese New Year ("Yuandan"), whose dates vary from year to year, when many businesses are closed.

- Starting business relationships with customers in the Pacific Rim usually requires a third-party contact because Asian executives prefer to do business with people they know. In addition, building personal relationships is important. Many business deals take place over informal activities in this part of the world. American entrepreneurs doing business in the Pacific Rim should avoid hard-sell techniques, which are an immediate turnoff to Asian businesspeople. Harmony, patience, and consensus make good business companions in this region. It is also a good idea to minimize the importance of legal documents in negotiations. Although getting deals and trade agreements down in writing always is advisable, attempting to negotiate detailed contracts (as most American businesses tend to do) would insult most Asians, who base their deals on mutual trust and benefits.

International Trade Agreements

LO4

Describe the trade agreements that will have the greatest influence on foreign trade in the twenty-first century.

With the fundamental assumption that free trade among nations results in enhanced economic prosperity for all parties involved, the last 50 years have witnessed a gradual opening of trade among nations. Hundreds of agreements have been negotiated among nations in this period, with each contributing to free trade around the globe. Although completely free trade across international borders remains elusive, the following trade agreements have reduced some of the barriers to free trade that had stood for many years.

World Trade Organization

The World Trade Organization (WTO) was established in January 1995 and replaced the General Agreement on Tariffs and Trade (GATT), the first global tariff agreement, which was created in 1947 and was designed to reduce tariffs among member nations. The WTO, currently with 164 member countries, is the only international organization that establishes rules for trade among nations. Its member countries represent more than 97 percent of all world trade. The rules and agreements of the WTO, called the multilateral trading system, are the result of negotiations among its members. The WTO actively implements the rules established by the Uruguay Round of negotiations of GATT from 1986 to 1994 and continues to negotiate additional trade agreements. The ninth round of negotiations, the Doha Development Agenda, began in 2001, but has still not reached full agreement. Through the agreements of the WTO, members commit themselves to nondiscriminatory trade practices and to reducing barriers to free trade. The WTO's agreements spell out the rights and obligations of each member country. Each member country receives guarantees that its exports will be treated fairly and consistently in other member countries' markets. The WTO's General Agreement on Trade in Services addresses specific industries, including banking, insurance, telecommunications, and tourism. In addition, the WTO's intellectual property agreement, which covers patents, copyrights, and trademarks, defines rules for protecting ideas and creativity across borders.

In addition to the development of agreements among members, the WTO is involved in the resolution of trade disputes among members. The WTO system is designed to encourage dispute resolutions through consultation. If this approach fails, the WTO has a stage-by-stage procedure that can culminate in a ruling by a panel of experts.

North American Free Trade Agreement

free trade area

an association of countries that have agreed to eliminate trade barriers, both tariff and nontariff, among partner nations.

The North American Free Trade Agreement (NAFTA) created a free trade area among Canada, Mexico, and the United States. A **free trade area** is an association of countries that have agreed to eliminate trade barriers, both tariff and nontariff, among partner nations. Under the provisions of NAFTA, these barriers were eliminated for trade among the three countries, but each remained free to set its own tariffs on imports from nonmember nations.

NAFTA forged one of the world's largest free trade areas, a unified United States–Canada–Mexico market of 493 million people with a total annual output of more than $22 trillion in goods and services.[63] This trade agreement binds together the three nations on the North American continent into a single trading unit stretching from the Yukon to the Yucatan. NAFTA's provisions called for the reduction of tariffs to zero on most goods traded among these three nations. NAFTA's provisions have enhanced trade among the United States, Canada, and Mexico. Since NAFTA's passage in 1994, total trade among the three countries has increased 348 percent.[64] It also has made that trade more profitable and less cumbersome for companies of all sizes and has opened new opportunities for many businesses. Recall that the top two destinations for small exporters are Canada and Mexico.[65] The United States, Canada, and Mexico now conduct more than $3.5 billion in trilateral trade each day.[66]

ENTREPRENEURIAL PROFILE: Drew Greenblatt: Marlin Steel Wire Products LLC Marlin Steel Wire Products LLC started in 1968 as a supplier of wire baskets to the baking industry. Drew Greenblatt purchased the company in 1998, and as the market for bagel baskets declined due to cheap imports from foreign countries, Greenblatt realized that he had to transform his company. He shifted its focus to highly engineered products, including steel racks, material handling baskets, and mesh baskets used by manufacturers in a multitude of industries, ranging from automotive and aerospace to machinery and pharmaceuticals. Marlin Steel Wire Products, now based in Baltimore, Maryland, began exporting in 2004 and today sells its products in 39 different countries. Exports account for 25 percent of the company's sales, and because of NAFTA, two of its most important markets are Canada and Mexico, which together account for 10 percent of sales. Greenblatt says that free trade agreements, such as NAFTA, level the playing field for small companies such as his and open global markets to U.S. exporters by eliminating tariffs and other trade barriers.[67] ∎

Dominican Republic–Central America Free Trade Agreement

The Dominican Republic–Central America Free Trade Agreement (CAFTA-DR) is to Central America what NAFTA is to North America. The agreement, which was implemented in stages between 2006 and 2008, is designed to promote free trade among the United States and six

Central American countries: Costa Rica, El Salvador, Guatemala, Honduras, the Dominican Republic, and Nicaragua. In addition to reducing tariffs among these nations, CAFTA-DR protects U.S. companies' investments and intellectual property in the region, simplifies the export process for U.S. companies, and provides easier access to Central American markets.

Conclusion

To remain competitive, small businesses must assume a global posture. Global effectiveness requires entrepreneurs to be able to leverage workers' skills, company resources, and customer know-how across borders and throughout cultures across the world. They also must concentrate on maintaining competitive cost structures and a focus on the core of every business—the *customer!* Although there are no surefire rules for going global, small businesses that want to become successful international competitors should observe these guidelines:

- Take the time to learn about doing business globally before jumping in. Avoiding mistakes is easier and less expensive than cleaning up the results of mistakes later.

- If you have never conducted international business, consider hiring a trade intermediary or finding a local partner to help you.

- Make yourself at home in all three of the world's key markets: North America, Europe, and Asia. This triad of regions is forging a new world order in trade that will dominate global markets for years to come.

- Appeal to the similarities within the various regions in which you operate but recognize the differences in their specific cultures. Although the European Union is a single trading bloc composed of 27 countries, smart entrepreneurs know that each country has its own cultural uniqueness and do not treat the more than 508 million people in the EU as a unified market.

- Develop new products for the world market. Make sure your products and services measure up to world-class quality standards.

- Familiarize yourself with foreign customs and languages. Constantly scan, clip, and build a file on other cultures: their lifestyles, values, customs, and business practices.

- Learn to understand your customers from the perspective of *their* culture, not your own. Bridge cultural gaps by adapting your business practices to suit their preferences and customs.

- "Glocalize." Make global decisions about products, markets, and management but allow local employees to make tactical decisions about packaging, advertising, and service.

- Recruit and retain multicultural workers who can give your company meaningful insight into the intricacies of global markets. Entrepreneurs with a truly global perspective identify, nurture, and use the talents and knowledge multicultural workers possess.

- Train employees to think globally, send them on international trips, and equip them with state-of-the-art communications technology.

- Hire local managers to staff foreign offices and branches.

- Do whatever seems best wherever it seems best, even if people at home lose jobs or responsibilities.

- Consider using partners and joint ventures to break into foreign markets you cannot penetrate on your own.

- Evaluate opportunities to become an expat entrepreneur.

By its very nature, going global can be a frightening experience. Most entrepreneurs who have already made the jump, however, have found that the benefits outweigh the risks and that their companies are much stronger because of it.

MyLab Entrepreneurship

If your instructor is using MyLab Entrepreneurship, go to **www.pearson.com/mylab/ entrepreneurship** to complete the problems marked with this icon ⭐.

Chapter Summary by Learning Objective

1. **Explain why "going global" has become an integral part of many small companies' marketing strategies.**

   - Companies that move into international business can reap many benefits, including offsetting sales declines in the domestic market; increasing sales and profits; extending their products' life cycles; lowering manufacturing costs; improving competitive position; raising quality levels; and becoming more customer oriented.

2. **Describe the principal strategies small businesses can use for going global.**

   - Perhaps the simplest and least expensive way for a small business to begin conducting business globally is to establish a Web site. Companies that sell goods on the Web should establish a secure ordering and payment system for online customers.

   - Trade intermediaries, such as EMCs, ETCs, MEAs, export merchants, resident buying offices, and foreign distributors, can serve as a small company's "export department."

   - In a domestic joint venture, two or more U.S. small companies form an alliance for the purpose of exporting their goods and services abroad. In a foreign joint venture, a domestic small business forms an alliance with a company in the target area.

   - Some small businesses enter foreign markets by licensing businesses in other nations to use their patents, trademarks, copyrights, technology, processes, or products.

   - Franchising has become a major export industry for the United States. Franchisers that enter foreign markets rely on three strategies: direct franchising, area development, and master franchising.

   - Some countries lack a hard currency that is convertible into other currencies, so companies doing business there must rely on countertrading or bartering. A countertrade is a transaction in which a business selling goods in a foreign country agrees to promote investment and trade in that country. Bartering involves trading goods and services for other goods and services.

   - Once established in international markets, some small businesses set up permanent locations there. Although establishing and maintaining them can be very expensive, international locations give businesses the opportunity to stay in close contact with their international customers.

   - Many small companies shop the world for the goods and services they sell. The intensity of price competition has made importing and outsourcing successful strategies for many small businesses.

   - Some entrepreneurs choose to exploit opportunities in foreign markets by moving to those countries and becoming expat entrepreneurs.

3. **Discuss the major barriers to international trade and their impact on the global economy.**

   - Three domestic barriers to international trade are common: the attitude that "we're too small to export," lack of information on how to get started in global trade, and lack of available financing.

   - International barriers include tariffs, quotas, embargoes, dumping, and political, business, and cultural barriers.

4. **Describe the trade agreements that will have the greatest influence on foreign trade in the twenty-first century.**

   - The WTO was established in 1995 to implement the rules established by the Uruguay Round of negotiations of GATT from 1986 to 1994, and it continues to negotiate additional trade agreements. The WTO has 164 member nations and represents more than 97 percent of all global trade. The WTO is the governing body that resolves trade disputes among members.

   - NAFTA created a free trade area among Canada, Mexico, and the United States. The agreement created an association that knocked down trade barriers, both tariff and nontariff, among the partner nations.

   - CAFTA-DR created a free trade area among the United States and six nations in Central

America: Costa Rica, El Salvador, Guatemala, Honduras, the Dominican Republic, and Nicaragua. In addition to reducing tariffs among these nations, CAFTA-DR protects U.S. companies' investments and intellectual property in the region, simplifies the export process for U.S. companies, and provides easier access to Central American markets.

MyLab Entrepreneurship

If your instructor is using MyLab Entrepreneurship, go to **www.pearson.com/mylab/entrepreneurship** for Auto-graded writing questions as well as the following Assisted-graded writing questions:

1. Outline the 10 strategies that small businesses can use to go global.
2. Describe the barriers businesses face when trying to conduct business internationally.

Discussion Questions

16-1. Why must entrepreneurs learn to think globally?

⭐ 16-2. What forces are driving small businesses into international markets?

16-3. What advantages does going global offer a small business owner?

16-4. What risks does going global offer a small business owner?

16-5. Describe the various types of trade intermediaries that small business owners can use.

16-6. What functions does each type of trade intermediary perform?

16-7. What is a domestic joint venture?

16-8. What is a foreign joint venture?

16-9. What are the advantages and disadvantages of taking on an international partner through a joint venture?

16-10. What mistakes are first-time exporters most likely to make?

16-11. Outline the steps a small company should take to establish a successful export program.

⭐ 16-12. What are the benefits and challenges of establishing international locations?

16-13. How can a small business owner overcome the obstacles of conducting business internationally?

16-14. What is a tariff?

16-15. What is a quota?

16-16. What impact do tariffs and quotas have on international trade?

16-17. What impact have agreements such as WTO, NAFTA, and CAFTA-DR had on small companies that want to go global?

16-18. Summarize the key provisions of the WTO.

16-19. Summarize the key provisions of NAFTA.

16-20. Summarize the key provisions of CAFTA-DR.

16-21. What advice would you offer an entrepreneur interested in launching a global business effort?

Beyond the Classroom . . .

16-22. Go to lunch with a student from a foreign country and discuss what products and services are most needed there.

16-23. Ask a student from a foreign country how business systems there differ from ours.

16-24. Ask a student from a foreign country about government regulation and how it affects business in his or her country.

16-25. Ask the student from a foreign country about the cultural differences between the United States and his or her country.

16-26. Ask the student from a foreign country about trade barriers that his or her government has erected.

16-27. Review several current business publications and prepare a brief report on which nations are the most promising for U.S. entrepreneurs.

16-28. What steps should a small business owner take to break into the most promising markets for U.S. entrepreneurs?

16-29. Identify the nations that are currently the least promising for U.S. entrepreneurs.

16-30. Describe why the least promising nations are not attractive markets.

16-31. Select a nation that interests you and prepare a report on its business customs and practices.

16-32. For the nation you selected, explain its similarities with business customs and practices in the United States.

16-33. For the nation you selected, explain its differences with business customs and practices in the United States.

Endnotes

[1] Patrick Delehanty, "Small Businesses Key Players in International Trade," Small Business Administration Office of Advocacy, Brief #11, December 1, 2015, p. 3.

[2] *2016 European SME Exporting Insights Survey*, UPS, 2017, p. 7.

[3] "Small Business Exporting Survey 2016," National Small Business Association and Small Business Exporting Association, 2016, p. 4.

[4] "Faces of Trade: Hampel Corporation," U.S. Chamber of Commerce, 2016, www.uschamber.com/faces-trade-hampel-corporation.

[5] Homi Kharas, "The Unprecedented Expansion of the Global Middle Class: An Update," Brookings Institution, February 28, 2017 p. 11.

[6] Stephen Dover and Mark Mobius, "Emerging Market Equity 2017 Outlook," Franklin Templeton Investments, December 20, 2016, http://mobius.blog.franklintempleton.com/2016/12/20/emerging-market-equity-2017-outlook/.

[7] "How the U.S. Economy Benefits from International Trade and Investment," *Business Roundtable*, 2012, p. 1.

[8] *World Trade Statistical Review*, Chapter 3, World Trade Organization, 2017, p.1.

[9] *Small and Medium-Sized Enterprises: Characteristics and Performance*, U.S. International Trade Commission, Publication 4189, November 2010, pp. 3–4.

[10] "Infographic: Small Business, Big Trade," Service Corps of Retired Executives, March 7, 2017, https://www.score.org/resource/infographic-small-business-big-trade; John Larsen, "Trade Promotion Coordinating Committee," U.S. Department of Commerce, International Trade Administration, 2011, p. 8; "New Markets, New Jobs: The National Export Initiative Small Business Tour," U.S. Department of Commerce, January 27, 2011, www.commerce.gov/blog/2011/01/27/new-marketsnew-jobs-national-export-initiative-small-business-tour.

[11] *Small Business Exporting Survey 2016*, National Small Business Association and the Small Business Exporters Association, 2016, p. 9.

[12] "Internet Users in the World by Region March 2017," *Internet World Stats*, 2017, www.internetworldstats.com/stats.htm.

[13] "Worldwide Retail Ecommerce Sales Will Reach $1.915 Trillion This Year," *eMarketer*, August 22, 2016, www.emarketer.com/Article/Worldwide-Retail-Ecommerce-Sales-Will-Reach-1915-Trillion-This-Year/1014369.

[14] Phred Dvorak, "Small Firms Hire Guides as They Head Abroad," *Wall Street Journal*, November 5, 2007, p. B3.

[15] "About Dorian Drake," Dorian Drake International, n.d., www.doriandrake.com/frameset.htm.

[16] "NuStep, Inc. Receives Presidential Award for Export Successes," *PRWire*, May 17, 2016, www.prnewswire.com/news-releases/nustep-inc-receives-presidential-award-for-export-successes-300269780.html; "About Us," NuStep, n.d., www.nustep.com/about-nustep/; "Faces of Trade: NuStep," U.S. Chamber of Commerce, n.d., www.uschamber.com/faces-trade-nustep.

[17] Zack O'Malley Greenburg, "Diddy Explains New Diageo Joint Venture, DeLeón Tequila," *Forbes*, January 8, 2014, www.forbes.com/sites/zackomalleygreenburg/2014/01/08/diddy-explains-new-diageo-joint-venturedeleon-tequila/.

[18] Josh Horwitz, "Starbucks Is Opening More Than a Store a Day in China and Only Plans to Get Faster There," *Quartz*, March 28, 2017, https://qz.com/943502/in-china-theres-starbucks-and-then-theres-everything-else/.

[19] William Edwards, "International Expansion: Do Opportunities Outweigh Challenges?" *Franchising World*, February 2008, www.franchise.org/Franchise-News-Detail.aspx?id=37992.

[20] "Subway Opens 600th Outlet in India," *NDTV*, March 11, 2017, http://profit.ndtv.com/news/corporates/article-subway-opens-600th-outlet-in-india-1668619; Boby Kurian, "Top Subway 'Agents' Consolidate India Ops," *Time of India*, June 15, 2016, http://timesofindia.indiatimes.com/business/india-business/Top-Subway-agents-consolidate-India-ops/articleshow/52755559.cms.

[21] "Brands," Jubilant FoodWorks, n.d., www.jubilantfoodworks.com/brand/dominos-pizza/; "Domino's 101: Basic Facts," Domino's, n.d., https://biz.dominos.com/web/public/about-dominos/fun-facts.

[22] Nancy Luna, "Creamistry Ramps Up Global Expansion with 70 New Stores This Year," *Orange County Register*, June 8, 2017, http://www.ocregister.com/2017/06/08/creamistry-ramps-up-global-expansion-with-70-new-stores-this-year/; "Irvine-based Creamistry to Grow at Home and Overseas," *Global Franchise Magazine*, June 12, 2017, http://www.globalfranchisemagazine.com/news/news/irvine-based-creamistry.

[23] "U.S. Export Fact Sheet," International Trade Association, April 5, 2016, p. 1.

[24] "The Facts About Exporting," International Trade Association, n.d., www.nist.gov/sites/default/files/documents/mep/data/NIST_Infographic_EXPORTING_08AUG14_FINAL_linked-1.pdf.

[25] Casey Coombs, "Location-Sharing Company Glympse Snags $11M to Expand Headcount," *Puget Sound Business Journal*, December 21, 2016, www.bizjournals.com/seattle/news/2016/12/21/app-glympse-snags-venture-capital-funding-hiring.html; "Glympse," Export Washington, n.d., www.exportwashington.com/why-export/success-stories/Glympse/Pages/default.aspx.

[26] "Alabama SBDC Network Success Story," Alabama International Trade Center, n.d., http://asbdc.org/wp-content/uploads/2012/05/Process-Barron-Success-Story-AITC.pdf.

[27] Joseph Zaritski, "15 Tips to Start Successful Export Business," *Australian Export Online: Export 61*, www.export61.com/export-tutorials.asp?ttl=tips.

[28] *Small Business Exporting Survey 2016*, National Small Business Association and the Small Business Exporters Association, 2016, p. 7.

[29] Anabel Guerra, "Blue Orange Pottery," University of Texas San Antonio International Trade Center, May 20, 2015, https://texastrade.org/blue-orange-pottery/.

[30] "Small Business Exporting Survey," National Small Business Association and Small Business Exporters Association, 2016, p. 6.

[31] "Western New York Company Enters Korean Market," Food Export Association, March 3, 2017, www.foodexport.org/who-we-are/success-stories/2017/03/03/western-new-york-company-enters-korean-market.

[32] *Small and Medium-Sized Enterprises: Characteristics and Performance*, U.S. International Trade Commission, Publication 4189, November 2010, pp. 6–8.

[33] "Missouri Supplier Gains Export Success on Focused Trade Mission," *Food Export*, June 12, 2017, https://www.foodexport.org/who-we-are/success-stories/2017/06/12/

[33] missouri-supplier-gains-export-success-on-focused-trade-mission; "United States of Trade—Missouri: U.S. International Foods," Office of the United States Trade Representative, 2017, p. 54.

[34] "More Than 40 Years of Export Success for This Chicagoland Manufacturer," SBA Illinois District Office, 2015, www.sba.gov/offices/district/il/chicago/success-stories/more-40-years-export-success-chicagoland-manufacturer.

[35] Ryan Underwood, "Going Global: Why Borders Still Matter," *Inc.*, May 2011, pp. 120–122.

[36] "Small Business Exporting Survey," National Small Business Association and Small Business Exporters Association, 2016, p. 10.

[37] Lee Gimpel, "Global Hot Spots," *Entrepreneur*, June 2008, pp. 62–70.

[38] Daniel Kaufmann and Shang-Jin Wei, "Does 'Grease Money' Speed Up the Wheels of Commerce?" World Bank, February 2, 2011, www.worldbank.org/wbi/governance/pdf/grease.pdf.

[39] "2017 in Charge—Technology," *Nashville Post*, March 29, 2017, www.nashvillepost.com/business/nashville-post-magazine/article/20856494/2017-in-charge-technology; Peter Marcum, personal communication, May 23, 2014.

[40] "Annual Trade Highlights," U.S. Census Bureau, 2016, www.census.gov/foreigntrade/statistics/highlights/annual.html.

[41] John Wiegand, "Nuvar Purchases New Facility to Address Capacity Constraints," *MiBiz*, November 8, 2015, https://mibiz.com/item/23048-nuvar-purchases-new-facility-to-address-capacity-constraints; Scott Kuyper, personal communication, May 21, 2014.

[42] Jamie McGee, "Arciplex to Expand in Nashville," *Tennessean*, February 25, 2016, www.tennessean.com/story/money/2016/02/25/arciplex-expand-nashville/80924016/; Tom Haarlander, personal communication, May 22, 2014.

[43] "Trade Recovery Expected in 2017 and 2018, Amid Policy Uncertainty," World Trade Organization, April 12, 2017, https://www.wto.org/english/news_e/pres17_e/pr791_e.htm; *World Trade Statistical Review*, Chapter 3, World Trade Organization, 2017, p. 1.

[44] "Tariff Rate, Applied, Weighted Mean, All Products," World Trade Organization, n.d., http://data.worldbank.org/indicator/TM.TAX.MRCH.WM.AR.ZS.

[45] *Harmonized Tariff Schedule of the United States, 2016*, U.S. International Trade Commission, www.usitc.gov/tata/hts/index.htm.

[46] "Tariff Rate, Applied, Weighted Mean, All Products," World Trade Organization, n.d., http://data.worldbank.org/indicator/TM.TAX.MRCH.WM.AR.ZS.

[47] Patrick Frater, "U.S. and China Struggle Over Film Quotas," *Variety*, February 9, 2017, http://variety.com/2017/biz/asia/u-s-and-china-struggle-over-film-quotas-1201979720/; Lilian Lin, "China Set to Top U.S. in Number of Movie Screens," *Wall Street Journal*, November 14, 2016, http://blogs.wsj.com/chinarealtime/2016/11/14/china-set-to-overtake-u-s-as-worlds-largest-cinema-market/.

[48] "Trade in Goods with Vietnam," United States Census Bureau, 2017, www.census.gov/foreign-trade/balance/c5520.html.

[49] Arthur Nelsen, "Europe Strengthens Ban on Seal Products After WTO Challenge," *The Guardian*, September 8, 2015, www.theguardian.com/environment/2015/sep/08/europe-strengthens-ban-on-seal-products-after-wto-challenge; Jaime Berkheimer, Stacey Cargile, Gabriel Richards, Erika Palsson, and Inbal Shem-Tov, "Issue Guide: Trade Embargoes, Seals, and More," University of California, Irvine, http://darwin.bio.uci.edu/~sustain/issueguides/Embargoes/index.html.

[50] Megan Geuss, "Chinese Solar Exports Fall in 2016 with Global Anti-Dumping Measures," *ARS Technica*, February 20, 2017, https://arstechnica.com/business/2017/02/chinese-solar-exports-fall-in-2016-with-global-anti-dumping-measures/; "China Rejects U.S. Solar Dumping Ruling, Companies Warn Tariffs Might Hurt Clean Energy Industry," *Washington Post*, May 18, 2012, www.washingtonpost.com/business/chinese-solarmakers-reject-us-dumping-ruling-saytariffs-might-hurt-clean-energy-industry/2012/05/18/gIQARwneXU_story.html; Steven Mufson, "U.S. Solar Manufacturers to File Dumping Charges against Chinese Firms," *Washington Post*, October 19, 2011, www.washingtonpost.com/business/economy/us-solarmanufacturers-to-file-dumping-charges-against-chinesefirms/2011/10/19/gIQAlkPrxL_story.html.

[51] Gary D. Bruton, David Ahlstrom, Michael N. Young, and Yuri Rubanik, "In Emerging Markets, Know What Your Partners Expect," *Wall Street Journal*, December 15, 2008, p. R5.

[52] Alexey Rashevskiy, personal communication, April 6, 2017; Alexey Rashevskiy, "A Fly in the Ointment: How Banking Red Tape Undermines Irish Startup Environment," *Financial Examiner*, June 5, 2015, https://medium.com/on-banking/a-fly-in-the-ointment-how-banking-red-tape-undermines-irish-startup-environment-1eb4f1cbded4.

[53] Lydia Dishman, "How U.S. Employee Benefits Compare to Europe's," *Fast Company*, February 17, 2016, https://www.fastcompany.com/3056830/how-the-us-employee-benefits-compare-to-europe.

[54] Lawrence Van Gelder, "It Pays to Watch Words, Gestures While Abroad," *Greenville News*, April 7, 1996, p. 8E.

[55] Malika Zouhali-Worrall, "Watch Your Language!" *FSB*, July/August 2008, pp. 71–72.

[56] Tyler Seymour and Caleb Jones, personal communication, May 23, 2014; Jamie McGee, "Pivot Point: Entrepreneurs Find Greater Success with the Unexpected," *Nashville Business Journal*, March 1, 2013, www.bizjournals.com/nashville/print-edition/2013/03/01/pivot-point-entrepreneurs-find.html.

[57] "Chile Business Etiquette, Culture, & Manners," International Business Center, n.d., www.international-business-etiquette.com/besite/chile.htm.

[58] "New Zealand Business Etiquette, Culture, & Manners," International Business Center, n.d., www.international-business-etiquette.com/besite/new_zealand.htm.

[59] "Spain Business Etiquette, Culture, & Manners," International Business Center, n.d., www.international-business-etiquette.com/besite/spain.htm.

[60] "India Business Etiquette, Culture, & Manners," International Business Center, n.d., www.international-business-etiquette.com/besite/india.htm.

[61] Aliza Pilar Sherman, "Going Global," *Entrepreneur*, December 2004, p. 34.

[62] Ibid.

[63] "List of Countries by Projected GDP," *Statistics Times*, April 23, 2017, http://statisticstimes.com/economy/countries-by-projected-gdp.php; "Countries in the World by Population," *Worldometer*, 2017, http://www.worldometers.info/world-population/population-by-country/.

[64] James McBride and Mohammed Aly Sergie, "NAFTA's Economic Impact," Council on Foreign Relations, January 24, 2017, www.cfr.org/trade/naftas-economic-impact/p15790; "The Facts on NAFTA: Assessing Two Decades of Gains, in Trade, Growth, and Jobs," U.S. Chamber of Commerce, March 8, 2017, https://www.uschamber.com/report/the-facts-nafta-assessing-two-decades-gains-trade-growth-and-jobs.

[65]*Small Business Exporting Survey 2016*, National Small Business Association and the Small Business Exporters Association, 2016, p. 6.

[66]James McBride and Mohammed Aly Sergie, "NAFTA's Economic Impact," Council on Foreign Relations, January 24, 2017, www.cfr.org/trade/naftas-economic-impact/p15790.

[67]Ken Monahan, "PP in Real Life: From Bagel Baskets to Highly Engineered Industrial Products, Why One Baltimore-based Small Business Says We Need to Pass TPP and Export Like Crazy," Shop Floor, October 25, 2016, http://www.shopfloor.org/2016/10/tpp-in-real-life-from-bagel-baskets-to-highly-engineered-industrial-products-why-one-baltimore-based-small-business-says-we-need-to-pass-tpp-and-export-like-crazy/; "Marlin Steel Wire Products LLC", *Faces of Trade*, U.S. Chamber of Commerce, p. 1.

17

Building a New Venture Team and Planning for the Next Generation

Tatiana Badaeva/123RF

Learning Objectives

On completion of this chapter, you will be able to:

1. Explain the challenges involved in the entrepreneur's role as leader and what it takes to be a successful leader.

2. Describe the importance of hiring the right employees and how to avoid making hiring mistakes.

3. Explain how to create a company culture that encourages employee retention.

4. Describe the steps in developing a management succession plan for a growing business that allows a smooth transition of leadership to the next generation.

5. Explain the exit strategies available to entrepreneurs.

MyLab Entrepreneurship

 Improve Your Grade!

If your instructor is using MyLab Entrepreneurship, visit **www.pearson.com/mylab/entrepreneurship** for videos, simulations, and writing exercises.

LO1

Explain the challenges involved in the entrepreneur's role as leader and what it takes to be a successful leader.

leadership

the process of influencing and inspiring others to work to achieve a common goal and then giving them the power and the freedom to achieve it.

Leadership: An Essential Part of an Entrepreneur's Job

To be successful, an entrepreneur must assume a wide range of roles, tasks, and responsibilities, but none is more important than the role of leader. Some entrepreneurs are uncomfortable assuming this role, but they must learn to be effective leaders if their companies are to grow and reach their potential. **Leadership** is the process of influencing and inspiring others to work to achieve a common goal and then giving them the power, the incentive, and the freedom to achieve it. Without leadership ability, entrepreneurs—and their companies—never rise above mediocrity. Entrepreneurs can learn to be effective leaders, but the task requires dedication, discipline, and hard work. In the past, business owners often relied on an autocratic management style, one built on command and control. Today's workforce is more knowledgeable, has more options, and is more skilled and, as a result, expects a different, more sophisticated style of leadership. Millennials, the 80 million Americans born between 1981 and 1997, now make up nearly 35 percent of the U.S. workforce and demand a more open, participative, inclusive, and flexible leadership typology.[1] Leadership is no longer about command and control; to attract the best and brightest people, leaders must create an environment in which they delegate authority to employees who have the freedom to use their intelligence and judgment to make decisions. When Gordon Bethune took over as CEO of Continental Airlines, the company was losing money, ranked last in the industry on almost every performance metric, and employed a workforce of disheartened, disengaged employees. Bethune, who had worked his way up the ranks at the company, immediately took steps to build trust and morale among employees, set challenging performance goals, and rewarded employees for accomplishing them. He created a profit-sharing plan, set aggressive goals for the company to become profitable, and gave employees the freedom to fix problems. His philosophy was "Everyone wins or no one does." In a little more than a year, Continental Airlines had some of the highest customer and employee satisfaction rankings in the industry and was earning a profit, and it went on to become one of the greatest turnaround stories in business history.[2]

The rapid pace of change shaping the economy also is placing new demands on leaders. Technology is changing the ways in which people work, the ways in which the various parts of an organization operate and interconnect, and the ways in which competitors strive for market dominance. To remain competitive, companies must operate at a new, faster speed of business, and that requires a new style of leadership. Leaders of small companies must gather information and make decisions with lightning-fast speed, and they must give workers the resources and the freedom to solve problems and exploit opportunities as they arise. Effective leaders delegate authority and responsibility and empower employees to act in the best interest of the business. In this way, leaders demonstrate trust in employees and respect for their ability to make decisions. Many entrepreneurs have discovered that the old style of leadership has lost its effectiveness and that they must develop a new, more fluid, flexible style of leadership that better fits the needs of modern workers and competitive conditions.

Until recently, experts compared a leader's job to that of a symphony orchestra conductor. Like the symphony leader, an entrepreneur made sure that everyone in the company was playing the same score, coordinated individual efforts to produce a harmonious sound, and directed the orchestra members as they played. The conductor (entrepreneur) retained virtually all of the power and made all of the decisions about how the orchestra would play the music, without any input from the musicians themselves. Today's successful entrepreneur, however, is more like the leader of a jazz band, which is known for its improvisation, innovation, creativity, and free-wheeling style. "The success of a small [jazz band] rests on the ability to be agile and flexible, skills that are equally central to today's business world," says Michael Gold, founder of Jazz Impact, a company that teaches management skills through jazz.[3] Business leaders, like the leaders of jazz bands, should exhibit the following characteristics:

Innovative. Leaders must step out of their own comfort zones to embrace new ideas; they avoid the comfort of complacency.

Passionate. One of entrepreneurs' greatest strengths is their passion for their businesses. Members of their team feed off of that passion and draw inspiration from it.

Willing to take risks. Playing it safe "is not an option in jazz or for any company that wants to be solvent ten years from now," says Gold.[4]

Adaptable. Although leaders must stand on a bedrock of resolute values, like jazz band leaders, they must adapt their leadership styles to fit the situation and the people involved.

Management and leadership are not the same, but both are essential to a company's success. Leadership without management is unbridled; management without leadership is uninspired. Leadership gets a small business going; management keeps it going. In other words, leaders are the architects of small businesses, and managers are the builders. Some entrepreneurs are good managers yet are poor leaders; others are powerful leaders but are weak managers. The best bet for the latter is to hire people with solid management skills to help them execute the vision they have for their companies. Stephen Covey, author of *Principle-Centered Leadership*, explains the difference between management and leadership in this way:

> Leadership deals with people; management deals with things. You manage things; you lead people. Leadership deals with vision; management deals with logistics toward that vision. Leadership deals with doing the right things; management focuses on doing things right. Leadership deals with examining the paradigms on which you are operating; management operates within those paradigms. Leadership comes first, then management, but both are necessary.[5]

Leadership and management are intertwined; one without the other means that a small business is going nowhere. Leadership is especially important for companies in the growth phase, when entrepreneurs are hiring employees (often for the first time) and must keep the company and everyone in it focused on its mission as growth tests every seam in the organizational structure.

Effective leaders exhibit certain behaviors:

- ***They define and then constantly reinforce the vision they have for the company.*** Effective leaders have a clear vision of where they want their companies to go, and they concentrate on communicating that vision to those around them. Unfortunately, this is one area in which employees say their leaders could do a better job. Clarity of purpose is essential to a successful organization because people want to be a part of something that is bigger than they are; however, the purpose must be more than merely achieving continuous quarterly profits. Effective leaders understand that a compelling vision is the first ingredient for any successful organization. The other requirements are a strategy for implementing the vision, a leader who sets a good example and develops principles and values that support the vision, and convincing others to buy into the vision and work together to achieve it.[6]

  In the 1930s, Walt Disney asked his team of animators to stay late one evening because he had a vision that would transform his company: Rather than continue making the short cartoons the company had become known for, he wanted to make the first full-length animated movie, a concept that at the time was revolutionary. Over the course of three and a half hours, Disney created an unmistakable vision for the young company by acting out all of the parts of the characters in *Snow White and the Seven Dwarfs*. Not only was the movie a commercial and critical success (becoming the top-grossing movie of all time until it was unseated in 1939 by *Gone with the Wind*) and winning a special Academy Award (a full-size Oscar accompanied by seven "dwarf" Oscars), it paved the way for dozens of other full-length animated films and transformed the entire company into an entertainment powerhouse.[7]

- ***They create a set of values and beliefs for employees and passionately pursue them.*** Values are the foundation on which a company's vision is built. Leaders should be like beacons in the night, constantly shining light on the principles, values, and beliefs on which they founded their companies. Whenever the opportunity presents itself, entrepreneurs must communicate with clarity the company's bedrock values and principles to employees and other stakeholders. Some entrepreneurs may not think that it is necessary to do so, but successful leaders know they must hammer home the connection between their companies' values and mission and the jobs workers perform every day.

- *They establish a culture of ethics.* One of the most important tasks facing leaders is to mold a highly ethical culture for their companies. They also must demonstrate the character and the courage necessary to stick to the ethical standards they create—especially in the face of difficulty. In a recent survey by Harvard University that asked leaders around the world to rate 74 leadership traits, two-thirds of the leaders ranked high ethical and moral standards as the most important competency.[8]

- *They develop a strategic plan that gives the company a competitive advantage.* Ideally, employees participate in building a successful strategic plan, but the leader is the principal strategic architect of the company. The leader also is responsible for implementing the plan with flexibility and the ability to adapt it to changing conditions.

- *They respect and support their employees.* To gain the respect of their employees, leaders must first respect those who work for them. Successful leaders treat every employee with respect. They know that a loyal, dedicated workforce is a company's most valuable resource, and they treat their employees that way.

- *They set the example for their employees.* Leaders' words ring hollow if they fail to "practice what they preach." Few signals are transmitted to workers faster than a leader who sells employees on one set of values and principles and then acts according to a different set. This behavior quickly undermines a leader's credibility among employees, who expect leaders to "walk their talk." That is why integrity is perhaps the most important determinant of a leader's effectiveness.

- *They are authentic.* Employees quickly see through leaders who only pretend to be what they are not. Authenticity does not make someone a leader, but a leader cannot be successful without it. Authenticity is a vital part in developing trust among employees. Successful leaders follow the philosophy of Popeye, the spinach-munching, crusty sailor who first appeared in a cartoon strip in 1929 and was famous for saying, "I yam what I yam, and that's all what I yam."[9]

- *They create a climate of trust in the organization.* Leaders who demonstrate integrity win the trust of their employees, an essential ingredient in the success of any organization. Honest, open communication and a consistent pattern of leaders doing what they say they will do build trust in a business. Research suggests that building trust among employees is one of the most important tasks of leaders.

- *They build credibility with their employees.* To be effective, leaders must have credibility with their employees, a sometimes challenging task for entrepreneurs, especially as their companies grow and they become insulated from the daily activities of their businesses. To combat the problem of losing touch with the problems their employees face as they do their jobs, many managers periodically return to the frontlines to serve customers. *Undercover Boss*, a popular television show, disguises CEOs and sends them to work in frontline jobs in their companies. In addition to seeing just how difficult many jobs can be, all of the CEOs get a superb refresher course in how important every worker's role is to the success of the company and how the policies they and other top managers create often make workers' jobs harder. Michael Rubin, founder and CEO of GSI Commerce, a company that provides distribution and call center services, learned so much from his frontline experience that he now requires all of GSI's executives to spend time working in the company's warehouses and call centers. The idea is that top managers will make better decisions about policies and procedures if they see firsthand the impact of those decisions on customers and frontline employees.[10] After appearing on *Undercover Boss*, Dan DiZio, founder of Philly Pretzel Factory, a Philly-style pretzel bakery with more than 150 franchised locations, said that he never intended to be a CEO who was isolated in the boardroom but admitted that he had become exactly that. During the show, DiZio was faced with the frustrations that franchisees and frontline employees experienced daily (such as an antiquated cash register system) and realized that most of their problems were the result of top managers' (including his) poor decisions. DiZio made a commitment to visit the company's stores more frequently, implemented a mystery shopper program to provide authentic feedback, and now includes frontline employees on conference calls with franchisees about store operations.[11]

- *They focus employees' efforts on challenging goals and keep them driving toward those goals.* When asked by a student intern to define leadership, one entrepreneur said, "Leadership is the ability to convince people to follow a path they have never taken before to a place they have never been—and upon finding it to be successful, to do it over and over again."[12] At Contently, a small company started by Joe Coleman, Shane Snow, and Dave Goldberg in 2011 that provides content marketing services to large businesses, Snow, who serves as the company's chief creative officer, constantly challenges employees to come up with what he calls "10X ideas"—ideas that can improve some aspect of the company by a factor of 10. Employees enjoy the challenge of coming up with big ideas, appreciate the intellectual stimulation, and have responded with game-changing ideas for Contently.[13]

- *They empower their employees to do their jobs well, trust their employees to do their work, and get out of the way.* Shawn Jenkins, cofounder of Benefitfocus, a benefits technology company, says that his leadership style is similar to that of a flight instructor (his first job). The instructor teaches the student pilot the skills required to fly and provides the resources to fly but knows that the pilot must take the controls to master the technique. The flight instructor must be willing to let the pilot experience failure, almost to the point of danger. A good instructor does not yank the controls away from the pilot; instead, he or she provides gentle nudges of correction along the way.[14] Unlike a good flight instructor, ineffective leaders are micromanagers who try to control everything their employees do, second-guess their decisions, and punish them when they fail. Jeff Lawson, founder of Twilio, a cloud-based communications platform that powers telephone calls, messaging and video for businesses in 40 countries, organizes his company's employees into small teams of no more than 10 people. Each team adheres to overall company standards and processes around their objectives but are empowered to make their own decisions and execute quickly. He says that success depends on making sure that every small team understands the company's mission of customer service and understands how their team measures success against that mission. He then trusts them to achieve it.[15]

- *They provide the resources employees need to achieve their goals.* Effective leaders know that workers cannot do their jobs well unless they have the tools they need. They provide workers not only with the physical resources they need to excel but also with the necessary intangible resources, such as training, coaching, and mentoring.

- *They communicate with their employees.* Leaders recognize that helping workers see the company's overarching goal is just one part of effective communication; encouraging employee feedback and then *listening* is just as vital. The goal of listening is not merely to be able to respond but to understand. In other words, they know that communication is a two-way street. Open communication takes on even greater importance when a company faces a difficult or uncertain future. Good leaders encourage employees to speak the truth, even if it means disagreeing with the boss.

- *They value the diversity of their workers.* Smart business leaders recognize the value of their workers' varied skills, abilities, backgrounds, and interests. When channeled in the right direction, diversity can be a powerful weapon in achieving innovation and maintaining a competitive edge. Good leaders get to know their workers and work to understand the diversity of their strengths. Achieving diversity is not only the right thing to do; it also is good business. A recent study by McKinsey and Company reports that companies at the 75th percentile or higher in gender diversity and in ethnic diversity are 15 percent and 35 percent, respectively, more likely to outperform financially those companies that are at the 25th percentile or lower.[16]

- *They celebrate their workers' successes.* Effective leaders recognize that workers want to be winners, and they do everything they can to encourage top performance among their people. The rewards they give are not always financial; in many cases, rewards are as simple as handwritten congratulatory notes.

- *They are willing to take risks.* Entrepreneurs know better than most that launching a business requires taking risks. They also understand that to remain competitive, they must constantly encourage risk taking in their companies. When employees try something innovative and it fails, they don't resort to punishment because they know that doing so would squelch creativity in the organization.

- **They encourage creativity among their workers.** Rather than punish workers who take risks and fail, effective leaders are willing to accept failure as a natural part of innovation and creativity. They know that innovative behavior is the key to future success, and they do everything they can to encourage it among workers.

- **They maintain a sense of humor.** One of the most important tools a leader can have is a sense of humor. Without it, work can become dull and unexciting for everyone.

Courtesy of GSOFT

ENTREPRENEURIAL PROFILE: Simon De Baene, Guillaume Roy, Dan Benoni, and Jeffrey Firmin: GSoft The cofounders of GSoft, a company based in Quebec, Canada, with more than 200 employees and sales of more than $45 million, instill a sense of humor and fun into their software company. Every new employee receives a Fitbit, and the entire workforce competes in the company Fit League to see who can log the greatest number of steps. Because many employees are hockey fans or former hockey players, the company sponsors a Winter Classic Hockey Tournament that builds team spirit, camaraderie, and good-natured competition. Whenever the company achieves an important goal, the entire team celebrates with champagne. Employees can take short breaks from work to play ping-pong or grab a cup of coffee at the in-house café, which is a popular place to gather and exchange ideas. The office also features a skateboard ramp and a sign that expresses the founders' philosophy: "Without fun, it sucks."[17] ∎

- **They create an environment in which people have the motivation, the training, and the freedom to achieve the goals they have set.** Leaders know that *their* success is determined by the success of their followers. The goal is to make every employee the manager of his or her job. The leader's role is to provide employees with the resources and support they need to be successful.

- **They create a work climate that encourages maximum performance.** Leaders understand that they play a significant role in shaping a company culture that sets high standards of performance. Anne Wojcicki, founder of 23andMe, a genetic testing company, says her primary role is to get everyone in the company to think bigger.[18]

- **They become a catalyst for change.** With market and competitive climates changing rapidly, entrepreneurs must reinvent their companies constantly. Although leaders must cling to the values and principles that form the bedrock of their companies, they must be willing to change—sometimes radically—the policies, procedures, and processes within their businesses. If a company is headed in the wrong direction, the leader's job is to recognize that and to get the company moving in the right direction.

- **They develop future leaders.** Effective leaders look beyond themselves to spot tomorrow's leaders and take the time to help them grow into their leadership potential. A vital component of every leader's job is to develop the next generation of leaders. Researchers at the Center for Creative Leadership say that the best leaders learn the most important lessons in three clusters of experience: completing formal coursework and training (10 percent), developing relationships (20 percent), and working on challenging assignments (70 percent).[19] Charlie Kim, founder of Next Jump, a technology company based in New York City that operates Web-based loyalty and rewards programs that connect employees at large companies (including 70 percent of Fortune 500 companies) to special discounts and other incentives at more than 30,000 merchants, has quite deliberately built his entire company and its culture around leadership development. The company, which Kim launched in his Tufts University dorm room in 1994, now generates more than $2 billion in annual sales and has an employee turnover ratio of virtually zero. Executives from around the globe have come to study Next Jump's unique culture, which Kim built on a simple yet profound formula:

Better Me + Better You = Better Us. Kim challenges all of the company's 200 employees to improve their own skills and to help someone else improve his or her skills.[20]

- *They keep their eyes on the horizon.* Effective leaders are never satisfied with what they and their employees accomplished yesterday. They know that yesterday's successes are not enough to sustain their companies indefinitely. They see the importance of building and maintaining sufficient momentum to carry their companies to the next level. "A leader's job is to rally people toward a better future," says Marcus Buckingham, who has spent nearly two decades studying effective leaders.[21] Just like winning athletes, good leaders visualize a successful future and then work to make it happen.

Table 17.1 presents 12 questions leaders should address if they want their companies to excel.

TABLE 17.1 **12 Questions That Every Leader Should Address**

Jim Collins, coauthor of business best-sellers *Good to Great* and *Great by Choice*, has spent 25 years researching great companies and has integrated the results of his research into 12 questions that leaders must address if they want their companies to excel. Collins advises leaders to discuss one of the following questions every month and repeat the process annually:

1. *Do we want to build a great company, and are we committed to doing the things that are required to make our company great?* Becoming a great company starts by making this fundamental choice, understanding the implications of choosing to build a great company, and making the commitment to take the necessary steps to achieve greatness.

2. *Do we have the right people on the bus and in the key seats?* Leaders must decide whether the people who will carry the company forward are the *right* people. Are they capable? Motivated? Committed? Leaders must answer this question before they decide *where* they want the business to go, and that sometimes means getting the *wrong* people *off* the bus.

3. *What are the brutal facts?* Leaders cannot make good decisions unless they have access to facts, both good and bad. Confronting the negative, most troubling issues is essential because ignoring them represents a serious threat not only to a company's success but also to its survival. The key is to confront the facts without losing faith.

4. *What are we best at, and what do we have an unbounded passion for?* By answering this question, leaders define their companies' fundamental economic engine. Isaiah Berlin wrote, "The fox knows many things, but the hedgehog knows one big thing."* In other words, a fox is easily distracted, but a hedgehog, like an outstanding company, is focused, determined, and relentless. A company's hedgehog combines its passion and its distinctive competence with what it can make money doing (its economic engine). What is the company's hedgehog?

5. *What is our company's 20-Mile March, and are we hitting it?* Collins refers to Roald Amundsen's successful attempt in 1911 to be the first person to reach the South Pole by committing to traveling 20 miles a day, no matter what the weather or other obstacles he and his team encountered. Every company has a specific performance goal it must hit year in and year out to be successful. Has the company identified that goal and committed to achieving it? How successful has the company been in achieving the goal? Measuring performance in the 20-Mile March means that leaders must develop a meaningful set of metrics and monitor them constantly.

(continued)

TABLE 17.1 12 Questions That Every Leader Should Address (*continued*)

6. *Where does empirical data tell us that we should be placing our big bets?* A company should invest major resources in a new initiative only if leaders already know that it is likely to succeed. That requires conducting low-cost, low-risk tests on a range of possible options ("shooting bullets") to figure out what works before unleashing the full power of the organization's resources on an initiative ("firing a cannonball"). The empirical evidence from the tests guides leaders' decisions about where to aim the cannon.

7. *What are the core values and core purpose on which we want to build this enterprise over the next 100 years?* The challenge is not only to build a company that can endure the long haul but also to build one that is *worthy* of enduring. Leaders must identify the core values and core purpose they would be willing to have their companies built around 100 years in the future, no matter what changes occur in the external environment.

8. *What is our 15- to 25-year BHAG?* A BHAG is "big hairy audacious goal." To build a great, enduring company, leaders must have a BHAG that is tangible, energizing, and highly focused and that people can understand immediately with little or no explanation. The BHAG should be linked to the company's core values and purpose. In addition, achieving the BHAG should require a company to make a quantum leap in its capabilities and its aptitude.

9. *What could kill our company, and how can we protect our flanks?* Paranoia is productive when it helps a business survive the inevitable bad surprises that come along and avoid the disasters they are capable of producing. The idea is for leaders *not* to be plagued by constant fear but to be sensitive to changing conditions in the environment and ask, "What if . . .?" Great leaders are always watching the horizon for the threat of storms—and opportunities. They also prepare for the inevitable stormy times by building up cash reserves.

10. *What should we stop doing to increase our discipline and focus?* Effective leaders are disciplined when it comes to pursuing business opportunities. They know that determining what their companies should *not* do is as important as determining what they *should* do. Although an "opportunity of a lifetime" may arise, excellent leaders know that pursuing it is meaningless (and downright dangerous) unless it fits inside the three circles of their "hedgehog."

11. *How can we increase our return on luck?* All companies are affected by both good luck and bad luck. What counts is what a company does with the luck it encounters—good *and* bad. How can the company glean the greatest benefit from good luck and minimize the damage that a run of bad luck causes?

12. *Are we becoming a Level 5 leadership team and cultivating a Level 5 management culture?* Collins calls the highest level of leadership Level 5, which builds enduring greatness in a company through a paradoxical blend of personal humility and professional will. "The central dimension for Level 5 is a leader who is ambitious first and foremost for the cause, for the company, for the work, not for himself or herself; and has an absolutely terrifying iron will to make good on that ambition," says Collins. Are you and your management team providing Level 5 leadership?

*Archilochus (c. 680 BC– c. 645 BC), Greek poet and mercenary. Translated by Isaiah Berlin, *The Hedgehog and the Fox: An Essay on Tolstoy's View of History*, © Isaiah Berlin 1953 (London: Weidenfeld and Nicolson Ltd., 1953).

Sources: Based on Bo Burlingham and Jim Collins, "Hedgehogs, Cannonballs, BHAGs, and Bullets," *Inc.*, June 2012, p. 71; Neil Phillips, "The Entrepreneur's Hedgehog," *The Coach Toolkit*, October 20, 2009, www.thecoachtoolkit.com/2009/10/the-entrepreneurs-hedgehog; Troy Schrock, "*Great by Choice* and Strategy Execution," *CEO Advantage*, December 8, 2011, www.ceoadvantage.com/blog/tag/jim-collins; Jim Collins, *Vision Framework*, 2002, p. 2; Stephen Blandino, "Productive Paranoia: Lesson #3 from Jim Collins' *Good to Great*," Stephen Blandino, January 3, 2012, http://stephenblandino .com/2012/01/productive-paranoia-lesson-3-from-jim-collins-great-by-choice.html; Jim Collins, "Jim Collins and Level 5 Leadership," *Management Issues*, January 3, 2006, www.management-issues.com/2006/5/24/mentors/jim-collins-and-level-5-leadership.asp; and "Roald Amundsen, Alone on the Ice," WGBH Educational Foundation, 1999, www.pbs.org/wgbh/amex/ice/peopleevents/pandeAMEX87.html.

Leading an organization, whatever its size, is one of the biggest challenges any entrepreneur faces. Yet for an entrepreneur, leadership success is one of the key determinants of a company's success. Research suggests that there is no single "best" style of leadership; the style a leader uses depends, in part, on the situation at hand. Some situations are best suited for a participative leadership style, but in others, an authoritarian style actually may be best. Research suggests that today's workers tend to respond more to adaptive, humble leaders who are results oriented and who take the time to cultivate other leaders in the organization.[22] The practice is known as **servant leadership**, a term coined by Robert Greenleaf in 1970. Humility is at the core of a servant leader's worldview. Servant leaders are servants *first* and leaders second, putting their employees and their employees' needs ahead of their own. They are concerned more about empowering others in the organization than about enhancing their own power bases. "Servant-leaders ask, 'What do people need? How can I help them to get it? What does my organization need to do? How can I help my organization to do it?'" explains Kent Keith, CEO of the Greenleaf Center for Servant Leadership. "Rather than embarking on a quest for personal power, servant-leaders embark on a quest to identify and meet the needs of others."[23] At ENGEO, a geotechnical and hydrologic engineering consulting firm in San Ramon, California, managers see themselves as servant leaders whose jobs are to "lead from the bottom" by supporting

servant leadership

a leadership style in which a leader takes on the role of servant first and leader second.

employees as they perform their daily work. That means managers train and empower workers to make decisions that in many other companies only managers are authorized to make.[24]

One business writer explains servant leadership this way:

> Real leadership is grounded in a higher level of self-interest that's tied to the interests of those who trust and follow their leader. It [creates] an atmosphere of confidence and light of clarity that flows from and surrounds the leader and that fills the room with the exhilaration of possibility.[25]

To tap into that exhilaration of possibility, an entrepreneurial leader must perform many important tasks, including the following:

- Hire the right employees for the entrepreneurial team and constantly improve their skills.
- Create a culture for motivating and retaining employees.
- Plan for "passing the torch" to the next generation of leadership.

 You Be the Consultant

What Happens When a CEO Loses His Voice and Changes His Leadership Style?

Kevin Hancock, 49, is the sixth-generation CEO of Hancock Lumber, a family business started in Casco, Maine, in 1848. In addition to owning 5,000 acres of forestland, the company operates 10 lumberyards across Maine and New Hampshire and three sawmills in Maine that turn out more board-feet of Eastern white pine lumber than any other company. Hancock Lumber, which exports 25 percent of its production, has received Maine International Trade Center's exporter of the year award, and the company is consistently listed as one of the best places to work in Maine. During the Great Recession, however, when home building and construction ground to a halt, Hancock Lumber's sales plummeted by 45 percent, and Kevin was forced to implement hiring freezes followed by painful layoffs at its sawmills and lumberyards to ensure the company's survival. He thought things could not get worse.

Then he contracted spasmodic dysphonia, a neurological disorder that causes throat spasms and is aggravated by stress, and it caused him to lose his voice.

He seriously contemplated stepping down as CEO of the company but decided against it. Today, both the construction industry and Hancock Lumber, now with 430 employees, have recovered, and Kevin remains CEO, a job he assumed at 32, after his father died. Despite his youth and the fact that he had worked only one year in the family business, Kevin was a natural leader and had a clear vision for Hancock Lumber. Employees and associates cite his authenticity and humility as two reasons for his success. Under his leadership, Hancock Lumber was one of the first companies in the industry to adopt lean manufacturing principles to ensure that it met the industry standard known as OTIF—delivering customers' orders "on time and in full." Hancock also focused on recognizing and rewarding employees for their accomplishments. He also did everything he could to shore up morale, especially during the recession.

By 2012, Kevin had steered Hancock Lumber back to financial stability, and he decided to step away from the company for a short time and go to Pine Ridge, South Dakota, to the Ogala Lakota Sioux Indian reservation, where he started a nonprofit organization, Seventh Power Foundation, to combat the poverty and social problems there. He also wrote a memoir, *Not for Sale: Finding Center in the Land of Crazy Horse*, about his self-discovery during this time. By unplugging from his duties as CEO and focusing on helping others, Hancock realized that losing his voice helped him become a better leader. Reinvigorated, he stepped back into his role as leader of Hancock Lumber but with a different perspective. Given the nature of his disability, he listened more than he talked. He began delegating decision making authority and sharing power with his employees and built a culture of individual responsibility. He was encouraged and somewhat surprised when he saw how many managers and employees had great ideas about ways to improve the company that they were willing to share—if someone simply asked. He also discovered that they were willing to work hard to make sure their ideas were successful. Kevin introduced a bonus program that rewards employees financially for hitting improvement targets on the accuracy of customers' orders, improving productivity, and increasing profits. In addition to earning cost-of-living raises, employees have seen their paychecks increase by more than 3 percent per year because of the bonus program. Increases in efficiency and productivity have allowed Hancock Lumber to shorten the average workweek from 47 hours to 41 hours. Overall, company sales are growing at an average of 8 percent per year. Looking back, Kevin says that losing his voice transformed his leadership style, which, in turn, transformed his company.

1. Identify at least three lessons that other leaders of small businesses can learn from Kevin Hancock's experience.

2. What other principles described in this chapter might Hancock Lumber benefit from? Explain.

Sources: Based on Jennifer Van Allen, "A Lumber Executive Loses His Voice and Finds a New Way of Working," *New York Times*, March 10, 2016, p. B7; "Hancock Named 'Best Places to Work' in Maine, 3 Years in a Row," Hancock Lumber, August 19, 2016, www.hancocklumber.com/hancock-named-best-places-work-maine-3-years-row/; "History of Hancock Lumber," Hancock Lumber, 2017, www.hancocklumber.com/culture/history/.

LO2

Describe the importance of hiring the right employees and how to avoid making hiring mistakes.

Building an Entrepreneurial Team: Hiring the Right Employees

As a company grows, the people an entrepreneur hires determine the heights to which the company can climb—or the depths to which it will plunge. Experienced managers understand that the quality of their workforce affects the company's ability to thrive. Acquiring that human capital, however, can be difficult. In a recent survey, 63 percent of employers say that they are concerned about a growing skills gap in the United States.[26] The problem is particularly acute for small companies, which usually cannot afford to match the salaries and benefit packages their larger rivals offer employees. Half of all small business owners say that they can find few or no qualified applicants for job openings (see Figure 17.1).[27] In addition, 42 percent of small business owners report that their companies have suffered negative impacts, including lower productivity (41 percent), lower quality of work (29 percent), and lost revenue (27 percent), due to extended job vacancies.[28]

The decision to hire a new employee is an important one for every business, but its impact is magnified many times in a small company. One new employee represents a significant investment and a significant risk. Adding just one or two employees can significantly increase a company's ability to generate sales. However, in a small company, one bad hiring decision can poison the entire culture, reduce employee productivity, and disrupt any sense of teamwork. Unfortunately, hiring mistakes in business are all too common: 75 percent of companies in the United States report that they made a "bad hire," a person who has a negative impact on the organization's productivity, performance, retention, or culture.[29] The culprit in most cases? The company's selection and hiring process.

Hiring mistakes are incredibly expensive, and no company, especially small ones, can afford too many of them. The higher the position is in an organization and the longer the tenure of the person who holds that position, the higher the cost associated with replacing a bad hire. Small business owners report that their hiring mistakes have a negative impact on employee morale (38 percent), result in lower productivity (36 percent), and produce both direct and indirect costs (25 percent), such as the cost of recruiting the bad hire, as well as recruiting and training another worker, compensation, and diminished customer satisfaction.[30] Replacing a bad hire often leads to burnout among existing employees, who must pick up the slack left by the vacancy. In addition, the poor work habits of bad hires are highly contagious, can infect everyone in the company (especially in a small company), and are difficult to eradicate. One study estimates the total cost of making a bad hire to be two to three times the employee's salary.[31] Even the best training program cannot overcome a flawed hiring decision. One study reported in the *Harvard Business Review* concludes that 80 percent of employee turnover is caused by bad hiring decisions.[32] The most common causes of a company's poor hiring decisions include the following:

- Managers relying on candidates' descriptions of themselves rather than requiring candidates to demonstrate their abilities.

- Managers failing to follow a consistent, evidence-based selection process. Employers often rely on intuition when making hiring decisions. In fact, 51 percent of managers say that

FIGURE 17.1

Percentage of Business Owners Who Cite Few or No Qualified Applicants for Job Openings

Source: Based on data from William C. Dunkelberg and Holly Wade, "NFIB Small Business Economic Trends," National Federation of Independent Businesses, July 2017, p. 9.

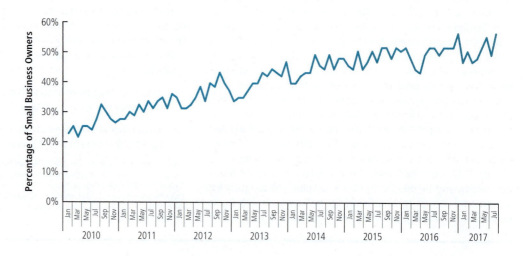

they know within the first five minutes of the start of an interview whether a candidate is a good fit for the position.[33]

- Managers failing to provide candidates with sufficient information about what the jobs for which they are hiring actually entail, which results in a job–skill mismatch.[34]

- Managers being so desperate to fill a position that they hire candidates who are not as qualified as they should be. The result is almost always an expensive hiring mistake for the company. Fifty-six percent of small business owners admit to committing this error.[35] Smart entrepreneurs maintain their hiring standards even when the pressure is on to fill a position. Jim Koch, who founded the Boston Beer Company in 1985, says that the worst hiring mistakes he has made in his career were "desperation hires" that inevitably were extremely costly to rectify.[36]

- Managers failing to check candidates' references.[37]

- A weak employer brand, which limits the size and quality of the applicant pool and reduces the probability of making a good hiring decision. Companies that invest in building a strong employer brand (e.g., becoming known as a great place to work) are three times more likely to make better hiring decisions.[38]

- Managers succumbing to pressure to fill a job quickly. The average time required to fill jobs across all industries in the United States is 27.8 days, a significant increase from 15.4 days in 2009.[39]

ENTREPRENEURIAL PROFILE: Dane Atkinson: SumAll Dane Atkinson, cofounder of SumAll, a business analytics company in New York City, believes that hiring "fast" increases the odds of hiring mistakes. At SumAll, every new employee goes through a 45-day probationary period, during which time he or she is assigned to a mentor and receives regular reviews from a dedicated selection committee. At the end of the probationary period, selection committee members vote on whether to hire the candidate permanently. If the candidate passes that vote, the remainder of the employees in the company vote, and one "no" vote sends the candidate packing. About 70 percent of candidates make it through the process and are hired permanently. The process works; in the two years since it has been in place, only one employee has left the company.[40] ∎

As crucial as finding good employees is to a small company's future, it is no easy task because entrepreneurs face a labor shortage, particularly among knowledge-based workers. The severity of this shortage will become more acute as Baby Boomers retire in increasing numbers and the growth rate of the U.S. labor force slows (see Figure 17.2). These demographic changes have created a skilled worker gap in which small businesses already find themselves pursuing the best talent not just across the United States but around the globe. A recent study by ManpowerGroup reports that 40 percent of companies around the world have difficulty

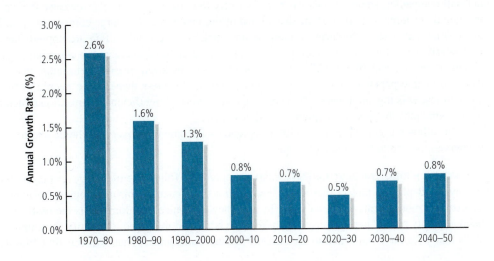

FIGURE 17.2

Annual Growth Rate in the U.S. Workforce by Decade

Source: Bureau of Labor Statistics, 2012.

filling jobs because of a lack of available talent, the highest level since 2007. The United States is above the global average, with 46 percent of companies having difficulty filling jobs because of a lack of talent.[41]

Unfilled jobs are expensive; the average company loses more than $14,000 for every job that is vacant for at least three months. Employers report that their extended job vacancies result in a negative impact on employee morale (41 percent), work not getting done (40 percent), delays in delivery times (34 percent), diminished customer service (30 percent), lower quality of work because the remaining employees are overworked (30 percent), and diminished employee motivation (29 percent).[42]

High employee turnover rates cost companies as well. The voluntary turnover rate for employees is 11.6 percent, which means the average employee's tenure at a company is slightly more than 8.5 years.[43] (A recent survey reports that the members of Generation Z, who are starting to enter the workforce, say that the appropriate amount of time to spend in their first job is no more than *three* years.[44]) The average cost that a company incurs when an employee leaves is 21.4 percent of the employee's annual salary for employees who earn less than $50,000 annually and 213 percent of the annual salary for an executive who leaves.[45] A company with 25 employees can expect to lose, on average, about 3 employees per year. If those employees earn an average of $45,000, the cost to the company is $28,890 per year ($45,000 × 21.4% = $9,630 per employee × 3 employees = $28,890). To reduce their employee turnover rates, companies can employ the following strategies:

- Provide rewarding and challenging work.
- Pay employees fairly.
- Provide training opportunities and mentoring relationships.
- Offer more and faster opportunities for upward mobility in the organization, which is especially important to Millennial workers.
- Offer flexible work schedules.
- Provide simple (and inexpensive) rewards such as thank-you notes for extra effort or "good job" notes for jobs well done.
- Conduct exit interviews when employees leave to determine areas that require improvement.

Smart business owners recognize that the companies that have the most talented, best-trained, and most motivated workforces will be the winners.

How to Hire Winners

Conducting job searches is time-consuming and expensive; the average cost for a company to fill an open position is $4,129.[46] Even though the importance of hiring decisions is magnified in small companies, small businesses are most likely to make hiring mistakes because they lack the human resources experts and the disciplined hiring procedures that large companies have. In many small businesses, the hiring process is informal, and the results often are unpredictable. In the early days of a company, entrepreneurs rarely take the time to create job descriptions and specifications; instead, they usually hire people because they know or trust them rather than for their job or interpersonal skills. As the company grows, business owners hire people to fit in around these existing employees, often creating a very unusual, inefficient organization structure built around jobs that are poorly planned and designed.

The following guidelines can help entrepreneurs become employers of choice and to hire winners as they build their team of employees.

COMMIT TO HIRING THE BEST TALENT Smart entrepreneurs follow the old adage "A players hire A players; B players hire C players." They are not threatened by hiring people who may be smarter and more talented than they are. In fact, they recognize that doing so is the best way to build a quality team. One recent survey asked CEOs around the globe to identify the employee skills that were most important to the success of their companies. What skill sets do CEOs say are essential to employees' success? Problem-solving skills, leadership ability, the capacity to collaborate with others, creativity and innovation, and adaptability.[47]

ELEVATE RECRUITING TO A STRATEGIC POSITION IN THE COMPANY The recruiting process is the starting point for building quality into a company. Assembling a quality workforce begins with a sound recruiting effort. By investing time and money in the crucial planning phase of the staffing process, entrepreneurs can generate spectacular savings down the road by hiring the best talent. Recruiting is so important that many entrepreneurs are actively involved in the process themselves. Visionary entrepreneurs *never* stop recruiting because top-quality talent is hard to find and is extremely valuable. Unfortunately, only 38 percent of hiring managers say they constantly recruit. Their principal barrier: lack of time.[48]

Attracting a pool of qualified job candidates requires not only constant attention but also creativity, especially among smaller companies that often find it difficult to match the more generous offers large companies make. With a sound recruiting strategy and a willingness to look in new places, however, smaller companies *can* hire and retain high-caliber employees. The following techniques help:

Look inside the company first. One of the best sources for top prospects is inside the company itself. A promotion-from-within policy serves as an incentive for existing workers to upgrade their skills and produce results. In addition, an entrepreneur already knows the employee's work habits, and the employee already understands the company's culture. Recruiters rank candidates hired from within their companies as the highest-quality employees.[49] Unfortunately, Only 48 percent of companies invest in training and developing existing employees to take on hard-to-fill jobs.[50]

Look for employees with whom your customers can identify. For an entrepreneur whose company sells women's shoes, hiring young women straight out of college to manage the company's social media presence makes sense; however, hiring young women for sales positions in a company that sells makeup to middle-aged women does not. At the Vermont Country Store, a business in Rockingham, Vermont, now in its fifth generation of family ownership, half of the employees are older than 50, which benefits the company because the average customer is in his or her 60s.[51]

Encourage employee referrals. To cope with the shortage of available talent, many companies are offering their employees (and others) bonuses for referring candidates who come to work and prove to be valuable employees. Employees serve as reliable screens because they do not want to jeopardize their reputations with their employer. Employee referrals have proved to be an excellent source of quality employees. In fact, recruiters rank candidates hired as a result of employee referrals second in quality only to internal hires.[52] Although employee referrals are the source of only 7 percent of applicants, they account for 40 percent of those hired. Employees hired through employee referrals also have higher retention rates (46 percent) than those hired through job Web sites and job boards (33 percent).[53] Workers hired as a result of employee referrals are a better fit with a company's culture and values and cost less to hire than those from other sources.[54] Salesforce.com, a company based in San Francisco that provides cloud-based customer relationship management software, finds 58 percent of its new hires through referrals from existing employees.[55] To encourage employee referrals, many companies offer incentives for successful hires. Rewards companies offer to employees for successful referrals range from cash and iPads to big-screen televisions and exotic vacations. Salesforce.com hosts Oktoberfest-inspired "bring a referral" happy hour events and awards employees free trips to a destination of their choice and $5,000 spending money for successful referrals.[56]

Make employment advertisements stand out. Getting employment ads noticed in traditional media is becoming more difficult because they get lost in the swarm of ads from other companies.

ENTREPRENEURIAL PROFILE: Amy Rees Anderson: MediConnect Global When Amy Rees Anderson was CEO of MediConnect Global, a fast-growing medical records retrieval and electronic document management company, she created several offbeat videos that featured brief, homemade clips of employees demonstrating their silly and unusual talents (for example, one employee balanced a toilet plunger on one finger and then suctioned it to his stomach) to make her company's recruiting ad stand out and to communicate the sense of fun in the company's culture. The videos opened with a graphic that said, "Featuring the Elite Talent of MediConnect Global" before showing the employees' "talents" and closing with a graphic that said, "What's your elite talent? Apply now." The low-cost ads were successful, not only producing many new hires that Anderson says the company would have missed otherwise but also improving employee morale.[57] ∎

Use multiple channels to recruit talent. Although newspaper ads still top employers' list of job postings, many businesses are successfully attracting candidates through other media, particularly the Internet. The goal is to spread wide a company's recruiting net. Posting job listings on the company's Web page; on career-oriented Web sites such as Monster, CareerBuilder, and others; and on its social media accounts not only expands a small company's reach far beyond ads in a local newspaper but also is very inexpensive. Currently, 84 percent of companies use social media to recruit employees, a significant increase from 51 percent in 2011. The most common social media recruiting tools are LinkedIn (96 percent), Facebook (66 percent), and Twitter (53 percent).[58] Mobile apps provide another mechanism for reaching job candidates. One recent survey reports that 41 percent of smart phone owners have used their phones as part of the job search process.[59] Despite candidates' job search expectations using mobile devices, 55 percent of companies do not offer mobile-friendly career Web sites.[60]

Recruit on campus. For many employers, college and university campuses remain an excellent source of workers, especially for entry-level positions. College campuses are prime recruiting grounds for small companies. In a recent survey, 44 percent of college graduates say a small or medium-size business is the ideal place to work (compared to 14 percent who prefer to work for a large corporation).[61] When properly planned, on-campus recruiting is efficient; after screening résumés, a recruiter can interview a dozen or more high-potential students in just one day by conducting on-campus interviews. Entrepreneurs must ensure that the recruiters they send to campuses are professional, polished, and prepared to represent their companies well because students' impression of a recruiter is the primary determinant of their perception of the company.

Forge relationships with schools and other sources of workers. Internships and co-op programs can be excellent sources of future employees. As colleges and universities offer students more internship and co-op opportunities, small businesses can benefit from hosting one or more students for a semester or for a summer. Internships and co-op programs offer companies low-risk opportunities to "test-drive" potential employees, observe students' work habits, and sell top performers on permanent positions after graduation. A recent study by the National Association of Colleges and Employers reports that employers offer full-time jobs to 72.7 percent of their interns, and 85.2 percent of student interns accept the job offers from the companies where they work.[62] Stephen Spielberg, the famous movie director behind hits such as *E.T., the Extraterrestrial*, *Raiders of the Lost Ark*, and *Jaws*, started his film career as an intern at Universal Studios, where he made his first film, *Amblin*.[63]

ENTREPRENEURIAL PROFILE: Ron Reichen: Precision Body & Paint Ron Reichen, owner of Precision Body & Paint, an auto body shop in Beaverton, Oregon, with more than $10 million in annual sales, realized that the master technicians who made his business successful were growing older. His attempts to recruit master technicians were mostly unsuccessful, so Reichen decided to launch a program based on a European apprenticeship model that brings in paid interns whom Reichen trains and, over the course of several years, develops into master technicians. Precision Body & Paint agrees to invest $20,000 ($4,000 per year for five years) into each employee's training and pay him or her while the employee learns auto body repair skills by working next to the company's most seasoned experts. After five years, the employees "graduate" from the program and become either midlevel or master technicians, positions in which they can earn as much as $100,000 annually. Since launching the program, the average age of

Reichen's employees has decreased by 20 percent, and the company's retention rate has increased to an impressive 89 percent.[64] ■

Recruit "retired" workers. The population (and, hence, the workforce) in the United States is aging, and life expectancies are increasing. In the United States, nearly one in five workers age 65 or older (roughly "retirement age") is working, but experts forecast that by 2022, that percentage will increase to nearly one in four workers.[65] Many of these Baby Boom Generation employees continue to work past their retirement ages to support their lifestyles, and small businesses should be ready to hire them. With a lifetime of work experience, time on their hands, and a strong work ethic, "retired" workers can be the ideal solution to many entrepreneurs' labor problems and can be valuable assets to small firms.

Consider using offbeat recruiting techniques. To attract the workers they need to support their growing businesses, some entrepreneurs have resorted to creative recruiting techniques. As part of its recruiting efforts, Range Resources Corporation, a natural gas company, sponsors a unique float in the local Fourth of July parade, invites prospective employees to mingle with current employees at cookouts, and sends employee representatives prepared to talk about working at the company to more than 1,000 community events each year.[66] Other ideas include the following:

- Sending young recruiters to mingle with college students on spring break. Deloitte, an accounting and consulting firm, takes dozens of college students to various locations for spring break. Rather than party on the beach, however, the students work alongside Deloitte employees in a program called Maximum Impact, focusing on community projects ranging from sprucing up community parks and repairing homes for the elderly to preparing taxes and assisting in soup kitchens. Sara Ferguson, who took part in a Maximum Impact trip to Galveston, Texas, while she was a college student, now works for Deloitte. Ferguson says the experience gave her unique insight into the company's culture and assured her that Deloitte was the type of company for which she wanted to work.[67]

- Using social networks, such as LinkedIn, Facebook, Twitter, and company blogs, to reach potential employees, especially young ones.

- Sponsoring a "job-shadowing" program that gives students and other prospects the opportunity to observe firsthand the nature of the work and the work environment.

- Inviting prospective employees to a company tailgating party at a sports event.

- Inviting potential candidates to participate in a company-sponsored event. Corey Reese, cofounder of Ness Computing, a company that makes practical apps for the iPhone, sponsors "hackathon" events on college campuses that attract the technologically savvy computer software engineers he must hire for the fast-growing company.[68]

- Posting "what it's like to work here" videos created by current employees on the company's Facebook page, YouTube, and other video sites.

- Inviting potential candidates to meet and mingle with a company's workforce at informal, fun events. Ness Computing regularly invites potential employees to company-sponsored barbecues and picnics.

- Keeping a file of all of the workers mentioned in the "People on the Move" column in the business section of the local newspaper and then contacting them a year later to see whether they are happy in their jobs.[69]

Offer what workers want. Adequate compensation and benefits are important considerations for job candidates, but other, less tangible factors also weigh heavily in a prospect's decision to accept a job. To recruit effectively, entrepreneurs must consider what a McKinsey and Company study calls the "employee value proposition," the factors that would make the ideal employee want to work for their businesses. It is particularly important for small businesses to understand what Millennial workers, who now make up the largest part of the

TABLE 17.2 Traditional Work Culture Versus Results-Oriented Work Environment (ROWE) Culture

Traditional Work Culture	ROWE Culture
Culture of entitlement	Culture of opportunity
Focus on schedules and time off	Focus on work
Subjective conversations	Objective conversations
Individual focus	Team/organization focus
Time as the currency of work	Results as the currency of work
Freedom without accountability	Accountability first
Managers saying "All hands on deck"	Results coaches fostering the attitude "Everyone on point"
Managed flexibility (permission-based)	100% autonomous and accountable
No results? No more flexible work.	No results? No job.

Source: Based on Ann Diab, "Five Flexible Work Strategies and the Companies That Use Them," *Fast Company*, March 30, 2016, www.fastcompany.com/3058344/5-flexible-work-strategies-and-the-companies-who-use-them.

workforce, consider important. After salary, the most important factors to Millennial workers when considering a job are proper work–life balance, opportunities for advancement, flexible work schedules or locations, and deriving a sense of meaning from their work.[70] Flexible work schedules and telecommuting that allow employees to balance the demands of work and family life attract quality workers to small companies. Employees agree; one-third of workers say they have left a job because it did not offer flexibility.[71] Research shows that workers who control their schedules have higher levels of job satisfaction, lower levels of stress, and lower absenteeism rates.[72] Flexible work schedules fit into companies in which the culture follows a "results-only work environment" (ROWE) that measures employees' results, output, and performance rather than the traditional input measures, such as the number of hours worked or physical presence in an office. Table 17.2 shows the differences in the philosophies of a traditional work culture and a ROWE culture.

Many of the companies on *Fortune*'s "100 Best Companies to Work For" list offer low-cost but valuable (from their employees' perspectives) benefits, such as take-home meals, personal concierge services that coordinate everything from dry cleaning to auto maintenance for employees, compressed workweeks, and onsite fitness centers.[73]

ENTREPRENEURIAL PROFILE: Cedric Savarese, FormAssembly FormAssembly, founded by Cedric Savarese, is headquartered in Bloomington, Indiana. The company, which allows users to create custom forms using drag-and-drop technology from any Web browser, considers itself to be a "remote-first" company. FormAssembly's 30-plus employees, most of whom are Millennials, work from seven countries and 12 different states in the United States. To attract the employees he needs, Savarese focuses on employees' results and gives them the flexibility to set their own schedules.[74] ∎

Table 17.3 provides examples of affordable alternative benefits that small businesses can offer employees.

Create Practical Job Descriptions and Job Specifications

Business owners must recognize that what they do *before* they interview candidates for a position determines to a great extent how successful they will be at hiring winners. The first step is to perform a **job analysis**, the process by which a firm determines the duties and nature of the jobs to be filled and the skills and experience required of the people who are to fill them. Without a proper job analysis, a hiring decision is, at best, a coin toss. The first step in conducting a job analysis is to develop a **job description**, a written statement of the duties, responsibilities, reporting relationships, working conditions, and methods and techniques as well as materials and equipment used in a job. A results-oriented job description explains what a job entails and

job analysis
the process by which a firm determines the duties and nature of the jobs to be filled and the skills and experience required of the people who are to fill them.

job description
a written statement of the duties, responsibilities, reporting relationships, working conditions, and methods and techniques as well as materials and equipment used in a job.

TABLE 17.3 Affordable Alternative Benefits

Although small companies typically cannot match their larger rivals on the employee benefits packages they offer, with some creativity, entrepreneurs can provide less expensive options that increase employee retention, motivation, and morale.

Perhaps You Cannot Offer . . .	But You Might . . .
Tuition reimbursement for college classes	Implement a flex-time schedule that allows employees to attend classes at a nearby college or university
Paid leave	Use job sharing so that two part-time employees share one full-time job
Comprehensive health insurance	Hold a wellness day in which a local health care provider performs basic health screens for employees
An onsite fitness center	Set up a basketball goal in a corner of the parking lot or a ping-pong table in the office or negotiate a reduced fee for employees at the local YMCA
401(k) retirement plan with employer match	Invite a local investment adviser to provide financial counseling and retirement advice to employees
Counseling services	Allow employees to bring their dogs to work; research shows that allowing pets in the workplace reduces stress and increases job satisfaction
Childcare subsidies	Negotiate discounts at a local preschool for employees' children or allow employees to telecommute from home several days a week

Sources: Based on Paula Andruss, "Affordable Alternatives," *Entrepreneur*, May 2012, p. 57; "Pets at Work Keep Workers Happy," *U.S. News and World Report*, April 2, 2012, http://health.usnews.com/health-news/news/articles/2012/04/02/pets-at-work-keep-workers-happy.

 You Be the Consultant

Avoid These Hiring Mistakes

One week after hiring a shipping manager for her online personalized gifts business, The Younique Boutique, Brina Bujkovsky knew something was wrong. Other employees saw the new hire slipping in and out of the building with a backpack. One day at lunch, he left to "make a personal call" but did not return for several hours. When he finally showed up, he was extremely intoxicated. Bujkovsky fired him immediately.

Hiring mistakes like the one Bujkovsky made are quite common and can be expensive, especially for small companies. The problem is intensified when job markets are tight; half of small business owners say that they can find few or no qualified applicants for the positions they are trying to fill. Spotting problem employees before they are hired, however, is not always easy because bad employees often are adept at hiding their problems until well after they are hired. What steps can entrepreneurs take to avoid making critical hiring mistakes? Consider these:

- **Know what you want.** Before hiring anyone, an entrepreneur should create a job description and a job specification. These important documents spell out the duties and responsibilities of the job and define the skills, traits, and experience of the ideal candidate.

- **Don't be in a hurry.** Rushing through the hiring process almost always guarantees a hiring mistake. Hiring a new employee is a long-term commitment; make sure you devote sufficient time to making the right decision. Employers should avoid rushing to conclusions in interviews;

50 percent of employers say that they need only five minutes to determine whether a candidate is a good fit for a position.

- **Involve others in the selection process.** Involving others in the selection process reduces the probability that "warning signs" about a candidate will go unnoticed. After her hiring mistake, Bujkovsky changed the selection process in her company to include her entire team in the interview process.

- **Prepare for the interview.** Job candidates know that they should prepare for an interview, and the same goes for the employer. After creating a job description and a job specification for the position, an entrepreneur should develop a series of questions designed to reveal candidates' skills, abilities, and fit for the job—and for the company.

- **Listen carefully to candidates' answers and observe their body language.** Once entrepreneurs have a set of prepared questions that are designed to probe each candidate's experience, personality, background, and work ethic, they listen carefully (even for what candidates don't say) and watch their body language during the interview.

- **"Test drive" candidates whenever possible.** Internships and apprenticeships allow employers to observe candidates to determine whether they are likely to make good full-time employees. When internships or apprenticeships are not practical, some companies use interviews that put

(continued)

You Be the Consultant *(continued)*

candidates into situations they are likely to encounter on the job to see how they handle them.

- **Check references—always.** Checking candidates' references takes time, but the payoff can be huge. Some companies check "one-off" references, people with whom a candidate worked but who are not listed as references on the application. Asking listed references for other potential references and searching social media sites such as LinkedIn and Facebook can produce these valuable unofficial references.

- **Look for candidates' profiles on social media platforms.** Social media can be useful not only for finding candidates but also for learning more about them. Although it is not a good idea to ask for candidates' social media passwords (it actually is illegal in 26 states), reviewing their social media profiles can be quite revealing. A study by Career-Builder reports that 60 percent of employers investigate job candidates' social networking sites (a significant increase from 22 percent in 2008) and that 49 percent have discovered something there that caused them to reject a candidate. Conversely, 32 percent of hiring managers say they

found information on social media that led them to hire a candidate.

1. Why are hiring mistakes so expensive for companies, particularly small businesses?

2. Suppose your best friend is about to hire someone to work in his or her company. List at least three other tips that will enable him or her to avoid making a hiring mistake.

Sources: Based on Nikoletta Bika, "Interviewing Techniques: 10 Mistakes Experienced Interviewers Avoid," *Workable*, March 15, 2016, https://resources.workable.com/blog/job-interview-techniques-10-mistakes-experienced-interviewers-learned-avoid; "Number of Employers Using Social Media to Screen Candidates Has Increased 500 Percent over Last Decade," CareerBuilder, April 28, 2016, www.careerbuilder.com/share/aboutus/pressreleasesdetail.aspx?ed=12/31/2016&id=pr945&sd=4/28/2016; "Employers Share Strangest Interview Mishaps and Biggest Body Language Mistakes," CareerBuilder, January 14, 2016, www.careerbuilder.com/share/aboutus/pressreleasesdetail.aspx?sd=1/14/2016&siteid=cbpr&sc_cmp1=cb_pr929_&id=pr929&ed=12/31/2016; "5 Ways to Spot Bad Employees Before They're Hired," *All Business Experts*, January 1, 2013, http://experts.allbusiness.com/5-ways-to-spot-bad-employees-before-theyre-hired/#.U6w6C0BrTOs; *2013 Social Recruiting Survey Results*, Jobvite, 2013, p. 2; Kristin Piombino, "Social Media Costs Candidates Their Jobs, Report Says," *Ragan*, July 9, 2013, www.ragan.com/Main/Articles/Social_media_costs_candidates_their_jobs_report_sa_46973.aspx; Greg Fisher, "Eight Reasons You Made a Bad Hire," *Perspectives*, June 24, 2013, http://blog.betterweekdays.com/blog/employers/324758/eight-reasons-you-made-a-bad-hire.

---

the duties the person filling it is expected to perform. A detailed job description includes a job title, job summary, primary responsibilities and duties, nature of supervision, the job's relationship to others in the company, working conditions, the job's location, definitions of job-specific terms, and a description of the company and its culture.

Preparing job descriptions is a task that most small business owners overlook; however, this may be one of the most important parts of the hiring process because it creates a blueprint for the job. Without this blueprint, managers tend to hire the person with experience whom they like the best. Sherri Comstock, owner of The Cheshire Cat and The Spotted Crocodile, two jewelry and gift boutiques in Grayslake, Illinois, admits to failing to write meaningful job descriptions. She says that if the position is not well defined before hiring someone to fill it, a bad fit is all but inevitable.[75]

Useful sources of information for writing job descriptions include the manager's knowledge of the job, the worker(s) currently holding the job, and the *Dictionary of Occupational Titles*, which is available online (www.occupationalinfo.org). This dictionary, published by the U.S. Department of Labor, lists more than 20,000 job titles and descriptions and serves as a useful tool for getting a small business owner started when writing job descriptions. Internet searches can also assist in finding resources for writing job descriptions. Entrepreneurs can find templates and descriptions they can easily modify to fit their companies' needs. Table 17.4 provides an example of the description drawn from the *Dictionary of Occupational Titles* for an unusual job, a worm picker.

job specification
a written statement of the qualifications and characteristics needed for a job, stated in terms such as education, skills, and experience.

The second objective of a job analysis is to create a **job specification**, a written statement of the qualifications and characteristics needed for a job stated in terms such as education, skills, and experience. A job specification shows the small business manager the kind of person to recruit and establishes the standards an applicant must meet to be hired. In essence, it is a written "success profile" of the ideal employee. Does the person have to be a good listener, empathetic, well organized, decisive, and a "self-starter"? Should he or she have experience in Python programming? One of the best ways to develop this success profile is to study the top performers currently working for the company and to identify the characteristics that make them successful. Before hiring new sales representatives, sales managers at Blackboard, Inc., a Washington, DC, company that sells software for the educational market, study their top sales producers to

TABLE 17.4 A Sample Job Description from the *Dictionary of Occupational Titles*

Worm Picker—gathers worms to be used as fish bait; walks about grassy areas, such as gardens, parks, and golf courses, and picks up earthworms (commonly called dew worms and nightcrawlers). Sprinkles chlorinated water on lawn to cause worms to come to the surface and locates worms by use of lantern or flashlight. Counts worms, sorts them, and packs them into containers for shipment. (# 413.687-010)

identify the characteristics they demonstrate in four areas—skills, experience, knowledge, and personality traits. Table 17.5 provides an example that links the tasks for a sales representative's job (drawn from the job description) to the traits or characteristics an entrepreneur identified as necessary to succeed in that job. These traits become the foundation for writing the job specification.

Plan an Effective Interview

Once an entrepreneur knows what to look for in a job candidate, he or she can develop a plan for conducting an informative job interview. Research shows that planned interviews produce much more reliable hiring results than unstructured interviews, in which interviewers "freewheel" the questions they ask candidates. Unstructured interviews produce no better results than flipping a coin to decide whether to hire a candidate, but structured interviews produce highly valid hiring results.[76] Employers say that a flawed interview process plays the most important role in poor hiring decisions.[77] Too often, business owners go into an interview unprepared, and as a result, they fail to get the information they need to judge the candidate's qualifications, qualities, and suitability for the job. A common symptom of failing to prepare for an interview is that the interviewer, rather than the candidate, does most of the talking.

Conducting an effective interview requires an entrepreneur to know what he or she wants to get out of the interview in the first place and to develop a series of questions to extract that information. The following guidelines will help entrepreneurs develop interview questions that will give them meaningful insight into an applicant's qualifications, personality, and character:

> ***Involve others in the interview process.*** Solo interviews are prone to errors. A better process is to involve other employees, particularly employees with whom the prospect would be working, in the interview process either individually or as part of a panel.

ENTREPRENEURIAL PROFILE: Richard Sheridan: Menlo Innovations At Menlo Innovations, a successful custom software company in Ann Arbor, Michigan, collaboration among workers is paramount because employees typically work together on projects in pairs all day. The company's hiring process reflects its emphasis on collaboration in what cofounder Richard Sheridan calls "extreme interviewing." Candidates team up in pairs to tackle three 20-minute exercises that are typical of the projects they would work on at Menlo Innovations, and employees and managers observe them. To drive home the company's focus on teamwork, each team of candidates shares a single pencil. After an extreme interviewing

TABLE 17.5 Linking Tasks from a Job Description to the Traits Necessary to Perform a Job Successfully

Job Task	Trait or Characteristic
Generate and close new sales	"Outgoing"; persuasive; friendly
Make 15 "cold calls" per week	"Self-starter"; determined; optimistic; independent; confident
Analyze customers' needs and recommend proper equipment	Good listener; patient; empathetic
Counsel customers about options and features needed	Organized; polished speaker; "other oriented"
Prepare and explain financing methods	Honest; "numbers oriented"; comfortable with computers and spreadsheets
Retain existing customers	Customer oriented; relationship builder

session, employees collectively decide which candidates to invite back. Those selected spend a day working for pay with two employees on a project. Those who pass that test come back for a three-week trial employment period. Only after completing the trial successfully do they become Menlo Innovations employees.[78] ■

Develop a series of core questions and ask them of every candidate. To give the screening process more consistency, smart business owners rely on a set of relevant questions they ask in every interview. Of course, they also customize each interview using impromptu questions based on an individual candidate's responses. "The most effective way to hire fantastic, loyal employees who will fit into your company culture and help you meet your goals is to hire them for their inherent abilities (which can't be taught), such as personality, learning style, and core values," says Mike Michalowicz, a successful serial entrepreneur who started his first business at age 24. "You do this by identifying behavior patterns during the interview process. If you ask questions designed to identify the patterns, you can predict how prospective employees will behave."[79]

Ask open-ended questions (including on-the-job "scenarios") rather than questions calling for "yes" or "no" answers. These types of questions are most effective because they encourage candidates to talk about their work and volunteer experience in a way that will disclose the presence or the absence of the traits and characteristics the business owner is seeking. Peter Bregman, CEO of Bregman Partners, a company that helps businesses implement change, says one of the most revealing questions that an interviewer can ask candidates is, "What do you do in your spare time?" The answer to this question offers unique insight that helps interviewers differentiate between those who are merely competent and those who are stars. Research shows that candidates who participate in the greatest number of activities outside work, especially volunteer tasks, are also the most innovative and most productive employees on the job.[80] Bregman points to the example of Captain C. B. "Sully" Sullenberger, the pilot who safely landed a disabled jet with 155 passengers on the Hudson River, using skills he learned from his hobby: flying gliders.[81]

situational interview
an interview in which the interviewer gives candidates a typical job-related situation (e.g., a job simulation) to see how they respond to it.

Create hypothetical situations that candidates would be likely to encounter on the job and ask (or better yet watch) how they would handle them. Building the interview around these kinds of questions gives the owner a preview of the candidate's actual work habits and attitudes. For example, someone hiring for a customer service position might ask candidates, "Tell me about a time when you failed to meet a customer's expectations and what you did about it." Some companies take this idea a step further and put candidates into a simulated work environment to see how they prioritize activities and handle mail, e-mail, and a host of "real-world" problems they are likely to encounter on the job, ranging from complaining customers to problematic employees. Known as **situational interviews**, their goal is to give interviewers keener insight into how candidates would perform in the work environment.

Courtesy of Twilio

ENTREPRENEURIAL PROFILE: Jeff Lawson: Twilio Jeff Lawson, CEO and cofounder of Twilio, a company based in San Francisco that provides a cloud-based communications platform that routes telephone calls, text, and multimedia messages for businesses, wants employees who will support the company's "Nine Things," the nine core values ("Live the spirit of challenge" and "Create experiences" are two of them) that sustain Twilio. Before receiving a job offer from Twilio, all prospective employees must resolve 20 customer service calls and figure out how to build an app using Twilio's platform, even if they have never written computer code before.[82] ■

Probe for specific examples in the candidate's past work experience that demonstrate the necessary traits and characteristics. A common mistake interviewers make is failing to get candidates to provide the detail they need to make an informed decision. Experienced interviewers use the phrase "Tell me more" to harvest meaningful information about candidates.

Ask candidates to describe a recent success and a recent failure and how they dealt with them. Smart entrepreneurs look for candidates who describe their successes and their failures with equal enthusiasm because they know that peak performers put as much into their failures as they do their successes and usually learn something valuable from their failures.

Arrange a "noninterview" setting that allows several employees to observe the candidate in an informal setting. Giving candidates a plant tour, setting up a coffee break, or taking them to lunch gives more people a chance to judge a candidate's interpersonal skills and personality outside the formal interview process. These informal settings can be very revealing.

ENTREPRENEURIAL PROFILE: Scott Lerner: Solixr Scott Lerner, founder of Solixr, an all-natural energy drink company, says that he learns a great deal about job candidates in noninterview settings and often invites candidates to several lunches or to accompany him on in-store demonstrations. These informal settings give Lerner better insight into candidates' qualifications and personalities and how well they will fit into his company's culture.[83] ■

Table 17.6 shows an example of some interview questions one business owner uses to uncover the traits and characteristics he seeks in a top-performing sales representative.

Conduct the Interview

An effective interview contains three phases: breaking the ice, asking questions, and selling the candidate on the company.

BREAKING THE ICE In the opening phase of the interview, the manager's primary job is to defuse the tension that exists because of the nervousness of both parties. Many skilled interviewers use the job description to explain the nature of the job and the company's culture to the applicant. Then they use "icebreakers," questions about a hobby or special interest, to get the candidate to relax and begin talking.

ASKING QUESTIONS During the second phase of the interview, the employer asks the questions from the question bank to determine the applicant's suitability for the job. The interviewer's primary job at this point is to listen. Effective interviewers spend about 25 percent of the interview talking and about 75 percent listening. They also take notes during the interview to help them ask follow-up questions based on a candidate's comments and to evaluate a candidate after the interview is over. Experienced interviewers also pay close attention to a candidate's nonverbal clues, or body language, during the interview. They know candidates may be able to say exactly what they want with their words, but their body language does not lie!

Some of the most valuable interview questions are designed to gain insight into a candidate's creativity and capacity for abstract thinking. Known as **puzzle interviews**, their goal is to determine how candidates think by asking them offbeat questions, such as, "You are shrunk to the height of a nickel and thrown into a blender. Your mass is reduced so that your density is the

puzzle interview
an interview that includes offbeat questions to determine how job candidates think and reason and to judge their capacity for creativity.

TABLE 17.6 Interview Questions for Candidates for a Sales Representative Position

Trait or Characteristic	Question
Outgoing; persuasive; friendly; self-starter; determined; optimistic; independent; confident	How do you persuade reluctant prospects to buy?
Good listener; patient; empathetic; organized; polished speaker; "other" oriented	What would you say to a fellow salesperson who was getting more than his share of rejections and was having difficulty getting appointments?
Honest; customer oriented; relationship builder	How do you feel when someone questions the truth of what you say? What do you do in such situations?
Other questions:	If you owned a company, why would you hire yourself?
	If you were head of your department, what would you do differently?
	How do you recognize the contributions of others in your department?
	If you weren't in sales, what other job would you be in?

same as usual. The blades start moving in 60 seconds. What do you do?" (This is a classic interview question at Google.) "How many golf balls can fit into a school bus?" is another favorite Google interview question.[84] Other companies use questions such as "A penguin walks through that door wearing a sombrero. What does he say, and why is he here?" (asked at Clark Construction Group), "If we came to your house for dinner, what would you prepare for us?" (a question asked by interviewers at Trader Joe's), "How would you design Bill Gates's bathroom?" (a favorite at Microsoft), or "What is the angle of the two hands on a clock when the time is 11:50?" (asked at Bank of America).[85] The logic and creativity that candidates use to derive answers to these questions is much more important than the answers themselves.

Entrepreneurs must be careful to avoid asking candidates illegal questions. At one time, interviewers could ask wide-ranging questions covering just about every area of an applicant's background. Today, interviewing is a veritable minefield of legal liabilities waiting to explode in an unsuspecting interviewer's face. Although the Equal Employment Opportunity Commission, the government agency responsible for enforcing employment laws, does not outlaw specific questions, it does recognize that asking some questions can result in employment discrimination. If a candidate files charges of employment discrimination against a company, the burden of proof shifts to the employer to prove that all pre-employment questions are job related and nondiscriminatory. In addition, many states have passed laws that forbid the use of certain questions or screening tools in interviews. To avoid trouble, business owners should keep in mind why they are asking a particular question. The goal of an interview is to identify individuals who are qualified to do the job well. By steering clear of questions about subjects that are peripheral to the job itself, employers are less likely to ask questions that will land them in court. Wise business owners ask their attorneys to review their bank of questions before using them in an interview. Table 17.7 provides a quiz for you to test your knowledge of the legality of certain interview questions.

SELLING THE CANDIDATE ON THE COMPANY   In the final phase of the interview, the employer tries to sell desirable candidates on the company. This phase begins by allowing the candidate to ask questions about the company, the job, or other issues. Experienced interviewers note the nature of these questions and the insights they give into the candidate's personality. This part of the interview offers the employer a prime opportunity to explain to the candidate why the company is an attractive place to work. Remember that the best candidates will have other offers, and it's up to you to make sure they leave the interview wanting to work for your company. Pointing out the benefits of working for a small company, such as a flexible work schedule, the ability to accomplish a meaningful social cause, the opportunity to contribute directly to a meaningful mission, and the chance for growth and advancement, can influence a candidate's decision. Finally, before closing the interview, the employer should thank the candidate and tell him or her what happens next (e.g., "We'll be contacting you about our decision within two weeks.").

Contact References and Conduct a Background Check

Entrepreneurs should take the time to conduct background checks and contact candidates' references. Conducting background checks costs a little money but can save companies many thousands of dollars by identifying red flags in candidates' backgrounds and helping avoid expensive hiring mistakes. Conducting background checks is relatively inexpensive, costing as little as $30, but the payoffs can be tremendous. One recent survey reports that 84 percent of employers who conduct background checks have discovered problems with candidates that they would not have been able to detect otherwise.[86] By performing a basic background check, employers can steer clear of candidates with criminal or other high-risk backgrounds. Criminal background checks are the most popular type of background check. Although some states ban the practice, conducting credit checks on job candidates (which legally require the candidates' written permission) also can be quite revealing, giving employers insight into candidates' dependability and trustworthiness. A recent study by CareerBuilder reports that 28 percent of businesses do not conduct background checks on job candidates, and small businesses are less likely to conduct background checks than large businesses.[87]

Andrey Popov/Shutterstock

TABLE 17.7 Is It Legal?

Some interview questions can lead an employer into legal problems. Test your knowledge concerning which questions are legal to ask in an interview by using the following quiz.

Legal	Illegal	Interview Question
☐	☐	1. Are you currently using illegal drugs?
☐	☐	2. When was the last time you used illegal drugs?
☐	☐	3. Have you ever been arrested?
☐	☐	4. Have you ever been convicted of a crime?
☐	☐	5. Do you have any children, or do you plan to have children?
☐	☐	6. Are you willing to travel as part of this job?
☐	☐	7. When and where were you born?
☐	☐	8. Is there any limit on your ability to work overtime or travel?
☐	☐	9. How tall are you? How much do you weigh?
☐	☐	10. Do you drink alcohol?
☐	☐	11. How much alcohol do you drink each week?
☐	☐	12. Would your religious beliefs interfere with your ability to do the job?
☐	☐	13. What contraceptive practices do you use?
☐	☐	14. Are you HIV positive?
☐	☐	15. Have you ever filed a lawsuit or workers' compensation claim against a former employer?
☐	☐	16. Do you have physical/mental disabilities that would interfere with doing your job?
☐	☐	17. Are you a U.S. citizen?
☐	☐	18. What arrangements do you have for childcare while you are at work?
☐	☐	19. What is your Facebook password?

Answers: 1. Legal. Employers can screen candidates on their current use of illegal drugs. **2.** Illegal. Employers cannot ask about a candidate's past drug addiction because drug addiction is covered by the Americans with Disabilities Act; casual drug use, however, is not covered. **3.** Illegal. Employers cannot ask about an applicant's arrest record, but they can ask whether a candidate has ever been *convicted* of a crime. **4.** Legal. Although employers cannot ask about a candidate's arrest record, they can ask whether he or she has been convicted of a crime. **5.** Illegal. Employers cannot ask questions that could lead to discrimination against a particular group (e.g., women, physically challenged, and so on). **6.** Legal. **7.** Illegal. The Civil Rights Act of 1964 bans discrimination on the basis of race, color, sex, religion, or national origin. **8.** Legal. **9.** Illegal. Unless a person's physical characteristics are necessary for job performance (e.g., lifting 100-pound sacks of mulch), employers cannot ask candidates such questions. **10.** Legal. **11.** Illegal. Notice the fine line between question 10 and question 11; this is what makes interviewing so challenging. **12.** Illegal. This question violates the Civil Rights Act of 1964. **13.** Illegal. What relevance would this have to an employee's job performance? **14.** Illegal. Under the Americans with Disabilities Act, which prohibits discrimination against people with disabilities, people who are HIV positive or have AIDS are considered disabled. **15.** Illegal. Workers who file workers' compensation suits are protected from retribution by a variety of federal and state laws. **16.** Illegal. This question also violates the Americans with Disabilities Act. **17.** Illegal. This question violates the Civil Rights Act of 1964. **18.** Illegal. This question could lead to discrimination by the employer. **19.** Currently legal (in all but six states)—and creates the possibility that employers would have access to information about which they cannot legally ask, such as religion, marital status, and so on, which creates a potential legal liability. Six states have banned employers from asking job candidates for their social media passwords.

One expert says failing to conduct background checks on potential employees is the equivalent of walking up to a stranger and handing him or her the keys to your house.[88] To avoid legal problems, employers must be able to show a connection between the type of background check conducted and the applicant's job duties and must conduct the background check for *all* applicants for the job. Employers also should have applicants sign a separate disclosure document, authorizing the employer to conduct a background check.

Checking potential employees' social networking pages on Facebook, Twitter, and LinkedIn also can provide a revealing look at their character. A study by CareerBuilder reports that 60 percent of employers investigate job candidates' social networking sites (a significant increase

FIGURE 17.3

Why Hiring Managers Reject Job Candidates After Checking Their Social Media Profiles

Source: Based on "Number of Employers Using Social Media to Screen Candidates Has Increased 500 Percent over Last Decade," Career-Builder, April 28, 2016, www.careerbuilder.com/share/aboutus/pressreleasesdetail.aspx?ed=12/31/2016&id=pr945&sd=4/28/2016.

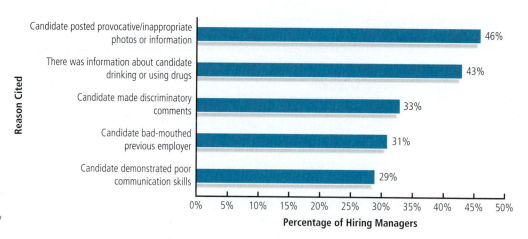

from 22 percent in 2008) and that 49 percent have discovered something there that caused them to reject a candidate (see Figure 17.3).[89]

Although many business owners see checking references as a formality and pay little attention to it, others realize the need to protect themselves (and their customers) from hiring unscrupulous workers. Is it really necessary? Yes! According to a recent survey, 77 percent of hiring professionals have detected false information or exaggerations on candidates' résumés (see Figure 17.4). At one company, an applicant claimed that he had worked at a federal prison, but when the interviewer conducted a background check, he discovered that the applicant actually had been *incarcerated* at the federal prison during that time![90] Checking references thoroughly can help employers uncover false or exaggerated information. Rather than contact only the references listed, experienced employers call applicants' previous employers and talk to their immediate supervisors to get a clear picture of the applicant's job performance, character, and work habits. At Bonobos, an online menswear company, managers conduct "off-list" reference checks, contacting people who have worked with a candidate but are not listed as references on the candidate's résumé. Andy Dunn, cofounder and CEO, says that in most cases, these off-list references enhance a candidate's application, but on occasion they have alerted the company to problem areas in a candidate's background. Using LinkedIn to find common connections to former employers, colleagues, or employees is an efficient way to expand a candidate's reference pool.[91]

Hiring employees who are a good fit with a company's culture also is crucial to its success. A recent survey by Jobvite reports that 60 percent of hiring managers say that candidates' cultural fit is an important consideration in hiring decisions, topped only by the candidate's job

FIGURE 17.4

Most Common Exaggerations on Candidates' Résumés

Source: "By the Numbers," *Workforce*, October 2014, p. 13.

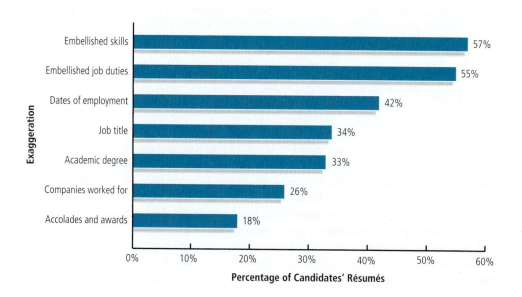

experience.[92] Another study shows that when considering recent college graduates' applications, hiring managers rank cultural fit higher than the applicant's references, coursework, and grades.[93] At Zappos, the online shoe retailer, veteran employees who serve as culture experts interview candidates and have the power to veto those whom they believe are not a good cultural fit. Talent acquisition managers estimate that one out of eight candidates fail the cultural fit criterion. One of the best ways to ensure that a candidate will be a good cultural fit is to hire him or her on a provisional basis for a short time. During the candidate's "audition," managers and employees have the opportunity to evaluate firsthand his or her work habits and capacity to fit into the company's culture. Doing so increases the probability that the company has found the right person for the job. After the first week of a four-week training program at Zappos, the company makes provisional hires "The Offer": Stay with the company or take a $3,000 payout to leave, no strings attached. About 90 percent of new hires stay, and the company says that those who remain are more likely to be a good fit for the company's unique culture.[94]

Experienced small business owners understand that the hiring process provides them with one of the most valuable raw materials their companies count on for success—capable, hard-working people. They know that hiring an employee is not a single event but rather the beginning of a long-term relationship. Table 17.8 features some strange but true incidents that employers have encountered during the selection process.

TABLE 17.8 Strange but True!

Human resource managers typically review résumés and job applications quickly. In fact, 68 percent of hiring managers say they spend less than two minutes, on average, reviewing a résumé or an application, and 17 percent of hiring managers spend no more than 30 seconds, on average, reviewing resumes. If you read enough résumés, conduct enough interviews, and check enough references, sooner or later you will encounter something bizarre. Consider the following examples (all true):

- During the interview, one candidate answered a phone call to set up an interview with a competitor of the company with which he was interviewing.
- During an interview, one applicant asked about the location of the nearest bar. Another one ate a pizza that he brought with him to the interview but never offered the interviewer a slice.
- One job candidate listed "taking long walks" as a skill on her résumé. Another candidate included "versatile toes" as a strength on her résumé.
- One applicant's résumé was written in Klingon, a fictional language spoken by humanoid warriors from *Star Trek*. Another candidate acted out a *Star Trek* role during the interview.
- When interviewing for a job that required working in Antarctica, one candidate claimed that he spoke "Antarctican."
- Under "Hobbies" on a job application, one candidate listed "Smoking."
- When an interviewer asked one candidate why she should become part of the team, she said, "Because my hair is perfect."
- After having lunch with a job candidate, a business owner took the applicant to her office for more discussion. The discussion ended, however, when the applicant dozed off and began snoring.
- One candidate decorated her résumé with pink rabbits. Another applicant revealed that her résumé was set up to be sung to the tune of "The Brady Bunch."
- One candidate walked into the interviewer's office, picked up the candy dish on her desk, and emptied its entire contents into her pocket.
- When asked what person, living or dead, he would most like to meet, one candidate replied, "The living one."
- One applicant checked his Facebook page during the interview, and another kept her iPod earbuds in her ears during the interview.
- One candidate popped his false teeth out of his mouth when discussing dental benefits with the interviewer.
- One candidate wore a Boy Scout uniform to his interview but never explained to the interviewers why.
- A candidate explained that promptness was one of her strengths—even though she showed up 10 minutes late for the interview.
- On his résumé, a candidate for an accounting position described himself as "detail oriented" and spelled the company's name incorrectly. Another claimed to have great attention to detail but misspelled "attention."
- During an interview, one candidate asked the interviewer, "What company is this again?" Another asked the interviewer if he could have a sip of the interviewer's coffee.
- During the interview, one candidate told the interviewer that he wanted a job that did not require him to "work a lot."

(continued)

TABLE 17.8 Strange but True! (*continued*)

- One candidate asked if he could bring his rabbit to work with him, adding that the rabbit was focused and reliable but that he himself had been fired before. Another applicant had his pet bird hidden in his shirt during the interview.
- One man who forgot to wear socks to his interview remedied the problem by coloring his ankles with a black felt-tip marker.
- One candidate applied lotion to her feet during the interview. Another candidate put her hand on the interviewer's chest to find a heartbeat so that they could "connect heart-to-heart."

Recommendations from previous employers can sometimes be quite entertaining, too. The following are statements from managers about workers:

- "Works well when under constant supervision and cornered like a rat in a trap."
- "This young lady has delusions of adequacy."
- "A photographic memory but with the lens cover glued on."
- "If you were to give him a penny for his thoughts, you'd get change."
- "If you stand close enough to him, you can hear the ocean."
- "He's so dense that light bends around him."

Sources: Based on "CareerBuilder Releases Annual List of Strangest Interview and Body Language Mistakes," CareerBuilder, January 12, 2017, www.careerbuilder.com/share/aboutus/pressreleasesdetail.aspx?ed=12%2F31%2F2017&id=pr984&sd=1%2F12%2F2017; "Career Builder's Annual Survey Reveals the Most Outrageous Resume Mistakes Employers Have Found," CareerBuilder, September 22, 2016, www.careerbuilder.ca/share/aboutus/pressreleasesdetail.aspx?sd=9%2F22%2F2016&id=pr967&ed=12%2F31%2F2016; Lydia Dishman, "These Are the Biggest Mistakes People Make During Interviews," *Fast Company*, January 14, 2016, www.fastcompany.com/3055458/these-are-the-biggest-mistakes-people-make-during-interviews; "Employers Share Most Memorable Interview Blunders," CareerBuilder, January 16, 2014, www.careerbuilder.com/share/aboutus/pressreleasesdetail.aspx?sd=1/16/2014&id=pr798&ed=12/31/2014; "CareerBuilder Releases Study of Common and Not-So-Common Resume Mistakes That Can Cost You the Job," CareerBuilder, September 11, 2013, www.careerbuilder.com/share/aboutus/pressreleasesdetail.aspx?id=pr780&sd=9/11/2013&ed=09/11/2013; "Hiring Managers Rank Best and Worst Words to Use in a Résumé in New CareerBuilder Survey," CareerBuilder, March 13, 2014, www.careerbuilder.com/share/aboutus/pressreleasesdetail.aspx?sd=3%2f13%2f2014&siteid=cbpr&sc_cmp1=cb_pr809_&id=pr809&ed=12%2f31%2f2014; "10 Strangest Job Interview Fails," *CBS News*, January 7, 2013, www.cbsnews.com/pictures/10-strangest-job-interview-fails/2/; "CareerBuilder Releases Study of Most Outrageous Resume Mistakes and Creative Techniques That Work," CareerBuilder, July 11, 2012, www.careerbuilder.com/share/aboutus/pressreleasesdetail.aspx?sd=7/11/2012&id=pr707&ed=12/31/2012; "Hiring Managers Share Most Unusual Résumé Mistakes in Annual CareerBuilder Survey," CareerBuilder, August 24, 2011, www.careerbuilder.com/share/aboutus/pressreleasesdetail.aspx?id=pr653&sd=8/24/2011&ed=8/24/2099; "Survey Reveals Wackiest Job Interview Mistakes," *SmartPros*, March 13, 2008, http://accounting.smartpros.com/x61115.xml; "Hiring Horrors," *Your Company*, April 1999, p. 14; Mike B. Hall, "From Job Applicants," Joke-of-the-Day, December 8, 2000, www.jokeoftheday.com; Karen Axelton, "L-L-L-Losers!," *Business Start-Ups*, April 2000, p. 13; "Great Places to Work: Interview Horror Stories," *Washingtonian*, November 1, 2005, www.washingtonian.com/articles/businesscareers/2159.html; and "Hiring Managers Share the Most Memorable Interview Mistakes in Annual CareerBuilder Survey," CareerBuilder, February 22, 2012, www.careerbuilder.com/share/aboutus/pressreleasesdetail.aspx?id=pr680&sd=2/22/2012&ed=12/31/2012.

LO3

Explain how to create a company culture that encourages employee retention.

culture

the distinctive, unwritten, informal code of conduct that governs an organization's behavior, attitudes, relationships, and style.

Creating an Organizational Culture That Encourages Employee Motivation and Retention

Culture

A company's **culture** is the distinctive, unwritten, informal code of conduct that governs its behavior, attitudes, relationships, and style. It is the essence of "the way we do things around here." In many small companies, culture is as important as strategy in gaining a competitive edge. Culture has a powerful impact on the way people work together in a business, how they do their jobs, and how they treat their customers. It also is a major determinant in a company's ability to retain quality employees. The companies that rank consistently in the "great places to work" lists have unique cultures that support and amplify their competitive strategies.

Company culture manifests itself in many ways—from how workers dress and act to the language they use. For instance, at some companies, the unspoken dress code requires workers to wear suits and ties, but at others, employees routinely come to work in jeans and T-shirts. At CustomInk, a company founded by three former college classmates, Marc Katz, Mike Driscoll, and Dave Christensen, that makes custom T-shirts and other imprinted items, the dress code includes jeans, flip-flops, and (no surprise) T-shirts. However, the company slogan, "Don't let the flip-flops fool ya," characterizes the company's strong work ethic and expectation of high performance. CustomInk reinforces a team spirit in its culture by sponsoring a formal recognition program at which employees (known as "Inkers") recognize each other for excelling at demonstrating the company's three core values: the Golden Rule, ownership, and innovation. CustomInk also provides learning opportunities for all employees through an in-house training program, InkyU.[95] Although it is an intangible characteristic, a company's culture has a powerful influence on everyone the company touches, especially its employees, and on the company's ultimate success.

An important ingredient in a company's culture is the performance objectives an entrepreneur sets and against which employees are measured. If entrepreneurs want integrity, respect, honesty, customer service, and other important values to be the foundation on which a positive culture can flourish, they must establish measures of success that reflect those core values. *Effective executives know that building a positive organizational culture has a direct, positive impact on the financial performance of an organization.* The intangible factors that make up an organization's culture have an influence, either positive or negative, on the tangible outcomes of profitability, cash flow, return on equity, employee productivity, innovation, and cost control. Research shows that companies that focus on building positive cultures generated an average rate of return of investment of 1,025 percent over a recent 10-year period, compared to 122 percent for the companies listed on the S&P 500.[96]

An entrepreneur's job is to create a culture that has a positive influence on the company's tangible outcomes. SAS, a company based in Cary, North Carolina, that provides business analytics software and services, is consistently listed on numerous "best places to work" lists. The company is situated on a beautiful campus that features onsite childcare, fitness, and medical facilities and offers employees job sharing, compressed workweeks, unlimited sick days, and college tuition reimbursement. At the heart of the company's culture is the concept of "We are family; spend your career here." Indeed, SAS benefits from an enviably low employee turnover rate of 3.6 percent. Online retailer Amazon has a very different culture than SAS. At Amazon, which is noticeably absent from the "best places to work" lists, the culture is much more intense and focused on productivity, with an "all hands on deck" expectation when problems arise. Managers expect employees to respond to e-mails and text messages at all hours. At the heart of Amazon's culture is the concept of "We are the Marines; if you can make it here, you can make it anywhere." Employees who stay reap the benefits of acquiring Amazon stock, but the high-pressure environment results in frequent burnout and a double-digit employee turnover rate. Both SAS and Amazon are highly successful companies because their cultures support their strategies, but their cultures are at opposite ends of the spectrum.[97]

Sustaining a company's culture begins with the hiring process. Beyond the normal requirements of competitive pay and working conditions, the hiring process must focus on finding employees who share the *values* of the organization. In winning workplaces, entrepreneurs build a culture of trust, treat their workers fairly, respect their personal lives, provide opportunities for growth and advancement, and provide them with jobs that are interesting, meaningful, and fun. The result is a team of people who give their best ideas and efforts to the business.

Creating a culture that supports a company's strategy is no easy task, but entrepreneurs who have been most successful at it understand that having a set of overarching beliefs serves as a powerful guide for everyday action. Culture arises from an entrepreneur's consistent and relentless pursuit of a set of core values that everyone in the company can believe in. "Values outlive business models," says management guru Gary Hamel.[98]

Nurturing the right culture in a company can enhance a company's competitive position by improving its ability to attract and retain quality workers and by creating an environment in which workers can grow and develop. As a new generation of employees enters the workforce, companies are discovering that more relaxed, open cultures have an edge in attracting the best workers. These companies embrace nontraditional, fun cultures that incorporate concepts such as casual dress, team-based assignments, telecommuting, flexible work schedules, free meals, company outings, and many other unique options.

Courtesy of LaSalle Network

ENTREPRENEURIAL PROFILE: Entrepreneurial Profile: Tom Gimbel: LaSalle Network Tom Gimbel founded LaSalle Network, a national staffing, recruiting and culture firm in Chicago, Illinois, in 1998, when he was just 26 years old. He started the company based on the foundation of treating employees right and showcasing appreciation. Although his company now employs nearly 300 people, Gimbel celebrates employees' accomplishments and work anniversaries (called "rebirthdays"). A slow clap starts at a random point in the day to give time for all employees in that given office to huddle around and sing happy rebirthday, which follows with brief speeches from the employee, Gimbel, and the employee's manager. Food is catered in to celebrate, and Gimbel also gives each employee a gift depending on the year they're celebrating, which ranges from padfolios to Nordstrom gift cards to iPads. Every August, to celebrate the anniversary of the company's founding, Gimbel throws a huge party called LaSallemas. In the past, he has taken the entire company to Las Vegas for an all-expenses-paid weekend, taken the company sailing, and rented the Adler Planetarium in Chicago to host LaSallemas. LaSalle Network has received numerous "Best Places to Work" awards, and employee ratings on the company atmosphere and culture are consistently in the upper 90 percent range.[99] ∎

Modern organizational culture relies on several principles that are fundamental to creating a productive, fun workplace that enables employees and the company to excel.

HIRING FOR CULTURAL FIT The best companies know that the only way to sustain a winning culture is to continue to hire people who fit into and support it. They make every hiring decision by looking through the lens of cultural fit. In one recent survey, 82 percent of global employers say that hiring for cultural fit is important.[100] Mike Weinberger, CEO of franchisor Maui Wowi, Hawaiian Coffees and Smoothies, says that hiring for culture is so important to the company that all 14 employees in the corporate office interview prospective new hires with a focus on cultural fit. Maintaining the company's unique culture is so important that Weinberger extends that same policy to prospective franchisees. A group of existing franchisees interviews franchise applicants with the goal of accepting applications only from those who fit into the company's relaxed, family-focused culture.[101]

RESPECT FOR WORK AND LIFE BALANCE Successful companies recognize that their employees have lives away from work. Generation X and Millennial workers, in particular, want to work for companies that erase the traditional barriers between home life and work life by making it easier for them to deal with the pressures they face away from their jobs. These businesses offer flexible work schedules, part-time jobs, job sharing, telecommuting, sabbaticals, and onsite day care and dry cleaning.

ENTREPRENEURIAL PROFILE: Pamela Noble: Noble-Davis Consulting Noble-Davis Consulting, a retirement plan administration and consulting service founded by Pamela Noble, not only attracts top-quality talent but also reaps the benefits of high productivity and employee retention by emphasizing work–life balance. The company provides its employees with flexible work schedules, self-determined vacations, and the opportunity to work from home when appropriate, benefits that allow employees to more easily balance their work–life demands. Meeting team goals calls for special celebrations, including bowling and movie nights or Whirly-Ball outings. Employees also can earn year-end performance bonuses, some of which have exceeded $20,000.[102] ∎

A SENSE OF PURPOSE As you learned in Chapter 5, one of the most important jobs an entrepreneur faces is defining the company's vision and then communicating it effectively to everyone the company touches. Effective companies use a strong sense of purpose to make employees feel connected to the company's mission. Mission-driven companies have 30 percent higher levels of innovation, and their employee retention rates are 40 percent higher than those of companies that are less mission focused.[103]

A SENSE OF FUN For some companies, the line between work and play is blurred. The founders of these businesses see no reason for work and fun to be mutually exclusive. In fact, they believe that a workplace that creates a sense of fun makes it easier to recruit quality workers and encourages them to be more productive and more customer oriented. "Healthy and sustainable organizations focus on the fundamentals: quality, service, fiscal responsibility, leadership—but they didn't forget to add fun to that formula," says Leslie Yerkes, a consultant and an author.[104] Karen Zuckerman, founder of HZDG, an award-winning integrated creative agency in Rockville, Maryland, acknowledges that creating a culture that includes a sense of fun is one of the reasons her business has been so successful. Zuckerman says that her employees spend most of their waking hours at work, so it is important for HZDG to be a place where they can work hard, play hard, and be inspired. The office incorporates plenty of natural light, bright colors, a layout that encourages employee interaction, and an "inspiration board" that features clippings, photos, fabrics, fashions, and other items to stimulate creativity. HZDG also encourages fun activities such as Nerf gun fights before meetings and monthly happy hours that feature an HZDG employee band. Celebrations, often spontaneous ones, are common, and the dress code is very casual.[105]

ENGAGEMENT Employees who are fully engaged in their work take pride in making valuable contributions to the organization's success and derive personal satisfaction from doing so. Although engaged employees are a key ingredient in superior business performance, just 33 percent of employees in North America are fully engaged in their work (compared to 70 percent at the world's top-performing companies), and 16 percent actually are disengaged.[106] Research shows that disengaged employees have higher turnover, accident, and absenteeism rates than the average employee, are more likely to steal from their employers, and are more likely to drive customers away. Disengaged workers also are less productive than engaged employees, costing U.S. companies between $483 billion and $605 billion a year.[107] Employees become disengaged when they are disconnected from the company's culture, when they lack opportunities for growth and advancement, when they don't believe the company values, and when they believe they are not compensated fairly for their contributions. What can managers do to improve employee engagement?

- Provide meaningful work for employees.

- Recognize and reward employees for top performance.

- Constantly communicate the purpose and vision of the organization and why it matters.

- Challenge employees to learn, grow, and advance in their careers and give them the resources and the incentives to do so.

- Encourage employees to try new ideas. Employees won't take the risks of new ideas if they know they will be punished for failure. To avoid that problem, Jay Steinfield, founder of Blinds.com, installed two 5-foot-tall test tubes in the company's office. Whenever employees implement a new idea, they drop a clear marble into one of the tubes. If their idea proves to be successful, they drop a colored marble into the tube. Steinfield proudly points out that the clear marbles outnumber the colored ones by a large margin. The tubes are visual reminders that taking risks is not only acceptable but expected.[108]

- Create a culture that empowers employees and encourages and rewards engagement.

Engaged employees *say* positive things about their companies, *stay* with their companies for the long haul, and *strive* to give their best efforts for the company.[109] Employees who are highly engaged act as advocates for their company; unfortunately, only 54 percent of employees are willing to recommend their company as a good place to work.[110] Engaged employees are half as likely as disengaged employees to leave the company, and as you have already learned, employee turnover is very costly.[111] Employees in companies with low engagement scores are less productive than employees in companies with high engagement scores.[112] Research also shows that companies with higher percentages of engaged employees generate higher earnings per share and faster growth in earnings per share than those with lower percentages of engaged employees.[113] Engaged employees are the drivers of innovative ideas and new customers and

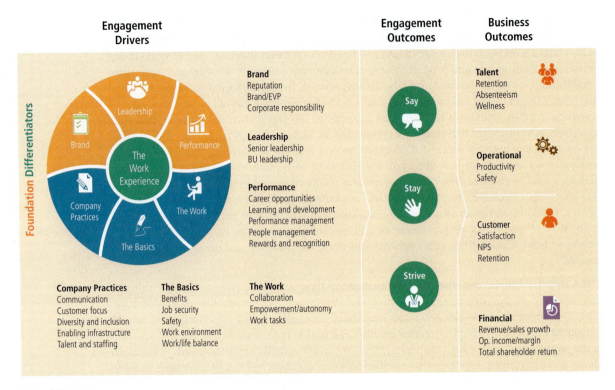

FIGURE 17.5

Drivers of Employee Engagement, Engagement Outcomes, and Business Outcomes

Source: 2017 Trends in Global Employee Engagement, Aon Hewitt, 2017, p. 2.

revenues that all companies, especially small ones, require to thrive. Figure 17.5 shows the factors that drive employee engagement and the positive business outcomes that high levels of employee engagement produce.

DIVERSITY Companies with appealing cultures not only accept cultural diversity in their workforces but embrace it, actively seeking out workers with different backgrounds. Today, businesses must recognize that a workforce that has a rich mix of cultural diversity gives the company more talent, skills, and abilities from which to draw. A study of the demographics of the United States reveals a steady march toward an increasingly diverse population. In fact, demographic trends suggest that by 2044, minority groups, including Hispanics, African Americans, Asians, and other nonwhite groups, will make up the majority (50.3 percent) of the U.S. population.[114] For companies to remain relevant in this environment, their workforces must reflect this diversity (see Figure 17.6). Who is better equipped to deal with a diverse, multicultural customer base than a diverse, multicultural workforce?

ENTREPRENEURIAL PROFILE: James Hartsell and Bryan Delaney: Skookum As founders of a fast-growing start-up, James Hartsell and Bryan Delaney, cofounders of Skookum, a software development company in Charlotte, North Carolina, focused on hiring recent college graduates with majors in computer science or related fields. They soon realized, however, that if their company were to thrive in a highly competitive industry, they would require people from diverse backgrounds with varied skill sets and experience. The entrepreneurs adjusted their hiring strategy, and Skookum, which recently opened an office in Denver, now boasts a highly diverse workforce of more than 50 employees.[115] ∎

INTEGRITY Employees want to work for companies that stand for honesty and integrity. They do not want to check their own personal values systems at the door when they report to work.

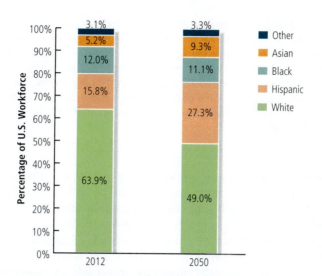

FIGURE 17.6

Composition of the U.S. Workforce

Sources: Based on Crosby Burns, Kimberly Barton, and Sophia Kerby, "The State of Diversity in Today's Workforce," Center for American Progress, July 12, 2012, p. 4; Steve H. Murdock, "Population Change in the United States: Implications for Education, the Labor Force, and Economic Development," Hobby Center for the Study of Texas at Rice University, November 10, 2011, p. 59.

Indeed, many workers take pride in the fact that they work for companies that are ethical and socially responsible. People want to work for a company that makes a difference in the world rather than merely make a product or provide a service. Autodesk, a company in San Rafael, California, that makes software for applications in 3D design, engineering, and entertainment, donates both money and time to the local community by giving its employees paid time off to volunteer at nonprofit organizations and matching employees' donations to nonprofits.[116]

PARTICIPATIVE MANAGEMENT Today's workers do not respond well to the autocratic management styles of yesteryear. Company owners and managers must learn to trust and empower employees at all levels of the organization to make decisions and to take the actions they need to do their jobs well. As a company grows, managers must empower employees at all levels to act without direct supervision. A study by consulting firm McKinsey and Company reports a strong correlation among the quality of a decision, clarity concerning the person responsible for implementing the decision, and that person's involvement in the decision-making process.[117] At W.L. Gore, the company that makes Gore-Tex, cables, guitar strings, and other products, participative management is standard practice. One of the company's values is "We don't manage people, we expect people to manage themselves." There is no formal organizational hierarchy or organizational chart at W.L. Gore, and employees come up with their own job titles.[118]

LEARNING ENVIRONMENT Progressive companies encourage and support lifelong learning among their employees. They are willing to invest in their employees, improving their skills and helping them reach their full potential. These companies are magnets for the best and the brightest young workers, who know that to stay at the top of their fields, they must always be learning. In 1998, the average number of training hours for managers and professionals at the companies listed on *Fortune*'s "100 Best Companies to Work For" list was 41 hours; hourly employees received an average of 33 hours of training. Today, those numbers have increased significantly, to 78 hours and 94 hours, respectively.[119]

ENTREPRENEURIAL PROFILE: Fred "Pal" Barger: Pal's Sudden Service At Pal's Sudden Service, a fast-food restaurant with 29 locations, all within an 80-mile radius of its headquarters in Kingsport, Tennessee, new employees receive 120 hours of training before they can begin work, and all employees receive training updates. In addition, all employees must be certified (and recertified) for every job they perform, from cooking hamburgers to serving customers—by taking tests. Every day, a computer randomly selects two to four employees per shift who must pass a recertification test; a score

of 100 percent is required. Employees who do not score 100 percent cannot work on that station until they regain their certification. Pal's focus on training pays off. Its turnover rate among employees is one-third of the industry average, and in 33 years, Pal's has lost only seven general managers. Customer service times are four times faster than the second-fastest quick-service restaurant in the United States, and order accuracy rates are 10 times better than the industry average (an average of only 1 error per 3,600 orders). The result is a cadre of loyal, happy customers. (Pal's also won a Malcom Baldridge National Quality Award, an impressive accomplishment for a small fast-food chain.)[120] ■

Job Design

Over the years, managers have learned that the job itself and the way it is designed is an important factor in a company's ability to attract and retain quality workers. In some companies, work is organized on the principle of **job simplification**, breaking down the work into its simplest form and standardizing each task, as in some assembly-line operations. The scope of jobs organized in such a way is extremely narrow, resulting in impersonal, monotonous, and boring work that creates little challenge or motivation for workers. Job simplification invites workers to "check their brains at the door" and offers them little opportunity for excitement, enthusiasm, or pride in their work. The result can be apathetic, unmotivated workers who don't care about quality, customers, or costs.

To break this destructive cycle, some companies have redesigned workers' jobs. The following strategies are common: job enlargement, job rotation, job enrichment, flextime, job sharing, and flexplace.

Job enlargement (horizontal job loading) adds more tasks to a job to broaden its scope. For instance, rather than an employee simply mounting four screws in computers coming down an assembly line, a worker might assemble, install, and test the entire motherboard (perhaps as part of a team). The idea is to make the job more varied and to allow employees to perform a more complete unit of work.

Job rotation involves cross-training employees so that they can move from one job in the company to others, giving them a greater number and variety of tasks to perform. As employees learn other jobs within an organization, both their skills and their understanding of the company's purpose and processes rise. Cross-trained workers are more valuable because they give a company the flexibility to shift workers from low-demand jobs to those where they are most needed. As an incentive for workers to learn to perform other jobs within an operation, some companies offer skill-based pay, a system under which the more skills workers acquire, the more they earn. Several years ago, when motorcycle manufacturer Harley-Davidson re-engineered the layout of its factory in York, Pennsylvania, the company also redesigned employees' jobs, giving them more complete units of work (enlargement) and allowing them to rotate through several different workstations during a shift (rotation) to reduce body strain and boredom.[121]

Job enrichment (vertical job loading) involves building motivators into a job by increasing the planning, decision-making, organizing, and controlling functions—traditionally managerial tasks—that workers perform. The idea is to make every employee a manager (at least a manager of his or her own job).

To enrich employees' jobs, a business owner must build five core characteristics into them:

- *Skill variety* is the degree to which a job requires a variety of different skills, talents, and activities from the worker. Does the job require the worker to perform a variety of tasks that demand a variety of skills and abilities, or does it force him or her to perform the same task repeatedly?

- *Task identity* is the degree to which a job allows the worker to complete a whole or identifiable piece of work. Does the employee build an entire piece of furniture (perhaps as part of a team), or does he or she merely attach four screws?

- *Task significance* is the degree to which a job substantially influences the lives or work of others—other employees or final customers. Does the employee get to deal with customers, either internal or external? One effective way to establish task significance is to put employees in touch with customers so they can see how customers use the product or service they make.

---

job simplification

the type of job design that breaks down work into its simplest form and standardizes each task.

job enlargement (horizontal job loading)

the type of job design that adds more tasks to a job to broaden its scope.

job rotation

the type of job design that involves cross-training employees so that they can move from one job in the company to others, giving them a greater number and variety of tasks to perform.

job enrichment (vertical job loading)

the type of job design that involves building motivators into a job by increasing the planning, decision-making, organizing, and controlling functions that workers perform.

- *Autonomy* is the degree to which a job gives a worker freedom, independence, and discretion in planning and performing tasks. Does the employee make decisions affecting his or her work, or must he or she rely on someone else (e.g., the owner, a manager, or a supervisor) to "call the shots"? One study shows that small businesses that give employees autonomy in their work grow four times faster and have employee turnover rates that are three times lower than companies that rely on command-and-control management styles.[122]

- *Feedback* is the degree to which a job gives the worker direct, timely information about the quality of his or her performance. Does the job give the employee feedback about the quality of his or her work, or does the product (and all information about it) simply disappear after it leaves the worker's station?

A study conducted by researchers at the University of New Hampshire and the Bureau of Labor Statistics concludes that employees of companies that use job enrichment principles are more satisfied than those who work in jobs designed using principles of simplification.[123]

Flextime is an arrangement under which employees work a normal number of hours but have flexibility about when they start and stop work. Most flextime arrangements require employees to build their work schedules around a set of "core hours," such as 10 A.M. to 2 P.M., but give them the freedom to set their schedules outside those core hours. For instance, one worker might choose to come in at 7 A.M. and leave at 3 P.M. to attend her son's soccer game, and another may work from 11 A.M. to 7 P.M. Flextime not only raises worker morale but also makes it easier for companies to attract high-quality Millennial workers who want rewarding careers without sacrificing their lifestyles. Companies using flextime schedules experience lower levels of tardiness, turnover, and absenteeism. A recent Gallup survey reports that 51 percent of employees would change jobs for one that offered them flextime.[124] Baker Donelson, a law firm in Memphis, Tennessee, offers flextime to its employees so that they can structure their work around their personal needs and goals.[125] The goal is to provide workers with the ability to achieve greater work–life balance.

> **flextime**
> an arrangement under which employees work a normal number of hours but have flexibility about when they start and stop work.

Flextime is becoming an increasingly popular job design strategy, especially among small companies. A recent study by the Families and Work Institute reports that 81 percent of U.S. businesses give at least some of their employees flexible schedules, up from 68 percent in 2005. However, 32 percent of small companies (fewer than 100 employees) offer most or all of their employees flexible schedules, compared to just 17 percent of large companies (more than 1,000 employees).[126] The number of companies using flextime will continue to grow as companies find recruiting capable, qualified full-time workers more difficult and as technology makes working from a dedicated office space less important. Research shows that when considering job offers, candidates, particularly young workers, weigh heavily the flexibility of the work schedule that companies offer.[127]

Nearly one-third of companies use **compressed workweeks**, an arrangement in which employees work 32 to 40 hours per week but concentrate those hours across 4 days rather than the typical 5 days.[128]

> **compressed workweeks**
> an arrangement in which employees work 32 to 40 hours per week but concentrate those hours across 4 days rather than the typical 5 days.

ENTREPRENEURIAL PROFILE: Ryan and Gillian Carson: Treehouse After graduating from college, Ryan Carson worked for a start-up company that required long days, little sleep, and almost constant exhaustion. When Carson and his wife, Gillian, launched their own business, Treehouse, an online learning platform in Portland, Oregon, he made a conscious decision not to impose long hours of strenuous work on his employees. Today, the growing company's 87 employees have a 32-hour, 4-day workweek. Everyone, says Carson, including him and his wife, has a better quality of life, and the thriving company is able to use its compressed workweek to attract talent for which much bigger companies vie.[129] ∎

Job sharing is a work arrangement in which two or more people share a single full-time job. For instance, two college students might share the same 40-hour-a-week job, one working mornings and the other working afternoons. Salary and benefits are prorated between the workers sharing a job. Because job sharing is a simple solution to the growing challenge of work–life balance, it is becoming more popular. Companies already using it are finding it easier to recruit and retain qualified workers.

> **job sharing**
> a work arrangement in which two or more people share a single full-time job.

flexplace

a work arrangement in which employees work at a place other than the traditional office, such as a satellite branch closer to home or at home.

telecommuting

an arrangement in which employees working remotely use modern communications equipment to connect electronically to their workplaces.

Flexplace is a work arrangement in which employees work at a place other than the traditional office, such as a satellite branch closer to home or, in many cases, at home. Like flextime, flexplace is an important tool for recruiting Millennial workers. One study reports that 95 percent of Millennial employees say that they want the option of working at home or some other location away from the office occasionally.[130] Flexplace is an easy job design strategy for companies to use because of **telecommuting**. Using modern communication technology, employees have more flexibility in choosing where they work. Today, connecting electronically to the workplace (and to all of the people and the information there) from practically anywhere on the planet is quite simple for many workers. One study estimates that 50 percent of all jobs in the United States are compatible with telecommuting at least some of the time, and 85 percent of employees in the United States say they would telecommute if their employers allowed it. However, only 2.8 percent of employees in North America telecommute at least half the time.[131] Telecommuting employees get the flexibility they seek, and they also benefit from lower stress levels, reduced commuting times and expenses, lower childcare costs, and less expensive wardrobes (bathrobes and bunny slippers compared to business suits and wingtips). Companies reap many benefits as well, including improved employee morale, less absenteeism, lower turnover, higher productivity, and more satisfied, loyal employees who are engaged in their work. Studies show that telecommuting can reduce employee turnover by 20 percent and increase productivity by 15 to 20 percent.[132] According to a study by technology conglomerate Cisco Systems, 67 percent of telecommuting employees say they produce higher-quality work, and 69 percent of telecommuters report higher productivity.[133] At Cisco Systems, which is based in San Jose, California, 95 percent of employees telecommute an average of two days per week.[134]

Motivating Employees to Higher Levels of Performance: Rewards and Compensation

Another important aspect of creating a culture that attracts and retains quality workers is establishing a robust system of rewards and compensation. The rewards that an employee gets from the job itself are intrinsic rewards, but managers have at their disposal a wide variety of extrinsic rewards (those outside the job itself) to attract, retain, and motivate workers. The keys to using rewards to motivate are linking them to performance and tailoring them to the needs and characteristics of the workers. Entrepreneurs must base rewards and compensation on what is really important to their employees. For instance, to a technician making $35,000, a chance to earn a $3,000 performance bonus would most likely be a powerful motivator. To an executive earning $195,000 a year, it may not be.

One of the most popular rewards is money. Not surprisingly, a recent survey by the Society for Human Resource Management reports that 95 percent of employees rated compensation as either important or very important to their job satisfaction; however, only 65 percent of employees say they are satisfied with their compensation.[135] Research shows that money is an effective motivator and can buy "happiness"—up to a point. Higher incomes increase satisfaction and emotional well-being for workers with modest earnings, but money begins to lose its effect once earnings reach $75,000.[136]

pay-for-performance compensation system

a compensation system in which employees' pay depends on how well they perform their jobs.

Some companies have moved to **pay-for-performance compensation systems**, in which employees' pay depends on how well they perform their jobs. In other words, extra productivity equals extra pay. By linking employees' compensation directly to the company's financial performance, a business owner increases the likelihood that workers will achieve performance targets that are in their best interest and in the company's best interest. Simple performance bonuses are a common reward at many companies. The closer the bonus payment is to the action that prompted it, the more effective it will be. Pay-for-performance systems work only when employees see a clear connection between their job performance and their pay, however. That's where small businesses have an advantage over large businesses. Because they work for small companies, employees can see more clearly the impact that their performances have on the company's profitability and ultimate success than their counterparts at large corporations. Hilcorp, an oil and gas company founded by Jeff Hildebrand in Houston, Texas, offers its employees impressive pay-for-performance bonuses that average one-third of employees' base pay for achieving challenging goals. In the past, when Hilcorp reached a five-year goal, the company rewarded employees with either a $50,000 voucher for a new car or $35,000 in cash. More recently, after the company hit its year-end performance targets, every employee received a $100,000 bonus![137]

Some companies offer their employees financial rewards in the form of **profit-sharing plans**, in which employees receive a portion of the company's profits. At Badger Mining, a family-owned sand extractor located in Berlin, Wisconsin, employees participate in a generous quarterly profit-sharing plan. The company also offers performance-based bonuses in addition to the profit-sharing program. The result is an employee turnover rate that is virtually nil, with 95 percent of employees saying they intend to retire from Badger Mining.[138] A few companies have gone even further, coupling profit sharing plans with **open-book management**, a system in which entrepreneurs share openly their companies' financial results with employees. The goal is to show employees how their job performances have a direct impact on profits and to give them an incentive to improve the company's bottom line. One long-time proponent and practitioner of open-book management says the practice gives employees the chance to see what they and the company must do to succeed.[139]

profit-sharing plan
a reward system in which employees receive a portion of the company's profits.

open-book management
a system in which entrepreneurs share openly their companies' financial results with employees.

ENTREPRENEURIAL PROFILE: Paul Saginaw and Ari Weinzweig: Zingerman's Deli Paul Saginaw and Ari Weinzweig, who in 1982 cofounded Zingerman's Delicatessen, now a multifaceted community of 10 businesses (many of them started by staff) that includes the original deli, a bakery, a creamery, a coffee company, a roadhouse, a farm, a Korean restaurant and Zingtrain, a business that teaches Zingerman's approaches to business and leadership. Zingerman's well-developed business philosophies combine open-book management and an employee stock ownership plan (more on these later in this chapter) to create a highly profitable and successful business. Each week, the staff gathers in "huddles," in which they review in detail their unit's key financial and quality metrics. Each line item at the huddle has "owners" who are responsible for managing it, presenting information about it, and leading discussions on how to improve it. Cooks, dishwashers, servers, and other staff—not the accountants—explain the company's financial statements, so that everyone understands how his or her role in the company affects the company's financial performance. The impact of employee involvement, engagement, and decision making on the company's performance is powerful.[140] ∎

Courtesy of Zingerman's Delicatessen

Money isn't the only motivator business owners have at their disposal, of course. In fact, money tends to be only a short-term motivator. In addition to the financial compensation they provide, most companies offer their employees a wide array of benefits, ranging from stock options and health insurance to retirement plans and tuition reimbursement. **Stock options**, a plan under which the employees can purchase shares of a company's stock at a fixed price, have become a popular benefit for employees. Employees at PCL Construction, a company founded in 1906 that owns construction firms across the United States, Canada, and Australia, receive stock options in the fast-growing company.[141] Stock options take on real value when the market price of a company's stock exceeds the exercise price, the price at which employees can purchase stock. (Note that if the fair market price of a stock never exceeds the exercise price, the stock option is useless.) When trying to attract and retain quality employees, many small companies rely on stock options to gain an edge over larger companies that offer bigger salaries. Stock options produce a huge payoff for employees when companies succeed. Workers at highly successful companies such as Microsoft, Google, and Dell have retired as multimillionaires thanks to stock options.

stock options
a plan under which employees can purchase shares of a company's stock at a fixed price.

Benefits packages also play an important part in attracting and retaining quality workers and achieving high productivity. A recent survey by MetLife shows that employees who are satisfied with their benefits demonstrate more loyalty to their employers and are less likely to leave than those who are not. The most important benefit? Health insurance.[142] Square Root, a company in Austin, Texas, that provides technology solutions for auto dealers and retailers, not only covers 100 percent of healthcare premiums (including coverage for alternative treatments such as acupuncture and homeopathy) for its employees and their families but also offers healthful breakfasts and lunches, wellness programs, and exercise classes designed to keep workers healthy.[143]

In an economy in which they must compete aggressively for employees, entrepreneurs must recognize that compensation and benefits no longer follow a "one-size-fits-all" pattern. The diversity of today's workforce requires employers to be highly flexible and innovative with the compensation and benefits they provide. To attract and retain quality workers, creative entrepreneurs offer employees benefits designed to appeal to their employees' particular needs. This diversity has led to the popularity of **cafeteria benefits plans**, in which employers provide certain base benefits and then allocate a specific dollar amount for employees to select the benefits that best suit their needs. A survey by MetLife reports that 72 percent of employees say that the ability to customize their benefits increases loyalty to their employer.[144] To provide the best package of benefits most efficiently, employers should survey their employees periodically to discover which benefits are most important to them and then build their benefits package to include them. Online shoe retailer Zappos, which consistently appears on *Fortune*'s "Top 100 Companies to Work For" list, conducts benefits surveys of its employees throughout the year and adjusts its benefits package accordingly.[145]

cafeteria benefits plan
a plan under which employers provide certain basic benefits and then allocate a specific dollar amount for employees to select the benefits that best suit their needs.

Beyond flexible benefits plans, many small companies are setting themselves apart from others by offering meaningful benefits customized to their employees, including the following:

- On its employees' six-year anniversaries, AgileCraft, an information technology company based in Georgetown, Texas, provides paid sabbatical leaves that enable employees to recharge and pursue an activity about which they are passionate. To keep its geographically dispersed employees connected, AgileCraft sponsors a virtual "happy hour" every Friday, during which employees "gather" to drink a beverage and talk about whatever is on their minds. Twice a year, employees go to interesting locations for a company retreat.[146]

- Talon Professional Services, an executive search and staffing company in Princeton, New Jersey, has a Staffing Slugger program that awards employees for successful placements with prizes such as ski trips, air travel, and hot tubs. Employees also receive rewards, including bonuses, dinners, and trips, when the entire company achieves a milestone objective. When staffers achieve individual goals, the company's Won on Won program allows them to earn salary increases. The Talys is a formal award ceremony the company hosts annually that follows the format of awards shows such as the Academy Awards.

- Wisetail, a company based in Bozeman, Montana, that provides an online learning management system for targeted industries, provides a dog-friendly office and caters organic lunches for employees twice a week. The company kitchen is always well stocked with healthful snacks and beverages, and Wisetail provides company bikes for employees to use on errands or to make "Hot Laps," loops on local trails that earn them free beverages at local restaurants. Every quarter, Wisetail awards an employee $1,000 for the best video submission of an adventure he or she wants to take.[147]

Many small business owners who think their companies cannot afford benefits find other creative ways to reward their employees, including vacation days on their birthdays, an occasional catered lunch (especially after completing a big project successfully), and free tickets to a local game, movie, or performance. Marc Zwerding, owner of Generation Z Marketing in New York City, hosts employee outings and events, including an annual steak dinner, and offers employees flexible work schedules, casual dress, and occasional tickets to sporting events.[148]

Besides the wages, salaries, and attractive benefits they use as motivators, creative entrepreneurs have discovered that intangible incentives can be more important sources of employee motivation. After its initial impact, money loses its effectiveness; it does not have a lasting motivational effect (which for small businesses, with their limited resources, is a plus). For many workers, the most meaningful motivational factors are the simplest ones—recognition, praise, feedback, job security, promotions, and so on—things that any small business, no matter how limited its budget, can provide. More than 90 percent of employees say that managers' recognition of employee job performance is important to them, yet only 63 percent say that they are satisfied with the recognition they receive at work.[149]

Praise is a simple yet powerful motivational tool. People enjoy getting praise, especially from a manager or business owner; it's just human nature. As Mark Twain said, "I can live for two months on a good compliment."[150] Praise is an easy and inexpensive reward for employees who produce extraordinary work. A short note to an employee for a job well done costs practically nothing, yet it can be a potent source of motivation. Barbara Corcoran, founder of The Corcoran Group, awarded her company's top performers each week with colored ribbons and annual "Salesperson of the Year" trophies, as if they had just won an Olympic event. Corcoran realized that recognition often is a better motivator than money after visiting her top salesperson's home and seeing a large cabinet in the middle of her living room in which she proudly displayed the five "Salesperson of the Year" trophies she had won.[151] How often has an employer recognized you and said "thank you" for a job you performed well?

Because they lack the financial resources of bigger companies, small business owners must be more creative when it comes to giving rewards that motivate workers. In many cases, however, using rewards other than money gives small businesses an advantage because they usually have more impact on employee performance over time. Rewards do not have to be expensive to be effective. At ENGEO, the engineering consulting firm in San Ramone, California, employees who provide extraordinary service to clients receive the coveted "ENGEO Rocks" traveling rock award, an actual rock (the company provides geotechnical and hydrologic consulting services) that the outstanding employee proudly displays at his or her workstation.[152] Managers are not the only ones who can provide rewards. At AcademicWorks, a company based in Austin, Texas, that provides scholarship management software for colleges and universities, employees submit compliments and praise about their coworkers to the Blue Box of Love. Managers read the submissions at quarterly meetings in front of the entire company.[153]

Entrepreneurs tend to rely more on nonmonetary rewards, such as praise, recognition, game tickets, dinners, letters of commendation, and so on, to create a work environment in which employees take pride in their work, enjoy it, are challenged by it, and get excited about it. In other words, the employees act like owners of the business.

Management Succession: Passing the Torch of Leadership

LO4

Describe the steps in developing a management succession plan for a growing business that allows a smooth transition of leadership to the next generation.

More than 80 percent of all companies in the world are family owned, and their contributions to the global economy are significant. Family-owned businesses account for 70 to 90 percent of global GDP. In the United States alone, family businesses account for 90 percent of all businesses, create 64 percent of the nation's gross domestic product, employ 62 percent of the private-sector workforce, and account for 65 percent of all wages paid. Not all family-owned businesses are small, however; 35 percent of Fortune 500 companies are family businesses. Family-owned companies such as Wal-Mart, Ford, Mars, Cargill, and Koch Industries employ thousands of people and generate billions of dollars in annual revenue.[154] Family firms also create 78 percent of the U.S. economy's net new jobs and are responsible for many famous products, including Heinz ketchup, Levi's jeans, and classic toys such as the Slinky and the Wiffle Ball.[155]

The stumbling block for most family businesses is management succession. Family businesses are most vulnerable when they are ready to make the transition from one generation of leaders to the next. Only about 30 percent of first-generation businesses survive into the second generation; of those that do survive, only 12 percent make it to the third generation, and just 3 percent make it to the fourth generation and beyond.[156]

Hands On . . . How To

Make Your Small Business a Great Place to Work

Smart entrepreneurs know that although they may be the driving force behind their businesses, their highly committed and engaged employees are the *real* keys to their companies' success. As a result, these entrepreneurs carefully select their employees, develop their talents through training and education, and create a culture that reflects the central role their employees play in the success of their businesses. Following are 10 lessons for creating a great workplace, drawn from small companies that have been recognized as some of the best places to work.

Lesson 1. Recognize your employees' stellar performances publicly, privately, and often. The best small businesses make recognizing employees' accomplishments a top priority and use a unique system of rewards to reinforce a positive company culture. Acknowledging employees' performances does not require a small company to spend a great deal of money. When their teams achieve a milestone accomplishment, some entrepreneurs give bonuses; others provide celebratory meals for their employees or take a "movie day," where everyone in the company goes to a movie together. At The Clymb, an online marketplace for outdoor gear and adventure travel in Portland, Oregon, employees can recognize one another's accomplishments by giving coworkers recognition cards called "Fist Bumps" that are posted in the kitchen for all to see. Company founders Kelly Dachtler and Cec Annett took their entire staff to Hawaii's North Shore on a "work-cation" as a reward for achieving an aggressive business goal. Employees worked shorter days and had the opportunity to take surfing lessons, snorkel, sight-see, and hang out on the beach. At Torch Technologies, recognition is not as elaborate, but it's no less effective. CEO Bill Roark recognizes employees' outstanding performances with a handwritten thank-you letter sent to their homes. Roark says that he get notes back from kids and spouses that bring tears to his eyes.

Lesson 2. Understand the rewards that matter most to each employee. This is an area in which small companies have an advantage over their larger rivals. In small businesses, entrepreneurs know their employees, their likes and dislikes, and the rewards that will mean the most to them. One worker's ideal reward may be tickets to a baseball game, but another employee may prefer tickets to a musical show. Jim Belosic, founder of ShortStack, a company that provides a platform for creating promotional campaigns for social media, mobile apps, and Web sites, takes his 16 employees (whose job titles include "Countess of Content Strategy," "Earl of Code," and "Baron of Booleans") out to lunch every Friday, where both business and informal conversations take place. It also is an ideal time for Belosic to get to know more about each person, which allows him to customize the rewards he gives. For instance, based on one of those lunch conversations, Belosic recently gave one employee who reached an important goal a new set of tires for her car. She was thrilled!

Lesson 3. Recognize your company's responsibility to society. The best small companies strive for more than profitability; they aim to make a difference in the world, both locally and globally, and they get their employees involved in their efforts. At Sage Rutty and Company, a business that provides financial services and insurance to individuals, families, and small businesses, the company provides support for community and nonprofit programs that are important to its 59 employees. Recently, the team assembled 100 Thanksgiving baskets for families in need. The company also makes donations to a variety of community charities and encourages employees to participate in Meals on Wheels deliveries to local residents. Zumasys, a cloud computing services company, donates 1 percent of its revenue to an array of local charities carefully selected by its 63 employees. Zumasys also matches its team members' donations to nonprofit organizations and gives them paid time off to encourage them to volunteer in local nonprofits.

Lesson 4. Honest, open, two-way communication helps your company in good times and bad times. Managers at these small companies recognize that good communication is a key to building trust with employees and to encouraging employees to participate in making decisions that improve the workplace. Leaders at Grantek Systems Integration, a provider of integrated manufacturing solutions, hold quarterly town hall meetings to provide important information to their 163 employees and to provide a forum for employees to ask questions. At Ideal Printers, a second-generation family-owned commercial printing company in St. Paul, Minnesota, sisters Lana Siewert-Olson and Joan Siewert-Cardona use open-book management, sharing with employees all of the company's financial statements and teaching them how to read them. They say opening the company's books allows employees to see how their jobs directly affect the company's profits and their compensation because Ideal Printers also offers a profit-sharing plan. During the Great Recession, when business slowed significantly, the company reduced everyone's pay by 10 percent (and has since restored the reduction) but did not resort to layoffs, unlike many of its competitors.

Lesson 5. Teamwork counts. Managers at leading small companies understand that a genuine team spirit leads to innovation, unparalleled productivity, and a fun atmosphere of camaraderie. They rely on team-based awards and recognition to encourage a team spirit and help employees understand how their jobs fit into the big picture. At Kayak, the online travel search engine, top-performing employees earn the right to serve on elite SWAT teams that tackle high-priority or high-risk projects and are free to go around normal organizational processes to achieve their goals or solve challenging problems. Several times during the year, the company sponsors SWAT Week, which challenges teams of employees to develop innovative ideas for improving customers'

(continued)

Hands On . . . How To

experience or some other aspect of Kayak. Winners receive a variety of rewards, but, most important, bragging rights.

Lesson 6. Investing in your employees is one of the best investments you can make. Great companies understand that enhancing their employees' skills benefits both the employee and the business. TDIndustries, a construction and facilities management firm in Dallas, Texas, provides 100 percent tuition reimbursement for employees who take college classes. In addition, the company encourages all of its employees (whom it calls "partners") to take at least 32 hours of training each year (either internally or externally), and the company pays for it. Managers at SmartPak, an online and catalog retailer of nutritional supplements, medicine, tack, and other equestrian supplies in Plymouth, Massachusetts, know that understanding the needs of horses and their riders is essential to the company's success. Although most of the company's employees own, ride, and show horses, not all do. SmartPak created SmartPak University, through which it offers a variety of courses to educate its employees about horses, their owners, and their unique needs. The company's New Hire Start Groups are designed to get new employees off to a good start, and its Barn Buddy program pairs non-riding employees with employees who are experienced equestrians to learn about horses—and to better understand the customers with whom they interact. Learning opportunities range from the informal Lunch and Learn program that provides employees with useful takeaways they can use immediately to the more elite Leadership Institute designed to develop the next generation of company leaders.

Lesson 7. Give your employees a real sense of ownership by making them owners. Every employer's dream is to have employees who act like owners of the company. The best way to achieve that is to make them owners of the company! When the company thrives, so do its employee-owners. Employees at TDIndustries, a construction and facilities management firm founded in 1946, own 100 percent of the company through an employee stock ownership plan (ESOP). One of the many benefits employee ownership produces is an employee turnover rate that is well below the industry average. Even in the leading small companies that do not offer ESOPs, employees receive some kind of performance-based compensation, such as profit sharing or stock options. The result is an ownership mentality and a workforce that is dedicated to making the company successful.

Lesson 8. Encourage your employees to stay healthy. With healthcare costs rising rapidly, smart business owners know that anything they can do to help their employees stay healthy not only lowers costs but also helps their employees lead better personal and work lives. Many of the leading small companies pay 100 percent of the cost of their employees' health insurance. Others provide incentives for employees to improve their health by quitting smoking, reaching and maintaining an ideal weight, or exercising regularly. Some companies provide onsite exercise facilities or pay for employees'

memberships at local gyms. At AgileCraft, an information technology company based in Georgetown, Texas, employees enjoy friendly competition in a Fitbit challenge, work from stand-up desks (because sitting is bad for one's health), and can help themselves to free healthful, organic snacks during the workday. Kayak, the online search engine, encourages employees to live healthy lives by providing fitness and yoga classes and providing dedicated space so that employees can exercise during the day.

Lesson 9. Let your employees have fun. Just because you are at work does not mean you cannot have fun. The best places to work allow their employees to take breaks from their work and have fun playing ping-pong, video games, or Nerf battles. At Disher, an engineering consulting company, every new employee receives a semi-automatic Nerf gun so that he or she can participate in the Nerf battles that frequently break out in the company's office. Disher also sponsors a monthly fun activity, such as Pinewood Derby races, Turkey Bowl flag football games, Ping-Pong March Madness, and a Living Healthy Challenge. OtterBox, a fast-growing company in Fort Collins, Colorado, that makes protective cases for smart phones, e-readers, and tablets, is known for its fun-based culture. The company's headquarters features a spiral slide in addition to stairs, scooters that employees can use to get around, a self-service latte machine and soda fountain, game rooms with pinball and foosball machines, and aquariums. Employees participate in impromptu events such as Flash Fitness Sessions and Star Wars Starship flying contests. There is a business purpose behind all of the fun these companies encourage. OtterBox CEO Brian Thomas says the goal is to create a culture that fosters innovation and inspires passion among employees.

Lesson 10. Give your employees the flexibility they need for work–life balance. Small companies that offer flextime, job sharing, telecommuting, and other flexible work arrangements have an edge when it comes to hiring the best workers. At engineering consulting firm Disher, the focus is on getting the job done, not on putting in a specific number of hours. Employees ("team members") have the flexibility to set their own schedules to accomplish their projects while taking into account the demands on their personal lives. The company offers flextime, job sharing, telecommuting, and compressed workweeks, and employees use all of these flexible job design tools. Employees have the flexibility to attend a child's school play, take a parent to a medical appointment, or have some personal time. The company has no formal vacation policy; employees take enough time off to stay energized about their jobs. Generous benefits such as health insurance, training and tuition reimbursement, and an employee stock ownership plan make working at Disher more than just a job.

Sources: Based on "Great Place to Work: Disher," 2017, http://reviews.greatplacetowork .com/disher; "Great Place to Work: AgileCraft," 2017, http://reviews.greatplacetowork .com/agilecraft; "Great Place to Work: Grantek Systems Integration," 2017, http://

(continued)

Hands On . . . How To (continued)

reviews.greatplacetowork.com/grantek-systems-integration; "Great Place to Work: Sage Rutty & Company," 2017, http://reviews.greatplacetowork.com/sage-rutty-co-inc; "Great Place to Work: Kayak Software Corporation," 2017, http://reviews.greatplacetowork.com/kayak-software-corp; Ed Frauenheim and Sarah Lewis-Kulin, "Giving Workers Paid Time Off to Volunteer Will Help Your Company Succeed," *Fortune*, April 26, 2016, http://fortune.com/2016/04/26/giving-workers-paid-time-off-to-volunteer-will-help-your-company-succeed/; Jim Belosic, "How to Give the Best Employee Perks—on Any Budget," *Forbes*, December 5, 2014, www.forbes.com/sites/dailymuse/2014/12/05/how-to-give-the-best-employee-perks-on-any-budget/#4b1774f61cf6; Milton Moskowitz and Robert Levering, "The 100 Best Companies to Work For," *Fortune*, March 15, 2015, p. 152; Paul Wozniak, "Fort Collins OtterBox Named Best Place to Work," Tri-102.5, October 26, 2012,

http://tri1025.com/fort-collins-otterbox-named-best-place-to-work/; "OtterBox," Great Rated, April 18, 2013, http://us.greatrated.com/otterbox; "The Clymb" Great Rated, September 12, 2013, http://us.greatrated.com/the-clymb; "CustomInk," Great Rated, August 6, 2013, http://us.greatrated.com/customink; "SmartPak," Great Rated, February 6, 2014, http://us.greatrated.com/smartpak; Todd Nelson, "Culture Helps Printing Firm Survive," *Star Tribune*, December 25, 2011, www.startribune.com/business/136171088.html#jlfMzZ7YOFeW2h5U.97; Gabrielle M. Blue, Dave Smith, and Drew Gannon, "2011 Top Small Company Workplaces," *Inc.*, June 2011, www.inc.com/top-workplaces/index.html; Kelly K. Spors, "Top Small Workplaces 2008," *Wall Street Journal*, February 22, 2009, http://online.wsj.com/article/SB122347733961315417.html; and *2008 Guide to Bold New Ideas for Making Work Work* (New York: Families and Work Institute, 2008), pp. 3–6, 42.

Jacques Lange/Paris Match Archive/Getty Image

ENTREPRENEURIAL PROFILE: Drouhin Family: Maison Joseph Drouhin Maison Joseph Drouhin, a winemaker based in the heart of France's famous Burgundy region, is a family business that has beaten the odds and survived into the fourth generation of family ownership. Frédéric Drouhin, now the president of the company, took over from his father in 2003. He is the great-grandson of Joseph Drouhin, who started the company in 1880, when he was just 22 and moved from Chablis to Beaune, where the company's headquarters remains to this day. Each generation of family owners has added value to the business, making it stronger for the succeeding generation. The current generation of owners, which, in addition to Frédéric, include Phillipe (vineyard manager), Laurent (North American sales and marketing director), and Véronique (winemaker), assumed complementary positions in the company that reflected their skills, abilities, and interests. One of the greatest contributions to the company that their father, Robert, now 83 (but still president of the board), made was expanding the family business into the United States by establishing vineyards in Oregon's lush Willamette Valley beginning in 1987. Now with an extensive portfolio of 90 different wines, Maison Joseph Drouhin's managers are busy grooming the next generation of family leadership.[157] ■

The average life expectancy of a family business is 24 years, although some last *much* longer.[158] For instance, the oldest family business in the world is Houshi Ryokan, an inn and spa that was built near a hot spring in Komatsu, Japan, in 718 by Gengoro Sasakiri. Today, the forty-sixth generation of Sasakiri's descendants operate the inn, which can accommodate 450 guests in its 100 rooms.[159]

Common causes of lack of continuity among family businesses are failure to create a management succession plan, inadequate estate planning, and lack of funds to pay estate taxes. In addition, sibling rivalries, fights over control of the business, and personality conflicts often lead to nasty battles that can tear apart families and destroy once thriving businesses. The best way to avoid deadly turf battles and conflicts is to develop a succession plan for the company. Numerous studies have found a positive relationship between the existence of a management succession plan and the longevity of family businesses. Figure 17.7 shows the eight characteristics that successful family businesses exhibit, including planning for the next generation, managing taxes, sustaining a supportive culture, and creating a mechanism for family governance.

Most of the family businesses in existence today were started after World War II, and their founders are ready to pass the torch of leadership on to the next generation. Experts estimate that between 2015 and 2045, $30 trillion in wealth will be transferred from one generation to the next, much of it through family businesses.[160] For these companies to have a smooth transition from one generation to the next, they must develop management succession plans. Unfortunately, only 57 percent of family business owners have created succession plans for their companies.[161] The most common reason that business owners give for not creating a succession plan is that they do not believe a succession plan is necessary (47 percent), they do not

FIGURE 17.7

Eight Characteristics of Successful Family Businesses

Source: Worldwide Inheritance and Estate Tax Guide, EY, 2016. p. v.

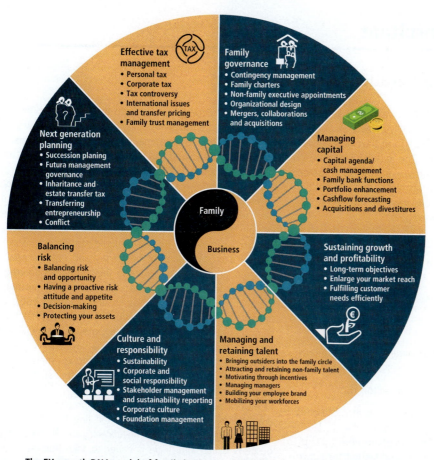

The EY growth DNA model of family businesses highlights the interlinked nature of the eight characteristics of a successful family business.

want to give up their life's work (14 percent), and they do not know how or when to create a plan (11 percent).[162] Another often unstated reason for failing to develop a succession plan is that entrepreneurs are unwilling to make tough and potentially disruptive decisions that involve selecting their successors. Family feuds often erupt over who is (and is not) selected as the successor in the family business. Without a succession plan, however, family businesses face an increased risk of faltering or failing in the next generation. Family businesses with the greatest probability of surviving are the ones whose owners prepare a succession plan well before it is time to pass the torch of leadership to the next generation. Succession planning also allows business owners to minimize the impact of estate taxes on their businesses and on their successors' wealth as well.

Succession planning reduces the tension and stress of a transition by gradually "changing the guard." A well-developed succession plan is like the smooth, graceful exchange of a baton between runners in a relay race. The concluding runner has already spent his or her energy by running at maximum speed, and the new runner still has maximum energy. The athletes never come to a stop to exchange the baton; instead, the handoff takes place on the move. The race is a skillful blend of the talents of all team members; the exchange of leadership is so smooth and powerful that the business never falters but accelerates, fueled by a new source of energy at each leg of the race.

How to Develop a Management Succession Plan

Creating a succession plan involves the following steps:

Step 1.   *Select the successor.* There comes a time for even the most dedicated company founder to step down from the helm of the business and hand over the reins to the next generation. The entire population of the Baby Boom Generation (born

You Be the Consultant

Time for the Next Generation?

A study by the Boston Consulting Group reports that family businesses financially outperform non-family-owned businesses during economic downturns but underperform their non-family-owned peers during economic booms. The reason? Family business strategies follow a longer perspective—a generation rather than just quarters—and focus more on resilience than performance. The study found that family businesses exhibit seven key differences from their non-family-owned peers:

1. They are more frugal.

2. They set the bar high for making capital investments.

3. They carry very little debt.

4. They acquire fewer and smaller companies.

5. They show a high level of diversification.

6. They are more ambitious about expanding into international markets.

7. They retain talent better than their competitors do.

Robinson Fans is a family business that has beaten the odds and survived to its sixth generation of family ownership. In 1892, Samuel Robinson and his son, J.R., both immigrants from England, left their jobs in the coal mining industry and started their own business, Robinson Machine Company, in Zelienople, Pennsylvania, to provide a line of equipment they designed for coal mines and mills. The company, which is now known as Robinson Fans because it specializes in manufacturing industrial fans that weigh as much as an 18-wheel tractor-trailer, is in its fifth and sixth generation of family ownership. Carl Staible, who assumed the reins of the company from his father-in-law, James Henderson, is Robinson Fans's CEO; Carl is 69 years old but has no immediate plans to retire from the company. His daughter, Tricia Staible, who is 36 and a former lawyer, will be Carl's successor when he decides to retire. For now, Tricia, who is president and is responsible for the company's daily operations, reports to her father.

Tricia joined the company in 2009 and began working in the company's Utah factory, where she learned about fans and their design, construction, and operation. She intentionally chose to start working in the family business away from Zelienople, where her father works, so that she could establish credibility and have a sense of independence. After four years, Carl, thinking about eventual management succession, asked Tricia to join him at the company's headquarters in Pennsylvania. Tricia, recognizing that her father, who had been with the company for more than 34 years, was accustomed to being in control, somewhat hesitantly accepted her father's invitation. Tricia had ideas about shifting to a team-based organization, giving employees more decision-making authority, and making the company more employee friendly. Carl, who was accustomed to a top-down approach to managing, was not convinced.

The father/daughter team do their best to resolve their differences, but it's not always easy or successful. A few years after Tricia moved to Pennsylvania, she proposed buying a small fabrication shop in Florida that had been one of Robinson Fans's long-time suppliers and was for sale. The Florida company served some of the same customers as Robinson Fans but with different products, such as piping and tanks. Tricia saw it as an ideal way to diversify the family business, increase sales, and provide more service to existing and new customers. Carl was hesitant because the purchase would require Robinson Fans to borrow a modest amount of money and enter a new line of business. She pitched the idea to the company's board of directors, which includes both her father and her mother. Board members required more research and planning but eventually approved Tricia's recommendation. Carl admits that the acquisition is going well and has great potential to increase Robinson Fans's revenue and profits. Tricia says she is interested in expanding the company's reach into foreign markets, but Carl has vetoed that, saying that she can take that step only after he has left the company.

Because their management styles and plans for the company are so different, Tricia and Carl often find themselves frustrated with one another. The two meet weekly to talk about important business issues, but Tricia is eager to take Robinson Fans in a direction that she defines. Carl is not yet ready to surrender control. He has no compelling hobbies to occupy his time, and when asked about retirement, says that he has not set a retirement date, although he does take longer vacations now. Tricia says that she does not want to push her father out of the company, but she is concerned about how to mesh their roles without causing major problems for the family business.

1. Are the issues that Carl and Tricia Staible face concerning management succession in the family business unusual? Explain.

2. Can Robinson Fans continue to be successful with two sometimes competing leaders at the helm? Explain.

3. One family business expert says that when it comes to management succession, a leader should pass the baton to the successor not when the leader is ready to leave but when the successor is ready to lead. Do you agree? How does this principle apply to Robinson Fans?

4. What specific advice can you offer Carl and Tricia Staible about management succession?

Sources: Based on Doug Bailey, "The Secrets of Success for Family-Owned Businesses," *Boston Globe*, February 23, 2016, http://sponsored.bostonglobe.com/rocklandtrust/the-secrets-of-success-for-family-owned-businesses/; "Robinson Fans Company History," Robinson Fans, 2017, www.robinsonfans.com/company/history; Claire Ansberry, "Two Generations, Both in Charge," *Wall Street Journal*, May 1, 2017, p. R1–R2; John A. Davis, "The Five Derailers of Effective Succession," Cambridge Institute for Family Enterprise, 2015, p. 3.

between 1946 and 1964), some 76.4 million people, will be 65 or older by 2030, and 60 percent of small business owners are Baby Boomers. A Baby Boomer business owner retires every 57 seconds, and as these Baby Boomers retire, they are creating a tidal wave of business transitions and sales as they look either to hand them over to the next generation or sell them.[163] Unfortunately, many of these soon-to-retire family business owners who intend to turn over their businesses to the next generation of family members have not yet identified their successors. They resist thinking about stepping away from the businesses they have built, but in the end, every business owner exits the company he or she created. Richard Branson, the brash founder of the Virgin Group, a collection of about 400 companies in industries that range from air travel and wine to balloon flights and space travel, waited until he was 65 to name a successor to the family business. Speculators thought that Branson's son, Sam, was the heir apparent; however, Branson eventually named his daughter, Holly, who left a career as a doctor to work for the Virgin Group as a special projects manager, as his successor. Holly admits that she has a great deal to learn about the vast collection of companies in the Virgin portfolio and is working hard to overcome her "dislike of numbers" and hone her financial management skills.[164]

Entrepreneurs should never assume that their children want to take control of the family business, however. It is critical to remember at this juncture in the life of a business that children do not necessarily inherit their parents' entrepreneurial skills and interests. By leveling with the children about the business and their options regarding a family succession, the owner will know which heirs, if any, are willing to assume leadership of the business.

When naming a successor, merit is a better standard to use than birth order or gender. More than one-third of family business founders say the next leader will be a woman, quite a change from just a generation ago.[165] The key to selecting the right successor is to establish standards of performance, knowledge, education, and ability and then identify the person who most closely meets those standards.

When considering a successor, an entrepreneur should consider taking the following actions:

- *Let family members, especially children, know that joining the business is not mandatory, and it's also not guaranteed.* Family members' goals, ambitions, and talents should be foremost in their career decisions, and the business does not owe jobs to people just because they are family members. Andrew Cornell, CEO of Cornell Iron Works, a family business that started in 1828 as a blacksmith shop and now makes overhead doors for industrial, commercial, and residential customers, says part of the company's success is its objective approach to hiring family members. He points out that successful family businesses cannot be homes for wayward family members.[166]

- **Do not assume that a successor must always come from within the family.** Simply being born into a family does not guarantee that a person will make a good business leader. Leon Gorman, the grandson of Leon Leonwood Bean, the founder of the iconic outdoor outfitter L.L.Bean, was the fourth-generation CEO of the family business for 33 years. When Gorman retired at 66, the company's board of directors, which the Gorman family controls, named long-time L.L.Bean manager Chris McCormick as the first CEO who was not a family member. When McCormick retired from the company in 2015, the board once again tapped a non-family member, Steve Smith, an outsider with significant retail experience, to be CEO.[167]

Kevin Galvin/Alamy Stock Photo

- **Give family members the opportunity to work outside the business first to learn firsthand how others conduct business.** This is a common strategy among family businesses; 70 percent of next-generation family business leaders work outside the family business before taking leadership roles in it so that they can gain useful knowledge and experience and overcome the credibility gap that comes from "being the boss's kid."[168] Marie-Christine Osterman knew even as a child that she eventually wanted to take over her family's grocery wholesale business, Rulko Großeinkauf. Osterman planned her career to prepare herself for the task of managing the family business, which is located in Hamm, Germany. Before earning a degree in business from the University of St. Gallen, she completed a banking internship at Commerzbank, a global banking company located in Frankfurt. After graduating, Osterman took a job at Aldi, a global discount supermarket chain with more than 10,000 stores in 18 countries, and was ultimately promoted to an area director position. With experience in the grocery business (but outside the family business), she joined Rulko Großeinkauf, where she learned its intricacies by starting at the bottom, loading boxes—something that won the respect of other employees. Her father, who had named Osterman as his successor, moved her into a management position so that he could groom her to become its CEO, a job she now proudly holds.[169]

One of the biggest mistakes entrepreneurs can make is to postpone naming a successor until just before they are ready to step down. The problem is especially acute when more than one family member works for the company and is interested in assuming leadership of it. Sometimes founders avoid naming successors because they don't want to hurt the family members who are not chosen to succeed them. However, both the business and the family will be better off if, after observing the family members as they work in the business, the founder picks a successor on the basis of that person's skills and abilities.

Step 2. *Create a survival kit for the successor.* After identifying a successor, an entrepreneur should prepare a survival kit and then brief the future leader on its contents, which should include all of the company's critical documents (wills, trusts, insurance policies, financial statements, bank accounts, key contracts, corporate bylaws, and so forth). The founder should be sure that the successor reads and understands all of the relevant documents in the kit.

Step 3. *Groom the successor.* Typically, founders transfer their knowledge to their successors gradually over time. The discussions that set the stage for the transition of leadership are time-consuming and require openness by both parties. In fact, grooming a successor is the founder's greatest teaching and development responsibility, and it takes time and deliberate effort. To create ability and confidence in a successor, a founder must be:

- Patient, realizing that the transfer of power is gradual and evolutionary and that the successor should earn responsibility and authority one step at a time until the final transfer of power takes place
- Willing to accept that the successor will make mistakes
- Skillful at using the successor's mistakes as a teaching tool
- An effective communicator and an especially tolerant listener
- Capable of establishing reasonable expectations for the successor's performance
- Able to articulate the keys to the successor's successful performance

Grooming a successor can begin at an early age simply by involving children in the family business and observing which ones have the greatest ability and interest in the company.

ENTREPRENEURIAL PROFILE: Tom, Kathy, Dan, and Bryan Nieman: Fromm Family Pet Foods Tom Nieman is the fourth-generation owner of Fromm Family Pet Foods, an artisanal pet food company based in Mequon, Wisconsin. Tom, his wife Kathy (with whom he has shared an office for more than 30 years), and their sons, Bryan (brand manager) and Dan (assistant operations manager), manage Fromm Family Pet Foods from a really long-term perspective. Rather than develop strategic plans across one or two years, as many non-family-owned businesses do, Nieman says the family's planning horizon is generational in scope. Bryan and Dan, the fifth generation of owners, work closely with their father and with other senior managers in the company, learning not only the technical aspects of running it but also the philosophical nuances of managing it.[170] ∎

Step 4. *Promote an environment of trust and respect.* Another priceless gift a founder can leave a successor is an environment of trust and respect. Fortunately, 88 percent of next-generation family business leaders say that the current generation of leaders has confidence in their abilities.[171] Trust and respect on the part of the founder and others fuel the successor's desire to learn and excel and build the successor's confidence in making decisions. Developing a competent successor typically requires at least 5 to 10 years. Dan Cathy, now chairman and CEO of Chick-fil-A, the highly successful chicken sandwich chain founded in 1967 by his father, Truett, started working in the family business at age 9. After graduating from college, he joined the company full-time, starting as a director of operations. Over the next several years, Dan opened 50 new stores and then moved up the ranks as vice president of operations and then senior vice president. In 2001, he became president and CEO. In 2013, as part of a long-planned succession, Dan assumed the mantle of chairman of the board from his then-92-year-old father. Cathy's sons, Andrew and Ross, who may represent the next generation of leadership, have been working in the family business for many years.[172]

Empowering the successor by gradually delegating responsibilities creates an environment in which all parties can objectively view the growth and development of the successor. Customers, creditors, suppliers, and staff members develop confidence in the successor. The final transfer of power is not a dramatic, wrenching change but a smooth, coordinated passage. The outgoing generation must be careful at this stage to avoid the "meddling retiree syndrome," in which they continue to report for work after they have officially stepped down and take control of matters that are no longer their responsibility. Doing so undermines a successor's authority and credibility among workers quickly.

Step 5. *Cope with the financial realities of estate and gift taxes.* The final step in developing a workable management succession plan is structuring the transition to minimize the impact of estate, gift, and inheritance taxes on family members and the business. Entrepreneurs who fail to consider the impact of these taxes may force their heirs to sell a successful business just to pay the estate's tax bill. Recent tax legislation may reduce the impact of taxation on the continuity of family businesses. Currently, without proper estate planning, an entrepreneur's family members incur a painful tax bite that can be as high as 40 percent (or more, if the state also imposes an estate tax) when they inherit the business (see Table 17.9). Entrepreneurs should be actively engaged in estate planning no later than age 45; those who start businesses early in their lives or whose businesses grow rapidly may need to begin as early as age 30. A variety of options exist that may be helpful in reducing the estate tax liability. Each operates in a different fashion, but their objective remains the same: to remove a portion of business owners' assets from their estates so that when they die, those assets will not be subject to estate taxes. Many of these estate planning tools need time to work their magic, so the key is to put them in place early on in the life of the business.

TABLE 17.9 Changes in the Estate and Gift Taxes

As this table illustrates, Congress is constantly tinkering with the often punishing structures of estate and gift taxes. The federal estate tax is actually interwoven with the gift tax; the impact of the two taxes began differing in 2004. Congress repealed the estate tax originally in 2010 but reinstated it in 2011. This table shows how the exemptions and the maximum tax rates for the estate and gift taxes have changed over time.

Year	Estate Tax Exemption	Gift Tax Exemption	Maximum Tax Rate
2001	$675,000	$675,000	55%
2002	$1 million	$1 million	50%
2003	$1 million	$1 million	49%
2004	$1.5 million	$1 million	48%
2005	$1.5 million	$1 million	47%
2006	$2 million	$1 million	46%
2007	$2 million	$1 million	45%
2008	$2 million	$1 million	45%
2009	$3.5 million	$1 million	45%
2010	Tax repealed	$1 million	35% (gifts only)
2011	$5 million	$1 million	55%
2012	$5.12 million	$5.12 million	35%
2013	$5.25 million	$5.25 million	40%
2014	$5.34 million	$5.34 million	40%
2015	$5.43 million	$5.43 million	40%
2016	$5.45 million	$5.45 million	40%
2017	$5.49 million	$5.49 million	40%

However the federal laws governing estate taxes may change over the next few years, entrepreneurs whose businesses have been successful cannot afford to neglect estate planning. Even though the federal estate tax burden has eased somewhat, some states have increased their estate taxes.

Source: Based on data from the U.S. Internal Revenue Service.

Buy–Sell Agreement

buy–sell agreement
a contract among co-owners of a business which states that each agrees to buy out the others in the event of the death or disability of one.

One of the most popular estate planning techniques is the buy–sell agreement. A **buy–sell agreement** is a contract that co-owners often rely on to ensure the continuity of a business. In a typical arrangement, the co-owners create a contract which states that each agrees to buy the others out in the event of the death or disability of one. That way, the heirs of the deceased or disabled owner can "cash out" of the business while leaving control of it in the hands of the remaining owners. The buy–sell agreement specifies a formula for determining the value of the business at the time the agreement is to be executed. One problem with buy–sell agreements is that the remaining co-owners may not have the cash available to buy out the disabled or deceased owner. To resolve this issue, many businesses purchase life and disability insurance for each of the owners in amounts large enough to cover the purchase price of their respective shares of the business.

Lifetime Gifting

The owner of a successful business may transfer money to his or her children (or other recipients) from the estate throughout his or her life. Current federal tax regulations allow individuals to make gifts of $14,000 per year, per parent, per recipient that are exempt from federal gift taxes. The recipient is not required to pay tax on the $14,000 gift he or she receives, and the donor must pay a gift tax only on the amount of a gift that exceeds $14,000. For instance, husband-and-wife business owners could give $1,680,000 worth of stock to their three children and their spouses over a period of 10 years without incurring any estate or gift taxes at all. To be an effective estate planning strategy, lifetime gifting requires time to work, which means that business owners must create a plan for using it early on.

Setting up a Trust

A **trust** is a contract between a grantor (the company founder) and a trustee (generally a bank officer or an attorney) in which the grantor gives to the trustee legal title to assets (e.g., stock in the company) that the trustee agrees to hold for the beneficiaries (the founder's children). The beneficiaries can receive income from the trust, the property in the trust, or both at some specified time. Trusts can take a wide variety of forms, but two broad categories of trusts are available: revocable trusts and irrevocable trusts. A **revocable trust** is one that a grantor can change or revoke during his or her lifetime. Under present tax laws, however, the only trust that provides a tax benefit is an **irrevocable trust**, in which the grantor cannot require the trustee to return the assets held in trust. The value of the grantor's estate is lowered because the assets in an irrevocable trust are excluded from the value of the estate. However, an irrevocable trust places severe restrictions on the grantor's control of the property placed in the trust. Although recent changes in tax laws have eliminated certain types of trusts as estate planning tools, business owners use several types of irrevocable trusts to lower their estate tax liabilities:

- *Irrevocable life insurance trust (ILIT).* This type of trust allows business owners to keep the proceeds of a life insurance policy out of their estates and away from estate taxes, freeing up that money to pay the taxes on the remainder of their estates. To get the tax benefit, business owners must be sure that the business or the trust (rather than the owners themselves) owns the insurance policy. The primary disadvantage of an ILIT is that if the owner dies within three years of establishing it, the insurance proceeds become part of the estate and *are* subject to estate taxes. Because the trust is irrevocable, it cannot be amended or rescinded once it is established. Like most other trusts, ILITs must meet stringent requirements to be valid, and entrepreneurs should use experienced attorneys to create them.

- *Irrevocable asset trust.* An irrevocable asset trust is similar to a life insurance trust except that it is designed to pass the assets (such as stock in a family business) in the parents' estate on to their children. The children do not have control of the assets while the parents are living, but they do receive the income from those assets. On the parents' death, the assets in the trust go to the children without being subjected to the estate tax.

- *Grantor retained annuity trust (GRAT).* A GRAT is a special type of irrevocable trust and has become one of the most popular tools for entrepreneurs to transfer ownership of a business while maintaining control over it and minimizing estate taxes. Under a GRAT, an owner can put property (such as company stock) in an irrevocable trust for a minimum of two years. While the trust is in effect, the grantor (owner) retains the benefits associated with the assets in the trust (e.g., the voting rights associated with the stock) and receives interest income (calculated at a fixed interest rate that is determined by the Internal Revenue Service [IRS]) from the assets in the trust. At the end of the trust, the property passes to the beneficiaries (heirs). The beneficiaries are required to pay a gift tax on the value of the assets placed in the GRAT. However, the IRS taxes GRAT gifts only according to their discounted present value because the heirs did not receive use of the property while it was in trust. The primary disadvantage of using a GRAT in estate planning is that if the grantor dies during the life of the GRAT, its assets pass back into the grantor's estate. These assets then become subject to the full estate tax. A GRAT is an excellent tool for transferring the appreciation of an asset such as a growing company to heirs with few tax implications.

ENTREPRENEURIAL PROFILE: Mark Zuckerberg: Facebook Mark Zuckerberg, founder of Facebook, and seven other major shareholders in the company recently created GRATs that will save an estimated $240 million in estate taxes in the future. By setting up a GRAT with 3.4 million pre-IPO shares of Facebook stock valued at just $1.85 per share, Zuckerberg alone will avoid nearly $68 million in estate taxes (at current estate tax rates).[173] ∎

Establishing a trust requires meeting many specific legal requirements and is not something business owners should do on their own. It is much better to work with experienced attorneys, accountants, and financial advisers to create them. Although the cost of establishing a trust can be high, the tax savings they generate are well worth the expense.

trust
a contract between a grantor (the company founder) and a trustee in which the grantor gives the trustee assets (e.g., company stock) that the trustee holds for the trust's beneficiaries (e.g., the grantor's heirs).

revocable trust
a trust that a grantor can change or revoke during his or her lifetime.

irrevocable trust
a trust in which a grantor cannot require the trustee to return the assets held in trust.

Estate Freeze

estate freeze

a strategy that minimizes estate taxes by creating two classes of stock for a business: preferred voting stock for the parents and nonvoting common stock for the children.

An **estate freeze** minimizes estate taxes by having family members create two classes of stock for the business: (1) preferred voting stock for the parents and (2) nonvoting common stock for the children. The value of the preferred stock is frozen, whereas the common stock reflects the anticipated increased market value of the business. Any appreciation in the value of the business after the transfer is not subject to estate taxes. However, the parent must pay gift taxes on the value of the common stock given to the children. The value of the common stock is the total value of the business less the value of the voting preferred stock retained by the parent. The parents also must accept taxable dividends at the market rate on the preferred stock they own.

Family Limited Partnership

family limited partnership (FLP)

a strategy that allows business-owning parents to transfer their company to their children (lowering their estate taxes) while still retaining control over it for themselves.

Creating a **family limited partnership (FLP)** allows business-owning parents to transfer their company to their children and lower their estate taxes while still retaining control over it for themselves. To create an FLP, the parents (or parent) set up a partnership among themselves and their children. The parents retain the general partnership interest, which can be as low as 1 percent, and the children become the limited partners. As general partners, the parents control both the limited partnership and the family business. In other words, nothing in the way the company operates has to change. Over time, the parents transfer company stock into the limited partnership, ultimately passing ownership of the company to their children.

One of the principal tax benefits of an FLP is that it allows discounts on the value of the shares of company stock the parents transfer into the limited partnership. Because a family business is closely held, shares of ownership in it, especially minority shares, are not as marketable as those of a publicly held company. As a result, company shares transferred into the limited partnership are discounted at 20 to 50 percent of their full market value, producing a large tax savings for everyone involved. The average discount is 40 percent, but that amount varies, depending on the industry and the individual company involved.

Because of their ability to reduce estate and gift taxes, FLPs have become popular estate planning tools in recent years. The following tips will help entrepreneurs establish FLPs that will withstand legal challenges:

- Establish a legitimate business reason other than avoiding estate taxes—such as transferring a business over time to the next generation of family members—for creating the FLP and document it in writing.

- Make sure that all members of the FLP make contributions and take distributions according to a predetermined schedule. Owners should not allow FLP funds to pay for personal expenses, nor should they time partnership distributions with owners' personal needs for cash.[174]

- Do not allow members to put their personal assets (such as a house, automobiles, or personal property) into the FLP. Commingling personal and business assets in an FLP raises a red flag to the IRS.

- Expect an audit of the FLP. The IRS tends to scrutinize FLPs, so be prepared for a thorough audit.[175]

Developing a succession plan and preparing a successor require a wide variety of skills, some of which the business founder will not have. It is important to bring experts into the process when necessary. Entrepreneurs often call on their attorneys, accountants, insurance agents, and financial planners to help them build succession plans that work for their particular situations. Because the issues involved can be highly complex and charged with emotion, bringing in trusted advisers to help improves the quality of the process and provides an objective perspective.

LO5

Explain the exit strategies available to entrepreneurs.

Exit Strategies

Most family business founders want their companies to stay within their families, but in some cases, maintaining family control is not practical. Sometimes, no one in the next generation of family members has an interest in managing the company or has the necessary skills and experience to handle the job. Under these circumstances, the founder must look outside the family for

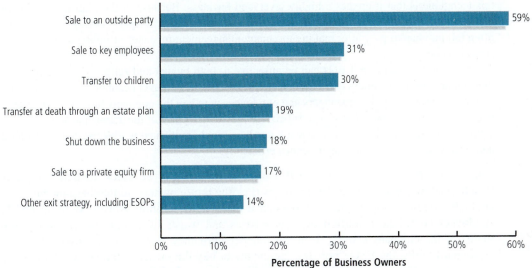

FIGURE 17.8

Exit Strategies Business Owners Are Considering

Source: Based on John Brown, "Out of the Woods: 4 Questions to Determine Your Exit Path," *Forbes*, April 27, 2017, www .forbes.com/sites/ johnbrown/2017/ 04/27/out-of-the- woods-4-questions-to- determine-your-exit- path/#5f3b6f723d19.

leadership if the company is to survive. Whatever the case, entrepreneurs must confront their mortality and plan for the future of their companies. Having a solid management succession plan in place well before retirement is near is absolutely critical to success. Entrepreneurs should examine their options once they decide it is time to step down from the businesses they have founded. Entrepreneurs who are planning to retire often use variations of two strategies: sell to outsiders or sell to (nonfamily) insiders (see Figure 17.8). We turn now to these two exit strategies.

Selling to Outsiders

As you learned in Chapter 7, selling a business to an outsider is no simple task. Done properly, it takes time, patience, and preparation to locate a suitable buyer, strike a deal, and make the transition. Advance preparation, maintaining accurate financial records, and timing are the keys to a successful sale. Too often, however, business owners, like some famous athletes, stay with the game too long, until they and their businesses are well past their prime. A "fire-sale" approach rarely yields the maximum value for a business.

A straight sale may be best for entrepreneurs who want to step down and turn over the reins of the company to someone else. However, selling a business outright is not an attractive exit strategy for those who want to stay on with the company or for those who want to surrender control of the company gradually rather than all at once.

ENTREPRENEURIAL PROFILE: Cindy Whitehead: Sprout Pharmaceuticals Serial entrepreneur Cindy Whitehead started Sprout Pharmaceuticals in Raleigh, North Carolina, and gained fame by developing the little pink pill designed to boost women's sex drives that became known as the "female Viagra." After two failed attempts, Whitehead finally succeeded in gaining approval for the drug by the Food & Drug Administration. The next day, she sold Sprout Pharmaceuticals to Valeant Pharmaceuticals, a Canadian pharmaceutical company that she had been negotiating with for about a month, for $1.1 billion. Whitehead then started her next venture, a business incubator aimed at women entrepreneurs called the Pink Ceiling.[176] ∎

Selling to Insiders

When entrepreneurs have no family members to whom they can transfer ownership or who want to assume the responsibilities of running a company, selling the business to employees is often the preferred option. In most situations, the options available to owners are a leveraged buyout and an employee stock ownership plan.

LEVERAGED BUYOUTS In a **leveraged buyout (LBO)**, managers and/or employees borrow money from a financial institution and pay the owner the total agreed-on price at closing; then they use the cash generated from the company's operations to pay off the debt. The drawback of

leveraged buyout (LBO)

a situation in which managers and/or employees borrow money from a financial institution to purchase a business and then use the money from the company's operations to pay off the debt.

this technique is that it creates a highly leveraged business. Because of the high levels of debt they take on, the new management has very little room for error. Highly leveraged businesses often fall into bankruptcy after making too many management mistakes or failing to cope with a slowing economy.

If properly structured, LBOs can be attractive to both buyers and sellers. Because they get their money up front, sellers do not incur the risk of loss if the buyers cannot keep the business operating successfully. The managers and employees who buy the company have a strong incentive to make sure the business succeeds because they own a piece of the action and some of their capital is at risk in the business. The result can be a highly motivated workforce that works hard and makes sure that the company operates efficiently.

employee stock ownership plan (ESOP)

an arrangement in which employees and/or managers contribute a portion of their salaries and wages over time toward purchasing shares of a company's stock from the founder until they own the company outright.

EMPLOYEE STOCK OWNERSHIP PLANS Unlike LBOs, **employee stock ownership plans (ESOPs)** allow employees and/or managers (i.e., the future owners) to purchase the business gradually, freeing up enough cash to finance the venture's future growth. With an ESOP, employees contribute a portion of their salaries and wages over time toward purchasing shares of the company's stock from the founder until they own the company outright. In leveraged ESOPs, the ESOP borrows the money to buy the owner's stock either all at once or over time. Then, using employees' contributions, the ESOP repays the loan over time (with pre-tax dollars), using the shares of the company's stock as collateral for the loan. An advantage of a leveraged ESOP is that the principal and the interest the ESOP borrows to buy the business are tax deductible, which can save thousands or even millions of dollars in taxes. Transferring ownership to employees through an ESOP is a long-term exit strategy that benefits everyone involved. The owner sells the business to the people he or she can trust the most, his or her managers and employees, and the managers and employees buy a business they already know how to run successfully. In addition, because they own the company, the managers and employees have a huge incentive to see that it operates effectively and efficiently. One study reports that private companies grow 2.4 percent faster after creating ESOPs than they would have been expected to grow without ESOPs.[177] Research also shows that creating an ESOP increases employees' productivity.[178] Approximately 7,000 ESOPs operate in U.S. companies, and they involve 14 million employee owners who own company stock worth an estimated $869 billion. In half of the companies, the ESOP controls a majority of the ownership.

ENTREPRENEURIAL PROFILE: Jeff Lebesch and Kim Jordan: New Belgium Brewing
Jeff Lebesch and Kim Jordan launched New Belgium Brewing in the basement of their home in Fort Collins, Colorado, in 1991 after taking a biking trip through Belgium. The company grew rapidly and today produces nearly 1 million barrels of beer annually that it sells in 46 states. For many years, New Belgium Brewing has provided its employees with many perks, including a bicycle on their first anniversary, a one-week trip to Belgium after 5 years of employment, and a month-long sabbatical after 10 years and then again after 20 years of employment. In 1996, Lebesch and Jordan created an ESOP through which they transferred 10 percent of the company's stock to their employees, a strategy that was only natural because the cofounders had been practicing open-book management for years. In 2013, Kim Jordan, then the company's CEO, surprised New Belgium Brewing's employees when she announced that she had sold the remainder of her shares (59 percent) of the company. Employees gasped. "To whom?" they wanted to know. Then she asked the employees to open the envelopes that had been placed on their chairs. Inside they found mirrors, which was Jordan's way of telling the employees who had played such an important role in New Belgium Brewing's success that they were the new owners of the company. Today, the employees own 100 percent of New Belgium Brewing, which continues to grow and expand across the United States.[179] ∎

MyLab Entrepreneurship

If your instructor is using MyLab Entrepreneurship, go to **www.pearson.com/mylab/ entrepreneurship** to complete the problems marked with this icon ⭐.

Chapter Summary by Learning Objective

1. **Explain the challenges involved in the entrepreneur's role as leader and what it takes to be a successful leader.**

   - Leadership is the process of influencing and inspiring others to work to achieve a common goal and then giving them the power and the freedom to achieve it.

   - Management and leadership are not the same, yet both are essential to a small company's success. Leadership without management is unbridled; management without leadership is uninspired. Leadership gets a small business going; management keeps it going.

2. **Describe the importance of hiring the right employees and how to avoid making hiring mistakes.**

   - The decision to hire a new employee is an important one for every business, but its impact is magnified many times in a small company. Every new hire a business owner makes determines the heights to which the company can climb—or the depths to which it will plunge.

   - To avoid making hiring mistakes, entrepreneurs should develop meaningful job descriptions and job specifications, plan and conduct an effective interview, and check references before hiring any employee.

3. **Explain how to create a company culture that encourages employee retention.**

   - Company culture is the distinctive, unwritten code of conduct that governs the behavior, attitudes, relationships, and style of an organization. Culture arises from an entrepreneur's consistent and relentless pursuit of a set of core values that everyone in the company can believe in. Small companies' flexible structures can be a major competitive weapon.

   - Job design techniques for enhancing employee motivation include job enlargement, job rotation, job enrichment, flextime, job sharing, and flexplace (which includes telecommuting).

   - Money is an important motivator for many workers, but it's not the only one. The key to using rewards such as recognition and praise to motivate involves tailoring them to the needs and characteristics of the workers.

4. **Describe the steps in developing a management succession plan for a growing business that allows a smooth transition of leadership to the next generation.**

   - As their companies grow, entrepreneurs must begin to plan for passing the leadership baton to the next generation well in advance. A succession plan is a crucial element in successfully transferring a company to the next generation. Preparing a succession plan involves five steps: (1) select the successor, (2) create a survival kit for the successor, (3) groom the successor, (4) promote an environment of trust and respect, and (5) cope with the financial realities of estate taxes.

5. **Explain the exit strategies available to entrepreneurs.**

   - Family business owners wanting to step down from their companies can sell to outsiders or to insiders. Common tools for selling to insiders (employees or managers) include LBOs and ESOPs.

MyLab Entrepreneurship

If your instructor is using MyLab Entrepreneurship, go to **www.pearson.com/mylab/entrepreneurship** for Auto-graded writing questions as well as the following Assisted-graded writing questions:

1. Explain the differences among job simplification, job enlargement, job rotation, and job enrichment. What impact do these different job designs have on workers?
2. Why is it important for a small business owner to develop a management succession plan? Why is it difficult for most business owners to develop such a plan? What steps are involved in creating a succession plan?

Discussion Questions

17-1. What is leadership? What is the difference between leadership and management?

17-2. What behaviors do effective leaders exhibit?

17-3. Why is it so important for small companies to hire the right employees? What can small business owners do to avoid making hiring mistakes?

17-4. What is a job description? A job specification? What functions do they serve in the hiring process?

17-5. Outline the procedure for conducting an effective interview.

17-6. What is company culture? What role does culture play in a small company's success? What threats does rapid growth pose for a company's culture?

17-7. Is money the best motivator? Explain.

17-8. How do pay-for-performance compensation systems work? What other rewards are available to small business managers to use as motivators? How effective are they?

17-9. Briefly describe the options a small business owner wanting to pass the family business on to the next generation can take to minimize the impact of estate taxes.

Beyond the Classroom . . .

17-10. Visit a local business that has experienced rapid growth in the past three years and ask the owner about the specific problems he or she had to face because of the organization's growth. How did the owner handle these problems? Looking back, what would he or she do differently?

17-11. Contact a local small business that has at least 20 employees. Does the company have job descriptions and job specifications? What process does the owner use to hire a new employee? What questions does the owner typically ask candidates in an interview?

17-12. Ask the owner of a small manufacturing operation to give you a tour of his or her operation. During your tour, observe the way jobs are organized. To what extent does the company use the job design concepts of job simplification, job enlargement, job rotation, job enrichment, flextime, and job sharing? Based on your observations, what recommendations would you make to the owner about the company's job design?

17-13. Find *Fortune*'s 100 Best Companies to Work For or *Inc.*'s Top Small Company Workplaces issue. Read the profiles of the companies included on the list and develop a list of at least five ideas you would like to incorporate into the company you plan to launch.

17-14. Contact five small business owners about their plans for passing their businesses on to the next generation. Do they intend to pass the business along to a family member? Do they have a management succession plan? When do they plan to name a successor? Have they developed a plan for minimizing the effects of estate taxes? How many more years do they plan to work before retiring?

17-15. Entrepreneurs say they have learned much about leadership from the movies. "Films beg to be interpreted and discussed," says one leadership consultant, "and from those discussions businesspeople come up with principles for their own jobs." A recent survey of small company CEOs by *Inc.* magazine[180] resulted in the following list of the best movies for leadership lessons: *Apollo 13* (1995), *The Bridge on the River Kwai* (1957), *Dead Poets Society* (1989), *Elizabeth* (1998), *Glengarry Glen Ross* (1992), *It's a Wonderful Life* (1946), *Norma Rae* (1979), *One Flew over the Cuckoo's Nest* (1975), *Twelve Angry Men* (1957), and *Twelve O'Clock High* (1949). Rent or download one of these films and watch it with a group of your classmates. After viewing the movie, discuss the leadership lessons you learned from it and report the results to the other members of your class.

Endnotes

[1]Richard Fry, "Millennials Surpass Gen Xers as the Largest Generation in the Workforce," *Pew Research Center Fact Tank*, May 11, 2015, www.pewresearch.org/fact-tank/2015/05/11/millennials-surpass-gen-xers-as-the-largest-generation-in-u-s-labor-force/.

[2]Rob Reuteman, "Value Lessons," *Entrepreneur*, March 2014, pp. 39–56.

[3]Michael Gold, "Jazzin' CEO," *Manage Smarter*, January 9, 2008, p. 1.

[4]Ibid.

[5]Francis Huffman, "Taking the Lead," *Entrepreneur*, November 1993, p. 101.

[6]Eric Schurenberg, "Born Leaders or Idea Machines?" *Inc.*, March 2015, p. 14; Brian O'Keefe, "Leader of the Crimson Tide," *Fortune*, September 24, 2012, pp. 150–160.

[7]"Sharing the Vision," *Fortune*, February 4, 2013, p. 24; Erin Glover, "Opening Night 1937: 'Snow White and the Seven Dwarfs' Premiers at Cathay Circle, Disney Parks Blog, December 21, 2011, http://disneyparks.disney.go.com/blog/2011/12/opening-night-1937-snow-white-and-the-seven-dwarfs-premieres-at-carthay-circle-theatre/.

[8]Sunnie Giles, "The Most Important Leadership Competencies, According to Leaders Around the World," *Harvard Business Review*, March 15, 2016, https://hbr.org/2016/03/the-most-important-leadership-competencies-according-to-leaders-around-the-world.

[9]Jack Welch and Suzy Welch, "What Do Great Leaders Have in Common? They're Authentic," *Fortune*, April 9, 2012, p. 58.

[10]Bill Briggs, "'Undercover Boss' Spurs Shop-Floor Changes," *MSNBC*, March 22, 2010, www.msnbc.msn.com/id/

35912818/ns/business-careers/t/undercover-boss-spurs-shop-floor-changes/#.T8eRpcqwX3Y.

[11]Jane M. Von Bergen, "Forman Mills' TV Makeover Was the Real Thing," *Philadelphia Inquirer*, May 22, 2015, www.philly.com/philly/business/20150522_Forman_Mills__TV_makeover_was_the_real_thing.html.

[12]John Mariotti, "The Role of a Leader," *IndustryWeek*, February 1, 1999, p. 75.

[13]Adam Bornstein and Jordan Bornstein, "What Makes a Great Leader? Build a Culture of . . . " *Entrepreneur*, March 2016, p.50.

[14]Adam Bryant, "Shawn Jenkins of Benefitfocus: A CEO Is Like a Flight Instructor," *New York Times*, March 15, 2014, www.nytimes.com/2014/03/16/business/shawn-jenkins-of-benefitfocus-a-ceo-is-like-a-flight-instructor.html?_r=0.

[15]Vanessa Richardson, "Hands Off," *Entrepreneur*, March 2014, pp. 52–53.

[16]Vivian Hunt, Dennis Layton, and Sara Prince, "Why Diversity Matters," McKinsey and Company, www.mckinsey.com/business-functions/organization/our-insights/why-diversity-matters.

[17]Ali Robins, "Why a Fun Culture Is Good for Business," *Office Vibe*, March 23, 2017, www.officevibe.com/blog/fun-company-culture-good-business.

[18]Anne Wojcicki, "The Way I Work," *Inc.*, June 2012, pp. 114–116.

[19]Paula Andruss, "3 Ways to Success," *Entrepreneur*, March 2014, p. 36.

[20]Meghan French Dunbar and Rachel Zurer, "How to Profit by Helping Your Workers Be Their Best Selves," *Conscious Company Media*, November 6, 2016, http://consciouscompanymedia.com/workplace-culture/developing-talent/how-to-profit-by-helping-your-workers-be-their-best-selves/; Jason Ankeny, "Human Capital Ideas," *Entrepreneur*, March 2014, p. 49.

[21]Bill Breen, "The Clear Leader," *Fast Company*, March 2005, p. 66.

[22]Ashley Merryman, "Leaders Are More Powerful When They Are Humble, New Research Shows," *Washington Post*, December 8, 2016, www.washingtonpost.com/news/inspired-life/wp/2016/12/08/leaders-are-more-powerful-when-theyre-humble-new-research-shows/?utm_term=.a7c7cad8d140.

[23]Kent M. Keith, "Servant Leaders Are the Best Leaders During Times of Change," *Branches*, January–February 2009, www.greenleaf.org/whatissl/BranchesMagazine.pdf.

[24]"ENGEO Incorporated," *Great Rated*, September 16, 2013, http://us.greatrated.com/engeo-incorporated.

[25]James Lea, "Leadership Is a Choice—One You Should Make Carefully," *Bizjournals*, July 16, 2007, http://sacramento.bizjournals.com/extraedge/consultants/family_business/2007/07/16/column267.html.

[26]"New CareerBuilder and Emsi Analysis Finds College Degrees Are Not Keeping Up with Demand in Critical Areas," CareerBuilder, March 3, 2016, www.careerbuilder.com/share/aboutus/pressreleasesdetail.aspx?sd=3%2F3%2F2016&siteid=cbpr&sc_cmp1=cb_pr937_&id=pr937&ed=12%2F31%2F2016.

[27]William C. Dunkelberg and Holly Wade, *NFIB Small Business Economic Trends*, National Federation of Independent Businesses, March 2017, p. 10.

[28]Pete Jansons, "Hiring for Your Small Business When There Is a Shortage of Skilled Labor," CareerBuilder, March 232, 2016, http://resources.careerbuilder.com/small-business/hiring-for-your-small-business-when-there-is-a-shortage-of-skilled-labor.

[29]"More Than One in Four Employers Do Not Conduct Checks of All New Employees, According to CareerBuilder Survey," CareerBuilder, November 17, 2016, www.careerbuilder.com/share/aboutus/pressreleasesdetail.aspx?sd=11/17/2016&site id=cbpr&sc_cmp1=cb_pr975_&id=pr975&ed=12/31/2016; Madeline Laurano, *The True Cost of a Bad Hire*, Brandon Hall Group, August 2015, p. 5.

[30]"The Cost of a Bad Hire Can Be Big for Small and Midsize Businesses," Robert Half, 2016, www.roberthalf.com/sites/default/files/Media_Root/images/rh-pdfs/rh_costs_of_bad_hire_us_infographic.pdf.

[31]"The Real Cost of a Bad Hire," Newton Software, July 7, 2016, http://newtonsoftware.com/blog/2016/07/06/the-real-cost-of-a-bad-hire/.

[32]Madeline Laurano, *The True Cost of a Bad Hire*, Brandon Hall Group, August 2015, p. 5.

[33]"CareerBuilder Releases Annual List of Strangest Interview and Body Language Mistakes," CareerBuilder, January 12, 2017, www.careerbuilder.com/share/aboutus/pressreleasesdetail.aspx?ed=12%2F31%2F2017&id=pr984&sd=1%2F12%2F2017.

[34]"Hiring Decisions Miss the Mark 50% of the Time," *Corporate Executive Board*, October 24, 2008, http://ir.executiveboard.com/phoenix.zhtml?c113226&pirol-newsArticle&ID1205091&highlight; "2 Out of 3 Managers Still Fear a Hiring Decision They'll Regret," DDI, March 16, 2009, www.ddiworld.com/about/pr_releases_en.asp?id211.

[35]"The Cost of a Bad Hire Can Be Big for Small and Midsize Businesses," Robert Half, 2016, www.roberthalf.com/sites/default/files/Media_Root/images/rh-pdfs/rh_costs_of_bad_hire_us_infographic.pdf.

[36]Scott Gerber, "Exit Interview: Jim Koch," *Inc.*, November 2015, p. 120.

[37]"More Than Two-Thirds of Businesses Affected by Bad Hire in the Past Year, According to CareerBuilder Survey," CareerBuilder, December 8, 2011, www.pitchengine.com/careerbuilder/more-than-twothirds-of-businessesaffected-by-a-bad-hire-in-the-past-year-according-tocareerbuilder-surveyheadline.

[38]Madeline Laurano, *The True Cost of a Bad Hire*, Brandon Hall Group, August 2015, p. 9.

[39]"DHI-DFH Vacancy Duration Measure," DHI Group, April 2017, http://dhihiringindicators.com/data-charts/.

[40]Issie Lapowsky, "The Quest for the Perfect Fit," *Inc.*, October 2013, pp. 52–53.

[41]"2016/2017 Talent Shortage Survey," ManPower, April 2017, www.manpowergroup.com/talent-shortage-explorer/#.WPfVaGe1vZ4.

[42]"Companies Losing Money to the Skills Gap, According to CareerBuilder Survey," CareerBuilder, March 6, 2014, www.careerbuilder.com/share/aboutus/pressreleasesdetail.aspx?sd=3/6/2014&id=pr807&ed=12/31/2014.

[43]"2015 Turnover Rates by Industry," *Compensation Force*, 2017, www.compensationforce.com/2016/04/2015-turnover-rates-by-industry.html.

[44]Amber Hyatt, "Generation Z," *Website Magazine*, April 2016, p. 12.

[45]"Turnover and Retention," *Catalyst*, August 12, 2016, www.catalyst.org/knowledge/turnover-and-retention.

[46]"Average-Cost-Per-Hire for Companies Is $4,129, SHRM Survey Finds," Society for Human Resource Management, August 3, 2016, www.shrm.org/about-shrm/press-room/press-releases/pages/human-capital-benchmarking-report.aspx.

[47]*The Talent Challenge: Harnessing the Power of Human Skills in the Machine Age*, PWC, 2017, p. 11.

[48]"Despite Extended Vacancies, Only 38 Percent of Employers Continuously Recruit," CareerBuilder, March 11, 2014, www.careerbuilder.ca/share/aboutus/pressreleasesdetail.aspx?sd=3%2F11%2F2014&id=pr808&ed=3%2F11%2F2099.

[49]*Jobvite Recruiter Nation Report*, 2016, Jobvite, 2016, p. 13.

[50]Roy Maurer, "This Is Why Finding Talent Is Getting Tougher in 2016," Society for Human Resource Management, June 20,

2016, www.shrm.org/hr-today/news/hr-news/pages/recruiting-gets-harder-in-2016.aspx.

[51]Matt Sedensky, "Oldies but Goodies: Some Employers Hire Boomers," *Greenville News*, September 14, 2013, p.7A.

[52]*Jobvite Recruiter Nation Report*, 2016, Jobvite, 2016, p. 13.

[53]Sarah Duke, "10 Employee Referral Program Fast Facts," *Recruiter*, March 31, 2015, www.recruiter.com/i/10-employee-referral-program-fast-facts/.

[54]Siofra Pratt, "The True Value of an Employee Referral," *Social Talent*, June 3, 2015, www.socialtalent.co/blog/the-incredible-true-value-of-an-employee-referral-infographic.

[55]Milton Moskowitz and Robert Levering, "The 100 Best Companies to Work For," *Fortune*, March 15, 2015, p. 144.

[56]Ibid.

[57]Amy Rees Anderson, "5 Unique Recruiting Ideas That Paid Off Big Time," *Forbes*, August 16, 2013, www.forbes.com/sites/amyanderson/2013/08/16/5-unique-recruiting-ideas-that-paid-off-big-time/.

[58]*Using Social Media for Talent Acquisition—Recruitment and Screening*, Society for Human Resources Management, 2016, p. 7.

[59]Aaron Smith, "Searching for Work in the Digital Era," Pew Internet Research Center, November 19, 2015, www.pewinternet.org/2015/11/19/2-job-seeking-in-the-era-of-smartphones-and-social-media/.

[60]*Jobvite Recruiter Nation Report*, 2016, Jobvite, 2016, p. 15.

[61]David Smith, Katherine LaVelle, Mary Lyons, and Yaarit Silverstone, *The Gig Experience: Unleashing the Potential of Your Talent and Your Business—Insights from the Accenture Strategy 2016 U.S. College Graduate Employment Study*, Accenture, 2016, p. 4.

[62]"2016 Internship and Co-op Survey 2016," National Association of Colleges and Employers, May 2016, p. 3.

[63]Áine Cain, "12 Famous People Who Started Their Careers as Interns," *Business Insider*, July 7, 2016, www.businessinsider.com/famous-people-who-paid-their-dues-as-interns-2016-7/#bill-gates-microsoft-founder-1.

[64]"Success Stories: Precision Body & Paint," Grads of Life, 2017, http://gradsoflife.org/success-stories/.

[65]Mark Mather, "Fact Sheet: Aging in the U.S.," Population Reference Bureau, January 2016, www.prb.org/Publications/Media-Guides/2016/aging-unitedstates-fact-sheet.aspx.

[66]Kris Maher, "A Tactical Recruiting Effort Pays Off," *Wall Street Journal*, October 24, 2011, p. R6.

[67]Susan Ladika, "Springing for Spring Break with Sun, Fun, and Recruiting All in One," *Workforce Management*, April 2013, p. 12.

[68]Jennifer Wang, "How to Build a Stellar Team at a High Potential Start-up," *Entrepreneur*, September 9, 2011, www.entrepreneur.com/article/220236.

[69]"Innovating Human Resources," *BrainReactions*, January 16, 2007, www.brainreactions.com/whitepapers/brainreactions_hr_innovation_paper.pdf, pp. 11–14; Christopher Caggiano, "Recruiting Secrets," *Inc.*, October 1998, pp. 30–42.

[70]"The 2016 Deloitte Millennial Survey: Winning Over the Next Generation of Leaders," *Deloitte*, 2016, p. 20.

[71]Brie Weiler Reynolds, "Survey: Only 7% of Workers Say They Are Most Productive in the Office," Flexjobs, August 26, 2016, www.flexjobs.com/blog/post/survey-workers-most-productive-in-the-office/.

[72]"Flextime Work Schedules Could Improve Loyalty and Profits," TrackSmart, November 29, 2016, http://blog.tracksmart.com/flextime-work-schedules-could-improve-loyalty-and-profits/.

[73]"100 Best Companies to Work For," *Fortune*, April 2017, http://beta.fortune.com/best-companies/.

[74]Ann Diab, "Five Flexible Work Strategies and the Companies That Use Them," *Fast Company*, March 30, 2016, www.fastcompany.com/3058344/5-flexible-work-strategies-and-the-companies-who-use-them; "Form Assembly Team," FormAssembly, https://www.formassembly.com/team/.

[75]Darren Dahl, "13 Most Common Mistakes Made When Hiring," *American Express Open Forum*, November 9, 2011, www.openforum.com/articles/13-most-common-mistakes-made-when-hiring.

[76]Michael A. McDaniel, Deborah L. Whetzel, Frank L. Schmidt, and Steven D. Maurer, "The Validity of Employment Interviews: A Comprehensive Review and Meta-Analysis," *Journal of Applied Psychology*, no. 79, August 1994, pp. 599–616.

[77]Madeline Laurano, *The True Cost of a Bad Hire*, Brandon Hall Group, August 2015, p. 8.

[78]Leigh Buchanan, "Core Value: Teamwork," *Inc.*, June 2011, pp. 68–69.

[79]Mike Michalowicz, "The Best Recruits May Not Be Who You Think They Are," *Wall Street Journal*, October 4, 2011, http://online.wsj.com/article/SB10001424052970204524604576610961317004204.html.

[80]Anne Fisher, "Want to Hire a Team Player? Ask About Volunteer Work," *Fortune*, January 27, 2016, http://fortune.com/2016/01/27/hiring-team-player-volunteer-work/.

[81]Peter Bregman, "The Interview Question You Should Always Ask," *Harvard Business Publishing*, January 27, 2009, http://blogs.harvardbusiness.org/cs/2009/01/the_interview_question_you_sho.html.

[82]Vanessa Richardson, "Value Lessons: Hands Off," *Entrepreneur*, March 2014, pp. 52–53.

[83]Minda Zetlin, "How to Hire Top Talent on a Small Budget," *Inc.*, June 18, 2013, www.inc.com/minda-zetlin/how-to-hire-top-talent-on-a-small-budget.html.

[84]Nicholas Carlson, "15 Google Interview Questions That Will Make You Feel Stupid," *Business Insider*, November 8, 2010, www.businessinsider.com/15-google-interview-questions-that-will-make-you-feel-stupid-2010-11.

[85]"25 Weirdest Job Interview Questions of 2012," *CBS News*, January 11, 2013, /www.cbsnews.com/news/25-weirdest-job-interview-questions-of-2012/; "Top 25 Oddball Interview Questions of 2011," *Glassdoor*, December 28, 2011, www.glassdoor.com/blog/top-25-oddball-interview-questions-2011; William Poundstone, "How to Ace a Google Interview," *Wall Street Journal*, December 24, 2011, http://online.wsj.com/article/SB100014240529702045523045771125229825505222.html.

[86]*2016 HireRight Employment Screening Benchmark Report*, HireRight, 2016, p. 6.

[87]"More Than One in Four Employers Do Not Conduct Checks of All New Employees, According to CareerBuilder Survey," CareerBuilder, November 17, 2016, www.careerbuilder.com/share/aboutus/pressreleasesdetail.aspx?sd=11/17/2016&siteid=cbpr&sc_cmp1=cb_pr975_&id=pr975&ed=12/31/2016.

[88]Chad Brooks, "Employee Background Checks: What's Legal and What's Not," *Business News Daily*, April 2, 2014, www.businessnewsdaily.com/6166-why-you-need-to-use-background-checks.html.

[89]"Number of Employers Using Social Media to Screen Candidates Has Increased 500 Percent Over Last Decade," CareerBuilder, April 28, 2016, www.careerbuilder.com/share/aboutus/pressreleasesdetail.aspx?ed=12/31/2016&id=pr945&sd=4/28/2016.

[90]"CareerBuilder's Annual Survey Reveals The Most Outrageous Resume Mistakes Employers Have Found," CareerBuilder, September 22, 2016, www.careerbuilder.com/share/aboutus/

pressreleasesdetail.aspx?sd=9%2F22%2F2016&id=pr967&ed=12%2F31%2F2016.

[91]Andy Dunn, "How to Stop Relying on the Job Interview," *Inc.*, November 2013, p. 51.

[92]*Jobvite Recruiter Nation Report*, Jobvite, 2016, p. 10.

[93]Rachel Feintzeig, "'Culture Fit' May Be Key to Your Next Job," *Wall Street Journal*, October 12, 2016, pp. B1, B6.

[94]Rachel Feintzeig, "'Culture Fit' May Be Key to Your Next Job," *Wall Street Journal*, October 12, 2016, pp. B1, B6; Susan M. Heathfield, "20 Ways Zappos Reinforces Its Company Culture," *The Balance*, June 28, 2016, www.thebalance.com/zappos-company-culture-1918813.

[95]"CustomInk," Great Places to Work, 2016, http://reviews.greatplacetowork.com/customink; Milton Moskowitz and Robert Levering, "The 100 Best Companies to Work For," *Fortune*, March 15, 2015, p. 144; "CustomInk," *Great Rated*, August 2013, http://us.greatrated.com/customink.

[96]Paul Spiegelman, "Does Corporate Culture Pay?" *Inc.*, May 18, 2011, www.inc.com/articles/201105/paul-spiegelman-does-corporate-culture-pay.html.

[97]Rich Karlgaard, "Do Jerks Always Win?" *Forbes*, December 29, 2014, p. 44.

[98]Damon Darlin, "When Your Start-up Takes Off," *Business 2.0*, May 2005, p. 127.

[99]Susan Adams, "Tough Lessons in Firing: Why It Took a Staffing Entrepreneur Eight Years to Let a Poor Performer Go," *Forbes*, January 17, 2017, www.forbes.com/sites/forbestreptalks/2017/01/17/tom-gimbel-of-staffing-firm-lasalle-network-explains-the-tough-lessons-hes-learned-about-hiring/#421dba5c5dad; Katherine Duncan, "Focused on Fun," *Entrepreneur*, March 2014, p. 50; "LaSalle Network," *Great Places to Work*, 2017, http://reviews.greatplacetowork.com/lasalle-network1.

[100]Kate Rockwood, "Beyond Fitting In," *Inc.*, December 2015/January 2016, pp. 112–113.

[101]Jason Daley, "Culture Club," *Entrepreneur*, January 2016, pp. 141–152.

[102]Psychologically Healthy Workplace Award: Noble-Davis Consulting," American Psychological Association Center for Organizational Excellence, 2014, www.apaexcellence.org/awards/national/winner/43.

[103]Kirsten Davidson, "A Best Workplace Takes Hard Work," *Workforce*, June 2016, p. 26.

[104]Nichole L. Torres, "Let the Good Times Roll," *Entrepreneur*, November 2004, p. 57.

[105]"We Are HZDG," *The Muse*, 2017, www.themuse.com/companies/hzdg; Holly E. Thomas, "Is This the DMV's Most Creative Office?" *Refinery 29*, October 23, 2012, www.refinery29.com/hzdg.

[106]*State of the American Workplace*, Gallup, 2017, pp. 174–183.

[107]Ibid., p. 19.

[108]Robin D. Schatz, "How Blinds.com Searched Its Soul—and Found Home Depot," *Inc.*, May 2014, p. 24.

[109]Josh Bersin, "Becoming Irresistible," *Deloitte Review*, Issue 16, 2015, p. 148.

[110]*2017 Trends in Global Employee Engagement*, Aon Hewitt, 2017, p. 2.

[111]*Engaging and Retaining Top Performers*, Aon Hewitt, August 2016, p. 1.

[112]Emma Seppala and Kim Cameron, "Proof That Positive Work Cultures Are More Productive," *Harvard Business Review*, December 1, 2015, https://hbr.org/2015/12/proof-that-positive-work-cultures-are-more-productive.

[113]*State of the American Workplace*, Gallup, 2017, p. 70.

[114]"New Census Bureau Report Analyzes U.S. Population Projections," U.S. Census Bureau, March 3, 2015, www.census.gov/newsroom/press-releases/2015/cb15-tps16.html.

[115]Kate Rockwood, "Beyond Fitting In," *Inc.*, December 2015/January 2016, pp. 112–113.

[116]"The 50 Best Workplaces for Giving Back," *Fortune*, February 9, 2017, http://fortune.com/2017/02/09/best-workplaces-giving-back/.

[117]"How Companies Make Good Decisions," McKinsey Global Survey Results, *McKinsey Quarterly*, January 2009, www.mckinseyquarterly.com/How_companies_make_good_decisions_McKinsey_Global_Survey_Results_2282.

[118]Milton Moskowitz and Robert Levering, "The 100 Best Companies to Work For," *Fortune*, March 15, 2015, p. 145.

[119]Ibid., p. 142.

[120]Leigh Buchanan, "Training the Best Damn Fry Cooks (and Doctors and Engineers) in the Country, *Inc.*, May 2014, p. 60; Bill Taylor, "How One Fast-Food Chain Keeps Its Turnover Rates Absurdly Low," *Harvard Business Review*, January 26, 2016, https://hbr.org/2016/01/how-one-fast-food-chain-keeps-its-turnover-rates-absurdly-low.

[121]James R. Hagerty, "Harley Goes Lean to Build Hogs," *Wall Street Journal*, September 21, 2012, www.wsj.com/articles/SB10000872396390044372020457800416419984545.

[122]*Gensler 2013 Workplace Study*, Gensler, 2013, p. 12.

[123]Robert D. Mohr and Cindy Zoghi, *Is Job Enrichment Really Enriching?* (Washington, DC: U.S. Department of Labor, U.S. Bureau of Labor Statistics, Office of Productivity and Technology, January 2006), pp. 13–15.

[124]*State of the American Workplace*, Gallup, 2017, p. 149.

[125]Milton Moskowitz and Robert Levering, "The 100 Best Companies to Work For," *Fortune*, March 15, 2015, p. 146.

[126]Kenneth Matos. Ellen Galinsky, and James T. Bond, *National Study of Employers*, Society for Human Resource Management, Families and Work Institute, and When Work Works, 2016, p. 19.

[127]"Flex at a Glance," When Work Works, www.whenworkworks.org/research/reports.html#gissues, p. 1.

[128]"SHRM Research: Flexible Work Arrangements," *Society for Human Resource Management*, 2015, p. 3.

[129]Richard Feloni, "This Tech CEO and His Employees Only Work 4 Days a Week," *Business Insider*, June 23, 2015, www.businessinsider.com/treehouse-ceos-32-hour-workweek-2015-6.

[130]Jennifer J. Deal and Alec Levenson, "Millennials Play the Long Game," *Strategy + Business*, October 5, 2015, www.strategy-business.com/article/00366?gko=c5472.

[131]"Latest Telecommuting Statistics," Global Workplace Analytics, January 2016, http://globalworkplaceanalytics.com/telecommuting-statistics.

[132]Meredith Levinson, "Survey: Telecommuting Improves Productivity, Lowers Cost," *CIO*, October 7, 2008, www.cio.com/article/453289/Telecommuting_Improves_Productivity_Lowers_Costs_New_Survey_Finds; Harriet Hagestad, "New Ways to Work: Telecommuting and Job Sharing," Career Builder, June 23, 2006, www.careerbuilder.com/JobSeeker/careerbytes/CBArticle.aspx?articleID369&cbRecursionCnt1&cbsid49944662f7b64dc38639d9a3ef87dd18-204624985-R5-4.

[133]John Rampton, "8 Expert Tips to Having a Healthy Company Environment," *Forbes*, February 18, 2015, www.forbes.com/sites/johnrampton/2015/02/18/8-expert-tips-to-having-a-healthy-company-environment/#2c5c38794dd7.

[134]Milton Moskowitz and Robert Levering, "The 100 Best Companies to Work For," *Fortune*, March 15, 2015, p. 150.

[135]"Employee Job Satisfaction and Engagement: Revitalizing a Changing Workforce," *Society for Human Resource Management*, 2016, p. 21.

[136]Raymond Fisman and Michael Luca, "The Flextime Paradox," *Wall Street Journal*, March 4-5, 2017, p. C3.

[137]Milton Moskowitz and Robert Levering, "The 100 Best Companies to Work For," *Fortune*, March 15, 2015, p. 145; "Company Gives Employees Six-Figure Bonus," *KTVU*, December 9, 2015, www.ktvu.com/news/56626557-story.

[138]Christopher Tkaczyk, "Small Businesses, Fantastic Employers," *Fortune*, October 7, 2013, p. 30; "Badger Mining Corporation," *Great Rated*, 2013, http://us.greatrated.com/badger-mining-corporation.

[139]Darren Dahl, "Open Book Management's Lessons for Detroit," *New York Times*, May 20, 2009, www.nytimes.com/2009/05/21/business/smallbusiness/21open.html.

[140]Lisa Jennings, "Giving Employees a Stake," *Restaurant Hospitality*, February 3, 2017, www.restaurant-hospitality.com/staffing/giving-employees-stake.

[141]Milton Moskowitz and Robert Levering, "The 100 Best Companies to Work For," *Fortune*, March 15, 2015, p. 150.

[142]*Work Redefined: A New Age of Benefits*, MetLife, 2017, pp. 27, 29.

[143]"Square Root," Great Places to Work, 2017, http://reviews.greatplacetowork.com/square-root.

[144]*Work Redefined: A New Age of Benefits*, MetLife, 2017, p. 13.

[145]Paula Andruss, "Perk Up Your Business," *Entrepreneur*, May 2012, pp. 54–58.

[146]"AgileCraft," Great Places to Work, 2017, http://reviews.greatplacetowork.com/agilecraft.

[147]"Wisetail," Great Places to Work, 2017, http://reviews.greatplacetowork.com/wisetail.

[148]"Client Profile: Generation Z Marketing," *Small Business Owner Report*, Bank of America, Spring 2015, p. 11.

[149]"Employee Job Satisfaction and Engagement: Revitalizing a Changing Workforce," *Society for Human Resource Management*, 2016, p. 29.

[150]Mark Twain, *Letter to Gertrude Natkin*, March 2, 1906.

[151]Christopher Hann, "A Leading Personality," *Entrepreneur*, March 2012, pp. 59–62; "Barbara Corcoran's 8 Lessons for Entrepreneurs," *Inc. Women's Summit*, December 1, 2011, www.inc.com/barbara-corcoran/eight-lessons-for-entrepreneurs.html.

[152]"ENGEO Incorporated," Great Rated, 2013, http://us.greatrated.com/engeo-incorporated.

[153]"AcademicWorks," Great Places to Work, 2017, http://reviews.greatplacetowork.com/academicworks-inc.

[154]"Family Owned Business Statistics," Statistics Brain, 2017, www.statisticbrain.com/family-owned-business-statistics/; "10 Surprising Facts About Family Businesses," Family Firm Institute, 2014, http://familybusinessinstitute.com/blog/10-surprising-facts-about-family-businesses/; "Family Business Facts," University of Vermont, School of Business Administration, 2014, www.uvm.edu/business/vfbi/?Page=facts.html; "Facts About Family Business," S. Dale High Center for Family Business at Elizabethtown College," 2014, http://familybizcenter.user-feedback.com/facts.cfm; Veronica Dagher, "Who Will Run the Family Business?" *Wall Street Journal*, March 12, 2012, p. R6; *Annual Family Business Survey General Results and Conclusions*, Family Enterprise USA, March 2011, p. 1; Karen E. Klein, "Fathers and Daughters: Passing on the Family Business," *Bloomberg Businessweek*, December 27, 2011, www.businessweek.com/small-business/fathers-and-daughters-passing-on-the-family-business-12272011.html.

[155]Chris Arnold, "Wiffle Ball: Born and Still Made in the USA," *National Public Radio*, September 5, 2011, www.npr.org/2011/09/05/140145711/wiffle-ball-born-and-still-made-inthe-usa.

[156]*Family Business Survey 2016: "The Missing Middle": Bridging the Strategy Gap in Family Firms*, PWC, 2016, pp. 4–5.

[157]Lettie Teague, "When French Winemaking Is a Family Affair," *Wall Street Journal*, April 23–24, 2016, p. D7; "Robert Drouhin & Family," *Wine Spectator*, 2016, www.winespectator.com/anniversary/leaders/id/Robert-Drouhin.

[158]"Facts and Perspectives on Family Business Around the World: United States," Family Business Institute, www.ffi.org/looking/fbfacts_us.pdf.

[159]Michelle Nati, "10 Oldest Companies Still in Business," *Oddee*, January 8, 2016, www.oddee.com/item_99566.aspx; "Family Business: The Oldest Family Businesses in the World," Family Business School, http://thefamilybusinessschool.com/node/60.

[160]Liz Skinner, "The Great Wealth Transfer Is Coming, Putting Advisers at Risk," *Investment News*, July 13, 2015, www.investmentnews.com/article/20150713/FEATURE/150719999/the-great-wealth-transfer-is-coming-putting-advisers-at-risk.

[161]*Family Business Survey 2016: "The Missing Middle": Bridging the Strategy Gap in Family Firms*, PWC, 2016, p. 5.

[162]"Nationwide Survey Finds Majority of Business Owners Don't Have a Succession Plan," Nationwide Insurance, February 7, 2017, www.nationwide.com/about-us/020717-nw-business-succession.jsp.

[163]Kevin Pollard and Paola Scommegna, "Just How Many Baby Boomers Are There?" Population Reference Bureau, April 2014, www.prb.org/Publications/Articles/2002/JustHowManyBabyBoomersAreThere.aspx; Karl Moore, "Family Business—Your Most Important Issue—Successfully Passing It On," *Forbes*, December 7, 2012, www.forbes.com/sites/karlmoore/2012/12/07/family-business-your-most-important-issue-successfully-passing-it-on/print/.

[164]Adam Helliker, "Holly's a Born-Again Virgin, Says Adam Helliker," *Express*, March 20, 2016, www.express.co.uk/comment/columnists/adam-helliker/654008/Holly-Richard-Branson-Virgin-Adam-Helliker-comment-celebrity.

[165]"10 Surprising Facts About Family Businesses," Family Business Institute, February 27, 2014, http://familybusinessinstitute.com/blog/10-surprising-facts-about-family-businesses/.

[166]Adriana Gardella, "Family Businesses Learn to Adapt to Keep Thriving," *New York Times*, April 4, 2012, www.nytimes.com/2012/04/05/business/smallbusiness/how-they-beat-the-odds-to-keep-family-businesses-healthy.html.

[167]Whit Richardson, "Leon Gorman, L.L. Bean's Leader for 45 Years, Steps Down as Chairman," *Bangor Daily News*, May 20, 2013, http://bangordailynews.com/2013/05/20/business/leon-gorman-l-l-beans-leader-for-45-years-steps-down-as-chairman/print/.

[168]*Great Expectations: The Next Generation of Family Business Leaders*, PwC, 2016, p. 1.

[169]*Bridging the Gap: Handing Over the Family Business to the Next Generation*, PwC, April 15, 2014, p. 16.

[170]Jenna Schnuer, "Next-Gen Nurturing," *Entrepreneur*, March 2014, p. 54.

[171]*Great Expectations: The Next Generation of Family Business Leaders*, PwC, 2016, p. 4.

[172]Lisa Jennings, "Chick-fil-A Names Dan Cathy CEO, Chairman," *Nation's Restaurant News*, November 7, 2013, http://nrn.com/people/chick-fil-names-dan-cathy-ceo-chairman; Margaret Reynolds, "CEO Interview: Dan Cathy, Breakthrough Masters," September 2010, www.breakthroughmaster.com/ceo-interviews/ceo-interview-dan-cathy/.

[173]Laura Saunders, "How Facebook's Elite Skirt Estate Tax," *Wall Street Journal*, May 12–13, 2012, p. B9.

[174]Gay Jervey, "Family Ties," *FSB*, March 2006, p. 60.

[175]Gay Jervey, "Family Ties," *FSB*, March 2006, p. 60; Tom Herman, "Court Ruling Bolsters Estate Planning Tool," *Wall Street Journal*, May 27, 2004, p. D1.

[176]Melia Robinson, "The Woman Behind 'Female Viagra' Sold Her Company for $1 Billion—See How She Spent the Money," *Business Insider*, February 1, 2017, http://nordic.businessinsider.com/photos-pinkcubator-cindy-whitehead-2017-1/; Mary Johnson, "ADDYI: Cindy Whitehead on the 'Disappointment' Over Libido Drug Launch," *Bizwomen*, April 29, 2016, www.bizjournals.com/bizwomen/news/profiles-strategies/2016/04/addyi-cindy-whitehead-on-the-disappointment-over.html?page=all.

[177]"ESOP Facts," National Center for Employee Ownership, 2017, www.esop.org.

[178]*Employee Ownership Month 2015: Press and Event Planning Kit*, The ASU Group, 2015, p. 42.

[179]Bo Burlingham, "Best Small Companies: New Belgium Brewing," *Forbes*, February 8, 2016, p. 90; Tony Kiss, "New Belgium Celebrates 25 Years," *Greenville News*, August 28, 2016, pp. 10A–11A; Tanza Loudenback, "Why Employee-Owned New Belgium Brewing Gives Workers Bikes, Travel Vouchers, and Paid Sabbaticals on Their Anniversaries," *Business Insider*, June 27, 2016, www.businessinsider.com/new-belgium-brewery-employee-perks-2016-6.

[180]Leigh Buchanan and Mike Hofman, "Everything I Know about Leadership, I Learned from the Movies," *Inc.*, March 2000, pp. 58–70.

Appendix

The Daily Perc Business Plan*

This sample business plan has been made available to users of *Business Plan Pro®*, business planning software published by Palo Alto Software, Inc. Names, locations, and numbers may have been changed, and substantial portions of the original plan text have been omitted because of space limitations and to preserve confidentiality and proprietary information.

You are welcome to use this plan as a starting point to create your own, but you do not have permission to resell, reproduce, publish, distribute, or even copy this plan as it exists here.

Requests for reprints, academic use, and other dissemination of this sample plan should be e-mailed to the marketing department of Palo Alto Software at marketing@paloalto.com. For product information, visit www.paloalto.com or call 1-800-229-7526.

*"The Daily Perc," Copyright Palo Alto Software, Inc., from Bplans.com Sample Plan Library.

1.0 Executive Summary

The Daily Perc (TDP) is a specialty beverage retailer. TDP uses a system that is new to the beverage and food service industry to provide hot and cold beverages conveniently and efficiently. TDP provides its customers the ability to drive up and order (from a trained Barista) their choice of a custom-blended espresso drink, freshly brewed coffee, or other beverage. TDP offers a high-quality alternative to fast-food, convenience store, or institutional coffee.

The Daily Perc offers its patrons the finest hot and cold beverages, specializing in specialty coffees, blended teas, and other custom drinks. In addition, TDP will offer soft drinks, fresh-baked pastries, and other confections. Seasonally, TDP will add beverages such as hot apple cider, hot chocolate, frozen coffees, and more.

The Daily Perc will focus on two markets:

The daily commuter. Someone who is traveling to or from work, shopping, delivering goods or services, or just out for a drive.

The captive consumer. Someone who is in a restricted environment that does not allow convenient departure and return for refreshments or where refreshments stands are an integral part of the environment.

The Daily Perc will penetrate the commuter and captive consumer markets by deploying drive-through facilities and Mobile Cafés in highly visible, accessible locations. The drive-through facilities are designed to handle two-sided traffic and dispense customer-designed, specially ordered cups of premium coffee in less time than is required for a visit to a locally owned café or one of the national chains.

In addition to providing a quality product and an extensive menu of delicious items, we will donate up to 7.5 percent of profits to local charities to increase customer awareness of and loyalty to our business and to generate good publicity coverage and media support.

The Daily Perc's customer service process is labor intensive, and TDP recognizes that a higher level of talent is essential to success. The financial investment in its employees will be one of the greatest differentiators between TDP and its competition. For the purpose of this plan, the capital expenditures of facilities and equipment are financed. We will maintain minimum levels of inventory on hand to keep our products fresh and to take advantage of price decreases when they should occur.

The Daily Perc anticipates an initial combination of investments and short- and long-term financing of $365,670 to cover start-up costs. This will require TDP to grow more slowly than might be otherwise possible, but our growth will be solid, financially sound, and tied to customer demand.

The Daily Perc's goal is to become the drive-through version of Starbucks between the mountains, eventually obtaining several million dollars through a private offering that will allow the company to open 20 to 30 facilities per year in metropolitan communities in the North, Midwest, and South with populations of more than 150,000. The danger in this strategy is that competitors could establish a foothold in a community before the arrival of TDP, causing a potential drain on revenues and a dramatic increase in advertising expenditures to maintain market share. Knowing these risks—and planning for them—gives TDP the edge needed to make the exit strategy viable.

By year 3, we estimate a net worth of $1,075,969, a cash balance of $773,623, and earnings of $860,428, based on 13 drive-throughs and four Mobile Cafés. At that point, a market value of between $3.5 million and $8.6 million for the company is reasonable. At present, coffee chains are trading in multiples of 4 to 10 times earnings. Using the midpoint of that range (7) provides an estimated value of $6 million by the end of year 3.

The figure on page 754 summarizes the forecasts for TDP's sales, gross profit, and net income for the first three years of operation.

1.1 Objectives

The Daily Perc has established three objectives it plans to achieve in the next three years:

1. Thirteen drive-through locations and four fully booked Mobile Cafés by the end of the third year

2. Gross profit margin of 45 percent or more

3. Net after-tax profit above 15 percent of sales

1.2 Mission

The Daily Perc's mission is threefold, with each being as integral to our success as the next.

- *Product mission.* Provide customers the finest quality beverages in the most efficient way

- *Community mission.* Support the local communities in which we operate

- *Economic mission.* Operate and grow at a profitable rate by making sound business decisions

1.3 Keys to Success

There are four keys to success in this business, three of which are virtually the same as in any food service business. It is the fourth key—the Community Mission—that gives TDP the extra measure of respect in the public eye.

1. The best locations, characterized by high visibility, high traffic counts, and convenient access

2. The best products, featuring the freshest coffee beans, cleanest equipment, premium serving containers, and most consistent flavor

3. The friendliest servers who are well trained, cheerful, skilled, professional, and articulate

4. The finest reputation that generates word-of-mouth advertising and promotes our community mission and charitable giving

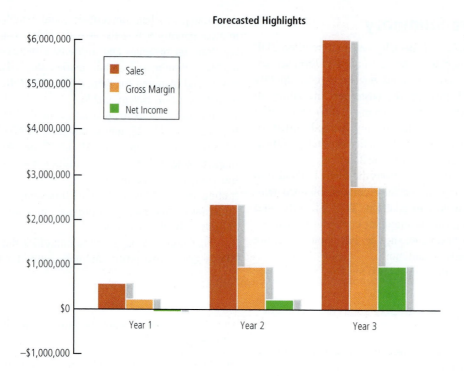

Forecasted Highlights

2.0 Company Summary

The Daily Perc is a specialty beverage retailer. TDP uses a system that is new to the beverage and food service industry to provide hot and cold beverages conveniently and efficiently. TDP provides its customers the ability to drive up and order from a trained Barista their choice of a custom-blended espresso drink, freshly brewed coffee, or other beverage. TDP offers a high-quality alternative to fast-food, convenience store, and institutional coffee.

2.1 Company Ownership

The Daily Perc is a limited liability company. All membership shares are currently owned by Bart and Teresa Fisher, who intend to use a portion of the shares to raise capital.

The plan calls for the sale of 100 membership units in the company to family members, friends, and private (angel) investors. Each membership unit in the company is priced at $4,250, with a minimum of five units per membership certificate, or a minimum investment of $21,250 per investor.

When TDP completes its financing, Bart and Terri Fisher will maintain ownership of 51 percent of the company.

2.2 Start-Up Summary

The Daily Perc's start-up expenses and funding are shown in the following tables and charts. The majority of these funds will be used to build the first facility, pay deposits, and provide capital for six months of operating expenses, initial inventory, and other one-time expenses. The Daily Perc also will need operating capital for the first few months of operation.

Table: Start-Up Expenses and Assets

Start-Up Requirements	
Start-Up Expenses:	
Legal	$3,500
Office Equipment	$4,950
Drive-Through Labor (6 months)	$65,000
Drive-Through Finance Payment (6 months)	$12,300
Drive-Through expenses (6 months)	$8,520
Land Lease (6 months)	$7,200
Vehicle Finance (6 months)	$3,700
Administration Labor (6 months)	$54,000
Web Site Development and Hosting	$5,600
Identity/Logos/Stationery	$4,000
Other	$5,000
Total Start-Up Expenses	$173,770
Start-Up Assets:	
Cash Required	$25,500
Start-Up Inventory	$35,000
Other Current Assets	$0
Long-Term Assets	$131,400
Total Assets	$191,900
Total Requirements	$365,670

Table: Start-Up Funding

Start-Up Funding	
Start-Up Expenses to Fund	$173,770
Start-Up Assets to Fund	$191,900
Total Funding Required	$365,670
Assets	
Noncash Assets from Start-Up	$166,400
Cash Requirements from Start-Up	$25,500
Additional Cash Raised	$0
Cash Balance on Starting Date	$25,500
Total Assets	$191,900
Liabilities and Capital	
Liabilities	
Current Borrowing	$9,000
Long-Term Liabilities	$131,400
Accounts Payable (Outstanding Bills)	$0
Other Current Liabilities (Interest Free)	$0
Total Liabilities	$140,400
Capital	
Planned Investment	
Partner 1	$10,000
Partner 2	$10,000
Partner 3	$10,000
Partner 4	$10,000
Partner 5	$11,500
Partner 6	$10,000
Partner 7	$11,500
Partner 8	$10,000
Partner 9	$11,500
Partner 10	$10,000
Partner 11	$11,500
Partner 12	$11,500
Other	$97,770
Additional Investment Requirement	$0
Total Planned Investment	$225,270
Loss at Start-Up (Start-Up Expenses)	($173,770)
Total Capital	$51,500
Total Capital and Liabilities	$191,900
Total Funding	$365,670

2.3 Company Locations and Facilities

The Daily Perc will open its first drive-through facility on Manchester Road in the Colonial Square Shopping Center. We will locate 12 more drive-through facilities throughout the metropolitan area over the next three years. The drive-through in the Colonial Square Shopping Center will serve as the commissary for the first mobile unit.

The demographic and physical requirements for a drive-through location are the following:

- Traffic of 40,000+ cars per day on store side
- Visible from roadway
- Easy entry, preferably with a traffic light
- Established retail shops in area

The founders identified TDP's first location with the help of MapInfo's Spectrum Location Intelligence Module, a mapping and geographic analysis software package that enables users to visualize the relationships between demographic and traffic count data and geography to produce maps that show the best locations for businesses. We will use this software to choose the company's future locations in the metropolitan area. As TDP expands into other cities, managers will supplement the insight that MapInfo provides with the tools in ZoomProspector, another useful location analysis tool, to identify the cities that are most likely to be home to other successful TDP locations.

3.0 Products

The Daily Perc provides its patrons the finest hot and cold beverages, specializing in specialty coffees and custom-blended teas. In addition, TDP will offer select domestic soft drinks, Italian sodas, fresh-baked pastries, and other confections. Seasonally, TDP will add beverages such as hot apple cider, hot chocolate, frozen coffees, and more.

3.1 Product Description

The Daily Perc provides its customers, whether at a drive-through facility or at one of the Mobile Cafés, the ability to custom-order a beverage that will be blended to their exact specifications. Each of TDP's Baristas will be trained in the fine art of brewing, blending, and serving the highest-quality hot and cold beverages with exceptional attention to detail.

Besides its selection of coffees, TDP will offer teas, domestic and Italian sodas, frozen coffee beverages, seasonal specialty drinks, pastries, and other baked goods. Through its Web site and shops, TDP will market premium items bearing the TDP logo, such as coffee mugs, T-shirts, sweatshirts, caps, and more.

3.2 Competitive Comparison

The Daily Perc considers itself to be a player in the retail coffeehouse industry. However, we understand that competition for its products range from soft drinks to milk shakes to adult beverages.

The Daily Perc's primary competition will come from three sources:

1. National coffeehouses, such as Starbucks and Panera

2. Locally owned and operated cafés

3. Fast-food chains and convenience stores

Two things make TDP stand out from all its competitors: The Daily Perc will provide products in the most convenient and efficient way, either at one of the two-sided drive-through shops or at one of the Mobile Cafés. This separates TDP from the competition in that its customers won't have to find parking places, wait in long lines, jockey for seats, and clean up the mess left by previous patrons. The Daily Perc's customers can drive or walk up, order their beverages, receive and pay for them and quickly be on their way.

The second differentiator is TDP's focus on providing a significant benefit to the community through a 7.5 percent contribution to customer-identified charities, schools, or other institutions.

3.3 Sourcing

The Daily Perc purchases its coffees from PJ's Coffee. It also has wholesale purchasing agreements for other products with Major Brands, Coca-Cola, Big Train, Al's Famous Filled Bagels, L&N Products, and Royal Distribution.

The drive-through facilities are manufactured by City Stations, and the Mobile Cafés are manufactured by Tow Tech Industries.

Fulfillment equipment suppliers include PJ's Coffee, City Stations, Talbert Ford, and Retail Image Programs. The Daily Perc's computer equipment and Internet connectivity are provided by NSI Communications.

3.4 Technology

The Daily Perc's delivery system uses state-of-the-art, two-sided drive-through facilities to provide convenience and efficiency for its clientele. An architectural exterior diagram of the drive-through building can be found in the appendix (not included in this sample plan).

The Daily Perc also has designed state-of-the-art Mobile Cafés that will be deployed on high school and college campuses, on corporate campuses, and at special events.

3.5 Future Products

The Daily Perc will offer products that reflect the changing seasons and customers' changing demand for beverages. During the warm summer months, TDP will offset lower hot beverage sales with frozen coffee drinks as well as soft drinks and other cold beverages. The Daily Perc will also have special beverages during holiday seasons, such as eggnog during the Christmas season and hot apple cider in the fall.

The Daily Perc's primary desire will be to listen to its customers to ascertain which products they want and to provide them.

4.0 Market Analysis Summary

The Daily Perc will focus on two markets:

1. *The daily commuter.* Someone traveling to or from work, out shopping, delivering goods or services, or just out for a drive

2. *The captive consumer.* Someone who is in a restricted environment that does not allow convenient departure and return while searching for refreshments or where refreshment stands are an integral part of the environment

4.1 Market Segmentation

The Daily Perc will focus on two different market segments: commuters and captive consumers. To access both of these markets, TDP has two different delivery systems. For the commuters, TDP offers the drive-through coffeehouse. For the captive consumer, TDP offers the Mobile Café.

Commuters are defined as anyone in a motorized vehicle traveling "from point A to point B." The Daily Perc's principal focus will be on attracting commuters heading to or from work and those on their lunch breaks.

Captive consumers include those who are tethered to a campus environment or to a restricted-entry environment where people's schedules afford limited time to make purchases. Examples include high school and college campuses, where students have limited time between classes, and corporate campuses, where the same time constraints are involved.

The following table and pie chart reflect the number of venues available for the Mobile Cafés and the growth we expect in those markets over the next five years. For an estimate of the number of Captive Consumers, we multiplied the total number of venues by 1,000. For example, in year 1, we estimate that there are 2,582 venues at which we might position a Mobile Café. That would equate to a captive consumer potential of 2,582,000 people.

Similarly, there are more than 2,500,000 commuters in the metropolitan area as well as visitors, vacationers, and others. Some of these commuters make not just one beverage purchase a day but, in many cases, two and even three beverage purchases.

The chart also reflects college and high school campuses, special events, hospital campuses, and various charitable organizations. A segment that the chart does not show (because it would skew the chart greatly) is the number of corporate campuses in the metropolitan area. There are more than 1,700 corporate facilities that employ more than 500 people, giving us an additional 1,700,000 potential customers, or a total of 2,582 locations at which we could place a Mobile Café.

Table: Market Analysis

Market Analysis		Year 1	Year 2	Year 3	Year 4	Year 5	
Potential Customers	Growth						CAGR
Public High School Campuses	1%	80	81	82	83	84	1.23%
Private High Schools	0%	88	88	88	88	88	0.00%
College Campuses	0%	77	77	77	77	77	0.00%
Golf Courses	0%	99	99	99	99	99	0.00%
Special Events	3%	43	44	45	46	47	2.25%
Nonprofits with $500K+ Budgets	2%	362	369	376	384	392	2.01%
Hospital Campuses	0%	100	100	100	100	100	0.00%
Total	1.10%	849	858	867	877	887	1.10%

CHART: MARKET ANALYSIS (PIE)

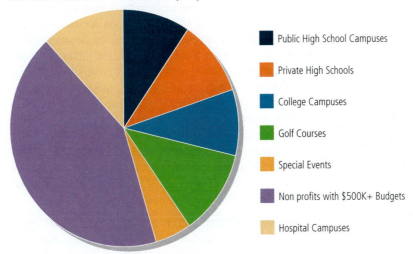

- Public High School Campuses
- Private High Schools
- College Campuses
- Golf Courses
- Special Events
- Non profits with $500K+ Budgets
- Hospital Campuses

Source: Based on data from the National Coffee Association.

4.2 Target Market Segment Strategy

The Daily Perc's target market is the mobile customer who has more money than time and excellent taste in the choice of a beverage but no desire to linger in a café. By locating the drive-throughs in high-traffic/high-visibility areas, these customers will patronize TDP and become our regular guests.

Our Mobile Cafés will allow TDP to take the café to the customer! By using the community support program that TDP is instituting, we will make arrangements to visit high schools, college campuses, or corporate campuses once or twice a month. (We also will offer to visit these facilities for special games, tournaments, recruiting events, or corporate open houses.) We will return a portion of the revenue from each beverage or baked goods sold to the high school or college, allowing the institution to reap a financial reward while providing a pleasant and fulfilling benefit to their students or employees.

4.2.1 MARKET TRENDS
Nearly 20 years ago, a trend toward more unique coffees began to develop in the United States.

There had always been specialty coffee stores, such as Gloria Jeans and others, but people began to buy espresso machines for their homes and offices. Coffee tastings in stores became popular, and later espresso bars began to appear. Then along came Starbucks, the quintessential bastion of upwardly mobile professionals who wanted to take control over how their beverages were made.

Since Starbucks arrived on the scene, people have become more pressed for time. The same customers who helped push Starbucks's sales to nearly $10 billion are now rushing to get their kids to soccer practice and basketball games, running to the grocery store, and trying to get to work on time and back home in time for dinner—or to get to the next soccer game. Yet they still have the desire for that refreshing, specially blended coffee each morning.

Recently, we have seen the introduction of beverage dispensers at convenience stores that spit out overly-sweet, poorly blended cappuccinos in flavors such as French vanilla or mocha, and consumers are paying as much as $3.00 for these substandard beverages.

The market is primed for the introduction of a company that offers a superior quality, specially blended product in a convenient, drive-through environment at a price that is competitive with national coffeehouses.

The Daily Perc is a member of the National Coffee Association and the National Specialty Coffee Association. These two trade associations provide useful information on the relevant trends in the industry, information for making comparisons to other companies on financial performance, and educational workshops and seminars.

4.2.2 MARKET GROWTH
The 183 million Americans who drink coffee consume 146 *billion* cups of coffee per year.

In addition, more than 173 million people in the United States drink tea. According to industry statistics, the consumption of coffee and flavored coffee products is growing rapidly, and 34 percent of coffee drinkers go to "premium" coffee outlets to purchase their beverages.

The segment of the market we are targeting is the commuter, and the number of people who commute to work is increasing by about 6 percent per year. In the metropolitan area, as with many metropolitan areas in the country, there is a migration away from the cities as people choose to live in quiet suburban areas and drive to work in the city.

The United States is home to 128.3 million commuters. Using census data, we estimate that more than 2.5 million commuters drive to and from work each day in our defined market. In addition, research shows that 54 percent of Americans drink coffee every day and that the typical coffee drinker consumes three nine-ounce cups of coffee per day. Nearly 65 percent of coffee consumption takes place in the morning, 30 percent occurs between meals, and 5 percent occurs with other meals. Therefore, TDP has a significant daily target for its beverages, particularly during the morning drive time.

4.2.3 MARKET NEEDS

The United States is a very mobile society. With the introduction of the automobile, we became a nation that thrived on the freedom of going where we wanted when we wanted. The population of the United States is 320 million people, and there are more licensed vehicles in the country than there are people. The population's mobility has created a unique need in our society for products available "on the go."

Our market is made up of consumers who have busy schedules, a desire for quality, and adequate disposable income. As much as they would like the opportunity to sit in an upscale coffeehouse and sip a uniquely blended coffee beverage and read the morning paper, they don't have the time. However, they still have the desire for a uniquely blended beverage as they hurry through their busy lives.

4.3 Industry Analysis

Consumers in the United States drink *450 million cups* of coffee per *day* and spend *$40 billion* a *year* on coffee-based drinks. The coffee industry in the United States has grown rapidly in the United States over the last five years. Sales of specialty coffees are growing at a rate of 20 percent per year. Even general coffee sales have increased, with international brands such as Folgers, Maxwell House, and Safari coffee reporting higher sales and greater profits. The United States is the leading coffee-consuming nation in the world, and the coffee industry is reaping the rewards.

4.3.1 DISTRIBUTION PATTERNS

The café experience comes from the Italian origins of espresso. The customer enters a beautifully decorated facility surrounded by wondrous aromas and finds himself or herself involved in a sensory experience that, more often than not, masks an average product at a premium price. However, the proliferation of cafés in the United States proves the viability of the market. It is a duplication of the same delivery process as currently exists in Europe.

4.3.2 COMPETITION AND BUYING PATTERNS

There are four general competitors in TDP's drive-through market. They are the national specialty beverage chains, such as Starbucks and Panera; local coffeehouses—or cafés with an established clientele and a quality product; fast-food restaurants; and convenience stores. There is a dramatic distinction among the patrons of each of these outlets.

Patrons of Starbucks or of one of the local cafés are looking for the "experience" of the coffeehouse. They want the ability to "design" a custom coffee, smell fresh pastries, listen to soothing Italian music, and read a newspaper or visit with a friend. It is a relaxing, slow-paced environment.

Patrons of fast-food restaurants or convenience stores expect just the opposite. They have no time for idle chatter and are willing to overpay for whatever beverage the machine spits out—as long as it's quick. They pay for their gas and are back on the road to work. Although they have the ability to differentiate between a good cup of coffee and a bad one, time is more valuable to them than quality.

Competitors of the Mobile Cafés on campuses include fast-food restaurants (assuming that they are close enough so that customers can get there and back in the minimal allotted time), vending machines, and company or school cafeterias. The customers in this environment are looking for a quick, convenient, fairly priced, quality beverage that allows them to purchase the product and return to work, class, or other activity.

Competitors of the Mobile Cafés at events such as festivals and fairs include all the other vendors who are licensed to sell refreshments. Attendees of these events expect to pay a premium price for a quality product.

4.3.3 MAIN COMPETITORS

The Daily Perc has no direct competitors in the drive-through segment of the market in the metropolitan area. The Daily Perc will be the first double-sided, drive-through coffeehouse in the city. However, we face significant competition from indirect competitors in the form of traditional coffeehouses, convenience stores, fast-food outlets, and other retailers.

National Chains: In 2013, Starbucks, the national leader, operated more than 11,400 retail outlets in the United States (and nearly 8,400 foreign outlets) that generated operating revenue of $14.9 billion, which represents an increase of 12 percent over 2012. The average annual revenue for a Starbucks outlet is $754,000, or $89,558 in revenue per employee.

Panera Bread had revenues of $2.11 billion, an increase of 12.2 percent over 2012. Annual sales at the average Panera Bread outlet are $2.5 million. Coffee beverages are not the primary focus of Panera Bread's menu.

Despite its name, Dunkin' Donuts's primary emphasis is on selling coffee. The company has more than 11,000 outlets worldwide, 7,000 of which are in the United States. Constructing a Dunkin' Donuts retail store costs about $500,000, and average sales at a Dunkin' Donuts outlet in the United States are $845,000. The company's stronghold on market share is greatest in the Northeast, where it originated.

The Daily Perc believes it has a significant competitive advantage over these chains because of the following benefits:

- Drive-through service
- Superior customer service
- Community benefit
- Mobile Cafés
- Greater selection
- Higher product quality

Local Cafés: The toughest competitor for TDP is the established locally owned café. The Daily Perc knows the quality and pride that the local café has in the products its customers purchase. Local cafés typically benefit from their loyal, highly educated customers. The quality of beverages served at an established café surpasses those of the regional or national chains.

The competitive edge TDP has over local cafés is based on the following:

- Drive-through service
- Supply discounts
- Mobile Café
- Consistent menu
- Community benefit
- Quality product

Drive-Through Coffeehouses: There are no drive-through specialty beverage retailers with a significant market presence in the central United States. The only company with similar depth to that of TDP is Quikava, a wholly owned subsidiary of Chock Full 'o Nuts. However, Quikava has limited its corporate footprint to the East Coast and the Great Lakes region.

In the drive-through specialty beverage market, TDP has a competitive edge over these competitors, including Quikava, because of the following:

- Mobile Cafés
- Consistent menu
- Community benefit
- Quality product
- Supply discounts
- Valued image
- Greater product selection

Fast-Food and Convenience Stores: Most national fast food chains and national convenience store chains already serve coffee, soda, and some breakfast foods. The national fast-food chains understand the benefits and value that drive-through service provides customers; 70 percent of the typical fast-food outlet's sales come from drive-through customers.

In addition, nearly 80 percent of the growth in the fast-food industry in the last five years has come through outlets' drive-through windows. Customers who buy coffee at fast-food and convenience stores shop primarily on the basis of price rather than quality and, therefore, are not TDP's primary target customers. The Daily Perc's advantage is that the quality of the products it sells is much higher than those sold at fast-food and convenience stores. Soft-drink sales for the typical quick-serve store account for a large portion of beverage sales. The Daily Perc believes that the quality of its products and the convenience of speedy drive-through service give it a competitive edge over fast-food and convenience stores.

Other Competition: The Daily Perc understands that once it has entered the market and established a presence, others will try to follow. However, TDP believes that although imitators will appear, they cannot duplicate its corporate mission, organizational design, or customer value proposition. The Daily Perc will constantly evaluate its products, locations, service, and mission to ensure that it remains a leader in the specialty beverage industry in its market segment.

4.3.4 INDUSTRY PARTICIPANTS There is only one national drive-through coffee franchise operation in the United States that poses a threat: a subsidiary of Chock Full 'o Nuts called Quikava. Quikava operates primarily on the East Coast and in the upper Great Lakes region. The East and West coasts and even some Mountain and Midwest states have smaller local drive-through chains such as Caffino, Java Espress, Crane Coffee, Java Drive, Sunrise Coffee, and Caffe Diva. However, other players in the premium coffee service industry include Starbucks, Gloria Jean's, Caribou Coffee, Panera Bread, and locally owned and operated coffee shops or "cafés."

5.0 Strategy and Implementation Summary

The Daily Perc will penetrate the commuter and captive consumer markets by deploying drive-through facilities and Mobile Cafés in highly visible, high-volume, accessible locations. The drive-throughs are designed to handle two-sided traffic and dispense customer-designed, specially ordered cups of specialty beverages in less time than required for a visit to the locally owned café or one of the national chains.

The Daily Perc has identified its market as busy, mobile people whose time is already at a premium but who desire a refreshing, high-quality beverage or baked item while commuting to or from work or school.

In addition to providing a quality product and an extensive menu of delicious side items, TDP pledges to donate up to 7.5 percent of profits from each cup sold in individual drive-throughs to the charities that its customers choose.

5.1 Strategy Pyramid

The Daily Perc's strategy is to offer customers quality products, convenient accessibility, and a community benefit. To execute this strategy, TDP is placing the drive-throughs and Mobile Cafés in well-researched, easily accessible locations throughout the metropolitan area. The Daily Perc is pricing its product competitively and training the production staff to be among the best Baristas in the country. Prices for TDP's products are at or slightly below the national average. Through coupons and display ads at its locations, TDP will involve customers in community support efforts by donating a portion of each sale to a charity of their choosing.

In so doing, TDP has accomplished the following:

1. Provided a customer with a quality product at a competitive price

2. Provided customers with a more convenient method for obtaining their desired products

3. Demonstrated how TDP appreciates their loyalty and patronage by donating money to a meaningful cause

5.2 Value Proposition

The drive-through facilities provide a substantial value proposition because our customers do not have to find parking places, exit their vehicles, stand in long lines to order, pay premium prices for average products, find places to sit, clean up the previous patron's mess, and then enjoy their coffee—assuming that they have sufficient time to linger over the cup.

The Daily Perc's concept is that the customer drives up, places an order that is filled quickly and accurately, receives a high-quality product at a competitive price, and drives away, having invested little time in the process.

The Daily Perc is also providing a significant community value on behalf of customers who patronize TDP. For every purchase a customer makes from us, TDP will donate up to 7.5 percent of profits to a local charity selected by our customers.

5.3 Competitive Edge

The Daily Perc's competitive edge is simple. TDP provides a high-quality product at a competitive price in a drive-through environment that saves customers valuable time.

5.4 Marketing Strategy

The Daily Perc will be placing its drive-through facilities in highly visible, easily accessible locations. They will be located on high-traffic commuter routes and near shopping centers and concentrations of complementary retail shops to catch customers who are traveling to or from work, going out for lunch, or venturing on a shopping expedition. The drive-throughs' design is very unique and eye-catching, which will be a branding feature of its own.

As the following chart indicates, TDP's target audience skews older.

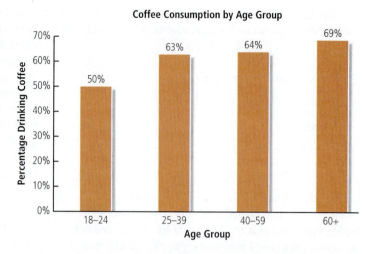

Coffee Consumption by Age Group

Therefore, TDP will implement a low-cost advertising campaign that includes traditional advertising media, such as drive-time radio and a few strategically located outdoor ads. However, because a significant portion of our target customers is younger than 40, we also will use social media tools extensively.

The Daily Perc will rely on building relationships with schools, charities, and companies to provide significant free publicity through its community support program. When TDP makes charitable contributions to these institutions, they will get the word out to their students/faculty/employees/partners about TDP. Word-of-mouth advertising has long been one of the greatest advertising techniques a company can use. In addition, we will encourage the media to cover the charitable aspects of TDP, giving the company the opportunity for more exposure every time TDP writes a check to a nonprofit organization.

The Daily Perc will use social media marketing tools such as Twitter and Facebook as well, particularly to promote the locations of its Mobile Cafés. We will send tweets to our followers to alert them to the location of our Mobile Cafés. We also will post the Mobile Cafés' locations on Facebook.

5.4.1 PROMOTION STRATEGY

The long-range goal is to gain enough visibility to expand the TDP brand into other regions and generate inquiries from potential inventors. To do that, TDP must employ the following:

- A public relations service at $1,000 per month for the next year to generate awareness of TDP among newspapers, magazines, bloggers, and reviews. We anticipate that the school fund-raising program will generate publicity on its own and eventually will minimize—or even eliminate—the need for a publicist.

- Advertising expenditures of $1,000 per month focused on drive-time radio and strategically selected billboards. The Daily Perc will experiment with different stations, keeping careful track of results. We will select billboards that are near our existing locations to serve as reminders of our locations for passing motorists. As with the school fund-raising program, TDP expects its storefronts and signage to be a substantial portion of our advertising.

- A social media presence on Facebook, Twitter, and YouTube. We can use these tools to reach our target customers at very little expense. We will promote daily specials on selected items on Facebook and Twitter and will post videos of our Best Barista Contest on YouTube. We also plan to involve our customers through a contest that offers free coffee for one year to the customer who posts the best YouTube video promoting TDP. We also will sponsor a "Fan of the Day" contest by randomly drawing one person who likes TDP on Facebook to receive a free cup of coffee and announcing the winner on Facebook and on Twitter.

5.4.2 DISTRIBUTION STRATEGY

The Daily Perc will locate its drive-through facilities in high-traffic areas of the city where it knows working commuters will be passing. Our first outlet will be located at the corner of Main Street and Broughton Road, which has a traffic count of 42,200 cars per day.

The Daily Perc will also make arrangements for the Mobile Cafés to be at as many schools, businesses, and events as possible every year to promote TDP to new customers.

5.4.3 MARKETING PROGRAMS

Distinctive Logo: Our logo, "Papo," is a very happy and conspicuous sun. The sun touches every human being every day, and TDP wants to touch its customers every day. Papo is already an award-winning logo, having won the "New Artist Category" of the 2013 Not Just Another Art Director's Club (NJAADC).

Distinctive Buildings: The Daily Perc is using diner-style buildings for its drive-through facilities and has worked closely with the manufacturer to make the building distinctive so that it is easy to recognize and functional.

The Mobile Café: The Mobile Café will be a key marketing tool for TDP. The similarities between the Mobile Cafés and the drive-through facilities will be unmistakable. The exposure that these units provide is difficult to measure directly but is extremely important to the company's growth. The Daily Perc will negotiate visits for its mobile units at schools, hospitals, companies, and special events. A portion of all sales made while at these locations will go to a nonprofit entity of the organization's choice. The organization will promote its presence to its constituency and encourage them to frequent TDP's drive-through establishments to support their charitable cause. This will give those patrons an opportunity to taste the products and become regular customers of the drive-through facilities. The Mobile Cafés will also appear at community events, such as fairs, festivals, and other charitable events.

Advertising and Promotion: In the first year, TDP plans to spend moderately on advertising and promotion, with the program beginning in June, prior to the opening of the first drive-through. This would not be considered a serious advertising budget for any business, but TDP believes that the exposure will come from publicity and promotion, so we will spend most of the funds on a good publicist who will get the word out about the charitable contribution program and how it works in conjunction with the Web site. The Daily Perc also believes that word-of-mouth advertising and free beverage coupons will be better ways to drive people to the first and second locations.

In the second year, TDP will increase the budget because it will need to promote several locations, with particular emphasis on announcing these openings and all the other locations. The Daily Perc will continue to use publicity as a key component of the marketing program because TDP could be contributing more than $70,000 to local schools and charities.

In the third year, TDP will double its advertising and promotion budget, with the majority of the advertising budget being spent on drive-time radio to reach our commuting target audience. As in the previous years, TDP will get substantial publicity from the donation of nearly $200,000 to local schools and charities.

5.4.4 PRICING STRATEGY

The national average price for a cup of brewed coffee is $1.38, and the average price of an espresso-based drink is $2.45. The Daily Perc's pricing will be slightly below those of the national chain coffeehouses but very similar to those of local cafés to reflect the value-added feature of immediate, drive-through service and convenience. Costs to make a 6-ounce cup of coffee are as follows:

Coffee	$0.25
Cup, lid, and sleeve	0.22
Milk	0.21
Total	$0.68

Additional ingredients add anywhere from $0.02 (sugar) to $1.08 (mocha syrup) to the cost of a single 6-ounce cup of coffee for a total cost that ranges from $0.70 for a basic cup of premium coffee to $1.76 for a café mocha.

5.5 Sales Strategy

We will rely on several in-store sales strategies, including posting specials on high-profit items at the drive-up window. The Daily Perc also will use a customer loyalty program that awards a free cup of coffee to customers who have accumulated the required number of points by purchasing 12 cups of coffee. Customers also can earn points by telling others about their purchases at TDP on Facebook, Twitter, and other social media sites. The Daily Perc will also develop window cross-selling techniques, such as the Baristas asking whether customers would like a fresh-baked item with their coffee.

5.5.1 SALES FORECAST

In the first year, TDP anticipates having two drive-through locations in operation. The first location will open on July 15. The second drive-through will open six months later. The Daily Perc is building in a few weeks of "ramp-up" time for each facility while commuters become familiar with its presence. The drive-throughs will generate 288,000 checks in the first year of operation.

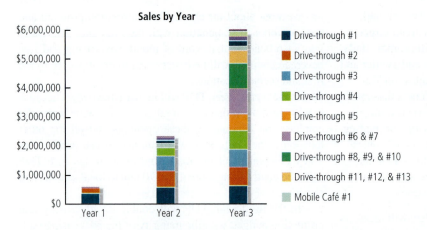

Sales by Year

Legend:
- Drive-through #1
- Drive-through #2
- Drive-through #3
- Drive-through #4
- Drive-through #5
- Drive-through #6 & #7
- Drive-through #8, #9, & #10
- Drive-through #11, #12, & #13
- Mobile Café #1

In the second year, TDP will add two more drive-throughs, and in the third year, TDP will add an additional nine drive-through facilities. The addition of these facilities will increase the revenue from drive-throughs with a total of more than 1,000,000 checks in the second year and 2,675,000 checks in the third.

In addition to the drive-throughs, TDP will deploy one mobile unit in the fourth quarter of the first fiscal year and expects this mobile unit to generate 10,000 checks at an average check of $2.45 (including baked goods).

In the second quarter of the second fiscal year, TDP will deploy its second and third mobile units and expects all three mobile units to generate a total of 150,000 checks in the second year. In the third fiscal year, with the addition of a fourth mobile unit, TDP expects to generate 264,000 mobile unit checks.

The Daily Perc also will generate revenue from the sale of "The Daily Perc" T-shirts, sweatshirts, insulated coffee mugs, prepackaged coffee beans, and other items. The Daily Perc is not expecting this to be a significant profit center, but it is an integral part of the marketing plan and an important part of developing our brand and building product awareness. The Daily Perc expects revenues from this portion, which will begin in the second fiscal year, to reach as much as $3,000 per month in the third fiscal year.

We forecast total first year unit sales will reach 298,402 cups. The second year will see unit sales increase to 1,177,400 cups. The third year, with the addition of a significant number of outlets, we will see unit sales increase to 2,992,000 cups.

Table: Sales Forecast

Sales Forecast			
	Year 1	Year 2	Year 3
Unit Sales			
Drive-Through 1	202,913	300,000	325,000
Drive-Through 2	85,489	300,000	325,000
Drive-Through 3	0	275,000	325,000
Drive-Through 4	0	150,000	325,000
Drive-Through 5	0	0	300,000
Drive-Throughs 6 and 7	0	0	450,000
Drive-Throughs 8, 9, and 10	0	0	450,000
Drive-Throughs 11, 12, and 13	0	0	225,000
Mobile Café 1	10,000	60,000	66,000
Mobile Café 2	0	45,000	66,000
Mobile Café 3	0	45,000	66,000
Mobile Café 4	0	0	66,000
Web Site Sales/Premium Items	0	2,400	3,000
Total Unit Sales	298,402	1,177,400	2,992,000
Unit Prices	Year 1	Year 2	Year 3
Drive-Through 1	$1.85	$1.90	$1.95
Drive-Through 2	$1.85	$1.90	$1.95
Drive-Through 3	$0.00	$1.90	$1.95
Drive-Through 4	$0.00	$1.90	$1.95
Drive-Through 5	$0.00	$1.90	$1.95
Drive-Throughs 6 and 7	$0.00	$1.90	$1.95
Drive-Throughs 8, 9, and 10	$0.00	$1.90	$1.95
Drive-Throughs 11, 12, and 13	$0.00	$1.90	$1.95
Mobile Café 1	$2.45	$2.50	$2.55
Mobile Café 2	$0.00	$2.50	$2.55
Mobile Café 3	$0.00	$2.50	$2.55
Mobile Café 4	$0.00	$2.50	$2.55
Web Site Sales/Premium Items	$0.00	$11.00	$12.00

Table: Sales Forecast (*continued*)

Sales Forecast			
	Year 1	Year 2	Year 3
Sales			
Drive-Through 1	$375,389	$570,000	$633,750
Drive-Through 2	$158,154	$570,000	$633,750
Drive-Through 3	$0	$522,500	$633,750
Drive-Through 4	$0	$285,000	$633,750
Drive-Through 5	$0	$0	$585,000
Drive-Throughs 6 and 7	$0	$0	$877,500
Drive-Throughs 8, 9, and 10	$0	$0	$877,500
Drive-Throughs 11, 12, and 13	$0	$0	$438,750
Mobile Café 1	$24,500	$150,000	$168,300
Mobile Café 2	$0	$112,500	$168,300
Mobile Café 3	$0	$112,500	$168,300
Mobile Café 4	$0	$0	$168,300
Web Site Sales/Premium Items	$0	$26,400	$36,000
Total Sales	$558,043	$2,348,900	$6,022,950
Direct Unit Costs	Year 1	Year 2	Year 3
Drive-Through 1	$0.64	$0.61	$0.59
Drive-Through 2	$0.64	$0.61	$0.59
Drive-Through 3	$0.00	$0.61	$0.59
Drive-Through 4	$0.00	$0.61	$0.59
Drive-Through 5	$0.00	$0.61	$0.59
Drive-Throughs 6 and 7	$0.00	$0.61	$0.59
Drive-Throughs 8, 9, and 10	$0.00	$0.61	$0.59
Drive-Throughs 11, 12, and 13	$0.00	$0.61	$0.59
Mobile Café 1	$0.64	$0.61	$0.59
Mobile Café 2	$0.00	$0.61	$0.59
Mobile Café 3	$0.00	$0.61	$0.59
Mobile Café 4	$0.00	$0.61	$0.59
Web Site Sales/Premium Items	$0.00	$6.50	$6.50
Direct Cost of Sales			
Drive-Through 1	$129,864	$183,000	$191,750
Drive-Through 2	$54,713	$183,000	$191,750
Drive-Through 3	$0	$167,750	$191,750
Drive-Through 4	$0	$91,500	$191,750
Drive-Through 5	$0	$0	$177,000
Drive-Throughs 6 and 7	$0	$0	$265,500
Drive-Throughs 8, 9, and 10	$0	$0	$265,500
Drive-Throughs 11, 12, and 13	$0	$0	$132,750
Mobile Café #1	$6,400	$36,600	$38,940
Mobile Café #2	$0	$27,450	$38,940
Mobile Café #3	$0	$27,450	$38,940
Mobile Café #4	$0	$0	$38,940
Web Site Sales/Premium Items	$0	$15,600	$19,500
Subtotal Direct Cost of Sales	$190,977	$732,350	$1,783,010

5.5.2 SALES PROGRAMS

Corporate Tasting Events. The Daily Perc plans to host at least one tasting event for customers each quarter. In addition, TDP will adjust its menu to reflect the changing seasons in the flavors it serves.

Drink Coupons. At fund-raising events for schools and corporate events, we will give away drink coupons as door prizes or awards. These giveaways are inexpensive and encourage new customers to come in to claim a free beverage and bring a friend or buy a baked item or a package of our premium coffee. The drive-through units will also distribute coupons for special menu items or new product introductions.

Chamber of Commerce and Professional Memberships. Because of the need to promote its drive-through locations and its Mobile Café services, TDP will be an active member in the regional and local chambers of commerce, food service associations, and two national coffee associations. The exposure and education that these organizations provide is outstanding, but equally important are the contacts and opportunities made available for deploying a Mobile Café—or even two—at a special event.

5.6 Milestones

The Milestone table reflects critical dates for occupying headquarters, launching the first drive-through and subsequent drive-throughs, and deploying the mobile units. The Daily Perc also defines our break-even month, our Web site launch and subsequent visitor interaction function, and other key markers that will help us measure our success.

Table: Milestones

Milestones					
	Start Date	End Date	Budget	Manager	Department
Launch Web Site	6/1/2015	8/15/2015	$5,600	COO	Marketing
Open First Drive-Through	7/15/2015	8/31/2015	$105,400	COO	Administration
First Break-Even Month	12/1/2015	12/31/2015	$0	COO	Finance
Open Second Drive-Through	12/15/2015	2/1/2015	$105,400	COO	Administration
Receive First Mobile Unit	3/1/2016	3/30/2016	$86,450	COO	Administration
Launch Web Site Voting	5/1/2016	6/1/2016	$12,500	COO	Marketing
Open Third Drive-Through	4/15/2016	6/1/2016	$105,400	COO	Administration
Receive Second and Third Mobile Units	7/15/2016	9/1/2016	$172,900	COO	Administration
Open Fourth Drive-Through	12/15/2016	2/1/2017	$105,400	COO	Administration
Install Point-of-Sale System	12/1/2016	2/1/2017	$21,000	CIO	MIS
Occupy Headquarters	4/1/2017	5/15/2017	$45,000	COO	Administration
Open Fifth Drive-Through	4/15/2017	6/1/2017	$105,400	COO	Administration
Receive Fourth Mobile Unit	4/15/2017	6/1/2017	$86,450	Equipment	Administration
Open Drive-Throughs 6 and 7	7/15/2017	9/15/2017	$210,800	COO/Director	Management
Open Drive-Through 8, 9, and 10	10/15/2017	12/15/2017	$316,200	COO/Director	Management
Open Drive-Throughs 11, 12, and 13	1/15/2018	3/1/2018	$316,200	COO	Administration
Expand to Kansas City	1/15/2018	6/1/2018	$176,943	COO	Management
Open First Franchise	10/31/2017	9/1/2018	$45,000	CFO	Finance
Initiate Exit Strategy	10/1/2018	1/1/2019	$100,000	CFO	Management
Totals			$2,122,043		

6.0 Management Summary

The Daily Perc will maintain a relatively flat organization. Overhead for management will be kept to a minimum, and all senior managers will be "hands-on" workers. We have no intention of creating a top-heavy organization that drains profits and complicates decision making.

At the end of year 3, TDP will have four executive positions: chief operating officer, chief financial officer, chief information officer, and director of marketing. There will be other midmanagement positions, such as district managers for every four drive-throughs and a facilities manager to oversee the maintenance and stocking of the Mobile Cafés and the equipment in the drive-through facilities.

6.1 Management Team

The Daily Perc has selected Mr. Barton Fisher to perform the duties of chief operating officer. Bart has an entrepreneurial spirit and has already started a company (NetCom Services, Inc.) that was profitable within three months of start-up and paid off all of its initial debt within six months. Bart's experience, leadership, and focus and three years of research in specialty drinks and drive-through service make him the ideal chief operating officer for TDP.

Ms. Mary Jamison will fill the position of bookkeeper and office manager. Mary has been the business administrator of Jones International, Inc., for the last four years. Jones is a $4 million company that retails vitamins and other nutritional products. During her four years with Jones International, Mary has written numerous corporate policies and directed the financial reporting.

Mr. Tony Guy will perform the duties of corporate events coordinator on a part-time basis. Tony has more than five years of experience in business-to-business sales. Last year he sold more than $250,000 of promotional material to corporate and educational clients.

Mr. Chuck McNulty will fill the position of warehouse/trailer manager. Chuck has worked for Nabisco, Inc., as a service representative for more than 10 years; before that, he was involved in inventory control for a Nabisco factory. His experience in account services, merchandising, and inventory control is a welcome addition to the TDP team. Chuck will use his knowledge to establish inventory and warehouse policies. The warehouse manager is responsible for the inventory of all products sold by TDP. In addition, knowledge of regulations and health requirements are important. Chuck will be responsible for ensuring that TDP maintains proper levels of inventory. He will work closely with the mobile and drive-through Baristas to make sure that all of the products they sell are fresh, appetizing, and available in the appropriate quantities at the right time.

6.2 Management Team Gaps

The Daily Perc will require several additional management team members over the next three years. We will hire one district manager for every four drive-throughs. These district managers will oversee the quality of the products sold, the training of the Baristas, inventory management, and customer satisfaction. Eventually, the goal is to promote from within, particularly from our Mobile Café and drive-through teams, for these positions.

By the beginning of the third year, TDP will have hired three key senior managers: a chief financial officer, a chief information officer, and a director of marketing. We will discuss the roles of each of these managers in subsequent sections of this plan.

6.3 Organizational Structure

The organization will be relatively flat; most of TDP's employees are involved in production, and our goal is to maintain a small core of qualified managers who empower employees to make decisions that are in our customers' best interest.

There are three functioning groups within the company: production, sales and marketing, and general and administrative. For purposes of this plan—and to show the details of

adding senior-level management—TDP has broken management down as a separate segment, but it is an integral part of the general and administrative function.

Production involves the Baristas, or customer service specialists, who will be staffing the drive-throughs and Mobile Cafés and blending the beverages for the customers. The sales and marketing staff will coordinate the promotion and scheduling of the Mobile Cafés as well as the promotion of the drive-throughs and the Community Contribution program. General and administrative personnel will manage the facilities, equipment, inventory, payroll, and other basic, operational processes for the company.

6.4 Personnel Plan

The Daily Perc forecasts its first year to be rather lean because we will have only two locations and one mobile unit, none of which will be in operation for the entire year. The total head count for the first year, including management, administrative support, and customer service (production) employees, is 15. The payroll expenditures are shown in the following table.

In the second year, with the addition of two drive-throughs and two mobile units, TDP will add customer service personnel, its first district manager, and some additional support staff at headquarters, including an inventory clerk, equipment technician, and administrative support staff. The head count will increase by nearly 100 percent in the second year to 29, causing a significant increase in payroll expense.

In the third year, we will see the most dramatic growth in head count—180 percent over year 2—because of the addition of nine drive-throughs and another mobile unit. Total payroll for the third year will reflect this increase as well as the significant increase in the senior management team with the addition of a chief financial officer, a chief information officer, and a director of marketing. The Daily Perc also will add two more district managers and a corporate events sales executive. Total personnel will reach 81.

The chief financial officer will be brought in to manage the growing company's finances. The chief information officer will be responsible for the expansion of our existing point-of-sale computerized cash register system that will make tracking and managing receipts, inventory control, and charitable contributions more robust. Ideally, this person will have both point-of-sale and inventory control experience that will allow him or her to provide real-time sales and inventory control information for accurate decision making at every level in the company. In addition, the chief information officer should begin building the foundation for an Internet-based information system that will support franchisees in the future.

The director of marketing will be charged with managing the relationships with advertising agencies, public relations firms, and the media; keeping the TDP Web site current; and coordinating the company's social media marketing efforts.

Personnel Plan

	Year 1	Year 2	Year 3
Production Personnel			
Drive-Through Team	$135,474	$439,250	$1,098,650
Mobile Café Team	$9,400	$172,800	$225,600
Equipment Care Specialist (Headquarters)	$0	$22,000	$77,000
Other	$0	$12,000	$24,000
Subtotal	$144,874	$646,050	$1,425,250
Sales and Marketing Personnel			
District Manager (Four Drive-Throughs)	$0	$22,000	$77,000
Corporate Events Sales Executive	$0	$0	$36,000
Director of Marketing	$0	$0	$72,000
Other	$0	$0	$0
Subtotal	$0	$22,000	$185,000
General and Administrative Personnel			
Bookkeeper/Office Administrator	$24,500	$46,000	$54,000
Warehouse/Site Manager	$7,000	$42,000	$48,000
Inventory Clerk	$0	$12,000	$42,000
Other	$0	$6,000	$12,000
Subtotal	$31,500	$106,000	$156,000
Other Personnel			
Chief Operating Officer	$66,000	$72,000	$78,000
Chief Financial Officer	$0	$0	$96,000
Chief Information Officer	$0	$0	$84,000
Other	$0	$0	$0
Subtotal	$66,000	$72,000	$258,000
Total People	15	29	81
Total Payroll	$242,374	$846,050	$2,024,250

7.0 Financial Plan

Although we forecast a loss of about $29,000 for TDP in its first year of operation, the company's long-term financial picture is quite promising. Because TDP is a cash business, its cash requirements are significantly less than other companies that must carry extensive amounts of accounts receivable. However, because our process is labor intensive, TDP recognizes that we must hire employees with more talent. The financial investment in our employees will be one of the greatest differentiators between TDP and its competitors. In this plan, we assume that we are financing the cost of our facilities and equipment. These items are capital expenditures and will be available for financing. We will maintain a minimum of inventory to ensure the freshness of our coffee products and baked goods and to take advantage of price decreases when and if they occur.

The Daily Perc forecasts that the initial combination of investments and long-term financing will be sufficient without the need for any additional equity or debt investment other than the purchase of additional equipment and facilities as it grows. This strategy will require TDP to grow more slowly than might be otherwise possible, but the company's expansion will be solid, financially sound growth based on its success in meeting customers' needs.

7.1 Important Assumptions

The following table shows the underlying assumptions used to build the financial forecasts for TDP:

- A slow-growth economy but no major recession.
- No unforeseen changes in public health perceptions of its products.
- Access to equity capital and financing sufficient to maintain its financial plan as shown in the tables.

Table: General Assumptions

General Assumptions			
	Year 1	Year 2	Year 3
Short-Term Interest Rate	8.00%	8.00%	8.00%
Long-Term Interest Rate	9.00%	9.00%	9.00%
Tax Rate (LLC)	0.00%	0.00%	0.00%

7.2 Key Financial Indicators

The following chart shows changes in key financial indicators: sales, gross margin, operating expenses, and inventory turnover. The expected growth in sales exceeds 250 percent each year. The Daily Perc forecasts its gross profit margin in year 1 to be 40 percent; by year 3, we expect it to reach 45 percent.

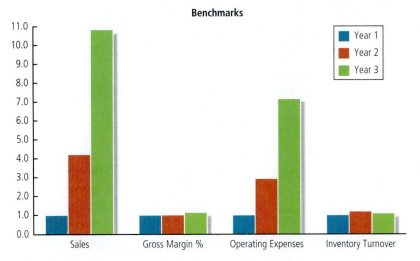

Benchmarks

Projections for inventory turnover show that TDP will maintain a relatively stable amount of inventory in its warehouse so that it has no less than one week of inventory on hand but no more than two weeks of inventory so that products stay fresh. The only time we will consider holding larger stores of inventory is if there is some catastrophic event that would cause shortages in the supplies of coffees or teas.

7.3 Break-Even Analysis

Assuming average revenue per unit of $1.87 and fixed operating costs of $19,457 per month, TDP estimates its break-even point to be $29,580 per month. This is the equivalent of selling 15,817 cups of coffee per month, or 527 cups per day.

Break-Even Analysis	
Monthly Units Break-Even	15,817
Monthly Revenue Break-Even	$29,580
Assumptions:	
Average Per-Unit Revenue	$1.87
Average Per-Unit Variable Cost	$0.64
Estimated Monthly Fixed Cost	$19,457

7.4 Projected Profit and Loss

The Daily Perc is expecting dramatic growth in the next three years, reaching strong sales and a healthy gross profit margin by the end of its first year of operation. Expenses during the first year will, however, produce a net loss of about $29,000.

Aside from production costs of 60 percent, which include actual purchases of products and commissions for sales efforts, the single largest expenditures in the first year are in the general and administrative (G&A) area, which total 23 percent of sales. G&A includes expenses for rents, equipment leases, utilities, and payroll for all employees.

Sales increase by nearly 400 percent in the second year because of the addition of two more drive-throughs and two more Mobile Cafés. Although operating expenses double in the second year, TDP forecasts a net profit of $217,000, which represents a net profit margin (net income ÷ sales) of 9.24 percent. In that same year, TDP will make substantial charitable contributions in the communities in which it operates.

The third year is when TDP has the opportunity to break into markets outside the metropolitan area. The Daily Perc will open nine additional drive-through facilities in the third year, which will increase sales faster than production costs, which improve the company's gross profit margin. Several expenses increase substantially in year 3, including advertising, charitable donations, and payroll (because TDP will add several key management team members). Once again, the company's two largest expenses are production costs and G&A expenses. However, the G&A expenses decrease from 23 percent of sales in year 1 to 18.5 percent of sales in year 2 and 15.0 percent of sales in year 3. By year 3, operating efficiencies push the company's net profit margin to 16 percent.

Pro Forma Profit and Loss			
	Year 1	Year 2	Year 3
Sales	$558,043	$2,348,900	$6,022,950
Direct Cost of Sales	$190,977	$732,350	$1,783,010
Production Payroll	$144,874	$646,050	$1,425,250
Sales Commissions	$1,416	$35,234	$90,344
Total Cost of Sales	$337,267	$1,413,634	$3,298,604
Gross Margin	$220,776	$935,267	$2,724,346
Gross Margin %	39.56%	39.82%	45.23%
Operating Expenses			
Sales and Marketing Expenses			
Sales and Marketing Payroll	$0	$22,000	$185,000
Advertising/Promotion	$18,000	$36,000	$72,000
Web site	$1,000	$15,000	$22,000

(continued)

Pro Forma Profit and Loss

	Year 1	Year 2	Year 3
Travel	$4,000	$7,500	$15,000
Donations	$3,332	$70,467	$180,689
Total Sales and Marketing Expenses	$26,332	$150,967	$474,689
Sales and Marketing %	4.72%	6.43%	7.88%
General and Administrative Expenses			
General and Administrative Payroll	$31,500	$106,000	$156,000
Sales and Marketing and Other Expenses	$0	$0	$0
Depreciation	$21,785	$92,910	$196,095
Leased Offices and Equipment	$0	$6,000	$18,000
Utilities	$9,640	$19,800	$41,100
Insurance	$12,570	$32,620	$63,910
Rent	$16,800	$50,400	$126,000
Payroll Taxes	$36,356	$126,908	$303,638
Other General and Administrative Expenses	$0	$0	$0
Total General and Administrative Expenses	$128,651	$434,638	$904,743
General and Administrative %	23.05%	18.50%	15.02%
Other Expenses:			
Other Payroll	$66,000	$72,000	$258,000
Consultants	$0	$0	$0
Legal/Accounting/Consultants	$12,500	$24,000	$36,000
Total Other Expenses	$78,500	$96,000	$294,000
Other %	14.07%	4.09%	4.88%
Total Operating Expenses	$233,483	$681,605	$1,673,431
Profit before Interest and Taxes	($12,707)	$253,662	$1,050,915
EBITDA	$9,078	$346,572	$1,247,010
Interest Expense	$16,165	$36,639	$77,102
Taxes Incurred	$0	$0	$0
Net Income	($28,872)	$217,023	$973,812
Net Income/Sales	−5.17%	9.24%	16.17%

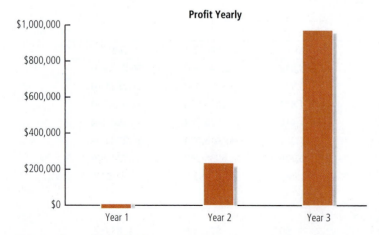

Profit Yearly

operating a cash business. Forecasts show that the business generates positive cash flow, even in year 1. The greatest challenge that TDP faces in managing cash flow results from the seasonal dips in coffee sales during warm weather, but TDP will attempt to offset those declines by adding seasonal menu items, such as iced cappuccinos, iced mochas, and others.

With sufficient initial financing, TDP anticipates no cash flow shortfalls for the first year or beyond. In year 1, the months of March and May produce the greatest cash drains because TDP will incur the cost of adding a second drive-through and a second mobile unit. In addition, TDP experiences heavier-than-normal cash disbursements

7.5 Projected Cash Flow

As in any business, TDP managers must manage cash extremely carefully; however, TDP has the benefit of in December and January because accounts payable come due then.

Pro Forma Cash Flow

	Year 1	Year 2	Year 3
Cash Received			
Cash from Operations			
Cash Sales	$558,043	$2,348,900	$6,022,950
Subtotal Cash from Operations	$558,043	$2,348,900	$6,022,950
Additional Cash Received			
Sales Tax, VAT, HST/GST Received	$0	$0	$0
New Current Borrowing	$0	$0	$0
New Other Liabilities (Interest Free)	$0	$0	$0
New Long-Term Liabilities	$181,463	$253,970	$729,992
Sales of Other Current Assets	$0	$0	$0
Sales of Long-Term Assets	$0	$0	$0
New Investment Received	$0	$0	$0
Subtotal Cash Received	$739,506	$2,602,870	$6,752,942
Expenditures			
Expenditures from Operations			
Cash Spending	$242,374	$846,050	$2,024,250
Bill Payments	$273,191	$1,236,069	$2,880,058
Subtotal Spent on Operations	$515,565	$2,082,119	$4,904,308
Additional Cash Spent			
Sales Tax, VAT, HST/GST Paid Out	$0	$0	$0
Principal Repayment of Current Borrowing	$1,500	$2,000	$5,000
Other Liabilities Principal Repayment	$0	$0	$0
Long-Term Liabilities Principal Repayment	$26,469	$27,000	$50,000
Purchase Other Current Assets	$0	$0	$0
Purchase Long-Term Assets	$191,850	$429,700	$1,356,993
Dividends	$0	$0	$0
Subtotal Cash Spent	$735,384	$2,540,819	$6,316,301
Net Cash Flow	$4,122	$62,051	$436,641
Cash Balance	$29,622	$91,673	$528,315

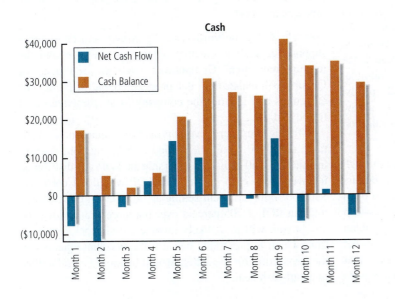

Cash

7.6 Projected Balance Sheet

The Daily Perc's projected balance sheet shows a significant increase in net worth in year 2, at which point the company will generate an impressive 90.5 percent return on investment (ROI). As the financial projections indicate, TDP expects to build a company with strong profit potential and a solid balance sheet that will be asset heavy and flush with cash at the end of the third year. The Daily Perc has no plan to pay dividends before the end of the third year; instead, the company will use the cash it generates to fuel its growth.

Pro Forma Balance Sheet

	Year 1	Year 2	Year 3
Assets			
Current Assets			
Cash	$29,622	$91,673	$528,315
Inventory	$35,159	$134,826	$328,253
Other Current Assets	$0	$0	$0
Total Current Assets	$64,781	$226,499	$856,568
Long-Term Assets	$323,250	$752,950	$2,109,943
Accumulated Depreciation	$21,785	$114,695	$310,790
Total Long-Term Assets	$301,465	$638,255	$1,799,153
Total Assets	$366,246	$864,754	$2,655,721
Liabilities and Capital			
Current Liabilities			
Accounts Payable	$49,724	$106,240	$248,402
Current Borrowing	$7,500	$5,500	$500
Other Current Liabilities	$0	$0	$0
Subtotal Current Liabilities	$57,224	$111,740	$248,902
Long-Term Liabilities	$286,394	$513,364	$1,193,356
Total Liabilities	$343,618	$625,104	$1,442,258
Paid-In Capital	$225,270	$225,270	$225,270
Retained Earnings	($173,770)	($202,642)	$14,381
Earnings	($28,872)	$217,023	$973,812
Total Capital	$22,628	$239,651	$1,213,463
Total Liabilities and Capital	$366,246	$864,754	$2,655,721
Net Worth	$22,628	$239,651	$1,213,463

7.7 Exit Strategy

There are three scenarios for the investors and managers to recover their investment, two of which produce significant returns on each dollar invested.

Scenario 1: The Daily Perc becomes extremely successful and begins selling franchises. When one considers the wealth that successful franchisers such as McDonald's, Wendy's, Five Guys Burgers and Fries, and others have created, the potential to franchise a well-run system is considerable. However, developing a franchise can be extremely costly, takes years to build, and can be diminished by a few franchisees who fail to deliver the consistency or value on which the founding company has built its reputation.

Scenario 2: The Daily Perc becomes the drive-through version of Starbucks, obtaining several million dollars through a private offering that allows the company to open 20 to 30 outlets per year in the region of the country between the mountain ranges in both metropolitan and micropolitan communities. This is the preferred exit strategy of the management team. The danger with this exit strategy is that once TDP becomes successful, competitors will attempt to enter high-potential markets with copycat concepts before TDP can expand into those markets, resulting in lower revenues and a dramatic increase in advertising expenditures to maintain market share. Understanding these risks—and planning for them—gives TDP the edge required to make this scenario work.

Scenario 3: By the third year, the growth and community support for TDP is creating a buzz in cities beyond the metropolitan area. Competitors such as Starbucks or Quikava will realize the value proposition that TDP offers its customers and identify the company as an attractive target for buyout.

Taking a conservative approach to valuation, we estimate that TDP would be valued at $7.5 million. Assuming that all 250 units of ownership in TDP are distributed to investors, a cash purchase of TDP would net each unit $30,000. With each unit selling at $4,250, that price constitutes an ROI of 705 percent over the three years. However, any buyout will most likely involve a cash/stock combination, which is preferable because the tax consequences of the transaction for the sellers would be more favorable than in an all-cash deal.

Pro Forma Cash Flow by Month

		Month 1	Month 2	Month 3	Month 4	Month 5	Month 6	Month 7	Month 8	Month 9	Month 10	Month 11	Month 12
Cash Received													
Cash from Operations													
Cash Sales		$0	$0	$0	$32,375	$42,637	$44,769	$42,530	$42,637	$77,144	$85,167	$95,392	$95,392
Subtotal Cash from Operations		$0	$0	$0	$32,375	$42,637	$44,769	$42,530	$42,637	$77,144	$85,167	$95,392	$95,392
Additional Cash Received													
Sales Tax, VAT, HST/GST Received	0.00%	$0	$0	$0	$0	$0	$0	$0	$0	$0	$0	$0	$0
New Current Borrowing		$0	$0	$0	$0	$0	$0	$0	$0	$0	$0	$0	$0
New Other Liabilities (Interest Free)		$0	$0	$0	$0	$0	$0	$0	$0	$0	$0	$0	$0
New Long-Term Liabilities		$0	$0	$5,300	$0	$0	$0	$0	$0	$98,184	$0	$77,979	$0
Sales of Other Current Assets		$0	$0	$0	$0	$0	$0	$0	$0	$0	$0	$0	$0
Sales of Long-Term Assets		$0	$0	$0	$0	$0	$0	$0	$0	$0	$0	$0	$0
New Investment Received		$0	$0	$0	$0	$0	$0	$0	$0	$0	$0	$0	$0
Subtotal Cash Received		$0	$0	$5,300	$32,375	$42,637	$44,769	$42,530	$42,637	$175,328	$85,167	$173,371	$95,392
Expenditures													
Expenditures from Operations													
Cash Spending		$5,500	$5,500	$5,500	$16,000	$18,100	$17,050	$18,800	$19,500	$28,624	$30,700	$38,200	$38,900
Bill Payments		$112	$3,349	$2,987	$7,228	$10,030	$17,719	$27,251	$24,342	$26,320	$54,407	$46,831	$52,615
Subtotal Spent on Operations		$5,612	$8,849	$8,487	$23,228	$28,130	$34,769	$46,051	$43,842	$54,944	$85,107	$85,031	$91,515
Additional Cash Spent													
Sales Tax, VAT, HST/GST Paid Out		$0	$0	$0	$0	$0	$0	$0	$0	$0	$0	$0	$0
Principal Repayment of Current Borrowing		$0	$0	$0	$0	$0	$0	$0	$0	$0	$0	$500	$1,000
Other Liabilities Principal Repayment		$0	$0	$0	$0	$0	$0	$0	$0	$0	$0	$0	$0
Long-Term Liabilities Principal Repayment		$2,500	$3,116	$0	$5,166	$0	$0	$0	$0	$0	$7,216	$0	$8,471
Purchase Other Current Assets		$0	$0	$0	$0	$0	$0	$0	$0	$0	$0	$0	$0
Purchase Long-Term Assets		$0	$0	$0	$0	$0	$0	$0	$0	$105,400	$0	$86,450	$0
Dividends		$0	$0	$0	$0	$0	$0	$0	$0	$0	$0	$0	$0
Subtotal Cash Spent		$8,112	$11,965	$8,487	$28,394	$28,130	$34,769	$46,051	$43,842	$160,344	$92,323	$171,981	$100,986
Net Cash Flow		($8,112)	($11,965)	($3,187)	$3,981	$14,507	$10,000	($3,521)	($1,205)	$14,984	($7,156)	$1,390	($5,594)
Cash Balance		$17,388	$5,422	$2,236	$6,217	$20,724	$30,724	$27,203	$25,998	$40,982	$33,826	$35,216	$29,622

Case 1

United Apparel Liquidators

Rather than remain the best-kept secret in fashion, how should a discount retailer of high-end clothing promote its unique inventory and incredibly low prices?

Bill and Melody Cohen met in 1968, when Melody was in high school and Bill was co-owner of a clothing boutique where Melody liked to shop. Several years later, the two married and opened a discount retail clothing store in Houma, Louisiana. Melody excelled at sales and customer service, and Bill was an expert at finding the right merchandise at bargain prices. Their store prospered until large chain retailers noticed the growth in the discount market and began selling inexpensive, mass-produced clothing. The Cohens failed to see the tidal wave of stronger competition until it washed over them. By 1979, their company was drowning in debt, and its sales were plummeting. They sold everything and moved in with Melody's mother in Mississippi.

The entrepreneurial couple was not willing to give up, however. The next year, they decided to open United Apparel Liquidators (U.A.L.), purchasing excess inventory of upscale fashions from other retailers and distributors. Melody operated the store in Hattiesburg, Mississippi, and Bill traveled to New York City's fashion district, where he built a network of contacts with retailers and designers, offering to buy any of their leftover merchandise.

The Cohens expanded U.A.L. into other small southern cities, such as Nashville, Tennessee, and New Orleans, all the while being careful not to take on debt. With fluorescent lights hanging from chains and concrete floors, their stores more closely resembled Goodwill stores than the luxurious department stores in the big cities that originally sold their merchandise. The first U.A.L. store was in a building that no other businesses would rent because it sat only 10 feet from a railroad track. Their newest store, their sixth, which is located in Brentwood, Tennessee, is in a strip mall in a building that formerly housed a car rental agency and includes a large deep freezer that no longer works, which the staff uses to store shoes. Although many have questioned their choices of locations, the Cohens' location decisions were intentional. Choosing small but growing southern cities minimized the competition from the large retail chains that had been the undoing of their first business and kept them off the radar of image-conscious fashion brands such as Balenciaga, Givenchy, Helmut Lang, Dolce & Gabbana, and others, whose clothing, shoes, and accessories they were selling at unbelievably low prices. Bill says that fashion brands

could generate sales from leftover goods without damaging their images by burying their goods in the rural South. For instance, one of the three Nashville U.A.L. stores had a Thierry Mugler gown that originally retailed for $2,960 priced at just $740. A pair of Manolo Blahnik leopard-print heels that listed at $1,000 sold for $224. An ivory-colored Oscar de la Renta dress trimmed with elaborate lace had an original price tag of $3,500; U.A.L.'s price: $733. Shipments arrive five days per week at the U.A.L. warehouse in Hattiesburg, and employees open the boxes with the enthusiasm of children on Christmas morning because they never know what—or how much—is in them. Because U.A.L. is a liquidator, the randomness and mystery of its constantly changing inventory adds to the sense of adventure that customers feel when they shop.

The Cohens had opened a store in Metairie, Louisiana, but Hurricane Katrina forced its closure, and they decided to venture into a higher-profile location in the New Orleans French Quarter. They also have a store in Austin, Texas, and they are ready to open new stores in other southern cities but are not sure which ones offer the best opportunities. The Cohens, who are semi-retired, now count on their former daughter-in-law, Stephanie Cohen, to manage U.A.L.'s operations. Although U.A.L. has a Web site, the company does not advertise but instead relies on word of mouth to draw customers. Some customers drive many hours and others fly from major cities across the United States just to shop at U.A.L.

Questions

1. What steps should the Cohens take to find other locations for new U.A.L. stores? What criteria should they use to screen potential cities?

2. Which of the three basic business strategies is U.A.L. using? Explain. How well are the Cohens executing their strategy?

3. Develop an outline of a marketing strategy for U.A.L. How should the company promote itself?

4. How should U.A.L. incorporate social media into its marketing strategy? Which social media tools should the Cohens use? What steps should they take to build a social media following?

Sources: Based on Steven Kurutz, "Is This Store the Best-Kept Secret in Fashion?" *New York Times*, March 15, 2017, https://www.nytimes.com/2017/03/15/fashion/best-kept-secret-in-fashion-shopping-nashville-ual.html; Liza Darwin, "Inside the Discount Designer Paradise You've Never Heard of," *Racked*, May 19, 2015, https://www.racked.com/2015/5/19/8621335/united-apparel-liquidators-discount-clothing-ual.

Case 2

Bark & Co.

Can a subscription service aimed at dog owners grow fast enough to satisfy the demands of the venture capital companies that have invested in it?

After Matt Meeker, Henrik Werdelin, and Carly Strife met through mutual friends, the trio decided to launch a business together. They noticed that consumer spending on pets in the United States had grown by 33 percent between 2006 and 2011 to $51 billion, two-thirds of which owners spent on dogs. The entrepreneurs also saw the success that Birchbox, a company that sells cosmetic and beauty supplies through a subscription model, had achieved and began soliciting valuable advice from that company's cofounders about their business model. In 2011, while still working in their day jobs, Meeker, Werdelin, and Strife used their own money and investments from family members and friends to launch Bark & Co., a business that for about $20 per month ships boxes of dog treats and toys to subscribers. In their first month, the trio shipped 94 boxes to friends and acquaintances who had signed up. To differentiate their company's products, the entrepreneurs scoured Etsy, The Grommet, and trade shows, looking for items that pet owners could not find at large chains such as PetSmart and PetCo. Each box follows a theme. For instance, one April, the BarkBox included baseball-shaped cookies and toys that resembled baseball caps and bats. The boxes have a gross profit margin of about 36 percent of sales, and the company has shipped more than 4.5 million of them.

Sales began to grow, and in 2012, Meeker, Werdelin, and Strife landed $1.7 million in venture capital; they received another $15 million from venture capital firms over the next two years. Meeker says that with its blend of unique products, Bark & Co., which is based in New York City, tapped into a large and growing segment of dog "parents" who treat their pets like children. Today, pet industry sales are $70 billion per year, and Bark & Co. has extended its product offerings beyond its original BarkBoxes to include BarkShop, an e-commerce site that allows dog owners to purchase a variety of products without committing to a subscription. The founders say that BarkShop has sold 25 million products. Its BarkPost blog, filled with dog news and feel-good stories, attracts 10 million unique visitors per month and is supported by advertisers such as American Express, Procter & Gamble, Subaru, and others. BarkLive sponsors events aimed at dogs and their owners, such as BarkFest, a day-long festival in cities across the United States that features live music and fun events. The company's product extensions carry gross profit margins that average 50 percent of sales,

but 75 percent of Bark & Co.'s revenue still comes from its BarkBox subscriptions.

Bark & Co.'s annual sales have doubled in each of the last two years and now total $100 million. The company employs 150 people but owns no warehouses, choosing instead to outsource the packing and shipping of its BarkBoxes. Although Bark & Co.'s subscription business is profitable, the company as a whole is not yet profitable but is cash-flow positive. The company has built its customer base primarily through social media, landing 1.2 million Instagram followers and 2.1 million Facebook likes.

In 2016, Bark & Co. raised an additional $60 million in funding from venture capital companies, including August Capital and Resolute Ventures, to fuel its growth. Competitors, including PetGiftBox and PawPack, have entered the market, but Bark & Co. remains the dominant player in the industry segment. The entrepreneurs recognize the importance of constant innovation and have created BarkBeta, a team that is charged with developing new business ideas for the company. BarkBeta's budget is 1 percent of the company's revenue. Several of the company's innovations have failed, including BarkCam, a mobile app designed to connect people with rescue dogs, and BarkCare, an in-home concierge veterinary service launched in New York City and San Francisco. Bark & Co. currently is exploring BarkAir, a chartered jet service that allows people and their dogs to fly together in comfort and style, and an Ancestry.com-style DNA test for dogs ("Any wolf in your genes?"). The company also is testing "pup-up" retail stores that will allow dogs, each equipped with RFID technology and unaccompanied by their owners, in shifts of five to enter the store and "shop" for their favorite toys and treats while their owners watch.

Meeker, Werdelin, and Strife are feeling pressure from the company's venture capital investors. Because of the risks associated with their investments in young companies, venture capital firms expect to receive returns of at least five times their original investments. For the venture capital firms that invested in Bark & Co. to get back five times what they invested, the company will have to grow to an estimated $500 million in sales within the next three or four years. Meeker says that the founders' goal is to give the investors a return of 100 times their investment by becoming the next "Disney for dogs." The question is: Can the entrepreneurs produce those challenging results, and, if so, how do they do it?

Questions

1. What advantages does a subscription pricing model offer a business?
2. Notice that several of Bark & Co.'s ideas for new businesses have failed. Is this unusual? Why is it important

for businesses to continue to innovate, even when their founders know that many of the innovations will fail? What steps can Meeker, Werdelin, and Strife take to encourage creativity in their company?

3. Explain the advantages and disadvantages of using venture capital to finance a company's growth.

4. Because of the risks associated with their investments, venture capital firms, which become part owners of the companies in which they invest, demand big returns within relatively short time frames. What impact do these expectations have on business founders such as Meeker, Werdelin, and Strife? Do investors'

expectations affect entrepreneurs' decisions about their businesses? Explain.

5. What strategies should Meeker, Werdelin, and Strife use to continue their company's impressive growth rate? Are there other related businesses that they should enter? Explain.

Sources: Based on Abram Brown, "The Alpha Pup," *Forbes*, July 26, 2016, pp. 46–48; Tomio Geron, "Bark & Co. Raises $60 M, Sets Sights on Global Brand for Dogs," *Wall Street Journal*, May 17, 2016, https://www.wsj.com/articles/bark-co-raises-60m-sets-sights-on-global-brand-for-dogs-1463482801; Donna Fenn, "How Bark & Co. Sold 20 Million Products and Dominated the Dog Subscription Space," *Inc.*, March 24, 2016, https://www.inc.com/donna-fenn/2016-30-under-30-bark-co.html.

Case 3

Cousins Maine Lobster

Sabin Lomac and Jim Tselikis launched Cousins Maine Lobster as a food truck in southern California. Would you purchase a franchise from this fast-growing franchisor?

Some of the fondest memories that cousins Jim Tselikis and Sabin Lomac have of their childhood days near Portland, Maine, are family picnics that featured fresh, locally caught lobster and lobster rolls. Eventually, both Tselikis and Lomac moved away, Tselikis to Boston and Lomac to Los Angeles. In 2011, Tselikis flew to the West Coast to visit his cousin, and over drinks one evening, the two began reminiscing about the wonderful fresh lobster meals they had enjoyed as kids. They also noted the popularity of food trucks and decided to pool their resources to launch a side business, Cousins Maine Lobster, that would serve lobster flown in from Maine in the form of lobster rolls (chunks of lobster meat served on split-top rolls topped with butter), lobster tacos, lobster bisque, and clam chowder. They invested $20,000 of their own money, bought a food truck, and began outfitting it as a rolling lobster wagon. In April 2012, on their first day in business, Tselikis and Lomac saw a line of customers that wrapped around the block. Business was so brisk that they ran out of food, and they knew that they were on to a business with real potential. Within six months, they quit their jobs to run the business as a full-time venture.

Local media coverage led to an appearance on ABC's *Shark Tank*, where the cousins pitched their idea to the sharks and endured intense questioning. During the eight weeks leading up to the show, Tselikis and Lomac practiced their elevator pitch, reviewed their company's financials to come up with a value for the business, and rehearsed answers to the questions they thought the sharks might ask. At the end of their segment, Barbara Corcoran agreed to invest $55,000 in return for 15 percent of the company (which established a value of $367,667 for Cousins Maine Lobster). Corcoran proved to be a valuable investor, helping Tselikis and Lomac land appearances on national television shows, including *The Today Show*, *Good Morning America*, *Master Chef*, and others, and helping them realize that franchising would be the ideal way to expand their business. Although Tselikis and Lomac had never envisioned franchising when they started Cousins Maine Lobster, they began working with the Franchise Development Group to create the Franchise Disclosure Document that the Federal Trade Commission requires every franchisor to provide to prospective franchisees. Because they had been operating their food trucks, which now numbered four, for only a year, they spent many long days developing training manuals and courses for franchisees. They were still learning about payroll, insurance, and maintaining quality control and were busy opening an e-commerce division focused on shipping lobster and other seafood products directly to customers across the country.

Once their Franchise Disclosure Document was completed, Tselikis and Lomac made a follow-up appearance on *Shark Tank*, where they announced that they were selling Cousins Maine Lobster franchises. Their appearance garnered more than 1,000 inquiries from would-be franchisees, and the flood of applications continues. Franchise Development Group conducts the initial screening of the applications, before Tselikis and Lomac interview the remaining applicants either by phone or Skype. They make the final decision about awarding franchises only after meeting candidates in person at one of the company's discovery days in Los Angeles. Every potential franchisee spends time in one of the company-owned food trucks, and Tselikis and Lomac have learned to include the chef's opinions in their final decisions about awarding franchises, pointing out that they are almost always right about which candidates will be successful. Currently, the company, which generates $20 million in annual sales, has 20 food trucks in 13 cities across the United States, with more on the way, including some in international markets. Cousins Maine Lobster estimates that franchisees' total investment ranges from $143,000 to $345,000. Franchisees pay an upfront franchise fee of $38,500, an ongoing royalty fee of 8 percent of their gross sales, and a 2 percent advertising fee. Looking back, Tselikis and Lomac say that although their journey into franchising has presented a steep learning curve and that relinquishing control to franchisees can be disconcerting, they are extremely satisfied with the path they have taken and the results so far.

Questions

1. Suppose that your best friend is considering purchasing a franchise such as Cousins Maine Lobster. What advice would you give him or her about the right way to go about purchasing a franchise?
2. What advantages do entrepreneurs who purchase a franchise get? What disadvantages do they encounter?
3. What is the Franchise Disclosure Document? How can it help prospective franchisees evaluate the various franchise operations in which they are considering investing?

4. Cousins Maine Lobster wants to expand its franchise internationally. How popular is franchising as an "export" to other nations? What steps should Tselikis and Lomac take to cultivate a successful international franchise operation?

Sources: Based on Jason Daley, "The Maine Course: A Case Study," *Entrepreneur*, March 2015, pp. 76-83; Jim Tselikis, "'Shark Tank' Success Story: How Lobster Truck Guys Turned $20,000 into $20 Million," *CNBC*, June 2016, http://www.cnbc.com/2016/06/30/shark-tank-success-story-how-lobster-truck-guys-turned-20000-into-20-million-commentary.html/; "Cousins Maine Lobster," *Entrepreneur*, 2017, https://www.entrepreneur.com/franchises/cousinsmainelobster/334512.

Case 4

ThinkImpact

Which business model is best for enabling a young social entrepreneur to engage college students in partnering with residents in developing nations to start businesses?

When Saul Garlick was a young boy, he traveled with his family to Delani, a rural community in Mpumalanga, South Africa, and was shocked by the antiquated conditions and lack of schools in which the residents of the small village lived. He pledged to do something to help. When he was 18, Garlick launched a nonprofit organization, Student Movement for Real Change (SMRC), and raised $10,000 to build a school in Delani. Over the next few years, Garlick's vision for the nonprofit expanded, and SMRC began to focus on sending college students to live with local families in South Africa and build entrepreneurial ventures with them. While attending graduate school at Johns Hopkins School of Advanced International Studies, Garlick took 18 undergraduate students on a five-week trip to Mpumalanga. He was dismayed when he saw that the school he had built years before was shuttered and in total disrepair.

It was then that Garlick realized that simply throwing money at a problem would not fix it.

He committed himself to finding a scalable, sustainable solution based on a social entrepreneurship model. Garlick began to reimagine SMRC. What if, he thought, he could take bright, enthusiastic college students from around the world to Africa and have them work with local people to develop new ideas and solutions to the most pressing local problems? He changed SMRC's name to ThinkImpact and began raising money to fund its mission. By 2009, Garlick was raising $400,000 annually to support ThinkImpact; unfortunately, costs were running higher. Like leaders of most other nonprofit organizations, he was frustrated because raising money is an ongoing process that demands a great deal of time and takes away from the time they spend on achieving their mission. Still, he was encouraged because ThinkImpact had gained traction and was beginning to make a difference in local communities in South Africa and Kenya. After missing a couple of payrolls for ThinkImpact's small staff, however, Garlick began to consider other ways that he could accomplish the organization's mission.

After attending a workshop with other social entrepreneurs, Garlick identified three options:

Option 1. Remain a nonprofit organization. ThinkImpact has contracts with two universities that generate $50,000 annually. In addition, Garlick expects that grants and donations will bring in up to $100,000 per year. However, if Garlick wants to realize ThinkImpact's mission, he estimates that he will need an additional $200,000 to $250,000. As he has learned, raising money for a nonprofit is never-ending and takes valuable time away from achieving the organization's mission.

Option 2: Shut down the nonprofit and start a for-profit company. Under this scenario, the for-profit company would purchase ThinkImpact's assets and pay off its debts, essentially giving Garlick and his employees a fresh start. To finance the new company, he could borrow money and approach family members and friends who have indicated that they would invest in a for-profit company if there is a chance of earning a return on their money. The for-profit business would generate revenue by charging colleges and universities a fee to provide students with meaningful, immersive international experiences that focus on social enterprise. Garlick estimates that the for-profit company would hit its breakeven point in three years. His primary concern is whether colleges and universities would be as open to working with a for-profit company as they are with a nonprofit such as ThinkImpact.

Option 3: Keep the nonprofit organization but start a for-profit business as a subsidiary. This hybrid model incorporates the advantages of the first two options. The nonprofit could still pursue grants and donations, and the for-profit operation could utilize traditional sources of financing, including debt, which would make ThinkImpact less dependent on somewhat unpredictable grants and donations. One concern that Garlick has is the potential for a conflict of interest if he is a stockholder in the for-profit subsidiary and the executive director of the nonprofit parent company.

Questions

1. Which organization structure should Garlick use for ThinkImpact? Explain.
2. If Garlick chooses to create a for-profit entity, either to replace the current nonprofit organization or as a subsidiary, what potential sources of funding might he be able to tap?
3. What steps should Garlick take before approaching some of the potential sources of funding you described in question 2?

Sources: Based on Esha Chhabra, "A Social Entrepreneur's Quandary: Nonprofit or For-Profit," *New York Times*, July 10, 2013, http://www.nytimes.com/2013/07/11/business/smallbusiness/a-social-entrepreneurs-dilemma-nonprofit-or-for-profit.html; Nicole Marie Richardson, "Transformative Thinking for Sale," *Inc.*, May 8, 2013, https://www.inc.com/30under30/nicole-marie-richardson/think-impact-saul-garlick-2013.html; "What We've Done," ThinkImpact, 2017, http://www.thinkimpact.com/about.

Case 5

Intertech Construction Corporation

How can this custom construction company improve its financial results?

General contractor Art Stadlen started Alamo Building Corporation in Hollywood, Florida, in 1971, taking on any residential and commercial work he could find. His specialty was "buildouts"—customized interior jobs. The company grew slowly, and in the early 1980s, Stadlen landed a contract for work on more than 100 locations for Hair Cuttery, a fast-growing chain of hair salons. In 1987, Stadlen changed the name of his company to Intertech Construction Corporation.

In 1996, Stadlen's son Joseph joined the company after graduating from the University of Florida with degrees in marketing, management, and economics. As Joseph moved up in the company, he took on more responsibility, ultimately guiding the business into the world of computers and automation. Joseph, who is now president of the company, was able to double the company's annual sales to more than $13 million. In 2001, Stadlen's other son, Aaron, joined Intertech after graduating from the University of Florida with a degree in fine arts. His acumen for business enabled him to become the company's chief financial officer.

Since Stadlen's sons have become part of the company, Intertech has carved out a niche in building out interiors for upscale retailers such as Hermès, Perry Ellis, Salvatore Ferragamo, Tumi, and others and food service companies ranging from Ben & Jerry's to Zinburger. About 75 percent of its jobs are in southern Florida. Intertech's sales are seasonal. The third quarter is busiest, typically with 15 to 17 projects; the remaining three quarters of the year generate six to eight projects. With 27 full-time employees, seasonal sales put a strain on the company's cash flow.

The average price of a job is $350,000, about $250 per square foot. The Stadlens say that their customers are good clients, but Intertech has more than the normal share of customers who do not pay invoices on time (and a few that have not paid the company at all). On several occasions, Intertech has had to file lawsuits to collect what customers owe, an expensive proposition that the Stadlens prefer to avoid. After a steep downturn during the Great Recession, sales rebounded; however, for the last several years, revenue has been stagnant, and profit margins have actually declined. To remain competitive, the company has invested more heavily in technology and training employees. Joseph points out that Intertech has been able to take on high-end jobs but is frustrated that its measures of profitability are declining.

Art Stadlen and his wife Ilene, who helped him build the company, are ready to retire and want to turn Intertech over to their sons. However, they do not have a management succession plan in place and have done no significant estate planning aside from creating wills. The Stadlens have never created a business plan for their company.

Questions

1. Identify possible causes that could explain Intertech's declining profitability. What steps can the Stadlens take to reverse this alarming trend?
2. What can the Stadlens do to manage their company's cash flow more effectively?
3. What steps should the Stadlens take to avoid problems with the company's accounts receivable? How dangerous is this threat? Explain.
4. What should Art and Ilene Stadlen do to ensure a smooth transition in handing over the Intertech reins to their sons? What tools can they use to transfer ownership? What are the implications for waiting as long as they have to address management succession issues?

Sources: Based on Julie Landry Laviolette, "Small Business Makeover: Building a Makeover for Hollywood Construction Company," *Miami Herald*, December 6, 2015, http://www.miamiherald.com/news/business/biz-monday/article48340830.html; "About," Intertech Construction Corporation, http://www.iccbuild.com/about/.

Case 6

Bluffton Pharmacy

Two New Pharmacy Owners Learn Valuable Lessons About Financial Statements and Analysis

It has been a little more than two years since Angela Crawford and Martin Rodriguez purchased the Bluffton Pharmacy from Frank White, the previous owner and founder, who had started the pharmacy in 1969. The two have spent many long hours in the store and have learned many valuable lessons as business owners that they had not had the opportunity to learn as employees of large chain pharmacies where they had previously worked.

Crawford and Rodriguez just received an e-mail from their accountant that contained the balance sheet and the income statement for Bluffton Pharmacy for the fiscal year that has just ended. The two financial statements appear below.

Bluffton Pharmacy

Balance Sheet, December 31, 20XX

	Assets
Current Assets	
Cash	$ 74,473
Accounts Receivable	$112,730
Inventory	$224,870
Supplies	$ 21,577
Other Assets	$ 10,202
Total Current Assets	$443,851
Fixed Assets	
Autos, net	$ 33,156
Equipment, net	$ 35,706
Furniture and Fixtures, net	$ 16,323
Total Fixed Assets	$ 85,185
Total Assets	$529,036

	Liabilities
Current Liabilities	
Accounts Payable	$ 29,585
Notes Payable	$ 70,902
Line of Credit Payable	$ 32,136
Total Current Liabilities	$132,623
Long-term Liabilities	
Note Payable	$170,880
Loan	$ 93,346
Total Long-term Liabilities	$264,226

	Owner's Equity
Crawford and Rodriguez, Capital	$132,187
Total Liabilities and Owner's Equity	$529,036

Bluffton Pharmacy

Income Statement December 31, 20XX

Prescription Sales Revenue		$2,228,767
All Other Sales Revenue		$ 167,757
Total Sales		$2,396,524
Cost of Goods Sold		
Beginning Inventory, 1/1/xx	$ 169,578	
+ Purchases	$1,938,097	
Goods Available for Sale	$2,107,675	
− Ending Inventory, 12/31/xx	$ 224,870	
Cost of Goods Sold		$1,882,805
Gross Profit		$ 513,719
Operating Expenses		
Utilities	$ 10,305	
Rent	$ 35,948	
Advertising	$ 9,586	
Insurance	$ 9,586	
Depreciation	$ 5,033	
Salaries and Benefits	$ 321,134	
Computer and E-commerce	$ 11,983	
Repairs and Maintenance	$ 28,758	
Travel	$ 4,793	
Professional Fees	$ 3,595	
Supplies	$ 5,991	
Total Operating Expenses		$ 446,712
Other Expenses		
Interest Expense	$ 24,879	
Miscellaneous Expense	$ 374	
Total Other Expenses		$25,253
Total Expenses		$ 471,965
Net Income		$ 41,754

To see how their pharmacy's financial position has changed since their first full year of operation, Crawford and Rodriguez want to calculate 12 financial ratios. They also want to compare Bluffton Pharmacy's ratios to those of the typical small pharmacy in the industry. The table below shows the value of each of the twelve ratios from last year and the industry median for small pharmacies.

Ratio Comparison

Ratio	Bluffton Pharmacy		Pharmacy Industry Median*
	Current Year	**Last Year**	
Liquidity Ratios			
Current ratio		3.41	4.71
Quick ratio		1.72	2.42
Leverage Ratios			
Debt ratio		0.70	0.62
Debt-to-Net-Worth ratio		2.23	2.1
Times Interest earned ratio		3.04	3.9
Operating Ratios			
Average Inventory Turnover ratio		10.90	11.7 times/year
Average Collection Period ratio		14.0	15.0 days
Average Payable Period ratio		5.0	14.0 days
Net Sales to Total Assets ratio		4.75	4.68
Profitability Ratios			
Net Profit on Sales ratio		1.94%	2.9%
Net Profit to Assets ratio		9.20%	8.2%
Net Profit to Equity ratio		29.21%	48.0%

*from Risk Management Association Annual Statement Studies and National Community Pharmacists Association

"Let's see how our ratios compare to last year's numbers," says Angela.

"I hope we're headed in the right direction," says Martin.

"There's only one way to find out," says Angela with a slight hint of tension in her voice.

Questions

1. Calculate the 12 ratios for Bluffton Pharmacy for this year.
2. How do the ratios you calculated for this year compare to those for the pharmacy last year?

What factors are most likely to account for these changes?
3. How do the ratios you calculated for this year compare to those of the typical company in the industry? Do you spot any areas that could cause the company problems in the future? Explain.
4. Develop a set of specific recommendations for improving the financial performance of Bluffton Pharmacy, using the analysis you conducted in questions 1–3.

Case 7

Bluffton Pharmacy, Part 2

How should the owners of a small pharmacy create a cash flow forecast for their business?

It has been a little more than two years since Angela Crawford and Martin Rodriguez purchased the Bluffton Pharmacy from Frank White, the previous owner and founder, who had started the pharmacy in 1969. Although Crawford and Rodriguez have prepared budgets for Bluffton Pharmacy and have analyzed their financial statements using ratio analysis, they have not created a cash flow forecast. During a recent meeting, their banker explained the importance of reliable cash flow forecasts, telling them that banks traditionally are "cash flow lenders." Bankers appreciate strong balance sheets and income statements, but they are most interested in a company's cash flow because they know that positive cash flow is required to repay a loan.

Crawford and Rodriguez expect sales to increase 4.5 percent next year, to $2,504,368. Credit sales account for 79 percent of total sales, and the company's collection pattern for credit sales is 11 percent in the same month in which the sale is generated, 63.5 percent in the first month after the sale is generated, and 22 percent in the second month after the sale is generated. The pharmacy's cost of goods sold is 77.4 percent, and vendors grant "net 30" credit terms, which means the pharmacy pays for the goods it purchases every month in the following month. Crawford and Rodriguez have been working with their accountant to develop estimates for their expenses for the upcoming year (see the accompanying table on page 783).

Actual sales for the last two months, November and December, were $272,357 and $315,458. The company's cash balance as of January 1 is $74,473. The interest rate on Bluffton Pharmacy's current line of credit is 8.25%, and whatever the pharmacy borrows must be repaid the following month (with interest), even if it must borrow again in that month. The entrepreneurs have established a minimum cash balance of $15,000.

Questions

1. Develop a monthly cash budget for Bluffton Pharmacy for the upcoming year.
2. What recommendations can you offer Angela Crawford and Martin Rodriguez to improve their pharmacy's cash flow?
3. If you were Bluffton Pharmacy's banker, would you be comfortable extending a line of credit to the pharmacy? Explain.

	Jan	Feb	Mar	Apr	May	Jun	Jul	Aug	Sep	Oct	Nov	Dec
Sales	$2,30,402	$2,37,915	$2,15,376	$1,77,810	$1,75,306	$1,72,801	$1,62,784	$1,67,793	$1,97,845	$2,47,932	$2,55,445	$2,62,959
Other Cash Receipts	105	55	60	75	85	55	65	60	65	85	95	110
Rent	3,083	3,083	3,083	3,083	3,083	3,083	3,083	3,083	3,083	3,083	3,083	3,083
Utilities	1,049	1,083	980	809	798	787	741	764	901	1,129	1,163	1,197
Advertising	1,150	1,188	1,075	888	875	863	813	838	988	1,238	1,275	1,313
Insurance	–	–	2,700	–	–	2,700	–	–	2,700	–	–	2,700
Salaries, Wages, and Benefits	27,404	27,515	27,182	26,627	26,590	26,553	26,405	26,479	26,923	27,663	27,774	27,885
Computer System and E-commerce	1,042	1,042	1,042	1,042	1,042	1,042	1,042	1,042	1,042	1,042	1,042	1,042
Repairs and Maintenance	2,000	2,000	2,000	2,000	2,000	2,000	2,000	2,000	2,000	2,000	2,000	2,000
Travel	–	–	150	–	5,000	–	–	–	200	–	–	–
Professional Fees	–	–	–	–	–	–	–	–	–	–	–	3,900
Supplies	644	665	602	497	490	483	455	469	553	693	714	735
Loan Payments	2,073	2,073	2,073	2,073	2,073	2,073	2,073	2,073	2,073	2,073	2,073	2,073
Other	50	50	50	40	40	40	40	45	50	50	50	50

Gitman Brothers

How can this classic American maker of quality shirts ramp up its e-commerce business?

In 1932, Max Gitman, a skilled shirt-maker, decided to move out of Brooklyn, New York, to the coal town of Ashland, Pennsylvania, where he established the Ashland Shirt and Pajama Factory. To satisfy the demands of his largest customer, the U.S. military, Gitman developed a shirt fabric that was softer and more comfortable, yet more durable, than shirts of the era. That fabric would become the foundation of the company's dress shirt business.

In 1950, Gitman's twin sons, Alfie and Shelly, joined the family business. Shelly managed the cut-and-sew operation, while Alfie handled the finishing department. Their hard work, emphasis on developing the best processes, and organizational skills produced shirts of superb quality with impeccable attention to detail. That same attention to detail carries through to the company's culture to this day. The factory remained a contract shop, making private-label shirts for upscale men's stores across the United States, until 1978, when a group of dedicated customers approached the Gitman brothers with the idea of selling shirts under their own label. Today, Gitman Brothers maintains its heritage of manufacturing its shirts (and now ties) in the United States, a rarity in the industry, right where Max Gitman started the company in Ashland. Many of the workers in the factory are third- and fourth-generation shirt-makers, whose knowledge and collective expertise are valuable assets. In fact, 90 percent of the company's shirt-makers have more than 20 years of experience.

Gitman Brothers is a boutique shirt-maker that sells through more than 800 independent men's shops across the United States and elsewhere around the globe as well as through its own Web site. Most of its shirts are ready-made in standard sizes, with an average retail price of $150, but Gitman recently began offering custom-made shirts at higher price points. All of its shirts are made of the highest-quality cotton fabrics. Some of Gitman's most famous customers include Al Pacino, former Pope Benedict, Drake, Gary Sinise, former Presidents George H.W. Bush and Barack Obama, Justin Timberlake, Adam Levine, TV's *Hawaii Five-O* series, Jonah Hill, Pharrell Williams, and several professional athletes, among many others. International customers are enamored with the quality of Gitman Brothers shirts and the "Made in the USA" label, but the only way for many of them to purchase shirts is through the company's Web site. Gitman Brothers knows that its Web site needs a makeover because it is not intuitive to users, does not reflect the company's heritage, and fails to promote the company's rich history and the superior quality of its shirts and ties. Building a shirt requires 80 minutes and 50 steps to turn the 25 pieces of fabric into a finished product; making the collar alone requires 12 detailed steps. Analytics show that when customers search for "men's shirts" using a search engine, Gitman Brothers does not show up on the first page of search results, which puts the company at a significant disadvantage online. With its history of making shirts for difficult-to-fit professional athletes, Gitman Brothers wants to use its Web site to promote a "Big & Tall" line of shirts. Once customers visit the Web site, managers want to ensure that they can easily find the items they are looking for and work through the steps to create their own custom shirts.

Questions

1. Develop a list of at least five search engine optimization strategies to help Gitman Brothers move up in search engine results.
2. Write a memo to the managers at Gitman Brothers that outlines the design for a new Web site that will achieve the goals they have established.
3. Identify at least three specific measures that Gitman Brothers managers can use to evaluate the quality of the company's Web site upgrade.
4. How can Gitman Brothers use social media to promote its line of quality shirts and ties?

Sources: Based on "Gitman Brothers," Go Marketing 2017, http://gomarketing.com/clients/gitman-brothers/; "12 Great Small Business Web Site Examples," Vintage, 2017, http://vintage.agency/blog/12-great-small-business-website-examples/; Andy Andrews, "Gitman Brothers: Made in the USA," *Reading Eagle Business Weekly*, March 1, 2016, http://www.readingeagle.com/business-weekly/article/gitman-brothers-made-in-the-usa; "Our Heritage," Gitman Brothers, 2017, https://www.gitman.com/pages/heritage

Case 9

Seabreeze Property Services

Should these young family members purchase a commercial landscaping and snow removal company in Portland, Maine?

James Higgins, 31, his wife Trish, 30, and his brother Palmer, 28, have grown weary of their work in the investment industry in Greenwich, Connecticut, and are searching for the right business to purchase. Like many other young people, they are looking to capitalize on a significant trend: purchasing a business from an entrepreneur of the Baby Boom Generation who has built a successful company and is ready to retire but has no one to whom to hand the reins. Trish says she has spent her career analyzing companies and crunching numbers but now wants to become a business owner so that she can contribute to and become a business leader in a community.

The trio started their search in the typical way: They typed "how to buy a business" into Google and discovered an astounding array of options. Initially, their search parameters were very broad, and their price range was between $3 and $10 million, which would enable them to use their own money and investments from family members and friends. They were willing to move almost anywhere in the United States, and they preferred a service business rather than a manufacturing or retail operation. They also wanted to purchase a company in which the current owner would be willing to stay on to help the new owners manage it.

As they researched potential candidates, they realized that their best option would be a business that has performed well financially over time, provides a service in a niche market, and faces little competition. They spent a year researching more than 1,000 potential companies, which they narrowed down to 75 prospects. After holding conference calls with the owners of those 75 companies, they filtered their list to 10 businesses that were spread across the country, from Nevada to Cape Cod, and were in industries as varied as event planning and conveyor belt maintenance. Most of the sellers fell into one of two groups: owners who were about to retire but had neglected to put into place a succession plan, and owners in their 40s or early 50s who had experience in their particular fields but lacked the management and financial acumen to grow their businesses in a significant way.

One of the most promising companies the three young entrepreneurs are considering buying is Seabreeze Property Services, a commercial landscaping and snow removal company in Portland, Maine. John and Pete Kelly, who have owned the company for 20 years, are not ready to retire (John is 51, and Pete is 46), but they want to see their company expand beyond the base of commercial customers that Seabreeze serves in a tight concentric area around Portland. Their asking price is within the range that the young entrepreneurs have set.

The Kellys have no database of their customers or the properties they serve; their job scheduling system is a whiteboard in the office. The Higginses note that most of the company's employees have been around for many years, know exactly what to do, and keep all of the knowledge in their heads. If they buy Seabreeze Property Services, they know that transferring all of that knowledge and information into a computer database will be essential.

The young entrepreneurs' approach to buying a business, which involves keeping the current owners around to manage its day-to-day operations, is unusual, but the Kellys are not bothered by it. In fact, the Kellys have talked to many potential buyers over the last several years but have not found a good fit with anyone who could take Seabreeze Property Services to the next level. They have been impressed with the Higginses' management and financial backgrounds and the vision and strategy they have described for increasing the company's sales.

The Higginses are moving forward with negotiations for purchasing Seabreeze Property Services, but they still have two other businesses in mind, a specialty advertising and publishing company in Atlanta and a food manufacturer in British Columbia, just in case they cannot strike a suitable deal.

Questions

1. What advantages do business buyers such as the Higginses gain over starting a business "from scratch"? What disadvantages do they typically encounter?

2. What steps do you recommend the Higginses take to conduct their due diligence on Seabreeze Property Services concerning the seller's motivation, asset valuation, legal issues, and the company's financial condition? Do you spot any "red flags" about this potential deal?

3. Explain the various methods that the Higginses can use to determine a reasonable value for Seabreeze Property Services.

4. In addition to investing their own money and tapping the capital of family members and friends, what other sources of capital should the Higginses explore if they decide to purchase Seabreeze Property Services?

5. What advice can you offer the Higginses about negotiating a deal with the Kellys to purchase Seabreeze Property Services?

Sources: Based on Alina Tugend, "Buying a Small Business? The Hard Work Is Only Just Beginning," *New York Times*, March 17, 2016, p. B4; Alina Tugend, "A Path for Entrepreneurs, When a Start-up Is Not the Goal," *New York Times*, September 9, 2015, https://www.nytimes.com/2015/09/10/business/smallbusiness/entrepreneurs-who-buy-small-companies.html?_r=0.

The Newark Nut Company, aka Nuts.com

Can this family-owned company achieve its young CEO's goal of becoming a $500 million business?

In 1929, Sol Braverman, the 22-year-old son of Jewish immigrants from Poland, had the opportunity to buy a small store at 99 Mulberry Street in his hometown, Newark, New Jersey. The store was just off Four Corners, one of the busiest intersections in the United States at the time. Braverman took the chance, and soon his company, The Newark Nut Company, was selling nuts and dried fruit to local customers. Through his street-smarts and sales know-how, Braverman built a successful business that supported his family and employed 30 people. Through the next several decades, The Newark Nut Company faced many challenges, including Sol leaving the company in his brother's hands while he served in World War II. Later, Newark began a long downward spiral, and the company, which at the time employed Sol's sons, Sandy and Kenny, struggled as well. In 1967, rioters burned the company's warehouse and many other buildings in the area to the ground. By 2002, Sandy and Kenny were running the company with just two employees, and annual sales had fallen to just $1.25 million.

In 1998, Kenny's son, Jeff, a freshman at the University of Pennsylvania, realized the potential of the Internet for reversing The Newark Nut Company's rapidly declining retail sales. Jeff purchased the URL Nutsonline.com and began building a Web site for the company, a task that was *much* more difficult in the early days of the Internet than it is today. Nutsonline.com was not the URL that Jeff wanted; in fact, he says that it was his seventh choice. His first choice was Nuts.com, but a cybersquatter in Guam already had registered that name. Porn sites owned his five other choices. Jeff's goal was for the site to generate 10 orders a day for the company. When the site went live, sales took off. (During one particularly busy holiday evening, when the entire family had pulled an all-nighter to fill customers' orders, Jeff's father, Kenny, bellowed across the warehouse floor, demanding that Jeff "turn that thing [the Web site] off," Jeff recalls with a laugh.) At the time, Jeff could not have known that his initial foray into e-commerce would transform the company.

After graduating from the University of Pennsylvania, Jeff took a job in the financial industry on Wall Street but hated it. In 2003, against his father's wishes, Jeff left his high-paying Wall Street job and took over The Newark Nut Company. He created a fresh business plan that focused on online sales. (An urban redevelopment project a few years before had bulldozed the company's warehouse and retail store in Newark, prompting a move to nearby Cranford, New Jersey.) Jeff began experimenting with Google AdWords, spending small amounts of money to purchase key words that would push the company's Web site to the top of Google's search engine results pages. He hired programmers to build a new, more robust Web site, installed modern warehouse fulfillment systems, and invested time in developing key analytics from the company's Web site, with the goal of continuously improving it. He also made a key decision about the company's URL after celebrity cook show host Rachael Ray said on national television, "I'd like to give special thanks to the folks at Nuts.com for providing the Jordan almonds for today's recipe." That error prompted Jeff to track down the person who owned the Nuts.com URL and offer him $200,000 to purchase it. The cybersquatter declined the offer; eventually Jeff paid him $700,000 to acquire the Nuts.com URL. Unfortunately, when he switched to the new domain name, the redirected links did not work properly, and Web traffic declined 70 percent, a loss of about 150 orders per day, until Jeff was able to resolve the problem.

Today, Nuts.com, the company's official corporate name, sells, in addition to nuts, more than 2,700 snack products that generate an impressive $35 million in annual sales. Jeff says that his biggest competitors are retail giants Amazon and Wal-Mart, to which $35 million in sales represents a rounding error. He points out that Amazon has spoiled customers into thinking that they can get free shipping on a $20 order, which for his company is impractical.

Jeff's goal is to increase the company's sales to $500 million, a 1,329 percent increase, but he knows that will take the family business into uncharted—and risky—territory. Research shows that only 0.03 percent of new companies achieve sales of $100 million. To reach $500 million in sales, Jeff knows that the company will have to move beyond Google AdWords and build a national brand name, something that is likely to cost many millions of dollars. He also believes that he will have to hire many more professional managers with experience in sales, marketing, distribution, and other areas. That, too, will be expensive. Growing that big would also require the company to establish a wholesale operation, which would increase sales but reduce its profit margin. Convincing the other family members who also own part of the company to sell shares to outsiders, perhaps a venture capital firm, will be challenging. Jeff recognizes that he could sell Nuts.com today and retire in his 30s quite wealthy, but he is driven by his desire to "go big."

Questions

1. What risks are present in Jeff Braverman's "go big" strategy? What benefits would it produce? How likely is the company to realize those benefits?
2. Considering the cost–benefit analysis you conducted in question 1, what recommendations can you offer Braverman about the strategic direction in which he should steer Nuts.com?
3. What other strategies, including e-commerce and marketing strategies, should Braverman pursue to increase Nuts.com's sales, recognizing that reaching $500 million in sales is an extremely aggressive goal?
4. Should Braverman sell Nuts.com? Explain.

Sources: Based on Ian Mount, "Going Nuts," *Forbes*, May 4, 2015, pp, 50–56; Christine Lagorio-Chafkin, "How Pop's Shop Became a $30 Million Business in Just Three Generations, *Inc.*, June 12, 2014, https://www.inc.com/christine-lagorio/three-generations-of-business-newark-nut-company.html; Patrick Clark, "Nuts.com Grows Like Crazy," *Bloomberg*, August 21, 2014, https://www.bloomberg.com/news/articles/2014-08-21/nuts-dot-com-the-web-fuels-a-family-shops-crazy-growth.

Name Index

Subject Index